S0-ADX-681

FROMMER'S
ENGLAND
ON $40 A DAY

by Darwin Porter

assisted by Danforth Prince
and Margaret Foresman

1988–89 Edition

Copyright © 1964, 1966, 1968, 1969, 1971, 1973, 1975, 1977, 1978, 1980, 1982, 1984, 1986, 1988 by Simon & Schuster, Inc.

All rights reserved
including the right of reproduction
in whole or in part in any form

Published by Prentice Hall Press
A Division of Simon & Schuster, Inc.
Gulf + Western Building
One Gulf + Western Plaza
New York, NY 10023

ISBN 0-13-279613-9

Manufactured in the United States of America

CONTENTS

MAPS

INFLATION ALERT: We don't have to tell you that inflation has hit England as it has everywhere else. In researching this book we have made every effort to obtain up-to-the-minute prices, but even the most conscientious researcher cannot keep up with the current pace of inflation. As we go to press, we believe we have obtained the most reliable data possible. Nonetheless, in the lifetime of this edition—particularly its second year (1989)—the wise traveler will add 15% to 20% to the prices quoted throughout these pages.

A DISCLAIMER: Although every effort was made to ensure the accuracy of the prices and travel information appearing in this book, it should be kept in mind that prices do fluctuate in the course of time, and that information does change under the impact of the varied and volatile factors that affect the travel industry.

BRITAIN'S VAT: On June 18, 1979, Great Britain raised its standard Value Added Tax (called VAT for short) from 8% to 15%. Most Common Market countries already have a tax similiar to VAT (France, for example, a paralyzing 23%). In Britain, hotel rates and meals in restaurants are now taxed 15%. This extra VAT charge will show up on your bill unless otherwise stated. It is in addition to the service charge. Should the service charge be 15%, you will, in effect, be paying 30% higher than the prices quoted. The service charges, if included as part of the bill, are also taxable!

As part of an energy-saving scheme, the British government has also added a special 25% tax on gasoline ("petrol")!

Introduction

ENGLAND ON $40 A DAY

The Reason Why

THE AIM OF THIS BOOK is to bring you closer to the heart of England.

In the pages that follow, I'll invite you to live—among other places—in a timbered, 17th-century home one hour from London; to sleep in a four-poster wooden bed; to enjoy festive, multicourse meals while seated at a polished black oak refectory table before a 15-foot-wide fireplace in which cherry logs burn brightly.

I'll take you to the cottage of an English sea captain where you can experience genial country hospitality and hear tales of the deep—or to a hillside farm, perched on a wild moor, where you'll be served a four o'clock tea accompanied by home-churned butter and crusty bread, warm from the oven, and thick cream piled high on a bowl of tiny strawberries that you yourself have just picked in a nearby field.

Such experiences as these have two characteristics in common: they represent the best way to live in England—and they are inexpensive, for the inns, guesthouses, and restaurants recommended in this book are those designed for and primarily patronized by Britishers, whose average wage is far below the North American standard.

You'll be taken to pubs dating back to the days of Shakespeare and Queen Elizabeth I that offer complete luncheons for £5.50 ($8.25). You'll be guided deep into the English countryside to a stone manor house which stands proudly at the end of an avenue of old trees. Here, for only £17 ($25.50) daily, you'll receive bed, breakfast, and a four-course evening dinner.

The budget details start in just a few pages. First, I'll outline the order of our discussion, then tell you a bit about the $40-a-day limit I've placed on basic expenditures.

THE ORGANIZATION OF THIS BOOK: Here's how *England on $40 a Day* sets forth its information:

Chapter I, directly ahead, deals with getting to England—mainly by air—and then with the various modes of transportation within the country. Naturally, our focus is on the least expensive means of transport—on such items as excursion fares and off-season discounts.

Chapter II discusses where you can go in England for the most interesting visits, as well as giving a condensed view of the country's history, its people, its culture, and its food and drink. It concludes with some vital data on the ABCs of life in this country that will help your adjustment to traveling here.

Chapters III through V turn the spotlight on London, giving some practical information and documenting first the budget hotels, then the restaurants, pubs, and wine bars, concluding with data on the major sights (including my personal list of the Top Ten), shopping bargains, inexpensive nightlife, and one-day trips within Greater London.

Chapter VI explores some of the most history-rich sights within easy reach of London: Windsor Castle, Woburn Abbey, and the university city of Oxford.

Chapters VII through XI move away from London to the south of England: Kent, Surrey, Sussex, then Hampshire and Dorset (Thomas Hardy country), followed by "The West"—Cornwall, Devon, Wiltshire, Somerset, and Avon. Here you'll find my descriptions of inexpensive thatched cottages, hillside farms, and Elizabethan manor houses, which you can use for exploring this varied English countryside.

Chapters XII and XIII do the same with respect to the most tourist-trodden district of England, the Shakespeare Country, and the sleepy hamlets of the Cotswolds.

Chapter XIV focuses on some less-visited, magnificent points for exploration— East Anglia (Cambridge, of course, but also Ely, Norwich, the fen and broads country), and the pink villages of Suffolk.

Chapter XV cuts through unknown England, ferreting out the attractions of the East Midlands, including the cathedral city of Lincoln.

Chapters XVI through XIX travel across the entire northern sweep of England, from the wilds of Northumbria to the cathedral city of York, to Liverpool and Cheshire, all the way to the beautiful Lake District, immortalized by the poets.

$40 A DAY—WHAT THAT MEANS: You can live in England on a number of price levels. The unknowing can lavish huge sums on sterile holidays, but comfort and charm are not necessarily priced so high at all. I aim to establish that fact by showing you exactly what you can get for $40 a day.

The specific aim of this book—as it is in all its companion books—is to show you clearly how to keep *basic living costs* (room and three meals a day) down to $40 per person per day. There is nothing gimmicky about this goal, as readers of my other books have found. Since the cost of entertainment, sightseeing, shopping, and transportation is all *in addition* to that basic $40-a-day figure, I prescribe reasonable standards for the budget-minded.

Half of this book is devoted to recommendations for comfortable rooms and well-prepared meals—within a $40-a-day budget. You'll find comfortable rooms in London and in the country, usually with innerspring mattresses and almost always with hot and cold running water. None of the rooms in this price bracket, unless otherwise stated, has a private bath.

The $40-a-day budget roughly breaks down this way—$23 per person (based on double occupancy) for a room and breakfast, $6 for lunch, and $11 for dinner.

You'll note also that I do include in these pages recommendations above our allowances—to enable you a wider range of choices where few budget establishments are available and also to give you opportunities for a good old fashioned splurge.

Many of the accommodations recommended were chosen because of a unique historical, cultural, or architectural feature that gives them special value. This is truer for the country than it is for London, where the $40-a-day hotels were selected more for their facilities, comfort, and conveniences than for any spectacular charm.

SOME DISCLAIMERS: No restaurant, inn, hotel, guesthouse, or shop paid to be mentioned in this book. What you read are entirely personal recommendations—in many cases, proprietors never knew that their establishments were being visited or investigated for inclusion in a travel guide.

A word of warning: Unfortunately, prices change, and they rarely go downward. England has no governmental control of hotel prices, as is the practice in countries such as Spain. "Mine host" can charge a guest anything he or she "bloody well chooses." Competition is what keeps the rate down. Always, when checking into a hotel or guesthouse, inquire about the price and agree on it. This can save much embarrassment and disappointment when it comes time to settle the tab.

Hotel owners sometimes complain that $40-a-day travelers have arrived at their establishments and demanded to be charged prices quoted in an earlier edition of this guide. Your chances of pulling off this stunt are about as good as they would be in the United States. *England on $40 a Day* is revised every other year at considerable expense, involving not only travel research but heavy typesetting and printing costs. It is foolish economy to travel with a copy that your brother-in-law and his wife used on their trip abroad some years ago. That cozy little family dining room of a year ago can change colors, blossoming out with cut-velvet walls and dining tabs that include the decorator's fee and the owner's new Bentley.

Finally, even in a book revised frequently, it may develop that some of the people, animals, or settings I've described are no longer there. Viennese chefs have nervous breakdowns, red-cheeked English maids elope with charming Italians, overstuffed sofas are junked in favor of streamlined modern ones, and 19-year-old dogs go to heaven—so any and all of these things may be different. But while people, dogs, and sofas come and go, many of the old inns and pubs recommended have weathered the centuries intact, and barring war, fire, or flood, should be standing proudly to greet you on your visit.

The $35-A-Day Travel Club—How to Save Money on All Your Travels

In this book we'll be looking at how to get your money's worth in England, but there is a "device" for saving money and determining value on *all* your trips. It's the popular, international $35-A-Day Travel Club, now in its 25th successful year of operation. The Club was formed at the urging of numerous readers of the $$$-A-Day and Dollarwise Guides, who felt that such an organization could provide continuing travel information and a sense of community to value-minded travelers in all parts of the world. And so it does!

In keeping with the budget concept, the annual membership fee is low and is immediately exceeded by the value of your benefits. Upon receipt of $18 (U.S. residents), or $20 U.S. by check drawn on a U.S. bank or via international postal money order in U.S. funds (Canadian, Mexican, and other foreign residents) to cover one year's membership, we will send all new members the following items.

(1) *Any two* of the following books

Please designate in your letter which two you wish to receive.

Frommer's $-A-Day Guides
    Europe on $30 a Day
    Australia on $25 a Day
    Eastern Europe on $25 a Day
    England on $40 a Day
    Greece on $30 a Day (including Istanbul and Turkey's Aegean Coast)
    Hawaii on $50 a Day
    India on $25 a Day
    Ireland on $30 a Day
    Israel on $30 & $35 a Day
    Mexico on $20 a Day (plus Belize and Guatemala)
    New York on $50 a Day
    New Zealand on $40 a Day
    Scandinavia on $50 a Day
    Scotland and Wales on $40 a Day
    South America on $30 a Day

Spain and Morocco (plus the Canary Is.) on $40 a Day
Turkey on $25 a Day
Washington, D.C., on $40 a Day

Frommer's Dollarwise Guides
Dollarwise Guide to Austria and Hungary
Dollarwise Guide to Belgium, Holland, & Luxembourg
Dollarwise Guide to Bermuda and The Bahamas
Dollarwise Guide to Canada
Dollarwise Guide to the Caribbean
Dollarwise Guide to Egypt
Dollarwise Guide to England and Scotland
Dollarwise Guide to France
Dollarwise Guide to Germany
Dollarwise Guide to Italy
Dollarwise Guide to Japan and Hong Kong
Dollarwise Guide to Portugal, Madeira, and the Azores
Dollarwise Guide to the South Pacific
Dollarwise Guide to Switzerland and Liechtenstein
Dollarwise Guide to Alaska
Dollarwise Guide to California and Las Vegas
Dollarwise Guide to Florida
Dollarwise Guide to the Mid-Atlantic States
Dollarwise Guide to New England
Dollarwise Guide to New York State
Dollarwise Guide to the Northwest
Dollarwise Guide to Skiing USA—East
Dollarwise Guide to Skiing USA—West
Dollarwise Guide to the Southeast and New Orleans
Dollarwise Guide to the Southwest
Dollarwise Guide to Texas
(Dollarwise Guides discuss accommodations and facilities in all price ranges, with emphasis on the medium-priced.)

Frommer's Touring Guides
Egypt
Florence
London
Paris
Venice
(These new, color illustrated guides include walking tours, cultural and historic sites, and other vital travel information.)

A Shopper's Guide to Best Buys in England, Scotland, and Wales
(Describes in detail hundreds of places to shop—department stores, factory outlets, street markets, and craft centers—for great quality British bargains.)

A Shopper's Guide to the Caribbean
(Two experienced Caribbean hands guide you through this shopper's paradise, offering witty insights and helpful tips on the wares and emporia of more than 25 islands.)

Bed & Breakfast—North America
(This guide contains a directory of over 150 organizations that offer bed & breakfast referrals and reservations throughout North America. The scenic attractions and major schools and universities near the homes of each are also listed.)

Dollarwise Guide to Cruises
(This complete guide covers all the basics of cruising—ports of call, costs, fly-cruise package bargains, cabin selection booking, embarkation and debarkation, and describes in detail over 60 or so ships cruising the waters of Alaska, the Caribbean, Mexico, Hawaii, Panama, Canada, and the United States.)

Dollarwise Guide to Skiing Europe
(Describes top ski resorts in Austria, France, Italy, and Switzerland. Illustrated with maps of each resort area plus full-color trail maps.)

Fast 'n' Easy Phrase Book
(French, German, Spanish, and Italian—all in one convenient, easy-to-use phrase guide.)

Guide to Honeymoon Destinations
(A special guide for that most romantic trip of your life, with full details on planning and choosing the destination that will be just right in the U.S. [California, New England, Hawaii, Florida, New York, South Carolina, etc.], Canada, Mexico, and the Caribbean.)

How to Beat the High Cost of Travel
(This practical guide details how to save money on absolutely all travel items—accommodations, transportation, dining, sightseeing, shopping, taxes, and more. Includes special budget information for seniors, students, singles, and families.)

Marilyn Wood's Wonderful Weekends
(This very selective guide covers the best mini-vacation destinations within a 175-mile radius of New York City. It describes special country inns and other accommodations, restaurants, picnic spots, sights, and activities—all the information needed for a two- or three-day stay.)

Motorist's Phrase Book
(A practical phrase book in French, German, and Spanish designed specifically for the English-speaking motorist touring abroad.)

Swap and Go—Home Exchanging Made Easy
(Two veteran home exchangers explain in detail all the money-saving benefits of a home exchange, and then describe precisely how to do it. Also includes information on home rentals and many tips on low-cost travel.)

The Candy Apple: New York for Kids
(A spirited guide to the wonders of the Big Apple by a savvy New York grandmother with a kid's eye view to fun. Indispensable for visitors and residents alike.)

Travel Diary and Record Book
(A 96-page diary for personal travel notes plus a section for such vital data as passport and traveler's check numbers, itinerary, postcard list, special people and places to visit, and a reference section with temperature and conversion charts, and world maps with distance zones.)

Where to Stay USA
(By the Council on International Educational Exchange, this extraordinary guide is the first to list accommodations in all 50 states that cost anywhere from $3 to $30 per night.)

(2) A one-year subscription to *The Wonderful World of Budget Travel*

This quarterly eight-page tabloid newspaper keeps you up to date on fast-breaking developments in low-cost travel in all parts of the world, bringing you the latest money-saving information—the kind of information you'd have to pay $25 a year to obtain elsewhere. This consumer-conscious publication also features columns of special interest to readers: **Hospitality Exchange** (members all over the world who are willing to provide hospitality to other members as they pass through their home cities); **Share-a-Trip** (offers and requests from members for travel companions who can share costs and help avoid the burdensome single supplement); and **Readers Ask . . . Readers Reply** (travel questions from members to which other members reply with authentic firsthand information).

(3) A copy of *Arthur Frommer's Guide to New York*

This is a pocket-size guide to hotels, restaurants, nightspots, and sightseeing attractions in all price ranges throughout the New York area.

(4) Your personal membership card

Membership entitles you to purchase through the Club all Arthur Frommer publications for a third to a half off their regular retail prices during the term of your membership.

So why not join this hardy band of international budgeteers and participate in its exchange of travel information and hospitality? Simply send your name and address, together with your annual membership fee of $18 (U.S. residents) or $20 U.S. (Canadian, Mexican, and other foreign residents), by check drawn on a U.S. bank or via international postal money order in U.S. funds to: $25-A-Day Travel Club, Inc., Frommer Books, Gulf + Western Building, One Gulf + Western Plaza, New York, NY 10023. And please remember to specify which *two* of the books in section (1) above you wish to receive in your initial package of members' benefits. Or, if you prefer, use the order form on the last pages of this book, simply checking off the two books you select and enclosing $18 or $20 in U.S. currency.

Once you are a member, there is no obligation to buy additional books. No books will be mailed to you without your specific order.

AN INVITATION TO READERS: Like all the books in this series, *England on $40 a Day* hopes to maintain a continuing dialogue between its author and its readers. All of us share a common aim—to travel as widely and as well as possible, at the lowest possible cost. In achieving that goal, your comments and suggestions can be of aid to other readers. Therefore, if you come across a particularly appealing hotel, restaurant, shop, or bargain, please don't keep it to yourself. And this applies to any comments you may have about the existing listings. The fact that a hotel or restaurant is recommended in this edition doesn't mean that it will necessarily appear in future editions if readers report that its service has slipped or that its prices have risen too drastically. You have my word that each and every letter will be read by me personally, although I find it well-nigh impossible to *answer* each and every one. Be assured, however, that I'm listening. Send your comments or finds to Darwin Porter, c/o Prentice Hall Press, Gulf + Western Building, One Gulf + Western Plaza, New York, NY 10023.

TIME OUT FOR A COMMERCIAL: Even in a book as fat as this one, I don't pretend to have covered the British Isles in just one volume. One book can hardly do justice to the treasures and lore of England. For that reason, we have since 1969 published a companion book, *Dollarwise Guide to England & Scotland,* for those visitors who often want to break up their economizing at times and patronize some of the more medium-priced hotels and restaurants of England, particularly its old manor houses and most charming restaurants. Over the years, thousands of readers have traveled with both guides, economizing in London, splurging in York, and so forth, since each guide offers a substantially different set of recommendations. Only the sights are the same in both guides. They don't change, regardless of what price bracket you travel in.

Many budget travelers to England, however, will want to venture beyond its borders and discover Scotland to the north and Wales to the west. With those people in mind, and after hundreds of written requests from readers, we now offer a separate guide, *Scotland and Wales on $40 a Day,* which covers the two countries sharing the same island with England. How close they are geographically, but how different they are once you get there!

Like its older sister guide to England, the book on Scotland and Wales is written on the same theme, describing hundreds of budget hotels and inns, B&B houses, restaurants, tea rooms, and pubs—often offbeat favorites that offer the most authentic and enriching travel experience.

In addition, budget-conscious travelers will find all the information needed on low-cost transportation, sightseeing, shopping bargains, and inexpensive nightlife throughout these other two fascinating countries.

So if you plan to travel not only to England, but also to "take the high road" north to Scotland, stopping off in such beautiful cities as Edinburgh, or if you intend to seek out that special magic that is Wales, take along our younger sister. You'll need her help.

Chapter I

GETTING TO AND AROUND ENGLAND

1. Plane Economics
2. By Ship
3. Traveling Within England

PRESIDENT CARTER'S DEREGULATION of the airline industry made world headlines in 1979, and ever since then, any vestiges of simplicity and uniformity in price structures for transatlantic flights have disappeared. Airlines now compete fiercely with one another, offering a confusing barrage of pricing systems and package deals, changing some of the public's preconceived ideas about the best available prices.

Travel agents laughingly refer to the masses of documentation they have received as "chaos." However, that can mean beneficial chaos to the alert traveler willing to study and consider all the choices available. The key to bargain air fares is to shop around.

1. Plane Economics

Latter-day pilgrims making the return trip to Britain will find the voyage a lot easier than their ancestors did, yet they will still have to overcome the hurdles of a complicated series of flight options. In what follows, I'll try to unravel the red tape of some attractive possibilities of air travel to England.

Of course, citing any actual fares in the fast-changing America-to-Britain routes would make this book obsolete before publication. All fares must be checked with the airline of your choice and/or your travel agent before departure.

Many **charter flights** exist to London with organizations which profit from group discounts. They are too numerous to describe here, and difficult to recommend because of the low capitalization of many of these companies and the changing legalities of the airline industry. Check with your travel agent for *legitimate* plans.

BRITISH AIRWAYS: The premier airline of the United Kingdom, British Airways, has more flights into Britain than any other airline. It also offers a wide variety of domestic flights within the British Isles, including connecting flights from London to most major destinations within the country. BA flies to London from such U.S. gateways as New York, Boston, Washington, D.C., Miami, Chicago, Detroit, Philadelphia, Seattle, Los Angeles, San Francisco, Anchorage, Orlando, Tampa, and Pittsburgh. It even maintains offices in additional cities not directly connected by BA to its other gateways. From Canada, BA services Toronto, Montréal, and Vancouver. It has added a service, a favorite with business travelers, a four-times-a-week nonstop flight between New York and Manchester. For the tourist, this can often serve as an efficient launching pad for tours of the Midlands, including the Shakespeare Country.

All transatlantic service is on wide-bodied jets laden with extra touches, which make an English vacation begin the moment you step aboard. Supersonic transport is available on BA's fleet of seven Concordes, any of which can whisk passengers across the Atlantic at twice the speed of sound.

British Airways offices and their staffs are unusually well qualified to discuss touring in Britain and to make whatever arrangements—hotels, sightseeing, escorted bus trips, and the like—you need. Also, the terminal used by BA at Heathrow (Terminal 4) is considered the most modern and up-to-date terminal at that airport.

LEAST EXPENSIVE "REGULAR" FARES: Currently, your cheapest option with regular airlines falls into two categories: Super APEX and Standby.

Super APEX Fares

This is now the most heavily used fare to London from North America. On most airlines, BA included, APEX tickets are valid for a stay abroad of from 7 to 180 days, and must be purchased at least 21 days in advance. Travel dates in both directions must be reserved at the time of purchase, with a $50 penalty assessed for alterations or cancellations.

For the purpose of APEX travelers (but not for certain other types of tickets), British Airways divides its year into three tariff schedules. The cheapest fares are offered in low season, stretching between November 1 and December 11 and from Christmas Day until the end of March. Shoulder season is slightly more expensive, lasting from April 1 until the end of May and for the entire month of October. High season is the most expensive (and also the most crowded), lasting from June 1 until the end of September. Travel just prior to Christmas (between December 12 and 24) is considered high season.

Standby Fares

Many airlines flying to London offer standby fares sold at the airport on the day of departure, and subject to availability. You'll have to risk waiting hours at the airport to find out whether you're confirmed, and you'll also risk being stranded at the airport for anywhere from one to several days on either leg of your trip if no seats become available. If you're emotionally prepared to hazard those risks, and your travel plans are flexible enough, then a standby ticket might be for you.

Experienced standby passengers usually phone their chosen airline before leaving for the airport in their locale. At British Airways, a standby fare, subject to change, costs $249 each way from New York to either Manchester or London. This type of fare is offered only during high season, when airplanes tend to be heavily booked. Standby hopefuls are served on a first-come, first-flown basis, depending on the availability of space just prior to takeoff.

Economy, First Class, and Supersonic

Anyone flying with a standby or APEX ticket will automatically be seated in the coach section of the well-upholstered aircraft. Passengers unable to meet the restriction imposed by BA on APEX tickets, and who still want to save money, select the regular economy-class fare. Costing more than an APEX ticket, it imposes no restrictions of any kind as to advance purchase or the duration of a passenger's stay.

Of course, first-class seating is considerably upgraded from that available in coach class. Seats are wider, roomier, and more comfortable, expanding into sleeperettes. Business class offers an option midway between coach and first class, making it the preferred choice of frequent travelers.

Finally, for the ultimate splurge, the definitive answer to Charles Lindbergh's 29-hour crossing of the Atlantic, British Airways offers the Concorde. For a hefty surcharge over a regular first-class passage, this supersonic bird will fly you to England and return you to your native shores in record-breaking time and in a style, as well as a price, that the Pilgrims would never have thought possible. Total in-flight time for the crossing is 3 hours and 40 minutes.

THE COMPETITION: Passengers to Britain from North America have a wider choice of airlines than they have to practically any other country in Europe. TWA offers daily service from New York from each of the more than 60 cities it services.

American Airlines offers daily service to Gatwick Airport from Dallas, a city not serviced by British Airways, as well as daily service from Chicago's O'Hare Airport to Manchester.

Pan American makes nonstop runs from New York three times a day, each of which lands at Heathrow Airport. Pan Am also offers daily nonstop service to Heathrow from Detroit, Miami, Los Angeles, and San Francisco, as well as five-times-a-week nonstop service from Seattle to London.

British Caledonian has a daily flight from JFK in New York to London's Gatwick. There are also daily flights to Gatwick from Houston, Dallas/Fort Worth, Los Angeles, and Atlanta.

Northwest Airlines flies nonstop from both Minneapolis and Boston to Gatwick Airport. Flights leave daily from both cities in summer, with slightly reduced service in winter.

Canadians, for the most part, prefer **Air Canada,** whose aircraft depart for London on nonstop flights from Vancouver, Calgary, Edmonton, Toronto, Montréal, and Halifax, after connecting with more than 31 Canadian cities.

THE NO-FRILLS FLIGHT: Only a few years ago, the price difference between the fares charged by the airline industry's giants versus those charged by no-frills new-comers was much wider than it is today. The days of the $99 one-way special to London have gone the way of the dinosaurs, cheap housing, and (regrettably) the safe and attractive $5-a-night hotel. Part of this is a result of the British government's reluctance to undermine their domestic flights with super-cheap competitors. Equally responsible are the rising prices of everything connected with air safety and maintenance.

Many passengers, faced with the bare-bones surroundings of the not-very-much-cheaper no-frills airlines, are opting for the slightly more expensive but much more comfortable flights on the world's better-established airlines.

If you insist on a bare-bones flight, you should investigate **Virgin Atlantic Airways,** which is owned by the same people (Virgin Atlantic Records) who gave the world Boy George and the Culture Club. At press time, the airline charged from $279 to $299 for a one-way passage between New Jersey's Newark Airport and London's Gatwick Airport. Fares depend on the season and the day of the week you intend to fly. Passage must be reserved and paid for at least 21 days before departure from the U.S. A $35 penalty is imposed for each leg of your round-trip ticket you alter or cancel up to 21 days before such departure. Passengers who can afford to be flexible with their scheduling can make a low-season reservation for around $219 each way, but only if they book their flight within seven days of their anticipated departure. The popularity of this ticket usually precludes there being any available space, so if you delay in anticipation of a cheaper fare, you might very easily not be able to make a reservation of any kind.

In 1985, Virgin Atlantic initiated service between Miami International Airport and Gatwick, with up to five flights a week. With a 21-day advance booking, one-way fares range from $297 to $320 each way, depending on the day of departure. In some cases, this is no less expensive than similar fares offered by British Airways. For more information, check with your travel agent or call 212/242-1330 in the New York area. From other parts of the U.S., call toll free by dialing 800/862-8621.

2. By Ship

Traveling by air sometimes brings cultures jarringly close to one another, allowing only a few hours to elapse before total immersion in a different lifestyle. Because of that, you might find sea travel in either direction a distinctive and restful way to collect your thoughts and feelings before or after the onslaught of your British experience.

This means of travel is for those who crave a sea experience, either on a luxury liner with resort-level facilities or else on a more relaxed, time-consuming freighter. Here is a description of the major service offered from the Atlantic seaboard to various ports in England (most often Southampton, where you'll pay a small debarkation fee):

The **Cunard Line,** 555 Fifth Ave., New York, NY 10017 (tel. 212/880-7500), boasts the *Queen Elizabeth 2* as its flagship—self-styled, quite accurately, as "the most advanced ship of the age." It is the only ocean-going liner providing regular transatlantic service—more than 20 sailings a year from April to December—between New York, Cherbourg, France, and Southampton, England. Designed for extended cruises, the *QE-2* is reaching a younger market, those leery of the traditional liner-type crossing. Hence, you'll find four swimming pools, a sauna, nightclubs, a balconied theater, an art gallery, cinemas, chic boutiques (including the world's first sea-going branch of Harrods), as well as four restaurants, a gymnasium, paddle tennis courts, and a children's playroom staffed with English nannies.

The tempting lifestyle available on the ship includes access to an on-board branch of California's Golden Door Health Spa, a computer learning center with 16 IBM personal computers, seminars by trained professionals on astrology, cooking, art, fitness, and medicine, and a Festival of Life series that introduces you to such personalities as Larry Hagman and Meryl Streep.

Fares are extremely complicated, based on the desirability of the cabin and the season of sailing. I suggest that you call your travel agent or a Cunard representative at their toll-free number (tel. 800/221-4770). In New York City, call 212/661-7777.

One of the most popular packages offered is the air/sea trip. On it, you cross in one direction by air and sail the other direction. The round-trip fares for this air/sea passage depend on the time of year and the size and opulence of your cabin. British Airways serves some 30 gateways in North America through which you can start or end your trip. However, conditions strictly state that the amount of time spent abroad cannot exceed 20 days for transatlantic-class passengers and 40 days for first-class passengers.

A series of maneuvers as to scheduling is possible, but in thrift season, roughly defined as early spring and late autumn, sailings usually cost a minimum of $1,350 in transatlantic class and around $2,500 in first class. Prices go up from there and can reach to a maximum of $6,555 per person. For a supplement of $699, you can fly the Concorde on one of the legs of your trip. All passengers pay a $70 port tax for each direction of sailing regardless of the options chosen.

The Cunard Line divides its sailing year into thrift, intermediate, and high season. The prices quoted by Cunard are per person, based on double occupancy.

3. Traveling Within England

BY AIR: Most of the airports of the United Kingdom are connected by **British Air-**

ways into one almost continuous network. The most popular routes (between London and Manchester, Glasgow, Edinburgh, and Belfast) benefit from shuttle services, leaving Heathrow Terminal 1 on more than 35 flights daily. More information, of course, can be obtained from a travel agent or by getting in touch with British Airways directly.

BY TRAIN: There is something magical about traveling on a train in Britain. You sit in comfortable compartments on upholstered seats, next to the British. You're served your meal in the dining car like an aristocrat, and the entire experience can be a relaxing interlude.

You should, of course, be warned that *your Eurailpass is not valid on trains in Great Britain*. The cost of rail travel here can be quite low, particularly if you take advantage of certain cost-saving travel plans, some of which can only be purchased in North America, before leaving for England.

BritRail Pass

This pass gives unlimited rail travel in England, Scotland and Wales, and is valid on all British Rail routes, with some 15,000 trains to more than 2,000 destinations. A seven-day economy-class pass, as of 1987, cost $115 for one person, rising to $160 in first class. A 14-day pass was $175 in economy, $245 in first class; a 21-day pass, $220 and $310; and a one-month ticket, $260 and $365.

Children up to 5 years of age travel free, and those from 5 to 15 travel at half the adult rate either with passes or regular tickets. The **youth rates** in economy class are $95 for 7 days, $150 for 14 days, $190 for 21 days, and $225 for a month.

BritRail also offers a **Senior Citizen Pass** to persons 65 or older. This is a first-class pass, but passengers pay less than the adult fare: $135 for seven days, $210 for 14 days, $265 for 21 days, and $310 for one month. Prices for BritRail Passes are higher for Canadian travelers.

BritRail Passes cannot be obtained in England, but should be secured before leaving North America either through travel agents or by writing to or visiting BritRail Travel International in the U.S. at 630 Third Ave., New York, NY 10017; Suite 603, 800 S. Hope St., Los Angeles, CA 90017; 333 N. Michigan Ave., Chicago, IL 60601; or Cedar Maple Plaza, 2305 Cedar Springs, Dallas, TX 75201. Canadians can write to 94 Cumberland St., Toronto M5R 1A3, ON, or 409 Granville St., Vancouver V6C 1T2, BC.

BritRail Passes do not have to be predated. Validate your pass at any British Rail station when you start your first rail journey. Travel can be made on all scheduled BritRail trains, including intercity high-speed 125 mph trains. The passes are all good for trips made on consecutive days from the time of validation. Seat reservations, usually obtainable on the day you travel, cost an additional $3 per person per trip. They are essential for some trains on certain peak days such as holidays and on Saturday in summer.

BritRail Seapass

In general terms, purchasers of a BritRail Pass wishing to travel one way or round trip between London and Ireland or London and continental Europe by Sealink services can purchase an extension of their BritRail Pass carrying one or two coupons, according to requirements. The one-way fare to continental Europe is $31 added to your BritRail Pass price, while a one-way ticket to take you to Ireland will cost $43 in addition to your pass price.

Furthermore, if the appropriate supplement is paid, the coupons are valid for all services operated by Sealink or Seaspeed and are not tied to the validity of the associated BritRail Pass. For example, a traveler may arrive in Ireland, use one coupon for the journey to London, stay several days, validate the BritRail Pass and travel for its duration, and then return to London for another period of time before traveling from London to a continental European port.

Special Bargain Fares

British Rail from time to time offers special round-trip fares for optional travel and weekend travel, which may only be purchased in Great Britain. Because of the changing nature of these fares and facilities, it is not possible to give information about them to travelers from abroad. Information may be obtained from travel agents and British Rail stations in Great Britain.

If you're in London, and want more information on transportation rates, schedules, or facilities, go to the **British Travel Centre,** Rex House, 4–12 Lower Regent St., S.W.1 (tel. 01/730-3400), only a few minutes' walk from Piccadilly Circus. This office deals only with inquiries made in person. Don't try to telephone for information. The office is open from 9 a.m. to 6:30 p.m. Monday to Saturday, 10 a.m. to 4:30 p.m. Sunday. You can also make reservations and purchase rail tickets there and at the British Travel Centres at Oxford Street, Victoria Station, the Strand, King William Street, Heathrow Airport, and the main London stations—Waterloo, King's Cross, Euston, Victoria, and Paddington—where each deals mainly with its own region. For general information, call the appropriate station. All numbers are listed in the telephone directory.

The Britainshrinkers

This is a bonanza for travelers who want to make several quickie trips into the heart of England without having to check out of their hotel room in London. Scheduled full-day tours are offered from April 1 to October 31, as well as several overnight excursions into Scotland and Wales. The journeys are operated by Road 'n' Rail Tours Ltd. in cooperation with British Rail. You're whisked out of London by train to your destination, where you hop on a waiting bus to visit the various sights during the day. You have a light lunch in a local pub, and there is also free time to shop or explore. A guide accompanies the tour from London and back. Your return is in time for dinner or the theater. Included in the rates are entrance fees and VAT.

On a one-day trip, you can visit Warwick Castle, Stratford-upon-Avon, and Coventry Cathedral at a cost of £43 ($64.50) for adults, £28 ($42) for children up to 16 years old. One of the most heavily booked tours is to Bath and Stonehenge, taking in Salisbury Cathedral, costing £44 ($66) for adults, £30 ($45) for children. A BritRail Pass can save you up to 45% on the prices quoted. For more information about Britainshrinkers, write to 10 Queen St., London WIX 7PD. You can also call 01/629-2525, even on weekends, providing you do so before 4:30 p.m.

CAR RENTALS: Once you get over the initial awkwardness of driving on the left-hand side, you'll quickly discover that the best way to see the real Britain is to have a car while you're there.

All you need to rent a car from most companies in England is to be older than 21 and in possession of a valid driver's license. You should also possess a major credit card or be prepared to make a cash deposit at the time of pickup. Underaged drivers will be happy to note that they can rent a car at age 18 from English branches of Hertz. But Hertz charges more for similar cars than does Budget Rent-a-Car, for example.

There are many car-rental services in England in addition to Budget and Hertz. These include Avis and a fine, lesser known company, Kemwel. There are also dozens of British-owned car-rental firms, including Godfrey Davis Europcar (affiliated with the U.S.-based National Car Rental). Most of these firms charge rates comparable to those of their American-affiliated competitors.

Among the major U.S.-based firms with branches in England, **Budget Rent-a-Car** is the most economical. As part of my continuing policy of using various firms and reporting on them, I recently used Budget in updating this guide. My prerental research revealed them to be less expensive than Avis, Godfrey Davis, or Hertz. The quality of the vehicle I rented was top-notch, while the number of days of advance reservation to qualify for Budget's lower rates was only two days instead of the seven required by their competitors. As of this writing, Budget's weekly rental of its cheapest car, a small vehicle (Ford Fiesta size), was £92.50 ($138.75) per week with unlimited mileage. You receive guaranteed price, whatever the rate of exchange, if you prepay the charge and get a voucher from Budget or at one of many travel agents in the United States and Canada. Reservations can be made in the United States by calling toll free 800/527-0700. All car-rental firms in England impose a 15% government tax. If you want a better car, Budget maintains sizable fleets of bigger and more luxurious cars at attractively competitive rates. If you encounter difficulties on the road, Budget maintains a 24-hour-a-day number within Britain that you can call for emergency assistance.

Car Insurance

The amount of public liability, personal liability, and property damage insurance written into most contracts seems adequate for the average driver. In general, most of the major firms have standard contracts. However, some small firms have different arrangements, and if you rent from one of them, it pays to ask questions.

I recommend that you purchase a "waiver"—usually about £6 ($9) per day—which will cover some £600 ($900) deductible should you be involved in an accident. Additional personal accident insurance, usually £1.25 ($1.88) per day, is another good idea.

Driver's License and Auto Clubs

To drive a car in Britain, your passport and your own driver's license must be presented along with your deposit; no special British license is needed. The prudent driver will secure a copy of the *Highway Code,* available from almost any stationer or news agent. It is now compulsory to wear a seatbelt if you're in the front seat of a car or minibus, either as a driver or passenger.

Although not mandatory, a membership in one of the two major auto clubs in England can be helpful: the **Automobile Association** and the **Royal Automobile Club.** The headquarters of the AA are at Fanum House, Basingstoke, Hampshire (tel. 0256/20123); the RAC offices are at RAC House, Lansdowne Road, Croydon, Surrey CR9 2JA (tel. 01/686-2525). Membership in one of these clubs is usually handled by the agent from whom you rent your car. Upon joining, you'll be given a key to the many telephone boxes you see along the road, so that you can phone for help in an emergency.

Fuel

Gasoline, called petrol by the English, is usually sold by the liter, with 4.5 liters making up their imperial gallon. Most pumps show a list of prices and measures. You'll probably have to serve yourself at the petrol station. In some remote areas, especially in Scotland, stations are few and far between, and many all over the country are closed on Sunday.

BUSES IN ENGLAND: For the traveler who wants to see the country as even a train cannot reveal it but who can't afford to rent a car or doesn't trust his or her driving skills on British roads, the old, reliable, and inexpensive (about half the cost of rail travel) bus, or "coach" as it's called here, offers a fine form of transportation. While the trains do go everywhere, passing through towns and villages, they rarely bring you into contact with country life, and they almost never carry you across the high (main) streets of the villages, as the buses do. Moreover, distances between towns in England are usually short, so your chances of tiring are lessened. Every remote village is reachable by bus.

The **express motorcoach network** covers the greater part of Britain. It links hamlets, towns, and cities with frequent schedules, convenient timetables, and efficient operation in all seasons. Most places off the main route can be easily reached by stopping and switching to a local bus. Fares are relatively cheap, making travel on the express motorcoach network economical.

The departure point from London for most of the bus lines is **Victoria Coach Station,** 164 Buckingham Palace Rd., S.W.1 (tel. 01/730-0202), which is a block up from Victoria Railroad Station. You'll be well advised to have reservations for the express buses. The locals can usually be boarded on the spot.

Britexpress Card

This offers one-third off all adult journey tickets purchased on Britain's Express Coach Network, valid for a 30-day period throughout the year. Travel where and when you wish with a choice of 1,500 destinations. All it costs is £10 ($15) for a discount card to travel around the network. Other bonuses are Flightline (Heathrow and Gatwick Airport services to London) and Jetlink (Heathrow to Gatwick Airport services) which offer similar discounts. The Britexpress Card can be purchased from your U.S. travel agent or on your arrival in London at the Victoria Coach Station. Examples of some approximate one-way fares and travel times are: London-Edinburgh, £12.50 ($18.75), time 9 hours; London–Stratford-upon-Avon, £8 ($12), time 3 hours 10 minutes; London-York (Rapide Service), £13.50 ($20.25), time 4½ hours; London-Cambridge, £6 ($9), time 1 hour 50 minutes.

British Bus Tourist Trail

Offered from June to October, the Tourist Trail connects ten towns and cities (London, Cambridge, Lincoln, York, Durham, Edinburgh, Windermere, Chester, Stratford-upon-Avon, and Oxford). You can make an unlimited number of trips within a 15-day period (from the date of your first journey), starting where you want to and stopping off as you choose. Nicer still may be the price: only £75 ($112.50). With a Britexpress Card, the holder can purchase a Tourist Trail ticket on arrival in the United Kingdom for £62 ($93).

Other Bus Service

For journeys within a roughly 35-mile radius of London, including such major attractions as Windsor, Hampton Court, Chartwell, and Hatfield House, try the **London Country Green Line** bus service. Personal callers can go to the Green Line Enquiry Office at Eccleston Bridge, Victoria, London, S.W.1 (off Buckingham Palace Road), where combined travel and admission tickets can be bought. Phone 01/668-7261 for more information.

Golden Rover tickets cost £3.95 ($5.93) per person, available for one day's travel on most London Country and Green Line routes, but not their Jetlink and Flightline buses connecting London and the airports. It is possible to cover quite a large area around London and into the country for a very small cost. For more precise information on routes, fares, and schedules, write to **London Country Bus Services Ltd.,** Lesbourne Road, Reigate, Surrey RH2 7LE (tel. 07372/42411). The Country Bus Lines ring the heart of London. They never go into the center of the capital, although they hook up with the routes of the red buses and the Green Line coaches that do. You can get free maps of Country Buses from the Lesbourne Road offices.

BICYCLES: If you choose this form of transportation, you may want to join the **Cyclists' Touring Club,** Cotterell House, 69 Meadrow, Godalming, Surrey (tel. 04868/7212). It costs £13.50 ($21) to join, with membership being good for one year. The club helps with information and provides maps, insurance, touring routes, and a list of low-cost accommodations, including farmhouses, inns, guesthouses, and even private homes that cater especially to cyclists.

MOTORCYCLES: These are real money-savers in this land of steep petrol (gas) prices, if you don't mind getting drenched occasionally. **Scootabout Limited,** 59 Albert Embankment, S.E.1 (tel. 01/582-0055), just a minute's walk from the Vauxhall Underground station, is the only motorcycle-rental company in London insured to rent to North Americans. They can also arrange for European travel on their vehicles. You can pick up a Moped by the day, week, or month. These are four-stroke, fully automatic motors with a kick-start and a twist throttle grip. They get more than 150 miles to the gallon, and prices are inclusive of VAT, insurance, helmet rental, and carrier, as well as unlimited mileage and RAC membership. A Moped costs £10.95 ($16.43) for the day, decreasing to £7.80 ($11.70) per day on a weekly rental. For vehicles from 125cc to 750cc, renters must possess valid motorcycle licenses from their own countries. A £50 ($75) deposit is required for vehicles of 50cc, 70cc, 125cc, and 200cc. A £100 ($150) deposit is required for vehicles of 500cc and 750cc. The deposit is refunded on a no-damage-done return of the vehicle:

BACKPACKING: For those who prefer to rely on their own two legs and savor the countryside at close quarters, the **Backpackers' Club,** 20 St. Michael's Rd., Tilehurst, Reading, Berkshire RG3 4RP (tel. 0734/428754), has information concerning the main routes—along Offa's Dyke, the border between England and Wales, the North and South Downs Ways, and the Pennine Way through the Yorkshire Dales and across Hadrian's Wall, to name only a few.

HITCHHIKING: It is not illegal and is normally quite safe and practical. It is, however, illegal for pedestrians to be on motorways. The cleaner and tidier you look, the better your chance. Have a sign with your destination written on it. It helps, of course, not to be overloaded with backpacks and luggage.

WHERE TO GO: It takes weeks to tour England thoroughly, and many readers do just that, either by car, train, or bus. However, others are much more rushed and will need to direct their limited sightseeing time carefully. **London** is targeted at the top of every first-time visitor's list. Even those on the most rushed of schedules generally fit in **Windsor Castle,** lying about an hour's train ride from central London. For many, that's it! Then they're off to Paris or other places on the continent.

However, those with more time will want to go to the south of England, the very cradle of English history, centering their exploration around the cathedral city of **Canterbury,** some 65 miles to the southeast of London. It can be done on a rushed day trip. I'd suggest two nights there, however: one day for Canterbury, another day for exploring some of the historic homes of Kent, including Knole, a showplace of England, lying in the village of Sevenoaks, about 25 miles from Central London, and Churchill's home, Chartwell, 1½ miles south of Westerham. Those with yet a third night to spend in the south can go to **Rye,** the old Cinque port near the English Channel, 65 miles south of London.

The second most popular jaunt is to **Stratford-upon-Avon** and the university city of **Oxford.** At the very minimum this should take up to two nights. The first night can be spent at Oxford, 57 miles northwest of London, and the second night at Stratford-upon-Avon, 40 miles northwest from Oxford, a total distance of 92 miles from London. Those with one or two more nights to spend in Stratford-upon-Avon can use it as a base for day trips to Warwick Castle, Kenilworth Castle, Sulgrave Manor (ancestral home of George Washington), and Coventry Cathedral.

My favorite tour—and perhaps yours too—might be to the fabled **West Country**

MILEAGE BETWEEN CITIES AND TOWNS
Distance in Miles

	Berwick-upon-Tweed	Birmingham	Blackpool	Bournemouth	Brighton	Bristol	Cambridge	Carlisle	Dover	Exeter	Gloucester	Great Yarmouth	Harwich	Kingston-upon-Hull	Land's End	Leeds	Leicester	Lincoln	Liverpool	LONDON	Newcastle upon Tyne	Norwich	Nottingham	Oxford	Plymouth	Portsmouth	Sheffield	Shrewsbury	Southampton	York
York	148	130	96	269	245	211	150	121	264	287	176	201	288	37	411	24	108	75	99	193	84	181	77	181	338	258	52	133	245	
Southampton	388	128	251	31	61	77	131	324	143	105	93	205	153	256	228	232	137	188	150	77	324	193	162	64	151	21	199	170		
Shrewsbury	265	45	98	185	208	103	145	176	221	179	79	225	220	146	303	109	84	119	58	150	205	205	82	106	225	185	82			
Sheffield	190	76	86	216	211	161	120	152	230	237	126	166	187	65	361	33	62	96	72	159	125	146	37	135	283	212				
Portsmouth	401	141	264	52	48	99	124	337	130	118	108	198	146	269	241	241	150	201	234	70	337	164	175	77	164					
Plymouth	474	203	328	128	212	122	263	399	289	46	157	343	294	355	79	316	242	293	283	218	410	343	267	185						
Oxford	324	64	187	90	99	74	83	260	128	142	52	156	126	192	274	168	73	124	157	57	260	145	98							
Nottingham	221	50	111	183	174	145	83	181	193	221	110	142	150	90	345	70	25	35	98	131	157	122								
Norwich	328	166	232	214	161	221	68	289	174	282	186	20	73	182	421	176	119	105	220	114	264									
LONDON	338	105	226	100	52	115	54	301	71	172	109	128	76	206	237	189	97	131	202											
Liverpool	219	93	49	234	234	161	168	120	273	237	126	240	235	130	361	55	100	118												
Lincoln	224	90	128	209	183	171	85	181	202	247	136	128	155	44	371	55	51													
Leicester	252	39	140	158	149	120	68	206	168	196	85	140	135	121	320	95														
Leeds	156	113	72	255	241	194	145	119	260	270	159	159	244	58	394															
Land's End	552	281	405	205	289	200	334	477	366	123	235	420	371	421																
Gloucester	318	56	174	99	133	35	123	237	180	111																				
Exeter	428	157	282	82	166	76	220	353	248																					
Dover	409	176	297	174	82	186	125	372																						
Carlisle	89	196	87	343	353	277	264																							
Cambridge	294	100	208	154	106	144																								
Bristol	352	81	204	82	137																									
Brighton	390	163	286	92																										
Bournemouth	412	147	270																											
Blackpool	193	121																												
Birmingham	264																													

of England, taking in Winchester, Salisbury, the New Forest, and the old spa at Bath. Bath is considered by many to be the most outstanding place to visit in the west of England. Your first night can be spent in Salisbury, which is a base for exploring the prehistoric ruins of Stonehenge on the Salisbury Plain. Salisbury is an 83-mile drive from London. From Salisbury, you can head north to Bath, that Georgian city on a bend of the River Avon, a distance of some 115 miles from London.

After that, those with three or four days remaining can either head southwest of Bath, taking in Devon and Cornwall, perhaps the single two most charming counties of England, or can head north to the Cotswolds, the rolling hills and old wool towns that always seem to enchant. I've left out the Lake District, Cambridge, East Anglia, the cathedral city of York, and many, many more places. But that's what this book is about. As I said, it will take weeks.

BARGAIN SIGHTSEEING TIPS: An organization similar to the National Trust, **English Heritage,** is a foundation set up by the government (but independent of it) to care for more than 400 sites open to the public throughout the country. On their books in London are such important attractions as the Tower of London, Kensington Palace, and Hampton Court. Membership in the society gives you an annual season ticket for free entrance to all their sites, together with a map and regular up-to-the-minute information on activities and innovations. Even if you don't plan to tour the country, membership will provide information and free entrance to a number of attractions in and around the London area. Membership is £9.50 ($14.75) for adults. You can also purchase a family ticket covering both parents and all children under 16 for £19.50 ($29.25) per year. Join when you are in England at any English Heritage property or write to English Heritage, Membership Department, P.O. Box 43, Ruislip, Middlesex HA4 OXW, England (tel. 01/734-6010).

An **Open to View ticket** sells for $24 (U.S.) for adults, $11.50 for children, and includes free admission to more than 500 properties in Britain, including Churchill's Chartwell, Woburn Abbey, Hampton Court Palace, and Windsor Castle. It is good for one month after you first use it, and covers all properties in care of Britain's National Trust and those run by the Department of the Environment. It is estimated that anyone visiting as many as seven of these sightseeing attractions will get back the initial outlay. In the U.S., inquire at BritRail Travel International at addresses listed above under BritRail Pass.

TOURS: Many questions arise for persons planning their first trip to the British Isles as well as to other European destinations. Sometimes a prospective traveler isn't sure what he or she really wants to see in England, aside, of course, from the Tower of London and Big Ben. Troublesome thoughts that arise often are: How do I plan my trip to be sure of seeing the most outstanding sights of the country? How much of a problem will I have in trying to get from place to place, complete with luggage? Am I too old to embark on such a journey, perhaps alone? Will I meet people who share my interests with whom to chat and compare notes?

My answer to all these questions, indeed, my advice to many people going to England and/or other European countries for the first time is simply: Go on a good tour. By this I don't mean simply a tour of one city or of one building. I refer to a vacation tour where you and your needs will be looked after from your arrival at Heathrow or Gatwick in England or wherever to your departure en route back to the United States. Choose a tour suited to the time you have for your trip, the money you can spend, and the places you want to go.

One of the best operators of such trips I have observed is **Trafalgar Tours Limited,** 15 Grosvenor Place, London SW1X 7HH, England (tel. 01/235-7090), with offices in the U.S. and Canada. The New York office is at 21 East 26th St., New York, NY 10010 (tel. 212/689-8977). In the U.S., you can call toll free, 800/854-0103.

Trafalgar has an exceptional schedule of tours of England, with Scotland, Wales, and/or Ireland included on some itineraries, with trips ranging from four to 22 days in length and at prices of anywhere from around $250 to $1,350, not counting your air fare. The prices, of course, vary with the destinations and the length of time spent.

When you return home, you can talk knowledgeably about Stonehenge, Coventry, the Rows of Chester, the Shambles in York, and the Lake District, beloved of poets and prose writers for generations. Perhaps you'll see where the Pilgrim Fathers embarked for the New World, baths where Roman aristocrats happily steamed and exchanged ideas, and the places where Shakespeare lived and loved. It will help you enjoy your tour more if you take along a copy of this guide, which gives the background of areas you'll see, where to shop, and other practical information. You may please your fellow tour members by taking them to a cozy pub you find recommended in these pages.

The great advantage of such tours, particularly for persons who are hesitant about setting out alone or as a couple to foreign shores, is that everything is arranged for you—transportation in Europe, hotels, services, sightseeing trips, excursions, luggage handling, tips and taxes, and many of your meals. But you're not led around like a little lamb. Plenty of time is provided on most trips for shopping, recreation, or brief side trips, perhaps to see the little town where your grandmother was born. I see many travelers on such tours clutching a Frommer guide to keep track of what they're seeing or want to see.

Whether you have a few days or several weeks for your trip, don't put off your England experience just because you're too timid or afraid to go. You're sure to meet some congenial people in your tour group, a number of whom may have had the very mental reservations you've had about setting off on such a journey. And you'll be glad you went.

Chapter II

INTRODUCING ENGLAND

1. The English
2. The Culture
3. Food and Drink
4. The ABCs of England

WHY GO TO ENGLAND? This is an easy and difficult question to answer. Millions of words have been written by some of the world's greatest writers who share my conviction that among all the countries of the world that one needs to savor and explore in a lifetime, England ranks near the top. I must speak of my own indelibly felt enthusiasm. I have cultural roots in the heritage of England—as do many other readers of this book—but my affection for England goes beyond my own "roots." In fact many of the world's greatest Anglophiles have no ancestral link to England at all.

The cultural side of England is a powerful lure. Once there, you can visit a people who have played a dynamic role in history. These islanders have shaped much of the character and customs of the world and have given it a great language. This in itself is surprising, since the English live in a cramped space and lack many natural resources. Perhaps for that very reason, they learned early to rely on a special resource: their wits.

Fortunately for latter-day pilgrims to England, the years and centuries have left a clear trail of former glory. Traveling around the country is similar to experiencing a living, illustrated history book. This is true whether you stop and ponder over the ancient mystery of Stonehenge, relive the days of the Romans when you walk through an excavated villa, hear the influence of the Celtic language in the accent of the Cornish people, or witness evidence of the cultures brought by the Danes, the Normans, the Germans, and now the Americans and Canadians. I find it amazing how these islanders have handled the outside forces brought to bear on them. In their own way and in their own time, they have absorbed them and made them distinctly English.

There is so much to thrill you. You can stand in the inner courtyard of the Tower of London and see where Lady Jane Grey was beheaded, or you can walk through Westminster Abbey, treading on the stone grave markers of such unforgettable men as Disraeli, Newton, Darwin, Chaucer, Kipling. You can visit the homes of many of the legendary figures of literary history, including Samuel Johnson, Charles Dickens, Shakespeare, and Emily Brontë. Attending an English court of law will give you a firsthand experience with one of the greatest systems of justice the world has ever known. The country's innumerable museums bring you quickly in touch with history-making events of the past. You can see and almost feel the treasures (plundered loot, as critics have called it) from Greece and Egypt; the important documents of musical, literary, and political figures. Here are the early Bibles, the Magna Carta, and the personal letters of Shelley. Here in England are two of the world's foremost universities, Oxford and Cambridge, which can be visited for a view of that unique educational system which has produced some of the world's greatest leaders and thinkers.

You will like the convenience of seeing so much in such a small area. America has treasures of history and geography, but the vastness of the United States can make it a lifetime project to visit them all. But in England, as you travel through fishing hamlets, villages, country lanes, cathedral cities, in an hour you have moved into a different region. For one thing, this is an island of widely varying geography, from the mountainous Lake District, the rolling hills of the Cotswolds, the Holland-like canals in Lincoln, the marsh areas of the Norfolk Broads, to the moody Lorna Doone country with its rugged hills and coastline.

England is marked by fascinating building styles, from the most imposing and romantic of moated castles to splendid country manor houses, with their highly cultivated gardens, to churches and cathedrals that are an art in themselves. The architecture of England is a direct reflection of the inner spirit. Soaring Gothic-arched churches with their stained-glass windows have been erected in nearly every city. People living in the country have built houses native to their surroundings that are sheer perfection in their combination of beauty and utility, be it a thatched cottage in a flower-filled lane in Devon or a half-timbered house in Stratford-upon-Avon.

Whether you're sports-oriented or a more contemplative traveler, you'll find the English calendar loaded with events. You can attend one of the Bard's plays at Stratford-upon-Avon, go on a canal ride through the Midlands, take a trip on a houseboat, or spend a week at a farm in the West Country, riding over hills and dales, perhaps joining a foxhunt. There is boat racing to watch at Cambridge and Henley-on-Thames, or you can walk across a Yorkshire moor. You can sample true English fare at hundreds of ancient inns and pubs or visit one of the stately homes of England, later strolling through spectacular gardens (the English, as the world knows, are great gardeners). Perhaps a swim in one of the hidden coves on the Cornish coast will lead you into a summer day. Whatever your interests or desires, England can usually accommodate you.

Best of all are the English people themselves. Like all the peoples of the world, they have their share of devils, but you are likely to be surprised by the warmth and graciousness of the average man or woman. Added to this is their amazing variety of artistic accomplishment—not only in their literature, but in their art, as exemplified by the sculpture of Henry Moore. The theater of London is stimulating and refreshing. You'll want to attend concerts, festivals, even country fairs, and you'll find that both the ballet and opera are alive, vital, and worth experiencing. You'll be fascinated by the English fascination with their sports—with cricket, football, racing, tennis, skating, sailing, hockey, or hiking.

Certainly you won't be able to do everything in just one trip. You'll want to come back for a second, a third, and most definitely a fourth visit.

1. The English

The British Isles have been a melting pot of races since prehistoric times, as attested by artifacts and traces of settlements.

HISTORY: Until about 6,000 years before Christ, Britain was probably part of the continent of Europe. It was split off by the continental drift and other natural forces, but even after the split people on the mainland could look across to what was now a big island. Pressed by marauders from the east or simply seeking living room for their increasing tribes, some brave souls made their way across the often wild waters of the channel. Some came, too, simply seeking plunder.

The earliest inhabitants of the British Isles of whom archeologists are certain were a small, dark people known as Iberians, also called pre-Celts. They are believed to have created Stonehenge before 500 B.C., when the early Celts, blond, often blue-eyed, poured in from the coastal areas of Europe, from Denmark to northern Italy. The Iberians who survived the bloody assaults of these invaders fled to the Scottish Highlands and the mountain fastholds of Wales, where some of their descendants live today.

In 54 B.C., the Romans, led by Julius Caesar, invaded Britain, where they believed they would find precious metals. The land was heavily wooded from the south of what is today England to the north coast of Scotland, with treeless areas around marshes and on hills and moors. The Britons resisted the onslaught of Roman troops but lacked the leadership and war experience to prevent the takeover. The Romans took all of the southern part of the island, from the Cheviot Hills in Scotland to the English Channel, and added it to the Roman Empire by A.D. 43. During almost four centuries of occupation, they built roads, villas, towns, walls, and fortresses, farmed the land, and introduced first their pagan religions and then Christianity. Agriculture and trade flourished, and the lives of the people were lastingly influenced.

After the withdrawal of Roman legions around A.D. 410, waves of Jutes, Angles, and Saxons flocked in from German lands, establishing themselves in small "kingdoms" throughout the formerly Roman colony. From the 8th through the 11th centuries, the old newcomers came into conflict with Danish raiders for control of the land.

The Battle of Hastings in 1066, when William the Conqueror invaded from Normandy and defeated the last Anglo-Saxon king, Harold, has probably become familiar to almost every American school child.

The Norman rulers were on the throne from 1066 to 1154, when the first of the Plantagenets, Henry II (that "friend" of Thomas à Becket), was crowned. That line held power until 1399. During this period, in 1215 King John was forced by his nobles to sign the Magna Carta, guaranteeing rights and the rule of law, and laying the foundations of the parliamentary system.

In 1399, the Lancastrians took the throne, their reign marked by defeat in the Hundred Years' War in which they tried to cement claims to lands in France. Opposing the Lancastrians at home and wanting the crown also was the House of York. Dissension between these claimants led to the War of the Roses, the red rose representing Lancaster and the white rose York. By 1461, the House of York had seized power, but the war continued. It was during this time that the boy king, Edward V, and his younger brother were murdered in the Tower of London, a crime still laid by some at the door of their uncle Richard III, who later became king.

In 1485 Richard III was slain at the Battle of Bosworth Field, ending the War of the Roses and placing the first Tudor on the throne. That king, Henry VII, was followed by his son, Henry VIII, whose daughter, Elizabeth I, eventually succeeded to the crown. Henry VII curbed the powers of the barons, established reforms of the legal system, gave more importance to the landed gentry, and improved England's economic situation. Henry VIII's excesses and exploits are well known: He married six times, and he split with the Roman Catholic Church, establishing the Church of England. Of his wives, two were beheaded, two were set aside, one died in childbirth, and one survived him. The dissolution of the monasteries brought the riches of the abbots and bishops pouring into the coffers of Henry and his associates and the property formerly owned by the church was placed mostly in lay hands.

Elizabeth I managed to walk a risky line between Catholic and Protestant dissidents but held to the latter faith. In her reign England became a major naval power, defeating the Spanish Armada, founding the first colonies in the New World, and establishing a vigorous trade with the Orient and Europe. Also Scotland was united with England, and the son of Mary Queen of Scots, whom Elizabeth had had beheaded, came to the throne as James I of England and James VI of Scotland.

Thus ended the Tudor dynasty. The Stuarts came to power in the year 1603, holding it until Charles I was beheaded in 1649. During this era, the *Mayflower* sailed for the New World, and dissatisfaction with the established Church of England, as well as with what many saw as Papist leanings by the monarchs, created a time of great stress in England. Parliament and the Stuart kings came into conflict, resulting in a bloody civil war between Parliamentarian troops led by Oliver Cromwell and Royalists who were on the side of King Charles. The Royalists lost the war, the king lost his head, and in 1649 the Puritan Commonwealth was established, with Cromwell as Lord Protector.

The Commonwealth lasted until 1660, when Stuart King Charles II came to the throne. The monarchy was restored, but troubles still beset the people of the country. The Great Plague wiped out thousands of lives in 1665–1666, and the Great Fire destroyed large portions of London in 1666.

In 1688, the so-called Glorious Revolution removed Catholic King James II from the throne and crowned in his place William of Orange and his wife, Mary, James's daughter. A Bill of Rights was signed by the monarchs, settling once and for all the question which had been at the very root of the Civil War: the king was king by will of Parliament, not by divine right from God.

The Hanoverian dynasty came into power in 1727. Britain had many ups and downs under the House of Hanover. Canada was won from the French, the British Indian Empire was firmly entrenched through the redoubtable Clive of India, the Boston Tea Party marked the start of the American Revolution, Captain Cook claimed Australia and New Zealand for England, and the British became embroiled in the Napoleonic Wars. This was the time of glory for two of the country's great leaders: Admiral Lord Horatio Nelson and the Duke of Wellington, the one at Trafalgar and the other at Waterloo.

Perhaps the single most important change in all this period, from the point of view of the "commoner," was the Industrial Revolution, which transformed the lives forever of the laboring class and brought great wealth to persons of the middle class. The loss of the American colonies probably had little effect on the day by day pursuits of the average English person.

The reign of Queen Victoria, which began in 1837, saw great progress in the country. Trade unions were formed, a universal public school system was developed, industrialization and urbanization spread, and railroads swept to almost every section of the British Isles. So impressed was Parliament with the glories of the empire that it declared Victoria empress, not just queen, reigning over large parts of Africa and Asia. When Edward VII succeeded to the throne in 1901, the country entered the 20th century with the advent of the telephone and the motorcar, which again changed the lifestyle and thinking of everybody.

In 1910 the Windsors took the sovereignty, leading the nation through World War I (George V), the abdication before his coronation of the man who would have been King Edward VIII (he became the Duke of Windsor in order to marry the American divorcee, Wallis Simpson), and on through World War II (George VI).

During these years came the blitz, the Dunkirk evacuation in 1941, and the successful D-Day operation which placed the Allies firmly on the road to defeating Hitler. These events have been kept alive through documentaries, movies, and the memories of those who participated. Winston Churchill had his finest hour as prime minister in those perilous times.

Queen Elizabeth II came to the throne on the death of her father in 1952. Since then, Britain has joined the NATO alliance and the Common Market—and Big Ben still chimes the hours outside the Houses of Parliament.

GOVERNMENT: The United Kingdom of Great Britain and Northern Ireland (that's its name), comprises England, Wales, Scotland, and Northern Ireland. It is governed by a constitutional monarchy, the head of state being Queen Elizabeth II. The head of government, however, is the prime minister, who is selected by the majority party in Parliament but is then requested by the queen to form a government, i.e., to take charge and name cabinet members to head the various branches of that government.

Parliament is technically three separate entities: the sovereign, the House of Lords, and the House of Commons. The "government" consists of the prime minister and the cabinet members (who must be members of Parliament). The queen's function is chiefly ceremonial. There are two main political parties, Conservative and Labour. The Conservatives present themselves as champions of free enterprise and freedom of the individual to make his or her own decisions, with some government support. Labour tends toward more state ownership and control, with the state providing a good deal of support for the individual. The Liberals and the Social Democrat Party have joined in an uneasy alliance to form the Social Democratic and Liberal Party, which is beginning to have some impact.

2. The Culture

The English are friendly people, happy to share their music, art, literature, and other cultural benefits with people who come from what was, after all, once a colonial possession of Great Britain (and Canada still is a member of the Commonwealth). With no language barrier—except for a dialect now and then—this is an opportunity for great cultural experiences.

LITERATURE: The most outstanding figure of all in England's literary tapestry is—who dare say me nay?—William Shakespeare (1564–1616). But if England had had no Shakespeare, that tapestry would still be a rich and glowing panoply of artists with words—oral, written, sung, in poetry, in prose, in drama. From the Old English epic poem, *Beowulf,* almost surely the result of centuries of verse recited down the ages by tribal bards, to the works of the post-World War II "angry young men," English literature is vast.

Old English poetry and prose yielded to the language now called Middle English, in which the culture and tongue of the Normans enriched the speaking and writing of the old Anglo-Saxon language. Middle English was used by philosophers, historians, and romance writers from the 13th and 14th centuries. Greatest of the writers of this period was Geoffrey Chaucer, whose *Canterbury Tales* are masterfully told. The literary highlight of the 15th century was *Morte d'Arthur,* Sir Thomas Malory's story about the legend of King Arthur and his court. Ballads were also popular story-telling devices in that century, a sort of continuation of the bardic epic tradition.

During the Tudor era, stars in the literary sky were Sir Thomas More (*Utopia*), Edmund Spenser (*The Faerie Queen*), and Christopher Marlowe (*The Tragical History of Dr. Faustus*). It was in this era that the sonnet form was adopted from an Italian verse model, attracting as users a number of poets, such as Sir Philip Sidney and the greatest of them all, Shakespeare (remember "Shall I compare thee to a summer's day"?).

With the coming to the throne of the Stuarts came "Rare Ben Jonson," writer of satirical comedies and leader of poets who met at the Mermaid Tavern in London, and

John Donne (". . . never send to know for whom the bell tolls . . ."). It was during this time that the great translation of the Bible, under the auspices of King James I and called the King James Bible, took its immortal position in literature. During this Jacobean period, the Cavalier poets, of whom Robert Herrick heads the list, wrote romantic verse and backed the king against Cromwell and Parliament.

The literary giant of the mid-17th century was John Milton, a pro-Parliamentarian who was also considered one of the country's great geniuses. In view of *Paradise Lost*, who will argue? This was a period—during the Commonwealth—when many writers were imbued with Puritanism (resulting in some rather dull reading), chief among them being John Bunyan (*Pilgrim's Progress*), who was imprisoned for his pains after the restoration of the monarchy but whose powerful writing transcends theological differences. After Charles II was returned to the throne, theaters closed by Cromwell reopened and literature took on a lighter, more lively tone, as reflected in such works as the famous *Diary* of Samuel Pepys.

Through the 18th century, the literary world of England was crowded with the output of geniuses and near-geniuses from the rising middle class, much of whose work was aimed at social reform. Among these were Defoe (*Robinson Crusoe* and *Moll Flanders*), Alexander Pope (*An Essay on Man*), and a host of essayists and novelists—Fielding (*Tom Jones*), Richardson (*Pamela*), and a number of others. Most memorable of this period, however, is Samuel Johnson, whose *Dictionary of the English Language* made him the premier lexicographer and man of letters. His association with James Boswell from Scotland resulted in Johnson's becoming a major figure in literary annals, albeit through Boswell's writings. In Johnson's circle of close friends was another notable literary figure of the time, Oliver Goldsmith.

To enter into a dissertation on the 19th-century literary scene in England and to try to expound on the stars in that galaxy in limited space would be to bog down utterly. So I'll just mention several names known to everyone who has ever studied literature in school: William Blake, William Wordsworth, Samuel Taylor Coleridge, Byron, Keats, Shelley, Jane Austen, and Charles Lamb—but there are so many more. As you travel through the country, you will see birthplaces, familiar haunts, habitations, and burial places of many such writers.

Now to a period that challenges a student of literature—the Victorian. The great middle class had learned to read, printing was flourishing, and the union of these forces produced a literary thrust that took the country at a gallop into the 20th century. In this letters-rich age, readers devoured the works of Charles Dickens, Thackeray, the Brontë sisters, Matthew Arnold, Alfred Lord Tennyson, the Brownings, Lewis Carroll, George Eliot, George Meredith, Thomas Hardy, Swinburne, and Oscar Wilde, with a little heavier reading from John Ruskin and Thomas Carlyle thrown in.

Coming at the turn of the century, but usually considered literary figures of modern times, are such notables as Kipling, H.G. Wells, Galsworthy, Arnold Bennett, Maugham, Houseman, and Walter de la Mare. Among the better known writers of the 20th century are Robert Graves, Stephen Spender, W.H. Auden, Rupert Brooke, Siegfried Sassoon, Virginia Woolf, D.H. Lawrence, Evelyn Waugh, Aldous Huxley, Kingsley Amis, J.B. Priestley, Graham Greene, George Orwell, E.M. Forster, A. A. Milne, Noël Coward, Daphne du Maurier, Nancy Mitford, C.P. Snow, Antonia Fraser, Norah Lofts, and, not to be forgotten, Winston Churchill. Although the literary merit of the many British writers we could name varies, they all provide "a good read," as the British say.

In this category—good reads—are some of the best mystery and suspense novels to be found. From these you can learn about life in England from cottages to castles, in the cities and in the remote country, in the past and in the present, and a lot about the police and the crime scene from even before the Bow Street Runners to today's New Scotland Yard. Ellis Peters makes you feel at home at Shrewsbury in the 12th century,

Dorothy Sayers places you in the fen country in the 1920s, and Agatha Christie brings to life village atmosphere in Miss Marple's St. Mary Mead. There are many other writers of this ilk, such as P.D. James, E.X. Ferrars, and Ruth Rendell, whose stories, whether you're a mystery fan or not, can enrich your visit to England by giving you a personal word tour of all the country.

I could, of course, go on and still manage to leave out your favorite English writer. In fact, I'm sure someone will ask, "But what about Jonathan Swift? George Bernard Shaw? Sir Walter Scott? Robert Burns? Robert Louis Stevenson? Dylan Thomas?" My answer is that although these novelists and poets are usually included and indeed made their mark in "English" literature, they are not English-born, being from Ireland, Scotland, or Wales, and I have tried to keep this within the limitations of literary figures of England. Even Sir Arthur Conan Doyle, creator of that quintessential Londoner, Sherlock Holmes, was born in Edinburgh.

No question about it—the British Isles are rich in literary greats, and I've only reminded you of *some* of them.

MUSIC: From the time the English monks' choirs surpassed those of Germany and France in singing the Gregorian chant (brought to this country by St. Augustine, Pope Gregory's missionary), and were judged second only to the choirs of Rome, music has been heard throughout England. Polyphonic music developed after the simple chant, and sacred vocal music was early accompanied by the organ. The first organ at Winchester was installed in the 10th century. One of the earliest written compositions was the polyphonic piece (a round), *Sumer is icumen in,* with six parts.

Instruments commonly used in the Middle Ages, besides the organ found only in churches, were the fiddle, the lute, and the rebeck, used in court circles for the entertainment of royalty and hangers-on. Kings had musicians at court through the Plantagenets and into the time of the Tudors, with Henry VIII in particular making himself known as a composer. The sonnets he wrote for his lady loves were set to music, the best known being *Greensleeves.* The British Museum contains some 34 manuscripts of Henry's compositions. So flourishing was music in England in the 16th century that Erasmus of Rotterdam reported, after one of his visits: "They are so much occupied with music here that even the monks don't do anything else."

Music among the common people of the time may have been less polished but no less enthusiastic, with ditties and rounds being composed and heard in taverns and fields, the richness of the tunes compensating for the frequent vulgarity of the words. Some of the songs Shakespeare had his characters sing attest to the coarseness of the lyrics.

It was during the Tudor dynasty that English cathedral music came into full flower. It was during these years, too, that the forerunners of the opera and operetta came into being, with spectacles, called masques, being accompanied by music. These combined instrumental and vocal music, dancing, satire, recitations, and elaborate scenic accompaniment—the beginning of stage design.

Musicians were persecuted in the 1600s during the Commonwealth, but they came back into glory with the restoration of the monarchy under the Stuarts, with Henry Purcell writing the first English opera, *Dido and Aeneas* in 1689. From this point on, a veritable galaxy of musical talent was inspired and appreciated in London and thence in all England. Operas were written, influenced by Italian works, with Sir John Gay satirizing such productions in *The Beggars' Opera* in 1728. Handel, who became an English subject, composed many oratorios here, including *Messiah,* and other musicians followed (sometimes haltingly) in his train.

All of this doubtless led to the totally English musical productions, the operettas of the 19th century, with those by Gilbert and Sullivan being at the top of the heap then and for all the years since.

Many great names in the music world are English: Sir Edward Elgar, Ralph

Vaughan Williams, Sir William Walton, Sir Benjamin Britten, to name just a few. But English music has not stood still. Paul McCartney and John Lennon of the Beatles, brought composition in the modern world into the annals of English musical history, whose pages have certainly not yet closed.

ART: From the first carved and jewel-bedecked baubles, utensils, and even weapons of prehistoric man, the craze for ornamentation continued and grew. Intricately wrought crosses, religious statuary, and illuminated manuscripts led the way to stained-glass windows, ecclesiastical paintings, and other art forms connected first with the abbeys and cathedrals that came into being over the centuries and over the country. Soon these were followed by decorative glorification and expansion of the homes of royal and noble personages. The same trend affected the gentry and whoever could afford to have their persons and structures beautified.

Ornate tombs with sculptured effigies of the dead marked the resting places of the nobility and the princes of the church in the Middle Ages, and the cathedrals became art galleries of awesome beauty. Medieval painting consisted mostly of illumination of manuscripts by monks who took as models work they had done in European monasteries. Other art by the 13th century was in the embroidering of tapestries, metalwork, and carving, with panel painting, stained glass, and frescoes being among the mediums of expression.

Art, and even beauty, were considered the work of the devil during the religious upheavals of the 16th and 17th centuries, but when peace of a sort returned, sculpture came into vogue again, and painting reached an enviable grandeur. The name of Grinling Gibbons looms large for his baroque work in the late 17th and early 18th centuries, but it was not really until the 20th century that sculpture became a serious competitor to painting in England. Names such as Henry Moore, Barbara Hepworth, Sir Jacob Epstein, and Kenneth Armitage are only a few of the greats connected with English sculpture of today.

By the time interest in art revived after the Reformation, painting in oils was being done on the continent, and from this arose the wealth of fine pictures, from miniatures to vast murals, which you can see today. This art reached great heights in England, and your visits to the many museums and galleries will make you conversant with the masters.

At first, portraiture was the "done thing" as the British put it, with everybody who was anybody being depicted—alone, with family, with pets, whatever. The early leader in this field was Hans Holbein the Younger, a Swiss-born artist who had moved to England and who became painter for Henry VIII. Among the leading painters of the Tudor and Stuart periods, two who were outstanding were Van Dyck and Lely, neither of them English-born.

Native English painters came into their own by the 18th century, during the same era that landscape and animal painting and social satire began to vie with portraiture as recognized art forms. A roll call of the greats of that time resounds even today: Gainsborough, Hogarth, Reynolds, Romney, and many more. It was in that era that the Royal Academy of Arts was formed (1768), which you can visit in Piccadilly. (The academy is considered old hat by many artists and art critics today.)

Painters of the 19th and 20th centuries whose supremacy is recognized include Constable, Turner, Aubrey Beardsley, Sir Edward Burne-Jones, Dante Gabriel Rossetti, W. Holman Hunt, Ben Nicholson, Augustus John, Francis Bacon, Graham Sutherland, to name a few. Some of these, it is true, are felt to be too cloyingly romantic or too iconoclastically avant garde for all tastes, but each has earned a place in art history.

Whatever your preferences may be—Old Masters or latter 20th-century artists— you can find something to please you (and probably something to complain about) in the hundreds of galleries large and small throughout England.

ARCHITECTURE: From ancient manmade ceremonial sites such as Stonehenge, seen as "prehistoric cathedrals," through the great minsters and more recognizable cathedrals of the Middle Ages up to the modern places of worship at Coventry and Liverpool, the art of man has ever sought to bring a functional shape to the site where a higher power is invoked, as well as to places of human habitation.

Architecture in England has moved through many periods, examples of most of which can be seen today in preserved, restored, and reconstructed form. Separate architectural periods came after untitled eons in which mankind made do with caves or huts of wattle and daub, and whatever was at hand to work with. These designated architectural periods embrace the Anglo-Saxon, 6th to mid-11th century; the Norman, 11th and 12th centuries; Gothic (actually including four phases: Early English, Decorated, Perpendicular, and Tudor), 12th to 16th centuries; Renaissance (including Elizabethan, Jacobean, Palladian, and Byzantine), mid-16th to early 18th centuries; Georgian, early 18th to 19th; Regency, early 19th; Victorian, mid-19th to 20th; and the architecture of the present century which has taken many forms.

Many examples exist of work from all these periods since the Norman, so that the interested visitor has little difficulty in finding them among the sights of England. The names of the architects responsible for many of these lasting monuments to human genius have not survived, but enough are known to make a formidable roster of greatness. From the monk, Gandulf, a stonemason credited with construction of the White Tower, the list reads through Inigo Jones, Sir Christopher Wren, Nicholas Hawksmoor, Sir John Vanbrugh, James Gibbs, John Nash, Sir Edwin Lutyens, and countless others. (Robert Adam, whose name is synonymous with handsome interiors and some exterior work was a Scotsman, but much of his work can be seen in England.)

Not a builder of houses but a landscape architect was Lancelot (Capability) Brown, whose work also lives on, framing the beauty of many palaces and manor houses.

The rich legacy of a millennium of builders is an integral part of the visitor's enjoyment of England.

3. Food and Drink

Understanding British traditional dishes will help you enjoy your visit even more. The following comments will explain a few; other "surprises" you must seek out for yourself. Many good old-fashioned dishes are available in restaurants, wine bars, and pubs—sometimes called inns or taverns, a name going back to the Middle Ages.

The most common pub meal is based on the food a farm worker took with him to work, a ploughman's lunch. Originally a good chunk of local cheese, a hunk of homemade crusty white or brown bread, some butter, and a pickled onion or two, it was washed down with ale. You will now find such variations as pâté and chutney replacing the onions and cheese. Cheese is still, however, the most common ingredient. There are many regional variations, the best known being Cheddar, a good, solid, mature cheese, as is Cheshire. Another is the semi-smooth–textured Caerphilly from a beautiful part of Wales, and also Stilton, a softer tangy cheese, more popular with a glass of port.

Dishes with names so perplexing you have no hint of their ingredients are found on the little tea shop menu or in pubs and the like. Perhaps the most popular is shepherd's pie, a deep dish of chopped cold lamb mixed with onions and seasoning and covered with a layer of mashed potato and served hot. Another version is cottage pie, which is minced beef covered with potatoes and served hot.

Traveling in the southeast part of England around Colchester, you will find a most prized British dish, the oyster, for which, it is suggested, Julius Caesar really invaded Britain in 54 B.C.

As you move about England, you will come across dishes that were developed to fill a particular need. The Cornish pasty was made from the remains of the family's Sunday lunch in a Cornish fishing village: minced meat, chopped potato, carrot, onion, and seasoning mixed together and put into a pastry envelope, ready to be taken to sea by the fisherman on Monday for his lunch. In Grasmere you can buy gingerbread cookies made from a recipe more than 125 years old, coming in the same alphabet shapes used to teach children to read in the 19th century. A "flitting dumpling," northern in origin, is made of dates, walnuts, and syrup mixed with other ingredients into a pudding. It was cut into slices and could feed a family when "flitting" from one area to another. It is said that "hurry pudding," or hasty pudding in some areas, was invented by men avoiding the bailiff. This dish from Newcastle uses up stale bread (some dried fruit and milk were added in a dish that was put into the oven). In the northeast you'll come across Lancashire hotpot, a stew of mutton, potatoes, kidneys, and onions (sometimes carrots). This concoction was originally put into a deep dish and set on the edge of the stove to cook slowly while the family went to work in a local mill.

Among the most known and traditional of English dishes is roast beef and York-shire pudding. The pudding is made with a flour base and cooked under the joint, al-lowing the fat from the meat to drop onto it. The beef could easily be a large "sirloin" (rolled loin) which, so the story goes, was named by King James I (not Henry VIII as some claim) when a guest at Hoghton Tower, Lancashire; "Arise Sir Loin," he cried as he knighted the joint with his dagger. Meat left over would be eaten the next day in "Bubble and Squeak," which is made with cabbage and potatoes chopped and fried together. Another dish which makes use of a batter similar to Yorkshire pudding is "toad-in-the-hole," in which sausages are cooked in batter.

On the west coast you'll find a delicacy not to be missed, the Morecambe Bay shrimp. Of course, the whole coast of Britain provides a feast of dishes, the champions being cod, haddock, herring, plaice, and the aristocrat of flat fish, Dover sole. Cod and haddock are the most popular fish used in the making of that curious British tradition, "fish and chips" (chips, of course, are fried potatoes or french fries). The true British cover this dish with salt and vinegar. In the past the wrapping was newspaper, but now hygiene has removed the added—some say, indispensable—taste of newsprint from the dish!

Kipper, a smoked herring, is a popular breakfast dish. The finest are from the Isle of Man, Whitby, or Loch Fyne in Scotland. Herrings are split open and placed over oak chips and smoked slowly to produce a nice pale brown smoked fish. The British eat large breakfasts, or at least many of them do. "Ham and eggs" is said to have originated in Britain. Kedgeree is another popular dish (haddock, egg, and rice). Some B&Bs still serve black pudding with breakfast items (it's made of pig's blood, oat-meal, barley, or groats and suet—rather repulsive sounding, but loved by many).

High tea, almost unknown in the south, is common in the north of England and in Scotland. It is a meal which is a mix of hot and cold, giving the worker on his return home a combination of tea and supper. The word "dinner," in the north describes the midday meal (lunch), while in the south it means the evening meal. Supper by tradition is a meal taken late at night, usually after the theater.

Incidentally, real English mustard is simply the fine ground seed mixed with water, nothing else.

The East End of London has quite a few interesting old dishes, among them tripe and onions. Dr. Johnson's favorite tavern, the Cheshire Cheese on Fleet Street, still offers a steak, kidney, mushroom, and game pudding in a suet case in winter and a pastry case in summer. The East Ender will be seen at the Jellied Eel stall on Sunday by Petticoat Lane, eating eel or perhaps cockles, mussels, whelks, and winkles, all small shellfish eaten with a touch of vinegar. The eel pie and mash shop can still be found in London. The name, eel pie, however, is misleading, because it is really a minced beef pie topped with flaky pastry and served with mashed potatoes and accompanied by a portion of jellied eel.

It is a misconception to believe that "everything" stops for tea. People in Britain drink an average of four cups of tea a day but mainly at work. The real delight is to visit the little country tea shops where you can enjoy a pot of tea, some toasted tea cake (currant bun), or a crumpet (sometimes confused with the rarely found muffin), bread and butter, or sandwiches and good homemade cakes, all enjoyed while listening to the conversation at the next table.

A word about the wine of the country: Britain does not produce much real wine. It does produce some very pleasant white wine on the medium sweet side and quite fruity in taste. The real "wines" are cider and beer, both of which go well with the traditional dishes mentioned earlier.

Beer is served in all pubs. Draft beer is traditionally served at cellar temperature; as the British like to taste their beer they prefer it on the warm side of cold. Most bottled beer, however, is similar to light lager beers and is served cold. Draft beer comes in several different tastes, the most common being called "Bitter," which is light in color and taste, not really bitter. A half pint is the equivalent in strength to a single measure of Scotch. Others are mild ale, which is full flavored, and brown ale which is dark and flavorsome. Stout is a strong, rich dark beer, often mixed with champagne to make "Black Velvet." Guinness is a black beer, strong tasting and very dark with a good white head (froth). Cider made from apples can be stronger than expected.

However, after reading all the above, you can still be assured that the food and drink (including French and Italian wines) served in most restaurants will be international in scope, with some traditional British dishes. The reputation that Britain had for years for its soggy cabbage and tasteless dishes is no longer deserved. If you pick and choose carefully, and use this guide to help you seek out the finer dining rooms, you can enjoy some of the finest food in Europe while touring the British Isles.

4. The ABCs of England

The aim of this "grab bag" section—dealing with the minutiae of your stay—is to make your adjustment to the English way of life easier. It is maddening to have your trip marred by an incident that could have been avoided had you been tipped off earlier. To prevent this from happening, I'll try to anticipate the addresses, data, and information that might come in handy on all manner of occasions.

For more specific information on London, refer to "Practical Facts" under the Orientation section on the British capital, Chapter III.

BABYSITTERS: These are very hard to find, and the only safe way would be to get your hotel to recommend someone—possibly a staff member. Expect to pay the going fee as well as the cost of travel to and from your hotel, although in suburban areas most babysitters have their own cars, in which case you will be expected to reimburse them for the gasoline used. A number of organizations advertised in the *Yellow Pages* of the telephone directory provide sitters, using registered nurses, infant teachers, housewives, and other experienced persons for this service.

BANKS: Hours, generally, are from 9:30 a.m. to 3:30 p.m., Monday to Friday. There are also Bureaux de Change, which charge for cashing traveler's checks or personal checks (limited to checks drawn on United Kingdom banks only). They also change dollars into sterling. Bureaux are often open 18 hours a day, seven days a week. There are also branches of the main banks at the international airports which offer a 24-hour service to travelers. As a word of warning, you should note that the little change bureaus have nothing to do with the main banks and tend to give lower rates of exchange. They are open for long hours, and you pay for this convenience. If you use one of the big banks—Midland, National Westminster, Barclays, Lloyds, Royal Bank of Scotland, Clydesdale, American Express, or Thomas Cook—you will get the best rate.

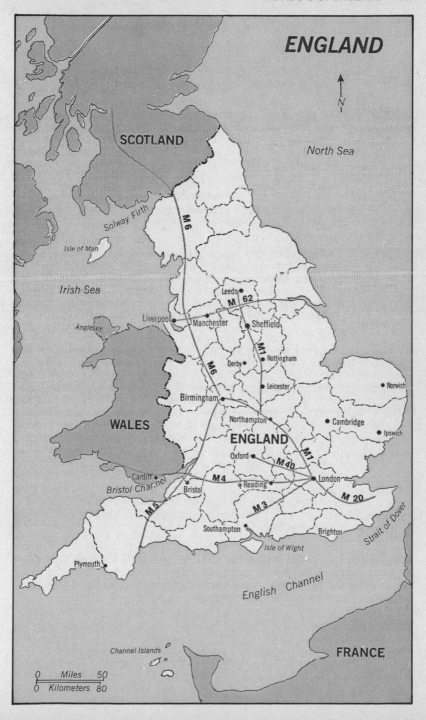

CIGARETTES: Most U.S. brands are available in major towns. Expect to pay more than £1.50 ($2.25) per pack.

Warning: Smoking is banned at an increasing number of places. Make sure you enter a "smoker" on the train or Underground, and smoke only on the upper decks of buses or in the smoking area of single-deckers, in theaters, and at other public places. Some restaurants restrict smoking.

CLIMATE: English temperatures can range from 30° to 110°F. It is, however, a temperate country with no real extremes, and even in summer evenings are cool. No Britisher will ever really advise you about the weather—it's far too uncertain. However, if you come from a hot area, bring some warm clothes. If you come from the cooler climes, you should be all right.

CRIME: Theft is not as bad, perhaps, as in the U.S. In the main, mugging is limited to the poor areas. Use discretion and a little common sense, and stay in well-lit areas. It's always wise to lock your car and protect your valuables.

CURRENCY EXCHANGE: As a general guideline, the price conversions in this book have been computed at the rate of £1 (one pound sterling) for each $1.50 U.S. There are now £1 coins as well as banknotes, plus coins of 20p, 10p, 2p, and 1p. The ½p coin has been officially killed, although they'll still be seen around for a while. Bear in mind, however, that international exchange rates are far from stable, and this ratio might be hopelessly outdated by the time you actually arrive in Britain.

CUSTOMS: Overseas visitors may import 400 cigarettes and one quart of liquor. But if you come from the Common Market (EEC) area, you're allowed 300 cigarettes and one quart of liquor, provided you bought them and paid tax in that EEC country. If you have obtained your allowance on a ship or plane, then you may only import 200 cigarettes and one liter of liquor. There is no limit on money, film, or other items that are for your own use. Obviously commercial goods, such as video films and nonpersonal items, will require payment of a bond and will take a number of hours to clear and deal with. Do not try to import live birds or animals. You may be subjected to heavy fines, and the pet will be destroyed. Upon leaving England, citizens of the United States who have been outside the country for 48 hours or more are allowed to bring back to their home country $400 worth of merchandise duty free—that is, if they haven't claimed such an exemption within the past 30 days. Beyond that free allowance, you'll be charged a flat rate of 10% duty on the next $1,000 worth of purchases. If you make purchases in Britain, it is most important to keep your receipts. On gifts, the duty-free limit has been increased to $50.

DENTISTS: You can find one listed in the *Yellow Pages* of the telephone book or else you can ask at your hotel. Appointments are usually necessary, but if you are in pain a dentist will generally fit you in. The **Emergency Dental Service** (tel. 01/584-1008) will put you in touch with a dentist in your area.

DOCTORS: Hotels have their own list of local practitioners, for whom you'll have to pay. (Look under "Hospitals" for 24-hour emergency service.) If out of town, dial "0" (zero) and ask the operator for the local police, who will give you the name, address, and phone number of a doctor in your area. Emergency treatment is free, but if you're admitted to a hospital, referred to an outpatient clinic, or treated for an already-existing condition, you will be required to pay. You will also pay if you visit a doctor in his or her office or if the doctor makes a "house call" to your hotel. Be safe. Take out adequate medical/accident insurance or extend your existing insurance to cover you while you're abroad.

DOCUMENTS FOR ENTRY: U.S. citizens, Canadians, Australians, New Zealanders, and South Africans all fall under the same category for entry into the United Kingdom. A passport is definitely required, but no visa is necessary. Immigration officers prefer to see a passport with two months' remaining validity. Much depends on the criteria and observations of immigration officers. The one checking you through will want to be satisfied that you have the means to return to your original destination (usually a round-trip ticket) and visible means of support while you're in Britain. If you are planning to fly from, say, the U.S. to the U.K. and then on to a country which requires a visa (India, for example), it's wise to secure the India visa before your arrival in Britain. Even the amount of time spent in the British Isles depends for holiday-makers on the immigration officer.

DRUGSTORES: In Britain they're called "chemist" shops. Every police station in the country has a list of emergency chemists. Dial "0" (zero) and ask the operator for the local police. Emergency drugs are normally available at most hospitals, but you'll be examined to see that the drugs you request are really necessary.

ELECTRICAL APPLIANCES: The electrical current is 240 volts, AC (50 Hz). Some international hotels are specially wired to allow North Americans to plug in their appliances, but you'll usually need a transformer plus an adapter for your electric razor, hairdryer, or soft contact lens sterilizer. Ask at the electrical department of a large hardware store for the size converter you'll need.

EMBASSY AND HIGH COMMISSION: The **U.S. Embassy** is at 24 Grosvenor Square, London W.1 (tel. 499-9000), and the **Canadian High Commission** is at Canada House, Trafalgar Square, London, S.W.1 (tel. 629-9492).

EMERGENCY: For police, fire, or ambulance, dial 999. Give your name and address, plus your telephone number, and state the nature of the emergency. Misuse of the 999 service will result in a heavy fine (cardiac arrest, yes; dented fender, no).

FILM: All types are available, especially in large cities. Processing takes about 24 hours, and many places, particularly in London, will do it almost while you wait. There are few restrictions on the use of your camera except when notices are posted, as in churches, theaters, and certain museums. If in doubt, ask.

HAIRDRESSING: Ask at your hotel. You should tip the "hairwasher" 50p (75¢) and the stylist £1 ($1.50), more if you have a tint or permanent. Hairdressing services are available in most department stores, and for men, at the main railway stations in London.

HOLIDAYS AND FESTIVALS: Christmas Day, Boxing Day (December 26), New Year's Day, Good Friday and Easter Monday, May Day, spring and summer bank holiday.

HOSPITALITY SERVICE: The **International Friendship League** is a highly commendable, nonpolitical organization with members in 54 countries throughout the world. The league's address is 55 Mount Vernon St., Boston, MA 02108, in the

United States, and Americans can also join through the British organization. For full details, please get in touch with (and enclose four international reply coupons): Miss Kathleen Suter, IFL Hospitality Service Organizer, 4 Wilton Close, Taunton, Somerset TA1 4EZ, England. There are 155 cities and towns in England, Scotland, and Wales that have IFL hospitality service. The IFL offers an excellent opportunity for Americans (and others) to meet the British, to visit with them in their homes, perhaps to have a meal with them, and sometimes to be accommodated with overnight lodging. A minimum of eight weeks notice is required.

LAUNDRY AND DRY CLEANING: Most places take two days to complete the job, and most hotels require the same length of time. London and most provincial towns have launderettes where you can wash and dry your own clothes, but there are no facilities for ironing. Many launderettes also have dry-cleaning machines. Otherwise, there are establishments that will do dry cleaning for you with one-day service.

LIBRARIES: Every town has a public library, and as a visitor you can use the reference sections. The lending of volumes, however, is restricted to local citizens.

LIQUOR LAWS: No alcohol is served to anyone under the age of 18. Children under 16 aren't allowed in pubs, except in special rooms. Hours vary, but as a general guide pubs are open from 11:30 a.m. to 2:30 p.m. and from 6 to 10:30 p.m., Monday to Saturday. Sunday hours are from noon to 2:30 p.m. and 7 to 10 p.m. Licensing laws have undergone some changes, and, at least in some places, you can have a late, late lunch that's not dry. That is, certain places that remain open will serve you a drink providing you order a meal—one that you must eat with a fork (in other words, not a sandwich). That could particularly affect diners at some pre-theater suppers or post-matinee meals. Remember, you must have a genuine meal in a table service restaurant.

Many general stores have "off licence" departments where you can buy liquor for home consumption, and hours are generally 9 a.m. to 5 p.m., depending on the store. There are also "off licence" shops which are usually open from 11 a.m. to 3 p.m. and from 5 to 9 p.m. (or later).

LOST PROPERTY: For help in finding items lost in London, see "Practical Facts," Chapter III. Wherever you are in England, report your loss to the nearest police station, which will help you if possible. For items lost on British Rail, go to the Euston Station Lost Property Office (tel. 01/922-6477).

For lost passports, credit cards, or money, report the loss and circumstances immediately to the nearest police station. For lost passports, you should then go directly to your embassy. The address will be in the telephone book (and see "Embassy and High Commission," above). For lost credit cards, report to the appropriate organization; the same holds true for lost traveler's checks.

LUGGAGE STORAGE: You may want to make excursions throughout Britain, taking only your essentials along. Very few B&B hotels in London have space to store lots of luggage, and you might want to return to a different hotel. It's possible to store suitcases at most railway stations. At stations you must be prepared to allow luggage to be searched for security reasons. Be warned that if you object, you could be viewed with suspicion.

MAIL DELIVERY: You can have your mail addressed Poste Restante at any of the big towns or give your hotel address. A letter generally takes about seven to ten days to arrive in the U.S. When claiming personal mail, always carry along identification.

MEDICAL SERVICES: Medical treatment is free only for unforeseen emergency conditions which arise during your stay in the United Kingdom. You'll need to consult a physician privately for any other medical treatment you require. The larger hotels will get in touch with their house doctor should you need one.

NEWSPAPERS: *The Times* is the top, then the *Telegraph*, the *Daily Mail*, and the *Guardian*, all papers carrying the latest news. Others have some news, but rely on gimmicks to sell. The *International Herald Tribune*, published in Paris, and an international edition of *USA Today* are available daily.

OFFICE HOURS: Business hours are from 9 a.m. to 5 p.m., Monday to Friday. The lunch break lasts an hour, but most places stay open all day.

PETS: See "Customs." It is illegal to bring in pets, except with veterinary documents, and even then they are subject to a quarantine of six months. Hotels have their own rules, but generally do not allow dogs in restaurants or public rooms and often not in the bedrooms either.

POLICE: The best source of help and advice in emergencies is the police (dial 999). If the local police can't assist, they will have the address of a person who can. Losses, theft, and other crimes should be reported immediately to the police.

POST OFFICE: Post offices and sub post offices are centrally situated and are open from 9 a.m. to 5 p.m. Monday to Friday. On Saturday, the hours are 9 a.m. to noon.

RADIO AND TELEVISION: There are 24-hour radio channels operating throughout the United Kingdom, with mostly pop music and talk shows during the night. TV starts around 6 a.m. with breakfast TV and educational programs. Lighter entertainment begins around 4 or 5 p.m., after the children's programs, and continues until around midnight. There are now four television channels—two commercial and two BBC without commercials.

RELIGIOUS SERVICES: Times of services are posted outside the various places of worship. Almost every form of worship is catered to in London and other large cities. But in the smaller towns and villages you are likely to find only Anglican (Episcopalian), Roman Catholic, Baptist, and Nonconformist houses of worship.

REST ROOMS: These are usually found at signs saying "Public Toilets." Expect to pay a 2p (3¢) to 5p (9¢) tip for women; men are free. Hotels can be used, but they discourage nonresidents. Garages (filling stations) also have facilities for use of customers only, and the key is often kept by the cash register. There's no need to tip except in hotels where there is an attendant.

SENIOR DISCOUNTS: These are only available to holders of a British pension book.

SHOE REPAIRS: Many of the large department stores of Britain have "Shoe Bars" where repairs are done while you wait.

STORE HOURS: In general, stores are open from 9 a.m. to 5:30 p.m. Monday to Saturday. In country towns, there is usually an early-closing day when the shops shut down at 1 p.m. The day varies from town to town.

TELEGRAMS: Inland telegrams have been replaced by telemessages which can be sent from most post offices. Such a message sent within the United Kingdom costs £4.50 ($6.75) for up to 50 words, including the address. An additional 50 words cost another £2.50 ($3.75), plus VAT. If your message is sent Monday to Saturday before 8 p.m., it will be included in the first mail delivery the next morning or you get your money back. Overseas cables can still be sent from main (not sub) post offices or by telephone. A telemessage sent to the U.S. costs a flat rate of £2.25 ($3.38), after which each word, including the address, is 36p (54¢). A less expensive way to send a telemessage is by using the overnight service. This will be transmitted at night, presumably when the lines are less busy. Fifty words cost £7.25 ($10.88), with each additional block of 50 words an extra £3.50 ($5.25). You'll probably be advised at the post office that it will be less expensive to call home, if you keep your message brief enough.

TELEPHONES: British Telecom is carrying out a massive improvement program to its public pay phone service. During the transitional period, you may encounter four types of pay phones. The old style (gray) pay phone is being phased out, but there are a few still in use. You will need 10p (15¢) coins to operate such phones, but you should not use this type for overseas calls. Its replacement is a blue and silver push-button model that accepts coins of any denomination. The other two types of phone require cards instead of coins to operate. The Cardphone uses distinctive green cards especially designed for it. They are available in five values—£1 ($1.50), £2 ($3), £4 ($6), £10 ($15), and £20 ($30)—and they are reusable until the total value has expired. Cards can be purchased from news agencies and post offices. Finally, the Creditcall pay phone operates on credit cards—Access, Visa, AMEX, and Diners—and is most common at airports and large railway stations.

Phone numbers in Britain outside of the major cities consist of an exchange number plus telephone number. To dial the number, you will need the code of the exchange being called. Information sheets on call box walls give the codes in most instances. If your code is not there, however, call the operator on 100. In major cities, phone numbers consist of the exchange code and number (seven digits in all). These seven digits are all you need to dial if you are calling from within the same city. If you are calling from elsewhere, you will need to prefix them with the dialing code for the city. Again, you will find these codes on the call box information sheets. If you do not have the telephone number of the person you want to call, dial 192 for any town within the U.K. except London. Give the operator the name of the town and then the person's name and address. Dial 142 for this information if the number you want is within the London postal code area.

The guide to telephone costs: A call at noon from London to Reading, 40 miles away, lasting three minutes costs 80p ($1.20). This charge is almost halved between 6 p.m. and 8 a.m. and on weekends. A local call costs 20p (40¢) for almost three minutes at all times. Unused coins are refunded at the end of a call. The charges quoted are for pay phones. You will have to pay far more if you use a hotel operator at any time.

TELEX: Telexes are more common in Europe than in the U.S., but are still mostly restricted to business premises and hotels. If your hotel has a Telex, they will send it for you. You may need to arrange the receipt of an expected message in advance.

TIME: England is based on Greenwich Mean Time with BST—British Standard Time (GMT + 1 hours)—during the summer (roughly April to October). When London is 12 noon, New York is 7 a.m., Chicago is 6 a.m., Denver is 5 a.m., and Los Angeles an early 4 a.m.

TIPPING: Many establishments add a service charge. If service has been good, it is usual to add an additional 5% to that. If no service is added to the bill, give 10% for poor service; otherwise, 15%. If service is bad, tell them and don't tip! Taxi drivers expect about 20% but never less than 15p (23¢) on a 60p (90¢) ride.

TOURIST INFORMATION: The British Tourist Authority has a **British Travel Centre** at Rex House, 4-12 Lower Regent St., London S.W.1 (tel. 01/730-3400). This center offers a full information service on all parts of England. For various sources of information on London, see Part I of Chapter III.

WEATHER: For London, telephone 01/246-8091; for Devon and Cornwall, 0392/8091; and for the Midlands, 021/8091.

Chapter III

SETTLING INTO LONDON

LONDON IS A HYBRID, a gathering place of people from the far corners of a once-great empire. The country gentleman and the blue-collar worker from the provinces visit London somewhat in the mood of going abroad.

The true Londoner, usually from the East End, is called a Cockney. He or she is a person born within the sound of "Bow Bells," the chimes of a church in Cheapside. But the city is also the home of the well-bred English lady who has had to sell her family estate of 400 years and take meager lodging in Earl's Court; of the expatriate Hollywood actress living in elegance in a Georgian town house; of the islander from Jamaica who comes seeking a new life and ends up collecting fares on one of London's red double-decker buses; and of the young playwright from Liverpool whose art reflects the outlook of the working class.

Cosmopolitan or not, Europe's largest city is still like a great wheel, with Piccadilly Circus at the hub and dozens of communities branching out from it. Since London is such a conglomeration of sections—each having its own life (hotels, restaurants, pubs)—the first-time visitor may be intimidated until he or she gets the hang of it. In this chapter, I'll concentrate on the so-called West End, although nobody has been able to come up with an explanation satisfactory to me as to what that implies. For the most part, a visitor will live and eat in the West End, except when he or she ventures into the old and historic part of London known as "The City" or goes on a tour to the Tower of London or seeks lodgings in the once remote villages such as Hampstead.

1. Orientation

London is a city that has never quite made up its mind about its own size. The "City of London" proper is merely one square mile of (very expensive) real estate around the Bank of England. All the gargantuan rest is made up of separate cities, boroughs, and corporations called Westminster, Chelsea, Hampstead, Kensington, Camden Town, and so forth, each with its own mayor and administration and ready to fight for its independent status at the drop of an ordinance. These started life as individual villages entirely, but through the centuries, the growth of Greater London has filled in the fields and woods which once separated them. Together, they add up to a mammoth metropolis—once the largest city on the globe, now dropped to 16th in a United Nations survey of population. The millions of people here live spread out over 609 square miles. Luckily, only a minute fraction of this territory need concern us—the rest is simply suburbs, stretching endlessly into the horizon, red-roofed and bristling with TV antennas.

But the heart, the brick-and-mortar core of this giant, is perhaps the most fascinating area on earth. For about a century, one-quarter of the world was ruled there. And with every step you take, you'll come across some sign of the tremendous influence this city has exerted over our past thoughts and actions—and still wields today.

HISTORY: London is a very old city, even by European standards. The Roman conquerors of Britain founded Londinium in A.D. 43 by settling and fortifying two small hills on the north bank of the River Thames and linking them via a military road network with the rest of the island.

More than a thousand years later, another conqueror turned the city into his capital. This was William of Normandy, who defeated the last Saxon ruler of England, Harold Godwin, in 1066. There isn't much left of the Roman period, but William the Conqueror left his imprint on London for all time to come. For a start, he completed and had himself crowned in Westminster Abbey. Every British monarch has been crowned there since, right up to the present Queen Elizabeth II. He also built the White Tower, which today forms part of the Tower of London. William did more to transform London (or rather, Westminster) into a royal capital. He and his nobles superimposed their Norman French onto the country's original Anglo-Saxon language and thus concocted English as we speak it today. Both the richness and the maddening illogicality of our tongue are direct results of that transplant.

The Normans weren't exactly gentle rulers, but the nation they created did pretty well. No one, for instance, has ever successfully invaded Britain since William's time —unless you count North American visitors and others from all over.

Royal but Democratic

London is a mass of contradictions, some of them dating way back in her history. On the one hand she's a decidedly royal city, studded with palaces, court gardens, coats-of-arms, and other royal paraphernalia. Yet she is also the home of mankind's second-oldest parliamentary assembly (Iceland has the oldest). When handsome and rash King Charles I tried to defy its representatives, he found himself swept off his throne and onto a scaffold long before the French got around to dealing likewise with their anointed monarch.

The huge, gray building that houses the "Mother of Parliaments," with its famous clock, Big Ben, is more truly symbolic of London than Buckingham Palace. For it was there that Prime Minister William Pitt intoned "You cannot make peace with dictators—you have to defeat them" at a time when England stood alone against the might of Napoleon. It was there too that Sir Winston Churchill repeated these sentiments in even better phrases when England—alone again—held out against Hitler. It was also in Parliament that "His Majesty's Loyal Opposition" stood up to give a rousing cheer for General Washington's army which had just whipped His Majesty's Hessian mercenaries—whom they detested every ounce as much as did the American colonists.

Nevertheless, London was largely shaped by the monarchs who ruled her—imposingly by the tough Tudors, beautifully by the wicked Georges, clumsily by the worthy Victoria.

Bouncing Back from Disasters

Much of London is also the result of disasters, both accidental and premeditated. The first was the Great Fire of 1666, which swept away most of the old wooden Tudor houses and resulted in a new city built of brick. The cause of the fire—like that of the great Chicago conflagration—remains unknown. Considering the fire hazards of those tightly packed timbered dwellings, the remarkable thing is that the town didn't burn down annually. As it was, the blaze gutted three-quarters of London—about 13,300 homes, churches, and public buildings. But it also gave England's greatest architect, Christopher Wren, the chance to design St. Paul's Cathedral as it stands today, as well as 51 other superb churches, plus the magnificent Royal Hospitals in Chelsea and Greenwich.

The blitz that Hitler unleashed on the city during 1940–1941 also had one beneficial result. Along with beautiful structures, the rain of incendiary bombs demolished vast patches of the pestilential slum areas around Whitechapel in the East End. The region—made equally famous by Charles Dickens and Jack the Ripper—had been London's festering sore, boasting possibly the worst housing conditions in the Western world. With slum clearance courtesy of the Luftwaffe, the L.C.C. rebuilt some of the area into rather drab, but infinitely superior, apartment blocks. There was something else the blitz gave London: a world image as the embattled fortress of freedom, caught unforgettably by the wartime news photo showing the white dome of St. Paul's silhouetted against the black smoke of a dozen simultaneous fires.

The postwar building boom may have made London a little less "quaint," but it also made her a very much healthier, happier place to live in, and it provided the overture of her present phase, which is that of a lively cosmopolitan city.

A BIT OF GEOGRAPHY: There is, fortunately, an immense difference between the sprawling vastness of Greater London and the pocket-size chunk that might be called "Tourist Country." For a start, all of the latter is *north* of the River Thames. Except for a couple of quick excursions, we'll never have to penetrate the southern regions at all.

Our London begins at Chelsea, on the north bank of the river, and stretches for roughly five miles up to Hampstead. Horizontally, its western boundary runs through Kensington while the eastern lies five miles away at Tower Bridge. Within this five- by five-mile square, you'll find all the hotels and restaurants and nearly all of the sights that are usually of interest to visitors. Make no mistake—this is still a hefty portion of land to cover, and a really thorough exploration of it would take a couple of years. But it has the advantage of being flat and eminently walkable, besides boasting one of the best public transport systems ever devised.

The local, but not the geographical, center of this area is **Trafalgar Square,** which we'll therefore take as our orientation point. The huge, thronged, fountain-splashed square was named after the battle in which Nelson destroyed the combined Franco-Spanish fleets and lost his own life. His statue tops the towering pillar in the center, and local residents maintain that the reason he's been up there all these years is that nobody has told him the lions at the base are made of stone. If you stand facing the steps of the imposing National Gallery, you're looking northwest. That is the direction of **Piccadilly Circus,** which, as mentioned, is the real core of tourist London, as well as the maze of streets that make up **Soho.** Farther north runs **Oxford Street,** London's gift to moderately priced shopping, and still farther northwest lies **Regents Park** with its zoo.

At your back—that is, south—runs **Whitehall,** which houses or skirts nearly every British government building, from the Ministry of Defence to the official residence of the prime minister on Downing Street. In the same direction, a bit farther south, stand the Houses of Parliament and Westminster Abbey.

Flowing southwest from Trafalgar Square is the table-smooth **Mall,** flanked by magnificent parks and mansions and leading to Buckingham Palace, residence of the Queen. Farther in the same direction lie **Belgravia** and **Knightsbridge,** the city's plushest residential areas, and south of them, **Chelsea,** with its chic flavor, plus **Kings Road,** the boutique-filled shopping drag.

Due west from where you're standing stretches the superb and distinctly high-priced shopping area bordered by **Regent Street** and **Piccadilly** (the street, *not* the Circus). Farther west lie the equally elegant shops and even more elegant homes of **Mayfair.** Then comes **Park Lane,** and on the other side, **Hyde Park,** the biggest park in London and one of the largest in the world.

Running north from Trafalgar Square is **Charing Cross Road,** past **Leicester Square** and intersecting with **Shaftesbury Avenue.** This is London's theaterland, boasting an astonishing number of live shows as well as first-run movie houses. A bit farther along, Charing Cross Road turns into a browser's paradise, lined with new and secondhand bookshops. Finally it funnels into **St. Giles Circus.** This is where you enter **Bloomsbury,** site of the University of London, the awesome British Museum, some of our best budget hotels, and erstwhile stamping ground of the famed "Bloomsbury Group," led by Virginia Woolf. Northeast of your position lies **Covent Garden,** known for its Royal Opera House.

Follow the **Strand** eastward from **Trafalgar Square** and you'll come into **Fleet Street,** the most concentrated newspaper section on earth, the place every reporter in the English provinces dreams about reaching one day. At the end of Fleet Street lies **Ludgate Circus**—and only there do you enter the actual City of London. This was the original walled settlement and is today what the locals mean when they refer to **"The City."** Its focal point and shrine is the Bank of England on Threadneedle Street, with the Stock Exchange next door and the Royal Exchange across the road.

"The City" is unique insofar as it retains its own separate police force (distinguished by a crest on their helmets) and lord mayor. Its 677 acres are an antheap of jammed cars and rushing clerks during the week and totally deserted on Sunday, because hardly a soul lives there. Its streets are winding, narrow, and fairly devoid of charm. But it has more bankers and stockbrokers per square inch than any other place on the globe. And in the midst of all the hustle rises St. Paul's Cathedral, a monument to beauty and tranquility. At the far eastern fringe of the City looms the Tower of London, shrouded in legend, blood, and history. It's permanently besieged by battalions of visitors.

Designed to Confuse

I'd like to tell you that London's thoroughfares follow a recognizable pattern in which, with a little intelligence, even a stranger can find his or her way around. Unfortunately, they don't and you can't. London's streets follow *no* pattern whatsoever, and both their naming and numbering seems to have been perpetrated by a group of xenophobes with an equal grudge against postmen and foreigners.

Be warned that the use of logic and common sense will get you nowhere. Don't think, for instance, that Southampton Row is anywhere near Southampton Street and that either of these places has any connection with Southampton Road. This is only a mild sample. London is checkered with innumerable squares, mews, closes, and terraces, which jut into or cross or overlap or interrupt whatever street you're trying to follow, usually without the slightest warning. You may be walking along ruler-straight Albany Street and suddenly find yourself flanked by Colosseum Terrace (with a different numbering system). Just keep on walking and after a couple of blocks you're right back on Albany Street (and the original house numbers), without having encountered the faintest reason for the sudden change in labels.

House numbers run in odds, evens, clockwise or counterclockwise as the wind blows. That is, when they exist at all—and frequently they don't. Every so often you'll come upon a square that is called a square on the south side, a road on the north, a park on the east, and possibly a something-or-other close on the west side. Your only chance is to consult a map or ask your way along. Most of the time you'll probably end up doing both.

But there are a couple of consoling factors. One is the legibility of the street signs. The other is the extraordinary helpfulness of the locals, who sometimes pass you from guide to guide like a bucket in a fire chain.

TRANSPORTATION IN GREATER LONDON: If you know the ropes, transportation within London can be unusually easy and inexpensive, because London enjoys one of the best Underground (subway) and bus systems in the world, operated by London Regional Transport, with Travel Information Centres at Victoria station (Underground and British Rail), King's Cross, Euston, Charing Cross, Oxford Circus, Piccadilly Circus, St. James's Park, West Croydon, and each of the Airbus/Underground terminals at Heathrow Airport.

Travelcards, for use on Underground and bus services and available in any combination of adjacent zones, and Capitalcards, good on British Rail, Underground, and bus services in Greater London and available also in any combination of adjacent zones, are offered by the transport service. The cost of a Travelcard good for seven days for adults is £5 ($7.50) in the central zone (no reduction for children); £6 ($9) for adults and £1.70 ($2.55) for children in two zones; £8.80 ($13.20) and £2.50 ($3.75), respectively, for three zones; £11.50 ($17.25) and £3.40 ($5.10) for four zones; and £14.50 ($21.75) and £3.40 ($5.10) for five zones.

Capitalcards for seven days of travel cost £7 ($10.50) for adults, £3.50 ($5.25) for children for two zones; £10.20 ($15.30) and £5.10 ($7.65), respectively, for two zones; £13.20 ($19.80) and £6.60 ($9.90) for four zones; and £16.30 ($24.45) and £8.15 ($12.23) for five zones.

To purchase a Travelcard, you must present a **Photocard.** For persons 16 years old or older, the Photocard is easy to get. Just take a passport-type picture of yourself when you buy your first Travelcard, and the Photocard will be issued free. Child-rate Photocards are only issued at main post offices in the London area, and in addition to a passport-type photograph, proof of age is required (for example, a passport or a birth certificate). Travelcards are not issued at child rates unless supported by a Photocard. Older children (14 or 15) are charged adult fares on *all* services unless in possession of one of the cards. A child-rate Photocard is not, however, required for child-rate London Explorer tickets or for tours.

Bargain Travel Passes: For travel within central London and the inner suburbs, a **London Explorer** ticket is available for unlimited bus and Underground travel for one, three, four, or seven days. The ticket costs £3.50 ($5.25) for adults and £1.30 ($1.95) for children for one day; £9 ($13.50) and £3 ($4.50), respectively, for three days; £11.50 ($17.25) and £3.50 ($5.25) for four days; and £16 ($24) and £4 ($6) for seven days. With this pass, you don't have to queue up at the ticket counter leading to the Underground: just flash your pass at the end of the run or when the bus conductor comes around. When you buy your ticket, you'll receive a free mini-guide showing you how to reach London's most famous sights, plus valuable discount vouchers saving you money at Madame Tussaud's, the London Zoo, the London Transport Museum, and many other attractions. To buy the London Explorer ticket, apply at the London Travel Information Centres, or at Underground stations.

For shorter stays in London, or for special excursions, you may want to consider the **One-Day Off-Peak Travelcard.** This ticket can be used on most bus and Underground services throughout Greater London after 9:30 a.m. Monday to Friday and at any time during the weekends and on bank holidays. The ticket is available from Underground ticket offices, bus garages, Travel Information Centers, and some news agencies. It costs £1.70 ($2.55) for a four-zone card (1, 2, 3a, and 3b), with no reduction for children. For an all-zone card, adults pay £2 ($3), children 70p ($1.05).

These fares, although valid at the time of writing, will very likely change during the lifetime of this edition and are therefore only presented for general background information so that you will know the range of travel options open to you.

The London Transport Information Centres provide information on a wide range of facilities and places of interest in addition to data on bus and Underground services. They sell special visitors' tickets, take reservations for London Transport's guided tours (see "Taking the Tours," Chapter V, Section 4), and have free Underground and bus maps and other information leaflets. A 24-hour telephone information service is available (tel. 222-1234).

In addition to the information obtainable from any of the Travel Information Centres, it is also available from London Regional Transport, Travel Information Service, 55 Broadway, London SW1H 0BD.

Airports

London has two main airports, **Heathrow** and **Gatwick.** It takes 35 to 45 minutes by Underground train from Heathrow Central to central London, costing £1.50 ($2.25) for adults and 40p (60¢) for children. From Heathrow, you can also take an airbus, which gets you into central London in about an hour. The cost is £3 ($4.50) for adults, £1.50 ($2.25) for children.

Gatwick Airport, where many charter and some scheduled flights come in, lies 30 miles south of London. Trains leave from there every 15 minutes until midnight and every hour after midnight. Also, there is an express bus from Gatwick to Victoria Station every half hour from 6:30 a.m. to 8 p.m. and every hour from 8 to 11 p.m. Flightline bus 777, it costs £3 ($4.50) per person.

The Underground, airbus, and train are, of course, far cheaper means of transport than a private taxi. For example, a taxi from Heathrow into central London is likely to cost more than £20 ($30).

A bus service connects the two airports, leaving every hour for the 70-minute trip. In addition, there is an expensive helicopter service that takes only 15 minutes between airports.

A service transporting passengers between both Heathrow and Gatwick airports and London is **Airliner** (tel. 759-4741), which has you and your luggage picked up and delivered in vans or cars. You'll be dropped off at your terminal forecourt, and you can be picked up there for the return trip. The one-way fares are: Heathrow-London, £4 ($6) for two or more passengers, £6 ($9) for a single passenger; Gatwick-London, £6 ($9) for two or more passengers, £8 ($12) for a single passenger.

When you arrive at the airport, call the Airliner people from the baggage collection hall, and you'll be directed to the vehicle. The Airliner headquarters is Argonaut House, Bath Road, London Heathrow, Hounslow, Middlesex TW6 2AL.

For flight information, telephone Heathrow at 01/759-4321 or Gatwick at 0293/31299.

The Underground

Londoners usually refer to the Underground as the "tube." Stations are identified by a distinctive sign, a red circle with blue crossbar, and the words "London Underground." (If you ask for a "subway," you risk ending up in a tunnel for pedestrians running beneath the road.) Destinations are listed on ticket machines, or you can buy your tickets from a booking office if you don't have the correct change. Maps showing the Underground network are displayed in every station, on each platform, and in Underground train cars. You can transfer as many times as you like so long as you stay in the Underground and don't leave the network on ground level.

The electric subways are, to begin with, comfortable, the cars having cushioned seats, no less. The flat fare for one journey within the central zone is 50p (75¢). Trips from the central zone to destinations in the suburbs range from 60p (90¢) to £2.40 ($3.60). *Be sure to keep your ticket;* it must be presented when you get off. If you owe extra, you'll be billed by the attendant. Each subway line has its own distinctive color, and all you need do is follow the clearly painted arrows, which are on every stairway and at every corridor turning.

Note: If you're out on the town and are dependent on the Underground, watch your time carefully. Many of the trains stop running at midnight (11:30 p.m. on Sunday).

The line serving Heathrow Airport to central London has trains with additional luggage space, as well as moving walkways from the airport terminals to the Underground station.

Buses

The comparably priced bus system is almost as good as the Underground—and you have a better view. To find out about current routes, pick up a free bus map at one of the London Transport Travel Information Centres listed above. The map is available to personal callers only, not by mail.

After you've queued up for the red, double-decker bus and selected a seat downstairs or on the upper deck (the best seats are on top, where you'll see more of the city), a conductor will come by to whom you'll tell your destination. He or she then collects the fare and gives you a ticket. As with the Underground, the fare varies according to the distance you travel. If you want to be warned when to get off, simply ask the conductor.

Bus Terminals: Victoria Coach Station, Buckingham Palace Road, S.W.1 (tel. 750-0202), is the main bus terminal. Tube: Victoria. Other bus stations are at King's Cross Coach Station and at Gloucester Road beside the Forum Hotel. The green, single-decker buses you see on London streets link the center with outlying towns and villages.

Taxis

You can pick up a cab in London either by heading for a cab rank, by hailing one on the streets, or by telephoning 253-5000, 272-0272, or 272-3030 for a radio cab. The minimum fare is 80p ($1.20). Each additional passenger is charged 20p (30¢) extra. On Saturday before 6 p.m., the minimum is £1.20 ($1.80), and from 6 p.m. Saturday to 8 a.m. Monday, the flag drops at a £1.40 ($2.10) minimum. Passengers are charged 10p (15¢) for each piece of luggage. All these tariffs include VAT. It's recommended that you tip about 20% of the fare and never less than 15%. If you have a complaint about the taxi service you get, or if you leave something in a cab, phone the Public Carriage Office, Panton Street, S.W.1 (tel. 278-1744). If your call is about a complaint, you must know the cab number which is displayed in the passenger compartment.

Be warned: If you phone for a cab, the meter starts running when the taxi receives instructions from the dispatcher. So you could find 80p ($1.20) or more on the meter when you get inside the vehicle. Cab-sharing is not done often.

Bikes

You can rent bikes by the day or by the week from a number of businesses, one of the most popular being **Savile's Bike Rental,** 97 Battersea Rise, Battersea, S.W.11 (tel. 228-4279), which has been renting out bicycles for some 75 years. Stan Savile's father started the company back in 1912. Prices are £15 ($22.50) per week, reduced to £10 ($15) after the first week, which is much lower than the charge of many of its competitors. The firm is not only one of the cheapest but also one of the most reliable bike companies I have found. A deposit of £15 ($22.50) is required with a passport. Padlocks are provided free, and insurance costs £2 ($3) for any one rental period. The shop is open daily except Sunday from 9 a.m. to 5 p.m. Take the Northern Line tube from central London to Clapham Common and change to bus 35 or 37, getting off at Clapham Junction.

PRACTICAL FACTS: In order to call **police, fire,** or **ambulance** in London, dial 999.

Among **hospitals** offering emergency care in London 24 hours a day are the **Royal Free Hospital,** Pond Street, N.W. 3 (tel. 794-0500) (Tube: Belsize Park), and the **University College Hospital,** Gower Street, W.C. 1 (tel. 387-9300) (Tube: Euston Square). The first treatment is free under the National Health Service. Many other London hospitals also have accident and emergency departments, including St. Mary's Hospital, Paddington; London Hospital, Whitechapel; King's College Hospital, Denmark Hill; Charing Cross Hospital; and St. Bartholomew's Hospital. Only emergency treatment is free.

If your **eyeglasses** get lost or broken, try **Selfridges Optical** in Selfridges Department Store, 400 Oxford St., W.1 (tel. 629-1234, ext. 3889). Most prescriptions can be filled within one or two hours. More complicated prescriptions may take up to 24 hours to prepare. Cost, including examination, will be around £45 ($67.50). You will pay more for elaborate frames. It's always wise to take a copy of your lens prescription with you when you travel. Tube: Bond Street.

Need a **dentist** for emergency treatment? To find the one nearest you, phone 677-6363 or 584-1008 in London. You will be directed to whichever dental surgery in or near your area can attend to your needs.

Doctors: Ask at your hotel, which probably has a list of practitioners available.

For **medical services,** you'll find **Medical Express,** Chapel Place, W.1 (tel. 499-1991), just off Oxford Street, almost equidistant between the Oxford Circus and Bond Street tube stations. It's a medical center where you can have a consultation and full medical/clinical examination, such as a blood-pressure check, an EKG, and X-rays. The cost is £35 ($52.50), plus £10 ($15) if you get a prescription. For £5 ($7.50), you can get the British equivalent of your U.S. prescription here, if they decide that it is bona fide. The center is open Monday to Friday from 8 a.m. to 8 p.m., Saturday from 9 a.m. to 6 p.m.

A 24-hour **drugstore** (chemist, in Britain) operation is maintained in London by **Bliss the Chemist,** 50–56 Willesden Lane, Kilburn, N.W.6 (tel. 624-8000) (Tube: West Hampstead), and 5 Marble Arch, W.1 (tel. 723-6116) (Tube: Marble Arch). Emergency drugs are normally available at most hospitals, but you'll be examined to see that the medication you request is really necessary.

The **telephone area code** for London is 01.

To make **telephone** calls: The **Westminster Communications Center,** 1A Broadway, S.W. 1, is open daily from 9 a.m. to 7 p.m., including Sunday. Here you can call all countries not available from a call box. Receptionists are available to help you in case of difficulty and to take your payment once your call is finished. You can pay in cash, check, credit card, or traveler's checks in pounds sterling. A range of other services is also available, including Telex and facsimile. Call 222-4444 for details. Tube: St. James's Park.

The **Chief Post Office** in London is on King Edward Street, E.C.1, near St. Paul's Cathedral. Tube St. Paul's. The **Trafalgar Square Post Office,** 24/28 William IV St., W.C.2, operates as three separate businesses: inland and international postal services and banking, open from 8 a.m. to 8 p.m. Monday to Saturday, 10 a.m. to 5 p.m. Sunday; philatelic sales, open from 8 a.m. to 7 p.m. Monday to Friday, 10 a.m. to 4:30 p.m. Saturday; and the post shop selling greeting cards and stationery, open 8:30 a.m. to 5:30 p.m. Monday to Friday, 8:30 a.m. to 4 p.m. Saturday. Tube: Charing Cross. Other post offices and sub-post offices are open from 9 a.m. to 5:30 p.m. Monday to Friday and 9 a.m. to 12:30 p.m. on Saturday.

To find a **babysitter** in London, your hotel may be able to help you. A good possibility is **Childminders,** 67A Marylebone High St., W.1 (tel. 935-9763). Tube: Regent's Park. Visitors to London can pay £3 ($4.50) temporary booking fee each time they hire a sitter from the agency, or, if they prefer, the annual membership fee is £16 ($24), plus VAT. The membership fee or booking charge is paid to the agency, while pay for the job goes to the employee. Evening babysitters cost £1.60 ($2.40) per hour Sunday to Wednesday nights; £1.70 ($2.55) per hour Thursday and Friday nights; and £1.95 ($2.93) per hour on Saturday evening and holidays. Day rates are £2.20 ($3.30) per hour (higher Christmas and New Year's Eve). (Guests of most major hotels are exempt from the membership charge.) **Universal Aunts,** 250 King's Rd., S.W.3 (tel. 351-5767), an old and respected organization, runs a comprehensive service, acting as substitute parents for children and assisting with problems where a granny or aunt may have been called on at home. Tube: Sloane Square.

American Express has its main office at 6 Haymarket, S.W.1 (tel. 930-4411). There are some ten other London locations. Tube: Piccadilly Circus.

Among the many laundry and dry cleaning establishments in London, the **Brunswick Launderette,** 1 Brunswick Centre, Bernard Street, W.C.1, opposite the Russell Square tube station (no phone), is a good bet right in an area of tourist hotels. The launderette is open daily from 7 a.m. to 8 p.m., including weekends, and there is always someone in attendance. If you wish, you can drop off your wash, go shopping or on a day tour, and pick it up that afternoon. A dry-cleaning machine and shirt service are also available.

For finding **lost property** in London on the tube or in a taxi—or elsewhere— report the loss to the police first, and they will advise you where to apply for its return. Taxi drivers are required to hand property left in their vehicles to the nearest police station. London Transport's Lost Property Office will try to assist personal callers only at their office at the Baker Underground station. For information on items lost on British Rail trains, lost passports, and lost credit cards, see "Lost Property" in the ABCs of England section of Chapter II.

The **American Church in London** (interdenominational) is at 79 Tottenham Court Rd., W.1 (tel. 580-2791) (Tube: Goodge Station), but almost every creed is catered to in London. Times of religious services are posted outside houses of worship.

Luggage shipping can relieve you of a lot of worry about how to get all your souvenirs home. **London Baggage Company Ltd.,** 262 Vauxhall Bridge Rd., S.W.1 (tel. 828-2400), offers worldwide service for shipping unaccompanied luggage, at rates usually below the normal excess baggage charges of airlines. They collect your extras from your London hotel and deal with all documentation and shipping. Prices vary according to weight and destination, but the charge for picking up your parcels, doing the paperwork, and delivering everything to the airport is about £20 ($30), plus insurance. Tube: Pimlico Station.

Help or information on particular subjects is available in London by telephone. **Alcoholics Anonymous,** 352-9779; **Gamblers Anonymous,** 352-3060; **Rape Crisis Centre,** 837-1600; **Gay Switchboard,** 837-7324; **Consumer Advice Centre,** 888-8442; **Law Society,** 242-1222; **Help Advisory Centre,** 937-6445 (this is for when you don't know where to get the sort of help you need); the **Samaritans,** 283-3400 (for the suicidal or depressed); **Traveline** (travel information), 246-8021; and **Weather,** 246-8091.

LONDON INFORMATION: Tourist information is available from the London Visitor and Convention Bureau's facilities. The **London Tourist Information Centre,** Victoria Station Forecourt, S.W. 1, can and will help you with almost anything of interest to a tourist in the U.K. capital. Staffed by courteous, tactful, sympathetic, patient, and understanding men and women, the center deals chiefly with accommodations in all size and price categories, from single travelers, family groups, and students to large-scale conventions. They also arrange for tour ticket sales and theater reservations and operate a bookshop. Hours are from 9 a.m. to 8:30 p.m. daily (8 a.m. to 10 p.m. in July and August). The bookshop is open from 9 a.m. to 7 p.m. Monday to Saturday and 9 a.m. to 4 p.m. on Sunday, hours being extended in July and August. For most types of service, you must apply in person.

The bureau also has offices at:

The Tower of London, West Gate, E.C.3, open from 10 a.m. to 6 p.m. daily from April to October (10:15 a.m. opening on Sunday). Tube: Tower Hill Station.

Selfridges Department Store, W.1, on the ground floor. Open during store hours. Tube: Bond Street.

Harrods Department Store, Knightsbridge, S.W.3, on the fourth floor. Open during store hours. Tube: Knightsbridge.

Heathrow Airport Information Center, Heathrow Central Underground Station, open from 9 a.m. to 6 p.m. daily.

Telephone inquiries may be made to the bureau by calling 730-3488 Monday to Friday from 9 a.m. to 5:30 p.m. (For riverboat information, call 730-4812.) Written inquiries should be addressed to the London Visitor and Convention Bureau, Central Information Unit, 26 Grosvenor Gardens, London SW1W ODU.

There are other information centers around The City and West End, providing particular data about certain areas. These centers know of exhibitions and places to visit which are seldom open to the public—the Livery Halls in The City, for example. The **City of London Information Centre,** St. Paul's Churchyard, E.C.4 (tel. 606-3030), is open Monday to Friday from 9:30 a.m. to 5 p.m., Saturday and holidays from 10 a.m. to 6 p.m. Tube: St. Paul's.

The British Tourist Authority has a **British Travel Centre** at Rex House, 4-12 Lower Regent St., S.W.1 (tel. 730-3400). This center offers a full information and hotel booking service on all parts of Britain, a British Rail ticket office, a travel agency, a theater ticket agency, hotel booking service, a bookshop, and a souvenir shop, all under one roof. Hours are from 9 a.m. to 6:30 p.m. Monday to Saturday, from 10 a.m. to 4:30 p.m. on Sunday. Tube: Piccadilly Circus.

B&B HOTELS—WHAT TO EXPECT: Since London is one of the gateway cities to Europe, some basic points about low-budget accommodations should be covered to avoid disappointing the first-timer abroad.

The majority of budget hotels aren't hotels at all (in the sense of having elevators, porters, private baths). Rather, they are old (averaging between 75 and 200 years), family-type guest houses masquerading under the name hotel. When the street pump ceased to supply the water, many of these homes for Victorian families were hastily, often badly, converted.

London still contains hundreds of these four- and five-story hotels, even though many blocks are being razed to make way for skyscrapers and commercial buildings. Some of the former town houses are attached in rows in the Georgian style and open onto a square. At first glance, most of them look the same, but, once inside, you'll find widely varying degrees of cleanliness, service, and friendliness.

Most bed-and-breakfast hotels (B&B) serve an English breakfast or at least a continental one, usually in a converted servants' room in the basement (rarely any other meal). The rooms on higher floors tend to be smaller. The rooms have sinks (except in the most rock bottom of establishments), innerspring mattresses (occasionally), closet and dresser space (hopefully), and a desk and armchair (maybe). The bathroom may be half a flight down, two flights down, or (miracle of miracles) on the same floor.

It can even be in your bedroom. There is no longer the shortage of baths and showers as in days of yore. Most B&B establishments now have adequate baths. Expect to pay around £5 ($7.50) to £12 ($18) extra on a room rate for a unit with private bath and toilet. Ask first what is included in the room rate, and in the case of a B&B, ask to see the room before accepting. You'll probably be asked to pay in advance in most B&B establishments. Incidentally, the designation of a private shower (or bath) on the tariff sheet presented to you doesn't always include a toilet in smaller places or in made-over old hotels.

A Traveler's Advisory

If you've arrived in London as a first-time visitor and, because of a limited budget, must seek low-cost lodgings, you should know that decent accommodations are hard to find. Since the last edition of this book was researched I have received more complaints about B&B hotels in London than any destination on the continent of Europe.

Chances are, you won't like what you get, and you will feel with some justification that you're being overcharged for a poor room, indifferent service, and often a surly reception.

I have selected a list of what I consider adequate lodgings for London. Most of them are presented without any particular enthusiasm. Dozens and dozens were rejected as being total disasters.

If you make out better than I have warned, then be happily surprised.

Because of the poor state of many of central London's B&B establishments and budget hotels, I have in this edition included a number of "big splurge," and in some cases "super splurge," choices where you'll break our very limited budget but will be assured of comfort and value. This was done at the request of hundreds of readers who did not want to compromise a certain standard of living—that is, moderate comfort and a private bath—when traveling to London. But, be warned, to get a good moderately priced hotel, especially a decent room with private bath, you may want to pay two to three times our room allowance. However, once you leave London, you can often find very good accommodations at low prices throughout all the counties.

For those who don't mind taking the tubes or trains for about 20 or 30 minutes every day, I've also included several B&B selections on the fringe of London where establishments offer low prices for quite good accommodations.

Reservations by Mail

Most hotels require at least a day's deposit before they will reserve a room for you. This can be accomplished either by an international money order or a personal check. Usually you can cancel a room reservation one week ahead of time and get a full refund. A few hotelkeepers will return your money three days before the reservation date. It's no trouble if you reserve well in advance, but if you send off several deposits at the last minute, you may lose money. Many hotel owners operate on such a narrow margin of profit that they find just buying stamps for airmail replies too expensive by their standards. Therefore it's most important that you enclose a prepaid International Reply Coupon. Mail bookings can be sent to **London Visitor and Convention Bureau,** Department HAS, 26 Grosvenor Gardens, London, SW1W 0DU. You must confirm it and send the required deposit directly to the hotel.

SOUTHWEST LONDON

During the most crowded periods already referred to, the wise budget visitor heads for the southwestern portion of the city—by which I mean the area south of Piccadilly and below Hyde Park, but still on the north bank of the Thames. Although the hotels here are not as numerous as in other sections of town, they are plentiful enough, and more likely than the others to have vacancies, even at the height of the season.

Most of the southwestern hotels are in the moderately expensive **Victoria** section (around Victoria Station) and in the less expensive **Earl's Court** area (where large numbers of Canadian and Australian visitors stay). Scattered, and most reasonably priced, hotels and guesthouses are also to be found in the museumland of **South Kensington** and the neighboring middle-class district of **Brompton.** I'll begin where you'll find most of the southwestern hotels.

2. Victoria

Directly south of Buckingham Palace is a section in Pimlico often referred to as Victoria, with its namesake, sprawling Victoria Station, as its center. Known as the "Gateway to the Continent," Victoria Station is where you get boat-trains to Dover and Folkestone for that trip across the Channel to France.

The section also has many other advantages from the standpoint of location, as the British Airways Terminal, the Green Line Coach Station, and the Victoria Coach Station are all just five minutes from Victoria Station. From the bus stations, you can hop aboard many a Green Line Coach fanning out to the suburbs. In addition, an inexpensive bus tour of London departs from a point on Buckingham Palace Road just behind the Victoria Railroad Station.

As you gaze down Belgrave Road, looking at the hotels that line the street, you'll find few recommendable choices, as many are now occupied by welfare recipients. With some exceptions, you'll find the pickings better on the satellite streets jutting off Belgrave Road.

Your best bet, however, is to walk about Ebury Street, which lies directly to the east of Victoria Station and Buckingham Palace Road. There you will find some of the best moderately priced lodgings in central London. My favorite recommendations along this street follow.

Collin House, 104 Ebury St., S.W.1 (tel. 730-8031), provides a good, clean B&B under the watchful eye of its resident proprietors, Mr. and Mrs. D. L. Thomas. Everything is maintained here, and all bedrooms have carpets, hot and cold running water, built-in wardrobes, and comfortable divan beds, and the majority have private showers and toilets. Single rooms with private bath/shower and toilet cost £26 ($39) per night; doubles rent for £32 ($48) without bath, rising to £36 ($54) with a private bath and toilet. All rates are inclusive of a full English breakfast, VAT, and the use of showers and toilets for those who don't have private facilities. There are also a number of family rooms. The main bus, rail, and Underground terminals are about a five-minute walk from the hotel. Tube: Victoria Station.

Ebury House, 102 Ebury St., S.W.1 (tel. 730-1350), is a simple, comfortable, and straightforward guesthouse where visitors are as likely to be greeted by Lola, the longtime manager, as by owners Marilyn and David Davies. All of the 13 bedrooms contain color TV and hairdryers, and there is one full bath per floor and a pay phone on

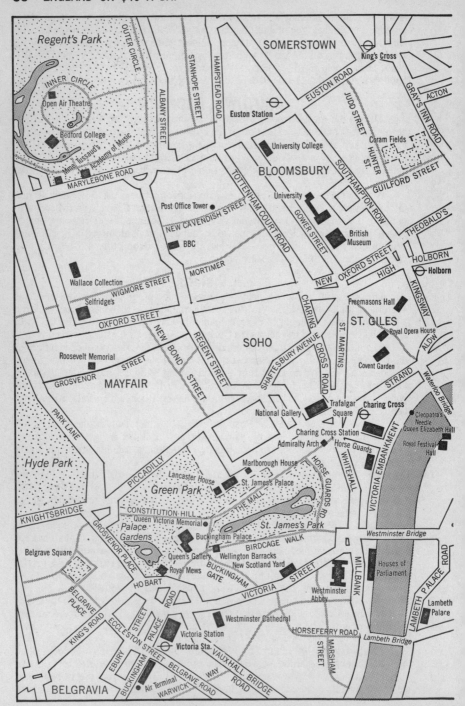

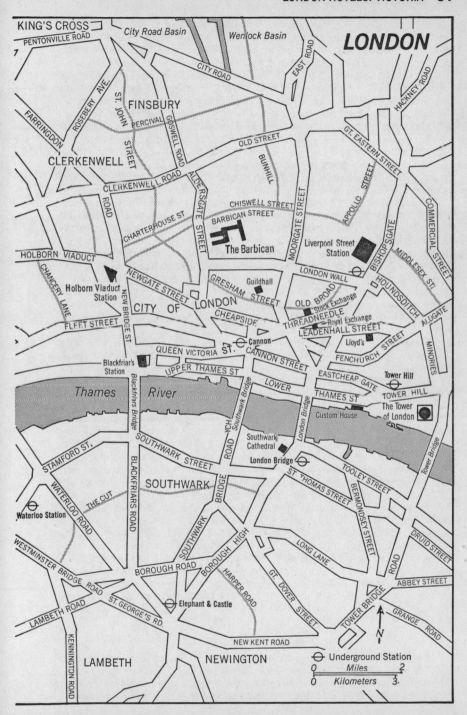

LONDON

KING'S CROSS

PENTONVILLE ROAD

7

City Road Basin

Wenlock Basin

CITY ROAD

EAST ROAD

HACKNEY ROAD

FARRINGDON

ROSEBERY AVE.

ST. JOHN STREET

PERCIVAL

GOSWELL ROAD

FINSBURY

OLD STREET

BUNHILL

GT. EASTERN STREET

APOLLO STREET

COMMERCIAL STREET

CLERKENWELL

CLERKENWELL ROAD

ROAD

CHARTERHOUSE ST.

ALDERSGATE STREET

CHISWELL STREET

BARBICAN STREET

The Barbican

MOORGATE STREET

Liverpool Street Station

BISHOPSGATE

MIDDLESEX ST.

HOLBORN VIADUCT

CHANCERY LANE

Holborn Viaduct Station

NEWGATE STREET

NEW BRIDGE ST.

GRESHAM STREET

Guildhall

LONDON WALL

HOUNDSDITCH

CITY OF LONDON

CHEAPSIDE

OLD BROAD

Stock Exchange

THREADNEEDLE

Royal Exchange

LEADENHALL STREET

ALDGATE

FLEET STREET

QUEEN VICTORIA ST.

Cannon

CANNON STREET

Lloyd's

FENCHURCH STREET

MINORIES

Blackfriar's Station

UPPER THAMES ST.

Southwark Bridge

LOWER

EASTCHEAP GATE

Tower Hill

Blackfriars Bridge

Thames   River

THAMES ST.

London Bridge

TOWER HILL

The Tower of London

STAMFORD ST.

SOUTHWARK   STREET

YCH ROAD

Southwark Cathedral

Custom House

Tower Bridge

Waterloo Station

WATERLOO ROAD

THE CUT

BLACKFRIARS ROAD

BRIDGE

London Bridge

ST. THOMAS STREET

TOOLEY STREET

BERMONDSEY STREET

SOUTHWARK

SOUTHWARK

BOROUGH HIGH

LONG LANE

ROAD

DRUID STREET

WESTMINSTER BRIDGE ROAD

BOROUGH ROAD

HARPER ROAD

GT. DOVER STREET

ABBEY STREET

LAMBETH ROAD

ST. GEORGE'S RD.

Elephant & Castle

TOWER BRIDGE

GRANGE ROAD

KENNINGTON ROAD

LAMBETH

NEWINGTON

NEW KENT ROAD

N

⊖ Underground Station

0   Miles   2

0   Kilometers   3

one of the stairwells. Accommodations, with breakfast included, cost £26 ($39) in a single, rising to £36 ($54) in a double. The pine-paneled breakfast room is the establishment's morning rendezvous point, where anyone wanting to discuss the weekend's rugby scores will find an avid connoisseur in David. Tube: Victoria Station.

Sir Gar House, 131 Ebury St., S.W.1 (tel. 730-9378), is one of a row of identical brick-fronted town houses along Ebury Street, convenient to Victoria Station (the nearest tube stop). What makes it unique is the reception and hospitality offered by two Welsh expatriates, Brian and Iris Howells. There's a basement-level breakfast room with a brick fireplace and lots of knickknacks. Unusual for the area, the small hotel has a walled-in, very manicured garden. The Howells offer a total of 11 comfortably furnished rooms, each with hot and cold running water, about half of them contain showers and toilets, for which you pay more: £40 ($60) for two persons, with VAT, service, and a full Welsh breakfast included. However, bathless rooms rent for £33 ($49.50) in a double, £25 ($37.50) in a single.

Elizabeth Hotel, 37 Eccleston Square, S.W.1 (tel. 828-6812), is an intimate, privately owned establishment overlooking the quiet gardens of a stately square. It is an excellent place to stay, convenient to Belgravia, Chelsea, and Westminster, and not far from Buckingham Palace. Of its 24 rooms, three have baths or showers, and good facilities are available for the bathless rooms, which have hot and cold water basins. Singles without bath cost from £24 ($36), and bathless doubles or twins go for £37 ($55.50). A double with a sink and shower but no toilet is priced at £41 ($61.50). A large double with a full bathroom, color TV, and refrigerator rents for £52 ($78). Prices include a full English breakfast and VAT. J.M.C. Maslinski, the proprietor, will help guests find good pubs and restaurants in the neighborhood. Tube: Victoria Station.

Chesham House Hotel, 64-66 Ebury St., S.W.1 (tel. 730-8513), has a stone facade flanked by a pair of old-fashioned carriage lamps, and its interior is more modernized than you'd expect from a glance at the outside. Each of the 23 rooms contains a TV and running water; none has a private bath. Coffee is served continuously after 5 p.m. every day, and breakfast is served in a functional basement room. The director, Major Eric J. Fletcher, rents singles from £20 ($30), doubles for £32 ($48) to £36 ($54), and family rooms for £42 ($63) to £48 ($72) per night. A full English breakfast is included in the room price. Tube: Victoria Station.

Victor Hotel, 51 Belgrave Rd., S.W.1 (tel. 828-6867), often attracts visitors who have just arrived from France via Victoria Station. A small hotel, it contains only 15 bedrooms, each of which is adequately furnished with wall-to-wall carpets, beds with innerspring mattresses, and hot and cold running water. A double rents for £22 ($33), a twin with shower or toilet for £30 ($45). There are some family rooms with bath at £34 ($51). The location is only a few minutes from coach and train stations. An English breakfast is included in the tariffs. Tube: Victoria Station.

Granada Hotel, 73 Belgrave Rd., S.W.1 (tel. 834-6560). Set into a row of identical houses, each with a protruding Adam-style porch, this renovated hotel offers comfortable accommodations. Each of the 16 bedrooms contains its own shower, TV and video, a phone, and radio and cassette. Most of them have complete baths. The Spanish-born owner, José Gil, has installed a ground-floor sauna, Jacuzzi, sunbed, and bar. Breakfast is the only meal served. The bedrooms rent for £24 ($36) in a single, £38 ($57) in a double, and £42 ($63) to £48 ($72) in a triple. Tube: Victoria Station.

3. Earl's Court

Another popular hotel and rooming-house district is the area in and around Earl's Court, below Kensington, bordering the western half of Chelsea. A 15-minute subway ride from the Earl's Court station will take you into the heart of Piccadilly, via either the District or Piccadilly Line. It is convenient to both the West End Air Terminal and the Exhibition Halls.

Incidentally, Earl's Court was for years a staid residential district, drawing genteel ladies who wore pince-nez, but I haven't seen one for a long time. Now a new young crowd is attracted to the district at night, principally to a number of pubs, wine bars, and coffeehouses. In summer, Australians virtually fill up all the cheap B&B houses.

The bulletin boards at 214 Earl's Court Rd. and the news agents next to the Earl's Court Underground station are still the best place to go for those seeking either a single overnight accommodation or a shared apartment (three women, for example, will advertise for a fourth to help meet expenses). At this type of do-it-yourself operation, rates and accommodations vary widely, according to availability.

The Beaver Hotel, 57–59 Philbeach Gardens, S.W.5 (tel. 373-4553), comprises 55 rooms on four floors. Built in the typical town house fashion, the hotel offers singles at £16 ($24) and doubles at £13 ($19.50) per person nightly for a bed and a full English breakfast, including service and tax. A few rooms have three or four beds, and these are suitable for families with children. Several of the rooms possess private baths and rent for £18 ($27) per person, based on double occupancy. But all the rooms are centrally heated and contain water basins, radios, and telephones. A bar serves drinks and snacks in the evening. Tube: Earl's Court.

Hotel Halifax, 65 Philbeach Gardens, S.W.5 (tel. 373-4153), is a well-appointed Victorian house which has been brought up to date with such amenities as central heating. Behind a neoclassical portico and an iron fence, the hotel rents out 15 bedrooms, each with hot and cold running water, color TV, and a radio and intercom unit. Some accommodations contain a private shower as well. Singles cost £18 ($27), doubles £28 ($42) to £33 ($49.50), depending on the plumbing. Guests are given their own keys. The hotel opens onto a tree-lined crescent near the Earl's Court tube stop.

Terstan Hotel, 29–31 Nevern Square, S.W.5 (tel. 373-5368), accommodates up to 90 guests in rooms that are centrally heated and have radio and phone. An elevator runs to all floors, and except for some singles, the bedrooms, which are simply furnished, contain private baths. Singles cost £19 ($28.50) without bath, from £23 ($34.50) to £28 ($42) with bath. Doubles or twins rent for £30 ($45) to £32 ($48). Ask about one of the three-bed family rooms with bath, costing from £39 ($56.55). All these tariffs include an English breakfast, VAT, and service charge. Rooms with private baths also contain color TV sets. In addition to a public lounge, there is a licensed bar and separate TV room. Mr. and Mrs. Tadaka are the hosts in this substantial brick structure, opening onto a square of similar dwellings, each fronting a private garden. London buses 74 and 31 pass within 100 yards of Nevern Square, and the Earl's Court Underground station is nearby.

Kensington Court Hotel, 33 Nevern Pl., S.W.5 (tel. 370-5151), lying just off Earl's Court Road, stands on a quiet residential street of Victorian era town houses. It presents one of the few modern facades on the street. The owners rent out a total of 35 clean, well-kept bedrooms, each with private bath, color TV, and coffee-making equipment. Singles cost £38 ($57), doubles or twins, £48 ($72). Some family units for three or four guests rent from £53 ($79.50) to £58 ($87). Bar snacks are available throughout the day and evening in the lounge bar. Tube: Earl's Court.

The Hogarth Hotel, Hogarth Road, S.W.5 (tel. 370-6831), is about 16 years old, which puts it in dramatic contrast to the Victorian houses in the neighborhood. Its vertical rows of windows betray its recent construction. Rising five floors near the Earl's Court Exhibition Centre, the hotel has a neat, streamlined lobby, along with a well-appointed restaurant. A large hotel, at least for a budget category choice, it contains 85 rooms, each with private bath, color TV, and coffee-making facilities. With a continental breakfast included, singles cost £42 ($63), doubles or twins, £55 ($82.50), and triples £65 ($97.50), including service and tax. Tube: Earl's Court.

Concord Hotel, 155 Cromwell Rd., S.W.5 (tel. 370-4151), offers one of the best values along this busy traffic artery. Frankly, many of the hotels along Cromwell

Road are disasters, but this one is suitable. It stands behind a brown brick facade with neoclassical detailing with a garden and children's sandboxes. There's a sunken TV lounge with leather couches. The front parlor has some of the original plasterwork around the coves, although the modern trappings are spartan. Rooms are modestly furnished but clean and comfortable. In all, Mrs. Hryniewicz, the owner, rents out 40 rooms, 15 of which contain a private shower or bath. Depending on the plumbing, singles cost £20 ($30) to £25 ($37.50), doubles £28.50 ($42.75) to £37 ($55.50). The hotel is not licensed for alcohol, but does offer breakfast. Tube: Earl's Court.

4. Brompton and South Kensington

Brompton and South Kensington (S.W.7), south of Kensington Gardens and Hyde Park, are essentially residential areas, not as elegant as bordering Belgravia and Knightsbridge. The section is, however, rich in museums—in fact, is often dubbed museumland—and it has a number of colleges and institutes, which draw large numbers of students.

Staying in this section of London has much to recommend it. In addition to the nearby Kensington museums, such as the Victoria and Albert, Albert Hall is within the district, and Kensington Gardens and Harrods department store are within walking distance. At the South Kensington Station, you can catch trains for Kew Gardens and Richmond in Surrey.

One of the best streets in London for hotels is the gracefully charming Sumner Place in South Kensington. However, most of these hotels are over our budget, but represent such good value, nevertheless, that I've decided to include them. Sumner Place was a rundown street filled with roughly similar Victorian houses, each of which was built during the early years of Victoria's reign. Today the street has been considerably upgraded. The rental income from the buildings along the street goes into a charitable trust, which was set up as a philanthropic institution after the death of the street's largest freeholder (landowner). Any of the street's hotels can be reached via the South Kensington tube stop or via buses 30, 45, and 14.

Number Sixteen, 16 Sumner Pl., S.W.7 (tel. 589-5232). This elegant luxury "pension" is the personal statement of its owner, Michael Watson, who has gradually acquired four early Victorian town houses and linked them together into a dramatically organized whole. As each house was added, the front and rear gardens expanded, until their flowering shrubs and tulips create one of the most idyllic spots on the street. The 32 rooms are identified by name (Aspen, Oak Room, etc.), and contain an eclectic mixture of English antiques and modern paintings. Light breakfasts are served in the rooms, and are included in the price of a night's stay. There's even an honor-system self-service bar in one of the elegantly formal sitting rooms, where a blazing fire is lit to take off the cold weather chill. Many of the clients of this place are tied into the arts in some way. Singles range from £37 ($55.50) to £47 ($70.50), with doubles going for £65 ($97.50) to £85 ($127.50). Tube: South Kensington.

Aster House, 3 Sumner Pl., S.W.7 (tel. 581-5888). The smallest hotel on this very unusual street of hotels is contained behind an early Victorian facade. Rachel and Peter Carapiet, both of whom are Armenian, are the charming owners of this hotel, whose patrons come from around the world. There's a square garden in back, plus a glassed-in conservatory where breakfast and afternoon teas are served. All of the hotel's dozen bedrooms contain private baths. Depending on the plumbing, singles rent for £48 ($72), and doubles or twins cost from £52 ($78) to £62 ($93). Room 1 is the largest and most sought after. Each unit has a small refrigerator, phone, and TV. Tube: South Kensington.

The **Alexander Hotel,** 9 Sumner Pl., S.W.7 (tel. 581-1591), is among the most expensive on the street, but also the best. Made up of four mid-18th-century town houses transformed into a single unit, it is an elegant hostelry, thanks to the refinements made by partners Martin Langdon and John Hodder. It's filled with an array of artwork, both modern and antique. Part of the Alexander seems more like a gallery than a hotel. English hunting scenes alternate with original theater posters of Mistinguette to create an ambience that made S. J. Perelman (the comedy writer for the Marx brothers) return again and again. The 39 rooms each contain a private bath, color TV, phone, and original art. Princess Louise awarded the 1985 "Brighter Kensington" hotel award to this thriving establishment, which added a garden studio apartment into the recesses of its well-tended garden. Singles are priced at £55 ($82.50), and doubles cost £70 ($105) to £85 ($127.50), with breakfast and VAT included. Prices tend to be about 10% lower in winter. Tube: South Kensington.

Sydney Place Hotel, 6 Sydney Pl., S.W.7 (tel. 584-5637), is run by Mr. and Mrs. C. J. Bygraves. It is centrally situated near the museumland of London, as well as the best shopping areas of Knightsbridge, King's Road, and Chelsea. It is also close to the private home of Margaret Thatcher. The tariffs are from £20 ($30) in a single, from £30 ($45) in a double, and from £14 ($21) per person in a triple. Half prices are quoted for children under 12. Units contain hot and cold running water, a gas or electric heater, and TV. There are showers or bathrooms on each floor, and rates include an English breakfast. Tube: South Kensington.

Eden Plaza Hotel, 68-69 Queensgate, S.W.7 (tel. 370-6111), set behind a well-maintained 1850s era facade, was opened as a hotel in 1972. Standing on a broad, tree-lined boulevard, which gets a lot of traffic, it is especially reasonable in price considering its fine neighborhood. Double-glazed windows help keep out the traffic noise. The hotel rents out 65 bedrooms, which, frankly, are quite small but well maintained. They are furnished with modern pieces, each with private bath or shower, direct-dial phone, color TV, and hairdryer. An elevator services all floors. A single rents for £45 ($67.50), doubles or twins from £56 ($84) to £60 ($90), and triples for £72 ($108). Breakfast is included in the price, along with VAT and service. A cocktail bar is a good rendezvous point, and a restaurant, the Plaza, serves both British and continental dishes. The hotel also has a sauna along with massage and solarium rooms. Tube: Gloucester Road.

Adelphi Hotel, 127–129 Cromwell Rd., S.W.7 (tel. 373-7177), is set within a brick-fronted structure which was originally constructed as two private town houses in the 1860s. Now transformed into one of the best value hotels in the neighborhood, it rents out about 60 comfortably furnished bedrooms which come in widely different shapes and dimensions. All but three of these contain private baths. Singles rent for £45 ($67.50), doubles or twins for £60 ($90), triples for £70 ($105), and four-bedded units for £79 ($118.50). Rates include an English breakfast, service, and tax, and all accommodations are equipped with phone, color TV, and radio. The large bow window of its front parlor has been transformed into a stylish lounge with a bar. Tube: Gloucester Road.

The Sorbonne Hotel, 39 Cromwell Rd., S.W.7 (tel. 589-6636), built in 1840, was once the private residence of the aunt of Sir Winston Churchill. Nowadays, standing opposite the Natural History Museum, and near Harrods department store, it is an appealing choice. The Sorbonne has a neoclassical facade appropriate to its French name. The owners rent out 20 pleasant rooms, a dozen of which contain private shower or bath, along with a phone and radio. The furniture is, in a word, practical. Accommodations, naturally, depend on the plumbing: singles from £18.50 ($27.75) to £29 ($43.50), doubles from £28.50 ($58.50), rising to a high of £39 ($58.50) in a twin with bath. Some triples with bath are also rented for £48 ($72), these tariffs including VAT and a continental breakfast. The hotel is not licensed for alcohol. Tube: South Kensington.

5. Knightsbridge

Adjoining Belgravia is Knightsbridge, a top residential and shopping district of London. Just south of Hyde Park, Knightsbridge is close in character to Belgravia.

Much of this section of the west of Sloane Street is older, dating back in architecture and layout to the 18th century. Several of the major department stores, such as Harrods, are here. Since Knightsbridge is not principally a hotel district, my recommendations are limited.

Knightsbridge Green Hotel, 159 Knightsbridge, S.W.1 (tel. 584-6274). This unusual establishment was constructed a block from Harrods in the 1920s. Later, when it was converted into a hotel, the developers were careful to retain the wide baseboards, cove molding, high ceilings, and spacious proportions of the dignified old structure. None of the accommodations contains a kitchen, but the result comes close to apartment-style living. Many of the doubles or twins are suites, each well furnished with access to the second-floor "club room" where coffee and pastries are available throughout the day. Each of the accommodations contains a private bath, phone, and TV set. Singles rent for £38 ($57) a night, and doubles cost £52 ($78). VAT and breakfast are extra. Tube: Knightsbridge.

Knightsbridge Hotel, 10 Beaufort Gardens, S.W.3 (tel. 589-9271), sandwiched between the restaurants and fashionable boutiques of Beauchamp Place and Harrods, still retains the feeling of a traditional British hotel. On a treelined square that is peaceful and tranquil, and free from traffic, it has a subdued Victorian charm. The place is small, only 20 bedrooms, and is personally run by the manager, Robert A. Novella. Each of the accommodations has phones, radios, and central heating, and there's a lounge with a color "telly" and a bar on the premises. Most expensive are the rooms with full or partial private bath, renting for £26 ($39) to £32.50 ($48.75) in a single and £49 ($73.50) to £53.50 ($80.25) in a twin. The best for the budget are the bathless units, priced at £23.50 ($35.25) in a single and £33.50 ($50.25) in a twin. Depending on the plumbing, triples range from £50 ($75) to £58.50 ($87.75). Each price includes a continental breakfast, VAT, and service. Tube: Knightsbridge.

6. Chelsea

This fashionable district stretches along the Thames, south of Hyde Park, Brompton, and South Kensington. Beginning at Sloane Square, it runs westward toward the periphery of Earl's Court and West Brompton. Its spinal cord is King's Road. The little streets and squares on either side of the King's Road artery have hundreds of tiny cottages used formerly by the toiling underprivileged of the 18th and 19th centuries. By now, except maybe for Mayfair or Belgravia, Chelsea couldn't be more chic. Hence, the tourist seeking reasonably priced accommodations should follow Greeley's sage advice to go west. However, those who can afford a splurge may want to settle in here.

Blair House Hotel, 34 Draycott Pl., S.W.3 (tel. 581-2323), is a good, moderately priced choice for those who'd like to anchor deep in the heart of Chelsea. An old-fashioned building of architectural interest, it has been modernized and completely refurnished. Rooms are usually small but still comfortable, and contain such conveniences as phone, radio, and facilities for making tea or coffee, along with a TV set. Most rooms contain a private bath or shower, and, naturally, these are more expensive. Singles range in price from £27 ($40.50) to £37.50 ($56.25), and twins or doubles cost from £38 ($57) to £49 ($73.50), including a continental breakfast and VAT. Tube: Sloane Square.

Eden House, 111 Old Church St., S.W.3 (tel. 352-3403), built in 1914 as the London residence of Lord Airedale, is today a pleasantly attractive guesthouse, the domain of Peter Johnson and his family. Some of the bedrooms spill into what used to be a separate adjoining house. Each of the 14 accommodations is reached via a carved stairwell. In back, accessible via a sitting room filled with Delft tiles and marquetry antiques, is a small garden. No meals other than breakfast are served; however, snacks and tea are available upon request. All but three of the accommodations have a private bath, and each is equipped with a phone and TV. Rates depend on the plumbing. Singles rent for £25 ($37.50) to £37 ($55.50), and doubles cost £26 ($39) to £47 ($70.50). Breakfast is included in the price, and VAT is extra. Tube: Gloucester Road.

Oakley House, 71–72 Oakley St., S.W.3 (tel. 352-7610), is contained within two nearly identical Victorian houses whose front stoop is accented with masses of potted ivy. Until they talk to the establishment's distinguished owner, Asif Ali, few visitors realize the cultural wealth of the neighborhood. He offers literary maps indicating the houses where such luminaries as Sir Thomas More and Oscar Wilde lived. Modern-day luminaries who own houses in the area include everybody from Margaret Thatcher to J. Paul Getty II. When visitors tire of pavement pounding, they can retire into the cool recesses of the Ali family garden, where a marble Buddha meditates between cascades of camellia and hydrangea. With his Pakistan-born wife, Kausar, and their son, Mr. Ali rents 24 well-maintained bedrooms, none of which contains a private bath, but each has hot and cold running water. There are showers and baths on each landing. A generous breakfast buffet is included in the prices: from £16 ($24) to £20 ($30) in a single, £23 ($34.50) to £27 ($40.50) in a twin, and £33 ($49.50) in a triple, and £40 ($60) in a quad. Take bus 11, 22, or 49 to reach the place.

WEST LONDON

A potential bonanza for finding a room. There are literally hundreds of private hotels scattered over a wide and attractive section of the West End. I'll first list the guesthouses in the Royal Borough of Kensington (west of Kensington Gardens and Hyde Park).

In the same vicinity is another hunting ground, Bayswater, encompassing within its undefined borders Queensway and Notting Hill Gate. The alreadymentioned Paddington district, surrounding Paddington Station, north of Hyde Park, is one of the major sections for budget hotels in London, with the prized Sussex Gardens in its lair. Finally, I'll conclude with St. Marylebone, a section that touches one corner of Hyde Park and is next to Regent's Park in the east, Edgeware Road in the west.

7. Kensington

The Royal Borough (W.8) draws its greatest number of visitors from shoppers (Kensington High Street), but it also contains a number of fine middle-class guesthouses, lying, for the most part, west of Kensington Gardens. The district can be a convenient place at which to stay—so near the Kensington Palace where Queen Victoria was once a resident. Of course, in Victoria's day the rows of houses along Kensington Palace Gardens were inhabited by millionaires (yet Thackeray also lived there). Today the houses are occupied in part by foreign ambassadors.

Hotel Lexham, 32–38 Lexham Gardens, W.8 (tel. 373-6471), is a Victorian terrace hotel opened in 1956. It is owner-operated, lying on an attractively quiet residential street with a cast-iron fence out front. Four connected town houses make up the hotel, and some rooms still have high ceilings and elaborate cove molding. Of the 60 comfortably furnished bedrooms, nearly half contain a private bath or shower. Depending on the plumbing, singles cost from £22 ($33) to £26.50 ($39.75), doubles or twins from £29.50 ($44) to £40 ($60). Units also contain phones, radios, electric shaver points, and central heating, and families with children receive a special welcome. Guests have use of two well-appointed lounges, and a restaurant overlooking a walled garden serves a traditional English breakfast (included in the tariffs) along with moderately priced lunches or dinners. Tube: Gloucester Road.

Atlas Hotel, 24–30 Lexham Gardens, W.8 (tel. 373-7873), along with the nearby Apollo Hotel (see below), offers a total of 130 rooms between the two, 70% of which contain private baths. Most of the bathless rooms are singles. This long-established hotel enjoys patronage by budget-conscious travelers from all over the world. They know they'll get good value in the rooms at prices ranging from £20 ($30)

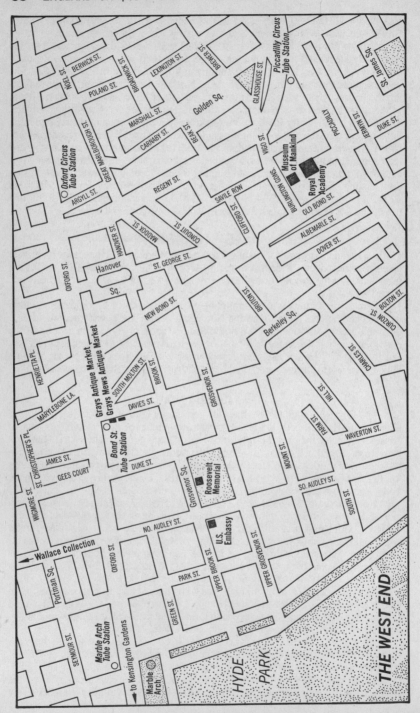

to £28 ($42) in a single, from £15 ($22.50) to £20 ($30) per person in a twin- or double-bedded unit. Three adults can also rent a triple-bedded room with bath at £16 ($24) per person. One child (that is, 12 or under) sharing a room with parents stays free. Tube: Gloucester Road.

Apollo Hotel, 18–22 Lexham Gardens, W.8 (tel. 373-3236), shares much in common with its just-recommended sister, the Atlas. There are differences in the accommodations, of course. For example, the Apollo has more rooms with baths; whereas, there are more showers at the Atlas. The tariffs are the same, however: from £20 ($30) to £28 ($42) in a single, from £15 ($22.50) to £20 ($30) per person in a twin- or double-bedded unit. The owner operates these Victorian buildings on a quiet residential street in Kensington, just off Cromwell Road. Dinner at the Apollo is a good buy at £6 ($9) per person, including VAT. Guests of both hotels use the dinner restaurant at the Apollo; however, there are bars at both hotels. An elevator services all floors. Tube: Gloucester Road.

Vicarage Private Hotel, 10 Vicarage Gate, W.8 (tel. 229-4030), is the domain of Eileen and Martin Diviney, who charge £14.50 ($21.75) in a single, £13 ($19.50) per person in a double, £10 ($15) per person in a triple, and £9 ($13.50) per person in a quad. All rates include breakfast, individually prepared by Mrs. Diviney. The rooms have pleasant furnishings, water basins, and shaver points, and there is a good supply of showers. The house is centrally heated. Vicarage Gate is handy for boutiques and restaurants on Kensington Church Street, and a laundromat is nearby. Parking is likely to be a major problem in case you bring a car into London. The nearest tube stops are Kensington High and Notting Hill Gate.

Clearlake Hotel, 19 Prince of Wales Terrace, W.8 (tel. 937-3274), is a family hotel on a residential street facing Kensington Gardens. Remodeled from a row of early Victorian houses, the hotel offers several conveniences for the traveler weary of typical hotel life. You can, of course, rent the comfortable single and double rooms, but the real finds here are the one-, two-, and three-room apartments with private baths and gas or electric kitchenettes. Some apartments also have a full-size kitchen and two bathrooms. The larger apartments can accommodate as many as eight, with plenty of closet space to go around. Rates range from £18 ($27) single up to £82 ($123) for a large apartment capable of housing four or more. All units have phones, color TV, and firm beds. Tube: Kensington High Street or Gloucester Road.

Avonmore Hotel, 66 Avonmore Rd., W.14 (tel. 603-4296), is easily accessible to West End theaters and shops yet is located in a quiet neighborhood, only two minutes from the West Kensington station of the Underground's District Line. It's also reached by bus number 9, 27, or 73. The Avonmore, a privately owned, bright, friendly place, boasts wall-to-wall carpeting, color TV sets, refrigerators, phones, radio alarms, and central heating in each room. An English breakfast, VAT, and service are included in the price of £35 ($52.50) for a double room or £20 ($30) for a single.

Abbey House, 11 Vicarage Gate, W.8 (tel. 727-2594), is managed by Mr. and Mrs. Nayach, who see that it's kept clean and comfortable. Although the interior of the brick house, built about 1860 on a typical Victorian square, is modern, thanks to renovations, the house contains original marble foyers, high ceilings, and the cast iron balustrade of its front entrance. The 15 spacious bedrooms have shaver points, vanity lights, and hot and cold water basins, and the hotel offers shared bathrooms, with one to each two to four lodging units. Singles rent for £18 ($27) and doubles for £30 ($45), with VAT and a hot breakfast included. Tube: Kensington High Street.

8. Shepherd's Bush

Gillett Hotel, 120 Shepherd's Bush Rd., W.6 (tel. 603-0784), is owned and operated by Mr. and Mrs. C. N. Gillett, whose place lies only 15 minutes by tube from Piccadilly Circus. The rooms have hot and cold water, television, and some have re-

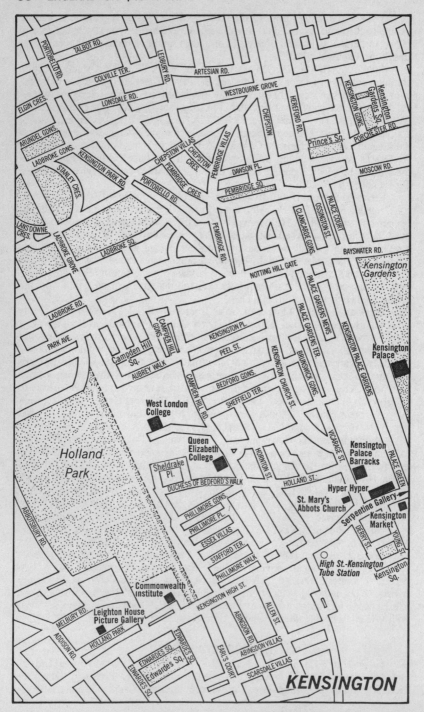

frigerators. There are shower stalls on two floors and the price is £12 ($18) per person, including breakfast. The rooms are clean and adequately furnished. The breakfast, served in the dining room, is a typical, filling English one. The hotel is a short distance to the Shepherd's Bush or Hammersmith Underground stations.

9. Notting Hill Gate

Increasingly gaining in fashion and frequented by such persons as the Princess of Wales, Notting Hill Gate is bounded on the south by Bayswater Road and on the east by Gloucester Terrace. It is hemmed in on the north by West Way and on the west by the Shepherd's Bush ramp leading to the M40. It has many turn-of-the-century mansions and small houses sitting on quiet, leafy streets.

The **Pembridge Court Hotel,** 34 Pembridge Gardens, W.2 (tel. 229-9977), presents a neoclassically elegant, cream-colored facade to a residential neighborhood that is making gains toward gentrification. Its brick-lined restaurant, where full meals with wine cost from £15 ($22.50), is a popular and well-recommended attraction, often filled with the owners of neighboring town houses taking a break from the broken plaster and rusty pipes of their renovations. Most of the 26 comfortably outfitted bedrooms contain at least one antique, as well as 19th-century engravings and plenty of warmly patterned fabrics. All units have private baths, color TV, direct-dial phones, and hairdryers. A full English breakfast is included in the price of £40 ($60) in a single, from £55 ($82.50) to £85 ($127.50) in a double. The building, which was constructed in 1852 as a private house, is ably administered by Paul Capra. Tube: Notting Hill Gate

10. Paddington / Bayswater

Another popular hotel area, jammed with budget housing, is the Paddington section, around Paddington Station, just to the northwest of Kensington Gardens and Hyde Park. Here, you'll be within walking distance of Marble Arch, a central entrance into Hyde Park. Lying just north of Bayswater Road and Kensington Gardens, slightly to the west of Hyde Park, Bayswater is an unofficial district with a number of decently priced lodgings. Many former town houses—converted into guesthouses or private hotels—date back to the days when Bayswater spelled the good life to a prosperous upper middle class. Some of these houses, often lined up in rows, open onto pleasant squares.

Again, you'd be well advised to telephone ahead before you make your search. If you have not obtained a reservation, then begin your trek by taking the Underground to either Paddington or Edgware Road, and then by walking to Sussex Gardens, a long avenue flanked by bed-and-breakfast houses, many of which, quite frankly, are dreadfully rundown and in need of a major overhaul. That's not all: Many of the budget hotels in the Paddington and Bayswater areas now deal mostly with homeless persons sent from the local authorities. Postbreakfast hours, when guests have just checked out, are your best time for finding a vacancy.

If you're unable to find a room on Sussex Gardens, then try the satellite Norfolk Square, which lies near Sussex Gardens (even closer to Paddington Station) and contains additional guesthouses. My recommendations on nearby Sussex Gardens follow.

Columbia Hotel, 95–99 Lancaster Gate, W.2 (tel. 402-0021), overlooks Kensington Gardens and Hyde Park. For the money, it offers one of the best deals in the neighborhood. Once an embassy, it was originally constructed as four town houses, and was the site of a well-known military club, the Columbia Club, in World War II. In fact, the U.S. military still gets a 10% discount off regular rates. About 12 years ago, it became a hotel, with 94 well-furnished bedrooms, each with private shower or bath and color TV. Obviously, the accommodations with views over Hyde Park are grabbed up first. Prices, including VAT, service, and an English breakfast, are from £33 ($49.50) to £37 ($55.50) in a single, £39 ($58.50) to £49 ($73.50) in a double or twin, and £59 ($88.50) in a triple. Guests enjoy the Regency-style residents' lounge or the Trafalgar Cocktail Bar. An in-house restaurant serves good, straightforward cookery, with dinners costing from £10 ($15). Tube: Paddington Station or Lancaster Gate.

Craven Gardens Hotel, 16 Leinster Terrace, W.2 (tel. 262-3167), lies right north of Kensington Gardens and Bayswater Road. Within a yellow-and-white neoclassical-style Victorian building, with a Doric portico, it offers a total of 45 modestly furnished but well-kept bedrooms, only four of which lack a private bath. Each unit has a color TV, phone, and radio. Singles cost from £33 ($49.50) to £37 ($55.50), doubles or twins from £39 ($58.50) to £49 ($73.50), and some triples from £59 ($88.50). Only breakfast is served. A few steps from the modern reception area is a bar outfitted with cane furnishings, that's popular with residents. Tube: Paddington Station or Lancaster Gate.

Hotel Parkwood, 4 Stanhope Pl., W.2 (tel. 402-2241), occupies one of the best locations for a good value hotel in London, standing right near Oxford Street and Marble Arch. Hotel entrepreneur Peter Evans acquired this desirable building—once the private residence of a wealthy Victorian—and now offers 18 well-furnished bedrooms, mainly with private baths. The location, on a fairly quiet street just 50 yards from Hyde Park, is in a section of London known as Connaught Village, with many Georgian and Victorian structures. Behind a cream-colored facade, guests are received in a pleasant high-ceilinged reception area which doubles as a TV lounge. Cozy, clean rooms await the visitor at the top of a winding staircase, where there are about three units per floor. Only breakfast is served, and tariffs include VAT. Singles cost £28 ($42) to £40 ($60), doubles or twins £40 ($60) to £50 ($75), and some triple-bedded units £55 ($82.50) to £63 ($94.50). All accommodations contain color TV and coffee-making equipment. Tube: Marble Arch.

The **Colonnade Hotel,** 2 Warrington Crescent, W.9 (tel. 286-1052), is an imposing town house in a pleasant residential area. Owned and managed for some 35 years by the Richards family, the hotel is run in a personal and friendly manner. The 53 bedrooms are spacious, some with balconies, and are equipped with either private baths/showers or hot and cold water basins. All have TV, radios, phones, hairdryers, and trouser presses. Seven have four-poster beds. The rates in rooms with private baths are from £32 ($48) to £35 ($52.50) in a single and from £50 ($75) to £85 ($127.50) in a double. Units without baths rent for £28.50 ($42.75) for a single and £40 ($60) for a double. A full English breakfast and VAT are included, but a 10% service charge is added to your bill. Mr. Richards emphasizes: "Every bedroom, bathroom, and corridor is centrally heated 24 hours a day of every day from the first chill wind of autumn until the last breath of retreating winter, even in summer if necessary." He's installed a water-softening plant as well. The hotel has a licensed restaurant and a garden bar. Tube: Warwick Avenue station.

Mornington Lancaster Hotel, 12 Lancaster Gate, W.2 (tel. 262-7361), brings a touch of Swedish hospitality to the center of London. Just north of Hyde Park and Kensington Gardens, the hotel has been completely redecorated with a Scandinavian-designed interior. The bedrooms, 70 in all, are not only tastefully conceived and comfortable, but each unit is complete with private bath and shower, color TV, a phone, and a radio. Rates are from £32 ($48) to £52 ($78) in a single, rising to £53 ($79.50) to £59 ($88.50) in a double or twin. If you're traveling with a child, the Swedish-speaking staff will place an extra bed in your room for an additional charge. Tariffs include a Scandinavian buffet breakfast, service, and VAT. Naturally, there's a genuine Finnish sauna. You can order snacks and even afternoon tea, if you're there at the right time, in the well-stocked bar. The library is a comfortable place for visitors to wind down. Tube: Lancaster Gate.

Camelot Hotel, 45 Norfolk Square, W.2 (tel. 723-9118), is a hideaway town house (now turned hotel), a remarkable bargain and a friendly oasis. It stands at the corner of an old, tree-filled square, only two minutes from Paddington Station. Peter

Evans purchased the property in 1981 and completely refurbished it from top to bottom, installing some new showers and redesigning the dining room. A lounge was also provided, and the hotel has been recarpeted throughout. All bedrooms have color TV, radio, and tea- and coffee-making facilities. Prices are fully inclusive of all facilities, and that means free luggage storage, ironing facilities, hair dryers, whatever. Mr. Evans's aim is to provide full hotel standards at a budget price. A single room rents for £21 ($31.50), a double or twin-bedded room for £15 ($22.50) per person. Families may be interested in one of the three- or four-bedded rooms, renting at a cost of £12 ($18) per person. These tariffs include VAT and as much as you can eat of an English breakfast. Wisely, Mr. Evans has hired Barbara Knox as his manager. She is helpful to guests.

St. David's Hotel, 16 Norfolk Square, W.2 (tel. 402-9061), is run by George Neokleous, who offers not only clean and comfortably furnished bedrooms, but good English breakfasts and pleasant service. Rates are from £15 ($22.50) per person in units which contain hot and cold running water. There is central heating, and rooms have TV as well. Guests have found the owner helpful and courteous. The hotel stands one minute from the Paddington and Lancaster Gate tube stations.

St. George, 46 Norfolk Square, W.2 (tel. 723-3560), rents pleasant rooms, with a bath on each floor. Each unit is equipped with hot and cold running water, and the hotel has central heating. Singles rent for £15 ($22.50), and doubles go from £25 ($37.50). Triples and quads are available for £12 ($18) per person. Children sharing their parents' room are granted a reduced rate. The tariffs quoted include an English breakfast. Tube: Paddington Station.

Piccolino House, 14 Sussex Pl., W.2 (tel. 723-9360), is a Victorian town house which was converted into a comfortable hotel. The guest rooms are clean, and the English breakfast the next morning is good. The management is acommodating. The hotel has 18 bedrooms, all furnished with TV, wall-to-wall carpets, innerspring mattresses, hot and cold running water, and razor points. Showers and toilets are found on all floors. A single goes for £16 ($24) a night, a double or twin for £22 ($33) to £23 ($34.50). A triple room costs from £28 ($42), and there are some family units at £35 ($52.50). Children 5 to 12 stay here for half price. A front-door key is provided, and the management will also arrange theater tickets. Tube: Paddington Station.

Lancaster Court Hotel, 202–204 Sussex Gardens, W.2 (tel. 402-8438), is one of the best and most highly rated hotels in this neighborhood of accommodations. It has been completely refurbished, with modern amenities, and now offers 42 bedrooms, about 14 of which contain a private shower or bath. The centrally heated units offer radio, intercom, electric shaver points, and color TV. A terrace hotel, it charges from £24 ($36) to £28 ($42) in a single, from £21.50 ($32.25) to £28 ($42) per person in a double or twin, and from £17 ($25.50) to £18.50 ($27.75) per person in a triple. A few family rooms are also rented, costing from £13.50 ($20.25) to £15 ($22.50) per person. All tariffs include a continental breakfast and VAT, with 10% reductions granted in winter. The hotel has a separate breakfast room and guest lounge, with limited overnight parking out front. It's at Lancaster Gate, the nearest tube stop, but is convenient to the Paddington underground as well.

Fairways Hotel, 186 Sussex Gardens, W.2 (tel. 723-4871), is easily recognized by its colonnaded front entrance with carved iron balustrade stretching across the front second-floor windows. The building is a black-and-white painted town house near Hyde Park. Jenny and Steve Adams are the congenial owners, maintaining the 15-room establishment in cozy comfort. Many of their bright and clean bedrooms contain private baths. You can also make tea or coffee in your room. An English breakfast, served in a blue-and-white dining room, is included in the prices. Singles cost from £20 ($30), while doubles run from £32 ($48) to £38 ($57) for two, depending on the plumbing. Tube: Paddington Station.

ABC Hotel, 121 Sussex Gardens, W.2 (tel. 723-3945), is run by two Londoners,

Mr. and Mrs. W. M. Landers, who try to make their guests comfortable. All their accommodations contain hot and cold running water, tea- or coffee-making facilities, color TV, and radio, and are pleasantly furnished and kept. The rate in a double- or twin-bedded room ranges from £13 ($19.50) to £16 ($24) per person, including an English breakfast and VAT. Some family rooms are available as well. There is no limit on the baths and showers you use. The Landers couple welcomes "our American cousins," and gives advice on how to see London in the easiest and cheapest way. Tube: Paddington Station.

Nayland Hotel, 134 Sussex Gardens, W.2 (tel. 723-3380), has been a family-run hotel for more than 30 years. The helpful management offers clean and comfortable rooms equipped with TVs, radios, and tea- and coffee-making facilities. They provide a traditional English breakfast. There is a lounge with a log fire during cold weather and full central heating. Rates are from £17 ($25.50) per person nightly. The hotel is one of the few in the whole area listed by both A.A. and R.A.C. Tube: Paddington Station.

Sass House Hotel, 11 Craven Terrace, W.2 (tel. 262-2325), is a centrally located accommodation. If you anchor here, you'll be able to easily reach all of London's main attractions by foot, bus, or tube. There is a lounge with color TV, and the place is centrally heated. All the 22 bedrooms have radio and intercom phone, but don't expect a private bath. Prices begin at £16 ($24) in a single, going up to £26 ($39) in a double—most reasonable for London. Tube: Lancaster Gate.

11. St. Marylebone

Below Regent's Park, lying northwest of Piccadilly Circus, is the principally Georgian district of St. Marylebone (pronounced Mar-li-bone), a residential section facing Mayfair to the south and extending north of Marble Arch at Hyde Park. A number of simple but gracious town houses in this section have been converted into private hotels, and little discreet bed-and-breakfast signs appear in the windows.

As you walk up and down some of these streets, you are certain to find them. For example, Upper Berkeley Street has some attractively priced accommodations. If you have arrived in London without a reservation in the peak months, then start at Edgware Road and walk past Seymour and Great Cumberland Place. Let the summer crowds fight it out in Bloomsbury.

Bryanston Court Hotel, 56–60 Great Cumberland Pl., W.1 (tel. 262-3141). Each of the three individual houses that were joined together into this hotel was built around 190 years ago. Today it's one of the most elegant hotels on the street, thanks partially to the decorating efforts of its owners, the Theodore family. There's a gas fire burning in the Chesterfield-style bar, plus a stairwell leading up to the 56 bedrooms. Each of these contains a private bath, color TV, phone, and radio. The opulently red dining room, the Brunswick Restaurant, is furnished in an early 19th-century style with antiques and oil portraits. After you pass through the iron gate in front, under the awnings, you'll be quoted a single rate of £47 ($70.50) or £60 ($90) in a double, with VAT and a continental breakfast included. Tube: Marble Arch.

Hotel Concorde, 50 Great Cumberland Pl., W.1 (tel. 402-6316), is a small hotel with style. The reception desk, the nearby chairs, and part of the tiny bar area were at one time a part of a London church. A display case in the lobby contains an array of reproduction English silver, each piece of which is for sale. This establishment was built as a private house and later converted into a 30-room hotel. Each of the accommodations is modern and stylish. They all have color TV, direct-dial phones, and private baths. Singles rent for £42 ($63) and doubles for £52 ($78), with VAT and a continental breakfast included in the tariffs. Breakfast is the only meal served, but guests can patronize the Bryanston Court Restaurant, next door at the hotel recommended above. To reach it, you exit onto the street and enter the doorway adjacent. The Concorde is owned by the Theodore family and managed by their capable son,

Martin. About half a block away, they rent eight studio apartments, each with a kitchenette, costing around £80 ($120) per night. Tube: Marble Arch.

The **Edward Lear Hotel,** 30 Seymour St., W.1 (tel. 402-5401), is a popular hotel, made all the more desirable by the bouquets of fresh flowers set up around the public rooms. It's a few blocks from Marble Arch in a pair of brick town houses, both of which date from 1780. The western house was the London home of the 19th-century artist and poet Edward Lear, whose illustrated limericks adorn the walls of one of the sitting rooms. Steep stairs lead up to the 30 bedrooms, 11 of which contain private bath. The cozy bedrooms are simply furnished, usually papered in flowery patterns, all with color TV, radios, beverage facilities, hair dryers, free luggage storage, and ironing facilities. The hotel, owned by Peter Evans, is managed by Duncan McGlashan, who rents singles starting at £26 ($39), doubles and twins at £37 ($55.50), and triples at £45 ($67.50). Tube: Marble Arch.

Hart House Hotel, 51 Gloucester Pl., W.1 (tel. 935-2288), is a well-preserved building, part of a group of Georgian mansions occupied by the French nobility during the French Revolution. The hotel is in the heart of the West End and is convenient for shopping, theaters, and sightseeing. It is within a few minutes' walking distance of Oxford Street, Selfridges, Marble Arch, Hyde Park, Regent's Park, and the zoo, as well as Madame Tussaud's and the Planetarium. Hart House is centrally heated, and all rooms have hot and cold running water, color TV, radio, and phone. This is a small family hotel with 15 bedrooms, all clean and comfortable. It is run by the proprietors, Mr. and Mrs. Bowden, and their son, Andrew, who offer their guests warm hospitality. Prices, which include an English breakfast, range from £20 ($30) for a single room, £30 ($45) for a twin or double, and £43 ($64.50) for a triple. With a private bath, a twin or double costs £36 ($54), and a triple £49 ($73.50). VAT is added. Tube: Marble Arch.

Hallam Hotel, 12 Hallam St., Portland Place, W.1 (tel. 580-1166), is a heavily ornamented stone and brick Victorian house, one of the only ones on the street to escape bombing in World War II. Today it's the property of one of the most charming families in the neighborhood, Earl Baker, who maintains it with his sons, Grant and David. The breakfast room is prettily done up in shades of pink and green, with a small patio visible through glass doors. There is also a bar for residents. An elevator leads to the 23 simple but comfortable bedrooms, each with TV, phone, radio, and 24-hour room service. VAT and a light English breakfast are included in the price of the rooms, costing from £35 ($52.50) in a single, £50 ($75) in a double. Tube: Oxford Circus.

NORTHERN LONDON

London's most numerous cluster of budget hotels is to be found in the northern part of the city, a geographical designation that shouldn't discourage you. By northern I refer to an area which has as its southern border Oxford Street, New Oxford Street, and High Holborn. Its western border touches Regent's Park; its northern border, the terminals of Kings Cross, St. Pancras, and Euston Stations; its eastern border, Farringdon Road, the beginning of Finsbury. Most of the accommodations are centered in the southern part, known as Bloomsbury.

During the warmer months, June through mid-September, the hotels here are heavily booked. It is for that reason I suggest you seek out your summertime accommodations in the southwestern area of the city. If, nevertheless, you crave to live in the well-situated north, be sure to obtain advance reservations, or phone the hotels that sound attractive to you before appearing on their doorsteps. A timely call can spare you fruitless searching.

12. Bloomsbury

Northeast of Piccadilly Circus, beyond Soho, lies a world within itself. It is, among other things, the academic heart of London, where you'll find London University, several other colleges, the British Museum, and many bookstores. Despite its student overtones, the section is fairly staid and quiet. Its reputation has been fanned by such writers as Virginia Woolf, who lived within its bounds (it figured in her novel *Jacob's Room*). The novelist and her husband, Leonard, were once the unofficial leaders of a group of artists and writers known as "the Bloomsbury group"—nicknamed "Bloomsberries." At times, this intellectual camaraderie reached out to embrace Bertrand Russell.

The heart of Bloomsbury is **Russell Square,** and the streets jutting off from the square are lined with hotels and bed-and-breakfast houses. If you have not found a hotel room by phoning first, and prefer to make your search on foot, you might try the following itinerary:

From the Russell Square Underground station (whose exit is on Bernard Street), walk first along Bernard Street, which contains many hotels. Then, one long block north of Bernard Street, try Coram Street, another hotel-lined block, and after that sample Tavistock Place, running one block north of Coram and parallel to it. North of Tavistock Place is Cartwright Gardens, which has a number of old converted town houses catering to overnight guests.

The Bernard Street–Coram Street–Tavistock Place hotels are, however, the most likely Russell Square establishments to be booked in summer. You'll have a better chance on the other side of Russell Square (opposite Bernard Street), where you'll find the relatively high-priced hotels of Bloomsbury Street (lined with publishing houses) and those on the less expensive Gower Street, where you'll be at the midpoint of the London University area. On Gower Street, for instance, you'll find the Royal Academy of Dramatic Art, across from which are a number of B&B houses.

Hotel President, Russell Square, W.C.1 (tel. 837-8844), is a larger and more substantial hotel than any of the B&B establishments I've recommended so far. Part of the Imperial Hotel grouping, it dates from the 1960s when it opened in Bloomsbury with a total of 450 rooms, each with private bath, shower, and phone. However, its rates are reasonable, costing £36 ($54) in a single, £50 ($75) in a double or twin, including a full English breakfast. Rooms are centrally heated and are reached by elevator. They are clean and comfortable, but not stylish in any way. If you can't find a room here, then the Imperial grouping takes in a total of 4,500 beds in other Central London establishments, including the Imperial and the Bedford. The hotel also has vast public areas, including an arcade of shops, a hairdresser, and a coffee shop serving till 2 a.m. Tube: Russell Square.

Bonnington Hotel, 92 Southampton Row, W.C.1 (tel. 2452-2828), dates from the Edwardian era, but it's kept abreast of the times. A large and substantial hotel, this longtime Bloomsbury favorite opened in 1911. Today it's run by the Frame family, who have substantially modernized it. It lies behind an ornate facade of red brick and floral-patterned sandstone. Of the 240 comfortably furnished bedrooms, some 44 don't have private baths, and these are cheaper, of course. Regular tariffs range from £31.50 ($47.25) to £51 ($76.50) in a single, from £52 ($78) to £68 ($102) in a double- or twin-bedded room. At certain times, "getaway weekends" at greatly reduced rates are featured. Guests meet in the pleasant lounge bar for drinks or to enjoy a bar buffet with both hot and cold dishes. They can also dine in the Bonnington Grill at moderate prices. Tube: Russell Square.

"Y" Hotel, 112 Great Russell St., W.C.1 (tel. 637-1333), is a modern 168-room hotel in the heart of London. Single rooms, with VAT and service included, rent for £32.50 ($48.75) a night, with doubles and twins going for £47.50 ($71.25). All the units have private showers, central heating, color TV, and radios. The furnishings are up-to-date and comfortable, and there's even wall-to-wall carpeting. Built at the Oxford Street end of Tottenham Court Road by the London Central Young Men's Christian Association for men and women of all ages, this "Y" Hotel may be unlike any you've ever seen. Its facilities include squash courts, a gymnasium, a swimming pool, a shop, and an underground parking garage. Other facilities are a lounge and bar, plus a restaurant. Tube: Tottenham Court Road.

Morgan Hotel, 24 Bloomsbury St., W.1 (tel. 636-3735), is one of a long row of similar buildings but distinguished by its gold-tipped iron fence railings. Several of the 17 rooms overlook the British Museum, and the whole establishment is very much part of the international scholastic scene of Bloomsbury. The lobby is a bit cramped, the stairs rather steep, but the rooms are pleasant and the atmosphere congenial. Consequently, the hotel is usually heavily booked. Bedrooms, three to a floor, vary in size, some being rather large. All are well carpeted, equipped with big beds (by British standards), hot and cold water basins, dressing tables with mirrors, and ample wardrobe space. There are no private baths in this centrally heated establishment, but showers and toilets have been installed on each floor. Singles cost £19 ($28.50), doubles going for £33 ($49.50), with a full English breakfast included. The nearest tubes are Russell Square and Tottenham Court Road.

Lonsdale Hotel, 9–10 Bedford Pl., W.C.1 (tel. 636-1812), is a Regency town house, within the shadow of the British Museum. It's positioned on an attractive tree-lined street Midway between Russell and Bloomsbury Squares. It is a particular favorite of professors and scientists from the continent who find it a convenient place to stay while researching at the museum. The B&B rate in a double or twin is £33 ($49.50); singles pay £20 ($30), including VAT. All rooms have razor outlets, and the hotel has central heating. The hotel is privately owned and has a little garden in the rear. Tube: Russell Square.

Crescent Hotel, Cartwright Gardens, W.C.1 (tel. 387-1515), is a good economy choice in Bloomsbury. Its success is based in large part on the long-time management of its owner, Mrs. Bessolo, who hires a pleasant staff. Her rooms are well maintained, costing £19 ($28.50) per day in a single, rising to £31 ($46.50) for a twin- or double-bedded room. These rates include a full English breakfast and tax. In addition, she also rents out family rooms, consisting of two single beds and one double bed beginning at £39 ($58.50) daily. Children under 14 years of age pay half price in a family room. There's a TV lounge as well. Tube: Russell Square.

George Hotel, 58–60 Cartwright Gardens, W.C.1 (tel. 387-6789), is part of this famous Georgian crescent. The hotel was made from a trio of three Georgian houses dating from the turn of the 19th century. Well run and decidedly well maintained, it is one of the best of the B&Bs along this highly competitive crescent. Many of its bedrooms, 40 in all, have been redecorated. Several are quite small with an exposed sink with hot and cold running water. Only three contain a private bath or shower, and there is no room phone or TV. Singles cost £18 ($27) to £20 ($30), doubles £33 ($49.50) to £35 ($52.50), triples £39 ($59.25) to £45 ($67.50), and quads £40 ($60) to £50 ($75), including VAT and an English breakfast. Tube: Russell Square.

Academy Hotel, 19 Gower St., W.C.1 (tel. 631-4115), was built in 1770 as three separate Georgian row houses. The original builders made use of Chippendale mahogany and teak, along with marble fireplaces. Now substantially modernized, and admittedly less grand, it is nevertheless one of the most appealing budget hotels in Bloomsbury. Even after its 1986 overhaul, it still contains interesting architectural features, including the original colonnades and intricate plasterwork on the facade. The hotel rents out nearly 35 bedrooms, about 70% of which have private showers. All units contain color TV, phone, and central heating, and often dark wood furniture. Rates, including a continental breakfast, range from £32 ($48) to £48 ($72) in a single, from £52 ($78) to £65 ($97.50) in a double or twin. An extra bed in a room costs another £10 ($15). The hotel has a pleasantly decorated dining room, and its bar remains open until 2 a.m. Tube: Euston Square.

Gower House Hotel, 57 Gower St., W.C.1 (tel. 636-4685), is a clean and suitable hotel run by P. and J. Borg, its owners, who cater to families. In all, they offer 14 bedrooms, including some large family rooms, adequate for three to five persons. In

No B,

these the rate is £12 ($18) per person nightly. Otherwise, singles pay £18 ($27), and doubles or twins go for £26 ($39). All tariffs include a full English breakfast and tax. Each room contains hot and cold running water, and there is a breakfast room as well as a TV lounge. Tube: Goodge Street.

Arran House Hotel, 77 Gower St., W.C.1 (tel. 636-2186), is run by Mr. W. J. Richards, an ex-army major, who commands a good place. He lives at the hotel too *No* along with his family. The rooms are well maintained, containing hot and cold running *B* water. All are centrally heated as well, and equipped with intercom. All bedrooms are near baths, toilets, and showers. A few contain private shower and color TV. Rates in a single are £16 ($24) per person daily, rising to £22 ($33) in a twin or double. Doubles with shower cost £26 ($39). The special family rooms, with three, four, and five beds, range in price from £25 ($37.50) to £30 ($45) daily, all tariffs including a full English breakfast. There is also a residents' lounge with a color TV. Tube: Euston Square.

Ruskin Hotel, 23–24 Montague St., W.C.1 (tel. 636-7388), stands next to the British Museum, within walking distance of London's shopping district and major West End theaters. A family-run business, the hotel has several modern amenities. All floors are serviced by an elevator. Listed as a building of historical interest, the hotel has retained many of its original architectural features. The television lounge has a mural ascribed to James Ward. The bedrooms have hot and cold running water, shaver points, intercoms, hot beverage facilities, and electrical outlets. The rooms also are centrally heated, and several contain showers. The cost of a room, including a full English breakfast served in the dining room, is £19 ($28.50) in a single, from £34 ($51) in a double, including VAT. Tube: Holborn or Tottenham Court Road.

13. In and Around Hampstead

Sandringham Hotel, 3 Holford Rd., N.W.3 (tel. 435-1569). You'd never guess this is a hotel, because it stands on a residential street in one of the best parts of London. After getting off at the Hampstead tube station, you walk up Heath Street, past interesting shops, pubs, and charmingly converted houses. Shortly, you turn right into Hampstead Square which leads you into Holford Road. A high wall and trees screen the house from the street (if you have a car, you can park in the driveway). It is a well-built, centrally heated house, and the comfortable rooms often house professional people who want to be near the center of London yet retain the feel of rural life. The charges for B&B, service, and VAT are £18 ($27) for a single, £32 ($48) for a double. Some rooms have private baths, and family rooms are available. The breakfast room overlooks a walled garden. From the upper rooms you can see past the heath to a panoramic view of the center of London. You'll find a home-like lounge furnished with a color TV. The owner, Mrs. Dreyer, lives on the premises.

Frognal Lodge, 14 Frognal Gardens, N.W.3 (tel. 435-8238). The easy-going and charming staff of this attractive hotel has been the subject of several glowing reader reports. A personal investigation found it worthy of its advance billings. It's housed within the brick walls of a late 19th-century house whose rear garden offers a quiet oasis after a day in London. Of the 17 rooms, seven are equipped with full private baths and have color TV. All accommodations have phones. A generous English breakfast and VAT are included in the prices quoted by Cathy Turner, manager. Singles cost £23.50 ($35.25) for a room and shared bath, £36 ($54) with private bath. Doubles rent for £37.50 ($56.25) to £47.75 ($71.63). The attic room, which has a sloped ceiling and exposed beams, is a favorite. Tube: Hampstead.

In West Hampstead, a somewhat offbeat accommodation is provided by the **Charlotte Restaurant,** 221 West End Lane, N.W.6 (tel. 794-6476), an old established and inexpensive restaurant with a tasteful decor which offers B&B and a three-course dinner for an inclusive rate of £13 ($19.50) per person. The food is really good, and the chef will give you enough of it, both an English and a continental cuisine. Accommodations are simple but comfortable. The house lies only one minute to British Rail, tube, and bus routes (17 minutes from the heart of London). The nearest Underground station is West Hampstead.

14. Blackheath

Stonehall House Hotel, 35–37 Westcombe Park, Blackheath, S.E.3 (tel. 858-8706), is so pleasant that guests are willing to undergo a little inconvenience in transportation to stay there. The owners, Tony and Kathleen Fagg, assisted by their son Matthew, who trained at Westminster hotel school and gained experience in large London hotels, offer rooms with phones, radios, color TV, and innerspring mattresses. Inclusive rates for B&B are £15 ($22.50) in singles, £28 ($42) in a double, and £50 ($75) in a large family room. Reductions are made for children under 12 sharing a room with their parents. For stays of seven nights, you're charged for only six nights. Guests are entitled to use of the prize-winning garden. Tony Fagg was managing director of an agricultural tractor company, and he has traveled extensively in England and the U.S., as well as the rest of the world. He has many useful tips for visitors. The hotel, which accommodates 50 guests, is near Greenwich Park, with its Royal Observatory. The hotel is only a short hike from Maze Hill Station (Southern Region), where you can catch trains for the City and the West End, a 20-minute ride. It is also convenient to bus stops, and for catching boats to Greenwich and the Tower of London.

Bardon Lodge Hotel, 15–17 Stratheden Rd., Blackheath S.E.3 (tel. 853-4051), is two Victorian residences built in 1869 that still retain their original grandeur. They have been linked together to form a 42-bedroom hotel where personal and friendly service is provided. All rooms are pleasantly appointed, having showers, TV, hot beverage facilities, and direct-dial phones. Most units have private baths. A double costs £40 ($60) per night. Prices include a substantial English breakfast and taxes. The hotel is in a quiet residential area a short walk from Greenwich Park, the National Maritime Museum, and the famous Royal Naval College. From Greenwich Pier, a boat will take you to the Tower of London and Westminster. Two minutes' walk from Bardon Lodge, the no. 53 bus will take you direct to Westminster, Trafalgar Square, Piccadilly Circus, and Oxford Street.

15. On the Fringe

The Cottage, Handel Close, Canons Drive, Edgeware in Middlesex (tel. 952-2104), provides a personal family style of London living, only 35 minutes by tube from the core of the theater and shopping areas. Handel, the composer, was a chapel master and musical director for two years in this area—hence Handel Close. The house is a detached corner structure in the Tudor style. For B&B on a daily basis, Mrs. Stein charges two persons from £23 ($34.50) to £26.50 ($39.75) in a double, from £15 ($22.50) to £17 ($25.50) in a single, plus service. There are tea-making facilities in each room. No private baths are available, but there are two bathrooms. The Cottage is attractively furnished in a personal style, some windows opening onto a landscaped garden with a sunken lawn and wishing well. Canons Drive has its own seven-acre lake, available to guests. Mr. Stein is pleased to offer free rides to guests when he drives into London. Otherwise, the closest tube stations are Edgware (Northern Line) and Canons Park (Jubilee Line).

Worcester House, 38 Alwyne Rd., Wimbledon, S.W.19 (tel. 946-1300). Built as a private home around 1910, this hotel has a red brick facade accented with white trim. It contains nine rooms, each of which has its own shower and toilet, color TV, radio, phone, and tea-making equipment. The owner, opera singer Tom Emlyn Williams, charges £26 ($39) to £30 ($45) in a single, £39 ($58.50) to £43 ($64.50) in a double, with VAT and a savory English breakfast included. Evening meals are prepared if notice is given in advance. Tennis fans will appreciate this establishment's location, only ten minutes from the tennis courts at Wimbledon. Tube: Wimbledon. A train goes directly to the Wimbledon station from Waterloo Station.

Justin James Hotel, 43 Worple Rd. (corner of Malcolm Road), Wimbledon, S.W.19 (tel. 947-4271). Named after the two sons who assist their father, Alf Jessiman, this century-old building has a steep tile roof and heavy overhanging eaves. Its location is only about 30 minutes by train from Waterloo or Victoria Stations (passengers coming from Victoria will have to change trains once). All but a few of the 12 bedrooms contain private bath. Bathless singles cost £20 ($30) a night; bathless doubles or twins, £34 ($51). Twins or doubles with private bath go for £40 ($60). Tube: Wimbledon Station.

Solana, 18 Golders Rise, Henson, N.W.4 (tel. 202-5321), is a small private guesthouse run by Mrs. L.M. Taylor for non-smokers only. In this clean, terraced house, most rooms have water basins, and there is a public shower/bathroom. Prices range from £9 ($13.50) in a single to £16 ($24) for two persons sharing a twin-bedded room. The rates cover bed and breakfast, which can be either continental or English. Guests can sit in the little garden in summer. The guesthouse is in a pleasant area off the main road, but there are parks, shops, restaurants, and pubs not far away, and it is possible to park your car if you stay at Solana. It's close to the end of the M1, A406, A41, and A1 motorways and is easily reached via the Northern Line Tube and buses from the city, ten minutes walk from Hendon Central tube stop.

Mrs. Betty Merchant, 562 Caledonian Rd., Hollaway, N.7 (tel. 607-0930), has a small, comfortable private guesthouse with unrestricted parking on the street for guests. The bedrooms—one single, one double, and one family unit—rent for £8.50 ($12.75) per adult, £6.50 ($9.75) for children under 12. A full English breakfast is included in the prices. The house has central heating, and electric blankets can add to the comfort on cool nights. Mrs. Merchant's house is connected to the West End by buses which stop quite near the house. The Piccadilly Line tube's Caledonian Road stop is only a few minutes' walk away.

16. Airport Hotels

Most regularly scheduled planes will land at Heathrow, and charter flights are likely to go to Gatwick, which more and more is becoming the gateway to London. If you need to be near either airport, close to your point of departure, consider some of the following suggestions instead of the well-advertised and more expensive operations at both airports.

HEATHROW: Close to the airport are several worthwhile suggestions.

The Swan, The Hythe, Staines (tel. 0784-52494), lies beside the Thames. It is an attractive old inn with a reputation for good food ranging from bar snacks to a limited à la carte choice of traditional English "fayre." A three-course meal can cost as little as £8.50 ($12.75) in the candlelit dining room overlooking the river. The bedrooms have central heating, color TV, and tea/coffee-making facilities. Singles start at £22.50 ($33.75), and a double begins at £32 ($48) per night, both rates including a full English breakfast and VAT.

Upton Park Guest House, 41 Upton Park, Slough, Berkshire (tel. 0753/28797), is about a 15-minute cab ride from Heathrow. Jan and Pete Jones, who run the place, can arrange for a local cab to meet you if you preplan. The rate is cheaper than taking a cab at the airport. All rooms have central heating, hot and cold running water, color TV, and complimentary tea and coffee. A pleasant bar is available for residents. Bed and a full English breakfast costs £20 ($30) per night.

Parkside Hotel, 1 Upton Court Rd., Slough, Berkshire (tel. 0753/22533), is a well-run place, offering B&B at a cost of £13 ($19.50) in a single, £21 ($31.50) in a double, plus VAT. All units have hot and cold running water and razor points. There is a TV lounge, plus another lounge which doubles as the breakfast room. Anna Edwards, the manager, can provide local information about train service to London and buses to Windsor.

GATWICK: Since this airport is so far from London, you may want to find a convenient perch nearby while waiting for the departure of your flight. Some suggestions follow.

Gatwick Skylodge Hotel, London Road, County Oak, Crawley, Surrey (tel. 0293/54411), is a busy airport hotel within easy reach of Gatwick by courtesy bus. The bus operates regularly from 6:15 a.m. to 11:45 p.m. All rooms have a private bath, color TV, tea- or coffee-maker, and direct-dial phone—useful if you need to call home. Rates, including VAT and a continental breakfast, are £32 ($48) in a single, £40 ($60) in a twin or double, and from £52 ($78) to £57 ($85.50) for three to four persons. Rooms are held on 6 p.m. release unless a deposit of £10 ($15) is prepaid. There is a restaurant where evening meals are served. An English breakfast is available if required.

Mr. and Mrs. A.A. Williams, 27 Boundary Way, Addington Village, Croydon (tel. 0689/41739), operate a pleasant guesthouse with central heating. Their tranquil, history-steeped village is surrounded by fields and golf courses, and the Williamses provide free transportation to the East Croydon railway station so that guests can catch trains into the center of London. Accommodations include a double-bedded room with a private bath, and its own sitting room with color TV, plus a single-bedded room. Rent is £17 ($25.50) per person for bed and breakfast. Mrs. Williams will provide an evening snack at the request of guests, for a reasonable charge.

Brooklyn Hotel, Bonnetts Lane, Ifield, Crawley (tel. 0293/546024), is an old, well-cared for Victorian house set in the lovely English countryside, only five minutes from Gatwick Airport. A phone call from the airport will bring a car from the hotel to collect you and your luggage free and take you to the hotel, or, if you're staying there prior to departure, they'll take you to Gatwick in time for your flight, another free service. The hotel, set in five acres of rural parkland, offers full central heating, color TV, and beverage-making facilities. Martin Davis charges £15 ($22.50) to £20 ($30) for a single, £26 ($39) to £30 ($45) in a double. An additional person in a room is charged £5 ($7.50). Breakfast is extra, and if a guest wishes, a light snack will be served in the evening. However, a free courtesy service takes guests to and from a nearby restaurant, and there are two pubs within about a ten-minute walk, both serving inexpensive meals. The hotel does not have a bar, but it is licensed, so that you can have drinks served in the lounge if you wish. The hotel staff will help guests plan trips into London by public transport.

17. An Accommodation Round-up

STAYING WITH A FAMILY: Many agencies in Britain can arrange stays with a private family, either in London or in the country. As much as is possible, interests are matched. This program is an intriguing way to involve yourself in the social life of a country, seeing it from the inside. Also it's a bargain when compared to hotels. Some agencies limit themselves to teenagers; others welcome older readers. Try one of the following:

Family Holidays, 42 Walton Rd., Sidcup, Kent, DA14 4LN (tel. 01/300-5444), under the direction of Michael and Geraldine Kenney, has a well-screened list of British families who will welcome you into their homes as paying guests. The choice includes numerous professional people and others who live in attractive town, country, and seaside locations all around Great Britain. Upon application, you'll receive information about your hosts such as interests, age, and family. The cost of accommodation is less than $100 (U.S.) per person per week for full board. There is a booking fee of

£10 ($15), and operating costs are covered by a 15% service charge. There's even an arrangement for what to do if you and your host don't get on too well!

Home from Home International Ltd. specializes in finding you genuine hospitality with a host family. Local knowledge and advice is readily given to make your stay enjoyable, whether it's in a country cottage, flat, farmhouse, or period house with antiques. Here is your chance to get to know the beautiful countryside of Surrey, Kent, Hampshire, Sussex, and the Cotswolds, or stay in London. B&B costs from £12 ($18) to £22 ($33) per person per night, and other meals are available on request. More information and brochures can be obtained from the 53 Smithbrook Kilns, Horsham Road, Cranleigh, Surrey GU8 8JJ (tel. 0483/276444).

Ball Tourist Services, 82 Newlands Rd., Norbury, London S.W.16 (tel. 653-8467), will arrange for accommodations with selected families living in the southwest suburbs of London, including Streatham, Norbury, and Thornton Heath. Only about 15 to 20 minutes by train to the center of London, the area is convenient for all sorts of recreational and sightseeing activities. Host-family accommodation is also available in Paignton (Devon), Edinburgh, Eastbourne, Canterbury, the Isle of Wight, Cambridge, and the Lake District. Accommodation with an English breakfast is from £8.50 ($12.75). With an English breakfast and an evening meal, £12.50 ($18.75). Prices include the booking fee and tax.

B&B IN PRIVATE HOMES:
Thea Druce, who has operated a B&B establishment, manages **London Homes,** 8 St. Dunstans Rd., Barons Court, W.6 (tel. 748-4947), which books visitors into private homes in the London area. These homes are in such districts as Swiss Cottage, Hampstead, Richmond, Putney, Chiswick, and Hammersmith. All the homes are well decorated, unlike the reputation of some London establishments as "Dickensian." Bedrooms offer subtle decoration, wall-to-wall carpets, wash basins, central heating, and a friendly atmosphere. All the homes are near the Underground system, so traveling around is easy. In addition to the sections mentioned, London Homes also offers some B&B establishments right in the center of London—Kensington, Knightsbridge, and Sloane Square in Chelsea. A key is provided so that visitors can come and go as they wish. Accommodations are cleaned daily, and every morning a choice of a continental or an English breakfast is provided. Best yet, there is a warm personal welcome waiting. Accommodations are in areas surrounded by good restaurants and typical pubs. Daily rates begin at £10 ($15) per person, ranging upward. Whether you wish to stay in a luxurious guest suite in a Georgian manor house or in a more modest room at a Victorian town house—with Mrs. Smith in Richmond or Lady Winn in Kensington—with a choice of more than 80 homes, there's a good selection of accommodation and prices to suit every pocket. Brochures can be obtained by writing directly to London Homes. Reservations should be made far in advance if you're contemplating a summer visit.

COTTAGES FOR RENT:
Outside London, there are many delightful and charming cottages for rents, as well as apartments. But you should book for at least a week or more. The range of accommodations varies from the wing of a 300-year-old cottage in Cornwall to a 16th-century cottage for two in Shottery, a place that rivals Anne Hathaway's Cottage for quaintness. You can also rent modern country houses. All places come fully furnished and equipped, and most will provide bed linen if you order it in advance (renters must provide their own towels). Heat is usually charged locally through a gas or electric meter. Babysitters are often available. If you're interested, get in touch with **Character Cottages,** 34 Fore St., Sidmouth, Devon (tel. 03955/77001). Prices range from around £80 ($120) to £170 ($255) a week, depending on the season and capacity. I found this is a remarkable bargain and a chance to get to know the real England.

A company which concentrates on the heart of England—so convenient to the

Cotswolds and Stratford-upon-Avon—is **Heart of England Cottages,** Ridlands Cottage, Briston, Melton Constable, Norfolk NR24 2LU (tel. 0263/861000). Typical properties include the magnificent Elizabethan Gatehouse to Upton Cressett Hall in Shropshire, going for around £330 ($495), or Crudwell House Cottage in the south Cotswolds, offering pretty and comfortable accommodation for around £250 ($375) per week in high season. They also have properties close to Bath, as far north as Shropshire for those who wish to visit historic Chester, the cider and cattle farms of Hereford, and the Potteries, plus Norfolk, Yorkshire, and the Borders (with easy access to Scotland).

Bargain Hotel for Students

Driscoll House, 172 New Kent Rd., Elephant and Castle, S.E.1 (tel. 703-4175), is an international hotel, offering accommodations for short or long terms. Some 200 rooms are offered, including many facilities and amenities. At a cost of £70 ($105) per week, a single room with full board is rented, among the least expensive accommodations in central London. Rooms are centrally heated, and there are TV and table-tennis areas, as well as a library and a laundry. And there are a dozen pianos. About a quarter of the residents are students, and the rest are composed of civil servants, teachers, secretaries, whatever. In all, Mr. Driscoll has been host to people from some 158 countries. The hotel is about 20 minutes by bus from Victoria. In the main building are sitting rooms, including three for television, another for laundry, and a library. Social and cultural activities are organized. The hotel was founded in 1913 and opened by H.R.H. the Princess Louise. Tube: Elephant and Castle.

YOUTH HOSTELS: In youth hostels, reservations are imperative—and must be made months or even a year in advance. In one season alone, the youth hostels of London turned away 33,000 written applications with deposits! You must, of course, comply with each hostel's restrictions, such as a membership card and in many cases a curfew. A great number also carry limitations on the number of nights you can stay.

Britain is an ideal choice for those who want to put some action in their holidays. The activities are widely varied, ranging from underwater swimming off the coast of Devon, to canoeing on the River Wye, climbing in Scotland, walking, and gliding.

One way to find out information about these adventure holidays is to go to the London office of the **Youth Hostels Association,** 14 Southampton St., W.C.2 (tel. 836-8541). The yearly membership fee is £6 ($9) for adults.

For a full list, write to YHA National, Trevelyan House, St. Stephens, St. Albans, Herts., England (tel. 0727/55215).

In the United States, you can join the **American Youth Hostels Association** (contact them at: American Youth Hostels, Inc., P.O. Box 37613, Washington, DC 20013-7613, or call 202/783-6161). To join, mail a check for the yearly membership fee of $20 if you're between the ages of 18 and 59. A three-year membership costs $50. If you're between the ages of 14 and 17 or over 60, you can apply for a junior or senior membership, each of which costs $10 per year. A Lifetime Membership costs $200, regardless of age. A family membership is available for $30 for one year and will include two parents and any accompanying children age 17 and under. Parents can use a family membership without being accompanied by children, although children under 17 who arrive without their parents are required to have a junior membership of their own. Membership in AYH is honored at Youth Hostels in England as well as in 60 other countries.

Quest Hotel, 45 Queensborough Terrace, W.2 (tel. 229-7782), is run by Katrina, an affable Australian woman, with an internatinal staff. The hotel is operated as a student hostel for travelers from all over the world. Fun and laughter can be shared with the staff, and worldwide budget travel hints are passed around by guests from all over, with a large Australian contingent. They cater mostly to young people in the 18 to 30 age range, but they also enjoy the company of spirited, more mature travelers. The hotel is in the heart of London, close to all major sights and attractions, only a stone's throw from Kensington Gardens and Hyde Park. The price per person is from £7.50 ($11.25) in a room shared with four to five other people and £12 ($18) in a twin-bedded room. A continental breakfast is included in the prices. Tube: Bayswater or Queensway.

Fieldcourt House, 32 Courtfield Gardens, S.W.5 (tel. 373-0152), keeps the student market firmly in mind, and is a hostel that is a favorite among economy tour operators. The residential hotel lies in a pleasant garden square near Cromwell Road, from which it's possible to obtain buses to all parts of London. The house is midway between the Gloucester Road and Earl's Court Underground stations (Piccadilly and District Lines). There is no curfew. Fieldcourt was formed by combining two large Victorian mansions. There are central heating, wash basins, hot water, and ample showers, baths, and toilets in the public hallways. Other amenities include a residents' lounge with color TV and a launderette. To keep hostel charges low, general cleaning is carried out by the staff, but residents are expected to make their own beds. Accommodation charges are payable daily or weekly, in advance. All prices include VAT and a continental breakfast. Beds in rooms accommodating three to six sleepers cost £8 ($12) to £9.50 ($14.25) each. Private singles cost £12.50 ($18.75), with twin-bedded units going for £20 ($30). None have private baths. A deposit of £10 ($15) is required on booking, and it's refundable on departure.

"73," 73 Oakley St., S.W.3 (tel. 352-5599), is in Chelsea, north of the Chelsea Embankment and best reached by buses. It offers bed and an English breakfast at £7 ($10.50) to £8.20 ($12.30) per person in a room shared with two other people. For a twin, the charge is £9 ($13.50) to £10.60 ($15.90) per person, rising to £10.50 ($15.75) to £11.70 ($17.55) in a single. There are no curfews, no age limits, and house telephones with extensions are provided in all rooms. A refrigerator and a cooker are in the kitchen for the use of guests, and everything but food is provided for preparing your own meals. In addition, a coin-operated washing machine and dryer are also available. If you ask for Roy or Eleanor, you'll receive a fine welcome. The establishment is in Chelsea, just off King's Road, north of the Embankment and best reached by buses. The nearest tube station is Sloane Square.

38 Bolton Gardens, Earl's Court, S.W.5 (tel. 373-7083), is a youth hostel providing dormitory-style living for £6 ($9) to £7.50 ($11.10), including breakfast. The premises are open from 8 to 10 a.m. and 5:15 to 11:30 p.m. each day. The building is an old five-story mansion. In all, they have 110 beds, plus ten bathrooms. Tube: Earl's Court.

J.D. House, 285 Pentonville Rd., N.1 (tel. 278-5385), is a hostel northeast of Bloomsbury. It provides beds at £5 ($7.50) to £6 ($9) nightly, including your linen. The weekly rate is £28 ($42) to £38 ($57). Accommodation is in multiple rooms, with a maximum of four persons housed in each. Amenities include ironing and cooking facilities, as well as heating and television, with hot and cold running water in the rooms. There is no curfew, as a key is provided. The nearest Underground station is Kings Cross, which is reached by at least seven buses that go near the student house.

LONDON: RESTAURANTS, PUBS, AND WINE BARS

1. West End
2. Westminster and St. James's
3. The City
4. Holborn and Bloomsbury
5. Belgravia and Knightsbridge
6. Chelsea
7. Kensington
8. West London
9. East End
10. South of the Thames
11. Hampstead Heath
12. Thames Dining
13. For Fish and Chips
14. Time Out for Tea
15. Almost-24-Hour Eateries

WITH THE PRESSURE of tourism and the influx of foreign chefs, the local cuisine picture has brightened considerably. There also exists now a current wave of English-born, bred, and trained chefs who have set a superb standard of cookery, using high-quality ingredients. One food writer called this new breed "the very professional amateur."

In the snackeries of suburbia the vegetables may still taste as if they had a grudge against you, and the soup remains reminiscent of flavored tapwater. But in the central sections of London—where you'll do your eating—the fare has improved immeasurably. This is largely because of intense competition from foreign establishments, plus the introduction of espresso machines, which made English coffee resemble—well, coffee.

In the upper brackets, London has always boasted magnificent restaurants, several of which have achieved world renown. But these were the preserve of the middling wealthy, who'd had their palates polished by travel abroad. The lower orders enjoyed a diet akin to parboiled blotting paper. For about a century the staple meal of the working class consisted of fish 'n' chips—and in my opinion they still haven't learned how to properly fry either the fish *or* the chips (potatoes).

There are some dishes—mostly connected with breakfast—at which the English have always excelled. The traditional morning repast of eggs and bacon (imported from Denmark) or kippers (smoked herring, of Scottish origin) is a tasty starter, and the locally brewed tea beats any American bag concoction.

It's with the other meals that you have to use a little caution. If you want to splurge in a big way, you have the London "greats" at your disposal. But if these eateries are too expensive for you, you'll find dozens of moderately priced restaurants and budget establishments.

The prevailing mealtimes are much the same as in the U.S. You can get lunch from about midday onward and dinner until about 11 p.m.—until midnight in the Soho area. The difference is that fewer Londoners go in for the "business-person's lunch." They'll either make do with sandwiches or take a snack in a pub. The once-hallowed custom of taking afternoon tea for many years became the preserve of matrons unworried about their waistlines. However, in the past few years it is having a renaissance. Viewed as a civilized pause in the day's activities, it's particularly appealing to those who didn't have time for lunch or who plan an early theater engagement. Some hotels, such as the Ritz, feature orchestras and tea-dancing in afternoon ceremonies, usually from 3:30 to 6:30 p.m.

What may astonish you is the profusion of international restaurants. London offers a fantastic array of Italian, Indian, Chinese, French, German, Swiss, Greek, Russian, Jewish, and Middle Eastern dineries, which probably outnumber the native establishments. You'll find them heavily represented on my list.

Most of the restaurants I mention serve the same meals for lunch or dinner, so they're easily interchangeable. Most—but not all—add a 10% service charge to your bill. You'll have to look at your check to make sure of that. If nothing has been added, leave a 12% to 15% tip.

All restaurants and cafés in Britain are required to display the prices of the food and drink they offer, in a place where the customer can see them before entering the eating area. If an establishment has an extensive à la carte menu, the prices of a representative selection of food and drink currently available must be displayed, as well as the table d'hôte menu if one is offered. Charges for service and any minimum charge or cover charge must also be made clear. The prices shown must be inclusive of VAT.

Finally, there's the matter of location. Once upon a time London had two traditional dining areas: Soho for Italian and Chinese fare, Mayfair and Belgravia for French cuisine.

Today the gastronomical legions have conquered the entire heart of the metropolis. You're likely to find any type of eatery anywhere from Chelsea to Hampstead. The majority of my selections are in the West End region, but only because this happens to be the handiest for visitors.

First, I'll survey the downtown district of London, by which I refer to a broad area embracing not only the theater district, but Piccadilly Circus, Soho, Covent Garden, the Strand, Trafalgar Square, and Leicester Square, as well as the elegant residential district of Mayfair and "Little America." South of here is the seat of government, Westminster and Whitehall, and the heart of royal and aristocratic London, St. James's (Buckingham Palace). To the east is the older part of London, which includes the financial square mile known as "The City," as well as the newspaper and publishing empire centered around Fleet Street.

Finally, I'll fan out to such residential districts as Bloomsbury (budget hotels and the British Museum), Chelsea, St. Marylebone, Brompton, and Kensington. And then, at the end of the chapter, I'll set forth my more remote recommendations —the pubs and bistros in Hampstead Heath, and a few scattered, but famous, inns, restaurants, and pubs either in the East End or along the Thames.

1. West End

PICCADILLY CIRCUS: Garish, overneoned, crowded, but exciting, Piccadilly Circus keeps time with the heartbeat of a mighty city. If you're intrigued by Times Square at night, you'll find that Piccadilly Circus carries an equal fascination. Here from all sections of the city come the aristocrat, the housewife, the punk, the government official, the secretary, the pimp, the financier. They converge around the statue of Eros, named for love, about the only thing that occasionally unites these diverse elements of life which descend on Piccadilly.

Much of your London activity will be centered in and around here. Finding the right restaurant is most important, as many establishments in this area are unabashed tourist traps, or sleazy little joints aimed more at the "bangers-and-mash" palate. The following restaurants and pubs have been selected not only for the quality of their food but because they offer the best value for the money.

The **Trocadero,** 7 Rupert St., near Piccadilly Circus, W.1 (tel. 439-8476), is a shopping, entertainment, restaurant, and café complex in the heart of London. The **International Village** restaurants offer lunch, dinner, or a snack at any time. The village comprises French and Italian café bars and restaurants on the lower ground floor of the Trocadero complex. The Trocadero also offers exhibitions, including the Guinness World of Records, a life-size display taken from the *Guinness Book of Records;* a multi-media extravaganza on the history of London; and Light Fantastic, a hologram exhibition. Numerous stores are also here. You can buy anything from souvenirs to records, clothes, children's toys, and teddy bears, even brass rubbings.

The Italian Piazza serves freshly made pizza and pasta dishes, as well as huge Italian ice cream coppas and cappuccinos. Seat yourself by the Venetian canal in this bubbly Venetian restaurant where the average cost is around £5 ($7.50) per person. The French Quarter of the International Village offers a Pâtisserie where light French snacks are available for around £2 ($3) per person, plus the Brasserie Montmartre where three-course French Provincial meals are served, costing an average of around £8 ($12) per person. Listen to the strains of the accordionist during lunchtime in the French Quarter, and for more intimate conversations, move along to the Montmartre Wine Bar and sample the French wines. The Italian Piazza is open from noon to midnight and the Brasserie Montmartre and Wine Bar from noon to 3 p.m. and 6 p.m. to midnight. All restaurants are open all year except on Christmas Day. Tube: Piccadilly Circus.

The **Carvery,** ground floor, Regent Palace Hotel, Glasshouse Street, W.1 (tel. 734-7000), just 20 feet from Piccadilly Circus, will fool you. Who'd think that for only £9.95 ($14.93) you could have all that your plate can hold of fabulous roasts and be able to go back for seconds—even thirds for those who suffer from one of the seven deadly sins? Yet that's the famous policy of this renowned, all-you-can-eat establishment; a winner with those seeking rib-sticking "joints," for which the English are known. For the first course, help yourself from a wide range of appetizers. After that, you can go to the horseshoe-shaped buffet carving table, where before you will be spread roast prime ribs of beef (choice of rare, medium, or well done), with Yorkshire pudding, roast leg of Southdown lamb with mint sauce, and a roast leg of English pork with apple sauce.

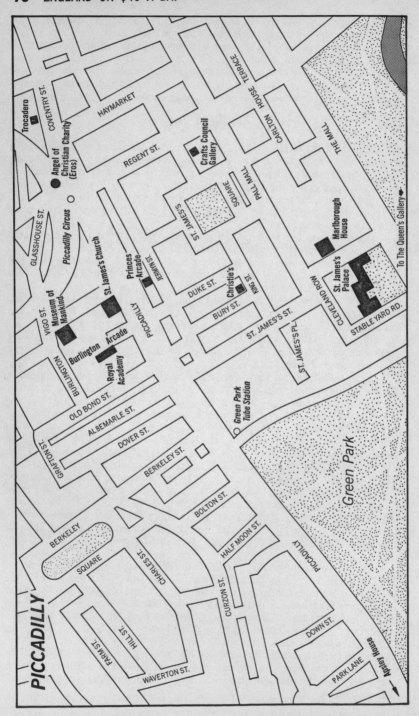

PICCADILLY

Trocadero
COVENTRY ST.
HAYMARKET
Angel of Christian Charity (Eros)
REGENT ST.
GLASSHOUSE ST.
Piccadilly Circus
VIGO ST.
Museum of Mankind
St. James's Church
Princes Arcade
JERMYN ST.
PICCADILLY
BURLINGTON
Burlington Arcade
Royal Academy
OLD BOND ST.
GRAFTON ST.
ALBEMARLE ST.
DOVER ST.
BERKELEY ST.
BERKELEY SQUARE
CHARLES ST.
FARM ST.
HILL ST.
WAVERTON ST.
BOLTON ST.
HALF MOON ST.
CURZON ST.
DOWN ST.
PARK LANE
Apsley House
PICCADILLY

ST. JAMES'S
Crafts Council Gallery
SQUARE
PALL MALL
CARLTON HOUSE TERRACE
THE MALL
Marlborough House
St. James's Palace
CLEVELAND ROW
STABLE YARD RD.
To The Queen's Gallery

DUKE ST.
Christie's
BURY ST.
KING ST.
ST. JAMES'S ST.
ST. JAMES'S PL.

Green Park Tube Station

Green Park

You carve the meat yourself, slicing off as much as you want. Carvers stand by to assist and give instructions on how to wield the knife. You may then heap your heated china plate with buttered peas, roast potatoes, new carrots, and gravy. In another area is a display of cold joints and assorted salads, whatever is in season. Select from the sweet trolley such desserts as meringue or chocolate and pineapple cake, perhaps a strawberry mousse. Well-brewed coffee for "afters" is included in the price. The Carvery is open Monday through Saturday from noon to 2:30 p.m. and 5:15 to 9 p.m., and on Sunday from 12:30 to 2:30 p.m. and 6 to 9 p.m. Tube: Piccadilly Circus.

The Crêperie, 56a South Molton St., W.1 (tel. 629-4794), is a pleasant and informal place, with bare wooden tables and chairs. The crêpes are cooked on the right as you enter, on pristine hotplates amid bubbling cauldrons of soup of the day. Main courses are buckwheat pancakes filled with a vast variety of goodies—onions, cheese, mixed salad, chicken, ratatouille, you name it. Prices range from £2.50 ($3.75) to £3 ($4.50) for a filling pancake, served with salad. For dessert, another pancake, made with plain flour this time, is filled with chestnuts, pineapple, bananas, or chocolate. In addition, a dish of the day—perhaps a Greek-style moussaka or a beef stew—bubbles alongside the soup. A two-floor restaurant, the Crêperie is in an alley off South Molton Street, amid many other eateries. A tortuous staircase leads up from the ground floor to the light airy dining room. The restaurant is open Monday to Wednesday from 9:30 a.m. to 8 p.m., Thursday to Saturday from 10 a.m. to 11:30 p.m., and closed Sunday. Tube: Bond Street.

The Granary, 39 Albemarle St., W.1 (tel. 493-2978), serves a variety of dishes, all of which have a real home-cooked flavor. The whole place is under the watchful eye of John Shah, who opened it in 1974. In winter 25 hot dishes and five cold ones are served, and in summer 20 hot dishes and ten cold ones, plus desserts, are offered. An inexpensive meal of, say, meat pie, vegetables, chocolate cake, a glass of wine, and coffee, will cost from £6 ($9). The fare is likely to consist of spiced chicken, paella, and beef burgundy. Desserts are tempting, especially the tipsy cake and the upside-down cake. All portions are large, and everything can be taken away in containers to eat elsewhere. Hours are from 11 a.m. to 8 p.m. weekdays (on Saturday from noon to 2:30 p.m.); closed Sunday. Tube: Green Park.

Wren at St. James's Coffee House, 35 Jermyn St., S.W.1 (tel. 437-9419). At this enterprising church, a two-minute walk from Piccadilly Circus, visitors can do brass-rubbings. It also boasts a cheerful coffeeshop right within its walls, offering good value. It's entered through a narrow door on Jermyn Street. It is possible also to enter from Piccadilly via the courtyard, where tables and chairs are placed in fair weather. Inside, you're greeted with bright paint, round café-style tables, white tables, metal chairs, and windows overlooking the courtyard. A glass counter groaning with appetizing dishes is served to the lined-up patrons by a pleasant, capable team. There is always a fresh soup of the day, along with cold appetizers such as avocado with prawns. They specialize in large potatoes baked in their "jackets," as the British say, and filled with a variety of stuffings such as cheese and tuna. A bill isn't likely to run more than £5.50 ($8.25). It's busy at lunchtime, particularly with local in-the-know office workers. Hot dishes are only served at lunchtime. Teatime specialties include homemade cakes and large scones with cream and jam. The establishment is open from 10:30 a.m. to 6 p.m. Monday to Saturday. Tube: Piccadilly Circus.

McDonald's, 57 Haymarket, S.W.1 (tel. 930-9302). Yes, the real thing from America long ago arrived, and there are some 50 chain sisters in and around London. All produce, including meat, is purchased locally and is of high standard. A Big Mac costs £1.14 ($1.70). The place is brash, brightly lit, and busy from 6 a.m. to midnight seven days a week. Tube: Piccadilly Circus.

AROUND LEICESTER SQUARE: Named for the second Earl of Leicester, and once the site of the home of Sir Joshua Reynolds, Leicester Square has changed its colors today, bursting out as the cinema center of London. The 19th-century square is a congested area of stores, theaters, cinemas, even churches. And beyond those, it has some inexpensive restaurants and pubs in its little offshoot lanes and alleyways, where West End actors discreetly select their "local."

There's now a large paved pedestrian precinct rivaling Piccadilly Circus and Eros as a meeting place for travelers and locals. It's less dangerous than Piccadilly Circus for many reasons, among which is that there's no traffic.

The **Stockpot,** 40 Panton St., S.W.1 (tel. 839-5142), suggests good wholesome fare and lives up to its promise. Penny for penny, I'd hazard a guess that this cozy little member of a popular chain offers one of the best dining bargains in London. (Others are at 6 Basil St., S.W.3, and at 98 King's Rd., S.W.3.) All the Stockpots are favored by a young crowd, who know by heart the low prices charged for the well-cooked meals, including a bowl of minestrone, spaghetti bolognese (the eternal favorite), a plate of braised lamb, and the apple crumble (or other desserts). Meals cost from £5 ($7.50) up. Offering two levels of dining in a Scandinavian-style atmosphere, the Stockpot has a share-the-table policy during peak dining hours. Hours are from 8 a.m. to 11:30 p.m. Monday to Saturday, from noon to 10 p.m. on Sunday. The little restaurant lies off Haymarket, opposite the Comedy Theatre. Tube: Piccadilly Circus.

If it's a charming ambience you're seeking, you'll find it in the heart of the theater district at the pubs and wine bars recommended below.

Slatters, 3 Panton St., S.W.1 (tel. 839-4649), lies off Haymarket, a split-level, wine bar and restaurant convenient for theater-goers. It makes a good rendezvous for before- and after-theater suppers. The owners, Bob and Henrietta Lewin, continue in the tradition of good food, such as tarragon spiced chicken or cold baked ham, served with a selection of salads (your choice), or you may prefer smoked salmon or gravlax. For those who like it hot, chili con carne, vegetarian curry, and beef bourguignon are among the dishes served on a bed of rice. Freshly made soups are another of the specialties, a selection of four or five always being available. French bread, brown or white, is included with every meal, or you can also have garlic bread for two. The average meal price is £7 ($10.50) for three courses. The wine list is extensive, with many selections offered by the half bottle. The house wine is from France, costing £1 ($1.50) per glass or £4.95 ($7.43) per bottle. The wine bar is open Monday to Saturday from 11:30 a.m. to 3 p.m. and 5:30 p.m. to midnight. Tube: Leicester Square or Piccadilly Circus.

Cork and Bottle Wine Bar, 44–46 Cranbourn St., W.C.2 (tel. 734-7807), is in the theater district, just off Leicester Square. Don Hewitson, the owner, devotes a great deal of love and care to this establishment. He has revitalized the food, with a wide range of hot dishes, so that it is not a typical glass-of-wine-and-a-slice-of-pâté type of bistro. The most successful dish is a raised cheese-and-ham pie. In just one week the bar sold 500 portions of this alone. It has a cream-cheesy filling, and the well-buttered pastry is crisp—not your typical quiche. Don also offers a mâchon Lyonnaise, a traditional worker's lunch in Lyon. He imports his own sauçisson from a charcuterie in Lyon, serving it hot with warm potato salad, a mixed green salad, spicy Dijon mustard, and french bread. You can also order an "American gourmet salad," consisting of lettuce, tomato, avocado, green beans, and croutons, in a spicy red stilton dressing. Meals cost from £8 ($12). Don has expanded the wine list, and he doubts if anyone in the U.K. has a better selection of Beaujolais cru and wines from Alsace. He also stocks a good selection of California labels. In fact, Don, a New Zealander, has been called "the Kiwi guru of the modern wine bar movement." The bar is open Monday to Saturday from 11 a.m. to 3 p.m. and 5:30 to 11 p.m., on Sunday from noon to 2 p.m. and 7 to 10:30 p.m. Tube: Leicester Square.

The **Salisbury,** 90 St. Martin's Lane, W.C.2 (tel. 836-5863), one of the most famous Victorian pubs of London, is ably run by Jerry Wynne. Its glittering cut-glass mirrors reflect the faces of English stage stars (and would-be stars) sitting around the curved buffet bar, having a cold joint snack. A plate of the roast leg of pork at the buffet, plus a salad, costs from £4 ($6). If you want a less prominent place to dine or to nibble oysters, choose the old-fashioned wall banquette with its copper-top tables and art nouveau decor. The light fixtures, veiled bronze girls in flowing robes holding up clusters of electric lights concealed in bronze roses, are appropriate. In the saloon, you'll see and hear the Oliviers of yesterday and tomorrow. The place is open Monday to Saturday from 11 a.m. to 3 p.m. and 5:30 to 11 p.m.; on Sunday from noon to 2 p.m. and 7 to 10:30 p.m. Tube: Leicester Square.

TRAFALGAR SQUARE AND THE STRAND: Between Leicester Square and Westminster, a former marshy meadow is known today as Trafalgar Square. The square is dominated by a monument honoring Lord Nelson, who died in the Battle of Trafalgar on October 21, 1805.

Beginning at the square, the Strand, south of Covent Garden, runs east into Fleet Street. Londoners used to be able to walk along the Strand and see the Thames, but the river, of course, has receded now. In the 17th century the wealthy built their homes on the Strand, and their gardens stretched to the Thames itself. But today it is in transition to something less grand—flanked as it is with theaters (the Savoy, for example), shops, hotels, and such landmarks as Somerset House.

Peaceful lanes jut off from the Strand, leading to the Victoria Embankment Gardens along the river. Opposite the gardens is Cleopatra's Needle, an Egyptian obelisk, London's oldest monument. If the weather permits, you might want to stroll along the river.

Because this is such a major geographic and tourist center, you'll probably want to take some of your meals here. My recommendations follow.

Lyons Corner House, 450 The Strand, W.C.2 (tel. 930-9381), is a whisper from the past, having figured in its earlier reincarnation in the writings of T.S. Eliot, Virginia Woolf, and Bertrand Russell. Once Lyons Corner Houses were much more prominent, having fed hungry Londoners for decades. This white-fronted place with gold trimmings offers a wide variety of fast food and traditional English dishes at reasonable prices. Meals are served by a new generation of waitresses known, as were their predecessors, as "Nippies," for the way they get around among the tables. Dressed in black frocks and natty white aprons, they serve hamburgers and brunches in the coffeeshops on the ground floor, along with soft drinks, tea, or coffee throughout the day. The Garden Restaurant serves more substantial meals, including steak-and-kidney pie and fried fish and chips. A set lunch or dinner, including dessert, costs only £5 ($7.50). The establishment is open from 10 a.m. to 7 p.m. daily. Tube: Charing Cross or Embankment.

The **Sherlock Holmes,** 10 Northumberland St., W.C.2 (tel. 930-2644), is for devotees of the legendary English detective and his creator, Arthur Conan Doyle. You can have your mug of beer and then look at the upstairs re-creation of the living room of 221B Baker Street, where get-togethers of "The Baker Street Irregulars" are held. The homemade food, served upstairs in the restaurant called Mrs. Hudson's Pantry, is simple and plain. The fare consists of grilled chops, steaks, fish such as sole or scampi, and a selection of desserts. All main dishes are served with three different potatoes and fresh vegetables. A meal will cost from £6 ($9) to £10 ($15). In the snackbar on the street level, you can order macaroni and cheese, hot pot (in cold weather), shepherd's pie, and other snackbar meals for around £3 ($3.50). Hot dishes include curry. Lunch is served from noon to 2:15 p.m. and dinner from 6 to 9:15 p.m. (from 7 p.m. on Saturday). No meals are served at lunchtime on Saturday nor all day Sunday. Pub hours are daily except Sunday from 11 a.m. to 3 p.m. and 5:30 to 11 p.m. Sunday hours for the pub are from noon to 2 p.m. and 7 to 10:30 p.m. Sir Arthur Conan Doyle used to visit this pub back when it was called the Northumberland Arms. He refers to it in *The Hound of the Baskervilles*. Tube: Charing Cross.

The **Clarence Inn,** 53 Whitehall, S.W.1 (tel. 930-4808), just down from Trafalgar Square, is the haunt of civil servants from the nearby ministry offices. They enjoy such lunchtime food as braised oxtail, Oriental pork chops, or traditional shepherd's pie. There are always at least four hot dishes of the day. There is also a wide range of cold dishes and salads at around the same price, and the same food is available in the evening when the workers have gone home. Managers Rodger and Christine Burston have also opened the upstairs room ("more civilized than the street level bar") for lunches. A serve-yourself buffet luncheon costs from £5.50 ($8.25) per person. The 18th-century inn offers a choice of six real ales in the bar, with its friendly bartenders, blackened beams, sawdust-strewn-floor, church pews, a food bar, and uncovered tables lit by flickering gaslights. Ancient farm tools and weapons decorate the smoke-blackened beams, and in the evening from Monday to Thursday a strolling minstrel makes light music in the bar. Lunch in the upstairs room is served weekdays from noon to 2:30 p.m. At the downstairs food bar, service is seven days a week from noon to 2:30 and, after a 15-minute restocking of the dishes, from 2:45 to 10 p.m. Tube: Charing Cross or the Embankment.

The **National Gallery Restaurant,** Trafalgar Square, W.C.2 (tel. 930-5210). You can have lunch in this comfortable basement before you explore the gallery. Juicy quiches and flans are presented before you, along with a line-up of fresh crisp salads. Hot daily specials are likely to include chili with rice, coq au vin, and beef bourguignon. Count on spending from £5 ($7.50). The restaurant opens at 10 a.m. and closes at 5 p.m. Hot food is served only at lunchtime, noon to 3 p.m. From 3 to 5 p.m., drinks and snacks are available. Tube: Charing Cross.

Val Taro, 32 Orange St., W.C.2 (tel. 930-2939), wedged between somber and massive neighboring buildings, is an angular, modern glass-fronted place, whose proximity to Piccadilly makes it popular as an after-theater dining spot. Named for an Italian valley southeast of Genoa, it offers an Italy-inspired menu which includes at least six superb veal dishes, grilled double filet of sole, excellent beefsteaks, and an array of pastas and antipasti. Meals are served daily except at lunch on Saturday and all day Sunday. Hours are noon to 3 p.m. and 6 to 11:15 p.m. The wine bar in the basement maintains the same hours as the upstairs restaurant, and you can order a plate of pasta or a salad to accompany your glass of vintage wine. Tube: Leicester Square.

COVENT GARDEN: In 1970, London's flower, fruit, and "veg" market celebrated its 300th anniversary. But "Auld Lang Syne" might have been the theme song. Once a district of gambling dens and bawdy houses, east of Piccadilly Circus and north of the Strand, the historic, but congested, market was transferred in 1974 to a $7.2-million, 64-acre site at Nine Elms, in the suburb of Vauxhall, South London, 2½ miles away, across the Thames.

Covent Garden dates from the time when the monks of Westminster Abbey dumped their surplus home-grown vegetables here. Charles II in 1670 granted the Earl of Bedford the right to "sell roots and herbs, whatsoever" in the district. The king's mistress, Nell Gwynne, once peddled oranges on Drury Lane (later appearing on the stage of the Drury Lane Theatre).

Before that, in the 1630s Inigo Jones designed the square, hoping to have a plaza in the Florentine style, but the work bogged down. Even his self-tabbed "handsomest barn in England," St. Paul's Covent Garden, burned down in the late 18th century and was subsequently rebuilt. The English actress, Dame Ellen Terry (noted in particular for her letters to G.B. Shaw), is buried here.

St. Paul's eastern face looks down on the market where Professor Higgins in *Pygmalion* met his "squashed cabbage leaf," Eliza Doolittle, and later got reacquainted in *My Fair Lady.* Also in the area is the Royal Opera House on Bow Street housing the Royal Ballet and the Covent Garden Opera Company. On nearby Russell Street, Samuel Johnson met his admirer, Boswell, and coffeehouses in the district were once patronized by Addison and Steele. Just as chicly dressed people of fashion once flocked to Les Halles in Paris to have onion soup with butchers in blood-soaked smocks, so London revelers have dropped in at Covent Garden's pubs to drink with Cockney barrow boys in the early dawn hours. The tradition will be sadly missed.

The old central market is reopened with expensive stores selling exclusive products jostled by the more temporary stalls in the center peddling unremarkable souvenirs, jewelry, baskets and wickerwork, clothing, and T-shirts. Occasional groups enliven the place with impromptu music.

The area attracts art galleries, such as the Acme, the Hammond Lloyd, the Covent Garden, and the William Drummond. It's appropriate that art galleries should be returning to Covent Garden. In the 18th century it was a beehive of artists, including Lely and Kneller (famous portrait painters, the latter of whom is buried at St. Paul's Church, around the corner). Others who lived there were Thornhill, Richard Wilson, Fuseli, Daniel Mytens, the sculptor Roubiliac, Zoffany, and Flaxman. The American painter Benjamin West also lived here after he got out of jail for trying to study in London during the Revolution.

In the popular Covent Garden complex is **Plummers Restaurant,** 33 King St., W.C.2 (tel. 240-2534). It is a friendly, informal sort of place where a woman can go on her own without attracting attention and where there is room enough between the tables so that you don't have to listen to someone else's conversation. The color scheme of cream and plum is enlivened by pretty print tablecloths and fresh flowers on the tables. Ferns and plants are reflected in mirrors around the walls. Appetizers include avocado vinaigrette or clam chowder. Then there is a wide selection of main dishes including halibut and spinach in a parmesan cheese sauce, traditional steak-and-kidney pie, vegetarian dishes including vegetable cottage pie, Californian chili with chef's salad and garlic bread, and cream cheese nut crumble. There are Scottish beefburgers (100% meat) ranging from plain to Plummers Superburger topped with bacon, egg, and melted cheese. All burgers come with french fries or baked potato with sour cream and chives or butter, or with the chef's salad, but other vegetables are extra. Desserts include various flavors of ice cream and sorbets, and there is apple and blackberry pie and cream. Coffee—as much as you can drink—finishes off the meal. A meal will cost around £14 ($21), but you can get away with £8 ($12) for a beefburger and coffee. VAT is included, but a 12% service charge is added to all bills. Hours are from 12:30 to 2:30 p.m. and 6 to 11 p.m. The place is closed at lunchtime Saturday and all day Sunday. Tube: Covent Garden.

Penny's Place, 6 King St., W.C.2 (tel. 836-4553), is a converted pub dating from 1660. However, it now has a real French ambience, serving customers from 11:30 a.m. to 3 p.m. and 5:30 to 11:30 p.m. A large range of wines is offered—I counted more than 40 French labels—along with selections from the vineyards of Spain, Yugoslavia, Italy, and Germany. Prices range from £1 ($1.50) for a glass of house wine to £1.50 ($2.25) for a smooth French château-bottled claret. The blackboard lists the dishes available, and is likely to offer whitebait, coq au vin, liver in wine and orange sauce, or garlic mushrooms. Most meals average £12 ($18). The menu changes daily and depends largely on the whim of the Cordon Bleu chef and the state of the market. Downstairs in the cellar bistro, there's often live music, especially on Friday. Penny's is closed Sunday. Tube: Covent Garden.

Diana's Diner, 39 Endell St., W.C.2 (tel. 240-0272), is a busy, noisy place, with no pretensions to elegance, but with a well-deserved reputation among local office workers for serving satisfying meals at very reasonable prices. The most expensive dish is the mixed grill, a grand selection of cutlet, steak, egg, sausages, mushrooms, and tomatoes. There are also massive three-egg omelets, steak pie, beef in cider, and a whole fried plaice served with the inevitable "chips." Meals cost around £8 ($12). It is open Monday to Friday from 9 a.m. to 7 p.m. and on Saturday from 9 a.m. to 2 p.m. only. Tube: Covent Garden.

Magno's Brasserie, 65a Long Acre, W.C.2 (tel. 836-6077), is useful for before- and after-theater meals if you're in the area. It offers a fixed-price menu of appetizer, a main course, a glass of wine, and coffee for only £8.50 ($12.75), including VAT and service. This meal is served from 6 to 7 p.m. However, should you miss the pretheater meal, your regular à la carte tab could easily rise to £18 ($27) or more. The brasserie is open Monday to Friday for lunch and dinner and on Saturday for dinner only, offering a selection of modern French cuisine, grills, and salads. It has a friendly atmosphere and good service. Hours are noon to 2:30 p.m. for lunch and 6 to 11:30 p.m. for dinner. Tube: Covent Garden.

Porter's English Restaurant, 17 Henrietta St., W.C.2 (tel. 836-6466), is owned by the Earl of Bradford, who is a frequent visitor. It has a friendly, informal, and lively atmosphere in comfortable surroundings. It is open daily from noon to 3 p.m. and 5:30 to 11:30 p.m. It specializes in classic English pies, including steak and kidney, lamb and apricot, chicken and asparagus, and steak, oyster, and clam. The traditional roast beef with Yorkshire pudding is served on weekends. Served with whipped cream or custard, the "puddings" come hot or cold, including bread and butter pudding, and most definitely a steamed syrup sponge. Count on a bill of around £10 ($15). The bar does quite a few exotic cocktails, and you can also order Westons Farmhouse Draught cider by the half pint, even English wines or the traditional English mead. Tube: Covent Garden.

Food for Thought, 31 Neal St., W.C.2 (tel. 836-0239), serves some of the best and least expensive vegetarian food in the neighborhood, with meals costing from £4 ($6). During the peak dining hours, it is likely to be crowded, so it's advised that you go after the rush. The place is small, a basement café in fact, but it's most central and especially convenient to the theater section. After leaving the tube at Covent Garden, stroll along Neal Street toward Shaftesbury Avenue. The restaurant is on the left in the second block. The food selections change twice a day, but include good soups with whole-meal bread, freshly made salads, quiches, curries, and casseroles, including hot pie or mushroom and zucchini with a sweet-sour sauce. It is open only from noon to 8 p.m. Monday to Friday. A fast and popular take-away service is also provided.

MAYFAIR: Mayfair (W.1), bounded by Piccadilly, Hyde Park, and Oxford and Regent Streets, is the elegant, fashionable section of London. Luxury hotels exist side by side with Georgian town houses and swank shops. Here are all the parks, names, and streets that have snob associations the world over. Grosvenor Square (pronounced Grov-nor) is nicknamed "Little America" because it contains the American Embassy and a statue of Franklin D. Roosevelt. Berkeley (pronounced Barkley) is the home of the English Speaking Union.

At least once you'll want to dip into the exclusive Mayfair section, or even make repeated trips to Carnaby, lying only one block from Regent Street.

Perhaps you'll prefer to have afternoon tea in Mayfair, or you might combine a luncheon with sightseeing. If so, you'll find that not all the establishments here charge rarefied prices. To prove my point, here are these budget recommendations:

Bubbles, 41 North Audley St., W.1 (tel. 499-0600), is an interesting wine bar near the American Embassy, owned by David and Susan Nichol. David offers numerous wines by the bottle and glass, including an American selection. The owners take a special interest in the food. David was a chef and restaurant owner in New Zealand before coming to London. He specializes in ballotines and terrines, including a ballotine of duck stuffed with veal and spinach and a game terrine. The bar has an ever-changing buffet of freshly made salads in unusual combinations, such as a broccoli salad in a dressing made with soya sauce and peanut butter. Try Susan's well-known chicken salad or roast leg of English lamb cooked rare. There is a lovely selection of both French and English cheese, as well as tempting desserts, including strawberry mousse. They also offer three hot dishes every day, the most popular of which is a layered hot ham-and-cheese pie. Meals begin at £8 ($12) and up. Live classical Spanish guitar music is played on Tuesday, Wednesday, and Friday night. Hours are Monday to Friday from 11 a.m. to 3 p.m. and 5:30 to 11 p.m.; on Saturday from 11 a.m. to 3 p.m. only. Tube: Bond Street.

The **Chicago Pizza Pie Factory,** 17 Hanover Square, W.1. (tel. 629-2669), specializes in deep-dish pizza covered with cheese, tomato, and a choice of sausage, pepperoni, mushrooms, green peppers, onions, and anchovies. The regular-size pizza is enough for two or three diners, and the large one is suitable for four or five persons. This restaurant was introduced to London by a former advertising executive, Bob Payton, an ex-Chicagoan. The atmosphere is pleasant and friendly even though they are quite busy. It's one of the few places where a doggy bag is willingly provided. There are smoking and nonsmoking tables. The menu also includes stuffed mushrooms, garlic bread, salads, and homemade cheesecakes served with two forks. The cost begins at £8 ($12). The restaurant also has a large bar with a wide choice of cocktails, including a specialty known as the St. Valentine's Day Massacre. A video over the bar shows continuous American baseball, football, and basketball games. The 275-seat restaurant is full of authentic Chicago memorabilia, and the waitresses wear *Chicago Tribune* newspaper-sellers' aprons. The factory is just off Oxford Street in Hanover Square, opposite John Lewis and within easy reach of Regent Street as well. The factory is open Monday to Saturday from 11:45 a.m. to 11:30 p.m. Tube: Bond Street.

Shampers, 4 Kingly St., W.1 (tel. 437-1692), is a joint venture of a New Zealander, Don Hewitson, who, along with Tom and Sue Glynn, have perked up the wine bar movement with their excellent and superb selection of wines and their imaginatively prepared food. You have a choice of seats: either upstairs or down. Or perhaps you'll prefer to perch on a stool alongside the bar. I prefer the cozy ambience of the downstairs. A meal for one person with wine comes to about £8 ($12). Salads are a star, and look for the hot dish of the day including, perhaps, grilled marinated rabbit with mustard sauce. The selection of wines range from California to Germany to Australia. This might make an especially good choice if you're shopping in the area. Hours are Monday to Friday from 11 a.m. to 3 p.m. and from 5:30 to 11 p.m. The bar also serves lunch on Saturday. Tube: Oxford Circus.

Cranks Health Food Restaurant, 8 Marshall St., W.1 (tel. 437-9431) (around the corner from Carnaby Street), took its name from "cranks." But instead of the colloquial meaning of an eccentric, impractical person, the restaurant defines the word as those "who have the courage to pursue a line of thinking against the general stream of orthodox belief." Their "line," by the way, is excellent—the best of natural soups, salads, and breads made from whole-meal, compost-grown, stone-ground English flour. Cranks became famous when it operated on Carnaby Street, and first drew its young health-conscious clientele. The food-reform restaurant even tempts full-fledged carnivores by its fresh-tasting selections—such as the mix-it-yourself salad platter at lunch. If you've got a small waist, you can order a small bowl of choice salads. If you've already lost the battle of the bulge, you may prefer a large plate. Homemade cakes are always featured. Meals cost from £7 ($10.50). Cranks serves the best tiger's milk and dandelion coffee in town. It's open Monday from 8 a.m. to 8:30 p.m., Tuesday to Friday from 8 a.m. to 11 p.m., and Saturday from 9 a.m to 11 p.m. Warning: At lunchtime, it gets crowded. Tube: Oxford Circus.

The **Widow Applebaum's Deli & Bagel Academy,** 46 South Molton St., W.1 (tel. 629-4649), is a useful place for those who don't wish to go to the East End of London to enjoy New York Jewish food in the strict environment of Bloom's. It's good for a before-theater meal, but avoid it during office lunch hours. The typists are mad about the salt (corned) beef sandwiches. The pastrami is flown in fresh daily from New York. Sandwiches, including roast beef and turkey, are topped with cole slaw and pickled cucumbers, and are accompanied by potato salad. You can enjoy the chopped liver or the chicken matzoh ball (dumpling) soup. An authentic 100% beef quarter-pound, charcoal-grilled hamburger on a toasted bun with lettuce, tomato, and french fries is also served. Count on spending from £8 ($12). The deli has a video system with a wide screen showing the latest hits in music and popular TV serials. Hours are daily except Sunday from 10 a.m. to 11 p.m. Tables for sit-down meals are in the rear, going deep into the back. South Molton Street is a pedestrian precinct, and tables are set outside in fair weather. Tube: Bond Street.

Justin de Blank, 54 Duke St., W.1 (tel. 629-3174), just off Oxford Street, offers breakfast, lunch, and dinner, and is a haven for tired shoppers. They serve a variety of hot dishes including lamb and eggplant casserole, barbecued spare ribs, cauliflower cheese, or you might like one of their many choices of salads. Desserts include fruit pie with cream, cheesecake, and fresh fruit salad. They bake their own breads and also have a "take-out" order department. A three-course meal is likely to average £8 ($12). Justin is open weekdays from 8:30 a.m. to 3:30 p.m. and 4:30 to 9 p.m. On Saturday they are open only from 9 a.m. to 3:30 p.m., and are closed on Sunday. Tube: Bond Street.

Hard Rock Café, on Piccadilly at Hyde Park Corner, W.1 (tel. 629-0382), is a down-home southern-cum-midwestern funky American roadside diner with good food at reasonable prices and service with a smile. A double burger in a sesame-seed bun with french fries and salad is one of the most popular items, or you can try hot chili served with tortilla chips, followed by homemade ice cream. Count on spending from £8 ($12). The café is on two levels, with color TV at the end of the room and nonstop rock music. The bar is for solace while you wait for a table. Almost every night there is a line waiting to get in, as this is one of the most popular places in town for young people. Hours are noon to midnight. Tube: Hyde Park.

Shepherd Market

One of the curiosities of Mayfair is Shepherd Market, a tiny village of pubs, two-story inns, book and food stalls, and restaurants, all sandwiched between the slices of Mayfair grandness. At one corner you might be contemplating whether to buy that antique Rolls-Royce, then you suddenly turn down a street and are transplanted to a remnant of a village of old England, where the peddlers are hawking their wares. While here, you may want to drop in for a drink at one of London's best known pubs.

Shepherds Tavern, 50 Hertford St., W.1 (tel. 499-3017), is a nugget, considered *the* pub of Mayfair. It attracts a congenial mixture. There are many fine luxurious touches, including an exceptional collection of antique furniture; supreme among these is a sedan chair which once belonged to the son of George III, the Duke of Cumberland (it's now fitted with a telephone for those very private ring-ups). Many of the local habitués recall the tavern's association with the pilots in the Battle of Britain. Bar snacks and hot dishes include shepherd's pie, curry, or fish pie with vegetables. Upstairs, the owners operate a cozy restaurant, the Sedan, offering a three-course lunch for £6.35 ($9.53), with à la carte dinners going for £14 ($21) and up. The menu is likely to offer such dishes as poached monkfish with cucumber in a pink peppercorn sauce, medallions of veal with a black currant and cranberry sauce, and roast breast of duck with apple and apricot sauce. For dessert, try the whisky soufflé with orange sauce, if featured. The room is Georgian style with cedar paneling and pink napery. It serves Monday to Saturday from noon to 2:30 p.m. and 6 to 10 p.m. and on Sunday from noon to 1:45 p.m. and 6:30 to 10 p.m. Tube: Green Park.

The **Bunch of Grapes,** 16 Shepherd Market, W.1 (tel. 629-4989), is a pub which is all bustle at lunchtime, when it's filled with local office workers. It's a period piece from 1882, with a fireplace, lace curtains, turn-of-the-century chandeliers, hunting trophies, and Staffordshire figurines. The place is so popular that in summer, the action spills out onto the pavement. Nevertheless, foreign visitors are welcome and expected to force their way with the locals toward the bar to order real ale at £1.50 ($2.25) a half pint. Lunch is served from noon to 3 p.m. in the restaurant upstairs. You can select from a vast array of cold meats, pies, salads (such as cole slaw with orange), and hot dishes including kidneys in sherry, braised brisket, and, in season, fresh poached salmon and oysters. Meals cost from £6 ($9). No food is served on Sunday or in the evening, but you can go for a drink. Evening hours are from 5:30 to 11 p.m. (10:30 p.m. on Sunday). Tube: Green Park.

SOHO: This wedge-shaped section (W.1) of crisscrossed narrow lanes and crooked streets is the main foreign quarter of London, site of many of the city's best foreign restaurants. The unanglicized life of the continent holds forth in Soho: great numbers of French people are found here, and so are Italians and all other European nationalities, as well as Orientals. Traditionally it has been known as the center of vice and prostitution in London.

Soho starts impudently at Piccadilly Circus, spreading out like a peacock and ending at Oxford Street. One side borders the theater center on Shaftesbury Avenue. From Piccadilly Circus, walk northeast and you'll come to Soho, to the left of Shaftesbury. This jumbled section can also be approached from the Tottenham Court Road tube station. Walk south along Charing Cross Road, and Soho will be to your right.

Of Gerrard Street, a correspondent wrote that "the smell of pickled ginger and roast duckling seeps from restaurant doors. The men scurry into stores from afternoon games of fan-tan and mah-Jongg. A lilting twang of Chinese rock 'n' roll envelops the downtown street." The East End's Limehouse made a small pretense, but Gerrard Street has succeeded in becoming London's first Chinatown. Strip shows have given way to Chinese restaurants and bookstores keeping you informed of the latest developments in Hong Kong or China.

Soho in a sense is a Jekyll and Hyde quarter. In daytime it's a paradise for the searcher of spices, continental food, fruits, fish, and sausages, with at least two street markets offering fruit and vegetables, often at knock-down prices. At night it's a dazzle of strip joints, gay clubs, porno movies, sex emporiums, and titillating bookshops, all intermingled with international restaurants which, because of the competition, are on their toes to offer value for money.

Red Fort, 77 Dean St., W.1 (tel. 437-2410), is considered one of the finest Indian restaurants in London where the competition is keen (there are Indian restaurants virtually on every street corner). Opened by Amin Ali, this elegant Soho dining room is decorated in trendy tones of aubergine, plum, and pink. If you're on the tightest of budgets, go only for their help-yourself Sunday buffet at £8.95 ($13.43) where a spread of Indian delicacies is placed before you. Otherwise, count on spending from £15 ($22.50) for a superb meal of the finest dishes of Southern India. You might begin your hot and spicy meal with masha (spicy beans in a scooped-out onion) and follow with one of the tandoori specials or else a lamb dish. The waiters are helpful in explaining the menu. Hours are from noon to 2:45 p.m. and 6 to 11 p.m. daily. Tube: Leicester Square.

Kettner's Restaurant, 29 Romilly St., W.1 (tel. 437-6437), has had a long and topsy-turvy history, dating back to 1869. Once it was patronized by King Edward VII, then Prince of Wales. Today it's pasta and pizza time, as this is the flagship restaurant of the Piazza Express chain. However, its standards of service and the quality of its food are far above the standards of a typical chain emporium. It's also a center for live jazz, usually offered on Friday and Saturday night and at lunch on Sunday. You can begin your evening by having a glass of something in the champagne bar on the ground floor. The restaurant is open seven days a week from noon to midnight. Tube: Leicester Square.

Maison Berlemont, 49 Dean St., W.1 (tel. 437-2799), is popularly known as "The French House," attracting in its day such notables as Charles de Gaulle and also Dylan Thomas and Brendan Behan. Run by Monsieur G. R. Berlemont, it once was the unofficial headquarters of the French resistance in exile in London during the war. Nostalgic Frenchmen still come here, talking about the old days and purchasing outstanding "vins" by the glass. The pub has a plain exterior, and the decor is not remarkable. However, the hospitality of the patron is laudable. Prices of wine by the glass begin at 90p ($1.35). A lot of authors, theater and film people are attracted here. Hours are 11 a.m. to 3 p.m. and 5:30 to 11 p.m. Tube: Tottenham Court Road, Piccadilly Circus, or Leicester Square.

The **Dumpling Inn**, 15a Gerrard St., W.1 (tel. 437-2567), in the small Chinese district of Soho, attracts a number of devoted regulars. Don't be fooled by the name or the Venetian murals—this is an elegant Chinese restaurant serving classical Mandarin dishes. The haute cuisine of China, Mandarin cooking dates back nearly 3,000 years and employs a number of unique cooking rituals. The fact that this restaurant serves somewhat small portions can be turned into an advantage because it gives you an opportunity to sample a variety of this delectable cuisine. You can savor the special tastes of Mandarin cooking in the shark's fin soup, the beef in oyster sauce, or the grilled pork or beef dumplings, and many Pekinese and Cantonese specialties are also served. Pancakes stuffed with discreetly flavored minced meat are a house specialty. Main dishes include prawns in chili sauce and dumplings. Meals cost from £8 ($12). Dinner reservations are recommended, and you should allow plenty of time for dining here since most dishes are prepared to your special order. Hours are nonstop, every day of the year except Christmas, from noon to 11:45 p.m. Tube: Leicester Square.

Pasticceria Amalfi, 31 Old Compton St., W.1 (tel. 437-7284), is a crowded, unusually good, bargain-priced Italian restaurant, one of the finest in Soho. It's popular with lunchers in an area where there are dozens of other luncheon possibilities. Cedric Melliss is "boss" around here, and he likes to hire Italian chefs who prepare dishes in the traditional way. That includes spaghetti, pizzas, veal in white wine, minestrone, and lasagne. Dinners cost from £10 ($15) to £12 ($18). A pâtisserie turning out Italian pastries is at the back of the restaurant on the ground floor. Hours are from noon to 2:45 p.m. and 6 to 11:15 p.m. daily except Sunday. On Sunday, it's open from noon to 9:45 p.m. Tube: Leicester Square.

The **Venus Kebab House**, 2 Charlotte St., W.1 (tel. 636-4324), is a zesty choice on a highly competitive street. It's a winner for Greek specialties and good food in the low-price range. Appetizers include taramasalata, hummus, tzatziki, and kalaman in wine sauce. Avgolemono, the Greek national soup, is made with chicken stock, rice, egg, lemon, and spices. You can have three lamb or pork kebabs or a large Greek salad, a main dish. The standard specialties are dolmades (vine leaves stuffed with lamb, beef, rice, tomatoes, and spices) and moussaka. A selection of fish dishes includes Dover sole. For dessert, try baklava (a light, flaky pastry made with blended honey and nuts). Four-course meals begin at £8 ($12). A corner restaurant, the Venus has outdoor tables in summer. It's open from noon to 11:30 p.m. Monday to Saturday. Tube: Goodge Street or Tottenham Court Road.

Triano Restaurant, 53 St. Giles High St., W.C.2 (tel. 240-2360), just off New Oxford Street, is good public relations for the Cypriots. It serves excellent dishes, but keeps the prices low. You can have the popular moussaka with rice and peas, or you may prefer the special shish kebab. One of the specialties of Triano is a seafood pilaf. For dessert, try the baklava. Meals average £10 ($12). The restaurant usually serves from noon to 3 p.m. and 5:30 to 11 p.m. However, it is closed on Saturday for lunch and all day on Sunday. Tube: Leicester Square.

Jimmy's, 23 Frith St., W.1 (tel. 437-9521), is across the street from Ronnie Scott's (see Chapter V). I recommend a dinner at Jimmy's, then a visit to Ronnie Scott's later, where you need order only drinks and not its high-priced food. Jimmy's is a basement bistro, with the menu posted outside. Scruffy waiters, an unswept floor, and empty bottles on the bar create an atmosphere that ages ago used to be called bohemian. The cooking is basically Greek-Cypriot, with an international flavor. Appetizers include soups, taramasalata, and the like. Chops, kebabs, moussaka, and chicken dishes are the main courses, along with stuffed vine leaves. The helpings are huge, a complete meal costing around £5.50 ($8.25). There's jukebox music. Hours are 12:30 to 3 p.m. and 5:30 to 10:45 p.m. daily except Sunday. Tube: Leicester Square.

Anemos, 32 Charlotte St., W.1 (tel. 636-2289), is the place for breaking plates, dancing, and joining the waiters in a rip-roaring Greek song. They also have a magic show and a floor show. A typical meal of taramasalata, hummus, and kebabs, plus dessert, cheese, coffee, and a half bottle of wine, will run as much as £10.50 ($15.75). However, a smaller meal with, say, two courses only and no wine, will average around £7 ($10.50). You'll need a good digestion for you will be expected to dance on the tables, gyrate to bouzouki music, and drink retsina or Cyprus wines (others are expensive). The restaurant is closed on Sunday so the staff can clean up the mess. Otherwise, it's open from noon to 2:45 p.m. and 6 to 10:30 p.m. Tube: Goodge Street.

Gabys Continental Bar, 30 Charing Cross Rd., W.C.2 (tel. 836-4233), is really just a snackbar but is open from 9 a.m. to midnight, and can satisfy your needs whatever the time of day, particularly after the theater. The service is quick and friendly. Salt beef (corned, to us) sandwiches are a featured selection, as are hearty soups such as bean and barley. The house specialties are doner kebabs, which are spit-roasted lamb served in pita bread with relish and shredded salad. Moussaka is another house specialty, and the chef also prepares many different types of omelets and vegetarian menus. Meals cost from £6 ($9). Tube: Leicester Square.

Le Beaujolais Wine Bar, 25 Litchfield St., W.C.2 (tel. 836-2277), stands at Cambridge Circus. People go here to enjoy wine and cold snacks in a friendly atmosphere. Joel deFaut has created this bar for those who like to chat and drink. House wines range from 95p ($1.43) to £1.20 ($1.80) per glass. By the bottle, prices start at £4.50 ($6.75) for the house wine, either white or red. He has cold food to accompany your wine, including French pâtés, cheeses, and chicken and ham. You might also prefer to order a hot dish such as a classic French coq au vin. Meals begin at £6 ($9), or you can do it for less if you settle for pâté and french bread. Le Beaujolais is open daily from 11:30 a.m. to 3 p.m. and 5:30 to 11 p.m. (closed Saturday at lunchtime and Sunday). Tube: Leicester Square.

North of Soho, in a section of London called "Fitzrovia," **Auntie's,** 126 Cleveland St., W.1 (tel. 387-1548), opened in 1969, having been a popular tearoom in the early part of that decade. Shaun Thomson and Ian Wild are dedicated to the art of English cookery, and they present an array of dishes that many of their diners remember from their childhood: beef and mushroom pie with Guinness gravy, "toad in the hole," even Auntie's bangers and mash. Rabbit hot pot is served with a white mustard seed sauce, and for dessert you can order a tipsy fruit trifle. A set dinner goes for £12.50 ($18.75), and meals are served Monday to Friday from noon to 3 p.m. and 6 to 11 p.m. (on Saturday, hours are only from 6 to 11 p.m.). The service, food, and surroundings make this a worthy choice. It's very intimate so reservations are imperative. Tube: Great Portland Station.

2. Westminster and St. James's

This section (S.W.1) has been the seat of the British government since the days of Edward the Confessor. Dominated by the Houses of Parliament and Westminster Abbey, Parliament Square is the symbol of the soul of England. Westminster is a big name to describe a large borough of London, including Whitehall itself, the headquarters of many government offices. In addition, the sprawling area in and around Victoria Station (with many budget hotels) is also a part of Westminster. Sections of it fall into Pimlico.

After you've been photographed with Big Ben in the background, chances are you'll be ready for lunch.

The **Westminster College,** 76 Vincent Square, S.W.1, is the luncheon find of the year. In a spacious dining room, with great windows opening onto a garden square, a complete midday meal, coffee included, is served for around £6 ($9), including VAT. The secret is that this is the finest school for hotel and restaurant catering in England, and the nonprofit meals are cooked and served by undergraduates. The young waitresses and waiters, with their efforts to do everything perfectly, give attentive service. It's really not amateur hour, as there is strict supervision. The food is of a high standard, but you must order whatever their "assignment" is for the day. You can reserve space by phone (tel. 828-1222) between noon and 2 p.m. only, up to ten days in advance, or just arrive around noon to see whether there is space, have a drink in the lounge if you wish, and then be shown to your seat. If you are alone, you'll probably have to share. Naturally, the dining room is closed on weekends and college holidays from July through September. Tube: St. James's Park.

Top Curry Centre, Tandoori House, 3 Lupus St., S.W.1 (tel. 821-7572), has the colossal advantage of listing the hotness and strength of the curries graded from one to nine, so you need not suffer the agonies if you prefer a mild dish. Nibble two bhajis with various fillings while you decide on your main curry dish. Curries include succulent chicken kurma, prawn and mushroom curry, egg or vegetable curry, beef or lamb curries. Side dishes include cauliflower or spinach bhajis and cucumber raita (in yogurt). Poppadums, chapatis, and, of course, rice accompany these, and the bill will come to around £7.50 ($11.25) per person for a highly satisfying meal. Drinks are available and you should certainly wash No. 9 curry down with lager unless you have an asbestos-lined palate. The center is open from noon to 3 p.m. and 6 p.m. to midnight Monday to Thursday. On Friday and Saturday it's open from noon to midnight. Tube: Pimlico.

Grandma Lee's Bakery and Restaurant, 2 Bridge St., S.W.1 (tel. 839-1319), is a bright and cheerful place across the street from the Houses of Parliament and the tower of Big Ben. Bread, buns, and rolls are freshly baked on the premises, later to appear at the ground-floor service counter filled with your choice of an array of ingredients. You can either take these sandwiches out or else carry them upstairs to consume at the lightwood varnished tables and chairs. Everything comes in a bun, including breakfast, a bacon-and-egg bun served from 7 to 11 a.m. Along with juice, tea, and coffee, it comes to £1.75 ($2.63). Try a Grandwich Plate, a huge, thick slice of bread with your choice of filling. It's topped with another gigantic slice, served with cole slaw on the side. They also serve beef casserole with bread and chili with bread. Meals cost from £4 ($6). It's open daily from 7 a.m. to 9 p.m. Tube: Westminster.

ST. JAMES'S: This section (S.W.1), the beginning of Royal London, starts at Piccadilly Circus, moving southwest. It's frightfully convenient, as the English say, enclosing a number of locations, such as American Express on Haymarket, many of the leading department stores, eventually encompassing Buckingham Palace.

But don't be scared off. There are luncheon bargains available in an atmosphere ranging from the world's most exclusive grocery store to a posh Victorian pub.

Fortnum and Mason, 181 Piccadilly, W.1 (tel. 734-8040). Pause, first, to look at the famous Fortnum and Mason clock outside, then enter the refined precincts of the world's most elegant grocery store (more about this in the shopping section coming up). It's well known historically that this store has supplied "take-out" treasures to everybody from the Duke of Wellington to Florence Nightingale in the Crimea, even Mr. Stanley while he pursued Dr. Livingstone. What is lesser known is that you can also order a sandwich here prepared by grocers who hold the Royal Warrant or else partake of a proper sitdown meal, and not just caviar, truffles, or rich chocolates.

There are three places at which to eat or dine, including the Fountain Restaurant which is open from 9:30 a.m. to 11:30 p.m. Monday to Saturday (when the store closes, you can enter this restaurant in the evening from Jermyn Street). Actually, you can come here when it opens for a properly cooked English breakfast for £4.25

($6.38), but mostly the Fountain is known for its ice cream sundaes, its celebrity watchers, and its afternoon teas, beginning at £4.95 ($7.43) and served from 3 to 5 p.m. At night, a grill menu is available costing from £8 ($12).

You can also patronize the Patio and Buttery on the mezzanine, any time from 9 a.m. to 5 p.m. Monday to Friday and from 9:30 a.m. to 4:30 p.m. on Saturday. It has the same menu as the Fountain (see above).

On the fourth floor is the St. James's Restaurant, which keeps the same hours as the buttery just mentioned. With its sea-green decor, this large restaurant offers conservative dining, with such specialties as roast beef with Yorkshire pudding and fresh grilled fish. Meals average £10 ($15). Tube: Green Park or Piccadilly Circus.

The **Red Lion,** 2 Duke of York St., St. James's Square, S.W.1 (tel. 930-2030), is only a short walk from Piccadilly Circus, near American Express on Haymarket. Ian Nairn compared its spirit to that of Edouard Manet's painting *A Bar at the Folies-Bergère* (see the collection at the Courtauld Institute Galleries). Try to avoid peak hours, so that you'll be able to introduce yourself to the friendly owners, Roy and Corinne Hamlin. They offer pub luncheons at noon: steak pie and a wide variety of sandwiches, all on healthful brown bread. A simple meal costs from £3.50 ($5.25). Roasts are also presented. Everything is washed down with a pint of lager or cider in their jewel-like little Victorian pub, with its posh turn-of-the-century decorations such as patterned glass, deep-mahogany curlicues that recapture the gin-palace atmosphere. It's open six days a week from 11 a.m. to 3 p.m. and 5:30 to 11 p.m., on Sunday from noon to 2 p.m. Single women can be at ease here, under the unofficial and kindly eye of the Hamlins. Tube: Piccadilly Circus.

NEAR VICTORIA STATION:

On one of London's most popular streets for budget hotels, **Ebury Wine Bar,** 139 Ebury St., S.W.1 (tel. 530-5447), is most convenient for dining or drinking in the area. This wine bar and bistro attracts a youthful crowd to its often crowded but always atmospheric precincts. Wine is sold by either the glass or bottle. A cold table is offered daily, and you can always get an enticing plat du jour, such as beef braised in beer, preceded by perhaps orange-and-carrot soup. The menu invariably includes grilled steaks and lamb cutlets. All the food is prepared fresh daily. Sunday lunch costs £6.50 ($9.75). Otherwise, meals go for around £12 ($18). The wine bar is open seven days a week, serving food from noon to 2:45 p.m. and 6 to 10 p.m. Monday to Saturday, from noon to 2:30 p.m. and 7 to 10 p.m. on Sunday. Tube: Victoria Station.

Methuselah's, 29 Victoria St., S.W.1 (tel. 222-1750). Don Hewitson, a New Zealander, is credited with changing the face of London wine bars, and all of them that have shown his magic touch over the years are recommended in this guide. Opposite New Scotland Yard, his latest venture, which is exclusively his, is popular with MPs from the House of Commons. Mr. Hewitson not only has an excellent cellar of wines, but he also believes in providing a sophisticated menu to back it up, along with attractive surroundings. He calls his food "Bourgeois," and it shows a devotion to Provence. The day's specialties are written on the blackboard. There is a ground floor bar, along with two cellar buffet and wine bars, plus a more formal restaurant, the Burgundy Room, on the mezzanine. Meals cost from £10 ($15), and are served Monday to Friday only from 11:30 a.m. to 3 p.m. and 5:30 to 11 p.m. Tube: Victoria.

The Albert, 52 Victoria St., S.W.1 (tel. 222-5577), once named "pub of the year," is a real bit of Victorian England, nestling among modern office blocks near Victoria Station (the nearest tube stop). From 8 to 10 a.m., it serves a traditional English breakfast for £4.95 ($7.43), including sausages, bacon, kidneys, tomatoes, mushrooms, kippers, and fried eggs. Toast with English marmalade, and plenty of coffee or tea, round out the repast. To reach this repast, head up the staircase, hung with pictures of prime ministers and Queen Victoria, past dark wood paneling, until you reach the dining room. You can come back for lunch at the Carvery Restaurant, with sumptuous roasts traditionally prepared and carved for you, or for dinner seven days a week. Hours are from noon to 2:30 p.m. and 6 to 9:30 p.m. The cost is £11.50 ($17.25) per person. Tube: Victoria.

PIMLICO: Still the choice for taking a maiden aunt to lunch, the **Tate Gallery Restaurant,** Millbank, S.W.1 (tel. 834-6754), is better than ever. Even if it weren't, it would still be a viable choice as the Whistler Room contains the famous murals by Rex Whistler. The menu undergoes seasonal changes, but you can count on good, wholesome food in the British tradition. Some recipes, I suspect, were in use in Victoria's time, and the lamb chops, for example, are likely to be named after Lord Nelson. The wine list is extensive, and the restaurant is widely praised for its moderate tabs on some excellent vintages. It's essential to reserve a table (many in-the-know locals call ahead and even order their wine so that it can be at the right temperature upon their arrival). Costing from £15 ($22.50) lunches in this highly unusual setting are served from noon to 3 p.m. Monday to Saturday. Tube: Pimlico.

3. The City

When the English talk about "The City" (E.C.2, E.C.3), they don't mean London. The City is the British version of Wall Street. Not only is it an important financial and business square mile, but it contains much worth exploring.

Here are the buildings known all over the world: the Bank of England on Threadneedle Street (entrance hall open to the public); the Stock Exchange, where you can watch from a special gallery as fortunes are made and lost; and Lloyd's of London, on Leadenhall, one of the world's great insurance centers. Lloyd's will insure anything from a stamp collection to a giraffe's neck.

Typical English food—shepherd's pie, mixed grills, roast beef—is dished up in dozens of the old pubs of The City. Here you can eat along with the English, whether it be the man in the bowler worried about the value of the pound, or a Cockney clerk who has stayed within the sound of the Bow bells.

Many of the old pubs and wine bars date back to Elizabethan days, and lay claim to having entertained literary celebrities. For the most part, the following recommendations have been selected not only because of their well-prepared and inexpensive food, but because the buildings themselves have interest. The pub might have been designed by Sir Christopher Wren, or Shakespeare might have performed in one of them . . . whatever.

Have a good lunch.

The **Barbican Centre,** The Barbican, E.C.2 (tel. 638-4141), offers a choice of eating and drinking establishments in several price ranges. On Level 5, the Waterside Cafeteria is a self-service restaurant, offering a range of hot meals, salads, sandwiches, pastries, tea, and coffee, along with wine and beer. It is open from 10 a.m. to 8 p.m. daily, Monday to Saturday (from noon on Sunday and public holidays). A variety of hot dishes is available, as well as a salad bar and bakery items, with meals costing from £5 ($7.50). It offers views over the lake, and in summer there are seats on the terrace. On Level 7, the Cut Above is a carvery-style restaurant which features roast joints, along with an array of cold meats, fish, and salads. Meals cost from £12 ($18), plus VAT and service. From the restaurant, windows open onto St. Paul's Cathedral, St. Giles Cripplegate, and the Barbican Lake. It is open daily from noon to 3 p.m. and from 6 p.m. until the last orders are taken half an hour after the last performance at the Barbican Hall Theatre. On Level 6, you might also want to patronize Wine on Six, which has an extensive list of bottled and draft wines and beers, accompanied by a variety of cold meats, fish, and salads, along with specialty breads and cheese. Light meals with drinks cost from £5 ($7.50). It is open from 5:30 p.m. before concerts Monday to Saturday. There are bars, along with coffee and snackbars, in the foyers of the Barbican Hall Theatre and Cinema One. Tube: Barbican.

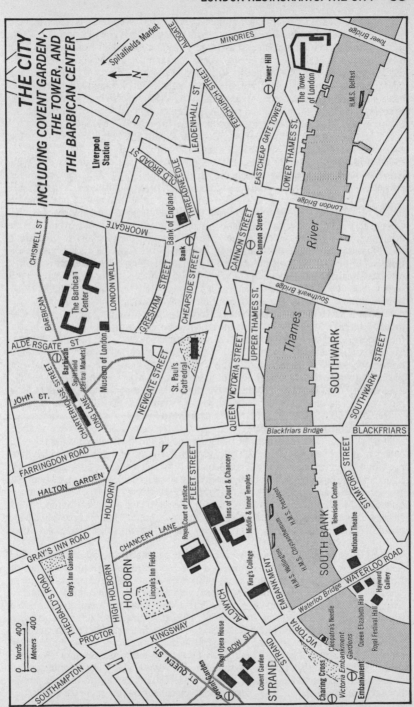

THE CITY
INCLUDING COVENT GARDEN,
THE TOWER, AND
THE BARBICAN CENTER

Wren's Bistro Upstairs, 29 Watling St., E.C.4 (tel. 248-6252), is rich in associations with Sir Christopher Wren. It was rebuilt after the Great Fire of London in 1666. In the intimate restaurant upstairs, meals are served on weekdays from noon to 2:30 p.m., under oak beams and on trestle tables. You can have a good choice of English food, with such traditional dishes as steak-and-kidney pie. Three or four hot dishes made on the premises daily are likely to include chicken-and-mushroom pie, moussaka, and chili con carne. Meals cost from £4 ($7.50). No food is served in the street level Old Watling Pub, filled with Wren memorabilia and open from 11:30 a.m. to 3 p.m. and 5 to 9 p.m. Monday to Friday only. Tube: Mansion House.

The **George & Vulture,** 3 Castle Court, Cornhill, E.C.3 (tel. 626-9710), is for the enthusiast of Dickens, ye olde Pickwickian hostelrie and the like. This chophouse, founded in 1660, makes the claim that it is probably the world's oldest tavern, with reference to an inn on this spot going back to 1175. The George & Vulture no longer puts up overnight guests (Dickens used to bed down here), but its three floors are still used for serving English meals. The Pickwick Club meets here now. Come here for lunch, Monday through Friday, noon to 3 p.m. In addition to the daily specials, the George & Vulture features a "loin chop, chump chop," fried filets of Dover sole with tartar sauce, or a more modest plaice. Every Thursday, the specialty is "Pickwick Pie," that is, steak-and-kidney pudding. On other days the specialty is various roasts. Potatoes or buttered cabbage are served with most platters. The apple tart is always reliable. Meals begin at about £9 ($13.50) for three courses. After lunch, explore the intricate nearby passageways, discovering for yourself the maze of shops, wine houses, pubs, and old buildings surrounding the tavern. Tube: Bank.

Slender's Health Food Restaurant (don't you just love that name?) is at 41 Cathedral Pl., E.C.4 (tel. 236-5974), a most convenient location as it is just across from the Underground station at St. Paul's. Usually attracting a young crowd, it offers an inviting ambience and friendly service. For an appetizer you might try one of their homemade soups, and for a main course, a selection of such dishes as lentil-and-egg pie or beans with chili and rice. The desserts, as the local office workers will testify, "are super," and likely to include plum crumble. Most diners enjoy the whole-food buns and scones which are freshly baked. Meals cost from £5.50 ($8.25), and the place is open only from 7:30 a.m. to 6:15 p.m. Monday to Friday.

Old King Lud, 78 Ludgate Circus, E.C.4 (tel. 236-6610), is a Victorian pub built in 1855 on the site of the Old Fleet Prison. The former dungeons are now the cellars of this old-world pub, which bills itself as the home of the original Welsh rarebit. However, it no longer serves that specialty for which it became famous. Rather, it offers a selection of pâtés which ranges from venison to duck with orange. Both hot and cold dishes are dispensed, with light meals costing from £4 ($6), served at lunch only from Monday to Friday. Wine is sold by the glass, and you can also order good Marlow Bitter here. The decor is in varying shades of green, including the tufted banquettes. Pub hours are 11 a.m. to 3 p.m. and 5:30 to 11 p.m. Tube: Blackfriars.

WINE BARS: My favorite of all **Mother Bunch's Wine House,** Arches F & G, Old Seacoal Lane, E.C.4 (tel. 236-5317), is a maze of vaults underneath the arches of Ludgate Circus. Mother Bunch's is one of the most atmospheric places for dining in The City, boasting a "well-stocked larder," with the best of hams and all manner of cheeses as well as game and other pies. Port wines of the most noted vintages are decanted daily "for gentlemen in the proper manner." In season, grouse, partridge, pheasant, and Scottish salmon are featured. Guests can dine in the mellow room downstairs or perhaps in the elegantly furnished upstairs room where many are seated around a large table and served family style. Sherry, port, and madeira "from the wood" begin at £1.20 ($1.80), as do the table wines by the glass. The favorite dish is a plate of smoked ham off the bone, and game pie is also served. Strawberries and raspberries in season make the finest dessert, and you can always order cheese with french bread. Meals begin at £9 ($13.50). The wine house is open from 11:30 a.m. to 3 p.m. and 5:30 to 8:30 p.m. Monday to Friday. Tube: Blackfriars.

Capataz Wine Store, 89 Old Broad St., E.C.2 (tel. 588-1140), is a City wine vault, under a shoe shop, that maintains a turn-of-the-century atmosphere, with sawdust covering the floors. You sit on simple wooden chairs grouped around wine cases and casks. At lunchtime a mainly business-oriented clientele patronizes this atmospheric cellar, selecting their favorite sherries or table wines. Wines, incidentally, are sold by the glass—a recently sampled red burgundy going for 90p ($1.35), Italian red and white wines for 75p ($1.13), and claret for 90p ($1.35). Food is not served. However, you can bring in and eat your own sandwiches and snacks, while enjoying a selection from some 70 different wines. The wine store has been under the management of the same family for more than a century. Hours are from 11:30 a.m. to 3 p.m. and 5 to 7 p.m. Monday to Friday. Tube: Bank, Liverpool Street, or Broad Street.

Bow Wine Vaults, 10 Bow Churchyard, E.C.4 (tel. 248-1121), has existed since long before the current wine fad. The atmosphere is staunchly masculine in the "Old Bar," but the clientele in the recently extended "New Bar" is fairly mixed. Sherries, port, and madeira are available by the glass, as are an assortment of table wines at prices ranging from £1 ($1.50) to £3 ($4.50). Sandwiches, cheeses, and fruitcake are available in the "Old Bar," varying salads and hot dishes in the "New Bar." A bustling restaurant downstairs and more formal private dining rooms complete the range of services. The bars are open from 11:30 a.m. to 3 p.m. and 5 to 7 p.m., the restaurant open only at lunchtime. They are closed weekends and bank holidays. Tube: Mansion House.

Jamaica Wine House, St. Michael's Alley, off Cornhill, E.C.3 (tel. 626-9496), lies in a tangle of City alleyways, and if you do manage to find it, you'll be at one of the first coffeehouses to be opened in England. In fact, the Jamaica Wine House is reputed to be the first coffeehouse in the Western world. Pepys used to visit it and mentioned the event in his *Diary.* The coffeehouse was destroyed in the Great Fire of 1666, rebuilt in 1674, and has remained, more or less, in its present form ever since. For years London merchants and daring sea captains came here to lace deals with rum and coffee. Nowadays the two-level house dispenses beer, ale, lager, and fine wines to appreciative drinkers. The oak-paneled bar on the ground floor is more traditional, as the downstairs bar has been modernized. You can order a glass of wine from £1.20 ($1.80), along with light snacks such as pork pie, stuffed baked potatoes with various fillings, and toasted sandwiches. Light meals cost from £3.50 ($5.25). It is open from 11:30 a.m. to 3 p.m. and 5 to 8 p.m. The Bank of England is only a stone's throw away. Tube: Bank.

Olde Wine Shades, 6 Martin Lane, off Cannon Street, E.C.4 (tel. 626-6876), is the oldest wine house in The City, dating from 1663. It was the only City tavern to survive the Great Fire of 1666, not to mention the blitz of 1940. Only 100 yards from the Monument, the Olde Wine Shades used to attract Charles Dickens, who enjoyed its fine wines. In the smoking room the old oil paintings have darkened with age, and the 19th-century satirical political cartoons remain enigmatic to most of today's generation. Some of the fine wines of Europe are served here, and port and sherry are drawn directly from an array of casks behind the counter. The owners, El Vino, the famous City wine merchants, boast that they can satisfy anyone's taste in sherry. A candlewick bar and restaurant is found downstairs, but upstairs, along with your wine, you can order french bread with ham off the bone, Breton pâté, and sandwiches, with light meals costing from £5 ($7.50). Hours are from 11:30 a.m. to 3 p.m. and 5 to 8 p.m. Men must wear a jacket and tie. The establishment is closed on Saturday, Sunday, and bank holidays. Tube: Monument.

FLEET STREET: This "street of ink" (E.C.4), as it is called, is a continuation of the Strand and is the gateway to The City, but it is famous as the center of London's newspaper and publishing world. The chances are that the person you are rubbing shoulders with in one of the old pubs is a writer or author, as people of letters gather in the historic pubs around here, just as they have been doing for centuries. Here you can eat steak-and-kidney pie.

Ye Olde Cock Tavern, 22 Fleet St., E.C.4 (tel. 353-3454), should inspire you to follow the long line of ghostly literary comrades, such as Dickens, who have favored this ancient pub with their presence. Downstairs you can order a pint as well as snackbar food. You can also order steak-and-kidney pie or a cold chicken-and-beef plate with salad. Light meals cost from £3 ($4.50). At the Carvery upstairs, a meal costs from £8.50 ($12.75) and includes a choice of five appetizers, such as soup or prawn cocktail, followed by all the roasts you can carve—beef, lamb, pork, or turkey. The Carvery serves only lunch, from 12:15 to 2:30 p.m., and the street-level pub's hours are from 11:30 to 2:30 p.m. and 5 to 9:30 p.m. The place is closed Saturday and Sunday. Tube: Temple or Chancery Lane.

Cheshire Cheese, Wine Office Court, 145 Fleet St., E.C.4 (tel. 353-6170), is one of the greatest of the old city chophouses, open and running since 1667. It is famous as the place where Dr. Johnson dined with his friends and entertained them with his acerbic wit. This is quite possible, and certainly Dickens was a customer. The first specialty is "ye famous pudding"—(steak, kidney, mushroom, and game)—and the other is roast beef, with Yorkshire pudding and horseradish sauce. The hot plate holds a giant joint of the roast beef, and the waiters will give you additional helpings, warning you "not to waste it." For dessert, there is "ye famous pancake." Meals cost from £10 ($15). Lunch is served from noon to 2:30 p.m. (last orders), and dinners from 6 to 9 p.m. Warning: The bars open at 11:30 a.m. and again at 5 p.m. Closed Saturday and Sunday. Tube: St. Paul's.

4. Holborn and Bloomsbury

HOLBORN: In "legal London," you can join barristers, solicitors, and law clerks for food and drink at the following recommendations.

The Spaghetti House, 20 Sicilian Ave., W.C.1 (tel. 242-2434), was known for its pasta dishes long before pasta became "the thing" in London. This large place, part of a chain, is seemingly always filled with hungry diners. It serves Monday to Wednesday from noon to 10:30 p.m. and Thursday to Saturday from noon to 11 p.m. The Italian-speaking waiters rush about, serving good, tasty, and reasonably priced food, with a wide selection of moderately priced Italian wines. Selections include pizzas and lasagne, and some of the pastas will please the vegetarian. The average meal comes to £8 ($12), very good value, and portions are generous. Children get a special welcome. Tube: Holborn.

My Old Dutch, 131 High Holborn, W.C.1 (tel. 242-5200), London's only Dutch restaurant, is a cheerful, friendly place, resembling a Dutch kitchen with scrubbed pine tables at which you can be served 101 different pancakes—all enormous —on huge Delft plates. Fillings and garnishes include cheese, meats, and vegetables, as well as sweet fillings, such as Pandora's Pleasure (pear, ginger, and ice cream with crème de cacao sauce). There is also a selection of waffles and ice cream. The cost is from £5 ($7.50) up, and one of these dishes makes a good meal. Tea and coffee are available, as well as wines and cocktails. My Old Dutch is open from noon to 11:30 p.m. Monday, Thursday, and Friday; to 12:30 a.m. Friday and Saturday. Tube: Holborn.

The Cittie of York, 22–23 High Holborn, W.C.1 (tel. 242-7670), stands near the Holborn Bars, the historic entrance to London marked by dragons holding the coat of arms of The City between their paws. Persons entering and leaving London were checked and paid tolls here. The gatehouse to Gray's Inn, one of the ancient Inns of Court in the Legal London of today. A pub has stood on this site since 1430. The present pub is named the Cittie of Yorke after a 16th-century hostelry later called the Staple Inn (now across on the other side of High Holborn). Its principal hall, said to have the longest bar counter in England, has handsome screenwork, comfortable little compartments, a long row of huge vats, and a high trussed roof. The place is popular with barristers and judges. Typical bar food is served along with fresh salads, grilled salmon, and steaks, meals costing £2 ($3) to £3 ($4.50). The pub is closed Sunday, but otherwise, hours are from 11 a.m. to 3:30 p.m. and 5:30 to 11 p.m. No food is served on Saturday evening. Tube: Holborn.

BLOOMSBURY: The Big Mamma of a chain of spaghetti and pizza houses is the **Spaghetti House**, 15 Goodge St., W.1 (tel. 636-6582). Chianti bottles enhance an inviting, Italy-oriented atmosphere on floor after floor.

A worthy main dish is veal escalope in butter, served with vegetables. The minestrone is flavorsome. For dessert, cassata siciliana makes a soothing selection. Expect to pay at least £9 ($13.50) for a complete meal. The Spaghetti House is open Monday to Saturday from noon to 11 p.m., and from 5:30 to 10:30 p.m. on Sunday. It's across Tottenham Court Road in the vicinity of Russell Square which is the nearest tube stop.

The **Museum Tavern**, 49 Great Russell St., W.C.1 (tel. 242-8987), directly across the street from the British Museum, is a turn-of-the-century pub, with all the trappings: cut velvet, oak paneling, and cut glass. Right in the center of the London University area, it is popular with writers and publishers. At lunch you can order real, good-tasting, low-cost English food. Such standard English fare is featured as shepherd's pie or "sausage and mash." Hot pies are another featured selection. A cold buffet is offered, including herring, Scotch eggs, and veal and ham pies, as well as salads and cheese. Meals cost from £5 ($7.50). It keeps regular pub hours from 11 a.m. to 3 p.m. and 5:30 to 11 p.m. Tube: Holborn or Tottenham Court Road.

Entrecôte, 124 Southampton Row, W.C.1 (tel. 405-1466), invites you to go downstairs to its Edwardian precincts. Attractive "resting" actresses are the waitresses, and they will serve you the house specialty, an entrecôte with french fries. Other daily specials are offered as well—perhaps coq au vin or beef bourguignon. A meal costs from £12 ($18). In fact, the food is generally French inspired, and the wine list includes some Haut Médoc selections. The food is made fresh every day—no deep-freeze. In the evening, a small disco atmosphere prevails, and usually there is dancing to live music. Hours are noon to 2:45 p.m. and 6 to 11:45 p.m. (to 10:45 p.m. on Sunday). Closed for lunch on Saturday and Sunday. Tube: Russell Square or Holborn.

Tagore, 8 Brunswick Centre, off Russell Square, W.C.1 (tel. 837-9397), is one of the finest Indian restaurants in London. It has an unobtrusive and rather unattractive entrance in this modern complex of apartments and shops. Hardly what you'd expect if you're seeking delicate Indian cookery, including the best of tandoori dishes. Colored lights inside illuminate a display of art objects and paintings. The wide-ranging menu includes gustaba (lamb) meatballs cooked in a yogurt sauce and northern Indian (Kashmir) dishes, lobster curry tandoori, and various kinds of freshly baked Indian breads, such as nan, châpiti, kulch (bread with onion stuffing and vegetables), paratha, and stuffed paratha (fried bread). Tagore is an ideal center for vegetarians who will find a special menu of tempting dishes. A set lunch is offered for £5 ($7.50), including dessert and coffee. The average à la carte meal will cost from £8.50 ($12.75), plus a lot more if you order a bottle of wine, beginning at £5 ($7.50). At the entrance is a large portrait of Rabindrinath Tagore (1861–1941), the Nobel Prize-winning Hindu poet and prose writer for whom the place was named. The restaurant is open daily, including Sunday, from noon to 3 p.m. and 6 to 11:30 p.m. Tube: Russell Square.

5. Belgravia and Knightsbridge

BELGRAVIA: Belgravia (S.W.1), south of Hyde Park, is the so-called aristocratic quarter of London, challenging Mayfair for grandness. It reigned in glory along with Queen Victoria. But today's aristocrats are likely to be the top echelon in foreign embassies, along with a rising new money class—or at least young fashion models or actresses clever enough to secure a most desirable flat here. Belgravia is near Buckingham Palace Gardens (how elegant can your address be?) and Brompton Road. Its center is Belgrave Square (take the Piccadilly Underground line to Hyde Park Corner), one of the more attractive plazas in London.

Upper Crust in Belgravia, 9 William St., S.W.1 (tel. 235-8444), is recommended by visitors and local business people alike. This very English restaurant, with a friendly staff, is an atmospheric place, evocative of a farmhouse setting. Its owners, the butchers, Wainwright & Daughter, guarantee a goodly supply of high quality game, fish, and meat. You can order very British fare here, including fisherman's pie or steak and pickled walnut pie, and, for dessert, perhaps Yorkshire pudding stuffed with sweet mincemeat. The restaurant serves breakfast from 10 a.m. to noon, lunch from 11:30 a.m. to 3 p.m. when a two-course meal costs from £7.50 ($11.25), tea from 2:30 to 6 p.m., and dinner from 6 to 11:30 p.m., averaging around £12 ($18). Tube: Knightsbridge.

The **Antelope,** 22 Eaton Terrace, S.W.1 (tel. 730-7781), is on the fringe of Belgravia, at the gateway to Chelsea. This eatery caters to a hodgepodge of clients, aptly described as "people of all classes, colours and creeds who repair for interesting discussion on a whole gamut of subjects, ranging from sport to medieval, mid-European, wicker-work, bed-bug traps, and for both mental and physical refreshment." You can take lunch in a ground-floor bar which provides hot and cold pub food. On the second floor (British first floor), food is served at a wine bar both morning and evening. The ground floor is devoted to drinks only at night. Meals cost from £10 ($15), plus the cost of your drinks. The food is principally English, with steak-and-kidney pie and jugged hare among the specialties. The place is open from 11 a.m. to 3 p.m. and 5:30 to 11 p.m.; however, meals are not served Saturday evening or Sunday. This is a base for English rugby aficionados (not to be confused with those who follow soccer). Rugby is a game not unlike American football, but it is played continuously for 80 minutes, and the players wear no bodily protection. The trappings have long since mellowed, as the Antelope goes back to about 1800. Tube: Sloane Square.

The **Grenadier,** Wilton Row, Belgrave Square, S.W.1 (tel. 235-3074), is an oldtime pub on a cobblestone street, sheltered by higher buildings and protected from the noise of busy traffic. The Grenadier is one of the special pubs of London—associated with the "Iron Duke." But today it's filled with a sophisticated crowd of Belgravia flatmates and chic stable-dwellers. English and continental dishes are served in front of fireplaces in two of the small rooms behind the front bar. Specialties include half an Aylesbury duckling; steak, kidney, and mushroom pie; and in honor of its former patron, filet of beef Wellington. A person can dine here in the range of £10 ($15) to £15 ($22.50) per person. However, snacks available include a plate of rare beef with salad and horseradish, rollmops, soup, sandwiches, Scotch eggs, or whatever. The grill room is open seven days a week for lunch from noon until 2:30 p.m. and for dinner from 7 to 10 p.m. At the entrance to Wilton Row (in the vicinity of Belgrave Square), a special guard ("good evening, guv'nor") was once stationed to raise and lower a barrier for those arriving by carriage. The guard's booth is still there. A gentle ghost is said to haunt the premises, that of a Grenadier guard who was caught cheating at cards and died of the flogging given as punishment. Pub enthusiasts are fanatic about the Grenadier. If anyone tries to tear it down, he may meet his Waterloo. Tube: Knightsbridge or Hyde Park Corner.

Motcomb's, 26 Motcomb St., S.W.1 (tel. 235-9170), opposite Sotheby's Belgravia, is one of the handsomest and most charming wine bars and restaurants in London. On two levels, the bar is decorated with family paintings and wooden paneling. A complete range of food is served, and there is an excellent choice of wine as well, including several sold by the glass. Dishes are cooked to order. Specialties include what may be the best calves' liver and bacon in London, sea bass grilled with oil and lemon, and salmon trout grilled or poached to perfection. Dinners begin at £15 ($22.50). Motcomb's is open from noon to 3:30 p.m. and 7 p.m. to midnight Monday through Saturday. Tube: Knightsbridge.

KNIGHTSBRIDGE: Adjoining Belgravia is Knightsbridge (S.W.1), another top residential and shopping section of London, just south of Hyde Park. Knightsbridge is close in character to Belgravia. Much of this section, to the west of Sloane Street, is older, dating back (in architecture and layout) to the 18th century. This is where many Londoners go to shop, as several of the major department stores, such as Harrods, are here (take the Piccadilly Line to Knightsbridge to patronize any of the restaurants below).

The Georgian Restaurant, Harrods Department Store, Brompton Road, S.W.1 (tel. 730-1234, ext. 3467), lies on the top floor of this fabled emporium, under elaborate ceilings and belle-époque skylights. It is one of the neighborhood's most appealing lunchtime restaurants. Breakfast, lunch, and afternoon tea are served. One of the rooms, big enough for a ballroom, contains a pianist, whose music trills between the crystals of the chandeliers. A member of a battalion of polite waitresses will bring you the first course of a fixed-price lunch, costing £12 ($18) per person. The second course is served from a sprawling buffet filled with cold meats and an array of fresh salads. Guests who want a hot meal can head for the carvery section, where a uniformed crew of chefs serves such dishes as Yorkshire pudding with roast beef, poultry, fish, and pork. Desserts are served tableside by your waitress. Harrods afternoon tea, costing £5.50 ($8.25) per person, is one of the most popular events. Breakfast is served from 9:30 to 11 a.m. and lunch from noon to 2:30. Tea time is 3:30 to 5:30 p.m.; but guests start lining up before 3 p.m. Sandwiches and pastries are served from the "Grand Buffet," which shuts down at 4:30 p.m. Everything is closed on Sunday. Tube: Knightsbridge.

Bill Bentley's, 31 Beauchamp Pl., S.W.3 (tel. 589-5080), stands on this restaurant- and boutique-lined street near Harrods. A small Georgian house, it offers tiny ground-floor rooms and a little sun-filled patio in back. Cozy and atmospheric, it presents a varied list of reasonably priced wines, including a fine selection of bordeaux. If you're in the neighborhood for lunch, you can enjoy a pub-style lunch, such as ham and salad. Hot main dishes are likely to include skate in black butter with capers and grilled lemon sole. Meals cost from £12 ($18). It's open daily from 11:30 a.m. to 3 p.m. and 5:30 to 11 p.m.; Saturday, from 6:30 to 11 p.m. Closed Sunday and bank holidays. Tube: Knightsbridge.

The **Chicago Rib Shack,** 1 Raphael St., Knightsbridge, S.W.7 (tel. 581-5595), serves real American barbecued foods—huge racks of baby back ribs, barbecued chicken, and barbecued beef sandwiches. The meat is cooked in imported smoking ovens and marinated in a barbecue sauce containing 15 secret ingredients. The shack is the creation of Bob Payton, an ex-Chicagoan who also owns the successful Chicago Pizza Pie Factory in Hanover Square. The menu also includes their famous onion loaf which *Harper's & Queen* described as "either a Brobdingnagian French fried onion or the Illinois equivalent of an onion bhaji." Stuffed potato boats, salads, cheesecake, pecan pie, and ice cream round out the menu. Visitors are encouraged to eat with their fingers, and bibs and hot towels are provided. The restaurant's vast bar has a special cocktail license for people preferring simply to drink without a meal. A video is suspended in the bar showing American sports games. There is an overwhelming number

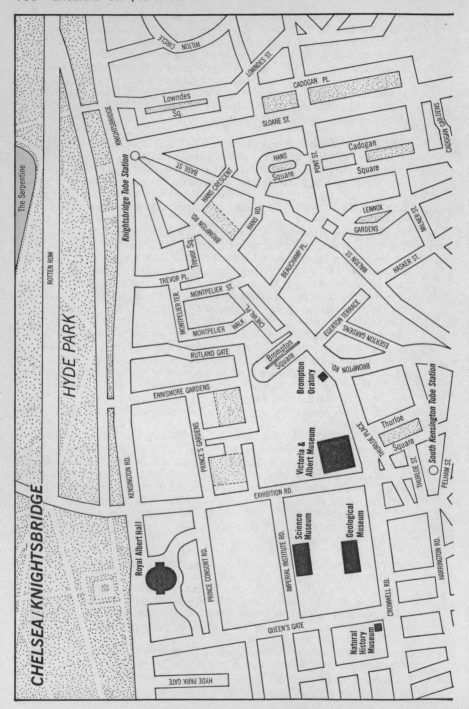

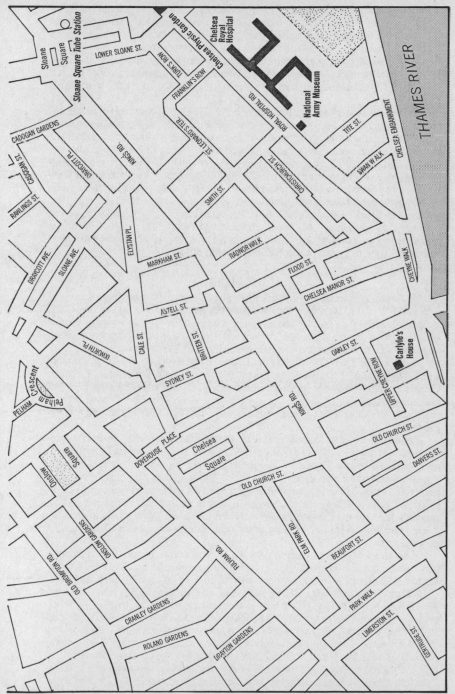

THAMES RIVER

Sloane Square Tube Station

Sloane Square

LOWER SLOANE ST.

Chelsea Physic Garden

Chelsea Royal Hospital

National Army Museum

ROYAL HOSPITAL RD.

TURK'S ROW

FRANKLIN'S ROW

ST. LEONARD'S TER.

CADOGAN GARDENS

CADOGAN ST.

DRACCOTT PL.

KING'S RD.

CHRISTCHURCH ST.

TITE ST.

SWAN WALK

CHELSEA EMBANKMENT

RAWLINGS ST.

DRACOTT AVE.

SLOANE AVE.

ELYSTAN PL.

SMITH ST.

MARKHAM ST.

RADNOR WALK

FLOOD ST.

CHEYNE WALK

CHELSEA MANOR ST.

ASTELL ST.

CALE ST.

IXWORTH PL.

BRITTEN ST.

SYDNEY ST.

OAKLEY ST.

UPPER CHEYNE ROW

Carlyle's House

PELHAM Crescent

Pelham Square

Onslow Square

DOVEHOUSE PLACE

Chelsea Square

KING'S RD.

OLD CHURCH ST.

DANVERS ST.

OLD CHURCH ST.

ONSLOW GARDENS

OLD BROMPTON RD.

FULHAM RD.

ELM PARK RD.

BEAUFORT ST.

PARK WALK

CRANLEY GARDENS

ROLAND GARDENS

DRAYTON GARDENS

LIMERSTON ST.

GERTRUDE ST.

of Victorian architectural antiques which have been salvaged from demolished buildings all over the country. The 45-foot-long ornate mahogany and mirrored bar was once part of a Glasgow pub, and eight massive stained-glass windows came from a chapel in Lancashire. The restaurant's walls are covered with an ever-increasing collection of pictures, posters, and pottery farmyard animals—pigs and cows especially. The average tab comes to about £11 ($16.50) per head. The restaurant, which lies just 100 yards from Harrods, serves daily from 11:45 a.m. to 11:30 p.m. Tube: Knightsbridge.

Luba's Bistro, 6 Yeomans Row, S.W.3 (tel. 589-2950), is an oasis of moderately priced dining in tab-happy Knightsbridge. The atmosphere here is strictly business —just a big, narrow room with family-style tables covered with plastic cloths. The posters and paintings on the walls evoke a nostalgic feeling of early Bohemia. The food is good, and the chef believes in giving you enough of it. The management isn't licensed, so you have to bring your own bottle. For openers, I'd suggest Luba's Russian borscht or else kapoostniak (braised cabbage with prunes and sour cream). Main courses include beef Stroganoff, chicken Kiev, hussar's steak, stuffed green pepper, and shashlik (marinated pieces of lamb grilled on a skewer, with onion sauce, served with rice and vegetables). My latest tab came to £9 ($13.50), plus a 10% service charge. Bring your own wine, as there is no corkage charge. Hours are noon to 3 p.m. and 6 to 11 p.m. daily except Sunday. Tube: Knightsbridge.

6. Chelsea

In this area, comparable to the Left Bank of Paris or the more elegant parts of Greenwich Village, even the simplest stable has glamour. Here the diplomats and wealthy-chic, the stars of stage and screen, and successful sculptors and painters now live alongside a decreasing number of poor and struggling artists. To reach the restaurants reviewed below, take the Circle or District Line to Sloane Square.

King's Road (S.W.3) (named after Charles II) is the principal avenue, the main street of Chelsea, and activity is lively here both day and night. On Saturday morning, Chelsea boutiques blossom with London's flamboyantly attired. What were once stables and garages, built for elaborate town houses nearby, have been converted and practically rebuilt, so that you see little alleyways with two-story houses, all brightly painted.

In the Mauve Era, Chelsea became popular with artists. Oscar Wilde found refuge here—so did Henry James, Whistler, and many more. The Chelsea Embankment, an esplanade along the Thames, is also found here. Homes of writers, such as the one once occupied by George Eliot, line the street. The best known and most interesting part of the embankment, Cheyne Walk (pronounced Chain-y), contains some Georgian town houses. It's a good place to go for a stroll around dusk. The most popular residents here are the Chelsea Pensioners, who live at the Royal Chelsea Hospital. These veterans and invalid soldiers, in uniform, can be seen perambulating up and down the riverfront.

This district boasts some of the city's finest restaurants, but not the cheap ones. Still, most readers will probably want to go to Chelsea. If so, they'll find the following restaurant, pub, and wine bar recommendations offering good and reasonable meals.

Henry J. Bean's (But His Friends All Call Him Hank) Bar and Grill, 195 King's Rd., S.W.3 (tel. 352-9255), is another venture of that Chicago-born entrepreneur, Bob Payton of Chicago Pizza Pie Factory fame. Nearly opposite the Fire Station in Chelsea, it has brought renewed vitality to the restaurant scene in Chelsea. With a 250-foot garden, impossibly crowded on sunny days, it is open seven days a week: Monday to Saturday from 11:30 a.m. to 11:45 p.m. (on Sunday from noon to 10:30 p.m.). Check the blackboard for Hank's daily specials, but know you can count on "chicken fried chicken," a smokehouse burger, nachos, and Henry J's own secret chili recipe. Meals costing from £8 ($12) are served against a backdrop of a late 1950s decor, American saloon style. Tube: Sloane Square.

The **Chelsea Kitchen,** 98 King's Rd., S.W.3 (tel. 589-1330), is a favorite of those who know they can get large portions of good, plain cooking at inexpensive prices. The atmosphere is Nordic inspired, with compact booths and tables and bright, strong colors. The minestrone is good tasting, as is the steak-and-kidney pie. A strictly economy dish, most filling, is the stuffed marrow (in season), or you might prefer the coq au vin. To finish off, try either the apple crumble or ice cream. An average three-course meal will cost from £6 ($9). The Kitchen is open from 8 a.m. to 11:45 p.m. Monday to Saturday, from noon to 11:30 p.m. on Sunday. In the evening, you are likely to hear classical tapes played as background music. Tube: Sloane Square.

King's Head & Eight Bells, 50 Cheyne Walk, S.W.3 (tel. 352-1820), is a historic Thames-side pub in a fashionable residential area of London. It's run by Mary Timmons, one of London's first pub landladies. It's popular with stage and TV personalities as well as writers. Many distinguished personalities once lived in this area. A short stroll in the neighborhood will take you to the former homes of such famous personages as Carlyle, Swinburne, and George Eliot. Press gangs used to roam these parts of Chelsea seeking lone travelers who were abducted for a life at sea. The snackbar has been upgraded to Cordon Bleu standards at pub prices. The best English beers are served here, as well as a goodly selection of wines and liquors. A large plate of rare roast beef is a favorite selection, followed by a choice of salad from the salad bar, celery and sultana, rice, beansprouts, for instance. Other tasty dishes include homemade game pie, if featured, or else steak-and-kidney pie. Everything is displayed on a large old table in the corner. Meals cost from £6 ($9). Open daily from 11 a.m. to 3 p.m. and 5:30 to 11 p.m., it's a long, long walk from the Sloane Square tube stop.

Blushes, 52 King's Rd., S.W.3 (tel. 589-6640), stands across from the Duke of York's headquarters. (That's not Fergie's husband but a long-ago ancestor. Built in 1801, it is now the barracks of several London regiments of the Territorial Army.) This is technically a wine bar, with exotic libations by the glass, but customers are required to order food as well. Behind its brown facade, it is usually busy in the evening, attracting a lively King's Road crowd, drawn to its array of salads, cold meats, and hot dishes, plus roast joints. Lunch is served from 11:45 a.m. to 3:30 p.m. and dinner from 7 to 11:30 p.m. seven days a week. Expect to pay around £10 ($15) for a meal. Tube: Sloane Square.

Charco's Wine Bar, 1 Bray Pl., S.W.3 (tel. 584-0765), has an entrance on two streets in Chelsea, lying right off King's Road. A very bright crowd patronizes this establishment, enjoying the reasonably priced wines and the good and inexpensive food. A blackboard lists daily specials, all good, home-cooked dishes, including roast rack of lamb, chicken suprême, steaks, and fresh fish. Meals cost from £12 ($18). Hours are from noon to 3 p.m. and 5:30 to 11 p.m. Monday to Friday, from noon to 3 p.m. and 7 to 11 p.m. on Saturday. In summer, you can sit at one of the streetside tables and, in the evening, dine by candlelight. Tube· Sloane Square.

Ziani, 45 Radnor Walk, S.W.3 (tel. 351-5297), on a street of mews houses, is one of the finest but least known Italian restaurants in the Chelsea area. It is decorated in a garden, greenhouse style, brightly adorned with paintings. If you follow an Italian expatriate in the area, he is likely to be heading for Ziani, named after a prominent and wealthy Venetian family. Meals cost from £12 ($18) and feature excellently prepared dishes, including fettuccine with "fruits of the sea," carpaccio, and deep-fried scampi and squid. Roast quail with polenta is a particular favorite. The restaurant can get crowded, so make sure you call for a table. Hours are from 12:30 to 2:45 p.m., dinner from 7 to 11:30 p.m. (Sunday, 7 to 11 p.m.). Tube: Sloane Square.

FULHAM: A typical Cockney delight is **Eel Pie and Mash Shop,** 140 Wandsworth

Bridge Rd., S.W.6 (tel. 731-1232), outside of the East End and therefore more accessible to visitors. You can feast on jellied or stewed eels with mashed potatoes, on succulent homemade beef pie and mashed potatoes, or on "bangers and mash" (sausages and mashed potatoes). Meals cost from £2 ($3). Served in simple pristine surroundings, it is something different, and you'll be sure to see some local color, for this sort of food is still much loved by Londoners. It's open from 11:45 a.m. to 6 p.m. on Tuesday and Wednesday, to 8 p.m. Thursday and Friday, and to 5 p.m. Saturday. It's closed Sunday and Monday. Your host is Mrs. Atkins. Tube: Fulham Broadway.

7. Kensington

Most smart shoppers in London patronize two busy streets: Kensington High, with its long string of specialty shops and department stores, and the abutting Kensington Church, with its antique shops and boutiques.

Twin Brothers, 51 Church St., W.8 (tel. 937-4152), is run by Detlef Schmidt who came to Britain with his twin brother, Helge, and opened this restaurant which is known for its good value. His staff offers excellent and friendly service, good continental food, and a relaxed atmosphere. Once only a small coffee shop, lying adjacent to the Carmelite Church, it is near the corner of Vicarage Gate. Cozy and intimate, with louvered doors and banquettes, it is ideal for a tête-à-tête dinner. You might begin with Bismarck herring ("our mother's recipe") and go on to either chicken Kiev or Wiener schnitzel. For dessert, try "mother's apple cake." That mother must have been some good cook. Every dish is freshly prepared for you. Hours are Monday to Saturday from 6:30 to 11 p.m. (Sunday, 7 to 10 p.m.), and the price of an average meal is £8 ($12). Tube: Kensington High Street.

Clarke's, 124 Kensington Church St., W.8 (tel. 221-9225), is named after Sally Clarke, who is justifiably proud of this excellent Anglo-French restaurant. Everything is bright and modern, with wood floors, discreet lighting, and additional tables in the basement. Here you get a set menu with a very limited choice, but the food is so well prepared "in the new style" that diners rarely object. A set two-course lunch costs £12.50 ($18.75), a table d'hôte dinner £22 ($33). Bargain tip: go after 10 p.m. when the set dinner is reduced in price to £16 ($24). Lunch hours are from 12:30 to 2 p.m. Monday to Friday, dinner or supper 7:30 to 11 p.m. Monday to Friday. It is closed Saturday and Sunday. You might begin with appetizers such as a hot cream soup of roasted red peppers with parmesan and rosemary breadsticks, then follow with pork filet marinated in sesame oil, ginger, and mint, which is grilled and served with a light mint sauce. Desserts are likely to include a strawberry and vanilla ice cream trifle. Tube: Notting Hill Gate or High Street Kensington.

Maggie Jones, 6 Old Court Pl., off Kensington Church St., W.8 (tel. 937-6462), is a longtime favorite, with dining on two levels (I prefer the basement), with plain pine furniture and candles stuck in bottles. Its atmosphere has been likened to that of a country kitchen. You get British fare here with a vengeance. That means grilled saddle of lamb with rosemary, baked mackerel with gooseberries, or Maggie's fish pie. In season, game is featured (try the rabbit and mustard casserole). Dinners cost from £15 ($22.50), but a set lunch goes for only £7 ($10.50). Desserts, including a treacle tart, are called "puds." Lunch is from 12:30 to 2 p.m., Monday to Saturday, from 12:30 to 2:45 on Sunday. Dinner is from 7 to 11:30 p.m. Monday to Saturday, from 6:30 to 11 p.m. on Sunday. Tube: High Street Kensington.

Texas Lone Star Saloon, 154 Gloucester Rd., S.W.7 (tel. 370-5625), should fit the bill if you're homesick for the great Southwest. Its food is "Tex-Mex," and that means enchiladas, hot chili, ribs, and burgers, everything washed down with beer or margaritas. The decor brings back memories of the Old West, and if it doesn't, then the video westerns surely will. Count on parting with £10 ($15) or more. Hours are noon to 11:30 p.m. Monday to Saturday, noon to 11:15 p.m. on Sunday. Tube: Gloucester Road.

SOUTH KENSINGTON: When you've grown weary of exploring this district's many museums, try a feast in one of the following recommendations.

Chanterelle, 119 Old Brompton Rd., S.W.7 (tel. 373-5522), used to be a part of the South Kensington Public Library. But times have changed. The smell is not of old books, but of highly original English and continental cookery in a restrained setting of wood paneling. The personable Stewart Grimshaw oversees the restaurant, and his partner, Fergus Provan, organizes the kitchen. They are open every day of the week for both lunch and dinner, including Sunday. Dinner is nightly from 7 to midnight. A three-course luncheon menu, costing £8.50 ($12.75), is changed every three days, and a fixed-price dinner menu, also consisting of three courses, is changed every two weeks, going for £11.50 ($17.25). Main courses at dinner are likely to include filets of sole stuffed with scallops and served with a champagne sauce, roast saddle of hare, and filet of veal sautéed in sage. Wines are limited but well selected. Reservations are advised. Tube: South Kensington or Gloucester Road.

Daquise, 20 Thurloe St., S.W.7 (tel. 589-6117), is a total anachronism, as it is a tea room sitting in the midst of the fast-food emporiums of South Kensington. It has long been a bastion of typical Polish food. Across from the South Kensington tube station, it is a good choice after your tour of the Victoria and Albert Museum. Here you get typically Eastern European cuisine, including stuffed cabbage and other Slavic specialties. It has excellent pastries for dessert. Meals cost from £6 ($9). Service is from noon to midnight, seven days a week. Tube: South Kensington.

8. West London

ST. MARYLEBONE: This area has quite a fine cross section of the best of what London has to offer in culinary treats.

The Baker & Oven, 10 Paddington St., W.1 (tel. 935-5072), may be in an out-of-the-way neighborhood, but it's a big success—a little corner bakery, with a sales shop converted into a tavern with a genuine pub atmosphere. The neighborhood people mingle with the fashionable West End visitors. Meals are served in the cellar kitchens, attractively done in a rustic style. The very English food often pleases the most critical; the portions are large, the tabs moderate. With a bit of luck, you'll be given a bare wooden table in one of the brick cove-ceilinged nooks, the former ovens. The onion soup is a fine beginning, as is the country pâté. For the main course, there are several good choices, including roast Aylesbury duckling with stuffing and apple sauce, and jugged hare with red currant jelly. All entrees include vegetables. For dessert, you can order a hot fruit pie and cream. Meals begin at £10 ($15), including wine. The restaurant is open Monday to Friday from noon to 3 p.m. and 6 to 11 p.m. On Saturday, it's open only in the evening. The same prices are charged for both lunch and dinner. Tube: Baker Street.

Light of India, 59 Park Rd., near Regent's Park, N.W.1 (tel. 723-6753), doesn't require you to don a turban or sari to dine, although many homesick Indians will be wearing theirs. Happily, you can order varying strengths of curry, so have no fear about burning your throat if you're inexperienced. If there are several in your party, you can select a wide variety of plates—and share them, Chinese style. The traditional soup, of course, is mulligatawny. Warning: Unless you'd like a sneak preview of Hades, avoid anything labeled *vindaloo*. The biryanis made in a variety of ways—chicken, mutton, prawn, even vegetable—are good for beginners. The restaurant also specializes in tandoori dishes cooked in a clay oven. Charcoal instead of the traditional gas fire is used. Some of these dishes include a tandoori chicken masala, a mixed grill, king prawns, and naan, a leavened bread, among others. Meals cost from £7 ($10.50). Service charge is not included in the prices. The Light of India is open from noon to 3 p.m. and 6 p.m. to midnight, including Sunday. Tube: Baker Street.

Garfunkels, Duke Street, W.1 (tel. 499-5000), is a coffeeshop operation with large glass walls which open onto the pavement onto which the tables spill in summer. The bright modern decor of plush benches and glass and chrome chairs and tables was designed to give a little privacy within the close quarters. There is a large, well-stocked salad bar from which you help yourself. Typical fare includes roast chicken, chili con carne, and hamburgers. With these, you might order jacket potatoes or fried potatoes. Desserts feature a magnificent banana split, about six inches high and oozing with cream, ice cream, nuts, and sauce. Meals cost from £6 ($9). There's also a children's menu for around £1.30 ($1.95). Garfunkels serves continuously from noon to 11 p.m. seven days a week. Tube: Bond Street. There are several branches of this operation around central London.

PADDINGTON: Many guests find themselves near Paddington Station, having booked into a B&B house on, say, Sussex Gardens or Norfolk Square. If so, it's best to go Oriental if you're seriously economizing.

Rasa Sayang Restaurant, Keio Hotel, 168 Sussex Gardens, W.2 (tel. 402-9142), two blocks from Paddington Station, stands on a corner and is a restaurant on two levels—street and basement. The executive chef/manager is Terry Tan, Singapore's best known chef, cookery teacher, and cookbook author *(Oriental Kitchen, Straits Chinese Cooking,* and *Cooking with Chinese Herbs).* The restaurant is both Chinese and Singapore in terms of cuisine. Singapore cuisine is derived from both Chinese and Indian, and is a spicy hybrid. Typical is satay, cubes of beef and chicken marinated in spices and barbecued over charcoal. Others are gado-gado, a Singapore salad bathed in a spicy peanut sauce, and rendang, a beef curry, along with laksa, spicy noodles in coconut milk, and the more familiar nasi goreng, spicy fried rice. Fully licensed, the restaurant serves a complete meal for £10 ($15). Orders are accepted in the kitchen from 11 a.m. to 2:45 p.m. and 6 to 10:45 p.m. seven days a week. Tube: Paddington Station.

Oodles, 128 Edgware Rd., W.2 (tel. 723-7548), is just beyond the Marble Arch tube station. This aptly named place (one of several around London) fulfills the promise with well-filled plates of stews, curries, pies, and a wide range of vegetables dishes —leeks au gratin, stuffed eggplant, macaroni and cheese. Desserts are equally substantial, including country-style apple pie served from a deep dish with cream. A three-course meal with wine is about £6 ($9). The place is white, bright, and clean with wood tables and bench seats. Hours are from 11 a.m. to 9 p.m. daily. Tube: Edgware Road.

9. East End

At least once you may want to plunge into the colorful East End. In restaurants it has a few potent drawing cards. The most famous one is surveyed below.

Bloom's, 90 Whitechapel High St., E.1 (tel. 247-6001), is worth crossing over to the wrong side of the tracks. Overcrowded, with frantic service, Bloom's continues to tempt with kosher delights supervised and inspected by a rabbi. Sunday lunch, however, is extremely busy, so try to schedule your visit at some other time. A chicken blintz might rest on your plate or borscht in your bowl. Main dishes include such specialties as boiled leg of fowl and salt beef (corned, to us). Try also the kreplach and kneidlach (dumplings) soup, very rich chopped liver and egg, sweet balls of chopped white fish (fried or boiled), and lockshen pudding. A good meal will cost around £9 ($13.50), but you can spend more. Don't forget that Bloom's is kosher, so don't expect milk in your coffee if you've ordered meat. Soup and sandwich customers are not allowed to sit down, that privilege being reserved for full-service dinner patrons. Hours are 11 a.m. to 9:30 p.m. Monday to Thursday and on Sunday. On Friday, it's open from 11 a.m. to 3:30 p.m. Closed Friday evening and all day Saturday. Tube: Aldgate East.

10. South of the Thames

The **George Inn**, 77 Borough High St. (tel. 407-2056), across the bridge in Southwark, S.E.1, is a National Trust property, the last of the old galleried coaching inns of London. Known to Charles Dickens *(Little Dorrit)*, the inn is a touch of olde England, tucked away in an alley. Some claim that Shakespeare and his troupe performed in an old inn that stood on the same ground. The George today is essentially late 17th century. You enter through a gateway into the Little Old Coffee Room. On the ground floor there are two bars and a wine bar where hot chili, sausages and mash, along with shepherd's pie and beans are served. There is a serve-yourself salad table, with some dozen different mixtures. Light meals here cost from £4 ($6). The restaurant upstairs serves meals Monday to Saturday from 6:30 to 9 p.m. Lunch is offered Monday to Friday only, from 12:30 to 2 p.m. From the à la carte menu, a three-course meal costs £11 ($16.50) to £15 ($22.50). Tube: London Bridge.

Royal Festival Hall Cafeteria, South Bank, S.E.1 (tel. 921-0810), is where you can get an inexpensive meal or snack in an unusual setting on the banks of the Thames. It's worth the five-minute trek over the bridge from the Embankment tube station to combine a meal with any of the activities at the Royal Festival Hall. The cafeteria is open from 10 a.m. to 8 p.m. Monday to Thursday, to 10 p.m. Friday to Sunday. There's a buffet upstairs open daily from noon to 2:30 p.m. and 5:30 p.m. to 10 p.m. The buffet is known for vegetarian dishes and salads, but you can also have fish, ham, or pâté. The basic cost is £3.50 ($5.25), each major addition costing around £1 ($1.50) extra. The buffet is served in a modern room with big windows. There's always a view of London's skyline. When it's high tide, you can enjoy the tops of the river boats and the ships on the Thames. Between June and September, free concerts are given in the Charing Cross Gardens, adjacent to the tube station.

Goose and Firkin, 47 Borough Rd., S.E.1 (tel. 403-3590), is a pub that brews its own beer. The owner of this enterprise is David Bruce, who worked as a brewer for one of the big companies for many years until his chance came to buy the pub that is known as the Goose and Firkin. He has now expanded his operation to include six other London pubs. A large mirror proclaims "Bruce's Brewery, established 1979." He brews four special strengths: Goose Bitter, Borough Bitter, Dogbolter, and for special occasions, Gobstopper, only served in halves. Be warned: this one is a real man's beer, worth the equivalent of three measures of whisky in strength. Food is also available in this lovely old London pub. Each day there is a different hot dish. Or you can order extra large baps (bread buns) filled with your choice of meat and salad. Meals cost from £4 ($6). The pub is open seven days a week from 11:30 a.m. to 3 p.m. and 5:30 to 11 p.m. Most evenings, there is a pianist playing all the old numbers in a good old "knees up" style. Tube: Elephant and Castle.

11. Hampstead Heath

This residential suburb of London, beloved by Keats and Hogarth, is a favorite excursion spot for Londoners on the weekend. The Old Bull and Bush, made famous by Florrie Forde's legendary song, is long gone (the pub bearing that name today is modern.) However, there are pubs up here with authentic historical pedigrees. Take the Northern Line of the Underground to the Hampstead Heath station, N.W.3.

Spaniards Inn, Spaniards Lane, N.W.3 (tel. 455-3276), is a Hampstead Heath landmark, site of the residence of the Spanish ambassador to the Court of James I. It's opposite the old tollhouse, a bottleneck in the road where people had to pay a toll to enter the country park of the Bishop of London. The notorious highwayman, Dick Turpin, didn't pay. He leaped over the gate on his horse when he was in flight from the law. The pub, opened by two Spanish brothers in 1630, was already a century old in Turpin's heyday. It still contains some antique benches, open fireplaces, and cozy nooks in the rooms with their low, beamed ceilings and oak paneling. Old muskets on the walls are mute survivors of the time of the Gordon Riots of 1780, when a mob stopped in for drinks on their way to burn nearby Kenwood House, property of Lord Mansfield. The innkeeper set up so many free drinks that when the Horse Guards arrived, they found many of the rioters *hors de combat* from too much libation and relieved them of their weapons. The pub serves traditional but above-average food. A light repast begins at £2.50 ($3.75). Hot dishes are served until half an hour before closing at lunchtime and until 9:30 p.m. Pub hours are from 11 a.m. to 3 p.m. and 5:30 to 11 p.m. Monday to Saturday, from noon to 2 p.m. and 7 to 11:30 p.m. on Sunday. In summer, customers can sit at slat tables on a terrace in a pleasant garden beside a flower-bordered lawn, with an aviary. The pub and garden were known to Byron, Dickens, Galsworthy, Shelley, and David Garrick. Tube: Hampstead or Golders Green.

Manna, 4 Erskine Rd., N.W.3 (tel. 722-8028), offers a fine array of strictly vegetarian dishes to tempt even the most skeptical nonvegetarian. On its blackboard menu, you can check out the offerings for the day. They are likely to include lentil soup or avocado with curd dressing as appetizers, followed by such main courses as vegetable goulash, stuffed pancakes, or a bean fricassee. For dessert, you face a choice of gorgeous fruit and yogurt desserts. A meal will cost from £5 ($7.50) for two courses. Hours are 6:30 a.m. to 11:45 p.m. daily. The place has somewhat the atmosphere of a country kitchen. The location is within a short walk of the Chalk Hill tube station. From Adelaide Road, cross the bridge at Regent's Park Road and go along King Henry's Road (Manna will be on the left at the corner of Erskine Road and Ainger Road).

12. Thames Dining

When much of the West End is closed on Sunday, you'll find life if you take a taxi, tube, or bus to Aldgate East and spend a hectic hour or so at **Petticoat Lane.** That's the street market where, even if you don't want to buy the goods, you can see the full wit and expertise of the Cockney street vendors. Look for the one who sells tea services, or buy a toffee apple or a hot dog.

Then a short walk will bring you down to the Tower of London and, right beside it, just below Tower Bridge, **St. Katharine's Dock.** This development was created out of the old London dock area where the "breakfast ships," carrying bacon and eggs from Holland, used to tie up. It has become a vast open-air pleasure area.

At the **Tower Thistle Hotel,** St. Katharine's Way, E.1 (tel. 481-2575), you can eat all you want for a set price of £11.50 ($17.25) in its Carvery restaurant, open from noon to 2:30 p.m. and 6 to 10 p.m. seven days a week. However, it's wise to reserve a table. You can select (rare, medium, or well done) from a standing rib of prime beef with Yorkshire pudding, horseradish sauce, and the juice, or from tender roast pork with crackling accompanied by a spiced bread dressing and apple sauce, or perhaps the roast spring Southdown lamb with mint sauce. Before or after dinner, you might want to visit the Thames Bar, which has a nautical theme and a full panoramic view of its namesake along with Tower Bridge and the river traffic. There's a small balcony outside for drinks in summer.

Nearby is the **Dickens Inn by the Tower,** St. Katharine's Way, E.1 (tel. 488-2208), a very carefully reconstructed 19th-century warehouse. Incorporating the original redwood beams, stock bricks, and ironworks, it is a balconied pub/restaurant on three levels. Sitting on a wooden chair at an old table, you can enjoy such bar snacks as cockles, mussels, and rollmops. Prices begin at £2.50 ($3.75) for some of the snacks. Hot dishes are served too. The pub, at street level, is open seven days a week from 11:30 a.m. to 2:30 p.m. and 5:30 to 11 p.m. The upstairs restaurant, specializing in fish, serves only lunch daily from 11:30 a.m. to 2:30 p.m. Tube: Tower Hill.

The **Prospect of Whitby,** 57 Wapping Wall, E.1 (tel. 481-1095), is one of London's oldest riverside pubs, having been founded originally in the days of the Tudors. In a traditionally pubby atmosphere, with a balcony overlooking the river, the Prospect has many associations—it was visited by Dickens, Turner, and Whistler, searching for local color. Come here for a tot, a noggin, or whatever it is that you drink. The Pepys room honors the diarist, who may—just may—have visited the Prospect back in rowdier days, when the seamy side of London dock life held sway here. Among the tempting appetizers are pâté country style and a hearty soup. Well-recommended main courses include poulet à la Kiev (breast of chicken stuffed and fried) and escalope of veal Cordon Bleu. Meals run about £12 ($18), unless you want to enjoy an inexpensive bar snack. If you're having lunch upstairs, you'll have to call for a reservation if you want a table in the bow window overlooking the river. The street-level pub is open from 11 a.m. to 3 p.m. and 5:30 to 11 p.m. six days a week, from noon to 2 p.m. and 7 to 10:30 p.m. on Sunday. The upstairs restaurant's hours are from noon to 2 p.m. and 7 to 10:15 p.m. daily. No lunch is served upstairs on Saturday and no dinner on Sunday evening. There's also live music almost every evening from 8:30 to 11 p.m. Take the Metropolitan Line to Wapping Station. When you emerge onto Wapping High Street, turn to your right and head down the road along the river. Wapping Wall will be on your right, running parallel to the Thames. It's about a five-minute walk. (It was around the area of Wapping Wall that lesser pirates were executed by tying them to rings in the wall at low tide and then letting the tide come up and finish the job.)

CRUISE AND DINE: The Regents Canal, which winds and twists through London, is the home of the *My Fair Lady* cruising restaurant, departing from her moorings at 250 Camden High St. at 8 p.m. Tuesday to Saturday. In comfortable surroundings, a three-course English dinner is offered for £16.50 ($24.75). Reservations are essential; telephone 485-4433. *My Fair Lady* also serves a Sunday lunch for £11.50 ($17.25), departing at 1 p.m. The location is 200 yards from Camden Town tube station, Northern Line.

R.S. (restaurant ship) *Hispaniola,* moored on the Thames at Victoria Embankment, Charing Cross, is a large and luxurious air-conditioned ship offering a splendid view of the heart of London from Big Ben to St. Paul's, armchair comfort at the tables, and two cocktail bars for other brands of comfort. Meals are served on both the upper and lower decks, and at night the sparkling lights along the bank turn the entire area into a romantic scene. The menu offers many meat and vegetarian dishes, and the cost without service is £12.50 ($18.75) for a set lunch, including dessert, with an average dinner going for £20 ($18), with the cover charge included. Lunch is served from noon to 2 p.m. Monday to Friday and on Sunday. Dinner is available seven days a week, from 7 to 10 p.m. Sunday and Monday, 7 p.m. to midnight Tuesday to Saturday. For reservations, telephone 839-3011. Tube: Embankment.

13. For Fish and Chips

With the wealth of restaurants of all persuasions, snackbars, sandwich shops, fast-food takeout establishments, what have you, visitors from the United States are, by and large, likely to miss that most English of all eateries and products—fish and chips. True, the once ubiquitous fish and chips shop, also known as chippies, have become few in London today, and even those that remain are of such varying quality that it's difficult for a foreigner to be able to sample good chippie output. The fish may not be absolutely fresh in the one you select at random. Many of them have combined with other food output, perhaps kebabs, the batter has been changed from the time-honored flour and water mixture of old, and some commit the unpardonable sin of using frozen fish and/or frozen chips.

Proper shops offer a selection of such deep-fried fresh fish, found by the proprietor at the New Billingsgate Market, as plaice, cod, haddock, skate, and rockfish. This is served with potatoes Americans consider french fries, with vinegar and salt on the table or counter to be applied by the customer. The purpose of the vinegar is to offset the grease in which the fish and potatoes have been fried. For years, you were served this food in a cone made of printed newspaper, but today, chippies must use paper without ink. However, the service is the same at the true dispensers of traditional fish and chips, and you can eat in the shop, usually at a communal table, or take your food outside, just so you eat it while it's hot. It's best to choose a fish and chips shop where a long queue of Londoners is to be seen at lunchtime awaiting what is unquestionably one of the earliest of the fast foods.

The recommendable fish and chips shops in London today are few, and they have yielded to progress in some aspects, such as perhaps having waitresses or smaller tables, but you can still get a filling and tasty serving at a low price.

My favorite, the **Upper Street Fish Shop,** 324 Upper St., N.1 (tel. 359-1401), is in Islington near the Camden Passage antiques center. Operated by Alan and Olga Conway, the shop is open from 11:30 a.m. to 3 p.m. and 5:30 to 10 p.m. Monday to Friday, with Saturday hours being 11:30 a.m. to 3 p.m. and 5:30 to 10 p.m. Expect to spend about £4 ($6) for your fish and chips, something to drink, and perhaps a home dessert such as jam roly-poly. Tube: Angel.

Geales, 2–4 Farmer St., W.8 (tel. 727-7969), is worth the investment in a subway ride to the western part of London if you're seeking some of the best fish and chips in the English capital, at prices for around £6 ($9) for a meal. The fish is bought fresh daily, and it's not greasy as it is in most London chippies. Cod, hake, and plaice are the featured mainstays of the menu. This corner restaurant, at the end of a mews street, is owned by Christopher A. Geale, who is proud of his offerings. The place is run on informal lines and is open from noon to 3 p.m. and 6 to 11:30 p.m. Tuesday to Friday, from noon to 3 p.m. and 6 to 11 p.m. Saturday. Tube: Notting Hill Gate.

Third in the trio of places for fish and chips that I think most worthy of recommendation is the **Sea Shell,** 49-51 Lisson Grove, N.W.8 (tel. 723-8703), one of the most popular places in London for fish and chips. In fact, Americans may find the chips more to their taste, since they are crisper than at other places, more like Stateside french fries. Also, the fish here, although dipped in batter made with milk and egg, is fried in peanut oil. What with waitress service and other marks of progress, expect to pay up to £5 ($7.50) for a filling repast. John Faulkner, the proprietor, offers other fish dishes, such as Dover sole, and there's even a wine list. Service is from noon to 2 p.m. and 5:15 to 10:30 p.m. Tuesday to Saturday. Tube: Marylebone.

14. Time Out for Tea

During the 18th century, the English from every class became enamoured of a caffeine-rich brew finding its way into London from faraway colonies. Tea-drinking became the rage of London. The great craftsmen of England designed furniture, porcelain, and silver services for the elaborate ritual, and the schedule of aristocrats became increasingly centered around teatime as a mandatory obligation. Even Alexander Pope found it expedient to be witty publicly as he satirized teatime as something uniquely English.

The taking of tea is having a renaissance in the lives of the English. Viewed as a civilized pause in the day's activities, it is particularly appealing to people who didn't have time for lunch or who plan an early theater engagement. Some hotels feature orchestras and tea-dancing in afternoon ceremonies, usually lasting from 3:30 to 6:30 p.m.

For an experience in a tradition that could have sparked the American Revolution (remember the 1773 Tea Party in Boston?), try the old-fashioned atmosphere of **Richoux,** where waitresses wear period dresses with frilly aprons and good-quality pastries are wheeled around on a cart. You might consider your tea there as a belated lunch (Richoux serves regular meals too). For £3.50 ($5.25) per person you can order four hot scones with strawberry jam and whipped cream, or six small sandwiches, perhaps sardine, anchovy, or egg salad. Of course, tea is obligatory. Always specify lemon or cream, and one lump or two.

There are three branches of Richoux in London. One stands opposite Harrods

Department Store in Knightsbridge, at 86 Brompton Rd., S.W.3 (tel. 584-8300), open from 9 a.m. to 7 p.m. (Tube: Knightsbridge). Another is at the bottom of Bond Street, 172 Piccadilly, W.1 (tel. 493-2204) (Tube: Green Park), and the last is at 41A South Audley St., W.1 (tel. 629-5228) (Tube: Hyde Park). The latter two are open from 8:30 a.m. to 11:30 p.m. The full menu is served all day long seven days a week at the three.

15. Almost-24-Hour Eateries

Sometimes you'll want to dine at odd hours, when most of the eating establishments in London are shut down. However, in a city as vast as London, some chef (not always a great one) is cooking. Here are some random selections.

Try **Canton Chinese Restaurant,** 11 Newport St., W.C.2 (tel. 437-6220), which is open 24 hours a day, an average meal costing £9 ($13.50). Tube: Leicester Square.

You might also visit the appropriately named **Up-All-Night Restaurant,** 325 Fulham Rd., S.W.10 (tel. 952-1998), a well-known Fulham café serving burgers, steaks, and pastas. A meal costs around £4 ($6) per person. Tube: Gloucester Road or Earl's Court.

At London's **Heathrow Airport,** all three terminals serve hot food 23 hours a day.

The **Wimpy Bar,** 27 London St., W.2 (tel. 723-4721), in Paddington, is also open 24 hours a day. Tube: Paddington.

The **24 Hour Supermarket,** 68 Westbourne Grove, W.2 (tel. 727-4927), near Paddington Station, never closes, serving the public seven days a week, 24 hours a day, 365 days a year. Tube: Royal Oak.

Chapter V

LONDON: WHAT TO SEE AND DO

1. Seeing the Sights
2. Shopping
3. London After Dark
4. Taking the Tours
5. London for Children
6. One-Day Trips from London

DR. JOHNSON SAID: "When a man is tired of London, he is tired of life for there is in London all that life can afford." "The Great Moralist" can say that again—even more so today.

Come along with me as I survey only a fraction of that life—ancient monuments, boutiques, debates in Parliament, art galleries, discos, Soho dives, museums, legitimate theaters, flea markets, and castles. Some of what we're about to see was known to Johnson and Boswell, even Shakespeare, but much of it is new.

1. Seeing the Sights

London is not a city to visit hurriedly. It is so vast, so stocked with treasures that, on a cursory visit, a person will not only miss many of the highlights but will also fail to grasp the spirit of London and to absorb fully its special flavor, which is unique among cities. But faced with an infinite number of important places to visit and a timeclock running out, the visitor will have to concentrate on a manageable group.

I will lead off with a survey of what I consider the indispensable **Top Ten** sights of London. Try to see them even if you have to skip all the rest, saving them for next time.

 1. THE TOWER OF LONDON: This ancient fortress and royal palace on the north bank of the Thames continues to pack 'em in because of its macabre associations with all the legendary figures who were either imprisoned or executed here, or both. James Street once wrote: ". . . there are more spooks to the square foot than in any other building in the whole of haunted Britain. Headless bodies, bodiless heads, phantom soldiers, icy blasts, clanking chains—you name them, the Tower's got them."

Back in the days of the axman, London was "swinging." Ranking in interest are the colorful attending Yeoman Warders, the so-called Beefeaters, in Tudor dress, who look as if they are on the payroll for gin advertisements (but don't like to be reminded of it).

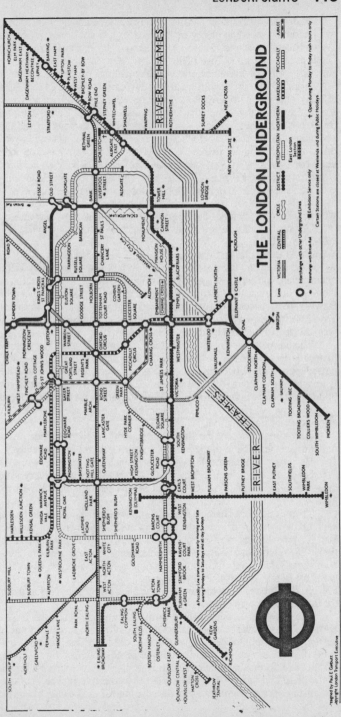

THE LONDON UNDERGROUND

Many visitors consider a visit to the Tower to be the highlight of their sightseeing in London, so schedule plenty of time for it. You don't have to stay as long as Sir Walter Raleigh (released after some 13 years), but give it an afternoon. Take either the Circle or District Line to Tower Hill station (the site is only a short walk away). Or on a sunny day why not take a boat instead, leaving from Westminster Pier?

Admission to the Tower, including the Jewel House, is £4 ($6) for adults, £1.50 ($2.25) for children from April 1 to December 31; £3 ($4.50) for adults, £1.50 ($2.25) for children in March, when the Jewel House costs 80p ($1.20) extra for adults, 40p (60¢) for children. In February when the Jewel House is closed for the annual cleaning and maintenance, admission to the tower is £2 ($3) for adults and £1 ($1.50) for children. Youngsters under five are admitted free. The Tower and all its buildings are closed on New Year's Day, Good Friday, the Christmas holidays, and on Sunday from November through February. The gates open at 9:30 a.m. weekdays all year and at 2 p.m. on Sunday from March to October (closed Sunday the remainder of the year). The last tickets are sold at 5 p.m. March to October and at 4 p.m. November to February, with actual closing being at 5:45 p.m. in summer, 4:30 p.m. in winter.

For further information about opening times and visiting privileges, telephone 709-0765, ext. 235.

Don't expect to find only one tower. The fortress is actually a compound, in which the oldest and finest structure is the White Tower, begun by William the Conqueror. Here you can view the Royal Armouries, the present collection dating back to the reign of Henry VIII. A display of instruments of torture and execution is in the Bowyer Tower, recalling some of the most ghastly moments in the history of the Tower. At the Bloody Tower, the Little Princes (Edward V and the Duke of York) were allegedly murdered by their uncle, Richard III.

The hospitality today far excels that of years ago, when many of the visitors left their cells only to walk to the headsman's block on Tower Hill. Through Traitor's Gate passed such ill-fated, but romantic, figures as Robert Devereux, a favorite of Elizabeth I, known as the second Earl of Essex. Elizabeth herself, then a princess, was once imprisoned briefly in Bell Tower. At Tower Green, Anne Boleyn and Katharine Howard, two wives of Henry VIII, lost their lives. The nine-day queen, Lady Jane Grey, also was executed here.

According to legend, the disappearance of the well-protected ravens at the Tower will presage the collapse of the British Empire (seen any around lately?).

By joining a Yeoman Warder's tour, which lasts an hour, you visit the Chapel Royal of St. Peter ad Vincula. The public is allowed free entry every Sunday morning to attend Holy Communion at 9:15 and Matins and sermon at 11, except during August.

There is no extra charge to visit the **Jewel House,** where the Crown Jewels are kept. Of the three English crowns, the Imperial State Crown is the most important—in fact, it's probably the most famous crown on earth. Made for Victoria for her coronation in 1838, it is today worn by Queen Elizabeth when she opens Parliament. Studded with some 3,000 jewels (principally diamonds), it contains the Black Prince's Ruby, worn by Henry V at Agincourt, the battle in 1415 when the English defeated the French. In addition, feast your eyes on the 530-carat Star of Africa, a cut diamond on the Royal Sceptre with Cross.

The Tower of London has an evening ceremony called the **Ceremony of the Keys.** It is, in fact, the ceremonial locking up of the Tower for yet another day in its 900 years. Nothing stops the ceremony. During World War II, a bomb fell within the castle walls during the ceremony, and nobody flinched—but the Tower was locked up two minutes late. Rumor has it that the guard that night was censured for tardiness, the pilot of the plane that dropped the bomb blamed as the culprit. The Yeoman Warder will explain to guests the significance of the ceremony. For free tickets, write to the Governor, Tower of London, London EC3N 4AB, England, requesting a specific date but also giving alternative dates you'd like to attend. At least six weeks' notice is required. All requests must be accompanied by a stamped, self-addressed envelope *(British stamps only)* or two International Reply Coupons. With ticket in hand, you'll be admitted by a Yeoman Warder around 9:35 p.m.

2. WESTMINSTER ABBEY: No less than such an illustrious figure as St. Peter is supposed to have left his calling card at the abbey. If it's true, I wouldn't be surprised —for nearly everybody else, at least everybody in English history, has left his or her mark. But what is known for certain is that in 1065 the Saxon king, Edward the Confessor, rebuilt the old minster on this spot, overlooking Parliament Square and founded the Benedictine abbey.

The first English king crowned in the abbey was Harold, in 1066, who was killed at the Battle of Hastings that same year. The man who defeated him, Edward's cousin, William the Conqueror, was also crowned at the abbey; the coronation tradition has continued to the present day, broken only twice (Edward V and Edward VIII). The essentially Early English Gothic structure existing today owes more to Henry III's plans than to any other sovereign, although many architects, including Wren, have contributed to the abbey.

Adults pay £1.40 ($2.10), students pay 70p ($1.05), and children, 40p (60¢), to visit the Royal Chapels, the Royal Tombs, the Coronation Chair, the Henry VII Chapel, and the transepts. Hours are 9:20 a.m. to 4:45 p.m. (last ticket sold at 4 p.m.), Monday through Friday; 9:20 a.m. to 2:45 p.m. (last ticket at 2 p.m.) and 3:45 to 5:45 p.m. on Saturday (last ticket, 5 p.m.). On Wednesday the abbey, including the Royal Chapels, is open with free admission from 6 to 7:45 p.m. Only during this time may photographers snap away. On Sunday the Royal Chapels are closed, but the rest of the church is open between services.

Built on the site of the ancient Lady Chapel, in the early 16th century, the Henry VII Chapel is the loveliest in Europe, with its fan vaulting, colorful Knights of the Order of the Bath banners, and Torrigiani-designed tomb of the king, in front of which is placed a 15th-century Vivarini painting, *Madonna and Child*. The chapel represents the flowering of the Perpendicular Gothic style. Also buried here are those feuding sisters, Elizabeth I and Mary Tudor ("Bloody Mary"). Elizabeth I was always vain and adored jewelry. The effigy that lies on top of her tomb has been fitted out with a new set of jewelry, a gilded collar and pendant, a modern copy derived from a painting now at Hatfield House. The originals were stolen by souvenir hunters in the early 18th century. In one end of the chapel you can stand on Cromwell's memorial stone and view the R.A.F. Chapel containing the Battle of Britain memorial stained-glass window, unveiled in 1947 to honor the R.A.F.

You can also visit the most hallowed spot in the abbey, the shrine of Edward the Confessor (canonized in the 12th century). In the saint's chapel is the Coronation Chair, made at the command of Edward I in 1300 to contain the Stone of Scone. Scottish kings were once crowned on this stone (in 1950 the Scots stole it back, but it was later returned to its position in the abbey). Nearby are the sword and shield of Edward III.

Another noted spot in the abbey is Poets' Corner, to the right of the entrance to the Royal Chapel, with its monuments to everybody from Chaucer on down—the Brontë sisters, Shakespeare, Tennyson, Dickens, Kipling, Thackeray, Samuel Johnson, "O Rare Ben Johnson" (his name misspelled), even the American Longfellow. The most stylized and controversial monument is Sir Jacob Epstein's sculptured bust of William Blake. One of the most recent tablets commemorates the poet Dylan Thomas.

Statesmen and men of science, such as Disraeli, Newton, and Charles Darwin, are also either interred in the abbey or honored by monuments. Near the west door is the 1965 memorial to Sir Winston Churchill. In the vicinity of this memorial is the Tomb of the Unknown Soldier, symbol of British dead in World War I. Surprisingly, some of the most totally obscure personages are buried in the abbey precincts, including an abbey plumber.

Many visitors overlook such sights as the 13th-century **Chapter House** where Parliament used to meet (special shoes must be worn to walk across the 700-year-old floor). The Chapter House in the Great Cloister is open from 9:30 a.m. till 6 p.m. (closed on Sunday from March through September). It shuts down at 3:30 p.m. off-season.

Even more fascinating is the **Museum of Abbey Treasures** in the Norman undercroft (crypt), part of the monastic buildings erected between 1066 and 1100. The collection includes effigies—figures in wax, such as that of Nelson, and woodcarvings of early English royalty. Along with the wax figures, the abbey's answer to Madame Tussaud, are ancient documents, seals, replicas of coronation regalia, old religious vestments (such as the cope worn at the coronation of Charles II), the sword of Henry V, and the famous Essex Ring that Elizabeth I is supposed to have given to her favorite earl. The museum, which charges 35p (53¢) for adults, 10p (15¢) for children, is open from 10:30 a.m. to 4:30 p.m. seven days a week.

For tours of the abbey with an expert guide, the cost is £3.50 ($5.25) per person. These tours operate Monday through Friday at 10, 10:30, and 11 a.m. and at 2, 2:30, and 3 p.m.; on Saturday at 10 and 11 a.m. and at 12:30 p.m. These are called Super Tours and are conducted by vergers, members of the abbey staff. They last about 1½ hours, and visitors are shown parts of the abbey not open to regular visitors. Along the way, they are given a witty, fascinating commentary by guides.

For information on religious services, tours, and special functions, telephone 222-5152 or write to the Chapter Office, Westminster Abbey, Deans Yard, London, S.W.1.

Off the Cloisters, **College Garden** is the oldest garden in England, under cultivation for more than 900 years. Surrounded by high walls, flowering trees dot the lawns, and park benches provide comfort where you can hardly hear the roar of passing traffic. It is open on Thursday throughout the year, from 10 a.m. to 4 p.m. in winter, to 6 p.m. in summer. In August and September, band concerts are held at lunchtime from 12:30 to 2 p.m. Admission is free. Tube: Westminster.

 3. HOUSES OF PARLIAMENT: These are the spiritual opposite of the Tower and the stronghold of Britain's democracy, the assemblies that effectively trimmed the sails of royal power. Strangely enough, both Houses (Commons and Lords) are in the formerly royal Palace of Westminster, the king's residence until Henry VIII moved to Whitehall.

Although I can't assure you of the oratory of a Charles James Fox or a William Pitt the Elder, the debates are often lively and controversial in the House of Commons (seats are at a premium during crises). The chances of getting into the House of Lords when it's in session are generally better than they are of going to the more popular House of Commons, where even the Queen isn't allowed. The old guard of the palace informs me that the peerage speak their minds more freely and are less likely to adhere to party line than their counterparts in the lower house.

The general public is admitted to the Strangers' Gallery in the House of Commons on "sitting days"—normally about 4:15 p.m. on Monday to Thursday and about 9:30 a.m. on Friday. You have to join a public queue outside the St. Stephen's entrance on the day in question. Often, there is considerable delay before the head of the public queue is admitted. You may speed matters up somewhat by applying at the American Embassy or the Canadian High Commission for a special pass, but this is too cumbersome for many people. Besides, the embassy has only four tickets for daily distribution, so probably you might as well stand in line. It is usually easier to get in after about

6 p.m. The head of the queue for the House of Lords is normally admitted to the Strangers' Gallery there after 2:40 p.m. Monday to Wednesday (often at 3 p.m. on Thursday).

The present House of Commons was built in 1840, but the chamber was bombed and destroyed by the German air force in 1941. The 320-foot tower that houses Big Ben, however, remained standing and the celebrated clock continued to strike its chimes—the signature tune of Britain's wartime news broadcasts. "Big Ben," incidentally, was named after Sir Benjamin Hall, a cabinet minister distinguished only by his long-windedness.

Except for the Strangers' Galleries, the two Houses of Parliament and Westminster Palace are presently closed to the public.

Further information about the work of the House of Commons is available by phoning 219-4272; House of Lords, 219-3107; or on the Post Office Prestel Viewdata system, frame 5,000.

In a fast-changing world, these details should be confirmed before planning a visit. Tube: Westminster.

4. THE BRITISH MUSEUM: Within its imposing citadel on Great Russell Street in Bloomsbury (tel. 636-1555), the British Museum shelters one of the most catholic collections of art and artifacts in the world, containing countless treasures of ancient and modern civilizations. To storm this bastion in a day is a formidable task, but there are riches to see even on a cursory first visit, among them the Oriental collections (the finest assembly of Islamic pottery outside the Islamic world), the finest collection of Chinese porcelain in Europe, the best holdings of Indian sculpture outside India and Pakistan, and the Prehistoric and Romano-British collections, among many others. Basically, the overall storehouse splits into the national collections of antiquities; prints and drawings; coins, medals, and bank notes; and ethnography.

As you enter the front hall, you may want to head first to the Assyrian Transept on the ground floor, where you'll find the winged and human-headed bulls and lions that once guarded the gateways to the palaces of Assyrian kings. Nearby is the Black Obelisk of Shalmaneser III (858–824 B.C.), tribute from Jehu, King of Israel. From here you can continue into the angular hall of Egyptian sculpture to see the Rosetta Stone, whose discovery led to the deciphering of the mysterious hieroglyphs, explained in a wall display behind the stone.

Also on the ground floor is the Duveen Gallery, housing the Elgin Marbles, consisting chiefly of sculptures from the Parthenon. The frieze shows a ceremonial procession that took place in Athens every four years. Of the 92 metopes from the Parthenon, 15 are housed today in the British Museum. These depict the to-the-death struggle between the handsome Lapiths and the grotesque, drunken Centaurs. The head of the horse from the chariot of Selene, goddess of the moon, is one of the pediment sculptures.

The classical sculpture galleries also hold a *Caryatid* from the Erechtheum, a temple started in 421 B.C. and dedicated to Athena and Poseidon. Displayed here, too, are sculptures from the Mausoleum at Halicarnassus (one of the Seven Wonders of the Ancient World) built for Maussollos, ruler of Caria, who died around 350 B.C. Look also for the blue and white Portland Vase, considered the finest example of ancient cameo carving, having been made in the first century B.C. or A.D.

The Department of Medieval and Later Antiquities has its galleries on the first floor (second floor to us Americans), reached by the main staircase. Of its exhibitions, the Sutton Hoo Anglo-Saxon ship burial, discovered in Suffolk, is, in the words of an expert, "the richest treasure ever dug from English soil," containing gold jewelry, armor, weapons, bronze bowls and cauldrons, silverware, and the inevitable drinking horn of the Norse culture. No body was found, although the tomb is believed to be that of a king of East Anglia who died in the seventh century A.D. You'll also see the bulging-eyed Lewis chessmen, Romanesque carvings in Scandinavian style of the 12th century, and the Ilbert collection of clocks and watches.

The featured attractions of the Upper Floor are the Egyptian Galleries, especially the mummies. Egyptian room 63 is extraordinary, looking like the props for *Cleopatra*, with its cosmetics, domestic utensils, toys, tools, and other work. Some items of Sumerian art, unearthed from the Royal Cemetery at Ur (southern Iraq), lie in a room beyond: a queen's bull-headed harp (oldest ever discovered); a queen's sledge (oldest known example of a land vehicle); and a figure of a he-goat on its hind legs, crafted about 2500 B.C. In the Iranian room rests "The Treasure of the Oxus," a hoard of riches, perhaps a temple deposit, ranging in date from the sixth to the third century B.C., containing a unique collection of goldsmith work, such as a nude youth, signet rings, a fish-shaped vase, and votive plaques.

If your visit to the museum makes you want to know more about this treasure trove, I recommend a book by Ms. M. L. Caygill of the museum director's office, *Treasures of the British Museum*, which gives detailed account of the major treasures and summaries of departmental collections.

The museum is open weekdays from 10 a.m. to 5 p.m. (on Sunday from 2:30 to 6 p.m.). (The galleries start to close ten minutes earlier.) It is closed Good Friday, December 24, 25, and 26, New Year's Day, and the first Monday in May. Admission to the entire museum is free. Tube: Holborn or Tottenham Court Road.

The British Library

Some of the treasures from the collections of the British Library (tel. 636-1544), one of the world's greatest libraries, are on display in the exhibition galleries in the east wing of the British Museum building. In the Grenville Library are displayed western illuminated manuscripts. Notable exhibits are the Benedictional (in Latin) of St. Ethelwold, Bishop of Winchester (963–984), the Luttrell Psalter, and the Harley Golden Gospels of about 800.

In the Manuscript Saloon are manuscripts of historical and literary interest. Items include two of the four surviving copies of King John's Magna Carta (1215) and the Lindisfarne Gospels (an outstanding example of the work of Northumbrian artists in the earliest period of English Christianity, written and illustrated about 698). Almost every major literary figure, such as Charles Dickens, Jane Austen, Charlotte Brontë, W. B. Yeats, is represented in the section given over to English literature. Also on display are historical autographs including Nelson's last letter to Lady Hamilton and the journals of Captain Cook.

In the King's Library, so-called because this is where the library of King George III is housed, the history of the book is illustrated by notable specimens of early printing, including the Diamond Sutra of 868, the first dated example of printing, as well as the Gutenberg Bible, the first book ever printed from movable type, 1455.

In the center of the gallery is an exhibition of fine bookbindings dating from the 16th century. Beneath Roubiliac's 1758 statue of Shakespeare is a case of documents relating to the Bard, including a mortgage bearing his signature and a copy of the First Folio of 1623. The library's unrivaled collection of philatelic items, including such things as the 1840 Great British Penny Black and the rare 1847 Post Office issues of Mauritius, are also to be seen.

The library regularly mounts special temporary exhibitions, usually in the Crawford Room off the Manuscript Saloon. The hours of the British Library's exhibition galleries are the same as those of the museum. Admission is free.

The Museum of Mankind

The Museum of Mankind, the Ethnography Department of the British Museum, is housed at 6 Burlington Gardens, W.1 (tel. 437-2224), where the galleries are open to the public during the same hours as those of the Bloomsbury museum. It has the world's largest collections of art and material culture from tribal societies. A dazzling selection of treasures from five continents is displayed, and a number of large exhibitions show the life, art, and technology of selected cultures. New exhibitions are mounted every year. There is a large anthropology library open to the public on weekdays. Weekday hours are 10 a.m. to 5 p.m., on Sunday from 2:30 to 6 p.m., and there is no admission fee. Film shows, lectures, and educational services are also available. Tube: Piccadilly Circus.

5. MADAME TUSSAUD'S: In 1770 an exhibition of life-size wax figures was opened in Paris by Dr. Curtius. He was soon joined by his niece, Strasbourg-born Marie Tussaud, who soon learned from him the secret of making lifelike replicas of the famous and the infamous. During the French Revolution, the head of almost every distinguished victim of the guillotine was molded by Madame Tussaud or her uncle.

After the death of Curtius, Madame Tussaud inherited the exhibition, and in 1802 she left France for England. For 33 years she toured the United Kingdom with her exhibition, and in 1835 she settled on Baker Street. The exhibition was such a success that it practically immortalized her in her day; she continued to make portraits until she was 81 (she died in 1850). The perennially popular waxworks are visited by some even before they check out Westminster Abbey or the Tower of London.

While some of the figures on display today come from molds taken by the incomparable Madame Tussaud, the exhibition continues to introduce new images of whoever is *au courant*. An enlarged Grand Hall continues to house years of royalty and old favorites such as Winston Churchill, as well as many of today's heads of state and political leaders. In the not-to-be-missed Chamber of Horrors, you can have the vicarious thrill of meeting such types as Dr. Crippen, in case you never had the dubious pleasure in real life. You can walk through a Victorian street where special effects recreate the atmosphere of the London of Jack the Ripper. The instruments and victims of death penalties contrast with present-day criminals portrayed within the confines of prison. You are invited to mingle with the more current stars in the Conservatory, as well as seeing the Beatles relaxing.

In 1985, an area opened where the latest technologies in sound, light, and special effects combine with new figures in a celebration of success in the fields of rock music, sports, and show business. On the ground floor, you can relive the Battle of Trafalgar on the gun deck of Nelson's flagship, *Victory*.

Madame Tussaud's, air-conditioned throughout, is open daily, including Saturday and Sunday, year round (closed on Christmas Day only). Hours are 10 a.m. to 5:30 p.m. weekdays and 9:30 a.m. to 5:30 p.m. on weekends. Doors open earlier throughout the summer season. Admission for adults is £3.95 ($5.93). Children under 16 pay £2.30 ($3.45). The London Planetarium is right next door, costing £2.20 ($3.30) for adults, £1.40 ($2.10) for children. A combined ticket for Madame Tussaud's and the Planetarium is priced at £5.15 ($7.73) for adults, £3.10 ($4.65) for children. Those under five years old are not admitted to the Planetarium. For information, phone 935-6861. The entrance to Madame Tussaud's is on Marylebone Road. Tube: Baker Street.

6. TATE GALLERY: This building, beside the Thames on Millbank, S.W.1 (tel. 821-1313), houses the best collection of British paintings from the 16th century on, as well as England's finest collection of modern art, the works of British artists born after 1860 together with foreign art from the impressionists onward. The Tate is open from 10 a.m. to 5:50 p.m. weekdays (on Sunday from 2 to 5:50 p.m.). To reach it, take the tube to Pimlico or bus 88 or 77A. The number of paintings is staggering. If time permits, try to schedule at least two visits, the first to see the classic English works, the second to take in the modern collection. Since only a portion of the collections can be shown simultaneously, the works on display vary from time to time. However, the most time-pressed individual may not want to miss the following, which are almost invariably on view:

The first giant among English painters, William Hogarth (1697-1764), is well represented, particularly by his satirical *O the Roast Beef of Old England, Calais Gate*, with its distorted figures, such as the gluttonous priest. The ruby-eyed *Satan, Sin, and Death* remains one of his most enigmatic works.

Two other famous British painters of the 18th century are Sir Joshua Reynolds (1723-1792) and Thomas Gainsborough (1727-1788). Reynolds, the portrait painter, shines brightest when he's painting himself (two self-portraits hang side by side). Two other portraits, that of Francis and Suzanna Beckford, are typical of his work. His rival, Gainsborough, is noted for his portraits too, and also landscapes ("my real love"). His landscapes with gypsies are subdued, mysterious; *The View of Dedham* is more representative. One of Gainsborough's most celebrated portraits is of Edward Richard Gardiner, a handsome boy in blue (the more famous *Blue Boy* is in California). Two extremely fine Gainsborough portraits have recently been acquired: *Giovanna Baccelli* (1782), who was well known both as a dancer and as the mistress of the third Earl of Dorset, and *Sir Benjamin Truman*, the notable brewer.

In the art of J. M. W. Turner (1775-1851), the Tate possesses its greatest collection of the works of a single artist. Most of the paintings and watercolors exhibited here were willed to the nation by Turner. Of his paintings of stormy seas, none is more horrifying than *Shipwreck* (1805). In the Petworth series, he broke from realism (see his *Interior at Petworth*). His delicate impressionism is best conveyed in his sunset and sunrise pictures, with their vivid reds and yellows. Turner's vortex paintings, inspired by theories of Goethe, are *Light and Color—the Mornings After the Deluge*, and *Shade and Darkness—the Evening of the Deluge*.

In a nation of landscape painters, John Constable (1776-1837) stands out. Some of his finest works include *Vale of Dedham* and *Flatford Mill, on the River Stour*, painted in 1817, both scenes from East Anglia.

American-born Sir Jacob Epstein became one of England's greatest sculptors, and some of his bronzes are owned and occasionally displayed by the Tate. Augustus John, who painted everybody from G. B. Shaw to Tallulah Bankhead, is also represented here with portraits and sketches.

The Tate owns some of the finest works of the Pre-Raphaelite period of the late 19th century. One of the best of the English artists of the 20th century, Sir Stanley Spencer (1891-1959), is represented by his two versions of *Resurrection* and a remarkable self-portrait (1913).

The Tate has many major paintings from both the 19th and 20th centuries, including Wyndham Lewis's portraits of Edith Sitwell and of Ezra Pound, and Paul Nash's *Voyages of the Moon*. But the sketches of William Blake (1757-1827) attract the most attention. Blake, of course, was the incomparable mystical poet and illustrator of such works as *The Book of Job, The Divine Comedy*, and *Paradise Lost*.

In the modern collections, the Tate contains Matisse's *L'Escargot* and *The Inattentive Reader*, along with the works by Dali, Chagall, Modigliani, Munch, Ben Nicholson (large collection of his works), and Dubuffet. The different periods of Picasso bloom in *Woman in a Chemise* (1905), *Three Dancers* (1925), *Nude Woman in a Red Armchair* (1932), and *Goat's Skull, Bottle and Candle* (1952).

Truly remarkable is the area devoted to the sculpture of Giacometti (1901-1966), and the paintings of two of England's most famous modern artists, Francis Bacon (especially gruesome, *Three Studies for Figures at the Base of a Crucifixion*), and Graham Sutherland (see his portrait of W. Somerset Maugham).

Rodin's *The Kiss* and Marino Marini's *Cavaliere*, both world-famous pieces of sculpture, are on show. In addition, sculptures by Henry Moore and Barbara Hepworth are displayed.

Downstairs is the internationally renowned, Rex Whistler-decorated restaurant and a coffeeshop.

The major Clore Gallery extension adjoining the Tate, opened in 1987, houses the Turner Bequest of more than 19,000 watercolors and nearly 300 oil paintings.

7. NATIONAL GALLERY: On the north side of Trafalgar Square, W.C.2, in an impressive neoclassic building, the National Gallery (tel. 839-3321) houses one of the most comprehensive collections of European paintings, representing all the major schools from the 13th to the 19th centuries. The largest part of the collection is devoted to the Italians, including the Sienese, Venetian, and Florentine masters.

Of the early Gothic works, the *Wilton Diptych* (French school, late 14th century) is the rarest treasure. It stands in a niche by itself, and depicts Richard II being introduced to the Madonna and Child by such good contacts as John the Baptist and the Saxon king, Edward the Confessor.

A Florentine gem, a Virgin and grape-eating Bambino, by Masaccio (one of the founders of modern painting) is displayed, as are notable works by Piero della Francesca, particularly his linear *The Baptism.*

In a specially lighted hall is the famous cartoon (in the fine arts sense) of *The Virgin and Child with Saint John and Saint Anne* by Leonardo da Vinci. Matter and spirit meet in the haunting nether world of the *Virgin of the Rocks,* a famous Leonardo painting. Also shown are two other giants of the Renaissance—Michelangelo (represented by an unfinished painting, *The Entombment*), and Raphael (*The Ansidei Madonna,* among others).

Among the Venetian masters of the 16th century, to whom color was paramount, the most notable works include a rare *Adoration of the Kings* by Giorgione; *Bacchus and Ariadne* by Titian; *The Beginning of the Milky Way* by Tintoretto (a lush galaxy, with milk streaming from Juno's breasts), and *The Family Darius Before Alexander* by Veronese (one of the best paintings at the National). Surrounding are a number of satellite rooms, filled with works by major Italian masters of the 15th century—artists such as Andrea Mantegna of Padua (*Agony in the Garden*); his brother-in-law, Giovanni Bellini (his portrait of the Venetian doge, Leonardo Loredano, provided a change of pace from his many interpretations of Madonnas); finally, Botticelli, represented by *Mars and Venus, Adoration of the Magi,* and *Portrait of a Young Man.*

The painters of northern Europe are well displayed; for example, Jan van Eyck's portrait of G. Arnolfini and his bride, and Pieter Brueghel the Elder's Bosch-influenced *Adoration,* with its unkingly kings and ghoul-like onlookers. The 17th-century pauper, Vermeer, is rich on canvas in a *Young Woman at a Virginal,* a favorite theme of his. Fellow Delft-ite Pieter de Hooch comes on sublimely in a *Courtyard of a House in Delft.*

One of the big drawing cards of the National is its collection of Rembrandts. Rembrandt, the son of a miller, became the greatest painter in the Netherlands in the 17th century. His *Self-Portrait at the Age of 34* shows him at the pinnacle of his life, his *Self-Portrait at the Age of 63* is more deeply moving and revealing. For another Rembrandt study in old age, see his *Portrait of Margaretha Trip.* His *The Woman Taken in Adultery* shows the artist's human sympathy. Part of the prolific output of Peter Paul Rubens is also to be seen, notably his *Peace and War* and *The Rape of the Sabine Women.*

Five of the greatest of the home-grown artists—Constable, Turner, Reynolds, Gainsborough, and Hogarth—share their paintings with the Tate. But the National owns masterpieces by each of them. Constable's *Cornfield* is another scene of East Anglia, along with *Haywain,* a harmony of light and atmosphere. Completely different from Constable is the work of Turner, including his dreamy *Fighting Téméraire* and *Rain, Steam, and Speed.* In what are essentially portrait galleries, you can see several works by Sir Joshua Reynolds, along with a Gainsborough masterpiece, *The*

Morning Walk, an idealistic blending of portraiture with landscape. Finally, in a completely different brushstroke, Hogarth's *Marriage à la Mode* caricatures the marriages of convenience of the upper class of the 18th century.

The three giants of Spanish painting are represented: Velázquez's portrait of the sunken-faced Philip IV; El Greco's *Christ Driving the Traders from the Temple;* Goya's portrait of the Duke of Wellington (once stolen) and his mantilla-wearing *Dona Isabel Cobos de Porcel.*

Other rooms are devoted to 18th-century French painters such as Watteau and Fragonard; 19th-century French painters such as Delacroix and Ingres; 19th-century French impressionists such as Manet, Monet, Renoir, and Degas; and 19th-century post-impressionists such as Cézanne, Seurat, and Van Gogh.

Important acquisitions in recent years include *Samson and Delilah* by Peter Paul Rubens, J. -L. David's portrait of Jacobus Blauer, Bassano's *Way to Calvary,* and *Balbi Children* by Van Dyck.

The National Gallery is open weekdays from 10 a.m. to 6 p.m., on Sunday from 2 to 6 p.m. Closed January 1, Good Friday, the three-day Christmas holidays, and bank holidays. Admission is free. Tube: Charing Cross.

8. KENSINGTON PALACE: Home of the State Apartments, some of which were used by Queen Victoria, this is another of the major attractions of London, at the far western end of Kensington Gardens, W.8 (tel. 937-9561, ext. 2). The palace was acquired by asthma-suffering William III (William of Orange) in 1689, and was remodeled by Sir Christopher Wren. George II, who died in 1760, was the last king to use it as a royal residence.

The most interesting chamber to visit is Queen Victoria's bedroom. In this room, on the morning of June 20, 1837, she was aroused from her sleep with the news that she had ascended to the throne, following the death of her uncle, William IV. Thus the woman who was to become the symbol of the British Empire and the Empress of India began the longest reign in the history of England. In the anteroom are memorabilia from Victoria's childhood such as a dollhouse and a collection of her toys.

In Queen Mary's bedroom, you can see her mid-17th-century writing cabinet with its tortoise-shell surface. Incidentally, Mary II reigned with William III, and is not to be confused with the late Queen Mary (1867–1953), who also has many relics at Kensington. The late Queen Mary was born in Victoria's bedroom.

A special attraction is the Court Dress Collection, which shows restored rooms from the 19th century, including Queen Victoria's birthroom and a series of room settings with the appropriate court dress of the day, from 1760 to 1950.

As you wander through the apartments, you can admire many fine paintings, most of which are from the Royal Collection. The State Apartments are open Monday through Saturday from 9 a.m. to 5 p.m., on Sunday from 1 to 5 p.m., throughout the year. They are closed New Year's Day, Good Friday, Christmas Eve, Christmas Day, and Boxing Day. Admission fees are as follows: adults pay £2.20 ($3.30) and children £1.10 ($1.65). You enter from the Broad Walk, and you can reach the building by taking the tube either to Queensway or Bayswater on the north side of the gardens, or High Street Kensington on the south side. You'll have to walk a bit from there, however.

The palace gardens, originally the private park of royalty, are also open to the public for daily strolls around Round Pond, near the heart of Kensington Gardens. The gardens adjoin Hyde Park. Also in Kensington Gardens is the Albert Memorial to Queen Victoria's consort. Facing Albert Hall, it reflects all the opulent overstatement of the Victorian era—it's fascinating, nonetheless.

9. ST. PAUL'S CATHEDRAL: During World War II, newsreel footage reaching America showed the dome of St. Paul's Cathedral lit by bombs exploding all around it.

That it survived at all is miraculous, as it was hit twice in the early years of the Nazi bombardment of London. But St. Paul's is accustomed to calamity, having been burned down at least three times and destroyed once by invading Norsemen. It was in the Great Fire of 1666 that the old St. Paul's was razed, making way for a new Renaissance structure designed (after mishaps and rejections) by Sir Christopher Wren.

The masterpiece of this great architect was erected between 1675 and 1710. Its classical dome dominates The City's square mile. Inside, the cathedral is laid out like a Latin cross, containing few art treasures (Grinling Gibbons choir stalls an exception) and many monuments, including one to the "Iron Duke" and a memorial chapel to American servicemen who lost their lives in World War II while stationed in the United Kingdom. Encircling the dome is the Whispering Gallery, where discretion in speech is advised. In the crypt lie not only Wren but the Duke of Wellington and Lord Nelson, as well as Wren's Great Model and the Diocesan Treasury. It was in this cathedral on July 29, 1981, that Prince Charles married Lady Diana Spencer amid much pomp and ceremony.

The cathedral is open daily from 8 a.m. to 6 p.m. The crypt and galleries, including the Whispering Gallery, are open only from 10 a.m. to 4:15 p.m. weekdays (from 11 a.m. on Saturday). Guided tours, lasting 1½ hours, and including the crypt and other parts of St. Paul's not normally open to the public, take place daily at 11 and 11:30 a.m., 2 and 2:30 p.m. when the cathedral is open (except Sunday) and cost £3.25 ($4.88) for adults and £1.60 ($2.40) for children.

St. Paul's is an Anglican cathedral with daily services held at 8 a.m. and at 5 p.m. On Sunday, services are at 10:30 and 11:30 a.m. and at 3:15 p.m. For more information, telephone 248-2705. In addition, you can climb to the very top of the dome for a spectacular 360-degree view of all of London, costing 85p ($1.28) per person. Tube: St. Paul's.

10. VICTORIA AND ALBERT MUSEUM: When Queen Victoria asked that this museum be named after herself and her consort, she could not have selected a more fitting memorial. The Victoria and Albert is one of the finest museums in the world, devoted to fine and applied art of many nations and periods, including the Orient. In many respects it's one of the most difficult for viewing, as many of the most important exhibits are so small they can easily be overlooked. To reach the museum on Cromwell Road, S.W.7 (tel. 589-6371), take the tube to the South Kensington stop. The museum is open weekdays, except Friday, from 10 a.m. to 5:50 p.m., on Sunday from 2:30 till 5:50 p.m.

There is space only to suggest some of its finest art. The early medieval art includes many treasures, such as the Eltenberg Reliquary (Rhenish, second half of the 12th century). In the shape of a domed, copper-gilt church, it is enriched with champlevé enamel and set with walrus-ivory carvings of Christ and the Apostles. Other exhibits in this same salon include the Early English Gloucester Candlestick, and the Byzantine Veroli Casket, with its ivory panels based on Greek plays. An area devoted to Islamic art contains the Ardabil carpet from 16th-century Persia (320 knots per square inch).

In the Gothic art exhibition, there are some fine pieces, such as the Syon Cope, made in the early 14th century, an example of the highly valued embroidery produced in England at that time; a stained-glass window from Winchester College (circa 1400); a Limoges enameled triptych for Louis XII. The Gothic tapestries, including the Devonshire ones depicting hunting scenes, are displayed.

Renaissance art in Italy includes such works as a Donatello marble relief, *The Ascension;* a small terracotta statue of the Madonna and Child by Antonio Rossellino; a marble group, *Samson and a Philistine,* by Giovanni Bologna; a wax model of a slave by Michelangelo. The highlight of the 16th-century art from the continent is the marble group, *Neptune with Triton,* by Bernini.

The cartoons by Raphael, which are owned by the Queen, may also be seen. These cartoons, conceived as designs for tapestries for the Sistine Chapel, include scenes such as *The Sacrifice of Lystra* and *Paul Preaching at Athens*.

A most unusual, huge, and impressive exhibit is the Cast Room, with life-size plaster models of ancient and medieval statuary and architecture, made from molds formed over the originals.

Of the rooms devoted to English furniture and decorative art during the period from the 16th to the mid-18th century, the most outstanding exhibit is the Bed of Ware, big enough for eight. In the galleries of portrait miniatures, two of the rarest ones are both by Hans Holbein the Younger (one of Anne of Cleves, another of a Mrs. Pemberton). In the painting galleries are many works by Constable. His *Flatford Mill* represents a well-known scene from his native East Anglia.

No admission is charged, but they suggest a donation of £2 ($3) for adults, 50p (75¢) for children under 12.

THE BEST OF THE REST: Now, for those with more time to get acquainted with London, we'll continue our exploration of a many-faceted city.

Royal London

From Trafalgar Square, you can stroll down the wide, tree-flanked avenue known as **The Mall.** It leads to **Buckingham Palace,** the heart of "Royal London" (English kings and queens have lived there since the days of Queen Victoria). Three parks—St. James's, Green, and the Buckingham Palace Gardens (private)—converge at the center of this area, where you'll find a memorial honoring Victoria.

London's most popular daily pageant, particularly with North American tourists, is the **Changing of the Queen's Guard** in the forecourt of Buckingham Palace (tube to St. James's Park or Green Park). The regiments of the Guard's Division, in their bearskins and red tunics, actually are five regiments in one, including the Scots, Irish, and Welsh. The guards march to the palace from either the Wellington or Chelsea barracks, arriving around 11:30 a.m. for the halfhour ceremony. To get the full effect, go somewhat earlier. There is usually no ceremony when the weather is what the English call inclement. But remember that your idea of inclement may not be a weather-toughened Londoner's idea of inclement. These ceremonies are curtailed in winter, between October 1 and March 31. During those months the official schedule is that the Changing of the Guard takes place on even calendar days in October, December, and February, and on odd calendar days in November, January, and March.

Any and all of this information might change suddenly without notice, depending on circumstances, so you should phone 730-3488 for the most up-to-the-minute details. That way, you won't necessarily miss out on this most important ceremony which every first- or even second-time visitor to London wants to see.

You can't visit the palace, of course, without an invitation, but you can inspect the **Queen's Gallery,** S.W.1 (entrance on Buckingham Palace Road) (tel. 930-4832). The picture gallery may be visited from 11 a.m. to 5 p.m. Tuesday through Saturday (from 2 to 5 p.m. on Sunday), including bank holidays (closed Monday), for an admission of £1.10 ($1.65), 50p (75¢) for children. As is known, all the royal families of Europe have art collections, some including acquisitions from centuries ago. The English sovereign has one of the finest, and has consented to share it with the public. Of course, I can't predict what exhibition you're likely to see, as they are changed yearly at the gallery. You may find a selection of incomparable works by Old Masters, and sometimes furniture and objets d'art. The Queen's collection contains an unsurpassed range of royal portraits from the well-known profile of Henry V through the late Plantagenets, the companion portraits of Elizabeth I as a girl and her brother, Edward VI, and the four fine Georgian pictures by Zoffany, to recent works including two portraits of

Queen Alexandra from Sandringham and paintings of Queen Elizabeth II and other members of the present royal family. Tube: Green Park or St. James's.

You can get a close look at Queen Elizabeth's coronation carriage at the **Royal Mews,** on Buckingham Palace Road, S.W.1 (tel. 930-4832). Her Majesty's State Coach, built in 1761 to the designs of Sir William Chambers, contains emblematic and other paintings on the panels. Its doors were executed by Cipriani. It is used by sovereigns when opening Parliament in person and on other state occasions. Queen Elizabeth used it upon her coronation in 1953 and in 1977 for her Silver Jubilee Procession. It is traditionally drawn by eight gray horses. Many other official carriages are housed here as well, including the Scottish and Irish state coaches. The Queen's horses are also sheltered here. The Mews is open to the public on Wednesday and Thursday from 2 to 4 p.m. and charges an admission of 30p (45¢) for adults, 15p (23¢) for children. It is closed during Ascot week in June. Tube: Green Park or St. James's.

Official London

Whitehall, S.W.1, the seat of the British government, grew up on the grounds of Whitehall Palace, which was turned into a royal residence by Henry VIII, who snatched it from its former occupant, Cardinal Wolsey. Beginning at Trafalgar Square, Whitehall extends south to Parliament (Houses of Parliament and Westminster Abbey, described earlier). On this street, you'll find the Home Office, the Old Admiralty Building, and the Ministry of Defence.

Visitors today can see the **Cabinet War Rooms,** the bomb-proof bunker, that suite of rooms large and small just as they were left by Winston Churchill in September 1945 at the end of World War II. Many objects were removed only for dusting, and the Imperial War Museum studied photographs to replace everything exactly as it was, including notepads, files, and typewriters—right down to pencils, pins, and paperclips. You can see the Map Room with its huge wall maps, the Atlantic map a mass of pinholes. Each hole represents at least one convoy. Next door is Churchill's bedroom-cum-office, reinforced with stout wood beams. It has a very basic bed and a desk with two BBC microphones on it for his broadcasts of those famous speeches that stirred the nation.

The Transatlantic Telephone Room, to give it its full title, is little more than a broom cupboard, but it had the Bell Telephone Company's special scrambler phone by the name of Sig-Saly. From here, Churchill and Roosevelt conferred. The scrambler equipment was actually too large to house in the bunker, so it was placed in the basement of Selfridges Department Store on Oxford Street. The actual telephone was still classified at the end of the war and was removed. Seventy feet below ground level, it was impossible to know the world's weather conditions. Therefore a system of boards, rather like old railway-station boards, was used with laconic phrases such as wet, very wet, hot and sunny, dry and dull.

The entrance to the War Rooms is by Clive Steps at the end of King Charles Street, S.W.1, off Whitehall near Big Ben (tube to Westminster). It is open Tuesday to Sunday from 10 a.m. to 5:50 p.m. (last admission at 5:15 p.m.). It is closed on Monday, New Year's Day, Good Friday, May bank holiday, and Christmas holidays. The rooms may be closed with short notice on state occasions. Admission is £2.50 ($3.75) for adults, £1.25 ($1.88) for children 5 to 16 and students. For further information, telephone 930-6961.

At the **Cenotaph** (honoring the dead in two World Wars), turn down unpretentious Downing Street to the modest little town house at **No. 10,** flanked by two bobbies. Walpole was the first prime minister to live here, Churchill the most famous.

Nearby is the **Horse Guards Building,** Whitehall, S.W.1, which is now the headquarters of the commander-in-chief of the British Home Forces. There has been a guard change here since 1649 when the site was the entrance to the old Palace of Whitehall. You can watch the Queen's Lifeguards in the mounted guard-change ceremony at 11 a.m. (10 a.m. on Sunday). You can also see the smaller change of the guard hourly when mounted troopers are changed. At 4 p.m. you can watch the evening inspection when ten unmounted troopers and two mounted troopers assemble in the courtyard. As mentioned, the main guard change takes place at 11 a.m. when 12 mounted troopers arrive from the Knightsbridge Barracks. Photographers can get a good view of the London traffic halted for this colorful troop to cross out of Hyde Park, past the Wellington Arch. They proceed down Constitution Hill and the Mall. If you are at Hyde Park Corner at 10:30 a.m., you can follow them. Tube: Westminster.

Across the street is Inigo Jones's **Banqueting House,** Palace of Whitehall, S.W.1 (tel. 930-4179), site of the execution of Charles I. William and Mary accepted the crown of England here, but prefered to live at Kensington Palace. The Banqueting House was part of Whitehall Palace, which burned to the ground in 1698. The ceremonial hall escaped razing. Its most notable feature today is an allegorical ceiling painted by Peter Paul Rubens. The Banqueting House may be visited weekdays from 10 a.m. to 5 p.m., except Monday (on Sunday from 2 to 5 p.m.). The admission fee is 70p ($1.05) for adults, 35p (53¢) for children. Tube: Westminster.

Finally, you may want to stroll to Parliament Square for a view of **Big Ben,** the world's most famous timepiece, the very symbol of the heart and soul of England. Big Ben is actually the deepest and loudest bell, although the common name for the clock tower on the Houses of Parliament. Opposite, in the gardens of Parliament Square, stands the statue of Churchill by Oscar Nemon.

Legal London

The smallest borough in London, bustling Holborn (pronounced Hoburn), W.C.1, is often referred to as Legal London, the home of the city's barristers, solicitors, and law clerks. It also embraces the university district of Bloomsbury. Holborn, which houses the ancient Inns of Court—Gray's Inn, Lincoln's Inn, Middle Temple, and Inner Temple—was severely damaged in World War II bombing raids. The razed buildings were replaced with modern offices, housing insurance brokers, realtors, whatever. But the borough still retains quadrangle pockets of its former days.

Going from the Victoria Embankment, Middle Temple Lane leads between Middle and Inner Temple Gardens in the area known as **The Temple,** E.C.4 (tel. 353-4366) (Tube: Temple), named after the medieval order of the Knights Templar (originally formed by the Crusaders in Jerusalem in the 12th century). It was in Temple Gardens that Henry II's barons are supposed to have picked the blooms of red and white roses and started the War of the Roses in 1430. Today only members of the Temples and their guests are allowed to enter the Inner Temple Gardens. The Middle Temple contains a Tudor hall completed in 1570 with a double hammer-beam roof. It is believed that Shakespeare's troupe played *Twelfth Night* here in 1602. A table on view is said to have come from timber from Sir Francis Drake's *The Golden Hind*. The hall may be visited from 10 a.m. to noon and from 3 to 4:30 p.m. weekdays.

Within the precincts of the Inner Temple, E.C.4 (Tube: Temple), is the **Temple Church,** one of three Norman "round churches" left in England. First completed in the 12th century, it has been restored. Look for the knightly effigies and the Norman door any time from 10 a.m. to 5 p.m. (4 p.m. in winter). Take note of the circle of grotesque portrait heads, including a goat in a mortar board. A caretaker can show you a "dungeon" one flight up. Continue north on Middle Temple Lane to about where the Strand becomes Fleet Street going east. Look for the memorial pillar called Temple Bar, marking the boundary of the City.

On to the north, across the Strand, stand the **Royal Courts of Justice,** E.C.4 (Tube: Temple). You can go through its main doorway on the Strand and on through the building which was completed in 1882 but designed in the style of the 13th century. This is the home of such courts as Admiralty, divorce, probate, chancery, appeals, and Queen's Bench. Leave the Royal Courts building by the rear door, and you'll be on

Carey Street, not far from New Square. From there, you're in the near vicinity of **Lincoln's Inn,** W.C.2 (Tube: Holborn), another of the famous inns of court, and **Lincoln's Inn Fields.**

Lincoln's Inn, founded in the 14th century, evokes colleges at Cambridge or Oxford. This ancient inn forms an important link in the architectural maze of London. Its chapel and gardens are open to the public between noon and 2:30 p.m., and they're well worth seeing. The chapel was rebuilt around 1620 by Inigo Jones. Cromwell lived here at one time. To the west of the inn lies the late 17th-century square, one of the few complete such areas left in London, called Lincoln's Inn Fields. It's a large square with a garden in the center and surrounded by buildings, including the Sir John Soane's Museum (see The Best of the Museums below). Near the south of the fields on Kingsway is the **Old Curiosity Shop,** immortalized by Charles Dickens.

If you proceed north on Chancery Lane to High Holborn, W.C.1, heading toward **Gray's Inn,** the fourth of the ancient Inns of Court still in operation, take a look at the old **Staple Inn,** near the Chancery Lane tube stop. This half-timbered edifice, and eight other former Inns of Chancery, are no longer in use in the legal world. Now lined with shops, it was built and rebuilt many times, originally having come into existence between 1545 and 1589. Dr. Johnson moved here in 1759, the year *Rasselas* was published.

Gray's Inn, on Gray's Inn Road north of High Holborn, is entered from Theobald's Road. As you enter, you'll see a late-Georgian terrace lined with buildings which, like many of the other houses in the inns, are combined residences and offices. Gray's has been restored after being heavily damaged by World War II bombings. Francis Bacon (not the modern artist) was the most eminent tenant who resided here in other days. The inn contains a rebuilt Tudor Hall, but its greatest attraction is the plane-tree shaded lawn and handsome gardens, considered the best in the inns. The 17th-century atmosphere exists today only in the square.

When Horace Rumpole, known to readers and TV audiences as *Rumpole of the Bailey,* leaves his chambers in one of the Temple Inns of Court to go to court, he usually heads not for the Royal Courts of Justice mentioned above, which are involved with civil cases, but to the **Central Criminal Court,** E.C.4, better known as Old Bailey. To reach it, go east on Fleet Street, which along the way becomes Ludgate Hill. Cross Ludgate Circus and turn left to the Old Bailey, a domed structure with the figure of Justice standing atop it. It fronts on a small street called Old Bailey, from which the court gets its common appellation. The courthouse replaced the infamous Newgate Prison, once the scene of public hangings and other forms of public entertainment. Tube: Temple or Chancery Lane.

The Best of the Museums

The present **Guildhall,** on King Street in Cheapside (The City, E.C.2; tel. 606-3030; tube to Bank), was built in 1411. But the Civic Hall of the Corporation of London has had a rough time, notably in the Great Fire of 1666 and the 1940 blitz. The most famous tenants of the rebuilt Guildhall are *Gog and Magog,* two giants standing over nine feet high. The original effigies, burned in the London fire, were rebuilt only to be destroyed again in 1940. The present giants are third generation. Restoration has returned the Gothic grandeur to the hall—replete with a medieval porch entranceway; monuments to Wellington, Churchill, and Nelson; stained glass commemorating lord mayors and mayors; the standards of length; a 13th-century crypt; and colorful shields honoring fishmongers, haberdashers, merchant tailors, ironmongers, skinners, and some of the major Livery Companies. The Guildhall and Crypt may be visited Monday through Saturday, 10 a.m. to 5 p.m. (on Sunday, May to September only, from 2 to 5 p.m.).

Sir John Soane's Museum, 13 Lincoln's Inn Fields, W.C.2 (tel. 405-2107), is the former home of an architect who lived from 1753 to 1837. Sir John, who rebuilt the

Bank of England (not the present structure, however), was a "spaceman" in a different era. With his multilevels, fool-the-eye mirrors, flying arches, and domes, Soane was a master of perspective, a genius of interior space (his picture gallery, for example, is filled with three times the number of paintings a room of similar dimensions would be likely to hold). That he could do all this and still not prove a demon to claustrophobia victims was proof of his remarkable talent. Even if you don't like Soane (he was reportedly a cranky fellow), you may still want to visit this museum to see William Hogarth's satirical series, *The Rake's Progress*, containing his much-reproduced *Orgy*, and the less successful satire on politics in the mid-18th century, *The Election*. Soane also filled his house with paintings (Watteau's *Les Noces*, Canaletto's large *Venetian Scene*), and classical sculpture. Finally, be sure to see the Egyptian sarcophagus found in a burial chamber in the Valley of the Kings. Soane turned his house over to his country for use as a museum. It is open Tuesday through Saturday from 10 a.m. till 5 p.m. Tube: Holborn or Chancery Lane.

The **Royal Academy of Arts,** Piccadilly, W.1 (tel. 734-9052), founded in 1768, is the oldest established society in Great Britain devoted solely to the fine arts. The academy is made up of a self-supporting, self-governing body of artists, who conduct art schools, hold exhibitions of the work of living artists, and organize loan exhibits of the arts of past and present periods. A summer exhibition is held annually, with contemporary paintings, drawings, engravings, sculpture, and architecture on display. This summer show has been held without a break since 1769.

In Burlington House, which was built in Piccadilly in the 17th century, the Royal Academy had as its first president Sir Joshua Reynolds. Purchases and gifts have provided a rich collection of artworks, and the ongoing program of loan exhibition provides opportunities to see fine art examples on an international scale. The Royal Academy Shop and a restaurant are open during exhibition hours, usually 10 a.m. to 6 p.m. daily. The framing department is open from 10 a.m. to 5 p.m. Monday to Saturday. Serious students may use the library by appointment from 2 to 5 p.m. Monday to Friday. You can see works of Gainsborough, Constable, Reynolds, Turner, Benjamin West, Angelica Kauffman, Landseer, and even Michelangelo here. Burlington House is opposite Fortnum and Mason. Tube: Piccadilly Circus or Green Park.

Just across the Thames in Lambeth Road, S.E.1, is the **Imperial War Museum** (tel. 735-8922; tube to Lambeth North or Elephant and Castle). This large domed building, built around 1815, the former Bethlehem Royal Hospital for the Insane, or Bedlam, houses the museum's collections relating to the two World Wars and other military operations involving the British and the Commonwealth since 1914.

A wide range of weapons and equipment is on display, along with models, decorations, uniforms, posters, photographs, and paintings. You can see a Mark V tank, a Battle of Britain Spitfire, a German one-man submarine, and the rifle carried by Lawrence of Arabia, as well as the German surrender document, Hitler's political testament, and a German flying bomb. The museum is open Monday to Saturday from 10 a.m. to 5:50 p.m., on Sunday from 2 to 5:50 p.m. It is closed on Good Friday, the three-day Christmas holidays, New Year's Day, and the May bank holiday. Admission is free.

The **Wellington Museum,** at Apsley House, 149 Piccadilly, Hyde Park Corner, W.1 (tel. 499-5676), takes us into the former town house of the Iron Duke, the British general (1769–1852) who defeated Napoleon at the Battle of Waterloo. Wellington's London residence was opened as a public museum in 1952. Once Wellington had to retreat behind the walls of Apsley House, even securing it in fear of a possible attack from Englishmen, outraged by his autocratic opposition as prime minister to reform. In the vestibule you'll find a colossal statue in marble of Napoleon by Canova—ironic, to say the least. Completely idealized, it was presented to the duke by King George IV. In addition to three good paintings by Velázquez, the Wellington collection includes Coreggio's *Agony in the Garden,* Jan Steen's *The Egg Dance,* and Pieter de Hooch's *A*

Musical Party. You can see the gallery where Wellington used to invite his officers for the annual Waterloo banquet (the banquets were originally held in the dining room). The house also contains a large porcelain and china collection—plus many Wellington medals, of course. Also displayed is a magnificent Sèvres porcelain Egyptian service, made originally for the Empress Josephine and given by Louis XVIII to Wellington. In addition, superb English silver and the extraordinary Portuguese centerpiece, a present from a grateful Portugal to its liberator, are exhibited. The residence was designed by Robert Adam and built in the late 18th century. The museum is open Tuesday, Wednesday, Thursday, and Saturday from 10 a.m. to 6 p.m.; Sunday, 2:30 to 6 p.m. Admission is 60p (90¢) for adults, 30p (45¢) for children. Tube: Hyde Park Corner.

The **Commonwealth Institute,** Kensington High Street, W.8 (tel. 603-4535), is a center of information on the 49 countries of the modern Commonwealth. There are continuous exhibitions on each country, and you can capture some of the atmosphere and flavor of places as different as Sri Lanka and Papua, New Guinea, Canada, and Kenya, India, and Jamaica. Admission is free. There is also an Arts Centre which runs programs of non-European arts events: dance, drama, music, and poetry; art galleries; a Flags Restaurant; a licensed bar; the "Soma" bookshop; and a library information service. Hours are 10 a.m. to 5:30 p.m. Monday to Saturday, on Sunday from 2 to 5 p.m. Tube: Kensington High Street. You can also take bus 9 from Piccadilly.

The **National Army Museum,** Royal Hospital Road, S.W.3 (tel. 730-0717), in Chelsea, traces the history of the British land forces 1485, to 1982, the Indian Army, and Colonial land forces. (The Imperial War Museum above concerns itself with World Wars I and II.) The army museum stands next door to Wren's Royal Hospital. The museum backers agreed to begin the collection at the year 1485, because that was the date of the formation of the Yeomen of the Guard. The saga of the forces of the East India Company is traced, beginning in 1602 and going up to Indian independence in 1947. The gory and the glory—it's all here, everything from Florence Nightingale's lamp to the French Eagle captured in a cavalry charge at Waterloo, even the staff cloak wrapped round the dying Wolfe at Québec. Naturally, there are the "cases of the heroes," mementos of such outstanding men as the Dukes of Marlborough and Wellington. But the field soldier isn't neglected either. One gallery traces British military history from 1914 to 1982. The museum is open weekdays from 10 a.m. to 5:30 p.m., on Sunday from 2 to 5:30 p.m. It is closed on New Year's Day, Good Friday, from December 24 to 26, and on the May bank holiday. Tube: Sloane Square.

In London's Barbican district near St. Paul's Cathedral, the **Museum of London,** 150 London Wall, E.C.2 (tel. 600-3699), allows visitors to trace the history of London from prehistoric times to the present through relics, costumes, household effects, maps, and models. Exhibits are arranged so that visitors can begin and end their chronological stroll through 250,000 years at the main entrance to the museum. You can see the death mask of Oliver Cromwell, but the pièce de résistance is the Lord Mayor's coach, built in 1757 and weighing in at three tons. This gilt-and-red horse-drawn vehicle is like a fairytale coach. Visitors can also see the Great Fire of London in living color and sound; a reconstructed Roman dining room with the kitchen and utensils; cell doors from Newgate Prison made famous by Charles Dickens; and perhaps most amazing of all, a shop display with pre-World War II prices on the items.

The museum overlooks London's Roman and medieval walls and, in all, has something from every era before and after, including little Victorian shops and recreations of what life was like in the Iron Age. Anglo-Saxons, Vikings, Normans—they're all there, arranged on two floors around a central courtyard. With quick labels for museum sprinters, more extensive ones for those who want to study, and still deeper details for scholars, this museum, built at a cost of some $18 million, is an enriching experience for *everybody*.

At least an hour should be allowed for a full (but still quick) visit to the museum. Free lectures on London's past are given during lunch hours. These aren't given daily, but it's worth inquiring at the entrance hall. In addition, the museum holds special exhibitions. You can reach the museum by going up to the elevated pedestrian precinct at the corner of London Wall and Aldersgate, five minutes from St. Paul's. The museum also has a licensed restaurant, Milburns, overlooking a garden. It is open Tuesday through Saturday from 10 a.m. to 6 p.m.; on Sunday from 2 to 6 p.m.; closed Monday. Admission is free. Tube: St. Paul's or Barbican.

The **London Transport Museum,** Covent Garden, W.C.2 (tel. 379-6344), is in a splendidly restored Victorian building which formerly housed the flower market. Horse buses, motorbuses, trams, trolley buses, railway vehicles, models, maps, posters, photographs, and audio-visual displays illustrate the fascinating story of the evolution of London's transport systems and how this has affected the growth of London. There are a number of unique working displays. You can "drive" a tube train, a tram, and a bus, and also operate full-size signaling equipment. The exhibits include a reconstruction of George Shillibeer's omnibus of 1829, a steam locomotive which ran on the world's first underground railway, and a coach from the first deep-level electric railway. The museum is open every day of the year except the three-day Christmas holidays from 10 a.m. to 6 p.m. Admission charges are £2.20 ($3.30) for adults and £1 ($1.50) for children.

The museum sells merchandise of London Transport, including maps of the London Underground system in its original size, books, souvenirs, photos, and reproductions of the famous London Transport poster collection in print and postcard form (see Shopping section). Tube: Covent Garden.

The **Royal Air Force Museum,** Grahame Park Way, Hendon, N.W.7 (tel. 205-2266), covers all aspects of the history of the Royal Air Force and its predecessors and much of the history of aviation in general. The museum lies on ten acres of the former historic airfield at Hendon. Its aircraft hall, which occupies two hangars dating from World War I, displays some 40 aircraft from the museum's total collection of more than 100 machines. Admission is free; hours are weekdays from 10 a.m. to 6 p.m. and on Sunday from 2 to 6 p.m. The nearest Underground is Colindale on the Northern Line. The entrance is via the M1, the A41 (Aerodrome Road off Watford Way), or the A5 (Colindale Avenue off Edgware Road).

On a site adjacent to the main building is the **Battle of Britain Museum.** It contains a unique collection of British, German, and Italian aircraft which were engaged in the great air battle of 1940. The museum is a national memorial to the victorious forces and especially to "The Few." Machines include the Spitfire, Hurricane, Gladiator, Defiant, Blenheim, and Messerschmitt BF109. A central feature of the exhibition is a replica of the No. 11 Group Operations Room at RAF Uxbridge. Equipment, uniforms, medals, documents, relics, works of art, and other memorabilia of the period are included in the permanent memorial to the men, women, and machines involved in the air battle. Admission is £1 ($1.45) for adults, 50p (75¢) for children.

Also in the same complex is the massive **Bomber Command Museum,** with its striking display of famous bomber aircraft including the Lancaster, Wellington, B-17 Flying Fortress, Mosquito, and Vulcan. Admission is £1 ($1.50) for adults, 50p (75¢) for children.

The **National Postal Museum,** King Edward Building, King Edward Street, E.C.1 (tel. 432-3851), attracts philatelists from all over the world—and even vaguely kindred spirits. Actually part of the Post Office, it features permanent exhibitions of the stamps of Great Britain and the world and special displays of stamps and postal history, changing every few months, according to certain themes. For example, one exhibition featured the 50th anniversary of the completion of airmail links throughout the Commonwealth, with the establishment of the through flight from London to Australia in 1934. The museum is open from 9:30 a.m. to 4:30 p.m. Monday through Thursday; to 4 p.m. on Friday. Admission is free. Tube: St. Paul's.

The **Science Museum,** Exhibition Road, S.W.7 (tel. 589-3456), traces the development of both science and industry, particularly their application to everyday life —meaning that there's a minimum of "pure science." Exhibits vary from models and facsimiles to the actual machines. You'll find Stephenson's original *Rocket,* the tiny locomotive that won a race against all competitors and thus became the world's prototype railroad engine. The earliest motor-propelled airplanes, a cavalcade of antique cars, and steam engines from their crudest to their most refined form may be seen here. The greatest fascination is with the working models of machinery (visitor operable by push buttons). The plastics gallery tells the story of plastic from its invention to the present day. The museum also has a "launch pad," a hands-on gallery of experiments and demonstrations in technology and science. The museum is open Monday to Saturday from 10 a.m. to 6 p.m.; on Sunday from 2:30 to 6 p.m. Admission is free. Take the tube to South Kensington or bus 14.

The Greatest of the Galleries

National Portrait Gallery, Orange Street, W.C.2 (tel. 930-1552; entrance around the corner from the National Gallery on Trafalgar Square, tube to Trafalgar Square), gives you a chance to outstare the stiff-necked greats and not-so-greats of English history. In a gallery of remarkable and unremarkable portraits, a few paintings tower over the rest, including Sir Joshua Reynolds first portrait of Samuel Johnson ("a man of most dreadful appearance"). Among the best are Nicholas Hilliard's miniature of a most handsome Sir Walter Raleigh; a full-length Elizabeth I (painted to commemorate her visit to Sir Henry Lee at Ditchley in 1592), along with the Holbein cartoon of Henry VIII (sketched for a family portrait that hung, before it was burned, in the Privy Chamber in Whitehall Palace). You'll see a portrait of William Shakespeare with a gold earring. The artist is unknown, but the portrait bears the claim of being the most "authentic contemporary likeness" of its subject of any work yet known. The John Hayls portrait of Samuel Pepys adorns one wall. Whistler could not only paint a portrait, he could also be the subject of one. One of the most unusual portraits in the gallery—a group of the three Brontë sisters (Charlotte, Emily, Anne)—was painted by their brother, Branwell. A turbaned, idealized portrait of Lord Byron (painted from life by Thomas Phillips) is pleased with itself. Treat yourself to the likeness of the incomparable Aubrey Beardsley. For a finale, Princess Diana is on the Royal Landing. The gallery is open from 10 a.m. to 5 p.m. Monday to Friday, from 10 a.m. to 6 p.m. on Saturday, and from 2 to 6 p.m. on Sunday. Special exhibitions are held throughout the year. Tube: Charing Cross.

The **Wallace Collection,** Manchester Square, off Wigmore Street, W.1 (tel. 935-0687), has an outstanding collection of works of art of all kinds bequeathed to the nation by Lady Wallace in 1897 and still displayed in the house of its founders. There are important pictures by artists of all European schools, including Titian, Rubens, Van Dyck, Rembrandt, Hals, Velázquez, Murillo, Reynolds, Gainsborough, and Delacroix. Representing the art of France in the 18th century are paintings by Watteau, Boucher, and Fragonard, and sculpture, furniture, goldsmiths' work, and Sèvres porcelain. Valuable collections also are found of majolica and European and Oriental arms and armor. Frans Hals's *Laughing Cavalier* is the most famous painting in the collection, but Pieter de Hooch's *A Boy Bringing Pomegranates* and Watteau's *The Music Party* are also well known. Other notable works include Canaletto's views of Venice (especially *Bacino di San Marco*), Rembrandt's *Titus,* and Gainsborough's *Mrs. Robinson (Perdita).* Boucher's portrait of the Marquise de Pompadour is also worthy. The Wallace Collection may be viewed daily from 10 a.m. to 5 p.m., on Sunday from 2 to 5 p.m. Closed Christmas holidays, New Year's Day, Good Friday, and the first Monday in May. Tube: Bond Street.

The **Courtauld Institute Galleries,** Woburn Square, W.C.1 (tel. 580-1015), is the home of the art collection of London University, noted chiefly for its superb impressionist and post-impressionist works. It has eight works by Cézanne alone, including his *A Man with a Pipe*. Other notable works include Seurat's *Young Woman Powdering Herself*, Van Gogh's self-portrait (with ear bandaged), a nude by the great Modigliani, Gauguin's *Day-Dreaming*, Monet's *Fall at Argenteuil*. Toulouse-Lautrec's most delicious *Tête-à-Tête*, and Manet's *Bar at the Folies Bergère*. The galleries also feature classical works, including a *Virgin and Child* by Bernardino Luini, a Botticelli, a Giovanni Bellini, a Veronese, a triptych by the Master of Flémâlle, works by Pieter Brueghel the Elder, Massys, Parmigianino, 32 oils by Rubens, oil sketches by Tiepolo, three landscapes by Kokoschka, and wonderful old master drawings (especially Michelangelo, Brueghel, and Rembrandt). The collection may be viewed Monday to Saturday from 10 a.m. to 5 p.m., on Sunday from 2 to 5 p.m. Admission is £1.50 ($2.25) for adults, 50p (75¢) for children. Tube: Euston Square, Goodge Street, or Russell Square.

The **Hayward Gallery,** South Bank, S.E.1 (tel. 629-9495), presents a changing program of major exhibitions organized by the Arts Council of Great Britain. The gallery forms part of the South Banks Arts Centre, which also includes the Royal Festival Hall, the Queen Elizabeth Hall, the Purcell Room, the National Film Theatre, and the National Theatre. Admission to the gallery costs about £2.50 ($3.75), with a one-day cheaper entry, usually on Monday, and in the evening Tuesday and Wednesday between 6 and 8 p.m. Hours are Monday to Wednesday from 10 a.m. to 8 p.m., Thursday to Saturday from 10 a.m. to 6 p.m., and on Sunday from noon to 6 p.m. The gallery is closed between exhibitions, so check the listings before crossing the Thames. Tube: Waterloo Station.

The **Serpentine Gallery,** Kensington Gardens, W.2 (tel. 402-6075). The Old Teahouse, near the Albert Memorial, was an inspired choice for the Arts Council's London platform for professional artists whose work has not been seen in commercial galleries. Its four large rooms, spacious and adaptable, are well suited to the experimental, and large-scale works are often shown here. The fact that the gallery is in popular parkland not only means that there are excellent adjacent outdoor facilities for sculpture and events, but that it draws a crowd who generally would not think of going to a Bond Street exhibition. Usually a minimum of four artists is shown at a time and given freedom to use the space as they wish. The exhibitions are principally for those interested in the most outstanding contemporary trends and tendencies, and are carefully watched by the more far-sighted commercial gallery owners. The gallery has a winter program as well, and stages some international shows, exhibitions by more established artists, and occasional retrospectives devoted to just one artist. The gallery is open daily from 10 a.m. to 6 p.m., April through October, and 10 a.m. to 15 minutes before dusk during November through March. Admission is free. Closed Good Friday, the three-day Christmas holidays, and New Year's Day. Tube: High Street Kensington.

Homes of Famous Writers

Dr. Johnson's House: The Queen Anne house of the famed lexicographer is at 17 Gough Square, E.C.4 (tel. 353-3745). It'll cost you £1 ($1.45), and it's well worth it. Students and children pay 50p (75¢). It was there that Dr. Johnson and his able copyists compiled his famous dictionary. The 17th-century building has been painstakingly restored (surely "Dear Tetty," if not Boswell, would approve). Although Johnson lived at Staple Inn in Holborn and at a number of other houses, the Gough Square house is the only one of his residences remaining in London. He occupied it from 1748 to 1759. It is open from 11 a.m. to 5:30 p.m. Monday through Saturday, May through September, closing half an hour earlier off-season. Take the tube to Blackfriars, then walk up New Bridge Street, turning left onto Fleet. Gough Square is a tiny, hidden square, north of the "street of ink."

Carlyle's House: 24 Cheyne Row, S.W.3 (tel. 352-7087), in Chelsea (bus 11, 19, 22, or 39). For nearly half a century, from 1834 to 1881, the handsome author of *The French Revolution* and other works, known as "the Sage of Chelsea," along with his letter-writing wife, took up abode in this modest 1708 terraced house, about three-quarters of a block from the Thames, near the Chelsea Embankment. Still standing and furnished essentially as it was in Carlyle's day, the house was described by his wife as being "of most antique physiognomy, quite to our humour; all wainscotted, carved and queer-looking, roomy, substantial, commodious, with closets to satisfy any Blue-beard." Now who could improve on that? The second floor contains the drawing room of Mrs. Carlyle. But the most interesting chamber is the not-so-soundproof "sound-proof" study in the skylit attic. Filled with Carlyle memorabilia—his books, a letter from Disraeli, a writing chair, even his death mask—this is the cell where the author labored over his *Frederick the Great* manuscript. The Cheyne (pronounced Chainey) Row house may be visited Wednesday to Sunday from the end of March to the end of October from 11 a.m. to 5 p.m. Admission is £1.40 ($2.10) for adults, half price for children up to 16 years of age. Closed November through March. Nearest tube, Sloane Square, is a long way off.

Dickens's House: In Bloomsbury stands the house of the great English author Charles Dickens, accused in his time of "supping on the horrors" of Victoriana. Born in 1812 in what is now Portsmouth, Dickens is known to have lived at 48 Doughty St., W.C.1 (tel. 405-2127; tube to Russell Square), from 1837 to 1839. Unlike some of the London town houses of famous men (Wellington, Soane), the Bloomsbury house is simple, the embodiment of middle-class restraint. The house contains an extensive library of Dickensiana, including manuscripts and letters second in importance only to the Forster Collection in the Victoria and Albert Museum. In his study are his desk and chair from the study at Gad's Hill Place, Rochester, on which he wrote his last two letters before he died (also the table from his Swiss chalet on which he wrote the last unfinished fragment of *The Mystery of Edwin Drood*). Dickens's drawing room on the first floor has been reconstructed, as have the still room, wash house, and wine cellar in the basement. The house is open daily, except Sunday and bank holidays, from 10 a.m. to 5 p.m. Admission is £1.50 ($2.25) for adults and 50p (75¢) for children.

Hampstead

Hampstead Heath, N.W.3, is hundreds of acres of wild and unfenced royal parkland about 4 miles north from the center of London, so elevated that on a clear day you can see St. Paul's Cathedral and even the hills of Kent south of the Thames. It is the scene of big one-day fairs in good weather, and it has for years drawn Londoners on such weekend pursuits as kite-flying, sunning, fishing in the ponds, swimming, and picnicking, and it is a favorite place for joggers. It was the common of Hampstead Manor in the time of King Charles II, a good ride out from London. Tube: Hampstead Heath.

Hampstead Village developed from the rural area around some of the substantial houses which were built in the area. From a village, a fashionable spa town developed in the 18th century, giving the name to Well Walk and other parts of the growing town. With the coming of the Underground in 1907, its attractions as a place to live even for those who went frequently into the City, became widely known, with writers, artists, architects, musicians, and scientists coming to join earlier residents, some of their own kind. The original village, on the side of a hill, still has pleasing features such as the old roads, lanes, places, alleys, steps, rises, courts, and groves to be strolled through and enjoyed.

Good Regency and Georgian houses were built in this village just 20 minutes by tube from Piccadilly Circus with its palatable mix of history-rich pubs, toy shops, and chic boutiques, as seen along Flask Walk, a pedestrian mall.

Many eminent figures in the literary world have lived in Hampstead, and some still do, either full- or parttime. Keats, D.H. Lawrence, Rabindranath Tagore, Shelley, Robert Louis Stevenson, Kingsley Amis, and John Le Carré, to name a few.

Keats's House: The darling of romantics, John Keats lived for only two years at Wentworth Place, Keats Grove, N.W.3 (tel. 435-2062; take the tube to Belsize Park or Hampstead or bus 24 from Trafalgar Square). But for the poet, that was something like two-fifths of his creative life, as he died in Rome of tuberculosis at the age of 25 (1821). In Hampstead Keats wrote two of his most celebrated *Odes*, in praise of a Grecian Urn and to the Nightingale. In the garden stands an ancient mulberry tree which the poet must have known. His Regency house is well preserved, and contains the manuscripts of his last sonnet (*"Bright star, would I were steadfast as thou art"*), a final letter to the mother of Fanny Brawne (his correspondence to his Hampstead neighbor, who nursed him while he was ill, forms part of his legend), and a portrait of him on his death bed in a little house on the Spanish Steps in Rome. Wentworth Place is open weekdays from 10 a.m. to 1 p.m. and 2 to 6 p.m.; Sunday, Easter, and spring and summer bank holidays hours are 2 to 5 p.m. Admission is free. Closed Christmas Day, Boxing Day, New Year's, Good Friday, Easter Eve, and May first Monday. Tube: Hampstead.

Kenwood House, Hampstead Lane, N.W.3 (tel. 348-1286), on the rim of Hampstead Heath, handsome with its columned portico, was built as a gentleman's country home around the start of the 18th century. It became the seat of Lord Mansfield in 1754 and was enlarged and decorated by the famous Scottish architect, Robert Adam, in 1764. All subsequent additions were done in the Adam style. In 1927, it was given to the nation by Lord Iveagh, together with his collection of pictures. The Adam stamp is strong in the restored oval library, painted in rose, blue, white, and gold, and in the Orangery and the music and arts rooms. The rooms contain some fine neoclassical furniture, but the main attractions are the Old Masters and the work of British artists. You can see paintings by Rembrandt (*Self-Portrait in Old Age*), Vermeer, Turner, Franz Hals, Cuyp, Crome, Gainsborough, Reynolds, Romney, Raeburn, Guardi, and Angelika Kauffmann, plus a portrait of the *Earl of Mansfield, Lord Chief Justice* who made Kenwood an important home. In the Coach House, where there is a cafeteria, stands a 19th-century family coach that carried 15 persons comfortably. The house is open daily from 10 a.m. to 7 p.m. April to September; from 10 a.m. to 5 p.m. in February, March, and October; and from 10 a.m. to 4 p.m. November to January. Admission is free. Closed Christmas Eve, Christmas Day, and Good Friday.

On the south lawn, looking toward the lake, symphony concerts are held in summer, and chamber music concerts are presented in the Orangery. A charge is made for the concerts. Tube: Hampstead.

The **Freud Museum,** 20 Maresfield Gardens, N.W.3 (tel. 435-2002), is a spacious, three-story red-brick house in which Sigmund Freud, father of psychoanalysis, lived after fleeing Vienna in 1938 because of the Nazis' persecution of the Jews. After his death at the age of 82, it was the home of his daughter, Anna, whose work in child psychiatry is widely known. During Freud's life and until the death of Anna in 1982, the house was visited by leading scientists, by noted Zionist Chaim Weizmann, and by writers and other persons eminent in their fields. Dali sketched Freud's portrait here. The two lower floors of the museum, opened in early 1986, contain his library, a collection of 1800s antiquities, and the couch covered with an Oriental carpet on which patients lay. The museum is open Monday to Saturday from 10 a.m. to 5 p.m. and on Sunday from 1 to 5 p.m. Admission is £1.50 ($2.25). Tube: Finchley Road.

The Parks of London

London's parklands easily rate as the greatest, most wonderful system of "green lungs" of any large city on the globe. Not as rigidly artificial as the parks of Paris, those of London are maintained with a loving care and lavish artistry that puts their American equivalents to shame. Above all, they've been kept safe from land-hungry building firms and city councils, and still offer patches of real countryside right in the heart of the metropolis. Maybe there's something to be said for inviolate "royal" property, after all. Because that's what most of London's parks are.

Largest of them—and one of the biggest in the world—is **Hyde Park,** W.2. With the adjoining Kensington Gardens, it covers 636 acres of central London with velvety lawns interspersed with ponds, flowerbeds, and trees. Hyde Park was once a favorite deer-hunting ground of Henry VII. Running through the width is a 41-acre lake known as the Serpentine, where you can row, sail model boats, or swim—providing you're not expecting it to be like Florida water temperatures. Rotten Row, a 1½-mile sand track, is reserved for horseback riding and on Sunday attracts some skilled equestrians.

Kensington Gardens, W.2, blending with Hyde Park, border on the grounds of Kensington Palace. Kensington Gardens also contain the celebrated statue of Peter Pan, with the bronze rabbits that toddlers are always trying to kidnap. It also harbors Albert Memorial, that Victorian extravaganza.

East of Hyde Park, across Piccadilly, stretch **Green Park** and **St. James's Park,** S.W.1, forming an almost unbroken chain of landscaped beauty. This is an ideal area for picnics, and you'll find it hard to believe that this was once a festering piece of swamp near the leper hospital. There is a romantic lake, stocked with a variety of ducks and some surprising pelicans, descendants of the pair that the Russian ambassador presented to Charles II back in 1662.

Regent's Park, N.W.1, covers most of the district by that name, north of Baker Street and Marylebone Road. Designed by the 18th-century genius John Nash to surround a palace of the prince regent that never materialized, this is the most classically beautiful of London's parks. The core is a rose garden planted around a small lake alive with waterfowl and spanned by humped Japanese bridges. In early summer the rose perfume in the air is as heady as wine. Regent's Park also contains an Open Air Theatre and the London Zoo.

Landmark Churches

St. Martin-in-the-Fields, overlooking Trafalgar Square W.C.2, is the Royal Parish Church, dear to the heart of many a Britisher, especially the homeless. The present, classically inspired church, with its famous steeple, dates back to 1726; James Gibbs, a pupil of Wren's, was its architect. But the origins of the church go back to the 11th century. Among the congregation in years past was George I, who was actually a churchwarden, unique for an English sovereign. Because of St. Martin's position in the theater district, it has drawn many actors to its door—none more notable than Nell Gwynne, the mistress of Charles II. On her death in 1687, she was buried there. Throughout the war, many Londoners rode out an uneasy night in the crypt, while blitz bombs rained down overhead. One, in 1940, blasted out all the windows. Tube: Charing Cross.

St. Etheldreda's, Britain's oldest Roman Catholic church, lies in Ely Place, Clerkenwell, E.C.1, leading off Charterhouse Street at Holborn Circus. Built in 1251, it was mentioned by the Bard in both *Richard II* and *Richard III*. It was one of the survivors of the Great Fire of 1666. The church was built and was the property of the Diocese of Ely in the days when many bishops had their episcopal houses in London rather than in the actual cathedral cities in which they held their sees. Until this century, the landlord of Ye Olde Mitre public house near Ely Place where the church stands had to obtain his license from the Justices of Cambridgeshire rather than in London, and even today the place is still a private road, with impressive iron gates and a lodge for the gate-keeper, all administered by six commissioners who are elected. St. Etheldreda, whose name is sometimes shortened to St. Audrey, was a seventh-century king's daughter who left her husband and turned to religion, establishing an abbey on the Isle of Ely. The name St. Audrey is the source of the word *tawdry,* from cheap trinkets sold at the annual fair honoring the saint. St. Etheldreda's is made up of a crypt and an upper church, catering to working people and visitors who come to pray. It has a distinguished musical tradition, with the 11 a.m. mass on Sunday sung in Latin. Other mass times are 9 a.m. and 6 p.m. on Sunday and at 8 a.m. and 1 p.m. Monday to Friday. For information about this historic church and the treasures to be seen within, get in touch with the Clerkenwell Heritage Centre, 33 St. John's Square, E.C.1 (tel. 250-1039). Tube: Farringdon.

Along the Thames

There is a row of fascinating attractions lying on, across, and alongside the River Thames. All of London's history and development is linked with this winding ribbon of water. The Thames connects the city with the sea, from which it drew its wealth and its power. For centuries the river was London's highway and main street.

Some of the bridges that span the Thames are household words. London Bridge, which, contrary to the nursery rhyme, has never "fallen down," but has been dismantled and shipped to the United States, ran from the Monument (a tall pillar commemorating the Great Fire of 1666) to Southwark Cathedral, parts of which date back to 1207.

Its neighbor to the east is the still-standing **Tower Bridge,** E.1 (tel. 407-0922), one of the city's most celebrated landmarks and possibly the most photographed and painted bridge on earth. Tower Bridge was built during 1886 to 1894 with two towers 800 feet apart, joined by footbridges that provide glass-covered walkways for the public who can enter the north tower, take the elevator to the walkway, cross the river to the south tower, and return to street level. It's a photographer's dream, with interesting views of St. Paul's, the Tower of London, and in the distance, Big Ben and the Houses of Parliament. You can also visit the main engine room with its Victorian boiler and steam-pumping engines, which raise and lower the roadway across the river.

Models show how the 1,000-ton arms of the bridge can be raised in 1½ minutes to allow ships passage upstream. These days the bridge is only opened once or twice a week, and you'll be lucky to catch the real thing. Admission is £2 ($3) for adults, £1 ($1.50) for children. It is open daily in summer from 10 a.m. to 6:30 p.m. (to 4:45 p.m. in winter). Tube: Tower Hill.

The piece of river between the site of the old London Bridge and the Tower Bridge marks the city end of the immense row of docks stretching 26 miles to the coast. Most of them are no longer in use, but they have long been known as the Port of London.

But the Thames meant more to London than a port. It was also her chief commercial thoroughfare and a royal highway, the only regal one in the days of winding cobblestone streets. Every royal procession was undertaken by barge—gorgeously painted and gilded vessels, which you can still see at the Maritime Museum at Greenwich. All important prisoners were delivered to the Tower by water—it eliminated the chance of an ambush by their friends in one of the narrow, crooked alleys surrounding the fortress. When Henry VIII had his country residence at Hampton Court, there was a constant stream of messenger boats shuttling between his other riverside palaces all the way to Greenwich. His illustrious daughter, Queen Elizabeth I, revved up the practice to such a degree that a contemporary chronicler complained he couldn't spit in the Thames for fear of hitting a royal craft. The royal boats and much of the commercial traffic disappeared when the streets were widened enough for horse coaches to maintain a decent pace.

Particular note should be taken of the striking removal of pollution from the Thames in the past three decades. The river, so polluted in the 1950s that no marine life could exist in it, can now lay claim to being "the cleanest metropolitan estuary in the world," with many varieties of fish, even salmon, back as happy denizens of these waters.

The Thames Flood Barrier

Since its official opening in 1984, the engineering spectacle known as the Thames Flood Barrier has drawn increasing crowds to the site, at a point in the river known as Woolwich Reach in east London, where the Thames is a straight stretch about a third of a mile in width. For centuries, the Thames estuary has, from time to time, brought tidal surges which have on occasion caused disastrous flooding at Woolwich, Hammersmith, Whitehall, and Westminster, and elsewhere within the river's flood reaches. The flooding peril has increased during this century from a number of natural causes. These include the unstoppable rise of tide levels in the Thames, surge tides from the Atlantic, and the down-tilt of the country of some 12 inches a century. Also London is sinking at about that same rate into its clay foundations.

All this led to the construction, beginning in 1975, of a great barrier with huge piers linking mammoth steel gates, smaller rising sector gates, and falling radial gates, all of which when in use make a solid steel wall about the height of a five-story building, which completely dams the waters of the Thames, keeping the surge tides from passage up the estuary. The gates are operated every month or so to remove river silt and be sure the operation is smooth.

London Launches offers trips to the barrier, operating from Westminster Pier. Four trips sail daily in summer at 10 and 11:15 a.m. and at 1:30 and 2:45 p.m. Except on the last trip, passengers can get off at the barrier pier, visit the Barrier Centre, and return by a later boat or by bus. An audio-visual show depicting the need for the barrier and its operation is presented at the center, where there are also a souvenir shop, a snackbar, and a cafeteria. Round-trip fare from Westminster Pier is £3.50 ($5.25) for adults, £2 ($3) for children. For further information, phone 740-8263.

2. Shopping

In London, "a nation of shopkeepers" displays an enormous variety of wares, and you can pick up values ranging from a still-functioning hurdy-gurdy to a replica of the crown jewels. For the best buys, search out the sensational clothing, as well as traditional and well-tailored men's and women's suits, small antiques and curios, woolens, tweeds, tartans, rare books, and Liberty silks, to name just a few.

Most stores are open from 9 a.m. to 5:30 p.m. Monday to Saturday, with late shopping until 8 p.m. on Thursday. In the East End, around Aldgate and Whitechapel, many shops are open on Sunday from 9 a.m. to 2 p.m. There are a few all-night stores, mostly in the Bayswater section.

Here's a brief survey of some of the attractive merchandise offered:

ANTIQUE MARKETS (FOR CURIOS): Billed as the world's largest covered antique market, **Chelsea Antique Market,** 245–253 King's Rd., S.W.3 (tel. 352-9695), is a gold mine where you can pan for some hidden little treasure. Sheltered inside a rambling old building, it offers endless browsing possibilities for the curio addict, stall after stall extending along a serpentine maze. In this ever-changing display you're likely to run across fur coats, Staffordshire dogs, shaving mugs, old books, prints, maps, paintings, Edwardian buckles and clasps, ivory-handled razors, old velours and lace gowns (most chic), wooden tea caddies, antique pocket watches, wormy Tudoresque chests, silver snuff boxes, and grandfather clocks. The market is open Monday through Saturday from 10 a.m. to 6 p.m. Closed Sunday. Tube: Sloane Square.

Grays and **Grays in the Mews Antique Markets,** 58 Davies St. and 1–7 Davies Mews, W.1 (tel. 629-7034), just south of Oxford Street and opposite Bond Street Tube Station, are in a triangle formed by Davies Street, South Molton Lane, and Davies Mews. The two old buildings have been converted into walk-in stands with independent dealers. The term "antique" here covers items from oil paintings to, say, the

1894 edition of the *Encyclopaedia Britannica*. Also sold here are exquisite antique jewelry, silver, gold, antiquarian books, maps and prints, paintings and drawings, bronzes and ivories, arms and armor, Victorian and Edwardian toys, furniture, art nouveau and art deco, antique luggage, antique lace, scientific instruments, craftsmen's tools, and Oriental, Persian, and Islamic pottery, porcelain, miniatures, and antiquities. There is also a whole floor of repair workshops and a Bureau de Change. Tube: Bond Street.

Alfie's Antique Market, 13–25 Church St., N.W.8 (tel. 723-6066), is one of the biggest and cheapest covered markets in London, and it's where many dealers come to buy. Alfie's is named after the father of Bennie Gray, the owner of Grays and Grays in the Mews Antique Markets and former owner of the Antique Hypermarket Kensington and Antiquarius. The market contains more than 200 stalls, showrooms, and workshops on 20,000 square feet of floor, plus an enormous, 70-unit basement area. Tube: Marylebone or Edgware Road.

Antiquarius, 135–141 King's Rd., S.W.3, echoes the artistic diversity of the street on which it is located. More than 200 standholders offer specialized and general antiques of all periods from ancient times to the 1950s, including statuary and metalwork, early domestic and craftsmen's tools, timepieces, silver and silver plate, precious and costume jewelry, period clothes, lace, theatrical items, porcelain, glass, early writing and travel accessories, tiles, ethnic items. Delft and faïence, antiquarian books and prints, fine paintings, and small furniture. It's open Monday to Saturday from 10 a.m. to 6 p.m. Tube: Sloane Square. Bus 11, 19, or 22 will also take you there, or you can travel on bus 137, alighting at Sloane Square.

ARTS AND CRAFTS: On a Sunday morning along **Bayswater Road,** for more than a mile, pictures, collages, and craft items are hung on the railings along the edge of Hyde Park and Kensington Gardens. If the weather is right, start at Marble Arch and walk and walk, shopping or just sightseeing as you go along. Along Piccadilly, you'll see much of the same thing by walking along the railings of Green Park on a Saturday afternoon.

The **Crafts Council,** 12 Waterloo Pl., S.W.1 (tel. 930-4811), is a public body that exists to promote crafts in England and Wales. It has galleries which offer a broad program of changing craft exhibitions from British domestic pottery to American traditional patchwork. Most exhibitions are free; otherwise concessions are available. Other facilities include a lively information center which can direct you to craft events throughout Britain, a slide library, a book stall, and a coffee bar selling excellent coffee. (Note: The Crafts Council runs a quality craft shop at the Victoria and Albert Museum, South Kensington.) The galleries and information center are open Tuesday to Saturday from 10 a.m. to 5 p.m. and on Sunday from 2 to 5 p.m. Tube: Charing Cross or Piccadilly Circus.

BEAUCHAMP PLACE: Of all the shopping streets of London, one has surfaced near the top. It's Beauchamp Place (pronounced Beecham), S.W.3, a block off Brompton Road, near Harrods department store. The *Herald Tribune* called it "a higgledy-piggledy of old-fashioned and trendy, quaint and with it, expensive and cheap. It is deliciously unspecialized." Whatever you're looking for—a place to revamp your old alligator bag, reject china, crystal, and pottery, secondhand silver, collages, custom-tailored men's shirts—you should find it here. It's pure fun even if you don't buy anything. Should you get hungry, you'll find some of the best-known restaurants in London here.

BOOKS: For a wide choice of reading matter, go to **W. & G. Foyle, Ltd.,** 113–119 Charing Cross Rd., W.C.2 (tel. 439-8501), which claims to be the world's largest bookstore, with an impressive array of hardcovers and paperbacks, including travel books and maps. The shop includes records and sheet music. Tube: Leicester Square.

Hatchards Ltd., 187–188 Piccadilly, W.1 (tel. 439-9921), is an old-fashioned looking place on the south side of Piccadilly stuffed with books ranging from expensive first editions through popular fiction and specialist reference book to paperbacks. There are shelves of guidebooks and atlases, cookbooks, and books of puzzles to occupy you on train and plane trips. Tube: Piccadilly Circus.

For history buffs, **The History Bookshop,** 2 The Broadway, corner of Friern Barnet Road and MacDonald Road, N.11 (tel. 368-8568), has thousands of affordable secondhand books on all aspects of history. Open Wednesday to Saturday from 9:30 a.m. to 5:30 p.m. Tube: Arnos Grove.

BRASS RUBBING: There is such a wealth of spectacular brasses in churches and cathedrals up and down the country that the pastime of brass rubbing is becoming more and more popular. The rubbing is made with a metallic wax on paper and can be done in about half an hour. The cost, depending on the size, ranges from around 50p (75¢) up to £10 ($15) for the largest and most important. Materials are provided at the centers which are in all parts of the country, including Stratford-upon-Avon, Oxford, York, Chester, Edinburgh, Coventry, and Chichester. It is wise to telephone ahead if you want to rub a particular brass. A complete list of centers is available from **Historycraft,** Cripps Road, Cirencester, Gloucestershire (tel. 0285/3971).

In London, the **Brass Rubbing Centre,** St. James's Church, Piccadilly, W.1 (tel. 437-6023), offers 70 exact copies of celebrated bronze portraits ready for use. The center furnishes the paper, rubbing materials, and instruction on how to begin your rubbing. It is open all year, except Christmas, from 10 a.m. to 6 p.m. Monday to Saturday, from noon to 6 p.m. on Sunday. Prices for rubbing here start at 50p (75¢) for a small, ten-minute brass, the average price being £3 ($4.50), while a life-size Crusader knight, taking about two hours to complete, costs as much as £9.55 ($14.33). Medieval music is played as you work, and a friendly team helps you make your own masterpiece from this traditional British craft. An enlarged gift area is open, selling brass-rubbing kits for children, budget-priced ready-made rubbings, plaques, a wide variety of books, souvenirs with a heritage theme, posters, and postcards. You can order a shield with your family coat-of-arms. Tube: Piccadilly Circus.

The same company operates a brass-rubbing center at **All Hallows Church by the Tower,** Byward St., E.C.3 (tel. 481-2928). This is run on the same basis as the one at St. James's Church, with material and instruction supplies, but with a smaller collection of brasses. It is open on the same schedule and the prices are the same as given above. Next door to the Tower, this center is a quiet place to relax. The church is a fascinating place with a crypt museum, Roman remains, and traces of early London, including a Saxon wall pre-dating the Tower. Samuel Pepys, famed diarist, climbed the spire of this church to watch the raging fire of London in 1666. Tube: Tower Hill.

BRITISH DESIGN: You can see representative collections of British goods at the **Design Centre,** 28 Haymarket, S.W.1 (tel. 839-8000). Apart from the exhibits, there is a gift shop where you'll find many items that are just right for your friends back home or for yourself to enjoy. You'll see everything from toys to fabrics to household goods to jewelry, all bearing the triangular black-and-white tag that says "Selected for the Design Centre London." Special exhibits of well-designed and often prizewinning items are frequently shown. There is a coffeeshop. The center is open from 10 a.m. to 6 p.m. Monday and Tuesday, from 10 a.m. to 8 p.m. Wednesday to Saturday, and from 1 to 6 p.m. on Sunday. Tube: Piccadilly Circus.

THE BURLINGTON ARCADE: A door west of the Royal Academy of Arts is the Burlington Arcade, W.1, a glass-roofed passage from Piccadilly north for several hundred feet to the next street. It houses dozens of shops, all with tiny upper floors, devoted solely to the sale of luxuries almost beyond imagination. You can take a short stroll through it, or spend a day wandering up and down, protected from the weather, no small item in rainy London. You will see some of the best that London has to offer in the way of jewelry, both antique and modern, clothing for both men and women, fine arts, linen, bric-a-brac, all in profusion. It is possibly the greatest single concentrated bit of luxury shopping in London. Pomp and ceremony may be departing, but if you linger in the arcade until 5:30 in the afternoon, you can watch the beadles, those ever-present attendants, in their black-and-yellow livery and top hats, ceremoniously put in place the iron grills that block off the arcade until 9 the next morning, when they just as ceremoniously remove them, marking the start of the new business day.

If you're in the arcade at 5:30 p.m., you'll see a British tradition of 150 years' standing. A hand-bell called the Burlington Bell is sounded, signaling the end of trading. It's rung by one of the beadles, a member of the smallest police force in England (there are only two members). He's responsible for seeing that shoppers behave in the arcade—no music, no singing, no riotous behavior! Tube: Piccadilly Circus.

CARNABY STREET: Just off Regent, Carnaby, W.1, is a legend, and legends take time to build. Often, by the time they are entrenched, fickle fashion has moved on elsewhere. Alas, Carnaby no longer dominates the world of pace-setting fashion as it did in the '60s. But it is still visited by the young, especially punkers, and some of its shops display lots of claptrap and quick quid merchandise. For value, style, and imagination in design, the Chelsea (King's Road) and Kensington boutiques have left Carnaby far behind. Tube: Oxford Circus.

CHILDREN: The Children's Book Centre Ltd., 229 Kensington High Street, W.8 (tel. 937-6314), trades as **Young World** and is thought to be the largest children's bookshop in the world. A feature of the shop is that fiction, both hardcover and paperback, is arranged according to age including the young-adult reader in the 14-to-16 age group. The large toy department, described as the most imaginative in London, offers a wide selection of toys, games, and stationery for all ages. The shop, open from 9:30 a.m. to 6:30 p.m. Monday through Saturday, also operates a sport and leisure department for the 6-to-14 age group. In the gift section are items suitable for children to give as gifts. Tube: High Street Kensington.

At 237 Kensington High Street, W.8 (tel. 937-7497), near the original store, the same people have a place called **The Tree House,** which is a gift shop for children, with a range of merchandise suitable for youngsters to give as presents to parents, friends, and relatives. It's open Monday through Saturday from 9:30 a.m. to 6 p.m. Tube: High Street Kensington.

Another Young World shop, open from 10 a.m. to 10 p.m., is in the Trocadero Centre, Piccadilly. Tube: Piccadilly Circus.

Hamleys of Regent Street, 188–196 Regent St., W.1 (tel. 734-3161), is an Ali Baba's cave of toys and games ranging from electronic games and Star Wars robots on the ground floor to different toys on each of the other floors—table and card games, teddy bears, nursery animals, dolls, and outdoor games. The Hamleys train races around the walls. Tube: Oxford Circus.

CHINA: The firm of **Lawleys,** 154 Regent St., W.1 (tel. 734-3184), offers a wide range of English bone china, as well as crystal and giftware. They specialize in Royal Doulton, Minton, Royal Crown Derby, Wedgwood, Denby, and Aynsley china; crystal by Webb Corbett, Stuart, Waterford, and Edinburgh; and Lladró figures. Tube: Piccadilly Circus or Oxford Street.

Wedgwood has a large shop at 249 Oxford St., W.1 (tel. 734-5656), at the corner of Regent Street. The staff there will explain their export plan to save you money on your souvenir buying. Besides selling tableware, the store offers inexpensive ashtrays in the traditional blue and white or in sage-green and white. It also carries a collection of china, jewelry, pendants, earrings, and brooches. Tube: Oxford Circus. There are also Wedgwood shops at 158 Regent St. and 173 Piccadilly.

CHOCOLATES: The best chocolates in the world are arguably those made by **Charbonnel et Walker Ltd.,** 28 Old Bond St., W.1 (tel. 491-0939). They'll send messages of thanks or love, spelled out on the chocolates themselves. Fiona Campus, who runs the bow-fronted shop on the corner of the Royal Arcade off Old Bond Street, will help you choose from a variety of centers. A box is priced according to what you decide to put into it. They have ready-made presentation boxes as well. Tube: Green Park. There is a City branch at 27b Throgmorton St., E.C.2 (tel. 588-1306). Tube: Bank.

Prestat, 40 South Molton St., W.1 (tel. 629-4838), is chocolate maker "to Her Majesty the Queen by appointment." Why not impress your friends by taking home a box of assorted Napoleon truffles or an assortment of connoisseur chocolates? Coffee or double mints and brandy cherries may tempt you. The boxes give Prestat products an extra touch of elegance. Tube: Bond Street.

COVENT GARDEN ENTERPRISES: In the Central Market Building, an impressive array of shops, pubs, and other attractions operates. For the shops listed below, take the tube to, of course, Covent Garden.

The **British Crafts Centre,** 43 Earlham St., W.C.2 (tel. 836-6993), is an association of craftspeople that is pioneering in its energetic encouragement of contemporary art work, both traditional and progressive. The galleries at the center are used to house a diverse retail display of members' work that includes glass, rugs, lights, ceramics for both use and decoration, fabric, clothing, papers, metalwork, and jewelry—all selected from the work of the most outstanding artisans currently producing in the country. There is also a program of special exhibitions that focus on innovations in the crafts. These are lone or small group shows from the membership. Many of Britain's best established makers are represented, as well as promising, lesser known ones. The center is open Monday to Friday from 10 a.m. to 5:30 p.m., from 10 a.m. to 5 p.m. on Saturday.

The **General Store,** 111 Long Acre, W.C.2 (tel. 240-0331), offers thousands of ideas for gifts and souvenirs with prices of a few pence to several pounds. It is ideally situated in Covent Garden, and because of the entertainment nature of the area, the store offers extended trading hours: from 10 a.m. to midnight Monday to Saturday, 11 a.m. to 7 p.m. Sunday. The store also features The Green & Pleasant soup and salad restaurant.

The **Market,** Covent Garden, W.C.2 (tel. 836-9136), is a specialty shopping and catering center with 40 stalls selling antiques on Monday and craft goods Tuesday through Saturday. Shopping hours are from 10 a.m. to 7 p.m.

The **Bead Shop,** 43 Neal St., W.C.2 (tel. 240-0931), specializes in loose beads and stones, providing the fittings, clasps, and strings to make necklaces and earrings.

Naturally British, 13 New Row, W.C.2 (tel. 240-0551), is owned and run by Jon Blake, who claims with total conviction that everything he sells is truly British—pottery, jewelry, knitwear, honey, toys, glass, woodwork, rocking horses, and wrought ironwork, products of Britain's Cottage Industry, fine for gifts.

The **Glasshouse,** 65 Long Acre, W.C.2 (tel. 836-9785), sells beautiful glass, and also invites visitors into the workshops to see the craftspeople producing their wares. At street level, passersby can see glassblowers at work. The Glasshouse is open from 10 a.m. to 5:30 p.m. Monday to Friday, from 11 a.m. to 4 p.m. on Saturday.

Penhaligon's, 41 Wellington St., W.C.2 (tel. 836-2150), established in 1870 as

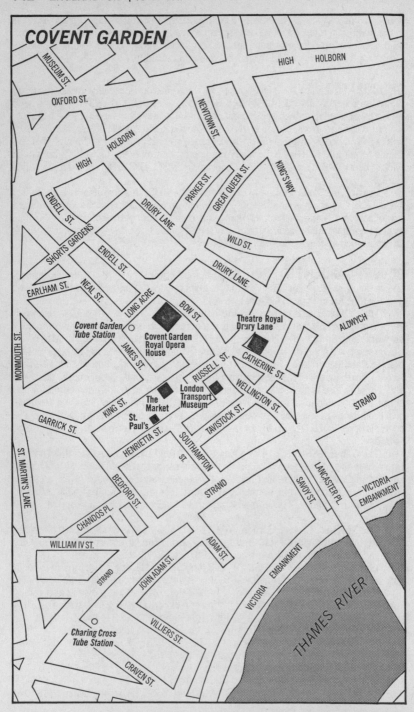

COVENT GARDEN

a Victorian perfumery, holds a Royal Warrant to H.R.H. the Duke of Edinburgh. It offers a large selection of perfumes, aftershave, soap, and bath oils for men and women. Perfect gifts include antique silver perfume bottles.

Behind the Warehouse off Neal Street runs a narrow road leading to **Neal's Yard,** a mews of warehouses which seem to retain some of the old London atmosphere. The open warehouses display such goods as vegetables, health foods, fresh-baked breads, cakes, sandwiches, and in an immaculate dairy, the largest variety of flavored cream cheeses you are likely to encounter.

Coppershop, 48 Neal St., W.C.2 (tel. 836-2984), offers a wide range of exclusively English-manufactured copper goods in the country for the kitchen, the fireplace, and the parlor. Copper pots and pans lined with nickel, stainless steel, or traditional tin are here along with tea kettles, coal scuttles, hods, buckets, and chestnut roasters. Cauldrons and jardinieres for plants, ships' lamps and copper oil lamps, vases and jugs in profusion—all these and many other gifts are to be found in the illustrated mail order catalog or at the Coppershop. It's run by Sally and Michael Crosfield and is an example of vendors of good English products at reasonable prices for those who don't want to go outside London and scour the countryside to find them.

There are a multitude of tiny shops, mostly of a specialized nature, where artists and craftspeople seem to have gathered to form a community. There are silversmiths, pewter, and copperware shops, and several small snackbars and restaurants. It's well worth making your own voyage of discovery finding odd shops and souvenirs to take home.

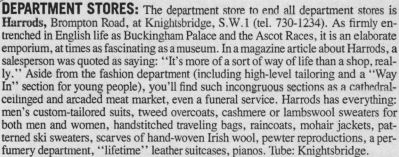

DEPARTMENT STORES: The department store to end all department stores is **Harrods,** Brompton Road, at Knightsbridge, S.W.1 (tel. 730-1234). As firmly entrenched in English life as Buckingham Palace and the Ascot Races, it is an elaborate emporium, at times as fascinating as a museum. In a magazine article about Harrods, a salesperson was quoted as saying: "It's more of a sort of way of life than a shop, really." Aside from the fashion department (including high-level tailoring and a "Way In" section for young people), you'll find such incongruous sections as a cathedral-ceilinged and arcaded meat market, even a funeral service. Harrods has everything: men's custom-tailored suits, tweed overcoats, cashmere or lambswool sweaters for both men and women, handstitched traveling bags, raincoats, mohair jackets, patterned ski sweaters, scarves of hand-woven Irish wool, pewter reproductions, a perfumery department, "lifetime" leather suitcases, pianos. Tube: Knightsbridge.

Much more economical, however, is **Selfridges,** 400 Oxford St. W.1 (tel. 629-1234), one of the biggest department stores in Europe, with more than 550 divisions, selling everything from artificial flowers to groceries. The specialty shops are particularly enticing, with good buys in Irish linen, Wedgwood, leather goods, silver-plated goblets, cashmere and woolen scarves. There's also the Miss Selfridge Boutique, for the young or those who'd like to be. To help you travel light, the Export Bureau will air-freight your purchases to anywhere in the world, completely tax free. On the ground floor, the London Tourist Board will help you find your way around London's sights with plenty of maps, tips, and friendly advice. Tube: Bond Street.

Liberty, on Regent Street, W.1 (tel. 734-1234), is famous for its fabrics, scarves, shawls, and Liberty Presents. On one floor is a choice of fabrics including Liberty's Tana lawn, Varuna wool, silks, cottons, and linens. There is an extensive knitting yarn department featuring among others Anny Blatt, Emu, Argyll, and Velentino, as well as designer kits by Kaffe Fassett and Sandy Black. Liberty is known worldwide for its distinctive shawls and scarves, found in wool, silk, and cotton in the scarf department on the ground floor. Liberty Presents includes gifts for everyone, from rag dolls to photo albums, all made in Tana lawn. The fashion department on the floor above features dresses and separates in Liberty fabrics, while the designer room has labels of couture names such as Christian Dior, Yves St. Laurent, Jasper Conran, and Jean Muir. There is also an extensive selection of furnishing fabrics, bed linens, and table napery on another floor. Other departments include treasures and jewelry from the East and from Africa, modern and arts and crafts furniture, books, pictures, china, and glass. Tube: Oxford Circus.

Marks & Spencer has many branches in London, attracting the British, who know fine buys, especially in woolen goods. The main department store is at 458 Oxford St., W.1 (tel. 935-7954), three short blocks from Marble Arch. There are 268 branches in Britain. This chain has built a reputation for quality and value, and now clothes about 70% of the British population—wholly or partially! It is said that one in every four pairs of socks worn by men in Britain comes from Marks & Spencer. The prices are competitive even when you go as far as cashmere sweaters for women. All goods can be changed if you keep the tab and return it with the goods. Tube: Marble Arch.

In addition, you might visit **BhS** (formerly British Home Stores), on Oxford Street, W.1 (tel. 629-2011), near the Oxford Circus tube station, between John Princes Street and Holles Street. Similar to Marks & Spencer, it is patronized almost exclusively by the English themselves, and is known for its buys in woolens. Look for bargains.

Simpson's, 203 Piccadilly, W.1 (tel. 734-2002), opened in 1936 as the home of DAKS clothing, and it's been going strong ever since. It is known not only for men's wear, but women's fashions, cosmetics, perfume, jewelry, and lingerie. Its basement level men's shoe department, for example, is a model of the way quality shoes should be fitted. Many of the clothes are lighthearted, carefully made, and well suited to casual elegance. More formal clothing is also sold, always by a staff who seems to be polite and thoughtful. Tube: Piccadilly Circus.

THE WORLD'S MOST ELEGANT GROCERY STORE: Down the street from the Ritz, **Fortnum and Mason**, 181 Piccadilly, W.2 (tel. 734-8040), draws the carriage trade, the well-heeled dowager from Mayfair or Belgravia who comes seeking such tinned treasures as pâté de foie gras or a boar's head. She would never set foot in a regular grocery store, but Fortnum and Mason, with its swallow-tailed attendants, is no mere grocery story: it's a British tradition dating back to 1707. In fact, the establishment likes to think that Mr. Fortnum and Mr. Mason "created a union surpassed in its importance to the human race only by the meeting of Adam and Eve." The chocolate and confectionery department is on the first floor (ground floor, to the British). Another of the many departments of interest is luxury leather goods, and there's an enchanting children's carousel on the second floor. In the basement, you can often pick up that odd gift to take home. For recommendations on the restaurant facilities here, see Chapter IV. Look for the Fortnum and Mason clock outside. Tube: Piccadilly Circus or Green Park.

IRISH WARES: Northern Ireland and Eire are united at the **Irish Shop**, 11 Duke St., W.1 (tel. 935-1366), by stocking so much stuff in such a small area. Directed by Charles Bruton and Anthony Tarrant, it is a useful place for those who missed buying souvenirs in Ireland. All products are genuine. Prices are reportedly as close to those you'd pay in Ireland as possible. Merchandise ranges from china to woolens, from tea-cozies to Celtic-design jewelry set with precious stones. Waterford and Galway crystal comes in all styles and types. Belleek china and Gaelic coffee glasses, single or in a set, are also featured. You can purchase handwoven tweed by the yard. A 45- by 45-inch Irish linen tablecloth, hand-embroidered, will be yours for £35 ($52.50). As the jerseys are all hand-knitted, you have to rummage to find the exact one to suit your particular shape and size. Also offered are Donegal tweed jackets and suits for men and women. Duke Street is off Wigmore, a street running alongside Selfridges from Oxford Street. Tube: Bond Street. The shop also has a branch at 80 Buckingham Gate, S.W.1 (tel. 222-7132). Tube: Victoria.

Ireland House Shop Limited, 150–151 New Bond St., W.1 (tel. 493-6219), can eliminate a trip to Ireland, if you were planning to go there just to pick up some of those wonderful Irish tweeds. Opened in conjunction with the Irish Tourism Bureau, this colorful shop provides fine hand-loomed tweeds, as well as hand-made apparel and accessories for both men and women. There is an interesting collection of long woven scarves in unusual colors. Tube: Bond Street.

JEWELRY: A family firm, **Sanford Brothers Ltd.,** 3 Holborn Bars, Old Elizabethan Houses, E.C.1 (tel. 405-2352), has been in business since 1923. They sell anything in jewelry, both modern and Victorian, silver of all kinds, and a fine selection of clocks and watches. The old Elizabethan buildings are one of the sights of Old London. Tube: Chancery Lane.

London Diamond Centre, 10 Hanover St., W.1 (tel. 629-5511), offers organized tours of a permanent exhibition showing how diamonds are mined, cut, polished, and made into exclusive jewelry, as well as a visit to the showroom where unmounted diamonds and ready-to-wear diamond jewelry, as well as other gem jewelry from costly to inexpensive can be purchased or ordered to your requirements. Hours are from 9:30 a.m. to 5:30 p.m. Monday to Friday, from 9:30 a.m. to 1:30 p.m. Saturday. Admission is £3.45 ($5.18) per person, the fee including a souvenir brilliant-cut stone (not a diamond) which you can have mounted in a 9-carat gold setting of your choice at modest cost.

KING'S ROAD: The formerly village-like main street of Chelsea, although still the cutting edge for fashion trends, has undergone yet another metamorphosis— the trendies of the '70s who replaced the hippies of the '60s have been pushed aside by the punk scene. Numerous stores sporting American clothes have sprung up along its length.

King's Road, S.W.3, starts at Sloane Square (with Peter Jones's classy department store) and meanders on for a mile before losing its personality and dissolving into drabness at a sharp bend appropriately known as World's End. Along the way you'll see the tokens of Chelsea's former claims to fame—cozy pubs, smart nightclubs and discos, coffee bars, cosmopolitan restaurants, and possibly the most casually attractive of London's beautiful people.

The leap of King's Road to the mod throne in the late '60s came with the advent of designer Mary Quant, who scored a bull's eye on the English as well as the world fashion target. Ms. Quant is no longer here, but what seems like a myriad of others have taken her place. More and more, however, King's Road is becoming a lineup of markets and "multistores," large or small conglomerations of in- and outdoor stands, stalls, and booths fulfilling half a dozen different functions within one building or enclosure. They spring up so fast that it's impossible to keep them tabulated. Tube: Sloane Square.

MEN'S CLOTHING: A tailormade British suit tends to be very, very expensive. A much cheaper alternative is to go to one of the **Burton** stores found all over Britain. There are some 66 branches in the Greater London are alone. The main store is at 214 Oxford St., W.1 (tel. 636-8040). Readymade suits, where a man selects first his jacket, then the trousers to match in his size, range from a low of £70 ($105) to a high of £125 ($187.50). Tube: Oxford Circus.

NEEDLEWORK: For those who like to do handcrafts, the **Royal School of Needle-**

work, 25 Princes Gate, S.W.7 (tel. 589-0077), offers in kit form many of the almost classic tapestry designs bequeathed to them by such designers as Burne-Jones and William Morris. The kits also include the appropriate wools and instructions. There are designs for cushion covers and fire screens, and plans for wall tapestries and work bags. If you have a particular object to cover, the school will draw a design especially for you. A good stock of books on the subject of needlework, as well as materials, are for sale. The school is open Monday to Friday from 9:30 a.m. to 5:30 p.m. Tube: Knightsbridge.

NOTIONS: In business since 1740, **Floris,** 89 Jermyn St., S.W.1 (tel. 930-4136), has floor-to-ceiling mahogany cabinets lining the walls that are architectural curiosities. They were installed relatively late in the establishment's history—1851—long after the shop had received its Royal Warrants as suppliers to the king and queen. The business was started by an 18th-century Minorcan entrepreneur, Juan Floris, who brought from his Mediterranean home a technique for extracting fragrances from local flowers. Fashionable residents of St. James's flocked to his shop, purchasing his soaps, perfumes, and grooming aids. Today, you can buy essences of flowers grown in English gardens, including stephanotis, rose geranium, lily of the valley, violet, Madagascar white jasmin, and carnation. Other items include cologne for men, badger-hair shaving brushes, ivory comb and brush sets, Chinese cloisonné, and combs made of both horn and bone. Tube: Piccadilly Circus.

OLD MAPS AND ENGRAVINGS: Antique maps, engravings, and atlases of all parts of the world are sold at **The Map House,** 54 Beauchamp Pl., S.W.3 (tel. 589-4325). The shop also has a vast selection of old prints of London and England, as well as engravings of flowers, birds, hunting scenes, lawyers, sports, and numerous other subjects. It's an ideal place to find an offbeat souvenir of your visit. The Map House is open from 9:45 a.m. to 5:45 p.m. Monday to Friday and from 10:30 a.m. to 5 p.m. on Saturday. Tube: Knightsbridge.

The **Record Office and History Library of the Greater London Council,** Northampton Road, E.C.1 (tel. 633-7193), near Clerkenwell, sells reproductions of old maps and prints of London. The office has archives, maps, history books, and photographs. Tube: Farringdon.

PHILATELY: A magnificent collection of postage stamps and allied material is at the **National Postal Museum,** King Edward Building, King Edward Street, E.C.1 (tel. 432-3851), open Monday to Thursday from 10 a.m. to 4:30 p.m., to 4 p.m. on Friday. It also sells postcards illustrating the collection and has a distinctive Maltese Cross postmark first used on the Penny Black. A letter mailed from Heathrow Airport is franked at Hounslow with an attractive Concorde cancellation. In country areas, the post office provides a postbus service between many remote and otherwise isolated villages. Often passenger tickets are cancelled with a special stamp of collector interest; and postcards, depicting places of interest along the routes, are issued and mailed from these buses. More specialized, many of the narrow-gauge and privately owned railways in the country issue and cancel their own stamps. Among these are the Ravenglass and Eskdale, the Keighley and Worth Valley Light Railway, and the Bluebell Railway, along with the Romney, Hythe, and Dymchurch Railway. Tube: St. Paul's.

POSTERS: A fine collection of posters is offered at the **London Transport Museum Shop,** Covent Garden, W.C.2 (tel. 379-6344), open daily from 10 a.m. to 5:45 p.m.

except the Christmas holidays. This unique shop carries a wide range of posters, costing from £1.50 ($2.25) to £5.95 ($8.93). The London Underground maps in their original size, as seen on every tube station, can be purchased here for £4.95 ($7.42). The shop also carries books, cards, T-shirts, and other souvenir items. Tube: Covent Garden.

PRINCES ARCADE: If you like "one-stop" shopping, you may be drawn to the Princes Arcade, which was opened by Edward VII when he was Prince of Wales in 1883. Between Jermyn Street and Piccadilly, in the heart of London, S.W.1, it has been restored. Wrought-iron lamps light your way as you search through some 20 bow-fronted shops, looking for that special curio (say, a 16th-century nightcap) or a pair of shoes made by people who have been satisfying royal tastes since 1847. A small sign hanging from a metal rod indicates what kind of merchandise a particular store sells. Tube: Piccadilly Circus.

SAINT CHRISTOPHER'S PLACE: One of London's most interesting and little-known (to the foreign visitor) shopping streets is Saint Christopher's Place, W.1. It lies just off Oxford Street—walk down Oxford from Selfridges toward Oxford Circus, ducking north along Gees Court across Barrett Street. There you will be surrounded by antique markets and good shops for women's clothing and accessories. The nearest tube is Bond Street.

SILVER: Looking for precious metal? The **London Silver Vaults,** Chancery Lane, W.C.2 (tel. 242-3844), were established in Victoria's day (1882), and soon became the largest silver vaults in the world. You can shop in vault after vault for that special treasure. The vaults are open Monday to Friday from 9 a.m. to 5:30 p.m., on Saturday to 12:30 p.m.; closed on bank holiday weekends. Tube: Chancery Lane.

SOUVENIRS: Charles Dickens enthusiasts can go to the **Old Curiosity Shop,** 13–14 Portsmouth St., off Lincoln's Inn Fields, W.C.2 (tel. 405-9891), used by the author as the abode of Little Nell. One of the original Tudor buildings still remaining in London and built in 1567, the shop crams every nook and cranny with general knick-knackery, what-nots, and souvenirs, including Charles Dickens first editions. A popular item is an unframed silhouette of Little Nell's grandfather for 60p (90¢), or horse brasses for £2 ($3) each. Old Curiosity Shop bookmarks cost £1.25 ($1.88), and ashtrays with Dickensian engravings go for £2.50 ($3.75) to £7 ($10.50). The shop is open every day of the week, including Sunday and holidays. Tube: Holborn.

STREET MARKETS: Colorful street markets have played an important part in the life of London. They are recommended not only for bric-a-brac, but as a low-cost adventure. In fact, you don't have to buy a thing. But, be warned, some of the stallkeepers are mighty convincing. Here are the best ones:

Portobello Road Market

This Saturday market is one of the city's most popular flea markets. Take bus 52 from Hyde Park Corner to Portobello Road (W.11). Here you'll enter a hurly-burly world of stall after stall selling curios to tempt even the staunchest penny pincher. Items include everything from the military uniforms worn by the Third Bavarian Lancers to English soul food. Some of the stallholders are antiquarians, with shops in fashionable Kensington, Belgravia, and Chelsea, and they know the price of everything. Feel free to bargain, however. A popular pastime is dropping in for a pint of ale at one of the Portobello pubs. The best time to visit is on a Saturday. The market is open Monday to Saturday from 9 a.m. to 5 p.m. (on Thursday until 1 p.m.)

New Caledonian Market

Commonly known as the **Bermondsey Market** because of its location, this street market is on the corner of Long Lane and Bermondsey Street, S.E.1. At its extreme east end, it begins at Tower Bridge Road. This is one of Europe's outstanding street markets in size and quality of goods offered. The stalls are well known, and many dealers come into London from the country. The market gets under way on Friday at 5 a.m. (take a flashlight as the light is poor at that early hour), before the Underground opens. Antiques and other items are generally lower in price here than at Portobello Road and the other street markets, but bargains are gone by 9 a.m. The market closes at noon. It's best reached by taking the Underground to London Bridge station, then bus 78 or walk down Bermondsey Street.

Petticoat Lane

On Sunday between 9 a.m. and 2 p.m. (go before noon), throngs of shoppers join the crowds on Petticoat Lane (also known as Middlesex Street, E.1). The lanes begin at Liverpool Street Station on the Bishopsgate side. Here you can buy clothing, food, antiques, and plenty of junk. Tube: Liverpool Street, Aldgate, or Aldgate East.

Camden Passage

This antique bric-a-brac market in Islington, N.1 (in back of the Angel), northeast of Bloomsbury, is open from 8 a.m. to 4 p.m. on Tuesday, Wednesday, and Saturday and from 9 a.m. to 5 p.m. on Thursday and Friday, which are the best days for books, prints, and drawings. The best time to visit otherwise is on Saturday market day. On all days, the emphasis is on paintings, antiques, and similar hard items. Prices are not inexpensive, but there are bargains to be found if you look carefully through the more than 50 shops and 20 boutiques. Take the Northern Line tube to the Angel stop.

Church Street

Along Church Street, N.W.8, you'll have to search through a wide assortment of junk, but you'll often come across a great buy. There's a lot of secondhand furniture that won't fit under your airplane seat, but you'll find smaller purchases as well. Business is conducted Monday to Saturday from early morning until evening (stalls may close earlier if trading is slow). Here's an opportunity to haggle and enter into a true market spirit, only don't forget that the vendor probably knows more about his or her merchandise than you and may give you an "earful" if you try some unfair or unnecessary bargaining. North of Marble Arch, Church Street crosses Edgware Road, one street beyond Harrow Road, and is reached by taking the tube to either Edgware Road or Marylebone.

Camden Lock

On Chalk Farm Road, Camden Lock is a five-minute walk from the Camden Town Underground station. It's a smaller and cozier version of Portobello. The stallkeepers sell old silver, jewelry, and other crafts, as well as unusual boots and shoes, even homemade cakes. This market is more out of the way than those previously recommended. Young women with spiky psychedelic hair stalk between the stalls, and you have the impression that sales are not vital to the stallkeepers, more a perk in life, the cream on the trifle. It's well worth a visit just for the atmosphere. They are open all day Saturday and Sunday.

Leather Lane

Leather Lane, E.C.1 (tube: Chancery Lane), is open from 11 a.m. to 2:30 p.m., Monday to Friday only. It provides a bewildering array of clothes, furniture, and food, plus plenty of atmosphere. The lane is patronized mainly by local office workers, but also is colorful to the foreign visitor as well.

Jubilee Market

At Covent Garden, W.C.2, this is a small general market that sells antiques on Monday, crafts on Saturday and Sunday, and various items Tuesday to Friday. It's open from 9 a.m. to 4 p.m. Tube: Covent Garden.

WOOLENS: One of the best and most obvious places in London for quality tweeds and woolens is **Scotch House,** 84 Regent St., S.W.1 (tel. 734-0203), with merchandise carefully crafted from the finest of Scotland's excellent woolen goods. Men's tweed blazers are a particular lure here, as well as woolens sold by the yard in patterns or plaids. There's also men's rainwear plus a good children's department for that tam o'shanter. The house stocks a full selection of sweaters and knitwear in cashmere and wool for both men and women. Tube: Piccadilly Circus.

Westaway & Westaway, near the British Museum at 62–65 Great Russell St., W.C.1 (tel. 405-0479), is a substitute for a shopping trip to Scotland. They stock an enormous range of kilts, scarves, waistcoats, capes, dressing gowns, and rugs in authentic clan tartans. What's more, they are knowledgeable on the subject of these minutely intricate clan symbols. They also sell superb—and untartaned—cashmere, camel-hair, and Shetland knitwear, along with Harris tweed jackets, Burberry raincoats, and cashmere overcoats for men. Another branch is at 92–93 Great Russell St., W.C.1. Tube: Tottenham Court Road.

3. London After Dark

London is crammed with change-of-pace nighttime entertainment. You'll have a wide choice of action, from the dives of Soho to the elegance of opening night on Shaftesbury Avenue. So much depends on your taste, pocketbook, and even the time of year. Nowhere else will you find such a panorama of legitimate theaters, operas, concerts, gambling clubs, discos, vaudeville at Victorian music halls, strip joints, jazz clubs, folk-music cafés, nightclubs, and dance ballrooms. For information about any of these events, ask a newsstand dealer for a copy of *Time Out. What's On* has now combined with *Where to Go* and contains listings of restaurants, theaters, and nightclubs.

THEATERS: The fame of the English theater has spread far and wide. In London you'll have a chance to see it on its home ground. You may want to spend a classical evening at the "Old Vic" (now the National Theatre Company), or you may settle for a new play by some unknown writer. You might want to catch up on that Broadway musical you missed in New York, or be an advance talent scout for next year's big Stateside hit. Production costs are lower in London, and sometimes it's easier for people in the legitimate theater there to experiment.

For the average production, you pay around £4 ($6) for upper circle seats, £15 ($22.50) to £20 ($30), sometimes more, for front stalls. You can either purchase your ticket from the theater's box office (the most recommended method), or from a ticket agency, such as the one operated from the reservations desk of American Express (agent's fee charged, however). In a few theaters you can reserve your spot in the gallery, the cheapest seats of all, but in some cases the less expensive seats are sold only on the day of performance. This means that you'll have to buy your gallery ticket early, then return about one hour before the performance and go around to the entrance to the balcony. Often you can rent a queueing stool from a man in charge. Occasionally, you can enjoy a preshow staged by strolling performers, called buskers, including next year's Chaplin—or last year's (the theater has its peaks and valleys).

It is also possible to telephone most of the theaters for reservations, quoting an American Express card number (if you possess such a thing). You then collect your tickets from the box office just before the performance.

If you want to see two shows in one day, you'll find that Wednesday, Thursday, and Saturday are always crammed with matinee performances. Many West End theaters begin their evening performances at 7:30.

Students and senior citizens get a break at most theaters (subject to availability) by being granted a discount at the local box offices. Currently, such discount tickets sell at a price beginning at £3.50 ($5.25) to £3.90 ($5.85) each.

The **Leicester Square Half-Price Ticket Booth,** Leicester Square, W.C.2, sells theater tickets on the day of performance for half price (cash only), plus an 80p ($1.20) service charge. Open from noon for matinee performances and from 2:30 to 6:30 p.m. for evening performances, they have a wide selection of seats available. Ask for the show you want to see, but it's a good idea to have a couple of choices. Tickets for "hits" are obviously not often available. There is often a long line, but it moves quickly and is well worth the effort if you want to take in a lot of theater while you're in London—and want to save money. All of the shows for which tickets are available are well displayed at the booth, so you can make up your mind on what to see as you wait in line (the queue, the English say). Tube: Leicester Square.

Of London's many theaters, these are particularly outstanding:

The **National Theatre,** South Bank, S.E.1, is a concrete cubist fortress, a three-theater complex that stands as a $32-million landmark beside the Waterloo Bridge on the south bank of the Thames, reached by the Waterloo Station tube. It was first suggested in 1848, and it took Parliament 101 years to pass a bill vowing government support. Flaring out like a fan, the most thrilling theater in this complex is the **Olivier,** named after Lord Laurence Olivier, its first director when the company was born in 1962. (Olivier was succeeded in 1973 by Sir Peter Hall, who created the Royal Shakespeare Company.) The Olivier Theatre bears a resemblance in miniature to an ancient Greek theater. It has an open stage and seats 1,160. The **Cottesloe** is a simple box theater for 400 people. Finally, the 890-seat **Lyttelton** is a traditional proscenium arch house that doesn't have one bad seat for any theater-goer. In the foyers there are three bookshops, eight bars, a restaurant, and two self-service buffets (some open all day except Sunday), and many outside terraces with river views. For everyone, with or without tickets for a play, there is live foyer music, free, before evening performances and Saturday matinees, and free exhibitions. The foyers are open 10 a.m. to 11 p.m. except Sunday. Also guided theater tours are available daily, including backstage areas, for £2 ($3).

Tickets generally range from £5.50 ($8.25) to £13 ($19.50), but midweek matinees are cheaper. Credit cards are accepted. You can book through a travel agent or with the theater in advance, but you must know the name of the particular auditorium in which the play you want to see is appearing. For general information, telephone 633-0880; for ticket information, 928-2252 or 928-8126. Matinee seats are available from 10 a.m. on the day of performance. Standby seats are available from two hours before a performance if there are any tickets left. These are sold at reduced prices. Student standby seats are available 45 minutes before the time of a performance, with any available tickets being sold for £4.50 ($6.75).

The National Theatre Restaurant will serve you a good meal for around £12 ($18), but at one of the coffee bars a snack will run only around £3.50 ($5.25). If the weather is good, you can sit to eat with a view of the river and the London skyline.

You may also be interested in the activities of the **National Film Theatre,** in the same South Bank complex, S.E.1 (tel. 928-3232). It runs a fascinating cinema program, ranging around the world. For instance, you might see avant-garde French films, American imports, or something fascinating out of Germany. A visitor can obtain a short-term membership for only 75p ($1.13). If booked in advance, tickets cost £2.75 ($4.13). Otherwise, you pay £2.50 ($3.75) if you line up right before a performance.

The Old Vic. This is a 165-year-old theater on Waterloo Road, S.E.1 (tel. 928-2651, or the box office at 928-7616). The facade and much of the interior were restored in their original early 19th-century style, and most of the modernization is behind the scenes. The proscenium arch was moved back, the stage trebled in size, and more seats and stage boxes added. It is air-conditioned and contains five bars. There are short seasons of varied plays, and several subscription offers have been introduced with reductions of up to £5 ($7.50) a seat if you purchase six tickets for different shows at once. Otherwise, top prices vary, with the best stalls or dress circle going for around £13 ($19.50) a ticket. Tube: Waterloo.

The **Royal Shakespeare Company** has its famous theater in Stratford-upon-Avon and is also housed in the Barbican Theatre, Barbican Centre, E.C.2 (tel. 628-8795—tube to Barbican or St. Paul's—or tel. 0789/295623). A program of new plays and Shakespearean and other classics is performed here. Plays run in repertoire and are presented two or three times a week each. The company also has two smaller theaters where new and experimental plays are performed as well as classics: **The Other Place** in Stratford-upon-Avon, and **The Pit,** also in London's Barbican Centre. There are tickets at varying prices, low rates for students, and some seats sold only on the day of the performance. Several packages are offered that include tickets, meals, and accommodations.

The **Royal Court Theatre,** Sloane Square, S.W.1 (tel. 730-1745; tube to Sloane Square). The English Stage Company has operated this theater since 1956. The emphasis is on new playwrights (John Osborne got his start here with the 1956 production of *Look Back in Anger*). Also on the premises is the Theatre Upstairs, a large room with an open stage suitable for unusual productions to supplement the main-house repertoire. Prices of tickets vary according to the play, those in the main theater averaging £5 ($7.50) to £12 ($18). At the Theatre Upstairs, the tickets go for £3 ($4.50) to £6 ($9). Shows are at 8 p.m. daily, 4 and 8 p.m. on Saturday downstairs, 7:30 p.m. daily and 3:30 and 7:30 on Saturday for the Theatre Upstairs.

The **Young Vic,** The Cut, Waterloo, S.E.1 (tel. 928-6363), houses the Young Vic Company, which offers a fascinating blend of modern, vivid, and vibrant interpretations of classic drama, with performances of works by new playwrights. Also here is the Studio, with a wide range of productions by visiting companies. The performances usually begin at 7:30 p.m. Seats cost £5.95 ($8.93). Reservations may be made by phone and paid for by credit card. Tube: Waterloo Station.

Sadler's Wells Theatre, Rosebery Avenue, E.C.1 (box office tel. 278-8916), is on a site where a theater has stood since 1683, a short walk from Camden Passage. Resident companies—Sadler's Wells Royal Ballet and the new Sadler's Wells Opera (producing light opera, operetta, and fresh productions of that most English of theatrical institutions, the work of Gilbert and Sullivan)—are complemented by a program of British and foreign dance, opera, and ballet. Seats are offered at prices ranging from £2.50 ($3.75) to £15 ($22.50). Performances generally begin at 7:30 p.m. Reach the theater by the Angel tube or bus 19 or 38 from Piccadilly, Charing Cross, or Holborn.

Lyric Theatre, 23 King St., Hammersmith, W.6 (tel. 741-2331), stands on the edge of the site where the old Lyric stood for 80 years until 1965. The elegant auditorium from the old theater, designed in 1895, has been restored and incorporated in the present building and offers a variety of productions, musical and dramatic. The theater is open Monday to Saturday from 10 a.m. to 8 p.m. for food in the buffet, and the bars are open during normal pub hours. Tube: Ravens Court Park.

Many theaters will accept bookings by telephone if you give your name and American Express credit card number when you ring. Then all you have to do is go along before the performance to collect your tickets which will be sold at the theater price. All theater booking agencies charge a fee. Once confirmed, the booking will be charged to your account even if you don't use the tickets. Only card holders can collect the tickets charged to their accounts.

The **Whitehall Theatre** at the top of Whitehall, S.W.1 (tel. 930-7765), just off Trafalgar Square, has recently been restored to its original 1930s art deco glory. To the splendid auditorium has been added continental seating (620 seats) to allow greater comfort and more leg room for the audience. Air conditioning has been installed and the bar areas considerably enlarged. In the foyer, a café-bar is open from noon to 3 p.m., and there's a Ticketmaster system where tickets for most shows, sports events, and concerts in London can be purchased. Tube: Charing Cross.

OPEN-AIR ENTERTAINMENT: Regent's Park, N.W.1 (tel. 486-2431), as the name indicates, is an outdoor theater, right in the center of Regent's Park. The setting is idyllic, and the longest theater bar in London provides both drink and food. Performances are given in June, July, and August only, evenings at 7:45, matinees on Wednesday, Thursday, and Saturday at 2:30 p.m. Presentations are mainly Shakespeare, usually in period costume. Both seating and acoustics are excellent. If it rains, you're given tickets for another performance. Prices are from £4 ($6) to £10 ($15). Tube: Baker Street.

The **Holland Park Open Air Theatre** is a charming stage in the park, W.8, close to the Commonwealth Institute. It really has the air of a court theater in some Renaissance palace yard. There is a weekly program in June, July, and August of opera and drama. Free band concerts are presented on Sunday at 3 p.m. Shows begin at 7:30 nightly, at 2:30 p.m. for Saturday matinees. The Dutch Garden is floodlit until midnight, and the theater is closed on Monday. For program inquiries, telephone 933-2542, ext. 52. Tube: Kensington High Street.

OPERA AND BALLET: On Bow Street, **London's Royal Opera House,** Covent Garden, W.C.2 (tel. 240-1066), provides performances of the highest caliber from September to August each year. It is the home of the Royal Opera and the Royal Ballet companies. The advance box office, 48 Floral St., W.C.2, is open from 10 a.m. to 8 p.m. Monday to Saturday. More than 800 seats in the amphitheater cost £8.50 ($12.75) or less for ballet and £12 ($18) or less for opera. Sixty-five rear amphitheater seats are held for sale on the day of performance and are available, one per person, from 10 a.m., but you may have to queue up well before this for the most popular productions. Tube: Covent Garden.

English National Opera, London Coliseum, St. Martin's Lane, W.C.2, just off Trafalgar Square (box office, tel. 836-3161). The London Coliseum, built in 1904 as a variety theater and converted into an opera house in 1968, is London's largest and most splendid theater. The English National Opera is one of the two national opera companies, and performs a wide range of works, from great classics through operetta to world premières, and every performance is in English. A repertory of 22 productions is performed five or six nights a week for 11 months of the year. The company has a large and enthusiastic following among young people. Balcony tickets are available for as little as £2 ($3), but many visitors prefer the Upper Circle or Dress Circle at about £8.50 ($12.75) to £18.50 ($27.75). During the opera season (usually from August to June), about 100 cheap seats in the balcony are held for sale on the day of performance, from 10 a.m. In early summer there are short guest seasons at the Coliseum by international ballet companies. Tube: Leicester Square.

Gilbert and Sullivan fans can patronize **Grim's Dyke Country Hotel,** Old Redding, Harrow Weald, Middlesex (tel. 954-4227), outside London. This building was once the home of W.S. Gilbert. There, in winter, the management sponsors Gilbert and Sullivan soirees every two weeks. These are increased to weekly in summer. The cost of a meal and entertainment is £19 ($28.50) per person, plus service.

The **Barbican Centre,** The Barbican, E.C.2, is considered the largest art and exhibition center in Western Europe. It was created to make a perfect setting in which to enjoy good music and theater from comfortable, roomy seating. The theater is the home of the Royal Shakespeare Company, already mentioned, which, of course, performs a wide range of works other than plays of the Bard. The Concert Hall is the permanent home of the London Symphony Orchestra and host to visiting performers. There are often lunchtime concerts where the admission is from £3 ($4.50) for the 45 minutes or so. Otherwise, seats for evening concerts cost from £3 ($4.50) to £15 ($22.50). Matinees in the theater start at £5 ($7.50), going up to £11 ($16.50), and evening seats range from £5 ($7.50) to £12.50 ($18.75). There are a number of bars and a self-service café.

The following numbers will be useful—628-8795 for the box office for seats for concerts and theatrical performances; 928-9760 for 24-hour information on performance of concerts; and 628-2295 for information about theatrical performances. Tube: Barbican or Moorgate.

CONCERTS: In recent years the musical focal point in London has shifted to a superbly specialized complex of buildings on the South Bank side of Waterloo Bridge, S.E.1. This Cultural Centre—including pleasure gardens and the National Film Theatre—houses three of the most stylish, comfortable, and acoustically perfect concert structures in the world: the **Royal Festival Hall,** the **Queen Elizabeth Hall,** and the **Purcell Room.** Here, more than 1,200 performances a year are presented, and it's not all classical music. Included are ballet, jazz, popular classics, pop, and folk. The Royal Festival Hall is open from 10 a.m. every day and offers an extensive range of things to see and do. There are free exhibitions in the foyers and free lunchtime music from 12:30 to 2 p.m., plus guided tours of the building, and book, record, and gift shops. The Festival Buffet has a wide selection of food at reasonable prices, and there are several bars throughout the foyers. Tickets are available from the Royal Festival Hall box office (tel. 928-3191); for credit-card bookings, phone 928-6544 or the usual booking agents. Tickets usually range in price from £3.50 ($5.25) to £10 ($15). Tube: Waterloo Station.

Royal Albert Hall, Kensington Gore, S.W.7 (tel. 589-8212). Acoustic improvements and other alterations have made this landmark Victorian building one of the world's finest auditoriums. The BBC Promenade Concerts are held here for eight weeks in summer. Throughout the year there are performances by top orchestras and artists, brass bands, and all manner of events ranging from covered court lawn tennis to the annual Royal British Legion Festival of Remembrance. Ticket prices vary according to the type of event. A tour and exhibition daily July through October costs £2 ($3). Tube: South Kensington, High Street Kensington, or Knightsbridge.

Wigmore Hall, 36 Wigmore St., W.1 (tel. 935-2141). At this intimate auditorium, you'll hear excellent recitals and concerts. There are regular series, master concerts by chamber music groups and instrumentalists, song recital series, Sunday morning coffee concerts, and concerts featuring special composers or themes throughout the year. In summer, Wigmore Summer Nights are featured. Many good seats are in the £3 ($4.50) range. A free list of the month's concerts is available from the hall. Tube: Bond Street or Oxford Circus.

MUSIC HALLS: A popular attraction is the **Players,** Villiers Street (formerly the famous Gatti's "Under the Arches"), W.C.2 (tel. 839-1134). Nowadays, the Players is a Victorian music hall variety club. Top-notch performers in London often use these two-week engagements as fill-ins. The presentation is professionally staged, with the appropriate settings and costumes. The master of ceremonies (he's called the chairman) asks members to introduce their guests who stand for a bow (and comments). Insults are exchanged in jest, especially if a guest is from one of the "colonies."

You can enjoy the entire show having drinks only (even toasting the Queen— Victoria, that is). Tuesday through Saturday, the theater opens at 6 p.m., with the show starting at 8:30 p.m. On Sunday, opening is at 6:30 p.m., and the performance starts at 8 p.m. It's best to make an entire evening of it, staying for the dancing session after the show. To do that, you can have a generous dinner, à la carte. Temporary membership is available for £6 ($9) per week or £12 ($18) for three months. Forty-eight hours must elapse before a membership becomes valid. Application must be made in person. While members do not have to pay for seats, they are charged £5 ($7.50) for each guest. Guests are limited to four at any time. The à la carte dinner offers fish, steaks, poultry, and the usual appetizers and desserts, and the average price for a three-course meal is £12 ($18). Performances are given every night except Monday, but check in advance by calling the box office. Take the tube to Embankment station. Directly across the street from the Players is a house with a plaque, commemorating the fact that Rudyard Kipling lived there between 1889 and 1891.

The Water Rats, 328 Grays Inn Road, W.C.1 (tel. 837-7269 for reservations), formerly The Pindar of Wakefield and Aba Daba, perpetuates the world of the Victorian music hall contained in a famous London pub that has operated since 1655. It is now the headquarters of the Grand Order of Water Rats, a charitable organization of Britain's top variety performers. The admission charge is £5 ($7.50) to the theater, where you can dine on traditional fare for £7 ($10.50) and remain at your table for the show. Tube: King's Cross Station.

The **Rheingold Club** thrives in a centuries-old wine cellar at Sedley Place, just off 361 Oxford St., W.1 (tel. 629-5543), and has a restaurant, two bars, and a good-size dance floor. The main attraction is a top-class band playing daily except Sunday and bank holidays from 9:30 p.m. to about 2 a.m. There is also an occasional cabaret, usually with big-time guest stars, but most of the entertainment is created by the patrons themselves. The Rheingold, founded in 1959, is the oldest and most successful "singles club" in London, existing long before the term had been coined. It is a safe place for men to take their wives or girl friends, and respectable single women are safe here. The temporary membership you purchase at the club's reception desk includes admission for the first visit and costs £5 ($7.50) for men and £4 ($6) for women. There is also a one-night membership (or admission charge) for £3.50 ($5.25).

The club offers a tasty German dish called champignon-schnitzel, a tender escalope of Dutch veal served with rice and peas in a cream and mushroom sauce, as well as typical German dishes such as bratwurst and eisbein (pickled pork knuckles) with sauerkraut. Meals cost £3.50 ($5.25) to £6.60 ($9.90). It has a strong German draft beer at 90p ($1.35) for a half pint and excellent French and German wines from £5 ($7.50) for an *appellation controlée* or *qualitaetswein* to £10 ($15) for a château-bottled Bordeaux or a Moselle Auslese. The club is open from 8 p.m. to 1:30 a.m. Monday and Tuesday, to 2 a.m. Wednesday, Thursday, and cabaret nights, and to 2:30 a.m. on Friday and Saturday. Take the tube to Bond Street station, use the main exit to Oxford Street, turn right, and turn right again to Sedley Place. It's only 40 yards from the station.

The luxury catamaran, *Naticia,* is a music hall showboat, leaving from Westminster Pier on Sunday at 7 p.m. for a 3½-hour cruise on the River Thames, returning at 10:30 p.m. There is a bar for drinks while you watch the landmarks slip by. Dinner is a three-course meal. At dinnertime, a first-class, oldtime music hall program entertains you. Advance dinner reservations are essential. Telephone Catamaran Cruisers Ltd., Westminster Pier, S.W.1 (tel. 839-2349). The dinner and cruise costs £27 ($40.50).

GAY NIGHTLIFE: The most reliable source of information on all gay clubs and activities is the **Gay Switchboard** (tel. 837-7324). The staff there runs a 24-hour service of information on places and activities catering openly to homosexual women and men. *Gay Times* is published monthly in a magazine format, and it's the best general guide to gay pubs, discos, and organizations in Great Britain. It can be found at newsstands throughout London.

For both men and women who aren't interested in bars or discos, the **London Lesbian & Gay Centre,** 67 Cowcross St., E.C.1 (tel. 608-1471), is the best bet. It is open Tuesday and Wednesday from 6 p.m. to midnight, Thursday and Sunday noon to midnight, and Friday and Saturday from noon to 2 a.m. It is closed on Monday. You can order food, enjoy the lounge, patronize the bookshop, and meet Londoners of similar interests. Nighttime action includes disco, occasional theater, and music. Membership is £15 ($22.50). Tube: Farringdon.

One club that welcomes overseas visitors, **The Heaven,** The Arches, Villiers Street, Charing Cross, W.C.2 (tel. 839-3852), is considered to be the largest and most high-energy gay disco in Europe, with fantastic lasers, lights, and sounds. There is no membership requirement and no dress code. The cover charge varies from £2 ($3) to £5 ($7.50). Hours are from 10 p.m. to 3 a.m. Only gay men can enter Heaven on Tuesday, Friday, and Saturday. On Wednesday, the requirement is still for gay people, but both men and women are welcomed. On Thursday, mixed (straight) men and women are permitted, and the place is closed Sunday and Monday. Tube: Charing Cross.

NIGHTCLUBS: The night scene of London changes so rapidly that it's difficult to keep abreast of it. There are several general situations to keep in mind:

First, the English are strongly addicted to jazz, and there are several clubs (dives) where you can fill up on a variety of jazz, whether it be the old-fashioned Louis Armstrong type or progressive. Many a rendezvous for jazz enthusiasts is found in Soho, right off Shaftesbury Avenue. Few are licensed for alcohol, so you'll have to adjust in some cases to soft drinks as you get lost in rhythmic forces.

There are several kinds of nightclubs where you can eat or drink, be entertained or allowed to dance—even gamble. Most often these clubs are private. To avoid the unpopular early closing hour (11 p.m.) for licensed public establishments, the private club has come into existence (many stay open till 3 and 4 a.m.). In most cases the clubs welcome overseas visitors, granting them a temporary membership with proof of identity and perhaps a nominal charge. Many clubs offer dinner, a show, and dancing. Inquire before you commit yourself. No visitor to London should be afraid to ask about membership in a private club. After all, most of the clubs are in business to make money—and welcome foreign patronage. I'll survey a range of jazz and disco clubs that charge a low membership and a nominal entrance fee, beginning with:

The **Cockney Cabaret,** 18 Charing Cross Rd., W.C.2 (tel. 408-1001), stands right in the heart of the West End, almost within the sound of the Bow bells. At the Cockney, the evening starts with a nip of Mother's Ruin (gin) or Gold Watches (scotch), while the honky-tonk piano turns out sing-along tunes. Then your Jim Skinner (dinner) will include loop (soup) and probably a Lillian Gish (fish), or else a feathered bird for the main dish followed by dessert. Unlimited beer and wines are provided during your meal, and it's finished off with a good old cuppa (tea). Then there's a cheerful, noisy cabaret, some time for dancing, followed by a second cabaret session before the end of the evening at midnight. From Sunday to Friday, the cost is £23.50 ($35.25), rising to £25.50 ($38.25) on Saturday. Hours are from 8 p.m. to midnight. Tube: Tottenham Court Road.

A unique theater restaurant in a unique setting, that's the **Talk of London** (tel. 408-1001), in the New London Centre, an entertainment complex at Parker Street, off Drury Lane, W.C.2, the heart of the city's theaterland. The restaurant is ingeniously designed so that every guest gets "the best seat in the house." By using a circular layout and varying floor levels, everyone has an uninterrupted view of the show. The

Talk of London offers a complete evening's entertainment from 8 p.m. to 1 a.m., a four-course dinner of your choice, dancing to an orchestra, and an international cabaret at 10:30 p.m. All this plus coffee, service, and VAT are included in the price of £20 ($30) Monday to Friday and £22 ($33) on Saturday. Drinks are extra. Phone for reservations, which are essential. Tube: Covent Garden or Holborn.

Eve, 189 Regent St., W.1 (tel. 734-0557), is London's longest established late-night club. Doyen of London's nightlife, owner Jimmy O'Brien launched it in 1953. Strip cabaret and erotic entertainment (at 1 a.m.) are presented, along with dancing to disco, alternating with live music of a high standard. Eve is open Monday to Friday from 10 p.m. to 3:30 a.m. Girls are available as dining or dancing partners for unaccompanied men, and an à la carte menu is available throughout the night. Admittance is by membership only. The annual subscription rate is £5 ($7.50), but a special temporary membership is granted for overseas visitors, valid for one night only, costing £1 ($1.50). Only one person in a party need be a member, and overseas visitors may be admitted on application without waiting for the customary 48 hours. After that, the entrance fee is £8 ($12) for a member and each guest. Tube: Oxford Circus.

THE DISCOS: A firmly entrenched London institution, the disco is, nevertheless, as vulnerable as the Stone of Scone. Many of them open, enjoy a quick but fast-fading popularity, then close. Some possible favorites that may still be going strong upon your arrival include the following:

Samantha's, 3 New Burlington St., W.1 (tel. 734-6249), just off Regent Street, has been one of London's most popular discos and nightspots since it opened some 25 years ago. However, it is very much a club of the '80s, and it has a good sound and light system and a new D.J. box. Now twice its original size, the club boasts a 30-foot cocktail bar with its own dance floor alongside, as well as Harry's Bar upstairs where you can relax to some quieter music. If electronic games are what you prefer, there's a room full of these to improve your skills. Admission is £4 ($6) Monday to Thursday, £7 ($10.50) on Friday, and £6 ($9) on Saturday. Food is served in Rocky's Restaurant from 6 p.m. to 6:30 a.m. Tube: Oxford Circus.

The **Marquee,** 90 Wardour St., W.1 (tel. 437-6603), is rightly considered one of the best-known centers for rock music in Europe, and is in fact the longest running rock club in the world. Its reputation goes back to the '50s, but it remains forever young, in touch with the sounds of the future. Famous groups, such as the Rolling Stones, played at the Marquee long before their names spread beyond the shores of England. Fortunately, you don't have to be a member—you just pay at the door. If you possess a student I.D. card from any country, it will cost you less to enter. The entrance fees vary, but usually fall in the £3 ($4.50) to £5 ($7.50) range, depending on who's appearing. Those 18 years of age or older can order hard drinks. Many well-known musicians are known to frequent the place regularly on their nights off. The quite-small and very crowded club is one of the few that features live music. Hours are 7 to 11 p.m. seven nights a week. Tube: Piccadilly Circus.

Studio Valbonne, 62 Kingly St., behind Regent Street, W.1 (tel. 439-7242), is a famous and popular disco and restaurant with a wide-ranging clientele. The decor is modern and stylish with the emphasis on comfort. There is continuous video entertainment shown on a cinema-size screen and 14 smaller screens around the club. This is a disco-theater with live acts, recording artists, surprise cabaret, and fashion shows. There are three bars, including a well-stocked cocktail bar which offers a variety of exotic drinks. You are sure to be delighted with the Gallery Restaurant where you can order from an à la carte menu or enjoy a table d'hôte dinner at £15 ($22.50) per person. Snacks and steak sandwiches are available all evening. Dress is smart and casual, but no jeans are allowed. Membership is not required, and normal admission prices are £5 ($7.50) for women Monday to Saturday, with men being charged £5 ($7.50) Monday to Wednesday, £7 ($10.50) on Thursday, and £8 ($12) on Friday and Saturday. If

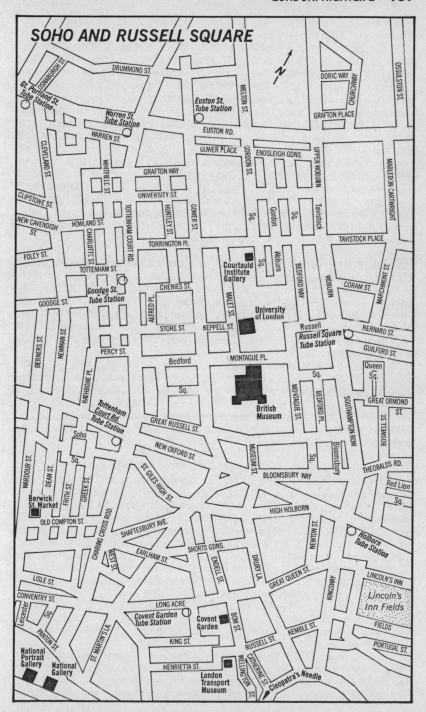

SOHO AND RUSSELL SQUARE

you're in the restaurant to dine before 11 p.m., there is no charge for admission to the disco-theater. Tube: Oxford Circus or Piccadilly Circus.

The Hippodrome, at the Hippodrome Corner of Charing Cross Road and Leicester Square, W.C.2 (tel. 437-4311). Peter Stringfellow has created one of London's greatest discos, an enormous place where light and sound beam in on you from all directions. Revolving speakers even descend from the roof to deafen you in patches, and you can watch yourself on closed-circuit video. The Vari-lites are a spectacular treat not to be missed. There are six bars, together with a balcony restaurant, where food is served. Lasers and a hydraulically controlled stage for visiting international performers are only part of the attraction of this place. Admission Monday to Thursday is £6 ($9). On Friday and Saturday, the charge is £7.50 ($11.25) before 11 p.m., £10 ($15) after. The Hippodrome is open Monday to Saturday from 9 p.m. to 3:30 a.m. Tube: Leicester Square or Covent Garden.

Le Beat Route, 17 Greek St., W.1 (tel. 734-1470), is a luxurious club with both live and disco music, open every day except Sunday. Top recording artists make personal appearances here. There's a superb sprung dance floor, as well as a pool room with its own bar. Admission ranges from £3.50 ($5.25) to £6 ($9). It opens at 9 p.m., closing at 3:30 a.m. Tube: Tottenham Court Road.

EROTICISM IN SOHO: When it comes to taking it off, London is one of the breeziest, barest capitals of Europe. Soho reigns supreme in the nude department, the dives lining whole sides of the streets (many of the strippers work several joints, hustling back and forth between engagements—sometimes doing a little street hustling on the side as well). Wardour, Frith, and Greek Streets are especially strong on disrobing. Some of the cheaper dens are really bleak—far removed from the humor and camp of such nudity emporiums as the Crazy Horse Saloon in Paris. Other, more lavish houses stage spectacular numbers.

The **Raymond Revuebar,** Walker's Court, Brewer Street, W.1 (tel. 734-1593). Proprietor Paul Raymond is considered the doyen of strip society, and his young, beautiful, hand-picked women are among the best in Europe. The stage show, Festival of Erotica, is presented Monday to Saturday at 8 and 10 p.m. There are licensed bars, and patrons may take their drinks into the theater. The price of admission is £12.50 ($18.75), and there is no membership fee. Whisky is around £1.50 ($2.25) per large measure. Tube: Piccadilly Circus.

JAZZ: A serious contender for the title of London's finest jazz center is the **100 Club,** 100 Oxford St., W.1 (tel. 636-0933). The emphasis here is strictly on the music, which begins each evening at 7:30 and lasts until midnight or later. On Tuesday and Thursday nights, rock and soul music are presented, but jazz—all kinds of jazz—is performed on the other five nights. The scheduled performers vary every night, so you'll have to phone ahead for that evening's program. However, you're sure to see the cream of jazz at the 100 Club, including such bands as Ken Colyer's All Star Jazzmen, Chris Barber's Jazz Band, and Mr. Acker Bilk and his Paramount Jazz Band. The club's menu features hamburgers and salads among other food. There's also a fully licensed bar, serving liquor, wine and beer. The club no longer requires membership, but imposes a door charge likely to range from £2.50 ($3.75) to £5 ($7.50), depending on which artist is appearing. Tube: Tottenham Court Road or Oxford Circus.

A much cheaper way to hear jazz is at one of the many pubs in the West End offering it on certain nights of the week. Some charge admission; others allow you to listen for the price of your drink.

Ronnie Scott's, 47 Frith St., W.1 (tel. 439-0747), has long held supremacy as the first citadel of modern jazz in Europe. Featured on almost every bill is an American instrumentalist, plus a top-notch singer (such as Carmen McRae or Blossom Dearie). The best of English and American groups are booked, including such names as Woody

Herman and his orchestra. In the heart of Soho, a ten-minute walk from Piccadilly Circus via Shaftesbury Avenue, it's worth an entire evening of your time. You can not only saturate yourself in the best of jazz, but get reasonably priced drinks and dinners as well. There are three separate areas: the Main Room, the Upstairs Room, and the Downstairs Bar. You don't have to be a member, although you can join if you wish. The entrance fee to the main room depends on who's appearing. The average price of admission for nonmembers is £6 ($9) to £7 ($10.50) Monday to Thursday, rising to £7 ($10.50) to £8 ($12) or more on Friday and Saturday. Students with a valid I.D. card pay only half price all evening from Monday through Thursday.

Open Monday to Saturday, 8:30 p.m. to 3 a.m., the Main Room is built like an amphitheater, with tiered tables, providing clear vision and good sound. You can either sit at the bar to watch the show or at the tables. The Downstairs Bar is more intimate—a pine-paneled rustic atmosphere, where you can meet and talk with the faithful habitués, usually some of the world's most talented musicians. The Upstairs Room is separate. It's a disco called The Maze, and is open Monday to Thursday from 8:30 p.m. to 2 a.m., from 8:30 p.m. to 3 a.m. on Friday and Saturday. Tube: Tottenham Court Road or Leicester Square.

The **Bull's Head,** 373 Lonsdale Rd., Barns, S.W.13 (tel. 876-5241), has presented live modern jazz concerts every night of the week for more than 25 years. One of the oldest hostelries in the area, it was a staging post in the mid-19th century where travelers on their way to Hampton Court and beyond could eat, drink, and rest while the coach horses were changed. The place is known today for its jazz, performed by musicians from all over the world. It's said by many to be the best in town. Two jazz concerts are presented on Sunday, at 8:30 and 11:30 p.m. From Monday to Saturday, you can hear the music at noon and at 2, 8, and 10:30 p.m. You can order good food at the Carvery in the Saloon Bar daily and dine in the 17th-century Stable Restaurant. The restaurant, in the original, restored stables, specializes in steaks, fish, and other traditional fare. It is open daily from 7 p.m. and on Sunday from noon. Meals cost from £8 ($12) up. To get there, take the tube to Hammersmith, then bus 9 the rest of the way.

While you're in the Covent Garden area, you might drop in at the **Rock Garden** on the Piazza, W.C.2 (tel. 240-3961), which offers two live bands every night. People such as Dire Straits, The Police, The Fixx, and the Thompson Twins played there regularly in their early days. Music is generally of a high standard and embraces everything from jazz to rock. Admission is around £2 ($3). Videotapes are shown in the club at night. In the restaurant, you can order a wide variety of dishes, including Louisiana Cajun blackened steak, hamburgers (meat or vegetarian), and a "Greenpeace" pasta salad. The average meal costs around £5.50 ($8.25). In summer, this is *the* place to dine al fresco, beneath the arcades designed by Inigo Jones. Open noon until very late seven days a week. Tube: Covent Garden.

Pizza on the Park, 11 Knightsbridge, S.W.1 (tel. 235-5550), is a good pizza parlor upstairs, but downstairs, two superb grand pianos provide almost nonstop music from 8:30 p.m. to 12:30 a.m. Entrance ranges between £3 ($4.50) and £5 ($7.50). Tube: Knightsbridge.

FOR DANCING: A legendary setting is the **Café de Paris,** off Piccadilly Circus, W.1 (tel. 437-2036). Once Robert Graves considered it a worthy subject for a book; the Duke of Windsor went there to see Noël Coward perform. Now part of the Mecca chain, it is elaborately decorated with chandeliers. Changing lights set the mood. Two bands alternate every night. Hours are from 8:30 p.m. to 1 a.m. Monday to Thursday, to 2 a.m. Friday and Saturday, and to midnight on Sunday. Tea dances are held from 3 to 5:45 p.m. Admission ranges from £2 ($3) in the afternoon to £3.60 ($5.40) to £3.90 ($5.85) in the evening. Don't expect to find many partners, as most people arrive in couples. Tube: Leicester Square.

The biggest and one of the best places to dance in London is the **Empire,** Leicester Square, W.C.1 (tel. 437-1446), a plushly ornate place operating on several levels centering around a magnificent dance floor. The bandstand is a leaping, revolving, and ever-changing spectrum of light. The largest dance hall of its type in Europe and situated in the heart of London's entertainment era, the establishment features live bands of top caliber, groups, and DJs seven nights a week. Hours are from 8 p.m. to 2 a.m. Monday to Wednesday, to 3 a.m. Thursday to Saturday, and to 1 a.m. on Sunday. Liquid refreshment is dispensed from no fewer than five bars, and the sign above the entrance says "Disco Dancing" in 14 languages. A wine bar is also in operation in the evening. According to the day of the week and the time (early is cheaper, of course), admission prices range from £3 ($4.50) to £5 ($7.50). Tube: Leicester Square.

A CULTURAL COMPLEX: Open seven days a week, **Riverside Studios,** Crisp Road, Hammersmith, W.6 (box office tel. 748-3354), is made up of theaters, gallery, bookshop, bar, and restaurant. The two theater spaces show a wide range of theater and dance, both English and foreign. The gallery holds many prestigious national and international exhibitions as well as those by local artists. Regular dance classes, theater workshops, and writers' groups are also held. The restaurant, open from noon to 8:30 p.m., serves a selection of hot and cold meals and salads, and a filling repast can be had for about £4 ($6). Coffee and cakes are served until 10 p.m. The bar is open normal licensing hours. Current programs are available throughout London. Tickets vary according to the show, ranging from £2 ($3) to £7 ($10.50). Dance classes are £2 ($3). The establishment lies a five-minute walk from the Hammersmith Underground.

A MEDIAEVAL FEESTE: If you'd like to eat, drink, and be merry in the style of the Middle Ages, try the **1520 A.D. Tudor Rooms,** 17 Swallow St., W.1 (tel. 340-3978). You get a banquet and medieval pageantry, with actors impersonating King Henry VIII, Anne Boleyn, Jane Seymour, the court jester, minstrels, and a dancing bear, while guests are served by "wenches." The feast is made up of game soup, pâté, a glass of Olde English mead, Henry's fish delight (puff pastry with a seafood filling), roast baby chicken with fresh vegetables, and, to finish, Master Edwarde's treat, made with fresh fruit, cream, and Grand Marnier. After the show, return to the 20th century with disco dancing until 12:30 a.m. The cost is £20 ($30) from Sunday to Thursday, £22 ($33) Friday and Saturday. Wine or ale is included with your meal. Tube: Piccadilly Circus.

GAMBLING: London was a gambling metropolis long before anyone ever heard of Monte Carlo and when Las Vegas was an anonymous sandpile in the desert. From the Regency period until halfway into the 19th century, Britain was more or less governed by gamblers. Lord Sandwich invented the snack named after him so he wouldn't have to leave the card table for a meal. Prime Minister Fox was so addicted that he frequently went to a cabinet meeting straight from the green baize table.

Queen Victoria's reign changed all that, as usual, by jumping to the other extreme. For more than a century games of chance were so rigorously outlawed that no barmaid dared to keep a dice cup on the counter.

The pendulum swung again in 1960 when the present queen gave her Royal Assent to the new Betting and Gaming Act. According to this legislation, gambling was again permitted in "bona fide clubs" by members and their guests.

Since London's definition of a "club" is as loose as a rusty screw in a cardboard wall, this immediately gave rise to the current situation, which continues to startle, amaze, and bewilder foreign visitors. For the fact is that you come across gambling devices in the most unlikely spots, such as discos, social clubs, and cabaret restaurants. All of which may, by the haziest definition, qualify as "clubs."

The most legitimate gambling clubs offer very pleasant trimmings in the shape of bars and restaurants, but their central theme is unequivocally Luck. There are at least 25 of them in the West End alone, with m the suburbs. And the contrasts between them are much sharpe Nevada casinos.

Under the law, casinos are not allowed to advertise, and if th to lose their licenses. Their appearance in a travel guide "advertising"—hence I can't recommend specific clubs as in th

However, most hall porters can tell you where you can gar not illegal to gamble, just to advertise it. You'll be required to become a member of your chosen club, and must wait 24 hours before you can play the tables, then strictly for cash. The most common games are roulette, blackjack, punto banco, and baccarat. Most casinos, as mentioned, have restaurants where you can expect a good standard of cuisine at a reasonable price.

4. Taking the Tours

In addition to the sites you can see in London by foot, or by utilizing the Underground, there are numerous attractions that can be reached via several coach tours. As an added bonus, there are dozens of fascinating trips that can be made on the Thames.

EASIEST WAY TO SEE LONDON: For the first-timer, the quickest and most economical way to bring the big city into focus is to take a two-hour, 20-mile circular tour of the West End and The City, the guided **London Transport Original Sightseeing Tour,** which passes virtually all the major places of interest in central London. Operated by London Transport, the city's official bus company, the journeys leave at frequent intervals daily from Piccadilly Circus (Haymarket), Victoria (Victoria Street), Marble Arch, and Baker Street. Departures are most frequent from 10 a.m. to 5 p.m. in July and August, with special late trips from Piccadilly Circus, until 9 p.m. Some of the journeys are by open-top buses. Every bus has an experienced, qualified guide on board, and passengers are given a photographic album of celebrated and historical scenes. Tickets cost £4.25 ($6.38) for adults and £3.25 ($4.88) for children and are available from the driver. Tickets can also be purchased from London Regional Transport Travel Information Centres, where you can get a discount of 50p (75¢) off each ticket. Locations of the travel information centers are given under "Transportation in Greater London," Chapter III of this book. In that section, you will also find information about **London Explorer** passes and **One-Day Off-Peak Travelcards,** which provide unlimited travel on red buses and the Underground.

LONDON'S WEST END AND THE CITY: If you prefer a more detailed look at the city's sights, **London Transport** offers highly regarded guided tours.

For a look at the West End, a three-hour tour is featured, passing Westminster Abbey (guided tour), the Houses of Parliament, Trafalgar Square, and Piccadilly Circus. A visit to the Changing of the Guard at Buckingham Palace or the Horse Guards Parade is also included. The cost is £9.50 ($14.25) for adults and £7 ($10.50) for children under 14.

London Transport's other popular three-hour tour is of The City, including guided trips to the Tower of London and St. Paul's Cathedral. The fare for this one is £12 ($18) for adults and £9 ($13.50) for children under 14, including admission charges.

These tours leave from Wilton Road Coach Station at 10 a.m. and 2 p.m., respectively. Departures are daily except Sunday. There is a connecting bus service from Kings Cross, Euston Bus Station, Russell Square, and Marble Arch. Seats may be reserved at the Travel Information Centres at St. James's Park, Piccadilly Circus, Kings Cross, Euston, Oxford Circus, Victoria, Charing Cross, West Croydon, and

...the Airbus/Underground desks in the terminals at Heathrow Airport. Reserva-
...may also be made at Wilton Road Coach Station or any national travel agents.

The guided 1½-hour nonstop tour leaves from Victoria Street (Underground station), Marble Arch (Speakers Corner), and Baker Street station forecourt, Piccadilly
Circus (Haymarket) at frequent intervals. The cost is £5 ($7.50) for adults and £3
($4.50) for children or £4.50 ($6.75) for adults and £2.50 ($3.75) if bought at any of
the Travel Information Centres.

Day and half-day tours start from Wilton Road Coach Station, and it is necessary
to reserve seats. This can be done at the Travel Information Centres at St. James's
Park, Oxford Circus, Piccadilly Circus, Victoria, Kings Cross, Euston, Heathrow,
and the Wilton Road Coach Station, as well as at any national travel agency.

CULTUREBUS: London's only hop-on, hop-off sightseeing service is operated by
Southend Transport Ltd., 87 London Rd., Southend-on-Sea (tel. 0702/355711).
Their blue-and-yellow double-decker buses will take you on an 18-mile, two-hour,
20-stop journey taking in Harrods, Albert Hall, and Hyde Park to the west, Madame
Tussaud's and the Planetarium to the north, and extending through The City to the
Tower of London and Tower Bridge in the east, after which the bus recrosses the river
past St. Paul's and then goes back to see the National Theatre and Lambeth Palace
before returning to the West End, past the Houses of Parliament and the Tate Gallery.
You can travel as far as you like, get off the bus at any of the stops on the route, spend
hours browsing in museums and art galleries, and rejoin a later bus—all for the price of
a day's ticket.

The service operates year round, coaches departing every 30 minutes between 9
a.m. and 6 p.m. daily. Taped and driver commentary are given. One-day tickets can be
purchased through your travel agent, at your hotel in London, or from the driver when
you board the bus on your first ride. Fare is £4 ($6) for adults, £2 ($3) for children
under 14.

BOAT CRUISES ON THE THAMES: Touring boats operate in profusion on the
Thames between April and September, with curtailed winter schedules, taking you
various places within London, and also to nearby towns along the Thames.

Main embarkation points are Westminster Pier, Charing Cross Pier, and Tower
Hill Pier, a system that enables you to take a "water taxi" to the Tower of London and
Westminster Abbey. Not only are the boats energy-saving, bringing you painlessly to
your destination, but they permit you to sit back in comfort as you see London from the
river's point of view.

A number of companies operate these boats, which vary from large launches to
smaller speedboats. Many have service every 20 minutes from 10:20 a.m. until dusk.
Because of tides, however, no exact schedule is given; you must simply go to the pier
and take your chance. But the wait is usually short.

The multitude of small companies operating boat services from Westminster Pier
have organized themselves into the **Westminster Passenger Service Association,**
Westminster Pier, Victoria Embankment, S.W.1 (tel. 930-4097). Boats leave the pier
for cruises of varying length throughout the day and evening. A selection follows.

The most popular ride is from Westminster to the Tower of London (also for St.
Katharine's Dock, H.M.S. *Belfast,* and London Dungeon). The cost is £1.40 ($2.10)
for an adult, 80p ($1.20) for children. You can also go from Westminster to Green-
wich. Adults pay £2.10 ($3.15) one way, £1.10 ($1.65) for children. From April to
October, the boat leaves Westminster for the Tower every 20 minutes and for Greenwich every 30 minutes. In winter, these services are combined, leaving Westminster
every 30 minutes.

Take the Westminster tube to Westminster Pier.

London Transport's evening tour of the city and the river by night departs on

Tuesday, Thursday, and Friday at 7:30 p.m. from Wilton Road. First you're taken on a short drive around the sights, including St. Paul's, the Tower of London, Buckingham Palace, and Trafalgar Square. Then you go for a leisurely cruise on the river, with a buffet and wine served on board. The return to Westminster Pier is approximately at 10:30 p.m. The cost, including the boat ride and the meal, is £18.50 ($27.75). Reservations for these and other tours operated by London Transport can be made at any of their travel information centers.

CANAL BOATS TO LITTLE VENICE: When you get tired of fighting the London traffic, you might want to come here and take a peaceful trip (1½ hours) aboard the traditionally painted narrow boat *Jason* and her butty boat *Serpens*. Come for lunch along the most colorful part of the Regent's Canal in the heart of London. The boat is moored in Blomfield Road, just off Edgware Road in Maida Vale. Little Venice is the junction of two canals and was given its name by Lord Byron.

To inquire about bookings, including the Boatman's Basket Luncheon Trip, get in touch with **Jason's Trip,** Opp. No. 60 Blomfield Road, Little Venice, W.9 (tel. 286-3428). Advance booking is essential during high season. If you come by tube, take the Bakerloo Line to Warwick Avenue. Face the church, turn left, and walk up Clifton Villas to the end and turn right (about two minutes). If you arrive early you can browse around the shop, which sells many brightly colored traditionally painted canal wares.

On the trip you'll pass through the long Maida Hill tunnel under Edgware Road, through Regent's Park, the Mosque, the Zoo, Lord Snowdon's Aviary, pass the Pirate's Castle to Camden Lock and return to Little Venice. The season begins on Easter weekend and lasts through to the middle of October. During April and May, the boats run at 12:30 and 2:30 p.m. In June, July, and August, they run at 10:30 a.m. and at 12:30, 2:30, and 4:30 p.m. During September and October, trips leaves at 12:30 and 2:30 p.m., but always telephone first. Refreshments are served on all trips, including a prebooked boatman's basket lunch on the 12:30 and 2:30 p.m. trips, and a cream tea on the 4:30 p.m. voyage. The fare for a day trip is £2.75 ($4.13) for adults and £1.50 ($2.25) for children.

Jenny Wren **Canal Cruises,** 250 Camden High St., N.W.1 (tel. 485-4433), will also take you aboard a traditionally designed and decorated canal narrow boat, along Regent's Park Canal from the Camden Town Lock, the Zoo, Regent's Park, and through the canal tunnel to Maida Vale, around the island at Little Venice, and then back to the point of embarkation. The cost is £1.85 ($2.78) for adults, £1.05 ($1.58) for children. On Friday and Saturday, there is a mystery cruise with a refreshment shop at a suitable hostelry, costing £3.75 ($5.60) per person. Tube: Mornington.

LONDON WALKS: An exciting way to see many parts of London is offered by **J.W. Travel,** 66 St. Michael's St., W.2 (tel. 262-9572). John Wittich, who owns J.W. Travel, started walking tours of London in 1960. He is a Freeman of the City of London and a member of two of the ancient guilds of London, as well as having written several books on London walks. He is also director of the London History Fellowship. There is no better way to search out the unusual, the beautiful, and the historic than to take a walking tour. The company concentrates on taking personal walking tours for families and groups that have booked in advance. John Wittich conducts all tours. The cost for 1½-hour walks is £7.50 ($11.25) for a family of up to five adults, while groups are charged £17.50 ($26.25) for up to 20 adults. Some of the trips include walks around London's villages (Hampstead, Highgate, Paddington, Chelsea, Kew, and elsewhere), the City of Westminster, sites which such people as Pepys and Jack the Ripper frequented, Legal London, and riverside walks. Tube: Paddington.

Hunt for ghosts or walk in the steps of Jack the Ripper, the infamous East End murderer of prostitutes in the 1880s. Discover the alleys and byways of Old London.

Investigate the London of Dickens, Shakespeare, and Sherlock Holmes, or taste the delights of an evening's drinking in four historic pubs. These and many other walks (the historic city from the Romans to the Blitz; Legal and Illegal London—Inns of Court) are included in the program of unusual and historical walks organized by **London Walks,** 139 Conway Rd., Southgate, London N14 7BH (tel. 882-2763). Walks take place on weekends all through the year and during the week throughout the summer. The cost is £2.25 ($3.38) for adults; children under 16 go free. No booking is required. Get in touch with the above address for details. Send an International Reply Coupon.

Another small and enthusiastic company offering a vast variety of London walks is **Discovering London.** It's operated by a Scot, Alex Cobban, a historian of some note who insists that his guides are knowledgeable and sympathetic and who, perhaps, looks at the London that Londoners take for granted. He is aided by Mrs. Cobban, also a highly qualified guide. Mainly on Sunday, but during the week as well, scheduled walks are planned, starting at easily found Underground stations—to the London Dickens Knew, Finding Roman London, Inns of Court—Lawyer's London, Belgravia "Upstairs and Downstairs," Ghost, and Jack the Ripper tours, some 70 different titles. Mr. Cobban's knowledge of Sherlock Holmes is immense. No advance booking is necessary for most tours, and the walks cost £2.25 ($3.38); children under 16 go free, and students with I.D. cards are charged £2 ($3). Each walk takes about 1½ to 2 hours. A selection of tours of museums, galleries, Westminster Abbey, St. Paul's, and Kensington Palace is also offered. Write, enclosing an International Reply Coupon, for a detailed sheet of the walks available during your stay in London. The address is Discovering London, 11 Pennyfields, Warley, Brentwood, Essex CM14 5JP (tel. 0277/213704).

Londoner Pub Walks set out every Friday evening from the Temple Underground Station at 7:30 p.m. to discover places full of interest and history. By exploring away from the more regular tourist areas, the walks offer a chance to meet the local people and to discover what it is that makes the English pub a unique institution. Reservations are not necessary, but further details may be secured from Peter Westbrook, 3 Springfield Ave., London, N.10 (tel. 883-2656). The charge is £2.50 ($3.75), and you buy your own drinks.

5. London for Children

It's hard to draw a clear distinguishing line between junior and senior brands of entertainment in many areas. In London, it's almost impossible. The British Museum, for example, is definitely rated as an adult attraction. Yet I've watched group after group of kids stand absolutely spellbound in front of the Egyptian mummies, still completely absorbed long after their parents were champing at the bit to trot along. Conversely, the Zoo is often supposed to be primarily for the younger set, but I've watched dignified daddies become so hypnotized by the ant colony and the nest-stitching Indian tailor bird that they had to be literally dragged away by their broods. One variation or another of the same scene is constantly enacted at the Tower, Madame Tussaud's, Billingsgate Market, Battersea Park, and a dozen other places.

I've seen small girls react with frozen unamusement to royal dollhouses that had their mothers cooing with delight. And I've observed those same little ladies aglow with enthusiasm before the oil painting of a particularly gruesome 17th-century massacre. Their spiritual brothers, meanwhile, disdained even to glance at a model car racetrack and preferred to give their total attention to the activities of a window cleaner. All of which goes to prove that children are at least as individualistic in their tastes as adults. It also goes to make my classification job difficult.

The attractions to follow are *not* meant specifically for children. They are general and universal fun places to which you can take youngsters without having to worry about either their physical or moral safety. There's nothing to stop you from going to any of them minus a juvenile escort. It is even possible that you'll enjoy them more thoroughly than any kid around. Many of the interesting sights, such as the Royal Mews, where you can see the Queen's horses and royal and state coaches, are described earlier in this chapter.

THE LONDON DUNGEON: The premises at 34 Tooley St., S.E.1 (tel. 403-0606), simulate a ghoulish atmosphere designed deliberately to chill the blood while reproducing faithfully the conditions that existed in the Middle Ages. Set under the arches of London Bridge Station, the dungeon is a series of tableaux, more grizzly than Madame Tussaud's, depicting life in medieval London. The rumble of trains overhead adds to the spine-chilling horror of the place. Bells toll, and there is constant melancholy chanting in the background. Dripping water and live rats (caged!) make for even more atmosphere. The heads of executed criminals were stuck on spikes for onlookers to observe through glasses hired for the occasion. The murder of Thomas à Becket in Canterbury Cathedral is also depicted. Naturally, there's a burning at the stake, as well as a torture chamber with racking, branding, and fingernail extraction.

If you survive, there is a souvenir shop selling certificates to testify that you have been through the works. The dungeon is open from 10 a.m. to 5:30 p.m. April through September, to 4:30 p.m. October through March, seven days a week. Admission is £3.50 ($5.25) for adults, £2 ($3) for children under 14, except in June, July, and August when prices are £3.80 ($5.70) for adults, £2.20 ($3.30) for children. Tube: London Bridge Station.

BATTERSEA PARK: The park is a vast patch of woodland, lakes, and lawns on the south bank of the Thames, S.W.1, opposite Chelsea Embankment. It boasts just about everything that makes for happiness on a dry day: a tree-lined boulevard, fountains, and a children's zoo with baby animals. The nearest tube at Sloane Square is a long, long way away and on the north bank of the Thames (you'll have to cross Chelsea Bridge). Better ask at your hotel for a convenient bus route.

THEATERS FOR CHILDREN: At the Arts Theatre, Great Newport Street, W.C.2, the **Unicorn Theatre** for children commissions several new plays each year as well as presenting dramatizations of classics such as *Beowulf* and *Gulliver's Travels.* Each play is presented for a specific age range within the 4-to-12 age group, which is indicated on all publicity. Visiting children's theater companies perform at the Unicorn during the spring, and in the summer months, the Unicorn Summer Tour goes to parks and playgrounds in the London area. Performances are given Tuesday to Sunday at 2 p.m., costing from £3 ($4.50) to £4 ($6). For additional information, such as how to secure temporary memberships for foreigners, telephone 379-3280. To reserve tickets, call the box office (tel. 836-3334). Tube: Leicester Square.

The **Little Angel Marionette Theatre,** 14 Dagmar Passage, Cross Street, N.1 (tel. 226-1787), is especially constructed for and devoted to presentation of puppetry in all its forms. It is open to the general public, and 200 to 300 performances are given each year. The theater is the focal point of a loosely formed group of some 20 professional puppeteers who work here as occasion demands, presenting their own shows or helping with performances of the resident company. In the current repertory, there are 25 programs. These vary in style and content from *The Soldier's Tale,* using eight-foot-high figures, to *Wonder Island* and *Lancelot the Lion,* written especially for the humble glove puppet. Many of the plays, such as Hans Christian Andersen's *The Little Mermaid,* are performed with marionettes (string puppets), but whatever is being presented, you'll be enthralled with the exquisite lighting and skill with which the puppets are handled.

The theater is beautifully decorated and well equipped. There is a coffee bar in the foyer and a workshop adjacent where the settings and costumes, as well as the puppets, are made. To find out what's playing and reserve your seats, call 226-1787. Performances are at 11 a.m. on Saturday, when the seats are £1 ($1.50) for children, £2 ($3) for adults; and at 3 p.m. on Saturday and Sunday, when the cost is £1.75 ($2.63) for children, £2.75 ($4.13) for adults. Take the tube to Angel Station, then walk up Upper Street to St. Mary's Church and down the footpath to the left of the church. You can go by car or taxi to Essex Road and then up to Dagmar Terrace.

LONDON ZOO: One of the greatest zoos in the world, the London Zoo is more than a century and a half old. Run by the Zoological Society of London, Regent's Park, N.W.1 (tel. 722-3333), with an equal measure of showmanship and scholarly know-how, this 36-acre garden houses some 8,000 animals, including some of the rarest species on earth. The most famous is the giant panda, Chia-Chia, a gift to Britain from the People's Republic of China. One of the most fascinating exhibits is the Snowdon Aviary. Separate houses are reserved for some species: the insect house (incredible bird-eating spiders, a cross-sectioned ant colony), the reptile house (huge dragon-like monitor lizards and a fantastic 15-foot python), and other additions, such as the Sobell Pavilion for Apes and Monkeys and the Lion Terrace.

Designed for the largest collection of small mammals in the world, the Clore Pavilion has a basement called the Moonlight World, where special lighting effects simulate night for the nocturnal beasties, while rendering them clearly visible to onlookers. You can see all the night rovers in action—leaping bush babies, rare kiwis, a fierce Tasmanian devil, and giant Indian fruit bats with heads like prehistoric dogs.

Many families budget almost an entire day to spend with the animals, watching the sea lions being fed, enjoying an animal ride in summer, and meeting the baby elephants on their walks. The zoo is open daily from 9 a.m. in summer and from 10 a.m. in winter, until 6 p.m. or dusk, whichever is earlier. Last entrance is half an hour before closing. Admission is £3.40 ($5.10) for adults, £1.70 ($2.55) for children 5 to 16 (under 5 free). On the grounds are two fully licensed restaurants, one self-service and the other with waitresses. Take the tube to Baker Street or Camden Town, then take bus 74 (Camden Town is nearer and an easy ten-minute walk).

NATURAL HISTORY MUSEUM: This museum, on Cromwell Road, S.W.7 (tel. 589-6323), is the home of the national collections of living and fossil plants, animals, minerals, rocks, and meteorites, with lots of magnificent specimens on display. Exciting exhibitions designed to encourage people of all ages to enjoy learning about modern natural history include "Human Biology—An Exhibition of Ourselves," "Dinosaurs and Their Living Relatives," "Man's Place in Evolution," "British Natural History," and "Discovering Mammals." Admission is free. The museum is open weekdays from 10 a.m. to 6 p.m., on Sunday from 2:30 to 6 p.m. Tube: South Kensington.

BETHNAL GREEN MUSEUM OF CHILDHOOD: On Cambridge Heath Road, E.2 (tel. 980-2415), this establishment displays toys over the past century. The variety of dolls alone is staggering, some of them dressed in period costumes of such elaborateness that you don't even want to think of the price tags they must have carried. With the dolls go dollhouses, from simple cottages to miniature mansions, complete with fireplaces and grand pianos, plus carriages, furniture, kitchen utensils, and household pets. It might be wise to explain to your children beforehand that—no—none of them is for sale. In addition, the museum displays optical toys, toy theaters, marionettes, puppets, and a considerable exhibit of soldiers and battle toys of both World Wars. There is also a display of children's clothing and furniture related to childhood. The museum is open weekdays except Friday from 10 a.m. to 6 p.m.; on Sunday from 2:30 p.m. Admission is free. Tube: Bethnal Green.

THE LONDON TOY AND MODEL MUSEUM: Two restored Victorian houses at 21/23 Craven Hill, W.2 (tel. 262-7905), off Bayswater Road, shelter one of the finest collections of commercially made toys and models on public display in Europe, with items by all the major toy and model manufacturers. The model and toy train collection is particularly comprehensive, tracing the development of the miniature train from the inception of railways in the early 19th century. There are several garden railway systems, including a child's ride-on train. The permanent collection details the rise of toys with the industrial revolution. There is a fine display of dolls, teddy bears, and a quarter-scale child's model of a Cadillac sports roadster made in 1916. Baywest City, one of the world's most stunning working miniature model cities, is a great attraction. The museum has a café and a large recreational garden area. It's open Tuesday to Saturday from 10 a.m. to 5:30 p.m., Sunday from 11 a.m. to 5:30 p.m., and on bank holiday Monday. Admission is £1.80 ($2.70) for adults, 60p (90¢) for children (free for children under 5 years of age). Nearest tube station is Lancaster Gate.

FUN ON HAMPSTEAD HEATH: This is the traditional playground of the Londoner, the 'Appy 'Ampstead of Cockney legend, the place dedicated "to the use of the public forever" by special Act of Parliament in 1872. Londoners might just possibly tolerate the conversion of, say, Hyde Park into housing estates or supermarkets, but they would certainly mount the barricades if Hampstead Heath were imperiled. This 800-acre expanse of high heath entirely surrounded by London is a chain of continuous park, wood, and grassland, bearing different names in different portions. It contains just about every known form of outdoor amusement, with the exception of deep-sea fishing and big game hunting. There's something here for children and grownups alike, with activities to include the entire family. There are natural lakes for swimmers (who don't mind goosebumps), bridle paths for horseback riders, athletic tracks, hills for kite flying, and a special pond for model yachting. You can catch bream and pike in several lakes, paddle your own boat on others, and feed the squirrels.

At the shore of Kenwood lake, in the northern section, is a concert platform devoted to symphony performances on summer evenings. In the northeast corner, in Waterlow Park, ballets, operas, and comedies are staged at the Grass Theatre in June and July.

At Easter, Whitsun, and August bank holidays, the heath becomes riotous with the noise and tunes of two fun fairs going full blast, and even sophisticated Londoners make a point of dropping in on them. It's all part of a tradition as deeply rooted as orderly queueing and Christmas decorations.

History-minded youngsters and adults should stand for a moment on top of Parliament Hill on the south side. It was from that vantage point that the ancient British (Iceni tribe) Queen Boadicea and her daughters watched the burning of the Roman camp of Londinium, which her tribesmen put to the torch in A.D. 61. Tube: Hampstead or Belsize Park.

5. One-Day Trips from London

It would be sad to leave England without ever having ventured into her countryside, at least for a day. The English are the greatest excursion travelers in the world, forever dipping into their own rural areas to discover ancient abbeys, 17th-century village lanes, shady woods for picnic lunches, and stately mansions. From London, it's possible to avail yourself of countless tours—either by conducted coach, boat, or via a do-it-yourself method on bus or train. On many trips you can combine two or more methods of transportation; for example, you can go to Windsor by boat and return by coach or train.

Highly recommended are the previously described Green Line Coaches, operated by London Country Bus Services Ltd. (see Chapter I, "Traveling Within England" section). For longer tours, say, to Stratford-upon-Avon, you will find the trains much more convenient. Often you can take advantage of the many bargain tickets outlined in Chapter I. For further information about trains to a specific location, go to the British Rail offices on Lower Regent Street.

The **London Regional Transport** system has conducted tours to places of interest in and around London. For example, a day tour to Windsor and Hampton Court goes seven days a week from the Wilton Road Coach Station, costing £26.50 ($39.75) for adults, £21 ($31.50) for children under 14, including admission prices and lunch at Windsor. Another tour to Canterbury and Leeds Castle is priced at £26.50 ($39.75) for adults, £19 ($28.50) for children. A Salisbury-Stonehenge-Longleat-Bath tour costs adults £29 ($43.50), children £24 ($36). For information on the transport system's information and ticket centers, see Chapter III under "Transportation in Greater London."

HAMPTON COURT: On the north side of the Thames, 13 miles west of London in East Molesey, Surrey, this 16th-century palace of Cardinal Wolsey can teach us a lesson: Don't try to outdo your boss, particularly if he happens to be Henry VIII. The rich cardinal did just that. But the king had a lean and hungry eye. Wolsey, who eventually lost his fortune, power, and prestige, ended up giving his lavish palace to the Tudor monarch. In a stroke of one-upsmanship, Henry took over, outdoing the Wolsey embellishments. The Tudor additions included the Anne Boleyn gateway, with its 16th-century astronomical clock that even tells the high-water mark at London Bridge. From Clock Court, you can see one of Henry's major contributions, the aptly named Great Hall, with its hammer-beam ceiling. Also added by Henry were the tiltyard, a tennis court, and kitchens.

Hampton Court had quite a retinue to feed. Cooking was done in the Great Kitchen, which may be visited. Henry cavorted through the various apartments with his wives of the moment, from Anne Boleyn to Catherine Parr (the latter reversed things and lived to bury her erstwhile spouse). Charles I was imprisoned at one time, and temporarily managed to escape his jailers.

Although the palace enjoyed prestige and pomp in Elizabethan days, it owes much of its present look to William and Mary of Orange, or rather to Sir Christopher Wren, who designed and had built the Northern or Lion Gates, intended to be the main entrance to the new parts of the palace. The fine wrought-iron screen at the south end of the south gardens was made by Jean Tijou around 1694 for William and Mary. You can parade through the apartments, filled with porcelain, furniture, paintings, and tapestries. The King's Dressing Room is graced with some of the best art, including Pieter Brueghel the Elder's macabre *Massacre of the Innocents*. Tintoretto and Titian deck the halls of the King's Drawing Room. Finally, be sure to inspect the Royal Chapel (Wolsey wouldn't recognize it). To confound yourself totally, you may want to get lost in the serpentine shrubbery Maze in the garden, also the work of Sir Christopher Wren.

The gardens, including the Great Vine, King's Privy Garden, Great Fountain Gardens, Tudor and Elizabethan Knot Gardens, Broad Walk, Tiltyard, and Wilderness, are open daily year round from 7 a.m. until dusk, but not later than 9 p.m., and can be visited free. Cloisters, courtyards, and State Apartments are open from 9:30 a.m. to 5 p.m. weekdays, from 2 to 7 p.m. Sunday, January 2 to March 31 and October 1 to December 31, with the same opening hours from April 1 to September 30, closing at 6 p.m. The Great Kitchen and cellars, Tudor tennis courts, King's private apartments, Hampton Court exhibition, and Mantegna Paintings gallery are open the same hours as the above, but only from April to September. Admission to all these attractions is £2.20 ($3.30) for adults, £1 ($1.50) for children 5 to 16 (under 5 free). To visit only the courtyards and cloisters, including the kitchens and cellars, costs 50p (75¢) for adults, 25p (38¢) for children 5 to 16.

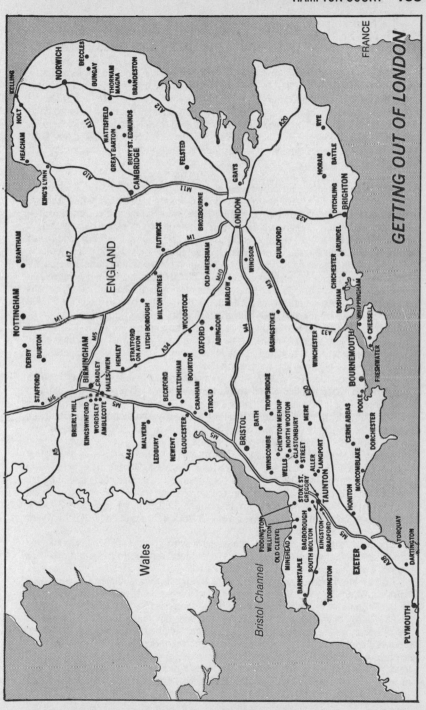

GETTING OUT OF LONDON

The Maze is open daily from 10 a.m. to 5 p.m. March 1 to October 31, costing 30p (45¢) for adults, 25p (38¢) for children 5 to 16 (under 5 free). For inquiries regarding the palace and its appurtenances, get in touch with the Superintendent of the Palace, Hampton Court Palace, East Molesey, Surrey KT8 9AU (tel. 977-8441).

You can go to Hampton Court by bus, train, boat, or car. London Regional Transport buses for routes 111, 131, 216, 267, and 461 make the trip, with Green Line buses (ask at the nearest London Country Bus office) for routes 713, 715, 716, 718, 726, and 728 offering service. Frequent trains from Waterloo Station (Southern Region) go to Hampton Court Station. Boat service is offered to and from Kingston and Richmond. Apply to Thames Passenger Services, Westminster Pier, London, S.W.1 (tel. 930-0921) or Turks Launches Limited, Thames Side, Kingston-upon-Thames, Surrey (tel. 546-2434).

KEW GARDENS: Nine miles southwest of central London at Kew, near Richmond, are the **Royal Botanic Gardens** (tel. 940-1171), among the best known in Europe, containing thousands of varieties of plants. But Kew is no mere pleasure garden—rather, it is essentially a vast scientific research center that happens to be beautiful. A pagoda, erected in 1761, represents the flowering of chinoiserie. One of the oddities of Kew is a Douglas fir flagstaff more than 220 feet high. The gardens cover a 300-acre site encompassing lakes, greenhouses, walks, garden pavilions, and museums, together with fine examples of the architecture of Sir William Chambers. At whatever season you visit Kew, there's always something to see: in spring, the daffodils and bluebells through to the coldest months when the Heath Garden is at its best. Among the 50,000 plant species are notable collections of arum lilies, ferns, orchids, aquatic plants, cacti, mountain plants, palms, and tropical waterlilies. The gardens are open daily except Christmas and New Year's Day from 10 a.m. to either 4 or 5 p.m., depending on the season. The entrance fee, although it has gone above the traditional "one penny" in effect for a couple of centuries, is only 25p (38¢).

Much interest focuses on the red-brick **Kew Palace** (dubbed the Dutch House), a former residence of King George III and Queen Charlotte. It is reached by walking to the northern tip of the Broad Walk. Now a museum, it was built in 1631 and contains memorabilia of the reign of George III, along with a royal collection of furniture and paintings. It is open only from April to September, 11 a.m. to 5:30 p.m. daily. Admission is 70p ($1.05) for adults, 40p (60¢) for children.

At the gardens, **Queen Charlotte's Cottage** has been restored to its original splendor. Built in 1772, it is half-timbered and thatched. George III is believed to have been the architect. The house has been restored in great detail, including the original Hogarth prints which hung on the downstairs walls. The cottage is open from mid-April to mid-October from 11 a.m. to 5:30 p.m. on Saturday, Sunday, and bank holiday Mondays. Admission is 40p (60¢) for adults and 20p (30¢) for children.

The least expensive and most convenient way to visit the gardens is to take the District Line Underground to Kew. The most romantic way to come in summer is via a streamer from Westminster Bridge to Kew Pier.

London's living steam museum, **Kew Bridge Engines,** Green Dragon Lane, Brentford, Middlesex (tel. 568-4757), houses what is probably the world's largest collection of steam-powered beam engines. These were used in the Victorian era and up to the 1940s to pump London's water, and one engine has a capacity of 700 gallons per stroke. There are six restored engines which are steamed on weekends, plus other unrestored engines, models, traction engines, and a working forge. The museum has a tea room, plus free parking for cars. It's open and in steam on Saturday, Sunday, and Monday when it falls on a holiday from 11 a.m. to 5 p.m. From Monday to Friday, you can see it as a static exhibition during the same hours. Admission on weekends is £1.60 ($2.40) for adults, 80p ($1.20) for children, with a family price of £4.50 ($6.75). On weekdays, adults are charged £1 ($1.50) and children 50p (75¢), with the family rate being £2.75 ($4.13).

The museum is north of Kew Bridge, under the tower, a ten-minute walk from Kew Gardens. You can reach it by a Southern Region British Rail train from Waterloo Station to Kew Bridge Station; by buses 27, 65, 237, or 267 (7 on Sunday), or by Gunnersbury or South Ealing tube and thence by bus.

RUNNYMEDE: Two miles outside Windsor is the meadow on the south side of the Thames, in Surrey, where King John put his seal on the Magna Carta (Great Charter). John may have signed the document up the river on a little island, but that's being technical. Today Runnymede is also the site of the **John F. Kennedy Memorial,** one acre of English ground given to the United States by the people of Britain.

The Pagoda you can see from the road was placed there by the American Bar Association to acknowledge the fact that American law stems from the English system. The John F. Kennedy Memorial is a large block of white stone, hard to see from the road on the edge of the treeline.

A HALF DAY IN GREENWICH: Greenwich Mean Time, of course, is the basis of standard time throughout most of the world, the zero point used in the reckoning of terrestrial longitudes since 1884. But Greenwich is also the home of the Royal Naval College, the National Maritime Museum, and the Old Royal Observatory. In drydock at Greenwich Pier is the clipper *Cutty Sark,* as well as Sir Francis Chichester's *Gipsy Moth IV.*

About four miles from "The City," Greenwich is reached by a number of methods, and part of the fun of making the jaunt is in the getting there. Ideally, you'll arrive by boat, as Henry VIII preferred to do on one of his hunting expeditions. In summer, launches leave at regular intervals from either the Charing Cross or Westminster Piers.

Actually, Westminster Pier is preferred because the boats from Charing Cross are usually filled with tour-group passengers. In addition, you can take the Underground to New Cross, then bus 171A or 177. Buses 70 and 188 run from Surrey Docks Underground station. The boats leave daily for Greenwich every 30 minutes from 10:30 a.m. to 4 p.m., costing £2.90 ($4.35) round trip for adults, half price for children. The trip takes 45 minutes.

Unquestionably, the *Cutty Sark*—last of the great clippers—holds the most interest, having been seen by millions. At the spot where the vessel is now berthed stood the Ship Inn of the 19th century (Victorians came here for whitebait dinners, as they did to the Trafalgar Tavern). Ordered built by Capt Jock Willis ("Old White Hat"), the clipper was launched in 1869 to sail the China tea trade route. It was named after the Witch Nannie in Robert Burns's *Tam o' Shanter* (note the figurehead). Yielding to the more efficient steamers, the *Cutty Sark* later was converted to a wool-clipper, plying the route between Australia and England. Before her retirement, she knew many owners, even different names, eventually coming to drydock at Cutty Sark Gardens, Greenwich Pier, S.E.10 (tel. 858-3445), in 1954. The vessel may be boarded, costing £1.20 ($1.80) for adults and 60p (90¢) for children, from 10 a.m. to 6 p.m. weekdays, from noon to 6 p.m. on Sunday. Closing time is 5 p.m. in winter. Of special interest is the completely refurbished lower hold housing the largest collection of figureheads known.

A neighbor to the *Cutty Sark*—and also in drydock—is Sir Francis Chichester's *Gipsy Moth IV* (also tel. 858-3445), in which he circumnavigated the world in 1967. He single-handedly fought the elements in his vessel for 119 days. For 20p (30¢) for adults and 10p (15¢) for children, you can go aboard (same hours as the *Cutty Sark*). It's usually closed Friday and from October to April.

The **Royal Naval College** (tel. 858-2154) grew up on the site of the Tudor palace in which Henry VIII and Elizabeth I were born. William and Mary commissioned

Wren to design the present buildings in 1695 to house naval pensioners, and these became the Royal Naval College in 1873. The buildings are a baroque masterpiece, in which the Painted Hall, by Thornhill (1708–1727), and the chapel are outstanding. Charging no admission, it is normally open to the public every day, except Thursday, Christmas, and Good Friday, from 2:30 p.m. until 5 p.m. (last entrance at 4:45 p.m.). However, it can be closed for security reasons.

The **National Maritime Museum** (tel. 858-4422), built around Inigo Jones's 17th-century Palladian Queen's House, portrays Britain's maritime heritage. Actual craft, marine paintings, ship models, and scientific instruments are displayed, including the full-dress uniform coat that Lord Nelson wore at the Battle of Trafalgar. In the west wing is a licensed restaurant. The museum is open from 10 a.m. to 6 p.m. in summer and from 10 a.m. to 5 p.m. in winter; from 2 to 6 p.m. on Sunday in summer, to 5 p.m. in winter. A combined ticket to the main buildings and the Old Royal Observatory (see below) costs £1.50 ($2.25) for adults, 75p ($1.13) for children. For one site only, a ticket costs £1 ($1.50) for adults, 50p (75¢) for children. A £4 ($6) family ticket admits two adults and up to five children.

On the same visit, you can explore the **Old Royal Observatory** (tel. 858-4422). Sir Christopher Wren was the architect—after all, he was interested in astronomy before he became famous. The observatory overlooks Greenwich and the Maritime Museum from a park laid out to the design of Le Nôtre, the French landscaper. Here you can stand with one foot in the west, the other in the east, as the Greenwich Meridian line is well marked to divide the world into hemispheres. See also the big red time ball used in olden days by ships sailing down the river from London to set their timepieces by. There is a fascinating bewilderment of astronomical and navigational instruments, and time and travel become more realistic after a visit here. Other curiosities include the chronometer (or sea watch) used by Captain Cook when he made his Pacific explorations in the 1770s. The observatory is open all year Monday to Saturday from 10 a.m. to 6 p.m. (to 5 p.m. in winter) and on Sunday from 2 to 6 p.m. (to 5 p.m. in winter). It is closed December 24, 25, and 26, January 1, Good Friday, and May Day bank holiday.

Where to Eat and Drink

The **Cutty Sark Free House,** Ballast Quay, Lassell Street, S.E.10 (tel. 858-3146), has plenty of local color on its Thames-side perch. About half a mile from the railway station, this English riverside tavern will dispense drinks in an atmosphere in which you can eavesdrop on the conversation of oldtime salts. "Mine host" is Derek Leach, a friendly, outgoing person who likes to see his guests happy. This riverside pub has lots of old beams, seats cut out of beer barrels, a flagstone floor, and real tradition. Bar snacks include everything from a ploughman's lunch to venison and vegetables. Upstairs is a more formal restaurant, serving à la carte steaks, game, fish, jugged hare, and the chef's specials. You can dine here for around £10 ($15) per person with some wine. Sunday lunch is a popular meal, costing £7 ($10.50). The upstairs restaurant is strict in its service hours for hot food, limiting order-taking to noon to 2 p.m. and 7 to 9:30 p.m. Downstairs, the place functions as a traditional pub. It's all closed on Sunday night and all day Monday.

SYON PARK: Just nine miles from Piccadilly Circus, on 55 acres of the Duke of Northumberland's Thames-side estate, is one of the most beautiful spots in all of Great Britain. There's always something in bloom. Called "The Showplace of the Nation in a Great English Garden," Syon Park was opened to the public in 1968. A nation of green-thumbed gardens is dazzled here, and the park is also educational, showing amateurs how to get the most out of their small gardens. The vast flower- and plant-studded acreage betrays the influence of "Capability" Brown, who laid out the grounds in the 18th century.

Particular highlights include a six-acre rose garden, a butterfly house, and the Great Conservatory, one of the earliest and most famous buildings of its type, built 1822–1827, housing everything from cacti to fuchsias. In it is also housed a walk-through aviary full of exotic and brilliantly colored birds. In the old dairy you will find an interesting seawater aquarium. There is a quarter-mile-long ornamental lake studded with waterlilies and silhouetted by cypresses and willows, even a huge gardening supermarket, and the Motor Museum, holding the Heritage Collection of British cars. With some 90 vehicles, from the earliest 1895 Wolseley to the present day, it has the largest collection of British cars anywhere.

Operated by the Gardening Center Limited, Syon was the site of the first botanical garden in England, created by the father of English botany, Dr. William Turner. Trees include a 200-year-old Chinese juniper, an Afghan ash, Indian bean trees, and a liquidambars. The gardens are open all year (except for Christmas and Boxing Day). The gates open at 10 a.m. and close at dusk or 6 p.m. In winter, after October 31, gates close at 4 p.m. Admission is £1.50 ($2.25) for adults, 80p ($1.20) for children.

On the grounds is **Syon House,** built in 1429, the original structure incorporated into the Duke of Northumberland's present home. The house was later remade to the specifications of the first Duke of Northumberland in 1762–1769. The battlemented facade is that of the original Tudor mansion, but the interior is from the 18th century, the design of Robert Adam. Basil Taylor said of the interior feeling: "You're almost in the middle of a jewel box." In the Middle Ages, Syon was a monastery, later suppressed by Henry VIII. Katharine Howard, the king's fifth wife, was imprisoned in the house before her scheduled beheading in 1542. The house is open from April until the end of September, daily except Friday and Saturday, from noon to 5 p.m.

If you want to visit the house as well as the park, ask for the combined ticket, costing £1.50 ($2.25) for adults and £1 ($1.50) for children. For more information, telephone 560-0882.

THORPE PARK: This is a 500-acre site built around four lakes in old gravel pits. A "theme" park, Staines Road at Chertsey, Surrey KT168 PN (tel. 09328-62633), it lies one and three-quarters of a mile north of Chertsey on the A320. The park is 20 miles west of London and can be reached by train from Waterloo Station or by London suburban bus from Victoria Station. Admission to the park is £6 ($9) for adults, £5.50 ($8.25) for children between 5 and 15. One area of the park includes scenes from British history, with full-size replicas of Roman and Viking ships built at the same Devonshire shipyard that produced a replica of Sir Francis Drake's *Golden Hind.* Other scenes include a Stone Age cave, a Norman motte and bailey castle (the type used by William the Conqueror), and King John's pavilion at the signing of Magna Carta. There's an entire section devoted to detailed reconstructions of World War I aircraft and the race-winning craft that took part in the Schneider Trophy Races for aircraft between 1913 and 1931. It is open April to September from 10 a.m. to 6 p.m. (from 10 a.m. to 9 p.m. in summer).

WINDSOR, OXFORD, AND THE HOME COUNTIES

WITHIN EASY REACH of London, the Thames Valley and the Chilterns are a history-rich part of England, and they lie so close to the capital they can be easily reached by automobile or Green Line coach. You can explore here during the day and return in time to see a show in the West End.

Here are some of the most-visited historic sites in England: the former homes of Disraeli and Elizabeth I, the estate of the Duke of Bedford, and, of course, Windsor Castle, 22 miles from London, one of the most famous castles in Europe and the most popular day trip for those visitors venturing out of London for the first time.

Of course, your principal reason for coming to Oxfordshire, our second goal, is to explore the university city of Oxford, about an hour's drive from London. But Oxford is not the only attraction in the county, as you'll soon discover as you make your way through Henley-on-Thames. The shire is a land of great mansions, old churches of widely varying architectural styles, and rolling farmland.

In a sense, Oxfordshire is a kind of buffer zone between the easy living in the southern towns and the industrialized cities of the heartland. In the southeast are the chalky Chilterns, and in the west you'll be moving toward the wool towns of the Cotswolds. In fact, Burford, an unspoiled medieval town, lying west of Oxford, is one of the traditional gateways to the Cotswolds (dealt with in a later chapter). The Upper Thames winds its way across the southern parts of the county.

The "Home Counties" are characterized by their river valleys and gentle hills. The beech-clad Chiltern Hills are at their most beautiful in spring and fall. This 40-mile chalk ridge extends in an arc from the Thames Valley to the old Roman city of St.

Albans in Hertfordshire. The whole region is popular for boating holidays, as it contains a 200-mile network of canals.

1. Windsor

A Green Line bus from London will deliver you in about an hour to Windsor, site of England's greatest castle and its most famous boys' school. Green Line buses 700, 702, and 704 leave from Eccleston Bridge behind Victoria Station (see "Buses in England," Chapter 1, Section 3). Buses 700 and 702 are express service, but these can only be used at reduced rates after 9 a.m. For the return journey, you can either go straight back into London or stop off at Hampton Court on the way. Take bus 726 or 718 from Windsor. For further information, telephone 01/668-7261.

Windsor was called "Windlesore" by the ancient Britons, who derived the name from the winding shore—quite noticeable as you walk along the Thames here.

THE SIGHTS: Your bus will drop you near the Town Guildhall, to which Wren applied the finishing touches. It's only a short walk up Castle Hill to the following sights:

Windsor Castle

It was William the Conqueror who founded a castle on this spot, beginning a legend and a link with English sovereignty that has known many vicissitudes. King John cooled his heels at Windsor while waiting to put his signature on Magna Carta at nearby Runnymede; Charles I was imprisoned here before losing his head; Queen Bess did some renovations; Victoria mourned her beloved Albert, who died at the castle in 1861; the royal family rode out much of World War II behind its sheltering walls. When Queen Elizabeth II is in residence, the Royal Standard flies. The State Apartments can be visited usually except for about six weeks at Easter, all of June, and three weeks in December, when the court is at Windsor. At other times, the apartments are open during January, February, early March, November, and early December from 10:30 a.m. to 3 p.m. daily except Sunday; July to late October from 10:30 a.m. to 5 p.m. weekdays, 1:30 to 5 p.m. on Sunday. Ticket sales cease about 30 minutes before closing, and last admissions are 15 minutes before closing time. The price of admission is £1.40 ($2.10) for adults, 60p (90¢) for children. It is always advisable to check what is open before visiting by telephoning 0753/868286, ext. 252.

The apartments contain many works of art, porcelain, armor, furniture, three Verro ceilings, and several Gibbons carvings from the 17th century. The world of Rubens adorns the King's Drawing Room and in his relatively small dressing room is a Dürer, along with Rembrandt's portrait of his mother, and Van Dyck's triple look at Charles I. Of the apartments, the grand reception room, with its Gobelin tapestries, is the most spectacular.

The castle precincts are open daily (except on the second or third Monday in June —official birthday of the Queen) between 10 a.m. and 4 p.m., charging no admission. The Changing of the Guard in many ways is more attractive than the London ceremony at Buckingham Palace. The castle backdrop lends itself to photographs, and you're able to get closer to the ceremony. The guard marches up through the town past Sir Christopher Wren's lovely Guildhall and into the castle for the ceremony daily except Sunday at 11 a.m. from May to August. In winter, the guard is changed at 11 a.m. every 48 hours except Sunday, so unless you plan to visit in summer, it is wise to phone in advance for information at the number listed above.

Old Master Drawings

The royal family possesses a rare collection at Windsor of drawings by old masters, notably Leonardo da Vinci. One Leonardo sketch, for example, shows a cat in 20 different positions; another is a study of a horse; still a third is that of Saint Matthew, a warmup for the head used in *The Last Supper*. In addition, you'll find sketches by

William Blake, Thomas Rowlandson, and 12 Holbeins (see in particular his sketch of Sir John Godsalve). The drawing exhibition may be visited at the same time as the State Apartments for an admission of 60p (90¢) for adults and 20p (30¢) for children. It remains open, unlike the State Apartments, when the Court is in residence.

Queen Mary's Dollhouse

Just about the greatest dollhouse in all the world is at Windsor. Presented to the late Queen Mary as a gift, and later used to raise money for charity, the dollhouse is a remarkable achievement and re-creation of what a great royal mansion of the 1920s looked like, complete with a fleet of cars, including a Rolls-Royce. The house is perfect for Tom Thumb and family, and a retinue of servants. All is done with the most exacting detail—even the champagne bottles in the wine cellar contain vintage wine of that era. There's a toothbrush suitable for an ant. A minuscule electric iron really works. For late-night reading, you'll find volumes ranging from Hardy to Housman. In addition, you'll see a collection of dolls presented to the monarchy from nearly every nation of the Commonwealth. The Dollhouse may be viewed for an admission of 60p (90¢) for adults, 20p (30¢) for children, even when the State Apartments are closed.

St. George's Chapel

A gem of the Perpendicular style, this chapel shares the distinction with West-minster Abbey of being a pantheon of English monarchs (Victoria is a notable exception). The present St. George's was founded in the late 15th century by Edward IV near the site of the original Chapel of the Order of the Garter (Edward III, 1348). You enter the nave first with its fan vaulting (a remarkable achievement in English architecture). The nave contains the tomb of George V and Queen Mary, designed by Sir William Reid Dick. Off the nave in the Urswick Chapel, the Princess Charlotte memorial provides an ironic touch. If she had survived childbirth in 1817, she—and not her cousin, Victoria—would have ruled the British Empire. In the aisle are the tombs of George VI and Edward IV. The Edward IV "Quire," with its imaginatively carved 15th-century choir stalls (crowned by lacy canopies and colorful Knights of the Garter banners), evokes the pomp and pageantry of medieval days. In the center is a flat tomb, containing the vault of the beheaded Charles I, along with Henry VIII and one of his wives (no. 3, Jane Seymour). Finally, you may want to inspect the Prince Albert Memorial Chapel, reflecting the opulent tastes of the Victorian era. St. George's Chapel is usually open from 10:45 a.m. to 3:45 or 4 p.m. Monday to Saturday, from 2 to 3:45 or 4 p.m. on Sunday. It is closed during services. Admission is £1.30 ($1.95) for adults, 60p (90¢) for children. It's advisable to telephone to check opening hours if you're going to be there at a time not given as a regular opening time (tel. 0753/865538).

Footnote: Queen Victoria died on January 22, 1901, and was buried beside her beloved Prince Albert in a mausoleum at **Frogmore** (a private estate), near Windsor (open only three days a year, in May). The Prince Consort died in December 1861.

The Royal Mews

Entered from St. Albans Street, the red-brick buildings of the Royal Mews and Burford House were built for Nell Gwynne in the 1670s. They were named for King Charles II's natural son by her, the Earl of Burford. When the child was 14 years old, he was created Duke of St. Albans, from which the street outside takes its name.

Housed in the mews is the exhibition of the Queen's Presents and Royal Carriages. Displayed are pictures of several members of the royal family, including those of Queen Elizabeth II as Colonel-in-Chief of the Coldstream Guards riding in the grounds of Buckingham Palace, the Duke of Edinburgh driving his horses through a water obstacle at Windsor, and the Queen Mother with Prince Edward, Viscount

Linley, and Lady Sarah Armstrong-Jones in the Scottish State Coach. There is also a full-size stable with model horses showing stable kit, harnesses, and riding equipment. In the coach house is a magnificent display of coaches and carriages kept in mint condition and in frequent use. The exhibition of the Queen's Presents includes unique items of interest given to Her Majesty and the Duke of Edinburgh throughout her reign. There is also a collection of pencil drawings of the queen and family with horses and dogs.

The exhibition is open in November and December and from January to March from 10:30 a.m. to 3 p.m. weekdays. From April to October, hours are 10:30 a.m. to 5 p.m. From May to October, it is also open on Sunday, 10:30 a.m. to 3 p.m., from May to October. Admission is 60p (90¢) for adults, 20p (30¢) for children.

Royalty and Empire

The famous company founded by Madame Tussaud in 1802 has taken over part of the Windsor Town railway station to present an exhibition of "Queen Victoria's Diamond Jubilee 1837–1897." It's at the Windsor & Eton Central Railway Station on Thames Street (tel. 0753/857837). At one of the station platforms is a replica of *The Queen*, the engine used to draw the royal coaches disembarking the life-size wax figures of guests arriving at Windsor for the Jubilee celebration. In one of the carriages, the Day Saloon, are Queen Victoria (in wax, of course) and her family. In the anteroom is her faithful Indian servant, Hafiz Abdul Karim, the Munshi. Among the famous guests portrayed are the Prince and Princess of Wales (Edward VII and Alexandra), the Empress Frederick of Prussia (Queen Victoria's eldest daughter), and the prime minister, Lord Salisbury.

The platform is busy with loyal servants, a flower seller and a newsboy, an Italian with a barrel organ, along with others who have come to see the arrival of the train. Drawn up in the courtyard are the troops of the Coldstream Guards and the horse-drawn carriage that will take the party to the castle. With the sounds of military music in the background and the commands of the officers to their troops, you really feel you are present in the courtyard yourself at Her Majesty, Queen Victoria's arrival.

Afterward, at the end of the walkway through the Victorian Conservatory, you reach the 260-seat theater for a short audio-visual presentation, with lifesize animated models giving further glimpses of life during Victoria's reign. The whole visit will only take 45 minutes. It is open daily except Christmas from 9:30 a.m. to 5:30 p.m., charging adults £2.50 ($3.75) for admission and children pay £1.80 ($2.70).

Sunday Entertainment

There are often polo matches in **Windsor Great Park**—and at **Ham Common** —and you can often see Prince Charles playing and Prince Philip serving as umpire. The Queen herself often watches. For more information, telephone 0753/860633.

Also, at the gates into the park are maps showing attractive paths for walking. You can circumnavigate Royal Lodge and walk through the Deer Park before enjoying a pint at one of the pubs outside the park (there's a pub at almost every gate).

The Town Itself

Windsor is largely a Victorian town, with lots of brick buildings and a few remnants of Georgian architecture. In and around the castle are two cobblestone streets— **Church and Market Streets**—with their antique shops, silversmiths, and pubs. One shop on Church Street is supposed to have been occupied by Nell Gwynne (she needed to be within beck and call of the king's private chambers). Church is also a good street on which to find low-cost tea room luncheons. After lunch or tea, you may want to stroll along the three-mile, aptly named, Long Walk.

Round Windsor Sightseeing Tour

A 35-minute tour of Windsor and the surrounding countryside is offered in an open-top, double-decker bus with commentary. The ten-mile drive starts from Windsor Castle and passes the Royal Mews, the Long Walk, the Royal Farms, Albert Bridge, Eton College, and the Theatre Royal. The departure point is Castle Hill, near the King Henry VIII Gateway to Windsor Castle. Adults pay £1.75 ($2.63) and children, £1.10 ($1.65). Tickets, along with information about dates of operation and departure times, are available from **Windsorian Coaches,** 17 Alma Rd. (tel. 0753/856841).

Guided Tours

A two-hour guided tour of Windsor Castle and the town leaves from the **Tourist Information Centre** (tel. 0753/852010) in the Central Station, the one opposite the castle. The walking tour includes a look at the Long Walk, then the Guildhall and Market Cross House, along with the changing of the guard when possible. In the castle precincts you'll visit St. George's Chapel, the Cloisters, and the Albert Memorial Chapel, finishing in the State Apartments where no guiding is allowed. Subject to demand, the tours leave at 10:20 and 11:30 a.m. and 1:30 p.m. Monday to Saturday and at 1:30 p.m. on Sunday, costing adults £3.50 ($5.25) and children £1.50 ($2.25). All tours are accompanied by a licensed guide.

Boat Trips on the Thames

From an embarkation point on the Promenade, at Barry Avenue, there are regular boat departures for 35-minute trips up to Boveney Lock. You pass the Windsor Horse Racecourse and cruise past Eton College's boathouses and the Brocas Meadows. On the return, you'll have one of the most perfect views of Windsor Castle to be captured by the camera's lens. The cost is £1.20 ($1.80) for adults, 60p (90¢) for children. However, you can also take a two-hour trip through Boveney Lock and up past stately private riverside homes, the Bray Film Studios, Queens Eyot, and Monkey Island at a cost of £2.80 ($4.20) for adults, £1.40 ($2.10) for children. The boats carry light refreshments and have a licensed bar. There are toilets on board, and the decks are covered in case of that unexpected shower. However, your view of the river will be unimpaired. Tours are operated by **Windsor Boats,** Clewer Boathouse, Mill Lane, Windsor (tel. 0753/862933).

WHERE TO EAT: Standing opposite the castle, the **Hideaway Bistro Grill,** 12 Thames St. (tel. 0753/842186), is operated by the prestigious Sir Christopher Wren's House Hotel. This is a far different place from their more formal restaurant, The Orangerie, which lies within the hotel itself. The Hideaway serves daily from 10 a.m. to 11 p.m., offering morning coffee, pastries, cakes, a wine and salad bar, cream teas, and informal candlelit dinners beginning at 6:30. It also features pre- and post-theater suppers. You can partake of the wine and salad bar for only £4.50 ($6.75) or else try one of their fresh sandwiches (I'd suggest the "Covent Garden"). At night dinners are priced from £8 ($12) and might begin with pâté of duckling and follow with a grill, perhaps stir-fry vegetables.

Dôme, 5 Thames St. (tel. 0753/864405), also across from the Castle, is another fetching choice. Decorated in a turn-of-the-century bistro style, it is one of the most popular and sophisticated cafés in town. Sometimes live music is a feature, and its happy hour is perhaps its most engaging time of the day. It keeps very long hours: 9 a.m. to 11 p.m. (until 10:30 p.m. on Sunday), and serves food throughout the day. The selections run to such fare as light omelets, salmon mousse, or steak sandwiches. Look for the daily specials on a blackboard menu.

The **William IV Hotel,** Thames Street, 100 yards from Eton Bridge (tel. 0753/

851004), a lovely old place (circa 1500) with its armor, beams, and log fire, invites visitors in with its friendly and local atmosphere. Just outside is the Chapter garden where the Windsor martyrs were burned at the stake in 1544 for their religious beliefs. It was from this pub that they received their last cups of strong ale "in gratification of their last wish." The house built by Sir Christopher Wren for his own use is opposite the William IV, and the great architect of St. Paul's was reputedly a regular visitor to the old tap room, as were diarists Evelyn and Pepys. The present landlord is Ken Gardner, award-winning journalist and writer. Rub shoulders here with newspapermen and actors (nearby is the Theatre Royal), artists and river folk, and drink traditional ale which is still pulled by old-fashioned beer engines. Food is home-cooked, and the portions are guaranteed to satisfy gargantuan appetites. Try a steak or one of the house regional specialties. A lunch—perhaps liver, bacon, and a vegetable—goes for £3.95 ($5.93) and is served from noon to 2 p.m. You can sit at a sidewalk table in a pedestrian area by the Eton Bridge, gazing up at the castle while enjoying your lunch. At night, this is one of the busiest drinking spots in town (go from 5:30 to 11 p.m.). The William IV lies at the bottom of Windsor Hill on the approach road to the bridge, which is open to pedestrians only.

Country Kitchen, 3 King Edwards Court, Peascod Street (tel. 0753/868681). Walk from the castle gateway down Peascod Street to King Edwards Court for a good, home-cooked, whole-food meal in this light, airy, self-service restaurant above the shops. They make their own scones, tea bread, flans, cheesecake, and dessert. The soups, pâtés, and quiches are homemade, and only good vegetable oils, honey, lemon juice, herbs, and spices are used in the preparation of the main dishes. There's always a vegetarian dish, along with some low-fat, low-calorie ones. Choose your own salad from the seven different, freshly made concoctions or else pick one as a side dish. Hot dishes include chicken curry, lasagne, and chili con carne, and you can choose from the display of scrumptious desserts, including passion cake. They offer five different teas and herbs—decaffeinated if you wish—and fine house wines by the carafe or glass. You can eat here for £5 ($7.50) and up, plus the cost of your drink. The Kitchen is open from 10 a.m. to 5:30 p.m. daily except Sunday.

The **Drury House Restaurant,** 4 Church St. (tel. 0753/863734). The very British owner states with pride that all luncheons served in this wood-paneled 17th-century restaurant, dating from the days of Charles II, are home-cooked "and very English." A visit here could be included in a tour of Windsor Castle, as the entrance to the restaurant is only a stone's throw apart. A typical meal could include soup followed by either roast beef and Yorkshire pudding or homemade steak-and-kidney pie, both served with vegetables and followed by a dessert such as apple pie. All this, and a dash of English history too, comes to about £6.50 ($9.75) per person. Owner Joan Hearne also serves a refreshing tea, including either homemade scones with jam and freshly whipped cream, or freshly made cream cakes, both offered with copious quantities of the obligatory tea. Drury House is open Tuesday through Sunday only from noon till 5:30 p.m.

Choices, 10 Thames St. (tel. 0753/866437), is a good "choice" following your visit to Windsor Castle. It is a bright cream- and green-painted place, aimed at budget catering. For its grills, it offers rump or sirloin steaks, burgers, fish, roast chicken, and homemade steak-and-kidney pie. A three-course meal costs from £6.50 ($9.75) to £8 ($12). Wine and chilled lager are available. The restaurant is open from 11 a.m. to 3 p.m. in winter, from 11 a.m. to 7 p.m. in summer.

The Court Jester, Church Lane (tel. 0753/864257), is one of the town's most popular pubs, especially with young people in the evening when loud music plays. The publican offers you a warm welcome as you savor traditional pub food during the day priced at £2.50 ($3.75) and up. During the winter, there is a selection of hot dishes, while in summer he provides an extensive buffet. As well as a wide range of English ales, a traditional Sunday lunch is a feature of the week. Hours are 11 a.m. to 2:30 p.m. and 6 to 11 p.m.

WHERE TO STAY: You can get help at the **Tourist Information Centre,** Central Station (tel. 0753/852010), in the railway station at the top of the hill opposite the castle. Here you can book a bed ahead if you're touring or else find an accommodation in and around Windsor. This is a very useful service, as many of the local guesthouses have no signs. There is also an information point in the Tourist Reception Centre at Windsor Coach Park.

Aurora Garden, 14 Bolton Ave. (tel. 0753/868686), is a spacious Victorian house which has been successfully converted and modernized to receive paying guests. It's one of the most substantial places at which to stay in Windsor, charging more than your typical B&B, but making up for it in quality. The location is in the vicinity of Long Walk and Windsor Great Park. The hotel's most notable feature is its water garden, and umbrella-shaded tables are placed outside in summer. Each well-furnished unit, 14 in all, contains a private bath or shower, direct-dial phone, an alarm clock radio, and color TV. Singles begin at £40($60), with doubles paying from £55 ($82.50).

The Christopher Hotel, High Street in Eton (tel. 0753/852359), is across the river from Windsor town. It has 25 self-contained chalettes. At one time this was a noted coaching inn, and the stable around the courtyard has been converted into modern bedrooms, fitted with shower room, color TV, radio, pay phone, trouser press, refrigerator, hair dryer, and all the ingredients for a self-catered continental breakfast. A traditional English breakfast is also available in the hotel. There are bar snacks, or you can be served in the Peacock Restaurant at lunchtime or in the evening for around £12 ($18). The cost of a room is from £34 ($51) to £40 ($60) for two persons. The Christopher is only a five-minute walk from Windsor Riverside Railway Station with a service to central London.

Trinity Guest House, 18 Trinity Pl. (tel. 9753/864186), offers one of the best values in town. B&B costs from £12 ($18) to £15 ($22.50) per person nightly, depending on the season. Operated by the Jackson family, the guesthouse also accommodates families in its larger units. Because of its limited number of accommodations it can fill up quickly. The management is polite and courteous, and the rooms are pleasantly furnished. You'll be within walking distance of Windsor Castle.

Fairlight Lodge, 41 Frances Rd. (tel. 0753/861207), emerges recently as about the most successful B&B inspected in Windsor. A well-appointed Victorian house, it rents out comfortably furnished bedrooms to overnight guests. Its major problem is lack of space, as it has only eight rooms to rent, and these are likely to go fast on a summer night. Two rooms are set aside for families. The cost for B&B is £18 ($27) to £20 ($30) in a single, £27 ($40.50) to £31 ($46.50) in a double or twin. The higher rates are for units with private baths. There is also limited parking.

Alma House, 56 Alma Road (tel. 0753/862983), drew praise from Helen Drew, a California reader, who proclaimed that in three years of ''B and B'ing'' in England she'd never found a more satisfactory place. The house is a well-built Victorian structure, about a five-minute walk from the castle. Many guests stay here and commute to Heathrow the following morning (depending on traffic, it's about a 20-minute ride). The hostess, Mrs. Brenda Licklay, is a wealth of information for travelers as well. She rents rooms for £13 ($19.50) to £16 ($24) in a single, £23 ($34.50) to £28 ($42) in a double. Two rooms contain private showers, and one is set aside for families.

ETON: To visit Eton, home of what is arguably the most famous public school in the world (Americans would call it a private school), you can take a train from Paddington Station, go by car, or take the Green Line bus to Windsor. If you go by car, you can take the M4 motorway, leaving it at exit 5 to go straight to Eton. However, parking is likely to be a problem, so I advise turning off the M4 at exit 6 to Windsor. You can park there and take an easy stroll past Windsor Castle and across the Thames bridge. Follow Eton High Street to the college.

From Windsor Castle's ramparts, you can look down on the river and on the famous playing fields of Eton.

Eton College

Largest and best known of the public (private) schools of England, Eton College was founded by a teenage boy himself, Henry VI, in 1440. Some of England's greatest men, notably the Duke of Wellington, have played on the fields of Eton. Twenty prime ministers were educated at Eton, as well as such literary figures as George Orwell and Aldous Huxley. Even Ian Fleming, creator of James Bond, attended. The traditions of the school have had plenty of time to become firmly entrenched (ask a young gentleman in his Victorian black tails to explain the difference between a "wet bob" and a "dry bob"). If it's open, take a look at the Perpendicular chapel, with its 15th-century paintings and reconstructed fan vaulting. Visits to the school are possible from Easter to the end of October from 2 to 5 p.m., with guided tours being given at 2:15 and 3:15 p.m. During the summer holidays, it is also open from 10:30 a.m. The guided tours of the school and the museum (see below) cost £2 ($3) for adults, £1 ($1.50) for children. In winter, you can sometimes visit parts of the school and see the museum for £1.50 ($2.25) for adults, £1 ($1.50) for children. For information regarding visits, telephone 0753/852010.

The Museum of Eton Life

The history of Eton College since its inception in 1440 is depicted in the museum in vaulted wine cellars under College Hall, which were originally the storehouse for use of the college's masters. The displays, running from formal to extremely informal, include a turn-of-the-century boy's room, schoolbooks, sports trophies, canes which were used by senior boys to apply corporal punishment they felt needful to their juniors, and birch sticks used by masters for the same purpose. Also to be seen are letters written home by students describing day to day life at the school, as well as samples of the numerous magazines produced by students over the centuries, known as *ephemera* because of the changing condition of writers and ideas. Many of the items to be seen were provided by Old Etonians, with collections formerly scattered throughout the various buildings of the school also being included.

The museum schedule is based on the school year, with hours varying widely (see above). For information, contact The Custodian, Eton College (tel. 0753/869991).

For Meals

Eton Wine Bar, High Street (tel. 0753/854921), is owned and run by William and Michael Gilbey of the Gilbey's gin family, even though no gin is served here. Just across the bridge from Windsor, it is a charming place set among the antique shops with pinewood tables and old church pews and chairs. There is a small garden out back. Hours are weekdays from 11:30 a.m. to 3 p.m. and 6 to 11 p.m.; on Friday and Saturday, from 11:30 a.m. to 3 p.m. and 6 t 11:30 p.m. Appetizers include borscht and a cheese-and-onion quiche. They also serve baked chicken with rosemary, Cornish smoked mackerel, cold roast beef, and salad. Each day several hot dishes are made, and desserts include pineapple and almond flan and damson crunch. Meals cost from £7.50 ($11.25). Wine can be ordered by the glass.

Eton Buttery, 73 High St. (tel. 0753/854479), is just on the Eton side of the bridge from Windsor, a building among the boathouses of the college with magnificent views over the river and up toward the town and castle. Open seven days a week from

9:30 a.m. to 10:30 p.m., it is decorated with plain red brick walls, brown carpets and tables, caneback chairs, and a mass of potted plants. This is an up-market self-service buffet owned by Doreen Stanton, owner of The House on the Bridge restaurant, opposite. Food is well displayed along spotless counters. There are waitresses to clear away and to bring you wine and drinks; otherwise you help yourself to a variety of quiches, cold sliced meats, and specialty salads and pâtés. There is also a hot roast of the day. A meal will cost from £5.50 ($8.25), including a glass of wine.

NEARBY SIGHTS: Attractions of interest are in the surrounding area.

One of England's Great Gardens

The **Savill Garden,** Wick Lane, Englefield Green (tel. 0753/860222), is in Windsor Great Park and clearly signposted from Windsor, Egham, and Ascot. Started in 1932, the garden is considered one of the finest of its type in the northern hemisphere. The display starts in spring with rhododendrons, camellias, and daffodils beneath the trees; then throughout the summer there are spectacular displays of flowers and shrubs all skillfully presented in a natural and wild state. It is open all year except at Christmas from 10 a.m. to 6 or 7 p.m., and the admission is £1.70 ($2.55) for adults, free for children. Prices are halved in winter.

Adjoining the Savill Garden are the **Valley Gardens,** full of shrubs and trees in a series of wooded natural valleys running down to Virginia water. It is open daily, free, throughout the year.

Windsor Safari Park and Seaworld

In the world-wide safari craze, even the Royal Borough of Windsor wasn't spared. The Safari Park and Seaworld, Winkfield Road (tel. 0753/869841), is open just two miles from Windsor Castle on a site 23 miles from London. There you can drive through reserves of lions, tigers, baboons, giraffes, camels, bears, and many other wild animals. The killer whale and dolphin show, the parrot show, and feeding of the big cats are popular features. By the time of your visit, work may be completed on new shows: birds of prey, sea lions, and an animated African "Tiki" presentation. A walk-through tropical plant and butterfly house and a Noah's Ark adventure playground are of interest. Burger Bar and Safari Lodge restaurants, fast-food cafeterias, licensed bars, and a refreshment kiosk provide service. You can ride around on the free safari coach or drive in in your own vehicle (if it's a hard-top). Admission, which includes all the shows, is £5 ($7.50) for adults, £4 ($6) for children under 14. The park is open every day except Christmas from 10 a.m.

The Wellington Ducal Estate

If you'd like to make an interesting day trip in Berkshire, I suggest **Stratfield Saye** (tel. 0256/882882), between Reading and Basingstoke on the A33. It has been the home of the Dukes of Wellington since 1817 when the 17th-century house was bought for the Iron Duke to celebrate his victory over Napoleon at the Battle of Waterloo. Many memories of the first duke remain in the house, including his billiard table, battle spoils, and pictures. The funeral carriage that since 1860 had rested in St. Paul's Cathedral crypt is now in the ducal collection here. In the gardens is the grave of Copenhagen, the charger ridden to battle at Waterloo by the first duke. There are also extensive pleasure grounds together with a licensed restaurant and gift shop.

A short drive away is the **Wellington Country Park** with the fascinating National Dairy Museum where you can see relics of 150 years of dairying. Other attractions include a riding school, nature trails, and boating and sailing on the lake. In addition, there are a miniature railway, the Thames Valley Time Trail, and a deer park.

The house is open Easter Saturday, Sunday, and Monday; on Saturday and Sunday in April; and daily except Friday from May 1 to the end of September. Hours are

11:30 a.m. to 5 p.m. Admission is £2.50 ($3.75) for adults, £1.25 ($1.88) for children. Wellington Country Park is open March to October from 10 a.m. to 5 p.m. Admission is £1.50 ($2.25) for adults, 70p ($1.05) for children. A combined ticket for the house and park costs £3.40 ($5.10) for adults and £1.60 ($2.40) for children.

Mapledurham House

The Elizabethan mansion home of the Blount family (tel. 0734/723350) lies beside the river in the unspoiled village of Mapledurham, which can be reached by car from the A4074 Oxford to Reading road. A much more romantic way of reaching the old house is to take the boat, leaving the Promenade next to Caversham Bridge at 2:15 p.m. on Saturday, Sunday, and bank holidays from Easter to the end of September. The journey upstream takes about 40 minutes, and the boat leaves Mapledurham again at 5 p.m. for the journey back to Caversham.

This gives you plenty of time to walk through the house, viewing the Elizabethan ceilings and great oak staircase. You'll see portraits of the two beautiful sisters with whom the poet Alexander Pope, himself a frequent visitor, was in love. The family chapel, built in 1789, is a fine example of "modern Gothick."

Cream teas with homemade cakes are available at the house, and on the grounds is the last working watermill on the Thames. It still produces flour—100% whole-meal flour which can be purchased. The house is open from 2:30 to 5 p.m. on Saturday, Sunday, and public holidays from Easter Sunday until the end of September. The mill is open from noon on the same days in summer and in winter on Sunday from 2 to 4 p.m. Entrance to the house costs £2 ($3) for adults, £1 ($1.50) for children. To visit the mill only, the charge is 90p ($1.35) for adults, 45p (68¢) for children.

The boat ride from Caversham costs £2.10 ($3.15) for adults, £1.20 ($1.80) for children. Further details of this boat ride and others operated from Caversham Bridge can be obtained by getting in touch with **D & T Scenics Ltd.,** Mapledurham Village, Reading, RG4 7TR (tel. 0734/724123).

2. Ascot

While following the Royal Buckhounds through Windsor Forest, Queen Anne decided to have a racecourse on Ascot Heath. The first race meeting at Ascot was inaugurated in 1711. Since then, the Ascot Racecourse has been a symbol of chic as pictures of the Royal Family, including the Queen and Prince Philip, have been flashed around the world. Nowadays, instead of Queen Anne, you are likely to see Princess Anne, an avid horsewoman.

Ascot lies only 36 miles west of London, directly south of Windsor (take the A332). There is frequent rail service in London from Waterloo to Ascot Station, which lies about 10 minutes from the Racecourse.

The **Ascot Racecourse** (tel. 0990/322211) is open throughout the year except for March and August. There are three enclosures: Tattersalls is the largest, Silver Ring the least expensive, and the third is the Members Enclosure. Plenty of bars and restaurants exist to suit a wide range of pocketbooks. Tickets cost adults from £2.50 ($3.75) to £13 ($19.50); children under 16 are admitted free if accompanied by an adult. The highlight of the Ascot social season is Royal Week, usually in mid-June.

FOOD AND LODGING: Chances are, you will not be spending the night in Ascot but will return to either London or Windsor. However, should you like to stay here, there is a good, moderately priced hotel, **Highclere House Hotel,** Kings Road, Sunninghill (tel. 0990/25220). Once an Edwardian private residence, this building has been successfully modernized and equipped to receive paying guests. It rents out a dozen well-furnished bedrooms, seven of which contain private baths. Singles range from £22 ($33) to £29 ($43.50), doubles £29 ($43.50) to £36 ($54). It's also possible to take half board, costing £24 ($36) to £32 ($48) per person nightly. If you stay here, you'll be only a 12-minute drive from Windsor Castle.

More likely you'll be in Ascot for lunch. If so, I suggest the **Stag,** 63 High St. (tel. 0990/21622), where Ann McCarthy enjoys a local reputation for her good, hearty, and healthy cookery. Right in the heart of town, this pub attracts diners who enjoy her homemade whole-meal pasta. Whenever available, she uses organically grown vegetables. Some guests make a lunch just out of her stuffed potatoes. Meals cost from £6 ($9), but you can get by for less. Lunch is daily from noon to 2 p.m., dinner from 6 to 10 p.m.

3. Henley-on-Thames

At the eastern edge of Oxfordshire, only 35 miles from London, Henley-on-Thames is a small town and resort on the river at the foothills of the Chilterns. It is the headquarters of the Royal Regatta held annually in July, the number one event among European oarsmen. The regatta dates back to the first years of the reign of Victoria.

The Elizabethan buildings, the tea rooms, and the inns along its High Street live up to one's conception of what an English country town looks like—or should look like. Cardinal Wolsey is said to have ordered the building of the tower of the Perpendicular and Decorated parish church.

Life here is serene, and Henley-on-Thames makes for an excellent stopover en route to Oxford. However, readers on the most limited of budgets will find far less expensive lodgings in Oxford. The fashionable inns of Henley-on-Thames (Charles I slept here) are far from cheap. Warning: During the Royal Regatta rooms are difficult to secure, unless you've made reservations months in advance.

WHERE TO STAY: Lying off the A423, **Thamesmead House Hotel,** Remenham Lane, Remenham, (tel. 0491/574745), is a Tudoresque and Victorian-style house, just over the bridge east of Henley-on-Thames near The Little Angel pub. Surrounded by a pretty garden, the house is of red brick with black and white timbers. A wing has been built in a style sympathetic to the spirit of the house, and there is a parking area. The hotel is owned and run by Mrs. Maisie Vallance, a charming French woman who learned to cook in Britanny. She has refurbished many bedrooms, adding showers and toilets. All rates include a full breakfast and VAT, and service is left to the discretion of a guest. Bathless singles cost £17.50 ($26.25). Bathless doubles go for £30 ($45), doubles with bath being priced at £35 ($52.50). Set lunches are offered for £6 ($9) and three-course dinners for £7.50 ($11.25). You can order an apéritif in the pleasant bar, and in winter you can enjoy log fires.

Flohr's Hotel and Restaurant, Northfield End (tel. 0491/573412), is a 16th-century inn at the edge of town, yet within walking distance of the center and the river. Formerly known as Sydney House Hotel, the establishment is now run by Susan and Gerd Flohr. Gerd trained in Switzerland as a hôtelier and worked for many years on the continent and in London as a hotel manager for major operators before acquiring his own place. He personally manages Flohr's and has kept the original charm, with oak beams and some period pieces, but still offers modern comforts. All rooms have hot beverage facilities as well as color TV. Many have private showers and toilets. Prices start at £21.50 ($32.25) for a single room, £39 ($58.50) in a double or twin. All tariffs include VAT and a full English breakfast. The restaurant boasts a creative continental menu, with many fish specialties. Expect to pay from £14.50 ($21.75) for a meal, VAT included.

WHERE TO EAT: Across the bridge on the London-Henley road (the A423) is a historic pub, **The Little Angel,** Remenham Lane, Remenham (tel. 0491/574165). Right on the highway, near the river, it serves ale brewed right in Henley and is also known for its fresh seafood. You can, in addition to fresh fish, get smoked salmon from

Scotland and freshly baked meat pies, perhaps, on occasion, barbecued spare ribs. In fair weather, guests can enjoy tables placed outside, but in winter they are more likely to retreat to an intimate alcove, enjoying softly flickering candlelight. Your host, Paul Southwood, offers food from 10 a.m. to 2:30 p.m. and from 6 to 11 p.m. The setting is warm and welcoming, with old beamed ceilings. Meals cost from £8 ($12).

Barnaby's, 2 New St. (tel. 0491/572421), at the corner of Bell Street, is a half-timbered Tudor building, with a dark and warmly decorated traditional interior. From noon to 2 p.m. and from 7 to 10:30 p.m. (no lunch on Sunday), it offers a menu that is wide ranging, everything from barbecued back ribs to swordfish steak, from chili con carne to beef bourguignon. Count on spending from £8 ($12).

From Henley-on-Thames it is only a 24-mile drive to Oxford.

4. Oxford

A walk down the long sweep of The High, one of the most striking streets in England; a mug of cider in one of the old student pubs; the sound of a May Day dawn when choristers sing in Latin from Magdalen Tower; the Great Tom bell from Tom Tower, whose 101 peals traditionally signal the closing of the college gates; towers and spires rising majestically; the barges on the upper reaches of the Thames; nude swimming at Parson's Pleasure; the roar of a cannon launching the bumping races; a tiny, dusty bookstall where you can pick up a valuable first edition. All that is Oxford—57 miles from London and home of one of the greatest universities in the world. An industrial city, the center of a large automobile business, as well as a university town, Oxford is better for sightseeing in summer. The students are wherever Oxford scholars go in the summer (allegedly they study more than they do at term time), and the many B&B houses—vacated by their gown-wearing boarders—will be happy to offer you an accommodation. But you'll be missing a great deal if you view Oxford without glimpsing its life blood.

However, at any time of the year you can enjoy a tour of the colleges, many of them representing a peak in England's architectural kingdom, as well as a valley of Victoriana. The Oxford Information Centre (see below) offers guided walking tours daily in summer and on Saturday in winter. Just don't mention the other place (Cambridge), and you shouldn't have any trouble.

The city predates the university; in fact, it was a Saxon town in the early part of the tenth century. And by the 12th century, Oxford was growing in reputation as a seat of learning at the expense of Paris. The first colleges were founded in the 13th century. The story of Oxford is filled with conflicts too complex and detailed to elaborate here. Suffice it to say, the relationship between town and gown wasn't as peaceful as it is today. Riots often flared, and both sides were guilty of abuses.

Nowadays the young people of Oxford take out their aggressiveness in sporting competitions, with the different colleges zealously competing in such games as cricket and soccer. However, all colleges unite into a powerful university when they face matches with their traditional rival, Cambridge.

Ultimately, the test of a great university lies in the persons it turns out. Oxford can name-drop a mouthful: Roger Bacon, Samuel Johnson, William Penn, John Wesley, Sir Walter Raleigh, Edward Gibbon, T. E. Lawrence, Sir Christopher Wren, John Donne, William Pitt, Matthew Arnold, Arnold Toynbee, Harold MacMillan, Graham Greene, A. E. Housman, and Lewis Carroll.

Many Americans arriving in Oxford ask, "Where's the campus?" If an Oxonian shows amusement when answering, it's understandable. Oxford University is, in fact, made up of 35 colleges, including three just for women (scholars in skirts in years past staged, and won, the battle for equal rights). To tour all of these would be a formidable task. Besides, a few are of such interest they overshadow the rest.

To help with an understanding of the university complex, Heritage Projects Ltd., United House, Piccadilly, York (tel. 0904/646411), has developed a new interpretation center, **The Oxford Tutorial,** in conjunction with Oxford University to provide an initial insight into the structure of the colleges, with a look behind the portals at some of the architectural and historical features that might otherwise be missed and a general background of the history and traditions of the colleges. Visitors are taken through a panorama of Oxford past and present, with both familiar and unfamiliar aspects, personalities, and architectural features of the famous university highlighted. Opening dates and hours for the Tutorial were not available at press time. Check with the tourist office.

For a bird's-eye view of the city and colleges, climb **Carfax Tower.** This is the one with the clock and figures that strike the hours. Admission is 40p (60¢) for adults, 10p (15¢) for children. The tower is open from 10 a.m. to 6 p.m. Monday to Saturday, from 2 to 6 p.m. on Sunday from mid-March to late October. The rest of the year, hours are 10 a.m. to 4 p.m. Monday to Saturday and 1 to 4 p.m. on Sunday.

Much of the city is either closed to motor traffic or is a maze of one-way streets. You might end up in Woodstock by mistake. Therefore, you might want to take advantage of the **Park and Ride** scheme. You leave your auto in one of the designated car parks, then take the free parking bus into the center of Oxford. Departures are every 10 to 15 minutes, and the cost of a bus ticket is 50p (75¢).

THE SIGHTS: The best way to get a running commentary on the important sightseeing attractions is to go to the **Oxford Information Centre,** St. Aldate's, opposite the Town Hall, near Carfax (tel. 0865/726871). Walking tours through the city and the major colleges leave daily most of the year in the morning and afternoon. They last two hours and cost £2 ($3) per person. Of all the tours I know in England, this ranks at the top, both for economy and information. There is a limit of 20 persons per tour so you should buy your ticket a little in advance.

At **Punt Station,** Cherwell Boathouse, Bardwell Road (tel. 0865/515978), you can rent a punt at a cost of £4 ($6) per hour, plus a £25 ($37.50) deposit. Similar charges are made on rentals at Magdalen Bridge Boathouse and at the Folly Bridge Boathouse.

A Word of Warning

The main business of a university, is, of course, to educate—and unfortunately this function at Oxford has been severely interfered with by the number of visitors who have been disturbing the academic work of the university. So, with deep regret, visiting is now restricted to certain hours and small groups of six or fewer. In addition, there are areas where visitors are not allowed at all, but your tourist office will be happy to advise you when and where you may "take in" the sights of this great institution. Admission charges are levied at some places.

Christ Church

Begun by Cardinal Wolsey as Cardinal College in 1525, Christ Church, known as The House, was founded by Henry VIII in 1546. Facing St. Aldate's Street, Christ Church has the largest quadrangle of any college in Oxford.

Tom Tower houses Great Tom, the 18,000-pound bell referred to earlier. It rings at 9:05 nightly, signaling the closing of the college gates. The 101 times it peals originally signified the number of students at the time of the founding of the college. The student body number changed, but Oxford traditions live on forever.

In the 16th-century Great Hall, with its hammer-beam ceiling, are some interesting portraits, including works by those old reliables, Gainsborough and Reynolds. Prime ministers are pictured, as Christ Church was a virtual factory turning out actual and aspiring prime ministers: men such as Gladstone and George Canning. There is a separate picture gallery.

The cathedral, dating from the 12th century, was built over a period of centuries.

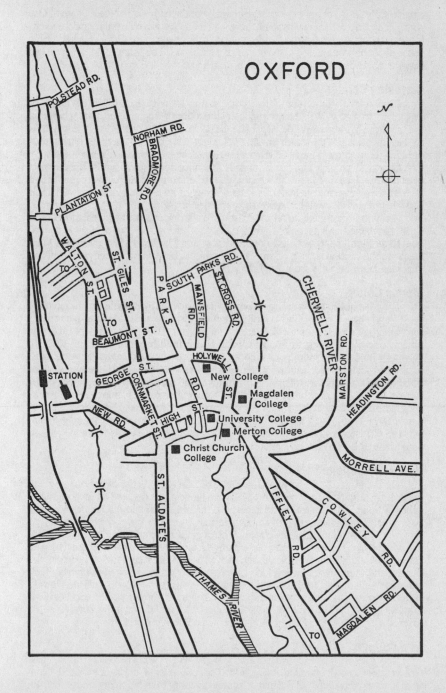

(Incidentally, it is not only the college chapel, but the cathedral of the diocese of Oxford.) The cathedral's most distinguishing features are its Norman pillars and the vaulting of the choir, dating from the 15th century. In the center of the Great Quadrangle is a statue of Mercury mounted in the center of a fish pond. The college and cathedral can be visited between 9:30 a.m. and 4:30 p.m. Entrance fee is 60p (90¢).

Magdalen College

Pronounced "maud-len," this college was founded in 1458 by William of Waynflete, bishop of Winchester and later chancellor of England. Its alumni range all the way from Wolsey to Wilde. Opposite the botanic garden, the oldest in England, is the bell tower, where the choristers sing in Latin at dawn on May Day. The reflection of the 15th-century tower is cast in the waters of the Cherwell below. On a not-so-happy day, Charles I, his days numbered, watched the oncoming Roundheads. But the most celebrated incident in Magdalen's history was when some brave Fellows defied James II. Visit the 15th-century chapel, in spite of many of its latter-day trappings. The hall and other places of special interest are open when possible.

A favorite pastime is to take Addison's Walk through the water meadows. The stroll is so named after a former alumnus, Joseph Addison, the 18th-century writer and poet noted for his contributions to *The Spectator* and *The Tatler*. The grounds of Magdalen are the most extensive of any Oxford college, containing a deer park. You can visit Magdalen each day from 2 to 6:15 p.m.

Merton College

Founded in 1264, this college is among the trio of the most ancient at the university. It stands near Corpus Christi College on Merton Street, the sole survivor of Oxford's medieval cobbled streets. Merton College (tel. 0865/249651) is noted for its library, one of the oldest in England, having been built between 1371 and 1379. In keeping with tradition, some of its most valuable books were chained. Now only one book is so secured, to show what the custom was like. One of the treasures of the library is an astrolabe (astronomical instrument used for measuring the altitude of the sun and stars), thought to have belonged to Chaucer. You pay only 30p (45¢) to visit the ancient library, as well as the Max Beerbohm Room (the satirical English caricaturist who died in 1956). Both are open from 2 to 4 p.m. from Monday to Saturday except between Christmas and the second week in February. You can also visit the chapel, dating from the 13th century, at these times.

University College

On the High, University College (tel. 0865/241661) is the oldest one found at Oxford, tracing its history back to 1249 when money was donated by an ecclesiastic called William of Durham. More fanciful is the old claim that the real founder was Alfred the Great! Don't jump to any conclusions about the age of the buildings when you see the present Gothic-esque look. The original structures have all disappeared, and what remains today represents essentially the architecture of the 17th century, with subsequent additions in Victoria's day, as well as in more recent times. For example, the Goodhart Quadrangle was added as late as 1962. Its most famous alumnus, Shelley, was "sent down" for his part in collaborating on a pamphlet on atheism. However, all is forgiven today, as the romantic poet is honored by a memorial erected in 1894. The hall and chapel of University College can be visited during university vacations from 10 a.m. to noon and 2 to 4 p.m. (otherwise, 2 to 4 p.m.).

New College

New College was founded in 1379 by William of Wykeham, bishop of Winchester and later Lord Chancellor of England. The college at Winchester supplied a constant stream of candidates. The first quadrangle, dating from before the end of the 14th century, was the initial quadrangle to be built in Oxford, forming the architectural design for the other colleges. In the antechapel is Sir Jacob Epstein's remarkable modern sculpture of *Lazarus* and a fine El Greco painting of St. James. One of the treasures of the college is a crosier (pastoral staff of a bishop) belonging to the founding father. In the garden you can see the remains of the old city wall and the mound. The college (entered at New College Lane) can be visited from 2 to 5 p.m. weekdays at term time (otherwise, 11 a.m. to 5 p.m.). On weekends, it is open from noon to 5 p.m.

Salter's River Thames Services

From mid-May until mid-September, Salter Brothers run daily passenger boat services on many reaches of the River Thames. Trips are to or from Oxford, Abingdon, Reading, Henley, Marlow, Cookham, Maidenhead, Windsor, Runnymede, and Staines. Combined outings from London can be made in conjunction with train or bus services. Full details can be obtained from **Salter Bros. Ltd.,** Folly Bridge, Oxford (tel. 0865/243421).

ACCOMMODATIONS: When the tourist rush is on, why tire yourself further. The **Oxford Information Centre,** St. Aldate's Chambers (tel. 0865/726871), operates a room-booking service for personal callers for a fee of 90p ($1.35) and a 7% refundable deposit. In addition, bed and breakfast accommodation can be arranged for visitors in most other areas of England for a £2 ($3) fee. If you'd like to seek out lodgings on your own, you may try one of the following recommendations:

Bed and Breakfast

The **Old Parsonage Hotel,** 3 Banbury Rd. (tel. 0865/54843), is so old it looks like an extension of one of the ancient colleges. Originally a 13th-century hospital named Bethleen, it was restored in the early 17th century. Today it's slated for designation as an ancient monument. Near St. Giles Church, it is set back from the street behind a low stone wall and sheltered by surrounding trees and shrubbery. However, most of the rooms are in a modern wing which is more institutional in character. The owners charge from £22.50 ($33.75) per person nightly for B&B in a single, £36 ($54) in a double or twin. Should you want a private shower, the price is increased to £45 ($67.50) for two persons. A family room for three rents for £48 ($72) nightly, including a full English breakfast, VAT, and service. Some of the large front rooms, with leaded-glass windows, are set aside for tourists. You have breakfast in a pleasant modern dining room, overlooking the garden. A licensed restaurant and bar are on the premises. In the restaurant you order à la carte. The cost of an average three-course meal is £9 ($13.50).

Green Gables, 326 Abingdon Rd. (tel. 0865/725870), was originally an Edwardian private residence before its transformation into a residence adapted to receive overnight visitors. The location is about a mile to the south of the university city, lying on the A4144. You might make it your center for exploring "the heart of England." Trees screen the house from the main road. Mr. and Mrs. Jelfs rent out eight comfortable bedrooms, three of which contain private baths. The charge for B&B is £13 ($19.50) to £16 ($24) in a single, £23 ($34.50) to £31 ($46.50) in a double. Limited parking is available.

Mr. and Mrs. Conrad Adams, 302 Banbury Rd. (tel. 0865/56118), operate a clean, comfortable guesthouse. They offer gracious hospitality, good beds, central heating, and an individually prepared English breakfast. Shower and bath facilities are available at no extra charge. Shopping amenities are nearby, and the city and university areas are a short bus ride away. Rates are from £12 ($18) per person per night, inclusive.

Lonsdale Guest House, 312 Banbury Rd., Summertown (tel. 0865/54872), is another pleasant accommodation. This one is run by Roland and Christine Adams, who have established a gem of a little guesthouse. A comfortable bedroom, with hot and cold running water, and free use of the corridor bath, plus an individually prepared breakfast, costs from £12 ($18) per person nightly (less for longer stays). A large family room has a private shower. All units have twin beds, lounge chairs, occasionally an antique chest of drawers, TV, innerspring mattresses, comforters of soft down, wall-to-wall carpeting, and central heating. A full English breakfast is served. If you arrive at term time, you may think you're in a fraternity house. Students of all races stay here (it's odd to hear a young Chinese speaking with a broad Oxonian accent). A heated indoor pool and several restaurants are about a two-minute walk from the house.

Mrs. K. Andrews, 26 St. Michael's St., off Cornmarket (tel. 0865/242101), has a few rooms which she rents to students from nearby St. Peter's College. But she always sets aside some rooms for tourists, charging them £12 ($18) per person nightly for B&B. Her little rooms are tidy, clean, and pleasingly comfortable. She takes care of the guests in a friendly, hospitable manner.

Mr. and Mrs. P. Durrant own the **Walton Guest House,** 169 Walton St. (tel. 0865/52137), lying at the city end of Walton Street, 100 yards from the bus station and half a mile from the rail station. It overlooks the grounds of Worcester College. All the pleasantly furnished rooms have hot and cold running water, shaver points, central heating, and TV. Terms are from £12 ($18) per person here, including a first-class English breakfast.

Belmont Guest House, 182 Woodstock Rd. (tel. 0865/53698), is the domain of Mr. and Mrs. Bellamy, who operate this house in a tree-shaded residential section of Oxford, at the junction of Woodstock Road and Moreton Road, about a mile from the heart of the city. Woodstock is the main road from the city leading north to Woodstock, Bladon (burial place of Sir Winston Churchill—about five miles away), Stratford-upon-Avon, Birmingham, and the Midlands. Belmont is an attractive house, once a private home. All rooms are centrally heated, and all have hot and cold running water basins. Baths and showers are available, some in private rooms. The rate for B&B, inclusive of taxes, is £10 ($15) to £12 ($18) in a single, from £20 ($30) to £25 ($37.50) in a double. Accommodations are pleasantly decorated, each overlooking the surrounding gardens.

Willow Reaches Hotel, 1 Wytham St. (tel. 0865/721545), lies on a cul-de-sac about a mile south from the center of Oxford. Attractively furnished bedrooms cost £15 ($22.50) to £21 ($31.50) in a single and from £26 ($39) to £32 ($48) in a double. The more expensive accommodations contain private baths. Excellent meals are served, and half board can be arranged at rates ranging from £21 ($31.50) to £28 ($42) per person daily. Children are especially catered for, and there is a boating lake just for them nearby. Guests can relax in the garden or follow a special footpath to a nearby village for a pub meal or an early-morning constitutional.

Brown's Guest House, 281 Iffley Rd. (tel. 0865/246822), is a year-round guesthouse run by the Brown family. The half-dozen rooms are pleasantly furnished, with hot and cold running water, central heating, color TV, and beverage-making facilities. Guests are charged from £11 ($16.50) for B&B. There are adequate showers outside the rooms. Families are catered for, with special breakfasts if requested. The Browns are hospitable people, helpful to their guests. The house is about a mile from the city center, with such nearby amenities as a post office, launderette, grocery store, drugstore, and bike rental shop.

Red Mullions Guest House, 23 London Rd. (tel. 0865/64727), outside the center, is nevertheless convenient because of good bus connections. It lies near the ring road, and a bus stop outside will whisk you to the heart of Oxford and the colleges. You can also use the place as a center for exploring the Cotswolds. Rooms are pleasantly and attractively furnished, especially the twins with private bath, color TV, and coffee-making equipment. The charge is from £15 ($22.50) per person nightly, including a breakfast for which your host, Mrs. Robinson, personally shops every day.

Lakeside Guest House, 118 Abingdon Rd. (tel. 0865/244725). Proprietors Kerry and Suzanne Bunt run this Victorian house overlooking open fields and parklands that leads to the University Boat Houses. It is about five minutes from Christchurch College. The house has been remodeled and updated. Their facilities include a twin room with a bath, a double with bath, a family unit for four, and another family unit for three. The charge for B&B is £11 ($16.50) to £13 ($19.50) per person nightly. There is hot and cold running water, tea- or coffee-making facilities, and color TV in all rooms. It is also centrally heated. Breakfast is served in a cozy dining room. Suzanne is a gracious hostess, and Kerry is warm and full of information about Oxford. He is a member of the fire department, and knows all the buildings of the city well. Outside is a good-sized car park. Nearby you'll find a playground, sports field, tennis courts, a pond for fishing, and four large swimming pools. Across the street is a field with horses and cows, a grocery store, and a flea market every summer.

The **Galaxie Private Hotel,** 180 Banbury Rd. (tel. 0865/515688), is owned by G. and M. Harries-Jones, whose rooms are spotlessly clean. A bus service on Banbury Road will take you the one mile to the center of town. All of the 33 bedrooms are equipped with reading lights, electric shaving points, hot and cold running water, central heating, and color TV. Many of the units have showers and toilets, for which you'll pay more, of course. For a bed and typical filling English breakfast, the cost per person daily for a single is from £18.50 ($27.75); a double is from £26 ($39). There is central heating, and parking space is available.

The **Pine Castle Hotel,** 290 Iffley Rd. (tel. 0865/241497), is a comfortable guest house operated by Peter and Marilyn Morris, with a host of amenities to make your stay happy. The hotel has central heating, with tea/coffee-making facilities and TV in all the rooms, plus a TV lounge if you prefer to watch in company. The Morrises can supply you with shoe-cleaning equipment, an iron, a hair dryer, current adaptors, and an alarm clock as needed, and there are laundry, dry-cleaning, and post office outlets across the street. For B&B, charges are £11 ($16.50) to £14 ($21) per person per day, with furniture for small children available.

In Iffley Village

The **Elms and Hawkwell Hotel,** Church Way in Iffley (tel. 0865/778529), just a few minutes' ride from the center of Oxford on a main road toward London, is suitable for motorists. The two buildings, several hundred feet apart, stand in three acres of lawns and gardens and were the private residences of English gentry until 1946. The Elms has nine bedrooms, each with TV and facilities for making tea or coffee. There are two bathrooms. The Tartan Bar, with more than 100 brands of whisky, is popular with both residents and the public. The price is £25 ($37.50) in a single, £35 ($52.50) in a double, including VAT, service charge, and a full English breakfast. The Hawkwell has one bath to each five bedrooms. Take bus 4 or 10A, or a taxi.

At Botley

Tilbury Lodge, 5 Tilbury Lane, Eynsham Road, Botley (tel. 0865/862138), lies on a pleasant country lane about two miles from the center of Oxford, less than a mile from the railway station. However, you don't need a car to stay here, because Eddie Trafford has been known to pick up guests at the station (however, I can't promise that). At the lodge, his wife, Eileen, welcomes guests, showing them to one of their well-furnished and comfortable rooms, three of which contain private baths. The B&B rate is from £13 ($19.50) in a single, £25 ($37.50) to £32 ($48) in a double, depending on the plumbing. Children are made welcome, and there is a large play garden for them. A bus which stops nearby takes visitors in the center of Oxford.

WHERE TO EAT: All Oxford undergraduates aren't the sons or daughters of wealthy dukes, as you'll soon discover when you see its numerous restaurants and cafés where you can get good food at reasonable prices. Here are my recommendations, which will be followed by my pub selections.

The **Cherwell Boathouse Restaurant,** Bardwell Road (tel. 0865/52746), is owned and run by Tony Verdin, with the help of a young crew. Everyone does anything that needs to be done, and preparation of menus and the cooking is taken in turns. Their menu contains items that have come from friends (the pork with mushrooms, for example). Two fixed menus are offered at each meal, and the cooks change the menu every two weeks to allow for the availability of fresh vegetables, fish, and meat. Appetizers include soups or fish or meat pâtés, followed by casseroles, pies, and hot pots, then some exotic dessert—cikolatak pasta, rum soufflé, or fruit fool. There is a very reasonable wine list, including brandy after dinner. The restaurant is open every evening from 8 to 10 p.m. and for Sunday lunch from noon to 2 p.m. For a regular dinner, the charge is £10.50 ($17), and Sunday lunch is £9.25 ($13.88), plus VAT. It's recommended that you make a reservation. Children, if they don't order a full meal, are granted half price. In summer, the restaurant also does an all-day cold buffet on the terrace.

Munchy Munchy, 6 Park End St. (tel. 0865/245710), is known for its food of Southeast Asia, including Indonesian and Malaysian dishes. Some Oxford students, who frequent this location near the station, consider that this restaurant offers the best food value in the city. The specialties of Ethel Ow are posted on her blackboard menu. Her dishes depend on her shopping for only the freshest ingredients in the marketplace. She is adept at herbs and seasoning, and often uses fresh fruit inventively, as reflected by such dishes as scallops sautéed with ginger, lamb with passion fruit sauce, and king prawns with nutmeg, lemon grass, and mace in coconut milk. Meals, costing from £5 ($7.50), are served Tuesday to Saturday from noon to 2 p.m. and from 5:30 to 9:30 p.m. It is closed on Sunday and for three weeks in August. The place is unlicensed so you have to bring your own bottle. Sometimes, especially on Friday and Saturday, long lines form at the door.

The **Nosebag,** 6–8 St. Michael's St. (tel. 0865/721033), is perhaps one of the most popular places to eat among students at Oxford. It's a self-service upstairs cafeteria on a side street off Cornmarket, opposite St. Michael's Church. Two floors of light wood-paneled furniture and cushioned benches greet you. But if you arrive at the busy main mealtimes, you'll probably have to queue (line up) on the stairs. The manager, Ray Hartman, keeps order out of the muddle. At lunch you can get a homemade soup, followed by the dish of the day, perhaps a moussaka. Baked potato with a variety of fillings is a good accompaniment, as is the hot garlic bread. Wine—white, red, or rosé—is available by the glass. A complete meal will cost from £5 ($7.50). The Nosebag is open Monday to Friday from 10 a.m. to 5:30 p.m., on Saturday from 9:30 a.m. to 6:30 p.m., and on Sunday from 10 a.m. to 6 p.m.

St. Aldate's Church Coffee House, 94 St. Aldate's (tel. 0865/245952), opened by the Archbishop of Canterbury in 1963, is almost opposite the entrance to Christ Church College, adjacent to St. Aldate's Church. An offbeat suggestion for eating, it is a bookshop/coffeehouse. The bookshop offers a wide range of first-class paperbacks suitable for holiday reading. Head for the back where you'll find a large restaurant with counter service run by the church. You receive value for money here, together with quantity. All the food is homemade, including soups and salads from fresh produce daily. The range of fresh baked scones and cakes brings the English fireside and cozy atmosphere right into the center of Oxford. Meals are priced around £3.50 ($5.25). The coffeehouse is usually open from 10 a.m. to 5 p.m. daily except Sunday.

Go Dutch, 18 Park End St. (tel. 0865/240686), opposite the railway station, is a bright and cheerful place where even the furnishings evoke the Netherlands, with clean wooden chairs and tables. Crêpes are served with savory fillings, such as bacon with apple or perhaps ham, corn, and green pepper. If you don't like the advertised stuffings, make up your own. To go with your crêpe, order one of the crisp, fresh salads as a side dish. Those intrepid diners who like their crêpes sweet will face a choice of such selections as black currant and mandarin. There is an extra-special concoction with banana ice cream, chocolate sauce, and Tía Maria. Count on spending from £5 ($7.50). Plenty of green plants have been placed about. The establishment is open from 6 to 10 p.m. Monday to Friday, from noon to 11 p.m. on Saturday and Sunday.

The above restaurant has opened **Go Dutch, Too,** at 43 St. Clements (tel. 0865/726286). It has the same pancake menu as Go Dutch but also offers a wide selection of homemade lunch snacks and meals. The furnishings, decor, and atmosphere are bright and cheerful. Expect to spend about £2.50 ($3.75) for lunch, £5 ($7.50) and up for dinner. It's open from 10 a.m. to 10 p.m. seven days a week.

Arts Centre Café/Bar, Old Fire Station Arts Centre, 40 George St. (tel. 0865/722115), is very much student oriented, and is most reasonable in price, as well as offering atmospheric dining and a chance to be with undergraduates. You can make your selection from the hot dishes of the day, both meat and vegetarian selections such as cheese, onion, and pepper quiche, steak-and-kidney pie, and the popular stuffed potatoes (try a filling of garlic or curry). These dishes are served after, perhaps, French onion or vegetable soup, accompanied by roll and butter and a side dish from the salad bar. If you still have room for dessert, try homemade flapjacks or sponge cake, perhaps a chocolate biscuit cake. A filling and wholesome meal will cost about £5 ($7.50) for three courses. They do some excellent teas, including Earl Grey and Ceylon, in addition to the regular Indian and herbal beverages. The café is open from 9 a.m. Monday to Saturday, with hot food being served from noon to 8 p.m. weekdays, from noon to 6 p.m. on Saturday. Closed Sunday.

Browns, 5–9 Woodstock Rd. (tel. 0865/511995), is a big, bustling brasserie "à l'anglaise," with music played in the background. It's popular with students who know of its quick snack meals. There is always a hamburger on the grill, and the staff will make you a hot pastrami on rye or perhaps a club sandwich. They also serve spaghetti with various sauces, including a Brighton seafood concoction. Salads include the usual chicken and tuna, and you can also order such main dishes as fish pie topped with cheddar cheese pastry. Check the blackboard for the day's specials. You'll spend from £8 ($12) for a meal, less if you're snacking. The decor is simple, with dark wood tables and potted plants. Browns is open seven days a week, from 11 a.m. (from noon on Sunday) to 11:30 p.m. Sometimes you'll see long lines of students waiting to get in, as this is the most popular dining place in Oxford.

Maxwell's, 36 Queen St. (tel. 0865/242192), is a big, airy room with steel supports set into the ceiling. It attracts homesick Americans with its cuisine. There is nothing corny, however, about Maxwell's, except for the grilled corn on the cob served as an appetizer. The Yankee theme is carried throughout the menu, which includes quarter-pound burgers served with practically anything. They also serve barbecue chicken and Tex-Mex chili. A large chef's salad makes a good lunch. Soda-fountain specials include malts, sundaes, and banana splits. Meals cost from £5 ($7.50). Maxwell's is open daily from noon to midnight. It's located on a busy shopping street across from Marks & Spencer (you climb the stairs to its second-floor setting).

Opium Den, 79 George St. (tel. 0865/248680), attracts only those "addicts" who desire good Cantonese food at reasonable prices. Sizable dinners can be ordered in special fixed-price menus for one, two, three, or four diners. There is a large selection from which to choose. A typical dinner might include grilled Chinese dumplings in soy sauce, followed by king prawns with baby corn in a sweet-and-sour sauce. This, plus an aromatic pot of Chinese tea, would bring the bill to £6.50 ($9.75). Budgeteers could select two courses at lunch from a wholesome variety of less expensive items for around £4.50 ($6.75). From Monday to Saturday, hours are noon to 2:30 p.m. and 6 p.m. to midnight. On Sunday, hours are 1 to 2:30 p.m. and 6 p.m. to midnight.

Raffles Tea Room, 90 High St. (tel. 0865/241855), is a branch of a tea-room chain system, part of the House of Tweed. In Oxford, the tea room, which opened in the summer of 1983, offers convenient refreshment for tired shoppers or visitors. The variety of beverages served reminds me of a Parisian café, but the ambience is definitely English. Teatime can be an event, particularly if you order two scones with jam and cream, along with a pot of Ceylon or Earl Grey tea. There's a wide choice of cakes and eclairs, and hot dishes and cold salads which could be a satisfying lunch or supper for around £4 ($6). For lighter appetites, Raffles offers Cona Toasties, a Scottish-derived formula for "closed toasted sandwiches," including ham and cheese with chutney. It is open from 9:30 a.m. to 5 p.m. (from 10:30 a.m. to 4:30 p.m. on Sunday in summer).

THE SPECIAL PUBS OF OXFORD: A short block from the High overlooking the northside of Christ Church College, the **Bear Inn,** Alfred Street (tel. 0865/244680), is an Oxford tradition. It's the village pub. Its swinging inn sign depicts the bear and ragged staff, old insignia of the Earls of Warwick, who were among the early patrons. Built in the 13th century, the inn has been known to many famous people who have lived and studied at Oxford. Over the years it's been mentioned time and time again in English literature.

The Bear has served a useful purpose in breaking down social barriers, bringing a wide variety of people together in a relaxed and friendly way. You might talk with a rajah from India, a university don, a titled gentleman—and the latest in a line of owners that goes back more than 700 years. Some former owners had an astonishing habit: clipping neckties! Around the lounge bar you'll see thousands of snipped portions of neckties, which have been labeled with their owners' names, the most famous of which is Lord Ismay, former head of NATO. For those of you who want to leave a bit of yourself, a thin strip of the bottom of your tie will be cut off (with your permission, of course) with a huge pair of ceremonial scissors. Then you, as the donor, will be given a free drink on the house. After this initiation, you may want to join in some of the informal songfests of the undergraduates. The shelves behind the bar are stacked and piled with items to nibble on: cheese, crisp rolls, cold meats, flans. Light meals cost from £3.50 ($5.25). Hours are 11 a.m. to 2:30 p.m. and 5:30 to 11 p.m.

The **Turf Tavern,** 4–5 Bath Place (tel. 0865/43235), is on a very narrow passage in the area of the Bodleian Library, off New College Lane. A 13th-century tavern, it is surely the find of the year. Thomas Hardy used the place for the setting of *Jude the Obscure*. It was "the local" of Burton and Taylor when they were in Oxford many years ago making a film, and today's stars include such names as Kris Kristofferson and John Hurt. At night, the old tower of New College and part of the old city wall are floodlit, enabling you, in warm weather, to enjoy an al fresco evening in a historical setting. In winter braziers are lighted in the courtyard and gardens which adds a beautiful atmosphere. Inside the low-beamed hospice, you can order traditional English food such as steak-and-kidney pie, baked potatoes, and old English casseroles and stews. More impressive, however, is a table about eight feet long and four feet wide, covered with meats, fish, fowl, eggs, cheeses, bread puddings, sausages, cakes, and salads (all cold), and a selection of hors d'oeuvres, freshly prepared daily. You can fill your plate for about £5 ($7.50). Old English brews from the wood, plus a range of country wines, are served all year, and a special punch is offered in winter to warm you through. Hours are from 10:30 a.m. to 2:30 p.m. and 5:30 to 11 p.m. It's reached via St. Helen's Passage between Holywell Street and New College Lane (you'll probably get lost, but any student worth his beer can direct you).

The **Trout Inn,** 195 Godstow Rd., near Wolvercote (tel. 0865/54485), lies on the outskirts of Oxford. Ask any former or present student of Oxford to name his or her most treasured pub, and the answer is likely to be the Trout. Hidden away from visitors and townspeople, the Trout is a private world where you can get ale and beer—and top-notch meals. Have your drink in one of the historic rooms, with their settles, brass, and old prints, or go out in sunny weather to sit on a stone wall, where you can feed crumbs to the swans that swim in the adjoining weir pool. Take an arched stone bridge, stone terraces, architecture that has wildly pitched roofs and gables, throw in the Thames River, and you have the Trout. If you don't have a car, take bus 520 or 521 to Wolvercote, then walk. Daily specials are featured for lunch. The seafood platter is popular, as is a tempting eight-ounce entrecôte. Soup of the day is hearty fare. For dessert, try the fruit tart with cream. Meal prices range from £7 ($10.50) to £10 ($15). The inn is open from noon to 2 p.m. and from 7 to 10 p.m. Salads are served during the summer, and grills in the winter. On your way there and back, look for the view of Oxford from the bridge.

DIDCOT: A little town ten miles south of Oxford near the Berkshire border, east of the A34, Didcot is served by trains from Paddington Station in London. Didcot Halt is a typical small country station. It would be called a flag stop in the U.S.

For the railway buff, this place is paradise, the home of the **Didcot Railway Centre** (tel. 0235/817200). In the engine sheds are steam locomotives, and on "steaming days" you can roll gently along in a Great Western Railway train running on a re-creation of Brunel's original broad-gauge Great Western track. In season, various other preserved railways in the country send visiting locomotives. The center is open Saturday, Sunday, and bank holidays from 11 a.m. to 5 p.m. March to October and daily from the end of July to the beginning of September. Admission charges are £1 ($1.50) to £2 ($3), depending on the event.

5. Woodstock (Blenheim Palace)

The small country town of Woodstock, the birthplace of the Black Prince, ill-fated son of King Edward III, in 1330, lies on the edge of the Cotswolds. Some of the stone houses here were constructed when Woodstock was the site of a royal palace, which had suffered the ravages of time, so that its remains were demolished when Blenheim Palace was built. Woodstock was once the seat of a flourishing glove industry.

Some 8 miles north of Oxford on the A34 road to Stratford-upon-Avon, Woodstock's main claim to fame today is—

BLENHEIM PALACE: This extravagant baroque palace regards itself as England's answer to Versailles. Blenheim is the home of the 11th Duke of Marlborough, a descendant of the first Duke of Marlborough (John Churchill), an on-again, off-again favorite of Queen Anne. In his day (1650–1722), the first duke became the supreme military figure in Europe. Fighting on the Danube near a village named Blenheim, Churchill defeated the forces of Louis XIV. The lavish palace of Blenheim was built for the duke as a gift from the queen. It was designed by Sir John Vanbrugh, who was also the architect of Castle Howard. Landscaping was carried out by Capability Brown.

The palace is loaded with riches: antiques, porcelain, oil paintings, tapestries, and chinoiserie. But more North Americans know Blenheim as the birthplace of Sir Winston Churchill. His birthroom forms part of the palace tour, as does the Churchill exhibition, four rooms of letters, books, photographs, and other Churchilliana. Today the former prime minister lies buried in Bladon Churchyard, near the palace.

Blenheim Palace is open every day from mid-March to the end of October from 11 a.m. to 6 p.m. (last admission to the palace at 5 p.m.). On spring bank holidays, Sunday, and Monday, charity events take place in the park, and different prices and times apply. Normally the admission fee is £3.50 ($5.25) for adults, £1.70 ($2.55) for children. In the park is the Blenheim Butterfly and Plant Centre. The complex contains a Butterfly House containing tropical moths and butterflies in free flight in a virtually natural habitat, an Adventure Play area, a Garden Café, a gift shop, and a shop for plants and gardening requirements, plus a putting green. For information, telephone 0993/811325.

From Oxford, there is a "Blenheim Palace and Historic Woodstock" open-top bus which runs every 70 minutes from Beaumont Street. Tickets, which include the palace tour, may be purchased on the bus or, including rail travel, at any main line railway station.

WHERE TO STAY: Much like a country house hotel, **The Kings Arms Hotel,** Market Street (tel. 0993/811412), was part of the properties that Queen Elizabeth I gave to Woodstock when she came to the throne. Behind a 19th-century stucco facade, the Kings Arms is run by the McEwen family, who welcomes travelers on the A34 between Stratford-upon-Avon and the south. Go early to enjoy a drink in the friendly bar, then later have a meal at Wheeler's St. James Restaurant. Since 1929 Wheeler's has been known in London for its seafood, and now they've opened a branch at Woodstock. Featuring the largest seafood menu in the area, they offer lunches for £9.50 ($14.25), dinners for £12 ($18). The bedrooms, 10 in all, are individually designed (one with a four-poster), each with private bath, direct-dial phone, hair dryer, coffee-making facilities, and color TV. Singles cost £28 ($42) to £35 ($52.50), doubles £44 ($66) to £52 ($78), including VAT and an English breakfast.

The **Marlborough Arms Hotel,** Oxford Street (tel. 0993/811227), is a pleasant 16th-century coaching inn, with an arched alleyway leading to the courtyard. Alistair McEwen and his staff of local help are used to passing travelers. Their bar snacks are ample and succulent. They also do a set lunch for £6.50 ($9.75) and a dinner for £10 ($15). Bedrooms are simple and comfortable, containing color TV. The charge in a single is £24 ($36), rising to £40 ($60) in a double or twin without bath. With a private bath, a double or twin rents for £48 ($72) nightly. Corridor baths are ample. This hostelry was called the George Inn in Sir Walter Scott's *Woodstock*.

WHERE TO EAT: Right in the heart of town, **Brothertons,** 1 High St. (tel. 0993/811114), is your best bet. Carefully chosen raw materials form one of the reasons for the success of this place, open from 10:30 a.m. to 10:30 p.m., which makes it convenient for a visit regardless of how much time you spend at Blenheim Palace. Meals cost from £8 ($12), and are likely to feature such dishes as a selection of crudités, smoked salmon, or game pie. There's always a vegetarian dish of the day, and families with small children are welcomed. Potted plants, pine chairs and tables, and gas mantles make for a simple but effective decor.

6. Hertfordshire

Like a giant jellyfish, the frontier of Greater London spills over into this country, once described by Charles Lamb as "hearty, homely, loving Hertfordshire." This fertile land lies northwest of London and supplies much of that city's food, in spite of encroachment by industry. Hertfordshire is sometimes called "the market basket of England."

Its most important attraction, which is usually visited on a day trip from London, follows.

HATFIELD HOUSE: One of the chief attractions of Hertfordshire, and one of the greatest of all English country houses, Hatfield House (tel. 07072/62823) is just 21 miles north of London. To build what is now the E-shaped Hatfield House, the old Tudor palace at Hatfield was mostly demolished. The Banqueting Hall, however, remains.

Hatfield was much a part of the lives of both Henry VIII and his daughter, Elizabeth I. In the old palace, built in the 15th century, Elizabeth romped and played as a child. Although Henry was married to her mother, Anne Boleyn, at the time of Elizabeth's birth, the marriage was later nullified (Anne lost her head and Elizabeth her legitimacy). Henry also used to stash away his oldest daughter, Mary Tudor, at

Hatfield. But when Mary became Queen of England and set about earning the dubious distinction of "Bloody Mary," she found Elizabeth a problem. For a while she kept her in the Tower of London, but she eventually let her return to Hatfield (Elizabeth's loyalty to Catholicism was seriously doubted). In 1558, while at Hatfield, Elizabeth learned of her ascension to the throne of England.

The Jacobean house that exists today contains much antique furniture, tapestries, and paintings as well as three much-reproduced portraits, including the famed ermine and rainbow portraits of Elizabeth I. The Great Hall is suitably medieval, complete with a minstrel's gallery. One of the rarest exhibits is a pair of silk stockings, said to have been worn by Elizabeth herself, the first lady in England to don such apparel. The park and the gardens are also worth exploring. The Riding School and Palace Stables contain a number of interesting historical exhibitions.

Hatfield is usually open from March 25 through the second Sunday in October, daily, except Monday, from noon to 5 p.m. (on Sunday from 2 to 5:30 p.m.). Admission is £2.50 ($3.75) for adults, £1.80 ($2.70) for children. You can reach Hatfield House by fast train from Kings Cross in London. The station faces the park gates. The new Moorgate to Hatfield electric train service has direct Underground links, via the Victoria Line at Highbury, Circle Line at Moorgate, or Piccadilly Line at Finsbury Park. For information on the house, call the curator, 07072/62823. Refreshments are available in a restaurant/cafeteria.

The **Old Mill House Museum,** Mill Green has displays of the history of the Hatfield area from the Stone Age to the present, including Mill Green Watermill. It's open Tuesday to Friday from 10 a.m. to 5 p.m.; weekends and bank holidays from 2 to 5 p.m. Admission is free.

FOOD AND DRINK IN OLD HATFIELD: One of the finest restaurants in the Home Counties is the **Salisbury,** 15 The Broadway (tel. 07072/62220). It's ideal for a stop-over if you're visiting Hatfield House. A brick-built structure, it is ruled by its owner-chef, Julian Waterer, who is remembered by many for his food served at Greywalls in Gullane in Scotland. A chef of much talent, he creates individual yet highly disciplined dishes. These might include filet of sea bass and scallops baked in foil, venison in a wine sauce, breast of chicken with a pistachio stuffing, and veal chops grilled with fresh herbs. His sauces are perfectly blended and a delight. A set lunch is offered at £10 ($15), a specialty dinner going for £22 ($33). Lunch is served from 12:30 to 2 p.m. and dinner from 7:30 to 9:30 p.m. The restaurant is closed for dinner on Sunday and all day Monday.

A fine place for light lunches and good lager is **Eight Bells,** a pub on Park Street (tel. 07072/66059). Dickens fans may like to know that this was the inn where Bill Sikes and his dog found temporary refuge after the brutal murder of Nancy. It's a rickety old corner inn with a central bar for drinks and dining nooks—in all, a forest of time-blackened beams, settles, and pewter tankards. A bowl of homemade soup is reasonably priced, and the cook's specialty is smoked mackerel filet. A light luncheon here will cost about £3.50 ($5.25). Hours are from 11 a.m. to 2:30 p.m. and 6 to 11 p.m.

HERTFORD: This old Saxon city is the country town, containing many fine examples of domestic architecture, some of which date back to the 16th century. Hertford is reached via the A1 or A10 from London. Samuel Stone, founder of Hartford, Connecticut, was born here. The town's Norman castle has long been in ruins, and part of the still-standing keep dates from the 16th century.

For food and lodgings, try the **Salisbury Arms Hotel,** Fore Street (tel. 0992/53091), which has been called "always Hertford's principal inn." For 400 years it's been feeding and providing lodgings to wayfarers, or giving a hot grog to the coachman, a stable for his horses. The stables have long given way to a car park, but a sense of history still prevails. In the cellar is medieval masonry predating the 16th-century structure around it. Cromwell is said to have lodged here, and both Royalists and Roundheads have mounted the Jacobean staircase. Bedrooms now spill over into a modern extension, a total of 22 functionally furnished rooms added to the 10 more antiquated original ones. Rates depend on the room occupied—singles, doubles, or twins. Singles start at £23.50 ($35.25), going up to £29 ($43.50) for those requiring a private bath. Two persons pay from £38 ($57) to £42.50 ($63.75). Family rooms rent for £50 ($75). Good, wholesome English "fayre" is provided. At lunch, when most visitors stop by, a cut from the roast of the day goes for £5.50 ($8.25) with vegetables. A paneled and intimately partitioned dining room provides traditional meals as well as a full Chinese menu. There is, as well, a well-stocked cellar. Dinners are from £12 ($18).

ST. ALBANS: This cathedral city, just 21 miles northeast of London, dates back 2,000 years. It was named after a Roman soldier, the first Christian martyr in England. Don't ask a resident to show you to the **Cathedral of St. Albans.** Here it's still known as "The Abbey," even though Henry VIII dissolved it as such in 1539. Construction on the cathedral was launched in 1077, making it one of the early Norman churches of England. The bricks, especially visible in the tower, came from the old Roman city of Verulamium at the foot of the hill. The nave and west front date from 1235.

The Chapter House, the first modern building beside a great medieval cathedral in the country, which also serves as a pilgrim/visitor center, was opened by the Queen in 1982.

The **Verulamium Museum** (tel. 0727/54659) at St. Michael's stands on the site of the Roman city. Here you'll view some of the finest Roman mosaics in Britain. Part of the Roman town wall, a hypocaust, and a theater and its adjoining houses and shops are still visible. Visit in summer from 10 a.m. to 5:30 p.m. weekdays (on Sunday from 2 to 5:30 p.m.), and in winter from 10 a.m. to 4 p.m. weekdays (2 to 4 p.m. on Sunday), paying 70p ($1.05) for adults, 40p (60¢) for children.

The **Clock Tower** at Market Place (tel. 0727/53301) was built in 1402, standing 77 feet high, a total of five floors. It is open from Easter to mid-September on Saturday and Sunday from 10:30 a.m. to 5 p.m.

From St. Albans you can see **Gorhambury House** (tel. 0727/54051), a classic-style mansion built in 1777, containing 16th-century enameled glass and historic portraits. It's open, May to September, only on Thursday (2 to 5 p.m.), charging adults £1.20 ($1.80) for admission; children pay 70p ($1.05). The location is 2½ miles west of St. Albans off the A414.

On the outskirts, the **Mosquito Aircraft Museum,** the oldest aircraft museum in Britain, lies on the grounds of Salisbury Hall, just off the M25 London to St. Albans road near London Colney, about five miles south of St. Albans. The hall is no longer open to the public, but the museum can be visited from Easter Sunday to the end of October on Sunday from 2 to 5:30 p.m. and on Thursday from 10:30 a.m. to 5:30 p.m. from July to the end of September (also on bank holiday Mondays). Displayed is the prototype of the the de Havilland "Mosquito" aircraft, which was designed and built at Salisbury Hall in World War II, plus 16 other aircraft of de Havilland origin, as well as memorabilia, and relics. Admission is 75p ($1.13) for adults, 25p (38¢) for children. For more information, telephone 0727/22051, or write Box 107, St. Albans.

Back in St. Albans, I offer the following recommendations for food and lodgings:

Melford House, 24 Woodstock Rd. North (tel. 0727/53642), is a 12–bedroom hotel-cum-guesthouse in the best residential area where it is quiet and away from the busy town center, charging moderate prices for B&B: £20 ($30) to £34 ($51) in a single, £28 ($42) to £37 ($55.50) in a double, and £37 ($55.50) to £44 ($66) for three persons in a family room. The higher prices are for rooms with showers and toilets. A full English breakfast is included in the tariffs. Each unit has its niceties, and each is immaculately kept, with full central heating. There is a spacious residents' lounge with color TV. The house is licensed for beer and liquor, and there is a car park and a garden. The resident owners are Yvonne and Cecil Green who are experienced hoteliers of long standing and have managed large luxury hotels abroad.

The best place in town for dining is **La Province,** 13 George St. (tel. 0727/52142), right in the heart of town, in the vicinity of the cathedral. Yet, for what it offers, it isn't expensive. Meals are served Tuesday to Saturday from noon to 2 p.m. and from 7 to 10 p.m., from £7 ($10.50) for the set lunch, £14.50 ($21.75) for a table d'hôte dinner. Some of the fish dishes recently sampled were excellent, as was a rabbit dish with a medley of fruit. Music soothes guests as they dine.

SHAW'S CORNER: Just southwest of Ayot St. Lawrence, three miles northwest of Welwyn, stands the home where George Bernard Shaw lived from 1906 to 1950. The house is practically as he left it at his death. In the hall, for example, his hats are still hanging, as if ready for him to don one. His personal mementos fill the four rooms that can be seen. The house is open April to October, Monday to Thursday from 2 to 6 p.m. It is also open on Sunday from noon to 6 p.m. From November to March, hours are 11 a.m. to 6 p.m. Sunday to Thursday. Admission is £1.40 ($2.10), half price for children. For information, telephone 0438/280307.

7. Buckinghamshire

This is a leafy county, lying north of the Thames and somewhat to the west of London. Its identifying marks are the wide Vale of Aylesbury, with its sprawling fields and tiny villages, and the long chalk range of the Chilterns. Going south from the range, you'll find what is left of a once-great beech forest.

CLIVEDEN: The former home of Nancy, Lady Astor, now a National Trust property, has been turned into a deluxe hotel, but the grounds and some of the sumptuously decorated rooms are on view to the public at certain times, so it's worth a visit, even if you can't afford to stay here. The garden features a rose garden, a magnificent box parterre, and an amphitheater where "Rule Britannia" was played for the first time. There are 375 acres of garden and woodland to explore. The house is open from the first of April to October only on Thursday and Sunday from 3 to 6 p.m. The grounds are open March to December daily from 11 a.m. to 6 p.m. or sunset if earlier. Admission to the grounds is £2 ($3); to the house, 60p (90¢). Children are admitted for half price. Cliveden is 20 miles west of London, lying two miles north of Taplow on the B476, off the A40.

AYLESBURY: Gourmets still speak of its succulent ducks, a prize-winning dish on any table. However, ducks bearing that name are usually raised elsewhere these days. The county town, Aylesbury has a number of timbered inns, old houses, and a wide Market Square. Less than 40 miles from London, it remains cozily old world.

Six miles northwest of Aylesbury on the Bicester road (A41), **Waddeson Manor** (tel. 0296/651211) contains an outstanding collection of French decorative art of the 17th and 18th centuries. Among the paintings are portraits by Reynolds, Gainsborough, and Romney. The manor was built in the late 19th century for Baron Ferdinand de Rothschild in the style of the French Renaissance. Now belonging to the National Trust, the manor stands in 150 acres of grounds with rare trees, an aviary, and a herd of Sika deer. Visiting times are from late March to late October, Wednesday to Sunday, from 2 to 6 p.m. (closed Wednesday after bank holidays). The admission to the house, grounds, and aviary is £2.50 ($3.75).

Back in Aylesbury, you can find big-splurge food and lodgings at the **Kings Head,** Market Square (tel. 0296/415158), a half-timbered hotel that was once a 15th-century coaching inn. It is one of the finest examples of Tudor architecture in Buckinghamshire. Its 24 bedrooms, about half of which have private baths, overlook a cobble courtyard. Bathless units cost £25 ($37.50) in a single, £35 ($52.50) in a double. Accommodations with bath cost £38 ($57) in a single, £48 ($72) in a double. A single with a shower but no toilet goes for £28 ($42). Meals in the restaurant, served from noon to 2:30 p.m. and 6:30 to 9:30 p.m., cost £10 ($15) on the fixed-price menu. Drinks are served in the cozy lounge bar in back, where you can see the chair used by Oliver Cromwell on his frequent visits to the inn. He slept in the Cromwell room upstairs with its extra-large bed. Some of his weapons are also on display here.

BUCKINGHAM: This old market town on the River Ouse was once the county town of Buckingham. It has a fine 13th-century Chantry Chapel and some 18th-century houses.

For food and lodging, try the **White Hart,** Market Square (tel. 0280/815151), a Trusthouse Forte property. This oldish market town hotel has 18th-century origins, but its plaster facade and portico are Victorian additions. In recent years, the hotel has been remodeled and equipped for modern comfort, its renovation bringing a workable efficiency to its interior. All of the hotel's 19 bedrooms contain a private bath or shower, with color TV and coffee-making facilities. Singles rent for £42.50 ($63.75), doubles or twins for £52 ($78), a worthy splurge choice considering the dearth of fine accommodations in the area. The hotel's dining room, the Georgian Room, has its own small dance floor, and there is a lounge bar as well. They also have Hathaways Kitchen, serving steaks and fish, with fresh salads and granary breads. Meals begin at £6.50 ($9.75).

JORDANS VILLAGE: A farm called **Old Jordans,** Jordans Lane, in Jordans Village near Beaconsfield (tel. 02407/4586), dates back to the Middle Ages. But its recorded history starts in the early 17th century when one Thomas Russell, sitting tenant, bought the freehold, signing the deed with his thumbprint. The house was added to over the years, and in the mid-17th century William Penn, founder of Pennsylvania, and other well-known Dissenters stayed here and worshipped.

Now the property of Quakers, the house is run as a guesthouse and conference center, with some 30 simply furnished rooms available for overnight guests at £20 ($30) in a single, £32 ($48) in a double, including breakfast. Morning tea or coffee with crackers and an afternoon tea of scones and jam are served in the kitchen-dining room of the hall. Lunch at £5 ($7.50) is served at 12:45 p.m.

On the grounds is the Mayflower Barn, built almost undisputably from timbers from the ship *Mayflower* in which the first Pilgrims sailed to the New World. These days the beams ring to the strains of concert music and recitals performed by top-notch artists.

It's a very peaceful place, full of history, and perhaps a little isolated from today's bustle. It is ideally situated midway between London and Oxford and makes a good first or last stop from Heathrow. Trains run frequently from Marylebone, London, to Seer Green Station three-quarters of a mile from Jordans Village. Taxis can usually be arranged to meet trains or buses if advance notice is given, or you may be able to find a taxi at Gerrards Cross or Beaconsfield.

MILTON'S COTTAGE: The modern residential town of Gerrards Cross is often called the Beverly Hills of England, as it attracts many wealthy persons who settle here in many beautiful homes. Surrounding this plush section are several tucked-away hamlets, including **Chalfont St. Giles,** where the poet Milton lived during the Great Plague in 1665. He completed *Paradise Lost* here, and the cottage he lived in contains a small museum of Miltoniana.

John Milton's Cottage, Deanway (tel. 02407/2313), is open daily except Monday from February 1 to October 31, 10 a.m. to 1 p.m. and 2 to 6 p.m. (on Sunday from 2 to 6 p.m.), charging an admission of £1 ($1.50) for adults, 40p (60¢) for children under 15. It is closed in November, December, January, and February. Allow time to visit the beautifully maintained garden.

West of Gerrards Cross, the town of Beaconsfield, with its broad, tree-lined High Street, enjoys many associations with Disraeli. Visitors pass through here en route to—

HUGHENDEN MANOR: Outside High Wycombe, in Buckinghamshire, sits a country manor that gives us not only an insight into the age of Victoria, but acquaints us with a remarkable man. In Benjamin Disraeli we meet one of the most enigmatic figures of 19th-century England. At age 21 Dizzy published anonymously his five-volume novel *Vivian Grey*. But it wasn't his shining hour. He went on to other things, marrying an older widow for her money. They developed, apparently, a most successful relationship. He entered politics and continued writing novels, his later ones meeting with more acclaim.

In 1848 Disraeli acquired Hughenden Manor, a country house that befitted his fast-rising political and social position. He served briefly as prime minister in 1868, but his political fame rests on his stewardship as prime minister during 1874-1880. He became Queen Victoria's friend, and in 1877 she paid him a rare honor by visiting him at Hughenden.

In 1876 Disraeli became the Earl of Beaconsfield: he had arrived. Only his wife was dead, and he was to die in 1881. Instead of being buried at Westminster Abbey, he preferred the simple little graveyard of Hughenden Church.

Hughenden contains an odd assortment of memorabilia, including a lock of Disraeli's hair. The letters from Victoria, the autographed books, and especially a portrait of Lord Byron, known to Disraeli's father.

If you're driving to Hughenden Manor on the way to Oxford, continue north of High Wycombe on the A4128 for about 1½ miles. If you're relying on public transportation from London, take coach 711 to High Wycombe, then board an Alder Valley bus (323, 324, 333, or 334). The manor house and garden are open daily from Wednesday to Sunday, April to October from 2 to 6 p.m. (noon to 6 p.m. on Sunday and bank holidays). In March they're open on Saturday and Sunday only from 2 to 6 p.m. Admission for adults is £1.80 ($2.70), half price for children. It is closed on Good Friday. For more information, telephone 0494/32580.

WEST WYCOMBE: Snuggled in the Chiltern Hills 30 miles west of London, the village of West Wycombe still has an atmosphere of the early 18th century. The thatched roofs have been replaced with tiles, and some of the buildings have been removed or replaced, but the village is still two centuries removed from the present day.

In the mid-18th century Sir Francis Dashwood began an ambitious building program at West Wycombe. His strong interest in architecture and design led Sir Francis to undertake a series of monuments and parks which are still among the finest in the country today. He also sponsored the building of a road using the chalk quarries on the hill to aid in the support of the poverty-stricken villagers. The resulting caves are said to have been used by "The Knights of St. Francis of Wycombe," later known as "The Hellfire Club." The knights consisted of a number of illustrious men drawn from the social circle surrounding the Prince of Wales. Its members "gourmandized," swilling claret and enjoying the company of women "of a cheerful, lively disposition . . . who considered themselves lawful wives of the brethren during their stay."

You can tour the caves today, wandering through a quarter mile of winding passages, past colorful waxwork scenes brought to life by sound and light effects.

A visit to **West Wycombe House,** home of the Dashwoods, is of both historical and architectural interest. Both George III and Ben Franklin stayed here, but not at the same time. The house is one of the best examples of Palladian-style architecture in England. The interior is lavishly decorated with paintings and antiques from the 18th century.

The house and grounds are open only in June, July, and August from Monday to Friday, 2 to 6 p.m. The caves, with the café and gift shop, are open Monday to Friday from early March to the end of May from 1 to 6 p.m., Monday to Saturday from early June to mid-September from 11 a.m. to 5 p.m., and on Sunday from the end of March to late October from 11 a.m. to 6 p.m. Admission to the house and grounds is £2 ($3) for adults, £1 ($1.50) for children, with the same entrance fee charged for visiting the caves. For more information, write to West Wycombe Park Office, West Wycombe, Buckinghamshire HP143AJ (tel. 0494/24411).

Other sights at West Wycombe include the **Church of St. Lawrence,** perched atop West Wycombe Hill and topped by a huge golden ball. Parts of the church date from the 13th century; its richly decorated interior was copied from a third-century Syrian sun temple. The view from the church tower is worth the trek up the hill. Near the church stands the Dashwood Mausoleum, built in a style derived from Constantine's Arch in Rome.

During your tour, you may also wander freely through the village, stopping for lunch at one of the public houses. Four miles of nature trails also meander about the village, through woods and farmlands.

8. Bedfordshire (Woburn Abbey)

This county contains the fertile, rich Vale of Bedford, crossed by the River Ouse. Most visitors from London head here on a day trip to visit historic Woburn Abbey (previewed below). Others know of its county town—

BEDFORD: On the Ouse, Bedford contains many riverside parks and gardens, but is better known for its associations with John Bunyan. On Mill Street stands the 1850 Bunyan Meeting Freechurch encompassing the **Bunyan Museum** (tel. 0234/58870), erected on the site of a barn where Bunyan used to preach. Panels on the doors illustrate scenes from *Pilgrim's Progress*. The Bunyan Museum contains the surviving relics of Bunyan and a famous collection of the *Pilgrim's Progress* in 169 languages. It is open Tuesday to Saturday, April to September, from 2 to 4 p.m., charging an admission of 30p (45¢) for adults and 20p (30¢) for children.

About 1½ miles south of Bedford lies Elstow, close to Bunyan's reputed birthplace. Here you can visit **Elstow Moot Hall,** a medieval market hall. In it is housed a collection of 17th-century relics associated with Bunyan. It is open April to October Tuesday to Saturday from 2 to 5 p.m. and on Sunday from 2 to 5:30, charging 30p (45¢) for adults, 15p (23¢) for children. For more information, telephone 0234/63222, ext. 30.

The **Swiss Garden,** Old Warden, near Biggleswade, is an unusual romantic site dating from the early 19th century. It contains original buildings and features, together with many interesting plants and trees, some of great rarity. A lakeside picnic area in adjoining woodlands is open at all times. Hours for the garden are 2 to 6 p.m. (last admission is at 5:15 p.m.) on Wednesday, Thursday, Saturday, Sunday, (except the last Sunday of each month), and bank holiday Monday, from April to October. The garden lies approximately 2½ miles west of Biggleswade adjoining the Biggleswade–Old Warden road about two miles west of the A1. For more information, telephone 0234/63222, ext. 2330.

Food and Lodging

If you've decided to stay in Bedford for the night, the best place to head for food is the **Greek Villager Restaurant,** a tavern and kebab house at the Mews, St. Peters St.

(tel. 0234/41798). It features dining and dancing to live Greek music on Friday and Saturday. Bouzouki and guitars, and a belly dancer, are featured, as well as Cypriot and Greek dancing. The restaurant is open six nights a week; until midnight Monday to Thursday, until 2 a.m. on Friday and Saturday (closed Sunday). A special feature of the chef is small portions of about 14 different Greek dishes served on separate plates at a cost of £10 ($15) per person. Otherwise, you get the usual appetizers such as hummus and taramosalata, followed by such typical Greek dishes as moussaka and dolmades (stuffed vine leaves). Regular meals begin at £12 ($18), plus the cost of your wine.

Homeleigh Guest House, 26 de Pary's Ave. (tel. 0234/59219), is near the center. A Victorian structure, with adequate car parking, it lies on a tree-lined street. Ken and Gianna White have renovated it and converted it into a place offering attractively furnished and pleasant rooms, many quite spacious. Only one room has a private bath, and that is more expensive, of course. Otherwise, if you don't mind sharing a bath, you'll find B&B rates costing from £11.50 ($17.25) in a single, rising to £19 ($28.50) in a double, including an English breakfast.

WOBURN ABBEY: Few persons visiting Bedfordshire miss the Georgian mansion
of **Woburn Abbey** (tel. 052525/666), the seat of the Dukes of Bedford for more than three centuries. The much-publicized 18th-century estate is about 42 miles from London outside of Woburn. Its State Apartments are rich in furniture, porcelain, tapestries, silver, and a valuable art collection, including paintings by Van Dyck, Holbein, Rembrandt, Gainsborough, and Reynolds. A series of paintings by Canaletto, showing his continuing views of Venice, grace the walls of the dining room in the Private Apartments (Prince Philip said the duke's collection was superior to the Canalettos at Windsor—but Her Majesty quickly corrected him!). Of all the paintings, one of the most notable from a historical point of view is the *Armada Portrait,* of Elizabeth I. Her hand rests on the globe, as Philip's invincible armada perishes in the background.

Queen Victoria and Prince Albert visited Woburn Abbey in 1841. Victoria slept in an opulently decorated bedroom (her stockings are still there). In 1954 another queen—this one of the cinema, Marilyn Monroe—slept in the same bed as a publicity stunt. Victoria's Dressing Room contains a fine collection of 17th-century paintings from the Netherlands. Among the oddities and treasures at Woburn Abbey are a Grotto of Shells, a Sèvres dinner service (gift of Louis XV), and a chamber devoted to memorabilia of "The Flying Duchess." Wife of the 11th Duke of Bedford, she was a remarkable woman, who disappeared on a solo flight in 1937 (the same year as Amelia Earhart). The duchess was 72 years old at the time.

In the 1950s the present Duke of Bedford opened Woburn Abbey to the public to pay off some $15 million in inheritance taxes. In 1974 he turned the estate over to his son and daughter-in-law, the Marquess and Marchioness of Tavistock, who reluctantly took on the business of running the 75-room mansion. And what a business it is, drawing more than a million visitors a year and employing more than 300 persons to staff the shops and grounds.

Today Woburn Abbey is surrounded by a 3,000 acre park containing many rare and exotic animals (ten varieties of deer). Some visit just to see the animals. In addition to many species of deer, there is also the Chinese Père David deer, saved here from extinction, as well as the Przewalski horse, yaks, bison, and camels, along with many other animals. While seated in one of 57 gondolas on the two-mile cable lift, you pass over lions, elephants, and giraffes. What would Humphry Repton, the designer of the estate's park in the 19th century, say?

Woburn Abbey is outside Woburn, near Dunstable. It is hard to reach by public transportation from London, so you may prefer to take one of the organized tours.

The abbey is open daily from the end of March to the first of November from 11 a.m. to 5:45 p.m. and on Saturday and Sunday only from early January to the end of

March from 11 a.m. to 4:45 p.m. The last entry is 45 minutes before closing. The abbey is closed in November and December. Admission is £3 ($4.50) for adults, £1.50 ($2.25) for children. If you wish only to explore the Deer Park, which opens at 10 a.m. in summer and 10:30 a.m. in winter, the charge is £1.50 ($2.25) for a car and passengers. The Deer Park charge does not apply to visitors who purchase their abbey tickets as they enter the park.

To visit the Woburn Wild Animal Kingdom and Leisure Park, the charge is £4.50 ($6.75) for adults and £3.50 ($5.25) for children. The animal kingdom is open March 16 to October 31 from 10 a.m. to 5 p.m.

A Pub at Woburn

Black Horse, Bedford Street, (tel. 052525/210), a former coaching inn, is the best-known pub in the area, serving good food. Many visitors come here for a pint after their visit to the abbey nearby. During the day you can order good-tasting bar food. In summer a cold buffet is featured which can be enjoyed in a walled garden. A good luncheon goes from £3.50 ($5.25), and in the evening you can dine in the restaurant for around £10 ($15), ordering such food as a seaman's platter or steaks. Wine is sold by the glass. Hours are from 10:30 a.m. to 2:30 p.m. daily and from 6 to 11 p.m. (on Sunday from noon to 2 p.m. and from 7 to 10:30 p.m.).

HISTORIC PLANES AND CARS: Should vintage airplanes and automobiles interest you, you can pay a visit to the **Shuttleworth Collection** at the Old Warden Aerodrome (tel. 076727/288). A classic glass aerodrome set in typically English countryside, it is the home of a unique selection of some 30 historic airplanes, maintained in a full flying status to illustrate the progress of aviation from a 1909 Bleriot XI to a 1941 Spitfire. An 1898 Panhard Levassor in which King Edward VIII once drove to Ascot is just one of the fascinating vehicles. The collection can be visited daily from 10:30 a.m. to 5:30 p.m. (to 4:30 p.m. in winter), with last admission an hour before closing time. It's closed for a week at Christmas. Admission is £1.75 ($2.63) for adults, £1 ($1.50) for children. There are special charges for flying displays. The aerodrome is some 2 miles west of the Al roundabout at Biggleswade.

WHIPSNADE PARK ZOO: This is the country breeding park of the Zoological Society of London (which also operates the London Zoo), where the animals roam free in large paddocks and certain species even wander among visitors. Situated on the edge of the Chiltern escarpment in Bedfordshire, Whipsnade (tel. 0582/872171) lays claim to being the world's first open-air zoo. Many endangered species are here, including the cheetah, Père David deer, oryx, and Indian and white rhinos. There are also 12 species of crane, including the rare and beautiful red-naped or Manchurian crane. There is a lot of walking here to see everything in a single day, but the opportunities for photography are second to none. Exhibits include dolphins, a steam railway, a birds of prey show, a habitats exhibition, and a family center. Animals are in geographical groupings. Cars are admitted for £3.50 ($5.25) in July and August and £2.50 ($3.75) at other times of year except from November 1 to February 28 when they are admitted free. In addition, you must pay £3 ($4.50) for adults and £1.50 ($2.25) for children. Children under the age of 5 are admitted free. The zoo is open daily from 10 a.m. to 6 p.m. or sunset, whichever is earlier. Take the train from St. Pancras to Luton, then a number 43 bus to Whipsnade Park.

Chapter VII

KENT, SURREY, AND SUSSEX

LYING TO THE SOUTH and southeast of London are the shires (counties) of Kent, Surrey, and the Sussexes. Combined, they form a most fascinating part of England to explore—and are easy to reach, within commuting distance of the capital.

Of all the tourist centers, **Canterbury** in Kent is of foremost interest, but the old Cinque ports of **Rye** and **Winchelsea** in East Sussex are almost equally exciting, as is the resort of **Brighton and Hove** in a completely different way. In and around these major meccas are dozens of castles and vast estates, monuments, homes of famous men (Churchill, for example), cathedrals, yachting harbors, and little villages of thatched cottages.

The range of accommodations varies from an old-world smugglers' inn in the ancient seaport of Rye to a clean, comfortable Georgian guesthouse in the heart of medieval Canterbury. Regardless of the price range in which you travel, you'll discover some superb bargains throughout the counties of the South Coast.

In the fog-choked cities of north England, the great dream for retirement is to find a little rose-covered cottage in the south, where the living's easier. The South Coast is also a potent magnet for London's East Enders. Come with me as we examine the lure, beginning with:

KENT

Fresh from his cherry orchard, the Kentish farmer heads for his snug spot by an inglenook, with its bright-burning fire, for his mellow glass of cherry brandy. The day's work is done. All's right with the world.

We're in what was once the ancient Anglo-Saxon kingdom of Kent, on the shirt-tails of London itself, yet far removed in spirit and scenery. Since the days of the Tudors, cherry blossoms have pinkened the fertile landscape. Not only orchards, but hop fields abound. The conically shaped oasthouses with kilns for drying the hops dot the rolling countryside. Both the hops and orchards have earned for Kent the title of the "garden of England." And in England the competition's rough for that distinction.

Kent suffered severe destruction in World War II, as it was the virtual alley over which the Luftwaffe flew in its blitz of London. After the fall of France, a German invasion was feared imminent. Shortly after becoming prime minister in 1940, Churchill sped to Dover, with his bowler, stogie, walking cane, and pin-striped suit. Once there, he inspected the coastal defense and gave encouragement to the men digging in to fight off the attack. But Hitler's "Sea Lion" (code name for the invasion) turned out to be a paper tiger.

In spite of much devastation, Kent is filled with interesting old towns, mansions, and castles. The country is rich in Dickensian associations, and for that reason Kent is sometimes known as Dickens Country. His family once lived near the naval dockyard at Chatham.

ROCHESTER: In the cathedral city of Rochester, 30 miles from London, you can visit the **Charles Dickens Centre** and **Dickens Chalet** in Eastgate House, built in 1590. This center, on High Street in Rochester, is open seven days a week from 10 a.m. to 12:30 p.m. and 2 to 5 p.m. Admission is £1.40 ($2.10) for adults and 80p ($1.20) for children. The museum has tableaux depicting various scenes from Dickens's novels, including a Pickwickian Christmas scene, then the fever-ridden graveyard of *Bleak House,* scenes from *The Old Curiosity Shop* and *Great Expectations,* along with *Oliver Twist* and *David Copperfield.* There is clever use of sound and light. Information is also available at the center on various other sights in Rochester associated with Dickens, including Eastgate House and, in the garden, the chalet transported from Gads Hill Place, where Dickens died, as well as the Guildhall Museum, Rochester Cathedral, and the mysterious "6 Poor Travellers' House." Pick up a brochure which includes a map featuring the various places and the novels with which each is associated. For further information, telephone 0634/44176.

Three miles from Rochester stands **Gads Hill Place,** which was the home of Dickens from 1858 to 1870. Standing on the A226, it can only be visited by prior arrangement.

At Broadstairs, the favorite seaside resort of the novelist—"our watering place" —the **Dickens House Museum** stands on the main seafront. This museum (tel. 0843/62853) was once the home of Mary Pearson Strong, on whom he based much of the character of Betsey Trotwood, David Copperfield's aunt. It is open April to October daily from 2:30 to 5:30 p.m. From July to September it is also open on Tuesday and Wednesday evening from 7 to 9 p.m. Admission is 40p (60¢) for adults and 20p (30¢) for children.

At Broadstairs, you can also visit **Bleak House** (tel. 0843/62224), high up on the cliffs. At the peak of his fame, this mansion was occupied by Dickens, and inspired the title of one of his greatest works, *Bleak House.* Here he entertained many men famous in art and literature, and he wrote the greater part of his novel *David Copperfield.* It is open seven days a week, Easter to November, from 10 a.m. to 6 p.m. From July through September it is open until 9 p.m. The property also contains a Maritime Museum and cellars once used by smugglers. Admission is £1 ($1.50) for adults and 55p (83¢) for children under 12.

An attraction especially for Canadian readers is the square, red-brick, gabled home where James Wolfe, the English general who defeated the French in the battle for Québec, lived until he was 11 years old. Called **Québec House** (tel. 0959/62206), a National Trust property, it contains an exhibition about the capture of Québec and memorabilia associated with the military hero, who was born in Westerham (Kent) on January 2, 1727. The house may be visited daily except Thursday and Saturday from April to the end of October from 2 to 6 p.m. Admission is £1.20 ($1.80) for adults, 60p (90¢) for children.

CHURCHILL'S HOME: For many years, Sir Winston lived at **Chartwell** (tel. 0732/866368), which lies 1½ miles south of Westerham in Kent. Churchill, a descendant of the first Duke of Marlborough, was born in grand style at Blenheim Palace on November 30, 1874. Chartwell doesn't pretend to be as grand a place as Blenheim, but it's been preserved as a memorial, administered by the National Trust. The rooms remain as Churchill left them, including maps, documents, photographs, pictures, and other personal mementos. In two rooms are displayed a selection of gifts that the prime minister received from people all over the world. There is also a selection of many of his well-known uniforms. Terraced gardens descend toward the lake with its celebrated black swans. In a garden studio are many of Churchill's paintings. Go if you want to see where a giant of a man lived and worked.

The house and garden are open April to November from noon to 5 p.m. on Tuesday, Wednesday, and Thursday; from 11 a.m. to 5 p.m. Saturday, Sunday, and bank holiday Monday. Closed Monday, Friday, and the Tuesday following a bank holiday. The house is also open Saturday, Sunday, and Wednesday in March and November from 11 a.m. to 4 p.m. Admission to the house and garden is £2.50 ($3.75), to the garden alone, £1.10 ($1.65). The self-service restaurant serves from the first of May on the days the house is open.

KNOLE: Begun in the mid-15th century by Thomas Bourchier, archbishop of Canterbury, Knole, Sevenoaks (tel. 0732/450608) is one of the largest private houses in England. It was an archbishop's palace from 1456 until the day Henry VIII's eye fell covetously upon it. He spent considerable sums of money on Knole, but there is little record of his spending much time there after extracting the gift from the reluctant Archbishop Cranmer. History records one visit only, in 1541. It was then a royal palace until Queen Elizabeth I granted it to Thomas Sackville, first Earl of Dorset, whose descendants have lived at Knole ever since. The building was given to the National Trust in 1946. The Great Hall and the Brown Gallery are Bourchier rooms, early 15th century, both much altered by the Earl of Dorset, who made other additions in about 1603. The earl was also responsible for the Great Painted Staircase. The house covers seven acres and has 365 rooms, 52 staircases, and seven courts. The elaborate paneling and plasterwork provide a background for the 17th- and 18th-century tapestries and rugs, the Elizabethan and Jacobean furniture, and the family portraits. Knole, in the village of Sevenoaks, on the A225, is five miles north of Tonbridge and 25 miles south of London. Frequent train service is available from London (about every 30 minutes), and then you can take a taxi for the remaining 1½ miles to Knole.

Knole is open from Good Friday to the end of October, Wednesday to Saturday, and bank holiday Monday from 11 a.m. to 5 p.m., on Sunday from 2 to 5 p.m. Closed November to March. Last admission is an hour before closing. Guided tours for pre-booked groups of 25 or more persons are given on Tuesday throughout the season (except after a bank holiday). Otherwise they are given only on Wednesday and Saturday in October (no reservations). The gardens are open May to September and may be visited on the first Wednesday. Admission to the house is £2 ($3) for adults, £1 ($1.50) for children. On Friday (except Good Friday), extra rooms in Lord Sackville's private apartments are shown, costing £2.50 ($3.75) for adults, £1.25 ($1.88) for children. To visit the gardens only costs adults 50p (75¢), children 25p (38¢). The park is open daily to pedestrians, with cars being allowed to enter for £2 ($3) per vehicle when the house is open.

IGHTHAM MOTE: A National Trust property, Ightham Mote, Ivy Hatch, Sevenoaks (tel. 0732/810378), is well worth a stop if you're in the area visiting other stately homes and castles. It was extensively remodeled in the early 16th century. The Tudor chapel with its painted ceiling, the timbered outer walls, and the ornate chimneys reflect that period. A stone bridge crosses the moat and leads into the central courtyard overlooked by the magnificent windows of the Great Hall. The rest of the house is built around the courtyard. From the Great Hall, a Jacobean staircase leads to the old chapel on the first floor, where you go through the solarium, with an oriel window, to the Tudor chapel.

Unlike many other ancient houses of England lived in by the same family for centuries, Ightham Mote passed from owner to owner, each family leaving its mark on the place. When the last private owner, an American who was responsible for a lot of the restoration, died, he bequeathed the house to the National Trust. It's open from 11 a.m. to 5 p.m. except Tuesday and Friday. Admission is £1.80 ($2.70) for adults, £1 ($1.50) for children.

SQUERRYES COURT: At Westerham, west of Sevenoaks on the A25, is Squerryes Court (tel. 0959/62345), a William and Mary period manor house built in 1691 and owned by the Warde family for 250 years. Besides a fine collection of paintings, tapestries, and furniture, in the Wolfe Room is a collection of pictures and relics of the family of General Wolfe. The general received his military commission in the grounds of the house at a spot marked by a cenotaph. The house and grounds are open from March to September (Sunday only during March). From April to September, you can visit on Wednesday, Saturday, Sunday, and bank holiday Monday from 2 to 6 p.m. Admission is £1.50 ($2.25) for adults, 80p ($1.20) for children.

DOWN HOUSE: North of the M25 motorway, Squerryes Court, and Chartwell, Down House, Luxted Road, Downe, Orpington (tel. 0689/59119), was the home of Charles Darwin for some 40 years. It was in this 18th-century house that he wrote *Origin of Species*. Visitors can see his memorial and museum containing articles including relics from the *Beagle* and other interesting items and pictures. Attractive gardens and the Sandwalk Wood are preserved. The house is open daily from 1 to 6 p.m. except Monday and Friday (open bank holidays). Closed in February. Admission is £1.20 ($1.80) for adults, 30p (45¢) for children. The village of Downe is 5½ miles south of Bromley off the A233.

HEVER CASTLE: Built at the end of the 13th century, Hever Castle was then just a fortified farmhouse surrounded by a moat. A dwelling house was added within the fortifications some 200 years later by the Bullen family. In 1506, the property was inherited by Sir Thomas Bullen, father of Anne Boleyn. It was here that Henry VIII courted Anne for six years before she became his second wife and later mother of Elizabeth, who became Queen Elizabeth I of England. In 1538, Hever Castle was acquired by Henry VIII, who granted it to his proxy (fourth) wife, the "great Flanders mare," Anne of Cleves, when he discovered that this mail-order bride did not live up to her Holbein portrait. This luckier Anne did not mind, however. She settled happily into this comfortable castle, living here for 17 years supported by Henry with plenty of money.

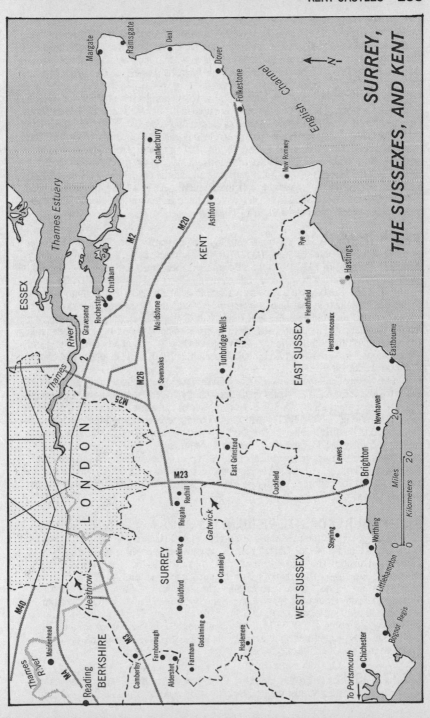

SURREY,
THE SUSSEXES, AND KENT

In 1903, the castle was purchased by William Waldorf Astor, who spent three years restoring and redecorating it, as well as building the unique village of Tudor-style cottages connected to the castle, for use by his guests. Astor was responsible also for the construction of the spectacular Italian gardens with fountains, classical statuary, a maze, and an avenue of yew trees trimmed into fantastic shapes. He also had a 35-acre lake put in, through which the River Eden flows.

The castle and its grounds have been used as locations for a number of motion pictures. The forecourt and the gardens were used in filming *Anne of a Thousand Days* in 1969. More recently, Hever Castle was used in *Lady Jane*.

The castle and grounds are open from Good Friday until the end of October. The gardens can be entered from 11 a.m. to 6 p.m. (last entry at 5 p.m.). The castle opens at noon. Admission is £3.20 ($4.80) for adults, £1.60 ($2.40) for children to both the castles and the gardens. To visit the gardens only, adults pay £2 ($3), children £1.20 ($1.80). For further information, call the Hever Castle Estate Office, Hever, near Edenbridge (tel. 0732/865224). The castle is three miles southeast of Edenbridge, midway between Sevenoaks and East Grinstead.

PENSHURST PLACE: A magnificent English Gothic mansion, Penshurst Place, at Penshurst, near Tonbridge (tel. 0892/870307), is one of the outstanding country houses in Britain. In 1338, Sir John de Pulteney, four times lord mayor of London, built the stone house whose Great Hall forms the heart of Penshurst still, after more than 600 years. The boy king, Edward VI, presented the house to Sir William Sidney, and it has remained in that family ever since. It was the birthplace, in 1554, of Sir Philip Sidney, the soldier-poet. In the first half of the 17th century, Penshurst was known as a center of literature, attracting such personages as Ben Jonson. Today it is the home of William Philip Sidney, the Viscount De L'Isle and Lady De L'Isle. Lord De L'Isle was in Winston Churchill's cabinet in the 1950s and Governor-General of Australia in the 1960s.

The Nether Gallery, below the Long Gallery which contains a suite of ebony and ivory furniture from Goa, houses the Sidney family collection of armor. Visitors can also see the splendid State Dining Room and Queen Elizabeth's Room. In the Stable Wing, there's an interesting Toy Museum. The place is open daily except Monday from April to the first Sunday in October. It is also open on Good Friday and all bank holiday Mondays. The gardens, home park, Venture Playground, nature trail, and countryside exhibition are open from 12:30 to 6 p.m., the house from 1 to 5:30 p.m. (last entry at 5 p.m.). Admission to the house and grounds is £2.50 ($3.75) for adults, £1.50 ($2.25) for children. Penshurst Place is 33 miles from London and 3½ miles west of Tonbridge.

SISSINGHURST CASTLE GARDEN: V. Sackville-West and her husband, Harold Nicolson, created the celebrated Sissinghurst Castle Garden, Sissinghurst, 2 miles northeast of Cranbrook (tel. 0580/712850), on view between the surviving parts of an Elizabeth mansion. The gardens are worth a visit at all seasons. There is a spring garden where bulb flowers flourish, a summer garden, and an autumn garden with flowering shrubs, as well as a large herb garden. The place is open Easter to mid-October, Tuesday to Friday from 1 to 6:30 p.m. and Saturday, Sunday, and Good Friday from 10 a.m. to 6:30 p.m. Admission is £3.30 ($4.95) for adults and £1.85 ($2.78) for children on Sunday, dropping to £2.75 ($4.13) for adults and £1.70 ($2.55) for children Tuesday to Saturday. Light meals are available in the Oast House Restaurant, open Good Friday to mid-October Tuesday to Sunday from 10 a.m. to 6 p.m.

LEEDS CASTLE: Once described by Lord Conway as the loveliest castle in the world, Leeds Castle, Maidstone (tel. 0622/65400), dates from A.D. 857. Originally built of wood, it was rebuilt in 1119 in its present stone structure on two small islands in the middle of the lake, and it was an almost impregnable fortress before the invention of gunpowder. Henry VIII converted it to a royal palace.

The castle has strong links with America through the sixth Lord Fairfax who, as well as owning the castle, owned five million acres in Virginia and was a close friend and mentor of the young George Washington. The last private owner, the Hon. Lady Baillie, who lovingly restored the castle with a superb collection of fine art, furniture, and tapestries, bequeathed it to the Leeds Castle Foundation. Since then, royal apartments, known as *Les Chambres de la Reine* (the chambers of the queen), in the Gloriette, the oldest part of the castle, have been opened to the public. The Gloriette, the last stronghold against attack, dates from Norman and Plantagenet times, with later additions by Henry VIII.

Within the surrounding parkland, there is a wildwood garden and duckery where rare swans, geese, and ducks can be seen. The redesigned aviaries contain a superb collection of birds, including parakeets and cockatoos. Dogs are not allowed here, but dog lovers will enjoy the Great Danes of the castle and the Dog Collar Museum at the Gatehouse, with a unique collection of collars dating from the Middle Ages. A nine-hole, 18-tee golf course is open to the public. The Culpeper Garden is a delightful English country flower garden. Beyond are the castle greenhouses and the vineyard, recorded in the Domesday Book and now again producing Leeds Castle English white wine.

Leeds Castle is open daily from 11 a.m. to 5 p.m. April to October; on Saturday and Sunday from noon to 4 p.m. November to March. It's closed one day in early July for the annual open air concert, and one day in early November for the grand fireworks spectacular. Admission to the castle and grounds is £3.85 ($5.78) for adults, £2.85 ($4.28) for children. If you want to visit only the grounds, the charge is £2.85 ($4.28) for adults, £1.85 ($2.78) for children. Car parking is free, with a free ride on a tractor-trailer available for persons who cannot manage the half-mile or so walk from the car park to the castle.

Snacks, salads, cream teas, and hot meals are offered daily at several places on the grounds, including Fairfax Hall, a restored 17th-century tithe barn with a self-service carvery restaurant and bar. On Sunday, you can feast on traditional roast beef lunch for about £12.50 ($18.75). Kentish evenings are presented in the tithe barn every Saturday throughout the year from 7 p.m. to 12:30 a.m., starting with a sherry cocktail reception, then a guided tour of the castle. Guests feast on Kentish pâté, followed by broth and roast beef carved at your table, plus seasonal vegetables. The meal is rounded off by dessert, cheese, fruit, and coffee. A half-bottle of wine is included in the overall price of £19.75 ($29.63) per person. During the meal, musicians play and sing songs suitable to the surroundings and the occasion. Advance reservations are required, made by calling the castle.

It is worth checking with British Rail and with London tour operators for the price of a package, unless you want to drive here yourself. The castle is 4 miles east of Maidstone at the junction of the A20 and M20 London-Folkestone roads.

The Leeds Castle Foundation also owns the Park Gate Inn, Hollingbourne (tel. 062780/582), built during the last year of the reign of Charles I, on the site of an earlier building dating back to the Middle Ages. The structure was originally a store and domestic quarters for Leeds Castle, being adjacent to the former entrance to the castle.

CHILHAM CASTLE GARDENS: In Chilham Village, 6 miles west of Canterbury, Chilham Castle Gardens (tel. 0227/730319), were originally laid out by Tradescant and later landscaped by Lancelot "Capability" Brown. On a former royal property, the gardens are visually magnificent, looking out over the Stour Valley. A Norman castle used as a hunting lodge once stood here. It was frequented by more than one royal personage until King Henry VIII sold it. The Jacobean castle, built between 1603 and 1616 by Sir Dudley Digges (whose descendant was governor-general of Virginia), was reputedly designed by Inigo Jones. It is one of the best examples extant of the architecture of its day and is built around a hexagonal open-ended courtyard. Medieval banquets are held in the Gothic Hall throughout the year at a cost of £23 ($34.50) per person.

The gardens are open daily from 11 a.m. to 5 p.m. mid-March to the end of October. Admission is £1.80 ($2.70) for adults, 90p ($1.35) for children weekdays, £2.40 ($3.60) for adults and £1.20 ($1.80) for children on Sunday when there is a medieval jousting display. On bank holiday Sunday and Monday, there is a jousting tournament for which admission is £3.50 ($5.25) for adults, £1 ($1.50) for children. Every afternoon except Monday and Friday there is a display of birds of prey from the Raptor Centre. You can also visit Petland and the old Norman castle keep.

The little village of Chilham has a lovely small square with a church at one end, the castle at the other, and a mass of half-timbered buildings interspersed with old red brick houses. It is on the A252 Canterbury-Maidstone road and the A28 Canterbury-Ashford road.

1. Canterbury

Under the arch of the ancient West Gate journeyed Chaucer's knight, solicitor, nun, squire, parson, merchant, miller, and cook—filled with racy tales. Straight from the pages of *The Canterbury Tales*, they were bound for the shrine of Thomas à Becket, archbishop of Canterbury, who was slain by four knights of Henry II on December 29, 1170. (It is said that the king later walked barefoot from Harbledown to the tomb of his former friend, where he allowed himself to be flogged in penance.) The shrine was finally torn down in 1538 by Henry VIII, as a part of his campaign to destroy the monasteries and graven images. Canterbury, then, has been an attraction of long standing.

The medieval Kentish city, on the Stour River, is the mother city of England, its ecclesiastical capital. Mother city is an apt title, as Canterbury was known to have been inhabited centuries before the birth of Christ. Julius Caesar once went on a rampage near it. Although its most famous incident was the murder of Becket, the medieval city has witnessed other major moments in English history, including Bloody Mary's order that nearly 40 victims be burned at the stake. Richard the Lion-hearted came back this way from crusading, and Charles II passed through on the way to reclaim his crown.

Canterbury was once completely walled, and many traces of its old fortifications remain. In the 16th century, weavers—mostly Huguenots from northern France and the Low Countries—fled to Canterbury to escape religious persecution. They started a weaving industry that flourished until the expanding silk trade with India sent it into oblivion.

The old city is much easier to reach today than it was in Chaucer's time. Lying 56 miles from London, it is within a 1½-hour train ride from Victoria Station. The city center is closed to cars, but it's only a short walk from several car parks to the cathedral or walking-tour starting point.

For information, check with the **Tourist Office,** 13 Longmarket (tel. 0227/66567).

Heritage Projects Ltd., United House, Piccadilly, York (tel. 0904/646411), has developed the **Canterbury Pilgrims Way** in conjunction with the Canterbury Archaeological Trust. Visitors can become pilgrims and follow the path to the shrine of the martyred St. Thomas à Becket, which demonstrates many aspects of the pilgrimage and includes live cameos taken from Chaucer's *Canterbury Tales*. Opening times and hours for the pilgrimage, starting in historic St. Margaret's Church close to the cathedral, were not available at press time. Check with the tourist board.

Now as in the Middle Ages, the goal of the pilgrim remains:

CANTERBURY CATHEDRAL: The foundation of this splendid cathedral (tel. 0227/472727), dates back to the coming of Augustine, the first archbishop, from Rome in A.D. 597, but the earliest part of the present building is the great Romanesque crypt built circa 1100. The monastic choir erected on top of this at the same time was destroyed by fire in 1174, only four years after the murder of Thomas à Becket on a dark December evening in the northwest transept, still one of the most famous places of pilgrimage in Europe. The destroyed choir was replaced by a magnificent Early Gothic one immediately, and first used for worship in 1180. The cathedral was the first great church in the Gothic style to be erected in England and set a fashion for the whole country. Its architects were the Frenchman, William of Sens, and "English" William who took Sens's place after the Frenchman was crippled in an accident in 1178 which later proved fatal.

This part of the church is noteworthy for its medieval tombs of royal personages such as King Henry IV and Edward the Black Prince, as well as numerous archbishops. To the later Middle Ages belongs the great 14th-century nave and the famous central "Bell Harry Tower." The cathedral stands in spacious precincts amid the remains of the buildings of the monastery—cloisters, chapter house, and Norman water tower, which have survived intact from the Dissolution in the time of King Henry VIII to the present day.

Becket's shrine was destroyed by the Tudor king, but the site of that tomb may be seen in Trinity Chapel, in the vicinity of the High Altar. Becket is said to have worked miracles. The cathedral contains some rare stained glass depicting those feats. Perhaps the most miraculous thing is that the windows escaped Henry VIII's agents of destruction and Hitler's bombs as well (part of the cathedral was hit in World War II). East of the Trinity Chapel is "Becket's Crown," in which is a chapel dedicated to "Martyrs and Saints of Our Own Time." St. Augustine's Chair, one of the symbols of the authority of the archbishop of Canterbury, stands behind the high altar. The cathedral is open from 8:45 a.m. to 7 p.m. in summer (closes at 5 p.m. in winter).

ROMAN PAVEMENT: This site is off High Street down Butchery Lane. It contains some fine mosaic pavement remains and treasures from excavations in the city. The Pavement is open daily from 10 a.m. to 1 p.m. and 2 to 4 p.m. (in winter, afternoons only). The entrance charge is 55p (83¢), which includes a ticket to the Westgate Towers Museum, which has the same hours. For information, call 0227/452747.

TOURS: Guided tours of Canterbury are organized by the **Guild of Guides,** Arnett House, Hawks Lane (tel. 0227/459779), costing 90p ($1.35), with daily tours, lasting 1½ hours, from April to October, usually at 2:15 p.m., sometimes oftener.

From just below the Weavers House, boats leave for half-hour trips on the river with a commentary on the history of the buildings you pass. The charge is £1.50 ($2.25) per person. Umbrellas are provided to protect you against inclement weather.

ACCOMMODATIONS: Before you can begin any serious exploring, you'll need to find a room. You have several possibilities within the city itself and on the outskirts, both budget guesthouses and splurge hotels.

Bed and Breakfast

Cathedral Gate Hotel & Restaurant, 37 Burgate (tel. 0227/464381), is for modern-day pilgrims who want to rest their bones at an inn shouldering up to the cathedral's gateway. In 1620 the former hospice became one of the earliest of the fashionable coffee and tea houses of England. Its facade was added in the 19th century, however. The interior reveals many architectural features of the 17th century. Mr. P.

Shingler, the proprietor, improved the amenities while retaining the hotel's old-world charm. Two curved bay windows in the living room overlook the little square in front of the gateway. The bedrooms and public rooms are warmed by gas central heating. Each of the 33 bedrooms has hot and cold running water, and some contain private baths. The single rate goes from £16.50 ($24.75) to £18.50 ($27.75); the double tariff, from £22.50 ($33.75) to £30.50 ($45.75). The ground-floor restaurant serves both luncheon and evening meals and is licensed.

The **Georgian Guest House,** 69 Castle St. (tel. 0227/61111), is a venture of Mrs. Mary Kennett, who has restored and preserved the old architectural features, including a minstrels' gallery, of a 1502 building near the center of Canterbury. She has updated it with water basins, baths, and heating. The home is gracious and pleasant, furnished with antiques. Your timbered bedroom may have either a half-tester Victorian bed, or a slim four-poster, making sleeping here a retreat to Pickwickian days. The cost of a sleep in a treasured bed plus an abundant breakfast is £9 ($13.50) per person. She rents out three singles, three doubles, and, most interesting for families traveling with children, two family rooms suitable for three to four persons. The back drawing room is made from the old cellar kitchen, overlooking the rear garden. Guests enjoy the restored Tudor exterior—wooden corbels, tile-hanging—at the back of the house and the garden. Mrs. Kennett is just the type for a stack of books beside a highbacked chair in front of the fireplace, ready for an evening's conversation on any subject. She's also considered one of England's authorities on Dr. Johnson.

Pilgrims Guest House, 18 The Friars (tel. 0227/464531), dates back in part more than 300 years, and is just a three-minute walk from the cathedral. Owners Patrick and Linde Martin believe in making guests feel thoroughly at home. Comfort is assured by such items as innerspring mattresses, hot and cold running water in all the rooms, some with their own toilet and shower, enough corridor baths and toilets, and a central heating system. The charge is from £10 ($15) nightly for B&B. The breakfast fortifies you for the day. In the evening, guests congregate in the lounge for conversation and to watch television. There's an adjoining concrete car park. Directly opposite is the Marlowe Theatre, which has many international personalities with top shows and plays.

Ersham Lodge, 12 New Dover Rd. (tel. 0227/463174), is a Tudor-style, 19thcentury building at the edge of town. The owners, Mr. and Mrs. Pellay, run this pleasant lodge, and the whole place has been redecorated and is as fresh as a country morning in Kent. All rooms contain TV, radio, telephone, and shower. Paying guests are accepted at a charge of £18 ($27) for B&B in a single room, £28 ($42) for two in a double. There are some rooms with TV, private bath, and toilet renting for £36 ($54) for two. A full English breakfast is included. The house is gracious in style—set back from the road and in the midst of many shade trees, with a back garden for children to play in. From the two-story living room, a winding staircase leads to the spacious and comfortably furnished corner bedrooms.

St. Stephens Guest House, 100 St. Stephens Rd. (tel. 0227/462167), is in a quiet part of the city, yet close to the main attractions. One of the most attractive buildings in Canterbury, St. Stephens is owned and managed by Richard and Jean Ganther, who give visitors a friendly welcome. The house, set in well-kept gardens and lawns, with its discreet extensions, has retained its character and yet also offers modern accommodations for the guests. There are nine bedrooms, all with central heating, shaver points, and hot and cold water. The house can also boast of its own water softener and sleeps up to 18 people. Tariffs include B&B and use of bath or shower. A single room rents from £12 ($18) nightly, a double room from £21 ($31.50). The guesthouse also has a residential liquor license, private parking, and a lock-up garage.

Kingsmead House, 68 St. Stephens Rd. (tel. 0227/60132), is a lovely 17thcentury house owned by Jan and John Clark, one of the most gracious and hospitable couples in Canterbury. The location of their timbered house is about six to eight minutes from the heart of Canterbury. They can accept only half a dozen guests, whom they put up in well-furnished rooms with private bath and central heating. The cost is from £12.50 ($18.75) per person nightly for B&B.

Ann's Hotel, 63 London Rd. (tel. 0227/68767), a family-owned enterprise, stands on an artery leading out of town. Its Victorian facade matches the grandiose houses lying nearby. Ample parking is found in front of the olive-green facade, and there is a low garden wall of brick. You enter into a Victorian hallway, where Hayden and Liz Clements rent out 19 bedrooms, each well furnished and comfortable, some with four-poster beds. A dozen of these have private baths, color TV, and coffee-making facilities. Singles without bath cost £15 ($22.50), doubles, also bathless, £24 ($36) to £26 ($39). With shower, two persons pay £32 ($48). VAT, service, and a full English breakfast are included.

Abbey Gate Guest House, 7 North Lane (tel. 0227/68770), offers friendly and personal service. The spotlessly clean rooms, although small, have central heating and lots of hot water. There are laundry facilities, and a bath or shower on the premises. If you need them, babysitting services are available. The Abbey is centrally located in Canterbury, and all fire regulations have been completed. Price (including a very good breakfast) per person daily is from £10 ($15). Children are most welcome. You can enjoy a three-course evening meal for £4 ($6).

Carlton Guest House, 40 Nunnery Fields (tel. 0227/65900), is operated by the very helpful Ian and Alison Williams, who enjoy meeting guests. All their rooms have TV, telephones, and tea/coffee-making facilities and are clean and comfortable, and some have private baths. The cost is £10 ($15) to £12 ($18) per person nightly for B&B. The road on which the guesthouse lies is quiet, and there is private parking. The town center is about a six-minute walk from Carlton, the cathedral about a ten-minute walk. The main station and the bus station also lie nearby. In the summer Mr. and Mrs. Williams will offer you an evening meal with traditional English cooking.

Yorke Lodge Guest House, 50 London Rd. (tel. 0227/451243), is spacious and comfortable, a Victorian guesthouse close to the center of town and the cathedral. The resident owner, Katrina Etheridge, is helpful to guests. The charge is from £12 ($18) per person for B&B. All units contain hot and cold running water, and there are two large shower rooms popular with American visitors. The house also has a comfortably furnished television lounge and a pleasant sun lounge looking onto the garden. An evening meal, offering traditional English fare with local produce when available, can be arranged.

Kingsbridge Villa, 15 Best Lane (tel. 0227/466415), is a bright, friendly, and spotless guesthouse run by Barbara Williams close to the cathedral in the oldest part of the city. She rents out a dozen rooms some with private baths, at a rate of £12 ($18) to £15 ($22.50) per person nightly. There's a small restaurant and bar in the basement which is reached through the house or else by area steps past a medieval well where they once found a coin dating from A.D. 163. Clay pipes adorn the red brick walls, and there are comfortable settle seats around the bar. All ingredients used in the kitchen are fresh. A set lunch of typically English fare goes for £5.50 ($8.25). Dinner, which is likely to include some continental dishes, costs about £8.50 ($12.75), including VAT.

Magnolia House, 36 St. Dunstan's Terrace (tel. 0227/65121), is a quiet and pleasant Canterbury guesthouse run by owner-managers Ann and John Davies. A Georgian building, it stands within easy walking distance of the major points of sightseeing interest in this historic old city. Families are catered to, with a trio of rooms set aside for them. The house is relatively small, so a reservation or call is important to get accommodation. The B&B rate ranges from £10.50 ($15.75) in a single to £18 ($27) in a double. There is limited off-street parking.

Alexandra House, 1 Roper Rd. (tel. 0227/67011), is an 11-room guesthouse only a few minutes from the old city center and the cathedral. The house is centrally heated, and all rooms have TV, hot beverage facilities, and cold and hot water basins.

Several also have shower units. The proprietor, M. Cain, charges £10 ($15) to £12 ($18) per person in high season, depending on the plumbing, and a full English breakfast is included. Even meals can be arranged, costing from £4.50 ($6.75) for three courses, with coffee. The house is known for its hospitality and comfort.

DINING IN CANTERBURY: Of special interest at **Queen Elizabeth's Restaurant,** 44-45 High St. (tel. 0227/464080), is the original room where Queen Elizabeth I entertained the Duke of Alençon, while she was trying to decide whether to marry him. The 16th-century interior, with its outstanding relief and wall paneling, recaptures the past admirably. The food is fresh and home-cooked—and very English as well, from the rich-tasting soups, such as cream of pea, to the roast pork with apple sauce and vegetables, to the deep-dish apple pie with heavy cream for dessert. A three-course meal costs around £5 ($7.50). If you go early enough, select the seat next to the window so you can look down the High Street. You can spot the restaurant easily by its gabled facade, which has plaster carving. Meals are served every day except Sunday, and the restaurant is open from 9:30 a.m. to 6 p.m. English afternoon tea is a specialty.

George's Brasserie, 71–72 Castle St. (tel. 0227/65658), is an attractive establishment run by a brother and sister, Simon Day and Beverly Holmes, who pride themselves on the cleanliness of their restaurant and the quality of their food, made only of fresh ingredients. They serve everything from coffee and a croissant to gourmet meals. You can order from the fixed-price menu, costing from £5.90 ($8.85), perhaps including, soup or savory tarts, fresh pasta and lamb chop, and coffee, to £10.50 ($15.75) for a choice of four appetizers, one of several meat dishes, and a choice of desserts, plus coffee. On the à la carte listing, numerous appetizers are offered, including a fresh anchovy salad and George's terrines, all served with a basket of french bread and being a satisfying meal for small appetites. The selection of main dishes changes with the season, but it always includes fish and meat dishes and is served with new potatoes or french fries. George's is open Monday to Thursday from 10 a.m. to 10 p.m., Friday and Saturday from 10 a.m. to 10:30 p.m., with last order time extended for theatergoers.

The **Mayflower Restaurant,** 59 Palace St. (tel. 0227/465038), stands on the corner of Palace and Sun Streets. The restaurant is well known in the area which is largely made up of junk-food eating houses. There are very few good English home-cooking establishments in the whole city, and the Mayflower is one of them. This is also an area of the city where many of the Pilgrim Fathers who sailed for America on the *Speedwell* and *Mayflower* came from. C. F. Byrom and his family run the establishment, offering good value on all their dishes. Their son, the chef, Colins, has a daily suggested menu. On the first floor is the Pilgrims Bar. Meals are also served here. The downstairs restaurant has been completely refurbished and decorated in keeping with the old-world surroundings of the building, which dates back to 1601. Breakfast and coffee are offered from 10 a.m., lunch and grills from 11:15 a.m. to 2:15 p.m., and dinner or light meals from 6 to 10 p.m. daily except Sunday. Specialty dishes include Mrs. Byrom's homemade individual beefsteak pudding or pie, roast topside of beef served with Yorkshire pudding, or roast chicken with a sage and onion stuffing. The family also serves two varieties of trout and a lemon sole cooked in wine and mushroom sauce. The portions of all dishes are large. Several continental dishes including coq au vin are also featured. The most expensive three-course dinner with wine and coffee costs around £13 ($19.50), and the cheapest full meal with wine and coffee goes for less than £6.50 ($9.75).

Alberrys Wine and Food Bar, 38 St. Margaret's St. (tel. 0227/452378), is fun —even the Victorian cartoons on its wine list claim that "Tomorrow morning you'il be able to perform great feats of strength if you drink plenty of wine tonight." Today, in the same area where slaves of the Romans once toiled (part of the exposed foundation was a section of a Roman amphitheater), there is jazz and rock/pop music performed live on Monday, Tuesday, Wednesday, and Thursday nights, completely free to customers. Alberrys offers an inexpensive and frequently changing repertoire of well-prepared food. Soup of the day, baked potato filled with chili con carne, followed by passion cake, costs £5.50 ($8.25). Pizzas and quiches are available. Beer and mixed drinks are served, and wine is available by the glass. It is open daily from noon to 2:30 p.m. and in the evening from 6:30 p.m. to midnight. Closed Sunday.

Cogan House, 53 St. Peter's St. (tel. 0227/472986), is a pleasantly inviting English brasserie, lying above a shop in the center of the city, about a block north of High Street. Climb a flight of steps to reach the second-floor dining room, housed in a building considered the oldest residence in the city, dating from 1170. The brasserie is owned by Ian and Jane McAndrew who enjoy far greater fame—and charge far higher prices—at their Restaurant Seventy Four, considered the best in Canterbury. Traditional English food, well prepared and served at attractive prices in generous portions, is the sustaining grace of this place. You might select from such offerings as venison sausages with onion gravy and potato cake or else a roast spring chicken baked whole. Desserts, especially their moist cakes, are also tempting. Food service is all day any time from 10:30 a.m. to 10:30 p.m. (Sunday from noon to 10:30 p.m.). A set lunch goes for £7 ($10.50), with dinner costing from £12 ($18). The restaurant usually closes from the middle of February for about two weeks.

Il Vaticano, 35 St. Margaret St. (tel. 0227/65333), is the best-known pasta parlor in Canterbury, bringing Italian flavor to wake up local tastebuds. All pasta is made on the premises, and you get a choice of sauces, including savory clam, carbonara, or a Pernod-spiked "fruits of the sea." The kitchen also does those three classics: lasagne, cannelloni, and ravioli. You might begin with a selection of antipasti or else Parma ham with melon. What's for dessert? Ever had chocolate pasta? Meals cost from £8 ($12), and the restaurant is decorated in a simple but sophisticated trattoria style, with bentwood chairs, small marble-topped tables, and exposed brick. Open from 11 a.m. to 11 p.m. Monday to Saturday (from noon to 10 p.m. Sunday), it lies on a pedestrian street in the commercial center of the city.

ELHAM: If you should arrive in Canterbury during the peak season, you might be better off to seek accommodation in a little English village such as Elham, on the B2065 road in the beautiful Elham Valley ten miles south from Canterbury and nine miles northwest from Folkestone.

The **New Inn,** High Street (tel. 030384/288), is an attractive traditional brick and tile building dating from 1820, its white walls, red doors, and black trim catching the eye of passersby on the main street of the village. Geoff and Pauline Cheshire operate an establishment with bedrooms, bars, a garden, and a parking area. In the public bar, guests can listen to the juke box, and play pool, billiards, or darts. The lounge bar has a small dining area, or you can go there or to the garden for a relaxing drink. The bedrooms rent for £29 ($30) to £24 ($36) double occupancy, with a reduction of £5 ($7.50) if occupied as a single. Prices depend on the season. All three rental units have showers, hot and cold water basins, and heaters. A full English breakfast is included in the rates.

The **Abbot's Fireside,** Elham (tel. 030384/265), has been a famous restaurant for many years. The inn is owned by Mr. and Mrs. Hill. The building is circa 1480, an example of pre-Renaissance architecture. Its wooden mullions and transoms have been well preserved. The whole structure leans forward, as if it's been standing too long. Latticed windows and grotesquely carved wooden brackets give an old-world aura. In one room is a great old fireplace, carved by a monk, from which the establishment takes its name. The Duke of Wellington made this his garrison headquarters when he was mustering his army for battle against Napoleon. Charles II and the Duke of Richmond are reported to have hidden in the chimney while pursued by Roundheads. The inn also has a rare Parliament Clock, thought to be 16th century, and in the restaurant is a "coat of chain mail" from the 14th century, reputedly worn by the Black Prince. Try to schedule at least a luncheon visit, from noon to 2 p.m., enjoying a set meal featuring standard English fare for about £6.50 ($9.75). If you fall in love with the place, you can stay over in one of the eight bedrooms. All units have private showers and toilets and are well furnished. B&B costs from £16.50 ($24.75) per person. There is a traditional English garden. They will also send a Rolls-Royce to pick up visitors from either the railway station or the airport.

KENT BATTLE OF BRITAIN MUSEUM: On a Battle of Britain airfield, a museum contains the most extensive collection of artifacts of this famous battle. It's at Hawkinge Airfield, Hawkinge, near Folkestone (tel. 030389/2779). On display are engines, pieces of downed aircraft, photographs, equipment, and letters from RAF pilots. These exhibits are presented in once-abandoned airfield buildings. Visits are possible from Easter until the end of October on Sunday from 11 a.m. to 5:30 p.m. From July and September, the museum is also open Monday to Saturday from 1 to 5 p.m. Admission is £1 ($1.50) for adults, 50p (75¢) for children.

A RAILROAD RIDE: A few miles to the south is the **Romney, Hythe & Dymchurch Light Railway Co.,** New Romney Station, New Romney (tel. 0679/62353), the world's smallest public railway. There are 12 passenger locomotives of which 11 are steam powered, more than 70 passenger coaches, most of which are fully enclosed, and a licensed observation saloon. The major difference between this and other tourist railways in Britain is in its size. The locomotives are all one-third scale versions of British, German, and North American engines of the 1920s and 1930s. They run on narrow-gauge tracks for 13½ miles across Kent's historic Romney Marsh from Hythe to Dungeness Lighthouse, via New Romney and Dymchurch. Fares depend on the length of your journey, a round trip over the entire line costing £4.95 ($7.43). Also, you can enjoy the freedom of the line for an entire day by buying a Day Rover Ticket, costing just over £7 ($10.50). Children are charged one-third of the adult rates. A round trip takes about three hours, and shorter journeys can be made to suit your available time.

The railway operates a daily service from Easter to the end of September, with only weekend service in March and October. The railway is easily reached from the south coast along the A259 and from London by using the M20/A20. The closest mainline railway station is Folkestone Central. You can take a bus from Folkestone Bus Station to the RH&D station at Hythe. Telephone for train times.

To get to Hythe from Canterbury, leave on the Dover Road and follow the signs for Hythe.

LYMPNE CASTLE: Near Hythe stands the small, medieval Lympne Castle (tel. 0303/67571), built in the 14th century on land that was given to the church at Lympne in the 18th century. There is mention of a Saxon abbey on the site in the *Doomsday Book* of 1085. Right on the edge of a cliff, the castle has magnificent views over the channel and across Romney Marsh to Fairlight. An ideal lookout against invasion, it has a Norman tower in the east and a medieval one to the west with turret stairways leading to the main rooms, including the Great Hall.

Besides the building and its furnishings, there are exhibits of toys and dolls and full-size reproductions of church brasses, as well as a small period costume display. The castle is open daily from 10:30 a.m. to 6 p.m. June to September and bank holidays. Admission is £1 ($1.50) for adults, 25p (38¢) for children 5 to 14 years of age.

Port Lympne Zoo Park, Mansion, and Gardens (tel. 0303/64646), near Hythe, has rare and endangered species among the animals housed in spacious enclosures in 270 acres of park and woodlands. Visitors can take a two-mile cross-country trek or a short main drive walk to see the animals in their natural settings. Included are chimpanzees, wolves, Siberian and Indian tigers, Atlas lions, leopards, cheetahs, monkeys, Indian gazelles, swamp and axis deer, elands, wapiti, buffalos, bisons, wild horses, rhinoceroses, sable and roan antelopes, elephants, wild dogs, and honey badgers.

You can also visit the historic house built in Dutch colonial style, called "the most historic house built in the United Kingdom in this century." Features include the Rex Whistler tent room, the Moroccan patio, and the hexagonal library where the treaty of Paris was signed. Owner John Aspinall's collection of wildlife paintings and other artworks are displayed in the galleries. The gardens have 15 acres of sculptured terracing, a remarkable Trojan stairway with 125 steps from which you can see across Romney Marsh to France on a clear day, a vineyard, a 125-foot-long herbaceous border, and striped, checkerboard, and clock gardens. The park dates from the 15th century. Open from 10 a.m. to 5 p.m. (or dusk). Admission to the entire complex is £3.50 ($5.25) for adults, £2.50 ($3.75) for children 4 to 14.

South along the A259 coastal road from Hythe lies Dymchurch, whose main attraction is the **Dymchurch Martello Tower** (tel. 0304/612013), one of the 74 artillery towers built along the coast between 1805 and 1812. The 24-pound gun on the roof of the Martello towers was to resist the expected invasion by Napoleon. A further discouragement for the French was the fact that there was no doorway at ground level, entrance being by a moveable outside ladder to an upstairs door. The tower can be visited from 9:30 a.m. to 6:30 p.m. Monday to Saturday, from 2 to 6:30 p.m. Sunday from the end of March to the end of September. Admission is 50p (75¢) for adults, 25p (38¢) for children.

2. Dover

One of the ancient Cinque ports, Dover is famed for its white cliffs. In Victoria's day it basked in popularity as a seaside resort, but today it is of importance mainly because it is a port for major cross-Channel car and passenger traffic between England and France (notably Calais). Sitting in the open jaws of the white cliffs, Dover was one of England's most vulnerable and easy-to-hit targets in World War II. It suffered repeated bombings that destroyed much of its harbor.

Hovering nearly 400 feet above the port is **Dover Castle** (tel. 0304/201623), one of the oldest and best-known in England. Its keep was built at the command of Becket's fair-weather friend, Henry II, in the 12th century. You can visit the keep all year, generally from 9:30 a.m. to 5:30 p.m. in summer (it closes earlier off-season), for an admission of £2 ($3); children pay £1 ($1.50). Admission to the castle grounds is free. The ancient castle was called back to active duty as late as World War II. The "Pharos" on the grounds is a lighthouse built by the Romans in the first half of the first century. The Romans landed at nearby Deal in 55 B.C. and 54 B.C. The first landing was not successful. The second in 54 B.C. was more so, but after six months they departed, and did not return until nearly 100 years later, A.D. 43, when they occupied the country and stayed 400 years.

The **Roman Painted House,** New Street (tel. 0304/203279), is a large section of a well-preserved Roman town house more than 1,800 years old. It contains the oldest and best-preserved Roman wall paintings north of the Alps. There are many other Roman remains. It is open from April until the end of October, Tuesday to Sunday from 10 a.m. to 5 p.m., charging an admission of 50p (75¢) for adults and 25p (38¢) for children.

ACCOMMODATIONS: Because Dover operates in a sellers' market, owing to the cross-Channel traffic, prices for lodgings tend to run high. But below you'll find some bargains.

St. Martins Guest House, 17 Castle Hill Rd. (tel. 0304/205938), stands a few blocks away from the cross-Channel ferries and the Hoverport, on the hillside leading up to Dover Castle. The house is more than 130 years old, and is maintained and furnished to high standards, with full central heating. Bedrooms with double-glazed windows also contain color TV sets and facilities for making hot beverages. Most have private showers. B&B only is provided, from £8 ($12) to £12 ($18) per person. The house has a lovely guest lounge and a residential license. Ample parking is available. The house is run by Mr. and Mrs. Morriss, who have proved to be very popular with their North American visitors. Mrs. Morriss had been connected with catering before taking over the guesthouse, and was in charge of some restaurants in London's West End. However, her dream always was to own her own guesthouse.

The dream of Mrs. Morriss has more than come true. The couple now also operates the guesthouse next door to the St. Martins, **Ardmore Private Hotel** (tel. 0304/205895), in a 200-year-old building which has undergone extensive redecoration under the Morriss ownership, offering double or twin rooms and family rooms with private baths. Prices for a double or twin, including breakfast and tax, are £10 ($15) to £13.50 ($20.25) per person. There is a communal reception area for the Ardmore and St. Martins.

To the east of Dover stands **Wallett's Court,** West Cliffe, St. Margarets-at-Cliffe (tel. 0304/852424), on about 3½ acres some three miles from Dover. A building has stood on this site for nearly 1,000 years and the present manor is a restored structure from the 17th century. Lea and Chris Oakley have renovated the historic structure and made it comfortable and cozy for paying guests. B&B costs £20 ($30) in a single, from £24 ($36) in a double. The more expensive rooms contain private baths, and two accommodations are set aside for families. Thoughtful extras such as fresh flowers in the rooms make this an exceptional choice. Dinner is served, with a three-course meal, from 6:30 to 7 p.m. Monday to Friday, costing £7 ($10.50), a four-course repast on Saturday at 8:30 p.m. going for £15 ($22.50). All prices include VAT.

Beulah House, 94 Crabble Hill, London Road (tel. 0304/824615), stands on the A256 (A2) road to London, and is run by its namesake, Beulah Abate, along with her husband, Donald. Their house is comfortably furnished, and their charge for B&B is from £12 ($18) per person nightly. What makes the house exceptionally appealing is its gardens in back, with sculptured yews and roses. They serve a bountiful breakfast as well.

Esmeralda Guest House, 273 Folkestone Rd. (tel. 0304/202873), is one of the best for the budget. The four accommodations—one suitable for families—share a central bath, and the rate ranges from £10 ($15) per person, including a full breakfast. The guesthouse, under the personal supervision of Ted and Sheila Wright, is some half a mile from the heart of town. It lies near sports fields fronting the A20. The owners are polite and helpful to visitors going to and from the continent.

Castle Guest House, 10 Castle Hill Rd. (tel. 0304/201656), is run by a friendly couple, Nona and Brian Howarth. They have taken a circa 1830 home and renovated it to receive paying guests. Bedrooms are pleasantly furnished and well kept, and each unit has a TV, hot and cold running water, private shower (some with toilets), and central heating. The tariffs run from £15 ($22.50) in a single and from £22 ($33) in a double or twin. Some family rooms cost from £31 ($46.50) nightly. They are convenient for cross-Channel ferries, and the house lies in the Leas of Dover Castle and the ruin of an old Saxon church.

Westbank Guest House, 239 Folkestone Rd. (tel. 0304/201061), is one of the best B&B houses in the area. Gwen and Bill Tennant welcome you, housing guests in one of their well-appointed, clean, and comfortable units, each with hot and cold running water and color TV. In season, the cost of a twin-bedded room is from £10.50 ($15.75) per person. That tariff includes a well-prepared breakfast. They also cater for stays of three days at reduced rates. For example, in the height of season (August), a family of four sharing a room can have bed, breakfast, and evening meal for £114 ($171) for three days. In all, they can accommodate 21 guests. Gwen is a cook of high standard, and if given a few hours' notice, she offers an evening meal at £5.50 ($8.25) per person. All guests receive a welcome tray of tea or coffee along with cookies on arrival.

WHERE TO EAT: Finding a good place to eat in Dover is not easy. One of the most reliable establishments is **Britannia,** Townwall Street (tel. 0304/203248), across from the Dover Stagecoachotel, near the seafront. It has a box window, along with gilt and brass nautical accents on its black facade. The restaurant is one floor above street level, with a popular pub on the ground floor. A vast array of international favorites are featured on the menu, including beef stroganoff, chicken Kiev, and duck à l'orange. Naturally Dover sole is on the menu (the chef grills it or prepares it verónique style). Meals cost from £8 ($12). Lunch is daily from noon to 2 p.m., dinner Monday to Saturday from 6 to 10 p.m. (from 7 to 10 p.m. on Sunday).

    Ristorante al Porto, 43 Townwall St. (tel. 0304/204615), brings a continental flair to Dover. One block from the landing dock of the ferry boats, this Italian-owned restaurant is decorated in a nautical style, with fishnets hanging from the ceiling. It offers one of the largest menus in town, featuring such specialties as steak in a black pepper, cream, and brandy sauce, along with cannelloni or succulent veal in a sauce of mushrooms, garlic, and tomatoes. Try the gelati misti (mixed ice cream) for dessert and a cup of espresso. Expect to pay from £10 ($15) for a meal here. However, an à la carte lunch goes for only £4.25 ($6.38). Hours are from noon to 2:30 p.m. and 7 to 10:15 p.m.; closed Sunday.

On the Outskirts

    Finglesham Grange, Finglesham, near Deal on the coast about 8 miles northeast of Dover (tel. 0304/611314), is a country house of style. It stands in 4½ acres of grounds about half a mile from the village. The house, run by Mr. and Mrs. R.W. Styles, is within easy reach of the Channel ports, beaches, golf courses, and the Kentish countryside. B&B is offered to no more than six guests at a time, each of whom is charged £14 ($21), with morning and afternoon tea and a goodnight drink. Three spacious double rooms are offered, each with its own facilities. A lounge with TV and a billiard room are also for the use of guests. Evening meals can be served if arranged in advance. The Stileses are an accommodating and helpful couple, and their English breakfast has been called "super."

TWO CASTLES: Just south of Deal on the Strait of Dover lie **Walmer Castle and Gardens** (tel. 0304/364288) and **Deal Castle** (tel. 0304/372762), about a mile apart.

    Walmer Castle and Gardens, about 6 miles north of Dover, was one of some 20 coastal forts built by Henry VIII to protect England from invasion from the continent. It is shaped like a Tudor rose, with a central three-story tower, and is surrounded by a moat now dry. In the early 18th century, it became the official residence of the Lords Warden of the Cinque Ports, among them William Pitt the Younger and the Duke of Wellington, who died here in 1852. The duke's furnished rooms and possessions, including a uniform and his telescope can be seen. Also preserved are rooms occupied by Queen Victoria and Prince Albert during visits. The magnificent formal gardens were laid out by Lady Hester Stanhope in 1805. A plaque at this location marks the spot where Julius Caesar is supposed to have landed in Britain in 55 B.C. The castle can be visited from 9:30 a.m. to 6:30 p.m. Tuesday to Saturday and 2 to 6:30 p.m. Sunday Mid-March to mid-October; from 9:30 a.m. to 4 p.m. Tuesday to Saturday and 2 to 4 p.m. Sunday mid-October to mid-March. Admission is £1.20 ($1.80) for adults, 60p (90¢) for children.

    Just a mile north of Walmer Castle is Deal Castle, standing a mile south of the Deal town center. A defensive fort built about 1540, is the most spectacular example of the low, squat forts constructed by Henry VIII. Its 119 gun positions made it the most powerful of his defense forts. Centered around a circular keep surrounded by two rings of semi-circular bastions, the castle was protected by an outer moat. The entrance was approached by a drawbridge with a portcullis. The castle was damaged by bombs during World War II but has been restored to its early form. An exhibition on coastal defenses is in the basement. Hours are the same as those for Walmer Castle. Admission is 75p ($1.13) for adults and 35p (53¢) for children.

For our next and final stopover in Kent, we go inland—37 miles from London—to a once-fashionable resort:

3. Royal Tunbridge Wells

Dudley, Lord North, courtier to James I, is credited with the discovery in 1606 of the chalybeate spring that started it all. His accidental find led to the creation of a fashionable resort 36 miles south of London, that reached its peak in the mid-18th century under the foppish leadership of "Beau" Nash. "Beau" or Richard Nash (1674–1761) was a dandy of a style-setter in his day, the final arbiter of what to wear and what to say—even how to act (for example, he got men to take off their boots and put on stockings). But, of course, most of his time was devoted to Bath.

Even so, Tunbridge Wells enjoyed a prime spa reputation from the days of Charles II through Victoria's time. Because so many monarchs had visited, Edward VII named it "Royal Tunbridge Wells" in 1909. Over the years "the cure" was considered the answer for everything from too many days of wine and roses to failing sexual prowess.

The most remarkable feature of Royal Tunbridge Wells is its Pantiles, a colonnaded walkway for shoppers, tea-drinkers, and diners, built near the wells. At the Assembly Hall, entertainment (opera, vaudeville) is presented.

Alas, there's nothing sadder in tourism than a resort that's seen its day: Royal Tunbridge Wells is more for Jane Austen than Jane Fonda. Still, it's worth a visit just for a fleeting glimpse at the good old days of the 18th century.

Canadians touring in the area may want to seek out the grave of the founder of their country's capital. Lt. Col. John By of the Royal Engineers (1779–1836) died at Shernfold Park in Frant, East Sussex, near Royal Tunbridge Wells, and is buried in the churchyard there. His principal claim to fame is that he built the Rideau Canal in Upper Canada and established what was later to be the capital of the Dominion of Canada, the city of Ottawa.

The Rideau Canal, some 124 miles long, links the city of Kingston on the St. Lawrence River with the city of Ottawa on the Ottawa River. Between 1826 and 1832 John By successfully constructed the canal through an unexplored wilderness for the British government. At the northern end of the canal he laid out "Bytown." Twenty years later this was renamed Ottawa, and it became the capital of the united Canada. His grave near Royal Tunbridge Wells is marked with a plaque erected by the Historical Society of Ottawa in 1979.

You can come to Royal Tunbridge Wells from London, via a fast express train service, taking about 40 minutes. The service is every 30 minutes. Many people have learned that because of the high cost of accommodations in London, it works out well for them to stay here and commute.

WHERE TO STAY: An unpretentious place to stay, **Thornedene Guest House,** 108 St. Johns Rd. (tel. 0892/21712), is moderately priced in a high-priced area. Mr. and Mrs. R. J. Jose, the owners, charge £11 ($16.50) per person daily for B&B. It's a simple place, but well kept.

Grosvenor Guest House, 215 Upper Grosvenor Rd. (tel. 0892/32601), is one of the better B&B houses at the spa. That's because it's owned by Paul and Jackie Tripley, who are fine hosts, seeing that each guest is made comfortable. They charge from £11 ($16.50) for a good bed and a "very fattening" English breakfast. They rent out three double bedrooms and two family rooms, and the house has full central heating and hot and cold running water in all units. In addition, there is parking space for five cars. They offer evening meals at moderate prices.

House of Flowers, 80 Ravenswood Ave. (tel. 0892/23069), takes its name not from the famous Broadway musical, but from a flower conservatory within the building. Near the heart of the old spa, it rents out a few rooms for paying guests, with a shared public bathroom. The charge, depending on the accommodation assigned, ranges from £10.50 ($15.75) in a single and from £17 ($25.50) to £21 ($31.50) in a double. The place is attractive and homey (or what the English call "homely").

For a real taste of English hospitality try **Birkfield,** 92 Ravenswood Ave. (tel. 0892/31776), in a quiet residential area within walking distance of the town. Mrs. Anne Kibbey offers pleasant, comfortable rooms overlooking landscaped gardens. Her English breakfast will fortify you for the day. She charges £9 ($13.50) per person, single or double.

Blinkbonnie, 4 Beltring Rd. (tel. 0892/27908), about seven minutes' walk from the town center, is Mrs. Hilda Marcroft's handsome white-painted brick Victorian house in which she rents three twin-bedded rooms, charging £10 ($15) for B&B. The units have hot and cold running water, and there are two bathrooms and a shower for the use of guests. The house is centrally heated, with a TV lounge and a small garden. An English breakfast is the only meal served. Accommodation in this homey place is available year round.

WHERE TO DINE: Most travelers are content with a luncheon stop in Tunbridge Wells, but you can also enjoy a good dinner here.

Thackeray's House, 85 London Rd. (tel. 0892/37558), serves the finest food in town, and you get a little history as well. This is the second oldest house in the spa, and it was once inhabited by the novelist, William Makepeace Thackeray. Bruce Wass, the owner-chef, once worked at one of my favorite restaurants in London, Odin's, before coming here to set up his own place. He has created an elegant atmosphere, backed up by attentive service, for his specialties which are served from 12:30 to 2:30 p.m. and 7 to 10 p.m. The place is closed Sunday and Monday and also for a two-week vacation sometime in summer. A table d'hôte lunch is modestly priced, beginning at £10 ($15), and a set dinner is offered for £16 ($24). Care goes into all his dishes, and many have great flair, including an occasional salad with fresh flowers! He reaches perfection with such dishes as tender duck breast served with citrus, or lamb with baby turnips, flavored with fresh herbs. For dessert, the chef is most often cited for his chocolate armagnac loaf served with a walnut liqueur sauce.

Less expensive is **Downstairs at Thackeray's,** 85 London Rd. (tel. 0892/37559), which is a brasserie under the just-recommended restaurant. Here traditional British cookery is presented, often with a certain flair. Try, if featured, medallions of pork in a Stilton cheese sauce. Sometimes fruit is cooked with meat dishes rather effectively. Meals cost from £6 ($9) and are served from 12:30 to 5 p.m. and 7 to 11 p.m. except Sunday and Monday.

Mayflower Chinese Restaurant, 37 Mount Ephraim (tel. 0892/510636), features a Peking, Szechuan, and Cantonese cuisine. A large menu, with many of the classic Chinese dishes the world is familiar with, is presented to you. Meals cost from £10 ($15), and are served Sunday to Thursday from noon to 2:15 p.m. and from 5:30 to 11:30 p.m. (on Friday and Saturday it stays open until midnight).

One of the most popular pubs in town is the **Hole in the Wall,** 9 The High (tel. 0892/26550), where Jack Muncer is "mine host" at this little place built in 1770. Most people come here to drink, but you can visit for pub lunches served from 11 a.m. to 2:30 p.m. The fare is simple, consisting mainly of stews, salads, and soups accompanied by crisp fresh bread. Meals cost from £3 ($4.50). If you're in the area at night, drop in for a drink from 6 to 11 p.m.

Instead of leaving London for Kent, you might head directly south of the capital to inviting Surrey.

SURREY

This tiny county has for some time been in danger of being gobbled up by the growing boundaries of London and turned into a sprawling suburb, catching the overflow of a giant metropolis. But although it is densely populated in the area bordering the capital, Surrey still retains much unspoiled countryside, largely because its many heaths and commons form undesirable land for post-war suburbanite houses. Essentially, Surrey is a county of commuters (Alfred Lord Tennyson was among the first), since a worker in the city can practically travel to the remotest corner of Surrey from London in anywhere from 45 minutes to an hour.

Long before William the Conqueror marched his pillaging Normans across its chalky North Downs, Surrey was important to the Saxons. In fact, early Saxon kings were once crowned at what is now Kingston-on-Thames (their Coronation Stone is still preserved near the Guildhall).

4. Richmond

Want to spend an afternoon in a Thames river town? Richmond in Surrey is only a 30-minute ride from London, and can be easily reached by the Underground trains, or by Green Line coaches 716 or 716a from Hyde Park Corner. The old town, popular in Victorian times, has good public rail links with London, and it offers the escape many seek from the rush and bustle of the metropolis. If you're feeling lighthearted, take the boat trip down the Thames. Turner himself, art materials in hand, came here for inspiration.

Richmond is only one mile from Kew and its botanical gardens. You may prefer a combined excursion to Kew Gardens and Richmond on the same day. One of the attractions of the Thames town is the 2,500 acre **Richmond Park,** first staked out by Charles I in 1637. It is filled with photogenic deer and waterfowl. Richmond has long enjoyed associations with royalty, as Henry VIII's Richmond Palace stood here (an even earlier manor was razed). Queen Elizabeth I died in the old palace in 1603. Somebody's short-sightedness led to the palace's being carried away, and only a carriageway remains.

If you want to be like the English, you'll climb **Richmond Hill** for a view of the Thames considered by some to be one of the ten best views in the world. The scene reminded William Byrd of a similar view near his home on the James River in Virginia, inspiring him to name the city founded there in 1737, Richmond.

There are good shops and an excellent theater facing the green on which, in summertime, cricket matches are played. Many locals go boating on the river. Richmond Park has a public golf course, and you can rent a horse from one of the local stables. The Richmond Ice Skating Rink has been the nursery of many of England's skating champions. Wimbledon and the Tennis Championships are within easy reach, as is Hampton Court Palace.

At Petersham, the 13th-century St. Peter's Church is the burial place of Capt. George Vancouver. The Queen Mother's parents, Lord and Lady Glamis, were married there. It also has some very old wooden box pews. At St. Anne's Church at Kew Green, the painters Gainsborough and Zoffany were buried.

From Richmond, you can take bus 65 or 71 to visit historic **Ham House** (disembark at the Fox and Duck Pub across from the grounds of the Ham Polo Club), eight miles from the heart of London. This historic house offers an amazing look into the lives of the aristocracy of 17th-century England. Unlike most such houses in Britain, this one has been maintained almost intact. Much of the house, especially the kitchen (modern for its time), was the work of Elizabeth Murray, Duchess of Maitland and

Countess of Dysart. Her aim was to create the most sumptuous private residence in Restoration England, complete from ceilings depicting mythological scenes to elegant French upholstered pieces. One of the first private bathrooms in England was installed at Ham House. The house is open daily from 2 to 6 p.m., charging an admission of £1.60 ($2.40) for adults, 80p ($1.20) for children. In summer, you can order tea in the 17th-century garden. For more information, phone 01/940-1950.

WHERE TO EAT: Londoners often go down to Richmond for the day, browse through its art galleries, and then dine out. The best bargain follows.

Mrs. Beeton, 58 Hill Rise (tel. 01/940-9561), was presumably named after the famous English cookbook writer. Decked out in pine, the restaurant is low-key and decidedly informal, and most reasonable in price, charging from £5.50 ($8.25) per person for lunch, served from 10 a.m. to 5 p.m., and dinner, offered from 6:30 to 10 p.m. It's owned by a women's cooperative, and each day a particular member displays her culinary wares—so you never know what you're going to get. The place doesn't have a liquor license, but you are allowed to bring a bottle. After dinner you may want to visit the antique shop in the basement.

5. Haslemere

A quiet, sleepy town, Haslemere attracts because Early English musical instruments are made by hand there. Ever hear a harpsichord concert? An annual music fesitival (see below) is the town's main drawing card. Over the years the Dolmetsch family has been responsible for the acclaim that has come to this otherwise unheralded little Surrey town, lying in the midst of some of the shire's finest scenery. Haslemere is only an hour's train ride from Waterloo Station in London, about 42 miles away.

THE FESTIVAL: It isn't often that one can hear such exquisite music played so skillfully on the harpsichord, the recorder, the lute, or any of the instruments designed so painstakingly to interpret the music of earlier centuries. Throughout the year, the Dolmetsch family makes and repairs these instruments, welcoming visitors to their place on the edge of Haslemere. They rehearse constantly, preparing for the concerts that are held in July and last eight days.

You can get specific information by writing to the **Haslemere Festival Office,** Jesses, Grayswood Road, Haslemere, Surrey, GU27 2BS (or telephone 0428/2161 between 9 a.m. and 12:30 p.m. daily). During the festival, matinees begin at 3:15 p.m., evening performances at 7:15 p.m. For seats in the balcony, prices range from £3 ($4.50) to £4.50 ($6.75), with stall seats going from £2 ($6) to £3.50 ($5.25).

WHERE TO EAT: The best-known pub in town, **Crowns,** Weyhill (tel. 0428/3112), serves substantial grub. In summer, guests take their drinks out into the garden. Look for daily specials, often fish, posted on a blackboard. Try, for example, grilled trout, poached salmon steak, or chicken in a peppery mustard sauce. Meals cost from £6 ($9). Portions are generous, and hearty soups are served from tureens. Vegetarians will also find specials, and you can bring your children at lunch. Hours are from 10:30 a.m. to 2:30 p.m. and from 6 to 11 p.m.

If you're seeking a more substantial restaurant, try **Shrimpton's,** Midhurst Road, Kingsley Green (tel. 0428/3539), lying on the outskirts. The setting is mellow, with beams, and the service is polite. The cookery is straightforward and honest, and the ingredients are fresh. The owner, Mrs. B.S. Keeley, turns to both her home country and the continent for inspiration in the dishes selected. For example, you might find a game fowl with berries on the menu or else beef cooked in a wine-flavored sauce. Save room for desserts, as they are worth it. A set lunch costs £9.50 ($14.25), a table d' hôte dinner going for £16 ($24). Hours are from 12:30 to 2 p.m. and 6:30 to 9:30 (last orders). It is closed for Saturday lunch and Sunday. Call for a table.

WHERE TO STAY: An attractive period house dating back some 300 years, **Houndless Water,** Bell Vale Lane (tel. 0428/2591), should get your attention by its name alone. Here you get inexpensive living English country style about 1¼ miles from the heart of town, lying off the A286. You'll be near the Sussex boundary if you find lodgings here. In one of the beauty spots of Surrey, you get comfortable rooms and a friendly welcome, for which you'll pay £13 ($19.50) to £17 ($25.50) per person. It's best to book in here on half-board terms, ranging from £21 ($31.50) to £25 ($37.50) per person nightly. Guests are not received in winter.

GUILDFORD: The old and new meet in the county town on the Wey River, 40 minutes by train from Waterloo Station in London. Charles Dickens believed that its High Street, which slopes to the river, was one of the most beautiful in England. The Guildhall has an ornamental projecting clock which dates back to 1683.

Lying 2½ miles southwest of the city, **Loseley House** (tel. 0483/571881), a beautiful and historic Elizabethan mansion visited by Queen Elizabeth I, James I, and Queen Mary, has been featured on TV and in five films. Its works of art include paneling from Henry VIII's Nonesuch Palace, period furniture, a unique carved chalk chimney piece, magnificent ceilings, and cushions made by the first Queen Elizabeth. The mansion is open from the end of May to the end of September on Wednesday, Thursday, Friday, and Saturday from 2 to 5 p.m., charging £1.60 ($2.40) for adults, 90p ($1.35) for children.

WHERE TO STAY: Back in Guildford, I suggest the following accommodations:

The **Carlton Hotel,** London Road (tel. 0483/575158), is used by some guests so as to be out of the big crush of London. It's just a three-minute walk to the London Road Station on the London (Waterloo) to Guildford line via Cobham. The tab here is £18 ($27) in a single, £14 ($21) per person in a double. If you require a private shower, a single is £23 ($34.50), and a double is £15 ($22.50) per person, including an English breakfast. You can spend the day visiting the London museums or theater and come home here to have an evening meal. All these prices include VAT and service. Bedrooms are centrally heated with hot and cold running water, and have a radio and intercom. For an evening's relaxation, a saloon bar beckons.

Mrs. Linda Atkinson, 129 Stoke Rd. (tel. 0483/38260), is most reasonable for B&B, considering the warmth of the welcome and the quality of the rooms. Mrs. Atkinson includes VAT, service, and the use of ironing facilities in her charge of £11.50 ($17.25) per person daily. All rooms have TV, tea/coffee-making facilities, central heating, and wash basins. Her breakfasts are plentiful and well prepared. Her house lies a ten-minute walk to the town center, opposite the scenic park with tennis courts and swimming pool.

WISLEY GARDEN: One of the great gardens of England and of the world, Wisley Garden in Wisley, near Ripley, off the A3, the main London to Portsmouth Road, is under the aegis today of the Royal Horticultural Society. Every season of the year, this 60-acre garden has a profusion of flowers and shrubbery, ranging from the Alpine House with its delicate blossoms in spring to the old Walled Garden with formal flowerbeds in summer to the Heather Garden's colorful foliage in the fall and a riot of exotic plants in the glasshouses in winter. This garden is the site of a laboratory where botanists, plant pathologists, and entomologists experiment and assist amateur gardeners. Open all year, hours are 10 a.m. to 7 p.m. (or sunset if earlier) Monday to Saturday, from 2 to 7 p.m. Sunday, closed only on Christmas Day. Admission April to October is £2.50 ($3.75) for adults, half price for children. The remainder of the year, adults pay £2 ($3). A licensed restaurant and cafeteria are in the garden.

DORKING: This town, birthplace of Lord Laurence Olivier, lies on the Mole River, at the foot of the North Downs. Within easy reach are some of the most scenic spots in the shire, including Silent Pool, Box Hill, and Leith Hill. Three miles to the northwest and 1½ miles south of Great Bookham, off the Leatherhead-Guildford Road, stands **Polesden Lacey** (tel. 0372/58203), a former Regency villa containing the Greville collection of antiques, paintings, and tapestries. In the early part of this century it was enlarged to become a comfortable Edwardian country house when it was the home of a celebrated hostess, who frequently entertained royalty here. The 18th-century garden is filled with herbaceous borders, a rose garden, and beech walks, and in all, the estate consists of 1,000 acres. It's open in March and November on Saturday and Sunday from 2 to 5 p.m.; April to the end of October Wednesday to Sunday from 2 to 6 p.m. The gardens are open daily from 11 a.m. to sunset. Admission to the gardens is £1 ($1.50), with the house costing an extra £1.20 ($1.80). Children 17 years of age or under are admitted for half price (under-5s get in free). A licensed restaurant on the grounds is open from 11 a.m. on the days the house can be visited. There is also a gift shop which sells the full range of National Trust goods.

Back in Dorking, you can find accommodations at the following:

The **Star and Garter Hotel,** Station Approach (tel. 0306/882820). Bill and June Smith, personally completed many of the renovations on what they call their "oldy worldly" establishment. It was originally built 150 years ago as the village's railroad inn. Today it is a popular pub and restaurant, serving such dishes as the traditional homemade steak-and-kidney pie. Pint after pint of ale and lager are dispensed to local residents. If you'd like such a pub-type accommodation, you'll find spacious and comfortable bedrooms, renting for £18 ($27) in a single, from £30 ($45) in a double, and from £38 ($57) in a family room, all prices including breakfast, VAT, and service. None of the dozen rooms contains a private bath, but the public facilities are adequate. The snooker tables in the pub usually draw a lively crowd of onlookers.

REDHILL: About eight miles east of Dorking, near Reigate, in the little town of Redhill, about 400 yards from the Redhill Railway Station on the A25 to Sevenoaks, stands the **Ashleigh House Hotel,** Redstone Hill (tel. 0737/64763), where Jill and Michael Warren receive guests in a lovely Tudor house, decorated and furnished in excellent taste. Michael is a retired TV executive, and Jill is a charming, gracious hostess who makes guests feel at home, serving a good English breakfast in the dining room overlooking a garden. Some of the accommodations have private baths and showers. Singles rent for £17.50 ($26.25) and doubles for £26 ($39) to £30 ($45) for B&B. There's a heated swimming pool for use of guests in summer, plus a TV lounge. The hotel is only about 15 minutes by car from Gatwick.

THE SUSSEXES

If King Harold hadn't loved Sussex so much, the course of English history might have been quite different. Had the brave Saxon waited longer in the north, he could have marshaled more adequate reinforcements before striking out south to meet the Normans. But Duke William's soldiers were ravaging the countryside he knew so well, and Harold rushed down to counter them.

Harold's enthusiasm for Sussex is understandable. The landscape rises and falls like waves. The country is known for its downlands and tree-thickened weald, from which came the timber to build England's mighty fleet in days gone by. The shire lies south of London and Surrey, bordering Kent in the east, Hampshire in the west, and opening directly onto the sometimes sunny, resort-dotted English Channel.

Like the other sections in the vulnerable south of England, the Sussexes witnessed some of the most dramatic moments in the country's history, notably invasions. Apart from the Norman landing at Hastings, the most life-changing transfusion of plasma occurred in the 19th century, as middle-class Victorians flocked to the seashore, pumping new spirit into Eastbourne, Worthing, Brighton, including old Hastings itself. The cult of the saltwater worshippers flourished, and has to this day. Although Eastbourne and Worthing are much frequented by the English, I'd place them several fathoms below Brighton and Hastings, which are much more suitable if you're seeking a holiday by the sea.

Far more than the resorts, the old towns and villages of the Sussexes are intriguing, particularly Rye and Winchelsea, the ancient towns of the Cinque Ports Confederation. No Sussex village is lovelier than Alfriston (and the innkeepers know it too). Arundel is noted for its castle, and the cathedral city of Chichester is a mecca for theater buffs. Traditionally, and for purposes of government, Sussex is divided into East Sussex and West Sussex. I've adhered to that convenient designation.

I'll begin in East Sussex, where you'll find many of the inns and hotels within commuting distance of London.

6. Rye and Winchelsea

"Nothing more recent than a Cavalier's Cloak, Hat and Ruffles should be seen in the streets of Rye," exuded Louis Jennings. He's so right. This ancient town, formerly an island, was chartered back in 1229. Rye, 65 miles below London, near the English Channel, and neighboring Winchelsea were once part of the ancient Cinque Ports Confederation. Rye flourished as a smuggling center, its denizens sneaking in contraband from the marshes to stash away in little nooks (even John Wesley's firm chastisements couldn't stop an entrenched tradition).

But the sea receded from Rye, leaving it perched like a giant whale out of water, still carrying its mermaid-like veil of antiquity 2 miles from the Channel. Its narrow, cobblestone streets twist and turn like a labyrinth, with buildings jumbled along them whose sagging roofs and crooked chimneys indicate the town's medieval origins. The old town's entrance is Land Gate, where a single lane of traffic passes between massive, 40-foot-high stone towers. The parapet of the gate contains holes through which boiling oil used to be poured on unwelcome visitors, such as French raiding parties.

Attacked several times by French fleets, Rye was practically razed in 1377. But it rebuilt sufficiently, decking itself out in the Elizabethan style. Queen Elizabeth I, during her visit in 1573, bestowed upon the town the distinction of Royal Rye. This has long been considered a special place, having attracted any number of famous persons, including Charles Lamb (who considered the smugglers "honest thieves") and Henry James who once lived in the **Lamb House,** West Street at the top of Mermaid Street, from 1898 to 1916. There are many James mementos in the Georgian house, which is set in a a walled garden. It is open from 2 to 5:30 p.m. Wednesday and Saturday from the end of March to the end of October, charging an admission of £1 ($1.50).

Today the city has any number of specific buildings and sites of architectural interest, notably the 15th-century **St. Mary's Parish Church,** with its clock flanked by two gilded cherubs, known as the Quarter Boys from their striking of the bells on the quarter hour. If you're courageous, you can climb a set of wooden stairs and ladders to the bell tower of the church, from which a striking view is afforded.

Rye Museum, 4 Church Square (tel. 0797/223254), is housed in the Ypres Tower, a fortification built circa 1250 by order of Henry III as a defense against French raiders. It's housed in an ancient building and contains collections of military objects, shipping artifacts, toys, Cinque Ports relics, Victoriana, inn lore, and pottery. Open from Easter to mid-October, hours are from 10:30 a.m. to 1 p.m. and 2:15 to 5:30 p.m. (open at 11:30 p.m. Sunday). Admission is 75p ($1.13).

The sister Cinque port to Rye, Winchelsea too has witnessed its waters ebbing away. It traces its history back to Edward I, and has experienced many dramatic moments, such as those from the sacking French. But today it is a staidly dignified residential town. In the words of a now-almost-forgotten 19th-century writer, Winchelsea is "a sunny dream of centuries ago." Its finest sight is a badly damaged 14th-century church, containing a number of remarkable tombs.

On the outskirts, you can visit **Smallhythe Place,** which for 30 years was the country house of Dame Ellen Terry, the English actress acclaimed for her Shakesperean roles, who had a long theatrical association with Sir Henry Irving. She died in the house in 1928. This timber-framed structure, of a type known as a "continuous-jetty house," was built in the first half of the 16th century. It is filled with Terry memorabilia. The house is on the B2082 near Tenterden, about 6 miles to the north of Rye. It's open April to October except from 2 to 6 p.m. except Tuesday and Friday. Admission is £1.10 ($1.65) for adults, 60p (90¢) for children. For more information, phone 05895/2334.

WHERE TO STAY IN RYE: A beautiful Georgian house, **Durrant House Hotel,** East Street (tel. 0797/223182), is set on a quiet residential street in the old town behind a cream-colored facade at the end of Market Street. Over the years it has attracted many famous personages, including John Wesley during his evangelical tours. In more recent times, the famous artist, Paul Nash, lived next door until his death in 1946. In fact, his celebrated view, as seen in his painting, *View of the Rother,* can be enjoyed from the River Room of the hotel. Sir William Durrant, a friend of the Duke of Wellington, acquired the house which is now named after him. In time, it was used as a relay station for carrier pigeons. These birds brought news of the victory at Waterloo. The hotel possesses much charm and is full of character. There is a cozy lounge with an arched brick fireplace, and, across the hall, a residents bar. The hotel rents out nine comfortably furnished bedrooms, seven of which contain private baths. Depending on the plumbing, singles range from £11 ($16.50) to £19.50 ($29.25) per person, including an English breakfast.

Little Saltcote, 22 Military Rd. (tel. 0797/223210), owned by Sally and Terry Osborne, is an attractive guesthouse five minutes from the town center, yet with a peaceful rural setting. The well-appointed rooms, complete with TV, central heating, razor points, and coffee- and tea-making facilities, cost from £10 ($15) per person nightly including an English breakfast with a good choice of menu. Guests are provided with forecourt parking and may wander freely in the large garden.

Little Orchard House, West Street (tel. 0797/223831), is among the most elegant and moderately priced accommodations in the old seaport. The Georgian house, built in the 18th century, was then the home of Rye's Mayor Thomas Proctor, who pursued his political life and engaged in smuggling at the same time. Others prominent in politics, if not in smuggling, also lived here through the years, even Prime Minister David Lloyd George 70 years ago. The house is tastefully furnished, using many antiques, and there is much Georgian panelling. A large open fireplace in the lounge-study has a blazing fire when it's needed, a big bouquet of dried flowers otherwise. From this room and the intimate breakfast room, you can see the old-style walled garden, with espaliered fruit trees. Geraldine and Robert Bromley welcome guests to the individually decorated bedrooms, all with color TV, hot drinks trays, and private baths, costing from £28 ($42) to £42 ($63) in a single, from £34 ($51) to £42 ($63) in a double, which is very good value. Tariffs include a hearty Sussex breakfast. You'll want to spend much time in the old-style walled garden.

Mizpah Guest House, 89 Military Rd. (tel. 0797/223657), is one of the most reasonably priced accommodations in town. The only problem is, it has so few rooms you may not have much of a chance of getting in unless you've reserved or called ahead. Rooms have private showers, and two are reserved for families. It's best to take the half-board rate, costing from £15 ($22.50) per person nightly. You'll be near the heart of Rye. Accommodations are comfortably cozy.

Cliff Farm, Military Road, Iden Lock (tel. 07978/331), is a different way to live in Rye, providing you show up between March and October. During those months, Jeff and Pat Sullivin receive guests on their nearly 4½ acres of property. Because of the elevated position of the farm, you'll have good views of the area, particularly over

Romney Marsh. Guests share the public bath, paying from £8.50 ($12.75) to £9.50 ($14.25) per person in a double. There's a sitting room where a log fire blazes when the weather is cool. Farm produce means a generous country breakfast, and you can see the farm animals as you stroll around. Cliff Farm is about two and a quarter miles from Rye. Fishing can be arranged.

DINING IN RYE: In an ancient vicarage converted into a tea room, **Fletcher's House,** Lion Street (near St. Mary's Church) (tel. 0797/223101), serves morning coffee, hot or cold luncheons, and afternoon tea from 10 a.m. to 5 p.m. seven days a week. Daily specials might include grilled trout with a side salad and freshly baked french bread. Meals cost from £6.50 ($9.75). The house is particularly noted for its Sussex cream teas, the scones for which are baked daily on the premises. John Fletcher, the Elizabethan dramatist and contemporary of Shakespeare, was born in the house in 1579, when his father was vicar of Rye. It still retains many of its original architectural features, such as the old hidden-away front door with its design of York and Tudor roses, and an impressive oaken room. Do look at the clock on that church. It contains animated figures.

The **Mermaid Inn,** Mermaid Street (tel. 0797/223065), is the most famous of the old smugglers' inns of England—known to the band of cutthroats, the real-life Hawkhurst Gang, as well as to Russell Thorndike's fictional character, Dr. Syn. One of the present bedrooms, in fact, is called Dr. Syn's Bedchamber, and is connected by a staircase, set in the thickness of a wall, to the bar. The Mermaid had been open for 150 years when Elizabeth I visited Rye in 1573. The inn has 30 comfortable bedrooms, three four-posters, and central heating. It is owned by the Gregory family. The inn, the most charming tavern in Rye, serves good food—English with frills. For £8 ($12), you can have a table d'hôte luncheon such as this typical one: a rich and heavy kidney soup, followed by poached sea trout with hollandaise sauce (superb), accompanied by three vegetables, including string beans. English cheese or traditionally made fruit pies, such as black currant and apple, round out the repast. Luncheon is served from 12:30 to 2 p.m. At the dinner, from 7:30 to 9 p.m., your tab for four courses may average around £12 ($18). The dining room, with its linenfold paneling, Caen-stone fireplaces, and oak-beamed ceiling, makes for an ideal setting. Even if you're not dining at the Mermaid, drop in to the old Tudor pub, with its 16-foot-wide fireplace (look for a priest's hiding hole).

For a splurge, the **Flushing Inn,** Market Street (tel. 0797/223292), is a family-run operation (since 1960), in a 16th-century inn on a cobblestone street. It has preserved the best of the past, including a wall-size fresco in the restaurant dating from 1544 and depicting a menagerie of birds and heraldic beasts. A rear dining room overlooks a carefully tended flower garden. A special feature is the Sea Food Lounge Bar, where sandwiches and plates of seafood are available from £3 ($4.50) to £9 ($13.50). In the main restaurant, luncheons are offered from £8 ($12), dinners from £12.50 ($18.75). Besides these lunches and dinners, gastronomic evenings are held at regular intervals between October and April. For one of these specially prepared meals, including your apéritif, wine, and after-dinner brandy, you pay £25 ($42) per person. Fine Wine evenings cost £28 ($42) per person. Hours are from noon to 1:45 p.m. and 7:15 to 9 p.m. The inn is closed Monday night, all day Tuesday, and for two weeks after Christmas. The Flushing Inn has been run by the Mann family for a quarter of a century, with the second generation now being fully active in the business in the persons of a daughter and son-in-law.

The **Durrant House Restaurant,** East Street (tel. 0797/223182), in a hotel of the same name previously recommended, requires reservations, even from residents. The Lampon family runs this pink-colored dining room, one of the most elegant choices in Rye. They serve only dinner (except on Wednesday and Thursday) from 7 to 8:30 p.m. Guests peruse a fixed price menu, costing £9.25 ($13.88) for five freshly prepared courses. While waiting for dinner, patrons of the restaurant enjoy a view of the rear garden. As befits a former seaport, the chef specializes in fresh fish. Only fresh vegetables are used, and desserts and ice creams are homemade. If you arrive early, have a drink in the Wellington Bar, which not only serves real ale but does light pub lunches from noon to 2 p.m. as well.

The **Swiss Patisserie and Tea Room,** 50 Cinque Ports St. (tel. 0797/222830), is where expatriate Swiss-born Claude Auberson concocts creamy Swiss cakes, cream meringues, buns, and pastries. Everything is very good and fattening, and it's to be washed down in a tiny tea room with coffee or Swiss-style hot chocolate. A cream tea goes for £1.50 ($2.25), and there is a selection of hot savory snacks baked daily on the premises. These are likely to include Cornish pasties, sausage and eggroll, or ravioli with cheese sauce. Hours are from 8 a.m. to 4:30 p.m. except Tuesday when it closes at 12:30 p.m. and all day Sunday.

The **Quayhole,** Strand Quay (tel. 0797/223638), is a restaurant and beefburger bar in three of the original warehouses, built as early as 1720, down by the Rother River. The owners have created a delightful establishment, keeping the rough brick walls and stone floors, along with dark-wood settles (comfortably cushioned) with tables to match. Pictures of Old Rye and articles used during the working life of the warehouses are an added spice of interest. You can generally eat and drink throughout the day. Hours are flexible, usually from noon to 10 p.m. (in winter, mainly on weekends). You can order such dishes as four kinds of steak, curries, burgers, mixed grills, and crêpes. Meals cost from £10 ($15).

FOOD AND LODGING IN WINCHELSEA: Sure to catch your eye is the **Strand House** (tel. 0797/226276), a weathered historic house and cottage set in a garden at the foot of a hill, and separated from the sea by meadows in which sheep graze. The house is a mixture of thick brick and stone walls with tiled roof, rambling roses, and a lawned garden with flowering shrubs and rockeries. The owners, Shane and Mary Redmond, are conscious of comforts, and their high standard includes complete baths in seven of the eight rooms, plus wall-to-wall carpeting, TV, hot beverage facilities, and central heating in all bedrooms. One of the rooms includes a four-poster bed. Reserved for the guests is a private dining room with a huge inglenook fireplace. There is ample parking for guests' cars within the hotel grounds. The house is open all year and charges from £20 ($30) for two, including a choice of a full English breakfast. The cottage can be hired on a self-catering basis for those wishing independence. The house is well over 500 years old and has irregular oak floors. The heavy oak ceiling beams have been taken from ships and are quite low, as are some of the doors (duck or bump your head). The stairs are much safer than they look! It is believed that a tunnel near the house leads up to Winchelsea Town and is a relic of the days when smuggling was one of the main industries of the area. In World War II the wooded bank at the rear of the house was used to store rifles and ammunition in the event of a Nazi invasion (the meadow below was flooded to deter foot soldiers bent on invasion).

Manna Plat Restaurant, Mill Road (tel. 0797/226317), is one of the most charming—and the best—restaurants in the area. It lies within a terracotta, tile-covered stone cottage dating from 1750. The vaults beneath the dining room are now a wine cellar, through which you can tour. Tina and Stewart Duggan-Palmer will welcome you into their restaurant, which serves an impeccable English cuisine, heavy with French overtones. You might begin with a watercress and celery soup or a Stilton soup and go on to grilled halibut steak with a prawn sauce or filet of beef stroganoff. For dessert, try if available the meringue boat with ice cream and chocolate sauce. Meals cost from £10 ($15) to £15 ($22.50). Since the place has only seven tables, reservations are important. Enjoy a pre-dinner drink beside an applewood fire if you should arrive on a winter's night. Lunch is Tuesday to Friday and on Sunday from noon to 2 p.m., dinner Tuesday to Saturday from 7 to 9 p.m.

Snailham House, Broad Street, Icklesham, near Winchelsea (tel. 0424/814556), was once honored by the Automobile Association as "guest house of the year." Irene and Denis Coxell run this country guesthouse which lies about three miles from the coast and Winchelsea, and half a mile off the A259, attracting those wanting to get off the main road. Surrounded by landscaped gardens, it has views from all its attractively furnished bedrooms which rent for £16 ($24) per person daily for half board. B&B is £11 ($16.50) per person nightly. This former farmhouse stands in the midst of a fruit and sheep farm. In colder weather, log fires burn in the lounges. The cookery is good and pleasantly served, and there is a residential license for drinks. They are open from late March to the end of October.

7. Hastings and St. Leonards

The world has seen bigger battles, but few are as well remembered as the Battle of Hastings—1066. When William, Duke of Normandy, landed on the Sussex coast and lured King Harold (already fighting Vikings in Yorkshire) southward to defeat, the destiny of the English-speaking people was changed forever. It was D-Day in reverse. The actual battle occurred at what is now Battle Abbey (seven miles away), but the Norman duke used Hastings as his base of operation.

Hastings suffered other invasions, being razed by the French in the 14th century. But after that blow an old Tudor town grew up in the eastern sector, and it makes for a good stroll today. The more recent invasion threat—that of Hitler's armies—never came to pass. The dragons' dentures were put up across the countryside to bite into Nazi tanks.

Linked by a three-mile promenade along the sea, Hastings and St. Leonards were given a considerable boost in the 19th century by Queen Victoria, who visited several times. Neither town enjoys such royal patronage or prestigious name guests today; rather, they do a thriving business with middle-class Midlands traffic who shun the wicked ways of the continent to bask in the highly unreliable English sun. Hastings and St. Leonards have the usual shops and English sea-resort amusements. Lying only 63 miles from London, the coastal resorts are serviced by fast trains from Victoria Station.

THE SIGHTS: This area has two major attractions of interest.

Hastings Castle

In ruins now, the first of the Norman castles to be built in England sprouted up on a western hill overlooking Hastings, circa 1067. Precious little is left to remind us of the days when proud knights, imbued with a spirit of pomp and spectacle, wore bonnets and girdles. The fortress was ordered torn down by King John in 1216, and later served as a church and monastery until it felt Henry VIII's ire. Owned by the Pelham dynasty from the latter 16th century to modern times, the ruins have been turned over to Hastings. From the mount, you'll have a good view of the coast and promenade. It is open from 10 a.m. to 5 p.m. daily from Easter to the end of September, charging 55p (83¢) for adults, 30p (45¢) for children. For information, phone 0424/424242.

The Hastings Embroidery

A commemorative work, the Hastings Embroidery (tel. 0424/424242) was first exhibited in 1966. It is a remarkable achievement that traces 900 years of English history through needlework. Depicted are some of the nation's greatest moments (the Battle of Hastings, the coronation of William the Conqueror) and its legends (Robin Hood). In all, 27 panels, each nine feet wide (243 feet total), depicting 81 historic scenes, are exhibited at the Town Hall. The history of Britain comes alive—the murder of Thomas à Becket, King John signing Magna Carta, the Black Plague, Chaucer's pilgrims going to Canterbury, the Battle of Agincourt with the victorious Henry V, the War of the Roses, the Little Princes in the Tower, Bloody Mary's reign, Drake's *Golden Hind,* the arrival of Philip's ill-fated Armada, Guy Fawke's gunpowder plot, the sailing of the *Mayflower,* the disastrous plague of 1665 and the great London fire of the following year, Nelson at Trafalgar, the Battle of Waterloo, the Empress of India, Victoria, the Battle of Britain, and the D-Day landings at Normandy. In the center is a scale model of the battlefield at Battle, depicting William's one-inch men doing in Harold's small soldiers. The embroidery may be viewed from October to May, Monday to Friday from 11:30 a.m. to 3:30 p.m. From June to September, it is open Monday to Friday from 10 a.m. to 5 p.m. and on Saturday from 10 a.m. to 1 p.m. and 2 o 5 p.m. An admission of 65p (98¢) is charged for adults and 30p (45¢) for children.

BED AND BREAKFAST: Overlooking the sea, **Seafoam Guest House,** 3 Pelham Crescent (tel. 0424/431903), is a small (two singles, six doubles) establishment with a winning location. It is one of a row of well-preserved Regency houses, complete with a half-moon balcony and the traditional wrought-iron decoration. Even in high season, the B&B rate is from £10 ($15) per person nightly. The owner, Mrs. C. Evans, believes in giving you your money's worth: soft beds, a fine breakfast, good-sized rooms, a friendly and pleasant ambience, and a roomy lounge opening onto the water.

The **Fairlight Lodge,** Fairlight Road (tel. 0424/812104), lies three miles from the center of Hastings on the coast road to Rye, 600 feet above sea level. It is set in more than three acres of private grounds, adjacent to the Country Park, with ample carparking facilities. Open all year, the premises are fully licensed, with central heating and hot and cold running water in all rooms. A warm welcome is given by the resident owners, the Cutler and Davidson families, who charge from £11.50 ($17.25) per person for B&B, £18 ($27) for half board.

Eagle House Hotel, 12 Pevensey Road (tel. 0424/430535), St. Leonards-on-Sea, is one of the best guesthouses in the area. A buff-colored, three-story mansion, it lies in a residential section about a 10-minute walk from the beaches. A pair of gilded eagles top the most central of the upper balconies. Originally built in 1860 as a palatial private home, it has been successfully converted into a hotel. The owners rent out a total of 15 well-furnished bedrooms, 12 of which contain private bath, each with phone, color TV, central heating, and coffee-making facilities. Depending on the plumbing, singles rent for £19 ($28.50) to £23 ($34.50), doubles £26 ($39) to £33 ($49.50). The hotel has an attractive lobby done in reds along with an elegant Victorian dining room complete with oil paintings. It has a full residential and restaurant license.

Glastonbury Guest House, 45 Eversfield Pl. (tel. 0424/422280), stands in the neighboring St. Leonards-on-Sea, on the seafront adjoining the harbor. For a long time it has been receiving guests in its small number of rooms, some with private baths and color TV, and all with facilities for making hot drinks. It's one of the better values in town, offering a good, comfortable room and an English breakfast at a rate of £11 ($16.50) in a single and from £22 ($33) in a double. Guests are accepted only in season, from April through September.

WHERE TO DINE: Hastings is a fishing center, with a multitude of very competitive small seafood restaurants along the street fronting the beach at the east side of the city (on the way to the old part of town).

Martlets, 11 Grand Parade, St. Leonards-on-Sea (tel. 0424/437589), is owned and run by Peter and Anne Sharrard, who named it after the Sussex coat-of-arms. He doesn't like any frozen food, so his vegetables are fresh and well cooked. The cuisine is award-winning. Lunch is served from noon to 2 p.m. Tuesday to Sunday, and dinner from 6:30 to 10 p.m. Tuesday through Saturday. A three-course luncheon or dinner costs from £4.95 ($7.43) to £8.50 ($12.75), including roll and butter as well as coffee.

There is also a full à la carte menu available, including Dover sole, filet steak stuffed with prawns and laced with madeira sauce, homemade pâtés, and roast duckling with orange sauce and Grand Marnier.

Judge's Restaurant, 15 High St., in Old Town Hastings (tel. 0424/427097), is run by Eileen Inwood, who does the cooking, using only fresh ingredients. There is a choice of a roast joint, chicken, steak-and-kidney pie, chicken pie, or shepherd's pie, and a variety of cold meats and salads. High Street is in the old town fishing quarter of Hastings, and local fish also appears on the menu daily. There are homemade desserts such as apple pie, fresh fruit salad, and a trifle. Meals cost around £6.50 ($9.75). Judge's is open from 10 a.m. to 5 p.m., to 2 p.m. on Wednesday. Closed Sunday, Monday, the last two weeks in May, and the first two weeks in October. The son of the owner runs a bakery adjoining the restaurant, where a variety of freshly baked bread, buns, and cakes are available.

Brant's, 45 High St., Old Town Hastings (tel. 0424/431896), a vegetarian restaurant run by Mr. and Mrs. Stevens, serves a wide variety of unusual salads with savoury pies or quiches, cheese and vegetable pie, and home-made desserts, fruit pies, and other rich confections. All the food is prepared and/or cooked on the premises. A meal will cost around £4.50 ($6.75), and the establishment is open 10 a.m. to 5 p.m., 2 p.m. on Wednesday, and 4 p.m. in winter. It closes for two weeks in April and two weeks in the fall.

If you have a car, you might leave Hastings and head for **Crossways,** corner of Waites Lane, at Fairlight, near Hastings (tel. 0424/812356), a country village restaurant about five miles away. It is known for its food, and many English residents in Sussex journey for miles around to enjoy the hospitality of Len and Babs Nevill. They offer a three-course luncheon for a fixed price of £3.25 ($4.88) weekdays, £3.75 ($5.63) on Sunday between 12:30 and 2 p.m., and a three-course à la carte evening meal for £6 ($9) to £8.50 ($12.75). You might select crab thermidor for an appetizer, followed by a 12-ounce T-bone steak or duck à l'orange among the main dishes. There's always a good dessert selection. Closed Monday. Evening meals are served Wednesday to Saturday from 7:30 to 9:30 p.m. and reservations are requested.

8. Battle

Nine miles from Hastings, in the heart of the Sussex countryside, is the old market town of Battle, famed in history as the setting for the Battle of Hastings in 1066. King Harold, last of the English kings, encircled by his housecarls, fought bravely, not only for his kingdom but for his life. In the battle Harold was killed by William, Duke of Normandy, and his body was dismembered. To commemorate the victory, William the Conqueror founded **Battle Abbey,** High Street (tel. 0426/3792), some of the stone for which was shipped from his own lands at Caen, in northern France.

During the dissolution of the monasteries in 1537 by King Henry VIII, the church of the abbey was largely destroyed. Some buildings and ruins, however, remain in what Tennyson called "O Garden, blossoming out of English blood." The principal building still standing is the Abbot's House, which is leased to a private school for girls and not open to the general public. Of architectural interest is the Gatehouse, with its octagonal towers, standing at the top of the Market Square. All of the north Precinct Mall is still standing, and one of the most interesting sights of the ruins is the ancient Dorter Range, where the monks once slept.

The town of Battle grew up around the abbey, but even though it has remained a colorful medieval market town, many of the town's old half-timbered buildings regrettably have lost much of their original character because of stucco plastering carried out by past generations. The abbey is generally open from 9:30 a.m. to 6:30 p.m. (to 4 p.m. in winter). On Sunday, hours are from 11 a.m. to 6:30 p.m., from 2 to 4 p.m. off-season. Admission is £1.25 ($1.88) for adults, 60p (90¢) for children (under 5 admitted free).

FOOD AND LODGING: Mainly French cuisine is offered at **La Vieille Auberge Hotel and Restaurant,** 27 High St. (tel. 04246/2255). It is housed in a structure rebuilt in 1688 using stones from the Battle Abbey kitchen, demolished in 1685. In the cozy restaurant is an inglenook fireplace where big logs are burned. Gourmet dishes with French provincial specialties are offered, as well as two fixed-price meals, all made with local products (fish, venison, and wild duck). The proprietors are Trevor Keith and Jean Woolley, who is also the chef. Lunch is served from noon to 2 p.m. and dinner from 7 to 9 p.m. The fixed-price, three-course dinner goes for £8.95 ($13.43), the five-course repast costing £10.95 ($16.43). Expect to pay from £10 ($15) for an à la carte evening meal. There is a pleasant bar lounge, in addition to the comfortable bedrooms. Each of the units has individually controlled central heating, radio, house phone, and hot and cold running water. Three of the nine units contain private baths. The charge for bed and an English breakfast is £16 ($24) to £22.50 ($33.75) in a single, £24.50 ($36.75) to £34.50 ($51.75) in doubles or twins, with service and VAT included.

Little Hemingfold, Telham (tel. 04246/2910) lies 1½ miles from Battle off the A2100. Mrs. Benton and Mr. Barnes rent out 13 well-furnished and comfortable bedrooms, some of which contain 19th-century antiques. The house abounds in art and objects, some a heritage from Ann Benton's celebrated sculptor father. Nine of the bedrooms contain private baths. The B&B rate (no advance bookings taken for that) is from £24 ($36) per person nightly, and stays of one night are not normally taken, but it's worth a call just in case. Normally guests book in for at least two nights in summer at a half-board cost of £68 ($102) per person. Four downstairs rooms have log-burning stoves, and one bedroom has a four-poster for which there is an extra charge. The house, reached by going down a steep road, is part 17th century and part early Victorian. At night some 20 guests gather around large Victorian tables for a sumptuous cuisine, much of the offerings grown locally on the farm. Food is likely to include duckling à l'orange, beef Wellington en croûte, or trout meunière (the fish comes from the nearby lake).

Pilgrims Rest Restaurant, Battle Village Green, High Street (adjacent to Battle Abbey; tel. 04246/2314), is an early 14th-century, black-and-white timbered house, the preferred place for morning coffee, lunch, or afternoon tea while in town. You'll not only receive good portions of homemade food, but you'll encounter an authentic atmosphere. The set lunch for £6 ($9) includes a choice of appetizers, a main-course choice, and a special English dessert. There is also a light-meal menu where the choice is wide and varied. The restaurant is licensed. You may have your meal in the Long Room, the Great Hall, or in the garden with its view of the ancient stones of Battle Abbey Gate. For afternoon tea you can have a pot of tea, a Sussex cream tea, cakes, or something more substantial. The Pilgrims Rest, with its inglenook fireplace and king-post supported roof, is an interesting example of its age. Hosts are Peter and Heather Randall-Nason. Hours are daily from 10 a.m. to 6 p.m.

The **Gateway Restaurant,** 78 High St. (tel. 04246/2856), offers meals costing from £4 ($6) for a simple lunch to £12 ($18) for a more elaborate meal. The menu is likely to feature such dishes as chicken breasts filled with leeks and Stilton, venison in red wine sauce, or duck in orange sauce. A tea garden is entered by walking through this fully licensed restaurant, which has a good wine list. It is open at 10 a.m. for coffee, closing after the last tea is served at 6 p.m. In mild weather you can sit out on the smooth lawn, smell the roses, and enjoy the view of the abbey across the road. The establishment is open seven days a week in summer; closed Sunday and Monday offseason.

Life at a 15th-Century Farmhouse

Kitchenham Farm, Bodiam, near Robertsbridge (tel. 058085/357), is a 15th-century farmhouse, owned and operated as a farm by Mrs. Daws and her family. Their house is typical of East Sussex: weather boarded, with an interior boasting old beams, a fireplace with an inglenook, and a well-kept garden that grows raspberries, red and black currants, and strawberries. The farm was originally called St. Christopher, because it was a resting place for pilgrims en route to Canterbury from Chichester. The homey farmhouse is comfortable, modestly furnished, with all the necessary amenities. You'll be charged from £11 ($16.50) per person for B&B. Try to call before 6 p.m. Breakfast is prepared farm style, including bacon, grilled tomatoes, freshly laid eggs, and homemade jam. The farm is on the Sussex border, half a mile from Bodiam Castle, built in 1386, the last military castle in Britain. That's only eight miles from Battle Abbey, the same distance from Rudyard Kipling's former home, and just 54 miles from London.

9. Alfriston and Lewes

ALFRISTON: Nestled on the Cuckmere River, Alfriston is one of the most beautiful villages of England. Its High Street, with its old market cross, looks like one's fantasy of what an English village should be. Some of the old houses still have hidden chambers where smugglers stored their loot. Alfriston has several old inns, the best known of which is the Star, now a Trusthouse Forte hotel with its heraldic carvings outside.

During the day, Alfriston is likely to be overrun by coach tours (it's that lovely, but that popular). The village lies about 60 miles from London, northeast of Seaford on the English Channel, in the general vicinity of the resort of Eastbourne and the modern port of Newhaven.

Guesthouses

Deans Barn Guest House (tel. 0323/870274) is at the edge of the village. An 18th-century farmhouse with a white picket fence, it is surrounded by gardens and a lawn shaded by tall trees. The B&B rate is £14 ($21) per person, inclusive of service charge and VAT, in rooms with TV and hot drink facilities. The hosts, Mr. and Mrs. Powell, long-timers in Alfriston, have adapted their spacious and interesting home to the needs of paying guests. They really enjoy sharing their English ways with responsive overseas visitors. ("They are usually so charming, so appreciative of our home. They seem to love our antiques and the old beams and timbers," to quote Mr. Powell). The Powells receive guests from February when the snowdrops and crocuses carpet the lawn until the end of October when the log fire crackles in the hall.

Riverdale Private Hotel, Seaford Road (tel. 0323/870397), is a family-run hotel with chimneys, bays, and gables, on the outskirts of the village, commanding views across the valley to the Downs. The owners, Rosalind and John Kebel, superview everything personally, making for a comfortable stay. Their well-furnished and carpeted bedrooms come with hot and cold running water, shaver sockets, color TV, beverage-making facilities, and some with private baths. Visitors are facinated by the stained-glass front doors. Daily B&B terms are from £17 ($25.50) per person, inclusive of VAT and with a minimum two-night stay required. A good, filling four-course evening meal is available at an extra charge of £6.50 ($9.75). Home-grown fruit and vegetables and fresh eggs are features of the cuisine.

Pleasant Rise Farm (tel. 0323/870545) is an attractive farmhouse on 100 acres of beautiful farmland adjoining an old-world village. Delightful downland views are provided from quiet, comfortable rooms, some with private baths. Indoor and outdoor tennis and badminton courts and country walks add to the pleasure of a stay here. Mr. and Mrs. Savage extend a warm welcome to all guests, and are happy to advise on places to eat, sightseeing, and leisure activities. Bed and a full English breakfast costs £11 ($16.50).

Where to Eat

George Inn, High Street (tel. 0323/870319), was first licensed as an inn in 1397, and in its time it's been a rendezvous for smugglers. Behind a facade with half timbering and stone masonry, this is a long, low, and inviting inn. They serve a three-course dinner for £9.50 ($14.25), one of the best food values in town. If you're there for lunch, you can help yourself to a salad bar at £3.75 ($5.63). Hours are from noon to 2:15 p.m. and 7:30 to 9:30 p.m. A garden is in back but most guests head for the restaurant with its Windsor chairs and beamed ceiling. The hotel also rents out eight pleasantly furnished bedrooms, five of which contain private baths. The B&B rate ranges from £16 ($24) to £28 ($42) per person, depending on the plumbing.

Drusilla's Thatched Barn, Drusilla's Corner (tel. 0323/870234), is an amusing complex, especially for families traveling with children. It's part of an English Wine Centre, containing a small zoo, a souvenir shop, a pottery, and a bakery serving freshly baked goods. From 10:30 a.m. to 5 p.m. (closed in winter), guests can enjoy fresh, healthy food served in a thatched cottage, with beamed ceilings and fireplaces. Here is your chance to sample English wine (an acquired taste in my opinion) but you can order ciders and ales as well. Traditional English cookery is featured (try their Sussex pie with a fresh salad). Meals cost from £5 ($7.50) at this family-run enterprise which has been in business since 1924.

LEWES: An ancient Sussex town, Lewes is worth exploring. Centered in the South Downs, Lewes lies 51 miles from London. Since the home of the Glyndebourne Opera is only five miles to the east, the accommodations of Lewes are often frequented by cultured guests.

The county town has many historical associations, listing such residents as Thomas Paine, who lived at Bull House, High Street, now a restaurant. The half-timbered **Anne of Cleves House,** so named because it formed part of that queen's divorce settlement from Henry VIII, is a Museum of Local History and is cared for by the Sussex Archaeological Society (tel. 0273/474379). Anne of Cleves never lived in the Anne of Cleves House, and there is no proof that she ever visited Lewes. The museum has a furnished bedroom and kitchen and displays of furniture, local history, the Wealden Iron Industry, and other local crafts. It is found on Southover High Street and is open weekdays from mid-February to November from 10 a.m. to 5 p.m.; on Sunday, April to October, from 2 to 5 p.m. Admission is 80p ($1.20) for adults and 55p (83¢) for children.

Lewes Castle is an early Norman construction of the "motte and bailey" type. It is unique in that it has two mottes—one at each end of the bailey or central courtyard. From the keep, you can obtain a fine view of the surrounding countryside. To visit **Lewes Castle and Museum** (tel. 0273/474379), a joint ticket costs adults 85p ($1.28); children, 45p (68¢). The castle is open Monday through Saturday from 10 a.m. to 5 p.m. or dusk throughout the year. It is also open on Sunday, April to October, from 11 a.m. to 5 p.m.

Also in Lewes Castle, you can visit **Lewes Town Modern and Living History Centre,** which has a "son et lumière" of the town and its history, showing every half hour from 10 a.m. to 5 p.m. Admission is 95p ($1.43) for adults, 50p (75¢) for children.

Where to Stay

Accommodations are difficult during the Glyndebourne Opera Festival, but adequate at other times.

Crown Hotel, High Street (tel. 02734/472391), will not please everybody, and it's not grand in any way, but many readers like it. It's a bit creaky, as it's one of the oldest bars in Lewes. Very basic, it is really a Georgian pub hotel, renting out only 10 modest bedrooms, one of which has a private bath. Singles cost £18 ($27), doubles without bath £28 ($42), and doubles with that bath £35 ($52.50). It is run by Brian and Gillian Tolton originally from New Zealand. Opposite the War Memorial, the hotel stands at a traffic circle. Pub lunches are always available, and evening meals can be made up on request.

Felix Gallery, 2 Sun St., Lancaster Street (tel. 0273/472668), is one of the best buys, although it has only two rooms to rent. Completely up-to-date, this inviting and pleasant cottage lies in a tranquil location a short walk from the heart of town and the already-previewed Lewes Castle. The welcome is friendly, and the comfort most adequate for an overnight stay. The rooms have TV and hot-drink facilities. Rates for B&B are reasonable: £10 ($15) to £12 ($18) in the single, depending on the season, and £18 ($27) to £22 ($33) in the twin-bedded room. Guests share the bath. Parking is available.

Where to Dine

The **Bull House,** 92 High St. (tel. 0273/473936), lies at the West Gate in the oldest part of the town. There is a car park opposite. A coaching inn in 1450, a knight's home in the 16th century, the scene of a fight between Cavaliers and Roundheads in the 17th-century English Civil War, the Bull House has had a checkered career. Thomas Paine, who coined the name United States of America, lived here from 1768 to 1774. The restaurant in this historic house specializes in traditional French cuisine, with three fixed-price menus, at £7.95 ($11.93), £10.45 ($15.68), and £13.95 ($20.93). A special Sunday lunch is available for £8.15 ($12.23). Justin Pepper, owner of the Bull House, has employed a French chef, who specializes in such dishes as beef bourguignon, éminicé de saumon marine au citron, and paupiette de turbot aux langoustines. The menus change frequently. Hours are from noon to 2:30 p.m. and 7 to 10:30 p.m. The place is closed for lunch Monday, on Sunday evening, and all day Tuesday.

Mike's, 197 High St. (tel. 0273/477879), is the most youth-oriented place in town, a popular wine bar decorated stylishly and attractively in a café-bistro style, with dark wood chairs and circular tables. Jazz is featured on Sunday evening. Meals, costing from £7 ($10.50), are likely to offer special platters for vegetarians, lasagne verdi, roast beef salad, or chili con carne. Of the desserts none is better than the hot chocolate fudge cake. The Sunday brunch from 11 a.m. to 2:30 p.m. is the most well-attended event in town. It is also open on Sunday night from 7 to 10. Weekdays its hours are from 10 a.m. to 2 p.m. and from 6 to 10:30 p.m.

RODMELL: This small Downland village lies midway between Lewes and the port of Newhaven on the C7 road. The chief claim to fame here is **Monks House** (tel. 0273/472385), a National Trust property which was bought by Virginia and Leonard Woolf in 1919 and was their home until his death in 1969. Virginia wrote of the profusion of fruit and vegetables produced by the garden and of the open water meadows looking out on the downs. Much of the furniture of the house was decorated by Virginia's sister, Vanessa Bell, and the artist, Duncan Grant. The house can be visited from the end of March to the end of October from 2 to 6 p.m. Wednesday and Saturday. Admission is £1.20 ($1.80).

Rodmell also has a 12th-century church, a working farm, and a tiny Victorian village often visited.

In the village, you can stay at a 16th-century thatched cottage, **Deep Thatch,** The Street (tel. 0273/477865), where Ian and Bernadette welcome guests to their white weatherboard home with small leaded windows and hanging baskets of geraniums. The bedrooms, with white walls and dark oak beams, are simply and tastefully furnished, costing £17 ($25.50) per person for B&B. Guests eat in the beamed dining room or the sunny breakfast room opening onto the garden. The lounge has an inglenook fireplace.

THE BLUEBELL RAILWAY: This railway is at Sheffield Park Station, near Uckfield in East Sussex (tel. 082572/2370) on the A275 from Lewes to Danehill. It takes its name from the spring flowers that grow alongside the track, running from Sheffield Park to Horsted Keynes. A railway buff's delight, the steam locomotives date from 1872 with Fenchurch to the 1950s and the end of steam in England. You can visit the locomotive sheds and works, plus a museum and a large buffet and bookshop. There's a carriage shed at Horsted Keynes. The Victorian room on the platform at Horsted Keynes offers refreshments while you wait for your train. The journey from Sheffield Park, climbing out of the Ouse Valley through lovely countryside, takes 15 minutes, costing adults £2.60 ($3.90), and children £1.30 ($1.95). There are several daily services from the end of May to the end of September. In spring and autumn service is restricted mainly to Wednesday and weekends, and in December, January, and February trains operate on Sunday only.

Only eight miles from Lewes is the royal resort of:

10. Brighton

Back in 1753, when Dr. Russell propounded the seawater cure—even to the point of advocating the drinking of an oceanic cocktail—he launched a movement that was to change the life of the average Britisher, at least his or her vacation plans. Brighton, 53 miles south of London, was one of the first of the great seaside resorts of Europe. The village on the sea from which the present town grew was named Brighthelmstone—so of course the English eventually shortened it to Brighton.

The original style-setter who was to shape so much of its destiny arrived in 1783, just turned 21; he was the then Prince of Wales, whose presence and patronage gave status to the seaside town.

Fashionable dandies from London, including Beau Brummell, turned up. The construction business boomed, as Brighton blossomed out with charming and attractive town houses, well-planned squares and crescents. From the Prince Regent's title came the voguish word "Regency," which was to characterize an era, but more specifically refers to the period between 1811 and 1820. Under Victoria—and in spite of her cutting off the patronage of her presence—Brighton continued to flourish.

Alas, in this century, as the English began to discover more glamorous spots on the continent, Brighton lost much of its *joie de vivre*. It became more aptly tabbed as tatty, featuring the usual run of fun-fair-type English seaside amusements ("let's go down to Brighton, ducky"). Happily, the state of affairs has changed, owing largely to the huge numbers of Londoners moving in (some of whom have taken to commuting, as Brighton lies only one hour's—frequent service—train ride from Victoria Station). It's London by the Sea. A beach east of the town has been opened for nude bathing, Britain's first venture into this sport. Introduction of real life attractions of the flesh has certainly made passé such pictorial representations as were once the big draw shown on penny machines by the sea front. These, however, still clank and grind away in a museum, where you can take a trip back in time by means of an old penny purchased at the museum's kiosk.

The Lanes, a closely knit section of alleyways off North Street in Brighton (many of the present shops were formerly fishermen's cottages), were frequented in Victoria's day by style-setting curio and antique collectors. Many are still there, although sharing space with boutiques.

At **Hove,** once a separate town but now a part of the Greater Brighton complex, of special interest is the **Engineerium,** in a building that used to house a waterworks. Here you can see a little steam launch, models of engines and steam trucks, old motorbikes, and the Victorian waterworks kept in operative condition.

Still, the eternal attraction remains—

THE ROYAL PAVILION: Among the royal residences of Europe, the Pavilion at Brighton (tel. 0273/603005), a John Nash version of an Indian mogul's palace, is unique. Ornate and exotic, it has been subjected over the years to the most devastating wit of English satirists and pundits. But today we can examine it more objectively as one of the outstanding examples of the Orientalizing tendencies of the romantic movement in England.

Originally, the Pavilion was built in 1787 by Henry Holland. But it no more resembled its present look than a caterpillar does a butterfly. By the time Nash had transformed it from a simple classical villa into an Oriental fantasy, the Prince Regent had become King George IV. He and one of his mistresses, Lady Conyngham, lived in the place until 1827.

A decade passed before Victoria, then queen, arrived in Brighton. Although she was to bring Albert and the children on a number of occasions, the monarch and Brighton just didn't mix. The very air of the resort seemed too flippant for her, and the latter-day sea-bathing disciples of Dr. Russell trailed Victoria as if she were a stage actress. Further, the chinoiseries of the interior and the mogul domes and cupolas on the exterior didn't set too well with her firm tastes—even though the pavilion would have been a fitting abode for a woman who was to bear the title Empress of India.

By 1845 Victoria and Brighton had had it. She began packing, and the royal furniture was carted off. Its tenants gone, the Pavilion was in serious peril of being torn down. By a narrow vote, Brightonians agreed to purchase it. It is gradually being restored to its former splendor, enhanced in no small part by the return of much of its original furniture on loan by the present tenant at Buckingham Palace.

Of exceptional interest is the domed Banqueting Hall, with a chandelier of bronze dragons supporting lily-like glass globes. Around the room and on the central banqueting table, there is a spectacular collection of silver-gilt and gilt-bronze of the Regency period. In the Great Kitchen, with its old revolving spits, is a collection of Wellington pots and pans, his *batterie de cuisine*, from his town house at Hyde Park Corner. In the State Apartments, particularly the domed Salon, dragons wink at you, serpents entwine, lacquered doors shine. You can walk through the world of crustacean ceilings, silk draperies, lacquered furniture, water-lily chandeliers, gilt dolphins, Chinese mythological figures, and serpents who hold everything up. The newly restored Music Room, with its scalloped ceiling, is a salon of water lilies, flying dragons, sunflowers, reptilian paintings, bamboo, silk, and satin. In the second-floor gallery, look for Nash's views of the Pavilion in its elegant heyday. There is also an exhibition of Pavilion history, illustrating the damage caused by rainwater, frequent alterations, and the impressive program of repair and reclamation in progress. The on-going program may conceal parts of the exterior during your visit as well as causing the temporary closure of certain rooms.

Currently the Royal Pavilion is undergoing an extensive program of structural and decorative restoration. This inevitably results in occasional inconvenience to visitors, although the work is, in its own right, absolutely fascinating. The pavilion is open daily from 10 a.m. to 5 p.m., October to May, and from 10 a.m. to 6 p.m. June to September. It is closed Christmas and Boxing Day. Admission is £2.25 ($3.38) for adults, £1.25 ($1.88) for children.

SEEING BRIGHTON: A walking tour costs 50p (75¢) for adults, 25p (38¢) for children. Tours take place from June to September every Monday at 2:30 p.m., every Tuesday at 10:30 a.m., and every Wednesday at 7:30 p.m. They start from the **Tourist Information Centre**, Marlborough House, 54 Old Steine (tel. 0273/23755), by the Royal Albion Hotel and the bus terminal. You can also get help here if you have accommodations problems.

WHERE TO STAY IN BRIGHTON: Hundreds of accommodations are to be found in all price ranges. I'll give you only a representative sampling in Brighton itself.

The **Adelaide Hotel,** 51 Regency Square (tel. 0273/205286), is a small hostelry in a beautifully restored Regency building which has been tastefully modernized and decorated without losing its early 19th-century ambience that harmonizes with the amenities of today. The owners, Ruth and Clive Buxton, pride themselves on their high standard of housekeeping in the hotel's 11 bedrooms. All the units have complete bathrooms (some with showers), hair dryers, direct-dial phones, color TV, and facilities for making hot beverages. Singles, with breakfast and VAT, cost £24 ($36), with doubles or twins going for £45 ($67.50) and family rooms for three persons for £55 ($82.50). An extra cot is available in a room for £1.50 ($2.25) per night. The Adelaide is in the center of Brighton, just behind the West Pier.

Twenty-One Hotel, 21 Charlotte St., Marine Parade (tel. 0273/686450), is one of the most sophisticated—perhaps the most sophisticated—of the smaller hotels of Brighton, and it also serves some of the best food (some say the best) at the resort. But, regrettably, the dining room isn't open to nonresidents. In other words, to enjoy the full experience of the place you'd better try to get a room here. Stuart Farquharson and Simon Ward rent out only seven bedrooms in this early Victorian white-fronted house a block from the sea. Five of their attractive and well-furnished bedrooms contain a private bath, and all of them offer color TV, direct-dial phone, radio, and coffee-making facilities. Each accommodation has a different color scheme, often in green, pink, or terracotta. The basement level garden suite opens directly onto an ivy-clad courtyard. Singles rent for £25 ($37.50) to £38 ($57), doubles £32 ($48) to £48 ($72), including VAT, breakfast, and service. A menu degustation of five courses, costing £18 ($27), is written in French but translated into English. Main courses are likely to include such subtle dishes as sliced breast of duck served pink with a lime sauce or wild poached salmon with fine strips of vegetables.

Marine House Hotel, 8 Charlotte St., Marine Parade (tel. 0273/605349), is one of the best accommodations in its price range at Brighton. This white-fronted town house sits about a block from the sea, near an interesting collection of antique shops. Built in the Regency Style, it has 11 rooms, eight of which contain showers. Singles (all bathless) rent for £15 ($23) per person, two guests paying £27 ($40.50) with shower, £29 ($43.50) with full bath. Many of the accommodations have high ceilings and elaborate plasterwork. Raji and Syd Jung are the owners, keeping their attractive place open all year. Visitors have free use of the elegant front parlor, and evening meals are available upon request.

Topps Hotel, 17 Regency Square (tel. 0273/729334), enjoys a diagonal view of the sea from its position beside the sloping lawn of Regency Square. Flowerboxes fill the windows of this cream-color town house, whose owners, Paul and Pauline Collins, have devoted years to upgrading it. The establishment contains 12 rooms, some of which have large bathrooms. Each accommodation is of a different shape and is furnished individually, sometimes with neo-Elizabethan pieces and early 19th-century moldings. Each contains a TV, radio, mini-bar, phone, and trousers press. Closed during most of January, the hotel charges £30 ($45) to £42 ($63) in a single and £60 ($90) in a double, with an English breakfast and VAT included. A small restaurant in the basement serves dinners to persons who reserve by noon.

The **Regency Hotel,** 28 Regency Square (tel. 0273/202690), is in a circa 1815 town house with bay windows, a carved door, and a canopied balcony facing south across the square toward the sea. Owners Mr. and Mrs. Simons have extensively renovated the establishment. The ground floor contains a high-ceilinged lounge with period furniture, Waterford chandeliers, and an original coal-burning fireplace. The 14 bedrooms, ten of which have private baths, rent for £20 ($30) to £32 ($48) in a single, £38 ($57) to £53 ($79.50) in a double with service, VAT, and a full English breakfast included. For a romantic splurge, you can reserve the Regency suite, whose canopied bed, private balcony, and formal furniture look like something out of the Royal Pavilion. The higher up you go, the simpler the bedrooms become. An elegant period dining room on the ground floor serves well-prepared meals which you might enjoy after a drink at the in-house bar.

Malvern Hotel, 33 Regency Square (tel. 0273/24302), only a stone's throw from the seafront, is an 1820 Regency building on this attractive square. It's run by Mr. and Mrs. Douglas Foster. He was a former engineer for Westinghouse, living in Kansas City and Pittsburgh. Their rooms are clean and brightly furnished, containing private showers and toilets, color TV, and tea- and coffee-making facilities. Singles rent for £20 ($30) and doubles for £36 ($54). There's a small lounge bar with a residential license.

Rowland House, 21 St. George's Terrace, Kemp Town (tel. 0273/603639), is open all year, has full central heating and units with shower, TV, room call, and courtesy coffee. Run by R. E. Davis and R. W. Smith, it is a well-furnished house of ten bedrooms, located just behind the Royal Crescent in Marine Parade, 250 yards from the beach. No rooms are higher than the second floor. Rates are from £13 ($19.50) for a bed and full English breakfast.

Downlands Hotel, 19 Charlotte St. (tel. 0273/601203), is a well-run small hotel, only a short walk from the Palace Pier and Royal Pavilion. The rooms are comfortably furnished and contain hot and cold running water, plus razor points and electric fires. The B&B rate ranges from £11 ($16.50) per person nightly. The hotel has central heating, and all rooms have TV. Some have private showers. Owners Barry and Betty Green attract many Americans to their pleasant hotel. When writing for a reservation, enclose a deposit of £5 ($7.50).

Lynton House, 14 Charlotte St. (tel. 0273/681854), is one of the better run guesthouses in the center. Set back from the water, it offers comfortable and pleasantly furnished accommodations, with a big breakfast you might expect to be served in the country. The more expensive units contain private showers, but each accommodation has hot and cold running water. The B&B rate ranges from £9.50 ($14.25) to £10.50 ($15.75) in a single and from £19 ($28.50) to £23 ($34.50) in a double.

Ascott House, 21 New Steine, Marine Parade (tel. 0273/688085), has sheltered many a satisfied reader. Personally run, it enjoys a heartbeat location, within a short walk of the Royal Pavilion. You'll also be near the pier and the famous Lanes, with their antique shops and boutiques. All the bedrooms have color TV, hot and cold running water, and central, and some contain private showers or full baths. Michael and Avril Strom charge from £11.50 ($17.25) to £12.50 ($18.75) in singles, from £20 ($30) to £30 ($45) in doubles and family rooms. All of the front bedrooms have a sea view.

Trouville Private Hotel, 11 New Steine, Marine Parade (tel. 0273/697384), offers rooms that are nicely furnished, bright, cheerful, and clean. Showers and bathrooms are also large and well kept. The proprietors are helpful, and their food is good. For a double room and breakfast, their charge is from £19 ($28.50) nightly. Most rooms have color TV, and four doubles have private showers.

DINING OUT IN BRIGHTON: Outside of London, in the south of England you'll find the best food, the widest choice of restaurants, in the resort of Brighton. New restaurants of widely varying cuisine and standards are popping up all the time, and the foreign invasion isn't confined solely to Chinese and Indian. My sampling represents the best of the budget eating establishments.

Trogs, 125 King's Rd. (tel. 0273/26302), is a charming restaurant in the semi-basement of the Granville Hotel and under the same ownership. Its name is short for *troglodytes* (cave dwellers), but the little bistro-style eating place is far from cave-like, being a sunny place with a continental patio overlooking the sea. Under an arched ceiling, bentwood chairs and potted palms against rough plaster walls provide a pleasing ambience in which to enjoy the French cuisine. Some dishes depend for their ingredients on the best produce found in the market that day. A fixed-price, three-course lunch costs £8.95 ($13.43), including VAT, and might offer such food as crêpes filled with cream mushrooms (for vegetarians) or lamb noisette gingered and grilled. A three-course dinner, costing £12.95 ($19.43), plus service, might include crudités and garlic dip, pâté, porc en croûte (filet of pork stuffed with pâté, wrapped in a puff pastry, and baked), and a dessert or cheeseboard selection. À la carte meals cost from £13 ($19.50) up. Lunch is served from noon to 2:30 p.m. and dinner from 7 to 10:30 p.m.

Browns Restaurant and Coffee House, 3–4 Duke St. (tel. 0273/23501), is a rather 1930s place with plain tables and hoop-backed chairs. Dishes have interesting accompaniments. For example, spaghetti dishes are served with hot garlic bread and a salad; pies, including steak, mushroom, and Guinness, come with baked potatoes rather than the ubiquitous chips. American sandwiches are featured as well, along with spare ribs, chili, stuffed trout, and invariably a special of the day such as braised oxtail or game in season. Salads and grills make up a small but tasty menu. Followed by thick, dark-chocolate cake and coffee, a meal will cost around £8 ($12). The place is open from 11 a.m. to 11 p.m. Monday to Saturday, from noon to 11:30 p.m. on Sunday.

Ceres Health Food Restaurant, 23 Market St. (tel. 0273/27187), may give you a "raw deal," but you'll love it. For those who like naturalism, it's unbeatable. Everywhere, the good basic value of the unadorned dominates, such as the natural pine settles, tables, and stools, or the simple hanging basket lamps. Food is served in handmade pottery. On the walls are Japanese paintings and prints. You help yourself, selecting from such offerings as freshly made soup or a fruit salad. The most imaginative entrees are the freshly made flans and salads. Meals cost from £6 ($9). It is also licensed to sell wine. The Ceres is open all day, serving coffee from 9:30 to 11:45 a.m.; luncheon, 11:45 a.m. to 3 p.m.; high tea from 3 to 5:30 p.m.

The **Market Wine House,** 20 Market St. (tel. 0273/23829), is a wine bar and restaurant, featuring soups, salads, steaks, cheeses, and continental dishes. Housed in a black-and-white Regency building in the center of a boutique district, the wine house, the oldest in Brighton, will serve you a whole plaice on the bone. The seafood platter is popular as well. Various chicken dishes, such as Kiev, are featured also. Pietro Addis owns and runs the establishment. He offers a three-course meal of, say, chilled melon or avocado with prawns, plus a choice of plaice, steak, and chicken with vegetables and potatoes, dessert, and coffee, for about £5.90 ($88.50). The decor of the cellar bar consists of natural wood booths, stacks of french bread, barrels of sherry, and candlelight—not to mention the talented instrumentalists and singers who entertain by flickering candlelight in the evening. The Market Wine House is open from noon to 2:15 p.m. and again from 6 to 10:30 p.m., seven days a week.

Nanking, 21 Market St. (tel. 0273/29404), is one of the best of the budget Chinese restaurants in Brighton. Right in the shopping district, it offers a three-course luncheon for £3 ($4.50). A choice of six dishes, different each day, is featured. In the evening, two people can order a dinner for £10 ($15), comprising chicken and mushrooms, pork with mixed vegetables, sweet-and-sour king prawn balls, cashew nuts with pork, and boiled rice. The Nanking, established for more than 30 years, also lists a number of tempting dishes on its à la carte menus. The fully licensed restaurant has a fine selection of European, Chinese, and Japanese wines. It is open from noon to midnight seven days a week.

Allanjohn's, 8 Church St. (tel. 0273/683087), is not a fish 'n' chips shop but a fascinating display of winkles, cockles, shrimp, crab, and lobster fresh from the sea to be eaten with brown bread and butter, salt, and vinegar. You can select a well-filled bowl of fresh crabmeat or a seafood plate with a salad. If you're lunching light, a smoked salmon sandwich will be prepared or perhaps a crab sandwich. Lobster and crab are only available in season. Hot food includes jumbo scampi, Chesapeake oysters, butterfly prawns, and shrimp royale, all served with salad and french fries. Meals cost from £2.50 ($3.75) up. John and Jackie Haslem, the hosts, keep the place open Monday to Thursday from 10 a.m. to 5:30 p.m., Friday from 9:30 a.m. to 6 p.m., Saturday from 9 a.m. to 6 p.m., and Sunday from 10:30 a.m. to 3 p.m.

STAYING AT HOVE: It may be small, but **Chatsworth Private Hotel,** 9 Salisbury Rd. (tel. 0273/737360), meets the tests of cleanliness, good food, sleep-producing beds, and a comfortable lounge with television—not to mention the Swiss-style personal services of Francis Gerber. The B&B rate is from £11 ($16.50) per person nightly. The bedrooms are large and suitably furnished, and there's a bathroom and toilet on every floor.

The **Albany Hotel,** corner of St. Catherine's Terrace and Albany Villas (tel. 0273/773807), is a small hotel on the Hove seafront on level ground, one mile from Brighton's West Pier, with a sea view from the lounge/diner and the front bedrooms. The King Alfred sports and entertainment complex is nearby. Bedrooms are on the ground, first, and second floors, and there is no elevator. The hotel contains central heating throughout, as well as a lounge with color television. All bedrooms have color TV, coffee-making facilities, and private showers or baths. The price per person, daily, including breakfast is £12.50 ($18.75), based on double occupancy. The resident proprietors are Mr. and Mrs. C. C. Wardle.

ST. MARY'S AT BRAMBER: A fine half-timbered house, St. Mary's (tel. 0903/816205), in the ancient village of Bramber, 10 miles northwest of Brighton, has been brought back to its original splendor through the work of the owner, Peter Thorogood, a musician, composer, and retired lecturer, and his curator, Roger Linton, a fine arts teacher at Brighton College. Former owners had made the historic house into a butterfly museum, with many of the beauties of the place obscured by dark paint and alterations, all of which Thorogood had to get rid of in order to restore the handsome interiors.

The foundations of St. Mary's go back to the 12th century when land at Bramber was granted to the Knights Templar. The present house was refashioned around 1470 by William of Waynflete, Bishop of Winchester, founder of Magdalen College at Oxford. This is classified as "the best example of late 15th-century timber-framing in Sussex." Fine paneled rooms include the unique "Painted Room," decorated for the visit of Elizabeth I. The "King's Room" has connections with Charles II's escape to France in 1651. Rare 16th-century painted wall-leather, carved fireplaces in wood and stone, English furniture, ceramics, pictures, and manuscripts enrich the house. The library contains the largest collection in existence of first editions and illustrated books by the celebrated 19th-century comic poet and artist, Thomas Hood. In the past century, during the ownership of Albert Musgrave, St. Mary's was the inspiration for the Sherlock Holmes story, *The Musgrave Ritual.* Morning coffee and afternoon tea are served in the Victorian Music Room. St. Mary's is open from early April to late October from 10 a.m. to 6 p.m. on Sunday, from 2 to 6 p.m. Monday and Thursday, and from 10 a.m. to 6 p.m. on bank holiday Monday. Admission is £1.50 ($2.25) for adults, £1 ($1.50) for children.

11. Arundel

This small and beautiful town in West Sussex, only 58 miles from London, four miles from the English Channel, nestles at the foot of one of England's most spectacular castles. The town was once an Arun River port, its denizens enjoying the prosperity of considerable trade and commerce. The harbor traffic is gone, replaced by coaches filled with visitors who come in summer to hike through the vastness of—

ARUNDEL CASTLE: The seat of the present Duke of Norfolk, this baronial estate is a much-restored mansion of considerable importance. Its legend is associated with some of the greatest families of England, the Fitzalans and the powerful Howards of Norfolk. But Arundel Castle traces its history back to King Alfred, while its keep goes back to the days before the Norman landing at Hastings.

Over the years Arundel Castle suffered destruction, particularly during the Civil War when Cromwell's troops stormed its walls, perhaps in retaliation for the 14th Earl of Arundel's (Thomas Howard) sizable contribution to the aid of the faltering king. In the early 18th century the castle virtually had to be rebuilt. In late Victorian times it was remodeled and extensively restored again. Today it is filled, as you'd expect, with a good collection of antiques, along with an assortment of paintings by old masters such as Van Dyck and Reynolds.

The castle is open April to October, Sunday to Friday, from 1 to 5 p.m. From June to August and bank holidays, it is open daily from noon to 5 p.m. For full details, get in touch with the Comptroller, Arundel Castle Trustees Limited, Arundel Castle, West Sussex, BN189AB (tel. 0903/883136). Admission is £2.60 ($3.90) for adults, £1.60 ($2.40) for children 5 to 15. Surrounding the castle is an 1,100-acre park (scenic highlight: Swanbourne Lake).

OTHER SIGHTS: A delightful and intriguing family collection is in the **Arundel Toy and Military Museum** at "Doll's House," 23 High St. (tel. 0903/88310), with displays spanning many generations of old toys and games, small militaria, dolls, doll-houses, tin toys, musical toys, Britain's animals and soldiers, arks, boats, rocking horses, and crested military models. Housed in a Georgian cottage in the heart of historic Arundel, it is open most days from Easter to October (winter, weekends only), or it may be seen at any time by arrangement. Admission is 75p ($1.13) for adults, 50p (75¢) for children. The museum is opposite Treasure House Antiques Market.

Arundel Cathedral (the Cathedral of Our Lady and St. Philip Howard), London Road (tel. 0903/882297), stands at the highest point in town. A Roman Catholic cathedral, it was constructed for the 15th Duke of Norfolk by A.J. Hansom, who invented the Hansom taxi. However, it was not consecrated as a cathedral until 1965. The interior includes the shrine of St. Philip Howard, featuring Sussex wrought ironwork. Admission free, it is open from 9 a.m. to 6 p.m. (closes at dusk in winter). Donations are appreciated.

WHERE TO STAY: The best of the small hotels in town, **Dukes,** High Street (tel. 0903/883847), is big on amenities, charm, and character. Mike and Valerie Moore are the guiding light behind this little gem of a place, with six elegantly decorated rooms in the main building and two additional units in a Victorian cottage in the rear garden. Most of the accommodations have a TV, coffee-making facilities, and sleekly modern baths, while a few still retain their Regency detailing and ornate plasterwork. Depending on the plumbing, singles range from £20 ($30) to £30 ($45), doubles £15 ($22.50) to £23 ($34.50) per person, with VAT and a full English breakfast included. The location is across a busy street from the crenellated fortifications surrounding the castle. The hotel's street-level restaurant is recommended separately.

Dating from the 17th century, **Arundel House,** 11 High St. (tel. 0903/882136), is a guesthouse and licensed restaurant. Only seconds away from the castle entrance, it offers clean, comfortable rooms costing from £12 ($18) nightly per person, including a full English breakfast. John and Christine Crowe are the resident owners. The house is open from 11 a.m. to 7 p.m. for morning coffee, hot meals, afternoon tea, and Sussex cream teas. A ham radio station (G4NHU) is available for persons with licenses.

The **Swan Hotel,** High Street (tel. 0903/882314), a Georgian inn on the River Arun, provides one of the best moderately priced accommodations in Arundel. Ken and Diana Rowsell offer pleasant, comfortably furnished bedrooms, all with bath or shower, color TV, and equipment for making hot drinks. Most of the rooms are twins or doubles. The charge for a double with full English breakfast is £30 ($45); £25 ($37.50) for single occupancy. You can enjoy drinks and bar snacks in the open bar space, with comfortable seats, in a warm atmosphere enhanced by pleasant background music. The restaurant serves meals with the freshest of ingredients, and the service is polite and attentive. A fixed-price dinner is offered at £5 ($7.50).

The Arden, 4 Queens Lane (tel. 0903/882544), has a few comfortably furnished rooms, some with private baths and all with hot and cold running water, color TV, and facilities for making hot drinks. Morag McCoubrey, the manager, is polite and considerate, charging B&B rates that range from £10 ($15) per person in a bathless room to £12 ($18) in a room with bath. A full English breakfast is served.

Portreeves Acre, Causeway (tel. 0903/883277). When this modern two-story house was built by a local architect within a stone's throw of the ancient castle, it caused much local comment. Today the glass-and-brick edifice is the property of Charles and Pat Rogers. The five guest rooms, all with TV, are on the ground floor, which opens onto a view of the flowering acre in back. The property's boundary is bordered on one side by the River Arun, near which rabbits and flowering trees flourish. Each of the pleasant accommodations contain a private bath. The Rogerses charge £12 ($18) per person for B&B in low season, £16 ($24) in high.

WHERE TO EAT: Already recommended as a hotel, **Dukes,** High Street (tel. 0903/883847), is also one of the leading restaurant choices. Valerie and Michael Moore, the owners, invite guests into their elegant dining room on the street level. It is noted for its 17th-century ceiling, which was originally from a baroque Italian palace. Part of this ceiling was once installed in the home of Douglas Fairbanks Jr. The ceiling is in gilt-carved walnut. Dinner is served Sunday to Thursday from 6 to 9 p.m., until 10 p.m. on Friday and Saturday. The restaurant is closed on Sunday and Monday in low season. Specialties include steak au poivre, trout with almonds, and sole meunière. À la carte meals range from £7 ($10.50) to £12 ($18) per person.

If you're just passing through, and are a bit rushed, **Partners,** High Street (tel. 0903/883847), may satisfy your needs. It is a sandwich bar and simple restaurant with a take-away service, lying across from the Swan Hotel. It does "freshly cut" sandwiches and light lunches. It also offers a selection of fresh salads. Light meals can be made up for £3 ($4.50). Service is daily from 9 a.m. to 6 p.m. May to October (closes at 5 p.m. otherwise).

On the Outskirts

George & Dragon, Houghton, about 3 miles north of Arundel (you turn off the A284 at Bury Hill onto the B2139) (tel. 079881/559), is an old English pub known for excellent food. In 1651, Charles II, fleeing Cromwell's wrath after being crowned king at Scone in Scotland, stopped at the George & Dragon for food and drink before escaping to France. (He returned in 1660, after the death of Cromwell, to take the throne.) Originally a farmhouse, the inn is made up of two timber and flint cottages dating from the 13th century, with huge inglenook fireplaces and a shared chimney. An ancient spit in one of them was once used for preparing the roast joints of which the English are so fond. In winter, log fires blaze, making the pub toasty warm. The main bar and smaller apéritif bar, both with tapestry-covered seating and beamed ceilings, overlook the restaurant, where the cows dined back in the 17th century. Lunch is served from noon to 2 p.m. when pub dishes are offered. Dinner, with a more ambitious menu, is from 7 to 10 p.m. Meals cost from £5 ($7.50) to £8.50 ($12.75). In summer, you can eat in the pleasant garden or on the terrace.

12. Chichester

According to one newspaper, Chichester might have been just a market town if the Chichester Festival Theatre had not been established in its midst. One of the oldest

Roman cities in England, Chichester is in vogue, drawing a chic crowd from all over the world who come to see its presentations.

Only a five-minute walk from Chichester Cathedral and the old Market Cross, the 1,400-seat theater with its apron stage stands on the edge of Oaklands Park. It opened in 1962 (first director: Lord Laurence Olivier), and its reputation has grown steadily, pumping new vigor and life into the former walled city. The Chichester theater has given fresh stimulus to the living theater in England.

THE FESTIVAL THEATER: Booking generally opens in the beginning of March, and the season starts in April or May (it continues until late September). The price range is from £2.50 ($3.75) for an unreserved seat bought at the time of the performance up to £4.50 ($6.75) for the cheapest reserved seat. The best seats cost about £11 ($16.50). Reservations made over the telephone will be held for a maximum of four days (call 0243/781312). It's better to mail inquiries and checks to the box office, **Chichester Festival Theatre,** Oaklands Park, Chichester. Matinee performances on Thursday and Saturday begin at 2:30 p.m., evening shows at 7:30 p.m.

To reach Chichester from London by rail takes about an hour and 40 minutes, with trains departing Victoria Station about 20 minutes past each hour, Monday to Saturday only (from 8:20 a.m. to 10.20 p.m.).

WHERE TO STAY: Representing the successful joining of two 18th-century town houses, **Clinchs Hotel** is on Guildhall Street (tel. 0243/789915). The hotel, managed by Nick Clinch, is set on a quiet street between some of the city's main pedestrian malls. Only seven bedrooms, each with its own small bath, are contained within this engagingly decorated town house close to the Festival Theatre. The lounge contains its own bar, while each of the bedrooms offers such extras as a wall safe, mini-bar, and quilts. Singles cost £40 ($60) a night, doubles £55 ($82.50), with a continental breakfast included. Long before her successful venture into TV soaps, Joan Collins spent significant time at this hotel while working in live theater in Chichester. The hotel also operates a coffeeshop serving tea, coffee, and light meals all day.

The **Bedford Hotel,** Southgate (tel. 0243/785766), is a 28-bedroom hotel tracing its origins to the 18th century. It has been considerably modernized and improved by Mr. and Mrs. David Winship, owners. It offers comfortable and quiet rooms, along with personalized service. Accommodations contain color TV and hot and cold running water, and some also have private showers and toilets. The charge of from £17 ($25.50) to £20 ($30) per person nightly also includes a full English breakfast. In summer advance reservations are strongly advised. One of the best all-around budget accommodations in Chichester.

Rawmere, Rew Lane, Summersdale (tel. 0243/527152), stands about a mile from the heart of the city. On the northern periphery of Chichester, it enjoys a tranquil and bucolic setting. Nonsmokers only are welcome, housed in pleasantly furnished accommodations. The rate ranges from £10 ($15) in a single and from £20 ($30) to £22 ($33) in a double, including a full English breakfast. The higher price is for a room with private bath.

WHERE TO EAT: Snacks and light meals are served at the **Roussillon Coffee Shop,** Dolphin & Anchor, West Street (tel. 0243/785121), from 10 a.m. to 10 p.m. daily. Those on the sightseeing run might settle happily for a cheese and bacon burger, although fish dishes and sirloin steak (ten ounces uncooked weight, served with french fries) are also featured. A complete hot meal is likely to cost from £8 ($12). Children under 14 may choose from the main menu at half price.

Noble Rot Brasserie and Wine, Little London, off East Street (tel. 0243/779922). Three cellars were converted to two eating areas, and very quickly this has become one of the most popular eating and drinking establishments in town. David Hickman and D.G. Hudson plastered the walls with posters of famous theater productions, and their wine bar and brasserie is the best-known place for after-theater dinners. Dinners, costing from £12 ($18), might include such appetizers as lobster bisque, then follow with roast duck in orange sauce, sirloin chasseur, or veal marsala. Everything is prepared with continental flair. Otherwise, you can visit for lunch, ordering meals with such fare as pizzas, burgers, and salads at a cost of £5 ($7.50). Hours are from noon to 2:30 p.m. daily and 6:30 to 11 p.m. Descend a flight of exterior steps from the street to the vaulted cellar.

Nicodemus, 14 Eastgate Square (tel. 0243/787521), near the cattle market, offers the best Italian cuisine in Chichester, and it's very reasonable in price, with meals costing from £10 ($15). To reach it, walk to the end of East Street to a roundabout. The atmosphere, especially during a candlelit evening, is often lively and bustling in the best trattoria tradition. Service is efficient and friendly. You might begin with a selection of antipasti, perhaps prosciutto with melon. You can then order various kinds of pasta with savory sauces or else three kinds of pizza. More substantial fare is offered as well, including a mixed fish casserole or brasato al barolo (beef casserole in red wine and mushroom sauce). Hours are from noon to 2 p.m. and from 7 to 10:30 p.m. (closes at 10 p.m. off-season). It is also closed for Monday lunch and all day Sunday.

On the Outskirts

The Hunters Inn, Lavant (tel. 0243/527329), dates back to the early 16th century, and its present facade was added in the 18th century by the Duke of Richmond. In the 1940s it was the center for the Goodwood motor-racing fraternity, and now with extensive modernization is an inn where you can find pleasant rooms and excellent meals, featuring fresh fish dishes. It's just two miles north of Chichester and, although on the roadway, its side and rear gardens have many old trees and flowering shrubbery. Another acre provides fruit and vegetables for the kitchen. The bedrooms overlook the garden, and are nicely appointed with hot and cold running water (most of them have private bath and TV), and the charge per person, including VAT, service, and a complete bacon-and-egg breakfast, is £22 ($33) per person.

The chef and patron, Allan Hope-Kirk, has two restaurants, a small à la carte dining room with an English and French cuisine, and the "Light Bite" bar, serving everything from sandwiches to steaks at reasonable prices, but still with waiter service. The bars, both the public bar and the lounge bar, serve no fewer than 40 different beers and lagers, including real ale, along with wines and such staples as scotch and bourbon. In winter an open fireplace provides cheer and warmth. Food service is available during regular hours.

WEALD AND DOWNLAND OPEN AIR MUSEUM: This museum stands on a 40-acre site at Singleton, six miles north of the cathedral city of Chichester on the A286 (London road). In a beautiful downland setting, rescued historic buildings dating from the Middle Ages to the 19th century are being reassembled. The museum is open every day from 11 a.m. to 5 p.m., April 1 to October 31. Admission for adults is £2 ($3). Children and students pay £1.10 ($1.65). Still developing, the museum shows the history of traditional buildings in southeast England. Exhibits include a Tudor market hall; timber-framed medieval houses dating from the 14th to the 16th centuries with wattle-and-daub walls; a working watermill producing stone-ground flour; a blacksmith's forge; plumbers' and carpenters' workshops; a toll cottage; a 17th-century treadwheel; agricultural buildings, including thatched barns and an 18th-century granary; a charcoal burner's camp; and a 19th-century village school. For further information, telephone 0243/63348.

FISHBOURNE: A trip well worth the taking and just a few miles away from

Chichester is to the largest Roman palace yet discovered. It's called the **Fishbourne Roman Palace and Museum,** Salthill Road (tel. 0243/785859). Built in A.D. 75, it is architecturally pure Italian, and you will be amazed to discover it has an underground heating system. Mosaic floors survive, and the first-century garden has been re-planted. There is good parking and a cafeteria on the premises that serves coffee and sandwiches. Admission is £1.30 ($1.95) for adults, 60p (90¢) for children.

OLD BOSHAM: A few miles west from Fishbourne is Bosham, one of the most charming villages in West Sussex. It was the site of the first establishment of Christianity on the Sussex coast. The Danish King Canute made it one of the seats of his North Sea empire, and it was the site of a manor (now gone) of the last of England's Saxon kings, Harold, who sailed from here to France on a journey which finally culminated in the invasion of England by William the Conqueror in 1066. Bosham's little church was depicted in the Bayeux tapestry. Near the harbor, it is reached by a narrow lane. Its graveyard overlooks the boats. A daughter of King Canute is buried inside. The church is filled with ship models and relics, showing the villagers' link to the sea. Bosham is principally a sailing resort, linked by good bus service to Chichester.

HAMPSHIRE AND DORSET

STONE FARMHOUSES—conjuring up images of Burke's *Landed Gentry*—all this belongs to the countryside of the 17th century: fireplaces where stacks of logs burn gaily; wicker baskets of apples freshly brought in from the orchard (ever had home-made apple butter?); chickens stuffed with dressing and roasted with strips of bacon on top to keep them tender and juicy; milk that doesn't come from bottles; and mellowed village houses, now run as hotels. Beyond the pear trees, on the crest of a hill, are the ruins of a Roman camp. And a village pub, with two rows of kegs filled with varieties of cider, is where the hunt gathers.

You're in Hampshire and Dorset, two shires guarded zealously by the English, who protect their special rural treasures. Everybody knows of Southampton and Bournemouth (Dorset), but less known is the undulating countryside lying inland. Your car will take you through endless lanes, revealing tiny villages and thatched cottages—untouched by the industrial invasion.

HAMPSHIRE

This is Jane Austen country—firmly middle class, largely agricultural, its inhabitants doggedly convinced that Hampshire is the greatest spot on earth. The English writer left six novels of manners, including *Pride and Prejudice* and *Sense and Sensibility*, that earned her a room at the top among 19th-century English novelists. Her books provided a keen insight into the solid middle-class English who were to build such a powerful empire. Although the details of the life she described have now largely faded ("at five o'clock the two ladies retired to dress, and at half-past six Elizabeth was summoned to dinner"), much of the mood and spirit of Hampshire depicted in her books remains.

Born in 1775, Miss Austen was the daughter of the Oxford-educated rector, the Reverend Mr. George Austen, a typical Hampshire country gentleman, who had much charm but little money. In keeping with a custom of the time, the Austens gave their second son, Edward, to a wealthy, childless family connection, Thomas Knight, whose heir the young man became. It was Edward who gave to his mother and sisters **Chawton Cottage**, near Alton (tel. 0420/83263), where visitors can see the surroundings in which the novelist of manners spent the last 7½ years of her life, her period of greatest creation. In the unpretentious but pleasant cottage, you can see the table on which Jane Austen penned new versions of three of her books and wrote three more, including *Emma* (her "handsome, clever, and rich" heroine, Emma Woodhouse). You can also see the rector's George III mahogany bookcase and a silhouette likeness of the Reverend Austen presenting his son to the Knights. It was in this cottage that Jane Austen became ill in 1817 of what would have been diagnosed by the middle of the 19th century as Addison's disease.

There is an attractive garden in which visitors are invited to have picnics and an old bakehouse with Miss Austen's donkey cart. About a mile and three-quarters from the station (take bus 214), the home is open daily including Sunday from 11 a.m. to 4:30 p.m. April to October. Admission is 85p ($1.38) for adults, 35p (53¢) for children under 14. It is closed Monday and Tuesday in November, December, and March. In January and February it is open only on Saturday and Sunday. Closed Christmas Day and Boxing Day.

Hampshire embraces the **New Forest** (don't expect anything in England labeled "new" to be new), the **South Downs,** the **Isle of Wight** (Victoria's favorite retreat), the passenger port and gateway city of **Southampton,** and the naval city of **Portsmouth.**

Going west from Southampton, you'll come to the New Forest, more than 90,000 acres selfishly preserved by William the Conqueror as a private hunting ground (poachers met with the death penalty). William lost two of his sons in the New Forest, one killed by an animal, the other by an arrow. Today it is a vast and unspoiled woodland and heath ideal for walking and exploring.

STOPS ON THE WAY: For those driving down to Winchester and the New Forest, there is a good lunch stop at **Selborne.** After traveling the A31 from London to Chawton to see Jane Austen's home, take the signposted B3006 to Selborne, five miles away.

"The Wakes," home of the Reverend Mr. Gilbert White, where his classic book, *The Natural History of Selborne* (1789), was written, is now open as the **Oates Memorial Library and Museum** and the **Gilbert White Museum** in Selborne (tel. 042050/275). You can see the historic house and five acres of garden. Inside, two furnished rooms and displays on Gilbert White trace the history and natural history of Selborne. Upstairs is the Oates museum with exhibits relating to the travels of the 19th-century naturalist, Frank Oates, in Central America (1872) and Africa (1873–1875), and of Capt. Lawrence Oates who was on Scott's last, ill-fated expedition to the South Pole. The house is open daily except Monday from noon to 5:30 p.m. March to October (last entrance at 5 p.m.). Admission is £1 ($1.50) for adults, 50p (75¢) for children.

At the **Queens Hotel** (tel. 042050/272), you can order either a pub luncheon of

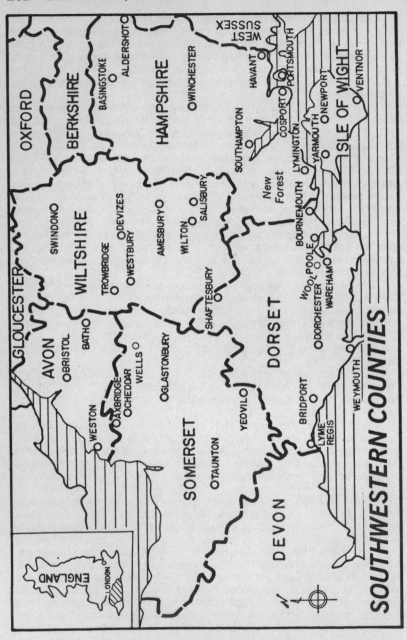

SOUTHWESTERN COUNTIES

homemade soup, Queensburger, and Welsh rarebit for £2.20 ($3.30), or eat in the fantastically decorated dining room under a canopy of brass jugs, bits of farm equipment, corn cobs, and God-whattery, hanging from old oak beams. The owner, David Paton, ladles out the special Peggy Paton's homemade soup (his mother's recipe) and large portions of freshly roasted beef with all the trimmings. That means Yorkshire pudding, roast potatoes, and properly cooked cabbage—just *al dente* with a little butter and some pepper. On other days there is lamb with mint sauce and red currant jelly. Desserts are homemade—fruit pies and cream, trifles, or a good cheeseboard with bread or crackers. Wines can be ordered by the glass, and peppermints and book matches are handed out with the coffee and the bill—which, including VAT, comes to around £5.50 ($8.25) per person.

The hotel is open for lunch from 12:30 to 1:45 p.m. and for dinner from 7:30 to 8:45 p.m. Mr. Paton also sells candy, fudge, chocolates, and honey, plus other local goodies. If you're not too stuffed to drive after dining here, Winchester is not too far away. Retrace your steps to the A31.

If you'd like to stay over, B&B terms in a double range from £24 ($36) to £29 ($43.50) a night, the latter for units with private bath or shower.

1. Portsmouth and Southsea

Virginia, New Hampshire, and Ohio may have their Portsmouths, but the daddy of them all is the old port and naval base on the Hampshire coast, about 70 miles south of London. German bombers in World War II virtually leveled the city, destroying or hitting about nine-tenths of its buildings. But the seaport has recovered admirably.

Its maritime associations are famous. From Sally Port, the most interesting district of the Old Town, "naval heroes innumerable have embarked to fight their country's battles." That was certainly true on June 6, 1944, when Allied troops set forth to invade occupied France.

Southsea, adjoining Portsmouth, is a popular seaside resort with fine sands, beautiful gardens, bright lights, and a host of holiday attractions. Many historic monuments can be seen along the stretches of open space where you can walk on the Clarence Esplanade and look out on the Solent, viewing the busy shipping activities of Portsmouth harbor.

THE SIGHTS: Some 400 years before D-Day, an English navy ship didn't fare as well. The *Mary Rose,* flagship of the fleet of wooden men-o'-war of King Henry VIII, sank in the Solent in 1545 in full view of the king. In 1982 a descendant of that monarch, and heir to the throne, Charles, Prince of Wales, watched the *Mary Rose* break the water's surface after almost four centuries spent lying on the sea bottom, not exactly shipshape and Bristol fashion but surprisingly well preserved nonetheless. Now the remains are on view, but the hull must be kept permanently wet. The hull and the more than 10,000 discoveries brought up by the divers constitute one of the major archeological discoveries of England in many years. Among the artifacts on permanent exhibit are almost the complete equipment of the ship's barber, with surgeon's cabin saws, knives, ointments, and plaster all ready for use; long bows and arrows, some still in shooting order; carpenters' tools; leather jackets; and some fine lace and silk. Close beside the dock where the hull lies is the *Mary Rose* Exhibition in Boathouse No. 5. The artifacts rescued from the ship are stored there. It contains an audio-visual theater and a spectacular two-deck reconstruction of a segment of the ship, including the original guns. A display with sound effects recalls the sinking of the vessel.

To see the *Mary Rose* Ship Hall and Exhibition, use the entrance to the Portsmouth Naval Base through the Victory Gate (as for H.M.S. *Victory),* and follow the signs. It is open every day from 10:30 a.m. to 5:30 p.m. (closed Christmas Day). Admission is £2.60 ($3.75) for adults, £1.50 ($2.25) for children, and £6.50 ($9.75) for a family ticket. The administrative offices of the *Mary Rose* Trust are at Old Bond Store, 48 Warblington St. (tel. 0705/750521).

Of major interest is Lord Nelson's flagship, H.M.S. *Victory,* a 104-gun, first-rate ship of the line, now at No. 2 Dry Dock in Portsmouth (tel. 0705/826682). She is Great Britain's foremost maritime monument. Although she first saw action in 1778, her fame was earned on October 21, 1805, in the Battle of Trafalgar when the British destroyed the combined Spanish and French fleets. It was in this battle that Lord Nelson lost his life. The flagship, after being taken to Gibraltar for repairs, returned to Portsmouth with Nelson's body on board (he was later buried at St. Paul's in London). It is open March to October, weekdays from 10:30 a.m. to 5:30 p.m., on Sunday from 1 to 5 p.m. From November to February, weekdays, hours are 10:30 a.m. to 4:30 p.m., on Sunday from 1 to 4:30 p.m. Admission is £1.80 ($2.70) for adults, £1 ($1.50) for children.

Portsmouth was the birthplace of Charles Dickens, and the small terrace house dated 1805 in which the future famous novelist made his appearance in the world on February 7, 1812, and lived for a short time, was restored and furnished to illustrate the middle-class taste of the early 19th century. Called the **Charles Dickens' Birthplace Museum,** it is at 393 Old Commercial Rd., Mile End (tel. 0705/827261). It is open daily from 10:30 a.m. to 5:30 p.m. (closed November to the end of February). Admission is 50p (75¢) for adults, 25p (38¢) for children. Family tickets (four persons) are available for £1.25 ($1.88). Last tickets are sold at 5 p.m.

The **Royal Naval Museum** (tel. 0705/822351) stands next to Nelson's flagship, H.M.S. *Victory,* and the *Mary Rose* in the heart of Portsmouth's historic naval dockyard. The only museum in Britain devoted exclusively to the general history of the Royal Navy, it contains relics of Nelson and his associates, together with unique collections of ship models, naval ceramics, figureheads, medals, uniforms, weapons, and other naval memorabilia. Special displays include the Victorian navy; the *Dreadnought, Polaris,* and the modern navy.

The museum is open daily from 10:30 a.m. to 5 p.m. (with some seasonal variations). An admission charge of 50p (75¢) for adults, 25p (38¢) for children is levied. There is a buffet and a souvenir shop in the museum complex.

On the Southsea front, you can see a number of naval monuments, including the big anchor from Nelson's ship, *Victory,* a commemoration of the officers and men of H.M.S. *Shannon* for heroism in the Indian Mutiny, an obelisk with a naval crown in memory of the crew of H.M.S. *Chesapeake,* and a massive column, the Royal Naval memorial honoring those lost at sea in the two World Wars, as well as a shaft dedicated to men killed in the Crimean War. There are also commemorations of persons who fell victim to yellow fever in Queen Victoria's service in Sierra Leone and Jamaica. The Southsea Common, between the coast and houses of the area, known in the 13th century as Froddington Heath and used for army bivouacs, is a picnic and play area today. Peaceful walks can be taken along Ladies' Mile if you want to be away from the common's tennis courts, skateboard and roller-skating rinks, and other activities.

Southsea Castle, built in 1545 as part of the coastal defenses ordered by King Henry VIII, and the **D-Day Museum,** devoted to the Normandy landings 399 years later, are next door to each other on the Clarence Esplanade of Southsea. The castle, a fortress built of stones from Beaulieu Abbey, houses a museum with displays tracing the development of Portsmouth as a military stronghold, as well as naval history and the archeology of the area.

The D-Day Museum contains the Overlord Embroidery, showing the complete story of Operation Overlord, as the D-Day action was designated, the men, and the machines that were featured in the invasion operation. The appliquéed embroidery, believed to be the largest of its kind (272 feet long and three feet high), was designed by Sandra Lawrence and took 20 women of the Royal School of Needlework five years to complete. There is a special audio-visual program with displays, including reconstructions of various stages of the mission with models and maps. You'll see a Sherman tank in working order, Jeeps, field guns, and even a DUKW (popularly called a Duck), that incredibly useful amphibious truck that operated on land and sea.

Southsea Castle and the D-Day Museum are both open seven days a week from 10:30 a.m. to 5:30 p.m. except during the three-day Christmas holiday. A ticket admitting visitors to both attractions costs £1.75 ($2.63) for adults, £1.25 ($1.88) for children. If visited separately, admission is 50p (75¢) for adults, 25p (38¢) for children. For information on both, phone the Visitors Services Organiser (tel. 0705/827261).

On the northern side of Portsmouth Harbour on a spit of land are the remains of **Portchester Castle** (tel. 0705/378291), built in the late 12th century by King Henry II, plus a Norman church. It is set inside the impressive walls of a third-century Roman fort built as a defense against Saxon pirates when this was the northwest frontier of the declining Roman Empire. By the end of the 14th century, Richard II had modernized the castle, making it a secure small palace. Among the ruins are the hall, kitchen, and great chamber of this palace. Portchester was popular with medieval kings who stayed here when they visited Portsmouth. The last official use of the castle was as a prison for French seamen during the Napoleonic wars. It is open from 9:30 a.m. to 6:30 p.m. weekdays, 2 to 6:30 p.m. mid-March to mid-October; with closing time being 4 p.m. the remainder of the year. Admission is 75p ($1.13) for adults, 35p (53¢) for children.

Cross Portsmouth Harbour by one of the ferries that bustle back and forth all day to Gosport. Some departures go directly from the station pontoon to H.M.S. *Alliance* for a visit to the **Royal Naval Submarine Museum** (tel. 0705/529217). On show is the Royal Navy's first submarine, which was launched in 1901. Thirteen years later she sank with nobody on board. Salvaged in 1982, she was towed to Plymouth Harbour for renovation. Also on view, H.M.S. *Alliance* is a much more modern vessel through which you can walk to see the torpedo tubes and stowage compartment, as well as the mess for seamen and stokers. The museum contains a vast collection of artifacts of submarine life, including wartime trophies. The entrance fee is £1.80 ($2.70) for adults and 90p ($1.35) for children.

Overnighting in Portsmouth? If so, I have the following recommendations.

LIVING IN OLD PORTSMOUTH: A charming small house, **Fortitude Cottage,** 51 Broad St. (tel. 0705/823748), in Old Portsmouth is on Camber inner harbor. It is a narrow, four-story structure, with a steep staircase, almost in Dutch fashion, that leads to the compact home of Carol Harbeck. There are several rooms available, and the charge is £12 ($18) nightly for B&B. Mrs. Harbeck has demonstrated her excellent taste in the designing and furnishing of the home. It is airy, colorful, modern, yet not too extreme, and the views from the rooms are good. Her breakfasts are on a "what you want" basis.

Keppel's Head Hotel, The Hard (tel. 0705/833231), is an impressive Victorian brick monument facing the train, bus, and ferry stations and overlooking the Solent. A prestigious hotel for generations, it has 27 comfortable, well-furnished bedrooms, all with private baths or showers, color TV, radios, phones, and facilities for making tea or coffee. Singles rent for £46 ($69) and doubles for £56 ($84) per night, including a full English breakfast and VAT. Dinners in the 19th-century-style restaurant of this Anchor Hotel cost from £12 ($18), and there's a friendly bar.

LIVING IN SOUTHSEA: Southsea abounds with moderately priced small hotels or B&B houses. One of the best is the **Bristol Hotel,** 55 Clarence Parade (tel. 0705/821815). This family-run hotel is small and inviting, occupying half of a twin-gabled Victorian house whose windows overlook a seaside park. It's run by Edward and Jean Fry (he spent 25 years in the Royal Navy before opening this place). They offer a total of 13 modernized rooms, nine of which have their own private bath. A single without bath costs from £14.50 ($21.75), going up to £20 ($30) with bath. Two persons pay

£29 ($43.50) in a bathless room, £36 ($54) with bath, including an English breakfast and VAT.

DINING AND DRINKING IN PORTSMOUTH: Head up Broad Street to the **Lone Yachtsman** (tel. 0705/24293), a revamped pub that is the center of much of the local life of Old Portsmouth. Decorated in a nautical theme, it commands a view of the harbor from its perch on the end of a promontory. You can drink in both the Sir Alec Rose bar (popular with yacht people) or dine at the Lively Lady (hot luncheons and evening meals seven days a week from noon to 2:30 p.m. and 7:30 to 10:30 p.m.). Among the usual entrees are such tempting items as soup of the day and steak, kidney, and mushroom pie. A set lunch costs £5 ($7.50). The Dover sole, depending on size, is excellent, as are many other seafood dishes. A tradition is the hot fruit pie, served with thick cream. Dinners cost from £10 ($15).

The Hungry One, 15 Arundel Way, Arundel Street (tel. 0705/817114). Owner Peter Clubley runs this coffee lounge with the help of his wife, Edna, offering excellent coffee and toasted sandwiches. You can eat a three-course meal for less than £5.50 ($8.25). Mr. and Mrs. Clubley keep the place open Monday to Saturday from 9 a.m. to 5 p.m. The Hungry One offers pleasant surroundings and a relaxing atmosphere. It is on a street off Commercial Road, close to the Guildhall and the town railway station, a short bus journey from the Dockyard, H.M.S. *Victory,* and the *Mary Rose*.

Between Portsmouth and Southampton lies an increasingly popular attraction in this part of the country—

BROADLANDS: The home of Earl Mountbatten of Burma until his assassination in 1979, Broadlands, Romsey (tel. 0794/516878), lies on the A31, 72 miles southwest of London. Lord Mountbatten lent the house to Princess Elizabeth and Prince Philip (now H.M. the Duke of Edinburgh), Mountbatten's nephew, as a honeymoon haven in 1947, and in 1981, Prince Charles and Princess Diana spent the first nights of their honeymoon here. Broadlands is now owned by Lord Romsey, Lord Mountbatten's eldest grandson, who has created a fine exhibition and audio-visual show depicting the highlights of the brilliant career of his grandfather as a soldier and statesman, who has been called "the last war hero."

The house, originally linked to Romsey Abbey, was purchased by Lord Palmerston in 1736. It was later transformed into an elegant Palladian mansion by Capability Brown and Henry Holland. Brown landscaped the parkland and grounds, making the river (the Test) the main object of pleasure. Broadlands has long been a center of hospitality for royal and eminent persons. This tradition continues, but it remains very much a home for Lord and Lady Romsey. The house, where you'll see four Van Dyck oil paintings plus grilles by Whistler, the Mountbatten Exhibition, and the Riverside lawns are open daily from 10 a.m. to 6 p.m. April to the end of September. Closed Monday except in August, September, and on bank holidays. Admission is £3 ($4.50) for adults, £1.60 ($2.40) for children.

If you'd like to stay over, the **Wessex Guest House,** 5 Palmerston St. in Romsey (tel. 0794/512038), is run by Mrs. Patricia Edwards. Her comfortable house stands close to Broadlands. It's a good base from which to tour the New Forest area or to make trips to Winchester and Salisbury. Bed and a good breakfast is £9 ($13.50) to £10 ($15) per person. Evening meals aren't provided, but there are one or two pleasant inns in the village.

2. Southampton

To many North Americans, England's premier passenger port, home base for the Cunard's *Queen Elizabeth 2,* is the gateway to Britain. Southampton is changed today, a city of wide boulevards, parks, and shopping centers. It was rebuilt after German bomb damage, which destroyed hundreds of its old buildings.

In World War II, some 3½ million men embarked from here (in the First World War, more than twice that number passed through Southampton). Its supremacy as a port has long been recognized and dates from Saxon times when the Danish conqueror, Canute, was proclaimed king here in 1017.

Southampton was of special importance to the Normans, keeping them in touch with their homeland. And it shares the dubious distinction of having "imported" the bubonic plague in the mid-14th century that wiped out a quarter of the English population. On the Western Esplanade is a memorial tower to the Pilgrims, who set out on their voyage to the New World from Southampton on August 15, 1620. Both the *Mayflower* and the *Speedwell* sailed from here but were forced by storm damages to put in at Plymouth, where the *Speedwell* was abandoned. The memorial is a tall column with an iron basket on top of the type used as a beacon before lighthouses.

If you're waiting in Southampton between boats, you may want to use the time to explore some of the major sights of Hampshire that lie on the periphery of the port—the New Forest, Winchester, the Isle of Wight, and Bournemouth in neighboring Dorset.

Finding an accommodation directly in Southampton isn't as important as it used to be. Very few ships now arrive, and the places to stay just outside the city are, in the main, superior to what one finds directly in the heartland. For accommodations in the area, refer to the New Forest section. However, I'll provide some budget accommodation listings for those who for transportation or other reasons may want to stay within the city center.

WHERE TO STAY: One of the most substantial of the moderately priced inns in the center is **The Star Hotel,** 26 High St. (tel. 0703/30426). Its origins are uncertain (it may date from 1601), and it was a fashionable rendezvous in Georgian times. The Victoria Room at the Star commemorates the visit of little Princess Victoria in 1831 at the age of 12. The Star has kept abreast of the times, and today it rents out 32 centrally heated and comfortably furnished bedrooms, with radio, phone, hot and cold running water, and (in many cases) private baths. Depending on the plumbing, singles rent for £28 ($42) to £39 ($58.50), doubles or twins from £46 ($69) to £49 ($73.50). However, if you can stay on a Friday, Saturday, or Sunday night, for at least two nights, you get substantial reductions except in September. Tariffs include a full English breakfast and VAT. There's an informal but popular pub facing the street, plus a gracious yet inexpensive restaurant on the premises.

Claremont Hotel, 33–35 The Polygon (tel. 0703/223112), is surrounded by other B&Bs about a block from a major traffic artery of town and a beautiful city park. Marilyn and Joe Jarman rent out 14 comfortably furnished bedrooms, charging guests £10 ($15) per person nightly, with VAT and breakfast included. All bedrooms are centrally heated with color TV. There's a TV lounge for guests, along with a licensed bar.

The Linden, 51 The Polygon (tel. 0703/225653), sits behind a forest-green facade and under an elaborate twin-gabled roof. This turn-of-the-century building is operated by Patricia and David Hutchins, who rent out 13 comfortably furnished bedrooms for £10 ($15) per person nightly. None of the accommodations has a private bath, but each is equipped with hot and cold running water. Only breakfast is served.

WHERE TO EAT: Southampton isn't distinguished for its gastronomy. However, some of the best meals are found at **Pearl Harbour,** 86A Above Bar St. (tel. 0703/225248), the finest Cantonese restaurant in the area. It's far superior to most Chinese restaurants you encounter on the southern coast. Concentrate on the fish specialties, such as braised lobster, for the finest dining sensations. Many dishes are rarely found in the typical Chinese restaurant, including steamed winter melon soup. Other specialties that are prepared with style and lots of flavor include barbecued Peking duck and beggar's chicken. Set menus begin at £7.50 ($11.25) and are served daily from noon to midnight. A set lunch is priced at only £3 ($4.50). The restaurant lies on the second floor of a building right in the heart of town.

La Lupa, 123 High St. (tel. 0703/331849), is a functional Italian restaurant and pizzeria, occupying a prominent position right in the heart of the city. A wide range of pizzas and pastas, all reasonable in price, are offered from noon to 2:15 p.m. and from 6:30 to 11:30 p.m. (stays open to midnight on Friday and Saturday). You can also order grilled steaks and veal dishes, as well as Dover sole, finishing off with the chef's dessert specialty, a tartufo (shades of the Piazza Navona in Rome). Meals begin at £6 ($9) but could run much higher.

The **Red Lion,** High Street (tel. 0703/333595), is one of the few architectural jewels to have survived World War II. This pub has its roots in the 13th century (a Norman cellar), but its high-ceilinged and raftered "Henry V Court Room" is in the Tudor style. The room was the scene of the trial of the Earl of Cambridge and his accomplices, Thomas Grey and Lord Scrope, who were condemned to death for treason in plotting against the life of the king in 1415. The Court Room is adorned with coats-of-arms of the noblemen who served as peers of the condemned trio. All this bloody history needn't deter you. The Red Lion is a friendly, fascinating place at which to stop in for a drink and a chat. Pub lunches, served from 11:30 a.m. to 2:30 p.m., cost from £4 ($6) and are likely to include homemade steak and kidney pie, chicken and mushroom pie, or grilled rumpsteak. In the evening you can go for drinks from 5:30 to 11 p.m.

3. New Forest

The New Forest came into the limelight in the times of Henry VIII, who loved to hunt here, as venison abounded. Also, with his enthusiasm for building up the British naval fleet, he saw his opportunity to supply oak and other hard timbers to the boatyards at Buckler's Hard on the Beaulieu River for the building of stout-hearted men-o'-war. Today you can visit the old shipyards, and the museum with its fine models of men-o'-war, pictures of the old yard, and dioramas showing the building of these ships, their construction, and their launching. It took 2,000 trees to build one man-o'-war.

Stretching for about 92,000 acres, New Forest is a large tract 14 miles wide and 20 miles long. William the Conqueror laid out the limits of this then-private hunting preserve. Those who hunted without a license faced the executioner if they were caught, and those who hunted but missed had their hands severed.

Nowadays New Forest is one of those places traversed by a motorway by those motorists bound for the southwest. However, I'd suggest you stop a moment and relax.

This used to be a forest, but now the groves of oak trees are separated by wide tracts of common land which is grazed by ponies and cows, hummocked with heather and gorse, and frequented by rabbits. Away from the main arterial roads, where signs warn of wild ponies and deer, there is a private world of peace and quiet.

BEAULIEU ABBEY-PALACE HOUSE: This stately home is in the New Forest (tel. 590/612345). The abbey and house, as well as the National Motor Museum, are on the property of Lord Montagu of Beaulieu, at Beaulieu, five miles southeast of Lyndhurst and 14 miles south of Southampton. A Cistercian abbey was founded on this spot in 1204, and the ruins can be explored today. The Palace House was the great gatehouse of the abbey before it was converted into a private residence in 1538. The house is surrounded by gardens.

In the grounds, the **National Motor Museum,** one of the best and most comprehensive motor museums in the world, with more than 200 vehicles, is open to the public. It traces the story of motoring from 1895 to the present. Famous autos include four land-speed record-holders, among them Donald Campbell's *Bluebird*. The collection was built on the foundation of Lord Montagu's family collection of vintage cars. A special feature is called "Wheels." In a darkened environment, visitors can travel in specially designed "pods," each of which carries up to two adults and one child, along a silent electric track. They move at a predetermined but variable speed, and each pod is capable of rotating almost 360°. This provides a means by which the visitor is dramatically introduced to a variety of displays, spanning 100 years of motor development. Sound and visual effects are integrated into individual displays. In one sequence, visitors experience the smell, noise, and visual thrill of being involved in a Grand Prix race.

All facilities are open daily from 10 a.m. to 6 p.m. (to 5 p.m. November to March). Admission to the museum, house, abbey ruins, and garden is an inclusive £4 ($6) for adults, £2.50 ($3.75) for children.

BUCKLER'S HARD: This historic 18th-century village on the banks of the River Beaulieu is where ships for Nelson's fleet were built, including the admiral's favorite, *Agamemnon,* as well as *Eurylus* and *Swiftsure.* The **Maritime Museum** (tel. 059063/203) reflects the shipbuilding history of the village. Its displays include shipbuilding at Buckler's Hard, Henry Adams, master shipbuilder; Nelson's favorite ship; Buckler's Hard and Trafalgar; and models of Sir Francis Chichester's yachts and items of his equipment. The cottage exhibits are a re-creation of 18th-century life in Buckler's Hard. Here you can stroll through the New Inn of 1793 and a shipwright's cottage of the same period or look in on the family of a poor laborer at home. All these displays include village residents and visitors of the late 18th century.

The museum is open daily from 10 a.m. to 6 p.m. Easter to May, 10 a.m. to 9 p.m. June to September, and 10 a.m. to 4:30 p.m. October to Easter. Admission is £1.50 ($2.25) for adults, £1 ($1.50) for children. The walk back to Beaulieu, 2½ miles along the riverbank, is well marked through the woodlands. During the summer, you can cruise on the River Beaulieu in the present *Swiftsure,* an all-weather catamaran cruiser.

FOOD AND LODGING: My recommendations for food and lodging in the New Forest include a few places for overnighting.

Whitley Ridge, Beaulieu Road, Brockenhurst (tel. 0590/22354), is a Georgian house built as a royal hunting lodge around the 18th century. The addition of an extension in Victorian times created a large and elegant home. It stands in nearly five acres of secluded grounds in the heart of the New Forest. Today, it is a 15-bedroom hotel run as a family business by Keith and Josephine Hamson, who are assisted by their son Stephen in making guests welcome and comfortable. The units, most of which have private baths or showers with toilets, also have color TV in the larger accommodations, as well as facilities for making hot drinks. Charges are £47 ($70.50) to £51 ($76.50) double occupancy in a twin or double, from £30 ($45) when the room is used for a single. The supplement for an extra bed in a room is £15 ($22.50), with children under 14 sharing the parents' room for £6 ($9). Prices include a full English breakfast and VAT. Special rates are quoted for stays of two nights or more.

The hotel is acclaimed for its food and interesting wines, offering different meals ranging from unusual and imaginative dishes to classic cuisine. You dine in a handsome restaurant that is a popular rendezvous for nonresident patrons as well as hotel guests. A table d'hôte dinner, costing £9.50 ($14.25), is served from 7:30 to 8:30 p.m. A comfortable and intimate bar is inviting, and there are two well-furnished lounges.

Grove House, Newtown Minstead, near Lyndhurst (tel. 0703/813211), is owned and run by Marion Dixon, who offers accommodations in her own family's home. She has a comfortable family room to accommodate from two to four persons, facing south and west and going for £11 ($16.50) per person per night, including a large breakfast. An evening meal can be arranged from £7 ($10.50) per person. This pleasant farmhouse lies at the rural end of the village with the New Forest a quarter mile away up a country lane.

Lyndhurst House, 35 Romsey Rd., Lyndhurst (tel. 042128/2230), is a solid, turn-of-the-century house opposite Pat's Garage in the town. It's the home of Sydney and Yvonne Renouf, who rent several rooms in their main house, plus three more in a chalet behind, at a cost of £9.50 ($14.25) per person nightly. Yvonne turns out an enormous breakfast of eggs, sausages, bacon, tomatoes, toast, jam, tea or coffee. The house is close to the New Forest and to shops.

Bentley, Sway Road, Brockenhurst (tel. 0590/22407), is a lovely New Forest house run by a friendly couple, Michael and Inez Lancaster. They offer rooms at £11.50 ($17.25) per person nightly, including a good hot breakfast. They rent out two family rooms, two doubles, one twin, and one single, and can provide bunk beds for kids. There is a warm lounge with TV, plus a car park, and the whole place is surrounded by a large garden. Wild forest ponies wander around, and the open forest is just around the corner. If given a warning in time, they'll prepare a dinner for you, the fare consisting mainly of chops, chicken, or roast. The cost is about £6 ($9) per person. They'll also make a picnic lunch for you if you want to go exploring the next day.

Rose & Crown Hotel, Lyndhurst Road, Brockenhurst (tel. 0590/22225), is an 18th-century coaching inn in the center of the New Forest, run by Brian and Daile Parkin. Rooms go from £12 ($18) per person, including a traditional English breakfast. A buffet bar serves hot and cold meals costing from £2 ($3), and in Roses, the charming à la carte restaurant, you can enjoy fine English cuisine in friendly surroundings, paying from £9.50 ($14.25) for three courses and coffee. Food service is during regular pub hours.

The **Old Well Restaurant and Guesthouse,** Copythorne (tel. 0703/812321). Pat and Laurie Martin's family used to own the village grocery store, and they are true forest folk. In 1960 they bought the Old Well, which opens at 9 a.m. and closes according to the departure of the last guest. Breakfast is a good meal of homemade bread and local eggs, bacon, and sausages; then morning coffee leads to lunch, a set meal going for £5 ($7.50). On Sunday they always have a traditional roast joint or something from the à la carte menu such as lamb chops. Cream teas at £1.75 ($2.63) take over after lunch. If you decide to stay over, they have five rooms to rent in the main house, and the charge is £10 ($15) per person, including that large and wholesome breakfast. This is a friendly place, offering excellent value.

Copythorne Lodge, Romsey Road, Cadnam, near Southampton (tel. 0703/812127), is a large country house with a small dairy farm which provides fresh produce for the substantial farm breakfasts which Mrs. Garrett serves. There is a cozy lounge with TV, and one of the bedrooms has its own bath. The others must share showers and a toilet. The overnight charge is £9 ($13.50) per person, a little bit more for the room with private plumbing.

The Vicarage, Church Corner, Burley, near Ringwood (tel. 04253/2303), is a quiet house set in an informal and secluded garden in a clearing in the New Forest, opposite the church in the village of Burley. The village lies between the A31 and the A35 main roads near Ringwood, and is a good center for seeing the forest and coastal resorts. The house is run by Mrs. Alan Clarkson, the vicar's wife, who can accommodate up to six people at £10 ($15) per person nightly. The units are pleasant and comfortable and a home-like atmosphere prevails.

Jack in the Basket, 7 St. Thomas St., Lymington (tel. 0590/73447), in a building dating back to the 17th century, consists of a restaurant and three bedrooms. The rooms rent for £13 ($19.50) per person for bed and breakfast. The restaurant, respected for its home-cooked food served in a pleasant and friendly atmosphere, is open from 9 a.m. to 5 p.m., except on market day, Saturday, when they open early for breakfast. The establishment is at the top end of Lymington High Street with a large, free car park behind.

4. Isle of Wight

Four miles across the Solent from the South Coast towns of Southampton, Lymington, and Portsmouth, the Isle of Wight is known for its sandy beaches and its ports, favored by the yachting set. The island, which long attracted such literary figures as Alfred Tennyson and Charles Dickens, is compact in size, measuring 23 miles from east to west, 13 miles from north to south. You can take regular ferryboats over. Hydrofoils cross the Solent in just 20 minutes from Southampton.

Visitors who'd like to explore the Isle of Wight for the day can take an **Around the Island Rover** ticket which may be purchased on the bus. This enables anyone to board and leave the buses at any stop on the island. The price is £3.80 ($5.70) for adults, £1.90 ($2.85) for children. For further information, telephone 0983/523831.

The ferry from Southampton to Cowes costs about £3.80 ($5.70) for a day round-trip ticket for foot passengers or £16.80 ($25.20) for an average size car, plus passengers.

The Lymington-Yarmouth (Isle of Wight) ferry charges £24 ($36) for the average size car, passengers included. Foot passengers are charged £3.40 ($5.10) for a cheap day round trip.

The more usual way of reaching the island from London is by ferry from Portsmouth Harbour or by Hovercraft from Southsea, both of which take you to Ryde, the railhead for the island's communications system. Arriving in Yarmouth, via Lymington, however, is something else—a busy little harbor providing a mooring for yachts and also for one of the lifeboats of the Solent area.

Long a favorite of British royalty, the island has as its major attraction **Osborne House** (tel. 0983/200022), Queen Victoria's most cherished residence, lying a mile southeast of East Cowes. Prince Albert designed the Italian-inspired mansion which stands in lush gardens, right outside the village of Whippingham with its much-visited church. The rooms have remained as Victoria knew them, right down to the French piano she used to play and with all the cozy clutter of her sitting room. Grief-stricken at the death of Albert in 1861, she asked that Osborne House remain as it was, and so it mainly has been. Even the turquoise scent bottles he gave her, decorated with cupids and cherubs, are still in place. It was in her bedroom in Osborne House that Victoria died on January 22, 1901. In the gardens are the Swiss Cottage where the royal children played and the queen's bathing machine. The house is open to the public from the first Monday in April to the last Friday in October from 10 a.m. to 5 p.m. daily. Admission is £2.20 ($3.30) for adults, £1.10 ($1.65) for children.

A completely different attraction, **Carisbrooke Castle** (tel. 0983/522107) is where Charles I was imprisoned by the Roundheads in 1647. This fine medieval castle is in the center of the island, 1½ miles southwest of Newport. Everybody heads for the Well House, concealed inside a 16th-century stone building. Donkeys take turns treading a large wooden wheel connected to a rope which hauls up buckets of water. The castle is open weekdays mid-March until mid-October from 9:30 a.m. to 6:30 p.m. (from mid-October to mid-March, to 4 p.m.). However, Sunday hours are different. From mid-March until March 31 and from October 1 to mid-October it is open on Sunday from 2 to 6:30 p.m. From April 1 to September 30 it is open on Sunday from 9:30 a.m. to 6:30 p.m., and from mid-October to mid-March Sunday hours are from 2 to 4 p.m. Admission is £1.70 ($2.55) for adults, 85p ($1.28) for children.

You have a choice of several bases on the Isle of Wight unless you're what the English call a "day-tripper."

Cowes is the premier port for yachting in Britain. Henry VIII ordered the castle built there, but it is now the headquarters of the Royal Yacht Squadron. The seafront, the Prince's Green, and the high cliff road are worth exploring. Hovercraft are built in the town, and it is also the home and birthplace of the well-known maritime photographer, Beken of Cowes.

Along the southeast coast are the twin resorts of **Sandown,** with its pier complex and theater, and **Shanklin,** at the southern end of Sandown Bay which has held the British annual sunshine record more times than any other resort. Keats once lived in Shanklin's Old Village.

Farther along the coast, **Ventnor** is called the "Madeira of England," because it arises from the sea in a series of steep hills.

On the west coast, the sand cliffs of **Alum Bay** are a blend of many different colors, a total of 21 claimed. The Needles, three giant chalk rocks, and the Needles Lighthouse, are further features of interest at this end of the island. If you want to stay at the western end of Wight, refer to my recommendations under **Totland Bay** and **Freshwater Bay.**

Newport is the capital, a bustling market town lying in the heart of the island.

RYDE: A good anchor for the Isle of Wight is the **Seaward Guest House,** 14–16 George St. (tel. Ryde 63168), as Ryde is a good center for exploring the island. Many tour buses leave from here, as well as the train from the ferry docks at Ryde. Harold and Margaret Gath, a helpful couple, receive guests into their century-old home, charging from £10.50 ($15.75) per person nightly for B&B, including a four-course breakfast. A four-course evening dinner will also be served for another £6 ($9). Everything is well kept in their pleasant home, and Mr. Gath works with the tourist board. Even if they can't accommodate you in their busy season, they'll have suggestions where you can find a room.

Some of the best dining on the island is at **Biskra House Restaurant,** 17 St. Thomas's St. (tel. 0983/67913), a Georgian mansion right near the center of town. Separated from a busy street by a stone wall, it opens onto the Solent. A table d'hôte lunch costs £4.95 ($7.43), a set dinner going for £10.95 ($16.43). The Sunday lunch costs £5.50 ($8.25). Considering the high quality of the food, these prices are very reasonable. Fresh lobster is often featured, and steak Diane is prepared at your table. Other specialties include duck with a fruit and cointreau sauce and venison steak with a black cherry sauce. The chef also specializes in such pastas as lasagne and cannelloni. Hours are from noon to 2 p.m. and 7 to 10:30 p.m. It is closed for dinner Sunday and on Monday. The hotel also rents out nine attractively furnished bedrooms, each with private bath or shower. The B&B rate in a single ranges from £21 ($31.50) to £29 ($43.50), in a double from £41 ($61.50) to £57 ($85.50).

SHANKLIN: A comfortable choice is **Afton Hotel,** Clarence Gardens (tel. 0983/ 863075), a substantial red brick hotel with ornate white Victorian trim under its gables. Owned by the enterprising John and Anita Williams, who have as their motto "Home Sweet Afton," they bring to their guests charm and consideration. They have brought flair and style to the decorations and furnishings, and sound comforts as well, including full double glazing. The dining room, opening onto a sun terrace, is furnished with mahogany armchairs set around polished tables, and an interesting wicker bird stand. The living room has an ornate kelly-green and mahogany Victorian sofa and armchairs, with rose medallion wallpaper and a white trim. The intimate drinking lounge, the Shakespeare Bar, also has the Victorian touch. The bedrooms have central heating, lots of hot water, plenty of clean towels, soap, reading lights, radio, tea/coffee trays, and color TV. Several units have private shower and toilet, and one has a four-poster bed. Anita does all the cooking, and if you have a special diet, she'll happily comply with your needs. There is a choice of menu, including traditional English specialties. Daily terms include B&B and a five-course evening dinner for around £24 ($36) per person, including VAT.

VENTNOR: Perhaps one of the nicest places to stay on the Isle of Wight is **Madeira Hall,** Trinity Road (tel. 0983/852624). In an estate garden of lawns, tall trees, and flowering shrubs stands this stone manor house, with mullioned windows, gables, and bay windows. It has housed interesting people, such as Lord Macaulay, who wrote some of his well-known essays here. And there are associations with Charles Dickens and some of his characters. On the grounds is a heated swimming pool and an 18-hole putting course. All bedrooms have color TV and facilities for making hot beverages. Most have private baths or showers. Mr. and Mrs. Waring quote a B&B rate of £16.50 ($24.75) per person nightly. The half-board rate is £19.50 ($29.25) to £23 ($34.50) per person daily.

Apse Manor Country House (tel. 0983/866651) is a superb 17th-century manor house situated in an acre of secluded gardens surrounded by woods and open country, yet only three minutes from Shanklin with all its amenities and safe sandy beaches. The manor, formerly a farmhouse, has been carefully converted to a high standard, with six bedrooms decorated in country-house style, with period furnishings. All units are comfortably furnished and have bathrooms, color TV, tea/coffee-making facilities, and views of the grounds. The cooking is done under the personal supervision of Mr. and Mrs. P. Boynton, proprietors, with a liberal and varied menu using fresh garden produce where possible. Bed, breakfast, and evening dinner cost from £18.50 ($27.75) per person per day.

FRESHWATER BAY: Some 300 yards from the beach and caves at Freshwater Bay, **Blenheim House,** Gate Lane (tel. 0983/752858), is a twin-gabled, brick-fronted house laden with gingerbread. Built in 1894 as a private house, it offers eight well-furnished bedrooms, most of which contain private showers, toilets, and color TV with full central heating. Hazel and Jon Shakeshaft, the owners, charge from £20 ($30) per person for half board, including VAT and service. In back is a heated swimming pool. Good meals are served in the dining room with French windows opening onto the patio and lawn. Fresh local produce is used whenever possible.

TOTLAND BAY: A pleasant stay will be yours at **Littledene Lodge Hotel,** Granville Road (tel. 0983/752411), which has the appearance of a two-story traditional suburban home built at the beginning of this century. Owned and managed by Mrs. Maureen Wright, the hotel is small enough that you receive plenty of personal attention. Each of the nicely furnished rooms has facilities for comfort. Some have private bath. There is a TV lounge for the use of residents, and the hotel is centrally heated. Maureen is proud of her reputation for good, well-presented food served in the spacious bar/dining room. The charge is £16 ($24) per person per day for B&B and dinner, while B&B only costs £12.50 ($18.75) per day. Children are welcome.

NEWPORT: In the center of the island, and worth a special trip, **Lugleys,** 42 Lugley St. (tel. 0983/521062), serves, in the view of many critics, the finest food on the Isle of Wight. It's small—only five tables—but "it's choice," as Spencer Tracy said about Katharine Hepburn. Attractively decorated, Lugleys is the domain of Angela Hewitt, who offers a variety of seasonal dishes throughout the year. Go only for dinner from 7 to 9:30 p.m. except Sunday. Meals cost from £12 ($18) and might include such delights as old English oyster stew, scallops in orange sauce, and grouse from Scotland with red currants. Wild pigeon breasts are served with a juniper berry glaze, and locally caught partridge is marinated for seven days, then cooked and served with a creamy garlic sauce. Desserts are luscious, including on one recent occasion banana cheesecake.

Twelve miles from Southampton is the ancient city of:

5. Winchester

The most historical city in all of Hampshire, Winchester is big on legends. It's even associated with King Arthur and the Knights of the Round Table. In the Great

Hall, the remains of Winchester Castle, a round oak table, with space for King Arthur and his 24 knights, hangs on the wall. But all that spells undocumented romance. What is actually known is that when the Saxons ruled the ancient kingdom of Wessex, Winchester was the capital.

The city is also linked with King Alfred, who is honored today by a statue and is believed to have been crowned there. The Danish conqueror, Canute, came this way too, as did the king he ousted, Ethelred (Canute got his wife, Emma, in the bargain). The city is the seat of the well-known Winchester College, whose founding father was the bishop of Winchester, William of Wykeham. Established in 1382, it lays claim to being the oldest public (private) school in England.

Traditions are strong in Winchester. It is said (although I've never confirmed the assertion) that if you go to St. Cross Hospital, now an almshouse, dating from the 12th century, you'll get ye olde pilgrim's dole of ale and bread (and if there's no bread, you can eat cake). Winchester, 65 miles from London, is essentially a market town, on the downs on the Itchen River.

WINCHESTER CATHEDRAL: For centuries Winchester Cathedral (tel. 0962/53137) has been one of the great mother churches of England. The present building, the longest cathedral in Britain, dates from 1079, and its Norman heritage is still in evidence. Early in this century when parts of the cathedral were breaking away and sinking into the log raft and peat bed on which it had been built in the 13th century, a diver, William Walker, worked in darkness for several years in the water below to build a brick and concrete base to support the massive structure. When a Saxon church stood on this spot, St. Swithun, bishop of Winchester and tutor to young King Alfred, suggested modestly that he be buried outside. When he was later buried inside, it rained for 40 days. The legend lives on; just ask a resident of Winchester what will happen if it rains on St. Swithun's Day, July 15.

Of the present building, the nave with its two aisles is most impressive, as are the chantries, the reredos (late 15th century), and the elaborately carved choir stalls. Of the chantries, that of William of Wykeham, founder of Winchester College, is perhaps the most visited (it's found in the south aisle of the nave). The cathedral also contains a number of other tombs, notably those of novelist Jane Austen and Izaak Walton (exponent of the merits of the pastoral life—*The Compleat Angler*.) The latter's tomb is to be found in the Prior Silkestede's Chapel in the South Transept. Miss Austen's grave is marked with a commemorative plaque. Winchester Cathedral contains in chests the bones of many of the Saxon kings and the remains of the Viking conqueror, Canute, and his wife, Emma, in the presbytery. The son of William the Conqueror, William Rufus (who reigned as William II in 1087), is also believed to have been buried at the cathedral. There are free guided tours on weekdays in the summer at 11 a.m. and 3 p.m.

The Crypt is flooded for a large part of the year, and at such times is closed to the public. When it's not flooded, there are regular tours at 10:30 a.m. and 2:30 p.m. The Library, in which is displayed the *Winchester Bible* and other ancient manuscripts, is open for limited hours throughout the summer (except Monday morning and Sunday) and on Wednesday and Saturday for the rest of the year (except January, when it's open only on Saturday). The Treasury is open during the summer season from 11 a.m. to 5 p.m. It is small and does not require a guide. No admission fee is charged, but a donation of £1 ($1.50) for the upkeep of the cathedral is suggested.

OTHER SIGHTS: The military displays at the **Royal Hussars Museum,** Southgate Street (tel. 0962/63751), trace the history of the famous regiment in tableaux and pictures. You go from the days when the original regiments, the 10th and 11th Royal Hussars, were engaged in the Peninsular War and fought at Waterloo, to their mechanization in 1928 and their amalgamation in 1969. All sorts of questions are answered, including why the 11th is known as "Cherrypickers." The answer to that one is that they had an engagement with the French in a cherry orchard during the Peninsular War. The word "Hussar," you'll learn, is a derivation from old Hungarian relating to the method of conscripting "one in twenty" from the men of each village. The museum is open from Easter until the end of October, Tuesday to Sunday from 10 a.m. to 4 p.m. Admission is 50p (75¢) for adults and 10p (15¢) for children.

The **Royal Green Jackets Museum,** Peninsular Barracks, Romsey Road (tel. 0962/63846, ext. 288). In the same military complex as the Royal Hussars Museum, this other exhibition hall has a collection of weaponry and uniforms illustrating the history of the Oxfordshire and Buckinghamshire Light Infantry. Along with that, you'll see other mementos of the King's Royal Rifle Corps and the Rifle Brigade, which together form the Royal Green Jackets. The museum is open in March from 10:30 a.m. to 12:30 p.m. and 2 to 4 p.m., Monday to Saturday. From April to September it's open Monday to Friday from 10:30 a.m. to 12:30 p.m. and 2 to 4:30 p.m. On Saturday hours are 2:30 to 4:30 p.m. Admission is free.

LODGING: Several 18th-century town houses have been joined and renovated to form the **Winton Court Hotel,** 49 Southgate St. (tel. 0962/53664). All accommodations have radios, phones, and hot and cold water basins, and the hotel is centrally heated. Depending on the plumbing, the B&B rate ranges from £15 ($22.50) to £21 ($31.50) per person nightly. All the floors are serviced by elevator. The pine-paneled and rugged stone drinking lounge has a rock garden and fountain, and there is a comfortable lounge with color TV. Meals are served in the paneled dining room, decorated in strong primary colors. Parking is available at the rear of the hotel, which lies a few minutes' walk from the city center.

The **Winchester Hotel,** St. Cross Road (tel. 0962/53507), is just outside the heart of the city, set back from the busy Southampton road. It is composed of two Edwardian brick houses. Hot and cold water and central heating are in all rooms. At present there are 22 singles, 11 doubles, five family rooms, and one twin. Singles range from £15.50 ($23.25) bathless to £21.50 ($32.55) with bath and twins or doubles cost £31 ($46.50) with private bath. Tariffs include breakfast, VAT, and service. Many public bathrooms are available, as is a comfortable television lounge. There is an excellent restaurant open seven days a week, but in the evening only. You must tell the staff if you want a meal before 4:30 p.m. The cost is £7.50 ($11.25) to residents.

Southgate Hotel, Southgate Street (tel. 0962/51243), is a brick house in the center of Winchester. It opens onto a rear garden with flowerbeds and an old walnut tree. Christopher Wren designed and built Southgate in 1715, and many of the original architectural details remain (note the front entry with the glass lights over the doorway). All the bedrooms are equipped with hot and cold running water, and some have private bath. The B&B rate is £18 ($27) per person, to which 10% is added for service. There is an excellent cuisine, from gourmet à la carte meals to economy bar grub.

Stratton House, Stratton Road, St. Giles Hill (tel. 0962/63919), is a lovely old Victorian house (circa 1890) set in an acre of ground in an elevated position on St. Giles Hill, overlooking the city. It is about a five- to ten-minute walk from the center. Single, double, twin-bedded, and family units are available throughout the year. The charge for B&B is about £14 ($21) per person. An evening meal can be arranged for another £7 ($10.50). All bedrooms have TV and hot-drink facilities, and there is ample parking in a private courtyard. Free pick-up is possible on arrival from train and bus station.

Ann Farrell, 5 Ranelagh Rd., St. Cross (tel. 0962/69555), offers one of the best values. Near the heart of the city, the house has only three rooms to rent, which contain hot and cold running water. A bathroom and shower are for exclusive use of guests. This is a Victorian house furnished in that period but with comfort. Rates are from £9.50 ($13.50) in a single, £18 ($27) in a double.

You might also try **Mrs. Lawrence,** 67 St. Cross Rd. (tel. 0962/63002), who will house you in comfort, giving you a complete English breakfast for £10 ($15) per person. One room is rented to families. The location is convenient, near the heart of the city.

FOOD AND DRINK: Just by the cathedral, the **Wessex Hotel,** Paternoster Row (tel. 0962/61611), has a bright coffeeshop, with a separate entrance from the street, where hot and cold snacks are available all day. A typical meal of soup, breaded plaice with fried potatoes, apple pie and cream, plus coffee, will cost about £6.50 ($9.75). They also do a traditional afternoon tea. From noon to 2 p.m. the cocktail bar in the hotel has a table where you can help yourself to a selection of English cheeses and pâté, pickles, and salad ingredients. The chef's homemade soup and freshly baked rolls are also offered. In the elegant Walton Restaurant, overlooking the cathedral, a full three-course lunch costs £9.25 ($13.88), a four-course dinner £12.50 ($18.75). The best time to go for dinner is from 7 to 9 p.m.

Spys, 9 Great Minster St. (tel. 0962/64004), has many prints in support of its name in the downstairs bar, where light meals are served, such as lasagne, pies, and fresh salads. Upstairs in the elegant restaurant overlooking the cathedral, a full à la carte menu is offered, mainly of French cuisine. You can choose from such dishes as roast partridge in season, fresh halibut, Dover sole, or English lamb cutlets, from among courses that change weekly. A complete meal will cost from £10 ($15). The better wines of France as well as of other countries are represented on the comprehensive *carte des vins* offered by Christopher and Anthea Coulson, the owners. Spys is open from 11:30 a.m. to 2:30 p.m. and 6 to 10:30 p.m. Monday to Saturday.

Minstrels, 2 Little Minster St. (tel. 0962/67212), serves a variety of functions: it's ideal for morning coffee and a pâtisserie, quick and reasonably priced lunches, and afternoon teas extending to light suppers suitable for family and friends. The menu is limited, simple fare such as homemade soup, leek and potato pie, fisherman's pie, and chili con carne. Continental dishes, however, also appear, and they cater to vegetarians. Thus on any given day you are likely to find ratatouille, quiche, moussaka, and lasagne. Expect to spend no more than £5 ($7.50), unless you're ravenously hungry. A hot menu is available all day, and there is take-away service. Hours are Monday to Saturday from 10 a.m. to 5:30 p.m.

Mr. Pitkin's Wine Bar & Eating House, 4 Jewry St. (tel. 0962/69630), is installed in a fine Victorian town house in the heart of the city. Peter and Alan Tucker run one of the most popular rendezvous points in Winchester. And with good reason. Bar snacks begin at £1.50 ($2.25) for the hot homemade soup and bread, going up to £3.25 ($4.88) for the various curries, chili, lasagne, and moussaka. A three-course lunch goes for £7.40 ($11.10), a three-course dinner for £9.50 ($14.25). They also have an extensive à la carte menu, with more than 100 different wines from vintners ranging from America to Africa. It is open from 11:30 a.m. to 2:30 p.m. and 6 to 9:30 p.m.

The Old Mill Restaurant, 1 Bridge St. (tel. 0962/63151) is a historic restaurant dating from 1744. On the river, it is charmingly situated next to the Winchester City Mill. Fully licensed, it offers some of the finest food in town, not only various versions of steak and grilled Dover sole, but more imaginative fare as well, perhaps Hampshire pheasant hot pot, wood pigeon casserole, and rabbit in red wine. A lunch costs from £6 ($9), dinner from £12 ($18), with a Sunday lunch tallying up at £7.50 ($11.25). Hours are from Tuesday to Sunday 10 a.m. to 3 p.m. for coffee and lunch and from 6:30 to 9:30 p.m. Monday to Saturday for dinner.

Raffles Tea Room, 12 The Square (tel. 0962/61736), is above the House of Tweed shop. It's a traditional English tea room, offering morning coffee with pastries or toasted buns, as well as light lunches, including sandwiches, salads, chicken pie, and quiche, costing around £3 ($4.50). Afternoon teas are a specialty. You can have warm scones with strawberry jam and clotted cream, plus a choice of five blends of tea, all costing less than £2 ($3). The place is open from 9:30 a.m. to 5 p.m. Monday to Saturday.

The Pick of the Pubs

Instead of lunching at one of the above restaurants, you may want to drop in at the **Royal Oak Pub,** Royal Oak Passage (tel. 0962/61136), which is to be found in a passageway next to the God Begot House in the High Street. This pub reputedly has the oldest bar in England. Luncheons are served at the bar from noon to 2 p.m. Monday to Saturday. Various hot dishes and snacks are available. Expect to pay from £5 ($7.50) for a full meal. A traditional Sunday lunch is served from noon to 1:30 p.m., costing around £6.50 ($9.75). John and Pat Coles, the publicans, offer assorted live music Sunday, Wednesday, and Thursday. Admission is free. This is a busy, friendly pub with plenty of atmosphere where the hosts and staff enjoy serving good food and drink. Hours are from 11:30 a.m. to 3 p.m. and 5:30 to 11 p.m.

Olde Market Inn, 34 The Square (at Market Street) (tel. 0962/52585), is ideal for those who enjoy a local pub. It offers a relaxed, friendly, un-self-conscious atmosphere, a proper background in which to drink a pint. The corner pub sits opposite the cathedral in the oldest, most historic district of Winchester. It's mellowed enough to have timbers galore, cozy nooks, and comfortable chairs. A good selection of hot and cold bar snacks is available at lunchtime, including home-cooked steak-and-kidney pie, cottage pie, and chicken-and-mushroom pie. Prices begin at £2 ($3). The owners don't think their establishment merits international publicity, but they welcome individual travelers who stray in. The place is open from 11:30 a.m. to 3 p.m. and 5:30 to 11 p.m.

If time remains, you might now continue your trip westward into the too-often-neglected county of:

DORSET

This is Thomas Hardy country. You may long ago have seen the films or read *Far from the Madding Crowd* or *Tess of the D'Urbervilles,* one of the most memorable of all Victorian heroines, and know that Dorset is the Wessex of Hardy novels. Some of the towns and villages, although altered considerably, are still recognizable from his descriptions—however, he changed the names to protect the innocent. Poole, for example became Havenpool; Weymouth converted to Budmouth. The last of the great Victorians, as he was called, died in 1928 at the age of 88. His tomb rests in a position of honor in Westminster Abbey, but his heart was cut out and buried in his beloved Dorsetshire.

One of England's smallest shires, Dorset stretches all the way from the Victorian seaside resort of Bournemouth in the east to Lyme Regis in the west (known to Jane Austen, who couldn't find where all the action was). Dorset is a southwestern county, bordering the English Channel. It's big on cows, and Dorset butter is served at many an afternoon tea. Mainly, it is a land of farms and pastures, with plenty of sand heaths and chalky downs.

The most prominent tourist center of Dorset is the Victorian seaside resort of Bournemouth. If you don't anchor there, you might also try a number of Dorset's other seaports, villages, and country towns. For the most part, I've hugged closely to the impressive coastline.

Incidentally, Dorset, as the vacation-wise Britisher might tell you if he or she wanted to divulge a secret, is a friend of the budget traveler.

6. Bournemouth

The South Coast resort at the doorsteps of the New Forest didn't just happen: it was carefully planned and manicured, a true city in a garden. Flower-filled, park-dotted Bournemouth contains great globs of architecture inherited from those arbiters of taste, Victoria and her mischievous boy, Edward. Its most distinguishing feature is its Chines (shrub-filled, narrow, steep-sided ravines) along the zigzag coastline. The walking English strike out at, say, Hengistbury Head, making their way past sandy beaches, both the Boscombe and Bournemouth Piers—finally reaching Alum Chine, a distance of six miles away, but a traffic-free walk to remember.

It is estimated that of the nearly 12,000 acres which Bournemouth claims for its own, about one-sixth is turned over to green parks, stage-setting-type waters, even flowerbeds, such as the Pavilion Rock Garden, through which amblers pass both day and night. The total effect, especially in spring, tends to be dramatic and helps explain Bournemouth's long-established popularity with the garden-loving English. Bournemouth was discovered back in Victoria's day, when sea-bathing became a firmly entrenched institution, often practiced with great ritual. Many of the comparatively elegant villas that exist today (now largely B&B houses and hotels) once privately housed eminent Victorians.

Bournemouth, which along with Poole and Christchurch forms the largest urban area in the south of England, is not as sophisticated as Brighton. Increasingly, it is retirement acres for widowed or spinster English ladies who have found their place in the sun by playing the wicked game of Bingo. Increasingly, too, Bournemouth and its neighbors have a floating population of some 20,000 students attending one of its schools or colleges and in their off-hours exploring places written about or painted by such poets and artists as Shelley, Beardsley, and Turner.

The resort's amusements are wide and varied. At the Pavilion Theatre, for example, you can see West End-type productions from London; the Bournemouth Symphony Orchestra is justly famous in Europe; and there's the usual run of golf courses, band concerts, variety shows, and dancing.

Bournemouth is about 104 miles from London, easily reached in about an hour and 40 minutes on an express train from Waterloo Station in London. It makes a good base for exploring a history-rich part of England. On its outskirts are the New Forest, Salisbury, Winchester, and the Isle of Wight (an island that lies 15 miles away, the former seaside retreat of Victoria).

WHERE TO STAY: One of the most dramatically situated hotels in Bournemouth is the aptly named **Cliff House,** 113 Alumhurst Rd., Alum Chine (tel. 0202/763003). This white-painted house, operated by the Clark family, is also one of the best B&Bs at the resort. The hotel faces the sea, and you can walk along the Promenade to the Pier, shops, and amusements. The interior of this gabled house has a modernized decor, and each accommodation has a sea view. All but one of the units offers a private bath or shower and a toilet. It's best to book in here on the half-board rate of £21 ($31.50) per person nightly. The hotel shuts down in October.

Hinton Firs Hotel, Manor Road, East Cliff, Bournemouth (tel. 0202/25409), near the sea, is a turn-of-the-century country house enjoying a tranquil setting in a pine grove. It is a substantial and inviting hotel, whose major attraction is a swimming pool in back. The Waters family rents out 56 bedrooms, each well furnished and the majority of which contain private baths. Six units are in an annex. The furnishings are modern, as the hotel has been considerably upgraded in recent years. It's best to take the half-board rate of £21 ($31.50) to £30 ($45) per person nightly, depending on the season and the plumbing. There's a comfortable array of public rooms, each painted in vivid but tasteful colors, including a bar, TV lounge, dining room, and a particularly lovely garden.

Chilterns Hotel, 44 Westby Rd. Boscombe (tel. 0202/36539), stands on the seaside of Christchurch Road. The setting is that of a turn-of-the-century street lined with B&Bs, of which this one is the most outstanding. It is a red-brick building with a gabled tile roof. The Anthony family rents out a total of 19 comfortably furnished bedrooms, five of which have full private baths. The B&B rate ranges from £12 ($18) to

£15 ($22.50) per person, and evening meals can be served but only to residents. The hotel has a sunny lounge with color TV, along with a bar.

Blinkbonnie Heights Hotel, 26 Clifton Rd., Southbourne (tel. 0202/426512). The name of this small, 1920s hotel means "good view" in Scottish. It is set in the resort of Southbourne, four miles to the east of the center of Bournemouth. In a quiet residential neighborhood, it stands on a half acre plot of land with flowering shrubs and a terraced garden. Family run, the hotel offers 11 comfortably furnished bedrooms, only one of which has a private bath. The B&B rate ranges from £9 ($15) to £12 ($18) per person, with VAT included. Residents can also arrange for an evening meal.

Park View Hotel, 27 Spencer Rd. (tel. 0202/28955), stands on a hillside, away from the bustle of Bournemouth center, with an impressive view of the resort. Zelda and Roy Swan and family welcome guests at a cost of £10 ($15) per person. Rooms come with hot and cold running water and are comfortably furnished. Dinner is an extra £4 ($6) per person. Parking is available in the forecourt.

Belgravia Hotel, 56 Christchurch Rd., East Cliff (tel. 0202/290857), is a gracious brick mansion in a posh section of the resort, set in its own garden, the pride of the owners. For from £11 ($16.50) per person daily, plus VAT, you can stay here and have B&B. Dinner is available on request at £7 ($10.50) per person. The Belgravia is a five-minute walk along a zigzag path to the water. It's a pleasant house, with a mansard roof and a multitude of bay windows. The bedrooms are sun-filled and roomy. The beds have innersprings, and the rooms contain built-in wardrobes, bedside lamps, and armchairs. Reservations of only a night or two are almost impossible to get during the summer season (when the one-weekers are given priority, of course).

Sunnydene, 11 Spencer Rd. (tel. 0202/22281), is a substantial, gabled house on a tree-lined road between the Central Station and Bournemouth Bay. This comfortable turn-of-the century private hotel has recently made many additions, including a cozy licensed bar and an enlarged dining room. Winter visitors also enjoy central heating. All bedrooms are carpeted and have hot and cold running water, and many contain private bathrooms. The cost for B&B is from £12 ($18) per person daily. An evening meal of four courses, with some choice of menu, will cost an extra £6.50 ($9.75) per person. The hotel is open all year, and daily accommodation is usually readily available during all months except July and August. Bill and Marion Jackson, the proprietors, are efficient and most solicitous in their attentions. They serve excellent meals, and seem to pride themselves on running a bright and welcoming hotel.

EATING OUT IN BOURNEMOUTH: A restaurant that lives up to its name in food and decor is the **Old England,** 74 Poole Rd., Westbourne (tel. 0202/766475). The Chaplins run a friendly, comfortable restaurant, offering good value, and their efforts have gained increasing attention in town. A set daily three-course lunch or supper menu goes for £5 ($7.50) or a child's portion for £3.50 ($5.25). This menu is served daily including Sunday. I recently enjoyed the roast Hampshire pork with a savory stuffing. You can also order from a large à la carte menu, including such well-prepared English fare as roast fresh Dorset chicken, roast Scottish beef, and the mixed grill "Old England." However, expect to spend from £10 ($15). For dessert, I'd suggest the homemade apple pie, served either with custard or cream. Hours are 10 a.m. to 3 p.m. and 6 to 10:30 p.m. daily (Tuesday to Saturday evening during the winter).

Below the restaurant is the Dickens Wine Cellar, serving bar snacks such as homemade curries, chili, casseroles, pies, and ploughman's lunches, costing from 95p ($1.43) to £2.50 ($3.75). A selection of wines is available at reasonable prices, and there's a large range of continental lagers.

Crust, Hampshire House, Bourne Avenue, The Square (tel. 0202/21430), is one of the best bistros in Bournemouth, waking up sleepy local tastebuds with some really good food at fair prices. Paul Harper and his wife, Tricia, the owners, keep their pleasant little place open from noon to 2:30 p.m. and 6:30 to 11 p.m., offering a set lunch for £6.50 ($9.75), with dinners priced from £12 ($18). Look for the daily specials on a blackboard menu. You might begin with a freshly made quiche, a hearty soup, or pâté, then follow with Moroccan lamb or fresh grilled fish cooked just right.

Coriander, 14 Richmond Hill (tel. 0202/22202), is a Mexican restaurant that brings South of the Border flair to staid Bournemouth. You get the usual range of Mexican specialties, including burritos, tacos, and enchiladas, but are also given some well-prepared vegetarian dishes made with fresh ingredients. Meals, costing from £5 ($7.50), are served from noon to 2:15 p.m. and 6 to 11 p.m. In the center of Bournemouth, the Coriander has a rustic decor. It is closed for lunch on Sunday.

The **Salad Centre,** Post Office Road (tel. 0202/21720), is for devotees of vegetarian and "whole-food." Against a sparkling, pristine backdrop, it places its emphasis on fresh ingredients. There is always a large selection of salads, and you can also count on a fresh soup every day. Various quiches are presented, as are vegetable flans. Instead of roast beef, you get a nut roast. There is no fixed menu, however, and the center is more or less cafeteria style. Meals begin at £3.50 ($5.25), and hours are Monday to Saturday from 9 a.m. to 8 p.m. The center is run by Mrs. Doreen Fisher, who provides a warm welcome.

ON THE OUTSKIRTS: Dating back to 1673, the **Fisherman's Haunt Hotel,** Winkton, Christchurch (tel. 0202/484071), is a wistaria-covered country house, run by James Bochan, of Ukrainian origin, who came to England with the Polish forces in 1943. He and his wife, Isobel, welcome guests all year, charging £17 ($25.50) for bathless singles, going up to £32 ($48) in a bathless double. Doubles with private baths and toilets cost £40 ($60), those with four-poster beds going for £44 ($66). Authentic regional British dishes are the fare of the dining room which overlooks the River Avon. Open from noon, the restaurant at Fisherman's Haunt Hotel offers a set luncheon for £6 ($9). Dinners on weeknights are served from 7 to 10 p.m. A special feature of the restaurant is the traditional Sunday midday meal. If you do stay over, you will be served a full English breakfast in the morning. All bedrooms have full central heating and tea- or coffee-making facilities. Bedroom windows afford views of the garden, the river, and the meadows. The hotel lies only seven miles from Bournemouth and a mile and a half from Christchurch.

7. Shaftesbury

The origins of this typical Dorsetshire market town date back to the ninth century when King Alfred founded the abbey and made his daughter the first abbess. King Edward the Martyr was buried there, and King Canute died in the abbey but was buried in Winchester. Little now remains of the abbey, but the ruins are beautifully laid out. The museum adjoining St. Peter's Church at the top of Gold Hill gives a good idea of what the ancient Saxon hilltop town was like.

Today ancient cottages and hostelries cling to the steep cobblestone streets, thatch roofs frown above tiny-pane windows, and modern stores vie with the street market in the High Street and the cattle market off Christy's Lane.

The town, right on the A30 from London, is an excellent center from which to visit the Hardy Country (it appears as Chaston in *Jude the Obscure*), Stourhead Gardens, and Longleat House.

FOOD AND LODGING: About half a mile from Shaftesbury, **The Old Rectory,** St. James (tel. 0747/2003), offers one of the most moderately priced accommodations in the area. A Georgian building, it stands on attractive grounds and offers well-furnished rooms with private bath. The welcome is polite and friendly, and the cost is £17 ($25.50) per person, double occupancy. All rooms have private baths. The hostess is a Cordon Bleu cook, serving excellent meals costing from £10 ($15) per person.

You might also consider **Vale Mount,** 17A Salisbury St. (tel. 0747/2991), which lies about two minutes from the heart of town. A comfortable, pleasantly furnished house, it is a very good bargain at £10 ($15) in a single and £18 ($27) in a double. You can also take half-board here at terms beginning at £15 ($22.50) per person daily. Baths are shared.

8. Wareham

On the Frome River, this historic little town is about a mile west of Poole Harbour. Many find it a good center for touring the South Dorset coast and the Purbeck Hills. It contains remains of early British and Roman town walls, plus the Saxon church of St. Martin has an effigy of Lawrence of Arabia (T.E. Lawrence).

Lawrence died in a motorcycle crash in 1935, and his former home, **Clouds Hill,** (no phone), near Wool, lies 7 miles to the northwest of Wareham near Wareham Forest, one mile north of Bovington Camp. The house is open Wednesday, Friday, and Sunday from 2 to 5 p.m. April to the end of September. It is open only on Sunday, from 1 to 4 p.m. the remainder of the year. Admission is £1 ($1.50) for either an adult or child, and no photography is allowed.

The sleepy hamlet of Wool is 19 miles west of Bournemouth on the River Frome. One of the most charming places in East Dorset, it has thatched cottages on either side of the road. It lies west of Wareham just off the A352 on the B3071 road leading to the channel.

FOOD AND LODGING: A riverside country pub, **The Old Granary,** The Quay (tel. 09295/2010), is near a double-arched bridge. You dine either inside or on a terrace overlooking the boats and swans. The interior dining room has a charm of its own, with bentwood chairs, saffron cloths, a wine rack, a natural wood sideboard, and white walls displaying a collection of locally painted watercolors. A gracious and informal atmosphere prevails. The secret behind the success of the Old Granary is its fine cuisine; the owners, Mr. and Mrs. Derek Sturton, try hard to stick to natural country foods. Homemade soups and pâtés are featured. Main dishes include filet of pork in a barbecue sauce and Dorset lamb chops with cheese and onion. A hefty portion of homemade fruit pie with cream finishes off the meal nicely. A five-course table d'hôte menu costs £12 ($18), and you can also order à la carte. The restaurant is open every day and serves food during regular pub hours. If you wish to overnight here, the charge per person is £17 ($25.50) without bath, £21 ($31.50) with bath, including a full English breakfast and VAT. Children are not accepted overnight.

9. Dorchester

Thomas Hardy, in his 1886 Victorian novel *The Mayor of Casterbridge,* gave it literary fame. But Dorchester was known to the Romans. In fact its Maumbury Rings, south of the town, are considered the best Roman amphitheater in Britain, having once resounded with the shouts of 12,000 spectators screaming for gladiator blood. Dorchester, the county town, was the setting of another blood-letting, the Bloody Assize of 1685, when Judge Jeffreys, suffering from "the stone," dispensed the ultimate in justice to the poor wretches condemned for supporting the Duke of Monmouth's ill-fated attempt to become the English monarch.

But it is mostly through Hardy that the world knows Dorchester. Many of his major scenes of love and intrigue took place on the periphery of Dorchester. The land was best known to Hardy, since he was born in 1840 at **Higher Bockhampton,** three miles northeast of Dorchester, off the A35. His home, now a National Trust property, may be visited by the public from March to October, from 11 a.m. to 6 p.m. or dusk, whichever is earlier. But to go inside, you must make an appointment with the tenant. You may write in advance to **Hardy's Cottage,** Higher Bockhampton, Dorchester, Dorset, England, or telephone 0305/62366. You approach the cottage on foot, a seven-minute walk after parking your vehicle in the space provided in the wood. The admission is £1.20 ($1.80). Within easy reach of the cottage is **Rainbarrow,** mentioned by Hardy in *Return of the Native.*

You may also want to browse around the **Dorset County Museum** on High West Street (next to St. Peter's Church; tel. 0305/62735), with memorabilia of Thomas Hardy and other famous inhabitants of Dorset. In addition, you'll find prehistoric and Roman relics, plus natural history exhibits and others pertaining to the geology of the region. There is also a rural craft section of bygones. Displays and finds from Maiden Castle, Britain's largest Iron Age hill fort can be seen, plus galleries on the geology and natural history of Dorset. The museum is open weekdays from 10 a.m. to 1 p.m. and 2 to 5 p.m. Admission is 80p ($1.20) for adults, 40p (60¢) for children 5 to 16 years of age (children under 5 free).

Five miles east of Dorchester, on the Dorchester-Bournemouth road (A35), one mile east of Puddletown, stands **Athelhampton** (tel. 030584/363), one of England's great medieval houses, considered the most beautiful and historic in the south. It was begun in the reign of Edward IV on the legendary site of King Athelstan's palace. It was Thomas Hardy's Athelhall. A family home for more than 500 years, it is noted for its 15th-century Great Hall, its Tudor Great Chamber, its state bedroom, and King's Room. The house stands on ten acres of formal and landscaped gardens, with a 15th-century dovecote, river gardens, fish ponds, fountains, and rare trees. It is open to the public on Wednesday, Thursday, Sunday, and bank holidays, from the Wednesday before Easter to the second Sunday in October, 2 to 6 p.m. In August it is also open on Monday and Tuesday. Admission is £1 ($1.50) to the garden and another £1 to the house.

WHERE TO STAY: Built on medieval foundations, the **Wessex Hotel,** High West Street (tel. 0305/62660), is an architecturally interesting Georgian structure. In the town center, the hotel offers 20 bedrooms with full residential services. Room rates range from £15 ($22.50) for a single room to £26 ($39) for a double or twin. Prices include a full English breakfast and VAT. The Wessex has a restaurant license and a popular public restaurant with an extensive menu and a good wine list.

East Linton, 7 Damers Rd. (tel. 0305/64547), is one of the best B&B houses in the town. A short walk from the heart of town, it is a Victorian building that has not been ruined by modernization. It is comfortable and pleasantly furnished, and one room is set aside for families. Guests are welcomed in every month except December, and are charged from £10 ($15) per person for B&B. Guests must share a bath, and the rate includes a full English breakfast.

WHERE TO EAT: Opposite the County Museum, **Judge Jeffreys' Restaurant,** 6 High West St. (tel. 0305/64369), built as a house in 1398, is an attractive stopover on your cross-country jaunt. It had the dubious distinction of lodging that "cantankerous alcoholic," Judge Jeffreys, during the Bloody Assizes. The place has an old English atmosphere of massive oak beams, a spiral staircase, stone-mullioned windows, and paneled rooms, along with Tudor fireplaces. It is open Monday to Saturday from 9 a.m. to 4 p.m. and on Sunday from 11 a.m. to 2 p.m. The menu offers curries, casseroles, filet of plaice, and steak and kidney pie, with meals costing from £4 ($6).

The Horse with the Red Umbrella, 10 High West St. (tel. 0305/62019). The window of this shop/coffeehouse is filled with appetizing cakes, doughnuts, bakewell tarts, and enormous, cream-filled eclairs. Inside you will find neat tables and chairs where you can watch the passing locals and enjoy quiche, savory rice, omelets, and various toasted snacks, finishing with a homemade fruit pie with cream or a sorbet. It is cheap and good. In winter they also have stuffed baked potatoes. Meals cost from £3.50 ($5.25). It's open from 8:30 a.m. to 5:30 p.m. Monday through Saturday.

Potter In, 19 Durngate St. (tel. 0305/68649), is a cheerful little place really known only to the local people who flock in for the whole-meal scones, home-baked rolls, flapjacks, and a spicy, moist carrot cake which is worth stopping in for. Two specials are offered at lunch, served noon to 2 p.m., which may be roast chicken and vegetables or a filling vegetable casserole. There are also omelets, whole-food pâtés, rarebits, and quiches from which to select. A meal cost from £($4.50) up. The establishment is open from 10 a.m. to 5 p.m. daily except Sunday.

On the Outskirts

Brace of Pheasants, Plush (tel. 03004/357). Jane and Geoffrey Knights run this charming country restaurant and inn which has beautiful views through its little dormer windows, opening onto a rural setting. To reach it, take the B3143 out of Dorchester to Piddletrenthide, turning off at the sign to Plush. The inn, open every day, is on your left. Geoffrey does the cooking, with an emphasis on traditional country dishes and game specialties. The restaurant and bar are done in cream color with chintz fabrics, old paintings, and antique tables, and are warmed by two open fires. Charcoal grills are the specialty of the bar, and not only steaks but cutlets and game dishes are available seven days a week. In summer, Jane and Geoffrey offer grilled lobster and prawns. They also have a covered patio in the garden which is fun in summer. The variety of food offered in this inn is enormous, including at least eight appetizers and six main courses, along with a large selection of desserts. The cost is about £14 ($21) per person, including VAT. It's open from 11 a.m. to 2:30 p.m. and 6 to 11 p.m. Reservations are advised.

Yarlbury Cottage, Lower Bockhampton, near Dorchester (tel. 0305/62382), is a thatch-roofed cottage with inglenook and beamed ceilings in a small country village in the heart of Hardy country and, in fact, within walking distance of Thomas Hardy's cottage at Higher Brockhampton and of Stinsford Church where his heart is buried.

The restaurant, particularly popular with locals and tourists alike in summer at lunchtime, has good food and a warm, friendly atmosphere. You might choose from cold dishes such as roast beef, fresh salmon, or ham, although a hot dish of the day and a ploughman's lunch are also offered. The à la carte menu in the evening is short but special. There are about half a dozen appetizers, a variety of main courses, and desserts to suit most tastes. A specialty is the English lamb. Good sauces and lightly cooked fresh vegetables are important. All the food is prepared on the premises from fresh ingredients and is served to please the eye and the palate. Lunches cost about £5 ($7.50) and dinners from £10 ($15). Reservations are required for dinner. The restaurant is open all year, but hours are shortened in winter, so check first. In summer, it's best to go from noon to 2 p.m. and 7 to 9 p.m.

FLEET AIR ARM MUSEUM: This museum at the Royal Naval Air Station, Yeovilton in Somerset (tel. 0935/840565), contains the largest collection of historic military aircraft in Europe, including the Concorde 002. It also displays scale models and other memorabilia associated with the RN Air Service and the Fleet Air Arm. Flying displays from the airfield can be viewed from the car park area. The museum, charging £2.20 ($3.30) for adults, £1 ($1.50) for children, is open daily from 10 a.m. until 5:30 p.m. or dusk. There are a tea room and a picnic area.

From Dorchester, we continue west 15 miles to:

10. Bridport

In Thomas Hardy's fictional Wessex terrain, Bridport was Port Bredy. The town lies inland, although there is a harbor one mile away at the holiday resort of West Bay, near the end of Chesil Beach. Ropes and fishing nets are Bridport specialties. Many a man dangled from the end of a Bridport dagger—that is, a rope—especially when some home-grown rebels were carted off to Dorchester to face Hanging Judge Jeffreys.

An interesting excursion from Bridport is to visit **Parnham** at Beaminster (tel. 0308/862204). One of the loveliest houses in Dorset, it stands in a wooded valley beside the River Brit. Since Tudor times it has been surrounded by sweeping lawns and magnificent trees, along with terraces and falling water. In 1976 John Makepeace, internationally known designer and furniture-maker, bought Parnham, made it his home, and set up his workshop in the former stables. Here his team of artisans make the unique pieces of exquisite commissioned furniture Makepeace designs and on which his reputation is based. The well-restored rooms of the great house display recently completed pieces from the workshop, and there are monthly exhibitions by Britain's leading contemporary artists, designers, and artisans. The ornate plastered ceilings, paneled walls, and stone fireplaces are a splendid setting for the best of 20th-century design and craftsmanship.

Light lunches and teas with homemade cakes and local clotted cream are served in the 17th-century licensed buttery. The house, gardens, exhibitions, and workshop are open from 10 a.m. to 5 p.m. on Wednesday, Sunday, and bank holiday from April to October. Admission is £2 ($3) for adults and £1 ($1.50) for children. Parnham is on the A3066, five miles north of Bridport.

FOOD AND LODGING: A 16th-century coaching inn, the **Bull Hotel,** 34 East Street (tel. 0308/22878), now houses modern wayfarers in its 27 bedrooms, all with hot and cold running water. A single ranges from £14 ($21) to £25 ($37.50), and a double goes for £25 ($37.50) to £45 ($67.50). The atmosphere is old-worldish, complete with a minstrels' gallery and enough bars to satisfy anybody. The bedrooms are simply but comfortably furnished. In 1939 George VI stopped off at the Bull. The hotel remains open all year, and nonresidents may patronize its restaurants, such as the Dorset Room, where table d'hôte luncheons cost £5.50 ($8.25) and a set dinner goes for £9 ($13.50).

If you're a nonsmoker, you may want to enjoy the B&B hospitality provided by **48 West Allington** (same address) (tel. 0308/25381). About one-third of a mile from the heart of town, this is a Georgian building. It rents out two pleasantly furnished rooms, one of which has a private bath. The bathless room rents for £8 ($12) per person, the one with bath costing £9.50 ($14.25). Limited parking is available.

Only one mile west of Bridport lies the little village of:

11. Chideock

A model village of West Dorset, Chideock is bathed in charm. In this mainroad hamlet of thatched houses, a mellowed stone is used for most of the buildings. A dairy farm is found in the village itself. About a mile from the coast, it's a gem of a place for overnight stopovers or even longer stays. The beautiful countryside, with its rolling hills, makes excursions a temptation.

By the time you visit, the Duke and Duchess of York will probably have moved into their new home, Chideock Manor, a handsome old stone structure. Perhaps you'll see Fergie somewhere around the village or countryside.

FOOD AND LODGING: Dating from 1685, the **George Inn** (tel. 0297/89419) is the oldest establishment in the village, right on the A35. The owners, Mike and Marilyn Tuck, extend a warm welcome to all and offer excellent food either in the bar or dining room during regular pub hours. Three-course meals can be obtained for prices from £4 ($6). B&B in the well-equipped bedrooms will cost £10.50 ($15.75) per person, the price including tea- and coffee-making equipment and TV. All bedrooms have hot and cold running water. The George Inn is fully licensed, with facilities for children, a game room, and a well-kept Beer Garden.

Betchworth House (tel. 029789/478) is a 17th-century guesthouse on the main road at the edge of the village. Owned by Mr. and Mrs. David Scott, it purveys accommodations that are immaculate, homey, and a good bargain—£12 ($18) to £14 ($21) per person for B&B. When evening dinner is included, add another £7.50 ($11.25) to the bill. The Scotts will point out the way to the beach, a mile walk along a quiet road. The house is open all year. There's a large free car park just opposite the house, and a pretty walled garden in back of the building where you can sit and enjoy the peace among the flowers.

Chideock House Hotel (tel. 0297/89242) is perhaps the prettiest thatched house in Chideock, a village of winners. Set near the road, with a protective stone wall, the house opens onto a rear garden of flowers, shrubs, and fruit trees. A driveway through the gardens leads to a large car park in the rear. You go directly into the beamed lounge, with its wide fireplace (wood-burning fires on cool days). You can stay here on a B&B basis at a cost beginning at £18 ($27) per person nightly. Most of the bedrooms have baths. The cuisine is a local favorite, with the best dessert table in town. In addition to the à la carte restaurant, a grill room offers a range of large steaks, fish, homemade dishes, and a salad table. Especially interesting is the Tudor part of the house, and the Adam fireplace in the lounge. The house quartered the Roundheads in 1645, and the ghosts of the village martyrs are still said to haunt, as their trial was held at the hotel. Resident owners are Barbara and Alf Way and Kevin and Alison Davies.

The **Thatch Cottage** (tel. 0297/89473). You'd never suspect that under the thatch of this 17th-century cottage are the comforts of home. The owner, Mrs. Pat Shayler, accepts paying guests all year. While this is essentially a summer resort, there are those who welcome the idea of staying winter weekends, snugly sitting in front of the fireplace after enjoying good home cooking. A table d'hôte dinner at £8 ($12) is featured. You may also order à la carte. Fresh local produce is a specialty. Most of the year, the charge is £10 ($15) per person for B&B. With dinner, the rate becomes £17 ($25.50) per person. If you want to walk to the beach, you can ask your hostess to pack a picnic lunch. It's best to make Chideock your center for a week, exploring the many sights in the area on day trips. Reservations are necessary from June to September.

A short ride and we're at:

12. Charmouth

On Lyme Bay, Charmouth is still another winner. A village of Georgian houses and thatched cottages, Charmouth contains some of the most dramatic coastal scenery in West Dorset. The village lies to the west of Golden Cap, which is—according to the adventurers who measure such things—the highest cliff along the coast of southern England.

The **Queens Armes Hotel** (tel. 0297/60339). Catherine of Aragon, the first of Henry VIII's six wives and the daughter of Ferdinand and Isabella of Spain, stayed in this hotel near the sea. A small medieval house, it also figured in the flight of the defeated King Charles, the Roundheads in hot pursuit. Since the Queens Armes is right on the road, you may not suspect its inner charm: a rear flower garden, oak beams, a dining room with dark oak tables and Windsor chairs, and the living room with its Regency armchairs and antiques. Out of 11 rooms, ten have private baths, and all have color TV. B&B costs £18 ($27) to £21 ($31.50) per person, depending on the season (higher during Christmas week). For an additional £6 ($9) per person, you can have dinner. The hotel specializes in well-prepared English fare, with some continental dishes, and there's a vegetarian menu. The owners, Mr. and Mrs. Peter G. Miles, have pleasantly added their own touches to the house.

Newlands House, Stonebarrow Lane (tel. 0297/60212), lies on the periphery of the village, within walking distance of the beach. It draws increasingly favorable reports from readers who are drawn to its comfortable and well-furnished bedrooms. The rate for B&B ranges from £12 ($18) to £15.50 ($23.25) per person nightly, depending on the accommodation assigned. It's also possible to take half-board terms here, costing from £19 ($28.50) to £22 ($33) per person nightly.

Two miles west is—

13. Lyme Regis

On Lyme Bay near the Devonshire border, the resort of Lyme Regis is one of the most attractive centers along the South Coast. For those who shun such big commercial holiday centers as Torquay or Bournemouth, Lyme Regis may be ideal—the true English coastal town, with a highly praised mild climate. Sea gulls fly overhead; the streets are steep and winding; walks along Cobb Beach brisk and stimulating; the views, particularly of the craft in the harbor, photogenic. Following Lyme Regis's career as a major seaport (the Duke of Monmouth landed here to begin his unsuccessful attempt to become king), one finds it was a small spa for a while, catering to such visitors as Jane Austen, who was also fond of nearby Charmouth.

The stone breakwater, the Cobb, was immortalized in *The French Lieutenant's Woman*. As you walk on the Cobb—and everybody does—the waves crash around you, and as a backdrop you have the Dorset cliffs which seem to tumble into the sea. The actors stayed in the town's two main hotels. John Fowles, its author, is a resident of Lyme Regis.

The town also boasts the 1979–1981 world champion and best dressed town crier. Richard Fox is just maintaining a tradition that has been handed down for 1,000 years in Lyme Regis when he announces the local news. He'll also take visitors on a two-hour tour of the resort on Tuesday and Thursday at 3 p.m. to see the Cobb, the harbor from which ships sailed to fight the Spanish Armada. The walks head up old Broad Street. Mr. Fox can be reached at Flat 2, 54 Broad St. Lr. (tel. 02974/3568).

The surrounding area is a fascinating place for fossilism. Mary Anning discovered in 1810 at the age of 11 one of the first articulated ichthyosaur skeletons. She went on to become one of the first professional fossilists in the country. Books telling of walks in the area and the regions where the fossils can be seen are available at the local information bureau in the Guildhall on Bridge Street.

WHERE TO STAY: On a ledge above the village, with a panoramic view of the coast, the **Kersbrook Hotel and Restaurant,** Pound Road (tel. 02974/2596), lives up to its boast of being the "dream house of the Dorset Riviera." Built of stone and crowned by thatch roof, the hotel has a century-old terraced garden in the rear. Major renovations have been done by Eric and Jane Stephenson, the resident proprietors, who offer bedrooms with private baths, costing from £15.50 ($23.25) to £19.50 ($29.25) per person. In the handsome restaurant, carefully looked after by Jane Stephenson, you can enjoy imaginative and interesting French-English and West Country dishes, a meal costing from £10 ($15) up. The Kersbrook has two lounges and an intimate cocktail bar. All the public rooms, fitted with some antiques, add to the individual "olde world" charm of the place.

The **Three Cups Hotel,** Broad Street (tel. 02974/2732), is on the main street close to the shops, about 100 yards from the sea. About 200 years old, it boasts a handsome columned entrance with a Regency bow window above, which was used in the film, *The French Lieutenant's Woman.* Inside the hotel, the rooms are light and airy, some with sea views, with features such as stained glass windows and sloping corridors giving added character. Rooms have hot and cold running water, tea- and coffee-making equipment, radios, and TV, as well as private toilet facilities if required. Accommodations cost from £20 ($30) per person for B&B, with VAT included. The hotel has a restaurant serving à la carte or table d'hôte meals from £11 ($16.50), as well as a paneled lounge bar with an open log fire, where you can enjoy bar snacks. Parking is available.

The **White House,** 47 Silver St. (tel. 02974/3420), is a friendly, small, centrally heated guest house run by John and Ann Edmondson. It is only a few minutes' walk from the harbor and the center of town. The house is attractively furnished and well maintained, offering B&B from £10 ($15) per person daily. Of the house's seven rooms, five are doubles and two have twin beds. Four have private shower, toilet, and basin, while one has a basin and shower, and two have basins only. All units have tea/coffee-making facilities, color TV, and digital clock radios. A large lounge with color TV is set aside for residents. The White House is fully licensed. There is a private car park.

Norman House, Coombe Street (tel. 02974/3191), is one of the best B&Bs in the area. Built in the 1500s, it opens onto a historic narrow street at the foot of Lyme Regis, a short walk from the Guildhall, the sea wall fronting the Channel, and the local museum. Readers James and Nancy Heldman, who found this place for me, write: "The owner, Mrs. Franklin, is gracious and cultivated; a warm lady who goes out of her way to make her guests feel that they are visiting her." She rents one double (with private bath), plus two other doubles and a single with a shared bath. The rate is from £9 ($13.50) per person for B&B.

WHERE TO EAT: Down by the Cobb, the **Cobb Arms** (tel. 02974/3242) is a pub right on the harborside where you can order bar snacks such as braised beef with vegetables. Or you can dine in the restaurant on fresh Lyme Bay plaice with a salad and vegetable, or local Dover sole. Fresh local scallops are often sautéed in herb butter and served with a salad and brown bread and butter. Appetizers include soups, pâtés, and smoked fish. There are also mixed grills, rump or T-bone steaks, served with baked potatoes and salads. Meals cost from £12 ($18) up. The restaurant is open from noon to 2 p.m. and 6:30 to 9 p.m.; closed Wednesday.

As you eat, you can look out over the harbor in very much the same way as the French lieutenant's woman did. It was in this pub, run by Sylvia and Steve Waller, that the members of the cast and the stars were dressed and made up for their parts in the film.

Next to the inn is the Lifeboat Station, with its boat ever ready to put to sea to rescue sailors in distress.

14. Donyatt

After Lyme Regis, you may want to journey to Donyatt, a village near Ilminster. Just outside the village, between the A303 and the A30 London-West Country roads, stands the following recommendation:

Thatchers Pond (tel. 04605/3210) is a 15th-century thatched hamstone (a local rock) farmhouse where David and Marlene Douglas, both experienced caterers, offer a vast cold table for lunch and dinner daily except Monday. The house is warm and welcoming, with old clocks, guns, and swords adorning the walls of the flagstoned hall and carpeted dining room. Meals are served from a vast table laden with fresh lobster, salmon, crab, prawns, cold roast beef, ham, tongue, homemade pâté, quiches, and mousse. After your choice from the buffet, you are invited to help yourself from a selection of 25 different salads. The main course is large enough, but if you're a gourmand, you can choose from a range of appetizers. The dessert trolley or the cheese board will supply the finish to your meal. The bar offers beers, wines, spirits, liqueurs, coffee, and tea. Lunch from the buffet costs £9 ($13.50), and dinner goes for £11 ($16.50). Thatchers is open from noon to 2 p.m. and 7 to 9 p.m. Closes Sunday evening and Monday.

15. Sherborne

A little gem of a town, with well-preserved medieval, Tudor, Stuart, and Georgian buildings, Sherborne is in the heart of Dorset in a setting of wooded hills, valleys, and chalk downs. It was here that Sir Walter Raleigh lived before the vicissitudes of power dislodged him forever.

Sherborne Old Castle (tel. 0935/812730), half a mile east of the town, was built in the early 12th century by the powerful Bishop Roger de Caen, but it was soon seized by the Crown about the time of the death of King Henry I in 1135 and the troubled accession to the throne of Stephen. The castle was given to Sir Walter Raleigh by Queen Elizabeth. The gallant knight built Sherborne Lodge in the grounds. The buildings were mostly destroyed in the Civil War, but you can still see a gatehouse, some graceful arcades, and decorative windows. The castle ruins can be visited from 9:30 a.m. to 6:30 p.m. mid-March to mid-October and from 9:30 a.m. to 4 p.m. the remainder of the year. On Sunday, hours are the same as weekdays from April to September, with a 2 p.m. opening otherwise.

Sherborne Castle (tel. 0935/813182) was built by Sir Walter Raleigh in 1594, when he decided that it would not be feasible to restore the old castle to suit him. His new home was an Elizabethan residence, a square mansion, which later owners gussied up with four Jacobean-style wings to make it more palatial. After King James I had Raleigh imprisoned in the Tower of London, the monarch gave the castle to a favorite Scot, Robert Carr, so that the Raleighs were banished from their home. It became the property of Sir John Digby, first Earl of Bristol, in 1617 and has been the Digby family home ever since. The mansion was enlarged by Sir John in 1625, and in the 18th century, the formal Elizabethan gardens and fountains of the Raleighs were altered by Capability Brown, who created a serpentine lake between the two castles. The 20 acres of lawns and pleasure grounds around the 50-acre lake are open to the public. In the house are fine furniture, china, and paintings by Gainsborough, Lely, Reynolds, Kneller, and Vandyck, among other artists. Easter Saturday to the end of September, the house is open on Thursday, Saturday, Sunday, and bank holidays from 2 to 6 p.m. Admission to the castle is £2.50 ($3.25) for adults, £1.20 ($1.80) for children; to the grounds only, 80p ($1.20) for adults, 40p (60¢) for children.

Sherborne Abbey is worth visiting to see the splendid fan vaulting of the roof, as well as the many monuments, including Purbeck marble effigies of medieval abbots and the Elizabethan marble four-posters and canopied Renaissance tombs. A baroque statue of the Earl of Bristol, standing between two wives, was carved in 1698. The church is open daily until dusk. Many of the abbey's medieval and Tudor monastic buildings are still in existence, used today to house a school. This British public school was the setting of a novel by Alec Waugh, *The Loom of Youth*.

WHERE TO STAY: Once one of the shire's mellow old tollhouses, Farthing Gate, Holnest, near Sherborne (tel. 096321/479), has a pleasant ambience and inviting, welcoming owners. They have only two double rooms which rent for £19 ($28.50). Guests are received only from April to October.

A more substantial hotel is Half Moon, Half Moon Street (tel. 0935/812017), centrally located in Sherborne. It rents out 15 well-furnished and comfortable bedrooms, with rates ranging from £24 ($36) to £32 ($48) in a single, £35 ($52.50) to £42 ($63) in a double. Tariffs depend on the plumbing. The restaurant has a carvery restaurant, offering one of the best food values in town, with a help-yourself selection of roast joints. Meals begin at £7 ($10.50).

Chapter IX

DEVON

1. Beer and Seaton
2. Exeter
3. Dartmoor
4. Chagford
5. Torbay (Torquay)
6. Totnes
7. Dartmouth
8. Salcombe
9. Plymouth
10. Clovelly
11. Combe Martin and Lynton-Lynmouth

THE GREAT PATCHWORK-QUILT area of the southwest of England, part of the West Countree, abounds with cliffside farms, rolling hills, foreboding moors, semitropical plants, and fishing villages—all of which combine to provide some of the finest scenery in England. The British from other parts of the country approach the sunny counties of Devon and Cornwall (see next chapter) with the same kind of excitement one would normally reserve for hopping over to the continent. Especially along the coastline, the British Riviera, many of the names of the little seaports, villages, and resorts have become synonymous with holidays in the sun: Torbay, Clovelly, Lynton-Lynmouth.

It's easy to involve yourself in the West Country life, as lived by the British vacationers. Perhaps you'll go pony-trekking across moor and woodland, past streams and sheep-grazing fields, stopping off at local pubs to soak up atmosphere and mugs of ale. Chances are your oddly shaped bedroom will be in a barton (farm) mentioned in the *Domesday Book* or in a thatch-roofed cottage neither straight, level, nor true.

Fishermen may catch their lunch (salmon and trout in such rivers as the Dart), then take it back to the kitchen of their guesthouse to be grilled. Life is often most informal. Your hosts, many being of farming stock themselves, don't like to muck about putting on airs for tourists. In the morning your landlady might be out picking string beans for your dinner. Later she'll bring up pails from the milk house, and you can watch her create her own version of clotted Devonshire cream cooked on the back of the stove. For dessert that night, you'll get a country portion heaped on your freshly picked gooseberries.

When a Devonian invites you to walk down the primrose path, he or she means just that. The primrose is practically the shire flower of this most beautiful of counties.

Devon is a land of jagged coasts—the red cliffs in the south facing the English Channel, the gray cliffs in the north opening onto the Bristol Channel. Sandwiched between them is some of the most widely varied scenery in England, ranging from heartlands and wooded valleys to buzzard-haunted combes. Aside from the shores, a great many of the scenic splashes appear in the two national parks, **Dartmoor** in the south, **Exmoor** in the north.

A SPECIAL BUS TICKET: The two main bus companies of Devon and Cornwall combine to offer a **Key West ticket,** granting unlimited travel anywhere on the two networks for any seven consecutive days at a cost of £12 ($18) for adults and £7 ($10.50) for children under 14. You can plan your journeys from the maps and timetables from any Western National/Devon General offices when you purchase your ticket. Further information may be obtained from Devon General Ltd., Belgrave Road, Exeter EX1 2LB (tel. 0392/39333).

SOUTH DEVON

It can be the lazy life in South Devon, as you recline in an orchard, enjoying the view of the coast from which native sons Raleigh and Drake set sail. Almost every little hamlet, on some level, is geared to accommodate visitors, who flock here in great numbers from early spring to late fall. There is much to see and explore. Mainly the tranquil life prevails.

Our adventure begins in:

1. Beer and Seaton

Only seven miles from one of our last stopovers, the coastal resort of Lyme Regis in Dorset, Beer no longer is a center for smugglers, but remains still colorful, with its small fleet of fishing craft, its sandy beach, white cliffs, and a pebbly cove. Tucked away into the only chalk cliffs on Devon's south coast, Beer offers safe boating and bathing, plus deep-sea fishing. The village has an interesting history, stretching back beyond the time when the Romans quarried stone here. Honiton lacemaking was introduced from Flanders, and Beer women made Queen Victoria's wedding dress. There are four golf courses within nine miles, and tennis and riding are available locally.

Almost incongruously in the small seaside town of Seaton is a lovingly preserved collection of open-topped double-decker tramcars painted with authentic advertising. The collection lies on Harbour Road and is called the **Seaton and District Electric Tramway Company** (tel. 0297/21702). The gentle ride to Colyton, three miles up the Axe Valley, passes through fields between hedgerows. There are several departures daily from May to October (also on Sunday from Easter to May).

FOOD AND LODGING: In Beer you can stay at **Durham House Hotel,** Fore Street (tel. 0297/20449), in the main street 500 yards from the sea. This small family hotel is run by Jenny and Brian Clinch, a friendly couple who offer accommodation all year in their 100-year-old granite house. You will find a comfortable lounge with color TV, a bar, and a dining room with an excellent reputation for good food and personal service. Some bedrooms have baths, and all have color TV. For B&B and an evening meal, you pay £14 ($21) per person nightly, plus VAT. Durham House is probably the best of the small, inexpensive hotels in the village, and makes an ideal base for touring.

In Seaton, "check out" the **Check House,** Beer Road, Seaton (tel. 0297/21858), which is exactly what its name implies, a checkered house with a steep slate roof and tall chimneys set in a large garden with a gate right on to the beach. There is a large lounge, plus comfortable bedrooms with central heating. Mrs. Lee charges from £10.50 ($15.75) to £12.50 ($18.75) per person nightly for B&B, and will provide a good-tasting dinner on request for another £6 ($9).

On the Outskirts

Kingswood Hotel, Esplanade, near Sidmouth (tel. 03955/6367), is an attractive place right on the seafront with a glazed balcony and potted plants overspilling the balcony railings. The hotel has won prizes in the Britain in Bloom competition. Colin Seward, the chef/patron, operates in the best French tradition and prides himself on the quality and variety of the cookery served in the attractive dining room where an evening meal begins at £7.50 ($11.25). The bedrooms are neat, decorated with fresh flowers and containing either a bath or shower, along with a toilet, color TV, phone, radio, and tea-maker. B&B costs from £12.50 ($18.75) to £15 ($22.50) per person.

2. Exeter

The county town of Devonshire, on the banks of the Exe River, Exeter was a Roman city founded in the first century A.D. Two centuries later it was encircled by a mighty stone wall, traces of which remain today. Conquerors and would-be conquerors, especially the Vikings, stormed the fortress in the centuries ensuing. None was more notable than William the Conqueror. Irked at Exeter's refusal to capitulate (perhaps at the sheltering of Gytha, mother of the slain Harold), the Norman duke brought Exeter to its knees in short order.

Under the Tudors the city grew and prospered. The cocky Sir Walter Raleigh and Sir Francis Drake cut striking figures strolling through Exeter's medieval and Elizabethan streets. Regrettably, in May of 1942 the skies over Exeter were suddenly filled with German bombers. When their merciless task was over, Exeter was in flames. One of the most beautiful and historic cities of England was a mere shell of its former self. Exeter grew back, of course, but the new, impersonal-looking shops and offices couldn't replace the Georgian crescents, the black-and-white timbered buildings with their plastered walls. Fortunately, much was spared, including the major architectural treasure—

EXETER CATHEDRAL: Owing its present look to the Decorated style of the 13th and 14th centuries, the Exeter Cathedral of St. Peter (tel. 0392/55573) actually goes back to Saxon times. Even Canute, the Viking conqueror, got in on the act of rebuilding around 1017. The Norman cathedral of Bishop Warelwast came into being in the early 12th century, and the north and south towers serve as reminders of that period. The remarkable feature of the present Gothic building is the interior, with its tierceron vaulting, stretching out for some 300 feet. The cathedral did suffer damage in the 1942 German bombings, which destroyed its St. James's Chapel (subsequently restored). But most of the treasures remain intact, including the rows of sculpture along the west front, the 14th-century Minstrels' Gallery, and the bishop's throne. The cathedral asks that visitors contribute at least 80p ($1.20) toward its upkeep for the future.

EXETER MARITIME MUSEUM: At the Quay (tel. 0392/58075), the maritime museum has a collection of more than 140 small craft, many of which are on display, and shelters the world's largest collection of English and foreign craft, ranging from the Congo to Corfu. The larger boats afloat in the canal basin can be boarded. There are canoes and boats that have been rowed across the Atlantic, and you can go aboard the oldest working steamboat or even picnic on a Hong Kong junk or an Arab dhow. This is an active museum, and the ISCA members who maintain the boats sail some of them during the summer months. Five colorful Portuguese chatas are available for rent at the museum from May to September, carrying a maximum of six passengers. The boats are rowed along the three miles of navigable water on the historic canal at a charge of £2 ($3) per hour. The museum is open every day of the year except Christmas and Boxing Day from 10 a.m. to 5 p.m. October to May, from 10 a.m. to 6 p.m. June to September. Adults pay an admission of £2.50 ($3.75), and children, £1.25 ($1.88).

Note: Occasionally, individual boats for special events or sailing may not be on display.

OTHER MONUMENTS: Much of the old remains. The **Exeter Guildhall, a** colonnaded building on the High Street (tel. 0392/77888), is regarded as the oldest municipal building in the kingdom. The earliest reference to the Guildhall is contained in a deed of 1160. The Tudor front that straddles the pavement was added in 1593. Inside is a fine display of silver in the gallery. It contains a number of paintings as well, including one of Henrietta Anne, daughter of Charles I (she was born in Exeter in 1644). The ancient hall is paneled in oak. The Guildhall is open throughout the year, Monday to Saturday from 10 a.m. to 5:30 p.m., when civic functions permit, and admission is free.

The present headquarters of the Devon County Council, **Rougemont Castle,** with its Norman gateway, is now largely a memory. Rougemont was created for William the Conqueror on the site of a Saxon fortification. Over the centuries the castle fell into ruins. Now there has been some small-scale restoration, and it is pleasant to stroll through Rougemont Gardens.

If time remains, see also **St. Nicholas Priory,** the Mint, lying off Fore Street (founded in 1080—now partially restored); **Tucker's Hall,** Fore Street, a 15th-century craft building; and the underground passageways of **Princesshay** (the subterranean water supply channels of medieval times).

On the Outskirts

Powderham Castle, Powderham (tel. 0626/890243), lies eight miles south of Exeter off the A379 Dawlish road. A castle here was built in the late 14th century by Sir Philip Courtenay, sixth son of the second Earl of Devon, and his wife, Margaret, granddaughter of Edward I. Their magnificent tomb is in the south transept of Exeter Cathedral. The castle suffered damage during the Civil War and was restored and altered in the 18th and 19th centuries, but its towers and battlements are still pure 14th century. The castle contains much fine furniture, including a remarkable clock which plays full tunes at 4, 8, and 12 o'clock, some 17th-century tapestries, and a chair used by William III for his first Council of State at Newton Abbot. The staircase hall contains some remarkable plasterwork set in bold relief against a brilliant turquoise background, more than two centuries old, as well as a detailed pedigree of the Courtenay family, a document more than 12 feet high. The chapel dates from the 15th century, with hand-hewn roof timbers and carved pew ends. Powderham Castle is a private house lived in by Lord and Lady Devon. From the Sunday of the late spring bank holiday to the second Thursday in September, the castle is open daily from 2 to 5:30 p.m. except Friday and Saturday when it's closed. Admission is £1.75 ($2.63) for adults, £1 ($1.50) for children 8 to 16.

WHERE TO STAY: On the outskirts of the town, the **Lea-Dene,** 34 Alphington Rd. (A377), St. Thomas (tel. 0392/57257), is a semi-detached Edwardian house with gardens. Mr. and Mrs. Rogers offer a lot of extras, including a large free car park mainly behind the house, a double garage, a choice of evening meals, family rooms (with cots and highchairs), full central heating, a public phone, a color TV lounge (the units also have private color TV sets), and free baths and showers. They'll also provide a babysitting service, and will even arrange for special diets if given advance notice. Each bedroom is carpeted and well furnished, and rates are from £11 ($16.50) to £13 ($19.50) per person for B&B. Regular bus service into the center of town goes right by the front door.

Trenance House Hotel, 1 Queen's Crescent, York Road (tel. 0392/73277), is one of the best B&Bs in town, lying just three minutes from the heart of town in the vicinity of the coach station. The resident owners, the Breading family, welcome guests to their 14 comfortably furnished bedrooms, some of which contain a private

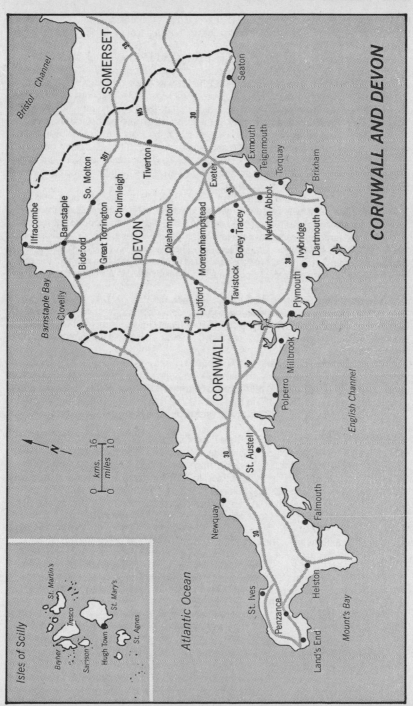

CORNWALL AND DEVON

SOMERSET

Bristol Channel

Seaton

M5

30

Exmouth
Teignmouth
Torquay
Brixham

Tiverton

So. Molton

Chulmleigh

Exeter

Ilfracombe

Barnstaple

Great Torrington

DEVON

Okehampton

Moretonhampstead

Bovey Tracey

Newton Abbot

Ivybridge

Dartmouth

Bide'ord

Barnstaple Bay

Clovelly

Lydford

Tavistock

Plymouth

Millbrook

Polperro

English Channel

CORNWALL

St. Austell

Newquay

Falmouth

Atlantic Ocean

St. Ives

Helston

Penzance

Land's End

Mount's Bay

0 kms. 16
0 miles 10

N

Isles of Scilly

St. Martin's

Tresco
Bryher

Samson

Hugh Town

St. Mary's

St. Agnes

bath or shower. Singles pay from £12 ($18) for B&B, two persons from £21 ($31.50). It's best to book in here on half-board terms, costing from £18 ($27) per person nightly.

If you're driving, your best bet might be the **Lord Haldon Hotel,** Dunchideock, near Exeter (tel. 0392/832483), which was constructed around 1720 as the center of the Lords of Haldon. The wing that is still intact was one of the shire's biggest and grandest mansions from the 1700s. In the rolling Devon hills, it is only a short drive into the center (the location is five miles southwest of the cathedral city and the M5). Mr. and Mrs. Preece welcome guests to their 14 well-furnished bedrooms, most of which have private baths or showers. Bedroom windows open onto beautiful scenes not only of their own grounds, but the surrounding countryside. The B&B rate costs £18.50 ($27.75) in a single, £36 ($54) in a double. The best rate is the half-board term, costing from £25 ($37.50) per person daily. The meals are reliable here, using fresh local produce in the very British dishes.

Sylvania House, 64 Pennsylvania Rd. (tel. 0392/75583), is a spacious Edwardian house that was designed by a sea captain for his retirement. Many of the original characteristics have been preserved in its conversion to a comfortable hotel. All rooms are large and most have private bathrooms. Each unit is well furnished and has color TV and beverage-making facilities. The charge is £11 ($16.50) per person per night, with a full English breakfast included. The establishment is about ten minutes from the center of Exeter, lying in a tranquil residential area in the vicinity of the university.

Rhona's Guest House, 15 Blackall Rd. (tel. 0392/77791), is tiny but the welcome is big. Guests in comfortable, well-maintained accommodations share the public bath or shower and toilet. The rate is £11 ($16.50) in a single, rising to £17 ($25.50) in a double, including a full English breakfast. The location is about ten minutes from the heart of Exeter.

Trees, 2 Queen's Crescent (tel. 0392/59531), is a "mini-hotel" run by Dick and Bridget Bigwood, about a five-minute walk from the city center, near the coach station. There are 12 bedrooms, all with washbasins and shaver points. Bed and a full English breakfast cost £10 ($15) in a single, £18 ($27) in a double, and £19 ($28.50) in a twin-bedded room. The Bigwoods welcome their guests with a smile and a pot of tea.

WHERE TO EAT: A short walk from the cathedral, **Ship Inn,** Martin's Lane (tel. 0392/72040), was often visited by Sir Francis Drake, Sir Walter Raleigh, and Sir John Hawkins. Of it Drake wrote: "Next to mine own shippe, I do most love that old 'Shippe' in Exon, a tavern in Fyssh Street, as the people call it, or as the clergie will have it, St. Martin's Lane." The pub still provides tankards of stout and lager and is still loved by both young and old. The reconstructed dining room on the second floor also retains the early English atmosphere: settles, red leather and oak chairs. The fare is hearty English, the service friendly. At either lunch or dinner, you can order onion soup, grilled rainbow trout, or grilled rump steak. Expect to spend from £6 ($9) to £9 ($13.50) up for a meal. The price of the main courses includes vegetables, roll, and butter. The portions, as in Elizabethan days, are large. The restaurant is open from noon to 2 p.m. and 6:30 to 10:30 p.m. Monday through Saturday; closed Sunday and all bank holidays. The bars are open from 11 a.m. to 2:30 p.m. and 5 to 10:30 p.m. weekdays, until 11 p.m. on Friday and Saturday.

The **Port Royal Inn,** The Quay (tel. 0392/72360), stands close to the **Maritime Museum,** along the edge of the River Exe, a two-minute walk from the quay. In fair weather, tables are placed outside overlooking the river. This is a real ale house, also known for its ports and sherries. With such a name, the pub reminds one of smugglers in the Caribbean, intrepid explorers, and the famous navigators. The bar food offered will revive the inner person in a more modern way. Salads are tempting, and you can also order a ploughman's lunch or pâté and toast. Sandwiches made from granary bread are filled with meat or cheese. There are also mini-loaves of white or granary bread filled with salad, cheese, or meat. Each day they do two or three hot specials such as seafood, roast chicken, and roast lamb. There are also desserts and coffee with cream, and the pub serves real ales from various breweries, including Flowers, Eldridge Pope, and Hall and Woodhouse. Meals cost from £5 ($7.50). Food is served year round from 11 a.m. to 2:30 p.m., and in summer dinner is also offered from 5 to 11 p.m. On Sunday, hours are noon to 2 p.m. and 7 to 10:30 p.m. The inn is open seven days a week.

Coolings Wine Bar, 11 Gandy St. (tel. 0392/34183). The family who runs this place welcomes guests as friends, even if they don't know you. It's a little hideaway that is both unpretentious and enjoyable. The beams overhead are familiar enough, and the bright tables create an English version of a bistro. You're also allowed to dine below in the cellar, which is most atmospheric. A blackboard informs you of the specials of the day, and I generally prefer these. Everything tastes fresh here. Try the steak-and-kidney pie, if featured, or one of the Italian pasta dishes, most tasty and filling. At the serve-yourself counter, you can make up your own smörgåsbord-inspired plate. Expect to spend from £6 ($9) up, depending on what you order. Hours are noon to 2 p.m. Monday to Saturday, and 5:30 to 10:30 p.m. for dinner.

LIVING ON THE OUTSKIRTS: Perhaps the finest way to enjoy the cathedral city of
Exeter, especially if you have a car, is to live on the outskirts, from 10 to 19 miles from the heart of the city.

At Whimple

Nine miles from Sidmouth, which lies on the South Devon coast, and ten miles from Exeter, **Down House** (tel. 0404/822860) is an ideal base for touring in Devon. Alan and Vicky Jiggins welcome visitors to their gracious Edwardian gentleman's farmhouse set in five acres of garden and paddocks. Guests can relax in the elegant lounge or on the terrace, and enjoy the fine cuisine in which garden fruit and vegetables and local eggs are used. B&B costs from £8.50 ($12.75) to £10.50 ($15.75) per person, with an evening meal served from £5 ($7.50).

At Bickleigh

In the Exe Valley, four miles south of Tiverton and ten miles north of Exeter, lies a hamlet with a river, an arched stone bridge, a mill pond, and thatch-roofed cottages —a cliché of English charm, one of the finest spots in all of Devon.

Bickleigh Cottage Guest House, Bickleigh Bridge (tel. 08845/230), is a thatched, 17th-century guesthouse, with a riverside garden leading down to a much-photographed Bickleigh Bridge. Add to this image swans and ducks gliding by to get your leftover crumbs from tea on the lawn. Mr. and Mrs. Stuart Cochrane, the friendly owners, charge from £11 ($16.50) to £13 ($19.50) per person nightly for B&B. In a room with a private bath, the rate is from £14 ($21) nightly. Meals are unforgettable. The raspberries and gooseberries come fresh from the garden, topped with generous portions of Devonshire cream. Dinner is priced from £7.50 ($11.25). Inside, the rooms are cozy, with oak beams and old fireplaces. The no. 354 bus runs between Exeter and Tiverton, if you don't have a car.

The Fisherman's Cot Hotel (tel. 08845/237) sits like a picture postcard across the way from Bickleigh Bridge and the Bickleigh Mill Craft Centre. It is rumored that Simon and Garfunkel wrote their famous hit song, "Bridge Over Troubled Water," while staying at this hotel which stands on the River Exe. A cocktail bar has recently been built, and most bedrooms have been completely redecorated. A number of units have private bathrooms. The B&B rate is £18 ($27) to £25 ($37.50) in a single, from £35 ($52.50) in a double with bath. The food served in the à la carte restaurant, evening only, is superb and includes many excellent fish dishes and chef's specials. A table d'hôte menu is available in the evening also, costing from £12 ($18). Around the bar and lounge, a good choice of bar snacks is offered at reasonable prices, including homemade soup, steak-and-kidney pie, and cottage pie. The Fisherman's Cot farmhouse grill is popular. Cold salads, ploughman's cheddar or stilton, and a variety of sandwiches freshly made are always available. The hotel is popular with fishermen, and many salmon and trout are caught within the hotel grounds. The place is fully licensed.

Trout, on the main Tiverton-Exeter road, the A396, four miles south of Tiverton (tel. 08845/339), is a former 17th-century coaching inn, transformed into a pub and a restaurant. The thatch roof is long and low, and there are tiny leaded windows. Former stables have been converted into rooms for dining. One of the favored rooms contains an old fireplace, made from the original bridge stone. A sign indicates that the inn was built in 1630 as a trout hatchery. The Trout is owned by Sir Fred Pontin, who gained fame as the founder and owner of British holiday camps. You may bump into Sir Fred in the bar. All year round they have hot and cold bar snacks, home-baked ham, homemade pies, and a selection of salads. The restaurant is open in summer for lunch from noon to 2 p.m. and for dinner from 7 to 11 p.m. (in winter for dinner only, from 7 to 9 p.m.). A buffet lunch, available all year, goes for £6 ($9). There are four twin-bedded rooms with wash basins to rent, plus two self-catering cottages. They overlook the river, and you can almost hear the trout jumping. There is no sitting room, but the bedrooms have easy chairs. Bed and a full English breakfast, VAT, and service cost £34 ($51) for two. No singles are available.

3. Dartmoor

Antiquity-rich Dartmoor lies in the southern part of the shire. The **Tors,** huge rock formations of this granite mass, sometimes soar to a height of 2,000 feet. The national park is a patchwork quilt of mood changes: gorse and purple heather, gorges with rushing water, a foreboding landscape for the experienced walker only. Look for the beautiful Dartmoor pony.

Some 13 miles west from Exeter, the peaceful little town of **Moreton Hampstead,** perched on the edge of Dartmoor, makes a good center. Moreton Hampstead contains much that is old, including a market cross and several 17th-century colonnaded almshouses.

The heavily visited Dartmoor village of **Widecombe-in-the-Moor** is only seven miles from Moreton Hampstead. The fame of the village of Widecombe-in-the Moor stems from an old folksong about Tom Pearce and his gray mare, listing the men who were supposed to be on their way to Widecombe Fair when they met with disaster: Bill Brewer, Jan Stewer, Peter Gurney, Peter Davy, Daniel Whiddon, Harry Hawke, and Old Uncle Tom Cobley. Widecombe also has a parish church worth visiting. Called the **Cathedral of the Moor,** with a roster of vicars beginning in 1253, the house of worship in a green valley is surrounded by legends. When the building was restored, a wall-plate was found bearing the badge of Richard II (1377–1399), the figure of a white hart.

The **National Park Authority** operates a summer bus service throughout the moor. Services have such inviting names as the Pony Express and the Transmoor Link, and are an ideal way to get onto the moor to hike the 500 miles of foot- and bridgepaths. The country is rough, and on the high moor you should always make sure you have good maps, a compass, and suitable clothing and shoes. Don't be put off, however. Unless you are a professional hiker, it is unlikely that you will go very far from the well-trodden paths. The park authority also runs guided walks from selected starting points.

Information on the bus links between various villages and towns on Dartmoor is available from Plymouth CityBus, Milehouse, Plymouth (tel. 0752/264888), and from Devon General, Exeter Bus Station, Paris Street, Exeter (tel. 0392/219911).

There are also guided walking tours of varying difficulty, ranging from 1½ hours up to six hours for a trek of some 9 to 12 miles. All you have to do is turn up suitably clad at your selected starting point, and there you are. Details are available from the Dartmoor National Park Information Centres or from the **Dartmoor National Park Dept.,** Parke, Haytor Road, Bovey Tracey, Newton Abbot (tel. 0626/832093). The charge for walks is between 70p ($1.05) to £2 ($3).

Throughout the area are stables where you can arrange for a day's trek on horseback across the moors. For horse-riding on Dartmoor, there are too many establishments to list. All are licensed, and you are accompanied by an experienced rider/guide. The moor can be dangerous, with sudden fogs descending without warning on treacherous marshlands. All horse-rental stables are listed in a useful free publication, the *Dartmoor Visitor*, obtainable from tourist and visitor centers or by mail. Send an International Reply Coupon to the Dartmoor National Park Dept. (address above). Prices are around £3 ($4.50) per hour, £6 ($9) for a half day, and £12 ($18) for a full day.

The **Museum of Dartmoor Life** is at the rear of 3 West St., Okehampton (tel. 0837/3020). The market town of Okehampton owes its existence to the Norman castle built by Baldwin de Bryonis, sheriff of Devon, under orders from his uncle, William the Conqueror, in 1068, just two years after the Conquest. The Courtenay family lived there for many generations until Henry VIII beheaded one of them and dismantled the castle in 1538. The museum is a number of authentic buildings grouped around a courtyard. These include two 19th-century cottages, an agricultural mill, and a printer's workshop. They display farm machinery and some old vehicles: a Devon box wagon of 1875, a 1922 Bullnose Morris motorcar, and a 1937 motorcycle. There is a reconstructed waterwheel, a wheelwright's shop, a farm kitchen, a dairy, and a courtyard featuring working craft studios, Victorian tea rooms, and a tourist information center. The museum is open all year from 10 a.m. to 5 p.m. Monday to Saturday (on Sunday from June to August). Admission is 60p (90¢) for adults, 30p (45¢) for children.

FOOD AND LODGING: In the heart of Dartmoor, **Lydgate House Hotel** at Postbridge (tel. 0822/88209), is an attractive residence run by Mr. and Mrs. Beale. The East Dart River runs through the grounds which cover about 35 acres. Guests are assured of a warm welcome, comfortable accommodation, and plenty of good English food. The rate for B&B, depending on the plumbing and time of year, ranges from £14.50 ($21.75) to £16 ($24) per person nightly. Dinner can also be arranged. Log fires burn on cold nights, but there is also central heating. The breakfasts are generous as are the dinners. The house is quite old, but it's been restored, the dining room extended out to the garden. Big windows allow views of the river. There are several comfortable lounges set aside for get-acquainted conversations or quiet retreats. In a snug bar, before-dinner drinks are served. From Exeter, take the A38 Plymouth road to Peartree Cross (signposted Ashburton to Dartmoor), follow the B3357 to Two Bridges and turn right onto the B3212. Postbridge is about three miles away.

Old Walls Farm, Ponsworthy, near Widecombe-in-the-Moor and Newton Abbot (tel. 03643/222), is a substantial, stone-colored plastered country home set remotely on a working farm and reached by very narrow lanes. Here you are comfortably in the heart of the moors, and in the safe, knowing hands of owner Bill Fursdon, an expert on the area. He is a genial, handsome, white-haired gentleman with a gracious smile who is by avocation a naturalist. He'll take you on a short walk around his farm, showing you his collection of cows, Jack Russell terriers, ducks, a pet goat (its milk is served at breakfast, but it's strictly optional), and a beautiful little river, which gives electric power to the house. He'll make handmade maps, pinpointing the places of interest within driving distance. His house is a living tribute to a fast-disappearing era. He is assisted by his wife, Elizabeth, who plays the organ on Sunday at the village church, and their son who lives in a separate home close by. Guests relax around a stone fireplace in the drawing room, or on a sunny day enjoy a crescent-shaped, all-glass sun room. From the latter, the view of the moorland is exceptional. The living room has an old grand piano, a Victorian card table, a soft arm sofa, and armchairs placed in a curving bay recess. The B&B rate is £11 ($16.50) per person. Breakfast is a special event in the dining room, and you can have as much food as you want.

Old Walls Farm is reached from the A38 dual carriageway between Exeter and Plymouth. Turn right past Ashburton onto the B3357, then right at Poundsgate onto the Ponsworthy–Widecombe road. Go through the hamlet of Ponsworthy, passing the all-purpose post office and store, and look for the B&B sign on the left about 600 yards on.

Dowerland Farm, Mary Tavy, near Tavistock (tel. 082281/345), is an immaculate, simple farmhouse, ideal for tranquility seekers. Near a little village, it lies only a few minutes via a country lane from the main highway, the A386. A 50-acre farm, Dowerland produces vegetables, including five different kinds of potatoes, sold in the local shops. The owner, Mrs. I. M. Hogg, is motherly and thoughtful, kindness itself —and a good cook! She charges from £9 ($13.50) per person for B&B. She opens her farm to paying guests all year, except in December, which she sets aside as "our family month." The living room is snug, with chairs for relaxing gathered around an open fire. On cold nights a hot-water bottle is placed in your bed.

Lydford House Hotel, Lydford, near Okehampton (tel. 082282/347), is a family-run country-house hotel, standing in some eight acres of gardens and pasture land on the outskirts of Lydford, just on the edge of Dartmoor. It was built in 1880 for the Dartmoor artist William Widgery, and several of his paintings hang in the residents' lounge. Owners Ron and Ann Boulter offer varied and interesting menus, all of which feature home-cooking using local produce. The rates are £18.50 ($27.75) per person per night for a room with private bath/shower and toilet, color TV, tea/coffee-making facilities, and a full English breakfast, while a table d'hôte dinner costs £8 ($12). Reductions are allowed for seven or more nights, especially off-season. All prices include taxes. The hotel is seven miles south of Okehampton, just off the A386, and it's on your right as you approach the hamlet of Lydford. Lydford House has its own riding stables in the hotel grounds under the personal supervision of daughter Claire Boulter, BHSAI. Superb riding on Dartmoor is available in small, escorted groups, and expert instruction is offered to beginners.

The **Castle Inn,** Lydford, near Okehampton (tel. 082282/242), is a 16th-century inn next to Lydford Castle. The low inn, with its pink facade and row of rose trellises and clematis, is the hub of the village, along with the all-purpose grocery store and post office. The inn's owners, David and Susan Grey, have maintained the character of the commodious rustic lounge, with its collection of old furniture and accessories, including wing chairs, a grandfather clock, a large collection of Victorian ribbon plates, and antique prints. One room is called the "Snug," containing a group of high-backed oak settles arranged in a circle. The inn is the home of the famous Lydford pennies, hammered out in an old Saxon mint in the reign of Ethelred the Unready (circa A.D. 1000). Seven of the pennies are displayed in the Foresters' Bar. It is in this bar, with its low, lamplit beams, vast collection of old plates, and great Norman fireplace, that meals are served buffet style, from noon to 2 p.m., a great spread set out on a long table. The cost depends on your selection of a main course. The salads are on a help-yourself basis. Snacks are available as well, and you can take your plate, along with a lager, and sneak off to an inviting nook. À la carte dinners are available in the evening, going for £8 ($9.20). For a bed and a large country-style breakfast, the charge is £25 ($37.50) for two persons nightly. The bedrooms, although not large, are well planned and attractively furnished, often with mahogany and marble Victorian pieces, each room with its own color scheme and color TV.

Higher Cadham Farm, Jacobstowe, near Okehampton (tel. 083785/647), just off the moor, is a typical Devon working farm where the period house offers accommodations from March to October. Four rooms are rented, each warm and comfortable, costing from £8.50 ($12.75) per person for B&B. Washing and ironing facilities are available, and there is a TV room. Jannay King, the farmer's wife, will provide an evening meal made with fresh local produce for £6 ($9). Fishing and shooting can be arranged if you want a bit of sport.

The Old Inn, Widecombe-in-the-Moor (tel. 03642/207), is a real traditional old country inn run by the Boults. There are the usual "olde world" bars, such as the Old Grey Mare Lounge, the Cobley Room, and the public bar, each well patronized by the local farming community. Traditional English country fare is always available, including Cornish pasties, ploughman's lunches, steak-and-kidney pie, and, on Sunday, a typical English roast lunch. The proprietors have expanded the menu to include a selection of superb steaks and many international dishes, including Mexican beef, beef bourguignon, sweet and sour pork, lasagne, and moussaka, always available, in addition to daily house specialties such as roast lamb in a rich gin sauce, suprême of chicken, and lamb chops in an orange, marmalade, and sherry sauce. A two-course meal will cost around £5.50 ($8.25). Hours are Monday to Saturday 11 a.m. to 2:30 p.m. and 6 to 11 p.m.; Sunday noon to 2 p.m. and 7 to 10:30 p.m.

The **Ring of Bells,** North Bovey (tel. 0647/40375), is a 13th-century inn in the moorland village, set just off the village green. Here you can sleep in a four-poster bed surrounded by three-foot-thick walls supported by time-blackened beams and have excellent meals in the pub. George and Cora Batcock, the proprietors, offer half board from £25 ($37.50) per person. Meals go for £12.50 ($18.75) and up. There's ample free parking, and a swimming pool is available during the summer. North Bovey is 1½ miles from Moretonhampstead.

The **White Hart Hotel,** Moretonhampstead (tel. 0647/40406), is a 300-year-old inn, a Georgian posting house on the main street, with a white hart on the portico over the front door. All rooms have bath, tea/coffee-making facilities, TV, and central heating. They vary in size, and some have beamed ceilings. Meals are taken in the polished dining room graced by a carved sideboard, antique grandfather clock, and magnificent silver candelabra. You may enjoy a drink or snack in the cheerful oak-beamed bar sharing the warmth of the log fire with the locals. Dinner might include chef's chicken liver pâté, grilled local trout, duck in orange sauce, beefsteak-and-kidney pie, home-cooked ham, or roast stuffed leg of pork, all served with fresh vegetables. Desserts include treacle tart, Dartmoor apple cake, and old-fashioned bread pudding, all served with Devon clotted cream. A three-course meal will cost about £11.50 ($17.25), or you can choose the tourist menu for £9.75 ($14.63). Dinner is served from 7 to 9 p.m. "Mine host" is Peter Morgan, hotelier in Devon for some three decades. Overnight rates are £19.50 ($29.25) per person for a room with bath, an English breakfast, and VAT. A special two-day bargain rate is offered for £56 ($84) and includes dinner, B&B, bath, and VAT.

The **Dancing Tree,** 8 Cross St., Moretonhampstead (tel. 0647/40265). This Dartmoor property is more than 200 years old and offers budget licensed restaurant facilities, with home-cooked cakes, snacks, sandwiches, and Devon cream teas. You can order good inexpensive meals here, including soup, roll and butter, fish and chips, fruit pie and cream, all for about £4 ($6). They also have a daily English roast served with potatoes and vegetables for £5 ($7.50). Upstairs, they have comfortable rooms to rent at a cost of £9.50 ($14.25) per person nightly, including a large English breakfast. Jennifer and Fred Green are the owners and managers.

4. Chagford

Six hundred feet above sea level, Chagford is an ancient Stannary Town. With the moors all around it, it is a good base for your exploration of the region of North Dartmoor. It is approximately 20 miles from Exeter, Torquay, and Plymouth. Chagford overlooks the Teign River in its deep valley, and is itself overlooked by the high granite tors. There's good fishing in the Teign (ask at your hotel). From Chagford, the most popular excursion is to **Postbridge,** six miles to the southwest, a village with a prehistoric clapper bridge.

Near Chagford stands **Castle Drogo,** in the hamlet of Drewsteignton (tel. 06473/ 3306). This massive granite castle was designed and built by Sir Edwin Lutyens and the castle's owner, Julius Drewe, in the early 20th century. It stands high above the River Teign, with gorgeous views over the moors. The family can trace its origins back to the Norman Conquest. Julius Drewe wanted to create a home worthy of his noble ancestors. He found the bleak site high above the moors. Between them, he and Lutyens created a splendid modern castle. The tour includes the elegant library, the drawing room, the dining room with fine paintings and mirrors, and a simple chapel, along with a vault-roofed gun room. There is a restaurant open daily from 11 a.m. to 6 p.m. The castle is open from April until the end of October from 11 a.m. to 6 p.m., charging an admission of £2.50 ($3.75) for adults. If you wish to visit only the grounds, the fee is £1.40 ($2.10). Children are admitted for half price.

FOOD AND LODGING: There are several good possibilities in the area.

The **Great Tree Country House Hotel,** Sandypark (tel. 06473/2491). Although you may have to consider this place as your luxury for a night or two, it is well worth the expense just to be able to walk in the 20 acres of grounds at eight o'clock in the morning and hear nothing but the birds and the sound of running water from the nearby stream, mingling with the occasional moo of a cow. Mr. Whyte, who manages the hotel, brings a very considerable experience to this attractive establishment. He offers a well-prepared, four-course dinner for £12 ($18). Bar snacks are varied at lunch. Try the home-cooked ham and a salad, preceded by a country soup. You pay only £3.50 ($5.25) for the lot. When the weather is fine, Devonshire cream teas are served on the terrace overlooking Dartmoor and the forest. If it rains, you can sit in the lounge and gorge yourself on scones, jam, cream, cakes, and tea. Bedrooms are simple and coun-trified. The beds are good, and all units have baths, radios, and TV, and some have phones. The rate of £29 ($43.50) per person includes a bountiful breakfast the next morning.

The **Three Crowns Hotel** at Chagford (tel. 06473/3444), is a granite inn of the 13th century built to withstand the rigors of the climate, with open fireplaces, roaring log fires, and firelight dancing on old oak beams. Much of the furniture is of the period. The old manor house has modern conveniences, central heating, hot water, and bath-rooms. Elizabeth and John Giles charge from £20 ($30) to £25 ($37.50) per person for B&B, the latter price for a room with bath and toilet. The bar snacks are very good. Served at lunch and in the evening too, they include basket meals of chicken, fried fish, or sausages, as well as steak-and-kidney pie with vegetables, home-cooked ham and pastries. They also do a set dinner from £10 ($15). Some specialty dishes include coq au vin, half a roast duckling with apple sauce, beef Stroganoff, and escalope of Devon veal. There are desserts and a good selection of cheese assortments to finish off with.

Glendarah Guest House at Chagford (tel. 06473/3270), is a clean, comfortable guesthouse run by Edward and Marian Willett. The house is on the edge of Chagford and makes a good base for exploring Dartmoor National Park. The Willetts offer good accommodations, with color TV in the residents' lounge and a licensed bar featuring a range of locally-grown wines. The two bathrooms in the house contain showers. There is also a cottage suite which has a four-poster bed, a complete bath, exposed oak beams, and color TV. It is in converted stables, only a short distance from the house. Mrs. Willett provides ample cooked breakfasts and an excellent four-course dinner every night. The B&B rate is £11 ($16.50) per person, and dinner, bed, and breakfast goes for £18 ($27) per person. The Glendarah has a quiet, respectable atmosphere.

Claremont Guest House at Chagford (tel. 06473/3304), is a family-run place with a warm welcome and excellent home cooking. Comfort is assured in the well-appointed rooms rented by the James family, each with color TV and two with private baths. Prices range from £9 ($13.50) to £11 ($16.50) for B&B, with an evening meal costing £5 ($7.50). They'll pack lunches for your excursions into neighboring Dartmoor National Park, if you request it.

Bly House, Nattadon Hill (tel. 06473/2404), is a country-house hotel converted from a former rectory. A short walk from the village of Chagford, it is set in five acres of grounds with sweeping lawns. The house is elegantly furnished with antiques, and some bedrooms have four-poster beds and private baths. Mr. and Mrs. G. B. Thompson welcome you, offering a total of five double bedrooms with bath, two doubles without, plus a single without. In all, they take a maximum of only 15 guests, which makes for a house-party atmosphere. For half board, the tariff ranges from £19 ($28.50) to £21.50 ($32.25) per person daily. When the weather's cool, a log fire burns in the comfortable lounge. The house, however, is centrally heated, and all bedrooms have hot and cold running water, along with coffee- or tea-making equipment. Small children are not accepted. The cuisine is good home-cooked food, using produce from Bly House's garden whenever possible. The hotel isn't licensed, but guests can bring their own wine or liquor.

A VISIT TO AN ABBEY: Of interest to visitors is **Sir Francis Drake's House,** Buckland Abbey, Yelverton (tel. 0752/668000), originally a Cistercian monastery, founded in 1278. It was dissolved in 1539 and became the country seat of Sir Richard Grenville and later Sir Francis Drake (two great sailors). It remained in the Drake family until 1946, when the abbey and grounds were handed over to the National Trust. The abbey is now a museum, housing portraits and mementos, including Drake's drum, banners, and a superb collection of model ships. The abbey lies three miles west of Yelverton off the A386. It is open Monday to Saturday from 11 a.m. to 6 p.m., on Sunday from noon to 6 p.m. Admission is £1.50 ($2.25) for adults, 75p ($1.05) for children.

The largest collection of hotels on the Devon coastline is found in:

5. Torbay (Torquay)

In 1968 the towns of Torquay, Paignton, and Brixham combined to form the County Borough of Torbay, as part of an overall plan to turn the area into one of the super three-in-one resorts of Europe. Escapees from the factories of the Midlands find it easier to bask in the home-grown Devonshire sunshine than to make the pilgrimage to Rimini or the Costa del Sol.

Torquay, set against a backdrop of the red cliffs of Devon, contains 11 miles of coastline, with many sheltered pebbly coves and sandy beaches. With its parks and gardens (including numerous subtropical plants and palm trees), it isn't hard to envision it as a Mediterranean-type resort (and its retired residents are fond of making this comparison, especially in postcards sent back to their cousins in Manchester). At night, concerts, productions from the West End (the D'Oyly Carte Opera appears occasionally at the Princess Theatre), vaudeville shows, and ballroom dancing keep the holiday-makers (and many honeymooners) regally entertained.

If you suddenly long for an old Devonshire village, you can always ride the short distance inland to **Cockington,** still in the same borough, which contains thatched cottages, an old mill, a forge, and a 12th-century church. Furthermore, if you want to visit one of the great homes of England, you can call on **Oldway,** in the heart of Paignton (tel. 0803/550711). Started by the founder of the Singer sewing-machine dynasty, Isaac Merritt Singer, and completed the year after he died (1875), the neoclassic-mansion is surrounded by about 20 acres of grounds and Italian-style gardens. Inside, if you get the feeling you're at Versailles, you're almost right, as many of the rooms were copied. It's open May to September, Monday to Saturday from 10 a.m. to 1 p.m. and 2:15 to 5 p.m. (on Sunday from 2:30 to 5:30 p.m.). In winter it's open Monday to Friday from 10 a.m. to 1 p.m. and 2:15 to 5:15 p.m. The gardens are always open. Admission is free.

BED AND BREAKFAST: For B&B accommodations, I've focused on one of the choicest hotel and residential districts of Torquay. The prices, especially the weekly partial-board terms, are moderate.

Glenorleigh, 26 Cleveland Rd. (tel. 0803/22135), is known in many circles as the "best B&B in Torquay." Lying in its own well-manicured grounds, it is a worthy choice if you can get in. The bedrooms, 16 in all, have been tastefully modernized, and they are well maintained. The B&B rate ranges from £15 ($22.50) to £16 ($24) per person nightly, with half-board terms going from £16 ($24) to £21 ($31.50) per person. In summer, many guests are booked in for the week, so you'll have to call and see if they have space for any short-time visitors. The hotel has a sauna, a solarium, and a small gym.

Cranborne Hotel, 58 Belgrave Rd. (tel. 0803/24100), is small but select, a family-run enterprise where guests get a personal welcome and warm hospitality from Mr. and Mrs. Dawkins. Conveniently located, the hotel has an inviting blue and white facade it turns to the world. Inside, the couple rents out a total of 14 comfortably furnished bedrooms, nine of which have private facilities. The B&B rate ranges from £9.50 ($14.25) to £11.50 ($17.25) per person nightly, with half board costing from £13.50 ($20.25) to £15.50 ($23.25) per person. Guests mix informally either in a lounge reserved for them or on the patio. It is closed in December.

Craig Court Hotel, 10 Ash Hill Rd., Castle Circus (tel. 0803/24400), gives guests a relaxing break in a homelike building facing a southern exposure, lying a short walk from the heart of town. Surrounded by a beautiful and well-kept garden, it has generous parking if you're a motorist. It also offers excellent value in its discreetly modernized bedrooms, 10 in all, many with private facilities. The owners, Ken and Christine Fallowfied, charge from £11 ($16.50) to £13 ($19.50) per person for B&B, from £12.50 ($18.75) to £16 ($24) per person for half board. The higher prices are for accommodations with private baths or showers. In addition to enjoying the good, wholesome food served here, guests can also make use of a well-appointed lounge or an intimate bar opening onto the grounds.

Kelvin House, 46 Bampfylde Rd. (tel. 0803/27313), is a former private home, and is within walking distance of the sea as well as the center of town. Beige with white trim, the guesthouse provides sunny rooms that are extra clean, sufficiently comfortable, and moderately priced, costing £9.50 ($14.25) per person for B&B. The cost of half board is from £12.50 ($18.75) per person. There's no skimping, since the bedrooms have innerspring mattresses and basins with hot and cold running water. Some have private showers and color TV. In addition, the resident owners, Mr. and Mrs. J. Dent, have provided a lounge for television.

Colindale, Rathmore Road (tel. 0803/23947), is a good choice. And it's about as central as you'd want, opening onto King's Garden, as well as lying within a five-minute walk of Corbyn Beach, and three minutes from the railway station. The B&B rate, set by Mr. and Mrs. A.C. Martin, is £12 ($18) per person in high season. But the best arrangement in one of their nine well-kept double rooms is to take the weekly half-board rate of £98 ($147) per person. The hotel has a cocktail bar and a resident's lounge and dining room. Colindale is one of a row of attached brick Victorian houses, with gables and chimneys. It's set back from the road, with a parking court in front.

Blue Haze Hotel, Seaway Lane (tel. 0803/607186), is an old home built for a wealthy Victorian family who wanted gracious holiday living near the sea. In a pleasant residential area overlooking Torbay, it is well built and large, with comfortably high-ceilinged rooms. For a room and a substantial English breakfast, you pay £11.50

($17.25) to £14.50 ($21.75) per person per day, depending on the season. Half board costs £15 ($22.50) to £18 ($27) per person per day for good home-cooking. You dine by an open fire at candlelit tables. All rooms have tea/coffee-making facilities, and some have toilets and showers. These cost an extra £3 ($4.50) per person per day. The hosts, Doug and Hazel Newton, will give you a warm welcome. There's a large private car park, and the hotel is licensed.

Castle Mount Hotel, Castle Road (tel. 0803/22130), is a little out of the way, but well worth the effort to reach it because of the reasonable prices and immaculate rooms. Mr. and Mrs. John C. Bruch, Santa Barbara, California, write: "An evening with the proprietors was a Torquay highlight!" Castle Mount is a converted private home, lodged high on a terrace and surrounded by lawns and gardens, just a few minutes' walk below to bus routes and the town center. Bay windows overlook the garden. The main rooms are centrally heated, and in chilly weather bedrooms have heaters and electric blankets. All accommodations have hot and cold running water and inner-spring mattresses. Room and breakfast is £8 ($12), per person, inclusive. Mrs. Bradbury or Mrs. Tapping, the resident owners, will pack lunches for £1.75 ($2.63). Evening meals, costing £4 ($6), are available by pre-arrangement. The hotel is approached from the harbor via the one-way system to Castle Circus. Castle Road is opposite the Town Hall.

Cresta Hotel, St. Agnes Lane (tel. 0803/607241), lies close to the waterfront and the train terminal. The hosts, John and Lucy Macmillan, are most helpful, offering ten comfortably furnished rooms, some with sea views. Seven of the units are usually set aside for families. In high season, the charge is from £12 ($18) per person nightly for B&B, but most guests prefer the half-board rate of £17 ($25.50) per person. Most of the accommodations have showers, and some rooms have both showers and toilets. The hotel is in a pleasant setting, with a sunny garden and ample parking.

At Cockington

The only hotel in this beautiful Devon village is well worth seeking out. It's **Lanscombe House** (tel. 0803/607556), a 250-year-old Georgian dower house with its own trout pond. It resembles a large church rectory, with lounges and dining rooms opening onto views, set in 3½ acres of gardens and adjoining the magnificent Cockington Court Estates. Only about three-quarters of a mile from the sea, this is a good base for country walks and otherwise touring the district without the fuss and noise of larger towns. The considerate hosts are Geof and Dianne Thomas, who do much to see that your stay is an enjoyable one. They rent out ten spacious bedrooms, all with color TV and one with a four-poster bed. Charges are from £12 ($18) per person for B&B. An evening meal is an extra £6 ($9), consisting of excellent food and good wines. There's a wood-beamed, cozy thatched bar in what was once the woodshed.

WHERE TO EAT: Serving inexpensive but gourmet lunches, **South Devon College of Arts and Technology,** Newton Road (tel. 0803/217583), is open during the school terms (closed June to August and the first two weeks in September as well as on weekends). You pay a set £6 ($9) for a meal, including coffee. Wines are inexpensive as well. The menu changes daily, and lunch is served at 12:15 p.m. (table reservations are made no more than ten days in advance; telephone between 10:30 a.m. and 2:30 p.m.). Special regional meals are offered on certain days, giving you a chance to try the Italian, German, and Provençal styles of cuisine. The usual bill of fare offers an hors d'oeuvre, soup, possibly an egg or farinaceous dish, followed by fish (perhaps filet of sole in white wine). The main course may be duck or an entrecôte steak chasseur, with vegetables, and finally you are served a dessert. The modern restaurant setting is enhanced by beautifully crisp table linen, sparkling silver and glassware, and the smartest of young students waiting at table. The college is well worth a visit.

Lisburne Restaurant, 7 Lisburne Square (tel. 0803/26968), isn't as well known as it should be. Dishes on its menu taste as good as they sound. The chef specializes in continental fare, and main courses such as trout with champignons are served with a selection of fresh vegetables. Robert and Anne McKinnon run this attractive, cozy dining room in a Regency terrace of structures opening onto this square, lying slightly outside the heart of Torquay. Lunch costs from £5 ($7.50) and up, with dinners beginning at £12 ($18). Hours are noon to 2 p.m. and 7 to 11 p.m. seven days a week (however, it is closed for lunch on Saturday and also Tuesday).

Remy's, 3 Croft Rd. (tel. 0803/22359), is considered by some as the finest independent dining spot in town. But its prices are reasonable. The name of this Victorian building comes from its owner and chef de cuisine, Remy Bopp of France. Here is a chef who puts great store by his raw ingredients, whether they be fresh fish from a native fisherman or fresh vegetables from the market. Food-wise guests also enjoy his carefully selected collection of French wines. Meals are served Monday to Saturday from 7 to 9:30 p.m., costing from £12.50 ($18.75) and up. It is closed Sunday, Monday, and for the first two weeks in August.

6. Totnes

One of the oldest towns in the West Countree, the ancient Borough of Totnes rests quietly in the past, seemingly content to let the Torbay area remain in the vanguard of the building boom. On the River Dart, 12 miles upstream from Dartmouth, Totnes is so totally removed in character from Torquay that the two towns could be in different countries. Totnes shelters a number of historic buildings (none worth making a special pilgrimage to, however), notably the ruins of a Norman castle, the ancient Guildhall, and the 15th-century church of St. Mary, made of red sandstone. In the Middle Ages, the old cloth town was encircled by walls, and the North Gate serves as a reminder of that period.

FOOD AND LODGING IN THE ENVIRONS: In and around the ancient Elizabethan town is some of South Devon's most beautiful scenery with valleys and hamlets, such as Harberton and Dartington, that are especially pleasing, and each motorist approaches them with the freshness of a personal discovery. To the southeast is the pleasant little village of Stoke Gabriel. You'll find intriguing living accommodations on both the economy and splurge price levels.

Farmhouses on the Outskirts

Ford Farm House, Harberton, near Totnes (tel. 0803/863539), is a 17th-century house in a rural village of South Devon. Near the moors, the house is capably managed by Mike and Sheila Edwards, who rent a single and a twin-bedded room with hot and cold water basins, plus a double with a private shower and toilet. B&B rates are from £12 ($18) to £14 ($21) per person, with VAT and service included. Sheila's culinary skills, sharpened by Cordon Bleu training, turn out tasty dinners by arrangement, costing £7.50 ($11.25). There is also a cottage for rent, as well as two apartments, available on a weekly basis.

About ten minutes' walk from Totnes, in a secluded valley with magnificent views of Dartmoor National Park, **Broomborough House Farm,** Broomborough Drive (tel. 0803/3134), is listed as an elegant gabled mansion. It was designed by Sir George Gilbert Scott, who also designed the Albert Memorial and other structures of architectural heritage in London. The house has central heating, spacious lounges, and the three bedrooms have tea/coffee-making facilities and electric blankets. One has its own bathroom. Bob and Joan Veale, who operate the house along with their 600-acre farm, charge £12.50 ($18.75) per person daily for B&B. An evening meal costs £7.20 ($10.80).

Keys Englebourne Farm (tel. 080423/729), in the peaceful Harbourne Valley, about five minutes' drive from Totnes, is run by Howard and Jackie Veale, son and daughter-in-law of the hospitable hosts at Broomborough House Farm. The lounge and dining room above the ground floor lead to a balcony overlooking the farm. The younger Veales rent a double bedroom and a twin-bedded unit with a private bathroom. B&B costs £10.50 ($15.75) per person per day, including a full English breakfast.

At Stoke Gabriel

About four miles southeast of Totnes sits the little village of Stoke Gabriel, one of the loveliest in Devon. Famous as a fishing hamlet, it lies on a creek of the Dart River. Dartmouth is only six miles to the south of the village (equidistant to Torquay).

For a splurge, the **Gabriel Court Hotel** (tel. 080428/206) is a manor that until modern times had been owned by one family since 1485. What must the ghosts have thought when Michael and Eryl Beacom acquired it and guests started to fill up the rooms, chasing away the cobwebs of the past? The gleaming white house is surrounded by gardens, hedges, and magnolia trees. A heated swimming pool is on the grounds. B&B rates are from £23 ($34.50) per person, including VAT, and what a breakfast! It's the old-fashioned English kind. You might get a room in the new wing, containing eight bedrooms, all with private bath, or one of the rooms in the old building which are tastefully decorated and furnished and most of which now have their own private shower or bathroom and toilet facilities, although a few feature hot and cold running water only. Gabriel Court holds a high reputation for its well-cooked English food. Game is often available, including Exmoor venison. Or you may be offered Brixham scallops, trout and salmon from the River Dart, and poultry from the nearby farms, enhanced with vegetables from the garden. The hotel has a bar/cocktail lounge. Wines are moderately priced. The hotel remains open all year.

At Dartington

For such a small hamlet, Dartington attracts a surprising number of international visitors, mainly because of **Dartington Hall** (tel. 0803/862271), an experimental Anglo-American alliance dating back to 1925. A Yorkshire man and his American-born wife (one of the Whitneys), Leonard and Dorothy Elmhurst, poured energy, courage, imagination, and money into the theory that such a village could be self-sufficient. They used historic Dartington Hall, built in the late 14th century and restored by them after 1925, as their center. In the surrounding acres of undulating hills and streams, several village industries were created: housing construction, advanced farming, milling of cloth, and an experimental school. One famous activity here is the College of Arts, in which students live and work in a series of modern buildings erected since the formation of the college in 1961. The Summer School of Music spends the month of August here, occupying the school and college buildings and giving numerous concerts. During the day, visitors are welcome to tour the extensive grounds and can make purchases of handmade crafts in the Cider Press Centre, a complex designed to provide a showcase for the work of leading British craftspeople. You'll find a craft gallery and shop, a print gallery, souvenir shop, toy shop, and a Cranks health food restaurant. One of the shops sells Dartington glass ''seconds,'' along with many interesting souvenirs. The center is open from 9:30 a.m. to 5:30 p.m. Monday to Saturday (also on Sunday in summer). Admission is by donation.

Cranks Health Food Restaurant, Dartington Cider Press Centre, Shinners Bridge (tel. 0803/862388), owes its concept to its parent restaurant in London, where it instantly became the leading health-food restaurant. Now, here among the creative craft center of Dartington, in an old Devonshire farmstead, it has found new dimensions. The center, with its handmade chairs, tables, and pottery, displays the work of various craftspeople. It's strictly self-service, and there's a buffet featuring salads. They use compost-grown vegetables when available, and serve freshly made vegetable soup, also live yogurts and freshly extracted fruit and vegetable juices. The Devonshire cream teas with Cranks' newly baked whole-meal scones are very popular. The restaurant is open Monday to Saturday from 10 a.m. to 5 p.m. Meals begin at £6 ($9).

The **Cott Inn** (tel. 0803/863777), on the old Ashburton-Totnes turnpike, is the second-oldest inn in England, built in 1320. It is a low, rambling, two-story building of stone, cob, and plaster, with a thatch roof and walls three feet thick. The owners, Steve and Gill Culverhouse and Margaret Yeadon, charge £18.50 ($27.75) per person, including VAT, for a full English or a continental breakfast and occupancy of one of their low-ceilinged old beamed rooms upstairs, where modern conveniences, including hot and cold running water, have been installed. The inn is a gathering place for the people of Dartington, and here you'll feel the pulse of English country life. Even though it is a lowly pub, it is sophisticated, and you'll hear good talk. In winter, log fires keep the lounge and bar snug. You'll surely be intrigued with the tavern, perhaps wanting to take a meal there. A buffet is laid out at lunchtime, priced according to your choice of dish. The menu is likely to include pork escalope, steak-and-kidney pie, Scottish rib of beef, home-cured ham, and local trout. Salads are crisp and fresh, the array of desserts appetizing. The evenings see the presentation of an à la carte featuring local produce prepared in interesting ways. Scallops, lobster, duck, chicken, filet steak, or fresh salmon may be available. Even if you're not staying over, at least drop in at the pub (seven beers on draft). Hours are from 11 a.m. to 2:30 p.m. and 6 to 11 p.m.

From Totnes, we head south to the old town of:

7. Dartmouth

At the mouth of the Dart River, this ancient seaport is the home of the Royal Naval College. Traditionally linked to England's maritime greatness, Dartmouth sent out the young midshipmen who saw to it that "Britannia ruled the waves." You can take a river steamer up the Dart to Totnes (book at the kiosk at the harbor). The scenery along the way is breathtaking, as the Dart is Devon's most beautiful river.

Dartmouth's 15th-century castle was built during the reign of Edward IV. The town's most noted architectural feature is the Butterwalk, lying below Tudor houses. The Flemish influence in some of the houses is pronounced.

WHERE TO STAY: A small guest house, **Ridgeway Cottage**, 27 Ridge Hill (tel. 08043/2799), owned by Mrs. Elizabeth Crotty, has one twin-bedded room facing the river and one single room fronting the Naval College. Both rooms have the exclusive use of Mrs. Crotty's own bathroom and shower, with a separate toilet. For B&B, per person, according to season and length of stay, the cost goes from £10 ($15) per person per day.

The **Victoria Hotel**, Victoria Road (tel. 08043/2572), is an unheralded little hotel just 150 yards from the harbor. The English family rents out a total of nine rooms ranging from £12 ($18) to £13 ($19.50) per person (the latter with shower). These tariffs include a full English breakfast, VAT, and service. A favorite place for before-dinner drinks is one of the Victorian slipper chairs in front of the lounge fireplace. The bedrooms are immaculate, tidy, and personal; the beds, fresh and restful.

The **Captains House**, 18 Clarence St. (tel. 08043/2133), run by Mrs. Norma Finn, lies near the waterfront, and is a well-run, clean, warm and inviting house. You get excellent hospitality and good beds, costing from £10 ($15) per person nightly. It's exceptional for Dartmouth.

WHERE TO EAT: Behind a former Victorian storefront, C.M. and E.A. Brendon Copp operate **Cranfords Restaurant**, 29 Fairfax Place (tel. 08043/2328), a typical English tea shop with cakes displayed for sale in the windows. Inside, it has wheelback chairs placed around dark mahogany tables. In summer, when business warrants, diners overflow to an upstairs room. Fully licensed for drinks, they serve dinners from £8 ($12), including steaks, lemon sole, curries, and an array of freshly made desserts. A light lunch costs from £4 ($6). You can also stop in for a Devonshire cream tea at £2.80 ($4.20). Summer hours ɛ ɔ daily from 9:30 a.m. to 9 p.m.; winter daily except Wednesday from 10 a.m. to 5:30 p.m.

An alternative possibility is the **Scarlet Geranium,** Fairfax Place (tel. 08043/ 2491), a charming old restaurant off the Quay. Built originally in 1333, it was once known as the Albion Inn. Try it for morning coffee or a three-course table d'hôte luncheon (noon to 2:30 p.m.) for £3.50 ($5.25), which features such temptations as roast leg of lamb or baked Wiltshire ham. When available, you can order the locally caught and dressed crab or fresh-caught salmon. From May to October the Scarlet Geranium blossoms at night, too, with dinner costing from £8 ($12), served from 7 to 9:30 p.m. except on Sunday when the place shuts down and on Monday. Two licensed bars are on the premises. It is open from March until November.

The **Cherub,** 13 Higher Street (tel. 08043/2571), was built around 1380 and maintains much of its original decor, the uniqueness of the old timbered building an attraction to North Americans. The owners of the attractive and friendly pub, Peter, Allison, and David Milne, serve bar meals at lunch from £2.50 ($3.75). In the evening they offer food in an intimate, candlelit restaurant, where the average meal costs around £15 ($22.50). Every item is home-cooked, and much local fish is on the menu, as well as steaks, chicken à la king, and game pies. Try the fresh scallops with tomato and cheese sauce, served with fresh vegetables. Bar snacks include jumbo sausages, cottage pies, and well-filled sandwiches such as fresh crab. Lunch is served from noon to 2 p.m. and dinner, except Sunday, from 7 to 10 p.m.

8. Salcombe

At the very tip of the southernmost part of Devon lies an estuary dominated today by the seaside resort of Salcombe. This is a place that became memorable to many Americans in military service during World War Two. The names of East Portlemouth, Strete Slapton, Torcross, even Kingsbridge are little known to many travelers, unless they happen to be boating people, but those names and that of Salcombe were the center of a world at war when the Salcombe estuary, known in ages past simply as the Haven, was selected as being an ideal point from which to launch many of the craft involved in the invasion of Normandy. The area around Slapton, on the east coast on the English Channel, a few miles from the main estuary, was found to be quite similar to the Normandy coastal point that would be called Omaha Beach.

At Salcombe, on the western side of the mouth of the estuary, a waterfront square is called **Normandy Way** commemorating the U.S. Navy's part in the splendid Allied D-Day effort, and at Slapton Cellars there is a **monument** presented by the U.S. Army to the people of the area, known as the South Hams, for their generosity in leaving their homes and property to provide a battle practice area in preparation for the assault in June 1944. Two books of interest to persons who want to know more about the circumstances and heroism of the local people and of the military Allies in this area are *The Land That Changed Its Face* by Grace Bradbeer and *The Magic Army* by Leslie Thomas.

Salcombe today is a beautiful and peaceful seaside resort, with fine beaches, a harbor that is almost completely landlocked, a good deep water port, excellent fishing facilities, and coastal walking paths in National Park coastal countryside.

The old market town of Kingsbridge is about five miles from Salcombe, at the head of the estuary. Market Day here is Tuesday, and tourists and country people alike crowd the market precincts. The A381 road runs between Salcombe and Kingsbridge, or, in summer, they are connected by a ferry service.

Salcombe's two principal beaches, North Sands and South Sands, can be reached by road. They have car parks and full catering facilities. On the eastern side of the estuary from across from Salcombe, a series of beaches is popular, partly because of their safety for children. These can be reached by car or boat, the area being served by the East Portlemouth passenger ferry.

Salcombe is accessible via the A391 south from Totnes, going through Kingsbridge. It is some 25 miles east of Plymouth and can be reached by train from London to Plymouth and then by public bus to Salcombe.

Overbecks Museum and Garden, Sharpitor, Salcombe (tel. 054884/2893), is a National Trust property 1½ miles southwest of Salcombe. The six acres of gardens have rare and tender plants and beautiful views over Salcombe estuary. Part of the house contains a museum of local interest, with emphasis on items that appeal to children. The gardens are open daily all year. The museum is open from the end of March to the end of October from 11 a.m. to 1 p.m. and 2 to 6 p.m. daily. Admission to the museum and garden is £1.30 ($1.95) for adults, half price for children. Admission to the gardens only is £1 ($1.50). There is a gift shop, and you can picnic in the grounds if you wish. Signs point the way to this site from both Malborough to the north and Salcombe.

FOOD AND LODGING: One of the best bargains at the resort is **Charborough House Hotel,** Devon Road (tel. 054884/2260). Jenny and Peter Sherlock welcome guests to their gabled house which lies near the center of town and the harbor, convenient to ferryboat connections and stores. Their rooms are comfortably furnished, and six units contain private showers and toilets. The rate is £10 ($15) to £11 ($16.50) per person for B&B. The food is good, the kitchen turning out both British and continental dishes, and whenever possible using fresh produce. Therefore, you may want to take the half-board rate of £14.50 ($21.75) to £16 ($24) per person. The hotel is closed from the middle of October until the middle of January.

Gara Rock Hotel, East Portlemouth (tel. 054884/2342), was once a Coast Guard station, protecting the Channel, but in Edwardian times it was turned into a hotel and has remained so until this day. Beautifully located on its own grounds, with good views of the coast, it is run by Colin Richard. He welcomes guests to one of his 40 bedrooms, each comfortably furnished. Thirty-one of the units contain a private bath. Depending on the plumbing, the B&B rate ranges from £21 ($31.50) to £23 ($34.50) per person nightly. The hotel also has a heated swimming pool and a tennis court, along with a children's play area. Fish from a local supplier regularly appears on the menu, and you may want to order dinner (served until 8:30 p.m.), costing from £7.50 ($11.25).

Thirty miles west from Dartmouth is my final stopover on the South Devon coast:

9. Plymouth

The historic seaport is more romantic in legend than in reality. But this was not always so. In World War II the blitzed area of Greater Plymouth lost at least 75,000 buildings. The heart of present-day Plymouth, including the municipal civic center on the Royal Parade, has been entirely rebuilt, the way it was done the subject of controversy.

For the old you must go to the Elizabethan section, known as the **Barbican,** and walk along the quay in the footsteps of Sir Francis Drake (once the mayor of Plymouth) and other Elizabethan seafarers, such as Sir John Hawkins, English naval commander and slave trader. It was from here in 1577 that Drake set sail on his round-the-world voyage. An even more famous sailing took place in 1620 when the Pilgrim Fathers left their final port in England for the New World. That fact is commemorated by a plaque at the harbor.

Legend has it that while playing bowls on Plymouth Hoe (Celtic for high place), Drake was told that the Spanish Armada had entered the Sound and, in a masterful display of confidence, finished the game before going into battle. A local historian questions the location of the bowls game, if indeed it happened, starring Sir Francis. I am told that the Hoe in the 16th century was only gorse-covered scrub land outside tiny Plymouth and that it is more likely that the officers of the Royal Navy would have been bowling (then played on a shorter green than today) while awaiting the Armada arrival at the Minerva Inn, Looe Street, 20 yards from the house where Sir Francis lived, about two minutes' walk from the Barbican. My informant says that other captains, knowing that it would take about 20 minutes to ready their ships to sail against the Spanish, may have sent their executive officers to prepare while they finished their drinks and game. Doubt is cast on Drake's display of such insouciance, however, the feeling being that "5 feet 2 inches of red-haired impetuosity as he was, he'd have been off like a flash!"

Of special interest to visitors from the U.S. is the final departure point of the Pilgrim Fathers in 1620, the already-mentioned Barbican. The two ships, *Mayflower* and *Speedwell,* that sailed from Southampton in August of that year, put into Plymouth after they suffered storm damage. Here the *Speedwell* was abandoned as unseaworthy, and the *Mayflower* made the trip to the New World alone. The Memorial Gateway to the Waterside on the Barbican marks the place, tradition says, whence the Pilgrims' ship sailed.

Here too is the **Black Friars Refectory Room,** dating from 1536, in Southside Street. The building is a national monument and one of Plymouth's oldest surviving buildings. It's now owned by Plymouth Gin Distillery, which welcomes visitors Monday to Friday to see the small exhibition of the history of the building. It was here that the Pilgrims met prior to setting sail for the New World.

Prysten House, Finewell Street (tel. 0752/661414), is another place with a strong U.S. connection. Built in 1490 as the priest's house of St. Andrews Church, it is now a museum. Rebuilt with help from the Daughters of the American Revolution, it contains a model of Plymouth as it was in 1620 and exhibits depicting the colonization of America. It is open from 10 a.m. to 4 p.m. Monday to Saturday April to October. Admission is 50p (75¢) for adults, 25p (38¢) for children.

The Barbican is a mass of narrow streets, old houses, and quayside shops selling antiques, brasswork, old prints, and books. Fishing boats still unload their catch at the wharves, and passenger-carrying ferry boats run short harbor cruises. A trip includes a visit to Drake's Island in the Sound, the dockyards, and naval vessels, plus a view of the Hoe from seaside.

A cruise of the Plymouth Harbour costs £1.50 ($2.25) for adults, 80p ($1.20) for children. Departures are from February through November, with cruises leaving every half hour from 10 a.m. to 4 p.m. daily. These **Plymouth Boat Cruises** are booked at the Phoenix Wharf, the Barbican (tel. 0752/822202).

The **Barbican Craft Centre,** White Lane (tel. 0752/662338), in the Barbican, has workshops and showrooms where you can watch and talk to people engaged in crafts. You'll see such sights as a potter throwing a special design or a glassblower fashioning a particular glass. Woodcarvers, leather workers, and weavers are also busy, and you can buy their products at reasonable prices, even commissioning your own design if you're lucky.

Still a major base for the British navy, Plymouth makes for an interesting stopover.

BED AND BREAKFAST: Present-day pilgrims from the New World who didn't strike it rich are advised to head for Smeaton Terrace, in one of the most colorful parts of Plymouth, West Hoe. Here they'll find a number of inexpensive B&B houses on a quiet, peaceful street near the water. My recommendations for overnighting follow:

The **Imperial Hotel,** 3 Windsor Villas, Lockyer Street (tel. 0752/227311), owned by Alan and Prue Jones, is an attractive and tastefully decorated Victorian hotel on Plymouth Hoe, with 23 bedrooms, 16 with private bath. It offers a friendly and homey atmosphere. Alan (Lieutenant-Commander Royal Navy Reserve, retired) was in the merchant navy for 13 years and is a former chairman of the Personal Service Hotel Group and a director of the Marketing Bureau in Plymouth. With their experience, Alan and Prue are more than able to help and advise overseas visitors with limited time on where to go and what to see, including the place where the Pilgrim Fathers embarked for the new world. The B&B rate is £19 ($28.50) per person, including service and VAT. Ground-floor rooms are available, and there is ample parking space on the premises.

The **Wiltun,** 39 Grand Parade, West Hoe (tel. 0752/667072), is set on Plymouth's historic foreshore overlooking Drake's Island and Plymouth Sound. This Victorian house has many modern facilities, but retains several of the architectural features of the 1850s. Len and Sandra Hirst, owner-proprietors, offer friendly service throughout the year. Family rooms are available. There's a private lawn to relax on and watch the ships go by. Major credit cards are welcome. The charge is £12.50 ($18.75) per person per day, including a large English breakfast. The well-prepared evening meal goes for £5.25 ($7.86), including VAT.

The **Anchorage,** Grand Parade, West Hoe (tel. 0752/668645), boasts a choice location, on the Grand Parade by the sea, overlooking Plymouth Sound. Owned by Mr. and Mrs. Willmott, the hotel is simply furnished in a modified modern style. Without flair or frills, it provides its own drama. The rooms have innerspring mattresses, hot and cold running water, beverage-making facilities, and electric heaters. The rate for B&B is from £9.50 ($14.25) per person.

St. Rita's, 76 Alma Rd. (tel. 0752/667024), is close to the Plymouth railway station in a row of blue-painted Victorian houses on the main bus route to the city center, approximately one mile away. The hotel furnishings aren't style setters, but the place is well kept and clean. Mr. and Mrs. Sheehan are only too willing to help. They offer 28 comfortable rooms, each with a wardrobe and chest. The tariff varies with the room, but averages £11 ($16.50) per person nightly, including breakfast. The accommodations at the back are quieter. Evening meals are offered only from October to May. However, you have to have something to eat if you want to drink because of license requirements. There is good parking at the rear of the hotel.

Camelot Hotel, Elliott Street, The Hoe (tel. 0752/669931), stands on a small road just off the grassy expanse of the Hoe. It is a neat tall house with a pleasant small bar and restaurant, with set menu meals and a short à la carte menu in the evening. There is a lounge with color TV and video, or else you can watch from your own set in your bedroom. Accommodations go for £20 ($30) in a single with bath. Two persons can stay here for £32.50 ($48.75) in a room with private bath. These tariffs include a full English breakfast, service, and VAT. There are facilities for laundry and dry cleaning, a boon when you're traveling.

Carnegie Hotel, 172 Citadel Rd., The Hoe (tel. 0752/25158), is a pleasant house open year round. The warm and pleasantly furnished bedrooms—ten in all—have hot and cold running water basins. B&B rates range from £13 ($19.50) to £14 ($21) per person (the latter with a private shower). For another £7 ($10.50), you'll be served a four-course dinner. There is unrestricted parking on the street, and keys are provided so that you will have access to the hotel at all times.

WHERE TO DINE: If you're pressed for time and are only passing through, try at least to visit the Barbican—perhaps for a meal. A good dining choice is the **Green Lanterns,** 31 New St., The Barbican (tel. 0752/660852). A 16th-century eating house on a Tudor street, the Green Lanterns lies 200 yards from the Mayflower Steps, about as close to the Pilgrim Fathers as you can get. Even to this day, it's a good restaurant. At lunchtime, an extensive menu of reasonably priced dishes is served from £5 ($7.50) up, including such items as farmhouse pâté, harvest home pie, beef in a blanket, and Lancashire hot pot. All courses at both lunch and dinner are served with the fresh vegetables of the day. Some unusual dishes are on the dinner menu, such as roast "gliny" (guinea fowl roasted with wine-flavored gravy), cider-baked rabbit, jugged steak (a casserole of chuck steak and celery flavored with spices, red currant jelly, and port wine), and chicken pepper pot (from an 18th-century recipe). Devonshire bass is good if it's available, or you might choose sole with herbs or one of the lamb dishes. Desserts include several tempting hot and cold selections, many served with Devon clotted cream. Expect to spend from £12 ($18) for a full dinner. Family owned, the Green Lanterns is run by Sally M. Russell and Kenneth Pappin, who are fully aware that voyaging strangers like the Elizabethan atmosphere, traditional English fare, and personal service. The restaurant is near the municipally owned Elizabethan House. Lunch is served from 11:45 a.m. to 2:15 p.m. and dinner from 6:30 to 10:45 p.m. daily except Sunday. Reservations for dinner are advised.

The Ship Tavern, The Barbican (tel. 0752/667604), is a stone-fronted building facing the marina. Its tables are placed to offer a view over the harbor. Take a flight of stairs one floor above street level where a well-stocked salad bar and a carvery await you. The carvery presents at least three roast joints, and you're allowed to eat as much as you want. Adults pay £6.95 ($10.43) for the privilege, children £4.25 ($6.38). The first course is from a help-yourself buffet, and a chef carves your selection of meats for your second course. Desserts are extra. This is one of the best food values in Plymouth, and it's available from noon to 2 p.m. and 6:30 to 10:30 p.m.

The **Barbican Wine Lodge,** Quay Road in The Barbican (tel. 0752/660875), lies right on the quayside, across the water from the Customs House. Owned and run by Peter Stadnyk, the lodge is an old building with wooden floors softened by sawdust. Vintage wines are stacked in racks behind the bar under an oak-beamed ceiling. There is a good ambience, plus a wide range of snacks, including avocado vinaigrette, pâtés, hot soups, quiches, salads, and cold plates of meat. They also feature fresh crab, baked red mullet with garlic and rosemary, and tournedos Rossini, as well as steaks. A lunch or dinner costs from £10 ($15). Each evening a live group plays in the bar, everything from folk to jazz. The wine lodge is open Monday to Saturday from noon to 2:15 p.m. (Sunday from noon to 1:45 p.m.) and from 7 to 10 p.m. daily. Parking is possible just outside if you can find a place among the local cars. This is a popular place.

The **Queen Anne Eating House,** 2 White Lane, The Barbican (tel. 0752/262101) stands next to the previously recommended Barbican Craft Centre. It's a bow-fronted, white-painted establishment open from 10:30 a.m. to 9:30 p.m., during which time you can order fresh coffee, tea, and other beverages. From noon till closing time, you can also order good wholesome food such as roast beef and Yorkshire pudding, steak-and-kidney pie, roast chicken, steak and chips, fish and chips, spaghetti bolognaise, and other hot meals. For an appetizer, I suggest the homemade pâté. Salads are available on request. Service is fast and friendly, but the homemade 8½-inch pizzas take about 15 minutes, costing from £2.20 ($3.30) to £3.70 ($5.55). Full meals, with the house wine or cooled lager, go for £3.50 ($5.25) to £6.75 ($10.13). There's a special Kiddies Corner on the menu, with meals costing from 80p ($1.20). If you're not looking for a full meal, try the Devonshire cream tea. It's served any time of the day for £1.30 ($1.95), and the homemade scones are half white and half wholewheat flour. White wood tables and chairs, along with white-paneled walls, make this a bright and cheerful place.

For a change of pace, try **China Garden,** 17 Derry's Cross (tel. 0752/664472), which is the finest Chinese restaurant in the area, charging remarkably low prices, considering the quality of its cookery. For example, a set lunch is priced at only £3.50 ($5.25), a table d'hôte dinner going for £7.50 ($11.25). The cooking is inspired by the cuisine of Peking (now Beijing), and you get the legendary Peking duck, along with tasty spare ribs and other delicacies—even that which is not so delicate (beef and red-hot peppers). Service is efficient and accurate, and lunch is from noon to 2:30 p.m., dinner 6 to 11:30 p.m. On Friday and Saturday, only dinner is served, 6 to midnight, and Sunday hours are only from 6 to 11 p.m. It's highly recommended, and located just outside the center of town.

Most tourists at this point will want to continue their trip into Cornwall. However, if you're entering Devon from Somerset, you may first want to explore:

NORTH DEVON

"Lorna, Lorna . . . Lorna Doone, my lifelong darling," is the wailing cry you're likely to imagine from your farmhouse bed in North Devon. A wildness seems to enter the air at night on the edge of the moody Doone Valley. Much of the district is already known to those who have read Victorian novelist R. D. Blackmore's romance of the West Country, *Lorna Doone*.

The coastline is mysterious. Pirates and smugglers used to find havens here, in crooked creeks and rocky coves. The ocean crashes against the rocks, and the meadows approach so close to the cliff's edge that you wonder why they don't go spilling into the sea, sheep and all. The heatherclad uplands of Exmoor spill over into North Devon from Somerset, a perfect setting for an English mystery thriller. Favorite bases are Clovelly, the twin resorts of Lynton and Lynmouth, and Combe Martin.

Our first stopover is the best:

10. Clovelly

This most charming of all Devon villages becomes overpopular in summer. Still, it remains one of the main attractions of the West Country. Starting at a great height, the village cascades down the mountainside, with its narrow, cobblestone High which makes travel by car impossible (you park your car at the top and make the trip by foot). Supplies are carried down by donkeys. Every yard of the way provides views of tiny cottages, with their terraces of flowers lining the main street. The village fleet is sheltered at the stone quay at the bottom.

If you don't want to climb back up the slippery incline, go to the rear of the Red Lion Inn and "queue up" for a Land Rover. In summer the line is often long, but considering the alternative it's worth the wait. Two Land Rovers make continuous round trips, costing 50p (75¢) per person each way.

Tip: To avoid the flock of tourists, stay out of Clovelly from around 11 in the morning till teatime. After tea, settle in your room, and have dinner, perhaps spend the night in peace and contentment. The next morning after breakfast, you walk around the village or go for a swim in the harbor, then visit the nearby villages during the middle of the day when the congestion sets in. Bideford, incidentally, is 11 miles away.

Be forewarned: It's not easy to get a room in Clovelly. Advance reservations, with a deposit, are imperative during the peak summer months. However, you can telephone in advance and *possibly* get a bed.

WHERE TO STAY: At the bottom of the steep cobble street, right on the stone seawall of the little harbor, the **Red Lion,** The Pier (tel. 02373/237), may well occupy the jewel position of the village. Rising three stories, with gables and a courtyard, it is actually an unspoiled country inn, where life centers around an antique pub, and village inhabitants, including sea captains, gather to satisfy their thirsts over pints of ale. Most of the bedrooms look directly onto the sea, and all of them contain hot and cold running water and adequate furnishings. The cost is from £12.50 ($18.75) per person nightly, including breakfast. Other meals are available in the sea-view dining room. Dinner goes for £10 ($15), with a choice of four main dishes, two of which are always fresh local fish, then a choice from the dessert trolley. The manager suggests that the Red Lion is not suitable for children under 7 years of age.

Midway House, 84 High St. (tel. 02373/382), offers some of the most charming accommodations in town in a 500-year-old house maintained by avid gardeners, Vic and Dot Smith. As its name implies, the house lies "midway" up (or down) the steep slope of the main street. The interior, which was enlarged by the Victorians, contains family antiques and freshly arranged flowers, the allure of a private English house. A grandfather clock in one of the reading rooms slowly marks time for the annual blossoming of the apple trees in the rear. In cool weather, Mrs. Smith is known to slip a hot-water bottle in a guest's bed before retiring. The three double rooms benefit from a sea view. The Smiths charge from £11 ($16.50) per person for B&B and receive guests from March until November.

Bed and Breakfast in Higher Clovelly

Overflow lodgings in summer are available in the tiny hamlet of Higher Clovelly, lying above the main village. Although Higher Clovelly has none of the charm of Clovelly, you don't have to face the problem of carting luggage down that steep cobblestone street. To get you started on your search for a room here, I'd recommend—

Jonquil House, Burscott Road, Higher Clovelly (tel. 02373/346). **Mrs. Grace Kelly** has been taking in guests for many years and is quite experienced in running this spotless home. Guests are welcomed with or without children at a rate of £8 ($12) per person. This includes a warm room, a comfortable bed, and a basin with hot and cold running water. Bathrooms are equipped with showers, and the house has panoramic views over the adjoining farmland.

The Four Poster, 5 Underdown (tel. 02373/224), is the most romantically named accommodation in the upper or lower villages. It's also one of the most reasonable in price, charging from £8 ($12) per person nightly for a good Devonshire breakfast and a comfortable bed. The price also includes a "wake-up" pot of tea and crackers served early in the morning if you like to get up early. A four-course evening meal is available, costing £8 ($12), if you order before 5 p.m. Mr. and Mrs. T.W.L. Clark are among the most accommodating hosts in Clovelly. Mr. Clark, a retired mariner, is a fount of information on local, regional, and nationwide attractions. He also makes all his own wine, beer, and cider. The immaculately kept stone house was built originally for use of the Coast Guard. It is adjacent to the main Clovelly car park.

11. Combe Martin and Lynton-Lynmouth

COMBE MARTIN: One of the best bases for excursions into Exmoor, Combe Martin is a lovely village, lying in a valley or combe. Cliffs, ideal for rambles, soar on both sides. After you've traversed its High Street, you've about seen the village. Its old church is built in the Early English and Perpendicular styles. The English like to sunbathe and swim nearby in the sheltered little coves, with their pebblestone beaches. Combe Martin lies six miles from Ilfracombe.

Staying over? I suggest the following accommodations:

Where to Stay

Saffron House, King Street (tel. 027188/3521), is an old farmhouse successfully adapted into a popular small, licensed, family hotel offering all-year accommodation with the benefit of full central heating for those early and late holidays. The hotel, which is set back from the road, is just a short walk away from the beach and harbor, and commands extensive views of the village and surrounding countryside, as well as the famous "Hangman Hill." The owners, Mr. and Mrs. Chantler, are sincerely interested in your comfort, being well traveled themselves, and from the moment of your friendly reception you know that you are going to have an enjoyable stay. The guest rooms vary in size and are clean and comfortable. You will find two lounges, a private heated swimming pool, a garden, and a sun terrace, as well as laundry and drying facilities. B&B rates are from £11 ($16.50) per adult, including VAT, with reductions for children. Most rooms have private showers. The Chantlers will point out the areas of interest and, if not too busy, will accompany you on a walk through the cliff paths.

The **London Inn** (tel. 027188/3409) is a roadside inn at the upper part of the village road, standing fresh and prim. The owner, Mrs. Denham, charges from £11 ($16.50), plus VAT, per person for B&B, based on double occupancy. The lounge tavern, heavy beams and all, is the meeting place for the nearby villagers, as well as residents. All are warmed by old features—four settles, a stone fireplace with logs on a raised hearth, a copper hood, and shelves of pewter and copper steins and mugs. The living room is comfortably furnished, as are the pleasantly decorated bedrooms. The emphasis is on comfort, good food, and cleanliness. On the rear lawn, you can sit quietly, listening to the movement of the nearby trout stream at the bottom of the garden, later enjoying music and dancing in the bar.

Twelve miles to the east is still another good base for exploring Exmoor—

LYNTON-LYNMOUTH: The north coast of Devon is set off most dramatically in Lynton, a village some 500 feet high. It is a good center for exploring the Doone Valley and that part of Exmoor that spills into the shire from neighboring Somerset. The Valley of Rocks, west of Lynton, offers the most spectacular scenery.

The town is joined by a cliff railway to its sister, Lynmouth, about 500 feet lower. The East Lyn and West Lyn Rivers meet in Lynmouth, a popular resort with the British. For a panoramic view of the rugged coastline, you can walk on a path halfway between the towns that runs along the cliff. From Lynton, or rather from Hollerday Hill, you can look out onto Lynmouth Bay, Countisbury Foreland, and Woody Bays in the west. This area offers the same kind of scenic excitement that Big Sur does in California.

Where to Stay

Countisbury Lodge, at Lynmouth (tel. 0598/52388), is a former vicarage overlooking Lynmouth and the West Lyn River. The hosts, Jan and Peter Patis, are enthusiastic innkeepers, providing for one's comfort. Their basic tariff is £13 ($19.50) per person for bed and a full English breakfast. Dinner is £8 ($12), these prices including VAT. The lodge offers eight double rooms, some with twin beds, some with matrimonial beds. Five rooms contain private baths. The lodge has a unique bar which was built into the rock face of Countisbury Hill.

Sandrock, Longmead, Lynton (tel. 0598/53307), is a substantial, three-story house on the edge of Lynton, one of the best economy oases in North Devon. The house is on the lower part of a hill beside the road, with most of its bedrooms opening onto views. You can see the beginning peaks of the Valley of Rocks. Fortunately, it's a hotel with many windows, and the rooms are sunny and bright. The bedrooms, generally quite large, are interestingly shaped; the third floor has dormer windows, which make the rooms even cozier. Each accommodation has its own water basin; the beds have innerspring mattresses, and there are plenty of spanking-clean bathrooms in which you can soak after those long walks. The high-season rate for your B&B and evening dinner ranges from £18.50 ($27.75) to £23.50 ($35.25) per person, depending on the plumbing. The owners, Mr. and Mrs. Harrison, manage everything at the Sandrock, and they do it well, taking a personal interest in the welfare of their guests. Their baked goods are a delight, especially the deep-dish apple and rhubarb pie, which are tasty, tart, and sweet at the same time. In the Anglers' Bar, foreign visitors meet the Lynton locals after dinner.

The **Rising Sun Hotel** (tel. 0598/53223) is perhaps one of the most colorful thatched inns in England, especially as it's right at the end of the quay at the mouth of the Lyn River. Not only is the harbor life spread before you, but you can bask in the wonder and warmth of an inn in business for more than 600 years. In bedroom after bedroom, with crazy levels and sloping ceilings, you'll have views of the water, the changing tides, and bobbing boats. Hugo Jeune, the owner, has skillfully worked matters out between Lynmouth regulars and voyagers from faraway lands. They charge

£14 ($21) to £21 ($31.50), plus service and VAT, per person nightly for B&B, with rooms facing the sea going at the higher rate and containing private baths. The inn is open all year. Even if you're not staying over, you may want to sample the English cuisine: dinners are from £11 ($16.50). It's a delight dining at the Rising Sun, as everything is 101% British in the dining room, with its deeply set window and fireplace. See the original 14th-century fireplace in the bar.

Bonnicott Hotel, Watersmeet Road in Lynmouth (tel. 0598/53346), was built 170 years ago as a rectory. John and Brenda Farrow who now own and run it as a private hotel are most helpful. Each of their nine bedrooms is distinctive and attractively decorated, most with private showers and views over Lynmouth Bay or the Lyn Valley. On cooler days a log fire burns in the lounge and bar. John and Brenda, who used to own a pub in London, offer excellent food, specialties being local fish and Scotch steak, served in the Bonnicott Grill. Sometimes a Cockney Night is held, with jellied eels, pie and mash, and a "knees up." Half board and a room costs from £21 ($31.50) per person per day. Special diets and vegetarian meals can be provided. John is glad to advise on walks, fishing, and riding, and to give details about the real-life locations of scenes from the novel *Lorna Doone*.

The **Denes Guest House,** Longmead, Lynton (tel. 0598/5373), is a tastefully decorated accommodation operated by Mr. and Mrs. Gay. The eight immaculate rooms are spacious, with hot and cold running water. B&B costs from £10 ($15) per person, plus another £7 ($10.50) if you want dinner. Tasty and filling meals are served in a cheerful dining room. Special rates are quoted for children.

Where to Dine (Lynmouth)

Ye Olde Cottage (Spinning Wheel Restaurant) (tel. 0598/53297) is a miniature quayside inn, centered in this tiny resort with an unspoiled view of the harbor. Here, under pleasant and homey circumstances, you can get teas and meals. For five generations the Wakeham family has been operating the inn. It's a favored spot for a Devonshire cream tea, served from 3 to 5 p.m. and costing £1.35 ($2.03), with all the trimmings. At lunch, noon to 2:30 p.m., you can order a three-course meal for £4.50 ($6.75), based on such traditional English "fayre" as roast beef or West Country chicken and homemade pies and tarts. From the à la carte menu you can select from such choice delights as rainbow trout, Lyn salmon, Lynmouth Bay lobsters, and a full range of prime steaks. Chef Peter Wakeham has introduced a line of dishes cooked in wine and cider, his own recipes. For a three-course dinner, expect to pay from £5.50 ($8.25). The cottage is open daily from 10:30 a.m. to 9:30 p.m. March to November.

Where to Dine (Lynton)

The **Green House Restaurant,** Lee Road (tel. 0598/53358), was originally the greenhouse on the grounds of an old hotel. The facade is green and cream colored, and inside, all is blue. Many of the overhead windows and skylights of the building have been replaced with solid walls and ceilings, for the sake of practicality, but the effect is still that of a greenhouse. Charming illustrations on the menus show Victorian times in the area. The restaurant is owned by Jean and Peter Williams, who bake their own bread and pastries on the premises daily. There is a wide range of dishes, all homemade, including steak-and-kidney pie, quiche Lorraine, lasagne, Cornish pasties, and meat dishes such as wienerschnitzel, and steaks. A three-course meal with drinks costs around £10 ($15). Vegetarian menus are also offered. Cooked meals, morning coffees, and afternoon teas are available from 10:30 a.m. to 8 p.m. in summer, from 10:30 a.m. to 5:30 p.m. in winter.

Chapter X

CORNWALL

THE ANCIENT DUCHY OF CORNWALL is the extreme southwestern part of England—often called the toe. But Cornwall is one toe that's always wanted to dance away from the foot. Even though a peninsula, it is a virtual island—if not geographically, then spiritually. Encircled by coastline, it abounds with rugged cliffs, hidden bays with fishing villages, sandy beaches, sheltered coves, and secluded creeks where the age-old art of smuggling was once practiced with consummate skill. Many of the hillside-clinging cottages in some of the little seaports are reminiscent of towns along the Mediterranean, although Cornwall retains its own distinctive flavor.

The true Cornish people are generally darker and shorter than the denizens with whom they share the country. These characteristics reflect their Celtic origin, which still lives on in superstition, folklore, and fairy tales. King Arthur, of course, is the most vital legend of all. When Cornish men speak of King Arthur and his Knights of the Round Table, they're not just handing out a line for the tourist. To them, Arthur and his knights really existed, romping around Tintagel Castle, now in ruins—Norman ruins, that is—lying 300 feet above the sea, 19 miles from Bude.

This ancient land had its own language up until about 250 years ago. And some of the old words ("pol" for pool, "tre" for house) still survive. As you move into the backwoods, you'll encounter a dialect more easily understood by the Welsh than by those who speak the queen's English.

The Cornish men, like the Welsh, are great miners (tin and copper), and they're fond of the tall tale. Sometimes it's difficult to tell when they're serious. One resident, for example, told me that he and his wife had been out walking in the woods near twilight but had lost their way. He claimed that the former owner of the estate (in Victoria's day) appeared suddenly in a dog-carriage and guided them back to where they'd taken the wrong turn. If this really happened I wouldn't be surprised, at least not in Cornwall.

Traditionally, the typical oldtimer in Cornwall is a man involved in a vendetta. I heard of one rich and wicked moneylender in Victorian times who wanted to live in total seclusion, but was frustrated in this ambition by two spinster sisters who kept a neighboring farm. So he bought a public chiming clock from Looe, placed it in the tower over the house, and set the quarter-only chimes going only at night—until he finally drove the good ladies out. The Cornish, they are a colorful lot.

The English come here for their holidays in the sun. I suggest anchoring in at one of the smaller fishing villages, such as East and West Looe, Polperro, Mousehole, or Portloe, where you'll experience firsthand the charm of the duchy. Many of the villages, such as St. Ives, are artists' colonies. In some of the pubs and restaurants frequented by painters, a wonderful camaraderie prevails, especially in the nontourist months. Recently, for instance, at one of the artists' hangouts, three young men who had finished dining brought out their guitars and spontaneously launched into folk songs for the rest of the evening. Detecting the accent of some visiting Americans, they sang (with appallingly perfect accents) several country music favorites, although it was their repertoire from Ireland and Wales that cast the greater spell. Living here with these artists is like going back 30 years, experiencing dependence upon yourself and your associates for entertainment. By all means, cross over the Tamar from Devon and see what Cornwall is up to.

Except for St. Ives and Port Isaac, most of my recommendations lie on the southern coast, the so-called Cornish Riviera, which strikes many foreign visitors as being the most intriguing. However, the North Coast is not without its own peculiar charm.

1. Looe

After your visit to Plymouth about 15 miles away, you can either take the Tamar Suspension Bridge to Cornwall, or cross by ferry from Plymouth. You'll soon arrive in the ancient twin towns of East and West Looe, connected by a seven-arched, stone bridge which spans the river. In the jaws of shrub-dotted cliffs, the fishing villages present a stark contrast to Plymouth. Houses scale the hills, stacked one on top of the other in terrace fashion.

In both fishing villages you can find good accommodations and meet interesting people. Fishing and sailing are two of the major sports, and the sandy coves, as well as East Looe Beach, make choice spots for sea bathing, as uniquely practiced by the British. Beyond the towns are cliff paths and downs worth a ramble.

In these villages are several levels of life, the most traditional of which is that followed by the Cornish villagers, many of whom are fishermen (go down to the harbor and watch the pilchard boats come in). Then there is a sophisticated group whose members enjoy the atmosphere. A large transient group, representative of no special class, trips down for a week or so, mostly in the summer months. But all year you can watch the artists and craftspeople who live and work here.

Looe is noted for its shark-angling, but you may prefer simply walking the narrow, crooked medieval streets of East Looe, with its colorful harbor and 17th-century Guildhall.

WHERE TO STAY: Spaces and prices are at a premium in Looe as in all of Cornwall in July and August.

Klymiarven Hotel, Barbican Hill, East Looe (tel. 05036/2333), is a Regency house standing in its own wooded and terraced gardens above the harbor. It is owned and run by the Goodenough family. Richard Goodenough has had wide experience in the hotel business and spent some years at sea as a purser in the Royal Fleet Auxiliary, traveling the world and studying hotel operations wherever he went, knowledge he puts to use since the family acquired the Klymiarven. This lovely old house is built on the foundations of an earlier dwelling and has cellars dating from the 16th century, the Tudor era. The main beams reputedly came from ships of the Spanish Armada. The cellars have been converted into a bar and games room. The restaurant features local produce, particularly the fresh fish from the local fishing fleet. The three-course table d'hôte dinner, with several choices for each course, costs £8 ($12). The hotel is small, with seven rooms in the Regency house (some with private showers, some family rooms) and six modern accommodations in a newer section, all with private baths. Rooms, with a full English breakfast included, cost from £12.50 ($18.75) per person off-season, from £15 ($22.50) to £22 ($33) in peak season.

New Barbican Farm, Barbican Road (tel. 05036/2773), overlooks the sea and the river. It is only open to guests from April to the end of September. There is a large garden where you can sit and enjoy the view. In the dining room, Mrs. Lawson Toms provides excellent breakfasts and evening meals, using as much local and home-grown produce as she can find. The charge for dinner, bed, and breakfast is from £14 ($21) per person. B&B alone costs £9.50 ($14.25).

Kantara Guest House, 7 Trelawney Terrace (tel. 05036/2093), is one of the best bargains of Looe, a comfortably appointed guesthouse looking out over the river. It lies about an eight-minute leisurely stroll from the water and the heart of the resort. Standing across from the spacious car park, it offers only six rooms, three of which are usually occupied by families. The two bathrooms are shared. From April to October, guests are received and charged from £9 ($13.50) in a single and from £16 ($24) in a double.

Sea Haze Guest House, Polperro Road (tel. 05036/2708), is immaculately kept, opening onto scenic vistas of the surrounding area. It lies on the road between Looe and Polperro. You get a lot of friendly service and always a polite welcome at this Cornish spot of hospitality. Bedrooms are pleasantly furnished and comfortable, and the two public baths must be shared. With a good Cornish breakfast included, the B&B rate, depending on the time of year, ranges from £11 ($16.50) to £16 ($24) in a single and from £15 ($22.50) to £18 ($27) in a double. Guests are accepted in every month except December.

Jesmond Guest House, Hannafore Road (tel. 05036/4156), has one of the best locations in town, lying only three minutes from the water. It is also the finest bargain if you take the daily half-board terms, ranging from £11.50 ($17.25) to £13.50 ($20.25) per person nightly. The hotel, operated by Carol Brown and Christopher Webb, has only six bedrooms, one of which has a private bath.

Lodgings on the Outskirts

Coombe Farm, Widegates (tel. 05034/233), about 3½ miles from Looe, is an eight-bedroom country house nestling in 10½ acres of lawns, meadows, woods, streams, and ponds, with views down a wooded valley to the sea. Alexander and Sally Low have furnished the centrally heated house with antiques, paintings, and other interesting objects. Open log fires blaze in the dining room and lounge in cool weather. The bedrooms, all with fine views of the countryside, have hot and cold water basins. For half board, the charges are £19 ($28.50) to £24 ($36) per person. Dinner, served in the candlelit dining room with views toward the sea, includes traditional English and Cornish dishes. The charming and friendly Lows invite guests to use the heated outdoor swimming pool in summer. One reader reports that every morning during her stay, a peacock displayed his colors right next to the dining room.

Just 1½ miles out of Looe on the east side is **Tregoad Farm Hotel,** St. Martins-by-Looe (tel. 05036/2718), a lovely old Georgian farmhouse owned by Kenneth Hembrow and his wife, Joyce. Set atop a hill, the house overlooks the sea, and you can sit in bed and watch the Looe fishermen in the bay. Joyce does the cooking and produces large, nourishing breakfasts and five-course dinners, as well as packed lunches. The charge for dinner, bed, and breakfast is £17 ($25.50) in high season, £14 ($21) in low. For B&B only, the rates are £10 ($15) and £8 ($12), according to the season. There are tea/coffee-making facilities in the rooms and color TV in the residents' lounge. The hotel is open from early April to the end of October.

The **Slate House,** Bucklawren, St. Martins-by-Looe, near Looe (tel. 05036/ 481), is a traditional old farmhouse which is beautifully kept by John and Betty-Ann Baynes-Reid. Arriving on a cool day in early autumn, you'll find a log fire burning. After a walk in the garden, you'll be ready for an evening meal before retiring to a comfortable room, costing from £8.50 ($12.75) to £9 ($13.50) per person for B&B, depending on the season. One reader found this place has "more than a touch of class."

WHERE TO EAT: Looe, both east and west, is another one of those gastronomic wastelands that one often encounters in England, surprisingly in major tourist centers. An exception or two to that is previewed below.

The **Flower Pot,** Lower Market Street in East Looe (tel. 05036/2314), has won the praise of many a reader. An old structure, typical of the port, it lies in the vicinity of the quay. James and Iris Ward open the place for morning coffee at 10:30 a.m., the day flowing through lunch until 3 p.m. They reopen for dinner from 7 to 10 p.m. The cookery is British, as represented by their well-baked and flavored meat pies, and, try, if featured, one of their fresh fish dishes. Meals cost from £6 ($9) and up.

On the outskirts, the **Talland Bay Hotel,** Talland Bay (tel. 0503/72667), lies four miles southwest of Looe by A387. An old country house, set on 2½ acres, it served the best food in the area. Yet a Sunday lunch with perfectly done roasts costs only £5.50 ($8.25), a set dinner going for £10.50 ($15.75). Meals are served from 12:30 to 2 p.m. and 7 to 9 p.m. It is closed for lunch Monday to Saturday in the off-season. A cold but enticing buffet of goodies is presented for lunch. Cornish seafood, of course, is the most preferred bill of fare, especially the locally caught crab and scallops.

If you wish, you can strike out from Looe on the cliff walk—a distance of 4½ miles—to Polperro. The less adventurous will drive.

2. Polperro

This ancient fishing village is reached by a steep descent from the top of a hill. Motorists in summer are forbidden to take their cars down unless they are booked in a hotel. Why? Because otherwise they'd create too much of a traffic bottleneck in July and August. The British have long known of the particular charm of this Cornish village.

At one time it was estimated that nearly every man, woman, and child in the village spent time salting down pilchards for the winter, or else was engaged in the art of smuggling. Today, tourists have replaced the contraband.

You'd have to search every cove and bay in Cornwall to come up with a village as handsomely mellowed as Polperro, which looks almost as if it had been removed intact from the 17th-century. The village is tucked in between some cliffs. Its houses—really no more than fishermen's cottages—are bathed in pastel-wash. A small river, actually a stream called the Pol, splits its way through Polperro. The heart of the village is its much-photographed, much-painted fishing harbor, where the pilchard boats, loaded to the gunnels, used to dock.

ACCOMMODATIONS: In and around Polperro, you'll find a number of quite good and colorful cottages and houses that receive paying guests.

Landaviddy Manor (tel. 0503/72210) is a 200-year-old manor house, built of gray Cornish stone, on a secluded ledge or a hill above the village on the west side of Polperro. The manor stands in a peaceful and attractive setting, commanding a view of

Polperro Bay and the coast. It adjoins National Trust land, giving access to cliff paths and coves along the coast. The Cornish moors and Dartmoor are easily accessible, as are numerous beaches nearby. Landaviddy retains its old character, yet all its bedrooms have hot and cold running water and innerspring mattresses. Some have private facilities. There is central heating as well, plus a comfortable lounge with TV, a cozy bar, and a licensed dining room. The owner, Mrs. Ros Morey, gives personal service and runs the place in a friendly and informal way. She charges from £10.50 ($15.75) in a single, from £20 ($30) in a double, including an English breakfast. For one-nighters, a surcharge of 10% is made. Dinner of four courses and coffee is £8 ($12) per person. All prices include VAT.

Penryn House Hotel, The Coombes (tel. 0503/72157), is a licensed, year-round guest hotel which is personally run and ideally located, lying right in the heart of town in the center of resort life. You are well taken care of here in one of the hotel's 14 bedrooms, five of which contain a full private bath. The best bargain is the half-board rate, costing from £12 ($18) to £15 ($22.50) per person nightly. Guests meet fellow guests in the sitting room, or can enjoy a drink in the bar. Several cars can be accommodated in the hotel's private zone as well.

New House, Talland (tel. 0503/72206), is a substantial guesthouse in a dramatic position overlooking the harbor and out toward the Eddystone light. Ken and Polly Perkins welcome guests warmly to their immaculate house. For a double room with a private bath and balcony, the charge for B&B is £22 ($33), bathless twin-bedded and doubles costing £18 ($27) for B&B. Among the attractions are a pleasant lounge with color TV and a lovely garden for the use of guests. With only four units for rent, it is important to reserve your room in advance.

On the outskirts, **Allhays Country House Hotel,** Talland Bay (tel. 0503/72434), stands at the edge of a narrow lane. It is a large country house, filled with character, with white stucco walls, cozy nooks, comfortable furniture, and imposing stone fireplaces. Linda and Brian Spring, urban refugees from London, purchased the place in 1985 and have considerably upgraded it. The house was built in 1930. They rent out seven attractively furnished bedrooms, some of which contain a private bath or shower. The cost ranges from £22.50 ($33.75) to £28.50 ($42.75) per person for half board. The good-tasting English food is served in an Edwardian conservatory. Dishes are likely to include duck with orange and lemon sauce or chicken in cider and honey. For lunch you can snack in the bar on their locally caught crab made into a salad. The house is surrounded by nearly two acres of gardens and grounds, with a greenhouse for growing flowers. From many of the bedroom windows, you'll have views of the Channel and a lighthouse. The hotel lies 2½ miles east of Looe, 2½ miles west of Polperro.

WHERE TO EAT: Good English cookery is offered at **The Kitchen,** Fish na Bridge (tel. 0503/72780), a pink cottage about halfway down to the harbor from the car park. Once a wagon builder's shop, it's now a restaurant, an extension of David and Judith Porter's house next door. David runs the 22-seat Kitchen, while Judith cooks in an area visible to diners. They use local produce from the sea and land. Specialties include local crab dishes, steaks, and Judith's luscious desserts. Various menus are offered at prices ranging from £8 ($12) to £12 ($18). Hours are noon to 2:30 p.m. and 7 to 9:30 p.m. daily except Monday in summer, only on Friday and Saturday in winter.

The Captain's Cabin, Lansallos Street (tel. 0503/72292), in one of the mellow antique structures of town, has long been known for its fresh seafood, all of which is caught locally. You're presented with an array of crab, lobster, oysters, and whitebait, each dish well-prepared and served by a friendly, helpful staff who aim to please. A three-course table d'hôte meal costs from £7.25 ($10.88), and you can also order four courses for £10.25 ($15.38). Lunch is from 12:30 to 2 p.m., dinner 7 to 9:30 p.m.

Nelsons Restaurant, Saxon Bridge (tel. 0503/72366), is owned and run by the Nelson family, not only Peter and Betty but Tony as well. Peter and Tony do the cooking, and Betty takes care of everything up front. They always have at least three soups —fish, crab, lobster, vegetable, meat. Each pot is homemade. Before your main course rests on your plate, it was probably swimming. However, you can also order home-cooked ham or beef, served with vegetable and a salad. A three-course menu goes for £10.50 ($15.75), and you can also order à la carte. For dessert, try one of their homemade ice creams using fresh fruit. They also offer many classic flans and pies. Hours are from noon to 2 p.m. and 7 to 9:30 p.m. except at lunchtime on Saturday. The place is richly decorated in reds with nautical trappings.

Crump's (tel. 0503/72312). It used to be hard to find an inexpensive place to eat in Polperro until this family-owned and -run bistro and wine bar opened in a farmhouse with heavy beams that is well on its way to three centuries of life. This pleasant little place always gives you a warm welcome. Most visitors seem to pass through here for lunch, enjoying fairly light fare such as quiches and good-tasting, crisp salads. You can also get a pizza. Expect to escape for around £5 ($7.50). If you're lucky enough to get to spend at least one night of your life in Polperro, you can partake of more substantial fare, ordering from a set menu. Count on spending at least £7.50 ($11.25) for a filling repast. It's well worth a visit anytime from Monday through Sunday—11 a.m. to 5:30 p.m. and 7:30 to last orders at 10 p.m.

THE VILLAGE PUB: Near the harbor, the **Three Pilchards** (tel. 0503/72233), is where the locals and sophisticates alike go for their evening pints of beer and social activity. It's a large L-shaped room with a fireplace that burns brightly at night. Black oak is used almost everywhere. Why don't you sit in the window-seat and listen to the talk of the villagers? That isn't really as rude as it sounds, as you may not be able to understand a word of their thick Cornish dialect. You may like the absence of quaint bits of decor in this honest, unvarnished pub, the center of life in Polperro. It's open from 11 a.m. to 2:30 p.m. and 6 to 11 p.m.

3. Fowey

Called the Dartmouth of Cornwall, Fowey is an old town of historical interest, one of the most ancient seaports in the West Country. Once the Fowey Gallants sailed the seas and were considered invincible when raiding French coastal towns. At the time of the Armada, Fowey sent more ships than London. With its narrow streets and whitewashed houses, the town has remained unspoiled over the years, enjoying a sheltered position on a deep-water channel. Its creeks and estuary attract sailors and fishermen. If you climb to St. Catherine's Point, you'll be rewarded with a view of the harbor. There are sandy beaches and coves to explore here, as well as an 18-hole golf course within easy reach of Carlyon Bay.

FOOD AND LODGING: Right in the heart of town, opening onto a quay, the **King of Prussia,** Town Quay (tel. 072683/2450), is a modest hotel and busy public house operated by Andy and Lesley McCartney. It's named after a local character who was a famous smuggler. Aside from having a rather formal appearance and a central exterior staircase, it is quite informal. It is the best low-priced hotel in Fowey. The charge is £9 ($13.50) per person for B&B, with a slight increase in July and August. Each room has hot and cold running water and TV. Everything is well kept. In a bar overlooking the river a variety of snacks are available at lunchtime, and you can also order Cornish ale "from the wood" (that is, from traditional wooden barrels).

Riverside, Passage Street (tel. 072683/2275), is the all-purpose ferry-landing hotel of Fowey, all under the watchful eye of T.B. Featherstone, the owner. Directly on the water as well as the main street at Fowey, the hotel is at the little car-ferry station where regular crossings leave for Bodinnick. The establishment has an individualistic decor. Most have views of the river, and from your window you can observe the passing river craft and ferries. All 14 of the hotel's bedrooms have hot and cold running water, but only six are equipped with private baths or showers. Rates are based on the time of the year, the plumbing, and the view. Bed and a full English breakfast costs from £17 ($25.50) to £23 ($34.50) per person daily. For stays of more than two nights, a half-board rate of £27 ($40.50) to £33 ($49.50) per person nightly will be quoted. The chef specializes in hot and cold salmon and lobster dishes; the produce caught locally is fresh and tasty.

At Bodinnick-by-Fowey

The **Old Ferry Inn** (tel. 072687/237). It's hard to believe that this warm, fresh, comfortable place has been standing here overlooking the Fowey Estuary for four centuries. The inn is easily reached by car-ferry from Fowey. Charming and spotless, it's filled with antiques, mostly 18th century, and paintings. Six comfortably furnished bedrooms are rented in the older section, plus another seven in a modern addition. Five contain private bath. The charge, depending on the plumbing, ranges from £18.50 ($27.75) to £20.50 ($30.75) per person. Dinner in the atmospheric restaurant is another £12 ($18). In the pub you can enjoy nautical prints and sea-going paraphernalia while sampling the good ale and drink.

4. Truro

This ancient town on the Truro River is the only cathedral city in Cornwall. As such, it is the ecclesiastical center of Cornwall. The Cathedral Church of St. Mary was begun in 1880 in the Early English style (the spires are in the Norman Gothic design). The town is within 8 to 20 miles of the Cornish beaches. It can be used as a base to explore the countryside, ranging from bleak Bodmin Moor to fertile farmland and the Winter Roseland of the Falmouth Estuary.

WHERE TO STAY: At a seven-room guest house, **Colthrop,** 46 Tregolls Rd. (tel. 0872/72920), you get a hearty welcome and a good bed and a large Cornish breakfast the next morning. It's even better if you arrive in time for dinner. That way, you can take the bargain half-board rate, costing from £14 ($21) to £17 ($25.50) per person nightly. Six of the rooms have a private shower, and one accommodation is reserved for families.

Outside of town, you might try **Greatwood,** Allet, near Shortlanesend (tel. 0872/76581), which stands on about six acres of land. It attracts seekers of tranquility to its precincts, where guests are housed comfortably. Three rooms are reserved for families, and the public bath is shared. The rate is among the best in the area: only £12 ($18) per person daily for a good bed, a Cornish breakfast, and a farm-style dinner. The guesthouse is closed in November and December.

At Tresillian

About three miles from Truro, the village of Tresillian lies along the River Fal. In the heart of the village, David Cocks has opened a guesthouse, **The Granary** (tel. 087252/279), with six bedrooms, all with hot and cold running water, and two communal bathrooms. He offers B&B for £8 ($12) to £9 ($13.50) per person, with evening meals available by arrangement, costing £4.50 ($6.75). David learned the basics of successful guesthouse operation from his parents, who run Colthrop in Truro, recommended above.

5. St. Mawes

Overlooking the mouth of the Fal River, St. Mawes is often compared to a port on the Riviera. Because it's sheltered from the northern winds, subtropical plants are found here. From the town quay, you can take a boat to Frenchman's Creek, Helford River, and other places. Mostly, St. Mawes is noted for its sailing, boating, fishing, and yachting. Half a dozen sandy coves lie within 15 minutes by car from the port. The town, built on the Roseland Peninsula, makes for interesting walks, with its color-washed cottages and sheltered harbor. On Castle Point, Henry VIII ordered the construction of St. Mawes Castle. Falmouth, across the water, is only two miles away.

FOOD AND LODGING SPLURGES: A colorful inn on the seafront, **The Rising Sun** (tel. 0326/270233), is made of a row of white fishermen's cottages, with a slate roof, and a flagstone terrace out front. Inside, every square inch oozes with tasteful charm. The locals gather in the pub, with its Windsor chairs grouped around the fireplace. The dining room has lush gold walls with paintings by Michael Oelman in the form of two poems, "Kubla Khan" and "Jacob's Ladder." English gentility reigns here. The proprietor, Mrs. Campbell Marshall, sets the gracious pace, and is known for her cuisine. If you're just dropping in for lunch, you can order hot or cold bar food. A three-course table d'hôte dinner costs £11.50 ($17.25), plus service. Without a private bath, the B&B rate begins at £23 ($34.50) per person, increasing to £25.88 ($38.82) to £34.50 ($51.75) with a bath.

Braganza, Grove Hill (opposite the Catholic church; tel. 0326/270281), is a Regency house, furnished with antiques and furniture of the period. It offers three twin-bedded rooms with private bath, and two without. All are centrally heated. Visitors gather in the lounge to watch television. The staircase is a perfect Regency one. The charge ranges from £12.50 ($18.75) to £14 ($21) per person per night. These tariffs include VAT and an English breakfast. The house, operated by Zofia Moseley, has an extensive garden overlooking the harbor of St. Mawes, where yacht racing takes place twice a week in the summer. Lord Byron, who stayed in Falmouth in 1809, may have visited this house, for he mentions its name in one of his poems. It's said that his limping step can be heard at the Braganza on windy nights.

The **Idle Rocks,** St. Mawes (tel. 0326/270771), is a solid old building right on the sea wall, with gaily colored umbrellas and tables lining the terrace. Water laps at the wall, and the site opens onto views over the river and the constant traffic of sailing boats and dinghies. The bar serves tasty lunchtime snacks, including fresh seafood caught locally. The bedrooms mostly have sea or river views, and they're equipped with central heating, tea- or coffee-making facilities, color TV, radio, and intercom. All of them contain private bath or shower, renting for £32 ($48) per person in winter, that tariff rising to £38 ($57) from May to September, including dinner, a full West Country breakfast. Considerable reductions are granted for stays of seven days or more.

PORTLOE: If you really want to get away from it all and go to that hidden-away Cornish fishing village, then Portloe may be for you. On the slope of a hill opening onto Veryan Bay, it is reached by a road suitable for cars.

Portloe might be an ideal stopover on the South Cornish coast if you're traveling to the West Country in July and August, which are the months when the popular tourist centers, such as Looe and St. Ives, are overrun with sightseers. Here, in Portloe, the living's more relaxed.

The **Lugger Hotel,** Portloe, near Truro (tel. 0872/501322), was built in the 17th century but has been carefully modernized since to provide some of the comforts expected in modern life. On the water's edge in this delightful cove, the Lugger is owned and run by Steve Powell and his family, who believe in making you feel welcome in their old smugglers' inn. There are 20 rooms, all with bath or shower, color TV, radios, phones, and tea- or coffee-making facilities. The accommodations in the main building and the 19th-century bedroom wing are traditionally furnished in Tudor or Victorian style. There is a cozy sitting room as an escape from the bar where life ebbs and flows through the french doors onto the terrace in summer. Meals include ingredients such as fish, shellfish, vegetables, and meat from the local stock. The daily rate includes dinner chosen from a four-course menu and a full West Country breakfast. The low-season tariff is £32 ($48) per person, rising to £38 ($57) from May to September, but there are reductions for stays of seven days or more. At lunch sandwiches and salads, hot potatoes with cheese or butter, or baked ham are served in the bar, along with soups and terrines. Fruit pies and ice cream complete your meal.

6. Falmouth

A lot of cutthroat smugglers used to live in the area. In fact, when John Killigrew, a leading citizen, started to build a lighthouse on Lizard Head, they protested that the beacon in the night would deprive them of their livelihood and "take awaye God's Grace from us." Falmouth, 26 miles from Penzance, is today a favorite base for the yachting set, which considers it one of the most beautiful harbors in Europe. On a small peninsula, Falmouth's old section overlooks the land-locked inner harbor. The newer part, center for most of the hotels, faces the bay and commands a panoramic sweep from St. Anthony's Lighthouse to Pendennis Castle. Warmed in winter by the Gulf Stream, Falmouth has become an all-year resort. Built on a promontory overlooking the fjord-like estuary of the Fal, it was once occupied in part by the captains of old mail-carrying packet ships. Many find it a good center for touring the rugged Cornish coastline. It's possible, for example, to take a ferry from Falmouth to St. Mawes, a 20-minute ride.

Pendennis Castle, now the Youth Hostels Association, was once part of Henry VIII's coastal defense system. It dates from 1544 when the central circular keep with semicircular bastions enclosed by a curtain wall was completed on the site of a prehistoric fortress. Since Tudor days it has protected the entrance to Falmouth Harbour. During the Civil War it suffered seige. Henrietta Maria, wife of Charles I, found shelter here as she fled to France. The castle was beseiged in 1646 by Parliamentary forces into surrender, but because of the bravery of the governor, his soldiers and citizens were allowed to march out with drums beating, colors flying, and trumpets sounding. Nowadays it is a more peaceful place, besieged only by tourists and sightseers. It is host to the Youth Hostels Association, who run a hostel in the old barrack block. The castle is open to visitors mid-March to mid-October from 9:30 a.m. to 6:30 p.m. (from 2 to 6:30 p.m. on Sunday). Off-season, hours are 9:30 a.m. to 4 p.m. (from 2 to 4 p.m. on Sunday). Admission is 75p ($1.13) for adults, 35p (53¢) for children. For information, phone 0326/313388.

During most of the year, sightseeing craft ply up and down the River Fal from the Prince of Wales Pier in Falmouth to the Town Quay in Truro. There are also morning and afternoon cruises to view the docks and the castle, St. Just, as well as romantic creeks, stately riverside mansions, and smugglers' cottages.

WHERE TO STAY: A family-run establishment, the **Tudor Court Hotel,** Melvill Road (tel. 0326/312807), is within a few minutes' walk of the beaches and the town center. Ron and Kay, assisted by their sons David and Robert, operate the hotel and the attractive lounge-bar leading into the dining room overlooking the garden. Bedrooms are comfortably furnished with hot and cold running water and a radio/intercom/baby monitoring system. Some units have private baths or showers. The cost for bed, a full English breakfast, and a four-course evening meal is £16 ($24) per person per day. Ron, an experienced chef, does the cooking. Trays of tea or coffee, bar snacks, sandwiches, and packed luncheon are available at a reasonable charge and can be obtained ·n request. Tudor Court is open all year, with special holiday packages offered.

Grove Hotel, 1 Grove Pl. (tel. 0326/319577), has a star position, overlooking the harbor. It is, in fact, a modest little hotel, offering sound value for your pound. Yet it's large enough to have a combination bar and guest lounge and a dining room with separate tables (most with a view of the water). The modestly furnished accommodations rent for £13.80 ($20.70) for B&B, plus £6 ($9) for your evening dinner. These are daily terms. The majority of bedrooms have bath/shower and toilet, and all have beverage-making facilities. There is a games room.

Maenheere Hotel, Grove Place (tel. 0326/312009), is a converted, stately 18th-century harborfront house, with Georgian windows and an attractive and popular bar. The furnishings are well chosen, and you get plenty of local atmosphere. It's a good buy, owing to its position. Highest rates are charged from June to August, when B&B costs £12 ($18) daily. You can get half board for £16.17 ($24.26) per person daily, plus VAT. Launderette service is available.

Harbour Hotel, 1 Harbour Terrace (tel. 0326/311344), is a small, family-run establishment, operated by Colin and June Larkin. It gives personal service and has a homey atmosphere. The cost of one of the six bedrooms is from £11.50 ($17.25) for B&B, including a toilet and shower. Half board costs £15 ($22.50) per person. The hotel has central heating throughout, and each unit has tea- or coffee-making facilities. The hotel has views overlooking Falmouth Inner Harbour and 4½ miles beyond. There is also a licensed bar.

WHERE TO EAT: Overlooking the harbor, **Secrets,** 6 Arwenack St. (tel. 0326/318585), is run with dedication by its hard-working owners. In summer they fill up with visitors but in winter they cater mainly to their reliable friends, the local residents who know they can get some of the best and most reasonably priced food in town here. No one puts on airs. The menu is straightforward, using fresh ingredients. Try, for example, the Cornish fishermen's pie or one of the posted changing daily specials. Crêpes and quiche, along with fresh salads, are regularly featured. In summer hours are from 10 a.m. to 4:30 p.m. (they do a brisk afternoon tea business) and 7 to 10 p.m. In winter they are open only from 11 a.m. to 2:30 p.m., and they serve dinner at that time only on Friday and Saturday from 7 to 10 p.m. They are also closed on Sunday in winter. Meals cost from £6 ($9).

The **Cornish Kitchen Café and Bistro,** 28 Arwenack St. (tel. 0326/316509), is a small tea shop and restaurant backing up to the water. Michael McDonald, and his wife, Connie, who own the establishment, open the kitchen at 10 a.m., closing at 10:30 p.m. In the café, you can order a hot soup and crusty bread or perhaps giant shrimps and mussels, certainly fried scampi (shrimps) and chips. My crab sandwich bulged, and I could also have ordered the local crab salad. A simple lunch costs from £4 ($6). A Cornish cream tea is also served, with Connie's homemade scones. For the bistro, open only in the evening from 6 to 10:30 p.m., Connie cooks excellent dishes, especially crab soup and French onion soup. Main dishes include local lemon sole grilled with prawns, Grecian lamb kebabs with rice, and pan-fried chicken with bacon, sage, and wine sauce and a baked potato. They also serve Falmouth Bay lobster and local oysters and clams in the evening. There are simple desserts as well. A three-course meal with a glass of wine costs about £6.50 ($9.75).

POLDARK MINE: Three miles north of Helston on the B3297 stands **Wendron** (tel. 0326/573173). As you have driven around Cornwall, the old workings of the tin mines will have been evident everywhere. Here you have the chance to visit a mine and walk through the old works which extend for several miles beneath the surface. Above ground is a museum of mining artifacts, mining equipment, steam engines, drills, and a history of mining. There is a souvenir shop and another selling good-quality local products, a snackbar, and a children's play area if they don't want to see the exhibits. Admission is £3 ($4.50) for adults, £1.80 ($2.70) for children. Tours last one hour. Open from 10 a.m. to 10 p.m. July to mid-August, from 10 a.m. to 6 p.m. April, May, June, September, and October.

The mine and surrounding area are of particular interest to readers and television viewers of the *Poldark* series, filmed from novels by Winston Graham.

A SIDE TRIP TO LIZARD: The most southerly point of England is Lizard, an unremarkable spot with jagged rocks reaching out into the sea where cormorants and gulls fish.

Right on the point, beneath the lighthouse, is the workshop of a man who must surely be one of the most perfect one-man cottage industries in the country. Mr. Casley runs **Lizard Point Serpentine Works** (tel. 0326/290706) in one of the small shacks by the car park. There he turns, polishes, and fashions into pots, vases, ashtrays, and dishes the serpentine stone found only in this part of the country. The veins in the stone can be green, gray, or sometimes red.

Ornamental barometers and clocks are a lot more, but these are absolutely genuine souvenirs made by a man who is entirely at peace with himself and the country he lives in. His two sons assist with the quarrying of the stone which comes from under Coonhilly Down close by, the site of the country's largest radio receiving and space-tracking station. Mr. Casley's son, another blue-eyed Cornishman, is fast learning the trade so there is every hope that in 50 years there will still be someone whistling happily in the tiny workshop at the tip of Lizard.

Mrs. Ingrid Sowden, Villa Clare, Lizard Point near Helston (tel. 0326/290300), must be the owner of the most southerly bedroom in England. Her home is definitely the most southerly house in the country, built on solid granite with a terraced garden. It opens onto fantastic views over the sea and the cliff edge from the garden fence some 170 feet above sea level. Despite this, the house is frequently showered by spray from the breakers below during storms. Mrs. Sowden, who settled here from Germany some 30 years ago, charges £7.50 ($11.25) per person for B&B. If she can't take you in, she'll recommend one of her friends in the village. If given advance notice, she will also prepare a four-course evening meal for £4 ($6).

7. Penzance

This little Gilbert and Sullivan harbor town is the end of the line for the Cornish Riviera Express. A full 280 miles southwest from London, it is noted for its equable climate (it's one of the first towns in England to blossom out with spring flowers), and summer throngs descend for fishing, sailing, and swimming. Overlooking Mount's Bay, Penzance is graced in places with subtropical plants, as well as palm trees.

The harbor is used to activity of one sort or another. *The Pirates of Penzance* were not entirely fictional. The town was raided by Barbary pirates, destroyed in part by Cromwell's troops, sacked and burnt by the Spaniards, and bombed by the Germans. In spite of its turbulent past, it offers tranquil resort living today.

The most westerly town in England, Penzance makes a good base for exploring Land's End, the Lizard Peninsula, St. Michael's Mount, the old fishing ports and artists' colonies of St. Ives, Newlyn, Mousehole, and the Isles of Scilly.

THE SIGHTS: Three miles east of Penzance, **St. Michael's Mount** is reached at low tide by a causeway. Rising about 250 feet from the sea, St. Michael's Mount is topped by a partially medieval, partially 17th-century castle. At high tide the mount becomes an island, reached only by motor launch from Marazion. A Benedictine monastery, the gift of Edward the Confessor, stood on this spot in the 11th century. The castle, with its collections of armor and antique furniture, is open on Monday, Tuesday, Wednesday, and Friday from 10:30 a.m. to 4:45 p.m. from April 1 to October 31. At other times of the year it can be visited on conducted tours leaving at 11 a.m., noon, and 2 to 3 p.m. on Monday, Wednesday, and Friday, weather and the tide permitting. It charges £2 ($3) for adults, £1 ($1.50) for children. From Penzance take bus 20, 21, or 22, then get off at Marazion, the town opposite St. Michael's Mount. To avoid disappointment, it's a good idea to telephone the office of St. Michael's Mount (tel. 0736/710507) to learn the state of the tides, especially during the winter months when a regular ferry service does not operate. After a longish walk over the causeway, be warned that there is quite a hard climb up cobblestreets to reach the castle. You must wear sensible shoes.

The **Minack Theater** in Porthcurno, nine miles from Penzance, is unique. It's carved out of the Cornish cliff face with the Atlantic as its impressive backdrop and was built almost entirely by one woman, Rowena Cade. In tiered seating, similar to that of the theaters of Ancient Greece, 550 persons can watch the show and the rocky coast beyond the stage. The theater is generally open to visitors who come sometimes just for sightseeing, although you may want to attend an evening performance. To reach Minack, leave Penzance on the A30 heading toward Land's End. After three miles, bear left onto the B3283 and follow the signposts to Porthcurno. For details, telephone 073672/471 during the season, lasting from the end of May to mid-September. Seats cost around £2.80 ($4.20) at the box office.

Roland Morris's Maritime Museum, 19 Chapel St. (tel. 0736/63324), is a fascinating collection of treasure recovered from many wrecks around the Isles of Scilly, among them the famous *Association,* flagship of Admiral Sir Cloudsley Shovell which foundered in 1707. Some of the gold coins are in mint condition. Roland Morris, a diver, has reproduced a section of a four-decker, 95-gun, first-rate ship-of-the-line of about 1730. You can inspect the gun decks, with their original cannon and guns, see where the surgeon and his assistants worked, and visit the admiral's great cabin where he slept among his treasured objects. The museum is open from 10 a.m. to 5 p.m. April to October. Admission is 80p ($1.20) for adults, 50p (75¢) for children.

WHERE TO STAY: Built in 1660, the **Abbey Hotel,** Abbey Street (tel. 0736/66906), is a well-preserved place that is frequented by discerning guests. The bonus is its situation—on a narrow side street on several terraces directly overlooking Penzance Harbour. Bedrooms and baths are stylishly furnished. You can take only your room and breakfast at the Abbey, or have dinner in the restaurant downstairs. Singles cost from £35 ($52.50) per day, a double or twin going from £40 ($60) to £60 ($90), including a full English breakfast and VAT. Behind the hotel, which is built close to the street, is a tiny formal garden on two tiers, each with a view of the water. Here the herbs are grown that are used to spice the delicately flavored meats in the restaurant downstairs. The owners, Michael and Jean Cox, have brought their vitality, style, and charm into the hotel business. Jean Cox is the former international model, Jean Shrimpton. Sample dishes from their dinner menu include homemade soups, mackerel paté, fresh local fish dishes, and generally a roast joint. Everything is fresh and delicately cooked, a dinner costing from £12 ($18).

The **Georgian House,** Chapel Street (tel. 0736/65664), once the home of the mayors of Penzance, has been completely renovated into a cozy, intimate hotel. Denise and Michael Hardman welcome guests to their bright, clean bedrooms, all with hot and cold water basins and beverage-making facilities. Bathless rooms are rented for £11 ($16.50) per person for B&B, rising to £13.50 ($20.25) to £14 ($21) per person in a unit with a private bath. The house is centrally heated, and you can watch color TV in the comfortable, carpeted lounge. In the dining room, with a nautical motif, you can enjoy good Cornish meals. The house is centrally located, with a courtyard at the rear where you can park your car.

Mincarlo, Chapel Street (tel. 0736/62848), is a guesthouse built directly on the sidewalk. Owned by Mrs. Welsh, it is near the Admiral Benbow restaurant. Mrs. Welsh tends to the large house herself, serving hearty Cornish breakfasts in her dining room, which is packed with antiques. Bright of spirit and most hospitable, she charges £8 ($12) per person daily for B&B. In one room a four-poster was installed by popular demand. Mincarlo is neat and adequate.

Richmond Lodge, 61 Morrab Rd. (tel. 0736/65560), is a comfortable early Victorian house with a nautical flavor, lying a few steps from Market Jew Street (the main street) and within an easy walk of the Promenade along the sea wall. The Morrab Gardens is across the street. The host-owners, Jean and Pat Eady, have warm courtesy, down-to-earth friendliness, and an unrehearsed charm. A Cornish woman, Mrs. Eady is an excellent cook, specializing in traditional English dishes. She provides faultless service in this clean, bright, homey place with full central heating to keep out the chill and a fully licensed bar for the occasional toddy. Some bedrooms have private bath. Charges are £8 ($12) per person for B&B or £56 ($84) to £70 ($105) per person weekly. Evening meals can be ordered daily at a charge of £4.50 ($6.75).

Kimberley House, 10 Morrab Rd. (tel. 0736/62727), lies between the promenade and the center of town, opposite Penlee Park and near the Morrab Gardens. Avril and Rex Mudway have run this house since his retirement after a long sea-going career. They are friendly and gracious to their guests, not only providing good food and accommodations but offering tips about what to see in the area. B&B costs around £10.50 ($15.75) per person, and a rather large dinner goes for £6 ($9).

Carnson House Hotel, East Terrace (tel. 0736/65589), is personally run by Trisha and Richard Hilder, two friendly owners. Close to the harbor, town center, station, and beach, their house is convenient for train, coach, and bus travelers. They charge from £10 ($15) daily for B&B, plus another £5.75 ($8.63) for dinner. At certain times of the year they also serve a light cooked supper from an à la carte menu as an alternative to a full three-course dinner. All bedrooms have automatic tea- or coffee-making equipment for your early-morning drink. Guests can also make use of a comfortable lounge with TV. The Hilders are also licensed to serve alcohol, and they provide a tourist information service on local "things to do." They are also ticket agents for local bus and coach tours as well as steamer trips to the Isles of Scilly.

Blue Dolphin, Alexandra Road (tel. 0736/63836). The Snells run a pleasant guesthouse on a tree-lined street just up from the promenade and the seafront. In the solid stone house, bedrooms, all with color TV, rent for £8.50 ($12.75) to £9 ($13.50) per person daily for B&B, prices depending on the season. An evening meal, costing £5.50 ($8.25), is served. A good and varied menu is provided in the attractive dining room. There is street parking, and the bus past the door goes to St. Ives, Land's End, and Mousehole.

On the Outskirts

Higher Trevorian Hotel, St. Buryan (tel. 073672/348), is a small, secluded, informal hotel ideally situated for exploring *"Poldark* Country," with all the beaches, coves, cliffs, harbors, and streams visited in novels and pictured in the *Poldark* TV series. Vivian and Paul Trimble receive B&B guests in their hotel in a section between Penzance and Land's End, just ¼ mile from the village of St. Buryan. The eight bedrooms are rented for £8.50 ($12.75) per person. Dinner is served for £6.50 ($9.75), or you can take half board for £14 ($21) per person per day. Home-cooked food is served, making use of much local produce. Guests can relax in the TV lounge or in the Grapevine Bar. There's plenty of free parking.

WHERE TO EAT: Down a narrow cobble street opposite Lloyds Bank, **Harris's Restaurant,** 46 New St. (tel. 0736/64408), is owned and run by a husband-and-wife team, Roger and Anne Harris. It's a pleasant, warm, candlelit place with a relaxed atmosphere. Light lunches, costing from £6 ($9), served upstairs, include crab florentine, lobster salad, and salade niçoise. Dinner is more elaborate, offering such dishes as breast of duckling in a port wine sauce, filet steak with red wine and wild mushroom sauce, or veal served with a marsala and cream sauce. Expect to pay from £12 ($18) for a complete dinner. Lunch is served from noon to 2 p.m. and dinner from 7 to 10 p.m. except on Monday in winter.

Olive Branch Vegetarian Restaurant, 3a The Terrace, Market Jew Street (tel. 0736/62438), is a second-floor dining room over a store that was the birthplace of Humphrey Davy. A plaque commemorates that event, and a statue of Davy stands on the square. Try for a chair with a view overlooking St. Michael's Mount. You might begin with a homemade vegetable soup, then follow with a "bean burger" or else parsnip and cashew patties. Snacks or sandwiches are made to order. Meals, costing from £5 ($7.50), are served from 10:30 a.m. to 2:30 p.m. and 6 to 8 p.m. except Sunday.

Turk's Head, Chapel Street (tel. 0736/63093), is reputed to be the oldest inn in Penzance, dating from 1233. It serves the finest food of any pub in town, far superior to its chief rival, the nearby Admiral Benbow. In summer drinkers overflow into the garden. Inside, the inn is decorated in a mellow old style, as befits its age, with flat irons and other artifacts hanging from its time-worn beams. Meals, costing from £6 ($9), include fishermen's pie, T-bone steaks, and chicken curry. Hours are Monday to Saturday from 11 a.m. to 2 p.m. and 6 to 10 p.m. (on Sunday from noon to 1:45 p.m. and 7 to 10 p.m.).

8. The Isles of Scilly

Perhaps the most interesting and scenic excursion from Penzance is a day trip to the Isles of Scilly, which lie off the Cornish coast about 27 miles west-southwest of Land's End. There are five inhabited and more than 100 uninhabited islands in the group, some consisting of merely a few square miles while others, such as St. Mary's, the largest, encompass some 30 square miles. Two of these islands attract tourists, St. Mary's and Tresco.

These islands were known to the early Greeks and the Romans, and in Celtic legend they were inhabited entirely by holy men. There are more ancient burial mounds in the islands than anywhere else in southern England, and artifacts found establish clearly that people lived here more than 4,000 years ago.

Today there is little left of this long history to show the visitor. Now these are islands of peace and beauty where early flowers are the main export and tourism the main industry.

St. Mary's is the capital, with about seven-eighths of the total population of all the islands, and it is here that the ship from the mainland docks, at Hugh Town. However, for the day visitor, I recommend the helicopter flight from Penzance to **Tresco,** the neighboring island.

HOW TO GET THERE: Daily departures are made by the **Isles of Scilly Steamship Company,** Quay Street, Penzance (tel. 0736/62009), from March to October, except Sunday. The trip from Penzance to Hugh Town, St. Mary's, takes about three hours. Steamships leave Penzance at 9:15 a.m. and return from Scilly at 4:55 p.m. In winter there is restricted service. Rates start with a walk-on single same-day round-trip fare of £15 ($22.50) for adults, £3.75 ($5.63) for children. To visit the other islands, go first to St. Mary's by steamship and take the small, inter-island boat. For information on inter-island launches, phone Kathy Stedeford at 0720/22886.

To reach **Tresco** from St. Mary's Quay, an inter-island boat charges £2.90 ($4.35) per person round trip. This amount includes the landing fee. Departures from St. Mary's are twice daily, at 10:15 a.m. and 2:15 p.m. Departures from Tresco are less rigidly scheduled, the shallow waters around the island making boat movements dependent on the tides. The inter-island boats leaving Tresco sail either from New Grimsby or Carn Near, depending on the tides and the seasons.

British Airways, at the Penzance Airport (tel. 0736/63871), operates a year-round helicopter service between Penzance and St. Mary's, as well as to Tresco from April to September. Flight time is 20 minutes. The standard fare from Penzance to either of the islands is £23 ($34.50) each way. There is also a round trip at £31 ($46.50) if you return the same day. Flights start at 7:50 a.m. in high season, July to September, and at 8:45 at other times. They continue regularly throughout the day, with the last flight back to Penzance at 6:15 p.m. in high season, 4:15 p.m. otherwise. For people arriving in Penzance on the overnight train from London, there is bus service between the railway station and the heliport. The cost is 60p (90¢) each way; the travel time, only five minutes.

Brymon Airways, City Airport, Crownhill, Plymouth (tel. 0752/707023), operates airplane flights from Heathrow and Gatwick via Plymouth to St. Mary's. The charge is £80 ($120) from Gatwick, £2 ($3) more from Heathrow per person one way from London to St. Mary's. Flying time is two hours and ten minutes, with a short stop at Plymouth. The one-way fare from Plymouth to St. Mary's is £40 ($60). There are no flights on Sunday.

Whatever the transportation you take, there is a £1.10 ($1.65) landing fee for Tresco.

British Rail runs express trains from Paddington Station, London, to Penzance. BritRail Passes can be used. Otherwise, the second-class round-trip fare is £74.80 ($112.20). Travel time is about five hours. There are special offers on the Night Riviera Express.

For those who wish to travel to Penzance by road, there is good express bus service. The Rapide costs £22.50 ($33.75) round trip for the journey from London, 6¾ hours each way. The buses are fitted with toilets and have reclining seats, TV, and a hostess who dispenses coffee, tea, and sandwiches. These buses are run by **National Express,** Victoria Coach Station, 172 Buckingham Palace Rd., London, S.W.1 (tel. 01/730-0202).

WHERE TO STAY ON TRESCO: You are welcomed to the **New Inn** (tel. 0720/ 22844) by Chris and Lesley Hopkins. Their pub, built of stone, has an outdoor area for those who wish to picnic and drink a glass of ale. The bar is a meeting place for tourists and locals alike. Lunch snacks are available. You can have what the English call "a good fill" for £5 ($7.50), and dinners cost from £13 ($19.50), with specials posted on the bar blackboard. The inn has 12 rooms, all twins or doubles with private bath. There is a wide range of prices, with special packages offered in spring and fall. Prices range from £28 ($42) to £35 ($52.50) per person, including a full English breakfast, a four-course dinner, and VAT. The inn has a heated outdoor swimming pool for use in the summer months.

WHAT TO SEE AND DO ON TRESCO: No cars or motorbikes are allowed on the island, but walking or bicycling is pleasant. Bikes can be rented for £3 ($4.50) per day. The hotels use a special wagon towed by a farm tractor to transport guests and luggage from the harbor.

The phone number for information to do with Tresco is 0720/22849. Call it to find out about boat schedules, possible changes in hours and prices at the abbey, and other matters.

The **Abbey Gardens** and **Valhalla,** mentioned above, are the most outstanding features of Tresco. Here you can enjoy a day's walk through the 735 acres, mostly occupied by the celebrated Abbey Gardens. These gardens were started by Augustus Smith in the mid-1830s. When he began work, the area was a barren hillside, a fact visitors find hard to believe.

The gardens are a collector's dream, with more than 5,000 species of plants from some 100 different countries. The old abbey, or priory, is a ruin said to have been founded by Benedictine monks in the 11th century, although some historians date it from A.D. 964. Of special interest in the gardens is Valhalla, a collection of nearly 60 figureheads from ships wrecked around the islands. There is a rather eerie atmosphere surrounding these gaily painted figures from the past, each one a ghost with a different story to tell. Hours are from 10 a.m. to 4 p.m. daily. Admission is £2.50 ($3.75).

After a visit to the gardens, walk through the fields, along paths, and across dunes thick with heather. Flowers, birds, shells, and fish are so abundant that Tresco is a naturalist's dream and a walker's paradise. Birds are so unafraid that they land within a foot or so of you and feed happily.

WHERE TO STAY ON ST. MARY'S: The only hotel in the islands that actually sits
at the water's edge is the **Atlantic Hotel** (tel. 0720/22417). From your seat in the restaurant, you can feel you're almost in the midst of the fishing boats bobbing about. The inn is old and rambling, with different sizes of bedrooms, many with views over the water and several with private bath and toilet. The charge ranges from £24 ($36) to £30 ($45) per person, for a comfortable room, a large breakfast, and a four-course dinner. The Shipwreck Bar and Cocktail Bar lead directly onto a patio from which you can climb down to the beach at low tide. The restaurant has a good choice for each course on its four-course table d'hôte, including grilled Cornish mackerel or freshly caught John Dory, a local fish.

Tremellyn Guest House (tel. 0720/22656) is a Victorian house on a hill behind Hugh Town with sheltered gardens and a beautiful view of the islands. Colin and Liz Ridsdale run a trim ship, offering comfortable rooms with hot and cold water and central heating. B&B costs from £12 ($18) per person nightly, rising to £15 ($22.50) in high season. Dinner is another £9 ($13.50).

Mincarlo Guest House (tel. 0720/22513). The Duncan family has owned this lovely house right on the edge of the harbor for 40 years. Colin and Jill Duncan charge £10 ($16.50) per person for B&B, or from £16 ($24) per person for half board, plus VAT. The cozy house has a variety of accommodations, including family rooms. Many overlook the harbor, only a five-minute walk away. Colin prepares and cooks the evening meal, featuring a selection of local produce, fish, and shellfish.

Evergreen Cottage Guest House, Parade (tel. 0720/22711), is one of the oldest cottages in the islands, originally the home for sea captains. Mr. and Mrs. Jenkins, whose name and family date back some 300 years in the islands, charge £11 ($16.50) per person for B&B, or £18 ($27) for half board. The bedrooms are warm and comfortable, all with hot and cold running water. There are adequate public bathrooms and toilets. Mr. Jenkins has written books on island maritime history and is fascinating to talk to.

Lyonnesse Guest House, The Strand (tel. 0720/22458), is another large family home in the quieter part of Hugh Town, but close to shops and the harbor. Derek and Melanie Woodcock are both young islanders, who take great pride in telling their guests about the Scillies. There is a large lounge, and the house is well appointed, the front rooms and lounge having views of the harbor and islands. All units have heating, hot and cold water basins, and shaver points. The daily half-board rate is £16.50 ($24.75) per person.

Carnwethers Country Guest House, Pelistry Bay (tel. 0720/22415), is a modernized, two-story farmhouse with a one-story extension, standing on top of a hill looking down to fields, beach, and the sea. Pelistry Bay is a secluded part of St. Mary's island, the sandy beach well sheltered. You can walk at low tide across to the nearby uninhabited island of Tolls. The hostelry is owned and operated by Roy and Joyce Graham, with Joyce personally supervising the kitchen. For dinner, although the choice is limited, traditional English fare is offered. Dinner, served at 6:30 p.m. (at 6 p.m. on Friday in high season), costs £6 ($9) for four courses. The ten bedrooms, some with private baths, cost £19 ($28.50) to £21 ($31.50) per person for full board in spring and fall, the rate depending on the plumbing. In high season, prices are £22 ($33) to £24 ($36). The main lounge is in two parts, one for conversation and reading, the other containing a library full of books about the islands. A heated outdoor swimming pool is in operation in summer.

WHERE TO EAT ON ST. MARY'S: May Duxbury, assisted by her daughter
Lisbet, runs a cheap and cheerful place, **The Café,** 8 Lower Strand, Hugh Town (tel.

0720/22124). They serve typical fare, including chicken and chips. May does most of the cooking, with meals costing from £5 ($7.50). Hours are from 9:30 a.m. to 7 p.m. in summer, from 10 a.m. to 5 p.m. in winter. The café, a little white-walled building, sits on a side of the harbor bay.

The **Gallery Restaurant,** Parade, Hugh Town (tel. 0720/22602), is a small two-floor establishment, run by Peter Thompson. On the street level, he sells take-away fish and chips, plus raw fish to be cooked at home. The upstairs restaurant is a light, wood-paneled room with pinewood tables and wheelback chairs, serving fresh local fish, such as cod, plaice, and crab. A specialty is the chef's tasty fish pie. Unusual dishes to order include megrim (a local sole), "skate wings," and John Dory. Meals cost from £5 ($7.50). The restaurant is open daily except Sunday from noon to 1:30 p.m. and 6 to 8:30 p.m.

WHAT TO DO AND SEE ON ST. MARY'S: Expert diver Mark Groves who runs **Underwater Island Safaris,** "Nowhere," Old Town, St. Mary's (tel. 0720/22732), has worked as a diver in both the Caribbean and the Red Sea. He can entertain both the experienced and the inexperienced diver. A diving safari costs from £17.50 ($26.25) for three hours of instruction and diving, including gear rental. Diving for qualified persons takes place on many of the historic wrecks and beautiful drop-offs. Waterskiing is also available.

The **Isles of Scilly Museum,** St. Mary's (tel. 0702/22337), is open daily in summer from 10 a.m. to noon, 1:30 to 4:30 p.m., and 7 to 9 p.m. In winter it is open on Wednesday from 1:30 to 4:30 p.m. Admission is 40p (60¢). The museum shows the history of the islands from 1500 B.C. with artifacts from wrecked ships, drawings, and relics discovered in the Scillies.

Cars are available, but hardly necessary.

The **Island Bus Service** has a basic charge of 80p ($1.20) for adults, 40p (60¢) for children.

Bicycles can be rented at **Buccabu Bicycle Rentals** (tel. 0720/22765) for about £3 ($4.50) per day.

The **Tourist Information Office** on St. Mary's offers friendly service (tel. 0720/22536).

WHERE TO SHOP ON ST. MARY'S: For a perfect and useful souvenir of the Scillies, visit the **Glassblowers** (tel. 0720/22900) and watch crystal glass blown from a furnace and handmade into goblets, vases, cream jugs, and ornaments. Then visit the Crystal Glass Shop and browse around. David Langsworthy is the designer and craftsman, and each piece is stamped and hand-engraved by the glassmaker.

The **Man of War** (tel. 0720/22563), is a nautical antique shop where you can buy ancient coins recovered from vessels around the island. They are made into pendants and cufflinks or just mounted.

Mrs. Hazel Harding on Garrison Hill (tel. 0720/22007) sells locally handmade woolen goods, hats, scarfs, and sweaters.

FOOD AND LODGING AT ST. AGNES: If you happen to find yourself at St. Agnes, try to stay overnight at **Coastguards** (tel. 0720/22373), the home of Wendy and Danny Hick, one of the islands' oldest names. St. Agnes people are called "Turks," and these people truly qualify for the appellation. Their cottage, white with black trim, stands in the middle of a row of coastguard cottages, on one of the highest parts of the island. For bed, breakfast, and an evening meal, Mrs. Hick charges £16 ($24) per person. Rooms have good views, and a large breakfast is served. Dinner (they call it supper here) is a tasty meal of homemade soup, homemade bread, and a Cornish roast. Mr. Hick is a traditional model shipwright by profession. His fine models are commissioned through Harrods and the Cunard Line.

The Turks Head (tel. 0720/22434) is run by Roger and Liz Harris, who offer bar lunches, including homemade soups and Cornish pasties. Meals cost from £2.50 ($3.25). Only lunch is served, from 11:30 a.m. to 2:30 p.m. The place is known throughout the islands.

Now we turn to the outlying district of Penzance, beginning first on the eastern side of the bay at St. Hilary, then heading south to Newlyn and Mousehole.

9. Newlyn, Mousehole, and Land's End

NEWLYN: From Penzance, a promenade leads to Newlyn, a mile away, another fishing village of infinite charm on Mount's Bay. In fact, its much-painted harbor seems clogged with more fishing craft than that of Penzance. Stanhope Forbes, now dead, founded an art school in Newlyn, and in the past few years the village has gained an increasing reputation for its artists' colony, attracting both the serious painter and the Sunday sketcher. From Penzance, the old fishermen's cottages and crooked lanes of Newlyn are reached by bus. For a dining or overnighting recommendation, try the following:

Panorama Guest House, Chywoone Hill (tel. 0736/68498), is run by Roy and Margaret Perry, who go out of their way to please their guests. They take care of them comfortably in a small collection of rooms ranging from a single to a family accommodation. The B&B rate runs from £9.50 ($14.25) per person nightly. Units have hot and cold running water, and several open onto a view of the sea. For another £5.50 ($8.25), you can enjoy a four-course dinner. There is space to park your car, and use of a heated outdoor swimming pool is available.

Smugglers Hotel and Restaurant, Fore Street (tel. 0736/64207), was chosen by the English Tourist Board to represent the "best of Cornish accommodation" in one of their campaigns. The choice was appropriate. It has a crooked beamed front, irregular windows, and an uneven roof. Most of the 12 accommodations open onto lovely views over the fishing boats in the harbor and across Mount's Bay. All have hot and cold running water, and many have private bath. Depending on the plumbing, singles rent for £16 ($24) to £20 ($30) and doubles for £14 ($21) to £16 ($24) per person nightly, including a continental or English breakfast. The Cellar Bar epitomizes the old inn's atmosphere and age. Here David Reeve, owner and manager, presides over the bar and generates conversation, dispensing drink and cheer in equal quantities. The restaurant enjoys a good local reputation, and you can sample some of the inn's specialties, including duck à l'orange, pork marsala, or beef bourguignon. Dinners, from 7 to 10:30 p.m., cost £12 ($18). No lunch is served.

MOUSEHOLE: Still another Cornish fishing village, Mousehole lies three miles south of Penzance (take bus 9), two from our last stopover in Newlyn. The hordes of tourists who flock here haven't changed it drastically—the gulls still squawk, the cottages still huddle close to the harbor wall (although they look as if they were built more to be photographed than lived in), the fishermen still bring in the day's catch, the salts sit around with their smoking tobacco talking about the good old days, and the lanes are as narrow as ever. About the most exciting thing that's occurred was the arrival in the late 16th century of the Spanish galleons, whose ungallant sailors sacked and burnt the village. In a sheltered cove, off Mount's Bay, Mousehole (pronounced mou-sel) today has developed the nucleus of an artists' colony. For rooms and meals, try the following recommendations, all within the village:

Food and Lodging
The Lobster Pot (tel. 0736/731251) is a country hotel and restaurant composed of a stone-walled complex of converted fishermen's cottages resting on massive foun-

dations sunk deep into the mud at the edge of the water. John and Susan Kelly, the likeable owners, rent 26 comfortable modern bedrooms scattered among the main buildings and outlying annexes. Each contains color TV, and most of them have bathrooms. Depending on the season, the view, and the plumbing, rates range from £14.50 ($21.75) to £28.50 ($42.75) per person for B&B. Half board costs an additional £9 ($13.50) per day. Guests can enjoy a pre-dinner drink under the heavy beams of the panoramic bar/lounge. As its seaside location suggests, shellfish and other seafood (perhaps the best in town) are the house specialty. Well prepared, sometimes by Mrs. Kelly, meals are reasonably priced at £6 ($9) for lunch, served from 12:30 to 2 p.m., and £11 ($16.50) and up for dinner from 7:30 to 10 p.m. The establishment is open from early March to early January.

Tavis Vor (tel. 0736/731306) is the only place in Mousehole with direct access to the sea through its own grounds. It has a marvelous view overlooking the harbor and St. Michael's Mount. Almost directly opposite is a small island on which there are the remains of a monastery. The first building on the sea side when you enter Mousehole, it accommodates 15 guests, costing £11.50 ($17.25) to £14.50 ($21.75) per person for B&B. The owners, John and Kathleen Hanley, keep the house open from mid-March to mid-October, offering rooms with sea views. Three have private showers. Mrs. Hanley does the cooking. Try her four-course dinner, costing £5 ($17.50).

Renovelle, The Parade (tel. 0736/731258), is a pretty little villa, all fresh blue and white, at the edge of the village. It's aptly perched right beside the sea, on a cliff, which makes the view memorable. Mrs. Stella Bartlett, the owner, has made it charming and comfortable. Her guests keep returning year after year, and pay a B&B rate of £10 ($15) per person nightly. Each bedroom is comfy, equipped with a water basin and shower, and they have good views of the sea. It's a pleasure to have breakfast set before you in the sunny little dining room.

Dolphins, Mousehole (tel. 0736/731828). A steep drive up to this house is rewarded with peace and quiet, plus a breathtaking view over Mount's Bay with the harbor and fishing boats below. Guests can relax and sunbathe in the suntrap garden, later enjoying the comfortable lounge before retreating to one of the well-furnished bedrooms (the doubles have private bath or shower). A good breakfast is provided, and the B&B costs range from £10 ($15) to £12 ($18) per person. It's run by Yvonne Lodge, who for many years was a naval nursing officer. Her whole place is neat and trim. Ask directions as you enter Mousehole.

Pam's Pantry, Mill Lane (tel. 0736/731532), is a small and cheerful café and kitchen which is open daily from 9 a.m. to 6 p.m. Some of the dishes here feature fish caught locally. You can order crab salad, a summer favorite, or smoked mackerel. To complete the meal, a homemade apple pie with Cornish clotted cream is served. The cost of a meal is £6.95 ($10.43).

On the Outskirts

Raginnis Farm is owned and run by the Harvey brothers, a 100-odd-acre tract of dairyland with a 70-strong Friesian herd. You get good local produce and views over the countryside to the far-off sea. The brothers' wives offer B&B. Tanya, wife of Robert, houses guests in her lovely thatched home, Thatch Cottage, Raginnis Farm, Mousehole (tel. 0736/731333), charging £8 ($12) per night. The early-18th-century place is not large enough to accommodate visitors with children. A double room with bath and toilet is a pleasant low-ceilinged room with a comfortable bed. An evening meal can be supplied. Also at Raginnis Farm (tel. 0736/731523), Penny Harvey has young children of her own and more space to welcome guests with families. She charges the same price.

LAND'S END: Craggy Land's End, where England comes to an end, is where you'll find the last of everything. It lies nine miles west of Penzance and is reached by bus 1 or 1B. America's coast is 3,291 miles away to the west of the rugged rocks that tumble into the sea beneath Land's End.

Publicity says that "Everyone should stand here, at least once." Given the romantic conception that this is the piece of England closest to America, the most distant point you can go on mainland England, this is so. It must still retain some of its mystique even if Big Business has now opened the Land's End Heritage Museum, the Man and the Sea Exhibition, the Worzel Gummidge Exhibition, not to mention a Video Theatre with continuous performances and the First and Last Craft Workshop from which to buy your first and "last" souvenirs.

True, the area needs an injection of money. As anyone standing on those jagged cliffs can see, the pounding they take causes much damage to the coastline. The debate continues for the time being as to the price of entry—whether there should be one at all. Better to ignore the commercial aspect and enjoy the cliff walks and spectacular views.

Food and Lodging

Old Success Inn, Sennen Cove, Land's End (tel. 073637/232). Just before you reach Land's End, turn right and follow the road down to Sennen Cove. The Old Success lies at the bottom, facing the sea and wide sandy beaches. Surfing rollers come in from the Atlantic almost to the foot of the sea wall beneath the 17th-century fishermen's inn. Over the years it has been extended and modernized, now offering bright, clean rooms, many with private bath, all with radio, tea and coffee maker, electric heater, and wash basin. Half board costs from £22 ($33) to £24.50 ($36.75) per person nightly. Downstairs, the inn has a lounge with color TV and panoramic views over the Atlantic, a cozy lounge bar, and Charlie's Bar where the locals and fishermen join the residents of the evening. Frank Carroll, resident manager, and his staff provide a varied dinner menu in the Seine Room, the house restaurant, for £8 ($12) and up. Hours are from 11:30 a.m. to 2:30 p.m. and 6:30 to 10 p.m. daily.

10. St. Ives

This north coast fishing village, with its sandy beaches, is England's most famous art colony. Only 20 miles from Land's End, ten from Penzance, it is a village of narrow streets and well-kept cottages. The artists settled in many years ago and have integrated with the fishermen and their families.

The art colony was established long enough ago to have developed several schools or splits, and they almost never overlap, except in pubs where the artists hang out, at an occasional café, and where classes are held. The old battle continues between the followers of the representational and the devotees of the abstract in art, with each group recruiting young artists all the time. In addition, there are the potters, weavers, and other artisans, all doing things creatively and exhibiting and selling in this area. There are several galleries to visit, with such names as the Sail Loft.

A *word of warning:* St. Ives becomes virtually impossible to visit in August, when you're likely to be trampled underfoot by busloads of tourists, mostly the British themselves. However, in spring and early fall, the pace is much more relaxed, and a visitor can have the true experience of the art colony.

PARK AND RIDE: During the summer months, many of the streets in the center of town are closed to vehicles. You may want to leave your car in the **Lelant Saltings Car Park,** three miles from St. Ives on the A3074, and take the regular train service into town, an 11-minute journey. Departures are every half hour. It's free to all car passengers and drivers, and the car-park charge is £2 ($3) a day. Or you can use the large **Trenwith Car Park,** close to the town center, for 25p (38¢) and then walk down to the shops and harbor or take a bus, costing 20p (30¢) for adults and 10p (15¢) for children.

WHERE TO STAY: Avoid the snug, suburban houses built on the edge of St. Ives and go instead to the end of the peninsula, or island as it's called (it's not actually). In these winding streets, you'll find the studios of the working artists, the fishermen, and the unusual places set aside to show and sell works of art. And you'll also find here a number of B&B guesthouses and cottages. For the most part, they are easy to find; simply look for B&B signs as you walk along the narrow streets.

Garrack Hotel, Higher Ayr (tel. 0736/796199), from its two-acre knoll, commands a panoramic view of St. Ives and Portmeor Beach. The vine-covered little hotel, once a private home, is reached by heading up a narrow lane. It's one of the friendliest and most efficiently run small medium-priced hotels on the entire coast, with every room furnished in a warm, homey manner. The atmosphere in the living room is inviting, with a log-burning fireplace, antiques, and comfortable chairs. The Garrack belongs to Mr. and Mrs. Kilby, who are proud of their meals. Most bedrooms have private bath and toilet, and some have shower also. Prices vary because of the view, the size of the room, and the season. B&B costs from £18 ($27) to £23 ($34.50) per person in a room without bath, rising to £22 ($33) to £28 ($42) in rooms with bath or shower. Half-board terms are quoted on stays of more than three days. A set dinner costs £9.50 ($14.25). There is a special shellfish menu with live lobster taken as required from a sea-water storage tank, prepared, cooked, and served as requested. An addition to the hotel contains a heated indoor swimming pool with a sauna and a solarium.

Kandahar, 11 The Warren (tel. 0736/796183), enjoys a waterfront location so that its rooms open onto the harbor and the bay. It's also near the town center and some 600 feet from the British Rail and bus terminals. Centrally heated rooms are pleasantly furnished, and the hotel is attractively decorated. The resident proprietors, Derek and Diana Mason, charge from £10 ($15) to £12 ($18) in a single and from £17 ($25.50) to £23 ($34.50) in a double. There's usually a place to park your car.

Dean Court Hotel, Trelyon Avenue (tel. 0736/796023), opens onto the harbor and beach, and naturally the most desirable accommodations here are those that have views over the water, seven in all. Each of the bedrooms has a private bath, and guests are accepted in every month except December. A family-run place, it takes guests for the half-board rate ranging from £23 ($34.50) to £30 ($45) per person nightly. You get good food and hospitality here.

Primrose Valley Hotel, Primrose Valley (tel. 0736/794939), lies on a private road in the vicinity of Porthminster Beach. It is a most desirable accommodation, offering pleasantly furnished and comfortable bedrooms. Family run, it quotes, half-board terms ranging from £15 ($22.50) to £24 ($36) per person nightly, which is very good value for the area. Children are welcome, the food is good, and there is plenty of parking.

Hobblers Guest House and Restaurant, The Wharf (tel. 0736/796439), is right on the harborside, a black-and-white building next to a shellfish shop. Paul Folkes has only three rooms to rent at £10 ($15) per person nightly. None of these has a private bath. His main interest is in his restaurant which is recommended separately. Because it's bull's-eye center, it may be hard to get a room here in high season. The house was built in the 17th century as a pilot's house.

The **Trecarrell Hotel,** Carthew Terrace (tel. 0736/795707), is housed in a 140-year-old building in a quiet quarter of St. Ives. The restaurant, bar, and kitchens are under the close supervision of the proprietor, Lynda D. Bayfield, who takes pride in the hotel. The best local produce and meats are used in the meals served here, along with fish caught from the ocean. Lobster and crab are specialties, plus many home-made desserts, with Cornish cream a specialty. The hotel is centrally heated and is small and friendly, with 16 bedrooms. Each unit is individually decorated, and most have private baths or showers. Rates start with a low season price of £12.50 ($18.75) to £15.50 ($23.25) per person for B&B in a bathless room, £14.50 ($21.75) to £17.50

($26.25) per person with bath. Dinner is from £6.50 ($9.75) per person for a table d'hôte meal. VAT is included in all tariffs.

Pondarosa Guest House, 10 Portminster Terrace (tel. 0736/795875), is a Victorian building enclosing some of the best rooms for the money in St. Ives. The owners rent out 10 well furnished and comfortable bedrooms, two of which are suitable for families. There is only one accommodation with a private bath, however. It's more economical to stay here on half-board terms, costing from £14 ($21) to £16 ($24) per person daily. Guests are received from April to October, and there is limited parking.

WHERE TO EAT: At this previously recommended guesthouse, **Hobblers Restaurant,** The Wharf (tel. 0736/796439), serves only lunch from noon to 2 p.m. from May to October, offering dinner from 6 to 10:30 p.m. April to October. At about £10 ($15) per person, you get some of the finest seafood in St. Ives. Dishes are likely to include scallops, halibut, scampi, and plaice, along with mussels and a cream of lobster bisque to begin with. If you don't want fish, you might settle happily for the chicken Kiev or a filet steak. Of course, the dishes come with "chips" and peas. The paneled rooms are decorated with pictures of ships and seascapes. It's cramped, nautical, and intimate.

Garrack Hotel, Higher Ayr (tel. 0736/796199), the domain of Mr. and Mrs. Kilby, is outstanding, producing an excellent cuisine and, when possible, using fresh ingredients from their own garden. The hotel dining room, open to non-residents, offers regular à la carte listings, plus a cold buffet or snacks at the bar, and a £9.50 ($14.25) dinner from 7 to 8:30 p.m. The menu features some of the finest of English dishes, such as roast shoulder of lamb with mint sauce, fried fillet of plaice, lobster and mussels from the live storage tank, oysters from Port Navas (if ordered before 10 a.m.), and a wide choice of continental fare, such as scampi Nantua, tournedos au poivre, or châteaubriand. VAT is included in the prices. Coffee is served in the lounge. The Kilby's son Michael has joined his parents in the operation of the hotel and restaurant after completing a training period with Claridges in London.

The **Sloop Inn,** The Wharf (tel. 0736/796584), is one of the most popular pubs—perhaps THE most popular—in St. Ives. The owner offers salad platters, chicken, ham, and turkey. The specialty, if there is one, is the seafood salad with prawn or crab. Count on spending around £4 ($6). Hours are from noon to 2:30 p.m. and 7 to 10:30 p.m. Monday to Saturday, noon to 2 p.m. and 7 to 10:30 p.m. Sunday.

The **Balancing Eel,** Black Lane (tel. 0736/796792), is almost a traditional fish and chips shop where you line up at the take-out counter and receive your supper wrapped—not in newspaper these days, pity!—or take it upstairs to eat in the restaurant. A bag of sole and chips is £1.60 ($2.40). There are the usual bottles on the counter—vinegar, catsup, chutney, and pickled onions. It's open from noon to 2 p.m. and 5:30 to 8 p.m. daily except Sunday. It's close to the Wharf Post Office and Chy-an-Chy Street.

The **Pudding Bag Restaurant,** in the Sloop Craft Market in St. Ives (tel. 0736/797214), is open daily from 10 a.m. to 10 p.m. A long, narrow cafeteria opens into a seating area, where gargantuan Cornish pasties are served. In one of the steak pies, the meat alone weighs a quarter pound. You're served vegetables too. There's always a soup and the inevitable mixed grill. A good and filling meal can be ordered here at a cost of £4 ($6), including a beer and coffee. If you don't enter through the Craft Market, you can go to the entrance on Back Road West.

BARBARA HEPWORTH MUSEUM: At Trewyn Studio and Garden, on Barnoon Hill (tel. 0736/796226), the former home of Dame Barbara Hepworth contains a museum of sculpture by the artist from 1929 until her death in 1975, together with photographs, letters, and other papers documenting her life and background. The garden also contains sculpture, and is well worth a visit. The museum is open year round from

10 a.m. to 5:30 p.m. Monday to Saturday. It is closed on Sunday and charges an admission of 50p (75¢) for adults and 25p (38¢) for children. There is limited parking some 200 yards away, but visitors may like to leave their cars at Lelant Station some three miles away and use the park-and-ride service into St. Ives.

11. Port Isaac

The most unspoiled fishing village on the north Cornish coastline is Port Isaac, nine miles from Wadebridge. This Atlantic coastal resort retains its original character, in spite of the intrusions of large numbers of summer visitors. You can wander through its winding, narrow lanes, gazing at the white-washed fishermen's cottages with their rainbow trims.

WHERE TO STAY: Considered the most desirable accommodation in Port Isaac, **Castle Rock Hotel** (tel. 0208/880300) is a carefully cared for pink house with a magnificent view over the coast to as far away as Tintagel. It is run by Brian and Margaret Firth, who offer 19 attractively furnished bedrooms, most of which contain private bathrooms. They charge from £27 ($40.50) to £31 ($47.25) per person for half board. Guests meet each other at the well-stocked bar before going into the dining room where home-cooked meals (Mrs. Firth is a Cordon Bleu cook) are served, using, whenever possible, local produce. The good food served here is part of the Castle Rock's attraction, along with that view.

Rogues Retreat, Roscarrock Hill (tel. 020880/566), is a licensed guesthouse run by Frank and Jill Gadman, who are marvelous hosts even though this is their first venture at innkeeping (perhaps that's why they're so good). They rent seven comfortable bedrooms, with hot and cold running water and coffee- or tea-making facilities. Their charge of £8.50 ($12.75) per person nightly is most reasonable. Reductions are granted off-season. The guesthouse has scenic views over the fishing village and harbor. It lies adjacent to a National Trust footpath where walkers can enjoy the scenery of the coast and deserted coves. An evening meal with a selection of fine wines is served from 7 p.m. in a cozy dining room. Table settings are color coordinated in royal blue and white. An evening meal costs £5 ($7.50). Unusual for Port Isaac, they have private parking.

The Old School, Port Isaac (tel. 020880/721), dates from 1875, a sentinel on a clifftop overlooking the harbor and out to sea over a pier built in the reign of Henry VIII. Sportsmen are drawn to the hotel, taking part in shark and deep-sea fishing, sailing, windsurfing, and waterskiing. Even if you're not interested in that, you'll surely enjoy the pleasant harbor view and a day or two's rest in comfortable bedrooms with bath. A night will cost from £9.50 ($14.25) per person in low season in a bathless double up to £20.50 ($30.75) per person in high season in a twin or double with bath or shower. Some of the suites have half-tester beds. Breakfast, included in the price, is eaten in the Refectory, a lovely long room with tall windows and tables with settle benches. A three- or four-course dinner costs from £7.50 ($11.25). Mike and Alicia Warner, the owners, are enthusiasts who go out of their way to make guests comfortable.

WHERE TO EAT: In the center of the village, **Harbour Café,** Fore Street (tel. 020888/237), has a special fame, featured several times on British television and once in scenes from the Sherlock Holmes thriller, *The Devil's Foot.* The unique café is designated as a building of architectural and historic interest, and is one of several buildings on this treacherous stretch of coast that used the timber of wrecked ships in construction. The owners offer complete meals as well as snacks. In addition they have a table-wine license. On the menu are such local dishes as crab and mackerel salads, plus a number of other homemade specialties. Meals begin at around £6 ($9). Perhaps you will arrive in the afternoon, when you can have a Cornish cream tea, and if your appetite is still unsatisfied, you may care to try a piece of homemade gâteau topped with a portion of clotted cream. The café is open from 11 a.m. to 9 p.m.

The **Golden Lion,** Fore Street (tel. 0208/880336), is perhaps the most handsomely positioned pub in the old fishing village, with a view of the harbor from a drinking patio. Mr. and Mrs. Spry, the owners, offer good drinks, snacks, and crab sandwiches. Light meals cost from £5 ($7.50). Hours are from 11:30 a.m. to 2:30 p.m. and 5:30 to 11 p.m.

Another good bet is the **Cornish Grill,** New Road (tel. 0205/880670), a licensed family restaurant owned by David Phelps. Port Isaac is known for its crabs and lobsters, used here in superb salads. They also prepare spicy curries along with grilled steaks. Meals begin at £5 ($7.50) for three courses. Lunch is served from 11 a.m. to 2 p.m. and dinner from 6:30 to 9 p.m. Closed in November.

12. Tintagel

On a wild stretch of the Atlantic coast, Tintagel is forever linked with the legends of King Arthur, Lancelot, and Merlin. The 13th-century ruins of Tintagel Castle (tel. 0840/770328), popularly known as King Arthur's Castle, stand 300 feet above the sea on a rocky promontory. They are open April to September from 9:30 a.m. to 7 p.m. (on Sunday from 2 to 7 p.m.). From October to March, hours are 9:30 a.m. to 4 p.m. (on Sunday, 2 to 4 p.m.). Admission is £1 ($1.50) for adults, 50p (75¢) for children. The colorful writing of Lord Tennyson in *Idylls of the King* greatly increased the interest in Tintagel, as did the writings of Geoffrey of Monmouth. The ruins, which date from Geoffrey's time, are what remains of a castle built on the foundations of a Celtic monastery from the sixth century, a long, steep, tortuous walk from the car park.

The **Old Post Office** at Tintagel is a National Trust property. It was once a 14th-century manor, but since the 19th century it has had connections with the post office. In the village center, it has a genuine Victorian post room which is open, April to October, daily from 11 a.m. to 5:45 p.m. or sunset if that is earlier. Admission is 80p ($1.20), plus 20p (30¢) for a guidebook.

In summer, many visitors make the ascent to Arthur's lair, 100 rock-cut steps. You can also visit Merlin's Cave.

If you become excited by legends of Knights of the Round Table, you can even go to **Camelford,** just five miles inland from Tintagel. The market hall there dates from 1790, but, more interestingly, the town claims to be Camelot.

FOOD AND LODGING: A family-run hotel, **Trenowan Hotel,** Treknow, near Tintagel (tel. 0840/770255), provides personal service and home-style cookery. Built in the late Victorian style as identical twin houses, it is now owned by Barbara and George Bond, who welcome guests and are helpful in telling them of nearby attractions. They rent out a total of nine comfortably furnished rooms, some with private shower and toilet. Their half-board rate is £15 ($22.50) per person. Mrs. Bond is a "proper English cook," using fresh vegetables grown by her husband. Their quiet retreat stands on its own grounds overlooking the coast near Trebarwith Sands. They are open year round.

Pennallick Hotel, Treknow, near Tintagel (tel. 0840/770296), is another small, family-run hotel, where the living is relaxed and homey. The Belmonte family welcomes you to their house on the coastline, about a mile from Tintagel. Their nine bedrooms contain hot and cold running water, and all double units have showers as well. In the peak summer months they charge £15 ($22.50) per person for half board. If you're touring the next day, a packed lunch will be provided. There is also a comfortable licensed lounge bar, a pool room, games room, and a TV room.

Belvoir House, Tregatta (tel. 0840/770265), was formed by combining two Cornish cottages with an old smithy. Joyce Martin welcomes guests into her delightful accommodation, charging them from £10.50 ($15.75) per person nightly for B&B. For another £6 ($9) per person, an evening dinner can be arranged. My favorite section is the old smithy, which now has a double bedroom with a shower and toilet. Other rooms are comfortably and tastefully furnished. Guests enjoy both a sun lounge and a TV lounge, and the hotel has a residential license. It's especially pleasant in chilly weather when I've found some of the other guesthouses to be underheated.

Trebrea Lodge, Trenale, near Tintagel (tel. 0840/770410), may appear a dignified stately home, but in truth it looks and feels inside like an old Cornish farmhouse. It dates back to 1315, and was lived in by the same family for more than 600 years. The house, owned by Ann and Guy Murray, looks straight out across fields to the sea, and each bedroom has a good view. Rooms are available in many sizes, and each has a private bath, color TV, radio, intercom, and even a baby-listening service. Evenings are cozy in the drawing room around an open fire. The original first-floor drawing room has been restored, and there is a traditional Victorian smoking room in addition to the bar. You can have drinks in another lounge with a fireplace. Dining is most informal, and all food is home-made by Mrs. Murray, who has mastered true English recipes. The cost is £20 ($30) per person for half board.

Bossiney House Hotel (tel. 0840/770240) stands in an inviting spot on the right as you approach Tintagel from Boscastle. Two brothers, John and Reg Wrightham, and their families operate the hotel, and everybody combines to make guests feel welcome. The hotel is comfortable, with a TV lounge and a well-stocked bar/lounge which has a fine view of surrounding meadows marching right up to the tops of the cliff as well as of the wide expanse of lawn with a putting green. Rooms are comfortably furnished and have private baths and central heating. The large dining room, where a big English breakfast is served and you can enjoy other well-prepared meals brought to you by smiling Cornish women, is so situated as to give a view of the front, side, and back lawns. Guests pay from £28 ($42) to £32 ($48) in a single, from £24 ($36) to £26 ($39) per person in a double, depending on the season, for a room with dinner, breakfast, and morning tea served in your room before breakfast. The Wrightams will direct you to interesting places you might otherwise miss seeing in the area. The hotel is closed from early October until spring. Look for the old phaeton in the front garden. A pine log chalet in the garden houses a heated swimming pool, a sauna, and a sun bed.

FARMHOUSES NEAR BUDE: A 250-year-old farmhouse, Forda Farm,

Morwenstow, near Bude (tel. 028883/275), is nestled in a wooded coombe about 1½ miles from the sea. Ruth Manfield likes to keep guests to a minimum so "they will feel more like a friend of the family than a paying guest." Guests, no more than four or five at a time, gather around the table at night, as the farm is noted for its excellent cuisine, using wholesome foods, including their own dairy products and home-grown vegetables. Breakfast is in the traditional Cornish style, and a picnic lunch will be provided if you want to go touring during the day. Daily rates, including bed, breakfast, early-morning tea, and a table d'hôte dinner, are from £22 ($33) per person, plus another £2.50 ($3.75) for a packed lunch. You can also go on guided tours at £6 ($9) per person. Readers Dr. and Mrs. William Douglas write, "We arrived in time for haying and milking. We pitched in with the family and later shared a warm evening and a wonderful meal together. One can walk through lovely meadows overlooking the sea to Ireland and share from the local inhabitants the charm of one of the loveliest parts of England."

Trenance Farm Guest House, Crackington Haven, near Bude (tel. 08403/273), has quite the best views you're likely to find in a B&B. There are a mass of cliff and farmland paths for walkers. Boscastle and Tintagel are near at hand for the sightseer, and when you return tired and hungry, Mrs. Redman will produce a fine evening meal with local produce and fresh vegetables for £6 ($9). Rooms are country style and comfortable, costing £8 ($12) per person for B&B. Washing and ironing facilities are available, and the guesthouse is open all year.

13. Bolventor

This village in central Cornwall, near Launceston, is visited by Daphne du Maurier, as it was the setting for her novel *Jamaica Inn* (see below). The inn is named for the Caribbean island where the one-time owner of the inn had become prosperous from sugar on his plantation. Opposite the inn, a small road leads to Dozmary Pool where the "waves wap and the winds wan" into which Sir Bedivere threw Excalibur at King Arthur's behest.

Jamaica Inn (tel. 056686/250) is a long, low building beside the main road across Bodmin Moor, an ideal spot on the desolate moor for a smuggler's den in other times. Busy throughout most of the day with passing trade, it has welcoming bars where food and soft drinks are dispensed along with local beer and cider. There are some simple bedrooms for which you pay around £16 ($24) per person for B&B. There is a large gift shop where most of the souvenirs are local.

WILTSHIRE, SOMERSET, AND AVON

FOR OUR FINAL LOOK at the West Countree, we move now into Wiltshire, Somerset, and Avon, the most antiquity-rich shires of England. When we reach this area of woodland and pastoral scenes, London seems far removed from the bucolic life here.

On cold, windswept nights in unrecorded times, the Druids used to steal across these plains armed with twigs. Sheltered by boulders, they'd burn their sloe with rosemary to ward off the danger of witchcraft.

Most people seem to agree that the West Country, a loose geographical term, begins at Salisbury, with its Early English cathedral. Nearby is Stonehenge, England's oldest prehistoric monument. Both Stonehenge and Salisbury are in Wiltshire.

Somerset is even more varied, the diet richer not only in historical cities, but in wild scenic grandeur, especially in Exmoor. The legendary burial place of King Arthur at Glastonbury and the cathedral city of Wells also await you on your visit to Somerset. The old Roman city of Bath is the main target in the county of Avon.

WILTSHIRE

When you cross into Wiltshire, you'll be entering a county of chalky, grassy uplands and rolling plains. Most of the shire is agricultural, and a large part is devoted to pastureland. Wiltshire produces an abundance of England's dairy products, and is noted for its sheep raising. In this western shire, you'll traverse the Salisbury Plain, the

Vale of Pewsey, and the Marlborough Downs (the last gobbling up the greater part of the land mass). Unquestionably, the crowning achievement of Wiltshire is:

1. Salisbury

Long before you've made the 83-mile trek from London, the spire of Salisbury Cathedral comes into view, just as John Constable painted it so many times. The 404-foot pinnacle of the Early English and Gothic cathedral is the tallest in England. But Salisbury is also a fine base for touring such prehistoric sights as Stonehenge.

Market days are generally Tuesday and Saturday. There is a general market in the Market Place, where stalls sell anything from meat by auction to clothes and household goods, plants, and sweets.

THE SIGHTS: Salisbury, or New Sarum, lies in the valley of the Avon River. Filled with Tudor-style inns and tea rooms, it is known to readers of Thomas Hardy as Melchester and to the Victorian fans of Anthony Trollope as Barchester.

Salisbury Cathedral

You can search all of England, but you'll find no purer example of the Early English, or pointed, style than Salisbury Cathedral. Its graceful spire has already been mentioned, but the ecclesiastical building doesn't depend totally on the tower for its appeal. Construction began on the structure as early as 1220, then took 38 years to complete, which was jet-age speed in those days (it was customary to drag out cathedral building for three centuries at least). The spire was to soar at the end of the 13th century. Despite an ill-conceived attempt at revamping in the 18th century, the architectural harmony of the cathedral was retained.

The cathedral's Chapter House (note the fine sculptures) is especially attractive, dating from the 13th century. It also contains one of the four copies of Magna Carta, together with treasures from the Diocese of Salisbury and manuscripts and artifacts belonging to the cathedral. There is a charge of 30p (35¢) to visit the Chapter House. The Cloisters enhance the beauty of the cathedral. The Close, with at least 75 buildings in its compound (some from the early 18th century, although others predate that), is exceptionally large, setting off the cathedral most fittingly. An interesting clock in the north transept is considered the oldest working mechanism in Europe. A voluntary contribution is asked to enter the cathedral.

The cathedral has a good **Brass Rubbing Centre** where you can choose from a selection of exact replicas molded perfectly from the original brasses. The small charge made for each rubbing includes the cost of materials and a donation to the church from which it comes. The center is open at the cathedral from early June to early September, Monday to Saturday from 10 a.m. to 5 p.m., from 2 to 5 p.m. on Sunday.

One of the houses in Cathedral Close is **Mompesson House and Garden,** built by Charles Mompesson in 1701. It was the home of the Townsend family for more than a century, and is well known for its fine plasterwork ceilings and paneling. There is also a magnificent collection of 18th-century drinking glasses. It is open April to October, daily except Thursday and Friday, from 12:30 to 6 p.m. or dusk, charging an admission of £1.20 ($1.80).

Also in the Close is the **Regimental Museum** of the Duke of Edinburgh's Royal Regiment (Berkshire and Wiltshire), The Wardrobe, 58 The Close (tel. 0722/336222, ext. 2683), in an elegant house, the origins of which date from 1254. Admission is £1 ($1.50) for adults, 20p (30¢) for children. It is open from 10 a.m. to 4:30 p.m. Monday to Friday; closed Christmas Day. It is also open on Saturday in July and August and on Sunday from April to October.

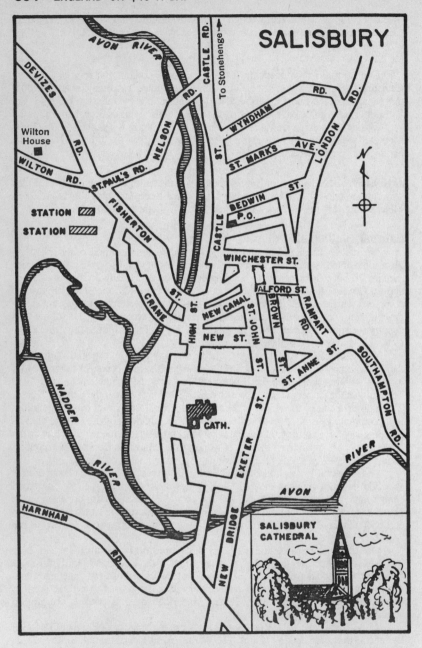

WHERE TO STAY: In a century-old structure, **Byways House,** 31 Fowlers Rd. (tel. 0722/28364), is in a residential area that consists mostly of Victorian houses. It is about a ten-minute walk to the cathedral. Turn to the right off Milford Hill, which is a continuation of Milford Street in the center of the city. The house is in very good condition, and the garden is well kept. Front windows look down onto the cathedral. Sue and Dick Shepherd are the owners. The accommodations vary in size and include six on the ground floor and ten with private shower and toilet. The cost is £11.50 ($17.25) per person, which includes tax, breakfast, heating, and baths. Rooms with private bath go for £13.50 ($20.25) per person.

White Lodge, 68 London Rd. (tel. 0722/27991), is the residence of Canada-born Barbara Smith who receives guests in her attractive brick-gabled house, charging £12 ($18) for a single, £20 ($30) per person for a double for B&B. The rooms are pleasant and the breakfasts personalized. The entrance to White Lodge is, in reality, a greenhouse, with lots of potted geraniums and trailing vines. The place is opposite St. Mark's Church, on the A30 at the edge of the city coming in from London.

Glen Lyn Guest House, 6 Bellamy Land, Milford Hill (tel. 0722/27880), is a large, comfortably furnished Victorian house in a quiet cul-de-sac a few minutes' walk from the city center. Tony and Jean Poat, the proprietors, rent out five rooms, two of which have private baths and all with central heating, beverage-making facilities, shaver points, and color TV. They charge £11 ($13.50) per person for bathless rooms and £13 ($19.50) per person in rooms with bath. All tariffs include a full English breakfast.

Stratford Lodge, 4 Park Lane, Castle Road (tel. 0722/25177), is run by Jill Bayly, who gives you a friendly welcome at her B&B, charging from £15 ($22.50) per person nightly. Her lodge stands in a residential area across from Victoria Park. The house is attractively furnished with pictures and antiques, and all bedrooms have their own bath or shower. Whenever possible home produce is offered, and the cookery is just fine—so good, in fact, that you should stay for dinner at £8.50 ($12.75) per person.

Hayburn Wyke Guest House, 72 Castle Rd. (tel. 0722/24141), next to Victoria Park, is a handsomely decorated house where you'll be welcomed by Mr. and Mrs. Marks. They offer six pleasantly furnished bedrooms, each with hot and cold running water. The charge is from £9.50 ($14.25) per person, including a full English breakfast. Two rooms can be rented by families.

In the vicinity, **Treetops Guest House,** 99 Castle Rd. (tel. 0722/22286), is a spacious house across from Victoria Park. From April to October it receives paying guests, charging them from £20 ($30) in a double. Rooms are pleasantly and comfortably decorated, and guests share the one public bath.

Richburn Guest House, 23 Estcourt Rd. (tel. 0722/25189), is one of the better bargains in Salisbury. A spacious Victorian home, it has been happily converted to receive paying guests. The rate, including a good Wiltshire breakfast, ranges from £10 ($15) to £12 ($18) in a single and from £18.50 ($27.75) to £19 ($28.50) in a double. A trio of family rooms is available. A large TV lounge is available to guests. The location is convenient to the monumental heart of Salisbury, and there is a place to park your car.

On the Outskirts

The **Mill House,** Berwick St. James (tel. 0722/790331), was built in 1785 and added to and modernized in 1960. Standing in a lovely garden, through which the River Till runs, the house is the pride of Mrs. Diana Gifford-Mead, who accepts paying guests into her six bedrooms, three of which have hot and cold water basins and one a complete bath. She charges £14 ($21) to £16 ($24) per person for B&B in the centrally heated units. You must walk over a bridge from the barns and garage to the house. The old mill with two large wheels is about 100 yards up the river from the bridge. The

12 acres in which the mill stands is a nature reserve where you can see birds and wild-flowers that have been destroyed elsewhere. Water for the farm is pumped by the mill. The pretty village of Berwick St. James, near Salisbury, has a population of about 150, a church, a pub, and a village shop. A short distance northwest of Salisbury on the A36, you turn right onto the B3083.

Mr. and Mrs. Spiller, at Nuholme, Ashfield Road (tel. 0722/336592), operate a fine B&B establishment in a large row house. The couple is warm and hospitable, and they rent three comfortably furnished rooms at a cost of £9 ($13.50) per person night-ly. For that, you get a good home-cooked breakfast. From Salisbury, follow the A30 road until you run into Wilton Road (still the A30). Ashfield Road turns off opposite the Horse and Groom Inn.

The **Cross Keys Hotel,** Shaftesbury Road at Fovant (tel. 072270/284), is ideal if you're motoring. A stone building, it dates from the late 15th century and is said to have been frequented by the notorious highwayman Jack Rattenbury. Pauline Story not only does B&B at £12 ($18) per person, but she prepares excellent English fare, including pheasant on occasion, along with venison, local trout, and duck in orange sauce. Cottage pie is regularly featured, and you can always get a steak. Usually there is a choice of a dozen main courses, along with about seven appetizers and the equiva-lent number of desserts. For a typical meal, expect to spend from £8 ($12). Hours are 8 a.m. to 10 p.m. every day; however, alcoholic beverages can only be served during regular licensing hours, in the stone stable bar.

Netton Old Farmhouse, Bishopstone (tel. 0722/780565), is a stone farmhouse under a thatch roof dating from 1637. It is believed that King Charles I stayed in the house during the early years of the Civil War. The house has been renovated to a high standard, and the accommodations available include two double bedrooms (one with its own bath) and a twin-bedded room. The house stands in 1½ acres of traditional English garden in the middle of the small village of Bishopstone, next to a trout stream. It is six miles southwest of Salisbury, and is convenient for exploring Stonehenge and Wilton House. The New Forest is only a half-hour drive from the house, and there are two golf courses nearby. B&B costs from £14 ($21) to £16 ($24) in a single, from £20 ($30) to £24 ($36) in a double. Dinner isn't offered, but there are a number of excellent thatched old pubs nearby, serving good meals at reasonable prices. The owner, Peter Burke, will direct you. Children are welcome, and the Burkes have children of their own who will let others ride their pet donkey. Guests are received April to October.

Holmhurst, Downtown Road (tel. 0722/23164), lies on the A338 Ringwood–Bournemouth road. Mr. and Mrs. Curley invite you to share their home, giving you a good, clean, well-furnished accommodation, along with an excellent breakfast, all for a cost of £10 ($15) per person nightly. Bath facilities are most adequate, and the hosts are helpful.

WHERE TO DINE: The best all-around tea room and pâtisserie in Salisbury is that of **Michael J.R. Snell,** 8 St. Thomas's Square (tel. 0722/336037). His specialty is tea and coffee along with handmade chocolates. Trained in Switzerland, Mr. Snell is a friendly, considerate owner-manager. He keeps his place open Monday to Saturday from 9 a.m. to 5:30 p.m. In fair weather the atmosphere becomes quite continental, with umbrella-shaded tables placed out on the square. In the afternoon you can enjoy a Wiltshire clotted cream tea with scones. Among the dessert specialties, I'd make a detour for a slice of his forêt noire gâteau, a Black Forest cake. Try also his black cherry cheesecake for the same price. A reasonable luncheon menu, which is likely to include everything from local smoked trout to pizza flan, is offered until 2:30 p.m., costing from £3.50 ($5.25) per person. Each main dish is served with a choice of sal-ads. Coffee is roasted right on the premises, and you can see the coffee-roasting room by the river. Children's portions are also available.

The **Old House Restaurant,** 47 New St. (tel. 0722/334651), is in an early 15th-century building. Denise Maidment, owner and manager, serves a traditional three-course luncheon for £3.50 ($5.25), or you can have a choice of à la carte dishes or bar meals. In the evening, roast beef and Yorkshire pudding are part of a three-course meal costing £6.50 ($9.75). An à la carte dinner of three courses goes for £7.50 ($11.25) and up. Hours are noon to 2 p.m. and 7 to either 9 or 10 p.m. Tuesday to Saturday. Only lunch is served on Sunday and Monday.

The **Haunch of Venison,** Minster Street (tel. 0722/22024), deserves its popularity. Right in the heart of Salisbury, this creaky-timbered, 14th-century chophouse serves some excellent dishes, especially English roasts and grills. Stick to its specialties and you'll rarely go wrong. Diners with more adventurous palates will sample a bowl of game soup. The pièce de résistance of the inn is its local New Forest haunch of venison, with chestnut puree and red currant jelly. A set lunch goes for around £6.50 ($9.75). If you avoid the à la carte menu in the evening, you can order a set dinner at £10 ($15). The Sunday spread at noon always has two different roasts at £6.50 ($9.75). For a bargain lunch, enjoy the bar snacks, including game pie made with venison. All this good food and hospitality are offered in a treasured building, dating back to 1320. The centuries have given a gleam to the oak furnishings, and years of polishing have worn down the brass. Twisting steps lead to tiny, cozy rooms (there is one small room with space for about four to sit where you can saturate yourself in the best of England's yesterdays and todays). Two windows of the barroom overlook St. Thomas's cloisters (naturally, it's called the Cloisters Chamber). Dancing fires are kept burning in the old fireplace; heavy beams are overhead; antique chairs encircle the tables. The restaurant is open daily for lunch from noon to 2 p.m. and in the evening from 7 to 10:30 p.m., except Sunday night when only the bar is open and no food is served.

The **Red Lion Hotel,** Milford Street (tel. 0722/23334), is too stately to roar. But since the 1300s it's been putting up wayfarers who rumbled in stagecoaches from London across the Salisbury Plain to the West Countree. Cross under its arch into a court-yard with a hanging and much-photographed creeper, a red lion, and a half-timbered facade, and you'll be transplanted back to the good old days. An à la carte luncheon costs from £6.50 ($9.75). The recommendable dinner ranges from £12 ($18) for a three-course meal. House specialties include jugged hare with red currant jelly, roast venison, steak-and-kidney pie, and roast beef with horseradish sauce. Meals are served from 12:30 to 1:45 p.m. and 7 to 9 p.m.

The **New Inn,** 43 New St. (tel. 0722/27679), isn't new at all. Backing up to the Cathedral Close wall, it's a bit of old England. The center of the inn is the serving bar, which is a common counter for three outer rooms—one, a tiny sitting area; another, a tavern with high-backed settles and a fireplace; the third, a lounge with a dart game. Snacks include a ploughman's lunch and sandwiches, with light meals costing from £2.50 ($3.25), perhaps accompanied by a half pint of draft cider. However, you can also order more substantial fare, with meals costing from £5 ($7.50) to £12 ($18). Typical dishes include chicken, ham, and mushroom pie, fresh grilled trout, and breast of chicken with mushrooms. Hours are 11:30 a.m. to 2:15 p.m. and 6:30 to 9:30 p.m. (on Sunday from noon to 2 p.m. and 7 to 9 p.m.).

Harper's Restaurant, 7-9 Ox Row, the Market Square (tel. 0722/333118), is run by its chef-patron, Adrian Harper, who prides himself on specializing in "real food," homemade and wholesome. The pleasantly decorated restaurant offers such à la carte selections as quiche maison garnished with salad, Harper's pâté with wholemeal toast, and keftedakia (lamb meatballs with a yogurt, mint, chili, and garlic dip) among the appetizers. Main dishes include sirloin and filet steaks, noisettes of lamb with apricot sauce, the captain's pie (cod in a creamy sauce topped with potato), and vegetarian food. Luscious desserts complete the menu. Expect to pay from £7.50 ($11.25) for an à la carte meal. Fixed-price menus are also offered, costing £6.95 ($10.43) and £9.95 ($14.93). Special menus for children, costing £1.95 ($2.93), include fish fingers, beefburgers, or sausage, all with french fries, beans, and ice cream.

Harper's is open from noon to 2 p.m. and 6:30 to 10:30 p.m. Monday to Saturday, as well as Sunday from 6:30 to 10 p.m. April to October. It's best to reserve a table.

Raffles Tea Room, Mitre House, 37 High St. (tel. 0722/333705), lies in the House of Tweed, offering convenient refreshment for visitors or shoppers. Light meals are served, including cona toasties, a Scottish-derived formula for closed toasted sandwiches, which include ham and pineapple. A refreshing English tea at Raffles includes two scones with jam and cream, and naturally a large pot of Earl Grey or Ceylon tea. There is a wide choice of cakes and eclairs, as well as hot dishes and cold salads—a satisfying meal in themselves—for around £3 ($4.50). Raffles is open from 9:30 a.m. to 5 p.m. (from 10:30 a.m. to 4:30 p.m. on Sunday) in summer, and from 9:30 a.m. to 5 p.m., Monday through Saturday only, in winter.

Mo's, 62 Milford St. (tel. 0722/331377), one of the most popular low-cost spots in Salisbury, is at its most bustling in the evening. It serves the type of food you are familiar with, and that means steaks, barbecue spare ribs, chili con carne, and burgers American style (try the one with mozzarella on a sesame bun). Of course, British food isn't neglected either, and you'll find steak-and-kidney pie and other such fare on the menu. Vegetarians are also catered to, with a selection of offerings. Meals, costing from £6 ($9), are served from noon to 2:30 p.m. and 5:30 to 11 p.m. (on Friday until midnight and 6 to 10:30 p.m. on Sunday). It is closed for Sunday lunch.

Mainly Salads, 18 Fisherton St. (tel. 0722/22134), is a self-service vegetarian restaurant. Fresh crisp salads, including slices of red pepper with peanuts, or leek, lentil, and mushrooms, are on display on a long counter. What makes the place—run by June and Ron Ceresa—interesting are these imaginative salad combinations, not your typical potato salad and cole slaw variety. You might also try their curried nut loaf and for dessert, if featured, a Dutch apple pie. The place can get exceptionally busy during the lunch break, but it remains open daily except Sunday from 10 a.m. to 5 p.m., charging £3 ($4.50) and up for a meal. It is unlicensed. You might also try it for morning coffee or afternoon tea.

SIDE TRIPS FROM SALISBURY: In this area rich in reminders of England's heritage, traces have been found of human occupation long beyond the dawn of history—Neolithic man, Iron Age habitation, Romans, Saxons, Danes, Normans, and English people of today, all have left their mark on the land and can be visited during your stay at Salisbury.

Old Sarum

About 2 miles north of Salisbury off the A345 is Old Sarum (tel. 0722/5398), the remains of what is believed to have been an Iron Age fortification. The earthworks were known to the Romans as Sorbiodunum, and later to the Saxons. The Normans, in fact, built a cathedral and a castle in what was then a walled town of the Middle Ages. Parts of the old cathedral were disassembled to erect the cathedral at New Sarum. It is open March to October from 9:30 a.m. to 6:30 p.m. weekdays and from 2 to 6:30 p.m. on Sunday. From October to March it has a shorter schedule: from 9:30 a.m. to 4 p.m. weekdays and 2 to 4 p.m. on Sunday. Admission is 75p ($1.13) for adults, 35p (53¢) for children.

Old Wardour Castle

The ruined 14th-century castle (tel. 0722/870487) stands in a lakeside setting in the landscaped grounds of New Wardour Castle, a 1770 Palladian mansion that now houses a girls' school. The old castle, built in 1392 by Lord Lovel, was acquired in 1547 by the Arundell family and modernized in 1578. After being besieged during the Civil War, however, it was abandoned. Today it houses displays on the war sieges and the landscape, as well as an architectural exhibition. It lies 1½ miles north of the A30 going west out of Salisbury, 2 miles southwest of Tisbury. From April to September, it is open from 9:30 a.m. to 6:30 p.m. Monday to Saturday, 2 to 6:30 p.m. on Sunday. In the winter season, it is open weekends only, from 9:30 a.m. to 4 p.m. on Saturday and 2 to 4 p.m. on Sunday. Admission is 75p ($1.13) for adults, 35p (53¢) for children.

Wilton House

In the small borough of Wilton, less than three miles to the west of Salisbury, is one of England's great country estates, Wilton House (tel. 0722/743115), the home of the Earl of Pembroke. The stately house in the midst of 20 acres of grounds dates from the 16th century, but has seen modifications over the years, as late as Victoria's day. It is noted for its 17th-century state rooms by Inigo Jones. Many famous personages have either lived at or visited Wilton. It is believed that Shakespeare's troupe entertained here. Plans for the D-Day landings at Normandy were laid out here by Eisenhower and his advisers, in the utmost secrecy, with only the silent Van Dycks in the Double Cube room as witnesses. The house is filled with beautifully maintained furnishings, especially a collection of Chippendale. Wilton House displays some of the finest paintings in England, including works by Rembrandt, Rubens, Reynolds, and the already-mentioned Van Dycks.

The estate lies in the midst of gardens and grounds, with Cedars of Lebanon, the oldest of which were planted in 1630. The Palladian Bridge was built in 1737. Wilton House may be visited Tuesday through Saturday and bank holidays from 11 a.m. to 6 p.m., and on Sunday from 1 to 6 p.m. Guided tours are conducted daily except Sunday from early April to mid-October. Admission is £2.50 ($3.75) for adults, £1.25 ($1.88) for children under 16, to the house and grounds only. An inclusive ticket to the house, grounds, and exhibitions costs £3.35 ($5.03) for adults, £1.90 ($2.85) for children.

The excellent, fully licensed, self-service restaurant is open during house hours and offers homemade cooking. Hot dishes can be had by ordering ahead. Don't miss a Wilton House cream tea. There is an Adventure Playground for children, plus an exhibition of 7,000 model soldiers and "The Pembroke Palace" dollhouse. You can also visit "Wiltshire in Miniature," a model railway in the 14th-century abbey building, and a historical tableau of dolls and toys through the ages.

Stonehenge

Two miles west of Amesbury on the junction of A303 and A344/A360 and about nine miles north of Salisbury is the renowned Stonehenge, believed to be anywhere from 3,500 to 5,000 years old. This huge oval of lintels and megalithic pillars is the most important prehistoric monument in Britain.

Some North Americans have expressed their disappointment after seeing the concentric circles of stones, which have been fenced off to protect the stones from the ravages of visitors. However, you can get within about 20 feet of the stones. Admittedly, they are not the pyramids, and some imagination has to be brought to bear on them. Pyramids or not, they represent an amazing engineering feat. Many of the boulders, the bluestones in particular, were moved hundreds of miles, perhaps from southern Wales, to this site by the ancients. If you're fanciful, you can always credit Merlin with delivering them on clouds from Ireland.

The widely held view of the 18th- and 19th-century romantics that Stonehenge was the work of the Druids is without foundation. The boulders, many weighing into the tons, are believed to have predated the arrival in Britain of that Celtic cult. Recent excavations continue to bring new evidence to bear on the origin and purpose of Stonehenge. The prehistoric site was a subject of controversy following the publication of *Stonehenge Decoded* by Gerald S. Hawkins and John B. White, which maintained that Stonehenge was in fact an astronomical observatory. That is, a Neolithic computing machine capable of predicting eclipses.

Others who discount Hawkins's decoding would prefer to adopt Henry James's approach to Stonehenge, which regards it as "lonely in history," its origin and purposes (burial ground, sun-worshipping site, human sacrificial temple?) the secret of the silent, mysterious Salisbury Plain.

Admission is £1.30 ($1.95) for adults, 65p (98¢) for children. From mid-March to mid-October it is open daily from 9:30 a.m. to 6:30 p.m. Off-season hours are 9:30 a.m. to 4 p.m. daily.

There is a small snackbar, offering fresh sandwiches, hot pies and cakes, soft drinks, tea and coffee. There's also a free car park.

If you don't have a car, getting to Stonehenge can be difficult unless you're athletic. First, take the bus to Amesbury, then walk about 2½ miles to Stonehenge. The British do this all the time, and they don't complain. But if that is too strenuous, you'd better take one of the organized coach tours out of Salisbury.

Nether Wallop

On a country road between the A 343 and the A30 east of Salisbury is the little village of Nether Wallop (not to be confused with Over Wallop or Middle Wallop in the same vicinity). Aficionados of television films about Agatha Christie's *Miss Marple* will be interested in this village, used as Miss Christie's fictitious St. Mary Mead, home of Miss Marple. Visitors to Nether Wallop easily identify the sites in many of the TV movies.

The village is about 12 miles from Stonehenge and about equidistant between Salisbury and Winchester. A stream winds through the valley in which Nether Wallop nestles, and there are many thatch cottages and a ninth-century church with medieval wall paintings.

You can stay in this inviting village at **Broadgate Farm** (tel. 0264/781439), a beautiful Georgian farmhouse with a walled garden, right in the center of Nether Wallop. Susan and Richard Osmond offer two spacious bedrooms and a good English breakfast for £14 ($21) per person. The house has full central heating, a dining room, and a well-furnished lounge. Susan's family has farmed in Nether Wallop since 1622, and the Osmonds still run the farm, with a pedigree herd of Friesian cows, 300 sheep, and grain crops.

Longleat House

Between Bath and Salisbury, Longleat House (tel. 09853/551) lies four miles southwest of Warminster, 4½ miles southeast of Frome on the A362. The first view of this magnificent Elizabethan house, built in the early Renaissance style, is romantic enough, but the wealth of paintings and furnishings within its lofty rooms is enough to dazzle. The Venetian ceilings were added in Queen Victoria's time by the fourth Marquess of Bath.

A tour of the house, from the Elizabethan Great Hall, through libraries, the State Rooms, and the Grand Staircase, is awe inspiring in its variety and splendor. The State Dining Room is full of silver and plate, and fine tapestries and paintings adorn the walls in rich profusion. The Victorian kitchens are open during the summer months, offering a glimpse of life below the stairs in a well-ordered country home. Various exhibitions are mounted in the Stable Yard, and the Safari Park contains a vast array of animals in open parklands. During the summer months, a program of outside events is arranged on weekends.

The house is open all year except Christmas Day. The Safari Park closes in winter. Admission to the house is £2.30 ($3.45) for adults, £1 ($1.50) for children. The Safari Park costs £3 ($4.50) per adult and £2.50 ($3.75) per child. There are many attractions within the grounds, including a 15-inch-gauge railway ride, safari boats, pets' corner, a doll's house, and a Dr. Who exhibition.

A maze, believed to be the largest in the world, was added to the attractions by Lord Weymouth, son of the marquess. It has more than 1½ miles of paths among yew trees. The first part is comparatively easy, but the second part is very complicated, with bridges adding to the confusion. It knocks the Hampton Court maze into a cocked hat, as the British say. The house also contains more than 39,000 magnificent books and rare manuscripts, some of which are on display to the public.

Stourhead

After Longleat, drive six miles south down the A3092 to Stourton, a village just off the A3092, three miles northwest of Mere (A303). Stourhead (tel. 0747/840348), a Palladian house, was built in the 18th century by the banking family of Hoare. On the site of an old Gothic house, called Stourton, the present mansion was designed by Colen Campbell, renowned early 19th-century architect. The furniture is mostly the work of Thomas Chippendale the Younger. Stourhead's landscaping, however, is the most outstanding thing about the property, now belonging to the National Trust. The pleasure grounds became known as *le jardin anglais,* in that they blended art and nature. Set around an artificial lake are temples, bridges, islands, and grottos. It is open April to October from 2 to 6 p.m. on Monday, Tuesday, Wednesday, Saturday, and Sunday. From May to the end of September it's open daily except Friday from 2 to 6 p.m. Admission is £2 ($3) for adults, £1 ($1.50) for children to the house and £1.50 ($2.25) for adults, 80p ($1.20) for children to the garden. The gardens are open daily from 8 a.m. to 7 p.m. or dusk.

Avebury

One of the largest prehistoric sites in Europe, Avebury lies about six miles west of Marlborough on the Kennet River. It is gaining in popularity with visitors now that the British have had to rope off the sarsen circle at Stonehenge. Explorers are able to walk the 28-acre site at Avebury, winding in and out of the circle of more than 100 stones, some weighing up to 50 tons. They are made of sarsen, a sandstone found in Wiltshire. Inside this large circle are two smaller ones, each with about 30 stones standing upright. Native Neolithic tribes are believed to have built these circles. The village of Avebury, taken over by the National Trust, bisects the prehistoric monument, and is worth exploring.

Dating from before the Conquest, **Avebury Manor** (tel. 06723/203) was built on the site of a Benedictine cell. An early Elizabethan manor house, it stands beside the great stone circle of Avebury. The manor is carefully restored and is now a family home which can be visited April to September from 11:30 a.m. to 6 p.m. weekdays (from 1:30 to 6 p.m. on Sunday). October to March, it is open only on Saturday and Sunday from 1:30 to 5 p.m. Admission costs £2 ($3) for adults, £1.65 ($2.48) for children. Inside are oak-paneled rooms and coved plasterwork ceilings. The state rooms were visited by Queen Anne and Charles II. Throughout is much early oak and fine furniture in a period setting. Portraits date from 1532. The Queen Anne bedroom, with its imposing state bed, is of particular note, as is the Cavalier bedroom, linked with tales of the supernatural recounted by more than one visitor staying at the manor. Tea and morning coffee are available in the South Library tea room. The surrounding garden and parkland are equally intriguing. The topiary—old yew and box— pleasantly emphasize the historic atmosphere. Outside attractions include the walled garden, herb border, wishing well, and a 16th-century dovecote. There's also a souvenir shop. Car parking is within the manor grounds. The **Avebury Museum** (tel. 06723/250), founded by Alexander Keiller, houses one of Britain's most important archeological collections. It began with Keiller's material from excavations at Windmill Hill and Avebury, it now includes artifacts from other prehistoric digs at West Kennet, Long Barrow, Silbury Hill, West Kennet Avenue, and the Sanctuary. From mid-March to mid-October it is open from 9:30 a.m. to 6:30 p.m. weekdays (on Sunday from 2 to 6:30 p.m.). Off-season hours are from 9:30 a.m. to 4 p.m. weekdays (from 2 to 4 p.m. on Sunday). Admission is 75p ($1.13) for adults, 35p (53¢) for children.

The **Great Barn Museum of Wiltshire Folk Life** (tel. 06723/555), housed in a 17th-century thatched barn, has displays on cheese making, blacksmithing, thatching, sheep and shepherds, the wheelwright, and other rural crafts. Regular craft demonstrations are held on Sunday. From April to October the barn is open daily from 10 a.m. to 5:30 p.m. Admission is 70p ($1.05) for adults, 30p (45¢) for children. Families are admitted for £1.70 ($2.55).

After sightseeing—and still in the same vicinity—you may be ready for a bite to eat.

Stones Restaurant, High Street (tel. 06723/514), has made an impact on the palates in the area since its opening in 1984 by Dr. Hilary Howard and Michael Pitts. They specialize in freshly made, original, high-quality food (no additives), served in friendly and attractive surroundings at reasonable prices. You can have a meal for around £5 ($7.50). A wide range of cakes, desserts, and cold savouries is available throughout the day, supplemented at lunchtime by a full hot-food menu which can be accompanied by the local, prize-winning ale, Wadworth's 6X. Other drinks are available, including coffee, tea by the pot, fruit juices, and bottled beer. Stones is open April to mid-October from 10 a.m. to 6 p.m. seven days a week.

Afterward, you can drop in for a drink at the **Red Lion** (tel. 06723/266), a typical English country inn complete with thatch roof and Tudor half-timbering. It even has its own resident ghost, Florrie, supposed to have been killed by her husband when he returned from the wars and discovered she had been unfaithful. Parts of the building are from the 1600s, but there isn't any record as to just how long Florrie has been on hand. The inn is open from 11:30 a.m. to 2:30 p.m. and 6 to 11 p.m.

On the A350 Blandford road, 20 miles from Warminster, stands **Milestones,** Compton Abbas, near Shaftesbury in Dorset (tel. 0747/811360), a 17th-century tea room right next to the church, with gorgeous views over the Dorset hills. This spotless little place is presided over by two delightful women who serve real farmhouse teas or a ploughman's lunch. Fresh sandwiches are also offered. Light meals and teas cost from £2 ($3). This is really the ideal English tea room, and the women who run it are charming and friendly. Morning coffee is served from 10 a.m. to 1 p.m. and afternoon tea from 2:30 to 5:30 p.m. except Thursday and November to March.

Lacock

Lacock is a National Trust village, with an abbey dating from 1232 and the famous **Fox Talbot Museum** (tel. 024973/459), tracing the history of photography. It's open daily from 11 a.m. to 6 p.m. March to October except Good Friday. Admission is £1 ($1.50) for adults, 50p (75¢) for children. Lacock is a good base for exploring Bath, Castle Combe, and Longleat.

Your best accommodations bet is **The Old Rectory,** Cantax Hill, Lacock, near Chippenham (tel. 024973/335). Mrs. Margaret Addison welcomes visitors to her old house built in 1866. The house stands in its own grounds of eight acres, with ample car parking space just off the A350 Chippenham–Melksham road. In comfortably furnished rooms, all with private baths, color TV, and beverage-making facilities, B&B is £12.50 ($18.75) per person. A TV lounge is offered for use of guests.

2. Castle Combe

Once voted Britain's prettiest village, Castle Combe was used for location shots for *Dr. Doolittle*. About ten miles from Bath, this little Cotswold village is filled with shops selling souvenirs and antiques. The village cottages are often set beside a trout stream, and are made of stone with moss-laden roofs. The church is unremarkable except for its 15th-century tower. An old market cross and a triple-arched bridge are much photographed.

No accommodation but plenty of local color is offered at the **White Hart,** on the main road through the village (tel. 0249/782295). It's a white-painted pub built of

Cotswold stone and covered with a stone tile roof. Dating from either the 13th or 14th century, it has low ceilings (in the cellars are Norman arches). The main bar is divided into two parts, with a cold buffet counter for meals. The garden is also open to visitors, and the parlor bar admits children. Catherine Wheeler and her daughters run the pub capably and hospitably. Home-cooked ham or beef, with cole slaw and bread and butter, is offered from £2.50 ($3.75). In winter, hot soups, chili, hot pasties, and toasted sandwiches are available. Bitter beer from traditional wooden barrels is popular with the locals. This is one of the few traditional English pubs in the Cotswolds recommended for evening life. It's open from 10 a.m. to 2:30 p.m. and 6 to 10:30 p.m.

You can stop for B&B at a place with a similar name, the **White Hart Inn,** at Ford, a short distance south of Castle Combe, on the A420 west of Chippenham (tel. 0249/782213). Here Ken Gardner and his wife, Lily, cater to the local population swelled during the summer months by passing tourists. The inn is a lovely old 16th-century building with gardens running down to the river. They have added a heated swimming pool to the amenities, but the bars remain low-ceilinged with blackened beams and open fires. Various local souls help in the bars and in the dining room, where residents can dine for £12 ($18) from a menu including braised venison (caught, matured, and marinated locally in port wine). If this is not enough, food offered in the old buttery can be anything from chicken casserole in cider to home-cooked ham or excellent steak-and-kidney pies made to order.

Bedrooms, some with four-poster beds, contain private baths. Singles begin at £31 ($46.50) and doubles at £45 ($67.50), including an enormous breakfast with lots of coffee.

GRITTLETON: Just three miles from Castle Combe, **Neeld Arms Inn** (tel. 0249/782470) is a charming 17th-century inn. The unspoiled village of Grittleton, in Beaufort hunt country, is built of the golden stone of Wiltshire. The inn is included on a map of 1760, but one section has been dated from the previous century. Sandie Nash, her husband, and sons make guests feel welcome whether they stay overnight or just stop in the pub, as many locals do, for a drink and perhaps a snack. When the young men are not in school, they cook, wait table, and otherwise participate in the smooth running of the inn. You can rent a double-bedded room with a complete bath for £30 ($45) per night or a twin or double with shower only for £26 ($39). Prices include a full English breakfast. The pleasant dining room is conveniently located just off the pub rooms, one of which has a large table in front of a big open fireplace, with window seats and chair cushions upholstered in cheery prints. You can dine from a large selection of dishes, including filet steaks, T-bones, chops, poultry, and seafood, and, of course, on game in season, this being hunt country. You can have a satisfying meal for £6.50 ($9.75).

In the mid-1600s an inn at Grittleton, the King's Arms, was closed down by Oliver Cromwell during the Reformation. For his forays in this area, Cromwell made his headquarters at nearby Fosscote Farm. The Neeld Arms Inn is a good base for visiting a number of interesting little towns and hamlets in Wiltshire, among them Lacock, only six miles away.

SOMERSET

When writing about Somerset, it's difficult to avoid sounding like the editor of *The Countryside Companion,* waxing poetic over hills and valleys, dale and field. In scenery, the western shire embraces some of nature's most masterly touches in England. Mendip's limestone hills undulate across the countryside (ever had a pot-holing holiday?). The irresistible Quantocks are the pride of the west, especially lovely in spring and fall. Here, too, is the heather-clad **Exmoor National Park,** a wooded area abounding in red deer and wild ponies, much of its moorland 1,200 feet above sea level. Somerset opens onto the Bristol Channel, with Minehead being the chief resort.

Somerset is rich in legend and history, and is particularly fanciful about its associations with King Arthur and Queen Guinevere, along with Camelot and Alfred the Great. Its villages are noted for the tall towers of their parish churches.

On the site of a Norman castle granted to the Mohuns by William the Conqueror shortly after the conquest is **Dunster Castle** (tel. 0643/821314), three miles southeast of Minehead above the village of Dunster, just off the A39. The 13th-century gateway built by the Mohuns is all that remains of the Norman castle. In 1376, the castle was bought by Lady Elizabeth Luttrell and belonged to her family until it was given to the National Trust, along with 30 acres of surrounding parkland, in 1976. The original castle was largely demolished during the Civil War, and the present Dunster Castle is a Jacobean house built in the lower ward of the earlier fortifications in 1620, then rebuilt by Salvin in 1870 to look like a castle. Terraced walks and gardens command good views of Exmoor, the Quantock Hills, and the Bristol Channel. Outstanding among the contents within are the 17th-century panels of embossed painted and gilded leather depicting the story of Antony and Cleopatra, and a remarkable allegorical 16th-century portrait of Sir John Luttrell shown wading naked through the sea with a female figure of peace and a wrecked ship in the background. The 17th-century plasterwork ceilings of the dining room and staircase and the finely carved staircase balustrade of cavorting huntsmen, hounds, and stags are also particularly noteworthy. The castle may be visited from April until the end of September every day except Thursday and Friday from 11 a.m. to 5 p.m. (last admission 4:30). In October it is open daily except Thursday and Friday from noon to 4 p.m. (last admission at 3:30 p.m.). The grounds only can be visited daily from April to the end of September from 11 a.m. to 5 p.m., from 2 to 4 p.m. daily in October. Admission to the castle and grounds is £2.50 ($3.75) for adults, £1.20 ($1.80) for children.

A quiet, unspoiled life holds forth in Somerset. You're likely to end up in a vine-covered old inn, talking with the regulars about staghounds. Or you may anchor at a large estate that stands in a woodland setting—surrounded by bridle paths and sheep walks (Somerset was once a great wool center). Maybe you'll settle down in a 16th-century, thatched, stone farmhouse, set in the midst of orchards in a vale. Somerset is reputed (and I heartily concur) to have the best cider anywhere. When you lounge under a shady Somerset apple tree, downing a tankard of refreshingly chilled, golden cider, everything you've drunk in the past tastes like apple juice.

My notes on Somerset, accumulated over many a year, would easily fill a book. But space and limited schedule being what they are, I confined the following comments in the main to the shire's two most interesting towns, Wells and Glastonbury. Still, I'll throw in a few farmhouse recommendations off the beaten path, for those who want rural atmosphere.

3. Wells

In Wells, we meet the Middle Ages. At the south of the Mendip Hills, the cathedral town is a medieval gem. It lies only 21 miles from Bath, but 123 from London. Wells was a vital link in the Saxon kingdom of Wessex—that is, important in England long before the arrival of William the Conqueror. Once the seat of a bishopric, it was eventually toppled from its ecclesiastical hierarchy by the rival city of Bath. But the subsequent loss of prestige has paid off handsomely in Wells today. After experiencing the pinnacle of prestige, it fell into a slumber, and for that reason much of its old look remains. Wells was named after wells in the town, which were often visited by pilgrims to Glastonbury in the hope that their gout could be eased by the supposedly curative waters. The crowning achievement of the town is:

WELLS CATHEDRAL: Dating from the 12th century, Wells Cathedral is a well-preserved, mellow example of the Early English style of architecture. The medieval sculpture (six tiers of hundreds of statues recently restored) of its West Front is without peer in England. The western facade was completed in and around the mid-13th century. The landmark central tower was erected in the 14th century, with its attractive fan vaulting attached later. The inverted arches were added to strengthen the top-heavy structure.

Much of the stained glass dates from the 14th century. The fan-vaulted Lady Chapel, also from the 14th-century, is in the Decorated style. To the north is the vaulted Chapter House, built in the late 13th century. Look also for a medieval astronomical clock in the north transept. There is no mandatory charge to enter the cathedral. However, visitors are asked to make voluntary donations of at least £1 ($1.50) for adults, 50p (75¢) for children and students. For information, telephone the cathedral offices (tel. 0749/74483).

After a visit to the cathedral, walk along its cloisters to the moated Bishop's Palace of the Middle Ages. In the moat, the swans ring a bell when they're hungry. Its former Great Hall, built in the 13th century, is now in ruins. Finally, the small lane known as the Vicar's Close is one of the most beautifully preserved streets in England.

WHERE TO STAY: You may want to base at Wells, as its budget establishments are better than equivalent-priced lodgings at Bath.

Ancient Gate House Hotel, Sadler Street (tel. 0749/72029). Its front is on Sadler Street, and the back overlooks the cathedral and the lovely open lawn in front of the cathedral's west door. It is run by Francesco Rossi, known as Franco to everyone. There are 11 rooms, three in the front. Two of these have showers and one a full bath. These doubles are £35.50 ($53.25) for B&B. Other rooms cost £31.50 ($47.25) in a double, £19 ($28.50) in a single, with a full English breakfast and VAT included. Most rooms have four-poster beds.

Franco also runs the Rugantino Restaurant attached to the hotel, where pastas and Italian dishes are a specialty. Popular dishes are scaloppine rustica (breadcrumbed veal escalope topped with tomato sauce and grated cheese and glazed) and tournedo chasseur (filet steak pan-fried with red wine, tomato, and mushroom sauce). There's also a list of interesting appetizers. Vegetarian dishes are offered, and fresh vegetables, including some imported items, are used when possible. A set dinner costs around £9 ($13.50).

The **Sherston Inn,** Priory Road (tel. 0749/73743), is a pleasant, friendly pub on the edge of the city, on the road to Glastonbury, with a car park and a beer garden. Part of the building is from the 17th century. Prices for B&B are £8 ($12) to £11 ($16.50) in a single, £19 ($28.50) in a double, and £24 ($36) in a triple, including VAT. The three bedrooms are comfortable and clean, with tea/coffee-making facilities. There is a small lounge with TV. Bar meals are served in the cozy Moat Bar or the more spacious Knights Bar, from an extensive menu, a meal costing from £4 ($6) to £8 ($12) and offering such dishes as chicken with cheddar cheese and chestnut filling in a cider and cream sauce. Daily home-cooked specials and the Sunday roast-beef lunch are especially popular. For the latter, it's advisable to reserve a table. Beer and wines are reasonably priced. The proprietors are Roy and Sheila Hampshire. Roy, a chef for many years, is in personal charge of the kitchen. The pub serves meals from 11:30 a.m. to 2 p.m. and 6:30 to 10 p.m.

The **Star Hotel,** High Street (tel. 0749/73055), is run by Mr. and Mrs. P. Nandi. This is a 16th-century coaching inn, with a cobble yard and low beamed ceilings. Some of the bedrooms have four-poster beds and all are equipped with color TV, coffee- or tea-making facilities, are centrally heated, and have showers or private bath. An overnight stay, including a full English breakfast, is £25 ($37.50) in a single, from £35 ($52.50) in a double. Bar meals are available seven days a week. In the restaurant, a three-course meal begins at £7.50 ($11.25) per person. These prices include VAT. All meals are served with fresh vegetables when possible.

Bekynton House, 7 St. Thomas St. (tel. 0749/72222), is a family-run guesthouse where you get a much more attractive price than at the more half-priced inns in the center of Wells, about a five-minute walk away. The nine rooms include some for families, some with private showers and toilets. All are clean and comfortable, renting from £10 ($15) per person for B&B. Evening meals can be arranged in the pleasant dining room, although several good restaurants are not far away.

Tor Guest House, 20 Tor St. (tel. 0749/72322), is where Adrian and Letitia Trowell receive lodgers in their 1610 house. From the front rooms, the view of the Bishop's Palace and the east face of the cathedral is an exciting prospect, and the delightful gardens of the guesthouse provide a handsome setting for what is claimed to be the oldest magnolia tree in Europe, a resplendent sight when it is in bloom in July. The Trowells rent out nine attractively furnished rooms, charging from £11 ($16.50) per person for B&B, from £17 ($25.50) per person for dinner, bed, and breakfast. Rates are inclusive of VAT and service.

WHERE TO EAT: The former city jail, the **City Arms,** 69 High St. (tel. 0749/ 73916), is now a pub with a pretty, open courtyard furnished with tables, chairs, and umbrellas. In summer it's a mass of flowers, and there is an old vine growing in the corner. Upstairs is a Barnaby Carving Restaurant, where for a set price of £7 ($10.50) you can help yourself to either homemade soup (the last time I ate there it was a tasty stilton soup) or pick up a plate and help yourself to a selection of the many and varied hors d'oeuvres displayed in crushed ice. The chef will carve for you from a choice of three roast joints, usually beef, turkey, and either ham, pork, or lamb. You can help yourself to a selection of fresh vegetables, Yorkshire pudding, and gravy made with juices of the meat. Following that, there is a large selection of desserts or cheeses. Barnaby's also has a good selection of wines at reasonable prices. The place is open from 11 a.m. to 2:30 p.m. and 6 to 11 p.m.

Penn Bar and Eating House, Crown Hotel, Market Place (tel. 0749/73457), has a sign outside which says that William Penn, founder of Pennsylvania, preached to a vast congregation from a window of the inn in 1685. Appetizers in the cozy dining room include pâté, watercross soup, butterfly prawns, and other good dishes, along with such main courses as escalope of salmon, trout, Scottish steaks, English lamb, and salads. The chef always has a special dish of the day, which might be curry, and there's the inevitable steak-and-kidney pie so beloved by the English. A set three-course dinner is presented for £12.95 ($19.43). Sunday lunch is £8.95 ($13.43), and a hot buffet lunch on weekdays costs £5 ($7.50). Hours are from 10 a.m. to 9 p.m. daily.

ON THE OUTSKIRTS: At Stoberry Park, only about a 15-minute walk from the center of Wells, **The Coach House** (tel. 0749/76535) stands in six acres of secluded grounds on the southern slope of the Mendip Hills. From College Road, you follow a quarter-mile drive through parkland dotted with ancient trees to the spacious, immaculate guesthouse run by Ian and Fay Poynter. They offer B&B at £13 ($19.50) to £19 ($28.50) per person. Half board, recommendable because of the quality of the meals served, costs £19 ($28.50) to £28 ($42) per person. From this pastoral setting, you can enjoy views over the city of Wells and the cathedral as well as Glastonbury in the distance.

Manor Farm, Old Bristol Road, Upper Milton, near Wells (tel. 0749/73394), is on the slopes of the Mendips. An Elizabethan manor house of stone, it is supported by the proceeds of 130 acres of farmland. Its owner, Mrs. Janet Gould, has renovated three corner rooms with the best views ("clear to the Bristol Channel on a day that's not misty"), and has made them comfortably suitable for B&B guests. And in an uninhibited moment, she transformed the attic room into a vivid bathroom. Mrs. Gould charges £8.50 ($12.75) per person for B&B. The full breakfast includes about five choices as a main course. Summer days and evenings are often spent on a flagstoned terrace, overlooking the meadow and enjoying the pale roses climbing over the stone walls. The manor lies about a mile from Wells. Take the A39 north out of Wells and turn left at the second turning after the mini-roundabout at the edge of the city, then turn right up the Old Bristol Road.

Crapnell Farm, Dinder, near Wells (tel. 0749/2683), is a 16th-century farmhouse on the south side of the Mendip Hills, three miles from Wells. The proprietor, Mrs. Pamela Keen, offers B&B for £10 ($15) per person. All bedrooms have hot and cold water basins and beverage-making facilities, and there is a guest lounge where you can watch color TV. A large snooker room and a swimming pool add to the enjoyment of a stay here. The food is traditional farmhouse cooking, using produce from the farm, freshly prepared and cooked. Evening meals, costing £7.50 ($11.25), are sometimes available.

Long House, at Pilton, near Shepton Mallet (tel. 074989/283), is a 17th-century building run by Paul Foss and Eric Swainsbury. Guests coming here for the first time, particularly Americans, comment on the comfortable beds, "the best coffee in England," the plentiful towels, and the excellent food. Paul, an experienced chef, shuns instant or so-called convenience foods. They treat their guests as they would wish to be treated—that is, with an easy graciousness. Bedrooms are attractively furnished, and most of the units have private bathrooms with showers. For half board the rate for a room with a private bath ranges from £13.50 ($20.25) to £16.50 ($24.75) per person nightly. Half board is £19.50 ($29.25) to £24 ($36) per person. Guests are encouraged to stay at least three nights, using Long House as a base for touring sights nearby. Facilities at Long House include a comfortably furnished lounge and dining room that's like that of a private home, plus a well-stocked bar. There your hosts are likely to talk to you about everything from architecture to zoology. As a word of warning, I caution that there are two Piltons in Somerset, and this has led to some confusion. Long House has a postal code of BA4 4BP.

The Old Vicarage, Pilton, near Shepton Mallet (tel. 074989/573), is an old stone vicarage, dated 1866, standing in 1½ acres of grounds, with commanding views of the countryside. Adjacent to the famous Pilton Manor vineyard and overlooking the 14th-century church, this charming family house is run by Roy and Lesley North and David and Bobby Appleby. It is ideally situated for visiting the historic sights of the area. The proprietors take pride in their cooking and are fast gaining a reputation for imaginative meals. The owners are particularly interested in antiques and are developing an antique shop on the grounds. Bed and a full English breakfast costs from £14 ($21), with a three-course dinner from £10 ($15). There are special rates for children.

Six miles southwest of Wells and we're at:

4. Glastonbury

The goal of the medieval pilgrim, **Glastonbury Abbey** (tel. 0548/32267), once one of the wealthiest and most prestigious monasteries in England, is no more than a ruined sanctuary today. But it provides Glastonbury's claim to historical greatness, an assertion augmented by legendary links to such figures as Joseph of Arimathea, King Arthur, Queen Guinivere, and St. Patrick.

It is said that Joseph of Arimathea journeyed to what was then the Isle of Avalon, with the Holy Grail in his possession. According to tradition, he buried the chalice at the foot of the conically shaped Glastonbury Tor, and a stream of blood burst forth. (You can scale this more than 500-foot-high hill today. A 15th-century tower rests atop it.)

At one point, the early saint is said to have leaned against his staff, which immediately was transformed into a fully blossoming tree. A cutting alleged to have survived from the Holy Thorn can be seen on the abbey grounds today. It blooms at Christmastime and in the early summer. Some historians have traced this particular story back to Tudor times.

Joseph, so it goes, erected a church of wattle (reeds and branches) in

Glastonbury. In fact, excavations have shown that the town may have had the oldest church in England.

The most famous link, fanned for Arthurian fans in the Victorian era by Alfred Lord Tennyson, concerns the burial of King Arthur and Queen Guinivere on the abbey grounds. In 1191 the monks dug up the skeletons of two bodies on the south side of the Lady Chapel, said to be that of the king and his queen. In 1278, in the presence of Edward I, the bodies were removed and transferred to a black marble tomb in the choir. Both their alleged burial spot and their shrine are marked today.

A large Benedictine Abbey of St. Mary grew out of the early wattle church. St. Dunstan, who was born nearby, was the abbot in the tenth century, later becoming archbishop of Canterbury. At its most powerful stage in English history, Edmund, Edgar, and Edmund (Ironside)—three early English kings—were buried at the abbey.

In 1184 a fire of unknown origin swept over the abbey, destroying most of it, along with what must have been vast treasures. It was eventually rebuilt after much difficulty, only to be dissolved by Henry VIII. Its last abbot, Richard Whiting, was hanged by the neck at Glastonbury Tor. For years after, the abbey, like the Roman Forum, was used as a stone quarry.

The modern-day pilgrim to Glastonbury can visit the ruins of the Lady Chapel, which is linked by an early English "Galilee" to the nave of the abbey. The best preserved building on the grounds is a 14th-century octagonal Abbot's Kitchen, where oxen were once roasted whole to feed the wealthier of the pilgrims (that is, the biggest donors). You can visit the ruins from 9:30 a.m. till dusk, for 80p ($1.20) for adults, 4.10 (60¢) for children under 16.

Glastonbury may be one of the oldest inhabited sites in Britain. Excavations have revealed Iron Age lakeside villages on its periphery. Some of the discoveries dug up may be viewed in a little museum in the High Street.

After the destruction of its once-great abbey, the town lost prestige. It is a market town today. The ancient gatehouse entry to the abbey, by the way, is a museum, its principal exhibit a scale model of the abbey and its community buildings as they stood in 1539, at the time of the dissolution. The above fees include entry to the abbey museum.

SOMERSET RURAL LIFE MUSEUM: The history of the Somerset countryside over the last 100 or so years is explained in a museum, Abbey Farm, Chilkwell Street (tel. 0458/32903). The main part of the exhibition is Abbey Barn, the home barn of the abbey, built in 1370. The magnificent timbered roof, the stone tiles, and the sculpture outside, including a head of Edward III, make it special. There are also a Victorian farmhouse and various other exhibits illustrating farming in Somerset during the "horse age" and domestic and social life in Victorian times. In summer they have demonstrations of buttermaking, weaving, basketwork, anything which has reference to the rural life of the country, now rapidly disappearing with the invention of the engine, the freezer, and the instant meal. The museum is open daily from 10 a.m. to 5 p.m. (2 to 6:30 p.m. on Saturday and Sunday; 2:30 to 5 p.m. in winter). Admission is 60p (90¢) for adults, half price for children. There is a snackbar for light meals and soft drinks.

ACCOMMODATIONS: Although I'll document some exceptional places to stay in the area, you might need emergency assistance if you arrive when all the rooms listed are taken. In that case, there is a nonprofit **Tourist Information Centre** run by volunteers. The center (tel. 0458/32954) is entered from Northload Street. Look for a narrow passage at the end of which is a pleasant terrace of flower-bedecked old brick cottages (the tourist office is in the first cottage). It is open Easter to mid-October from 9:30 a.m. to 5 p.m. daily except Sunday and can deal with accommodations inquiries.

Tor Down, Ashwell Lane (tel. 0458/32287), is a well-cared-for house on the edge of the town (half a mile from Glastonbury on the A361, toward West Pennard). The landlady, Miss Parfitt, charges from £9.50 ($14.25) to £10.50 ($15.75) per person for a comfortable bed in a centrally heated room and a large breakfast. There's an expansive view from the Tor of the Isle of Avalon. Miss Parfitt will pack lunches, if asked, and dinner can be served if a prior arrangement is made. She caters to vegetarians. Guests gather in the parlor in the evening for tea and crackers.

Little Orchard, Ashwell Lane (tel. 0458/31620), on the A361 Glastonbury to Shepton Mallet road, is a Tyrolean-type brick structure at the foot of Glastonbury Tor, with striking views over the Vale of Avalon. Rodney and Dinah Gifford rent centrally heated bedrooms with hot and cold water basins accommodating up to ten guests. Rates are £8.50 ($12.75) per person for B&B, with a full English breakfast served. The house has a fire certificate, and there is a color TV lounge. In summer, guests can enjoy the sun patio and large garden. Note the attractive stained-glass window in the staircase.

The **Market House Inn,** Magdalene Street (tel. 0458/32220), is a two-story building with Georgian detailing behind a red-brick facade. It enjoys a superb location across from the ruined abbey in an 18th-century building. Geoff and Barbara Pease operate not only this small inn, but also have a popular restaurant, beer garden, and skittle alley. They charge £15 ($22.50) per person in a room with bath and color TV, with breakfast included. Rates in a bathless unit are only £12 ($18) per person. However, they offer only five rooms, and in summer they tend to go quickly. There are two areas for eating and drinking. Both are cozy, rustic, and pleasantly old fashioned. Meals are served daily from noon to 2 p.m. and 6:30 to 9:45 p.m. (no dinner on Tuesday). Try the smoked mackerel filet or homemade Somerset pie (diced pork and apple cooked in cider).

Berewall Farm Country Guest House, Cinnamon Lane (tel. 0458/31451), is operated by Mrs. Nurse on the periphery of Glastonbury. From this piece of property, a panoramic sweep of Glastonbury Tor unfolds. Here is good, country living on a dairy with almost 150 acres. Her rooms are attractive and comfortable, with many amenities. In fact, out of nine of them, four contain full private baths along with color TV in all accommodations. Because of the good home cooking, it's best to book in here on half-board terms, costing from £20 ($30) to £23 ($34.50) per person.

Woodlands, 52 Bove Town (tel. 0458/32119), is an attractive and cozy residence lying within easy access to the ruins of Glastonbury Abbey. Guests receive a warm welcome and are housed in one of three twin-bedded rooms, the occupants of which share a well-maintained public bath. The charge for B&B ranges from £25 ($37.50) to £31 ($46.50) for two persons, these tariffs including a full English breakfast. The small property has a garden, and the owners maintain animals and poultry. Woodlands, like the previous recommendation, also opens onto a view of Glastonbury Tor. There is limited parking.

WHERE TO EAT: For centuries, pilgrims have been welcomed at **The George & Pilgrims,** High Street (tel. 0458/31145), one of the few pre-Reformation hostelries still left in England. The inn has a facade that looks like a medieval castle, with stone-mullioned windows with leaded glass. Its rooms are over our budget; however, in its downstairs section it serves some of the most reasonably priced food in town. You may be drawn to the old kitchen, which is now the Pilgrims' Bar with its old oak beams. Lunches cost from £5 ($7.50), dinners from £11.50 ($17.25). Food is served from noon to 2:30 p.m. and 6 to 9:30. However, the pub remains open until 11 p.m.

Rainbow's End Café, 17A High St. (tel. 0458/33896). The vegetarian side of you will be satisfied by the whole-food served here in one of the town's most charming and attractive cafés, where changing art exhibitions are held. You get good food, reasonably priced, in attractive surroundings. In summer, food is served on a patio when the weather's not acting up. Daily specials are posted, meals costing from £5 ($10.50).

Hours are Monday to Thursday (Saturday too) from 10 a.m. to 4:30 p.m., and on Tuesday from 9:30 a.m. to 4:30 p.m. It is closed on Wednesday but lunch is offered on Sunday from noon to 2 p.m. For the decor, you get Laura Ashley prints and stripped pine.

LIVING IN THE ENVIRONS: About two miles from Glastonbury, **Cradlebridge Farm,** Cradlebridge (tel. 0458/31827), is a secluded farmhouse where you can get not only B&B, but an evening meal as well. In this unsophisticated atmosphere, Mr. and Mrs. Henry Tinney will go out of their way to make you comfortable and will prepare old-fashioned meals. They have three doubles and one single for which they charge £9.50 ($14.25) per person nightly for B&B. All bedrooms have hot and cold running water, and one bedroom has its own private bath. You reach the farm by taking the A39 road from Glastonbury. Turn at the second right after passing the Morlands Shoe Factory, then take the first left, and Cradlebridge Farm will be at the end of the road.

For a deeply rural setting, head five miles south of Glastonbury to **The Vicarage,** Compton Dundon (tel. 0458/72324). Run by Joy Adams, it was built of local stone in 1867 on the site of a medieval manor and next to a medieval church. A well in the vicarage cellar is part of the ancient house. There are two double bedrooms, one with private bath. Both units have views over the unspoiled hills where deer can sometimes be seen. In the house are some interesting antiques, including a grandfather clock and a Welsh dresser. In addition to central heating, log fires burn on cooler days. For a bed and a full English breakfast, the charge is from £9 ($13.50) per person. The two-acre garden surrounding the property includes a Somerset orchard.

5. The Exmoor National Park

The far west of Somerset forms most of the Exmoor National Park. In addition to the heather-clad moor, the park includes the wooded valleys of the Rivers Exe and Barle, the Brendon Hills, and the sweeping stretch of coast from Minehead to the boundary of Devon. This is more of the land of Blackmore's *Lorna Doone*. You can walk up Badgworthy Water from Malmsmead to Doone Valley, divided by the Somerset-Devon line, or visit tiny Oare Church and see the window through which Carver Doone shot Lorna at her wedding. The moors, which rise to 1,707 feet at Dunkery Beacon, are inviting to walkers and pony trekkers, with ponies and wild deer roaming freely.

Visit England's smallest complete church at Culbone and the centuries-old clapper bridge over the River Barle at Tarr Steps. Some of England's prettiest villages are within the national park, and some lie along its borders. Selworthy, an idyllic little town, is in Exmoor, as is Allerford, with its pack-horse bridge and its walnut tree, both of them owned and preserved by the National Trust.

Minehead, a fine resort, is just outside the park's northeastern boundary, but in some ways, the little villages which have that town as a focal point have more charm.

On the eastern edge of Exmoor, you can visit **Combe Sydenham Hall,** Combe Sydenham, Monksilver (tel. 098/56284), which was the home of Elizabeth Sydenham, wife of Sir Francis Drake. It stands on the ruins of monastic buildings which were associated with nearby Cleeve Abbey. At the hall, you can see a cannonball legend says halted the wedding of Lady Elizabeth to a rival suitor to Sir Francis in 1585. The gardens include Lady Elizabeth's Walk, around ponds originally laid out when the knight was courting his bride-to-be, and Long Meadow with its host of wildflowers. Also to be seen are a deserted hamlet whose population was reportedly wiped out by the Black Death, plus High Viewpoint, accessible to the energetic who climb 1,000 feet for views over the Quantock woods and moors and the Bristol Channel, across Exmoor to Dunkery Beacon and North Hill. The hall is 5 miles north of Wiveliscombe and 3 miles south of Watchet on the B3188. It is open from 11 a.m. to dusk April to October. Admission is £1.80 ($2.70) for adults, 80p ($1.20) for children.

Incidentally, it was from Watchet, a few miles east of Minehead along the coast, that Coleridge's Ancient Mariner sailed.

For places to stay in Exmoor National Park, I suggest a trio of villages in the heart of the park, all to the southwest of Minehead.

WITHYPOOL: In this charming little village on the River Barle, **Westerclose Country House Hotel** (tel. 064383/302) was built as a hunting lodge more than 60 years ago. Now a hotel, it is surrounded by unspoiled countryside and stands in nine acres of gardens and paddocks overlooking the village. John and Judith Kelly offer a variety of bedrooms, some with private baths and color TV. All units have fine views of the moors. Charges for B&B are £16 ($24) per person, rising to £18 ($27) in a suite with a four-poster bed. For half board, prices are £25 ($37.50) to £27 ($40.50). Traditional English and classic French dishes are served, with à la carte and fixed-price dinners skillfully prepared using local products. Coffee and tea are served on the south-facing terrace and lawn in summer. To reach Westerclose, take the A361 Taunton-Barnstaple road at Bampton and then the B3222 road through Exebridge to Dulverton. From Dulverton, the B3223 Lynton road goes across the moor, where, after about seven miles, you'll see the signs for Withypool.

EXFORD: On the River Exe, at the junction of the B3224 and B2223 roads, a very short distance north of Withypool, lies **Edgcott House** (tel. 064383/495), a large old country house with a sheltered garden, close to the village of Exford. It offers comfortable bedrooms, some with private baths, and a warm lounge with an open fire in cool weather. A typical country atmosphere prevails. Enormous breakfasts are served, and dinners if prearranged. Your hostess, Mrs. Lamble, is a friendly person and a good cook. She charges from £10 ($15) per person for B&B and from £15 ($22.50) for half board.

SIMONSBATH: Another village in the heart of Exmoor National Park, Simonsbath, is about 12 miles to the west of Exford on the B3223 road. **Emmetts Grange Farm** (tel. 064383/282) is a hill stock farm standing beside the road, that leads from Dulverton to Lynton. This large country house, in a beautiful and quiet position, is where Mrs. Brown provides well-furnished rooms, all with hot and cold water basins. There are adequate bathroom facilities as well, plus a residents' lounge with color TV to watch before the log fire. Breakfast and the four-course dinner include much local produce, cream, butter and meat. A bed and full breakfast go for £14 ($21) per person, the cost of full board increasing to £24 ($36) per person.

6. The Caves of Mendip

The Caves of Mendip are two exciting natural sightseeing attractions in Somerset —the great caves of Cheddar and Wookey Hole, both easily reached by heading west out of Wells. After leaving Wells, you'll first come to **Wookey Hole** (tel. 0749/72243), less than two miles away, the source of the Axe River. In the first chamber of the caves, you can see, as legend has it, the Witch of Wookey turned to stone. These caves were believed to have been inhabited by prehistoric man at least 60,000 years ago. Even in those days there was a housing problem, with hyenas moving in and upsetting real-estate values! A tunnel opened in 1975 leads to chambers unknown to early man and previously accessible only to divers.

Leaving the caves, you follow a canal path to the mill, where paper has been made by hand since the 17th century. Here you can watch the best quality paper being made by skilled men according to the traditions of their ancient craft. Also in the mill is housed a Fairground by Night exhibition, an extraordinary and colorful assembly of relics from the world's fairgrounds, and Madam Tussaud's Cabinet of Curiosities, a re-creation of her traveling exhibition. Adults pay £2.95 ($4.43) and children under 16 pay £1.95 ($2.93) for a guided tour which lasts about 1½ hours. Free car parking is provided, and there are a cafeteria and picnic area. Wookey Hole is open every day from 9:30 a.m. to 5:30 p.m. in summer, from 10:30 a.m. to 4:30 p.m. in winter.

At **Cheddar,** eight miles from Wells, stands an attractive village, famous for its cheese and an underground river (the Yeo), powerful enough to hollow out the spectacular Cheddar Gorge, a two-mile-long pass through 450-foot-high limestone cliffs. It's unlawful to try to mount the cliffs, except by way of Jacob's Ladder, an exhausting 322 steps to the top. Your "heavenly" reward will be panoramic views of the Mendip Hills and the Somerset moors. The cost of the climb is 30p (45¢) for adults, 20p (30¢) for children. The main attractions of the gorge, however, are below the limestone cliffs, in **Gough's Cave** and **Cox's Cave,** with their stalactites and unique rock formations. Supplementing these are **Fantasy Grotto,** a mixture of animated children's characters, and a hologram display, three-dimensional pictures reproduced by using laser technology. The museum is unique for the serious student, as it holds rich finds still only a few yards from where they lay for thousands of years. Real caving trips are available. The Gough's Cave Adventure Caving Expedition takes visitors beyond the normal show cave, supplying them with helmets, lamps, and boiler suits. The minimum age for a caving trip is 12 years. Participants should be reasonably fit for the 1- to 1½-hour trip. Reservations should be made in advance, as only ten persons may go in a group, and only four trips are made per day.

Admission prices are £1.50 ($2.25) for adults, 75p ($1.13) per child for Gough's Cave; 90p ($1.35) for adults and half price for children for Cox's Cave. Fantasy Grotto costs 60p (90¢) for adults, 30p (45¢) for children, and admission to the museum is 35p (53¢) for adults and 20p (30¢) for children. A discount ticket for all of the above, including Jacob's Ladder, costs £2.70 ($4.05) for adults, £1.40 ($2.10) for children. Adventure Caving costs £3.50 ($5.75) per person. For more information or reservations for caving, telephone 0934/742343.

THE CHEESE TOUR: Still making Cheddar in the traditional way is the **Chewton Cheese Dairy,** Priory Farm, Chewton Mendip (tel. 076121/666). The dairy is owned by Lord Chewton, and visitors are welcome to watch the cheese-making process that takes place every morning. You should allow about an hour for the interesting tour. The best time to visit is usually at noon. After the tour, you can purchase a "truckle" (or wheel) of mature Cheddar to send home. A six-pound wheel costs about £21 ($31.50), including shipping. There is also a restaurant with viewing gallery looking onto the cheese dairy, offering coffee, snacks, farmhouse lunches, and cream teas.

WHERE TO STAY: In and around this area you'll find some interesting accommodations, as typified by the **George Hotel** (tel. 0934/712124) which lies three miles south of the Cheddar Gorge in the modest village of Wedmore. Here, King Alfred made peace with the Danes and their ruler, Guthrum, in A.D. 878, forcing him to be baptized. Faced with such antiquity, nothing but an old-world coaching inn will do. The George, part of which dates back to the 1350s, has for centuries been giving strangers a refreshing pint of ale and a restful night's sleep in one of the 12 upstairs bedrooms. The B&B rate is £13 ($19.50) per person nightly. There is no set lunch, but you can compose a two-courser of bar snacks for £3 ($4.50) to £4.50 ($6.75). In the evening you're presented with an à la carte menu and are likely to spend from £7.50 ($11.25). Behind the cellar bar are barrels of ales and beer, and rows of mugs hang from an overhead, time-blackened beam. Everywhere there is a sense of living in the past. It was in 1926 that the custom of holding "court leet of Wedmore" (a special type of manorial court) was abandoned, but the inn still functions as the center of village life. Kenneth and Valerie James, who own and manage the inn, are aware of this heritage—and its responsibilities.

In Cheddar, the best base is the **Gordons Hotel,** Cliff Street (tel. 0934/742497), which lies at the foot of Cheddar Gorge. Mr. and Mrs. J. P. Barker welcome visitors to their licensed hotel, offering 14 bedrooms, some with bathrooms, and all with hot and cold running water, TV, tea makers, and views of the Mendip Hills. For B&B, they charge from £10 ($15) daily. There is a comfortable lounge with color TV, plus a well-stocked bar where not only drinks but bar snacks are sold. The beamed restaurant, definitely "olde worlde," offers game when available. Dinner ranges from £5 ($7.50) to £8 ($12) for three courses. Outside is a garden with lawns and a heated swimming pool, and there's plenty of room for children to play.

A 16th-Century Farm

Churchill Green Farm, Churchill Green, Churchill (tel. 0934/852438), is a good base for exploring the Mendips. Janet Sacof has modernized this 16th-century farmhouse without endangering its old-world charm and character. But down-on-the-farm life has never been better since she added a swimming pool. She charges £18.50 ($27.75) per person daily for half board, or £12.50 ($18.75) per person for B&B. Children sharing a room with two adults are granted reductions. She offers a number of reasons for you to stay with her: a pleasant lounge with plenty of books (she is university educated herself); a large and ancient dining room; plenty of hot water; good beds (particularly the canopied Edwardian tester-bed hung with red brocade); cots for children; central heating throughout the house; log fires to sit by on those dull days; and Somerset cider or wine and spirits served in her "ye olde world bar."

If these aren't reasons enough, she suggests some more: she will babysit; horseback-riding is available (and it's beautiful riding over the ancient British encampment on Dolebury Hill and among the young pine forests of Mendip); and the gardens face due south, looking out onto the foothills. If you still aren't satisfied, she grows most of the food, including beef, and she bakes bread fresh every day. Although she doesn't provide midday meals, she will pack you a lunch. The house is furnished with well-selected antiques.

A Farm Near Bridgwater

Pear Tree Guest House, 16 Manor Rd., Catcott, near Bridgwater (tel. 0278/722390), is a 300-year-old converted farmhouse standing in a history-rich part of England. David and Sheila Horsell, the owners of Pear Tree, offer good, wholesome, farm-style living. Their B&B rate is £9.50 ($14.25). If you take evening dinner (highly recommended), the charge is £13 ($19.50).

The village of Catcott, on the slopes of the Polden Hills halfway between Glastonbury and Bridgwater on the A39, was once the camping ground of the Danes in 610. Facing Pear Tree Farm is a 13th-century church and tarry house, once used by the pilgrims on their way to Glastonbury, seven miles away. On the crest of the hill, you can look down on the battleground of Sedgemoor, the last major battle on English soil, between supporters of James II and forces loyal to the Duke of Monmouth.

Bridgwater itself was the home of Admiral Robert Blake (now turned into a museum). Near Bridgwater, at the little hamlet of Nether Stowey, on the A39 you can visit **Coleridge Cottage** (tel. 0278/732662), home of Samuel Taylor Coleridge when he wrote *The Rime of the Ancient Mariner*. During his 1797–1800 sojourn here, he and his friends, William Wordsworth and sister, Dorothy, enjoyed exploring Quantock woods. The cottage, at the west end of Nether Stowey on the south side of the A39 and 8 miles west of Bridgwater, has its parlor and reading room open to visitors from April to the end of September from 2 to 5 p.m. Tuesday to Thursday and on Sunday. Admission to the National Trust property is 70p ($1.05) for adults 30p (45¢) for children.

AVON

Avon is the name that has been given to the area around the old port of Bristol, an area that used to be in Somerset.

7. Bath

Victoria didn't start everything. In 1702 Queen Anne made the 115-mile trek from London to the mineral springs at Bath, thereby launching a fad that was to make the city the most celebrated spa in England. Of course, Victoria hiked up too, in due time, to sample a medicinal cocktail (which you can still do today), but Bath by then had passed its zenith.

The most famous personage connected with Bath's scaling the pinnacle of fashion was the 18th-century dandy, Beau Nash. Dressed in embroidered white, he was the final arbiter of taste and manners (as one example, he made dueling déclassé). The master of ceremonies of Bath, he cut a striking figure as he made his way across the city, with all the plumage of a bird of paradise. Dispensing (at a price) trinkets to the courtiers and aspirant gentlemen of his day, Beau was carted around in a liveried carriage.

The gambler was given the proper setting for his considerable social talents by 18th-century architects John Wood the Elder and his son. These architects designed a city of stone from the nearby hills, a feat so substantial and lasting that Bath today is the most harmoniously laid out city in England.

This Georgian city on a bend of the Avon River has, throughout history, attracted a following among leading political and literary figures, among them Dickens, Thackeray, Lord Nelson, and William Pitt. Canadians may know that General Wolfe lived on Trim Street, and Australians may want to visit the house at 19 Bennett St. where their founding father, Admiral Philip, lived. Henry Fielding came this way, observing in *Tom Jones* that the ladies of Bath "endeavor to appear as ugly as possible in the morning, in order to set off that beauty which they intend to show you in the evening."

Bath has had two lives. Long before its Queen Anne, Georgian, and Victorian popularity, it was known to the Romans as Aquae Sulis. The foreign legions founded their baths (which may be visited today) here, so they might ease their plight of rheumatism in the curative mineral springs.

That Bath retains its handsome look today is the result of remarkable restoration and careful planning. The city suffered devastating destruction from the infamous Baedeker air raids of 1942, when Luftwaffe pilots seemed more bent on bombing historical buildings, such as the Assembly Rooms, than in hitting any military target.

The major sights today are the rebuilt Assembly Rooms, the abbey, and the Pump Room and Roman baths. But if you're intrigued by architecture and city planning, you may want to visit some of the buildings, crescents, and squares. The North Parade, where Goldsmith lived, and the South Parade, where Fanny Burney (English novelist and diarist) once resided, represent harmony, the work of John Wood the Elder. The younger Wood, on the other hand, designed the Royal Crescent, an elegant half-moon row of town houses copied by Astor architects for their colonnade in New York City in the 1830s. Queen Square is one of the most beautiful (Jane Austen and Wordsworth used to live here, but hardly together), showing off quite well the work of Wood the Elder. And don't miss his Circus, built in 1754, as well as the shop-flanked Pulteney Bridge, designed by Robert Adam and compared aptly to the Ponte Vecchio of Florence.

THE SIGHTS: Since Bath suffers from a proliferation of one-way streets and traffic congestion, it is best to park in the heart of the city and explore its wonders on foot.

Bath Abbey

Built on the site of a much larger Norman cathedral, the present-day abbey is a fine example of the late Perpendicular style. When Queen Elizabeth I came to Bath in 1574, she ordered that a national fund be set up to restore the abbey. The west front is the sculptural embodiment of a Jacob's Ladder dream of a 15th-century bishop. When you go inside and see its many windows, you'll understand why the abbey is called the "Lantern of the West." Note the superb fan vaulting, achieving at times a scalloped effect. Beau Nash was buried in the nave and is honored by a simple monument totally out of keeping with his flamboyant character.

Pump Room and Roman Baths

In A.D. 75 the Romans founded their baths, dedicated to the native goddess Sul (similar to Minerva). Like many of their other baths, the one in Bath was in its day an engineering feat, and even today it is considered the finest Roman remains in the country. It is still fed by the original hot spring, which rises under the King's Bath. When the Romans departed, the baths decayed, and were buried until mid-18th century. Late in Victoria's day, major excavations were undertaken. A museum connected to the baths contains the most interesting objects from the digs (look for the head of Minerva). You can have coffee in the Pump Room or a drink at the licensed restaurant on the terrace. The Pump Room and the Roman Baths Museum (tel. 0225/61111) are open daily in summer from 9 a.m. to 6 p.m. (to 7 p:m. in July and August). In winter weekday hours are 9 a.m. to 5 p.m., on Sunday from 10 a.m. to 5 p.m. Admission is £1.75 ($2.63) for adults, £1 ($1.50) for children. A combined ticket to the Roman Baths Museum and the Museum of Costume (see below) costs £2.40 ($3.60) for adults, £1.20 ($1.80) for children.

The Assembly Rooms and Museum of Costume

Lying right off the Circus on Alfred Street, the Assembly Rooms (tel. 0225/61111) were originally designed by John Wood the Younger in 1769. Damaged by 1942 air raids, the rooms have been restored to the height of their 18th-century elegance, when the fashionable beaux and their ladies paraded about. Today they house a Museum of Costume, founded by the collection of Mrs. Doris Langley Moore, and greatly enlarged and enriched by donations from many sources. The display of clothes covers more than 400 years of fashion history—Madame Recamier's lounging ladies, Jane Austen's upper-middle-class look, styles right out of Watteau paintings, the Alice B. Toklas post-World War I garb, up to Dior haute couture and a mini by Mary Quant.

Men's apparel isn't neglected in the exhibition and ranges from a splendid silver-embroidered brown cloth coat, with matching silk stockings, of the early 18th century, another in green velvet decorated with sequins (which Liberace would have loved), right up to today's jeans. The museum is open weekdays in summer from 9:30 a.m. to 6 p.m., on Sunday from 10 a.m. to 6 p.m. Winter hours are 10 a.m. to 5 p.m. weekdays, 11 a.m. to 5 p.m. on Sunday. Admission is £1.35 ($2.03) for adults, 80p ($1.20) for children. A ticket for joint admission to the Roman Baths Museum and the Museum of Costume is £2.40 ($3.60) for adults, £1.20 ($1.80) for children.

Bath Festival

This annual festival of the performing arts lasts 17 days and takes place at the end of May and beginning of June. Concerts are held in the Assembly Rooms, the Guildhall, the Theatre Royal, the Abbey, Wells Cathedral, and many other historic houses and churches in the area. The varied program includes concerts by the major British and foreign choirs and chamber orchestras, opera, dance, an international lineup of soloists and chamber groups, exhibitions, lectures, garden and church tours, and jazz festival. A recent innovation is the festival's literary program with talks and readings by famous authors. Bath Festival holds a contemporary art fair—a four-day exhibition of modern visual art. The festival runs its own art gallery which provides exhibitions of paintings, sculpture, and crafts throughout the year, with a special exhibition by an artist or group of artists of international standing during the period of the festival. All information can be obtained from the Bath Festival Office, 1 Pierrepont Pl., Bath, BA1 1JY (tel. 0225/62231; box office, 0225/63362).

The Theatre Royal

The Theatre Royal, Sawclose, has been restored and refurbished with plush red-velvet seats, red carpets, and a painted proscenium arch and ceiling. It is a 1,000-seat theater with a small pit and then grand circles rising to the upper circle. Beneath the theater, reached from the back of the stalls or by a side door, are the theater vaults. There you will find a pleasant bar in one of the curved vaults with stone walls. In the next vault is the Theatre Vaults Brasserie, where lunch and pre-performance meals are served, costing from £10 ($15). It's open all day from morning coffee to dinner. For table reservations, phone 0225/65074, ext. 46. The theater also boasts a Japanese restaurant, Chikako's, with an entrance on St. John's Place, which is open daily from noon to 2:30 p.m. and 6 to 11:30 p.m., including Sunday. The menu is Japanese but geared to Western tastes (for reservations, phone 0225/64125). The theater advertises a sophisticated list of forthcoming events with a repertoire that includes, among other offerings, West End shows. The box office (tel. 0225/62065) is open from 10 a.m. to 8 p.m., Monday to Saturday. In addition to evening performances, the theater runs Thursday "Lunch and Listen" with a changing program of events. The cost of £2.95 ($4.43) includes a sandwich and a glass of wine, or you can pay £1 ($1.50) just to listen.

A Georgian House

No. 1 Royal Crescent (tel. 0225/28126) was given to the Bath Preservation Trust by Bernard Cayzer in 1968. By 1970 it had been carefully restored and the main rooms decorated and furnished to create an authentic 18th-century interior. Thus visitors may see for themselves what the inside of a house in Bath looked like in its heyday. It is open March to mid-December, Tuesday to Saturday from 11 a.m. to 5 p.m.; on Sunday, from 2 to 5 p.m. (closed Monday). Admission is £1.30 ($1.95) for adults, 70p ($1.05) for children.

Claverton Manor

Some 2½ miles outside Bath, you get a glimpse of life as lived by a diversified segment of American settlers until Lincoln's day. It was the first American museum established outside the United States. A Greek Revival house, designed by a Georgian architect, Claverton Manor sits proudly in its own extensive grounds above the Avon Valley. Among the authentic exhibits shipped over from the States are a New Mexico room, a Conestoga wagon, an early American beehive oven (ever had gingerbread baked from the recipe of George Washington's mother?), the dining room of a New York town house of the early 19th century, and (on the grounds) a copy of Washington's flower garden at Mount Vernon. You can visit the museum from March to October daily except Monday from 2 to 5 p.m., 11 a.m. to 5 p.m. on Sunday. Adults pay £2.25 ($3.38); children, £1.75 ($2.63). For more information, telephone 0225/60503.

Walking Tours

The **Mayor's Corps of Honorary Guides** conducts free walking tours of the city of Bath. The guides are all unpaid volunteers acting in an honorary capacity to point out the beauties of their city. They don't accept tips. Tours, lasting about 1¾ hours, leave from the abbey churchyard, outside the Pump Room. Visitors see the historical and architectural features of the city but are not shown into any buildings. From May to October, tours are offered at 10:30 a.m. Sunday to Friday, at 2:30 p.m. Sunday and Wednesday, and at 7 p.m. Tuesday and Friday except in October. Saturday tours are at 6 p.m. except in October. From November to April, the walks are Sunday to Friday at 10:30 a.m. and on Sunday at 2:30 p.m. The tours are arranged by the guides corps in conjunction with the Bath City Council (tel. 0225/61111, ext. 327). For further information, get in touch with the Tourist Information Centre, Abbey Churchyard, Bath, Avon (tel. 0225/62831).

WHERE TO STAY: A Georgian private home, **Dorset Villa,** 14 Newbridge Rd. (tel. 0225/25975), with a front garden and car park, has been converted by Mr. and Mrs. Ivor Ham into a well-operated hotel. A double-decker bus will whisk you into the heart of Bath in about ten minutes. The Hams charge £19 ($28.50) for a double, in a spacious, tidy, and pleasant room with hot and cold running water. No singles are offered except in off-season, when doubles are sometimes rented out to lone travelers. The atmosphere is personal, the owners genial and charming. There's a pleasant lounge with TV, a bright and cheerful breakfast room, and a place to park your car.

Arden Hotel, 73 Great Pulteney St. (tel. 0225/66601), is owned by Eric and Jacqueline Newbiggin, whose aim is to operate the pleasantest small hotel in Bath. A Georgian building, the hotel is licensed and has a dozen bedrooms. It stands on one of the city's most famous streets, a few minutes' walk from the abbey, the Roman Baths, and the Royal Crescent. The hotel has attractive rooms, often with private facilities. The rate in a single is £18 ($27), lowered to £15 ($22.50) per person in a double or twin without bath, rising to £17 ($25.50) to £18 ($27) per person with private bath. Guests can enjoy a cocktail in the bar or relax in the lounge, watching color TV.

Jane's Hotel, Manvers Street (tel. 0225/65966), a center for young people, is just down the road from the railway station and within a two-minute walk of the abbey and the Roman remains. There is ample car parking at the rear. The hotel is a Victorian building welded from a row of terrace houses. It provides clean rooms with comfortable beds, color TV, and plenty of hot water, at a cost of £16 ($24) per person, including breakfast. A double with private bath rents for £40 ($60). Jane's is run by Christopher Bradshaw, who, along with his partners, has spent the last few years improving the hotel.

Under the hotel is Jane's Speakeasy, Bath's top nightclub and disco. Entry for nonmembers is from £3 ($4.50), but it's free to residents of Jane's Hotel. The club is ideal for the over-20s looking for late evening entertainment. For £5 ($7.50), you are admitted to Jane's Roman Health Spa, which has a Jacuzzi, sauna, cold pool, steam room, and solarium.

Grove Lodge Guest House, 11 Lambridge (tel. 0225/310860), is a typical Georgian home dating from 1787, with well-furnished and spacious rooms, most with large windows overlooking a stone terrace, attractive garden, and the surrounding wooded hills. Just a few minutes from the city center, the lodge is serviced by frequent buses at the front gate. A warm welcome and personal attention are guaranteed by the owners, Alec and Diana Thompson, who have made many improvements in the house to increase service and comfort. There is a selection of single, twin, and double rooms, as well as large family rooms sleeping three or four persons. All units are equipped with TV, hot and cold running water, and wall-to-wall carpeting. There are ample shared bathroom and shower facilities. Drinks of all kinds are served until 10:30 p.m. The basic cost of a room, including a full breakfast and VAT, is £12 ($18) per person, but reductions are available for the larger rooms shared by three or more persons.

Chesterfield Hotel, 11 Great Pulteney St. (tel. 0225/60953), stands on a street laid out by Thomas Baldwin in 1798. It leads to the Pulteney Bridge with its shops on either side, built over the River Avon. The hotel is within a few minutes' walk of the center of Bath. It is a listed Georgian building, centrally heated, and has 28 bedrooms, with views from both front and back. All units are comfortably furnished, some with four-poster beds and antiques. Many units have private bathrooms, and color TVs are installed in the lounge and all principal bedrooms. Depending on the plumbing, singles range from £16 ($24) to £20 ($30); doubles, from £28 ($42). A room with a four-poster bed costs from £22 ($33) per person nightly. Breakfast is typically English, ample and well prepared. Garage parking is available at a small charge.

Highways House, 143 Wells Rd. (tel. 0225/21238), is an elegant Victorian family home within minutes of the historic center. There is private, off-street parking for guests, a rare facility within a city built when the sedan chair and coach and horses reigned supreme. Highways is the home of David and Davina James and their family. For 13 years, they were the owners of a much larger hotel in Wales and have brought their knowledge to Bath. They offer two twin-bedded and two double-bedded rooms, all with private showers and/or toilets, as well as beverage-making facilities. Prices are from £26 ($39) to £30 ($45), including service, VAT, and a full English breakfast. Both David and Davina know a lot about Bath and its environs and always show a willingness to help guests in their planning. Their ironing facilities may come in handy in an emergency, and drinks and snacks can be arranged. Ice is always available here, and there's a color TV in the sitting room.

Millers Hotel, 69 Great Pulteney St. (tel. 0225/65798), stands on a residential street of Georgian buildings, close to the heart of the city. Run by M.J. Miller, it offers 14 colorful, relaxing rooms, six of which have private baths. The hotel is centrally heated, and each unit can be controlled to a desired temperature. A single rents for £16 ($24), a twin for £27 ($40.50), and a double for £26 ($39). With bath, a twin costs £39 ($58.50), a double £38 ($57) per night. Some accommodations house three persons at rates ranging from £32 ($48) to £44 ($66), some housing four persons for £38 ($57) to £50 ($75). All these tariffs include a full English breakfast and VAT. There is a comfortable dining room with an adjoining licensed lounge bar. The hotel is well managed.

Charnwood House, 51 Upper Oldfield Park (tel. 0225/334937), is a charming example of the elegant and substantial style of Victorian Bath. The home of Linda and Robert Cooney (she's English, he's from Iowa) is a comfortable hotel with spa facilities and a sauna. The individually decorated bedrooms, most with private baths, all have color TV, beverage-making facilities, and other amenities of a good hotel. For B&B, the price, based on double occupancy, is from £14 ($21) to £20 ($30) per person, providing a choice of breakfast and VAT. The elegant sitting room is furnished with some antiques. To find Charnwood from the city center, within easy walking distance, follow the A36 signs toward Bristol, then take the A367 Wells to Exeter road for about ½ mile up the hill, and turn right into Upper Oldfield Park.

Oldfields, 102 Wells Rd. (tel. 0225/317984), is an elegant and traditional bed and breakfast accommodation, occupying two semi-detached Victorian houses dating from 1875. Anthony and Nicole O'Flaherty joined their family home to the one next door, restoring the facilities so that now they offer comfortably appointed rooms with color TV and beverage-making facilities. Eight of the units have private showers and toilets. The rates begin at £14 ($18) per person in a bathless room, rising to £18 ($27) per person if you want private plumbing. A full English breakfast and VAT are included in the tariffs. The house has a spacious lounge with decorated plaster ceilings and tall windows with lace curtains. Fine views of the hills and the city are part of the attraction. Parking is available at Oldfields, which lies about a 12-minute walk from the heart of Bath.

Glenbeigh, 1 Upper Oldfield Park (tel. 0225/26336), is a restored Victorian residence owned by Dorothy and Cyril Burton and their son John, who is helpful in advising guests about what to see in Bath. On the southern slopes of the city, Glenbeigh is within a 10- to 15-minute walk of the city center. Many of the furnishings of the house are antiques, and most bedrooms have good views. Some have canopied beds, and all have beverage-making facilities. For bed and a full English breakfast, singles are charged £17 ($25.50), doubles £25 ($37.50) bathless, and £32 ($48) for a double with bath. VAT and service are included in the prices.

Harington's Hotel and Restaurant, Queen Street (tel. 0225/61728), is known primarily as a place to eat, but the proprietors, Sally and Anthony Dodge, also offer comfortable overnight accommodations consisting of twin-bedded, double, and family rooms, some with showers and toilets. The rates are from £24 ($36) to £28 ($42) for a double or twin and £34 ($51) to £38 ($57) in a family room. These prices include a full English breakfast and VAT. Rooms are centrally heated and have hot and cold water basins, TV, and radio intercoms. Harington's is in an attractive cobbled street within easy walking distance of the major points of interest in Bath.

Harington's, formerly Mr. Smith's Steak & Chophouse, consists of several 19th-century buildings on the corner of Harington Place and Queen Street, on land owned by the Harington family after the Dissolution of the Monasteries. Sir John Harington, a godson of Queen Elizabeth I, whose main claim to fame is his invention of the water closet (flush toilet).

Orchard House, Warminster Road, Bathampton, outside Bath (tel. 0225/66115), provides excellent B&B, and all rooms have baths and showers, tea/coffee-making facilities, color TV, radio, central heating, and double glazing. Built in 1984, the hotel has a sauna, solarium, and spa in a special health facility. There's also a place to do your laundry. A double room costs £20 ($30) per person per night. A large traditional English breakfast is served, and the place is kept neat and clean. The owners, Keith and Barbara Reynolds, make guests feel welcome and comfortable. You can reach the place on the A36, just five minutes' drive from the heart of Bath. It's conveniently situated on a local bus route. In semi-rural surroundings, this is a peaceful and tranquil choice, and there is off-street parking.

Arden Hotel, 73 Great Pulteney St. (tel. 0225/66601), has only a dozen rooms, each pleasantly decorated and inviting. Family run, this is a most central hotel where you receive polite hospitality and several amenities, including a well-appointed lounge bar. B&B costs £18 ($27) in a single, £15 ($22.50) per person in a double. For a double with private bath, the charge is £17 ($25.50) to £18 ($27) per person.

The **Tasburgh Hotel,** Warminster Road, Bathampton, a mile outside Bath (tel. 0225/25096), is a spacious Victorian country house built in 1890. Set in pleasant gardens, the red-brick structure has a lounge and a residential license. Most rooms have private baths, and all contain TV, wash basins, and beverage-making facilities. For B&B, singles cost from £15 ($22.50) to £18 ($27), doubles from £26 ($39) to £34 ($51), and family rooms from £34 ($51) to £50 ($75), VAT included. The Avon and Kennet Canal runs along the rear of the property, and guests enjoy summer walks on the towpath. Audrey B. Archer is the gracious hostess.

WHERE TO DINE: An excellent choice is **Harington's Hotel and Restaurant,** Queen Street (tel. 0225/61728), recommended above for lodgings, the kind of dining establishment known to locals who have resided in the city for some time. It's hidden from the casual visitor on a narrow street in the heart of Bath. The protruding bay window lets in the sun, and you can sit in the front and watch the passing parade. The fully licensed restaurant offers English and French cuisine, the house specialties including Harington's Dover sole and chateaubriand. Other fish dishes are seafood pancakes (crêpes), grilled pink trout, and smoked haddock en papillotte. Of course, they serve steaks, chops, and ham. Set lunches are offered, costing from £2.75 ($4.13). For dinner from the à la carte menu, you'll pay from £8 ($12). The restaurant is open for lunch from noon to 2 p.m. and for dinner from 6:30 to 11 p.m.

Evans Fish Restaurant, 7–8 Abbeygate St. (tel. 0225/63981), only a three-minute walk from the abbey, features superb fish dinners at moderate cost. Created by Mrs. Harriet Evans in 1908, it is a family-style restaurant where you can have a three-course luncheon for as little as £5 ($7.50). The set meal might include the soup of the day, fried filet of fish with chips, and a choice of desserts. Mrs. Hunt carries on today in the fine traditions established by the Evans family. Only the freshest of fish is served in this restaurant, but—just so it won't smell fishy—the staff comes in extra early on Monday morning, when every square inch is scrubbed clean. The lower floor has a self-service section for quickies. On the second floor is an Abbey Room catering to families. The preferred dining spot is the Georgian Room—so named after its unspoiled arched windows and fireplace. You can order a number of crisply fried fish specialties, such as deep-fried scampi with chips, and many other main-dish fish courses from the take-out section. Sit-down dinners cost from £7.50 ($11.25). The restaurant is open Monday to Saturday from 11:30 a.m. to 2:30 p.m., reopening from 6 to 8:30 p.m. in summer. Self-service and take-out counters are open Monday to Saturday from 11:30 a.m. to 8:30 p.m.

Theater Vaults Brasserie, Saw Close (tel. 0225/65074). It required an imaginative entrepreneur to convert the stone vaults beneath the Theatre Royal into an engagingly decorated brasserie. Its late closing makes it a favorite of an after-theater crowd. However, daytime people can drop in to enjoy morning coffee, lunch, or afternoon tea. Menu specialties include chicken with a garlic-flavored cream-and-lemon sauce, juicy steaks, an array of soups and quiches, steak-and-kidney pie, and fresh English lamb. Meals cost from £10 ($15). The restaurant is open daily except Sunday from 12:30 to 7:30 p.m. After a short cleanup, it reopens from 8:30 to 11 p.m. Every Thursday to Saturday, it opens at 10 a.m. for coffee.

Binks Restaurant (downstairs) **and Coffeeshop** (upstairs), Abbey Churchyard (tel. 0225/66563), stands across the pavement from the Roman Baths and the abbey. Inside, the bakers start early in the morning preparing fresh croissants and *pain au chocolat* for breakfast, together with the renowned Bath buns, made from a recipe handed down from a Dr. Oliver to his coachman. Bread, cakes, and ice cream are sold in the coffeeshop, according to the season. Also served are early morning breakfast, light lunches, traditional cream teas, and early evening meals. The restaurant provides a variety of meals from pies to salads, gâteaux to lemon meringue, all at reasonable prices. A three-course meal will average £6.50 ($9.75). The restaurant is open from 7:30 a.m. to 9 p.m.

Tranter's Restaurant, 2 Saracen St. (tel. 0225/60868). One of our readers called this seafood restaurant "a magical place," and a quick visit here might confirm that impression. Owners Tina Tranter and Geoff Glover once worked as photographers and movie-camera operators (he worked on *Star Wars* and *The Empire Strikes Back*). Today the city of Bath benefits from their successful transition from the visual to the culinary arts, although both partners continue their former career as well. Lobster and crab bisque or a roulade of prime Scottish smoked salmon might be followed by quenelles of pike served with a cucumber, fresh dill, and cream sauce or perhaps Tranter's seafood soup, enough for two persons, served in a large tureen with crab claws, scallops, langoustine, prawns, and mussels. Game dishes are also a specialty. Lunch, served from noon to 2:30 p.m., costs £3 ($4.50) to £6 ($9), and dinner from 7 p.m. "until late" goes for £8 ($12) to £15 ($22.50). On Sunday, dinner is served from 7 to 9:30 p.m. VAT is included in the prices.

The Walrus & the Carpenter, 28 Barton St. (tel. 0225/314864), is a French bistro style place, lying a block from the Theatre Royal, off Queens Square. An appealing choice and youth oriented, it offers a wide array of well-prepared dishes at attractive prices. You pay £7.50 ($11.25) for a full meal. You get not only well-prepared steaks and fresh, crisp salads, but beef burgers and vegetarian specialties as well. You can enjoy its candlelit atmosphere from 6 to 11 nightly. There's a bar upstairs.

The Pump Room (tel. 0225/61111; see the sightseeing attractions, already previewed) serves morning coffee to the strains of the famous Pump Room trio. You can munch a traditional Bath Bun with your drink. At lunch, served from noon to 2:30 p.m., guests gravitate to the Four Seasons Restaurant in the adjoining Concert Room, where they face an attractive buffet of soups, pâté, and salads, followed by meat dishes such as pork with apples. The cold table has many delicacies, including game pie. For three courses and coffee, expect to pay around £8 ($12). Afternoon tea in the Pump Room, once frequented by Beau Nash and by Jane Austen and her mother, includes a choice of teas with sandwiches, cakes, and scones.

Clarets Restaurant and Wine Bar, 7a Kingsmead Square (tel. 0225/66688), near the Theatre Royal, is a cellar with whitewashed walls beneath one of Bath's Georgian houses. Head chef Steven Breese, with his individual style of culinary expertise, has helped Clarets become one of Bath's most popular eating and meeting places. The extensive lunch menu, offered from noon to 2:30 p.m. Monday to Saturday, changes daily. In the evening, you order à la carte from an imaginative and varied list, according to what is fresh, best, and in season. Dinner hours are from 6 to 11 p.m. Expect to pay from £1.95 ($2.93) for lunch, from £9.75 ($14.63) for a dinner of three courses. Bar snacks are available, and there is a good wine list. In season, tables are placed in the square for persons wishing to eat al fresco. Restaurant bookings are recommended. The establishment is closed on Sunday.

Sally Lunn's House, 4 North Parade Passage (tel. 0225/61634), is a tiny gabled licensed coffeehouse and restaurant, with a Georgian bay window set in the "new" stone facade put up around 1720. Original Tudor fireplaces and secret cupboards are inside. The house is a landmark in Bath, the present wood-frame building dating from about 1482 being the oldest in the city. If that was not enough, it is built on the site of the monastery kitchen that dated from around 1150, which itself was constructed on the site of a Roman mansion erected in about A.D. 200. Visitors to Bath have been eating here for more than 1,700 years. Sally Lunn, the person, is a legend in Bath, where she baked her buns in the cellar from 1680. They were so popular that the house took her name. It's like going back 500 years to visit the cellar bakery and then to peer at the excavations showing the earlier buildings.

On the ground floor, the Sally Lunn buns are served sweet or savory, fresh from the modern oven now on the third floor. Excellent coffee and toasted Sally Lunn buns with "lashings" of butter, whole fruit strawberry jam, and real clotted cream is everybody's favorite and is described by the owners, Mike and Angela Overton, as "heaven on a plate." You can have a bun served with meat salad, hot with Welsh rarebit, with venison or game, or many other ways. The all-day menu is easy for travelers. Light meals cost less than £5 ($7.50). The place is easy to find—near the abbey between Abbey Green and the Fernley Hotel. Hours are from 10 a.m. to 6 p.m.

A Favorite Pub

Crystal Palace, Abbey Green (tel. 0225/23944), is reached via Church Street, around the corner from Bath Abbey. On a small square, it is one of the few places in England where you can order Thomas Hardy ale, an expensive drink with the highest alcohol content of any beer in the world. In summer the managers, Marshall and Janet Ewart, place tables outside. In cooler weather guests retreat inside, enjoying the dark beams and the paneled fireplace. Come here for both food and drink, including sandwiches, baked potatoes, or a ploughman's lunch, along with traditional English fare such as steak-and-kidney pie. Meals cost from £5 ($7.50). Hours are from 10:30 a.m. to 2:30 p.m. and 6 to 10:30 p.m.

ON THE OUTSKIRTS: A high-grade accommodation in a converted barn and stables, the **Wheelwrights Arms,** Monkton Combe, 3 miles south of Bath (tel. 022122/2287), lies in the beautiful Midford Valley. This unique place of character is run by Ric and Monica Gillespie as a "free house," but it was once a pub which was in competition with the local monastery that brewed its own ale. The pub was refurbished and became the Wheelwrights Arms, a charming hostelry. Homemade snacks, luncheons, and steak dinners, costing from £8 ($12), are served in the bar. Warmed by a huge log fire in winter, it is here that the locals play darts, cribbage, and bar-type cricket. You have a choice of four real ales. The eight bedrooms are equipped with showers, toilets, wash basins, color TV, and beverage-making facilities. Rates are £24 ($36) in a single, £34 ($51) in a double. To reach the place, take the A36 out of Bath in the direction of Warminster, turning off toward Monkton Combe.

Fern Cottage Hotel, 9 Northend, Batheaston, some 3 miles northeast of Bath (tel. 0225/858190), lies at the end of St. Catherines, the most southerly of the Cotswold valleys. The hotel, in a quiet spot with plenty of car parking, has modern amenities, but its furnishings and decor are in keeping with its age, some 250 years. All rooms have hot and cold running water basins, TV, and facilities for making tea or coffee. Some have private bathrooms. Prices range from £14 ($21) to £19 ($28.50) per person per day, depending on the plumbing and the room placement. The hotel has a TV lounge, a dining room where evening meals are available, and a bar lit with the original gas lights installed in Fern Cottage around 1890. Mr. and Mrs. Goodhind welcome guests to this pleasant establishment, nestling at the foot of Little Solsbury Iron Age Hill Fort (the location of Bath before the Romans). To find the hotel, take the A4 from Bath toward Chippenham. In Batheaston, the turning to Northend is second on the left. Fern Cottage is about 400 yards along from the turn, on the left opposite School Lane.

8. Bristol

Bristol, the largest city in the West Country, is a good center for touring western Britain. Its location is 10 miles west of Bath, just across the Bristol Channel from Wales, 20 miles from the Cotswolds, and 30 miles from Stonehenge. This historic inland port is linked to the sea by seven miles of the navigable Avon River. Bristol has long been rich in seafaring traditions and has many links with the early colonization of America. In fact, some claim that the new continent was named after a Bristol town clerk, Richard Ameryke. In 1497 John Cabot sailed from Bristol which led to the discovery of the northern half of the New World.

In Bristol, the world's first iron steamship and luxury liner basks in her 1843 glory. She's the 3,000-ton S.S. *Great Britain*, and was created by Isambard Brunel, a Victorian engineer. Visitors can go aboard this "floating palace" at Great Western Dock, Gas Ferry Road, off Cumberland Road (tel. 0272/260680). She is open daily in summer from 10 a.m. to 6 p.m. (until 5 p.m. in winter). Admission is £1.50 ($2.25) for adults, 70p ($1.05) for children.

At the age of 25 in 1831, Brunel began a Bristol landmark, a suspension bridge over the 250-foot-deep Avon Gorge at Clifton.

Bristol Cathedral, College Green (tel. 0272/24879), was begun in the 12th century and was once an Augustinian abbey. The central tower was added in 1466. The Chapter House and Gatehouse are good examples of late Norman architecture, and the choir is magnificent. The cathedral's interior was singled out for praise by Sir John Betjeman, the late poet laureate.

Another church, **St. Mary Redcliffe,** 10 Redcliffe Parade West (tel. 0272/291962), was called "the fairest, the goodliest, and most famous parish church in England" by such an authority as Elizabeth I. Built in the 14th century, it has been carefully restored. One of the chapels is called "The American Chapel," where the kneelers show the emblems of all the states of the U.S.A. The tomb and armor of Admiral Sir William Penn, father of the founder of Pennsylvania, are in the church.

Cobbles King Street is known for its **Theatre Royal** (tel. 0272/24388), the smallest English playhouse and the oldest in continuous operation. It is the major home of the Bristol Old Vic.

Guided walking tours are conducted in summer, and these last about 1½ hours, leaving from the Exchange on Corn Street. The tour departs daily at 11 a.m. and 2:30 p.m. On Sunday, guided tours are also conducted through Clifton, a suburb of Bristol which has more Georgian houses than the just-previewed Bath.

Additional information on special walks is provided by **Bristol Tourist Information,** Colston House, Colston Street (tel. 0272/293891).

LODGINGS: Instead of finding lodgings in the center of Bristol, many visitors prefer to seek out accommodations in the leafy Georgian suburb of Clifton, near the famous suspension bridge, already mentioned.

There you'll find **Oakfield Hotel,** Oakfield Road, Clifton, off Whiteladies Road (tel. 0272/735556), an impressive guesthouse that would be called a town house in New York, with an Italian facade. It's on a quiet street, and everything is kept spic and span under the watchful eye of Mrs. D. L. Hurley. Every pleasantly furnished bedroom has hot and cold running water and central heating. The charge is £14 ($21) per person for B&B. For another £5 ($7.50), you can enjoy a good dinner.

The **Glenroy Hotel,** Victoria Square (tel. 0272/739058), stands across from a park in a gracious Regency neighborhood. Built of honey-colored limestone, the house has lawns and flowering shrubs. There's a big bow-windowed breakfast room, along with an adjacent bar lounge. You can still see many of the elaborate ceiling and cove moldings from the house's original construction. In Clifton, the hotel is within walking distance of the Suspension Bridge. Jean and Mike Winyard, the owners, rent out some 40 comfortably furnished bedrooms, most of which have private baths. Each accommodation has color TV, phone, a radio, and coffee-making equipment. In one of two buildings, you'll be assigned a single, costing from £21 ($31.50) to £26 ($39), a twin or double from £30 ($45) to £36 ($54). The hotel is considered one of the finest B&Bs in the Clifton/Bristol area.

Westbury Park Hotel, 37 Westbury Rd. (tel. 0272/620465), is a small, privately owned and run hotel on the A4018, one of Bristol's main arteries, linking the city center with the M4 and M5 motorways. The hotel stands about three miles from Exit 17 on the M5 and about two miles from the city center. After a two-minute walk, you'll be at the Durdham Downs, which are acres of open park stretching from the Avon Gorge to Brunel's suspension bridge. Heather Jenkins, the owner, maintains a personal style of service and a high standard of innkeeping. The hotel is an elegant Victorian house with a comfortable drawing room, a pretty sitting room where drinks are served, and well-appointed bedrooms with color TV. In a single, the B&B rate is £18.50 ($27.75), rising to £26.50 ($39.75) in a double. VAT and a good English breakfast are included. Rooms are available with private bath or shower and toilet, costing £24 ($36) in a single, £32 ($48) in a double. Only fresh food, including vegetables, is used in the kitchen, and interesting dishes are prepared for lunch and dinner daily. The table d'hôte dinner menu is £8 ($12). Sunday lunch is a traditional affair with English lamb and local pork costing £6.45 ($9.68).

Alandale Hotel, Tyndall's Park Road, Clifton (tel. 0272/735407), is an elegant early Victorian house that retains a wealth of its original features, including a marble fireplace and ornate plasterwork. Note the fine staircase in the imposing entrance hall. The hotel is under the supervision of Mr. Johnson, who still observes the old traditions of personal service. For example, afternoon tea is served, as are sandwiches, drinks, and snacks in the lounge (up until 11:15 p.m.). A continental breakfast is available in your bedroom until 10 a.m., unless you'd prefer the full English breakfast in the dining room. Terms are from £14 ($21) per person nightly in a twin-bedded unit, including VAT.

Washington Hotel, 11-15 St. Paul's Rd., in Clifton (tel. 0272/733980), makes up in quality for its smallness. It is on a quiet street, just north of the city center, with space for cars to park. Of the 34 bedrooms, 18 have private baths, and all contain TV, radios, electric blankets, and central heating. Depending on the plumbing, singles cost £18 ($27) to £25 ($37.50), and doubles go for £27 ($40.50) to £35 ($52.50). Guests congregate in the pleasant lounge for conversation.

The **Clifton Hotel,** St. Paul's Road, Clifton (tel. 0272/736882), has been improved greatly. On a peaceful street near the University of Bristol, it offers attractively furnished rooms that contain color TV, tea- or coffee-making facilities, and often a private bath or shower. Doubles range in price from £28 ($42) to £32 ($48), and singles cost from £19 ($28.50) to £22.50 ($33.75). The hotel has an intriguing vaulted bar converted from the old cellars and a fully licensed 1930s-style restaurant with an excellent chef providing good cooking.

Orchard House, Bristol Road, Chew Stoke, about 10 miles from Bristol (tel. 027589/3143), is run by a hospitable couple, Ann and Derek Hollomon. Their rooms are very comfortable and immaculately clean, with coffee-making facilities. Their baths are well kept, and they serve an excellent breakfast, B&B costing from £11 ($16.50) per person. Evening meals with the family cost from £4.50 ($6.75). They're cooked with care and imagination, using local produce. House wines are served. Chew Stoke is a good center for touring the area. Orchard House is more than 200 years old, and there is a nearby lake for trout fishing.

WHERE TO EAT: Right in the heart of town, **Guild Restaurant,** 68–70 Park St. (tel. 0272/291874), forms a section of the Bristol Guild Shop. While traffic in the distance roars down Park Street, you dine here in a secluded atmosphere of style and comfort. A covered terrace opens in fine weather onto a secluded garden. The restaurant is open from 9:30 a.m. (drop in for coffee) to 5 p.m. Monday to Friday; however, it shuts down at 4:30 p.m. on Saturday and is closed all day on Sunday. Soups at lunch are hearty and homemade, although you might prefer one of the pâtés or quiches to launch your repast. Salads are outstanding here, and casseroles are hot, good tasty and filling. Many of the dishes are inspired by the continental kitchen. Expect to spend from £7.50 ($11.25) for a complete meal.

La Romanina, 25 The Mall, in Clifton (tel. 0272/734499), is ideal if you, like most readers, are staying in Clifton and don't want to venture into the city center to dine. In recent times, a trattoria and pizzeria craze seems to have swept over Bristol, and La Romanina has surfaced near the top. It serves Monday to Saturday from noon to 2:30 p.m. and reopens for dinner at 7 p.m. (last orders around 11 p.m.). Homemade pastas and pizzas draw a crowd of all ages, and you can order a simple meal or a savory Italian feast, depending on your appetite and pocketbook. The waiters, at least on my latest rounds, have sunny dispositions, in keeping with the bright, florid atmosphere. For pasta or pizza, the charge begins at around £4 ($6), going up. Of course, if you order one of the main courses, such as a tender veal, the cost will rise. Still, you are likely to escape for around £9 ($13.50). Fresh vegetables are included with all main dishes.

Flipper, at 6 St. James Barton (no phone), at the edge of Broadmead, is said to serve the best fish 'n' chips in town. If you want to take out your dinner, it'll cost only £1.75 ($2.63), a little more if you prefer to sit down and eat it on the premises. Good-tasting cod or halibut, served with crisp chips, is freshly prepared daily. Open noon to 9 p.m.

Behind a Georgian facade, **51 Park Street** (tel. 0272/28016) caters for a wide range of tastes. Open Monday to Saturday from 10 a.m. to 11 p.m. and on Sunday from 11 a.m. to 11 p.m., the place has a simple, clean, and stylish ambience. The variety of food is such that you can have a snack or a three-course meal, depending on your needs, at any time. The food is real, fresh, and continental in outlook. The service is fast and friendly, and above all, the menu is good value for the money. The average price for a meal is £7 ($10.50), VAT and service included.

A Local Pub

Fleece and Firkin, St. Thomas Lane (tel. 0272/277150), is Bristol's only pub/brewery, a good place for the real ale aficionado, as the whole place is dedicated to the brewing and serving of ales. One of the specialties is Dogbolter. A huge converted wool warehouse has a long bar with the traditional brass rail, as well as tables and chairs for the more sedentary. At lunchtime daily, they also serve substantial bar food, with meals costing from £3.50 ($5.25). Baked potatoes with various fillings and large bread baps stuffed with cheese, ham, or beef are featured, all served with a salad. Evenings are the real drinking time, with a young, friendly crowd listening to live music. No food is served in the evening. The pub is open from 10:30 a.m. to 2:30 p.m. and 5:30 to 10:30 p.m.

Chapter XII

THE COTSWOLDS

1. Wotton-under-Edge
2. Tetbury
3. Malmesbury
4. Cirencester and Painswick
5. Cheltenham
6. Royal Sudeley Castle
7. Bibury
8. Burford and Minster Lovell
9. Shipton-under-Wychwood
10. Chipping Norton
11. Bourton-on-the-Water
12. Stow-on-the-Wold and Lower Swell
13. Moreton-in-Marsh
14. Broadway
15. Chipping Campden

THE COTSWOLDS, a once-great wool center of the 13th century, lie mainly in the county of Gloucestershire, with parts dipping into Oxfordshire, Warwickshire, and Worcestershire. If possible, try to explore the area by car. That way you can spend hours surveying the land of winding goat paths, rolling hills, and sleepy hamlets, with names such as Stow-on-the-Wold, Wotton-under-Edge, Moreton-in-Marsh, Old Sodbury, Chipping Campden, Shipton-under-Wychwood, Upper and Lower Swell, and Upper and Lower Slaughter (often called the Slaughters). These most beautiful of English villages keep popping up on book jackets and calendars.

Cotswold lambs used to produce so much wool that they made their owners rich, wealth they invested in some of the finest domestic architecture in Europe, made out of the honeybrown Cotswold stone. The wool-rich gentry didn't neglect their church contributions either. Often the simplest of villages will have a church that in style and architectural detail seems to rank far beyond the means of the hamlet.

"Come on in through the kitchen" is all you need hear to know that you've found a home-like place where naturalness and friendliness prevail. Many readers will want to seek out comfortable (even though unchic) accommodations in little stone inns that exist in the midst of the well-known and sophisticated hotels that advertise heavily. Perhaps you'll be served tea in front of a two-way fireplace, its walls made of natural Cotswold stone. Taking your long pieces of thick toasted bread, saturated with fresh butter, you'll find the flavor so good you won't resist putting on more chunky cherry jam.

Or maybe you'll go down a narrow lane to a stately Elizabethan stone manor, with thick walls and a moss-covered slate roof. Perhaps you'll arrive at haying time and watch the men at work in the fields beyond, as well as the cows and goats milked to produce the rich double cheese you'll be served later. Your dinner that night? Naturally, a roast leg of Cotswold lamb. If you arrive at a different season, you can enjoy the warmth and crackle of the logs on the fire in the drawing room.

Or you may want to settle down in and around Cheltenham, where the view from your bedroom window of the Severn Valley to the Malvern Hills to the Welsh mountains is so spectacular that old King George III came for a look. The open stretches of common, woodlands, fields, and country lanes provide the right setting for picnics. Life inside your guesthouse may be devoted to comfort and good eating—baskets of fresh eggs, Guernsey milk, cream, poultry, and a variety of vegetables from the garden.

If your tastes are slightly more expensive, you may seek out a classical Cotswold manor (and there are dozens of them) featuring creamy fieldstone, high-pitched roofs, large and small gables, towering chimneys, stone-mullioned windows, a drawing room with antique furnishings, a great lounge hall, an ancient staircase, and flagstone floors. Such Cotswold estates represent England at its best, with clipped hedges, rose gardens, terraces, stone steps, sweeping lawns, age-old trees, and spring flowers. You can revel in a fast-disappearing English country life, perhaps rent or borrow a pink coat (actually, it's red), and go on a genuine hunt, chasing a sly fox.

After leaving Bristol (our last stopover), we will head north, with Stratford-upon-Avon as our eventual goal. However, along the way, I've picked out what I consider the most rewarding Cotswold villages. Perhaps you'll find others equally enchanting on your own.

The adventure begins in:

1. Wotton-under-Edge

At the western edge of the Cotswolds, in Gloucestershire, Wotton-under-Edge is in the rural triangle of Bath (23 miles), Bristol (20 miles), and Gloucester (20 miles). Many of its old buildings indicate its former prosperity as a thriving wool town. One of its obscure claims to fame is that it was the home of Sir Isaac Pitman, who invented shorthand. Its grammar school is one of the oldest in England, founded in 1384 and once attended by Dr. Edward Jenner, the discoverer of the vaccine against smallpox.

WHERE TO STAY: In the heart of the village, the **Falcon,** Church Street (tel. 0453/842138), is a typical plastered Cotswold stone inn, with attractively priced accommodation rates. B&B costs £11 ($16.50) per person, inclusive of VAT and service. The owners are Irene and Bill Suffell and Cath and Tony Stephenson, who watch after the needs of their guests very well. They run their 17th-century coaching house as a family concern and will provide bar meals and snacks as well as evening meals upon request.

2. Tetbury

In the rolling Cotswolds, Tetbury was never in the mainstream of tourism (like Oxford or Stratford-upon-Avon). However, ever since an attractive man and his lovely bride moved there and took the Macmillan place, a Georgian building on nearly 350 acres, it is now drawing crowds from all over the world.

Charles and Diana will, of course, doubtless one day be King and Queen of England. Their nine-bedroom mansion, Highgrove, lies just outside the town on the way to Westonbirt Arboretum. The house cannot be seen from the road, but you might see the Princess of Wales shopping in the village.

Princess Anne, an avid horsewoman, and her husband, Mark Phillips, also live in the vicinity.

The town has a 17th-century Market Hall and lots of antique shops along with trendy boutiques (one called Diana's).

FOOD AND LODGING: Right in the commercial but attractive center of town, **The Gentle Gardener,** Long Street (tel. 0666/52884), offers a beer garden in back. Run by Malcolm and Julie McClellan, it was in its early days a coaching inn known as "The Lamb" before the Jacobite patrons of the place renamed it "The Ormond's Head." A mellow old place, it has a stone walled garden with ancient apple trees, along with herbs and Victorian roses. Inside, 18 well-furnished bedrooms are rented, 14 of which contain private facilities. The charge is £21 ($31.50) in a single, £41 ($31.50) in a twin or double. You can also stay here on half-board terms at a cost of £31 ($46.50) per person. Its restaurant features fresh local produce, and there is a wine bar serving not only fine and reasonably priced wines but also selections from a charcoal grill. The hotel serves a three-course dinner for £14 ($21).

The Crown Inn, Gumstool Hill (tel. 0666/52469), one of the best bargains in this very expensively priced Cotswold town, is a stone-built structure with three gables. A friendly pub is found downstairs, serving fine wines and good beer and ale which in fair weather can be enjoyed in a garden. Bar snacks are available, and you can also order full dinners costing from £8 ($12). Rooms are small but comfortable, often with beamed ceilings. Singles rent for £16 ($24), doubles for £26 ($39). Units contain hot and cold running water, and there is central heating.

On the outskirts, **The Hare & Hounds Hotel,** Westonbirt (tel. 066688/233), lies 2 ½ miles southwest of Tetbury on the A433. One of the more substantial buildings in the area, it has stone-mullioned windows and gables and is set in its own 10 acres of private grounds with two hard tennis courts. Originally a farmhouse in the 19th century, the Hare & Hounds was turned into a Victorian inn, and the lounge and country bars remain from those days. However, the main hotel building was added as late as 1928 but it was constructed so faithfully in the original stone that it looks much older. This traditional country hotel, often favored as a site of conferences, is run by the Price brothers, and they do a good job welcoming and entertaining guests, making the place a worthy splurge choice. Only three of their 27 well-furnished bedrooms don't have private baths, but all of them are comfortable, with many amenities. The cost ranges from £35 ($52.50) in a single to a high of £57 ($85.50) in a double. Under a hammerbeam ceiling, the restaurant serves a combination of British and continental dishes, with seasonal specialties. A four-course table d'hôte dinner goes for £12 ($18).

3. Malmesbury

At the southern tip of the Cotswolds, the old hill town of Malmesbury in the county of Wiltshire is moated by the Avon River. In the center of England's Middle West, it makes a good base for touring the Cotswolds. Cirencester is just 12 miles away; Bibury, 19 miles; and Cheltenham, 28 miles. Malmesbury is a market town, with a fine market cross. Its historical fame is reflected by the Norman abbey built there on the site of King Athelstan's grave. You can walk around the ruins and go through the cloister gardens.

Malmesbury is considered the oldest "borough" in England, as it was granted its charter by Alfred the Great in 880. In 1980, it celebrated its 1,100th anniversary. Some 400 years ago the Washington family lived there, leaving their star-and-stripe coat-of-arms on the church wall. In addition, Nancy Hanks, Abraham Lincoln's mother, came from Malmesbury. The town still has members of the family, noted for their lean features and tallness. The Penns of Pennsylvania also originally came from Malmesbury.

FOOD AND LODGING: A Cotswold cottage in a tranquil setting, **The Chestnuts,** Cleverton, near Chippenham (tel. 06662/3472), lies about 3¼ miles to the east of Malmesbury. Mrs. Sandra McDowell rents out two comfortable rooms, each with color TV, a radio, and beverage-making facilities in the centrally heated house. Half board costs £17 ($25.50) per person and includes a traditional English breakfast and a choice of dinner, with good English cookery. Log fires and two acres of land in the heart of the country make staying here a worthwhile experience.

The **Apostle Spoon Restaurant,** Market Cross (tel. 06662/3129), nestling between the abbey and the octagonal market cross, was built in the 13th century as the abbey hospice. The original well can be seen incorporated into the bar. Owned and operated by Dan and Ann Walker, the Quality Cuisine restaurant offers morning coffee, lunches, bar lunches, afternoon teas, and dinners. The dinner menu has such delicacies as a ramekin of boiled crab sautéed with mushrooms, white wine, brandy, and cream and topped with grated cheese. As a main course, try the filet steak Apostle Spoon, marinated in brown ale, filled with oysters and Stilton, and cooked to your order. Lunches cost around £4 ($6), with dinners going for £10 ($15) and up. The Spoon is open Tuesday to Saturday: morning coffee, 10:30 to 11:40; lunch, noon to 2 p.m.; afternoon tea, 3 to 5:30; and dinner, 7 to 9:15 p.m. Sunday lunch is from 12:15 to 1:45 p.m. This building is reputed to be the oldest house in the oldest borough in England

4. Cirencester and Painswick

CIRENCESTER: Don't worry about how to pronounce the name of the town. Even the English are in disagreement. Just say "siren-cess-ter" and you won't be too far wrong. Cirencester is often considered the unofficial capital of the Cotswolds, probably a throwback to its reputation in the Middle Ages when it flourished as the center of the great Cotswold wool industry.

In Roman Britain, five roads converged on Cirencester, which was called Corinium in those days. In size, it ranked second only to London. Today it is chiefly a market town, a good base for touring, as it lies 34 miles from Bath, 16 from the former Regency spa at Cheltenham, 17 from Gloucester, 36 from Oxford, and 38 from Stratford-upon-Avon. The trip from London is 89 miles.

Corinium Museum

On Park Street, the museum houses the archeological remains left from the Roman occupation of Cirencester. The mosaic pavements found on Dyer Street in Cirencester in 1849 are the most important exhibit. And the provincial Roman sculpture (Minerva, Mercury), the pottery, the bits and pieces salvaged from long-decayed buildings, provide a remote link with the high level of civilization that once flourished here. The museum has been completely redeveloped and modernized. It's open from 10 a.m. to 5:30 p.m. weekdays, 2 to 5:30 p.m. on Sunday. Admission is 55p (83¢) for adults; children, 25p (38¢). For information, telephone 0285/5611.

Cirencester Lock-Up

The restored 19th-century, two-cell jail, or lock-up as it was called in its heyday, on Trinity Road (tel. 0285/5611), is open daily by arrangement, so visitors can see interpretive displays including architectural conservation in the Cotswolds. Details of the exhibits here may be acquired at the Corinium Museum.

Cirencester Parish Church

Dating back to Norman times and Henry I, the Church of John the Baptist overlooks the Market Square. (Actually, a church may have stood on this spot in Saxon times.) In size, the Cirencester church appears to be a cathedral, not a mere parish church. It is in fact one of the largest parish churches in the country. The present building represents a variety of styles, largely Perpendicular, including its early 15th-century tower. Among the treasures inside are a 15th-century pulpit and a silver-gilt cup given to Queen Anne Boleyn two years before her execution.

Where to Stay

La Ronde Guest House, 52–54 Ashcroft Rd. (tel. 0285/4611), is run by Mr. and Mrs. N. E. Shales, who have family rooms as well as doubles, twins, and singles. In the town center, within walking distance of Cirencester Park, the abbey grounds, and the museum and parish church, the small hotel is licensed. The dining room offers a varied menu and an extensive wine list. Dinner is from £9 ($13.50), and midday bar snacks are available. The hotel has central heating and hot and cold water basins in all the rooms.

Bathless singles rent for £18.50 ($27.75) and singles with private baths for £20.50 ($30.75). Doubles cost from £28.50 ($42.75) to £32.50 ($48.75), depending on the plumbing. There's a color TV lounge, and visitors find the cocktail bar cozy and attractive. La Ronde can serve as your center for touring the Cotswolds. The owners will give you a printed leaflet, describing in detail 14 different tours that can easily be done in one day while based at their premises.

Wimbourne Guest House, 91 Victoria Rd. (tel. 0285/3890), is a Cotswold stone house, built in the Victorian era (1886). It is near the town center and marketplace which is dominated by the parish church. Nearby lie Cirencester Park, with 3,000 acres of beautifully wooded parkland, the abbey grounds, and the Corinium Museum. A friendly and welcoming atmosphere is provided by the owners, Dianne and Marshall Clarke. All the bedrooms have private baths, color TV, beverage-making facilities, clock radio-alarms, and are centrally heated. Rates are £10 ($15) to £12.50 ($18.75) per person for B&B, with an evening meal costing £6.50 ($9.75). There's a free car park.

Raydon House Hotel, 3 The Avenue (tel. 0285/3485), is only five minutes from the town center, in a peaceful residential area adjoining an attractive garden complex. This Victorian mansion is owned by W.R. and A. Peniston, who rent 16 large bedrooms, charging £15 ($22.50) in a bathless single, £25 ($37.50) in a single with private bath, and £35 ($52.50) in a double with private facilities. A full English breakfast is included in the rates. All the units have tea/coffee-making equipment. The hotel has an excellent restaurant and bar. If you are driving, there is space for your car in the parking area. From Market Place, drive along Cricklade Street and Watermoor Road, turning left on The Avenue.

Warwick Cottage Guest House, 75 Victoria Rd. (tel. 0285/66279), is a small B&B operated by Dave and Pat Gutsell, within easy walking distance of the town center. The four bedrooms have hot and cold water basins, color TV, radios, and beverage-making facilities. Two of them have private bathrooms. They rent for £10 ($15) to £12 ($18) per person for B&B. A range of snack-type meals is available, and a four-course dinner goes for £6.50 ($9.75). The Gutsells can provide such amenities as bike rental, babysitting, women's hairdressing, and transportation to and from the train and bus stations.

Cottage of Content, 117 Cricklade St. (tel. 0285/2071), is a delightful little restaurant owned and run by Mr. and Mrs. Pugh, who cook, serve, and even do the washing up. Serving only in the evening, they have a variety of succulent meals, or T-bone steaks, all served with fresh vegetable, salads in season, and a dessert. Meals begin at £10 ($15). They are open daily (except Sunday, Monday, and bank holidays) from 7:30 to 9:30 p.m. to 10:30 p.m. Saturday.

Where to Eat

Shepherds Wine Bar, Fleece Hotel, Market Place (tel. 0285/68507). Its half-timbered facade hints at its origins as an Elizabethan coaching inn. Inside, a handful of open fireplaces warm the beamed interior whenever it's chilly. This establishment has an attractive and more upmarket restaurant, but it also presents a congenial wine bar where local residents shuffle through a dusting of sawdust. Under a low ceiling, the decor consists of dividing curtains and wood panels. Hours are from 10:30 a.m. to 2:30 p.m. and 7 to 11 p.m., and meals cost from £6 ($9). Try one of their usually reliable daily specials, and, to finish, one of their selections of English cheese. Or else sample everybody's favorite dessert: raspberry and hazelnut meringue. The location is across the courtyard from the hotel.

Crown, 17 West Market Place (tel. 0285/3206), is the best-loved pub in town. A coaching inn since the 14th century, it stands opposite the lovely parish church. Many of its original architectural features have been preserved, and the old beams tell a story of long ago. The Crown serves pub food that's far above the usual offerings, and daily specials are written on a blackboard menu. Try such dishes as grilled sardines or calves liver with bacon and avocado. Meals are from £8 ($12). The setting is one of log fires, country chairs, cushioned pews, and plain stonework. The hotel has as its core a courtyard. Hours are from 11 a.m. to 2:30 p.m. and 6 to 11 p.m.

PAINSWICK: The sleepy little town of Painswick, four miles northeast of Stroud, is considered a model village. All its houses, although erected at different periods, blend harmoniously, because the former villagers used only Cotswold stone as their building material. The one distinctive feature on the Painswick skyline is the spire of its 15th-century parish church. The church is linked with the legend of 99 yew trees, as well as its annual Clipping Feast (when the congregation joins hands and circles around the church as if it were a Maypole, singing hymns as they do). Ancient tombstones dot the churchyard.

Where to Stay

Falcon Hotel, New Street (tel. 0452/812189), is a limestone Georgian era building across from the village churchyard. Originally built in 1554, then reconstructed in 1711, the hotel is owned by the Kimber family, who have 12 rooms, the majority of which contain private baths or showers and are comfortably furnished. Each unit has hot and cold running water, tea-making equipment, and shaver points. A single costs £25 ($37.50), a double or twin-bedded unit £38 ($57). Special reduced rates are sometimes quoted on Friday and Saturday nights. Guests enjoy use of a cocktail lounge, very English with flowery wallpaper, and twin limestone fireplaces illuminate the dining room. Even if you're not staying at the hotel, you may want to consider a meal here at a cost of £12 ($18). Dishes include tournedos Rossini, roast lamb with mint sauce, and cuts from their own Aberdeen Angus beef. Meals are served from noon to 2 p.m. and 7:15 to 10 p.m. The dining room is closed on Sunday night.

Where to Dine

Johnstone's Restaurant, Canton House, New Street (tel. 0452/812092), is one of the finest restaurants in the area, the creation of owner Andrew Johnstone who used to live in America. The food is prepared with style, and fresh ingredients are handled with expertise in kitchen. Fish, meat, and poultry are prepared in both English and continental ways, and, for dessert, you might happily face an iced walnut parfait with chocolate sauce. Lunches cost from £5 ($7.50), dinners from £9 ($13.50) and up. A traditional Sunday lunch is presented from noon to 2 p.m., costing £6.75 ($10.13). Otherwise, hours are Tuesday to Sunday noon to 2 p.m. and 7 to 10 p.m.

5. Cheltenham

In a sheltered area between the Cotswolds and the Severn Vale, a mineral spring was discovered by chance. An interesting legend is that the people of this Cotswold stone village noticed pigeons drinking from a spring, and observed how healthy they were. As a result of this story, the pigeon has been incorporated into the town's crest.

Always seeking a new spa, George III arrived in 1788 and launched the town. In trouble because of a liver disorder, the Duke of Wellington also is responsible for fanning its praise. Lord Byron came this way too, proposing marriage to Miss Millbanke.

Some 100 miles from London, Cheltenham is one of England's most fashionable spas. Its architecture is mainly Regency, with lots of ironwork, balconies, and verandas. Attractive parks and open spaces of greenery make the town inviting.

The main street, the Promenade, has been called "the most beautiful thoroughfare in Britain." Rather similar to the Promenade are such thoroughfares as Lansdowne Place and Montpellier Parade. The design for the dome of the Rotunda was based on the Pantheon in Rome. Montpellier Walk, with its shops separated by caryatids, is one of the most interesting shopping centers in England.

Guided walking tours of Cheltenham leave from the **Tourist Information Centre,** Promenade (tel. 0242/522878). However, an advance notice of at least two days is required.

WHERE TO STAY: In the heart of Cheltenham, **Carr's Hotel,** 42 Clarence St. (tel. 0242/524003), is a Georgian Hotel, taken over and redecorated by Mr. and Mrs. Douglas and their son, John. Carr's is close to the National Coach Station and the local bus station. It is opposite the art gallery, museum, and library. The Douglas family are warm and friendly, creating an inviting atmosphere. The hotel has 15 bedrooms, renting for £13 ($19.50) in a single, and from £22 ($33) to £23 ($34.50) in a double or twin. Special rates will be quoted for the family rooms. There is an extensive menu for a traditional English breakfast (included in the room prices), and a choice from the table d'hôte or a grill menu if you'd like to take dinner at your hotel.

Eveleigh, 56 Prestbury Rd. (tel. 0242/512692), is a large Victorian guesthouse run by Mrs. Luker, who charges £13 ($19.50) per person nightly for B&B. The house is well kept, tastefully decorated, and furnished with firm and comfortable beds. There are facilities for making tea and coffee. This is a suitable choice for those seeking budget accommodations. Rooms contain hot and cold running water, and there is access to the showers and toilets on the landing. A bus leads to the center of Cheltenham, a ten-minute walk away (six, if you're speedy).

North Hall Hotel, Pittville Circus Road (tel. 0242/20589), is a substantial and attractive 19-bedroom house, which lies close to the center of town as well as the race course and Pittville Park. There's free parking in the private forecourt. The house is nicely appointed, with full central heating. Rooms, well furnished and comfortable, contain color TV, beverage-making facilities, central heating, hot and cold running water, and razor plugs. In a double, the rate is £20 ($30), dropping to £13 ($19.50) in a single. Children are granted reductions. There's a lounge and dining room which serves good but simple English-style food, such as roast chicken with savory stuffing or roast beef with horseradish sauce, a complete meal costing from £5.50 ($8.25).

The **Lawn Hotel,** 5 Pittville Lawn (tel. 0242/526638), is a well-maintained Regency house built within the iron gates leading to Pittville Gardens and Pump Room. The house is one of 300 constructed around the same town as well as one of the few in the neighborhood that are still single units. Theresa and Steve Boyle rent nine rooms to guests, each of whom pays £11 ($16.50) for B&B or £16 ($24) for half board. The rooms have tea/coffee-making facilities and some have color TV. In addition to an evening meal, a variety of snacks is available and afternoon tea is served. The Boyles keep a bulletin board and information counter with details of nearby cultural events. The house is only four minutes' walk from the town center and bus station.

On the Outskirts

The **Cleeve Hill Hotel,** 3 miles north of Cheltenham, near Bishops Cleeve (tel. 024267/2052), is a 12-bedroom family-run hotel on the edge of the Cotswold Way, looking out over the Vale of Gloucester. Simeon J. Collins is the capable resident proprietor of this hotel, which is in an excellent position to be a base for seeing the Cotswolds. The bedrooms all have hot and cold water basins, two having complete baths and one with its own shower facilities. You can have a TV set placed in your room on request. B&B is priced at £13 ($19.50) to £16 ($24) per person, depending on the plumbing. The brick building housing the hotel sits above the A46 road and has its own car park. You can enjoy visiting the bar, dining in the restaurant, or watching TV in the lounge. The hotel is centrally heated.

DINING IN CHELTENHAM: An imposing Regency building, **Montpelier Wine Bar and Bistro,** Bayshill Lodge, Montpelier Street (tel. 0242/527774), was converted from an old established shop to a cellar bistro and a first-floor wine bar. Very busy at lunchtime, but worth the effort to get in, it offers a choice of some 12 wines by the glass. Then you can select a hot meal from the blackboard menu. A hot soup is always featured among the various appetizers, then cold meats and salad, hot meat pies, smoked fish, lasagne, interesting salads, and a good selection of desserts. You'll pay around £6 ($9) for a satisfying meal either in the cellar or, in good weather, on the terrace. It is open Monday to Saturday from noon to 2:30 p.m. and 6 to 10:30 p.m.

Forrest Wine Bar, Imperial Lane (tel. 0242/538001). Wines are sold here by the glass, which you can sip while admiring the lofty ceilings of this room, a former bakery. The menu changes daily but could include carrot and Brazil nut soup, followed by a dish of the day of pork and bacon kebabs marinated in barbecue sauce, lamb steak with Dijonnaise sauce, or chicken cacciatore. All this, plus fresh peach trifle, would come to only £5.50 ($8.25). A variety of less expensive dishes, such as eggplant and tomato gratin with salad or fresh spinach and cheese crêpes served with salad, are available for £2.50 ($3.75). VAT is included in all prices. Hot food is served from 12:30 to 2:15 p.m. and 6:30 to 10:30 p.m.

Retreat, 10 Suffolk Parade (tel. 0242/35436), is centrally located, a friendly, often crowded oasis, popular with young people, who come here for fine wine and reasonably priced, freshly prepared food. Its most distinctive feature is its plant-filled garden courtyard. Frankly, lunch from noon to 2:15 p.m. can get a little rushed, but the atmosphere is more mellow in the evening from 6 to 9 p.m. (closed Sunday). Meals cost from £6 ($9) and are likely to include an array of fresh salads—usually good, healthy ingredients often blended into a medley of imaginative combinations. The bread also carries out the health theme, as it's most often granary or pita. Hot dishes are likely to include whole-wheat spaghetti with a tomato and meat sauce or curried crab puffs. Save room for the equally rewarding desserts.

Below Stairs Restaurant, 103 Promenade (tel. 0242/34599), in the heart of the spa, is, as suggested by its name, below street level. You can enter from the Promenade through a basement doorway. But this is no dank, Dickensian cellar: it's one of the best and most rewarding targets for food and drink in Cheltenham. The international menu caters to local and foreign tastes alike. For example, crêpes filled with ratatouille is a trendy selection, and you'll nearly always do well to order one of the fresh fish dishes, most likely rushed in from the seacoast of southern England. Game is a seasonal feature. Set lunches cost from around £6 ($9), with dinners going for £9 ($13.50), but a lot depends on your appetite and what you order. Lunch is from noon to

3 p.m. Monday to Saturday, dinner from 6 p.m. to midnight Thursday through Saturday only.

6. Royal Sudeley Castle

In 1962 Elizabeth Chipps of Lexington, Kentucky, met and married Mark Dent-Brocklehurst, the wedding taking place in the 16th-century chapel of Royal Sudeley Castle. In 1970 her husband died, and Elizabeth inherited the 15th-century castle in the Cotswold village of Winchcombe, six miles northeast of Cheltenham. The history of the castle dates back to Saxon times, when the village was the capital of the Mercian kings.

Elizabeth remarried in 1979 and now lives at Sudeley as Lady Ashcombe. The castle remains in trust for her two children, Henry and Mollie Dent-Brocklehurst. Lady Ashcombe first reopened the castle to visitors shortly after her first husband's death. As one of England's finer stately homes, Sudeley Castle attracts visitors from all over the world. There are works of art by Constable, Turner, Rubens, Van Dyck, and many others. The ancient dungeon tower houses a unique collection of toys and dolls spanning four centuries. Exhibits include the rocking horse that once belonged to the beheaded King Charles I.

Peacocks strut in the formal gardens which are set in a landscape of rolling farmland and parks. Water fowl abound on the lake beside the castle. The exquisite herb garden dates from the time when Queen Catherine Parr, sixth and surviving wife of King Henry VIII, lived here after the death of the monarch. She died and was buried at Sudeley Castle. (Of Henry's six wives, only Catherine Parr and Anne of Cleves, whom he divorced, outlived him.)

The castle also has a coffeeshop good enough to participate in the "Taste of England" scheme, offering a variety of cold salads and home-cooked meats. A selection of desserts is also available. The cream teas are mouthwatering.

The castle is open daily from noon to 5 p.m. April 1 to October 31. The grounds are open from 11 a.m. Admission prices are £2.95 ($4.43) for adults, £1.80 ($2.70) for children.

A telephone call to the secretary at Sudeley Castle (tel. 0242/602308) will provide you with any up-to-the minute information you may wish before visiting.

If you'd like to stay near the castle, **Isbourne House,** Castle Street, in Winchcombe (tel. 0242/602281), is an excellent choice. Edward Saunders and his friend and colleague, Dick Whittamore, receive guests in a part Georgian, part Elizabethan Cotswold stone house surrounded by a well-kept garden, stone walls, and wrought-iron gates. They operate an extremely high standard B&B, providing a full platter English breakfast in the morning. Charges are from £25 ($37.50) to £35 ($52.50) in a double, depending on whether you have the room with complete bath or with just a shower. On 24 hours notice, elegant dinners can be provided. Sometimes guests can be introduced to country pastimes such as horse, country, or lurcher shows or fox hunting English style.

7. Bibury

Bibury, on the A433 road from Burford to Cirencester, is one of the loveliest spots in the Cotswolds. In fact, the utopian romancer of Victoria's day, poet William Morris, called it England's "most beautiful village." On the banks of the Coln River, Bibury is noted for **Arlington Row,** a gabled group of 15th-century cottages, its biggest and most-photographed drawing card. The row is protected by the National Trust.

Arlington Mill Museum (tel. 028574/368) dates from the *Domesday* survey and was in use until the outbreak of World War I. There are four floors in the mill and three in the cottage, with 16 exhibition rooms. It contains a collection of 19th-century mill machinery, along with agricultural and domestic bygones, Victorian costumes, toys, and furniture, and changing exhibitions of contemporary art. The mill is open March to October and winter weekends from 10:30 a.m. to 7 p.m., charging £1 ($1.50) for adults, 50p (75¢) for children for admission.

FOOD AND LODGING: If you want to stay in this famed village, you will have to pay big-splurge prices at the inns previewed below.

Bibury Court Hotel (tel. 0285/74337) is a Jacobean manor house built by Sir Thomas Sackville in 1633 (parts of it date from Tudor times). Its eight acres of grounds are approached through a large gateway, the lawn extending to the encircling Coln River. The structure is built of Cotswold stone, with many gables, huge chimneys, leaded-glass stone-mullioned windows, and a formal gravel entryway. Inside there are many country manor furnishings and antiques, as well as an open stone log-burning fireplace. In a double with bath, the rate ranges from £38 ($57) to £42 ($63), dropping to £22 ($33) to £25 ($37.50) in a single, the latter with bath. Many of the rooms have four-poster beds, original oak paneling, and antiques. Meals are an event in the stately dining room, with lunchtime bar meals priced from £3.50 ($5.25) and dinners costing from £13 ($19.50).

The Swan Hotel (tel. 0285/74204) is a scene-stealer. Before you cross over the arched stone bridge spanning the Coln, pause and look at the vine-covered facade. Yes, it's the same view that has appeared on many a calendar. The former coaching inn will bed you down for the night in one of its handsomely appointed chambers, all with bath or shower, costing £30.50 ($45.75) in a single, £52.50 ($78.75) in a double nightly for B&B. A traditional English breakfast and VAT are included. All the rooms have been modernized, and there are many comforts. The special feature of the Swan is the small stretch of trout stream reserved for guests. The restaurant serves an English and French cuisine, with lunches costing from £10.25 ($15.38) and dinners from £13.75 ($20.25).

8. Burford and Minster Lovell

BURFORD: In Oxfordshire, Burford is the gateway to the Cotswolds. This unspoiled medieval town, built of Cotswold stone, lies 19 miles to the west of Oxford, 31 miles from Stratford-upon-Avon, 14 miles from Blenheim Palace, and 75 miles from London. Its fame rests largely on its early Norman church (c. 1116) and its High Street, lined with coaching inns. Oliver Cromwell passed this way, as (in a happier day) did Charles II and his mistress, Nell Gwynne. Burford was one of the last of the great wool centers, the industry bleating out its last breath as late as Victoria's day. You may want to photograph the bridge across the Windrush River where Queen Elizabeth I once stood. Burford is definitely equipped for tourists, as the antique shops along the High will testify.

Food and Lodging

The Bull, High Street (tel. 099382/2220), today a 14-bedroom three-star hotel in the Cotswolds, has a long history, as it is the oldest hotel in Burford. The building—or at least its core—dates from around 1475, but it may be older than that. Establishment of a rest house for Burford Priory was authorized by Papal Bull (hence the name) sometime before 1403. The priory was given by Henry VIII to his barber-surgeon in 1544 after the monasteries were dissolved, and from 1603, when John Silvester became inn holder, the history of the Bull can be traced. Such visitors as the king's troops in the battle with Cromwell's Parliament Dragoons, Cromwell himself, and later King Charles II and Nell Gwynne have been lodged here. During the 18th century, the Bull was an important stop on the road, with 40 coaches passing through Burford each day. The hotel is distinguished by its brick-and-stone front dating from 1658, when the "new" additions increased the size of the hostelry. Today, old-world charm blends with modern comfort. Eleven of the bedrooms have private baths, and all have central heating. Depending on the plumbing, singles cost £24 ($36) to £28 ($42), and double or twins go for £37.50 ($56.25) to £42.50 ($63.75). Even if you don't stay here, drop in for a drink in the pub or for a good meal.

The **Corner House Hotel,** High Street (tel. 099382/3151), is informally run by Mr. and Mrs. Bateman, who like company. Actually, their hotel is an extension of their home. They've taken over this 15th-century Cotswold stone-and-timbered village residence, adding bathrooms to all the bedrooms. The units are attractive and comfortable. B&B costs from £17 ($25.50) per person nightly. You can also take your meals at the Corner House. At noon, an à la carte luncheon menu is served for £2.50 ($3.75) and up, or you can order bar snacks. Dinner, also à la carte, costs from £5 ($7.50). The Corner House is closed from mid-November to mid-February.

The **Boltons,** 9 Windrush Close (tel. 099382/2051), is Mrs. E. Barrett's three-bedroom guesthouse made of Cotswold stone with a natural state roof. From many of the windows, you can look out over gardens, green fields, hills, and sheep. The units are kept clean and neat. Singles cost from £12 ($18) and doubles from £17 ($25.50). Mrs. Barrett is a friendly hostess whose warmth, added to that of a cup of tea in the pleasant living room, takes the chill off a cool Cotswold day.

A MUSEUM AT NORTHLEACH: Opened in 1981, the **Cotswold Countryside Collection,** Fosseway (Cotswold District Council) (tel. 0451/60715), is a museum of rural life displays. You can see the Lloyd-Baker collection of agricultural history, including wagons, horse-drawn implements, and tools, as well as a "seasons of the year" display. A Cotswold gallery records the social history of the area. "Below Stairs" is an exhibition of laundry, dairy, and kitchen. The museum's home was a House of Correction, and its history is displayed in the reconstructed cellblock and courtroom. The museum is open daily from 10 a.m. to 5:30 p.m. (from 2 to 5:30 p.m. on Sunday). Admission is 55p (83¢) for adults, 25p (38¢) for children. Northleach lies off the A40 between Burford and Cheltenham.

MINSTER LOVELL: From Oxford along the A40, you pass through Witney. Soon after, you turn right at the Minster Lovell signpost, about half a mile off the highway between Witney and Burford. Long since passed by the main road, the village is visited because of **Minster Lovell Hall and Dovecot** (tel. 0993/75315). In ruins, the hall dates from the 1400s. The medieval dovecot with nesting boxes survives. An early Lovell is said to have hidden in the moated manor house and subsequently starved to death after a battle in the area. The hall and dovecot can be visited from 9:30 a.m. to 6:30 p.m. mid-March to mid-October weekdays, from 2 to 6:30 p.m. on Sundays. Off-season hours are 9:30 a.m. to 4 p.m. weekdays and 2 to 4 p.m. on Sundays. Admission is 75p ($1.13) for adults, 35p (53¢) for children.

It was in the village that the legend of the mistletoe bough originated by the Windrush River. Minster Lovell is mainly built of Cotswold stone, with thatch or stone-slate roofs. It's rather a pity that there is a forest of TV aerials, but the place is still attractive to photographers.

Where to Stay

Mrs. Brown, Hill Grove Farm, Crawley Road (tel. 0993/3120), accepts paying guests with a warm welcome at her stone farmhouse set on about 75 acres 1½ miles east of Minster Lovell in the direction of the village of Crawley. This family-run place has views over the Windrush Valley which is traversed by a river. She accepts a handful of guests for £20 ($30) to £22 ($33) in a double or twin-bedded room, including a country breakfast.

Mr. and Mrs. Woodin, The Olde Farm, Asthall Leigh, near Minster Lovell (tel. 099387/608), also accept paying guests at their 15-acre site. The origins of this sheep farm go back to the 1600s. Guests get plenty of conveniences and good food and comfort at prices ranging from £21 ($31.50) to £27 ($40.50) in a double or twin-bedded room, including a hearty breakfast. The higher price is for an accommodation with a private bath.

9. Shipton-under-Wychwood

Taking the A361 road, en route from Burford to Chipping Norton, you arrive after a turnoff at the little village of Shipton-under-Wychwood, in Oxfordshire. It's about four miles north of Burford, but don't blink—you'll pass it right by. The monks of Bruern Abbey used to run a hospice in the village.

Trips providing an insight into Cotswold life of the past and present are offered by **Guy's Tours** (tel. 0993/831532), with headquarters at Gales Green guesthouse, recommended below. Guy Brady supplies cars and guides for individual or group tours of little Cotswold villages, Oxford colleges, houses and gardens, and the places where such literary figures as Nancy and Jessica Mitford, Restoration poet and wit John Wilmot, second Earl of Rochester, and other writers once lived. You can look at antiques, architectural treasures, and other sights that make the Cotswolds so attractive. Prices vary, so telephone for information.

FOOD AND LODGING: A small Cotswold stone inn, **The Lamb,** High Street (tel. 0993/830465) is perfect if you're seeking a simple village stopover serving an excellent cuisine. It's owned by Hugh and Lynne Wainwright, who give a cordial welcome. Singles cost £25 ($37.50), twins or doubles going for £37.50 ($56.25), breakfast and VAT included. The inn is in the country style, and each accommodation has a private bath. Main dishes in the dining room are based on the season and the day's marketing. They are likely to include roast pheasant, grilled trout with almonds, and duck cooked in various ways. A set menu is £10.75 ($16.13). A Sunday roast beef or lamb lunch is traditionally offered with all the trimmings for £7 ($10.50). The restaurant is closed on Sunday evening.

Hunters Lodge (tel. 0993/830400) is a large house of Cotswold stone, where Janet and Jim Taylor receive B&B guests with a warm welcome. The lodge and its various outbuildings and barns have been listed as of historical and architectural interest, dating them from the early 1600s or before. The comfortable, carpeted bedrooms have either showers and hot and cold water basins or else complete private baths. They rent for £11 ($16.50) to £13 ($19.50) per person, double occupancy preferred, the price depending on the plumbing. Guests are given their own keys to the house so that they are free to come and go at their leisure. A cozy sitting room with TV is a good place to relax. You're sure to enjoy the big English breakfast. Among the attractions of Hunters Lodge are the original oak beams. The Taylors have many pictures painted by local artists which you can purchase if you wish.

Gales Green (tel. 0993/830072), now deep into its third century, is one of the most charming places to stay in this old Oxfordshire village. For those seeking a guesthouse of personality, this is it. Charging from £20 ($30) per person for B&B, it is inviting, welcoming, and comfortable. Only trouble is, there are so few rooms you might not get in in peak season unless you've reserved well in advance.

10. Chipping Norton

Just inside the Oxfordshire border, Chipping Norton is another gateway to the Cotswolds. Since the days of Henry IV it has been an important market town. Its main street is a curiosity in that it follows along a slope, making one side terraced over the lower part. The highest town in Oxfordshire, at 650 feet, Chipping Norton was long noted for its tweed mills. Seek out its Guildhall, its church, and its handsome almshouses. If you're touring, you can search for the nearby Rollright Stones, more than 75 stones forming a prehistoric circle 100 feet in diameter, the Stonehenge of the Cotswolds. Chipping Norton lies 11 miles from Stratford-upon-Avon.

WHERE TO STAY: Originally a coaching inn, the **Crown and Cushion Hotel,** High Street (tel. 0608/2533), dates back to 1497. All 18 bedrooms are centrally heated and have private baths, color TV, and tea/coffee-making facilities. Some have phones and four-poster beds. They rent for £21.50 ($32.25) per person, a full English breakfast and VAT included. Only fresh food is used in the cuisine, with à la carte or table d'hôte meals being served in the comfortable dining room or, in winter, in the cozy lounge bar, with its oak beams and open log fire. Jim and Margaret Fraser, the proprietors, can arrange for guests to make use of the local squash club, a few minutes' walk from the hotel, where a sauna, solarium, and Jacuzzi are featured. An outdoor beer garden at the hotel is a lure for summer visitors.

Hill View Guest House, 1 London Rd. (tel. 0608/2682), is the domain of Elizabeth and Roy Horobin, a warm, friendly, chatty couple. They charge £10 ($15) per person for B&B in rooms with facilities for making hot beverages. The big English breakfast they serve will keep you going for your excursions into the country roundabout. It's only about a 3½-mile walk to the Rollright Stones.

WHERE TO EAT: For good food at reasonable prices, try **Nutters,** 10 New St. (tel. 0608/41995). The owner, Elizabeth Arnold, sees that everything is homemade with fresh ingredients—no additives, artificial colorings, or flavorings used. Menus are low in salt, fat, and sugar, but high in fiber. A bright, refreshing stopover, with a small garden in back, it offers the best food in town for the price. However, it serves only from 10 a.m. to 6 p.m., Tuesday to Saturday, with meals costing from £5 ($7.50). If you go early for morning coffee, try one of their potato scones. Main dishes are likely to include beef in red wine, vegetable lasagne, or cheese cauliflower. You order what you want at a counter, then carry your tray to one of the tables.

AN OLD INN AT BLEDINGTON: On the B4450 across country from Chipping Norton to Stow-on-the-Wold, in the heart of the Cotswolds, nestles the **Kings Head Inn & Restaurant,** The Green, Bledington (tel. 060871/365). This 16th-century inn, occupying a beautiful position right on the village green complete with brook and ducks, has been catering for travelers since time immemorial. If you are just passing through, you can stop for real ale to be quaffed in the beer garden or in the low-ceilinged, timbered bars with inglenook fireplaces. Hot and cold buffet bar "fayre" is available at lunchtime, with hot bar food and a full à la carte menu served in the evening. Prices are from £3.50 ($5.25) to £8 ($12). You can also spend the night in one of the lovely double bedrooms here, all with private baths, color TV, and beverage-making facilities. The cost of £36 ($54) per night in a double includes a full breakfast. The bar here is noted for its King Henry punch.

11. Bourton-on-the-Water

In this most scenic Cotswold village, you can be like Gulliver, voyaging first to Brobdingnag, then to Lilliput. Brobdingnag is Bourton-on-the-Water, lying 85 miles from London, on the banks of the tiny Windrush River. Its mellow stone houses, its village greens on the banks of the water, and its bridges have earned it the title of the Venice of the Cotswolds. But such a far-fetched label as that tends to obscure its true charm.

To see Lilliput, you have to visit the **Old New Inn** (tel. 0451/20467). In the garden is a near-perfect and most realistic model village. It is open daily from 8:30 a.m. till dusk, and costs 70p ($1.05) for adults, 50p (75¢) for children. (The Old New Inn is also recommended as a lodging place, below.)

Among the attractions in the area, **Birdland** (tel. 0451/20689) is a handsomely designed garden set on about five acres, containing from 1,200 birds of 362 different species. Exotic birds and flowers include the most varied and largest collection of penguins in any zoo, with underwater viewing and a tropical house. In the latter are hummingbirds. Many of the birds are at liberty for the first time in the world. Hours are March to November from 10 a.m. to 6 p.m.; otherwise, from 10:30 a.m. to 4 p.m. Admission is £1.75 ($2.63) for adults and 90p ($1.35) for children to 14 years.

Also in the area, the **Windrush Trout Farm** stands on Rissington Road (tel. 0451/20541). On the River Windrush, it offers you a chance to wander among the ponds and enjoy your own picnic while watching the trout which can be fed with food obtained at a shop. It is open daily from 10:30 a.m. to dusk from March to November. Admission is 70p ($1.05) for adults and 35p (53¢) for children.

If you're coming to the Cotswolds by train from London, you'll find the nearest rail station is Moreton-in-Marsh, eight miles away. However, buses make connections with the trains.

WHERE TO STAY: Built of sturdy Cotswold stone, **Brookside Hotel,** Riverside (tel. 0451/20371), was originally a 17th-century manor house in the center of the village, standing on the banks of the River Windrush. All of its original character has been retained, and it has the atmosphere of a gracious country home. It is owned and managed by Jane and Neil Hardie. Even the dining room, with its dark polished wood, time-blackened Windsor chairs, and bright and cheery fabrics, is an ideal setting for an English cuisine. Homemade soups, pies, and pastries, with liberal amounts of fresh produce, even trout and local game when in season, are offered. Every bedroom is centrally heated, with emphasis on comfort and simplicity rather than sophistication. All rooms have hot and cold running water, radio, and intercom, and some of the larger rooms have a private bathroom. Depending on the plumbing, B&B costs from £19 ($28.50) per person nightly. VAT is included, but not service. You can have a typical English dinner in the dining room for £8 ($12), or, if you wish, bar snacks are available.

Duke of Wellington Inn, Sherbourne Street (tel. 0451/20539), provides comfortable accommodations in a centuries-old former coaching inn. Heavily beamed ceilings and stone walls give a warm Old English atmosphere. Guests in the three bedrooms (who share two public bathrooms) pay from £25 ($37.50) to £27 ($40.50) per night in a double room. Bar snacks are available in the bistro, or you can also have evening meals. Car parking is available. You can relax with fellow guests in the residents' TV lounge.

Chester House Hotel & Motel, Victoria Street (tel. 0451/20286), is a weathered, 300-year-old Cotswold stone house, built on the banks of the Windrush River. Owned and managed by Mr. J. Davies, the hotel is a convenient place at which to stay. A double room without bath rents for £32 ($48), increasing to £42 ($63) with bath, TV, and phone.

The **Old New Inn,** High Street (tel. 0451/20467), can lay claim to being the leading hostelry in the village. Right in the center, overlooking the river, it's a good example of Queen Anne design. But it is mostly visited because of the miniature model village in its garden (referred to earlier). Hungry or tired travelers are drawn to the old-fashioned comforts and cuisine of this most English inn. The B&B rate is from £19 ($28.50) per person nightly, including service charge and VAT. The rooms are comfortable, with homey furnishings, soft beds, and eight with private bath. Packed lunches at £4 ($6) will be provided for your excursion jaunts.

On the outskirts, **Farncombe,** Clapton (tel. 0451/20120), lies about 2½ miles from Bourton-on-the-Water. The little hamlet is a "secret address" known to the discerning English who stay here when the more popular and more famous place is overrun with tourists. The helpful owners receive guests from April to October. They rent out only three rooms, each suitable for two persons, charging from £19 ($28.50). Considering the hospitality and the comfort, the rooms are worth far more. Try to make this place your center for touring the Cotswolds, branching out on day trips. The property opens onto views of the Windrush Valley.

WHERE TO EAT: Previously recommended, the **Old New Inn,** High Street (tel. 0451/20467), with its popular beer garden, is one of the best places for food in Bourton-on-the-Water. You can dine here on different price levels. Local residents know of its good, fresh, and very reasonably priced bar snacks (which can easily be turned into a full meal), or else you can partake of more formal dinners in the evening. At lunchtime, guests not only enjoy the snacks, but can play darts or chat with the villagers. Lunch from noon to 2:30 p.m. costs from £4.50 ($6.75). At night you can order from 6 to 8:30 p.m., enjoying good English cookery, with meals costing from £10.50 ($15.75).

Also previously recommended, the **Chester House Restaurant,** Chester House Hotel and Motel, Victoria Street (tel. 0451/21522), is another good place to go for food. Part of this popular motel which was constructed around what had been a stable for horses, the dining room serves good-tasting food from noon to 2 p.m. and 7 to 9:30 p.m. In the off-season, no lunches are offered. The chef relies on quality ingredients in turning out a selection of English and continental dishes, with lunches costing from £7.50 ($11.25), dinners from £10.50 ($15.75).

A VISIT TO THE "SLAUGHTERS": Midway between Bourton-on-the-Water and Stow-on-the-Wold are the twin villages of **Upper** and **Lower Slaughter.** Don't be put off by the names, because these are two of the prettiest villages in the Cotswolds. Actually the name "Slaughter" was a corruption of "de Sclotre," the original Norman landowner.

The houses are constructed of honey-colored Cotswold stone, and a stream meanders right through the street, providing a home for the ducks that wander freely about, begging scraps from kindly visitors.

12. Stow-on-the-Wold and Lower Swell

STOW-ON-THE-WOLD: This is an unspoiled Cotswold market town, in spite of the busloads of tourists who stop off en route to Broadway and Chipping Campden, nine to ten miles away. The town is the loftiest in the Cotswolds, built on a wold (rolling hills) about 800 feet above sea level. In its open market square, you can still see the stocks where offenders in days gone by were jeered at and punished by the townspeople throwing rotten eggs. The final battle between the Roundheads and the Royalists took place in Stow-on-the-Wold. The town, which is really like a village, is used by many for exploring not only the Cotswold wool towns, but Stratford-upon-Avon, 21 miles away. The nearest rail station is at Moreton-in-Marsh, four miles away.

Where to Stay

The **White Hart,** The Square (tel. 0451/30674), is a limestone fronted building on the main square of town. You register at the bar of the street-level pub, which is laden with brass accents and open fireplaces. Since 1698, this has been a thriving coaching inn, welcoming wayfarers from all over the world. There is a healthy respect for the traditional around here, and the place has a mellow old atmosphere of uneven floors and low doorways. The innkeeper offers only four bedrooms, none with private bath, but they have color TV and coffee-making equipment. Half-board rates (the most economical way of staying here) range from £15 ($22.50) to £20 ($30) per person. The food, especially the steaks, are good tasting, and you can also order such specialties as steak and kidney pie and grilled local trout.

The **Old Stocks Hotel,** The Square (tel. 0451/30666), in spite of its ominous name, is one of the most inviting inns of Stow-on-the-Wold. Alan and Caroline Rose run this mellow limestone-fronted inn overlooking the market place which has been the scene of so much violence and bloodshed, although all is peaceful today except for the hordes of tourists who pass through. The hotel is made up of a trio of buildings from the 1500s and 1600s, which were constructed in part with natural stone and oak timbers from sailing vessels. The bedrooms, a total of 21, all with private bath, are tastefully decorated with many amenities. The charge is £22.50 ($33.75) per person for a bed and a full English breakfast. Even if you're not staying here, you may want to order a three-course table d'hôte dinner, costing £9.50 ($14.25). In winter you can warm yourself by a log fire, retreating to a walled garden in summer.

Limes, Tewkesbury Road (tel. 0451/30034), is a Georgian building of character which lies about a five-minute walk from the heart of this famed Cotswold village. It has a lovely garden, and in chilly weather log fires make it warm and inviting. Bedrooms are pleasantly and comfortably furnished, all with washbasins. One room with an early Victorian four-poster bed has a private shower. Rates are £20 ($30) for two people in a standard room, £26 ($39) for two in the four-poster unit. The owners, Mr. and Mrs. Keyte, personally supervise the operation of the Limes.

West View, Fosseway (tel. 0451/30492), is run by Nancy White, who charges from £7.50 ($11.25) to £8 ($12) for a comfortable bed and a good English breakfast. The shared bathroom has a shower with plenty of hot and cold running water. Mrs. White has furnished the place attractively, in part with antiques. She is most gracious as a hostess, serving a large breakfast. The location is about a block from the center of Stow.

South Hill Farmhouse, about ½ mile outside Stow-on-the-Wold (tel. 0451/31002), is a large period structure of Cotswold stone, where John and Sue Gilbert offer hospitality to travelers. They have three rooms each with a double and a single bed and one room with twin beds. One of the two shared baths has a tub, the other a shower. The charge is from £10.50 ($15.75) per person night for bed and a substantial English breakfast, with top-quality meat from the shop John runs. The Gilbert family is helpful with tour suggestions, and the daughters will saddle a horse for children to ride.

Where to Eat

St. Edwards, The Square (tel. 0451/30351), is a little tea room that's easy to spot, as it opens onto the market square. It has a formal facade with fluted stone pilasters. Inside, you can have morning coffee, lunches, or afternoon tea, while sitting on Windsor chairs in front of an open fireplace. Lunch is served from noon to 2:30, for £6 ($9) for three courses. A typical one, prepared with care, might include homemade soup, a steak "pastie," apple pie with fresh cream, and coffee. The set afternoon tea is £2.40 ($3.60) and includes freshly baked muffins and cake.

Prince of India, Park St. (tel. 0451/31198), has awakened the tastebuds of Stow-on-the-Wold with spices skillfully used in a wide range of dishes. If you have an asbestos palate, try the meat vindaloo, but you can also order less tongue-wilting fare, including tandoori chicken or hot and sour prawns Madras. Leavened bread is served, and there are many vegetarian dishes. A savory beginning is the lentil soup. Meals cost from £8 ($12) and are served from noon to 3 p.m. and 6 to 11:30 p.m. seven days a week.

Flower City, Park Street (tel. 0451/31989), is the local gathering place for those seeking Cantonese and Peking cuisine. The menu offers no great surprises, but each dish is well prepared. Main courses include roast duck Canton style, king prawns with cashews, and beef with bean sprouts in an oyster sauce. A dinner for two costs only £12 ($18) and is served from noon to 2:30 p.m. and 6 to 11:30 p.m. (closed Sunday, Monday, for lunch on Wednesday, and all day Tuesday).

LOWER SWELL: Near Stow-on-the-Wold, Lower Swell is a twin. Both it and Upper

Swell, its sister, are small villages of the Cotswolds. The hamlets are not to be confused with Upper and Lower Slaughter.

Where to Stay and Eat

Old Farmhouse Hotel (tel. 0451/30232) is a small, intimate hotel in the little village, with the comfortable and informal air of its 16th-century farmhouse origins. It is owned by Rollo and Rosemary Belsham, who have a reputation for excellent food and a warm, friendly atmosphere. The hotel is pleasantly furnished, and the cocktail bar (which only has a restaurant-and-residential license) and restaurant are popular with locals and visitors alike. Light lunches (soup, smoked salmon, deep-fried fish, sandwiches, and ice cream among other foods) are served Monday to Saturday from noon to 2 p.m., and on Sunday a traditional English lunch is featured. Dinner, from 7 to 9:30 p.m. daily, is likely to be a mouthwatering, filling repast. A table d'hôte meal goes for £9.25 ($13.88), with à la carte dinners cost around £12 ($18). The bedrooms are comfortable and have central heating and color TV. Most units contain private baths, and two are equipped with beautiful four-posters. For B&B in high season, the price is from £38.50 ($57.75) to £48 ($72) for two persons, VAT included. The latter price is for the rooms with the four-poster beds.

13. Moreton-in-Marsh

Connected by rail to Paddington Station in London (83 miles away), Moreton-in-Marsh is an important center for British Rail passengers headed for the Cotswolds because it is so near many villages of interest—Bourton-on-the-Water (8 miles), Stow-on-the-Wold (4 miles), Broadway (8 miles), Chipping Campden (7 miles), Stratford-upon-Avon (17 miles away).

Each of the stone Cotswold towns has its distinctive characteristics. In Moreton-in-Marsh, look for a 17th-century Market Hall, an old Curfew Tower, and then walk down the High, where Roman legions trudged centuries ago. The town once lay on the ancient Fosse Way. Incidentally, if you base here, don't take the name "Moreton-in-Marsh" too literally. Marsh derives from an old word meaning border.

WHERE TO STAY: Set on the main street of town, Moreton House, High Street (tel. 0608/50747), is perhaps the most desirable budget accommodation in the center of this popular Cotswold village. Chris and Chic Dempster own this mellow old house which has a Tudor facade of honey-colored sandstone. It has a very correct and attractive tea room on its street level. You register at a small reception desk inside this room. There are 12 attractively furnished and comfortable bedrooms upstairs, four of which contain private showers. The rate ranges from £11.50 ($17.25) to £13 ($19.50) per person in a double, depending on the plumbing, and from £13 ($19.50) in a bathless single. One suite at £15 ($22.50) per person is available, and tariffs include an English breakfast. Dinner will be served if arranged in advance at this family-run place, which has been in the same line of owners for a century.

The Rectory (tel. 0608/50389) offers B&B in the attractive manor home of Bridget and Tom Ekin, a charming couple with a vast fund of information about the Cotswolds. Their rooms are well cared for and comfortably furnished. One room has a private living room overlooking their garden and a private entrance. Each morning a full English breakfast is served. The charge is £16 ($24) per person per day for B&B. The Rectory is open May to October.

Townend Cottage and Coach House, High Street (tel. 0608/50846), is a 17th-century coach house in the heart of the Cotswolds, combining old world charm with modern comforts, including central heating. Several of the bedrooms have private showers and toilets. Doubles cost from £26 ($39) to £40 ($60) per night, breakfast included. Dinners, prepared by the owner, cost from £10.50 ($15.75). The house has good parking space and an attractive garden.

The Cottage (tel. 0608/50370) is where Helen Procter accepts guests in her house dating from the 1600s. The cottage has been modernized inside, providing comfortable rooms. B&B is priced at £10 ($15) per person nightly, accommodation being in either a double or a twin-bedded room with a shared bath. The reception here is gracious.

A Farmhouse in Dorn

A mile from Moreton-in-March, just off the A429, **New Farm,** Dorn (tel. 0608/50782), is mainly a dairy farm of about 250 acres and 90 Friesian milk cows. The farmhouse, built about 300 years ago of Cotswold stone, is where Mrs. C.M. Righton accepts B&B guests in three bedrooms, all with hot and cold water basins, accommodating no more than six to eight persons per night. She charges £10 ($15) per person for bed and a full English breakfast, served in the dining room where a blaze in the large fireplace keeps things cozy on cool days. The full English breakfast, the only meal served, comes with fresh, hot, crispy bread. Mrs. Righton accepts guests from Easter to mid-October.

WHERE TO EAT: In the center of the village, **Market House,** 4 High St. (tel. 0608/50767), is an ideal choice for morning coffee, a good-tasting lunch, afternoon tea, or a reasonably priced and well-prepared dinner. In summer, service is from 9 a.m. to 10 p.m., but in winter it operates on a more limited schedule—10 a.m. to 6 p.m. In this cozy tea room atmosphere, you can enjoy grills, such main dishes as chicken Kiev or fried plaice (perhaps haddock or cod), followed by a piece of moist cake or some other dessert. Sandwiches and fresh salads are also served, with meals costing from £5 ($7.50).

14. Broadway

This is the best-known Cotswold village. Its wide and beautiful High Street is flanked with honey-colored stone buildings, remarkable for the harmony of their style and design. Overlooking the Vale of Evesham, Broadway, a major stopover for bus tours, is mobbed in summer. That it retains its charm in spite of the invasion is a credit to its character.

Broadway lies near Evesham at the southern tip of Worcestershire, more than just a sauce familiar to steak lovers. Many of the prime attractions of the Cotswolds as well as the Shakespeare Country lie within easy reach of Broadway: Stratford-upon-Avon is only 15 miles away. The nearest rail stations are at Evesham and Moreton-in-Marsh.

For lodgings, Broadway has the dubious distinction of sheltering some of the most expensive inns in the Cotswolds. The guesthouses can also command a good price—and get it.

BED AND BREAKFAST: In the heart of an expensive village, **Olive Branch Guest House,** 78–80 High St. (tel. 0386/853440), is a budget oasis. You can get an English breakfast and a comfortable bed, as the guest of Peter and Sylvia Riley, from £12 ($18) per person nightly. They have eight bedrooms (two singles, one double, and five large family rooms), all with running water. Two showers are available, and two bedrooms have private baths. Behind the house is a large walled English garden and car park. The house, dating back to the 17th century, retains its old Cotswold architectural features. Guests are allowed a discount in the owners' attached antique shop.

Half Way Guest House, 89 High St. (tel. 0386/852237), is a little treasure in this picture-postcard village. True to its name, it lies halfway between the village green and the edge of town. Formerly a coaching inn, built in 1600, it has a carriage passageway to a rear courtyard. It is now a first-rate guesthouse, owned by the salty and dynamic Mrs. Brodie, who used to operate one of Broadway's fine antique shops. She is assisted by her daughter, Gillian, and they rent out six bedrooms. They charge from £15

($22.50) to £17 ($25.50) per person for B&B. In the olden days you'd have come out for less, as an old inn sign they display will testify—"4 pence a night for bed, 6 pence with pot luck. No more than five to sleep in one bed." For the antique-lover, the house is sheer heaven, as Mrs. Brodie brought with her an excellent collection of furniture and bric-a-brac, enough to make each bedroom as well as the living room special and tasteful. Even the bathroom, opening onto the rose garden, has a gilt cherub and a Cromwellian chair.

Milestone House, 122 High St. (tel. 0386/853432), is the kind of place to be found only in England. Richard and Gloria Walton have created a home-like atmosphere in this little private hotel. Once an inn, known as the Fox & Dog, it now receives B&B guests. The rooms have soft, downy beds and are immaculately kept. Nor have modern comforts been neglected; there is central heating and plenty of hot and cold running water. Singles cost £27 ($40.50), and doubles go for £17 ($25.50) per person, including a full breakfast and VAT. Rates depend on the room location, time of year, and plumbing. Excellent English breakfasts are prepared. In addition, you can order dinner at £10 ($15), served from 7 to 8:30 p.m., and they are licensed to sell drinks.

Helen and Alan Richardson, Whiteacres, Station Road (tel. 0386/852320), operate one of the best B&Bs in this high-priced town. A Victorian house, it rents three comfortably furnished doubles, plus another unit with twin beds, each equipped with private showers and toilets. A single costs from £14 ($21), while a double goes for £21 ($31.50). Guests gather in the lounge to have afternoon tea with Mr. and Mrs. Richardson.

Pathlow House, 82 High St. (tel. 0386/853444), places you right in the heart of the action of this model village of the Cotswolds. From spring through autumn, guests from around the world are received at this house of character, which rents out doubles (two on the ground floor), a twin, and a family room. Guests share three bathrooms. The rate for B&B is from £22 ($33) for a double, which is quite reasonable considering the heartbeat location of the property. The house is centrally heated, and all bedrooms have TV and beverage-making facilities. The house, run by William and Kay Brown, has parking in the rear.

East Bank, Station Drive (tel. 0386/852659), is a bargain for Broadway. The stone house where Anne and Ken Evans receive B&B guests is in a tranquil location, about a 12-minute walk from the center of the town, with unlimited parking in the grounds of the house or on the approach drive. The comfortable rooms, all with private baths, cost £17 ($25.50) to £20 ($30) for single occupancy of a double unit, £22 ($33) to £25 ($37.50) for a double or twin-bedded accommodation, and £30 ($45) to £35 ($52.50) for a family room. The house is centrally heated, but in addition a log fire blazes in the guest lounge during cooler weather. With prior notice, a selection of evening meals can be provided, costing £6 ($9) to £7.50 ($11.25) each.

The **Crown and Trumpet,** Church Street (tel. 0386/853202), might be ideal if you're seeking an old English inn with pub action which also rents out a few rooms. The B&B rate here ranges from £12 ($18) to £13 ($19.50) per person in a double. It's far more economical, however, to take the half-board rate, costing from £15 ($22.50) to £16 ($24) per person nightly. There are no private baths. Good English "fayre" is served, and the location is right near the old village green of Broadway.

Mill Hay, Snowshill Road (tel. 0386/852498), the home of the owner of Broadway Tower and Country Park, accepts a small number of B&B guests in this Queen Anne country house in a secluded position in the village. In a garden setting, the house has a spacious lounge where guests watch color TV. All the bedrooms, which vary greatly in position and furnishings, have hot and cold water basins and tea/coffee-making equipment, and some have private baths. For B&B, the price in rooms with queen- or king-size beds, one with a four-poster, is £35 ($52.50) for two people. Others rent for £20 ($30) in a four-poster single room to £30 ($45) for a couple in a large twin unit. The house is centrally heated. Smoking is prohibited in the bedrooms. The house is closed from mid-January until March. Mary Loggie is the courteous manager of Mill Hay.

WHERE TO DINE: Set back from the long High Street, **Hunter's Lodge Restaurant** (tel. 0386/853247), is surrounded by its own lawns, flowerbeds, shady trees, and flowering shrubs. The stone gables are partially covered with ivy, and the windows are deep-set with mullions and leaded panes. There is a formal entrance, with a circular drive and a small foyer furnished with antiques. The restaurant serves outstanding food, prepared by its chef-patron. The menu, which is changed every month, features high-quality seasonal food and fresh vegetables. Also, homemade chocolates are available. Lunches are served from 12:30 to 2 p.m., and dinners from 7:30 to 10 p.m. Lunch with a wide menu is reasonably priced, costing from £8 ($12) per person, and dinners begin at £13 ($19.50) per person. The Lodge is closed on Sunday night and all day Monday.

  Goblets Wine Bar, High Street (tel. 0386/852255), is a 17th-century inn built of Cotswold stone, with black-and-white timbered walls. It is filled with antiques which are much enjoyed by the people of Broadway themselves, who frequent the place along with tourists. Additions to the menu, which is changed every six weeks, are marked on the blackboard, and orders should be placed at the bar. The menu is limited but tasty. It begins with such appetizers as taramasalata and goes on to such daily specials as chicken marengo or duckling in orange sauce. About four desserts appear daily, including, for example, a hot gingerbread pudding. The coffee is well made, and the welcome is warm and friendly. The house wine goes for £5 ($7.50) a bottle, and dinner costs from £6 ($9). Hours are 11:30 a.m. to 2:30 p.m. except Sunday when Goblets is open from noon to 2 p.m. In the evening the doors open at 6, closing at 10:30 p.m. (until 11 p.m. on Friday and Saturday). The location is next to the Lygon Arms.

  Cotswold Restaurant, The Green (tel. 0386/853395), is an old favorite. Mrs. Susan Webb keeps the same high standards, serving meals all day. She specializes in good English food, offering a two-course lunch for £4.50 ($6.75) that is likely to include roast beef, or pork or chicken. Fresh vegetables are served with it, along with a homemade dessert. The homemade ice cream has been a feature of the establishment for decades. Each customer gets personal service as well. Hours are Monday to Friday from 10 a.m. to 6 p.m. In summer Mrs. Webb keeps her place open for suppers, the last booking at 8 p.m. (closing at 8 p.m. Saturday and Sunday). From soup to coffee, including a glass of French wine, the charge is from £8 ($12). At the high tea you are likely to find the Broadway locals. In season ask for a "fruit tea," which is likely to include fresh strawberries or raspberries along with homemade ice cream or fresh cream.

15. Chipping Campden

  The English, regardless of how often they visit the Cotswolds, are attracted in great numbers to this town, once a great wool center. It's neither too large nor too small. Off the main road, it's easily accessible to major points of interest, and double-decker buses frequently run through here on their way to Oxford (36 miles away) or Stratford-upon-Avon (12 miles away).

  On the northern edge of the Cotswolds above the Vale of Evesham, Campden, a Saxon settlement, was recorded in the *Domesday Book*. In medieval times, rich merchants built homes of Cotswold stone along its model High Street, described by the historian G.M. Trevelyan as "the most beautiful village street now left in the island." The houses have been so well preserved that Chipping Campden to this day remains a gem of the Middle Ages. Its church dates from the 15th century, and its old Market Hall is the loveliest in the Cotswolds. Look also for its almshouses. They and the Market Hall were built by a great wool merchant, Sir Baptist Hicks, whose tomb is in the church.

WHERE TO STAY: Recent renovations have given **Seymour House Hotel & Restaurant,** High Street (tel. 0386/840429), more style than ever. A Georgian house built of honey-colored Cotswold stone, it is attractively managed by David Hallett along with his wife, Jean. He is very familiar with the hotel business, as he was the former deputy director of the leisure division of British Transport Hotels. Their property contains a half acre walled garden, with ancient yews and a mulberry tree, plus a car park. They offer 15 pleasantly furnished bedrooms. The charge is from £15 ($22.50) per person in a bathless room, £18 ($27) per person with full shower or bath. The dining room is filled with red walls, wheel-backed chairs, and illustrations, everything resting under a beamed ceiling. A table d'hôte dinner, open to non-residents, costs £10 ($15) and is served from 7:30 to 9 p.m.

Sandalwood House, Back-Ends (tel. 0386/840091), offers comfortable accommodation and a friendly welcome for nonsmokers. Peacefully situated just a five-minute walk from the center of town and surrounded by a beautiful garden, this is one of three similar houses on a short lane. Each of the rooms has a wash basin with hot and cold water, and the bathroom has a bath and shower. There are two dining rooms and a lounge where the owner, Mrs. D. Bendall, serves a hot evening drink. With accommodation for only six people, the atmosphere is one of warmth and friendliness. There is a breakfast menu with a good choice of dishes to start the day. You'll find easy parking right in the drive, and the price is right for such a popular area: £12 ($18) per person, with reductions for four or more nights.

At the far north end of Chipping Campden's High Street **Two Ways,** Leysbourne (tel. 0386/840505), is a restored 18th-century Cotswold stone town house, with lots of exposed beams, stone walls, and flagstone floors comfortably combined with the conveniences of modern living. Mrs. Diana Knight rents a total of six beds in a double room and a twin/family unit, each of which has a hot and cold water basin. Rates are £11 ($16.50) to £13 ($19.50) per person for B&B. The house has central heating and a private lounge with color TV for use of guests. Unrestricted parking for cars is available on a service road, and bikes are secure at the rear of the property.

Mill Cottage, Calf Lane (tel. 0386/840594), is a 15th-century Cotswold stone cottage with a thatch roof, on a quiet street but within a one-minute walk of the center of town. Miss E.M. Forrester accommodates up to five guests in comfortable rooms, costing £11 ($16.50) per person for B&B. It's preferable to call in advance, as the cottage is not always open to guests. Readers Tippins and Marinez Goldston of Dothan, Alabama, say staying here is like "sleeping in a fairytale cottage."

The Dragon House, High Street (tel. 0386/840734), stands close to the Market Place. It is run by a pleasant and friendly Yorkshire proprietor, Mrs. Valerie James, who serves you tea in the evening as well as an excellent and plentiful breakfast the next morning. Rooms are attractively decorated and quite comfortable, costing from £9 ($13.50) per person for a bed and filling breakfast, quite a bargain for high-priced Chipping Campden. A separate house out in the backyard contains two double bedrooms and one modern bath. There's also a living/dining room area with TV.

Trinder House, High Street (tel. 0386/840869), is where Mrs. Dorothy Hart rents out two rooms at a rate of £9 ($13.50) per person for B&B. She is friendly and attractive, and runs her house like a real home. The front door is an often-open stable door with hanging flowers framing the woodwork. Rooms are comfortable and pleasantly furnished.

WHERE TO EAT: A full restaurant and pub are in the **Kings Arms,** The Square (tel. 0386/840256), as well as hotel accommodations. Even if you don't stay here, try to visit for the best bar snacks in Chipping Campden. You're likely to be tempted with artichokes and stilton dressing, baked eggs, crab with gruyère cheese and cream, fresh filet of mackerel with a mustard cream sauce, and taramasalata with hot toast, these items vying with the more prosaic soups and pâtés, all in the £1.20 ($1.80) to £5 ($7.50) range. Bar lunches are served from noon to 2 p.m., dinner from 7:30 to 9 p.m. In the formal dining room, you can order a complete evening meal for £14.50 ($21.75) per person. Main dishes include such continental fare as roast duck in a piquant orange sauce, beef Stroganoff, and filet of pork Calvados. Alexander S. Guthrie, the proprietor of the hotel, also rents comfortably furnished and pleasant bedrooms. Singles cost £25 ($37.50), and twins go from a low of £20 ($30) to a high of £52 ($78).

The **Badger Bistro and Wine Bar,** High Street (tel. 0386/840520), is a very attractive little Cotswold shop with a bar and tables all made of pinewood. A comfortable, cheerful place, it offers such items as grilled local trout, chicken fricassée hunter style, and wholefood lasagne and salad. In fair weather tables are placed in the garden. Colin and Diane Clark, who run the Badger, serve food daily except Thursday from 11 a.m. to 2:30 p.m., 3 to 5 p.m. (afternoon tea), and 7 to 11 p.m. Meals cost from £6 ($9).

Island House/Bagatelle French Restaurant, High Street (tel. 0386/840598), is a tiny restaurant with a handful of rooms to rent. In the center of town, it has inviting outdoor tables, and makes an excellent place for a stopover if you can get in. The owners have only two bedrooms to rent, each fitted with carpeting, color TV, central heating, a shower, and a wash basin. The charge is around £26 ($39) for two persons. This includes a continental breakfast. In the basement restaurant, excellently prepared meals are served, costing from £12 ($18) and including such delectable fare as monkfish in the style of Provence, lambs liver in onion sauce, or skate in black butter. Dinner is served from 7 to 9:30 p.m.

Of the more expensive hotels in town, the **Noel Arms** (tel. 0386/840317) is good if you want a splurge meal in more elegant surroundings. A three-course meal will cost about £12 ($18) and is likely to include such good-tasting English fare as grilled plaice, roast leg of lamb, ham steaks, or a carbonnade of beef. A selection of vegetables is served with the main dishes. Appetizers include the usual soups and prawn cocktails. Desserts are served from a selection of fruit pies and gâteaux. Lunch is served from 12:30 to 2 p.m., dinner 7 to 9 p.m. If you decide to stay here, singles rent for £25 ($37.50) to £28 ($42) for B&B, doubles going for £33.50 ($50.25) to £43.50 ($65.25), prices depending on the plumbing.

Bantam Tea Rooms, High Street (tel. 0386/840386), is a lovely, bow-windowed, 17th-century stone house where old-fashioned English afternoon teas are served. Tea can be just a pot of the brew and a teacake, or you can indulge in home-made scones, crumpets, sandwiches, and homemade pastries and cakes. Lunches are served, with a selection of local ham and salad, chicken pie, pâtés, omelets, and salads. Cream teas cost from £1.50 ($2.25) and meals from £5 ($7.50). The place is open daily from noon to 2 p.m. for lunch and 3 to 5:15 p.m. for tea in summer (opens at 3 p.m. on Sunday). In winter, it is closed on Monday. Other days, a log fire roars out its welcome from the house's original fireplace.

Chapter XIII

STRATFORD AND THE HEART OF ENGLAND

1. Stratford-upon-Avon
2. Warwick
3. Kenilworth Castle
4. Coventry
5. Hereford and Worcester

SO CLOSE TO LONDON, so rich in fascination, the Shakespeare Country in the heart of England is that district most visited by North Americans (other than London, of course). Many who don't recognize the county name, Warwickshire, know its foremost tourist town, Stratford-upon-Avon, the birthplace of England's greatest writer.

The county and its neighboring shires form a land of industrial cities, green fields, and sleepy market towns dotted with buildings, some of which have changed little since Shakespeare's time. Here are many of the places that have magic for overseas visitors, not only Stratford-upon-Avon, but also Warwick and Kenilworth Castles, as well as Coventry Cathedral.

Those who have time to penetrate deeper into the chapter will find elegant spa towns, such as Great Malvern, and historic cathedral cities such as Hereford and Worcester. Scenery ranges from untamed borderlands to gentle plains which give way in the north to wooded areas and meres.

1. Stratford-upon-Avon

The magnitude of traffic to this market town on the Avon River, the oldest and most attractive in Warwickshire, is one of the phenomena of tourism. Actor David Garrick really got the shrine launched in 1769 when he organized the first of the Bard's birthday celebrations. It is no secret by now, of course, that William Shakespeare was born in Stratford-upon-Avon.

Surprisingly little is known about his early life, as the frankest of his biographers concede. Perhaps because documentation is so lacking about the writer, much useless conjecture has arisen (did Elizabeth I really write the plays?). But the view that Francis Bacon authored Shakespeare's body of work would certainly stir up *The Tempest* if suggested seriously to the innkeepers of Stratford-upon-Avon. Admittedly, however, some of the stories and legends connected with Shakespeare's days in Stratford are largely fanciful, invented belatedly to amuse and entertain the vast number of literary fans making the pilgrimage.

Today's magnet, in addition to Shakespeare's Birthplace, is the Royal Shakespeare Theatre, where Britain's foremost actors perform during a long season that lasts from Easter until late October. Stratford-upon-Avon is also a good center for trips to Warwick Castle, Kenilworth Castle, Sulgrave Manor (ancestral home of George Washington), Compton Wynyates, and Coventry Cathedral. The market town lies 92 miles from London, 40 from Oxford, and 8 from Warwick.

THE SIGHTS: In addition to all the attractions on the periphery of Stratford, there are many Elizabethan and Jacobean buildings in this colorful town, many of them administered by the Shakespeare Birthplace Trust Properties. One ticket, costing £4.50 ($6.75) for adults, £2 ($3) for children, will permit you to visit the five most important sights. You should pick up the ticket if you're planning to do much sightseeing (obtainable at your first stopover at any one of the Trust properties). Shakespeare's Birthplace and Anne Hathaway's Cottage are open all year except Good Friday morning and December 24, 25, and 26. From April to October hours are weekdays from 9 a.m. to 6 p.m. (often till 7 p.m. in summer but only until 5 p.m. in October). On Sunday the in-season hours are 10 a.m. to 6 p.m. From November to March the weekday hours are 9 a.m. to 4:30 p.m.; on Sunday, 1:30 to 4:30 p.m. Mary Arden's House, New Place, and Hall's Croft are open all year except Good Friday morning and December 24, 25, and 26. From April to October, weekday hours are 9 a.m. to 6 p.m. (only until 5 p.m. in October); on Sunday, 2 to 6 p.m. From November to March, these three properties are open on weekdays only from 9 a.m. to 4 p.m.

For further information concerning the Trust's activities, send a stamped (English postage, please), self-addressed envelope to the Director, the Shakespeare Centre, Henley Street, Stratford-upon-Avon, CV37 6QW (tel. 0789/204016).

Shakespeare's Birthplace

On Henley Street, the son of a Glover and Whittawer was born on St. George's day (April 23) in 1564, and died 52 years later on the same day. Filled with Shakespeare memorabilia, including a portrait, and furnishings of the writer's time, the Trust property is a half-timbered structure, dating from the early years of the 16th century. The house was finally bought by public donors in 1847 and preserved as a national shrine. You can visit the oak-beamed living room, the bedroom where Shakespeare was born, a fully equipped kitchen of the period (look for the "baby-minder"), and a Shakespeare Museum, illustrating his life and times. Later, you can walk through the garden out back. It is estimated that some 660,000 visitors pass through the house annually. If visited separately, admission is £1.50 ($2.25) for adults, 60p (90¢) for children. Next door to the birthplace is the modern Shakespeare Centre, built to commemorate the 400th anniversary of the Bard's birth. It serves both as the administrative headquarters of the Birthplace Trust and as a library and study center. An extension to the original center, opened in 1981, includes a Visitors' Centre providing reception facilities for all those coming to the birthplace.

Anne Hathaway's Cottage

One mile from Stratford in the hamlet of Shottery is the thatch, wattle, and daub cottage where Anne Hathaway lived before her marriage to the poet. In sheer charm it is the most interesting and most photographed, it would seem, of the Trust properties. The Hathaways were yeoman farmers, and aside from its historical interest, the cottage provides an insight into the life of a family of Shakespeare's day. If the poet came a-courtin', he must have been treated as a mere teenager, as he married Miss Hathaway when he was only 18 years old and she much older. Much of the original furnishings,

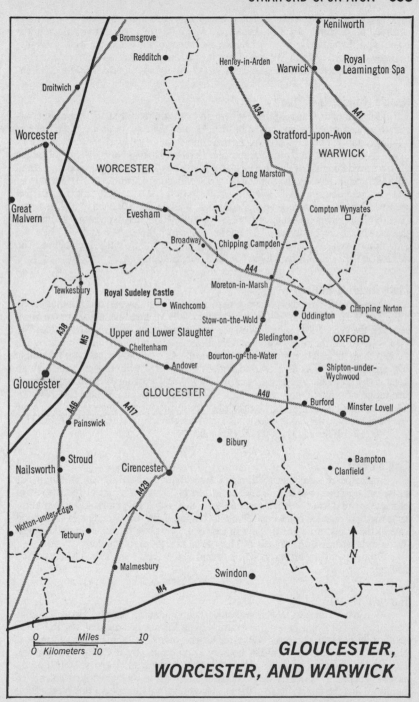

GLOUCESTER, WORCESTER, AND WARWICK

including the courting settle, and utensils are preserved inside the house, which was occupied by descendants of Shakespeare's wife until 1892. After a visit through the house, you'll want to linger in the garden and orchard. You can either walk across the meadow to Shottery from Evesham Place in Stratford (pathway marked), or take a bus from Bridge Street. The admission is £1.40 ($2.10) for adults, 50p (75¢) for children.

Nash's House/New Place

This site is on Chapel Street, where Shakespeare retired in 1610, a prosperous man to judge from the standards of his day. He died there six years later, at the age of 52. Regrettably, only the site of his former home remains today, as the house was torn down. You enter the gardens through Nash's House (Thomas Nash married Elizabeth Hall, a granddaughter of the poet). Nash's House has 16th-century period rooms and an exhibition illustrating the archeology and later history of Stratford. The heavily visited Knott Garden adjoins the site and represents the style of a fashionable Elizabethan garden. New Place has its own Great Garden, which once belonged to Shakespeare. Here the Bard planted a mulberry tree, so popular with latter-day visitors to Stratford that the cantankerous owner of the garden chopped it down. The mulberry tree that grows there today is said to have been planted from a cutting of the original tree. The admission is £1 ($1.50) for adults, 40p (60¢) for children.

Mary Arden's House

Shakespeare's mother, Mary Arden, and her family owned this building in the village of Wilmcote, four miles from Stratford. It is an attractive timber-frame farmhouse of the early 16th century, with herringbone struts on the wing to one side. The plan is usual for the time, with a screened passage from front to back, dividing the kitchen from the hall or main living room, which was originally open to the full height of the roof. A floor was later inserted to give two stories. The rooms are furnished with 16th- and 17th-century pieces. The farm here was still working in 1930, and there is a fine range of outbuildings, including a stone dovecote contemporary to the house. These now contain a large and fascinating collection of objects connected with farming and rural life, and this has been extended into a neighboring farm complex. Admission is £1.40 ($2.10) for adults, 50p (75¢) for children.

Hall's Croft

Shakespeare's daughter, Susanna, lived with her husband, Dr. John Hall, in this house in Old Town, not far from the parish church. This is a beautiful Tudor house of character with a lovely walled garden. Dr. Hall was widely respected and built up a large medical practice in the area. Exhibits illustrating the theory and practice of medicine in the Halls' time are on view in the house, which is furnished in middle-class Tudor style. Admission is £1 ($1.50) for adults, 40p (60¢) for children.

Other interesting sights not administered by the Trust foundation include the following:

Harvard House

Not just of interest to Harvard students and alumni, Harvard House on High Street (tel. 0789/204507) is a fine example of an Elizabethan town house. Rebuilt in 1596, it was once the home of Katherine Rogers, mother of John Harvard, founder of Harvard University. In 1909 the house was purchased by a Chicago millionaire, Edward Morris, who presented it as a gift to the American university. With a profusion of carving, it is the most ornate house in Stratford. Its rooms are filled with period furniture, and the floors, made of the local flagstone, are authentic. Look for the Bible

Chair, used for hiding the Bible during the days of Tudor persecution. Harvard House, charging admission of 75p ($1.13) for adults, 25p (38¢) for students and children, is open April through September from 9 a.m. to 1 p.m. and 2 to 6 p.m. on weekdays, 2 to 6 p.m. on Sunday; November through March, 10 a.m. to 1 p.m. and 2 to 4 p.m. Thursday, Friday, and Saturday only.

Holy Trinity Church

In an attractive setting near the Avon, the parish church of Stratford-upon-Avon is distinguished mainly because Shakespeare was buried in the chancel ("and curst be he who moves my bones"). The Parish Register records his birth and death (copies of the original, of course). No charge is made for entry into the church, described as "one of the most beautiful parish churches in the world," but visitors wishing to view Shakespeare's tomb are asked to donate a small sum, at least 30p (45¢), toward the restoration fund.

A Motor Museum

Stratford-upon-Avon Motor Museum, 1 Shakespeare St. (tel. 0789/69413). Just around the corner from Shakespeare's birthplace is a small but interesting museum, started in 1974 by Bill Meredith-Owens, internationally known motor rally driver; it is now run by his son. The Roaring '20s era is portrayed and consists of many Rolls-Royces (specially built for the maharajas of India, among others), Bugattis, early Jaguars, and many others. They also have a reconstructed garage of the '20s and a specialty bookshop where maintenance books on the old models and vintage cars are for sale, as well as a collection of car badges (not for sale). Admission is £1.35 ($2.03) for adults, 65p (98¢) for children. The museum is open daily from 9 a.m. to 6 p.m. April to October, from 10 a.m. to 4 p.m. November to March. Closed Christmas.

A Theater of History

The World of Shakespeare, Waterside (tel. 0789/69190), opposite the River Avon and the Royal Shakespeare Theatre, is a 25-minute multimedia presentation under the auspices of Heritage Theatre Series Ltd. The show takes you back to the flamboyant England of 1575, following Queen Elizabeth I on her spectacular Royal Progress from London to Kenilworth Castle (ten miles from Stratford-upon-Avon). The performance combines life-size tableaux, with dramatic lighting and sound techniques bringing to life one of the most exciting periods in history. Presentations are given half hourly from 9:30 a.m. to 5:30 p.m. seven days a week year round, except Christmas Day and Boxing Day. Admission is £2 ($3) for adults, £1.50 ($2.25) for children. Facilities include a gift shop, a Bureau de Change, and a cinema.

GETTING THERE: A service allowing you to spend the entire day in Stratford and Shakespeare's Country is the **Shakespeare Connection "Road and Rail Link,"** leaving from London's Euston Station Monday to Friday at 8:35 and 10:40 p.m. and 5:10 p.m.; on Saturday at 8:35 and 10:40 a.m. and 4:40 p.m. This is a safe, sure way for you to attend the Royal Shakespeare Theatre and return to London on the same day. If you only want to attend the evening performance at the theater, again the Shakespeare Connection is your best bet, trains leaving London at 5:10 p.m. Monday to Friday and 4:40 p.m. on Saturday. Returns to London are timed to fit theater performances, normally with departure at 11:30 p.m. from either the Guide Friday Ltd. office, the Civic Hall, 14 Rother St., or just opposite the theater. The service is the fastest way of reaching Stratford from London, journey time averaging two hours. It is operated by **British Rail** and **Guide Friday** (tel. 0789/294466). Prices are £12 ($18) for a single fare, £13 ($19.50) for a same-day round trip, and £19 ($28.50) for a round trip ticket valid for one month. Ask for a Shakespeare Connection ticket at London's Euston Station or at any British Rail London Travel Centre. BritRail pass holders using the service simply pay the bus fare to Stratford-upon-Avon from Coventry.

TOURS AND TOURIST SERVICES: A tourist reception center for Stratford and Shakespeare's Country is operated by **Guide Friday Ltd.**, the Civic Hall, 14 Rother St. (tel. 0789/294466). Their office dispenses free maps and brochures on the town and area and operates tours. Also available is a full range of tourist services, including accommodation reference and car rental. In summer, the office is open daily from 9 a.m. to 7:45 p.m. In winter, hours are 9 a.m. to 5:30 p.m. Monday to Friday, 9 a.m. to 2 p.m. Saturday and Sunday.

Guided tours of Shakespeare's Country leave the Guide Friday office daily. In summer, aboard open-top double-decker buses, departures are every half hour from 9 a.m. to 5 p.m. on the hour and half hour. The tour can be a one-hour panoramic ride, or you can get off at any or all of the Shakespeare Birthplace Trust properties. Anne Hathaway's Cottage and Mary Arden's House are the two logical stops to make outside the town. The price of these tours is £2.50 ($3.75) per person. Tours also are offered to Warwick Castle, Kenilworth Castle, and Charlecote Park, costing £4 ($6) per person; Cotswold Country Villages, £7 ($10.50) per person; Cotswold Country Pubs, £5.50 ($8.25) per person, and Blenheim Palace and Bladon (the Churchill story tour), £7 ($10.50) per person. Tour prices do not include entrance fees at stops made.

ATTENDING THE THEATER: On the banks of the Avon, **Royal Shakespeare Theatre** (tel. 0789/295623), is the number one theater for Shakespearean productions. The season runs for nine months from March to January, with a winter festival of music and ballet in February. The present theater was opened in 1932, after the old Shakespeare Memorial Theatre, erected in Victoria's day, burned down in 1926. The theater employs the finest actors and actresses on the British stage. In an average season, five Shakespearean plays rotate in repertory.

Usually, you'll need reservations: there are two successive booking periods, each one opening about two months in advance. You can best pick these up from a North American or an English travel agent. If you wait until your arrival in Stratford, it may be too late to get a good seat. Tickets can be booked through New York agents Edwards and Edwards or Keith Prowse or direct with the theater box office with payment by major credit card. There are eight lines in, and the number to call is listed above. The price of seats generally ranges from £4.50 ($6.75) to £16.50 ($24.75). A small number of tickets are always kept back for sale on the day of a performance. You can phone from anywhere and make a credit card reservation, picking up your ticket on the day it is to be used, but there is no cancellation once your reservation is made, and you must produce your credit card to collect your ticket. The rules are strict, so be sure you only reserve with your own card and pick up your tickets yourself. You cannot sign up ahead for tickets for someone else to pick up.

In the Victorian Wing of the old Memorial Theatre, spared by the fire of 1926, is the **New Swan Theatre,** opened in 1986, built in the style of an Elizabethan playhouse. Here the Royal Shakespeare Company presents plays from the 1570–1750 period (Elizabethan, Jacobean, and Restoration), which once packed the playhouses of London's Bankside. Tickets cost from £3 ($4.50) to £12 ($18). For information about performances, phone the box office number for the Royal Shakespeare, 0789/295623. This building also houses the company's **Collection,** an exhibition of stagecraft from medieval mummers to the present day, with costumes and props from Royal Shakespeare Company productions. Backstage/RSC Collection tours are available. The Collection is open April to January from 9 a.m. to 6 p.m. weekdays, from noon to 5 p.m. Sunday. Admission is 80p ($1.20) for adults, 40p (60¢) for children.

The company has a third theater in Stratford, **The Other Place,** seating just over 100 persons. New plays are presented, tickets costing £6 ($9).

The Royal Shakespeare Theatre has a package program, the Shakespeare Stop-Over. The packages are available in five categories, beginning at £46.50 ($69.75) for a one-night program of activities, peaking at £108.50 ($162.75) for a two-night package. The programs include dinner at the Box Tree Restaurant in the theater, a seat (either stalls or circle) for any Monday to Saturday performance at the Royal Shakespeare Theatre and the New Swan Theatre (two night or a matinee/evening "Blockbuster" package), and an overnight stay in a choice among 16 hotels, three guesthouses, a period cottage, and a town house. The selection of the hotel determines the cost of the package. Reservations are made by calling Val Mellini at the Royal Shakespeare Theatre, Waterside (tel. 0789/67262) from 9:30 a.m. to 9 p.m.

CAUGHT WITHOUT A ROOM? During the long theater season, the hotels in Stratford-upon-Avon are jam-packed, and you may run into difficulty if you arrive without a reservation. However, if you should visit from April to October during regular office hours (9 a.m. to 5:30 p.m. weekdays, 2 to 5 p.m. on Sunday) you can go to the **Information Centre** at the Judith Shakespeare House, 1 High St. (tel. 0789/293127).

Here a staff person, who has had much experience with travelers on all budgets, will get on the telephone and try to book a room for you in the price range you are seeking.

It is also possible to reserve accommodations if you write well enough in advance. By writing to the Information Centre, you'll be spared having to get in touch with several hotels on your own and running the risk of getting turned down. If you do write, specify the price range and the number of beds required. The center often gets vague letters, and the staff doesn't know whether to book you into a private suite at the Shakespeare Hotel or lend you a cot to put in front of the Royal Shakespeare Theatre. Don't be surprised. Stratford-upon-Avon visitors are a varied group.

BED AND BREAKFAST: A Victorian family house, the **Marlyn Hotel,** 3 Chestnut Walk (tel. 0789/293752), has been welcoming B&B guests since 1890. It is pleasantly and conveniently situated near Hall's Croft, the former home of Shakespeare's daughter, and is within a five-minute walk of the town center and the Royal Shakespeare Theatre. The hotel is centrally heated throughout, each bedroom contains tea- and coffee-making facilities, and there is a small lounge with TV. If you don't want to pack your Shakespeare, don't worry. A copy of the complete works of the Bard is available for reference in every bedroom. Free and unrestricted parking is available under the chestnut trees opposite the hotel. The owners, Mr. and Mrs. Cedric Allen, who have run the hotel since 1973, endeavor to provide guests with comfortable accommodation throughout their stay. Daily rates are £12 ($18) per person for bed and an English breakfast, inclusive of tax.

Midway Guest House, 182 Evesham Rd. (tel. 0789/204154), has four good double rooms, all with hot and cold running water, electric heaters, razor sockets, color TV, and beverage facilities. Two of them have private baths. Janet and Keith Cornwell charge from £9 ($13.50) per person for B&B (less for longer stays). The rooms are homelike and comfortable.

Penny Acres, 183 Evesham Rd. (tel. 0789/299652), is one of the brightest and cheeriest places on this road, operated by Mr. and Mrs. J.M. Taylor, who can accommodate six guests in comfortable and tastefully decorated rooms. Singles, which are hard to find in Stratford-upon-Avon, rent for £9.50 ($14.25), and doubles go for £18 ($27) for B&B. Mrs. Taylor prepares a full English breakfast every morning at the time you prefer. Tea/coffee-making facilities are provided, and the Taylors will arrange for your transportation to and from the train or bus station if you wish.

Lemarquand, 186 Evesham Rd. (tel. 0789/204164), is run by Anne Cross, who offers three bedrooms—two doubles and one twin—each comfortably equipped and containing hot and cold running water. The shared bathroom has a shower much appreciated by her American visitors. Rates of £10 ($15) per person nightly include a full English breakfast and pots of tea. She gives friendly service, and her location is close to the theater and town center.

Ashburton House, 27 Evesham Pl. (tel. 0789/292444), is a guesthouse with a restaurant license and is one of the better selections in Stratford. Evening dinners, particularly pretheater ones, are a specialty. Rooms are handsomely furnished and well equipped with color TV in all units and two with private baths. The establishment is centrally heated, and hot water is available for baths and showers at all times. Hosts are Steve and Bridget Downer, who are delighted to receive foreign visitors, charging them £12.50 ($18.75) per person for bed and a full menu breakfast. Dinners are optional and cost £12 ($18) for the four-course pretheater repast served at 6 p.m., in good time before the eight-minute walk to the Royal Shakespeare Theatre. A six-course dinner at a more leisurely hour for non-theater-goers cost £16 ($24) per person. Advance reservations by letter with a £5 ($7.50) deposit are strongly recommended. All charges are inclusive of service charge and tax.

Aidan Guest House, 11 Evesham Pl. (tel. 0789/292824), is a large Victorian family house, belonging to Kari and Barry Coupe. It has retained some of the best features and character of its architectural period. Close to the town center, the house lies within a five-minute walk of the theater and railway station. All rooms have central heating as well as hot,and cold running water and beverage-making facilities. Some units have private showers. The place is particularly recommended for parents traveling with small children, as babysitting can be arranged. Children's cots are also available. Charges are £11 ($16.50) per person nightly, including breakfast, service, and taxes. The Coupes keep their place impeccably clean and have tastefully furnished it. Fresh flowers abound.

The Hollies, 16 Evesham Pl. (tel. 0789/66857), is a welcoming B&B establishment run by a mother and daughter, Mrs. Mavis Morgan and Mrs. L. Burton. Their guesthouse is in a renovated three-story building which was once a school, although it looks like a stately old home. The bedrooms have plenty of wardrobe and breathing space, and beds have good, firm mattresses. The rate for rooms and plentiful breakfast served in a sunny dining room, decorated with hand-cut crystal, is £16 ($24) per person.

Grosvenor Villa, 9 Evesham Pl. (tel. 0789/66192), is owned and run by Mr. and Mrs. John Wells (he used to run a pub). Eight spotless rooms are available, and the nightly rate is £9.50 ($14.25) per person, including an English breakfast. They will serve an evening meal by arrangement, for £5 ($7.50). There is a comfortable lounge with color television and a small licensed bar. On the second floor, hot tea, coffee, and soups are available. Each room has a wash basin and hot running water, and there are several bathrooms. There's parking for six cars. The house is on the main road toward Evesham, and is only a few minutes from Market Place and about eight minutes from the theater.

Stratheden Hotel, Chapel Street (tel. 0789/297119), is a small, tuck-away hotel, in a weathered building dating back to 1673, with a tiny rear garden and top-floor rooms with slanted, beamed ceilings. Owned by Mr. and Mrs. Wells (she's from Northern Ireland, he's a native of Warwickshire), the house has improved in both decor and comfort, with fresh paint, new curtains, and good beds. The charge for B&B ranges from £11.50 ($17.25) to £16.50 ($24.75). Some rooms have private bath/shower and toilet along with color TV. The entry hallway has a glass cupboard, holding family heirlooms and collector tidbits. The house is sprinkled with old pieces. The dining room, with a bay window, has an overscale sideboard that once belonged to the "insanely vain" Marie Corelli, the eccentric novelist, poet, and mystic who wrote a series of seven books, beginning with *A Romance of Two Worlds* and ending with *Spirit and Power and Universal Love*. Queen Victoria was one of her avid readers. The Victorian novelist (1855–1924) was noted for her passion for pastoral paintings and objets d'art. In one room you can see an example of her taste in bedchamber furniture: a massive mahogany tester bed.

Ravenhurst Hotel, 2 Broad Walk (tel. 0789/292515), is a seven-bedroom, Victorian guesthouse in a quiet street of the Old Town, in easy reach of the historic town center. Richard and Brenda Workman welcome guests to their lodgings, all of which have color TV and beverage-making facilities. Some units have private baths. Bed and a full English breakfast are priced from £9.50 ($14.25) to £13 ($19.50) per person, depending on the plumbing. The Workmans are Stratfordians, whose extensive local knowledge can add to the pleasure of your visit.

Parkfield Guest House, 3 Broad Walk (tel. 0789/293313). Pauline Rush is the hostess with the mostest, having drawn more reader recommendations than any other place in Stratford-upon-Avon. She runs an immaculately kept and conveniently located guesthouse, charging only £10.50 ($15.75) per person nightly. Rooms are well furnished with adequate facilities, such as color TV and tea/coffee-makers. Some have private showers. Rates include a superb English breakfast better than in most guesthouses. Mrs. Rush, if possible, will help guests obtain theater tickets.

Newlands, 7 Broad Walk (tel. 0789/298449), is where Sue and Rex Bolton welcome B&B guests to their two double and one single rooms, which have hot and cold water basins, color TV, tea/coffee-making facilities, and central heating. A full English breakfast is included in the prices that range from £8.50 ($12.75) to £10.50 ($15.75) per person, depending on the season.

The Croft, 49 Shipston Rd. (tel. 0789/293419), is a B&B guesthouse that has been in business many years and is kept up-to-date. A visitor's book testifies to all those who have been pleased. The Croft stands on the A34 not far from the center of town and the Memorial Theatre. Fully modernized, the house has central heating and hot and cold running water in all units. Patricia and Russell Andrews are your friendly hosts, offering a freshly cooked breakfast and comfortable beds. A bathless single costs £13.50 ($20.25) nightly, a bathless double going for £11.50 ($17.25) per person. Twin- or double bedded rooms with private bath are rented for £15 ($22.50) per person, and family rooms, suitable for three to five persons, cost from £30 ($45) to £45 ($67.50) per night.

Craig House Guest House, 69 Shipston Rd. (tel. 0789/297473), is a family-run place, under the management of its owners, Mr. and Mrs. Giles. There is a comfortable guest lounge with TV and just five bedrooms to rent, costing from £9 ($13.50) per person per day for B&B, VAT included. Two showers are available. The house lies across the old Clopton Bridge from Stratford, a span that was there in Shakespeare's time. The theater is no more than ten minutes' walk from the guesthouse if you use the old tramway-bridge across the river.

Salamander Guest House, 40 Grove Rd. (tel. 0789/205728), one of the better guesthouses of Stratford-upon-Avon, is well maintained and homelike, fronting a woodsy park. Maurice and Ninon Croft rent out eight comfortably furnished rooms, including one for families, and the two public bathrooms are shared. The B&B rate in a single is from £9.50 ($14.25) and from £19 ($28.50) in a double. Evening meals, prepared by Maurice who is a qualified chef, can be ordered, costing £5 ($7.50) per person for three courses. Serving is timed so that patrons can get to the theater for the evening performances. The house is about a five-minute walk from the center of town.

Courtland Hotel, 12 Guild St. (tel. 0789/292401), is a Georgian building with much character, lying about a six-minute walk from the Shakespeare Theatre. It offers comfortably appointed and pleasantly decorated bedrooms, with color TV, two of which are set aside for families. There are no private baths, but rates are compensatingly modest: from £11 ($16.50) to £13 ($19.50) in a single, from £22 ($33) to £25 ($37.50) in a double.

Wayside Hotel, 11 Warwick Rd. (tel. 0789/292550), is a small six-bedroom hotel, at the edge of town in the direction of Warwick (a convenient five-minute walk to the theater). The owners, John and Madeleine Hainel, charge from £13.50 ($20.25) per person per night for B&B, including VAT and service. The rooms are comfortable and have color TV, tea/coffee-making facilities, and hot and cold water basins. Three rooms have their own private shower. Run separately from the hotel is the Cellar Bar Restaurant. Open nightly, except Monday, from 7 to 11:30 p.m., this fully licensed restaurant features an à la carte menu or a choice of meals of three courses, including coffee and VAT, for £8 ($12). The cost of your wine is extra. The hotel and restaurant have free car parking close by.

Hunters Moon, 150 Alcester Rd. (tel. 0789/292888), is a family-owned and -operated guest house on the fringe of Stratford. The owners, John Monk and his daughter, Mrs. Rosemary Banner, who have run it for 30 years, also operate another guesthouse just a few doors away, so you may be housed there. Hunters Moon has been completely modernized and extended. Shower rooms have been built, and in most cases there are showers and toilets in the bedrooms, along with tea- or coffee-making facilities. Between the two guesthouses Hunters Moon can accommodate 40 persons. There is a very good selection of rooms (singles, doubles, twins, or family rooms), and the price is from £12 ($18) per person nightly, including breakfast. I have received many letters of praise concerning Hunters Moon's cleanliness, neatness of the rooms, and general helpfulness. Guests arriving in Stratford without transportation can telephone and a car will be sent free.

Moonraker House, 40 Alcester Rd. (tel. 0789/67115), is a pleasant B&B where hard-working, competent Mike Spencer receives guests in rooms with showers, toilets, color TV, hair dryers, and beverage-making facilities. He charges from £19 ($28.50) for two persons. A luxury suite with a bedroom, lounge, and kitchenette is more expensive, of course. The house is five minutes by car from the heart of town.

Victoria Spa Lodge, Bishopton Lane (tel. 0789/67985), is a large house, dating from 1830, lying about a mile from the center of town. The lodge actually was a spa in its early days and once had Queen Victoria as a guest. Paul and Dreen Tozer are accommodating and friendly hosts. Their bedrooms are tastefully decorated with Laura Ashley wallpaper and matching bedspreads, as well as hot-beverage facilities. Only one unit has a private bath, but the public bathrooms are modern and clean. B&B rates are £11 ($16.50) in a single, £21 ($31.50) in a double. A full English breakfast is served in a cheerful, pleasantly furnished dining room.

A Town House Complex

Lysander Court, a project of the Royal Shakespeare Restaurants Company, Waterside (tel. 0789/67262 for information and reservations), is a new concept in "home from home" accommodations. Six Elizabethan-style town houses grouped around a charming and private courtyard, are luxuriously furnished and can house two to six persons. Each has a pleasant lounge, kitchen and dining area, bathroom, toilet, three bedrooms, color TV, metered telephone and car parking. Linen and toiletries are provided, and full service is supplied if required. A full English breakfast is included in the rates of £17 ($25.50) to £23 ($34.50) per person per night, depending on the number accommodated. Right in the heart of Stratford, Lysander Court is within easy walking distance of the theater, shops, and other attractions.

WHERE TO EAT: In the best position in town, the **Box Tree Restaurant,** Royal

Shakespeare Theatre, Waterside (tel. 0789/293226), is in the theater, with walls of glass providing an unobstructed view of the Avon and its swans. The meals and service are worthy of its unique position. The restaurant is open on matinee days from noon to 2 p.m., when a two-course table d'hôte luncheon costs £6.50 ($9.75). Evening hours are 5:45 p.m. to midnight, a three-course pretheater dinner being featured. During intermission, there is a snack feast of smoked salmon and champagne. After each evening's performance, you can dine by flickering candlelight. Classical French, Italian, and English cuisine is served. Dinner and supper are à la carte and cost from £13.75 ($20.63) to £16.50 ($24.75) per person. Be sure to book your table in advance, especially on the days of performances (there's a special phone for reservations in the theater lobby).

Also overlooking the Avon, the **River Terrace Restaurant** in the theater is open to the general public as well as to play-goers. A colorful coffeeshop and licensed restaurant serves typical English and pasta dishes, morning coffee, and afternoon teas, which are offered on a self-service basis. Meals cost from £4 ($6) to £8.50 ($12.75). It is open from 10:30 a.m. until after the performances. Sunday hours are from 11 a.m. to 5 p.m. The restaurant has the same phone as the Box Tree (above).

Cobweb Restaurant & Confectionery, 12 Sheep St. (tel. 0789/292554), is a black-and-white timbered building, with a high gabled wing, dating from the early 16th century. It's steeped in associations with the days of Shakespeare. On the ground floor are cases of goodies for sale, but you may want to go to the second floor, where there's a maze of three rooms filled with antique oak tables, Windsor chairs, and settles. The shop is noted as one of the finest in England for its cakes, pastries, cream gâteaux (especially chocolate and sherry), meringues, apple strudel, and cheesecake, offering at least 60 varieties of English and continental cakes. The luncheons and dinners of traditional English "fayre" are excellent. A special two-course lunch costs £4.25 ($6.38), and a £6.95 ($10.35) pre-theater menu is served. Otherwise, à la carte dinners cost from £10 ($15), featuring such main course selections as chicken Kiev and lamb ragoût. Monday to Saturday, lunch is available from noon to 2 p.m., pretheater dinners from 6 to 7 p.m., and regular dinners from 6 to 11 p.m. The Cobweb is also open for teas on Sunday from 3 to 6 p.m.

Thatch Restaurant, Cottage Lane, Shottery (tel. 0789/293122), is two doors from Anne Hathaway's Cottage and two miles from Stratford-upon-Avon. Almost hidden by the entrance to the big coach park, this tea room provides a relaxed meal away from the hurly-burly of the town of Stratford. Apart from morning coffee and afternoon cream teas, the Thatch offers a four-course roast beef lunch for £6.50 ($9.75). The staff also offers soup, a sandwich, and a dessert for £2.50 ($3.25). Wine, liquor, or beer is available to have with your meal. You might like to sit outside on the covered patio and watch the visitors lining up to see Anne Hathaway's house, or just listen to the chirping of the birds. The food is good, the prices reasonable, and the atmosphere pleasant. Hours are 9:30 a.m. to 5:30 p.m. daily; it is closed from October to Easter.

Hathaway Tea Rooms, 19 High St. (tel. 0789/292404), is housed in a mellowed 380-year-old building, timbered and rickety as is its across-the-street neighbor, Harvard House. You pass through a bakery shop up to the second floor, into a forest of olden beams. Sitting at the English tables and chairs you can order wholesome food made from time-tested recipes. The soup of the day is homemade. Usually, you have a choice of six main dishes, such as roast beef with Yorkshire pudding or steak-and-kidney pie. The classic steaming hot fruit pies round off most meals. Hathaway is recommended as a luncheon stop, with meals served from noon to 2 p.m., costing from £6 ($9). You might also want to visit it for afternoon cream tea from 3 to 5 p.m., costing £2.50 ($3.25).

The **Dirty Duck,** Waterside Street (tel. 0789/297312), is also known as the Black

Swan. By whatever bird it's called, it's been popular since the 18th century as a favorite hangout of Stratford players. Autographed photographs of its patrons, such as Lord Laurence Olivier, line the wall. The front lounge and bar crackles with intense conversation. The choices change daily, and in the bar you'll find good value and quick service, everything washed down with mellow beer. In the Dirty Duck Grill Room meals are served from noon to 2:30 p.m. and 6 p.m. to midnight. Typical English grills, among other dishes, are featured. You're faced with a dozen appetizers, most of which would make a meal in themselves. Main dishes include braised kidneys. Meals cost from £12 ($18).

The **Horseshoe Buttery and Restaurant,** 33–34 Greenhill St. (tel. 0789/292246), is a family-run business offering good old-fashioned, straightforward English cookery at reasonable prices. Centrally situated opposite the Safeway store, the café is open daily from 9 a.m. to 9 p.m., serving grills, snacks, salads, sandwiches, along with burgers and pizzas. In the restaurant, open from noon to 3 p.m. and 5 to 9 p.m. daily, the fare runs to steaks, chops, cutlets, scampi, fish, chicken, and salads. A two- or three-course luncheon is served daily for £3 ($4.50). The best dish to order is a homemade steak-and-kidney pie, or a roast joint, each served with fresh vegetables, creamed or boiled potatoes. Because of their 50% patronage by Americans or Canadians, ice water is always available. But you can also order iced lagers, beer, ales, and wines by the glass. The owner, Mr. G. J. Roughley, also rents out two bedrooms, offering B&B at a cost of £10 ($15) per person nightly. Rooms are attractively furnished and comfortable, with TV, central heating, and sliding doors to a roof garden.

Marlowe's Restaurant, Marlowe's Alley, 17–18 High St. (tel. 0789/204999), is made up of the Elizabethan Room, a 16th-century oak-paneled dining room, and the Loose Box Tavern, once the hayloft of this ancient house. The tavern meals start at £3.95 ($5.93), those in the Elizabethan Room costing from £11.50 ($17.25). The garden patio overflows with flowers, and the owners, George and Judy Kruszynskyj, invite you to have a drink or even an al fresco meal here. Hours are from 6 to 10:30 p.m. Monday to Friday, 6 to 11 p.m. Saturday. A traditional Sunday lunch is served from noon to 2:30 p.m.

Slug & Lettuce, 38 Guild St. (tel. 0789/299700), is a brick building with a cozy pub atmosphere of wood tables along with good food and ale. In fair weather, tables open onto Gloucester Court. Standing on a busy highway, it draws a lot of local business as well as tourists. The menu is robust, prepared whenever possible from fresh ingredients, and you get excellent value here, with meals costing from £8 ($12). You might begin with a hearty soup or a fresh crisp salad before going on to one of the specials which change daily. For example, you might try pork chops cooked with apples and flavored with Calvados. Hours are noon to 2 p.m. and 6 to 10 p.m. (on Sunday noon to 1:30 p.m. and 7 to 9:30 p.m.).

Pinocchio, 6 Union St. (tel. 0789/69106), standing next to the previously recommended Slug & Lettuce, is a pizza and pasta restaurant, one of the best in town. North of Bridge Street, it is cozy and welcoming. Your host is Gina Scimeca who brings a taste of Sicily to Stratford. Meals cost from £6 ($9), but could go far higher, depending on what you order. For example, one of the chef's specials is a grilled spring chicken flavored with herbs. There is also a wide range of pastas in various sauces (try the one with baby clams), along with the inevitable pizzas. Veal dishes are also good, and for dessert you might like a smooth zabaglione. Hours are daily except Sunday from noon to 2:30 p.m. and 6 to 11:30 p.m.

The **Vintner Wine Bar,** 5 Sheep St. (tel. 0789/297259). Wine bar dining is all the rage in England, even in Stratford-upon-Avon, as reflected by this place. The Elizabethan decor is fitting in the town of Shakespeare, and the name comes from a wine merchant, John Smith, who occupied this address early in the 17th century. Around the corner from the Shakespeare Hotel, the popular drinking and dining spot offers meals from £6 ($9). Daily specials are posted on the blackboard. Many guests prefer one of the tempting cold plates at lunch. You can also order a vegetable dish of the day, a grilled sirloin, or a salmon steak. Hours are from 11:30 a.m. to 11:30 p.m. daily.

A TUDOR PUB: A black-and-white timbered Elizabethan pub, the **Garrick Inn,** High Street (tel. 0789/296816) was named after one of England's greatest actors, David Garrick. It has its own kind of unpretentious charm. The front bar is decked out with tapestry-covered settles, an old oak refectory table, and an open fireplace where the locals gravitate. The back bar has a circular fireplace with a copper hood—plus a buffet bar serving ploughman's lunches and steak-and-kidney pie, among other dishes. A buffet menu is served daily from 11:45 a.m. to 2:15 p.m., costing from £5 ($7.50). At night, regular pub hours are kept from 5:30 to 11 p.m. The Garrick is across from the Town Hall next to Harvard House.

AT LOXLEY: The nearby village of Loxley, just 3½ miles from Stratford-upon-Avon, is an ancient community, boasting one of the oldest Saxon churches in England, the parish church of St. Nicholas. This quiet country village, claimed by some to be the original home of Robin Hood (Sir Robin of Loxley), is a quiet little place with a delightful old pub.

The **Old Rectory** (tel. 0789/842312), a Georgian-listed building standing in four acres of grounds, was built for the Vicars of Loxley, using funds donated by the bounty of Queen Anne. Sold by the Church of England in 1934, it is now an excellent B&B, where Paula Loake accommodates up to four persons, charging from £11 ($16.50) per person. You can make your own tea or coffee in your room, with breakfast being served in the Old Dining Room overlooking the churchyard. The house has a TV lounge for guests and ample parking space.

At historic **Loxley Farm** (tel. 0789/840265) Roderick and Anne Horton live in a real dream of a thatched cottage with windows peeping from the thatch and creeper climbing up the old walls. The garden is full of apple blossom, roses, and sweet-scented flowers. A stone path leads across the grass and into the flagstone hall, with nice old rugs and a roaring fire. Accommodations are in the main house and in the remodeled thatch-covered barn. Prices are from £11 ($16.50) to £16 ($24) per person, including an English breakfast and VAT. If you ask Anne in advance, she will prepare you a packed lunch or an evening meal, costing £7 ($10.50), served in the dining room on a table made from a panel from the wall of the Royal Mint in London.

ELSEWHERE IN THE ENVIRONS: In the home village of Shakespeare's mother, Mary Arden, **Pear Tree Cottage,** Church Road, Wilmcote (tel. 0789/205889), is a late-16th-century farmhouse (with later additions). Period charm has been preserved with exposed beams and antique furniture, while such things as modern plumbing and central heating add 20th-century comfort. No longer a farmhouse, the cottage stands in nearly an acre of lawn and gardens. Mr. and Mrs. Mander rent three bedrooms, accommodating up to seven guests. Two of the rooms have private baths and rent for £12 ($18) per person for B&B. The bathless unit costs £10 ($15) per person. A sitting room for guests has color TV and comfortable chairs. Mary Arden's birthplace is visible across the field from the house.

A privately owned 16th-century inn, **Broom Hall Inn** (tel. 0789/773757), stands in the little hamlet of Broom on the River Alne, shortly before it empties into the Avon. It's near Bidford-on-Avon, about six miles from Stratford-upon-Avon and ten miles from Broadway in the Cotswolds. The building is a black-and-white timbered Elizabethan structure in a rural location away from main roads. Tina and Robin Barrett own the inn and manage it, assisted by their daughter and her husband, Nina and George Downie. George is the resident chef, offering a wide range of inexpensive bar meals, plus an impressive restaurant menu with a limited but select number of à al carte specialties, including duckling à l'orange and steak au poivre. Restaurant meals cost from around £9 ($13.50). A special Sunday family luncheon is also offered. There are four double or twin-bedded rooms and two singles, of which three of the former have private bath. Rates are from £15.50 ($23.25) in a single, from £28 ($42) in a twin, including a full English breakfast and VAT.

Grafton House Farm, Temple Grafton (tel. 0789/772289), is near Alcester, five miles from Stratford-upon-Avon between the A439 and the A422 roads. The Fisher family rents six good-size rooms, charging £9.50 ($14.25) per person in a double, £11.50 ($17.25) in a single, the prices including an English breakfast and VAT. Rooms with private baths cost £13.50 ($20.25) per person in a double. The farm is quite old, but the bedrooms have been modernized. A small restaurant and licensed bar, adapted from the old stable and blacksmith forge, offer facilities for evening meals costing from £7.50 ($11.25).

King's Lodge, Long Marston (tel. 0789/720705), lies six miles from Stratford-upon-Avon. From Stratford, take the A34 Oxford road; on the outskirts of town, fork right on to the A46 Cheltenham road and continue for 4½ miles. Turn right at the signpost to Long Marston and proceed to a "T" junction, turning right. Once a manor house, which has now partly disappeared, it was a place where Charles II hid out as a manservant after the Battle of Worcester. George and Angela Jenkins welcome guests to comfortably furnished and centrally heated bedrooms, with hot and cold water basins. One bedroom features a traditional four-poster bed hewn from timber grown on the estate. Besides the bedrooms in the lodge, there are three self-contained apartments on the grounds, equipped for self-catering, but when the other accommodations are full, the Jenkinses will rent any unoccupied apartments on a B&B basis to one couple or a party. The charges per night are from £20 ($30) to £25 ($37.50) (in the four-poster room) for two persons, with a full English breakfast included. Singles are charged £11 ($16.50) per night. For £6 ($9), you can enjoy a three-course dinner with coffee at an oak table in what was once part of the manor's Great Hall. The restored room is dominated by a large stone inglenook fireplace. Mullioned windows frame vistas of green lawns and stately trees.

The Goodwins, Long Marston (tel. 0789/720326), six miles from Stratford-upon-Avon, five miles from Chipping Campden, is where you can submerge yourself in the best traditional "Olde Worlde" England. A 17th-century stone farmhouse, with four front gables, beams throughout, and mullioned windows, this is a true gem in the Bard's countryside, complete with a pond, a gaggle of geese, and sheep grazing in the meadow. Mr. and Mrs. Hodges, the owners, have double- and twin-bedded rooms, each with a hot and cold water basin, TV, beverage-making facilities, and shaver points. The price ranges from £12.50 ($18.75) per person, with a reduction for stays of three or more nights. There is a guest lounge with TV, where you can enjoy an English "cuppa." The farm aviation club offers gliding, parachute jumping, and microlight flying at moderate prices, by prior arrangement. Other attractions at the farm are private trout fishing and a Sunday morning antique market. The local Equestrian Centre and Stratford and Broadway golf courses are nearby.

Kingsmead Farm, Charlecote, near Wellesbourne on the Stratford Road (tel. 0789/840254), stands in seven acres of wooded grounds. In addition to receiving guests, the owner, Jennifer Secombe, runs a country furniture business specializing in antique stripped pine, fitted kitchens, dressers, cupboards, tables, chairs, wall racks, and mirrors. She has comfortably furnished double rooms available, with private bath. The charge is from £11 ($16.50) per person for B&B. You can also order an evening meal to be served in time for you to attend the theater in Stratford-upon-Avon.

The Old Rectory, Stratford Road, Sherbourne, near Warwick (tel. 0926/624562), just off the A46 between Warwick and Stratford-upon-Avon, is a 300-year-old farmhouse. It has been lovingly restored and decorated with antiques by the owners, Sheila and Martin Greenwood. There are seven double bedrooms, six of which have private baths or showers, in the main house, as well as a converted carriage house suitable for a family. Several bedrooms have antique brass beds. The cost is £12 ($18) per person for B&B, and the English breakfast is bountiful.

AN ATTRACTION AT ALCESTER: A magnificent, 115-room Palladian country house, **Ragley Hall** (tel. 0789/762090), built in 1680, is the home of the Marquess and Marchioness of Hertford and their family, lying 9 miles from Stratford-upon-Avon. The house has been lovingly restored and appears as it probably looked during the early 1700s. Great pains were taken to duplicate color patterns and in some cases even the original wallpaper patterns. Ragley Hall's vast and spacious rooms boast priceless pictures, furniture, and works of art that have been collected by ten generations of the Seymour family. While possessing a museum-like quality in the sense that its artifacts are properly displayed, lighted, and have great historical importance, Ragley Hall is indeed a private home.

Perhaps the most spectacular attraction is the lavishly painted south staircase hall. The present marquess commissioned muralist Graham Rust to paint the modern trompe l'oeil work on the subject *The Temptation,* but this religious theme stops with the lavishly evil Devil offering a gold circlet to Christ in the central ceiling medallion. The walls of the halls are decorated with a striking garden vista, with temples and trees, plus a far view over the countryside. Exotic birds and other creatures crouch above doorways while flamingos spar on a balcony. Up the stairs and toward the ceiling are painted balconies on which the Marquess of Hertford and his family and friends lean and talk, feed the birds, and look back at the interested observer. Depicted far above are the servants' quarters with Ragley's cook and butler peering down at the scene below. This is a fascinating work of art that blends with the ease of trompe l'oeil into the old house.

Ragley Hall, its garden, and the park are open from Easter Saturday to October daily except Monday and Friday (open on bank holidays). The house can be visited in April, May, and September from 1:30 to 5:30 p.m.; in June, July, and August from noon to 5 p.m. on Tuesday, Wednesday, and Thursday and from 1:30 to 5:30 p.m. on Saturday and Sunday. The garden and park, with the Adventure Wood and Country Trail, are open in April, May, and September from noon to 5:30 p.m. and in June, July, and August from 10 a.m. to 6 p.m. The licensed snackbar is open from noon to 5 p.m. when the park is open. Admission to the house, garden, and park is £2.90 ($4.35) for adults, £1.90 ($2.85) for children. The garden and park only can be entered for £1.90 ($2.85) for adults, 90p ($1.35) for children.

Most travelers approach our next stopover, Warwick, via the A46 from Stratford-upon-Avon, eight miles away. The town is 92 miles from London and is on the Avon.

2. Warwick

Visitors seem to rush through here to see Warwick Castle; then they're off on their next adventure, traditionally to the ruins of Kenilworth Castle. But the historic center of medieval Warwick deserves to be treated with greater respect. It has far more to offer than a castle.

In 1694 a fire swept over the heart of Warwick, destroying large segments of the town, but it still retains a number of Elizabethan and medieval buildings, along with some fine Georgian structures from a later date. (Very few traces remain of the town walls except the East and West Gates.) Warwick looks to Ethelfleda, daughter of Alfred the Great, as its founder. But most of its history is associated with the Earls of Warwick, a title created by the son of William the Conqueror in 1088. The story of those earls—the Beaumonts, the Beauchamps (such figures as "Kingmaker" Richard Neville)—makes for an exciting episode in English history, but is too detailed to document here.

WARWICK CASTLE: Perched on a rocky cliff above the Avon, this magnificent

14th-century fortress encloses a stately mansion in the grandest late 17th-century style.

The importance of the site has been recognized from earliest times. The first important work at Warwick was the Mound, built by Ethelfleda, daughter of Alfred the Great, in A.D. 915. The same Mound was enlarged at the time of the Norman Conquest, and a Norman castle of the motte and bailey type was built. There are now no remains of the Norman castle, sacked by Simon de Montfort in the Barons War of 1264.

The Beauchamp family, the most illustrious medieval Earls of Warwick, was responsible for most of the castle as it is seen today, and much of the external structure remains unchanged from the mid-14th century. When the castle was granted to the ancestors of the Greville family in 1604, Sir Fulke Greville spent £20,000 constructing a mansion within the castle fortifications, although this has been much altered over the years. The Grevilles have held the Earl of Warwick title since 1759, when it passed from the Rich family.

The State Rooms and Great Hall house fine collections of paintings, furniture, arms, and armor. The armory, dungeon, torture chamber, ghost tower, clock tower, and Guy's tower give vivid insights into the castle's turbulent past and its important part in the history of England. The private apartments of Lord Brooke and his family, who in recent years sold the castle to Madame Tussaud's company, of waxworks fame, are open to visitors to display a carefully constructed Royal Weekend House Party of 1898. The major rooms contain wax models of celebrities of the time: Winston Churchill, the Duchess of Devonshire, Winston's widowed mother, Jennie, and Clara Butt, the celebrated singer, along with the Earl and Countess of Warwick and their family. In the Kenilworth bedroom, the Prince of Wales, later to become King Edward VII, reads a letter, and in the red bedroom, the Duchess of Marlborough prepares for her bath. Among the most lifelike of the figures is a little uniformed maid, bending over a bathtub into which the water is running, to test the temperature.

Surrounded by gardens, lawns, and woodland, where peacocks roam freely, and skirted by the Avon, Warwick Castle was described by Sir Walter Scott in 1828 as "that fairest monument of ancient and chivalrous splendor which yet remains uninjured by time."

Don't miss the re-created Victorian Rose Garden, originally designed by Robert Marnock in 1868. It fell into disrepair, and a tennis court was built on the site among the trees. In 1980, it was decided to restore the garden, and as luck would have it, Marnock's original plans were discovered in the County Records Office. Close by the rose garden is a Victorian alpine rockery and water garden. The romantic castle is, throughout the year, host to various special events, colorful pageants such as those created by the members of the Sealed Knot and the French Foot Grenadiers. There are regular appearances of the magnificent Red Knight on his splendid warhorse, and international Morris Dancers perform on the lawns. Some form of live entertainment is presented almost every day on the grounds in summer.

Warwick Castle, Castle Hill (tel. 0926/495421), is open daily except Christmas Day. From March 1 through October 31, hours are 10 a.m. to 5:30 p.m.; November 1 through February 28, 10 a.m. to 4:30 p.m. All-inclusive admission is £3.50 ($5.25) for adults, £2.25 ($3.88) for children.

OTHER SIGHTS: Other nearby sights worth exploring include the following:

St. Mary's Church

This church was destroyed, in part, by the fire of 1694, and is characterized by its rebuilt battlemented tower and nave, considered among the finest examples of the work of the late 17th and early 18th centuries. The striking aspect of St. Mary's is that it's unusually lofty, dominating the surrounding countryside. The Beauchamp Chapel, spared from the flames, encases the Purbeck marble tomb of Richard Beauchamp, a well-known Earl of Warwick who died in 1439 and is commemorated by a gilded latten effigy. The most powerful man in the kingdom, not excepting Henry V, Beauchamp has a tomb considered one of the finest remaining examples of Perpendicular-Gothic as practiced in England in the mid-15th century. The tomb of Robert Dudley, Earl of Leicester, a favorite of Elizabeth I, is against the north wall. The choir, another survivor of the fire, dates from the 14th century. It too is built in the Perpendicular-Gothic style. The Norman Crypt is another fine example of this period, as is the 14th-century Chapter House. For more information, get in touch with the Parish Office, Warwick (tel. 0926/491132).

Lord Leycester Hospital

At the West Gate, this group of half-timbered almshouses was also spared from the Great Fire. The buildings were erected about 1400, and the hospital was founded in 1571 by Robert Dudley, the Earl of Leicester, as a home for old soldiers. It is still in use by ex-servicemen today. On top of the West Gate is the attractive little chapel of St. James, dating from the 12th century but much restored. The hospital, High Street (tel. 0926/491422), may be visited weekdays from 10 a.m. to 5:30 p.m. (closed Sunday) for £1 ($1.50) for adults, 50p (75¢) for children. Off-season it closes at 4 p.m.

Warwick Doll Museum

Housed in one of the most charming Elizabethan buildings in Warwick, this doll museum, Oken's House, Castle Street (tel. 0926/495546), near St. Mary's Church. Its seven rooms house an extensive private collection of dolls in wood, wax, and porcelain. The house once belonged to Thomas Oken, a great benefactor of Warwick. The house is open daily from 10 a.m. to 5 p.m. March to November; on Saturday and Sunday only from 10 a.m. to 5 p.m. December, January, and February. Admission is 70p ($1.05) for adults, 50p (75¢) for children.

Warwickshire Museum

At the Market Place, this museum (tel. 0926/493431, ext. 2500) was established in 1836 to house a collection of geological remains, fossils, and a fine grouping of British amphibians from the Triassic period. There is also much for the natural historian. The history collections include church plate, coins, firearms, and the famous Sheldon tapestry map of Warwick. It is open weekdays from 10 a.m. to 5:30 p.m., on Sunday in summer from 2:30 to 5 p.m. Admission is free.

St. John's House

At Coten End, not far from the castle gates, there is a display of domestic life and costumes. St. John's House (tel. 0926/493431, ext. 2132) in which these exhibitions are displayed is a thing of beauty itself, dating from the early 17th century. A Victorian schoolroom is furnished with original 19th-century school furniture and equipment. During term time, Warwickshire children dressed in replica costumes can be seen participating in Victorian-style lessons. Groups of children also use the Victorian parlor and the kitchen. As it is impossible to display more than a small amount at a time, a study room is available where you can see objects from the reserve collections. The costume collection is a particularly fine one, and visitors can study the drawings and photos that make up the costume catalogue. These facilities are available by prior appointment only. For more information and appointments, telephone the Keeper of Social History (tel. 0926/493431, ext. 2021).

Upstairs in St. John's House is a Military Museum tracing the history of the Royal Warwickshire Regiment from 1674 to the present day. The house is open Tuesday to Saturday from 10 a.m. to 12:30 p.m. and 1:30 to 5:30 p.m. and also on Sunday from 2:30 to 5 p.m. May to September. Admission is free.

BED AND BREAKFAST: A friendly B&B, the **Warwickshire Licensed Hotel,** 82 Emscote Rd. (tel. 0926/492927), is run by Christine Merrett. All rooms have color TV, tea/coffee-making facilities, central heating, hot and cold running water, and comfortable beds. The cost of £10 ($15) includes a full English breakfast. This is an informal place, close enough to Stratford-upon-Avon to be a base for touring Shakespeare Country. The area is full of pubs and restaurants that serve good "English fayre" at reasonable prices.

The **Woolpack Hotel,** Market Place (tel. 0926/496191), started life as a coaching inn and managed to survive the Great Warwick Fire of 1694. So today it is an authentic part of the old town. Comfortable modern bedrooms are available, and prices include a full English breakfast and VAT. The more expensive units contain private baths. Singles range in price from £19 ($28.50) to £30 ($45), and doubles or twins are priced from £30 ($45) to £45 ($67.50). In the bar and restaurant you can order set dinners or make selections from an à la carte menu. Sunday lunch is an event here. You sit down to an appetizer of fruit or pâté, then follow with a roast rib of beef with a selection of vegetables. The cost, including a glass of wine, is £5.45 ($8.18) per person seven days a week.

The **Avon Guest House,** 7 Emscote Rd. (tel. 491367), is a B&B in a handsome blue brick building standing in its own grounds with gardens to the front and rear. Mrs. Lyn Bolton extends a friendly welcome to her comfortable family-run accommodations, offering B&B plus an evening meal if you wish. She charges £9.50 ($14.25) per person in rooms with hot and cold water basins, shaver points, and beverage-making facilities. The house is centrally heated and has a TV lounge and a car park for guests. Near the center of town, the guesthouse is on the lefthand side of the A445 Leamington Road, opposite a park and the River Avon, about a five-minute walk from Warwick Castle.

40 The Butts, at that address (tel. 0926/400249), is a 16th-century black-and-white cottage residence with lots of genuine oak beams and "olde world" charm. The plumbing, however, is entirely new. In her private home in the town center, close to the castle, Mrs. Mackey provides accommodations for paying guests. Prices range from £15 ($22.50) to £18 ($27) in a single, from £20 ($30) in a bathless double, and from £25 ($37.50) in a double with bath. An English breakfast is included in the rates.

Tudor-House Inn & Restaurant, West Street (tel. 0926/495447), was built in 1472. It's at the edge of town, on the main road from Stratford-upon-Avon leading to Warwick Castle. It is a stunning black-and-white timbered inn, one of the few buildings to escape the fire that destroyed the High Street in 1694. Off the central hall are two large rooms, each of which could be the setting for an Elizabethan play. In the corner of the lounge is an open turning staircase, waiting for the entrance of a minstrel player. A regular meal in the restaurant and steak bar costs from £8 ($12). The inn has ten bedrooms, all with wash basins, and some have baths. The cost ranges from £19 ($28.50) to £36 ($54) per double room nightly. Two of the rooms have doors only four feet high. There's the usual resident ghost—an old man who gets up early in the morning, leaving the front door open and heading toward Stratford-upon-Avon, without paying his bill to innkeeper Eddie Bush. In addition, the old priest's hiding hole has become the Priest Hole Bar.

WHERE TO DINE: Near the East Gate, the **Porridge Pot,** Jury Street (tel. 0926/491641), serves good English food in an old-world setting. This historic building was originally a trader's dwelling, erected circa 1420 and refaced in 1694 after the Great Fire of Warwick destroyed many neighboring dwellings. The owners, Ken and Jackie Smith, provide excellent meals, many of the recipes taken from a 1717 cookbook. Especially recommended is the English beefsteak pie. Lunches cost from £6 ($9) up. The Pot is open six days a week for lunch from noon to 2 p.m., and from Tuesday to Saturday a full à la carte menu is offered in the evening, beginning at £12 ($18) per head. Dinner hours are 7:15 to 10 p.m. The unique setting with its crooked beams, brass pots and pans, and a collection of oil paintings and prints gives you a glimpse of life in old England.

Olde Saxon Mill, Guy's Cliffe (tel. 0926/492255), is a mill that predates the Norman Conquest, and it still has a turning water wheel. The old mill has gone through a lot of changes in fortune, but has emerged as a cheerful and economical roadhouse, offering a very good bar-snack menu during the day. Fresh salads are accompanied by home-cooked meats. Hot dishes are also available. Bar specials include chili con carne, lasagne, and chicken curry. For a more relaxed lunch in the restaurant, or for dinner, the cost will be about £7 ($10.50) for lunch and £10 ($15) for dinner. Appetizers are likely to include prawn cocktail, and a choice from the carvery of meats and poultry. An à la carte menu includes some good fish, such as trout and Dover sole, and you can also order a T-bone. Food is not served Saturday at lunchtime or all day Sunday. Otherwise, hours are from 11 a.m. to 2:30 p.m. and 7 to 11 p.m. The Olde Saxon Mill is about one mile outside Warwick on the old road to Coventry.

Bar Roussel, 62a Market Place (tel. 0926/491983), is a bistro and wine bar that is open daily for lunch from noon to 2:15 p.m. (no lunch on Sunday) and for dinner from 7 to 9:45 p.m. daily. There is a choice of 53 wines, beers, and "spirits." Every day there is a freshly made soup, followed by a homemade dish of the day, a hot casserole or a meat pie. The cheese board features nine different selections with crackers and bread. Meals cost from £5 ($7.50).

Nicolinis Bistro, 18 Jury St. (tel. 0926/495817), brings a touch of Italy and its savory cuisine to staid Warwick. Lynne and Nicky, as they are known, welcome you to their attractive restaurant, which is made most inviting with much greenery. Pause at the enclosed counter to check out the crisp salads and luscious Italian desserts. The lighting is also kind. You're faced with an array of appetizers, pizzas, pastas, salads, and desserts, and I haven't even gotten to the main courses. Pizzas come in sizes of 6½ to 9 inches, and Nicolinis choice includes "everything." For a main course you can order chicken Kiev with potatoes, although the lasagne would be more typical. Full meals cost around £10 ($15). The restaurant serves Tuesday through Sunday from 9:30 a.m. to 10:30 p.m.

3. Kenilworth Castle

In magnificent ruins, this castle, the subject of Sir Walter Scott's romance *Kenilworth,* in the county of Warwickshire, once had walls that enclosed an area of seven acres. It lies 5 miles north of Warwick, 13 from Stratford-upon-Avon. In 1937 Sir John Davenport Siddely purchased the castle and placed it in the care of the Office of Works (now English Heritage).

The castle dates back to the days of Henry I, having been built by his chamberlain, Geoffrey de Clinton. Of the original castle, only Tower Keep, with its 16-foot-thick walls, remains. Edward II was forced to abdicate at Kenilworth in 1326, before his murder at Berkeley Castle in Gloucestershire in 1327. Elizabeth I in 1563 gave the castle to her favorite, Robert Dudley, Earl of Leicester, who built the Gatehouse. Elizabeth I, surrounded by courtiers, visited on several occasions after Leicester moved in. Parts of the castle were destroyed on orders from Parliament after the Civil War. The castle is open from March 15 to October 15 on weekdays from 9:30 a.m. to 6:30 p.m. and on Sunday from 2 to 6:30 p.m. From October 16 to March 14 hours are 9:30 a.m. to 4 p.m. on weekdays, 2 to 4 p.m. on Sunday. Admission is £1 ($1.50) for adults, 50p (75¢) for children.

WHERE TO STAY: A homelike, family-run B&B, **Hollyhurst Guest House,** 47 Priory Rd. (tel. 0926/53882), is under the personal supervision of Peter and Chris Tolan. Charges are from £11 ($16.50) per person, including a full English breakfast. All rooms are well furnished and have central heating and hot and cold water, as well as tea/coffee-making facilities. Hollyhurst has a comfortable TV lounge and a licensed bar. By prior arrangement, home-cooked, three-course evening meals can be provided for £5.50 ($8.25).

The Magnolias, 58 Priory Rd. (tel. 0926/56173), is a pleasant small Victorian guesthouse where one has to reserve a room in July or August. The owner, Mrs. Peggy Watkins, is an interesting personality, and makes her guests very much at ease. She charges £10 ($15) per person nightly, whether in a single or double room. In the height of the season she can't offer dinners in the evening but can provide coffee, tea, and sandwiches if needed.

WHERE TO DINE: If you're passing through on a sightseeing expedition for the day, try to get a seat for lunch at **George Rafters,** 42 Castle Hill (tel. 0926/52074), whose name is very similar to the old movie gangster, George Raft (remember *Some Like It Hot* with Marilyn Monroe?). Here, there is no relation. This is an intimate candlelit restaurant in the vicinity of Kenilworth Castle, and it's the obvious choice for lunch. It serves from noon to 2 p.m., with dinner from 7 to 10 p.m. Meals cost from £5 ($7.50) to £8 ($12), depending on what you order. Many of the dishes are continental in style or from the Cordon Bleu kitchen, while others depend on the imagination of the chef. Of course, good English food is always featured.

If you're in Kenilworth for the night, go over to **Ana's Bistro,** 121 Warwick Rd. (tel. 0926/53763), for dinner, any time from 7 to 10:30 p.m. (closed Sunday and Monday and for three weeks in August). Its location is downstairs under the Restaurant Diment (which some consider is the finest in Kenilworth for those willing to spend the extra money). However, at Ana's you get food that is almost equal in taste and flavor, but at a better price. The menu is wisely limited, and the hearty cookery is straightforward, with occasional innovations. Specials change daily based on the shopping for the day. Meals cost from £6.50 ($ 9.75) to £9.50 ($14.25).

4. Coventry

The city of Coventry, in the county of West Midlands, home of motorcar and cycle manufacturing, is principally industrial, but you'll want to pay it a visit to see Sir Basil Spence's controversial **Coventry Cathedral,** 7 Priory Row (tel. 0203/27597), consecrated in 1962. The city was partially destroyed during the blitz bombing in the early '40s, but the rebuilding was miraculous. No city symbolizes more dramatically England's power to bounce back from adversity.

Before the war, Coventry was noted in legend as the ancient market town through which Lady Godiva made her famous ride, giving birth to a new name in English: Peeping Tom. The Lady Godiva story is clouded in such obscurity that the truth has probably been lost forever. It has been suggested that the good lady never appeared in the nude, but was the victim of scandalmongers, who, in their attempt to tarnish her image, unknowingly immortalized her.

The cathedral grew up on the same site as the 14th-century Perpendicular building. Many Coventry residents maintain that the foreign visitor is more disposed to admiring the structure than the Britisher, who perhaps is more tradition-laden in his concept of cathedral design.

Outside is Sir Jacob Epstein's bronze masterpiece, *St. Michael Slaying the Devil.* Inside, the outstanding feature is the 70-foot-high altar tapestry by Graham Sutherland, said to be the largest in the world. The floor-to-ceiling abstract stained-glass windows are the work of the Royal College of Art. The West Window is most interesting, with its engraved glass and rows of stylized saints and monarchs with jazzy angels flying around among them.

In the undercroft of the cathedral is a Visitor Centre, "The Spirit of Coventry." There you can see the Walkway of Holograms, three-dimensional images created with laser light, depicting the Stations of the Cross. It is an exciting walk through sound, light, and special effects, tracing the history of Coventry and the cathedral from its foundation to the present day. The treasures of the cathedral are on show. An audio-visual on the city and church includes the fact that 450 aircraft dropped 40,000 fire bombs on the city in one day.

The cathedral is open in summer from 8:30 a.m. to 7:30 p.m., closing at 5:30 p.m. in winter. The 14th-century Tower of the old cathedral costs 50p (75¢) for adults to visit, 25p (38¢) for children. Admission to the Visitor Centre is £1.25 ($1.88) for adults, 75p ($1.13) for children 6 to 16.

After visiting the cathedral, you may want to have tea in a nearby patio, listening to the chimes.

St. Mary's Guildhall, Bayley Lane (tel. 0203/25555, ext. 2874). Up a flight of steps leading from a small yard off Bayley Lane is one of the most attractive medieval guildhalls in England, dating from 1342. It was originally built as a meeting place for the guilds of St. Mary, St. John the Baptist, and St. Catherine. It is now used for the solemn election of the lord mayors of the city and for banquets and civic ceremonies. Below the north window is an arras (tapestry), added in the 15th century, and a beautiful oak ceiling with its original 14th-century carved angels which was rebuilt in the 1950s. There is a Minstrel's Gallery and a Treasury, and off the Armoury, Caesar's Tower where Mary Queen of Scots was imprisoned in 1569. By appointment only, you can also see a magnificent collection of 42 original watercolors by H. E. Cox, depicting Coventry before the bombings of 1939. The guildhall is open from 10 a.m. to 5 p.m. Monday to Saturday, from noon to 5 p.m. on Sunday May to October. Admission is free.

Ford's Hospital, Greyfriars Lane, is a house built in the very early 16th century to house the poor of the city. Today it is a wealth of old beams and mullioned windows restored during 1953. It is now the home once more of elderly Coventry residents. There is a beautiful inner courtyard surrounded by timbered walls hung with geraniums, ferns, and ivy. It is open from 10 a.m. to 5 p.m. daily throughout the year and is well worth a visit.

The **Museum of British Road Transport,** St. Agnus Lane, Hales Street, is some five minutes' walk from Coventry Cathedral in the city center. It houses the largest municipally owned collection in the United Kingdom, possibly in the world. The oldest car is an original Daimler, dating from 1897 (the first English Daimler was built in Coventry only one year before). The museum also displays some of the most antique vehicles still running, six of them regular participants in the annual London–Brighton run (only vehicles manufactured before 1905 are eligible). Curiosities include a 1910 Humber taxi whose mileage is listed at more than one million. Exhibits are diversified, as the museum has the ambitious task of covering the total history of transport in the Midlands, internationally recognized as the home of the British transport industry. Indeed, Coventry has been the home of some 116 individual motor vehicle manufacturers, many of whom are represented in the collections. Among the military vehicles is the staff car in which Montgomery rode into Berlin after the defeat of the Nazis. Memory Lanes, Royalty on the Road, and the History of the Cycle are three popular displays. The museum is open daily throughout the summer (Easter to September) and on Friday, Saturday, and Sunday from October to March. Admission is £1 ($1.50) for adults, 50p (75¢) for children. For further information, telephone 0203/25555, ext. 2086.

Coventry is 19 miles from Stratford-upon-Avon, 11 from Warwick, and 6 from Kenilworth.

WHERE TO STAY: A 12-bedroom licensed Victorian hostelry, **Croft Hotel,** 23 Stoke Green (tel. 0203/457846), is just ten minutes from the city center and the cathedral. Owned by Peter and Loraine Llewellyn, it's an all-purpose hotel, where single travelers are as welcome as families. The daily rate is £16.10 ($24.15) in a single room

and £30.47 ($45.71) in a double or twin-bedded accommodation. A single with color TV and a shower rents for £20.12 ($30.18), while a twin with those conveniences costs £33.35 ($50.03). The units are centrally heated and have radios and alarm clocks. Mr. Llewellyn prepares a hefty breakfast, and Mrs. Llewellyn offers evening meals at £6 ($9) per person. She also provides a selection of bar meals, which are served up to 10:30 p.m. All vegetables used in the cuisine are home-grown. You are invited to sit in the gardens or relax in the solarium.

The **Fairlight Guest House,** 14 Regent St., off Queens Road (tel. 0203/24215), is a late Victorian, three-story, red-brick building with a courtyard decorated in summer with pots of bright flowers. Betty and Brian Smith provide 11 rooms where guests can stay for £11.50 ($17.25) in a single, £10.50 ($15.75) per person in a double for B&B. All rooms in this centrally heated establishment have beverage-making facilities, hot and cold water basins, and showers. Color TV is provided in a pleasant lounge. The house is about five minutes from the city center.

The **University of Warwick,** Gibbet Hill (tel. 0203/523279). David Wilson is the man to speak to if you want to stay at this modern university campus where rooms are available for summer rental when the students are gone. It is landscaped in beautiful Warwickshire farmland on the southern boundary of Coventry. Rooms are mostly single, but there are twins, some with private facilities. All units are well but simply furnished, with access to the usual student facilities, washing machines, dryers, swimming pool, tennis courts, and games room. The cost is from £14 ($21) per person, including a full breakfast, VAT, and service. If you're traveling with children and would like to stay four or more nights, ask about the self-catering flats, a five-bedroom unit being available at £23 ($34.50) per night.

WHERE TO EAT: A traditional dining place, **Ostlers Eating House,** 166 Spon St. (tel. 0203/26603), lies some five to eight minutes from the cathedral. Spon Street itself is being restored to its original state as it was in medieval England, with some adjustments to the 20th century of course. A very satisfying meal will cost around £6 ($9). You're presented with a choice of appetizer, then perhaps roast chicken with baked potato or a grilled steak with salad and potato. Chili con carne or a meat-and-potato pie are also available. Ostlers is open from 11 a.m. to 10:30 p.m. Monday to Thursday, closing at 11:30 p.m. on Friday and Saturday. Sunday hours are 7 to 10:30 p.m. The place is good for atmosphere in a city that has had to be almost totally rebuilt.

Herbs, 28 Lower Holyhead Rd. (tel. 0203/555654). Remember dull vegetarian meals in health food restaurants where everything tastes bland? Forget that unfortunate memory here in Robert Jackson's place. He turns vegetarian cookery into an art. In a small private hotel, the Trinity House, Herbs enjoy an enviable reputation, even among meat-eaters who visit to see what the excitement is about. Some of the sauces use wine and cream, and that enlivens the fare considerably. Only dinner from 6:30 to 9:30 p.m. (except Sunday) is served, with meals costing from £7.50 ($11.25). Everything is super fresh. Dishes include red lentil lasagne or pine nut loaf, and desserts are also luscious. If you like the place so much you'd like to stay over, ask about one of the good, clean basic bedrooms, seven in all, where the cost ranges from £13.50 ($20.25) in a single to £23 ($34.50) in a double.

Corks Wine Bar & Restaurant, 4–5 Whitefriars St. (tel. 0203/23628), is both a wine bar and bistro, plus an intimate à la carte restaurant. The wine bar evokes a stylized belle époque atmosphere, with its dark colors and antique lighting fixtures. Daily fixed-price menus are displayed on chalkboards, costing anywhere from £1.60 ($2.40) to £3 ($4.50). From the handwritten à la carte menu, you can select a filling meal of soup, pâté salad, or lasagne, along with a dessert, for around £5 ($5.75). If you're really hungry for something to sink your teeth into, try the entrecôte bordelaise with a salad or french fries. In the more expensive restaurant, you can dine well for £12 ($18), perhaps beginning with frogs' legs in garlic butter, then going on to stuffed rainbow trout or sirloin steak with a pâté sauce. Monday to Saturday lunches are served from 11 a.m. to 2:30 p.m. Dinner is offered Monday to Thursday from 6 to 10:30 p.m., until 11 p.m. on Friday and Saturday, and on Sunday from 7 to 10:30 p.m.

5. Hereford and Worcester

The Wye Valley contains some of the most beautiful river scenery in Europe. The river cuts through agricultural country, and there is no population explosion in the sleepy villages. Wool used to be its staple business, and fruit growing and dairy farming are important today.

The old county of Herefordshire has now combined with Worcestershire to form "Hereford and Worcester"-shire. Worcestershire's name, of course, has become famous around the world because of its sauce familiar to gourmets. It is one of the most charming of Midland counties, covering a portion of the rich valleys of the Severn and Avon.

Herefordshire's Black Mountains border the Welsh Brecon Beacons National Park, and between the two cathedral cities of Hereford and Worcester the ridge of the Malverns rises from the Severn Plain.

The heart of England is the best point to travel to by train from Paddington Station in London if you wish to use your BritRail Pass. The train takes you through many of the previously mentioned towns and villages, and you can stop and visit Windsor, Henley-on-Thames, and Oxford, not to mention the numerous Cotswold villages such as Chipping Campden. It must be one of the best train rides in the country, and you can also take a side trip by bus from Evesham to Stratford-upon-Avon too. Or else take the bus back from Stratford to Oxford via Woodstock, then the train back into London.

HEREFORD: One of the most colorful old towns of England, the ancient Saxon city of Hereford, on the Wye River, was the birthplace of both David Garrick and Nell Gwynne. Dating from 1079, the red sandstone **Hereford Cathedral** (tel. 0432/59880) contains all styles of architecture, from Norman to Perpendicular. One of its most interesting features is a library of chained books—more than 1,600 copies—as well as one of the oldest maps in existence, the Mappa Mundi of 1290. There is also a Treasury in the crypt.

Hereford is surrounded by both orchards and rich pasturelands. Hence it has some of the finest cider in the world, best sampled in one of the city's mellow pubs. Hereford cattle sold here are some of the finest in the world too.

The Old House, High Street (tel. 0432/68121, ext. 207), is preserved as a Jacobean period museum, with the appropriate furnishings. The completely restored half-timbered structure, built in 1621, also contains superb 17th-century wall paintings and local history items. On Monday, hours are 10 a.m. to 1 p.m.; on Tuesday and Friday, 10 a.m. to 1 p.m. and 2 to 5 p.m. On Saturday in summer, hours are 10 a.m. to 1 p.m. and 2 to 5:30 p.m. (on Saturday in winter, 10 a.m. to 1 p.m.). Admission is 40p (60¢) for adults, 20p (30¢) for children.

The Museum of Cider, Pomona Place, off Whitecross Road (tel. 0432/54207), tells the fascinating story of traditional cider-making, from farmhouse to modern factory methods. Displays include a 350-year-old enormous French beam press, a reconstructed 17th-century farm ciderhouse, a working cooper (barrel-maker), traveling cider-makers' tack (equipment), and the original champagne cider cellars where huge stacks and bottles can be seen, together with the old oak vats dating back to Napoleonic times. The museum's King Offa Distillery produces cider brandy and royal cider, long known as the wine of England, which you can buy in the museum shop. Also on sale is locally produced cider at £1.80 ($2.70) a liter, pure apple juice, apple apéritif, perry (made from pears), cider barrels, pottery, recipe books, tea cloths, postcards, and a wide variety of gifts. Entrance costs £1 ($1.50) for adults, 60p (90¢) for children. The museum is open from 10 a.m. to 5:30 p.m. seven days a week April to October (November to March by appointment only). To reach the museum, take the A438 Hereford to Brecon Road, turning off left ¼ mile from the city ring road.

Where to Stay

Alexander House Hotel, 61 Whitecross Rd. (tel. 0432/274882), offers moderately priced accommodations for 15 guests in a lovely house, half a mile from the city center. It's on the A438 Hereford–Brecon road, and easy to spot. Owners Sylvia and Peter White charge £10.50 ($15.75) per person nightly whether in a single or double, and for an additional £5 ($7.50) to £8 ($12) you can have one of their home-produced dinners. The cooking is family style, with fresh vegetables used whenever available. They are licensed for alcoholic beverages as well. They'll even prepare packed lunches for you. Each bedroom is commodious, with hot and cold running water, color TV, bedside lights, and central heating. On each floor there is a bathroom with toilet and shower. Early-morning tea or coffee is served in the bedrooms, and substantial snacks are available for those guests who don't require a three-course dinner.

Ferncroft Hotel, Ledbury Road (tel. 0432/265538), is a simple, comfortable hotel with no pretensions, offering an economy accommodation. The B&B rate in a single is £15 ($22.50), rising to £27 ($40.50) in a double. There is central heating, and each of the nicely furnished bedrooms contains hot and cold running water. The location is off St. Owens Street, a short walk from the railway station and the Wye River.

Bowes Guest House, 23 St. Martins St. (tel. 0432/267202), is just across the River Wye, about a five-minute walk from the cathedral. John and Eileen Bowes own a nice old town house, leading straight from the street into the hallway. The 19th-century listed building was built by the Duke of Norfolk to accommodate his fishing retinue, and there is a large public park at the back. Parking is close by. There are ten bedrooms, with hot and cold running water and central heating. Baths are down the hall. Singles rent for £10.75 ($16.13), with doubles and twins ranging from £16.50 ($24.75) to £17.50 ($26.25). Some family rooms are available at £21 ($31.50) a night. These rates include a large breakfast that features haddock or kippers in addition to the regular bacon and eggs. They'll pack a picnic lunch for you if you give them warning. Eileen Bowes is a local person and will recommend tourist sights and give directions to places farther afield.

Westdene, 200 Whitecross Rd. (tel. 0432/50438). Harvey and Myfanwy Payne are real Herefordshire locals. They love the city and surrounding countryside and welcome guests into their comfortable home to share their enjoyment of the region. Their Victorian house is about five minutes from the center of the city by car, and there is a lounge with TV. Myfanwy provides teas and light evening meals. Bed and a large English country breakfast, along with morning and evening coffee, cost £8.50 ($12.75) to £9.50 ($14.25) per person. Mrs. Payne will pack a picnic lunch for another £2.50 ($2.88). The house is centrally heated.

Staying in the Environs

If you're motoring, you can seek out a farmhouse accommodation. Gladys and Frank Lee own and run **Cym Craig** at Little Dewchurch in Hereford (tel. 0432/70250). This is a mixed farm, 180 acres around a solid Victorian farmhouse where bed and a farm breakfast costs £8 ($12) per person in rooms with hot and cold water basins. The large, spotless bedrooms have snug beds, and a bath and toilet facilities are down the passage. Guests can use the comfortable sitting room with TV, a grander drawing room, or, during the day, walk around the farm. Son Anthony provides an interesting guide when he's not away driving heavy trucks around the country. To get there from Hereford, take the Ross road, the A49, over the river and turn left at the traffic lights by the church. Follow this road to a pedestrian crossing, turning right and driving for four miles to the village. Once there, turn left. Cym Craig is the first farm on the left.

The **Green Man Inn,** at Fownthorpe (tel. 043277/243), is an attractive country inn with black-and-white beams, gables, and leaded windows, lying in the center of this village outside Hereford. An archway leads into the inn yard. Dating from the 15th century, it was once known as Naked Boy. It fulfilled its role as a hospice and inn during the Civil War when Colonel Birch and his Roundhead troops stayed here before occupying Hereford. In the 18th and 19th centuries the Petty Sessional Court was held here, and you can still stay in the judge's room overlooking the courtyard (nowadays it has a modern shower and toilet). There is a four-poster room with bath, plus a garden room with bath with views over the meadows and the River Wye. The bars are low beamed, and the dining room and sitting room also have low beams, cottage-style furnishings, wheel-back chairs, and bench tables. The inn is run these days by Arthur and Margaret Williams, who offer good bar snacks and traditional English food in their dining room. A single goes for £17.50 ($26.25), a double for £29 ($43.50), including a full English breakfast and VAT.

Apple Tree Cottage, Mansel Lacy (tel. 098122/688), lies in a charming hamlet in the heart of beautiful country. The cottage in the Marches, near the Welsh border, is actually two farm cottages, one built in 1450 and the other in 1600, now joined and modernized inside to make for comfort but with the old beams and "cruck" construction still visible. It is centrally heated, and the two bedrooms contain facilities for making morning tea or coffee. Monica Barker offers B&B for £10 ($15) per person nightly, with an evening meal costing £7 ($10.50). Good home cooking is enhanced by use of fresh garden produce. To reach Mansel Lacy, take the A438 Brecon Road out of Hereford to the junction with the A480. Mansel Lacy is about 5 miles from the turn, just off the A480.

Food and Drink

Cathedral Restaurant, 17 Church Street (tel. 0432/265233), is, as its name suggests, quite close to Hereford Cathedral. At lunch they offer a choice of roast beef, steak-and-kidney pie, fried plaice, or rump steak, all with fresh vegetables. Lunches cost from £6.50 ($9.75). For the evening meal they have a cozy "olde worlde" cellar which has a menu different from that offered at lunch. You might choose grilled plaice with parsley butter or beef Stroganoff. A three-course meal for two with wine costs around £15 ($22.50). The place is open for coffee at 10:30 a.m., staying open for afternoon tea at 4:30 p.m. (5:30 p.m. on Wednesday, Market Day). The cellar is open Thursday and Friday from 7 to 10 p.m. and Saturday from 7 to 11 p.m. In high season it's also open on Tuesday and Wednesday. You'll find this a relaxing place, whether you come in for lunch, dinner, coffee, or tea, and you'll be waited on by a courteous staff.

Effy's, 96 East St. (tel. 0432/59754). It is generally conceded that this friendly, inviting place serves the best food in town, yet it doesn't charge high prices to those who partake of its refined offerings. Its set lunch at £7 ($10.50) is good value. A professionally run place near the Town Hall, Effy's has a selection of what the British often call "accomplished starters" (that's tasty appetizers to us), followed by well-prepared main dishes that rely on fresh ingredients and a subtle use of herbs for their flavoring. Portions are adequate, not overpowering, and you may have room for one of their excellent desserts. A simpler menu is offered at lunch from noon to 3 p.m., with their best bill of fare being presented in the evening from 6 to 11, costing from £12 ($18). The restaurant is shut all day Sunday and on Monday night.

Marches, 24 Union St. (tel. 0432/55712). In a health-conscious era, Marches is outstanding for the area. Reportedly, it is the biggest health food emporium in the country, with not only a health food store but a dining room on two floors. Service is from 8:30 a.m. to 5:30 p.m. except Sunday. Mrs. Vale is the guiding force behind the success of the place, where meals cost from £5 ($7.50). She's a specialist in "wholefood cookery," and you're faced with a dozen different and tempting salads "made with good things." Vegetable flans are far better than the usual bland fare, and you can also order chicken and ham cold plates (it's not wholly vegetarian). Save room for one of the fruity pies.

Gaffers, 89 East St. (no phone) is an interesting place, useful for many purposes. After a visit to the cathedral, a short walk brings you to this cheerful café, noisy with enthusiastic young people. A light meal goes for £2.50 ($3.75). This unlicensed place is open daily except Sunday from 10 a.m. to 4:30 p.m.

A Country Hotel Near Ledbury

Ledbury is a charming old-world market town and center for the Malvern Hills. From here you can explore Eastnor Castle, two miles to the east, which has a collection of paintings, tapestries, and armor. If you'd like accommodations in the area, you'll find them at—

The Verzons, Trumpet, near Ledbury (tel. 053183/381). Robin Pollock and Carolyn and Edward Henson welcome you to their establishment, which is a free house, bistro bar, restaurant, and B&B hotel. It is a beautiful Georgian house, standing on four acres overlooking the Malvern Hills. It lies on the A438 road, some two miles from Ledbury. Most of the bedrooms have private baths or showers en suite and are pleasantly furnished, costing £16 ($24) for a single, £30 ($45) for a twin or double for B&B. Much of the food served here is homemade, with pies, stews, and creamy sweets. A three-course meal in the bistro costs from £7 ($10.50). Table d'hôte and à la carte menus are served in the Garden Restaurant, which specializes in flambé dishes such as steak au poivre. You can enjoy a three-course meal for £9 ($13.50) and up.

An Inn on the Border

The **Rhydspence Inn,** Whitney on Wye, Hereford (tel. 04973/262), is a timbered inn right on the border of England and Wales, dating from the 16th century. It has a fascinating gabled porch through which you enter the gleaming bar where a log fire crackles in the chimney. Excellent meals and snacks prepared by the chef, Ray Grosvenor, are served, including thick home made soups. Specialties are "hammy," a soup made with chopped ham and eggs, and "fishy," made with smoked haddock, anchovies, mushrooms, and cream. In addition to the bar food, there is a restaurant where the chef applies himself to grills, roasts, and tasty country dishes. Dinner costs about £9 ($13.50), and wine can be ordered by the glass. The hosts, Peter and Pamela Glover, have six rooms to rent, all with private bathrooms, color TV, beverage-making facilities, and central heating. For B&B, the charge is from £18 ($27) per person. The inn is open seven days a week, and you're assured of a warm welcome from the Glovers. The local customers are friendly, too, and you can join them in the bar in the evening for a game of darts or quoits. Try the local cider as an alternative to beer.

WORCESTER: This historic cathedral city, famous for its gloves and porcelain, lies 27 miles from Birmingham and 26 miles from Stratford-upon-Avon.

Offering views of the Malvern Hills, **Worcester Cathedral** stands high on the banks of the River Severn. Dating from 1084, it contains the Quire (rebuilt in 1224) which shelters King John's Tomb from 1216. The Chapter House, with its massive central supporting column, is considered one of the finest in England. A refreshment room and gift shop are in the cloisters. The cathedral is open from 7:45 a.m. to 7:30 p.m. in summer, 9 a.m. to 6 p.m. otherwise. There is no charge for entry, but donations are invited. You can usually climb the tower and see the view over the city and countryside. The tower door is open from 11 to 11:30 a.m., noon to 12:30 p.m., 2 to 2:30 p.m., and 3 to 3:30 p.m. The reason for the fixed times is that the traffic up and down has to be one way. Cost is 50p (75¢) for adults, 25p (38¢) for children.

A visit to the **Royal Worcester Porcelain Factory,** Severn Street (tel. 0905/23221) is worthwhile. There is a short tour for £1.90 ($2.85), allowing you to see the craftspeople at work. Unfortunately it's necessary to book ahead if you wish to take a tour, but everyone can enjoy browsing in the shops at the factory. There you can buy examples of their craft. Many pieces are "seconds," all marked as such and sold at low prices. Most of the time you won't be able to tell why. There is a magnificent museum as well.

The city is rich in other sights as well, including the **Commandery,** Sidbury (tel. 0905/355071), founded in the 11th century as the Hospital of St. Wulstan, becoming over the years a fine 15th-century timber-frame structure that was the country home of the Wylde family. Charles II used the house as headquarters for the 1651 Battle of Worcester. The Great Hall has a hammerbeam roof and a minstrels' gallery. England's premier **Civil War Centre** is now situated here, with audio-visual displays and regular "living history" enactments with 17th-century costumes and crafts. Also in the building are workshops making fine porcelain dolls. The house is open from 10:30 a.m. to 5 p.m. Monday to Saturday and from 2 to 5 p.m. Sunday. Admission is £1 ($1.50) for adults, 50p (75¢) for children.

You can also see **Queen Anne's Guildhall,** built in 1723, with statues honoring Charles I and Charles II, erected by the Royalists. Walking tours of the city are offered during the summer months. Ask at the **Worcester Tourist Information Centre,** the Guildhall (tel. 0905/23471) for details.

Food and Lodging

The **Talbot Hotel,** 8 Barbourne Rd. (tel. 0905/21206), most certainly is a bit of old England—a long, half-timbered coaching inn, with tiny dormers, a tower bay window, and leaded-glass windows. It's owned by Ray and Daphne Cross, who welcome overnight B&B guests at reasonable rates—£13.50 ($20.25) in a single, £23 ($34.50) for a double, VAT included. Ask about a family room, renting for £29 ($43.50) nightly. Each bedroom has hot and cold running water, heating, intercom, and a radio. All other meals are extra and available in the timbered, old-style dining room. À la carte meals are served in the evening. Snacks are offered in the pub lounge as well.

Chatsworth, 80 Barbourne Rd. (tel. 0905/26410), is a good clean guesthouse with car parking, where an overnight stay will cost £10 ($15) per person, including a full breakfast. All bedrooms have color TV and tea/coffee-making facilities. It's run by Patricia Grinnell, whose husband, Dennis, is a radio ham. His call sign is G4MKO, so if you care to make your advance reservations by radio, give him a call. Incidentally, a licensed ham will be allowed to use Dennis's equipment.

Park House Hotel, 12 Droitwich Rd. (tel. 0905/21816), is a neat guesthouse with pleasantly decorated, centrally heated rooms, with radio and hot and cold running water. There is a TV lounge as well. The charge is £13.50 ($20.25) in a single and from £11.50 ($17.25) per person, based on double occupancy, including VAT and an English breakfast. There is a residents' license for serving alcoholic drinks, and they provide a good range of snacks and light meals. Dinner can be provided by arrangement for £6.50 ($9.75). David and Brenda Garrod are the owners.

For meals, I suggest **Bottle's Wine Bar & Bistro,** 5 Friar St. (tel. 0905/21958), perhaps the favored rendezvous right in the historic center, particularly among young people. It's managed by Chris Powell. The decor is handsomely subdued, with mahogany tables, and the selection of cold foods is very good. I prefer the clove-studded freshly baked ham, along with a nice crisp salad. In addition, the good-tasting soups are also homemade. The roast joints, seafood dishes, and at least one hot specialty every day are also recommended. You might end your meal with a brie or a stilton cheese. Meals cost from £5 ($7.50). The wine bar is open from noon to 2:30 p.m. (last orders at 2 p.m.) and from 6:15 to 11 p.m. (last food orders at 10 p.m.); on Friday and Saturday it's open until 11 p.m. Closed Sunday at lunchtime.

Heroes, 26 Friar St. (tel. 0905/25441). Good food and fun go hand in hand here at this popular youth-oriented place. Locals who have never been much beyond Wales often get a dash of international flavor, most recently from Mexico with spicy tacos and chili con carne with just the right amount of "fire." Vegetarians will always find something on the menu for them. You can order full meals or else tasty snacks at virtually any time of the day or night, as it's open from noon to midnight daily. A set menu is offered for a modest £4.50 ($6.75). You can also order hamburgers, pizzas, pastas, and kebabs fresh from a sizzling grill. Some good and inexpensive wines back up these offerings. The setting for such a modern menu is definitely "olde world," in an Elizabethan structure with time-worn beams and ceilings designed only for short people.

Staying in the Environs

Oaklands Farm, Main Evesham Road, near Pershore off the A44 southeast of Worcester (tel. 0386/860323), is a horticultural farm of five acres, specializing in summer flowering plants. The owners, John Ownsworth and his wife, Marlene, dispense good food and comfort to overnight guests. Their home is superbly furnished and decorated, and they allow guests to share in the pleasure of using solid-silver cutlery, fine crystal glass, and Worcester porcelain. The three double rooms have twin beds, and there are ample bathroom facilties down the landing. Rooms cost £19 ($28.50) for a double, £12 ($18) for a single, including a big breakfast. They prefer guests to stay more than one night if possible. Dinner at £8 ($12) is four courses, generally including a roast joint with the usual trimmings. They have a collection of china and another of horse brasses. Tea is served from a silver teapot before the fire under a glistening chandelier.

Museums on the Outskirts

Sir Edward Elgar's Birthplace, Crown East Lane, Lower Broadheath (tel. 090566/224), about 3 miles west of Worcester, is a brick cottage surrounded by stables and a coach house built by his father and uncle in the early 19th century. Nowadays the house contains a museum of photographs and drawings, original scores of his music, and mementos of his youth. Musicians and conductors come from afar to check his music and their interpretations of it. To reach the house, drive out of Worcester on the A44 toward Leominster. After two miles, turn off to the right at the sign. The house is in the village, half a mile along a side road. Admission is £1.50 ($2.25) for adults, 50p (75¢) for children. Open daily except Wednesday from 10:30 a.m. to 6 p.m. in summer, from 1:30 to 4:30 p.m. in winter. It's closed from mid-January to mid-February.

Avoncroft Museum of Buildings, Stoke Heath, Bromsgrove (tel. 0527/31886), is 11 miles from Worcester and 21 miles from Stratford-upon-Avon. It is open daily from 11 a.m. to 5:30 p.m. in June, July, and August. Hours are the same in April, May, September, and October, but it's closed Monday. In March and November, it's open from 11 a.m. to 4:30 p.m. daily except Monday and Friday; closed altogether in December, January, and February. Admission is £2 ($3) for adults, £1 ($1.50) for children.

The museum is an open-air site where a variety of historic buildings have been saved from destruction and reconstructed. Among them are a windmill in working order; a timber-frame merchant's house from the 15th century; an Elizabethan house; cockfight theater, a stable, and a wagon shed, all from the 18th century; chain- and nail-making workshops; a blacksmith's forge; an ice house; and a three-hole outdoor toilet. The displays give a fascinating insight into the construction of the buildings erected by English forefathers. The 14th-century Guesten Hall roof from Worcester has been reconstructed at ground level so that you can see how the joints were made by the skill of artisans of the past.

The museum's cafeteria is open from 11 a.m. for coffee, lunch, and afternoon tea. Lunch includes quiches, pâtés, and a selection of salads with cold meats. Snacks are also available. Free car parking is available, and there is also a picnic area.

The **Jinney Ring Craft Centre** (tel. 052784/272) is in the village of Hanbury, on the B4091 from Bromsgrove, northeast of Worcester and only 15 miles from Stratford-upon-Avon. A number of old timbered farm buildings have been carefully restored by Richard and Jenny Greatwood into small studio workshops, housing a jeweler, an artist, a woodcarver, a woodturner, a leather worker, a fashion designer, and a stained-glass artist. Many examples of their work can be purchased from the Craftsmens Gallery, and there is also a large gift shop. Coffee, tea, and lunches are served in the 200-year-old Barn Restaurant. There is a display of old farm tools and implements including the Jinney Ring from which the center gets its name. The ring was one of the first implements in the mechanization of farming. A series of complicated cogs and drives linked the cider press or the chaff-cutter with the patient horse who plodded ever onward around the ring to drive the grinding wheels. In season, there's a press for do-it-yourself cider making. Admission is free, and there's ample parking. The center is open from Easter to Christmas from 10:30 a.m. to 5 p.m. Wednesday to Saturday and 2 to 5:30 p.m. on Sunday. They do tasty lunchtime snacks from noon to 2:30 p.m., a light meal costing about £2.50 ($3.75).

Also in the area, **Hanbury Hall** (tel. 052784/214) is a Wren-style red brick building erected in the early 18th century. It is remarkable for its outstanding painted ceilings and magnificent staircase by Thornhill. It is open April to October, Saturday and Sunday (and also Easter Monday), from 2 to 5 p.m. From May until the end of September, it is open Wednesday to Sunday and bank holidays from 2 to 6 p.m. The admission charge is £1.60 ($2.40) for adults and 80p ($1.20) for children. Teas are served in the hall.

THE MALVERNS: The beautiful, historic Malverns, once part of the ancient kingdom of Mercia, lie to the west of Worcester. Great Malvern became important in the 19th century as a spa town, and much of the Victorian splendor remains. The Malvern Hills stretch for nine miles, with six townships lying along their line, making this a splendid walking center for your visit to the shire of Hereford and Worcester. The largest Priory Church in the area dates from the 15th century and has some fine stained glass. The monks' stalls have superb misericords and medieval titles. You can wander through Great Malvern, Malvern Link, West Malvern, Malvern Wells, Little Malvern, and several other hamlets on a walking tour.

Two miles out of Great Malvern to the left as you leave on the Ledbury Road is **St. Wulstan's Church** where Sir Edward Elgar, who lived throughout his life in the Malvern area, is buried with his wife and daughter. There is a bronze bust to the composer in Priory Park, and he lived at Craeglea on the Malvern Wells road and at Forli in Alexandra Road. It was here that he composed the *Enigma Variations, Sea Pictures,* and the *Dream of Gerontius.*

Water is still bottled at **Holy Well,** above Malvern Wells, and you can visit the place where monks are reputed to have wrapped the infirm in clothes steeped in the waters to cure their ills. St. Anne's Well is also open to view above the town, but you have to be hardy to climb the 200-odd steps to taste the waters.

Food and Lodging

Walmer Lodge, 49 Abbey Rd. (tel. 06845/4139), is a small, relatively simple hotel whose food is considered the finest at the resort. Rooms are comfortably and pleasantly furnished, costing £16.50 ($24.75) in a single, £30 ($45) in a double. But, as mentioned, the main reason most guests visit the place is for the award-winning food. Go only for dinner from 7 to 9 p.m. and expect to pay from £12.50 ($18.75) for a satisfying meal. The à la carte menu which is changed every season or so is backed up by daily specials which depend on the marketplace. The popularity of the food is based on the use of quality ingredients prepared with skill. Sometimes these dishes are allowed to speak for themselves, and sometimes they are accompanied by zesty sauces. Look for the gourmet nights as well. It's essential that you call and book a table as soon as you can. French and Italian wines appear on the wine card, some interesting English varieties as well.

Sidney House, 40 Worcester Rd. (tel. 06845/4994), is a Georgian building whose owners rent out seven attractively and comfortably furnished bedrooms, four of which contain a private bath. B&B costs from £15 ($22.50) to £21 ($31.50) in a single, £27 ($40.50) to £31 ($46.50) in a double. It's also possible to book in here on half-board terms, costing from £23 ($34.50) to £25 ($37.50) per person daily. It's a lovely place for a tranquil and relaxed stay, opening onto views of the countryside of Hereford and Worcester. Convenient to the town center, the hotel is run in an attentive and considerate manner.

Chapter XIV

CAMBRIDGE AND EAST ANGLIA

"WE ARE FARMERS, great animal lovers," say two spinster sisters who run a small farm in Essex. They delight in receiving paying guests at their old farm, feeding them fresh vegetables and home-grown fruit. They are not atypical of the East Anglians. The four counties of East Anglia—Essex, Suffolk, Norfolk, and Cambridgeshire—are essentially low-lying areas, where the bucolic life still reigns supreme.

East Anglia was an ancient Anglo-Saxon kingdom, under heavy domination of the Danes for many a year. Beginning in the 12th century it was the center of a great cloth industry that brought it prosperity, as the spires of some of its churches testify to this day. In part it is a land of heathland, fens, marshes, and "Broads" in Norfolk.

Cambridge is the most-visited city in East Anglia, but don't neglect to pass through Suffolk and Essex, the Constable country, containing some of the finest landscapes in England. Norwich, the seat of the Duke of Norfolk, is less visited, but the fortunate few who go that far toward the North Sea will be rewarded.

1. Cambridge

A young man and woman lying in an open green space between colleges, reading the romantic poets . . . rowing under the Bridge of Sighs . . . spires and turrets . . . droopy willows that witness much punting . . . dusty second-hand bookshops

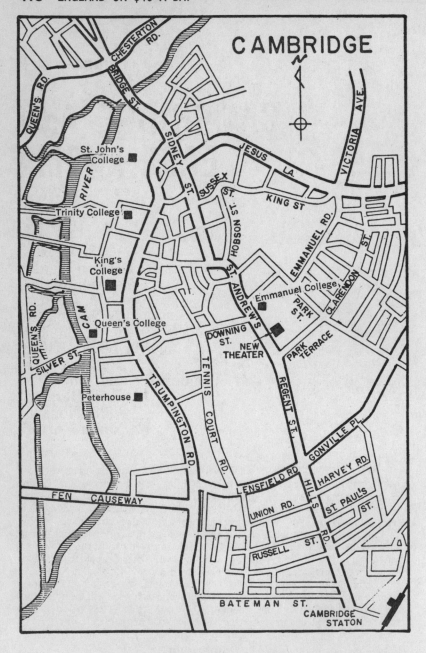

. . . daffodils blowing in the meadows . . . carol singing on Christmas Eve in King's College Chapel . . . dancing till sunrise at the end of the school year balls . . . the sounds of Elizabethan melodies from the throats of madrigal balladeers . . . the purchase of horse brasses at a corner in the open market . . . narrow lanes where Darwin, Newton, and Cromwell also trod . . . a protest demonstration . . . The Backs, where the lawns of the colleges sweep down to the Cam River . . . the tattered black robe of an upper-classman, rebelliously hanging by a thread to his shoulder as it flies in the wind.

We're in the university city of Cambridge, which, along with Oxford, is one of the ancient seats of learning in Britain. The city on the banks of the Cam River is also the county town of Cambridgeshire, 55 miles northeast of London, 80 miles from Oxford. In many ways the story of Oxford and Cambridge is similar, particularly the age-old conflict between "town and gown." But Oxford is an industrial city, sheltering a thriving life beyond the campus. Cambridge has some industry too. Yet if the university were removed, I suspect it would revert to an unpretentious market town.

There is much to see and explore in Cambridge, so give yourself time to wander, even aimlessly. For those pressed, I'll offer more specific directions.

A *Word of Warning:* Unfortunately, because of the disturbances caused by the influx of tourists to the university, Cambridge has regretfully had to limit visitors, and even exclude them from various parts of the university altogether, and in some cases, even charge a small fee for entrance. Small groups of up to six persons are generally admitted with no problem, and you can inquire from your local tourist office about visiting hours here.

A SELF-GUIDED TOUR: The center of Cambridge is closed to cars. There is good parking at the Anchor Pub in Silver Street, so why not leave your car there and then go for a walk around to some of the colleges?

Cross Silver Street Bridge, and you'll see the entrance to Queens College. Go into the college, crossing over the mathematical wooden bridge, so called because of its geometrical design. Then enter the older part of the college into the center of a quadrangle, and you'll see much of the Elizabethan architecture and also the doors around the quad, leading to the "staircases" of tiny studies and bedrooms for undergraduates within the college itself. Those who cannot get an accommodation here are boarded out around the city.

Exit through the fine Elizabethan arch into the new part of the college; turn right and, just past the Chapel, take the doorway open to the road. Turn left and at the end of the road the archway leads to King's College Chapel and the college. Just inside is a very well-defined "staircase." This is also a beautiful college with lawns sweeping to the Cam. Visit the Chapel to see the *Adoration of the Magi* by Rubens hanging over the High Altar. You can attend evensong at King's almost every night at 5:30. There are services every Sunday at 10:30 a.m., 3:30 p.m., and again at 6 p.m.

Leave by the Porter's Lodge and walk to the Church Tower of the 800-year-old parish church of St. Edward Saint and Martyr. Within its walls the reformers of the 16th century preached and ministered the gospel. Turn right into the main Market Square, where there is a daily market for fruit, vegetables, and other produce.

From here, follow Wheeler Street, leading on to Benet Street. Opposite St. Benet's Church in St. Benet's Lane you will see two doors leading to a passage which will bring you to the Eagle Pub on the grounds of Corpus Christi, reputedly the only galleried inn in Cambridge. It is little known by visitors but much frequented by locals.

Without stops, this walk will take you about one hour of leisurely observation. This tour is best done when the colleges aren't in session. Otherwise, many colleges at term time are, of course, closed in the morning.

GUIDED TOURS OF THE CAMBRIDGE COLLEGES: Leisurely walking tours of about two hours' duration take place daily from April to early November (Saturday only in winter). They start from the **Tourist Information Centre,** Wheeler Street (tel. 0223/322640). With a qualified and knowledgeable guide you will explore the small streets and courts of the major colleges. These are places of work, and at term time some of the buildings may be in use or closed. King's College Chapel, for example, may be in use for a choir practice. Only Fellows and their guests may walk on the grass, and staircases lead to the accommodations of students and are private. The cost of these tours is £1.75 ($2.63) per person. Tours vary in direction, but always contain as much of interest as is available at the time. Departure times also vary according to demand, but there are usually four departures a day during July to September, when the colleges are "down" in any case.

CAMBRIDGE UNIVERSITY: Oxford University predates the one at Cambridge. But in the early 13th century scholars began coming up to Cambridge. The choice of the market town as a seat of learning just happened, perhaps coming about because a core of important masters, dissatisfied with Oxford, elected to live near the fens. Eventually, Cambridge won partial recognition from Henry III, rising and slumping with the approval or disdain of subsequent English monarchs. In all, the University of Cambridge consists of 29 colleges, most of which are for both men and women. But if you have time for only one sight, then make it:

King's College Chapel

The teenage Henry VI founded the college on King's Parade in 1441. But most of its buildings today are from the 19th century. The Perpendicular chapel is not only its crowning glory, but one of the architectural gems in England inherited from the Middle Ages. The chapel, owing to the altogether chaotic vicissitudes of English kings, wasn't completed until the early years of the 16th century. Its most characteristic features are its magnificent fan vaulting, all of stone, and its Great Windows, most of which were fashioned by Flemish artisans between 1515 and 1531 (the west windows, however, dates from the late Victorian period). The stained glass, in hues of blues, reds, and ambers, reflects biblical stories. The long range of the windows, reading from the first on the north side at the west end, right around the chapel back to the first on the south side, tell the story of the birth of the Virgin, the Annunciation, the Birth of Christ, the Life, Ministry, and Death of Christ, the Resurrection, the Ascension, the Acts of the Apostles, and the Assumption. The upper range contains Old Testament parallels to the New Testament stories—that is, the logic of the windows derives from the story of Christ. The rood screen is from the early 16th century. Henry James called King's College Chapel "the most beautiful in England."

It is open during vacation time on weekdays from 9:30 a.m. to 5 p.m., and on Sunday from 10:30 a.m. to 5 p.m. During term time, the public is welcome to choral services which are at 5:30 p.m. on weekdays (service said on Monday) and at 10:30 a.m. and 3:30 p.m. on Sunday. In term the chapel is open to visitors from 9:30 a.m. to 3:45 p.m. on weekdays, from 2 to 3 p.m. and from the end of evensong (approximately 4:30) to 5:45 p.m. on Sunday. The chapel may be closed at other times of the year for special events. Closed December 26 to January 4.

Peterhouse

This college on Trumpington Street is visited largely because it is the oldest seat of learning at Cambridge, having been founded as early as 1284. The founding father was Hugo de Balsham, bishop of Ely. Of the original buildings, only the Hall remains. This was restored in the 19th century and now contains stained-glass windows by William Morris. Old Court was constructed in the 15th century, but refaced in 1754, and the chapel dates from 1632. Parties of not more than 12 at a time may visit the college between 1 and 5 p.m. Ask at the porter's lodge.

Trinity College

On Trinity Street, Trinity College, the largest at Cambridge (not to be confused with Trinity Hall), was founded in 1546 by Henry VIII from a number of smaller colleges that had existed on the site. The Great Court is the most spacious court in Cambridge, built when Thomas Nevile was master. Sir Christopher Wren designed the library. This college has Sir Isaac Newton, Lord Byron, and Prince Charles among its former members. For admission to the college, apply at the porter's lodge or telephone 0223/358201 for information.

Emmanuel College

On St. Andrew's Street, Emmanuel was founded in 1584 by Sir Walter Mildmay, chancellor of the exchequer to Elizabeth I. John Harvard, founder of that university, studied here. With its attractive gardens, it makes for a good stroll. You might visit the chapel designed by Sir Christopher Wren and completed in 1676. The chapel is open daily, except when in use, from 9:30 a.m. to 12:15 p.m. and 2 to 6 p.m. The gardens and paddock are open daily from 9 a.m. to 6 p.m.

Queens' College

On Queens' Lane, Queens' College (tel. 0223/335511) is considered by some old Cantabrigians as the loveliest in the architectural galaxy. Dating back to 1448, it was founded, then refounded, by two English queens—one the wife of Henry VI, the other the wife of Edward IV. Its second cloisters are the most interesting, flanked with the half-timbered President's Lodge, dating from around 1595. The college may be visited during the day. An admission fee of 35p (53¢) is charged and a short printed guide issued. Normally, individual visitors are admitted between 1:45 and 4:30 p.m. only, but during July, August, and September the college is also open to visitors from 10:15 a.m. to 12:45 p.m. Entry and exit is by the Old Porters' Lodge in Queens' Lane only. The college is closed between mid-May and mid-June. The Old Hall and chapel are normally open to the public when not in use.

St. John's College

On St. John's Street, the college was founded in 1511 by Lady Margaret, mother of Henry VIII. A few years earlier she had founded Christ's College. Before her intervention, an old monk-run hospital had stood on the site of St. John's. The impressive gateway bears the Tudor coat-of-arms, and Second Court is a fine example of late Tudor brickwork. But its best-known feature is the Bridge of Sighs, crossing the Cam, built as late as the 19th century, patterned after the bridge in Venice. It connects the older part of the college with New Court, a Gothic revival, on the opposite bank, from which there is an outstanding view of the famous Backs. Wordsworth was an alumnus of this college. The Bridge of Sighs is open from October till Easter but is best viewed from the neighboring Wren Bridge. The chapel is open from 10 a.m. to noon and 2 to 4 p.m. daily except Monday. The college is closed to visitors from late April until late June.

Other College Sights

The preceding form only a representative selection of some of the more interesting-to-visit colleges. **Magdalene College** on Magdalene Street was founded in 1542; **Pembroke College** on Trumpington Street was founded in 1347; **Christ's Col-**

lege on St. Andrew's Street was founded in 1505; and **Corpus Christi College** on Trumpington Street dates from 1352. Only someone planning to anchor into Cambridge for a long time will get around to them. Magdalene is open daily from 9 a.m. to 6:30 p.m.; Pembroke, daily till dusk; Christ's College, weekdays. For Corpus Christi times, inquire at the porter's lodge.

Colleges aren't the only thing to see in Cambridge, as you'll assuredly agree if you explore the following attractions:

THE FITZWILLIAM MUSEUM: On Trumpington Street, near Peterhouse, this museum (tel. 0223/332900) was the gift of the Viscount Fitzwilliam, who in 1816 gave Cambridge University his paintings and rare books, along with £100,000 to build the house in which to display them. He thereby knowingly or unknowingly immortalized himself. Other gifts have since been bequeathed to the museum, and now it is one of the finest in England. It is noted for its porcelain, old prints, archeological relics, and oils (works by such masters as Titian and Veronese). The museum is open weekdays from 10 a.m. to 5 p.m., on Sunday from 2:15 till 5 p.m. However, only half of the exhibits are open in the morning, the other half in the afternoon, owing to the lack of staff. Closed Monday, Good Friday, and December 24 to January 1 inclusive. Admission is free.

GREAT ST. MARY'S: Great St. Mary's (tel. 0223/350914), opposite King's College Chapel on King's Parade, is the university church. It is built on the site of an 11th-century church, but the present building dates largely from 1478. It was closely associated with events of the Reformation. The cloth that covered the hearse of King Henry VII is on display in the church. A fine view of Cambridge may be obtained from the top of the tower. Admission to the top of the church tower is 30p (45¢) for adults, 15p (23¢) for children.

BOAT RENTALS: Punting on the Cam (nothing to do with football) is a traditional pursuit of students and visitors in Cambridge, but there are other types of boating available if you don't trust yourself to stand up and pole a punt under and around the weeping willow trees. Up river, you can go all the way to Grantchester, a distance of about 2 miles, made so famous by Rupert Brooke. Downstream, you pass along the Backs behind the colleges of the university.

Scudamore's Boatyards, Granta Place (tel. 0223/359750), by the Anchor Pub, has been in business since 1910. Costs are by the hour: £3.20 ($4.80) for a punt, £3 ($4.50) for a rowboat, and £2.80 ($4.20) for a canoe. A deposit is required, £3 ($4.50) payable by cash, check or major credit card), refundable if you don't wreck the boat.

BICYCLE RENTALS: The most popular way of getting around in Cambridge, next to walking, is bicycling. **Geoff's Bike Hire,** 65 Devonshire Rd. (tel. 0223/65629), has bicycles for rent for £3 ($4.50) per day or £7 ($10.50) per week. A deposit of £15 ($22.50) is required.

PERSONALIZED TOURS: The person to know if you're in the Cambridge area is **Mrs. Isobel Bryant,** who runs Heritage Tours from her 200-year-old cottage, Manor Cottage, Swaffham Prior, Cambridge (tel. 0638/741440). A highly qualified expert on the area, she will arrange tours, starting from, say, your Cambridge hotel to Saffron Walden, Thaxted, and Audley End, for example, or to the U.S. military cemetery at Madingley, then Ely, Anglesey Abbey, and the lovely timbered villages of Suffolk. The day's trip costs around £60 ($90) for three people. Lunch and admission charges are extra—probably about £5 ($7.50) per person more. Mrs. Bryant can arrange accommodations with local families in their lovely country houses. The charges range from £20 ($30) to £50 ($75) for two persons per night in double rooms with private baths, these tariffs including a full English breakfast. Often dinner with the family can be arranged at around £9 ($13.50) per person, including wine.

There are also walking tours around the colleges of Cambridge, a tour of the Fitzwilliam Museum, and if you can make up a party of 15 or more persons, a fascinating tour of Newmarket, center of the horse-racing industry. On that tour, you visit a racing stable, sales paddock, and the elegant rooms of the Jockey Club, headquarters of racing since 1771, as well as a stud farm and other places of interest connected with racing. A whole day costs £12 ($18) per person; a half day, £7 ($10.50). If you want lunch arranged at a private house with Cordon Bleu cookery, the cost is around £8 ($12) per person.

ACCOMMODATIONS: During vacation periods, there are rooms available for tourists which are used by students in term time. The **Tourist Office** (tel. 0223/322640), on Wheeler Street, opposite the Arts Theatre and behind the Guildhall on Market Place, will give you information on available accommodations through their booking service, charging 90p ($1.35) per person for finding a room in or around Cambridge. If you have no reservation and want to try it on your own, check your luggage and go to the beginning of Chesterton Road, knocking on front doors as you proceed.

I'll survey the pick of B&B lodgings scattered around the city.

Regent Hotel, 41 Regent St. (tel. 0223/351470), reopened in 1985 to receive paying guests in its 12 attractively and comfortably furnished bedrooms, nine of which contain private baths. All units have a color TV and radio. Only breakfast is served, but there's a cocktail bar on the street level. It's one of the nicest of the moderately priced small hotels of Cambridge. Depending on the plumbing, singles cost £20 ($30) to £29 ($43.50), doubles or twins £30.50 ($45.75) to £40 ($60). Right in the city center, overlooking Parker's Piece, the house was built in the 1840s as the original site of Newham College. When the college outgrew its physical plant, the building became a hotel.

Ashley Hotel, 74 Chesterton Rd. (tel. 0223/350059), is one of the best B&Bs in Cambridge. However, it rents out only 10 rooms, and its good reputation is known far and wide, so reserve a room early if you wish to stay here. Accommodations cost £17.50 ($26.25) in a single, £28 ($42) in a double. It is within walking distance of the center of the university town and the colleges, lying near the River Cam and Jesus Green. Guests of the Ashley can use the dining and drinking facilities of the Arundel House Hotel at 53 Chesterton, which is right nearby, but cut down considerably on their room costs by staying at the Ashley.

Helen Hotel, 167–169 Hills Road (tel. 0223/246465), run by Gino and Helen (its namesake) Agodino, lying about a mile from the center of the university town. It's much bigger than most hotels considered in this section, containing a total of 29 well-furnished bedrooms, most of which have a private shower or toilet. Units contain phones and color TVs as well. The single rate is £21 ($31.50), a double or twin going for £38 ($57). The hotel has many amenities, including a pleasant garden along with a TV lounge and cocktail bar. You can also order dinner here for £10 ($15), the cooking a mixture of British and continental fare.

May View Guest House, 12 Park Parade (tel. 0223/66018), was the family home of Roger Stock's grandparents from 1922. When they died, he converted the pleasant house into one of the most charming B&Bs in the county. It sits on a street corner of the old city, across from the rolling expanse of Jesus Green. Its brick exterior was built by the Victorians, but the elegantly molded front door is an antique salvaged from a Georgian house slated for demolition. This concern for the past fills every corner of Mr. Stock's guesthouse. The three bedrooms he rents all have hot and cold running water and a view of the park. The charge is from £28 ($42) to £32 ($48) for double occupancy, with VAT and an English breakfast included. The morning meal is served in a dining room ringed with antiques or in a small Italianate courtyard.

Ayeone Cleave Guest House, 95 Gilbert Rd. (tel. 0223/63387), is a well-run B&B in a quiet part of the city with its own private car park and gardens. All the well-furnished rooms are centrally heated and contain hot and cold running water, color TV, radios, tea/coffee-making facilities, and razor sockets. There is a public shower. Rates, which include a full English breakfast, are £13 ($19.50) in a single. A twin or double with private shower and toilet is from £28 ($42) to £30 ($45). Cold drinks and sandwiches are served on request. Your hostess is Mrs. E. Humphries, who is helpful in providing information.

Parkside Guest House, 25 Parkside (tel. 0223/311212), is one of the better guesthouses, and it's run by Mr. and Mrs. John Sutcliffe, who do much to make guests enjoy their stay in the well-preserved 1850 building. Their 11 rooms, costing from £17.50 ($26.25) to £19 ($28.50) per person, the higher price for a unit with a private bath, all with a full breakfast. Meals can be served in your room or in an attractive breakfast room. Laundry facilities provided are part of several conveniences. They also help the tourist to Cambridge, renting bicycles, providing information, whatever.

Mr. and Mrs. D. Griffiths, 51 Jesus Lane (tel. 0223/66801), welcome you into their home, charging £9.50 ($14.25) per person for B&B. They offer clean, comfortable rooms, with convenient facilities. Although accommodation is limited during university terms, a room is always kept for transient guests.

Suffolk Guest House, 69 Milton Rd. (tel. 0223/352016), was built as the home of a well-known Cambridge doctor, but it has been converted into a contemporary guesthouse owned by Mr. and Mrs. Ball. Although they have retained some of the qualities of the old house, they have installed such modern conveniences as central heating, razor points, tea/coffee-makers, and color TV in the rooms. Singles rent for £14 ($21) nightly for B&B. Doubles cost £22.50 ($33.75) bathless, rising to £27.50 ($41.25) to £32 ($48) with private shower or bath and toilet. Children up to 10 years of age sharing a double room with their parents are charged £10 ($15). The helpful hosts will offer you their garden in summer for tea or coffee.

The Bridge Guest House, 151–153 Hills Rd. (tel. 0223/247942), is owned and run by Mr. and Mrs. Dalla-Libera. Their guesthouse stands a mile from the city center, and they offer rooms that are comfortable and agreeable. Fully licensed, their establishment charges from £14 ($21) to £16 ($24), in a single, the cheaper price for guests ordering the continental breakfast, the higher tab for the English breakfast. A double costs from £26 ($39). You can also order a three-course evening meal for £6.50 ($9.75).

Miss M. A. Sampson, 7 Malcolm St. (tel. 0223/353069), can accommodate tourists only when her university students go on vacation: that is, from mid-June till mid-September. Her home is a convenient place at which to stay, in the center of Cambridge, just off Jesus Lane. Her B&B rate ranges from £9 ($13.50) per person, and you'll be nestling down at one of the finest lodging choices on this Street.

Portugal Street is only a stone's throw from the most interesting colleges and the center of Cambridge—yet the street is a good choice for finding an inexpensive B&B. **Mrs. Clough,** 22 Portugal St. (tel. 0223/357769), opens her private home to paying guests. She charges from £9.50 ($14.25) per person for B&B. Normally modest, she does pride herself on the abundance of her English breakfast. The extensively modernized rooms she offers are small and tidy, containing comfortable beds. All units have basins with hot and cold running water. Mrs. Clough has a large and varied collection of antique dolls, and she is also quite an authority on monumental brass rubbing and where to find the best ones around Cambridge. Just ask.

WHERE TO EAT: In a building reputedly the oldest in Cambridge, **Belinda's Wine and Coffee Bar,** 14 Trinity St. (tel. 0223/356213), occupies two floors behind the black-and-white timbered facade. Upstairs, it serves coffee, tea, cakes, cold snacks, and soups as well as breakfasts from 8:30 to 11 a.m. The cellar Granary serves a range of drinks and hot meals. Belinda's is open seven days a week from 8:30 a.m. to 6 p.m. From noon to 2 p.m., there is a minimum charge of 75p ($1.13). Meals cost about £4 ($6). Both floors of the establishment are licensed.

Varsity Restaurant, 35 St. Andrew's St. (tel. 0223/356060). The Greek dishes offered here are eaten in a bare whitewashed room with black beams and pictures of boats and islands on the walls. Kebabs are served with rice and salad, and there are other Greek dishes along with some continental ones for less adventurous palates. A meal, including a glass of wine and coffee, will cost about £5 ($7.50). Service is fast and cheerful, and hours are from noon to 3 p.m. and 5:30 to 11 p.m. daily.

Browns, 23 Trumpington St. (tel. 0223/461655), firmly entrenched at Oxford, is now a sensation at Cambridge. Fronted with a neoclassical colonnade, it has all the grandeur of the Edwardian era. It was actually built in 1914 as the outpatient department of a hospital dedicated to Edward VII. Today it is the most lighthearted place for dining in the university city, with wicker chairs, high ceilings, pre-World War I woodwork, and a long bar laden with bottles of wine. Hours are Monday to Saturday from 11 a.m. to 11:30 p.m. (on Sunday from noon to 11:30 p.m.). The long bill of fare includes various renditions of spaghetti, fresh salads (even Mrs. Browns' vegetarian), several selections of meat and fish (from leg of lamb chargrilled with rosemary to fresh fish in season), hot sandwiches, and the chef's daily specials posted on a blackboard. Meals range from £5 ($7.50) to £12 ($18). If you drop in in the afternoon, you can also order thick ice cream milk shakes or pure fruit juices.

Hobbs Pavilion, Park Terrace (tel. 0223/67480), opens onto Parker's Piece in the vicinity of the University Arms Hotel. A delightful place, and deservedly popular, it is called "a crêperie with a difference." The location is the historic brick-built Cricket Pavilion constructed to honor Sir Jack Hobbs. You get a choice of nearly two dozen crêpes, both for a main course and as a dessert. The stuffings range from smoked haddock with egg to curried chicken. This savory list is backed up by a selection of freshly prepared soups and salads. Meals cost from £5 ($7.50) and up, and hours are Tuesday to Saturday, from noon to 2:30 p.m. and 7 to 10:30 p.m. (on Thursday it doesn't open until 8:30 p.m. for dinner). It is closed on Sunday and Monday and takes a vacation from mid-August to mid-September.

Shao Tao, 72 Regent St. (tel. 0223/353942), on a commercial street right near the center of town, is a specialist in the cuisine of Canton, Szechuan, and Peking. Some critics consider this operation of chef-owner Shao Tao the best Chinese restaurant in Cambridge; other food critics have different favorites. The menu, served in a choice of two inviting rooms, presents a wide array of dishes, including "three kinds of meat" soup, followed with beef with orange sauce and a host of other dishes. But if you're confused, you can order the "leave it to us feast" at £9.50 ($14.25) per person, and are likely to be happily surprised. Hours are daily from noon to 2:30 p.m. and 6 to 11 p.m. (until 11:30 p.m. on Friday and Saturday).

Free Press, 7 Prospect Row (tel. 0223/68337). Recently several Cambridge students directed me to a small back street Victorian pub which is reputed to offer some of the best grub in town. After sampling its fare, I agree. Costing from £5 ($7.50), meals are served only from noon to 2 p.m. You get a good range of food here, freshly made soups, flavorsome meat pies, and a hot chef's special of the day such as moussaka as well as some vegetarian meals. It's self-service, and the two outside tables go quickly in summer. Desserts are homemade and tempting as well. You can come back in the evening for a pint any time from 6 to 11:30 p.m. (until 10:30 p.m. on Sunday).

Shades Wine Bar & Restaurant, 1 King's Parade (tel. 0223/359506), opposite King's College, gives you a choice of having either a full meal in the restaurant or bar snacks from the wine bar buffet, which consists of pâtés, salads, cold meats, smoked fish, cheeses, and seasonal specialties, to be accompanied by excellent wines sold by the glass or bottle. It is open seven days a week: from 11:30 a.m. to 2:30 p.m. and 6 to 11 p.m. Monday to Saturday, from noon to 2 p.m. and 7 to 10:30 p.m. on Sunday. The restaurant is open from 6:30 to 10 p.m. Tuesday to Saturday. Appetizers include prawns in the shell with garlic mayonnaise, escargots, soup, and smoked oysters. For a main course, you might choose filet steak Madagascar, salmon steak tsar, or scampi marinière au riz. There is also a good selection of desserts and cheeses. The menu is good and imaginative, and portions are ample. A meal costs around £14 ($21).

The **Anchor Pub,** Silver Street (tel. 0223/353554), right beside the Silver Street Bridge, has a bar and terrace right on the waterside, where you can get snacks—a ploughman's lunch, french bread and pâté, ham salad, and various cold meats in sandwiches. Upstairs is a restaurant where you can enjoy a prawn cocktail, soups, lamb cutlets with mint sauce, peas, baked potato, plus vanilla meringue surprise, or grilled rump steak with potatoes, followed by dessert. A beefburger is another popular item. A three-course meal will cost about £10 ($15). Hours are from noon to 2 p.m. and 5 to 11 p.m. On Sunday, it's open from noon to 2 p.m. and 7 to 10:30 p.m. The pub is by Scudamore's, where you rent boats.

Martin's Coffee House, 4 Trumpington St. (tel. 0223/361757), is just past the Fitzwilliam Museum. It's a small coffeehouse, but has high standards, offering some of the best filled sandwiches in Cambridge. Whole-meal rolls are filled with turkey, ham, beef, salad, cheese, and eggs, for a mouth-filling snack. Homemade cakes and doughnuts are also sold. You can have steak-and-kidney pie and two vegetables, as well as casseroles, curries, pâtés, and omelets. Meals cost from £4 ($6). All marketing is done daily so everything is fresh and wholesome. The place is open from 8:30 a.m. to 7:30 p.m. Monday to Friday, from 9 a.m. to 5:30 p.m. Saturday, and from 10 a.m. to 5:30 p.m. Sunday.

Pentagon and **Roof Garden,** 6 St. Edwards Passage (tel. 0223/355246), is in the center of Cambridge, overlooking medieval cottages and the historic churchyard. Cold buffet meals and four hot specialties are served daily at the Pentagon, with meals costing from £7.50 ($11.25). There is a fine wine list and fully licensed bar. Connected to and run by the Arts Theatre, the restaurant has a strong artistic atmosphere and is patronized by many stars of the English stage. It's open for lunch Monday to Saturday from noon to 3 p.m. and for supper from 6 to 10:30 p.m. The Roof Garden, perched above the theater, is popular in summer as it offers al fresco meals, self-service lunch, afternoon tea, and supper, with a view of the Cambridge spires. You select from an array of hot and cold buffet dishes, with meals averaging around £6 ($9). Wines are available by the glass, and there's a fully licensed bar. Local artists exhibit their work here. The Roof Garden is open Monday to Saturday from 9:30 a.m. to 8 p.m.

Strudel's Restaurant, University Pitt Club Building, 7a Jesus Lane (tel. 0223/311678), occupies part of an edifice that was originally constructed as an elegant Turkish bath. Since 1866 it has been used by the exclusive University Pitt Club, a young gentlemen's dining club founded in memory of William Pitt. Part of the building, including the original club dining room, with its high ceiling, huge central glass dome, and oak paneling, is now Strudel's Restaurant. Tables are draped in white, with fresh flowers and candles. In colder weather, a large, glowing fire makes a warm, inviting atmosphere. The restaurant is run by Christopher Ryan, who likes everything fresh insofar as possible, does most of the cooking and shops in the market daily for fresh vegetables. Meals cost from £7.50 ($11.25) to £15 ($22.50). The restaurant specializes in continental dishes, often using old family recipes, many of which date back more than 100 years. When available, fish and game such as Sussex pheasant are featured. Only dinner is served (except for lunch by reservations on Sunday), and it's offered from 6 to 10 p.m. Monday to Thursday, from 7 to 11 p.m. on Friday and Saturday. Reservations are advisable.

ENTERTAINMENT: An outstanding attraction in Cambridge is the **Arts Theatre,** 6

St. Edward's Passage, with its entrance on Peas Hill, fitted into a maze of lodging houses and shops. It provides Cambridge and the surrounding area with its most important theatrical events. Almost all of the leading stars of the British stage have performed here at one time or another. Call 0223/352000 to find out what's playing. Seats for most productions are £6 ($9) and £6.50 ($9.75).

Nearby, on Market Passage, you'll find the principal film house, the **Arts Cinema,** which usually has three separate showings daily. Seats for the evening performances are bookable by telephone 0223/352001.

On the pub crawl, the **Eagle,** Bene't Street (tel. 0223/53782), at the point where King's Parade meets Trumpington, is near the top of everyone's list. A coaching inn with a history going back to the 1500s, it is entered through an arched doorway into a courtyard of cobblestones, with a galleried coachyard. Inside, look up at the ceiling where British and Yankee soldiers in World War II left graffiti (often bits of gum). You can enjoy bar food, such as fresh salads and Lancashire hot pot here, with meals costing from £5 ($7.50). Meals and bar snacks are served from noon to 2 p.m. and 6 to 8 at night except Sunday. However, the pub is open for drinkers until 11 p.m.

Cambridge Arms, 4 King St. (tel. 0223/359650), is a popular student haunt in the center of town. The place has plenty of atmosphere and doesn't neglect its food in favor of dispensing beer and ale. In fact, it has good lunchtime meals, including pâté as an appetizer and the chef's daily specials such as grilled steaks and cold buffet dishes. Meals cost from £5 ($7.50) and hours are from 10:30 a.m. to 2:30 p.m. and 6 to 11 p.m. (closes at 10:30 p.m. on Sunday). Jazz is a feature on Sunday through Tuesday nights. Ever played a game of shove-ha'penny?

Perhaps the most popular pub outing you can take from Cambridge is to the hamlet of Grantchester, lying two miles from the university city and reached by taking the A603. One of the most beautiful villages in the shire, Grantchester has an old church and gardens leading down to water meadows. It was made famous by Rubert Brooke, the famed pre-World War I English poet, who is best known today for his sonnet, *The Soldier.* He was a charming and romantic character, and his life, which ended prematurely in 1915, has inspired many books. His reputation isn't what it was, but literary fans still pay a pilgrimage to Grantchester. Even if you've never heard of Brooke, you may enjoy spending a late afternoon there, wandering through its old church, and then heading, as everybody does, including Cambridge students and their professors, to **The Green Man,** 59 High St., Grantchester (tel. 0223/841178), a coaching inn with a history of some four and a half centuries. On a winter's night, the mellow old pub welcomes you with an open fire. But in summer you may want to retreat to the beer garden in back, and, from there, you can stroll down to the river. If you're in Grantchester at lunch, you can enjoy a good spread, including fresh salads, pâtés, English cheese, and desserts, with filling meals costing from £5 ($7.50). Hours are from 11 a.m. to 2:30 p.m. and 6 to 11 p.m.

LODGINGS ON THE OUTSKIRTS: For those who prefer the peace and quiet of village life, try for rooms with **Mrs. Buckle,** St. Andrews, 16 Church St., Little Shelford (tel. 0223/842254), five miles south of the university city and three miles from Duxford Museum. Mrs. Buckle has a large, pleasant house, including some rooms with balcony overlooking a typical English garden. One of her comfortable bedrooms rents for £10 ($15) per person for B&B. Rare in such a place, you have a choice of breakfast items if you order the night before.

2. Ely

The top attraction in the fen country, outside of Cambridge, is **Ely Cathedral.** The small city of Ely lies 70 miles from London, but only 16 miles north of Cambridge. Ely used to be known as the Isle of Ely, until the surrounding marshes and meres were drained, forcing the sea to recede. The last stronghold of Saxon England,

Ely was defended by Hereward the Wake, until his capitulation to the Normans in 1071.

ELY CATHEDRAL: The near-legendary founder of the cathedral was Etheldreda, the wife of a Northumbrian king, who established a monastery on the spot in 673. But the present structure dates from 1083. Seen for miles around, the landmark octagonal lantern tower is the crowning glory of the cathedral. A remarkable engineering achivement, it was erected in 1322, following the collapse of the old tower. Four hundred tons of lead and wood hang in space, held there by timbers reaching to the eight pillars.

You enter the cathedral through the beautiful Galilee West Door, a good representation of the Early English style of architecture. The already-mentioned lantern tower and the Octagon are the most notable features inside, but don't fail to visit the Lady Chapel. Although it's lost much of its decoration over the centuries, it still is a handsome example of the Decorated style, having been completed in the mid-14th century. The cathedral is open from 7 a.m. to 7 p.m. in summer, from 7:30 a.m. to 6 p.m. on weekdays in winter, and from 7:30 a.m. to 6 p.m. on Sunday. Visitors are asked to make a donation of £1.60 ($2.40) to help save the cathedral from ruin. For information, telephone 0353/2078.

The city, really a market town, is interesting—at least momentarily so—as it seems to be living in the past. Nevertheless, the attractions of Cambridge are close by, too alluring for most visitors to want to spend much time in Ely, once they've experienced the lace-like cathedral. Still, here are my recommendations, which take in overnight guests should you succumb to the charm of Ely.

FOOD AND LODGING: In a quiet residential section of Ely, **Nyton Guest House,** Barton Road (tel. 0353/2459), is an attractive twin-gabled guesthouse, surrounded by a two-acre flower garden with lawn and trees. Additional beauty is gained from the adjoining 18-hole golf course (on which reduced greens fees are available), with uninterrupted views over a wide area of fenland. Arthur and Rosalyn Setchell, the owners, are rightly proud of the list of pleased clients shown in the guest book. The house is licensed for alcoholic drinks. Only B&B is provided, a double room costing £30 ($45) per night, and a single going for £20 ($30). All these tariffs include a full English breakfast. Each bedroom has a private bath, hot beverage facilities, and a clock radio-alarm. Barton Road is easily accessible from the cathedral and railway station. It's on the A142 Ely–Newmarket road, off the A10 Ely road.

The **Old Fire Engine House,** St. Mary's Street (tel. 0353/2582), opposite St. Mary's Church, is one of the finer restaurants in East Anglia, worth a detour. It enjoys an interesting setting, in a complex of buildings with an art gallery. The restaurant was converted from a fire station, and it has a walled garden in which you can dine or order a cream tea in summer. All the good English cooking is the result of the staff, a harmonious combination of unusual people who really care about food preparation. Food materials are all fresh. The menu is large and varied, including soups such as "lovage" (in season only). Main courses are likely to include such seasonal and other dishes as hot game pie, eel pie, pigeon casserole in red wine, casserole pheasant, jugged hare, and beef braised in beer. Expect to pay from £12 ($18) for a complete meal. The place is open for lunch weekdays from 12:30 to 2 p.m. and for dinner from 7:30 to 9 p.m. Sunday hours are from 12:30 to 5:30 p.m.

A TOUR TO GRIME'S GRAVES: On the B1108, off the main A1065 from Swaffham to Mildenhall road east of Ely, you can visit Grime's Graves (tel. 0842/810656), 3 miles northeast of Brandon. This is well worth the short detour, as it is the largest group of Neolithic flint mines in the country. This is fir-wooded country with little population, and it's easy to imagine yourself transported back to ancient times.

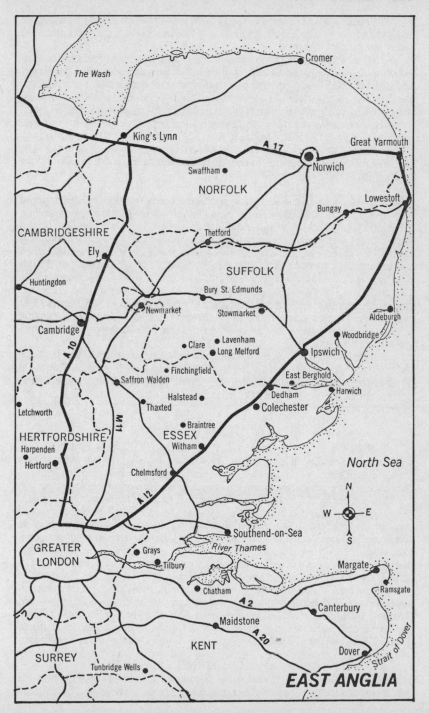

EAST ANGLIA

The mines are well signposted, and you soon find yourself at a small parking lot presided over by a custodian who will open up one or several of the shafts, allowing you to enter ancient Britain.

Climb down the ladder of the pit and imagine what must have been going on even before the time of the Anglo-Saxons. Restoration has been carried out during the intervening years, and it is now possible to see where work took place and, if you're lucky, you may find a worked flint of your own to present to the custodian. It's best to have a flashlight handy. The climb down is perpendicular, so it's only for the stout-hearted.

The mines are close to the air force bases so well known to countless American air crews during World War II. Hours are from 9:30 a.m. to 6:30 p.m. mid-March to mid-October on weekdays, from 2 to 6:30 p.m. on Sunday. Off-season hours are 9:30 a.m. to 4 p.m. weekdays, from 2 to 4 p.m. on Sunday. Admission is 75p ($1.13) for adults, 35p (54¢) for children.

AN AIRCRAFT MUSEUM: In hangars that date from World War I, the **Imperial War Museum** (tel. 0223/833963), on the A505 Newmarket–Royston road at junction 10 on the M11 motorway, is housed at Duxford Airfield, the former Battle of Britain station. Displayed is a huge collection of historic civil and military aircraft, including the B-17 Flying Fortress, the Super Sabre, and Concorde 01, Britain's preproduction specimen of the controversial jet. Other exhibits include midget submarines, British and German tanks, and a variety of field artillery pieces, plus such additions as a P-51 Mustang and a prototype TSR-2. The museum is open daily except Good Friday and the first Monday in May from mid-March to early November from 10:30 a.m. to 5:30 p.m. or dusk if earlier. Last admissions are 45 minutes before closing time. Admission is £2.50 ($3.75) for adults, £1.25 ($1.88) for children. Special charges apply for special events. Parking is free.

Duxford was also a U.S. Eighth Air Force fighter station in World War II. There are now more than 90 aircraft on display, including the only B-29 Super-fortress in Europe, plus a BE2c and an RE8 from World War I. Other exhibits include a giant 140-ton coastal artillery gun from Gibraltar and a special historical display on the U.S. Eighth Air Force in World War II.

ESSEX

Even though it borders London, and is industrialized in places, Essex still contains unspoiled rural areas and villages. Most motorists pass through it on the way to Cambridge. What they find, after leaving Greater London, is a land of rolling fields. In the east are many seaside towns and villages, as Essex opens onto the North Sea.

The major city is Colchester, in the east, known today for its oysters and roses. Fifty miles from London, it was the first Roman city in Britain, the oldest recorded town in the kingdom. It's a rather dull-appearing city today, although parts of its Roman fortifications remain. A Norman castle has been turned into a museum, containing a fine collection of Roman Britain. Among the former residents of Colchester were King Cole, immortalized in the nursery rhyme, and Cunobelinus, the warrior king, known to Shakespearean scholars as "Cymbeline."

However, Colchester is not in the pathway of most visitors, so I have concentrated instead on three tiny villages in the western part of Essex—Saffron Walden, Thaxted, and Finchingfield, all three representative of the best of the shire. You can explore all of them quite easily on your way to Cambridge or on your return trip to London. Roughly, they lie anywhere from 25 to 30 miles south of the university city.

3. Thaxted

Some 43 miles north of London, the Saxon town of Thaxted sits on the crest of a hill. It contains the most beautiful small church in England, whose graceful spire can be seen for miles around. Its bells are heard throughout the day, ringing out special chimes to parishioners who attend their church seriously. Dating back to 1340, the church is a nearly perfect example of religious architecture.

Thaxted was well known to newspaper and magazine readers because of the late iconoclastic Conrad Noel, the so-called Red Vicar.

During the summer, folk dancing is performed by the townspeople, both in and out of the church. The London Philharmonic Orchestra comes up to play. The vicar has encouraged the church to use music, and you can hear both the old and the experimental. The denizens of Thaxted are divided about the activities of the church, but one thing they like: their town is alive and flourishing because of it.

Thaxted also has a number of well-preserved Elizabethan houses and a wooden-pillard Jacobean Guildhall.

FOOD AND LODGING: A 14th-century coaching inn, **The Swan Hotel,** Watling Street (tel. 0371/830321), is right in the middle of everything. From several of the bedroom windows, you can see the church and have a box seat if a procession should pass by. For many centuries, the townspeople have patronized the Swan for drinks and gossip. It is owned by Pamela and Frank Brown, who respect the heritage of the inn. Single rooms cost from £20 ($30) to £24 ($36) and doubles from £30 ($45) to £34 ($51), the higher prices charged for units with baths. There is a bistro restaurant with à la carte meals in the evening, costing around £10 ($15), and a carvery serving meals for £8.50 ($12.75). During the day, you can order bar snacks.

The **Recorder's Restaurant,** Town Street (tel. 0371/830438), near the Guildhall, was built in 1450 and is believed to have incorporated part of the medieval Thaxted Manor House. It derived its name from the recorder who used to live there, collecting taxes for the crown. Apparently, there were objections to these taxes, as the winding staircase was built with steps that pitch outward, so that an attacking swordsman would be thrown off balance. As you dine in front of an inglenook fireplace (where Edward IV did when he brought his queen here for their honeymoon), you'll surely be pleased with the linenfold paneling, the carefully preserved wide oak floors, and the candlelight at night. The food, reflecting a continental influence, is the best in the area. At luncheon, a three-course table d'hôte is offered from 12:30 to 2:30 p.m. for an inclusive price of £7.50 ($11.25). Dinner, from 7 to 9:30 p.m., includes fine steaks and seafood cooked on the charcoal broiler, in addition to the small but well-planned à la carte menu. Prices begin at £12 ($18) for a three-course meal. Specials could include roast haunch of venison. The owner, Roy Hawkins, serves as much homemade cookery as possible, including the bread rolls.

4. Saffron Walden

In the northwestern corner of Essex, a short drive from Thaxted, is the ancient market town of Walden, renamed Saffron Walden because of the fields of autumn crocus that used to grow around it. It lies only 44 miles from London. Some residents of Cambridge, 15 miles to the north, escape to this old borough for their weekends.

One mile west of Saffron Walden (B1383 road) is **Audley End House** (tel. 0799/22399), considered one of the finest mansions in all of East Anglia. This Jacobean estate was begun by Sir Thomas Howard, Treasurer to the King, in 1603, built on the foundation of a monastery. James I is reported to have said, "Audley End is too large for a king, though it might do for a Lord Treasurer." The house has many outstanding features, including an impressive Great Hall at whose north end is a screen dating from the early 17th century, considered one of the most ornamental in England. Rooms decorated by Robert Adam contain fine furniture and works of art. A "Gothick" chapel and a charming Victorian ladies' sitting room are among the attractions. The park surrounding the house was landscaped by Capability Brown. It has a lovely rose garden, a river and cascade, and a picnic area. In the stables built at the same time as the mansion is a collection of agricultural machinery, a Victorian coach, old wagons, and the estate fire wagon. It's all open from April to the end of September, daily except Monday from 1 to 6 p.m. (last entry at 5:30 p.m.), for an admission of £2 ($3) for adults, £1 ($1.50) for children.

Many of the houses in Saffron Walden are distinctive in England, in that the 16th- and 17th-century builders faced their houses with parget, a kind of plasterwork (sometimes made with cow dung) used for ornamental facades.

In accommodations, Saffron Walden innkeepers charge fairly high prices, but at least the buildings are romantic.

FOOD AND LODGING: Opposite the post office, **Cross Keys Hotel,** The High (tel. 0799/22207), is a museum piece of black-and-white architecture built in 1449. Mr. and Mrs. Knott not only tend to locals at their neighborhood pub, but provide overnighters with pleasant and adequate lodgings in their upper-floor bedrooms. They have partially restored the interior, discovering an inglenook fireplace with a priest hole. In a single the charge is £15 ($22.50) without bath. Bathless doubles start at £28 ($42), going up to £34 ($51) with facilities. All these tariffs include a hearty English breakfast, service, and VAT.

For food and drink, head for **Eight Bells,** Bridge Street (tel. 0799/22790), right outside the center of Saffron Walden on the B184 in the direction of Cambridge. This black-and-white timbered Tudor building is both a restaurant and pub, the most frequented in town (Cambridge students often visit it). You can enjoy well-prepared meals here at both lunch and dinner: noon to 2 p.m. and 6:30 to 9:30 p.m. daily. Saturday hours are noon to 2 p.m. and 6:30 to 10 p.m., and Sunday noon to 1:45 p.m. and 7 to 9:30 p.m. For drinkers, however, the pub stays open until 11 p.m. Fresh fish is brought in and prepared in proper ways in the kitchen, along with poultry and meat dishes. Meals cost from £6 ($9) and are served in the bar areas or else in a candlelit restaurant, which is a timbered hall with oak furniture. Children are allowed into the pub's family room and the restaurant. The Eight Bells also rents out two comfortable bedrooms, costing £18 ($27) in a single, £29 ($43.50) in a double. The bedrooms rest under a beamed ceiling, and the occupants share the bath.

5. Finchingfield

This little village, only a short drive east of Thaxted, puts in a serious claim for being the model village of England. Even though you may have another personal favorite, you still must admit it's a dream village, surrounded by the quiet life of the countryside. If you're staying in either Saffron Walden or Thaxted, you might want to motor over here. It makes for an interesting jaunt.

FOOD AND LODGING: A small, six-bedroom guesthouse, the **Manse** (tel. 0371/ 810306), overlooks the village pond in the center of one of the prettiest villages in Essex. All rooms have central heating, wall-to-wall carpeting, hot and cold running water, shaving points, and TV. Joe and Joan King bend every effort toward making their visitors comfortable and welcome. The cost, including VAT and a full English breakfast consisting of farm produce, is £12 ($18) per person per night.

The **Fox Inn** (tel. 0371/810151) stands near the edge of the pond on the village green. It's an attractive 200-plus year-old pub, with authentic pargeting (raised plaster) design on the facade. Bruce Bullwinkle, owner, offers snacks and bar lunches, served from noon to 2 p.m. daily and costing from £5.50 ($8.25). The inn also contains six bedrooms, none with private baths. They rent for £24 ($36) in a single, £36 ($54) in a double, with breakfast included. No meals are served at the Fox at night, but there is a restaurant next door.

6. Dedham

Remember Constable's *Vale of Dedham*? In this little Essex village on the Stour River, you're in the heart of Constable country. Flatford Mill is only a mile farther down the river. The village, with its Tudor, Georgian, and Regency houses, is set in the midst of the water meadows of the Stour. Constable immortalized its church and tower. Dedham is right on the Essex-Suffolk border, and makes a good center for exploring both North Essex and the Suffolk border country.

In the village is **Castle House** (tel. 0206/322127), home of Sir Alfred Munnings, the president of the Royal Academy (1944–1949), and painter extraordinaire of racehorses and animals. The house and studio contain sketches and other works, and are open from May to October, Wednesday and Sunday from 2 to 5 p.m. (also Thursday and Saturday in August), charging adults an admission of £1 ($1.50); children pay 25p (38¢).

LODGING: Half a mile from the village, **Mrs. E. M. Watson,** Upper Park (tel. 0206/323197) does B&B in her attractive private home, with fine views over Constable country. To reach her place, you pass Dedham church on your left, driving through the village and up the hill. Some 200 yards from the top of the hill by a letter box on the corner, turn right. Travel another 100 yards and Upper Park will be the first house on the right. Her charge for B&B is £14 ($21) for a bathless single, £13 ($19.50) per person in a twin-bedded bathless room, and £15 ($22.50) per person in a twin with bath.

Barn Cottage, Long Road, West Dedham (tel. 0206/322329), receives guests to Constable country from April to October. The place is small, only four bedrooms, but it's in a desirable location, and the accommodations are comfortable and homelike. Guests share the one public bath, and rates range from £9 ($15) in a single to £16.50 ($24.75) and up in a double. The owners are helpful to visitors.

SUFFOLK

The easternmost county of England, a link in the four-county chain of East Anglia, is a refuge for artists, just as it was in the day of its famous native sons, Constable and Gainsborough. Many of the Suffolk landscapes have ended up on canvas.

A fast train can make it to East Suffolk from London in approximately an hour and a half. Still, its fishing villages, dozens of flint churches, historic homes, and national monuments remain relatively unvisited by overseas visitors.

The major towns of Suffolk are Bury St. Edmunds, the capital of West Suffolk, and Ipswich in the east, a port city on the Orwell River. But to capture the true charm of Suffolk, you must explore its little market towns and villages. Beginning at the Essex border, we'll strike out toward the North Sea, highlighting the most scenic villages as we move easterly across the shire.

7. Newmarket

This old Suffolk town, 62 miles from London, has been famous as a racing center since the time of King James I. Visitors can see Nell Gwynne's House, but mainly they come to visit Britain's first and only **National Horseracing Museum,** 99 High St. (tel. 0638/667333).

The museum is housed in the old subscription rooms, early 19th-century rooms used for placing and settlement of bets. Visitors will be able to see the history of horseracing over a 300-year period. There are fine paintings of famous horses, pictures on loan from Queen Elizabeth II, and copies of old Parliamentary acts governing races. There is also a replica of a weighing-in room, plus explanations of the signs used by the ticktack men who keep the on-course bookies informed of changes in the price of bets.

There is also a 53-minute audio-visual presentation showing races and race-horses, running continuously. At a shop at the entrance, you can buy from an interesting collection of small souvenirs, along with books, tankards, a Derby chart showing the male descent line of every winner of the celebrated race since 1780, and silk scarves with equine motifs. You can visit the garden and wine bar. Caroline Agar is the curator of the museum, which is open daily except Monday from 10 a.m. to 5 p.m., 2 to 5 p.m. on Sunday April to early December (from 10 a.m. to 5 p.m. Monday to Saturday and 2 to 5 p.m. on Sunday in August). Admission is £1.50 ($2.25) for adults, 75p ($1.13) for children. It's closed in December, January, and February, but those with a special interest in seeing it can telephone.

WHERE TO STAY AND EAT: A gabled building, one of the most historic inns in town, the **White Hart Hotel,** High Street (tel. 0638/663051), rises three stories in the center of town, opposite the Horseracing Museum. It was constructed on the site of an inn dating from the 1600s. The 21 well-furnished hotel rooms and the bars are decorated with racing pictures and prints. The cost in a single unit is £21 ($31.50), a double (with bath) going for £49 ($73.50). Bar snacks, such as a hot dish of the day, salads, cold meats, homemade soup with crusty bread, and cheese and apple pie, are offered. Two dishes cost about £6.40 ($9.75). In the hotel restaurant, you can order a three-course dinner for around £11 ($16.50).

The **Rutland Arms Hotel,** High Street (tel. 0638/664251), is an imposing Georgian coaching inn dating in part from the reign of Charles II. The hotel is at the clock end of the High Street. There are 45 rooms, large and comfortably furnished, most with private bathrooms. Prices are £40 ($60) for a single with bath, £50 ($75) for a double, also with bath. An English breakfast, service, and VAT are included. A good three-course lunch, costing £8.50 ($12.75), is served between 12:30 and 2 p.m., and a set dinner, for £12 ($18), is available from 6:30 to 9 p.m.

8. Clare

Lying 58 miles from London but only 26 miles east from Cambridge, the small town of Clare holds to the old ways of East Anglia. Many of its houses are bathed in Suffolk pink, the facades of a few demonstrating the 16th- and 17th-century plasterwork technique of pargeting. The Stour River, which has its source a few miles away, flows by, marking the boundary of Suffolk and Essex. The little rail station has fallen to the economy axe. The nearest station is now at Sudbury, where Gainsborough was born. The journey by road from London takes about two hours, unless you succumb to the scenery and the countryside along the way.

The **Ancient House Museum** (tel. 0842/2599), directly across from the churchyard, is a splendid example of pargeting and has many notable architectural features and numerous fascinating exhibits. It gives visitors an understanding and appreciation of the rural life of Suffolk. The museum is open from Easter to mid-October from 2:30 to 4:30 p.m. Wednesday to Sunday and on bank holidays, as well as from 11 a.m. to 12:30 p.m. on Sunday. Admission is 40p (60¢) for adults, 20p (30¢) for children.

FOOD AND LODGING: One of the oldest inns in England is the **Bell Hotel,** Market Hill (tel. 0842/277741). Once known as the Green Dragon, it served the soldiers of Richard de Clare, one of William the Conqueror's barons. Later it became a posting house, but in time the old stable gave way to a car park. Its owner, Brian Miles, is responsible for its recent facelift. He maintains 18 bedrooms, 13 of which have private baths. B&B rates range from £32 ($48) for a single, £40 ($60) for a double, plus service and tax. The rooms have a fresh, pleasant style, and the beds are soft. The beamed dining room, with its high-back chairs and large fireplace, is ideal for winter dining. Lunch, from noon to 2 p.m., costs £8 ($12) and dinner, from 7 to 9:30 p.m., goes for around £12 ($18).

9. Long Melford
Long Melford has been famous since the days of the early clothmakers. Like its sister, Lavenham (coming up), it grew in prestige and importance in the Middle Ages. Of the old buildings remaining, the village church is often called one of the glories of the shire. Along its High Street are many private homes erected by wealthy wool merchants of yore. While London seems far removed here, it is only 61 miles to the south.

EATING AND SLEEPING: If you're passing through, try to visit the **Bull Hotel** on Hall Street (tel. 0787/78494), one of the old (1540) inns of East Anglia. It was built by a wool merchant, and is considered Long Melford's finest and best preserved building. Incorporated into the general inn is a medieval weavers' gallery and an open hearth with Elizabethan brickwork. The dining room is the outstanding portion of the Bull, with its high-beamed ceilings, trestle tables, settles, and handmade chairs, as well as a ten-foot fireplace. You can order a set four-course lunch for £7.50 ($11.25) and a dinner for £11.50 ($17.25), all prices inclusive of VAT and service. On the dinner menu, you can expect such dishes as salmon and crayfish mousse, chilled vichyssoise, grilled Dover sole argenteuille, roast leg of lamb en croûte, and steak au poivre. Hours of food service are from noon to 2:30 p.m. and 6:30 to 9:30 p.m.

The **Countrymen Restaurant**, Hall Street (tel. 0787/79951), is a pretty Suffolk pink, 15th-century restaurant with pink and brown awnings, standing on the main street. Inside, the dining room is oak beamed with a huge inglenook fireplace. The tables have pink napery. Fixed-price menus are available for lunch and dinner, menus changing weekly. Prices range from £7 ($10.50) for lunch to £18.75 ($28.13) for the top price gastronomic dinner menu. All prices include VAT and unlimited coffee. A typical midweek lunch might include homemade soup, chicken chasseur with fresh garden vegetables, a choice of desserts from the chilled trolley, and coffee. The middle-price dinner, at £12 ($18), offers such specialties as deep-fried whitebait to start, a delicate poached filet of sole as a middle course, sirloin steak with a piquant sauce to follow, with fresh market vegetables or crisp salad, a choice of dessert or a selection of English and continental cheeses, and coffee. Janet and Stephen Errington, who operate the establishment, serve a recommendable traditional Sunday lunch with prime English roast beef. During summer afternoons, teas with fresh homemade scones, jam, and cream are served in the gardens and in the Stables Tea Room at the rear of the restaurant every Sunday. Food is served at the Countrymen from noon to 1:30 p.m. and 7 to 9 p.m. daily except for dinner on Sunday. On Saturday, it remains open to 9:30 p.m.

If you're staying over, consider the following recommendation:

The **Crown Inn**, Hall Street (tel. 0787/77666), is an attractive Suffolk inn on the main village road. Its restaurant and bedrooms, some with private bath, open onto a small but lovely garden kept private from the road by a high stone wall. It's owned and run by Mr. and Mrs. M. Wright, who will assure you of a warm personal welcome and will help you with your tour. While not ancient, the Crown has a country-cottage flavor, with a sitting room for guests filled with comfortable armchairs. The charge for B&B, including VAT, in one of the pleasantly furnished, well-kept bedrooms ranges from £20 ($30) to £25 ($37.50) in a single, depending on the plumbing. Doubles or twins run from £15 ($22.50) to £17.50 ($26.25) per person. Fixed-price lunches and dinners cost £6.50 ($9.75), £9.50 ($14.25), and £13.50 ($20.25). You might have pâté, fish mousse, or crab mornay, followed by trout meunière or suprême of salmon van den Berg, veal Marsala, pork chasseur or carbonnade of beef, perhaps a slice of lamb, pork, or beef from a joint. Real ale brewed locally is served from original hand pumps. Many fine wines are stored in the pre-Tudor cellars. Lunch is served from noon to 2:30 p.m. and dinner from 6:30 to 9:30 p.m. Of special interest in the lounge is a stained-glass panel depicting a scene from Shakespeare's *A Midsummer Night's Dream*.

10. Lavenham

Once a great wool center, Lavenham is filled with a number of beautiful, half-timbered Tudor houses, washed in the characteristic Suffolk pink. Be sure to visit the church, with its landmark tower, built in the Perpendicúlar style. Lavenham lies only 7 miles from Sudbury, 11 from Bury St. Edmonds.

WHERE TO STAY: The best little B&B in town is the **Angel Hotel,** Market Place (tel. 0787/247388). Mr. and Mrs. Graves welcome you, giving you a good bed and a bountiful breakfast the next morning, all at a cost of £16 ($24) per person nightly. It's also possible to order a three-course dinner from the inn's à la carte menu, paying from £6 ($9).

WHERE TO DINE: Popular with villagers and visitors alike, the **Timbers Restaurant,** High Street (tel. 0787/247218), is run by a splendid team who provide an agreeable setting. Traditional English-style meals at moderate prices are served, costing from £10 ($15). You'll come out less for lunch by ordering one of the blackboard specials. Portions are generous. On Sunday, the traditional roast beef and Yorkshire pudding is served. In the evening you can order such classic dishes as rack of English lamb flavored with rosemary, grilled trout, or beef Wellington. Desserts are rich and tempting. Hours are from noon to 2 p.m. and 7:30 to 9:30 p.m. Call for a table.

FOOD AND LODGING IN THE ENVIRONS: Off the A11 road from Lavenham to Hadleigh, the **Bell Inn** at Kersey (tel. 0473229/823), is in an attractive village with a watersplash right in the middle of the main street. Presided over by Arnold and Jeannette Fineman, the Bell offers good bar snacks in the timbered bar with glinting horse brasses. In the grill room, lunches and dinners start with appetizers. Then there is a selection of main courses, good-tasting English fare such as steak-and-kidney pie (individually prepared), game pie, honey-roasted ham, or a filet steak. Meals cost from £10 ($15). The grill room operates during pub hours. Cream teas are served from 3 to 5 p.m.

Also off the A1141, on the B1115, is Chelsworth, which is typical of the villages of the area. There the **Peacock Inn,** The Street (tel. 0449/740758), spreads its feathers. The inn is run by Tony and Lorna Marsh. It dates back to the 14th century, a genuine oak timbered inn, with inglenook fireplaces and its own unique character. It stands just across the road from the banks of the Brett River. At lunchtime they have a hot and cold table with a fresh soup, cold ham, chicken curry, homemade game pie, and salads, a meal costing from £4 ($6). A three-course evening dinner, beginning at £9 ($13.50), is also featured. Seasonal specialties are afternoon teas (from May onward) and spit beef roasted over an open log fire in winter. Most of the food is homemade on the premises, and is available seven days a week. The Peacock also offers five bedrooms, consisting of four doubles and one single, each with hot and cold running water. All are furnished traditionally. The cost is £15 ($22.50) per person.

11. Woodbridge and Aldeburgh

WOODBRIDGE: A yachting center, 12 miles from the North Sea, Woodbridge is a market town on a branch of the Deben River. Its best known, most famous resident was Edward Fitzgerald, the Victorian poet and translator of the *Rubáiyàt* of Omar Khayyám (some critics consider the Englishman's version better than the original). The poet died in 1883 and was buried nearly four miles away at Boulge.

Woodbridge is a good base for exploring the East Suffolk coastline, particularly the small resort of Aldeburgh, noted for its Moot Hall. The town is also a good headquarters for excursions to Constable's Flatford Mill, coming up.

Where to Dine

The **Captain's Table,** 3 Quay St. (tel. 03943/3145), is a good choice for intimate dining run by Tony Prentice. The food, mainly seafood, is well prepared, the atmosphere near the wharf colorful. The facade of this cozy nook is painted a Suffolk pink. The licensed restaurant serves a number of specialties, including Dover sole. Many of the main dishes are traditionally English, especially scallops cooked in butter with bacon and garlic. Vegetables are extra, and desserts are rich and good-tasting. A three-course bar lunch is likely to cost around £6.50 ($9.75), a dinner in the restaurant going for £14 ($21). The day's specials are written on a blackboard—oysters, sea salmon, turbot in lobster sauce, plaice, sole, whatever. Hours are noon to 2 p.m. and 6:30 to 9:30 p.m.

The **Lane O'Gorman Wine Bar,** 17 Thoro'fare, upstairs (tel. 03943/2557). The homemade food (cooked in the bar) is offered from a seasonal menu that changes weekly and might include garlic mushrooms, stuffed pepper, game pie, and an inventive display of help-yourself salads, plus desserts such as chocolate roulade or apple and apricot Brown Betty. Vegetarians can almost always be satisfied. Meals cost from £6 ($9) up. Of course, customers are not obliged to eat, as this is not a restaurant. You are welcome to sit with a glass or bottle of wine, a beer, or just a cup of coffee. The wine bar is open from noon to 2:30 p.m. and 7 to 11 p.m. It's closed Sunday and Monday.

Lodgings at Orford

For lodgings, try the nearby village of Orford, which is known for the ruins of its 12th-century castle. At this ancient town, once a port, you can stay at the **King's Head Inn,** Front Street (tel. 03945/450271), reputedly a 14th-century inn with a smuggling history, lying in the shadow of St. Bartholomew's Church. A wealth of old beams and a candlelit dining room add to the ambience of this small (five-bedroom) inn. Phyl and Alistair Shaw rent the bathless units for £25 ($37.50) nightly in a double, with a full English breakfast and VAT included. Alistair, who is also the chef, prepares a tasty evening meal, using fresh produce from the sea.

ALDEBURGH: Pressed against the North Sea, Aldeburgh is a favorite retreat of the in-the-know traveler, even attracting some Dutch people who make the sea crossing via Harwich, the British entry point for those coming from the Hook of Holland. Sir Benjamin Britten, the renowned composer (1913–1976) produced some of his most famous works while he lived here (*The Turn of the Screw, Gloriana,* and *Billy Budd*), but the festival he started at Aldeburgh in 1948 is held at Snape in June, a short drive to the west. A second festival, sponsored by Benson & Hedges, is now held in early autumn, featuring major international singers. Less than 100 miles from London, the resort was founded in Roman times, but legionnaires have been replaced by fishermen, boatmen, and fanciers of wildfowl. A bird sanctuary, Havergate Island, lies about six miles south of the town in the River Alde.

Constructed on a shelf of land at the level of the sea, the High or main street of town runs parallel to the often turbulent waterfront. This main street sits below a cliff face that rises some 55 feet. It has been turned in part into terraced gardens' which visitors can enter. Some take time out from their sporting activities (a golf course stretches 3½ miles) to visit the 16th-century **Moot Hall Museum** (tel. 072885/2158). The hall dates from the time of Henry VIII, but its tall, twin chimneys are Jacobean additions. The timber-frame structure contains old maps and prints. It's open from

2:30 to 5 p.m. on Saturday and Sunday only, Easter to June and seven days a week from July to September. Admission is 25p (38¢) for adults, free to children.

Aldeburgh also contains the nation's northernmost Martello tower, erected to protect the coast from a feared invasion by Napoleon.

In August, the time of the regatta and a carnival, accommodations tend to be fully booked.

Where to Stay

Uplands Hotel, Victoria Road (tel. 072885/2420), is as untouristy a retreat as you are likely to find. It's more like a private home run, by Robert, Patricia, and Nichola Tidder, who take in paying guests. The inn dates from the 18th century. At one time it was the childhood home of Elizabeth Garrett Anderson, the first woman doctor in England. Uplands provides personally decorated bedrooms and excellently planned and well-prepared meals. Once inside the living room, you sense the informality and charm. They have furnished it with some good antiques, a few comfortable upholstered chairs, paintings, and books. The prices range from £19 ($28.50) per person for B&B. Half board costs from £35 ($52.50) to £41 ($61.50) per person. There are seven twin-bedded chalets in the garden, with private bath and TV. In the hotel are 12 individually designed units. The chef, who has won many cooking awards, offers an à la carte dinner for about £12 ($18) and up. A typical meal might include escalope de veau "Uplands" or roast Aylesbury duck. You can have coffee in front of the fireplace or, in fair weather, in the garden.

Cotmandene Guest House, 6 Park Lane (tel. 072885/3775), is considered the best guesthouse in the area (as opposed to the more expensive hotels). A Victorian double-fronted structure, it stands in a tranquil neighborhood. If you go for a walk before breakfast, you will undoubtedly be following not only in Britten's footsteps, but those of frequent visitor E.M. Forster who liked Aldeburgh but called it—not very accurately—"a bleak little place, not beautiful." The owners of this pleasantly furnished and comfortable guesthouse rent out six bedrooms, none with private bath, for which they charge from £13 ($19.50) per person nightly for B&B. It's also possible to stay here on half-board terms for £18.50 ($27.75) per person. The cookery is wholesome English and very hearty.

Fish and Chips

Aldeburgh has two well-known fish and chips cafés, each with devotees claiming their favorite to be the best in town. You make up your own mind.

Aldeburgh Fish & Chip Shop, 226 High St. (tel. 072885/2250). Britten and his longtime friend, Peter Pears, used to bring visitors from London or America here to sample locally caught fish, notably plaice and cod. You can get a generous portion for around £1.35 ($2.03). Many guests pick up their treat here and take it to the sea wall, where they enjoy not only the fish but the smell of salt air from the sea from which their dinner came. The shop is open daily except Sunday and Monday from 11:45 a.m. to 1:45 p.m. and 5 to 9 p.m.

Hammersley's, 171 High St. (tel. 072885/2011), is the major rival, and, as mentioned, some like it better. This operation is run by Barry and Brenda Hammersley, and they must have a deal with local fishermen, because they seem always to have the best "catch in town." Certainly the freshest, and they know how to prepare the fish just right. A meal here will cost about £5 ($7.50), and service is from 10 a.m. to 4 p.m. and 7 to 9 p.m. The place is closed Sunday and Monday and on Tuesday only for dinner. They also operate an herb and spice shop attached.

The Local Pub

Ye Olde Crosse Keys, Crabbe Street (tel. 072885/2637), is a genuine 16th-century pub, with the real atmosphere of a Suffolk seaside local. In the summer, everyone takes his or her real English ale or lager out and sits on the seawall, sipping, talking, and thinking. The pub is favored by local artists, who in the cooler months sit beside an old brick fireplace and eat plates of oysters or smoked salmon. Meals cost from £5 ($7.50) and are served from noon to 2 p.m. and 7 to 9 p.m. (no dinner on Sunday). However, drinkers can stay here until 11 p.m.

12. East Bergholt

The English landscape painter, John Constable (1776–1837), was born at East Bergholt. Near the village is **Flatford Mill,** subject of one of his most renowned canvases. The mill, in a scenic setting, was given to the National Trust in 1943, and since has been leased to the Fields Studies Council for use as a residential field center, which offers a wide-ranging program of week-long courses in all aspects of the countryside and the environment, including painting and photography. Visitors of all ages and degrees of experience are welcome to apply to attend these courses. Details can be obtained from The Warden, Flatford Mill Field Centre, East Bergholt, Colchester, Essex, CO7 6UL (tel. 0206/298283).

Nearby, the National Trust has furnished a 16th-century cottage with a display on the life and work of John Constable, plus a shop for refreshments.

THE LOCAL PUB: Cited by numerous writers as one of the unmarred inns of East Anglia, the **Red Lion Inn,** Gaston Street (tel. 0206/298332), traces its ancestry back to around 1500. The friendly, family-run pub has an enclosed children's garden. There is a wide range of bar meals, costing from £1.50 ($2.25) to £5 ($7.50), including the best ploughman's lunch in the area. Steaks are offered in the evening. Hours are from 11:30 a.m. to 2:30 p.m. and 6 to 11 p.m. A short stroll from Flatford Mill and the heart of Constable land, the inn is opposite a historic church with a bell cage on the ground, where the bells are hand-rung. The Red Lion is reached by turning off the A12 Colchester–Ipswich road.

NORFOLK

Bounded by the North Sea, Norfolk is the biggest of the East Anglian counties. It's a low-lying area, with fens, heath, and salt marshes. An occasional dike or windmill makes you think you've been delivered to the Netherlands. One of the features of Norfolk is its network of Broads, miles and miles of lagoons, shallow in parts, connected by streams.

Summer sports people flock to Norfolk to hire boats for sailing or fishing. From Norwich, **Wroxham,** the capital of the Broads, is easily reached, only eight miles to the northeast. Motorboats regularly leave from the resort, taking parties on short trips. Some of the best scenery of the Broads is to be found on the periphery of Wroxham.

13. Norwich

Some 20 miles from the North Sea, Norwich still holds to its claim as the capital city of East Anglia. The county town of Norfolk, Norwich is a charming and historic city, despite encroachments by industry.

Norwich is the most important shopping center in East Anglia and is well provided with hotels and entertainment. In addition to its cathedral, there are more than 30 medieval parish churches built of flint.

There are many interesting old houses in the narrow streets and alleyways, and a big open-air market, busy every weekday, where fruit, flowers, vegetables, and other goods are sold from stalls with colored canvas roofs.

The **Assembly House** (see below) is a Georgian building (1752) restored to provide a splendid arts and social center. The **Maddermarket Theatre,** the home of the Norwich Players, is an 18th-century chapel converted by Nugent Monck in 1921 to an Elizabethan-style theater. On the outskirts of the city, the buildings of the University of East Anglia are strikingly modern in design and include the Sainsbury Centre (1978).

There is a **Tourist Information Centre** at the Guildhall Gaol Hill (tel. 0603/666071).

THE SIGHTS: In the center of Norwich, on a partly artificial mound, sits **Norwich Castle,** formerly the county gaol (jail). Its huge 12th-century Norman keep and the later prison buildings are used as a civic museum and headquarters of the county-wide Norfolk Museums Service (tel. 0603/611277, ext. 279). The museum houses an impressive collection of pictures by artists of the Norwich School, of whom the most distinguished were John Crome, born 1768, and John Sell Cotman, born 1782. The castle museum also contains a fine collection of Lowestoft porcelain and Norwich silver. These are shown in the rotunda. Two other displays are the Ecology Gallery, showing Norfolk's flora and fauna, and the Ceramics and Glass Gallery, including a fine collection of teapots. There are two sets of dioramas, one showing Norfolk wildlife in its natural setting, the other illustrating scenes of Norfolk life from the Old Stone Age to the early days of Norwich Castle. You can also visit a geology gallery and a permanent exhibition in the keep, "Norfolk in Europe." The castle museum is open weekdays from 10 a.m. to 5 p.m. and on Sunday from 2 to 5 p.m. Adults pay 70p ($1.05) in summer, 35p (53¢) in winter, children being charged 10p (15¢) year round. A cafeteria and licensed bar are open from 10:30 a.m. to 2:30 p.m.

The **Norwich Cathedral** (tel. 0603/626290), principally of Norman design, dates back to 1096. It is noted primarily for its long nave, with lofty columns. Its spire, built in the late Perpendicular style, rises 315 feet, and shares distinction with the keep of the castle as the significant landmarks on the Norwich skyline. On the vaulted ceiling are more than 300 bosses (knob-like ornamental projections) depicting biblical scenes. The impressive choir stalls with the handsome misereres date from the 15th century. Edith Cavell—"Patriotism is not enough"—the English nurse executed by the Germans in World War I, was buried on the cathedral's Life's Green. The quadrangular cloisters go back to the 13th century, and are among the most spacious in England. The cathedral can be visited from 7:30 a.m. to 7 p.m. daily. A donation of 50p (75¢) is requested.

A short walk from the cathedral will take you to **Tombland,** one of the most interesting old squares in Norwich.

The **Sainsbury Centre for Visual Arts** (tel. 0603/56161, ext. 2470) was the gift in 1973 of Sir Robert and Lady Sainsbury, who contributed their private collection to the University of East Anglia. Along with their son, David, they gave an endowment to provide a building to house the collection. The center, designed by Foster Associates, was opened in 1978, and since then the design has won many national and international awards. A feature of the structure is its flexibility, allowing solid and glass areas to be interchanged, and the superb quality of light which allows optimum viewing of the works of art. The Sainsbury Collection is one of the foremost in the country, including modern, ancient, classical, and ethnographic art. Other displays at the center include the Anderson collection of art nouveau and the university aggregation of 20th-century abstract art and design. There is also a regular program of special exhibitions. The center is open from noon to 5 p.m. daily except Monday. Admission is 50p (75¢) for adults, 25p (38¢) for children. The restaurant on the premises offers a self-service buffet from 10:30 a.m. to 2:30 p.m. Monday to Friday. A Conservatory coffee bar serves light lunches and refreshments from noon to 4:30 p.m. Tuesday to Friday.

The **Mustard Shop,** 3 Bridewell Alley (tel. 0603/627889), first opened in 1973, on the 150th anniversary of Jeremiah and James Colman's partnership. This delightful Victorian shop is a wealth of mahogany and shining brass. There is an old cash register to record your purchase, and the standard of service and pace of life also reflect the personality and courtesy of a bygone age. In the Mustard Museum is a series of displays illustrating the history of the Colman company and the making of mustard, its properties and origins. There are old advertisements, as well as packages and "tins." You can browse in the shop, selecting whichever of the mustards you prefer. Really hot, English-type mustards are sold, as well as the continental blends. Besides mustard, the shop sells aprons, tea towels, chopping boards, pottery mustard pots, and mugs, all of which are also available by mail order from the attractive free brochure provided. The shop and museum are open from 9 a.m. to 5:30 p.m. Monday to Saturday (closed all day Thursday).

A Memorial Room honoring the **Second Air Division of the Eighth United States Army Air Force** is part of the Central Library, Bethel Street (tel. 0603/611277). A Memorial Fountain, also honoring the United States airmen who were based in Norfolk and Suffolk in World War II, many losing their lives in the line of duty, is in the library courtyard. The fountain incorporates the insignia of the Second Air Division and a stone from each of the United States. Books, audio-visual materials, and records of the various bomb groups are in the library. There is no admission charge, but contributions are used for the upkeep of the memorial.

Persons interested in a tour of the old air bases in East Anglia used by the Eighth United States Army Air Force during World War II, should see **Tony North,** 62 Turner Rd. (tel. 0603/614041), who is connected to the Second Air Division Association, the Liberator Club, the American Aviation Historical Society, and the Eighth Air Force Historical Society. He works just across the road from Le Bistro on Exchange Street and can be reached through the restaurant as well as at the address given above.

Before I begin my recommendations for finding lodgings, I'll lead off with a tip about how to find a room in a hurry.

ACCOMMODATIONS: Norwich is better equipped than most East Anglian cities to handle guests who arrive without reservations. The **Norwich City Tourist Information Centre** maintains an office at the Guildhall, Gaol Hill, opposite the market (tel. 0603/666071), and the friendly personnel there will help. Each year a new listing of accommodations is drawn up, including both licensed and unlicensed hotels, as well as B&B houses, and even living arrangements on the outskirts.

A street called **Earlham Road** abounds in budget hotels and guesthouses. To drive there, go west along St. Giles Street from the north side of City Hall. The guesthouses were mostly built at the turn of the century, and they offer widely varying prices.

Bed and Breakfast

Marlborough House Hotel, 22 Stracey Rd. (tel. 0603/628005), is a comfortable and welcoming hotel where guests are housed in one of a dozen pleasantly furnished bedrooms. A family-run place, it offers only three units with private bath. The B&B tariff in a single goes from £11 ($16.88) to £15 ($22.50), the double- or twin-bedded rate, £21 ($31.50) to £26 ($39). There is a licensed bar for guests, along with a lounge for color TV. Evening meals will be provided—in fact, it's more economical to check in here on the half-board rate of £15 ($21) to £18 ($27) per person nightly. There is limited parking as well.

Wedgewood Guest House, 42–44 St. Stephens Rd. (tel. 0603/625730), in the vicinity of the bus station, is not only convenient for exploring many of the attractions of Norwich, it offers good rooms at a fair price. The hotel rents out 11 comfortably furnished bedrooms, three of which contain private baths. The B&B rate in a single goes from £11.50 ($17.25) to £12.50 ($18.72), in a double or twin from £20 ($30) to £26 ($39). The owners are conscious of the needs of visitors.

Heathcote Hotel, 19/23 Unthank Rd. (tel. 0603/625639), is managed by Mrs. Grace Pendle, a Norwich woman whose pleasant personality will soon make you feel at home. Established in 1904, the hotel is only a few minutes' walk from the city center. The heated rooms, which are well furnished, have hot and cold running water, color TV, radios, and tea-making facilities. The charge in a single ranges from £17 ($25.50) to £22 ($33) nightly, and doubles go for £30 ($45) to £36 ($54), the latter with private bath. A three-course evening meal is available at £7 ($10.50). Prices are subject to VAT, but there is no service charge. The hotel has a large car park.

Santa Lucia Hotel, 38–40 Yarmouth Rd. (tel. 0603/33207), is one of the best for value of the hotels outside Norwich, only 1½ miles from the center. The hotel offers not only an inexpensive accommodation, but an attractive setting and a friendly atmosphere. You pay from £10 ($15) nightly for B&B. The food is quite good too, costing from £3.50 ($5.25) for a dinner. Each room has running water, color TV, and a clock radio. There are sun terraces for relaxing, modern bathrooms and showers, and plenty of parking space. Two buses pass by the door heading for the center of the city.

DINING IN NORWICH: In the heart of the old city, the **Briton Arms Coffee House,** Elm Hill (tel. 0603/623367), overlooks the most beautiful cobbled street in Norwich. Over the years it's had several names, and traces its history back to the days of Edward III. Now it's one of the least expensive eating places in Norwich, certainly one of the most intimate and informal. The coffeehouse has several rooms, including a back one with an inglenook. You'll find old beamed ceilings and Tudor benches. It is open daily, except Sunday, from 10 a.m. to 5 p.m. The procedure here is to go to the little counter, where you purchase your lunch and bring it to the table of your choice. Everything I've tried was well prepared, and the items are homemade. Every day a different kind of soup is offered. You're likely to pay about £4 ($6) for a substantial, two-course meal. It's a good place to stop after your inspection of the cathedral, only a block away.

The **Assembly House,** Theatre Street (tel. 0603/626402), is a good example of Georgian architecture. You enter the building through a large front courtyard, which leads to the central hall, with its columns, fine paneling, and crystal chandelier. The restaurant is administered by H. J. Sexton Norwich Arts Trust. On your left is a high-ceilinged room with paneling, fine paintings, and a long buffet table ready for self-service. After making your selection, take your plate to any one of the many tables. Often you'll share—perhaps with an artist. There is an unusually varied selection of hors d'oeuvres. A big bowl of homemade soup might get you started. Hot main courses are made with fresh ingredients. Meals cost from £5 ($7.50). The restaurant is open first for coffee, 10 a.m. to noon; then lunch, between noon and 2 p.m. Teatime is from 2 to 5 p.m., and the supper hour is from 5 to 7:30 p.m. After dining, you may want to stroll through the rest of the building. Art exhibits are usually held regularly in the Ivory and Hobart Rooms, open from 10 a.m. to 5:30 p.m. Concerts are sponsored in the Music Room, with its chandeliers and sconces. There's even a little cinema.

Café la Tienda, 10 St. Gregory's Alley (tel. 0603/629122), is a relaxed, friendly two-story restaurant. Fresh, natural flavors are the hallmark of this place, serving from 10:30 a.m. to 5 p.m., with meals costing from £5 ($7.50). On Friday and Saturday, it is also open for dinner from 7 to 10:30 p.m. but is closed Sunday. Some of the offerings on your table were organically grown (the owners of the café have a small garden of their own). Vegetarians are king (or queen) here, as reflected by their daily offerings, which might include a vegetable and brown rice casserole or a rich but meatless soup, along with sandwiches and freshly baked items. However, some fish dishes are also served.

Le Bistro, 2a Exchange St. (tel. 0603/624452), in terms of value, is among the best establishments in Norwich. Mr. Squires offers a three-course English and French lunch for £5 ($7.50). In the evening you can enjoy a three-course English and French dinner for £7.50 ($11.25). On a typical menu you are likely to find frogs' legs, snails in their shells, roast leg of pork (with a sage-and-onion stuffing), and roast duck, perhaps chicken Maryland. French fries and seasonal vegetables are served with the main dishes. At least ten desserts are offered, perhaps raspberry sorbet with black currants and cream. All prices include VAT. Lunch is served Monday to Saturday from 11:30 a.m. to 2 p.m. Evening meals are served from 5 to 9:30 p.m. Tuesday to Saturday.

14. North Norfolk

This part is already well known by members of the American Eighth Air Force, as many Liberators and Flying Fortresses took off and landed from this corner of the country. Their captains and crews sampled most of the local hostelries at one time or another. Now it is mainly feathered birds that fly overhead, and the countryside is quiet and peaceful.

THE SIGHTS: The area is of considerable scenic interest, as the Queen of England herself will surely agree. It's extremely convenient for a weekend out of London, as it lies only a three-hour drive away.

Sandringham Estate

In the Norfolk countryside, some 107 miles northeast of London, Sandringham Estate (tel. 0553/772675) is the famous country home in East Anglia where the British royal family spends many of its holidays. The gardens plus a section of the interior are open to the public. The house and grounds are open from Easter Sunday until the last Thursday in September, inclusive, from Sunday through Thursday of each week. The house is closed for a certain period during the summer (normally the last two weeks in July and the first week in August). The house is open from 11 a.m. (noon on Sunday) to 4:45 p.m., and the grounds can be visited from 10:30 a.m. (11:30 a.m. on Sunday) to 5 p.m. For a combined ticket to the house and grounds, adults pay £1.80 ($2.70) and children are charged £1 ($1.50). The grounds are not open when the Queen or any member of the royal family is in residence.

The house dates from the mid-19th century and stands on the site of one bought for Edward VII when he was Prince of Wales. There are picnic areas, a souvenir shop, and a cafeteria. The museum, first opened in 1973, includes cars and a fire engine, big-game trophies, and a gallery of local archeological finds. The cars include a 1900 Daimler Tonneau of Edward VII, which was the first car bought by a member of the royal family. It still works!

Traditionally, the royal family welcomes in the new year at Sandringham. Sandringham lies eight miles northeast of the ancient port and market town of King's Lynn.

On the estate, the **Royal Station Museum** (tel. 0485/40674) in the village of **Wolferton** is where generations of royal visitors arrived for Sandringham until the line from King's Lynn to Hunstanton was closed in 1969. Now, the downside platform and its buildings are the home of Eric Walker, who has opened the paneled retiring rooms as a museum of royal railway travel. In one corner nestles Queen Victoria's traveling bed, made for her when a young girl in 1828. The museum is open from 11 a.m. to 1 p.m. and 2 to 6 p.m. Monday to Friday (2 to 6 p.m. on Sunday) April to September. Admission is 80p ($1.20) for adults, 30p (45¢) for children.

Blickling Hall

A long drive, bordered by massive yew hedges towering above and framing your first view of this lovely old house, leads you to Blickling Hall, near Aylsham (tel. 0263/733084). Rose-red and pinnacled, the hall is a near-perfect example of a historic English country house. The present building, erected during the reign of King James I by his chief justice, Sir Henry Hobart, has ornate staterooms mainly in late 18th-century style. The long gallery houses a fine library and has an elaborate 17th-century ceiling. The Blickling Estate, given to the National Trust by Lord Lothian, once British Ambassador to the United States, has an orangery with plants and statuary. The gardens are known for the great yew hedges and herbaceous borders, a Doric Temple, a woodland garden, and a secret garden. It is open from April to October from 1 to 5 p.m. daily except Monday and Thursday. Admission to the house and gardens is £2.50 ($3.75) for adults, £1.25 ($1.88) for children.

Norfolk Lavender Ltd.

At **Caley Mill** at Heacham (tel. 0485/70384), you can see how lavender is grown, the flowers harvested, and the essence distilled before appearing prettily packaged as perfume, aftershave, potpourri, and old-fashioned lavender bags to slip between your hankies. Much of the lavender is grown on the nearby Sandringham royal estate, so you may end up with a regal product. The grounds and shop are open from 10 a.m. to 6 p.m. from May to September, from 9 a.m. to dusk in winter. The tour costs 75p ($1.13) for adults, free for children. The **Miller's Cottage Tea Room** serves cream teas with homemade cakes, scones, and buns, from late May to September. The best time to see the lavender in bloom is July to mid-August.

Sutton Windmill and Broads Museum

At Sutton (1½ miles southeast of Stalham off the A149) is the tallest mill in the country. But its main claim to fame, in a county where many of the windmills still work, is the exceptional quality and interest of the working machinery. Chris Nunn, who owns the mill, decided it was time he put something back into the country instead of taking it out. So he left the construction business and now devotes his days to restoring the mill. When money runs short, he works on North Sea oil rigs for a time. He hopes shortly to be grinding corn again, but the lower floors—there are nine in all—house a collection of bygones reflecting the mill's 100 years of history.

A recently constructed building on the car park houses the Broads Museum, based on the private collection of the Nunn family. Chris, Marian, and Robyn invite you to see the craft tools once used in woodworking, leather trades, farming, working the marshes, and cooperage. A large collection of kitchen and domestic memorabilia, animal traps, bank notes, and many more items from the past are displayed. In the tea rooms, you can enjoy tea, coffee, soft drinks, ice cream, and sorbets. The entire complex can be visited April to mid-May Sunday to Wednesday from 1:30 to 5:30 p.m.; mid-May to the end of September from 10 a.m. to 6 p.m. daily except Saturday (open Saturday in July and August). Admission is 85p ($1.28) for adults, 45p (68¢) for children. There is a telescope on the top floor, and the view over the countryside is magnificent. Crafts, pottery, books, and gifts are on sale. Telephone 0692/81195 for more information.

The Thursford Collection

Just off the A148 which runs from King's Lynn to Cromer, at **Laurel Farm,** Thursford Green, Thursford, near Fakenham (tel. 032877/477), George Cushing has been collecting and restoring steam engines and organs for more years than you'd care to remember. His collection is now a trust, and the old painted giants are on display, a paradise of traction engines with impeccable pedigrees such as Burrells, Garretts, and the Ruston Proctors. There are some static steam engines, the sort that run merry-go-rounds at fun fairs, but the most flamboyant exhibits are the showman's organs, the Wurlitzers and concert organs with their brilliant decoration, moving figures, and mass of windpipes. The organs play at 3 p.m. There is a children's play area, and a Savages Venetian Gondola switchback ride with Gavoili organ, which operates daily. It was built at nearby King's Lynn, and Disneyland has been after it for years. On many days during the summer, the two-foot-gauge steam railway, the Cackler, will take you around the wooded grounds of the museum. There is a refreshment café and a souvenir shop where one can buy photographs, books, and records of the steam-organ music.

The collection is open daily from 2 to 5:30 p.m. from the beginning of April until the end of October. In March, it is open on Sunday. Admission is £2.20 ($3.30) for adults and 95p ($1.43) for children. There are live Wurlitzer concerts every Tuesday evening at 8 p.m. from June to September.

The North Norfolk Railway

This steam railway plies from Sheringham to Weybourne. The station at Sheringham (tel. 0263/822045) opens daily at 10 a.m. from Easter to October. Admission to the station and museum is free between October and March. From Easter until the end of September, admission is 30p (45¢) for adults and 15p (23¢) for children. There are two museums of railway paraphernalia, steam locomotives, and historic rolling stock. The round trip to Weybourne by steam train takes about 45 minutes through most attractive countryside. Days and times of departure vary, so you should telephone between 10 a.m. and 5 p.m. before you go there. A ride on a steam train between Weybourne and Sheringham is £1.90 ($2.85) for adults for a round trip, £1 ($1.50) for children.

KING'S LYNN: This ancient port and market town on the banks of the Great Ouse has a wealth of historic buildings dating from as far back as the 14th century. In spite of modern buildings, it also has many quaint streets.

One of its more recent attractions is the **Wedgwood Crystal Ltd.,** Oldmeadow Road (tel. 0553/765111). The custom of watching craftsmen at work is spreading throughout the country, and Wedgwood, whose Jasper pottery is so famous, has opened the glass factory to show the processes involved in making fine crystal, from the first gather of molten glass from the furnace at the end of a pipe, through the blowing and shaping. Conducted tours are available Monday through Friday from 9:30 a.m. to 2 p.m., but you must reserve in advance. The tour lasts half an hour, costing 70p ($1.05) for adults and 35p (53¢) for children. There is a well-stocked gift shop with Wedgwood Crystal and Dartington Glass where factory seconds and discontinued lines are sold at reduced prices. They also stock Wedgwood and Coalport pottery of first-grade quality.

Where to Eat

Antonio's Wine Bar, Baxters Plain (tel. 0553/772324), in the heart of King's Lynn, not far from the museum, is a small, bistro-style wine bar offering a combination of fast, friendly service and simple but excellent food and wine. Antonio's Italian flair is reflected in the menu as well as the decor and congenial atmosphere. Among the appetizers are several home-smoked dishes, and the antipasto misto, costing £3.50 ($5.75), is a meal in itself. There are usually specials for main dishes, and the pizzas, made of fresh dough, are outstanding. The calzone is an epicurean delight. A good meal can be enjoyed here for less than £10 ($15), and the coffee is arguably the best in town. You can partake of a drink at the bar or have a simple snack, but you're likely to be tempted by the main dishes when you see them. The place is open from noon to 2 p.m. and 7 to 10:30 p.m. daily except Sunday, Monday, and two weeks in August. This is the best watering hole for miles around, handy for visitors to Royal Sandringham and the Norfolk Lavender fields.

Staying on the Outskirts

Oakwood House, on Route A10 near Tottenhill, just four miles south of King's Lynn (tel. 0552/810256), is a country house of Tudor origin, with all the amenities of a modern hotel. The house was enlarged some 200 years ago and refaced with a typical Georgian exterior. Within a short drive of the Norfolk seacoast, Oakwood House offers visitors a peaceful alternative to the bustling seaside resorts and market towns. Nestled in its own two acres of gardens, the hotel and its annex have 12 guest rooms with color TV, tea/coffee-making facilities, hot and cold running water, individually controlled heating, and pleasant views over the Norfolk countryside and the gardens. Four rooms are equipped with private showers and toilets. The comfortably furnished guest lounge has a color TV, and the spacious dining room adjoins the well-stocked period bar. The menu is carefully chosen to make the best use of local and home-grown produce whenever possible, and all the cooking is under the personal supervision of Marjorie Rhodes, who, with her husband, Geoff, sees that the needs of guests are attended to. Rates per person for B&B begin at £15 ($22.50). A two-course dinner costs £7.25 ($10.88), a three-course repast going for £8.25 ($12.38). VAT is included in the price, and there is no service charge. Ample parking facilities are within the grounds.

Chapter XV

EAST MIDLANDS

1. **Northamptonshire**
2. **Leicestershire**
3. **Derbyshire**
4. **Nottinghamshire**
5. **Lincolnshire**

THE EAST MIDLANDS contains several widely varied counties, both in character and scenery. This part of central England, for instance, offers miles of dreary industrial sections and their offspring row-type Victorian houses, yet the district is intermixed with some of Britain's noblest scenery, such as the Peak District National Park, centered in Derbyshire. Byron said that scenes there rivaled those of Switzerland and Greece. There are, in short, many pleasant surprises in store for you, from the tulip land of Lincoln to the 18th-century spa of Buxton in Derbyshire, from George Washington's ancestral home at Sulgrave Manor in Northamptonshire to what remains of Sherwood Forest.

1. Northamptonshire

The shire of which the city of Northampton has long been the administrative center, lying in the heart of the Midlands of England, has been inhabited since Paleolithic times. Traces have been found of the Beaker and other Bronze Age people, and a number of Iron Age hill-forts existed here, remains of which can still be seen. Two main Roman roads—Watling Street and Ermine Street—ran through the county, and relics of Roman settlements have been discovered at Towcester, Whilton, Irchester, and Castor. A racial mix was contributed by the invasion in the seventh century by West Saxons and Anglians. Also in that century, in 655, the first abbey was established at Medehamstede, now Peterborough.

The Danes took over late in the ninth century, and although their stay was not long as history goes, it was under their aegis that Northampton became the seat of administration for a borough with almost the same boundaries as the shire has today and as recorded in the *Domesday Book*.

In the Middle Ages, castles and manor houses dotted the country, rich in cattle and sheep farming and leatherwork, particularly the production of boots and shoes.

SULGRAVE MANOR: On your way from Oxford to visit the Warwickshire area of Stratford-upon-Avon, Warwick, and Coventry, if you take the A34 road north, you can visit Sulgrave Manor, the ancestral home of George Washington. First, you'll come to Banbury (still in Warwickshire), a market town famed in the nursery rhyme immortalizing "a fine lady upon a white horse." The old Banbury Cross was destroyed by the Roundheads in the Civil War but was replaced in Victoria's day. Follow the A422 road east from Banbury into Northamptonshire, toward Brackley, but turn off to the left after a short distance onto the B4525 road which will take you to the hamlet of Sulgrave.

As part of Henry VIII's plan to dissolve monasteries, he sold the priory-owned manor in 1539 to Lawrence Washington, who had been mayor of Northampton. George Washington was a direct descendant of Lawrence (seven generations removed). The Washington family occupied Sulgrave for more than a century. In 1656, Col. John Washington left for the New World.

In 1914 the manor was purchased by a group of English people in honor of the friendship between Britain and America. Over the years major restoration has taken place (a whole new wing had to be added), with an eye toward returning it as much as possible to its original state. The Colonial Dames have been largely responsible for raising the money. From both sides of the Atlantic the appropriate furnishings were donated, including a number of portraits—even a Gilbert Stuart original of the first president. On the main doorway is the Washington family coat-of-arms, two bars and a trio of mullets, which is believed to have been the inspiration for the "Stars and Stripes."

The manor is open from February to December, daily except Wednesday, from 10:30 a.m. to 1 p.m. and 2 to 5:30 p.m. (till 4 p.m. in winter). Admission is £1 ($1.50) for adults, 50p (75¢) for children. For more information, telephone 029576/205.

Food and Lodging

Across from Sulgrave Manor is the **Thatched House Hotel** (tel. 029576/232), a long, low group of 17th-century cottages, with a front garden full of flowers. Even if you're just passing through, it's a good place to stop for tea following your visit to Sulgrave Manor. Afternoon teas cost from 90p ($1.35) to £2.85 ($4.28) for a great spread with sandwiches, homemade cakes, scones with thick cream and jam, and strawberries in season. Tea is served at a table in either the beamed living or dining room, furnished with antiques. If you're lucky enough to stay over, Ron Walpole, the owner and manager, has modernized the bedrooms, installing private baths or showers to accommodate overnight guests. They are charged £25 ($37.50) in a single and £40 ($60) in a double, including a full breakfast and VAT. Set lunches start at £5 ($7.50), and a table d'hôte dinner is served for £7 ($10.50) and up. At night, you can feast on such dishes as medallion of English lamb flavored with herbs or roast guinea fowl in a sherry sauce. Service is from 10:30 a.m. to 11 p.m. A traditional English roast is always served Sunday at lunch.

NORTHAMPTON: The administrative and political center of Northamptonshire was a favorite meeting place of Norman and Plantagenet kings, fortified after 1066 by Simon de Senlis (St. Liz). Here King John was besieged by the barons trying to force the policy changes that finally resulted in the Magna Carta. During the War of the Roses, Henry VI (before he achieved that note) was defeated and taken prisoner, and during the Civil War, Northampton stuck with Parliament and Cromwell. The town, on the River Nene, has long been an important center for the production of boots and shoes, as well as other leather craft, pursuits that are traced in two of the city's museums.

The **Central Museum & Art Gallery**, Guildhall Road (tel. 0604/34881), displays collections of footwear through the ages, plus a re-created cobbler's shop. It also houses local archeological artifacts and English ceramics, Old Masters, and modern paintings. It is open from 10 a.m. to 6 p.m. daily except Sunday. Admission is free.

The **Museum of Leathercraft,** The Old Blue Coat School, Bridge Street (tel. 0604/34881), traces the history of leather use from ancient Egyptian times to the present. Missal cases, 16th-century caskets, and modern saddles are displayed, with exhibits of costumes, luggage, and harnesses. Open Monday to Saturday from 10 a.m. to 1 p.m. and 2 to 5:30 p.m., with no admission charge.

Where to Stay

The **Coach House,** 8–10 East Park Parade (tel. 0604/250981), lies slightly outside the heart of the city. Once it was a row of Victorian town houses, but now it has been turned into a well-run little hotel, with a wide selection of rooms, including family accommodations. Those with private bath are more expensive, of course. The single rate ranges from £18 ($27) to £28 ($42), and doubles cost from £28 ($42) to £38 ($57). Arrangements can be made for dinner. The location opens onto the old racecourse of the city which is now a park.

Birchfields, 17 Hester St. (tel. 0604/28199), is an immaculate guesthouse run by Mrs. S. Smithson. All her rooms have color TV and facilities for making hot beverages, and the house's baths are modern, with warm showers. For a bed and full English breakfast, the charge is £11 ($16.50) per person.

Where to Eat

Sun Rise, 18 Kingsley Park Terrace (tel. 0604/711228), was built to attract business in a shopping complex about a mile from the heart of Northampton. But many "downtown diners" make the effort to drive out here, as they consider that this place serves some of the best food in the area. The Wan family, your hosts, welcome guests from noon to 2 p.m. and 5:30 to 11:30 p.m. seven days a week. A set lunch is offered at £3.50 ($5.25), a fantastic bargain, and you also get exceptional value if you order the table d'hôte dinner at only £5 ($7.50). You can also dine à la carte. Both the Peking and Canton kitchens are represented in the vast array of specialties. I find the duck and chicken preparations the most interesting. There's a sophisticated modern decor.

Buddies Food Factory, Old Mission School, Drychurch Lane (tel. 0604/20300), is inspired by life in these United States. That means big fresh salads, rib steaks, hamburgers done as you like 'em, milk shakes, and even Budweiser. All this food will make you homesick, and, if it doesn't, then you have everything served against a backdrop of posters of the Manhattan skyline, Disney creatures, or whatever. Meals cost from £6 ($9), and hours are noon to 2 p.m. and 6 to 10:30 (open till 11 p.m. on Friday and Saturday but closed Sunday).

THE SPENCER HOME: The mansion that was the girlhood home of the Princess of Wales, **Althorp,** Northampton (no phone calls allowed), is the residence of the Earl and Countess Spencer, parents of the former Lady Diana Spencer who married Prince Charles. The entrance lodge is five miles northwest of Northampton, beyond the village of Harlestone. Althorp is about a 1½-hour drive from London on the A428 from Northampton to Rugby. Built in 1508 by Sir John Spencer, the house has undergone many alterations over the years.

It contains a fabulous collection of pictures by Van Dyck, Reynolds, Gainsborough, and Rubens, as well as fine and rare French and English furniture, along with Sèvres, Bow, and Chelsea porcelain. The collection is quite as magnificent as that in better-known stately homes. The house is open daily all year from 1:30 to 5:30 p.m., Wednesday being Connoisseurs' Day, when extra rooms are shown and the tour is longer. Admission to the house and grounds on regular days is £2.50 ($3.75) for adults, £1.25 ($1.88) for children, rising to £3.50 ($5.75) for adults and £1.75 ($2.63) for children on Connoisseurs' Day. The grounds and lake can be visited separately for

50p (75¢) for adults, 25p (38¢) for children. A gift shop, wine shop, and tea room are maintained at Althorp. The present countess helps in the gift shop, and Lord Spencer's own favorite sideline is the excellent cellar and wine store.

STOKE BRUERNE: On the Grand Union Canal, the **Waterways Museum,** at Stoke Bruerne, near Towcester in Northamptonshire (tel. 0604/862229), is just south of the Blisworth Tunnel (take the A508 from the M1 junction 15 and the A5). The three-story grain warehouse has been lovingly restored and adapted to give an insight into the working lives of canal boatmen and their families. On display is a full-size replica of a "butty" boat cabin, complete with cooking range, brassware, and lace curtains, along with the traditional painted ware, tools, and teapots. There is also an early semidiesel Boliner boat engine, a boat-weighing machine once used to determine canal toll charges, and a shop where you can buy posters, books, illustrations of canal life, hand-painted miniatures of traditional canalware, models, and badges. The museum is open from 10 a.m. to 6 p.m. It is closed on Monday from October to Easter but open otherwise until 4 p.m. Admission is £1 ($1.50) for adults and 50p (75¢) for children. A family ticket costs £2.25 ($3.38).

If you find yourself in the area, you'll be able to partake of one of the most delightful dining adventures in Northamptonshire.

The **Boat Inn,** Stoke Bruerne, near Towcester (tel. 0604/862428), started as a row of humble cottages in the 17th century and has gradually progressed without losing its original character. It is still a limestone building with a thatched roof overlooking the Grand Union Canal and the Stoke Bruerne Waterways Museum. The Public House is the oldest part, with stone floors and open fires, along with pictures depicting canal boats and life. Bar food includes the usual soup of the day, steak-and-kidney pie, and ploughman's lunch. You can also order sandwiches, salads, and basket meals. Count on spending around £5 ($7.50). Hours are from 11 a.m. to 2:30 p.m. and 6 to 11 p.m. Next to the pub is a traditional Northamptonshire skittles room where you can try your skill at throwing the "cheese," the flattened puck used to knock the skittles down.

The restaurant offers a full range of dishes, including smoked salmon, snails in garlic butter, and an interesting apple and stilton soup. There are several fish dishes, including a whole lobster thermidor, and guinea fowl and grouse are served in season, along with such elegant continental dishes as tournedos Rossini or steak Diane. A three-course meal, finished off with a choice from the dessert trolley or the cheese board, then coffee and mints, will cost around £12 ($18), including VAT but excluding the service charge. That is, unless you started with poached oysters, followed by lobster thermidor, and rounded off with roast grouse! On Sunday they do a great British Sunday lunch, costing £6.50 ($9.75) for adults and £4 ($6) for children. There is also a traditional cream tea in the afternoon, costing £1.95 ($2.93). The Woodward family has owned and run the Boat Inn since 1877.

Cruises are available on the Woodwards' canal narrow boat, *Indian Chief*. The boat has a fully-stocked bar, soft drinks, tea, coffee, and snacks. A 25-minute trip to Blisworth Tunnel Mouth and back costs 70p ($1.05) for adults, 45p (68¢) for children. Other, longer cruises are offered, requiring a minimum of 30 persons.

BRACKLEY: This is an ancient market town mentioned in the *Domesday Book*. It lies on the A43 road about halfway between Oxford and Northampton. This is a handy base for touring such sights as Sulgrave Manor (6 miles) and Oxford (24 miles).

If you're in the area, I suggest a stop at the **Old Crown Inn,** Market Place (tel. 0280/702210), is an old-world posting house, parts of which date back to the 12th century. The Duke of Wellington stopped here in 1814, a year before the Battle of

Waterloo. Recent improvements have increased the size of the public rooms, but the original character of the Old Crown has been preserved. There are heavy, time-aged beams, open brick fireplaces, and oak paneling in the lounge. The bar has a Tudor-style fireplace. Each of the inn's 14 bedrooms has a private bathroom, color TV, a phone, and a radio. A single costs £30 ($45) and a double £44 ($66), all prices including VAT and a full English breakfast. Meals, served in the inn's dining room from noon to 2 p.m. and 7 to 9:30 p.m., include a traditional Sunday roast beef lunch. You can also have soup, steaks, and desserts in the bar.

2. Leicestershire

Virtually ignored by most North American tourists, this eastern Midland county was, according to legend, the home of King Lear. Whatever the truth of that, Leicestershire is rich in historical associations. It was at Bosworth Battlefield that the last of the Plantagenet kings, Richard III, was killed in 1485, irrevocably changing the course of English history.

LEICESTER: The county town is a busy industrial center, but it was once a Roman settlement and has a Roman wall and bath site that remind one of those days.

It also has a Norman castle-hall, a period museum, a costume museum in a late medieval building, a 15th-century Guildhall (Shakespeare is said to have played here), and many interesting gardens. On its abbey park and grounds are the remains of Leicester Abbey, Cardinal Wolsey's grave, a boating lake, paddling pool, riverside walks, a miniature railway, ornamental gardens, and an aviary.

You can ask at the **Leicester Information Bureau,** 12 Bishop St. (tel. 0533/556699), for details of guided walks around the city.

Where to Stay

Daval Hotel, 292 London Rd., Stoneygate (tel. 0533/708234), is a historical building of architectural interest, built in 1889 during the reign of Queen Victoria. There are rooms of all sizes: singles, doubles, twins, and family size. All are modern with hot and cold running water, shaver points, radio, intercom, and wall-to-wall carpeting. Charges, which include a full English breakfast and all taxes, are £15.50 ($23.25) in a single, £24 ($36) for two persons in a room with a double bed, and £25.50 ($38.25) for two persons in a twin-bedded room. Some units contain private shower and cost an extra £3 ($4.50) per night. Family rooms with three or four beds are offered on a pro rata basis. There is a cozy restaurant where home-cooked evening meals are available, including steaks, chicken, duckling, scampi, and other specialties. Emphasis is on personal and friendly service, and the owners, Mr. and Mrs. Navarro, will make you feel welcome. The hotel has its own licensed bar with a TV lounge. The Daval is ideally situated for touring and visiting the Midlands. It is on the main A6 trunk road. For those traveling by train or bus, it is just a few minutes' ride away from the stations.

Alexandra Hotel, 342 London Rd. (tel. 0533/703056), is a modest hotel owned by Mr. and Mrs. Andrew and Terri Warzynski, who not only provide B&B but will offer a four-course dinner for £7.50 ($11.25) per person. Mr. Warzynski will also prepare a light snack for you when required. Bedrooms have TV, baths with showers, and toilets. Singles begin at £16 ($24), doubles go for £25 ($37.50), and family rooms cost £36 ($54).

Where to Eat

Water Margin, 76–78 High St. (tel. 0533/56422). There is near universal agreement that this is the best place to eat in Leicester where the gastronomy has improved amazingly in recent years. From the Canton kitchen comes an array of familiar and inventive dishes to intrigue you—everything from pork with plum sauce to eel prepared with flavor and skill. In other words, you can stick to the familiar here or else be a little adventurous with your palate. The business lunch at £2.20 ($3.30) is one of the food bargains of Leicester. At night count on spending from £8 ($12) and up. Some diners go here just for the selection of dim-sum. Hours are daily from noon to 11:30 p.m.

One of the healthiest places to dine in the city is **Blossoms,** 17b Clark St. (tel. 0533/539535), which is a vegetarian second-floor restaurant popular with shoppers. It is at its most bustling at lunchtime, but opens at 9:30 a.m. (go for morning coffee) until 4 p.m. (try it for afternoon tea). The selections of the day, ranging from an all-veg hot pie to a "two-bean goulash," are displayed on a counter. Meals cost from £4 ($6), and are not served on Sunday. The salads are crisp and fresh, the bakery goodies homemade. Of course, drinkers and nonsmokers don't go here.

Joe Rigatoni (don't you love that name?), 3 St. Martins Square (tel. 0533/533977), is a two-floor restaurant in a contemporary store complex. Bright and inviting, it serves some of the best Italian viands in town. Of course, most of the young diners come here for pizza and pasta, but you can get more substantial fare as well. Scampi and veal dishes are the most expensive items on the menu. You can dine for as little as £5 ($7.50), depending on what you order. Service is from noon to 2:30 p.m. and 6:30 to 11 p.m. On Saturday, however, it stays open until 2:30 a.m.

TOURING THE COUNTRY: As long as people continue to read Sir Walter Scott's *Ivanhoe,* they will remember **Ashby-de-la-Zouch,** a town that retains a pleasant country atmosphere. Mary Queen of Scots was imprisoned in an ancient castle here. Other places of interest are:

Belvoir Castle

On the northern border of Leicestershire, **Belvoir** (pronounced beaver) **Castle** has been the seat of the Dukes of Rutland since Henry VIII's time, overlooking the Vale of Belvoir. Rebuilt by Wyatt in 1816, the castle contains paintings by Holbein, Reynolds, and Gainsborough, as well as tapestries in its magnificent state rooms. The location is seven miles west-southwest of Grantham, between the A607 to Melton Mowbray and the A52 to Nottingham. The castle was the location of the films *Little Lord Fauntleroy* and Steven Spielberg's *Young Sherlock Holmes,* and in summer it is the site of medieval jousting tournaments. From mid-March to October it is open on Tuesday, Wednesday, Thursday, and Saturday from noon to 6 p.m. On Sunday its hours are noon to 7 p.m. After October 1, it is open until the end of that month only from 2 to 6 p.m. Admission is £2.40 ($3.60) for adults and £1.20 ($1.80) for children. Further details are available from Jimmy Durrands, Estate Office, Belvoir Castle, Grantham, Lincolnshire (tel. 0476/870262).

The Bosworth Battlefield

The **Battle of Bosworth Visitor Centre,** Sutton Cheney (tel. 0455/290429), lies between the M1 and the M6, close to Nuneaton. The 1485 battle it commemorates is considered one of England's three most important battles (the other two being the one at Hastings in 1066 and the Battle of Britain in 1940). The Battle of Bosworth ended the War of the Roses between the Houses of York and Lancaster, ending with the death of King Richard III, last of the Plantagenets, and the proclamation of the victor, Henry Tudor, a Welsh nobleman who had been banished to France to thwart his ambition. Henry landed at Milford Haven and marched across country to Leicestershire where King Richard was encamped, defeated the monarch, and became King Henry VII, first of the Tudor dynasty. Today, the appropriate standards fly where the opponents had their positions, and in a mile and a quarter walk along the marked battle trails, you can see the whole scene of the fighting. In the center are exhibitions, models, book and gift shops, a cafeteria, and a film theater where an audio-visual introduction with an excerpt from a Lord Laurence Olivier film, is presented.

The center is open from mid-April to late October Monday to Saturday from 2 to 5:30 p.m., Sunday and bank holiday Mondays from 1 to 6 p.m. Admission is £1 ($1.50) for adults, 60p (90¢) for children. The battle trails can be visited all year during daylight hours.

Melton Mowbray

Other interesting towns to visit in Leicestershire include **Melton Mowbray,** a fox-hunting center and market town which claims to be the original home of stilton cheese and is renowned for its pork pies.

The **Melton Mowbray Museum,** Thorpe End (tel. 0664/69946), depicts the past and present life of the area, with special exhibits on Stilton cheese and Melton pork pies. It's open Easter to September from 10 a.m. to 5 p.m. Monday to Saturday, from 2 to 5 p.m. on Sunday. October to Easter, opening is from 10 a.m. to 4 p.m. Monday to Friday and 10:30 a.m. to 4 p.m. on Saturday. Closed Christmas Day, Boxing Day, January 1, and Good Friday.

3. Derbyshire

The most magnificent scenery in the Midlands is found within the borders of this county, lying between Nottinghamshire and Staffordshire. Derbyshire has been less defaced by industry than its neighbors. The north of the county, containing the **Peak District National Park,** is by far the most exciting for touring. In the south the land is more level, and the look becomes, in places, one of pastoral meadows.

Some visitors avoid this part of the country, because it is ringed by the industrial sprawl of Manchester, Leeds, Sheffield, and Derby. To do so, however, would be a pity, as this part of England contains the rugged peaks and leafy dales which merit a substantial detour, especially Dovedale, Chee Dale, and Millers Dale.

HISTORIC HOMES: Near Bakewell, ten miles north of Matlock, stands one of the great country houses of England, **Chatsworth,** the home of the 11th Duke of Devonshire and his duchess, the former Deborah Mitford (sister of Nancy and Jessica). With its lavishly decorated interiors and a wealth of art treasures, it takes in 175 rooms, the most spectacular of which are open to the public, who can visit daily from 11:30 a.m. to 4:30 p.m. March to October (tel. 024/6882204 for information). Admission to the house and garden is £3.20 ($4.80) for adults and £1.75 ($2.63) for children. The eccentric Bess of Hardwick built a house on this spot which eventually held Mary Queen of Scots prisoner upon orders of Queen Elizabeth I. Most of that structure was torn down, and the present building, with many, many additions, dates from 1686. Capability Brown (who seems to have been everywhere) worked on the landscaping at one time. But it was Joseph Paxton, the gardener to the sixth duke, who turned the garden into one of the most celebrated in Europe. Queen Victoria and Prince Albert were lavishly entertained here in 1843. The house contains a great library and such paintings as the *Adoration of the Magi* by Veronese and *King Uzziah* by Rembrandt. On the grounds you can see spectacular greenhouses and fountains, and there is a playground for children in the farmyard.

Hardwick Hall (tel. 0246/850430), near Chesterfield, was built in 1597 for Bess of Hardwick, a woman who acquired four husbands and an estate from each of them. It is particularly noted for its architecture, fine tapestries and needlework. It is open from

April to the end of October on Wednesday, Thursday, Saturday, Sunday, and bank holiday Monday from 1 to 5:30 p.m., charging £2.80 ($4.20) for adults and £1.40 ($2.10) for children.

Melbourne Hall, at Melbourne (tel. 03316/2502), 8 miles south of Derby, originally built by the Bishops of Carlisle (1133), stands in one of the most famous formal gardens in Britain. The ecclesiastical structure was restored in the 1600s by one of the cabinet ministers of Charles I and enlarged by Queen Anne's vice chamberlain. It was the home of Lord Melbourne, who was prime minister when Victoria ascended to the throne. He was born William Lamb, and Melbourne Hall was also the home of Lord Byron's friend, Lady Caroline Lamb. Lady Palmerston later inherited the house, which contains an important collection of pictures, antique furniture, and works of art. A special feature is the beautifully restored wrought-iron pergola by Robert Bakewell, noted 18th-century ironsmith. The house is open on Wednesday from 2 to 6 p.m. from early June to early October, costing £1.50 ($2.25) for adults, 75p ($1.13) for children. The garden can be visited Wednesday, Saturday, Sunday, and bank holiday Mondays from 2 to 6 p.m. April to September. Admission to the garden is £1 ($1.50).

OTHER PLACES TO SEE: In addition to majestic scenery, you may want to seek out the following specific sights:

Royal Crown Derby Porcelain Co. Ltd., 194 Osmaston Road, in Derby (tel. 0332/47051). In case this is your special favorite in the pottery world, I suggest a trip into the center of Derby to take the two-hour tour of the only factory allowed to use both the words "royal" and "crown" in its name, a double honor granted by George III and Queen Victoria. At the end of the tour, you can treat yourself to a bargain in the gift shop and visit the Royal Crown Derby Museum from 9 a.m. to 12:30 p.m. and 1:30 to 4 p.m. Monday to Friday. Tours take place at 10:30 a.m. and 1:45 p.m. Monday to Friday, costing £1.50 ($2.25). The factory shop is open Monday to Saturday from 9 a.m. to 4 p.m.

National Tramway Museum, Crich, near Matlock (tel. 077385/2565). One young 65-year-old whom I know spends as much of his free time as his wife will allow in the paradise of vintage trams—electric, steam, and horse-drawn from home and overseas, including New York. Your admission ticket is £2.20 ($3.30) for adults and £1 ($1.50) for children. This ticket allows you unlimited rides on trams which make the two-mile round trip to Glory Mine with scenic views over the Derwent Valley via Wakebridge, where a stop is made to visit the Peak District Mines Historical Society display of lead mining. It also includes admission to various tramway exhibitions and displays and to the tramway period street which is an ongoing project. Hours are 10:30 a.m. to about 6 p.m. It's open weekends and bank holidays from early April to November; Monday to Thursday from mid-April to late September; and on Friday from late April to the end of May and late July to early September.

Peak District Mining Museum, the Pavilion, Matlock Bath (tel. 0629/3834), is open year round, daily (except for Christmas), from 11 a.m. to 4 p.m. Admission is 75p ($1.13) for adults and 50p (75¢) for children. The main exhibit of this display of 2,000 years of Derbyshire lead mining is a giant water-pressure engine, used to pump water from the mines and itself rescued from 360 feet underground by members of the society before being brought to the museum. The most popular feature is the children's climbing shaft, a twisting tunnel through which they crawl.

Magpie Mine, at Sheldon, near Bakewell, has been the site of much desperate toil, murders, vendettas, and enormous financial losses. In summer the surface remains of the lead mine (the underground workings are dangerous) are open to view anytime. Guides are available for prebooked parties, at a charge of £10 ($15) minimum per group. For information and reservations, get in touch with the Peak District Mining Museum, visited above (tel. 0629/3834).

The **Clock Warehouse,** London Road, Shardlow (tel. 0332/792844), was built in 1780 on the Trent and Mersey Canal at the junction with the navigable River Trent. It became part of the inland port where merchandise was stored on arrival by narrow boat and river barge. Nowadays the old building houses the Canal Story exhibition which fills its three floors. There are life-size models of boats and barges, historic photographs, artifacts, and a diorama showing the history of the canal system and the flourishing trade carried on along the waterways. The Canal Shop will sell books, souvenirs, and mementos. Look out for the authentic canal boat painted buckets, jugs, and boxes. The Clock Warehouse Restaurant is a simple beamed room decorated with dozens of authentic "laceplates" peculiar to the canals. It serves snacks and refreshments throughout the day. Admission is 90p ($1.35) for adults, 50p (75¢) for children. The warehouse is open during most of the year, but telephone to make sure. It's also possible to take short trips on the canal on an authentic narrow boat or to rent canal boats with four to ten berths on a weekly basis. This is an ideal way of seeing the countryside, but the boats must be reserved well in advance.

BUXTON: One of the loveliest towns in Britain, Buxton was developed in the 18th century to rival the spa at Bath. However, long before that, its waters were known to the Romans, whose settlement here was called Aquae Arnemetiae. The thermal waters were pretty much forgotten after that until during the reign of Queen Elizabeth I, when the baths were reactivated, and even Mary Queen of Scots was brought here by her caretaker, the Earl of Shrewsbury, to "take the waters." Buxton today is mostly the result of the 18th-century development carried out under direction of the Duke of Devonshire.

The Crescent, modeled on the one in Bath but with more elegant classical lines, was originally a hotel complex, but it is now occupied by a hotel and the county library. The Pump Room of the spa has become the **Buxton Micrarium** (tel. 0298/78662), a world of microscopic animals and plants, a popular attraction in The Crescent. Open from 10 a.m. to 5 p.m. Admission is £1.50 ($2.25) for adults, 80p ($1.20) for children. Perhaps the most outstanding feature of recent restoration in Buxton is the Victorian opera house, for years the local movie palace, now restored in all its marble, velvet, and ornamental plaster opulence. The annual Opera Festival held here bids fair to become a rival of Glyndebourne.

The waters from the nine thermal wells is no longer available for spa treatment except in the hydrotherapy pool at the Devonshire Royal Hospital. It is also used in the swimming pool at the beautiful 23-acre **Pavilion Gardens,** but if you want a drink of spa water, you can purchase it at the Tourist Information Centre or help yourself at the public fountain across the street.

Poole's Cavern, Buxton Country Park, Green Lane, in Buxton (tel. 0298/6978), is a cave that was once inhabited by Stone Age man, who may have been the first to marvel at the natural vaulted roof bedecked with stalactites. Explorers walk through the spacious galleries, viewing the incredible horizontal cave, electrically illuminated. It is open from Easter until the first week in November, from 10 a.m. to 5 p.m., charging £1.50 ($2.25) for adults, 80p ($1.20) for children.

Some 20 minutes away in Grin Low Woods is **Solomon's Temple,** a folly built in 1895, on a tumulus which dates from the Neolithic Age. Climb the small spiral staircase inside the temple for impressive views over Buxton and the surrounding countryside.

The **Tourist Information Centre,** The Crescent (tel. 0298/5106), arranges guided walks each week from May to the end of August. They vary in length from 1½ hours for the Spa Heritage Trail around the conservation area of the town, including The Crescent and the Pavilion Gardens, to 3 hours for the Town and Country Trail, that includes the conservation area of Buxton and either Solomon's Temple or Corbar Cross. The Spa Heritage Trail tour is offered on Monday morning and Wednesday and Saturday afternoon, costing 75p ($1.13) for adults, 50p (75¢) for children. The Sunday afternoon Town and Country trail costs £1.50 ($2.25). Walking tours of the High Peak can be arranged with an experienced guide, costing £7 ($10.50) for 1½ hours, £14 ($21) for a 3-hour trip.

Accommodations

Ashwood Park Hotel, Bakewell Road (tel. 0298/3416), is an impressive stone building in the heart of the spa, owned by M. Jean Howarth. It's set back from the busy roads, facing the well-tended public gardens with a small stream and lawns. It's more of a country inn, and the entire ground floor is a bar-lounge, decorated in oranges and browns with a collection of glittering brass and copper. The charge for B&B in a double is £11 ($16.50) per person daily, and there are no evening meals. The hotel is open only from May 1 until the end of October.

The **Old Manse Guest House,** 6 Clifton Rd., Silverlands (tel. 0298/5638), is one of the lovely old buildings in a quiet area, yet close to everything. Owner Kathie Fuller accepts guests on either a B&B or half-board arrangement. For B&B she charges £9.50 ($14.25) and offers another bargain, £14 ($21) daily for bed, breakfast, and evening meal (served at 6 p.m.). The menu is varied, with use of local products when possible, and the dining room is licensed. In the lounge, guests congregate for either friendly chats or viewing TV. Rooms have hot and cold running water, with central heating. There's space for parking cars.

The **Egerton Hotel,** 36 St. John's Rd. (tel. 0298/6770), is a dignified stone building surrounded by its own gardens. It is a simple square Victorian, with a pair of bay windows. Its location is fine, opposite the Pavilion Gardens. The Egerton has been well adjusted for guests, with an elevator and central heating. There is a bar lounge decorated in pink pastel fabric with Austrian blinds. All the bedrooms have private baths, TV, and facilities for making tea and coffee. B&B costs from £12 ($18) per person, with full board starting at £18 ($27) per person. Horseback riding is arranged for guests.

Thorn Heyes Private Hotel, 137 London Rd. (tel. 0298/3539), is a solid Victorian stone house with a sweeping drive and large gardens. It has been much modernized to make for comfortable bedrooms with central heating. All have showers, toilets, color TV, and beverage facilities. Rooms are prettily decorated with continental quilts and flowery curtains. Downstairs is a lounge overlooking the garden, plus a dining room where fresh local produce is served whenever possible. David and Pat Green love to meet their guests, and David is delighted to pass on his lifetime of knowledge of Buxton and the Peaks. They charge from £14.50 ($21.75) per person for B&B, £21.25 ($31.88) for half board, VAT included.

On the Outskirts

Crewe & Harpur Arms Hotel, Longnor, near Buxton (tel. 029883/205), is set in a village in the hills of the Peak District 6 miles from Buxton. The valleys of the Rivers Dove and Manifold are a couple of miles away. On the village square with its cobble street and market hall, you are linked quickly with the past when Longnor stood at the crossing of the old wagon trails from Leicester to Liverpool. The hotel is tastefully furnished. All bedrooms have hot and cold water basins and showers. Ron King and Keith Williams, the hosts, charge £15 ($22.50) per person for B&B. An evening meal costs from £6.50 ($9.75). The Georgian dining room is a fine background for both table d'hôte meals and steaks. You can also have bar meals if you wish. Fishing is available for £2 ($3) per day.

ASHBOURNE: This old market town has a 13th-century church, a 16th-century grammar school, and ancient almshouses.

For accommodations, I recommend—

The Green Man and Black Head's Royal Hotel, St. John Street (tel. 0335/ 43861), in the town center, has many historical connections going back to 1710. In 1777 Dr. Samuel Johnson and his biographer, James Boswell, stayed at the inn, and Boswell writes, "I took my postchaise from the Green Man, a very good inn." In the Tap Room you can still see the chairs of Boswell and Johnson. Princess Victoria and her widowed mother, the Duchess of Kent, halted here and gave the inn the right to add "Royal" to its name. This red-brick posting inn has retained its traditional character, yet modern amenities have been added. There are 17 bedrooms, ten of which have private baths. Each is well decorated, and prices include a full English breakfast and early-morning tea or coffee, as well as VAT and service charge. The owner, John Clowes, charges from £22.50 ($33.75) to £25 ($37.50) in a single, from £35 ($52.50) to £40 ($60) in a double, the higher prices being for rooms with bath. Luncheons and evening dinner, from £9 ($13.50) to £10 ($15), are offered in the Shrovetide Restaurant, selections made from an à la carte menu.

On the Outskirts

Roston Hall Farm, Roston, near Ashbourne (tel. 033524/287). Mrs. Enid Prince has a lovely old farmhouse where she and her farmer husband take in a few guests. On 90 acres, the house and farm are clean and neat as a new pin. B&B costs from £8.50 ($12.75) per person, and another £4.50 ($6.75) will bring you an evening meal of homemade farm-style food.

ALSTONFIELD: This is a pretty village on the edge of Dovedale, a perfect center from which to tour the Peaks and Dales. It lies off the A515 road from Ashbourne to Buxton, and it's actually just across the Derbyshire line in Staffordshire.

If you're in the neighborhood, drop in at the **George Inn** (tel. 033527/205), a 16th-century pub with oak beams and open fires, run by Richard and Sue Grandjean, who have been here for about a quarter of a century and know everything worth knowing about the place. The inn is right off the village green and is the only place for locals to gather for an evening. Food is served from noon to 1:45 p.m. and 7 to 10 p.m., featuring such dishes as filet steak and fried plaice with french fries. Meals cost around £5 ($7.50). The bars, ringing with local chitchat, are open from 10:30 a.m. to 2:30 p.m. and 6 (7 in winter) to 11 p.m.

If you want to spend the night, try the following.

Overdale, Alstonfield, near Ashbourne (tel. 033527/206), lies on the outskirts of the tiny village. Mrs. Leason, along with her husband, has a lovely Derbyshire house kept absolutely spotless and set on immaculate grounds. She has five bedrooms plus two family rooms to rent, which are large and comfortable, costing from £8.50 ($12.75) per person. That includes a large cooked breakfast. An extra charge of £5 ($7.50) gets you an evening meal, three courses with coffee.

4. Nottinghamshire

"Notts," as it is called, was the county of Robin Hood and Lord Byron. It is also Lawrence country, as the English novelist, author of *Sons and Lovers* and *Lady Chatterley's Lover,* was also from here, born at Eastwood.

Sherwood Forest is probably the most famous woodland in the world. It isn't the greenwood haven it used to be, but it did provide in its time excellent cover for its world-famous bandit and his band, Robin Hood and his Merry Men, including Friar Tuck and Little John. Actually very little of it was forest, even in its heyday. The area consists of woodland glades, fields, and agricultural land, along with villages and hamlets.

The **Sherwood Forest Visitor Centre,** Sherwood Forest Country Park at Edwinstowe, near Mansfield (tel. 0623/823202), stands in the area just by the Major Oak, popularly known as Robin Hood's tree. It's the center of many marked walks and footpaths through the woodland. There's an exhibition of life-size models of Robin Hood and the other well-known outlaws, as well as a shop with books, gifts, and souvenirs. The center, some 18 miles north of Nottingham city off the A614, will provide as much information as remains of Friar Tuck and Little John, along with Maid Marian and Alan-a-Dale, as well as the other Merry Men. Little John's grave can be seen at Hathersage, Will Scarlet's at Blidworth. Robin Hood is believed to have married Maid Marian at Edwinstowe Church, close to the Visitor Centre. Nearby is the Major Oak, 30 feet in circumference, where the outlaws could easily have hidden in the hollow trunk.

Robin Hood's Larder offers light snacks and meals. There is a full program of events taking place on the center site and in the area. The center also contains a Tourist Information Centre, one of the national network in England. It's open daily from 11 a.m. to 5 p.m. in April; May to September, hours are 11 a.m. to 5 p.m. Monday to Saturday, to 6:30 p.m. on Sunday. In March and October it's open Monday to Sunday from 11:30 a.m. to 4:30 p.m. November and December hours are Tuesday to Thursday and Saturday and Sunday from 11:30 a.m. to 4 p.m., while in January and February it is open only on Saturday and Sunday at those same hours. The Larder is open at various hours, depending on the center opening days and times.

There is no admission charge to the center which is on the B6034 north of Edwinstowe village, seven miles east of Mansfield. In summer the Sherwood Forester bus service links Nottingham, the Visitor Centre, and other sights in the area, including Clumber Park and Rufford Country Park. In fine weather, several open-top buses are on the route, so you can get far closer to the atmosphere of the forest and Robin Hood.

Nottinghamshire is so rarely visited by foreign tourists that its beautiful landscapes could almost be called "undiscovered." British trippers, however, know of its hidden villages and numerous parks.

NOTTINGHAM: The county town is a busy industrial city, 121 miles north of London. On the north bank of the Trent, Nottingham is one of the most pleasant cities in the Midlands.

Overlooking the city, **Nottingham Castle** (tel. 0602/411881) was built by the Duke of Newcastle on the site of a Norman fortress in 1679. After restoration in 1878, it was opened as a provincial museum, surrounded by a charmingly laid-out garden. See, in particular, the collection of medieval Nottingham alabaster carvings. The works of Nottingham-born artists are displayed in the first-floor gallery. The castle is open April to September, daily from 10 a.m. to 5:45 p.m. Otherwise, its hours are daily from 10 a.m. to 4:45 p.m. Admission is free except on Sunday and bank holidays, when a small fee is charged. Closed Christmas Day.

For 50p (75¢), you'll be taken on a conducted tour at the castle of Mortimer's Hole and underground passages. King Edward III is said to have led a band of noblemen through these secret passages, surprising Roger Mortimer and the Queen, killing Mortimer, and putting his lady in prison. A statue of Robin Hood stands at the base of the castle. The museum shop has a wide range of British crafts.

The **Brewhouse Yard Museum,** Castle Boulevard, consists of five 17th-century cottages at the foot of Castle Rock, presenting a panorama of Nottingham life in a series of furnished rooms. Some of them, open from cellar to attic, have much local historical material on display, and visitors are encouraged to handle some exhibits. The most interesting features are in a series of cellars cut into the rock of the castle instead of below the houses, plus an exhibition of a Nottingham shopping street, 1919-1939, with 11 shops or services which are local to the city. This is not a typical folk museum, but attempts to be as lively as possible, involving both visitors and the Nottingham community in expanding displays and altering exhibitions on a bimonthly basis. Open all year, the admission-free museum (tel. 0602/411881, ext. 48) may be visited from 10 a.m. to 5 p.m. except during the lunch hour from noon to 1 p.m. It is closed Christmas Day. Donations to help with the upkeep are welcomed.

An elegant row of Georgian terraced houses, the **Museum of Costume and Textiles** at 51 Castle Gate (tel. 0602/411881), presents collections of costumes, textiles, and lace, one of the city's great industries. You'll see everything from the 1632 Eyre map tapestries of Nottingham to "fallals and frippery." The admission-free museum is open daily from 10 a.m. to 5 p.m.; closed Christmas Day.

On the outskirts of Nottingham, at Linby, **Newstead Abbey** (tel. 0623/792822) was once Lord Byron's home. It lies 11 miles north of Nottingham on the A60 (the Mansfield road). Some of the original Augustinian priory, bought by Sir John Byron in 1540, still survives. In the 19th century the mansion was given a neo-Gothic restoration. The poet's bedroom is as he left it. Mementos, including first editions and manuscripts, are displayed inside, and later you can explore a parkland of some 300 acres, with waterfalls, rose gardens, a Monk's Stew Pond, and a Japanese water garden. Admission to the grounds and gardens is 75p ($1.13) for adults, 25p (38¢) for children. To visit the abbey costs adults £1 ($1.50); children, 40p (60¢). There is an additional charge if you take the special tour around the abbey, which is open from Good Friday to September 30 from 1:45 to 6 p.m. (last admissions at 5 p.m.). The gardens are open all year from 10 a.m. to dusk.

Also on the outskirts of Nottingham, **Wollaton Hall** (tel. 0602/281333) is a well-preserved Elizabethan mansion, the most ornate in England (finished in 1588), housing a natural history museum, with lots of insects, invertebrates, and British mammals, along with reptiles and crustaceans, some a long way from their former home in the South Seas. The mansion is open, April to September, daily from 10 a.m. to 7 p.m. and on Sunday from 2 to 5 p.m. In October and March its hours are 10 a.m. to 5:30 p.m. (on Sunday, 1:30 to 4:30 p.m.). From November to February it is open from 10 a.m. to 4:30 p.m. (on Sunday, 1:30 to 4:30 p.m.). Admission is free except on Sunday and bank holidays when a modest charge is made. The hall is surrounded by a Deer Park and gardens. See the camellia house with the world's earliest (1823) cast-iron front. The bird dioramas here are among the best in Britain.

Where to Stay

The **Rufford Hotel,** 53 Melton Rd., West Bridford (tel. 0302/811233), is approximately 1½ miles from the city center, in a relatively quiet suburb, and within easy access of the M1. It's an adaptation of a clean-cut, rather attractive private house, fully converted to receive overnight guests. Owners Mr. and Mrs. Michael Fellows charge £30 ($45) for a double and £20 ($30) for a single, including breakfast. All rooms have private shower and toilet, color TV, phones, and beverage-making facilities. From Monday through Thursday an evening meal is also available. Over the weekend inexpensive bar snacks are on hand.

Cotswold Hotel, 330-332 Mansfield Rd. (tel. 0602/623547), is a comfortable private hotel, owned by Faune and John Kite. They've given the lounge, dining room, and bedrooms a fresh look with decorations and pleasant furniture. There is full central heating and hot and cold running water in each bedroom. In the invitingly home-like residents' lounge, color TV is offered. They charge a set fee of £15 ($22.50) per person nightly, which includes an English breakfast. Many of the rooms have their own shower, toilet, and color TV, plus tea- and coffee-making facilities. Daily except Sunday, you can order moderately priced evening meals. A carvery restaurant offers real English roast beef and yorkshire pudding. The hotel is easy to find, on the A60, one mile north of Nottingham center. It is on the road and has a Tudor-style facade.

The **Flying Horse Hotel,** Poultry (tel. 0602/502831), is one of the hotels owned by Barni Inns, and in this case provides adequate accommodation near St. Peters Church. The public rooms have been modernized, and many have a private bath. Depending on the plumbing, singles range from £18 ($27) to £23.50 ($35.25) and doubles go for £30.50 ($45.75) to £36 ($54). Lunch or dinner in one of the two restaurants costs from £8.50 ($12.75). There are nine bars (count them), including a wine bar. The inn celebrated its 500th birthday in 1983.

Food and Drink

Eviva Taverna, 25 Victoria St. (tel. 0602/580243). The political squabbles between Greece and Britain are over, at least during a meal in this joyful tavern. Do you like to watch Greek dancing and smash plates? If so, this is the place, although you'll be charged extra for the plates demolished. Chef's specialties include stefado, a Greek stew of beef, onion, and herbs, cooked in wine vinegar; and kleftico, a thick piece of lamb cooked very slowly in the oven with herbs. Of course there are the inevitable dolmades, stuffed vine leaves. The owner, J. Kozakis, runs a kebab house above the tavern, offering kebabs of lamb, pork, and steak. A meal here will cost from £5 ($7.50), plus your wine. And plate smashing! Hours are Monday through Saturday evening from 7 p.m. till 2 a.m.

Ben Bowers Restaurant, 128 Derby Rd. (tel. 0602/413388), is a four-in-one complex, all part of the same chain. The same phone number is valid for each member of the group: Ben Bowers Piano Restaurant, and Betty's Buffet Bar, as well as Ben Bowers Bar where a wide range of snacks is offered, costing from 65p (98¢). The ground-floor Ben Bowers Restaurant offers good value for your money, serving a three-course luncheon menu for £4.95 ($7.43) and set dinners for £8.50 ($12.75), rising to £8.95 ($13.43) on Saturday night. The cuisine features dishes from around the world. À la carte is also available, a meal costing from £12 ($18). Downstairs in the evening, the Piano Restaurant serves à la carte meals by candlelight, a complete repast, including wine, costing around £15 ($22.50). A resident pianist performs Monday to Saturday, playing a selection of love songs and classical music. Betty's Buffet Bar serves a large selection of fresh meats, fish, and pâté with imaginative salads, costing from £2.25 ($3.38). Hours are 11 a.m. to 2:30 p.m. and 6 to 10:30 p.m. Monday to Saturday, noon to 2 p.m. and 7 to 10:30 p.m. on Sunday.

Shogun, 95 Talbot St. (tel. 0602/475611). Someone, anybody, just had to come up with a name like this for a Japanese restaurant. Although relatively new, Shogun is now considered the leading restaurant in the Nottingham district. Yet, unlike the prices in Japan, the tariffs here are very reasonable. For example, a table d'hôte lunch goes for only £5 ($7.50), a set dinner costing from £9 ($13.50). Of course, you can spend a lot more by ordering à la carte. Service is Monday to Saturday from noon to 1:45 p.m. and 7 to 11 p.m. The chef is also the owner: Keiji Tomiyama. While admiring the samurai armor, you can order the classic dishes of the Japanese kitchen. The menu offers an imaginative choice of interesting, well-prepared dishes. Service is the most professional in the city. The location *could* be more convenient. It's on a road leading out of the city in the direction of the motorway (the M1) in a red-brick turn-of-the-century warehouse setting with a sophisticated decor.

Ye Olde Trip to Jerusalem, Brewhouse Yard, Castle Road (tel. 0302/43171), claims to be the oldest inn in England. It was a traditional stopover for the Crusaders on their way to the Holy Land. Founded in the 12th century, it was built right into the castle rock, and served, because of its coolness, as the castle brewery. Scientists can't fathom how the speaking tube, cut through the rocks, works—but it does. The two bars are literally cut out of the rocks, and the fireplace chimney is nearly 45 feet high, also cut out of the rock. You can order ginger wine or draft cider here, along with various sandwich rolls at lunchtime. Light snacks cost from £1 ($1.50). The pub is open from 10:30 a.m. to 2:30 p.m. and 5:30 to 10:30 p.m.

About a half-hour drive from Lord Byron's Newstead Abbey leads to—

SOUTHWELL: This ancient market town is a good center for exploring the Robin Hood country. Byron once belonged to a local amateur dramatic society here. An unexpected gem is the old twin-spired cathedral, **Southwell Minster,** which many consider among the most beautiful churches in England. James I found that it held up with "any other kirk in Christendom." Look for the well-proportioned Georgian houses across from the cathedral.

East of Southwell, near the Lincolnshire border, is—

NEWARK-ON-TRENT: Here is an ancient riverside market town, on the Roman Fosse Way, lying about 15 miles across flatlands from Nottingham. King John died at **Newark Castle** in 1216. Constructed between the 12th and 15th centuries, the castle, now in ruins, survived three sieges by Cromwell's troops before falling into ruin in 1646. From its parapet, you can look down on the Trent River and across to Nottingham. The delicately detailed parish church here is said to be the finest in the country. The town contains many ancient inns, reflecting its long history.

On the banks of the River Trent, a short walk from Newark Castle, is **Millgate Folk Museum** (tel. 0636/79403), in a building that housed a 19th-century oil-seed mill and then a warehouse. Today, it contains portrayals of social and industrial life in the area from the turn of the century to World War II. Agricultural, malting, and printing implements are displayed, and a series of furnished rooms depicts domestic life in those times. The museum, for which there is no admission fee, is open from 10 a.m. to 5 p.m. Monday to Friday all year and from 2 to 6 p.m. on Saturday and Sunday from Easter to September.

On the outskirts, I'd suggest the following for food and lodgings:

Newcastle Arms Hotel, Tuxford (tel. 0777/870208), has been a village inn since 1701, welcoming such guests as Margaret Tudor, Charles II, and Mr. Gladstone. It's a Georgian-style, two-story corner building, with a plain facade, except for a pair of bay windows flanking the small pillared entrance. Furnishings are in the style of an English country inn. A single without bath rents for £20 ($30) to £22 ($33), a single with bath going for £22.50 ($33.75) to £28 ($42). Bathless doubles cost £23 ($34.50) to £25 ($37.50), and doubles with bath go for £30 ($45) to £36 ($54), all prices including breakfast and VAT. The lower prices quoted in each category are weekend rates. All units contain phones and television sets. Fully licensed, the hotel offers good food and wine. The chef does not only good-tasting English dishes, but classically continental ones along with many Asian specialties. Luncheons run from £8 ($12), and dinner is from £9 ($13.50). The location is on the A1, 12 miles north of Newark, 20 miles south of Doncaster.

THE DUKERIES: In the Dukeries, portions of Sherwood Forest, legendarily associated with Robin Hood, are still preserved. These are vast country estates on the edge of industrial towns. Most of the estates have disappeared, but the park at **Clumber,** covering some 4,000 acres, is administered by the National Trust, which has preserved its 18th-century beauty, as exemplified by Lime Tree Avenue. Rolling heaths and a peaceful lake add to the charm. You can visit Clumber Chapel, built in 1886–1889 as a chapel for the seventh Duke of Newcastle. It is open from 2 to 7 p.m. Monday to Friday April to the end of September, noon to 6:30 p.m. on weekends. Off-season hours are daily from noon to 3:30 p.m. There is no admission charge, but car entry to the park costs £1.40 ($2.10). There are stables with a tower clock dated 1763, a classical bridge over the lake, lodges and pleasure grounds, as well as fishing, bicycle rental, a shop, and a restaurant. The park is open all year. Clumber Park is five miles southeast of Clumber Park Stableyard, Worksop (tel. 0909/486411).

A few miles south of Clumber stands the greatest Victorian house in the Midlands, **Thoresby Hall,** at Mansfield (tel. 0623/822301), a fine mansion in the heart of Sherwood Forest. Built by Salvin in 1864, this is the only palatial home in the Dukeries still occupied by the original owners' descendants. The hall is open only on bank holidays and on Sunday from 1 to 5 p.m. May through August. Admission to the house and gardens is £1.70 ($2.55) for adults, 80p ($1.20) for children. For further information, telephone the estate office, Thoresby Park (tel. 0623/822301). It lies four miles north of Ollerton, just west of the Bawtry road, the A614.

EASTWOOD: Because of the increased interest in D. H. Lawrence these days, many literary fans like to make a pilgrimage to Eastwood, his hometown. The English novelist was born there on September 11, 1885. Mrs. Brown, a member of the D. H. Lawrence Society, conducts parties of visitors around the "Lawrence country." At the end, you can make a donation to the society. If you're interested in taking a tour, write her in advance—Mrs. M. Brown, D. H. Lawrence Society, c/o 8a Victoria St., Eastwood, Nottingham (tel. 0773/718139).

The Lawrence birthplace at 8a Victoria St. has been turned into the **D. H. Lawrence Information Centre and Museum** (tel. 0773/763312), now authentically depicting a miner's home as it was in 1885. The Eastwood Library houses a unique collection of Lawrence's works and the headstone from his grave on the French Riviera. Hours are 10 a.m. to 5 p.m. daily; from 10 a.m. to 4 p.m. in winter. Admission is 35p (53¢) for adults, 15p (23¢) for children.

SCROOBY: This is a tiny village of some 260 inhabitants where in 1566 William Brewster, a leader of the Pilgrim Fathers, was born. His father was bailiff of the manor and master of the postes, so it may have been in the Manor House that the infant Brewster first saw the light of day. The original house dated from the 12th century, and the present manor farm, built on the site in the 18th century, has little except historical association to attract.

Brewster Cottage, with its pinfold where stray animals were impounded, lies beside the village church of St. Wilfred. But it's uncertain whether the Pilgrim Father ever lived there.

The village also contains Monks Hill on the River Ryton, now almost a backwater but once a navigable stream down which Brewster and his companions may have escaped to travel to Leyden in Holland and on to their eventual freedom.

In the 18th century the turnpike ran through the village, and there are many stories of highwaymen, robberies, and murders. The body of John Spencer hung for more than 60 years as a reminder of the penalties of wrongdoing. He'd attempted to dispose of the bodies of the keeper of Scrooby toll-bar and his mother in the river.

Search for Pilgrim Roots

Many North Americans who trace their ancestry to the Pilgrim Fathers come to this part of England to see where it all started. The Separatist movement had its origin in an area north of Nottingham and south of York, and the towns from which its members came are all in a small area. They include **Blyth** (the one in Nottinghamshire, not the one in Northumberland), **Scrooby, Austerfield, Bawtry,** and **Babworth.** Besides William Brewster, who is identified with Scrooby, as mentioned above, William Bradford's birthplace was a manor house in Austerfield, lived in and well maintained today. It can be visited by arrangement with the occupant. The churches at Scrooby and Babworth welcome North Americans.

Blyth is the most beautiful of the villages, with a green surrounded by well-kept old houses, looking a lot like a New England village, which is no surprise. The parish church was developed from the 11th-century nave of a Benedictine priory church. On the green is a 12th-century stone building which was once the Hospital of St. John.

5. Lincolnshire

This large East Midlands county is bordered on one side by the North Sea. Its most interesting section is Holland, in the southeast, a land known for its fields of tulips, its marshes and fens, and windmills reminiscent of the Netherlands. Much of the shire is interesting to explore. Foreigners, particularly North Americans, generally cross the tulip fields, scheduling stopovers in the busy port of Boston before making the swing north to the cathedral city of Lincoln, lying inland.

BOSTON: This old seaport in the riding of Holland has a namesake that has gone on to greater glory, and perhaps for this reason it is visited by New Englanders. At Scotia Creek, on a riverbank near Boston, is a memorial to the early Pilgrims who made an unsuccessful attempt in 1607 to reach the promised land. They were imprisoned in the Guildhall in cells that can be visited today. A company left again in 1620 and fared better, as anybody who has ever been to Massachusetts will testify. Part of the ritual here is climbing the Boston Stump, a church lantern tower with a view for miles around of the all-encircling fens. In the 1930s the people of Boston, U.S.A., paid for the restoration of the tower, known officially as St. Botolph's Tower. Actually, it's not recommended that you climb the tower, as the stairs aren't in good shape. The tower, as it stands, was finished in 1460. The city fathers were going to add a spire, making it the tallest in England. But because of the wind and the weight, they feared the tower would collapse. Therefore the tower became known as "the Boston Stump." An elderly gentleman at the tower assured me it was the tallest in England—that is, 272½ feet tall. Boston is 116 miles north from London, and 34 miles southeast of Lincoln.

Accommodations

The attractive **White Hart,** Bridge Foot, 1-5 High Street (tel. 0205/64877), is a Berni Inn in a Regency-style building right by the bridge, with some rooms overlooking the river. Of the 31 bedrooms, nine have private baths. B&B rates are £25 ($37.50) to £32 ($48) in singles, £45.50 ($68.25) to £53 ($79.50) in doubles. The difference in price depends on the room's location and whether or not it has a private bath. The location is right in the center, near the Boston Stump and the courthouse and prison. The inn has two restaurants. The Steak and Duck is a self-service salad bar, with prices about 10% higher than in the Steak and Chicken, where you can order soup, fish, vegetables, and a dessert. A meal costs from £10 ($15). There is good car parking here.

Fairfield Guest House, 101 London Rd. (tel. 0205/62869), is an economy oasis where you can spend the night in a stone Victorian house set in its own garden. Built originally for a large family, it has been adapted to receive overnight guests. Yet the personal quality hasn't been sacrificed. At the edge of Boston, it is reached by a driveway leading to a formal entry. The bedrooms have hot and cold running water and are centrally heated and pleasantly furnished. For B&B, the owners, the Pages, charge £10 ($15).

Fydell Lodge Guest House, 27 Norfolk St. (tel. 0205/62804), is one of the best of the B&Bs, lying about a six- or seven-minute walk from the heart of town. Guests are well taken care of here, in one of nine comfortably furnished bedrooms, none of which contains a private bath. The charge in a single is £12.50 ($18.75), rising to £24 ($36) in a double. The half-board tariff, the best bargain, is about £17 ($25.50) per person nightly. The management, which is most helpful, has totally updated the house, providing several amenities.

Where to Dine

The Carving Table, New England Hotel, Wide Bargate (tel. 0205/65255), offers the best food value in town. In its carving room guests are invited to choose their main dish from a selection of freshly roasted joints of prime meat, carved by the hotel chef. You help yourself to vegetables or else decide on a good-tasting cold meal served direct from a buffet. The roast of the day costs from £6.25 ($9.38), and children are charged half price. A choice of desserts from the trolley include fruit salad and fruit pie, all served with fresh cream. A cheese board is also presented. Appetizers are priced extra, but I found that one is unnecessary considering the amount of food offered at the fixed price. Carving room hours are noon to 2 p.m. and 7 to 10 p.m. seven days a week. In addition the hotel also serves bar snacks Monday to Saturday from noon to 2 p.m.

LINCOLN: One of the most ancient cities in England, and only 135 miles north of London, Lincoln was known to the Romans as Lindum. Some of the architectural glory of the Roman Empire still stands to charm the present-day visitor. The renowned Newport Arch (the North Gate) is the last remaining arch left in Britain that still spans a principal highway. For a look at the Roman relics excavated in and around Lincoln, head for the **Greyfriars City & County Museum,** Broadgate (tel. 0522/30401), open daily from 10 a.m. to 5:30 p.m. (2:30 to 5 p.m. on Sunday). Admission is 25p (38¢) for adults, 10p (15¢) for children.

Two years after the Battle of Hastings, William the Conqueror built **Lincoln Castle** on the site of a Roman fortress. Used for administrative purposes today, parts of the castle still remain, including the walls, the 12th-century keep, and fragments of the gateway tower. In addition, you can visit the High Bridge over the Witham River, with its half-timbered houses (you can have a meal in one of them). This is one of the few medieval bridges left in England that has buildings nestling on it.

Visit also the **Museum of Lincolnshire Life,** Burton Road (tel. 0522/28448), the largest folk museum in the area, with displays ranging from a Victorian schoolroom to locally built steam engines. It's open daily from 10 a.m. to 5:30 p.m. (from 2 to 5:30 p.m. on Sunday). Admission is 40p (60¢) for adults, 20p (30¢) for children.

Lincoln Cathedral

Towering over the ancient city, the Minster forms a grand sight, with its three towers. The central one is 271 feet tall, making it the second tallest in England, ranking under the Boston Stump, mentioned earlier. However, the central tower at Lincoln was once the tallest spire in the world (525 feet) until it blew down in 1549. The Norman cathedral was consecrated in 1092, but only the west front remains. The cathedral represents the Gothic style, particularly the Early English and Decorated periods. The nave was built in the early 13th century. In the Early English Great Transept, you can see a rose medallion window, known as the Dean's Eye. The rose window at the opposite end of the transept, in the Decorated style, is known as the Bishop's Eye. The Angel Choir, in the eastern end, completed in the 13th century, was named after the sculptured angels displayed in it. The exquisite carving in the choir dates from the 14th century. The black font of Tournai marble is from the 12th century.

In the Seamen's Chapel is a window commemorating Lincolnshire-born Capt. John Smith, one of the pioneers of early settlement in America and the first governor of Virginia.

The Library, in the Cloister, was designed in 1674 by Sir Christopher Wren. It contains many fine books and manuscripts, some of which are on view in the adjoining Medieval Library, together with one of the four remaining original copies of Magna Carta of 1215 and the Cathedral Charter of 1072. The Library is open Monday through Saturday, 10:30 a.m. to 1 p.m. and 2 to 4:30 p.m. May through September, and in winter by appointment (tel. 0522/44544), at a small charge.

In the Treasury (open weekdays from 2:30 to 4:30 p.m., May through September), there is fine gold and silver plate from churches in the diocese.

In line with many other great churches, the cathedral suggests donations. If you refuse, you will still not be excluded, however. Adults are asked to contribute £1

($1.50); children, 20p (30¢). All monies gathered are devoted to maintenance and repair of the ancient structure. There is a Minster Shop where you can contribute more funds by purchasing the attractive souvenirs, and the Coffee Shop run at the entrance to the library stairs also helps out.

Where to Stay

Hillcrest Hotel, 15 Lindum Terrace (tel. 0522/26341), is a fine red-brick house built in 1871 as the private home of a local vicar. And although it has been converted into a comfortable small licensed hotel, it retains many of the features of its original use. It is suitable for those who appreciate a cozy atmosphere where personal tastes can be accommodated. It is in a quiet tree-lined road overlooking 26 acres of parkland, in the old high town and within easy walking distance of Lincoln Cathedral and the Roman remains. It is the home of the proprietors, Mr. and Mrs. Mitchell, who have carried on improvements made in recent years. There are color TVs, radios, tea-making facilities, and wash basins in all rooms, and private showers and toilets are also available. The charge is from £21 ($31.50) in a single and from £30 ($45) in a double, with a £5 ($7.50) supplement for a room with shower and toilet. The à la carte restaurant serves a three-course meal for around £8 ($12). Snack meals are also available.

Castle Hotel, Westgate (tel. 0522/38801), constructed of red brick, rises three stories high, lying within a three-minute walk of the Cathedral in Old Lincoln. When it was built around 1858, it was the North District National School, but it has been successfully converted into a hotel of character and comfort. The management rents out 21 bedrooms, some of which are located within a nearby annex. Each is comfortably furnished, containing a private bath or shower. The charge for B&B in a single is £31 ($46.50), rising to £36 ($54) in a double. A warmly masculine bar, laden with Chesterfield-style leather sofas, sits a few steps from the reception desk. Good English-style cooking is served in the Westgate Restaurant, where dinners cost from £10 ($15).

The **Duke William Hotel,** 44 Bailgate (tel. 0522/33351), is in the heart of historic Lincoln near the Roman arch, within walking distance of the cathedral. Although the structure has seen many architectural changes since its establishment in 1791, care has been taken to preserve the atmosphere of an 18th-century inn. Many of the 11 bedrooms still have their original heavy timbers. All of them contain TV. Singles rent for £20 ($30) to £27 ($40.50) bathless, £24 ($36) to £29 ($43.50) with showers. Bathless doubles are priced at £30 ($45) to £36 ($54), those with showers costing £34 ($51) to £39 ($58.50). The hotel has both a good restaurant and a cozy bar. A tasty luncheon, costing from £5 ($7.50), is served from noon to 2:30 p.m. Monday to Saturday. Only cold snacks are served on Sunday, from noon to 1:45 p.m. Dinners are more elaborate, served Monday to Saturday from 7:30 to 9:30 p.m. An evening meal, with a main dish of rumpsteak, trout with almonds, or Mexican chicken, costs from £8 ($12).

The **Hollies Hotel,** Carholme Road (tel. 0522/22419), owned by the Williams family, provides clean, comfortable accommodations at fair prices. Including VAT and a tasty breakfast, the per-person rate in a single or double is £12 ($18) nightly. Each room is centrally heated, with hot and cold running water and a radio. During the day it's possible to obtain a light meal, but no evening meal is served. There's a free car park as well.

Fircroft Private Hotel, 398 Newark Rd. (tel. 0522/26522). Val and Clive Hummerstone Vasey run a very friendly, clean, and comfortable B&B house. All rooms have color TV, and out of 15 bedrooms six now have private toilets and showers. Depending on the plumbing, the rate ranges from £15.50 ($23.25) to £23.50 ($35.25) in a single and from £23.50 ($35.25) to £31 ($46.50) in a double or twin. All these charges include a full English breakfast and VAT. All their pleasantly furnished rooms have color TV, tea- and coffee-making facilities, and are heated. They have a Tudor-style dining room and a small cocktail bar, serving an evening meal for £7

($10.50) per head. Sandwiches are usually available at most times when the dining room is closed.

Delph Guest House, 177-179 Carholme Rd. (tel. 0522/29578), is run by Mrs. Dorr, who offers clean, pleasantly furnished rooms with beverage-making facilities, charging £8.50 ($12.75) per person for B&B, including the service charge and VAT. An evening meal can be ordered in advance for only £4.50 ($6.75). The house has a private car park.

On the outskirts, you'll find **The Graffoe,** Hall Lane, at Branston (tel. 0522/791452), less than five miles from the center of Lincoln at Branston on the B1188. Mrs. Jean Stevenson offers B&B in her charming country house. A bed and a large, cooked-to-order breakfast costs only £7.50 ($11.25) per person. An evening meal, a three-course family type, costs £5 ($7.50). Drive to Branston, then turn right at the Waggon and Horses for Mrs. Stevenson's red-brick house.

Dunston Manor, Dunston, near Lincoln (tel. 0526/20463), is a lovely old 18th-century stone manor house, warm and comfortable with a sitting room, dining room, and ample bathroom facilities. Ann Higginbottom charges from £13.50 ($20.25) per person for B&B. Light suppers and bedtime drinks are provided, and an evening meal can be arranged. You can wander through the large manor gardens and, if you feel like it, arrangements can be made for you to play the local golf course or fish the local river. This is a no-smoking establishment.

Where to Dine

High Bridge, 207 High St. (tel. 0522/23548), is a 16th-century tea room built over the medieval bridge that is one of the sightseeing attractions of Lincoln. If you're seeking only tea and coffee, R. W. Stokes & Sons are specialists. The building is timbered with black-and-white beams. From the room on the top floor there is a view of the river and bridge. You reach the tea room by going through a little shop on the bridge level. Food here is a bargain. A complete luncheon, including a main course such as roast beef with Yorkshire pudding, vegetables, and a dessert (perhaps steamed blackberry and apple pudding), costs around £4 ($6). Lunch is served from 11:50 a.m. to 2:15 p.m. (no dinners).

The **Grand Hotel,** St. Mary's Street (tel. 0522/24211), opens its restaurant to nonresidents—in fact, it seats 150 diners who know that they're getting good, well-prepared fare. The waitresses serve with a personal touch. From 7 to 9 p.m. a table d'hôte dinner is offered for £7.50 ($11.25). Meals are inclusive, priced according to the main dish. The food is not only typically English, but the portions are ample. The first course usually consists of a bowl of soup. Then comes the meat course, such as a roast leg of pork with apple sauce and a big bowl of vegetables, served family style. For dessert you can select desserts from the trolley. But that's not all: even cheese and biscuits (crackers) are included in the price. You can also lunch at the Grand from noon to 2 p.m. A buttery is open from 10:30 a.m. to 10 p.m.

Wig & Mitre, 29 Steep Hill (tel. 0522/35190), run by Michael and Valerie Hope, is not only one of the best pubs in Old Lincoln, but it also serves a bill of fare better than that found in most restaurants. Sitting on the aptly named Steep Hill, it serves food from 8 a.m. to midnight. Decorated in an old English atmosphere, the place operates throughout the day somewhat like a café-brasserie. It is on two levels; the main restaurant is behind the drinking section on the second floor. This restaurant has oak timbers, Victorian armchairs, and settees. This 14th-century pub, which has been much restored over the years, also has a summer beer garden. If the restaurant is full, all dishes can be served in the bar downstairs. Blackboard specials change daily, and you are likely to be offered such fare as leek and potato soup, chicken livers in red wine, even "Alabama chili." Meals cost from £5 ($7.50). Everybody's favorite dessert seems to be the chocolate roulade.

Green Dragon, Broadgate (tel. 0522/24950), has been dispensing food and drink for some two centuries from its location near the river, about a block from The High. One of the most attractive buildings in Lincoln, in shelters both pubs and a dining room decorated in a format of brass and exposed wood. Actually, it's composed of a row of 16th-century houses, black-and-white timbered, joined together and heavily reconstructed to create an inviting ambience. In its latest incarnation, under ownership of the Falstaff hotel chain, it offers a steak menu, serving excellent cuts of beef. Meals cost from £12 ($18), and are served from noon to 2:30 p.m. and 6:30 to 10:30 Monday to Thursday (stays open till 11 p.m. on Friday and Saturday). On Sunday it operates from 7 to 10 p.m.

Crust, 46 Broadgate (tel. 0522/40322), is a century-old building, an olde-worlde-style restaurant that occupies a site on the Old Roman Road. The chef-patron, Malta-born Victor Vella, has won a number of gold and silver medals for his cookery. He is assisted by his wife, Sylvia. They offer one of the best restaurant bargains in Lincoln, a fixed-price lunch for only £2.50 ($3.75). For that, you get three courses of well-prepared food. Other fixed-priced luncheon menus cost £4.50 ($6.75) and £5.50 ($8.25). The à la carte dinner menu is more elaborate, including such specialties as escalope of veal maréchale and steak Diane. You'll spend a lot more too, from £12 ($18) and up. A special luncheon menu, served from noon to 1:45 p.m. on Sunday, costs only £5.50 ($8.25) and includes the traditional roast beef and Yorkshire pudding. Morning coffee and cake are served from 10 a.m. to 2:30 p.m., lunch from 11:30 a.m. to 2:30 p.m., and dinner from 7 to 10:15 p.m., Tuesday to Thursday. On Friday and Saturday last orders are taken at 11:15 p.m. Sandwiches and bar snacks are served in the coffee lounge.

STAMFORD: This is a charming stone market town lying 89 miles from London and visited chiefly for the following attraction.

Burghley House

This magnificent Elizabethan house (tel. 0780/52451), the home of the Marquess of Exeter, was built in the 16th century by William Cecil, the first Lord Burghley, who was lord high treasurer to Queen Elizabeth I. His descendants were created Earls of Exeter in 1605, and the house has remained in the family ever since. It contains a fabulous collection of old masters, but it is perhaps the marvelous painted ceilings for which the house is best known. The ceiling of the great drawing room and the ceiling and walls of the Heaven Room by Verrio are a masterpiece of color and depth. Queen Elizabeth I's bedroom contains a four-poster bed covered in its original material. The kitchens are in the oldest part of the house and have been restored and decorated exactly as they were originally. The house and the vast park around it—the latter landscaped by Capability Brown—are open daily April to September from 11 a.m. to 5 p.m. Admission to the Deer Park and a guided tour of the house and special exhibitions costs £2.90 ($4.35) for adults, £1.60 ($12.40) for children.

Food and Lodging

The **Crown Hotel** in Stamford (tel. 0780/63136) stands on All Saints Place, a cobbled street near the church. It's a reasonable alternative to the much higher priced George of Stamford Hotel, and the establishment is also useful to those visiting Burghley House. Modest bedrooms rent for anywhere from £22 ($33) to £26 ($39) in a single and from £30 ($45) to £36 ($54) in a double, including breakfast. Meals served in the bar include fish dishes and roast beef from the trolley.

If you're passing through for the day, consider a stopover at **Mr. Pips Coffee Shop and Restaurant,** 11 St. Mary St. (tel. 0708/65795), on the second floor of a china store near the heart of town. From 9:30 a.m. to 4:30 p.m. daily except Sunday, you can get good-tasting food here, a meal costing £5 ($7.50) or even less. Some diners make a light lunch out of one of its stuffed potatoes, but you can get more substantial fare as well, including homemade soups, meat and poultry dishes, perhaps fresh fish. It's also a popular place for afternoon tea (also morning coffee) when one of the desserts might tempt you.

GRANTHAM: This market town stands in the middle of rich farming country. A corner site on North Parade was the childhood home of Britain's first woman prime minister, Margaret Thatcher. Her father, Alfred Roberts, ran a busy greengrocers shop on the ground floor, and the family lived in rooms above the business. Daughter Margaret was born there on October 13, 1925. The family moved to a nearby house in 1944, but Mr. Roberts continued with the store until he sold it in 1959.

In the Middle Ages, Grantham was a prosperous wool trade town. Isaac Newton attended King's School here in the 17th century, and his initials can still be seen on the wooden sill of the Old Schoolroom built of Ancaster stone. The 283-foot spire of St. Wulfram's Parish Church rises as a local landmark and can be seen for miles around. The town has many old inns and a medieval market cross. Its most important historic attraction is—

Belton House, a National Trust property 2½ miles north of Grantham (tel. 0476/66116), is one of the finest Restoration country houses in Britain, having been built in 1684 for Sir John Brownlow. The original architect was probably William Wynde, whose decorative plasterwork and woodwork resemble that of Wren. The house today appears very much as it did at its creation. The saloon and red drawing room are particularly finely carpeted, and the Tyrconnel room has a rare painted floor apparently from the early 19th century. The library contains a fine barrel-vaulted ceiling by James Wyatt. Oriental porcelain and chinoiserie are part of the attractions. Throughout the house hang portraits of the family by Reynolds. It is open April to October, Wednesday to Sunday from 1 to 5:30 p.m., charging adults an admission of £2.40 ($3.60) and children, £1 ($1.50).

Food and Lodging

Kings Hotel, North Parade (tel. 0476/65881), stands on the street where Margaret Thatcher was born. Of the three major hotels in town, it is the best for the budget. It is small but well run, a Georgian-style private residence constructed in the 1880s. It has made a successful transformation to a small hotel of character, now offering 16 comfortably furnished bedrooms. Thirteen of these are equipped with private bath. The B&B rate in a single is £21·($31.50) to £29 ($43.50), in a double £31 ($46.50) to £40 ($60). It's also possible to stay here on half-board terms, ranging from £29 ($43.50) to £37 ($55.50) per person daily. Bar meals are popular at lunch, and you can eat in the hotel's Buttery from 7:30 a.m. to 11 p.m. whose long hours have made it one of the most popular places in town. The hotel stands on the old A1, which in Dickens's day was known as the Great North Road leading out of town. However, there is a more modern A1 nowadays.

If you want an even better price, try the **Lanchester Guest House,** 84 Harrowby Road (tel. 0476/74169), which is about the best B&B in town. It's small, only four rooms (one with private bath), and its prices are modest and appealing. The B&B rate ranges from £11 ($16.50) to £13.50 ($20.25) in a single, £19 ($28.50) to £22 ($33) in a double. It's also possible to stay here on half-board terms costing £14 ($21) per person daily. The management is attentive at this Edwardian structure which was once a private home.

If you're looking for a good and reasonably priced place to eat, try **Knightingales,** Guildhall Court, Guildhall Street (tel. 0476/79243), which is open only during the day (9:30 a.m. to 4:30 p.m. daily except Sunday). On a small back street, this is an attractive dining room specializing in vegetarian cookery. Instead of beef stroganoff, you get mushroom stroganoff, and nuts such as cashew are often used to give protein where meat might normally be used. The daily specials appear on the blackboard, and be assured that Anne Knight insists that ingredients be fresh and good before she serves them. You can also order certain fish and poultry dishes, including an excellent chicken liver pâté. A "carob slice" is a favorite, healthy dessert.

Chapter XVI

CHESHIRE, SHROPSHIRE, AND THE POTTERIES

1. Chester
2. Nantwich
3. Shrewsbury
4. Stoke-on-Trent
5. Stafford
6. Lichfield

EXCEPT FOR CHESTER, the cities, towns, and villages in this chapter were once little visited by tourists. But all that has changed now, and this section of western England is coming in for long overdue attention.

Chester is the capital of Cheshire—known for its cheese—and most visitors may want to anchor there because of its wealth of accommodations. Nantwich, an old salt town also previewed, is another possibility.

Shropshire, on the border with Wales, has had a history of battles, sieges, and feuds. But the countryside is peaceful today and well worth a visit. One of the best centers for overnighting is Shrewsbury.

The county of Staffordshire lures because of its Potteries, which produce porcelain and china by such famous names as Spode and Wedgwood.

CHESHIRE

This county is low lying and largely agricultural. The name it gave to a cheese (Cheshire) has spread across the world. This northwestern county borders Wales, which accounts for its turbulent history. The towns and villages of Cheshire are peaceful and quiet, forming a good base for touring North Wales, the most beautiful part of that little country. For our headquarters in Cheshire, we'll locate at:

1. Chester

Chester is ancient, having been founded by a Roman legion on the Dee River in the first century A.D. It reached its pinnacle as a bustling port in the 13th and 14th centuries, declining thereafter following the gradual silting up of the river. The upstart Liverpudlians captured the sea-trafficking business. The other walled medieval cities of England were either torn down or badly fragmented, but Chester still retains two miles of fortified city walls intact.

The main entrance into Chester is Eastgate, itself dating back to only the 18th century. Within the walls are half-timbered houses and shops. Of course, not all of them came from the days of the Tudors. Chester is freakish architecturally in that some of its builders kept to the black-and-white timbered facades even when erecting buildings during the Georgian and Victorian periods, with their radically different tastes.

The Rows are double-decker layers of shops, one tier on the street level, the others stacked on top and connected by a footway. The upper tier is like a continuous galleried balcony. Shopping upstairs is much more adventurous than down on the street. Rain is never a problem. Thriving establishments operate in this traffic-free paradise: tobacco shops, restaurants, department stores, china shops, jewelers, and antique dealers. For the most representative look, take an arcaded walk on Watergate Street.

At noon and at 3 p.m. daily at the City Cross, the world's champion town crier issues his news (local stuff on sales, exhibitions, and attractions in the city) at the top of his not-inconsiderable voice, to the accompaniment of a hand bell, at the junction of Watergate, Northgate, and Bridge Streets.

After exploring The Rows, focus your attention on:

CHESTER CATHEDRAL: The present building, founded in 1092 as a Benedictine abbey, was created as a cathedral church in 1541. Considerable architectural restorations were carried out in the 19th century, but older parts have been preserved. Notable features include the fine range of monastic buildings, particularly the cloisters and refectory, the chapter house, and the superb medieval woodcarving in the quire (especially the misericords). Also worth attention are the long south transept with its various chapels, the consistory court, and the medieval roof bosses in the Lady Chapel. A free-standing bell tower, the first to be built in England since the Reformation, was completed in 1975 and may be seen southeast of the main building. The cathedral is open daily in summer from 7:45 a.m. to 7 p.m.; closes at 6 p.m. off-season. For more information, telephone 0244/25920.

DISCOVER CHESTER: In a big Victorian building opposite the amphitheater, the **Chester Visitor Centre,** Vicars Lane (tel. 0244/318916), only minutes from the city center, offers a number of services to visitors from 9 a.m. to 9 p.m. daily. A full Tourist Information Centre, part of the national network, provides a wide range of services including local and national accommodations booking, guide books, maps, free leaflets, guided tours, and reservations for local attractions. You are introduced to Chester by a map and print presentation of video film. A visit to a life-size Victorian street complete with sounds and smells helps your appreciation and orientation to Chester. The center has a gift shop, a licensed tea shop, and a currency exchange. The center is privately owned, operated by the Wilson family who operate Gibby's Restaurant and are familiar with the interests of visitors. A fee of 50p (75¢) for adults and 25p (38¢) for children is charged for the audio-visual presentation and exhibition areas.

A WALK ON THE WALL: In the center of town, you'll see an interesting old clock mounted on a wall. Climb the stairs near it that lead up to the top of the city wall, and you can follow it on a walk looking down on Chester today from a path of the past. The wall passes through centuries of English history. You pass a cricket field, see the River Dee which was formerly a major trade artery, and get a look at many old buildings of the 18th century, some undergoing renovation. Flower-filled back gardens are lovely from this height. The wall also goes past some Roman ruins, and it is possible to leave the walkway to explore them. The walk is charming and free.

CHESTER ZOO: Just off the A41 on the outskirts of Chester, the Chester Zoo (tel. 0244/380280), 2 miles from the center of the city, is world famous for its wide collection of mammals, birds, reptiles, and fish, as well as for its 110 acres of gardens. Many rare and endangered species breed freely in spacious enclosures, and the zoo is particularly renowned for the most successful group of chimpanzees and orangutans in Europe. The gardens are worth seeing in any season, with 160,000 plants in the spring and summer bedding displays alone. A waterbus, a popular summer feature, allows you to observe the hundreds of waterbirds who make their home here. The zoo has several facilities if you get hungry or thirsty during your visit: the licensed Oakfield Restaurant, the Jubilee self-service cafeteria, the Oasis snackbar, and the Rainbow kiosk, for either meals or snacks and drinks. The zoo is open from 10 a.m. to dusk daily except Christmas Day. Admission is £3 ($4.50) for adults, £1.50 ($2.25) for children 3 to 15.

ACCOMMODATIONS: A well-restored and elegantly furnished Edwardian residence, the **Cavendish Hotel,** 44 Hough Green (tel. 0244/675100), is attractive and reasonable. It stands on the A549 coast road leading to North Wales. There is a large car park, and the city center is about a mile away. Each bedroom is equipped with a hot and cold water basin and color TV, and the hotel has central heating. The B&B charge £20.50 ($30.75) to £30.50 ($45.75) in a single, £31 ($46.50) to £40.50 ($60.75) in a double. The lounge re-creates the mood of the Edwardian era, both in its decor and the antiques that furnish it. The dining room serves a limited but select menu, with dinner around £8 ($12), and packed lunches are available upon request. There's also a small residents bar. In all, it has a lot of cozy charm.

    Ye Olde King's Head, 48–50 Lower Bridge St. (tel. 0244/24855), is a 16th-century museum piece of black-and-white architecture. From 1598 to 1707, it was occupied by the well-known Randle Holme family of Chester, noted heraldic painters and genealogists (some of their manuscripts have made it to the British Museum). Since 1717, the King's Head has been a licensed inn. The host rents out a dozen handsome bedrooms, all with private baths or showers, color TV, and facilities for making hot beverages. The place has central heating. The charges are £27 ($40.50) in a single, £45 ($67.50) in a double or twin, and £55 ($82.50) in a double with a four-poster bed. A full English breakfast is included. The bedchambers are linked with the past. Many of the walls and ceilings are sloped and highly pitched, with exposed beams. The upstairs dining room, specializing in fish and seafood, with its massive beams overhead, boasts a Tudor fireplace and authentic furnishings, including an elaborate grandfather clock, an octagonal card table, high-backed Jacobean oak chairs, and soft, upholstered pieces. The main bar has wall settles, barrel tables, wood paneling and a Tudor fireplace. One room is a showcase of timberwork, with old furnishings, such as a Welsh cupboard and pewter and copper pieces. The hotel owner, Richard Casson, has a popular eating place, too, downstairs in the main bar, where real ale is sold. Here you can get bar snacks daily all year, and the salad bar in summer is excellent. Randles Restaurant is open daily except Christmas Day, offering a variety of traditional meals. Lunch, served from noon to 2 p.m., costs around £6 ($9), and dinner, from 6:30 to 9 p.m., goes for £10 ($15) and up.

    Riverside Pensione, 19 City Walls (tel. 0244/311498), lies off Lower Bridge Street and is not to be confused with the Riverside Hotel nearby at 22 City Walls. A small 10-room guesthouse, one of the best B&Bs in town, it has been recently modernized. On the old Roman Wall, it enjoys an enviable location, within easy walking distance of the main attractions in the center of town. Some of the comfortably furnished accommodations open onto views of the River Dee, and the licensed hotel also has a garden in front (in the rear is a car park). T.A. Astbury and P.S. Huxley welcome guests, housing them at rates ranging from £15.50 ($23.25) to £22 ($33) in a single, £20.50 ($30.75) to £27 ($40.50) in a double. These accommodations have either private baths or showers.

Redland Private Hotel, 64 Hough Green (tel. 0244/671024), standing on its own grounds, is a Victorian town house of character and charm, with oak paneling and stained-glass windows. This fine old mansion receives guests year round except in January and February. The house is large and well appointed, with a number of amenities. It lies about a mile from the center of Chester in the direction of the Welsh border, and many guests use it as a base for exploring North Wales. Ten pleasant bedrooms are rented, two of which contain private baths. The B&B charge in a single ranges from £20 ($30) to £25 ($37.50), in a double £31 ($46.50) to £35 ($52.50). There is a residential license for serving alcohol.

The **Eversley Private Hotel,** 9 Eversley Park (tel. 0244/373744), lies off Liverpool road, about a mile from the heart of old Chester. Bryn and Barbara Povey have fully modernized the select 11-bedroom hotel, where they charge £16 ($24) in a single, £28 ($42) in a bathless double or twin, £30 ($45) for a double or twin with bath, and from £30 ($45) in a family room. Most units have private baths or showers, and all have color TV, hot beverage facilities, hot and cold water basins, razor sockets, and radios, as well as intercoms. A full English breakfast is included in the rates. Evening meals are available in the candlelit dining room, and you can enjoy snacks in the Deva Bar. The hotel stands in a peaceful residential section.

The **Gables Guest House,** 5 Vicarage Rd., off Hoole Road, Hoole (tel. 0244/23969), is a nice Victorian house, lying in a quiet residential area of Chester, just off the main bus route into the city center, where cars are not permitted in any case. David R. Bawn charges £8.50 ($12.75) to £10 ($15) per person for a comfortable bed and a full breakfast, including VAT and service. All rooms have hot and cold running water, and there is a bathroom and shower room.

Mrs. James, 1 Queens Rd. off City Road (tel. 0244/28703), gives good value. Its location is about a block and a half from the rail station, and if you lodge here, you can walk to the heart of Chester. The guesthouse is tranquil and well kept. Mrs. James is a pleasant hostess, offering comfortable bedrooms at £8.50 ($12.75) per person nightly, capped the next morning with a good and hearty English breakfast that often includes fresh grapefruit and fresh mushrooms along with bacon and eggs.

Derry Raghan Guest House, 54 Hoole Rd. (tel. 0244/318740), lies about a mile from the heart of Chester and some three miles from the zoo. Bill and Doris Millar welcome guests to their pleasantly furnished rooms, charging them from £10 ($15) per person nightly. Each unit has a TV. Often guests are served tea or coffee with cookies upon their arrival. Drivers will find parking space.

WHERE TO EAT: Originally a stable courtyard, now a restaurant, is the **Courtyard,** 13 Werburgh St. (tel. 0244/21447), opposite the south transept of the cathedral. The owner, Pamela Stanarought, has covered in the cobblestone yard with a clear roof, air-conditioned it, and put in lots of greenery. The narrow entrance, with a black-and-white decorative motif, sets the stage for a two-in-one restaurant, with an ingeniously designed split-level bistro. Meals at lunchtime are meant to be fast, and they are. You can get a choice of filled crêpes, baked potatoes with a variety of stuffings, and salads. All lunches are priced from £5 ($7.50). In the evening, a meal costs from £10 ($15) and up. As many of the dishes possible are homemade, with lots of fish specialties, nine poultry and meat courses, and a fondue bourguignon. Lunch is served from noon to 2:30 p.m. and dinner from 7 p.m. The Courtyard is open nightly for dancing Monday to Friday. The restaurant is open Monday to Saturday and is closed on Sunday and bank holidays.

Lilian's Downstairs Restaurant, 49 Lower Bridge St. (tel. 0244/21139). On the day Pat Cowie opened the pretty little Upstairs Downstairs guesthouse she took over in Lower Bridge Street, a friend from the past, Lilian Rawlingson, stopped by to wish her luck, took her coat off, and stayed—to open with Pat the delightful restaurant in the vaulted basement of the house in what had been the Georgian below-stairs kitchen. A dancer by profession, Lilian had worked in many kitchens and restaurants while "resting" between engagements, and she used the time wisely to expand her natural gift for cooking. Appetizers here include shrimp with herbs, cream, and lemon cooked in garlic butter and served with crusty bread, roast spare ribs with barbecue sauce, and pâté with hot toast. Among main dishes are two lamb cutlets with mint sauce and fresh vegetables, duckling à l'orange with dauphinoise potatoes, and beef Stroganoff with green salad or ratatouille. Tracy's vegetarian salad is a selection of as many vegetables, greens, and fresh fruit as they can find, served with a dip and crusty french bread and butter. A two-course steak and salad special at lunch goes for £5 ($7.50). Dinner is from £15 ($22.50). The restaurant is so popular that unless you are a guest "Upstairs," you should make a reservation. The place is closed Monday, but otherwise service is from noon to 2 p.m. and 5:30 to 9:30 p.m.

The **Witches Kitchen,** 19 Frodsham Street (tel. 0244/311836), is in the center of town, just a short walk from the station. It seats 100 and has old-world charm and good service. The ground-floor restaurant is 15 yards from the city walls and Chester Cathedral. It is open every day for morning coffee (10 a.m.); luncheon (11:30 a.m. till 5:30 p.m.), high tea (5 to 6:30 p.m.), afternoon tea (3 to 5 p.m.) and dinner (7 to 10:30 p.m.). À la carte meals are served all day, and the Kitchen is open seven days a week. Luncheon is a three-course meal, costing from £3.50 ($5.25), beginning with juice or soup, a choice of three different roasts (beef, pork, or chicken), fried fillet of plaice or a salad, vegetables, and a choice of potatoes, ending with a dessert or coffee. And for £5.50 ($8.25), a traditional three-course Sunday luncheon is served which includes soup or fruit juice, roast beef and Yorkshire pudding with horseradish sauce, vegetables, and a choice of dessert. The Cheshire chicken is a favorite dish. Traditional roasts are served all day every day, a dinner costing from £12 ($18).

Pierre Griffe Wine Bar, 4-6 Mercia Square, Frodsham Street (tel. 0244/312635), owned by four graduate scientists, comes on to be arguably the best wine bar in Chester. A simple place inside with a long bar and blackboards to announce the dishes of the day, outside on the covered patio, it has tables and chairs in continental style. The daily menu may offer homemade cream of leek and potato soup, chili with a baked potato, Hawaiian chicken with rice, oriental beef with rice, or a choice from a cold buffet with a selection of salads. Meals cost from £6 ($9). The place is open daily except Sunday from 11:30 a.m. to 3 p.m. and 5:30 to 10:30 p.m. (later on Friday and Saturday), on Sunday from 7 to 10:30 p.m. as well as from noon to 2 p.m. on Sunday in summer. The choice of food is limited in the evening and is only available until 9 p.m.

The **Gallery Restaurant,** 24 Paddock Row, Grosvenor Precinct (tel. 0244/47202), is festooned with masses of green plants which make walking in here a little like going into an indoor garden. J.P. Lautrete, the host and owner, has created a conservatory atmosphere by the use of green-and-white walls and curtains, along with the plants and hanging baskets. A varied menu is displayed on a chalkboard: Three courses with wine can be enjoyed for £5 ($7.50) to £11 ($16.50). Hours are 10 a.m. to 5 p.m. Monday to Saturday.

Dukes Wine Bar and the **Carriage Restaurant and Pump Room,** Mercia Square (tel. 0244/23469). On the first floor of this Mercia Square building and convenient for a meal or a snack during a day's sightseeing, the Wine Bar and the Pump Room are drinking establishments with excellent bar food at lunchtime. In summer, it is possible to spill out onto the terrace overlooking the cathedral. The Carriage Restaurant is a more formal affair with waitress service and a lunchtime menu costing about £6 ($9) for three courses. At dinner, an à la carte meal might consist of an appetizer, scampi, coq au vin, steak-and-kidney pie, grill meats, fish, or roast chicken with stuffing. A complete dinner will cost from £7 ($10.50). Hours are noon to 2:30 p.m. and 5:30 to 10 p.m. Monday to Saturday.

Claverton's Wine Bar, Lower Bridge Street (tel. 0244/319760), is very popular with the locals in the evening, a good way to see—if not to meet—the people of Chester. The imposing building of which Claverton's occupies the lower part began life as a private residence in 1715, becoming the Albion Hotel in 1818. Since then, the building has seen many changes. The wine bar is attractively decorated, the food good and reasonable. No wonder it's such a popular choice. Begin, perhaps, with the leek-and-potato soup, followed by fisherman's pie (cod, mushrooms, and potatoes in a white sauce), or a selection from the cold buffet. A large salad is included with the meal, and this, along with homemade apple pie with cream, would come to only £5.50 ($8.25). The buffet, incidentally, is exceptional, in that it often includes game pie and fish mousse. An unusual dish, at least to Americans, is the fresh trout served with a gooseberry sauce. Chicken roulade is a specialty. In addition to the regular mixed drinks, wines are available by the glass, as are "mocktails" for drivers or those nursing a hangover from the day before. In summer, the tables outside are popular. Claverton's is open Monday to Saturday from 11 a.m. to 3 p.m. and 5:30 to 10:30 p.m. (to 11 p.m. Friday and Saturday). From June to September, afternoon teas with fresh baked scones are served daily from 3:30 to 5:30 p.m.

The **Farmhouse Serve-Yourself Kitchen,** 9-13 Northgate St. (tel. 0244/311332), offers some of the most inexpensive—and best—meals in the city in a friendly setting above a sporting-goods outlet. There is no menu, but lots of plants frame a blackboard where daily specials are written. Chicken in wine sauce or a Greek-inspired moussaka, accompanied by a fennel or beansprout salad, are featured items. At least 16 different, freshly made salads are displayed daily, ranging from Waldorf to pineapple and celery. A selection of homemade hot dishes is also offered daily, including a wide range of what they call "old favourites." A host of desserts completes a satisfying meal, which is likely to cost from £5 ($7.50). Hours are 9 a.m. to 5 p.m. (till 5:30 p.m. in summer).

Gibby's Restaurant, 12 Eastgate St. (tel. 0244/314669), run by Keith Wilson and his two brothers, is a bright and cheerful place. You get good simple food and low prices. Unelaborate service throughout the day starts at 8 a.m., lasting until 8 p.m. (on Sunday from 10 a.m. to 8 p.m.). You get such traditional English dishes as roast beef with Yorkshire pudding and home-baked steak-and-kidney pie. Fish dishes, hamburgers, salads, and a children's menu are also available. Expect to pay about £4 ($6) for a meal. Breakfast is served daily.

SOME LOCAL PUBS: The former town house of the Earls of Shrewsbury, built in 1644, houses the **Bear and Billet,** 94 Lower Bridge St. (tel. 0244/321272). With its intricately timbered and highly decorative facade, this is one of the most famous buildings in Chester. Although recently renovated, it still preserves its traditional atmosphere. A time-tested English menu is served, and that means such classic dishes as cockles and mussels, the original "Sir Loin" (that's sirloin steak), and old dessert favorites such as bread pudding and syllabub. Much research went into the menu which a reader, Roscoe E. Hill, dean at the University of Denver, called "the most authentic in the kingdom." Expect to spend £8 ($12) or a lot more for your dinner. Midday snacks and lunches are available for £1 ($1.50) to £2.50 ($3.75). The pub is open from 11 a.m. to 2:30 p.m. and 6 to 11 p.m.

An alternative for drinking is the **Boot Inn,** Eastgate Row (tel. 0244/314540), established in 1643, with timbered walls, high-back benches, and low ceilings. This is the smallest and most unspoiled pub in Chester, familiar only to oldtimers and those in the know. It's reached by entering a passageway along the upper Rows of Eastgate Street. The publican has a multitude of mementos cluttering the walls. Cold bar snacks here cost from £1.25 ($1.88). The Boot is open from 11 a.m. to 2:30 p.m. and 6 to 11 p.m.

2. Nantwich

The old market town on the Weaver River lies only 15 miles southeast of the county town of Chester, and can easily be tied in with a visit to that city. The town is particularly outstanding because of its black-and-white timbered houses. The most spectacular one, Churche's Mansion, is a dining recommendation.

FOOD AND LODGING: The most enchanting old restaurant in Cheshire, **Churche's Mansion Restaurant,** 150 Hospital St. (tel. 0270/625933), lying in Nantwich at the junction of Newcastle Road and the Chester bypass. Many years ago the late Dr. and Mrs. E. C. Myott learned that this historic home of a wealthy Elizabethan merchant had been advertised for sale in America, and asked the town council to step in and save it. Alas, no English housewife wanted such a gloomy and dark home, so the Myotts attended the sale and outbid the American syndicate who wanted to transport it to the United States. They sought out the mysteries of the house: a window in the side wall, inlaid initials, a Tudor well in the garden, a long-ago love knot with a central heart (a token of Richard Churche's affection for his young wife). Today the house, now run by the Myotts' son, is widely known and recommended for its quality meals. Lunch is offered daily, Monday to Friday, for £6 ($9), increasing to £7 ($10.50) on Saturday and Sunday. Dinner, Monday to Friday, costs £12 ($18), going up to £13 ($16.50) on Saturday. Tariffs include VAT and coffee. Lunch is served from noon to 2 p.m. and dinner from 7 to 9:30 p.m. The mansion restaurant is closed on Sunday night. You need to reserve a table, especially for dinner. Guests dine at candlelit tables. The mansion is "open to view" throughout the day for 50p (75¢), and refreshments are available.

Lamb Hotel, Hospital Street (tel. 0270/625286). For some two centuries, this mellow old place in the heart of Nantwich has been welcoming wayfarers who made it through the portals. The tradition continues. The hotel is small, with only 16 comfortably furnished bedrooms, eight of which contain private baths. Depending on the plumbing requested, the single rate ranges from £20 ($30) to £26 ($39), the double from £31 ($46.50) to £38 ($57). There is ample parking outside as well. Visitors and locals alike mingle in the pub of the hotel, and meals are served daily. Pub fare is offered from noon to 2 p.m., with lunches costing from £5.50 ($8.25), and full dinners from 7:30 to 9:30 p.m. go for £9.50 ($14.25). The cooking is both English and continental in preparation.

York Cottage, 82 Broad Lane, Stapeley, near Nantwich (tel. 0270/628867), is a 19th-century cottage with rural views, where Mrs. P. M. Winfield accepts guests. She has modernized and extended the place, until she can now offer two doubles and one single at a rate of £9.50 ($14.25) per person for B&B. Tariffs include a full English breakfast, and arrangements can be made for dinner. Rooms are comfortably and pleasantly furnished. The cottage is on the A529 Nantwich–Andlem road, 1½ miles outside Nantwich.

SHROPSHIRE

Immortalized by A. E. Housman's *A Shropshire Lad,* this hilly county borders Wales, which accounts for its turbulent history. The bloody battles are over today, and the towns, with their black-and-white timbered houses, are peaceful and quiet. It makes a good base for touring in the Welsh mountains.

When Parliament redistricted and even renamed some of the shires of England in 1973, the name of Shropshire was changed back to a much older name—Salop. However, in this case the name just didn't catch on, and you'll find the county still called Shropshire on recent maps and by most of its inhabitants.

3. Shrewsbury

Lying within a horseshoe bend of the Severn River, Shrewsbury is the capital of Shropshire. The river almost encloses the town. Known for its cakes and ale, Shrewsbury contains one of the best-known schools in England. It was also the birthplace of Charles Darwin.

Considered the finest Tudor town in England, Shrewsbury is noted for its black-and-white buildings of timber and plaster, including Abbot's House from 1450 and the tall gabled Ireland's Mansion from 1575 standing on High Street. It also has a number of Georgian and Regency mansions, some old bridges, and handsome churches, including the Abbey Church of Saint Peter and St. Mary's Church.

Shrewsbury Castle, built by the Norman Earl Roger de Montgomery by 1083, stands in a dominating position where the River Severn almost surrounds the town. It houses the Shropshire Regimental Museum, including the collections of the King's Shropshire Light Infantry, the Shropshire Yeomanry Cavalry, and the Shropshire Royal Horse Artillery. The collections represent more than 300 years of regimental service and include a lock of Napoleon's hair and an American flag captured when the White House was seized and burned in the War of 1812 (in 1814). The castle is open daily from 10 a.m. to 5 p.m. Admission is 60p (90¢). For more information, phone 0743/52234.

Rowley's House Museum, Barker Street (tel. 0743/61196), is housed in a fine 17th-century timber-frame house and an adjoining brick mansion. This museum includes displays on art, local history, Roman and prehistoric archeology, geology, costumes, and natural history. The great treasures include the fine Hadrianic forum inscription and silver mirror, both from the nearby Roman city of Viroconium (Wroxeter). The museum is open Monday to Saturday from 10 a.m. to 5 p.m., as well as on Sunday from noon to 5 p.m. Easter to mid-September. Admission is £1 ($1.50) for adults, half-price for children.

Clive House Museum on College Hill (tel. 0743/54811), town house of Clive of India as Mayor of Shrewsbury in 1762, contains period rooms and splendid local pottery and porcelain, early watercolors, and textiles and has a lovely garden. Hours are from 2 to 5 p.m. on Monday, from 10 a.m. to 1 p.m. and 2 to 5 p.m. Tuesday to Saturday. Admission is 30p (45¢).

At **Coleham Pumping Station,** Longden Coleham (tel. 0743/61196), you can see displayed compound rotative pumping engines from 1900. Open daily except Sunday from 2 to 5 p.m., it charges an admission of 30p (45¢) for adults, 15p (23¢) for children.

WHERE TO STAY: A small, well-kept hotel, **Abbey Court House,** 134 Abbey Foregate (tel. 0743/64416), is owned by Mr. and Mrs. Turnock, who charge £10 ($15) per person in a room with B&B, rising to £13 ($19.50) per person in a room with private bath. Mrs. Turnock provides a complete breakfast, and if you ask, she'll make your bacon "crispy."

The White House, Hanwood, near Shrewsbury (tel. 0743/860414), is a lovely, half-timbered, beamed country house supposedly dating back to the 16th century. It is to be found on the A488, 3½ miles from Shrewsbury near the mid-Wales border and famous Ironbridge with its museums. Rates are from £12 ($18) per person nightly, including a full English breakfast. There is an extensive menu and wine list, a meal costing £6 ($9) and up. There are five guest bedrooms, a comfortable TV lounge, and a fully licensed bar. The bar and lounge are for the use of guests only. The hotel is centrally heated.

Glyndene, Abbey Foregate (tel. 0743/52488), is an attractive guesthouse, providing B&B for £9 ($13.50) per night. Hot and cold running water and tea/coffee-making facilities are in each room, and TV is provided. A full English breakfast is served under the personal supervision of the owner, Judy McRea.

WHERE TO DINE: A good place to find good food is the **Cavalier Restaurant,** Prince Rupert Hotel, Butcher Row (tel. 0743/52461). The hotel has three restaurants, of which the Cavalier is the most outstanding choice. White tablecloths, oil paintings, and a beamed ceiling live up to the tourist's conception of the heart of England. A fixed-price lunch menu, costing £8 ($12), includes a tempting choice of a well-prepared cuisine, such as a mortadella salad, followed by poached filet of plaice mornay, with potatoes and two vegetables, plus cheese. A fixed-price dinner might include smoked mackerel with horseradish sauce, poached sweetbreads mexicaine, along with vegetables and a freshly prepared dessert. This restaurant is popular with local residents, as well as clients of the hotel. Lunch is daily from noon to 2:30 p.m. Dinner is served from 7 to 10:30 p.m. Guests can also patronize the Steak Bar and the Royalist Restaurant.

Delany's Vegetarian Restaurant, St. Julians Craft Centre, St. Alkmonds Square (tel. 0743/60602), is a whole-food vegetarian restaurant set in the vestry of a church which is now used as a craft center. The restaurant is open Monday to Saturday from 10:30 a.m. to 3:30 p.m., serving morning coffee, afternoon teas, and a selection of home-baked cakes and tasty fruit slices. At lunchtime, 11:30 a.m. to 2:30 p.m., a wide range of hot food is available. Spicy lentil and tomato soup with freshly baked bread and butter is a favorite. There is always a choice of a savoury bake or a casserole. For example, Chilean marrow and sweet corn bake is a seasonal selection. There are also burgers, quiches, and loaves to choose from. To complement your choice of hot food, there are six delicious salads to try out, or try a combination of them. If there's any room left, the desserts are a delight. Pear and lemon cashew crumble or chocolate orange pudding may tempt you. Reasonably priced wine is available by the glass or bottle. Meals cost from £5 ($7.50).

Cornhouse, 59a Wyle Cop (tel. 0743/241991), is both a restaurant (on the second floor) and a wine bar (at ground level). A major rendezvous point in town, it attracts a flow of loyal patrons who walk down a steep street to partake of its fine food and drink. They do so daily from noon to 2:30 p.m. and 6:30 to 9:30 p.m. Many of the dishes, such as stuffed dolmadas (vine leaves) and a Greek-inspired moussaka, look to the Mediterranean kitchen for their inspiration. Daily specials are posted on a blackboard menu, with meals costing from £6 ($9).

WHITTINGTON: Many motorists in Shropshire drive across the county to eat at the **Whittington Inn,** at Whittington, near Stourbridge on the main Kidderminster–Wolverhampton road (tel. 0384/872496). The inn is the original manor house of Sir William de Whittington, Dick Whittington's grandfather, who built it in 1310. Dick Whittington, of course, was the enterprising lad from a merchant family who became one of the principal bankers to English kings and later lord mayor of London, elected three times between 1398 and 1420.

Today the ancestral home boasts an attic bistro and wine bar. The interior is white-painted brick, and the menu offers a selection from a cold buffet along with such hot food as chili con carne, cottage pie, and stews. You can also order sandwiches and a wide selection of English cheeses. Meals cost from £6 ($9). Hours are noon to 2:30

p.m. (on Sunday, noon to 2 p.m.) and 7 to 10:30 p.m. In addition to the bistro, the inn operates three oak-paneled and beamed bars with fires burning in wintertime, and a Tudor walled garden, where traditional real ale is served. The restaurant part of the operation is open from Monday to Saturday in the evening and for Sunday lunch, offering both a table d'hôte menu and a more expensive à la carte menu than that served in the wine bar.

LUDLOW: Looking down on the Teme River, this is a mellow old town with a historic Norman castle. Many Georgian and Jacobean timbered buildings stand on its quiet lanes and courts. The most colorful street is known as "Broad," rising from the old Ludford Bridge to Broadgate, the one remaining gateway from walls erected in the Middle Ages. See, in particular, the Church of St. Laurence, Butter Cross, and Reader's House.

Bed and Breakfast
Wadboro Thatch, Thriftwicket Lane, Hayton's Bent, near Ludlow (tel. 058475/249), is a genuine 16th-century thatched cottage. It is in a completely secluded position in beautiful countryside, yet only a five-minute drive from Ludlow, the historic market town with a castle. Take Fishmore Road out of Ludlow, turning left up a lane shortly after you pass a telephone kiosk (on the right).

The cottage has been fully restored, yet its original features have been maintained —in fact, it's a perfect example of an old English country cottage. Not large, it's very traditional, with its upper rooms tucked under the thatch, latticed windows, oak beams, and an inglenook fireplace with a bread oven. Accommodation comprises two doubles with private baths. Constructed of stone, the walls are nearly two feet thick. This, together with the thatch roof, keeps it cool in summer, warm in winter. The cottage is owned by Mrs. Pamela Allcock-Brown. She loves people and is very used to meeting them and making them feel at home. A room with bath and an English breakfast rents for £12.50 ($18.75) per night per person, plus another £6.50 ($13.23) per person charged for an evening meal. The owner specializes in good traditional English food, including local Hereford beef and Welsh lamb, as well as fresh vegetables and fruits from her own half-acre garden.

Bromfield Manor, Bromfield, near Ludlow (tel. 058477/279), is a stone manor house with six gables, three groups of tall chimneys, and a surrounding park-like garden well back from the A49, three miles from Ludlow. Bromfield Manor is owned by Norman and Joy Cooke, who have been happily welcoming Canadian and American guests into their home at a moderate rate. Mrs. Cooke charges £11 ($16.50) per person daily, including VAT, for B&B in a single or double. Her bedrooms have hot and cold running water and tea- or coffee-making facilities. The living room is pleasantly furnished, and you can arrange for an evening meal. Mrs. Cooke also can direct you to several very good eating houses in Ludlow.

CRAVEN ARMS: A few miles north of Ludlow, on the A49, is the little village of Craven Arms in this "area of outstanding natural beauty," lying on the River Onny.

Hillside, Twitchen, Clunbury (tel. 05887/485), a short distance west of Craven Arms, just south of the B4368 road, is a good place to stay to explore the south Shropshire hills and visit major attractions of the area. Hillside is a 200-year-old stone country cottage, in which Veronica M. Oates accommodates guests in one single room, one double, and two twin-bedded rooms. All have hot and cold water basins and facilities for making tea and coffee. There is one bathroom and two toilets. A comfortable sitting room has a large inglenook fireplace where log fires blaze in inclement weather. Maps and guides of the area are kept here for the use of guests. The charge for B&B is

£10 ($15). With dinner added, the rate goes up to £14 ($21) per person. In the dining room, at separate tables, Mrs. Oates serves either a light or a full English breakfast, depending on the desires of guests. A 50p (75¢) surcharge is asked of persons spending only one night here. Children are not accommodated.

IRONBRIDGE: Ironbridge George is the location of an intriguing complex of museums, said to be the birthplace of the Industrial Revolution.

The **Ironbridge Gorge Museum** (tel. 095245/3522) includes the Blists Hill Open Air Museum with a re-creation of a 19th-century township with costumes demonstrators, the Coalbrookdale Furnace and Museum of Iron with a sound and light display, the Coalport China Museum, the Jackfield Tile Museum, the Severn Warehouse (now the museum visitor center), and many other smaller museums, including the Bedlam Furnaces, the 1779 Iron Bridge (first in the world) with its original Toll House, Rosehill House (the restored 18th-century home of the Darby family), the Long Warehouse Library and Archives, and the Elton Gallery with changing exhibitions. A ticket to all the attractions is £3.95 ($5.93) for adults, £2.50 ($3.75) for children. A family ticket (two adults and up to five children) costs £9.95 ($14.93). Hours are from 10 a.m. until 6 p.m. daily from March to October.

For an accommodation in the area, I suggest **The Hall,** Hope Bowdler, near Church Stretton (tel. 0694/722041), which charges £10 ($15) per person for B&B. Hope Bowdler, on the B4371, is only 1½ miles from Church Stretton, an attractive small resort in the Shropshire Hills. Turn off the road in the village onto an unpaved lane leading past the church. The Hall entrance is on the left at the end of the lane. The house has been modernized, providing two twin-bedded and one single room for guests. There are two baths with showers, plus hot and cold running water and central heating in each unit. The house is really the home of the Inglis family, direct descendants of Bishop Charles Inglis, rector of New York's Trinity Church at the time of the War of Independence, and later the first bishop of Nova Scotia. The house contains many interesting historical family pictures and possessions.

BRIDGNORTH/WORFIELD: The thriving town of Bridgnorth is accessible by a number of roads, chief among them being the A442 and the A458, as well as by the Severn Valley Railway. It is near the confluence of the Rivers Severn and Worfe. The Danes are known to have come to this area late in the ninth century, building a camp at Cwatbridge, which may be the present-day Quatbridge, a hamlet a short way down the Severn from Bridgnorth. At the beginning of the 10th century, a castle was erected here for King Alfred's daughter, Ethelfleda. Bridgnorth was first known to history when a castle was built here by Robert de Belleme at the end of the 11th century, but he was soon forced out by the army of King Henry I in 1102. The keep of the castle is all that remains, its tilted appearance reminiscent of the Leaning Tower of Pisa. The castle and the town which grew up around it, known as the High Town, were mainly destroyed during the Civil War, in the siege of 1646.

Surviving the depredations of war is the North Gate, dating from 1265 and now the site of **Bridgnorth Museum,** containing mainly local artifacts from Bronze Age tools to Civil War weapons and up to today. It is open from 2 to 4 p.m. April to September on Saturday and mid-July to August and bank holidays Monday, Tuesday, and Wednesday. Admission is free, but donations are welcomed.

In 1652, a new Town Hall, a little magpie half-timbered structure, was built over an archway in the middle of the wide main street. The Low Town is at the foot of the hill on the other side of the Severn, linked to the High Town by funicular.

At **Bridgnorth station,** you can see railway sheds housing steam locomotives from the 1930s and 1940s restored and kept in working order by Severn Valley Railway buffs. In summer, it's possible to take a ride on a train pulled by one of the glistening engines operating daily.

For information on these and other sights in the area, see the **Bridgnorth Library and Information Centre,** Listley Street (tel. 07462/3358).

If you're seeking accommodation in the area, your best bet is **The Croft Hotel,** St. Mary's Street (tel. 07462/2416), in Bridgnorth. Many people use this hotel as their base for exploring not only Bridgnorth but the beautiful Severn Valley. And an excellent choice it is, renting out a dozen comfortably and pleasantly furnished bedrooms to paying guests. Of these, 10 have private baths or showers. The charge for B&B, depending on the plumbing, ranges from £15 ($24) to £25 ($37.50) in a single, from £29 ($43.50) to £33 ($49.50) in a double. The hotel is one of character, with much charm, as reflected by its time-worn beams. The family who runs it are most welcoming, and will guide you to attractions in their area, such as the Wenlock Edge, Wyre Forest, and Clee Hills. Their food is good, and they will also quote half-board terms, ranging from £24 ($36) to £33 ($49.50) per person daily.

THE POTTERIES

In Staffordshire, Stoke-on-Trent is the name of the five towns called the Potteries, the "Five Towns" of Arnold Bennett's novels. The Potteries are known throughout the world for the excellence of their fine porcelain and china.

The so-called "Black Country" of steelworks and coal mines has almost disappeared, but you can visit a coal mine and descend in the "cage" to the worked-out seams.

Within easy reach of the industrial town of Dovedale is a valley with some of England's most beautiful scenery, forming part of the Peak District National Park.

4. Stoke-on-Trent

Because of the worldwide interest in the making of pottery, this Staffordshire town has found itself a tourist attraction. It's the home of the pottery made famous by Josiah Wedgwood, along with other well-known names such as Coalport, Minton, and Spode.

THE SIGHTS: The **Wedgwood Visitor Centre,** at Barlaston (tel. 078139/4141), charges £1 ($1.50) for adults and 50p (75¢) for children, and is open from 9 a.m. to 5 p.m. Monday to Friday except over Christmas. It is also open on Saturday from 10 a.m. to 4 p.m. April to October. In the demonstration hall you can watch the slip, the clay, built up on the potter's wheel, see how the raised motifs so well known on Wedgwood blue pottery are made and added to the pieces, as well as witness how delicate flowers are made and painted and plates turned and fired, then painted.

The young people working at the benches are often apprentices, but the work they produce is of the highest quality. They are happy to answer your questions about their special occupation.

There's a continuous film show in the large cinema, and the beginning of the movie is announced on the public address system. In the shop you can see samples of all the sorts of items made at the factory, and purchase souvenirs. Prices are the same as elsewhere, but they do sometimes have items of discontinued lines and some "seconds" available at reduced prices.

The fascinating museum has exhibits of more than 200 years of craftsmanship, showcases of old bills, working details, experimental pots and goblets, and drawings of machines invented by Josiah Wedgwood two centuries ago and still used daily in the factory.

Royal Doulton, Nile Street, Burslem, near Stoke-on-Trent (tel. 0782/85747).

You will have walked nearly a mile and negotiated some 250 steps during the tour of this pottery, but you will have seen exactly how plates, cups, and figures are made from basic raw materials. The gift shop has slightly imperfect articles on sale alongside quality goods, and you can browse through the Sir Henry Doulton Gallery, tracing the company's history since 1815 and containing a full collection of Doulton's historical figures. Tours of the factory are at 10:15 a.m. and 2 p.m., costing £2 ($3). The gallery is open Monday to Friday from 9 a.m. to 12:30 p.m. and 1:30 to 4:15 p.m. Advance reservations are necessary. Call Sandra Baddeley, the tour organizer.

John Beswick, Gold Street, Longton, near Stoke-on-Trent (tel. 0782/313041). Since 1896, the John Beswick Studios of Royal Doulton have built a reputation for fine ceramic sculpture. Most renowned for its authentic studies of horses, birds, and animals, the studio also creates the famed Character and Toby Jugs of Royal Doulton. You may be lucky enough to see Peter Rabbit, Gandalf, or Dick Turpin in the making during a tour. The 1½ hour tour ends in the factory shop so you can indulge your shopping whims. Tours depart at 10:15 a.m. and 2 p.m. Monday to Friday, costing £1.50 ($2.25). Advance reservations are essential (call Joan Barker).

It is recommended that you make reservations to visit any of the Royal Doulton facilities, either by writing or telephoning. All the premises date back to the 19th century and are not suitable for the elderly or disabled. Also, for safety reasons, they do not accommodate children under the age of 14.

Spode, Church Street, Stoke-on-Trent (tel. 0782/46011), is yet another factory to offer guided tours Monday to Friday at 10 a.m. and 1:30 p.m. Again, advance reservations are essential. The cost is £1 ($1.50). The shop is open Monday to Friday from 8:30 a.m. to 5 p.m. (on Saturday from 9 a.m. to 1 p.m.).

Staffordshire Potteries Limited Factory Shop, Meir Park, Stoke-on-Trent (tel. 0782/315251), is the largest mug manufacturer in the world. It is open from 9:30 a.m. to 5:30 p.m. Monday to Saturday, offering a wide range of tableware, mugs, vases, pots, and ovenware. In addition to perfect examples, they also sell "seconds" where the flaws are so minor that the untrained eye can't detect them. And the prices are very reasonable.

Moorcroft Pottery, W. Moorcroft Ltd., Sandbach Road, Burslem, near Stoke-on-Trent (tel. 0782/24323), is an interesting alternative to the world-famous names. Founded in 1898 by William Moorcroft who produced his own special brand of pottery and was his own exclusive designer until his death in 1945, the pottery is special in that decoration is part of the first firing, giving it a higher quality of color and brilliance than, say, Spode. Today, design is in the hands of William's son Walter, who carries on the personal traditions of the family firm, creating clear floral designs in bright, clear colors for what has been described as the art nouveau of the pottery world. There is much to admire and buy in the Factory Seconds Shop. The factory and the restored bottle oven is open Monday to Friday from 10 a.m. to 4 p.m. and on Saturday from 9:30 a.m. to 12:30 p.m. There is always someone around to explain the various processes and to show you around the museum, with its collections of early Moorcroft.

Afterward, a visit to the past is in order. The **Gladstone Pottery Museum,** Uttoxeter Road at Longton (tel. 0782/319232), is a 19th-century pottery factory restored as a museum, with craftsmen demonstrating daily in original workshops. There are galleries of the rise of the Staffordshire pottery industry, tile history, sanitaryware with washstand bowls and jugs plus toilets of all shapes and sizes, and colors and decoration. There is a replica of a potter's house and a factory manager's office. The area around the museum is known as Potters Acre because of the number of shops specializing in rejects and discontinued lines. Admission to the museum is £1.50 ($2.25) for adults, 70p ($1.05) for children. It is open from 10:30 a.m. to 5:30 p.m. Monday to Saturday, 2 to 6 p.m. on Sunday (closed Monday in winter).

The **Stoke-on-Trent City Museum and Art Gallery,** on Broad Street in

Hanley (tel. 0782/273173), surely must contain the most comprehensive collection of ceramics in the world. The enthusiastic curator tells me that they have eight times as much stored away as they can possibly show at any time. Even those who aren't museum buffs must find this a beautiful collection. There are also exhibitions of modern art as well as prehistoric local remains, all housed in a delightful contemporary building. The museum is open Monday to Saturday from 10:30 a.m. to 5 p.m., Sunday from 2 to 5 p.m.

After all that, sustenance is required, and where better than at **Heath's Wine Bar,** Albion Street, at Hanley (tel. 0782/272472), almost opposite the museum? The long bar groans beneath great dishes of pâté, cold meats, pies (veal, ham and egg, steak and kidney), chili, salads (several varieties), dressed crab, and hot soup. Mounds of french bread are stacked up, and jacket potatoes are a favorite item. For dessert, try the cheesecake or a fruit salad. Everything is fresh, and all pies, quiches, and flans are homemade. Order and collect your meal and repair to one of the low coffee tables surrounded by sofas or the wheel-backed-chair-surrounded tables. The music is soft, the atmosphere warm and red. A two-course meal will cost around £3.50 ($5.25) to £5 ($7.50). Only lunch is served, from 11:30 a.m. to 2 p.m.

The **Minton Museum** at London Road, Stoke-on-Trent (tel. 0782/49171), is the starting place for a 1½-hour tour through the major departments of the factory, where they specialize in heavily decorated work. A phone call or a letter in advance is needed to join the £1.50 ($2.25) tour, but your understanding of the processes will be complete when you have seen how to raise patterns and scour and burnish gold relief. It takes 45 minutes to finish the decoration on one plate, so you can see how much a dinner service would cost. Free-hand-painting from some 1,800 patterns is also shown during the tour. It is here that you can get that unique souvenir, a personalized free-hand-painted plate or other piece of china. Simply arrange to discuss with one of the artists the photo or picture you wish to have, and they'll do the rest. It'll take from 2 to 12 months to complete, depending on the demand for orders. But you'll have an elegant and totally different souvenir. For more information, see Mrs. Ann Hughes, the tour organizer, from 10 a.m. to 2 p.m. Monday to Friday.

The **Chatterley Whitfield Mining Museum,** at Tunstall, Stoke-on-Trent (tel. 0782/813337), is a unique museum of mining with an underground gallery showing the history of mining from early times to the modern day. Tours underground are led when possible by ex-miners who vividly relate their experiences working in a coal mine. Visitors are "kitted out" with lamp and helmet, and stout shoes are recommended. Chatterley Whitfield was the first colliery to produce one million tons of coal in a year. Coal was mined for 140 years before its transformation into a museum in 1979. Other displays and attractions include a steam-winding engine, pit ponies, locomotives, and a colliery canteen and museum shop. Hours are from 10 a.m. to 5 p.m. daily, with a reduced schedule in winter, depending on the demand. Tours cost £2.95 ($4.43) for adults, £1.85 ($2.78) for children.

Alton Towers, North Staffordshire (tel. 0538/702200), lies on the B5032 four miles east of Cheadle and 15 miles east of Stoke-on-Trent. It must be the nearest thing to Disneyland on this side of the Atlantic. The house, once the home of the Earls of Shrewsbury, now shelters the Planetarium, gift shop, and banqueting hall. The beautiful gardens, laid out in the 1800s, become a riot of rhododendrons in early summer. There are lakes and streams, formal terraces, and an Italian garden with sculptures, rock gardens, and topiary. In the park are many "white knuckle" rides, including the famous corkscrew and the black hole, along with railways and cable cars. The attractions are open from mid-March until the end of October daily. The grounds open at 9 a.m., and the rides are operated from 10 a.m. until 5, 6, or 7 p.m., depending on the time of year. Admission is £5.99 ($8.99). All rides and shows, including those performed at the Alton Theatre, are free once you enter.

WHERE TO STAY: Because of the long commercial history of Stoke-on-Trent, it has never been much of a tourist town so far as accommodations are concerned. However, there are several recommendations I can make within a radius of some ten or 12 miles from the heart of town where you might choose to settle in for your tours of the Potteries. Newcastle-under-Lyme, about 3 miles to the west of the main city, has some B&B places you might like, but the other suggestions I will make are to the east and north, toward the Peak National Park and along the valley of the River Churnet.

In the Environs

Clayton Farm, at Clayton, outside Newcastle-under-Lyme (tel. 0782/620401), is run by Mrs. Kathleen Varley. She has refurbished an old farmhouse handy to the factories of Wedgwood, Spode, Royal Doulton, and many more. You get good value for money here, along with cleanliness, warmth, and friendliness. The charges are from £10 ($15) per person for B&B.

Grove Court Hotel, 100 Lancaster Rd., Newcastle-under-Lyme (tel. 0782/614406), is operated by Mr. and Mrs. M.S. James. Set in a residential area, their small hotel is built of old red brick, and they have restored it and fixed it up quite well. In honor of the nearby Potteries, they have decorated their lounge in a Wedgwood style, and their dining room is also warm and inviting. All the bedrooms have showers or baths, toilets, color TV, tea/coffee-making facilities, radio alarms, and hairdryers. The price in a double is £14 ($21) per person, including a full English breakfast and VAT.

In the village of Cheddleton, on the A520, about 6 miles from Stoke-on-Trent, Mrs. Elaine Sutcliffe operates **Choir Cottage** and **Choir House,** Ostlers Lane (tel. 0538/360561), a guesthouse and adjoining restaurant, which is in the Sutcliffes' own home. The 300-year-old cottage was once used as a resting place for ostlers, caretakers of horses which traveled on Ostlers Lane when it was the main road between Alton and Manchester. The name Choir Cottage comes from the fact that this was at one stage used as a house for the choir at the local church. Mrs. Sutcliffe has well-furnished bedrooms with private showers and toilets, color TV, and beverage-making facilities. One unit has a four-poster, and one on the first floor is suitable for people who can't manage stairs. The charge for a bed and a full English breakfast are £13 ($19.50) per person for an overnight stay, £11 ($16.50) per person for stays of two or more nights. Meals are served in the Choir House, with evening dinner available on request.

The village of Cheddleton, on the River Churnet, has a Steam Railway Museum, a working flintmill, beautiful walkways including the Deep Hayes Nature Park, and interesting waterways. It is a short distance from Leek.

Micklea Farm, Micklea Lane, Longsdon, near Leek (tel. 0538/385006), is where Mrs. Barbara White welcomes paying guests, offering them good food and comfortable beds. The delightful stone house is furnished with taste, and the food is excellent. B&B costs from £9 ($13.50) per person nightly. Guests have use of the lounge and large garden. An evening meal will be served on request. Longsdon, not to be confused with Longton which is larger and much closer to Stoke-on-Trent, is on the A53 road to the northeast about eight miles toward Leek. The farm is just off the A53.

In the same district, **Glenwood House Farm,** Ipstones, on the B5053 (tel. 053871/294), stands right on the edge of the Peak National Park, with fine views over the Churnet Valley, yet is still close enough to explore Stoke-on-Trent and the Potteries. This is the home of Joyce and Keith Brindley, and it is very much a working farm in the British tradition. Joyce has several rooms to rent, including a family one. The charge of £10 ($15) per person per night includes a large cooked breakfast. You'll pay another £6 ($9) if you want a three-course evening meal. If the color TV doesn't amuse, perhaps a games room with darts will. There is both a children's play area and tennis courts.

Between Stoke-on-Trent and Leek on the A53 road, Endon is a large village long famous for its Welldressing Festival. It is fast becoming a center for visitors spending a night or two for explorations of the Potteries, museums, the Staffordshire Moorlands, and Alton Towers, Britain's Disneyland. **The Hollies,** Clay Lake (tel. 0782/503252), is a delightful Victorian house in a quiet location off the B5051, with a large secluded garden and ample space for parking. Mrs. Anne Hodgson rents three spacious bedrooms with hot and cold water basins, shaver points, and beverage-making facilities. B&B costs £10 ($15) per person. The house is centrally heated and has a TV lounge and pleasant breakfast room. Smoking is prohibited.

Long known as a silk manufacturing town, Leek lies in the River Churnet Valley, within easy reach of the Potteries, the Peak District, and Dovedale. The **Peak Weavers Hotel,** 21 King St. (tel. 0538/383729), is a former convent, now offering 11 comfortable rooms, many with private baths, costing £12.50 ($18.75) per person nightly for B&B, VAT included.

5. Stafford

The county town of Staffordshire was the birthplace of Izaak Walton, the British writer and celebrated fisherman. Long famous as a boot-making center, it contains many historic buildings, notably St. Chad's, the town's oldest church; St. Mary's, with its unusual octagonal tower; and the William Salt Library, with its interesting collection of folklore.

In the Staffordshire countryside, at Shallowford, between Stafford and Eccleshall, lies **Izaak Walton Cottage** (tel. 0785/760278). He is best remembered as the author of *The Compleat Angler*. The period garden of his cottage has been planted with 17th-century herbs and flowers, as well as plants, which are for sale. Admission is 25p (38¢) for adults, 15p (23¢) for children. It is open from 12:30 to 5:30 p.m. mid-March to October Friday to Tuesday. In winter, it is open only on weekends, from 12:30 to 4:30 p.m.

FOOD AND LODGING: In the quiet part of the market town of Stafford, **The Vine Hotel,** Salter Street (tel. 0785/51071), is believed to be the oldest licensed premises in the borough. The hostelry has an atmosphere enhanced by blackened beams and sloping floors. The 25 refurbished bedrooms rent for £27 ($40.50) to £29 ($43.50) in a single, depending on whether the bathroom has a shower or a tub, with doubles renting for £35 ($52.50) to £37 ($55.50). Each unit has color TV, a phone, beverage-making facilities, trouser press, and hairdryer. Rates include a full English breakfast, VAT, and service. The hotel restaurant offers lunch Monday to Saturday from noon to 2 p.m. and dinner from 7 to 9 p.m., with a choice of a grill menu or table d'hote meals. Steaks are a specialty. Expect to pay from £8.50 ($12.75) for a complete meal. The Vine's oak-beamed lounge bar is a good place to relax.

Bailey Hotel, 63 Lichfield Rd. (tel. 0785/214133), offers about the best value of any B&B in the area. Guests exploring this part of the West Midlands seek out this little place which has been totally restored, with many amenities provided. The location is on the A34 (the Lichfield Road), lying less than a mile south of the heart of the historic district of Stafford. Their location is near the intersection of St. Leonard's Avenue. The hotel also provides parking. Nine comfortably furnished bedrooms, none with private bath, are rented at rates of £12 ($18) to £17 ($25.50) in a single, £22 ($33) to £26 ($39) in a double. The hotel will also provide dinner in the evening, charging from £17.50 ($26.25) to £21 ($31.50) for half board. Accommodations contain color TVs and are centrally heated.

6. Lichfield

Fans of Samuel Johnson pay a pilgrimage here to this historic city where he was born in 1709, son of an unsuccessful bookseller and parchment maker. The city is noted for its **cathedral,** whose three spires are known as "Ladies of the Vale." The tallest spire rises more than 250 feet, and the west front of the cathedral was built from about 1280. You can walk around the beautiful close and see a bit of the Vicars Close, with its half-timbered houses, along with the 17th-century Bishop's Palace.

Dr. Johnson's Birthplace on Breadmarket Street (tel. 0543/264972) contains mementos and pictures of the author and his contemporaries. It is open from 10 a.m. to 5 p.m. Monday to Saturday May to September, from 2:30 to 5 p.m. on Sunday. Off-season hours are from 10 a.m. to 4 p.m. Monday to Saturday. Admission is 50p (75¢) for adults, 25p (38¢) for children.

Across the street from Dr. Johnson's Birthplace stands the **Heritage Centre & Treasury** in Lichfield's Market Square (tel. 0543/256611). The former parish church has been transformed into a treasury and exhibition room with coffeeshop and gift shop. The exhibition tells the story of Lichfield through its people and events including an audio-visual presentation of the Civil War. The treasury displays examples of the silversmithing art, showing civic, regimental, and church plate. It's open daily from 10 a.m. to 5 p.m. Admission is 70p ($1.05) for adults, 30p (45¢) for children.

You can also visit the **Guildhall** (across the road from Heritage Centre), over the city dungeons dating from the Middle Ages. The Guildhall was rebuilt in 1846. Prisoners were jailed here before they were burned at the stake in Market Square.

Incidentally, market days are Friday and Saturday in Lichfield.

WHERE TO STAY: A modest town house of historic and architectural interest, **Mrs. Pauline Duval's Guest House,** 21/23 Dam St. (tel. 0543/264303) is owned and kept tidy by its friendly landlady. She charges £10 ($15) for B&B in her two single, two double, and two twin-bedded accommodations, all with hot and cold water basins, each with TV and beverage-making facilities. The house is centrally heated, with a separate residents' lounge. Off-street parking is available. Dam Street, which is for pedestrians only, on which her guesthouse stands was mentioned in the *Domesday Book* of 1086. Opposite the guesthouse stands Brooke House, where a general in Cromwell's army was shot in 1647. A plaque on the street commemorates where Johnson was taught English in 1714 at Dame Oliver's school.

Gaialands, 9 Gaiafields Rd. (tel. 0543/263764), is a well-kept, small guesthouse within walking distance of the cathedral and Minster Pool. Mr. and Mrs. Robert White give their guests a true Staffordshire welcome in a quiet, secluded environment. If you ask her, Mrs. White will prepare a home-cooked four-course dinner for £6 ($9). She charges £12.50 ($18.75) single, £10 ($15) per person in a twin-bedded for B&B. Units have central heating, pedestal hand basins, and the bathrooms are adjacent.

Oakleigh Hotel House, 25 St. Chad's Rd. (tel. 0543/262688), is a country house standing on its own grounds adjoining a sailing lake, Stowe Pool. The owners have greatly improved the house both in decor and comfort. Visitors are assured a high standard of cleanliness and service. Guests are accommodated at one time in the spacious rooms with full central heating. Rates are £22 ($33) in a single, from £17.50 ($26.25) per person in a double. You might also enjoy an evening meal at a cost of £8 ($12) and up per person.

WHERE TO STAY: The town's best-known pub is **Scales,** Market Street (tel. 05432/24526), which is comfortable and well run. Guests enjoy the wood paneling while seated on leather seats or else retreat to the courtyard in back. While you drink your lager, stop to admire the collectin of Delftware. Bar food, with light meals costing from £4 ($6), are served from noon to 2:30 p.m. except on Sunday. Hearty soups and meat pies will tempt you along with a roast of the day and freshly made salads. Or else you might settle for a sandwich or a hamburger. Ask about the annual conker competition. You can also go for drinks in the evening from 5:30 to 11 p.m.

If you're in the area for dinner, one of the most substantial places is **Fradley Arms,** Rykneld Street, at Fradley (tel. 0283/790186). This Georgian building is on the A38, about three miles to the northeast of Lichfield, so you'll need a car. Standing in about 4½ acres of private grounds, against a country background, it is a small, family-run place that serves good food. In an inviting atmosphere, dinners from 7:30 to 10 p.m. are served for £7 ($10.50) to £10 ($15). Fresh seafood is invariably featured, and you get a selection of British and continental cookery here. You can also visit for lunch from noon to 2 p.m., with meals costing from £7 ($10.50).

Chapter XVII

LIVERPOOL AND BLACKPOOL

1. Liverpool
2. Blackpool

THE GREAT INDUSTRIAL SHADOW of the 19th century cast such darkness over much of England's northwest that it has been relatively neglected by the foreign visitor. At best, Americans rush through it heading for the glories of the Lake District and Scotland. Cities such as Manchester have evoked grim, Victorian sprawls, the ugly scars left over from the Industrial Revolution.

However, the area is receiving some belated tourist attention. Chester, which is on the remote southwestern fringe of this district, is covered in another chapter, as is Derbyshire, which contains the great scenic beauty of the Peak District. Liverpool has done much in recent years to revitalize its tourist industry, and Blackpool, the resort to the north, has for decades been the place to which workers from the Midlands go to frolic along the seashore. It's like the old Atlantic City in New Jersey (before its gambling heyday), but with a distinctive English flavor.

The northwest, in spite of its industry and bleak commercial areas, also has much beauty for the tourist willing to seek it out. Manchester, Lancaster, Morecambe, and Southport—to name only a few—are all interesting cities with good-quality accommodations, and much of the countryside is beautiful, filled with inns, restaurants, and pubs, along with sightseeing attractions worth a visit. Because of space limitations, I will confine our visit to the two most popular destinations, Liverpool and Blackpool.

1. Liverpool
Liverpool, with its famous waterfront on the River Mersey, is a great shipping port and industrial center that gave the world everybody from Fannie Hill to the Beatles. King John launched it on its road to glory when he granted it a charter in 1207. Before that, it had been a tiny 12th-century fishing village, but it quickly became a port for shipping men and materials to Ireland. In the 18th century, it grew to prominence as a port as a result of the sugar, spice, and tobacco trade with the Americans. By the time Victoria came to the throne, Liverpool had become Britain's biggest commercial seaport. Recent refurbishing of the Albert Docks, establishment of a Maritime Museum, and the converting of warehouses into little stores, similar to those in Ghirardelli Square in San Francisco, have made this an up and coming area once again, with many attractions for visitors.

Liverpudlians, as they are called, are rightly proud of their city, with its new hotels, two cathedrals, shopping and entertainment complexes (as exemplified by St.

John's Centre, a modern pedestrian precinct), and the parks and open spaces (2,400 acres in and around the city, including Sefton Park with its Palm House). Liverpool's main shopping street, Church, is traffic free for most of the day.

Liverpool is easily reached by car, following the M1, the M6, the M62, and the A5080 from London right to the coast city in the west where the River Mersey joins the Irish Sea. Trains go from Euston or Kensington Olympia Stations from London or the Rapide bus from Victoria Coach Station direct to Liverpool.

THE SIGHTS: Liverpool today has a wealth of things for the visitor to see and enjoy —major cathedrals, waterfront glories restored, cultural centers, even the places where the Beatles began their meteoric rise to fame and fortune.

The Cathedrals

Attracting many Liverpool visitors is the great new Anglican edifice, the **Cathedral Church of Christ,** Mount Pleasant (tel. 051/709-6271), largely completed 74 years after it was begun in 1903. On a rocky eminence overlooking the Mersey River, the cathedral might possibly be the last Gothic-style one to be built on earth. Dedicated in the presence of Queen Elizabeth II in 1978, it is the largest church in the country (the fifth largest in the world). England's poet laureate, Sir John Betjeman, hailed it as "one of the great buildings of the world." Its vaulting under the tower is 175 feet high, the highest in the world, and its length of 619 feet is second only to that of St. Peter's in Rome. The architect, who won a competition in 1903 for the building's design, was Giles Scott. He later went on to rebuild the House of Commons, gutted by bombs after World War II. He personally laid the last stone on the highest tower pinnacle. The organ of the world's largest Anglican cathedral contains nearly 10,000 pipes, the biggest found in any church. The tower houses the highest (219 feet) and the heaviest (31 tons) ringing peals of bells in the world, and the Gothic arches are the highest ever built.

In 1984 a Visitor Centre and Refectory was opened, the dominant feature being an aerial sculpture of 12 huge sails, with a ship's bell, clock, and lights that change color on a 76-hour basis. Full meals may be taken in the charming refectory. The cathedral can be visited from 9 a.m. to 6 p.m. daily. In August, tours of the tower are offered Monday to Saturday from 10:30 a.m. to 12:30 p.m. and 2 to 4:30 p.m. and on Sunday from 4 to 5 p.m. The tours cost adults £1.50 ($2.25), children (accompanied by an adult) 50p (75¢).

Half a mile away from the Anglican cathedral stands the Roman Catholic **Metropolitan Cathedral of Christ the King,** St. James Road (tel. 051/709-9222), but any notion that they glower at each other from that distance is dismissed by the name of the road that joins them: Hope Street. The sectarian strife of earlier generations has been ended, and a change in attitude, called by some the "Mersey Miracle," was illustrated clearly in 1982 when Pope John Paul II drove along Hope Street to pray in both cathedrals. The Metropolitan Cathedral is so called because Liverpool is, in Catholic terms, the mother city, the "metropolis" of the north of England. Construction of the cathedral to the design of Sir Edwin Lutyens was started in 1930, but when World War II halted progress in 1939, not even the granite and brick vaulting of the crypt was complete. At the end of the war it was estimated that the cost of completing the structure as Lutyens had designed it would be some £27 million. Architects throughout the world were invited to compete to design a more realistic project to cost about £1 million and to be completed in five years. Sir Frederick Gibberd won the competition and was commissioned to oversee construction of the circular cathedral in concrete and glass, pitched like a tent at one end of the piazza that covered all the original site, crypt included. Between 1962 and 1967 the construction was completed, providing seating for a congregation of more than 2,000, all within 50 feet of the central altar. Above the altar rises a multicolored glass lantern weighing 2,000 tons and rising to a height of 290 feet. It has been called a "space age" cathedral.

The Metropolitan Cathedral is open daily except Sunday from 8 a.m. to 6 p.m. (to 5 p.m. in winter). It has a bookshop, a tea room, and tour guides.

On the Waterfront

Albert Dock, Albert Dock Co. Ltd (tel. 051/709-7373), is the showpiece development on Liverpool's Waterfront. Built of brick, stone, and cast iron, it opened in 1846, saw a long period of decline, and has been renovated and refurbished so that the magnificent dockland warehouses now contain quality shops, restaurants, cafés, and a cellar wine bar. One block houses the main building of the Merseyside Maritime Museum (see below) and another is being fitted out as the home of the Tate Gallery Liverpool, which may be open by the time of your visit, with collections of artworks rivaling the London Tate Gallery displays. Albert Dock is open daily from 10 a.m. to 8 p.m. There's no charge for going there and strolling around, and car parking is available.

The **Merseyside Maritime Museum,** Pier Head (tel. 051/709-1551), has a blend of floating exhibits, craft demonstrations, working displays, and special events. Visitors can follow the quayside trail and visit restored buildings, including the Piermaster's House, the old Pilotage, and the Albert Dock Warehouse. A Liverpool pilot cutter and a schooner are among the floating exhibits visitors can board. Of special interest is an emigration gallery telling the story of how millions of people passed through Liverpool en route to the New World. The museum is open daily from 10:30 a.m. to 5:30 p.m. (last admission at 4:30 p.m.). Admission is £1 ($1.50) for adults, 50p (75¢) for children. Facilities include a café, restaurant, gift shop, and car parking area.

You can take a **Mersey Ferry** from the Pier Head to both Woodside and Seacombe, operating on a regular 20-minute schedule on weekdays from early morning to late evening. Special afternoon cruises are offered along Liverpool's historic waterfront. For information about times and prices, get in touch with the **Merseyside Transport Ferries Office,** Victoria Place, Seacombe, Wallasey (tel. 051/630-1030).

Where the Beatles Began

Whether they're Beatles fans or not, most visitors who come to Liverpool want to take a look at where Beatlemania began in the Swinging '60s. Mathew Street is the heart of Beatleland, and **Cavern Walks** (tel. 051/236-9082) is a shopping development and tour service built on the site of the former Cavern Club where the Beatles performed almost 300 times. John Doubleday's controversial statue of the group is in the central piazza of the Cavern complex, surrounded by shops and restaurants. The outside of Cavern Walks was decorated by Cynthia Lennon, John's first wife. Another controversial statue of John, Paul, George, and Ringo, this one by Liverpool sculptor Arthur Dooley, is opposite the building facade. Farther along Mathew Street is the John Lennon Memorial Club and the **Beatles Shop,** 31 Mathew St. (tel. 051/236-8066), open from 9:30 a.m. to 5:30 p.m. daily except Sunday. Around the corner on Stanley Street is a statue of Eleanor Rigby, seated on a bench.

For information about tours following in the footsteps of the Beatles, to see where they lived, their schools, and many other connections, such as Strawberry Field and Penny Lane, a number of possibilities exist: minibus tours of Beatle sites from May to September, costing £3.50 ($5.25); a guided car tour for £16.50 ($24.75); a Beatle walk for £11 ($16.50); or on a self-guided Beatle trail following a route you can purchase for 85p ($1.28) or in a Beatle book, £1.50 ($2.25).

Details on Beatles' attractions and events, such as a convention held every September, are available from the main **Tourist Information Centre,** 29 Lime St. (in front of the main train station) (tel. 051/709-3631).

Beatle City, P.O. Box 12, Seel Street (tel. 051/709-0117), in the heart of Liverpool, near the Liverpool Central Underground Station, is a permanent exhibition of Beatlemania, where a maelstrom of lights and sounds recreates the '60s and the story of the Beatles. Reconstructions of settings include the Cavern Club and a collection of original instruments, clothing, and photographs. A small souvenir shop sells Beatle records, books, and souvenirs, and a café offers light refreshments. It is open from 10:30 a.m. to 8:30 p.m. except over Christmas. Admission is £2.50 ($3.75) for adults, £1.25 ($1.88) for children.

Parks of Liverpool

To the surprise of many a visitor, about a ninth of the land mass of Liverpool is devoted to parks. In the limelight today is **Festival Park** on the western side of Riverside Drive (tel. 051/728-9888), to the south of the city on the banks of the River Mersey. On the site of the 1984 International Garden Festival in the Aigburth section, not far from the airport, it can be reached from the M62 and the city center by following the signposts. St. Michael's Station on the Merseyrail line is a few minutes' walk away. Within the 45 acres are the Magic Garden in the Festival Hall, Oriental gardens, picnic and play areas, free rides for children, and the Yellow Submarine. The park is open daily from 11 a.m. to 6 p.m. Admission is £1.50 ($2.25) per person.

Sea captains of the 18th century brought exotic plants back to Liverpool, and this led to a series of botanical gardens. The largest is **Sefton Park,** with a Palm House from 1896 built in an octagonal style. To the east of Sefton, in a residential section, is **Calderstones Park,** which has one of the most beautiful botanical gardens in the city. To the east of Sefton is the appropriately named **Riverside Park,** opening onto the River Mersey. This park, which grew out of a garbage dump and abandoned oil tanks, encompasses 125 acres. A tunnel leads under the river to Birkenhead Park, said to be the oldest free-entry city-owned park in the world.

About five miles from the city center is **Croxteth Hall** and **Country Park,** Muirhead Avenue East (tel. 051/228-5311), a 500-acre working country estate. Home of the Molyneux family, the Earls of Sefton, the hall, Walled Garden, and Home Farm are open from 11 a.m. to 5 p.m. daily mid-April to late September. Admission is £1.50 ($2.25) for adults, 75p ($1.13) for children. The parkland can be visited free all year.

Other Sights

The **Museum of Labour History,** former County Sessions House, William Brown Street (tel. 051/227-5234, ext. 2079), traces what it was like to live and work in Merseyside over the last 150 years, with people struggling for legal and political rights, establishing trade unions, and improving their working conditions. Open from 10 a.m. to 5 p.m. Monday to Saturday, 2 to 5 p.m. Sunday. Closed New Year's Day, Good Friday, and the three Christmas holidays. Admission is free.

The **Liverpool Museum and Planetarium,** William Brown Street (tel. 051/207-0001), has displays on antiquities, archives, botany, decorative arts, geology, zoology, physical sciences, social industrial history, and a transport gallery, as well as an aquarium and a vivarium. Open Monday to Saturday from 10 a.m. to 5 p.m., Sunday from 2 to 5 p.m. except New Year's Day, Good Friday and the Christmas holidays, the museum admission is free. To visit the planetarium, adults pay 80p ($1.20), children 40p (60¢).

The **Walker Art Gallery,** William Brown Street (tel. 051/227-5234, ext. 2064), has the largest collection of paintings outside London. It is known for its European pictures and sculpture from 1300 to the present. Open Monday to Saturday from 10 a.m. to 5 p.m. Monday to Saturday, 2 to 5 p.m. Sunday, it is closed New Year's Day, Good Friday, and for the Christmas holidays. Admission is free.

Bluecoat Chambers, School Lane (tel. 051/709-5297), once a charity school in a beautiful Queen Anne building, now houses a center for the arts, including a gallery, craft center, film theater, and café. It's open from 10 a.m. to 5 p.m. Monday to Saturday. Admission is free.

Among Liverpool's historic buildings, **St. George's Hall,** designed by a 24-year-old architect who never saw it realized, was completed in 1854. It has been called "England's finest public building." It contains law courts, and in the rear are pleasantly laid-out gardens.

Speke Hall, The Walk, Speke (tel. 051/427-7231), on the north bank of the Mersey, 7 miles from Liverpool's city center, is a National Trust property not far from Liverpool Airport. This lavishly furnished, half-timbered black-and-white Tudor house was built between 1490 and 1612. It is rich in ghost stories and priest holes, and two ancient yew trees stand in the courtyard. Hours are 1 to 5:30 p.m. Tuesday to Saturday, noon to 6 p.m. Sunday and bank holidays. Closed Good Friday. From November to mid-December, hours are from 1 to 5 p.m. Saturday and Sunday. Admission is £1.50 ($2.25) for adults, 70p ($1.05) for children.

WHERE TO STAY: Just a few minutes from the central railway station, **Hanover Hotel,** 62 Hanover St. (tel. 051/709-5035), is an all-purpose, modernized hotel right in the center of the city. Hanover Street adjoins Church Street and Ranelagh Street in the center of the Liverpool shopping complex, and is at the heart of the entertainment district. This has been a family hotel for more than 50 years and has undergone constant upgrading, providing 32 bedrooms with built-in units for hot and cold running water, drawers, and wardrobes. There is a finger-tip heating control, intercom, and radio. Bathless singles are £13.80 ($20.70); with bath, £16.10 ($24.15). Bathless doubles or twins rent for £23 ($34.50); with bath, £25.30 ($37.95). Rates include an English breakfast and all taxes. The hotel has a homey lounge with black leather chairs, a fireplace, and a TV set.

Solna Hotel, Ullet Road, Sefton Park (tel. 051/733-1943), is a rambling turn-of-the-century house converted to a hotel on the outskirts of Liverpool. It's 2½ miles from the heart of the city and three miles from the airport, standing in its own gardens overlooking Sefton Park. The B&B rate is £17.50 ($26.25) to £19.50 ($29.25) in a single, £30 ($45) to £34 ($51) in a double or twin. The 41 bedrooms (25 with private baths) have push-button radios, hot and cold water basins, and color TV. With your room, you get a good breakfast. The hotel is centrally heated and has plenty of parking space.

Aplin House Private Hotel, 35 Clarendon Rd., Garston (tel. 051/427-5047), is a well-kept B&B hotel run by Mr. and Mrs. Atherton, who have a good many repeat guests. Mrs. Atherton makes breakfast "as you want it." Her charges include VAT and service. Singles cost from £14 ($21) nightly, the rate in a twin-bedded room being from £11 ($16.50) to £12 ($18), rising to £12 ($18) to £13 ($19.50) per person in a large, double-bedded unit. Evening meals are offered, costing from £5 ($7.50). The hotel is about ten minutes by train from the city center.

Orrell Park Hotel, 109 Orrell Lane (tel. 051/525-4018), while five miles from the true city center, is only a five-minute walk from the railway station. The M57 motorway is two miles from the hotel. The terms for B&B are £14.50 ($27.75) in a single, £27 ($40.50) in a double, all bathless. There are a few rooms with private bath, renting for £17.50 ($26.25) in a single and from £33 ($49.50) in a double. Some family rooms can also be negotiated. There are 21 bedrooms in all, eight with bath, five with toilet. Monday through Thursday you can get a full evening meal for £6 ($9). Guests, often business representatives, gather in the licensed bar or TV lounge.

Aachen Hotel, 89–91 Mount Pleasant (tel. 051/709-3477), has a variety of rooms with a variety of plumbing. Singles range from £15 ($22.50) to £18 ($27), and doubles cost from £26 ($39) to £34 ($51). You tip as you see fit. Mr. F. P. Wilson, the owner, provides complete English breakfasts. Each of his modernized bedrooms has hot and cold running water, hair dryer, color TV, in-house movies, radio alarm, beverage-making facilities, and trouser press. The hotel has a bar. Mr. Wilson will help you with your Liverpool visit, as he knows the city well. The location is about five minutes from the center of the city.

EATING AND DRINKING: For some really good old-English cooking, go to the **Feathers Hotel,** 119–125 Mount Pleasant (tel. 051/709-9655), a long-standing favorite, moderately priced. Here you can sample the famous Lancashire hot-pot, a casserole where the lamb chops are layered with onions and potatoes. It's traditionally eaten with pickled red cabbage. Meals costing from £7.50 ($11.25) are served in the Peacock Restaurant, which features "old English specialty menus." It's open from noon to 2 p.m. and 6:30 to 8:30 p.m. The Feathers also rents out 80 comfortably furnished bedrooms, 22 with private baths. Singles cost £13.95 ($20.93) to £19.10 ($28.65), doubles and twins from £23.55 ($35.33) to £28.60 ($42.90), and some family rooms for four persons at £35 ($52.50).

La Grande Bouffe, 48a Castle St. (tel. 051/236-3375), sports a menu that illustrates what might be an Englishwoman and a Frenchman discreetly embracing, which is perhaps a symbol of the way the British residents of Liverpool have embraced the Gallic cuisine of the patronne, Juliet Shield. An inexpensive luncheon menu is written on a blackboard, and might consist of a chilled yogurt-and-cucumber soup, followed by a bacon-and-mushroom quiche. This could be finished off with a slice of nectarine and lemon curd tart, all for a deliciously low total of £3.50 ($5.25). Dinner is more elaborate and much more expensive, although a pretheater supper is served early in the evening for just £6.95 ($10.43). An à la carte dinner, costing from £10 ($15), might include La Bouffe's coarsely chopped chicken liver pâté (the menu warns that it's "very alcoholic"), followed by sautéed breast of chicken stuffed with cream cheese and a herb pâté, then homemade ice cream for dessert. As in France, a 10% service charge is automatically added. Hours are Monday from 10 a.m. to 4:30 p.m.; Tuesday through Friday, to 11:30 p.m.; and Saturday only from 6 p.m. till midnight. Teas, coffee, and cakes are served on weekdays before noon and after 3 p.m.

The **Mandarin Restaurant,** 40 Victoria St. (tel. 051/236-8899), Liverpool is particularly famous for its Chinese restaurants, not surprising as the city has one of the largest Chinese populations in Europe and its own "Chinatown." In a former warehouse, now converted, the Mandarin is reported to be the finest Chinese dining room in town. Yet its prices are very reasonable: £3 ($4.50) for a set lunch, £8 ($12) for a table d'hôte dinner. The cuisine is from the kitchens of Canton or Peking. Try the steamed spare ribs, the pork dumplings with a spicy hot chili sauce, or squid and green peppers in a black bean sauce. It is open Monday to Saturday from noon to 11:30 p.m. and on Sunday from 5:30 to 11:30 p.m. The location is near the Municipal Buildings.

Armadillo Restaurant, 20 Mathew St. (tel. 051/236-4123), a self-service place, stands across from the site of the famous Cavern, where the Beatles got their start. The selection of fresh, good-tasting food tilts toward the vegetarian, but meat and poultry are also served. This place, owned by Martin Cooper, seems to be near the top of everybody's favorite restaurant list in Liverpool. During the day you can make selections from a well-stocked buffet, paying from £5 ($7.50) for a satisfying meal. If you return in the evening, and especially if you make a selection from one of the excellently prepared fish courses, such as Scottish salmon in citrus, you'll pay at least £12 ($18), maybe more, for a meal here. Hours are from 10:30 a.m. to 3 p.m. and 5 to 10:30 p.m. except Sunday.

St. George's Carvery, St. John's Precinct, Lime Street (tel. 051/709-7090), lies in one of the best-known hotels in the city center, a modern structure, where you can enjoy a before-dinner drink in the Dragon Bar. Or, if you're in this bar from noon to 2 p.m., Monday to Saturday, you can make selections from a hot and cold buffet for only £1.50 ($2.25), truly one of the best food values in Liverpool. Or else you can go to the Carvery where you can help yourself to excellent roasts, including beef, leg of lamb, and pork, along with seasonal specials and vegetarian dishes. On the cold table you'll find honey-baked ham and turkey. This special food bargain is served seven days a week from noon to 2 p.m. and 7 to 10 p.m. A two-course lunch costs £5.50 ($8.25), and you can order "the works" at night for just £8.65 ($12.98).

Kismet Restaurant, 105 Bold St. (tel. 051/709-8469), is a well-patronized restaurant that has some of the best Indian food in Liverpool, specializing in tandoori dishes. Among these are their tandoori masala (lamb, chicken, or king prawns cooked in special gravy in the clay ovens). The Kismet special is a mild curry with prawns, chicken, meat, and pineapple with an omelet garnished with tomato, raisins, and coconut. Rogan josh (lamb spiced with herbs and cashew nuts) and sag gosht (beef cooked with fresh leaf spinach) are tasty selections. They also prepare English dishes. Lunch, served from noon to 2:30 p.m., costs from £3.50 ($5.25). Dinner, from 5:30 p.m. to 2:30 a.m., comes to £7.50 ($11.25) and up. The Kismet is open seven days a week.

Bistro Everyman, 9 Hope St. (tel. 051/708-9545), is informal, crowded on weekends, fun, and prices are reasonable. A buffet is offered with a wide range of pâtés, quiche, pizzas, soups, meat and vegetarian main courses, seasonal salads, cheeses, desserts, and pastries. The menu is changed twice daily and is influenced by the season and the weather, with only fresh produce from the local market being used. A typical three-course meal might consist of carrot soup with french bread, chicken pie with new potatoes and green salad, strawberries, in white wine with cream, and coffee, costing £5 ($7.50). On Sunday, only quiche, pizza, and salad are served, and live music predominates. The bistro, managed by Pauline Gaitskill, is open from noon to 11:30 p.m. daily. The bistro is part of the Everyman Theatre complex.

Everybody's favorite pub is at the **Philharmonic Hotel,** 36 Hope St. (tel. 051/709-1163), which has all those splendid turn-of-the-century architectural decorative features that are now so much in vogue—stained glass, carving, plasterwork, you name it. You pass through wrought-iron gates into a selection of several bars, some with rosewood paneling. Some of the private-seeming rooms are named after famous composers such as Liszt and Brahms. The heart of the pub is the Horseshoe Bar, with a mosaic floor and stained glass, fine Edwardian flamboyance. You can have a few pints and play dominoes. The feeling is like a private club, and almost any regular will advise a stranger what kind of local ale is good. The habitués refer to it as "The Phil," and it attracts art, drama, and music students as well as actors. If you're a man, I suggest you pay a visit to the gent's urinal, even if you don't need to go. It's a work of art! Hot and cold food is served in the cocktail lounge at lunch, with meals costing from £3.50 ($5.25). Hours are from 11:30 a.m. to 3 p.m. and 5 to 10:30 p.m. Live music is presented four times a week.

2. Blackpool

The custom began in 1720 when wealthy families, complete with children, maiden aunts, cousins, and servants, arrived to breathe the sea air. Hotels were built to accommodate them, and Blackpool, north from Liverpool, began its long and often rocky history as a resort. It's had good times and bad times. Nowadays it's working hard to restore itself with a fresh new image and many more attractions.

It has survived because of its **beaches,** called "the magnificent seven" and stretching for seven miles. The most athletic of visitors walk the seven-mile stretch every day; others prefer to take an easier and shorter ride on one of the famous donkeys that go up and down the beachfront. The so-called Golden Mile stretches for only 500 yards, from the Tower of Blackpool south to the Foxhall Hotel. It takes in such pleasure centers as the Golden Mile, Coral Island, and the Palatine Precinct. It is a world of discos, dining spots, cabaret shows, and the inevitable Tussaud waxworks (Louis, not Madame).

Particularly in summer, there is always something going on at Blackpool, and it's trying hard to beef up its winter business when the beaches are no longer a lure. Events range from strutting brass bands to dog shows and hockey tournaments. There's even an annual Coal Queen contest.

The landmark of Blackpool is its **Tower.** Soaring 519 feet into the air, it is illuminated at night by 10,000 lightbulbs. Brighton turned down the idea of such a Tower, but in 1891 Blackpool went for it, and it's been a tradition every since. The plan was to erect a small Eiffel-like tower on the Lancashire coast. Under the giant four legs of the tower is an indoor circus active both day and night. These include the Tower Ballroom (one of the great Victorian ballrooms of Britain), the Tower Circus, the Occan Room cabaret, and a Tower Aquarium, plus many other amusements, some designed for children. Those who ascend the tower are rewarded with a view of up to 60 miles on a clear day.

The best place for shopping is behind the Tower in the Hounds Hill Center. In red brick, it has glass arcades as in the days of King Edward VII. You can see buskers perform.

AMUSEMENTS: For Coney Island–type amusement, head for **Pleasure Beach,** built in 1904, 40 acres of amusements, including what the English refer to as "white-knuckle" rides. Featured is a 360-degree "loop the loop" roller-coaster. Its flagship is the Wonderful World Building, which is like an ocean liner with dining places, attractions, and a nightclub. You'll have an Atlantic City déjà vu as you walk along the seaside piers, three in all, each filled with restaurants (often fast food) and attractions to amuse.

And when you want to retreat from thriller rides and other amusements, there is **Stanley Park,** a 26-acre park setting, filled with motor and rowing boats and such facilities as six bowling greens, 32 tennis courts, and two 18-hole putting greens (plus a special playground set aside for children).

If the seawater off the beach is too cool for your tastes, you can plunge into an Olympic-size pool at the **Derby Baths,** a large indoor pool standing adjacent to the Pembroke Hotel on the North Shore. It has saunas, massages, even vapor and aeratone baths.

The easiest way to see Blackpool is to ride along the sea in one of the single- or double-decker trams. Established in 1885, it is Britain's only city tramcar system.

Blackpool is famous for its **illuminations,** lasting from the end of August until the end of October. This razzle-dazzle attraction features hundreds of illuminated figures, such as butterflies, 175 miles of wiring in all, with 375,000 lamps. Called the biggest single tourist attraction in the north of England, it draws some eight million visitors a year (hotel owners raise their prices at that time).

Some locals will tell you their **nightlife** outdazzles that of Las Vegas. In the past a lot of big names, such as Sarah Bernhardt, have performed at Blackpool. Today you are likely to see scantily clad showgirls in sequins and feathers. The major after-dark diversions take place at such establishments as the Horseshoe Bar at Pleasure Beach, the Gaiety Bar, the Yellow Submarine, and the Lion Showbar. Other nightlife attractions include the restored Grand Theatre, which was reopened by Prince Charles in 1981 after it had been allowed to become a Bingo hall. You can also attend a revue at the Ice Drome or patronize the modernized 1889 Opera House. Discos by the dozens are combined with lively pier shows and ballroom dancing. In all, there are some 50 cabaret spots and clubs.

Blackpool also has a modern **zoo,** with lions and elephants, along with a miniature railway and picnic areas.

It is also one of the least expensive places to go for a holiday in the United Kingdom.

WHERE TO STAY: Still retaining its Victorian facade, the **Dukeries Hotel,** 86–88 Adelaide St. (0253/22468), has been modernized inside. The Switzerland-born proprietors of this centrally located hotel, Rudolf and Carole Muller, welcome guests with a smile. Each of the 37 bedrooms contains contemporary furniture, tea/coffee-making facilities, TV, radio-intercoms, and baths. Bed, breakfast, and evening dinner costs £17.50 ($26.25) per person, based on double occupancy. B&B rates are from £14.50 ($36.75) per person. Reductions are granted for children. The hotel has a bar and a lounge.

Lansdowne Hotel, 256–262 North Promenade (tel. 0253/24476), has a sea view from many of the rooms. Each of the 75 bedrooms has beverage-making facilities and color TV. B&B costs from £14.50 ($21.75) per person, and half board is offered priced from £18.50 ($27.75) per person. Day and night porter service is available. The hotel has three bars and an elevator. The Hackett family, proprietors, sometimes offer discounts for stays during winter and early spring.

The **Seymour Hotel,** 60–62 Queen's Promenade (tel. 0253/51463), is a red-brick building which occupies a prominent position in the center of the resort. There are 72 bedrooms, many with private bath. All of them have hot and cold running water and central heating. B&B costs £11.50 ($17.25) per person. If you prefer half board, the charge is from £17 ($25.50). The Mayhew and Arnett families, the owners, welcome children. Guests congregate in the TV lounge, the games room, or the cocktail bar. In high season, entertainment is provided.

The **Sherwood Private Hotel,** 414 North Promenade (tel. 0253/51898), is one of the best bets for a reasonably priced smaller hotel with a desirable position on the promenade. The dining room allows a sea view. Each of the 17 simple but comfortable modern bedrooms has central heating, and most of them have private bath. The charge is from £14 ($21) per person for B&B.

Strathdene Private Hotel, 49 Woodfield Rd. (tel. 0253/46440), is a small private hotel with a residential license to serve drinks. Adjacent to the promenade, it is open all year, welcoming guests into comfortable rooms. The charge for B&B is from £9 ($13.50) per person nightly. The hotel is well maintained, and Mrs. I. Rowland, its owner, makes you feel welcome. Arrangements can be made to have an evening dinner as well. There is full central heating.

WHERE TO EAT: The place to go for fish and chips is **The Cottage,** 31 Newhouse Rd. (tel. 0253/64081). Some of the fish arrives on trawlers from the Irish Sea and the Faroes. You get a wide choice, including haddock, cod, hake, salmon, swordfish, and halibut, along with such delicacies as crab and prawns. Everything is very reasonably priced and has a homemade taste. A basic three-course meal starts at £3 ($4.50), the price increasing according to the size of fish you order. They also serve other food if you don't want fish. Desserts are good too, including an English trifle. Food is served weekdays from noon to 2 p.m. Dinner is served from 5 p.m. to midnight Tuesday to Sunday (on Monday from 8 p.m.). Margaret Stansfield is the proprietor of this licensed restaurant.

White Tower Restaurant, Blackpool Pleasure Beach, at Promenade and Balmoral Road (tel. 0253/46710), occupies a position on the third floor of the Wonderful World Building, on the South Shore adjacent to Pleasure Beach. It offers both set meals and à la carte dinners, along with a good view of the sea. Traditional roast beef carved from the trolley is a standard feature on Sunday at lunch, when the place is likely to be crowded. When available, try one of the lobsters from the Isle of Man. Lunch costs from £7 ($10.50), dinner from £10 ($15) to £12 ($18). Service is Tuesday to Saturday from 7:30 p.m. to midnight. The place is closed all day Monday and on Sunday night, but serves Sunday lunch from noon to 4 p.m.

Danish Kitchen, 95 Church St. (tel. 0253/24291), a self-service enterprise, offers food that is fresh and consistently well cooked. Against a pristine Scandinavian background, with pine furnishings, you can partake of the kitchen's daily offerings from 9:15 a.m. to 5:30 p.m. Monday to Saturday. A set lunch costs only £2.50 ($3.75), with most meals averaging £3 ($4.50) or so. Open-faced sandwiches, Danish style, are a powerful lure, and you can also order crisp salads, along with pizzas and quiches. Wine can be ordered by the carafe.

Robert's Oyster Bar, 92 Promenade (tel. 0253/21226), has long been a landmark on the dining scene. Grandparents who spent seaside holidays at Blackpool and ate here now their take their grandchildren to sample the delights of the sea. Of course, oysters are the piéce de rèsistance, but you can also select from an array of cockles and mussels, in the best of the Cockney tradition, along with whelks. Many diners can be seen sampling the wares right on the Promenade, finger-sampling their favorite morsels, and watching the passing parade. For £4 ($6) or so, you can get a good fill here any time from 9 a.m. to 10:30 p.m. (it closes at 5:30 p.m. off-season).

Chapter XVIII

THE LAKE DISTRICT

ONE OF ENGLAND'S MOST POPULAR summer retreats in Queen Victoria's day was the Lake District in the northwest. It enjoyed vogue during the flowering of the Lake Poets, including Wordsworth, who was ecstatically moved by the rugged beauty of this area. In its time the district has lured such writers as Samuel Taylor Coleridge, Charles Lamb, Shelley, Keats, Alfred Lord Tennyson, Matthew Arnold, and Charlotte Brontë.

The Lake District is a miniature Switzerland condensed into about 32 miles, principally in Cumbria, although it begins in the northern part of Lancashire.

The northwest of England is one of the special parts of the country, and more and more it is visited by foreign tourists, especially Americans, who view its remoteness as part of its charm. Have you ever seen one of those English-made films depicting the life of the Lake District? A soft mist hovers over the hills and dells, sheep graze contentedly on the slope of the pastures—and a foggy enchantment fills the air.

Driving in the wilds of this northwestern shire is fine for a start. But the best activity is walking, which is an art best practiced here by both young and old with a crooked stick. Don't go out without a warning, however. There is a great deal of rain and heavy mist, and sunny days are few. When the mist starts to fall, try to be near an old inn or pub, where you can drop in for a visit and warm yourself beside an open fireplace. You'll be carried back to the good old days, as many places in Cumbria have valiantly resisted change. If you strike up a conversation with a local, you must make sure you know something about hounds.

The far northwestern part of the shire, bordering Scotland, used to be called Cumberland. Now part of Cumbria, it is generally divided geographically into a trio of segments: the Pennines dominating the eastern sector (loftiest point at Cross Fell, nearly 3,000 feet high), the Valley of Eden, and the lakes and secluded valleys of the west, by far the most interesting. The area, so beautifully described by the romantic Lake Poets, enjoys many literary associations. Wordsworth ("when all at once I saw a crowd, a host of golden daffodils") was a native son, born at Cockermouth.

The largest town is **Carlisle** in the north—not a very interesting tourist center, but a possible base for explorations to Hadrian's Wall. The wall stretches from Wallsend in the east to Bowness on the Solway, a distance of about 75 miles. It was built in the second century A.D. by the Romans.

Brockhole National Park Centre, between Ambleside and Windermere, is well worth a visit.

A traditional gateway to the district is from the south, approached via:

1. Kendal

A simple market town, Kendal contains the ruins of a castle where Catherine Parr, the last wife of Henry VIII, was born. With its 13th-century parish church, Kendal makes for a good stopover en route to the lakeside resort of Windermere, beginning about nine miles away. Kendal is 270 miles from London.

The town was also associated with George Romney, the 18th-century portrait painter (Lady Hamilton his favorite subject), who used to travel all over the Lake District trying to get someone to sit for him. He held his first exhibition, married, and raised a family in Kendal. He deserted them in 1762, not returning until the end of his life. He died in Kendal in 1802.

Abbot Hall, Kirkland, a handsome stone Georgian mansion, houses the **Abbot Hall Art Gallery** and the **Museum of Lakeland Life and Industry** (tel. 0539/22646), operated by the Lake District Art Gallery and Museum Trust. The gallery, laid out in 18th-century rooms, contains portraits by Romney and Gardner and Lake District watercolors. The museum's exhibits include period rooms, costumes, printing, weaving, and local industries, as well as Queensgate, a reconstructed Victorian street scene, and a farming display. The gallery and museum are open weekdays from 10:30 a.m. to 5:30 p.m., weekends from 2 to 5 p.m. They are closed for two weeks at Christmas and on Good Friday. Admission is 70p ($1.05) for adults, 40p (60¢) for children.

The **Kendal Museum of Archaeology and Natural History,** Station Road (tel. 0539/21374), one of the oldest museums in Britain, now administered by the Abbot Hall Art Gallery, traces the story of people of the area since the Stone Age, as well as Kendal's development as a wool town. Realistic constructions take the visitor on a tour of the major wildlife habitats in the district. The museum also contains a world wildlife gallery with specimens of birds, animals, and insects, pointing out the ecological problems of the modern world. The museum is open Monday to Friday from 10:30 a.m. to 5 p.m., Saturday from 2 to 5 p.m., and closed Sunday, two weeks at Christmas, and on Good Friday. Admission is 40p (60¢) for adults, 20p (30¢) for children 6 to 16.

FOOD AND LODGING: A comfortable guesthouse, **Hillside,** 4 Beast Banks (tel. 0539/22836), is just two blocks from the main street of Kendal. Carl and Brenda Denison are the gracious and helpful owners of this neat, clean accommodation. There is a lounge with color TV, and all rooms have beverage-making facilities and modern sinks with plenty of hot water. The toilets are separate from the shower and bathrooms. The charge is £9.50 ($14.25) per person per night.

Brantholme, 7 Sedbergh Rd. (tel. 0539/22340), is an interesting Victorian house standing on its own grounds. A Lake Country family welcomes you into their limited but well-furnished accommodations, which include a room usually reserved for families. The meals are so good here, and so abundant, that it's best to take the half-board rate ranging from £21 ($31.50) to £26 ($39) per person nightly. They are closed in December.

The **Brewery Arts Centre,** Highgate (tel. 0539/25133), is set in a 150-year-old converted brewery and may be found just off Highgate. Morning coffee is served with freshly made scones from 10 a.m. in the restaurant, and on the sun terrace in summer. Lunches, between 11:30 a.m. and 2 p.m., cost from £5 ($7.50). In addition to a variety of fresh salads, the restaurant offers a range of hot dishes, plus a homemade dish of the day. The local specialty is Cumberland sausage. A warm welcome is always extended in the licensed Vats Bar, which is open lunchtime and in the evening. As its name suggests, the Vats Bar has been created out of the brewery's fermentation room where the cedar-wood vats provide unique seating for that quiet drink. Not everybody can boast that they have had a drink *in* a vat.

The **Cherry Tree,** 24 Finkle St. (tel. 0539/20547), is a tuck-away restaurant that's worth the search to find. Ian English (how British can your name get?) runs this friendly and atmospheric 120-seat establishment, serving from 10 a.m. to 8 p.m. seven days a week. Appetizers are limited and the usual sort, but the fish dishes include a goodly assortment of scampi, rainbow trout, halibut, plaice, and haddock. The meat and poultry salads are made to order and are quite fine, especially the roast beef. He offers savory lunches and dinners from £6 ($9). For lighter appetites, snacks such as hamburgers or the local Cumberland sausages are served.

Outside Kendal

Garnett House Farm, at Burneside (tel. 0539/24542), is a working farm with a large dairy herd and many sheep grazing the fells. The farmhouse dates from the 15th century, and its walls are thick, the beams low, and the windows deep set. Guests enjoy an oak-paneled sitting room, and in a pleasant dining room Mrs. Beaty serves large country meals, using home-grown produce and fresh vegetables. One of the bedrooms is in the bell tower (the bell, once tolled to call farmhands to meals, is long gone). All have electric heat, hot and cold running water, and shaver points. The cost is from £9 ($13.50) per person nightly, including breakfast, and the set dinner goes for £3.75 ($5.63).

2. Windermere

The grandest of the lakes is Windermere, the largest one in England, whose shores wash up against the town of Bowness, with Windermere in close reach. Both of these resorts lie on the eastern shore of the lake. A ferry service connects Hawkshead and Bowness. Windermere, the resort, is the end of the railway line. From either town, you can climb up **Orrest Head** in less than an hour for a panoramic view of England's lakeland. From that vantage point, you can even see **Scafell Pike,** the peak pinnacle in all of England, which rises to a height of 3,210 feet.

Windermere Steamboat Museum, Rayrigg Road (tel. 09662/5565), is one of the most delightful working museums it has been my lot to visit for many years. It was founded and developed by George Pattinson, who discovered the fascination of steam many years ago and now has probably the best and most comprehensive collection of steamboats in the country. The wet boatsheds house some dozen boats, including the veteran *Dolly,* probably the oldest mechanically powered boat in the world, dating from around 1850. It was raised from the lake bed in the early 1960s and was run for several years with the original boiler and steambox.

Also displayed is the *Espérance,* an iron steam yacht registered with Lloyds in 1869, as well as many elegant Victorian steamlaunches and ferryboats. Attached to the boathouses is the speedboat *Jane,* dating from 1938, the first glider-plane to take off from the water in 1943, and the hydroplane racer *Cookie*—all jostling Beatrix Potter's rowing boat and other Lakeland craft for position.

There's a small shop selling books, postcards, and souvenirs of historic craft. The

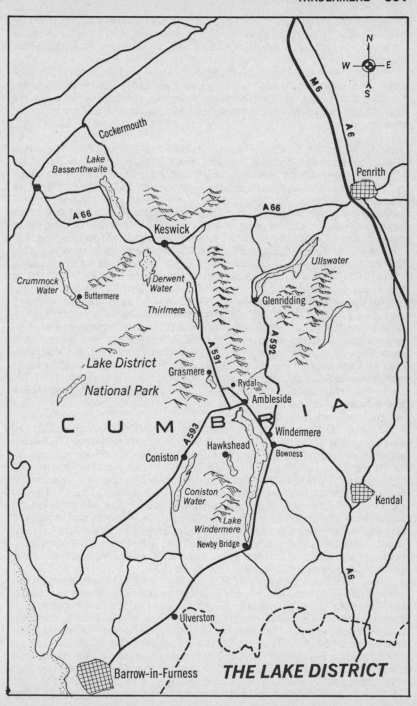

N
W — E
S

Cockermouth

Lake Bassenthwaite

M 6

A 6

Penrith

A 66

Crummock Water

Buttermere

Derwent Water

Keswick

A 66

Thirlmere

Ullswater

Glenridding

A 591

A 592

Lake District

National Park

Grasmere

Rydal

Ambleside

C U M B R I A

A 593

Windermere

Hawkshead

Bowness

Coniston

Kendal

Coniston Water

Lake Windermere

Newby Bridge

A 6

Ulverston

Barrow-in-Furness

THE LAKE DISTRICT

museum can be visited from 10 a.m. to 5 p.m. for an admission of £1.50 ($2.25) for adults and 85p ($1.28) for children. The *Osprey* is regularly in steam, and visitors can make a 40-minute trip on the lake at £1.95 ($2.93) for adults and £1.40 ($2.10) for children.

It's also possible to make trips on Ullswater and on Coniston, and there is regular steamer service around Windermere, the largest of the lakes, which serves the outlying villages as well as operating for visitors in summer. Nigel Dalziel is curator. He retired there in recent times, and is totally absorbed in the craft and concept of the museum.

WHERE TO STAY: About a ten-minute walk from the railway station and the shops, **Willowsmere Hotel,** Ambleside Road (tel. 09662/3575), is a handsome Edwardian stone hotel along the A591. Willowsmere is owned by David F. Scott, who is assisted by his daughter, Heather, the fifth generation of the Scott family to be catering in the Lake District. Heather's husband, Alan Cook, also helps run the business. Regular guests say that it is most appropriate that Heather's married name is now Cook, as her father receives many glowing compliments on her culinary abilities. The best way to stay here is to request the dinner and B&B rate of £24.50 ($36.75) per person nightly. The evening meal is a well-prepared four-courser. Bedrooms contain hot and cold running water, shaver points, and unmetered heat. For just B&B, expect a rate ranging from £15.25 ($22.88). Guests gather at night to socialize and watch the "telly." If you want to go on a lakeside ramble the next day, Heather will pack you a lunch.

Hideaway Hotel, Phoenix Way (tel. 09662/3070). Tim and Jackie Harper own this typical Lakeland house surrounded by neat lawns where tea is served on balmy summer evenings. The house is solid and comfortable, with a pleasant bar with an open fire and oak settles, along with a cheerful sitting room and an attractive dining room. The bedrooms are brightly and lightly decorated. Dinner, bed, and breakfast in a room with private bath and toilet, color TV, radio, and tea- and coffee-making equipment, costs from £25 ($37.50) per person. The hotel has a Switzerland-trained chef and has received awards many times for its cuisine, which includes roast meats, game pies, local trout, homemade soups, and exciting desserts. Breakfasts include Cumberland sausage, black pudding, and haggis.

Prospect House Guest House, High Street (tel. 09662/4205), is an old Lakeland stone house right in the center of town. It's a family home where Marjorie Clarke manages to offer a warm welcome to guests while lovingly dealing with her husband, Albert, and her daughters. All her rooms are centrally heated and contain hot and cold running water, TV, and tea- or coffee-making facilities. There is a small dining room, plus a comfortable lounge with color TV and video. Marjorie and Albert had always spent holidays in the Lake District, and now that they live here, are only too anxious to pass on local information on walking, riding, and sailing. Open throughout the year, their guesthouse charges from £9 ($13.50) per night for a bed and a large Lakeland breakfast. Packed lunches can be arranged, and you can return to a well-cooked meal, beginning with soup and followed by perhaps a braised steak or coq au vin, along with a dessert, at a cost of £6 ($9) per person, including VAT.

Rockside Guest House, Ambleside Road (tel. 09662/5343), is run by Neville and Mavis Fowles, who came to live in this area with their two daughters several years ago, thus achieving their ambition to live in "the most beautiful corner of England." They have since made Rockside one of the best establishments for B&B in the area. It is a licensed guesthouse full of character, offering singles, twins, doubles, and family rooms from £9.50 ($14.25) to £15.50 ($23.25) per person for B&B. The standard rooms have hot and cold running water basins, while those listed as "top choice" contain private showers and toilets, color TV, and beverage-making facilities. The house is centrally heated. Guests can choose from among six breakfasts big enough to start the day well whether you are walking or driving around the area. At the rear of the house is a car park for 12 vehicles, but Rockside is only two minutes' walk from the bus, train, or village of Windermere.

The Waverly, College Road (tel. 09662/5026), built in 1870, retains much of its Victorian charm as a hotel on a quiet road near the shops of Windermere, as well as the bus routes and train station. The comfortable bedrooms, all with private baths, color TV, and beverage-making facilities, are rented by the owners of Waverly, Jack and Judith Ashcroft, for £12.50 ($18.75) per person for B&B, VAT included. The hotel has its own car park.

Kenilworth Guest House, Holly Road (tel. 09662/4004). Brian and Jean Gosling offer a good bargain in a house noted for its cleanliness and comfort. Centrally heated, it has pleasant bedrooms, each with hot and cold running water. They receive guests March to October, charging them only £9 ($13.50) per person nightly for B&B. An informal atmosphere prevails. Prices include a full Lake Country breakfast, and an evening meal can be arranged upon request.

Townend House (tel. 0966/32172) lies in the little village of Troutbeck, about three miles north of Windermere. This building was previously a farmhouse, built of Lakeland stone in 1889. The two guest rooms have views of the valley. Mrs. A.E. Wilson charges £8.50 ($18.75) per person for B&B, and that's a full English breakfast. The house is approached from the A591 road at Troutbeck Bridge, about a mile past Windermere, where the village road turns only to the right. Townend House is not to be confused with "Townend" National Trust property nor with Townend Farm, nearby.

WHERE TO EAT: In the center of town, **Millers Restaurant,** 31-33 Crescent Rd. (tel. 09662/3877), has a simple tea-room decor and offers good, inexpensive food. Special lunches and dinners are offered for £4 ($6), including such dishes as homemade steak-and-kidney pie, two vegetables, new potatoes, and a choice of dessert. A three-course fish dinner is featured from £6 ($9). When available, char, a fish from Lake Windermere, is offered. The restaurant is owned and run by Mr. Lord, who is responsible for the carefully prepared, traditional dishes. It's best to go from noon to 9 p.m.

Village Restaurant, Victoria Street (tel. 09662/3429), stands near the rail station at Cross Street. The decor is pleasant and inviting, and fresh, natural flavors are the hallmark of the kitchen of this place. Lunches cost from £5 ($7.50), but in the evening the fare and the price are better, with dinners from £8 ($12). You are likely to be tempted by such selections as sautéed chicken chasseur, burgundy beef, grilled lake trout, or fishermen's pie. It is open in summer from 11:30 a.m. to 10 p.m., in the spring and fall from 11:30 a.m. to 12:30 p.m., and in winter only for dinner from 5 to 10 p.m. It is also closed on Monday in winter.

Gibbys, 43 Crescent Rd. (tel. 09662/5001), in the heart of the resort, is suitable for simple meals if you're looking for low prices. It is especially popular with traveling families, who can enjoy its food from March to November. Hours are 11:30 a.m. to 2:30 p.m. and 5:30 to 10 p.m. daily. Built in a mock Tudor style, the restaurant serves special dinners for ($9) and up. Meals include roast chicken, sirloin steak, and rainbow trout.

BOWNESS-ON-WINDERMERE: A short way south of Windermere, on Bowness Bay of the lake, the attractive town of Bowness has some interesting old architecture. This has been an important center for boating and fishing for a long time, and you can rent boats of all descriptions to explore the lake.

Lindeth Howe, Storrs Park (tel. 09662/5759), is a country house hotel in a superb position above Lake Windermere, standing in six acres of lovely grounds. The house, part stone and part red brick with a roof of green Westmorland slate, was built for a wealthy mill-owner in 1879, but its most famous owner was Beatrix Potter who installed her mother here while she lived across the lake at Sawrey. The present owners, Eileen and Clive Baxter, have furnished it in elegant style and offer 14 bedrooms, most of which have lake views. They are comfortably furnished, with private baths or showers, color TV, in-house movies, beverage-making facilities, and central heating. Two of them have handsome four-poster beds. Prices for B&B are from £19 ($28.50) to £22 ($33) per person, with half board costing from £27.50 ($41.25) to £31.50 ($47.25) per person. The dining room has two deep bay windows overlooking the lake. The lounge contains a brick fireplace with solid oak mantel set in an oak-framed inglenook.

Lindeth Fell Hotel, ½ mile south of Bowness on the Lyth Valley (tel. 09662/3286), high above the town and the lake, is a traditional large Lakeland house of stone and brick, with many of its rooms overlooking the handsome gardens and the lake. The owners, the Kennedys, run the place more like a country house than a hotel, achieving an atmosphere of homey comfort in pleasingly furnished surroundings. For B&B, they charge from £22 ($33) per person nightly, the price going up to from £30 ($45) per person for dinner, bed, and breakfast. All 15 bedrooms have private baths or showers, color TV, and beverage-making facilities. Prices include VAT. The cooking is under the supervision of Diana Kennedy and a resident chef, with local produce used when possible to prepare a variety of Lakeland and traditional English dishes. In pursuit of the country house atmosphere, the Kennedys offer tennis, croquet, and putting on the lawn, as well as a private tarn for fishing.

Belsfield Guest House, 4 Belsfield Terrace, Kendal Road (tel. 09662/5823), is a small, family-style guesthouse near the lake. It's owned by Joan and Jack Jackson, who have modernized the house. Their welcome is personalized, and they offer cleanliness and a friendly atmosphere. Their B&B rate is from £10 ($15) to £12 ($18) per person per night, depending on the facilities and the season. Some units have showers, and all have color TV. The Jacksons offer family rooms, doubles, and twins, receiving guests from Easter week until November.

Craig Foot Country House Hotel, Lake Road (tel. 09662/3902), is one of the stately homes in the area, dating from 1848 when it was built for a retired admiral. Standing on its own grounds, this Lake Country house opens onto views of the lake and the mountains in the distance. Most of its pleasantly furnished and comfortable bedrooms have private baths. The resident proprietors, Audrey and Gordon Shore, charge £29 ($43.50) per person per night for dinner, bed, and a full English breakfast. All accommodations have TV and hot drink facilities. Most have views of the lake.

LAKE DISTRICT TOURS: For a rewarding visit to this area, **Mountain Goat Holidays,** Victoria Street, Windermere (tel. 09662/5161), offers two types of holidays in the Lake District, based in Windermere and Keswick: Touring Holidays or, for the more energetic, the Valley or Mountain Walking Holidays.

Touring Holidays start at approximately £168 ($252) per week in guesthouses going up to about £236 ($354) per week in hotels. The price includes dinner, bed, a full English breakfast, and five Mountain Goat tours, plus such other extras as a welcome drink, transfers to and from the station, a welcome pack, and comprehensive insurance.

Walking Holidays start at about £168 ($252), rising to about £236 ($354), and include seven nights of half board in a hotel or guesthouse and four full-day walks with a guide. Introductory mountain walking weeks and gentle walking for over 55s are also available, as well as short breaks for two nights and up costing from £50 ($75).

Mountain Goat Tours, available on a day-to-day basis, can be bought on the spot at the Mountain Goat offices in Windermere and Keswick. Most of the full-day and half-day tours are in minibuses seating 12 to 16 persons, with fully qualified driver/guides. Prices start at £6.50 ($9.75) for a half-day tour, going up to £12 ($18) for a full-day tour. Half-day picnic tours cost £12 ($18), including the picnic.

Mountain Goat/British Rail Short Break to the Lakes is a package that can be purchased from any British Rail Travel Centre in London, in the south of England, and in Manchester. The price, from £76.50 ($114.75), includes two nights' B&B in a guesthouse or hotel, a cruise on Lake Windermere, a full-day Mountain Goat Tour, a taxi transfer from the station to your hotel and your train fare.

3. Ambleside

A good and idyllic retreat, Ambleside is one of the major centers of the Lake District, attracting pony-trekkers, fell-hikers, and rock-scalers. The charms are here all year, even in late autumn when it's fashionable to sport a mackintosh. Ambleside is superbly perched, at the top of Lake Windermere. Traditions are entrenched, especially at the Rushbearing Festival, an annual event.

WHERE TO STAY: Nestled in the sheltered valley of the Rothay, the **Rothay Garth Hotel,** Rothay Road (tel. 0966/32217), on the edge of Ambleside, is an elegant, century-old country house set in beautiful gardens. All bedrooms are tastefully decorated, warm, and comfortable, with private baths, color TV, beverage-making facilities, and hair dryers. Doreen and David Clark charge £28.50 ($42.75) per person for dinner, bed, and breakfast, or £22 ($33) per person for B&B. Fresh flowers are arranged throughout the hotel daily, and guests can enjoy a sunny garden room or the cozy lounge with its seasonal log fire. A wide choice of connoisseur bar lunches are served all year in the Loughrigg Bar. The special Ploughman's Lunch has received much praise. The hotel's 20-foot, fixed-keel yacht, sailboard, and canoe can be rented. Tennis courts, a pitch and putt golf area, and a croquet lawn are adjacent to the hotel. Laundry and ironing facilities are available.

Crow How Hotel, Rydal Road (tel. 0966/32193), along a private drive off the A591 north of Ambleside, is only a few minutes' walk from Rydal water. This was originally a large farmhouse of Lakeland stone. The proprietors, Mark and Glenise Heywood, offer bedrooms with a variety of plumbing, some with private baths and toilets and some with only hot and cold water basins. Charges are from £12 ($18) to £13 ($19.50) per person for B&B in bathless accommodations, from £15 ($22.50) to £16 ($24) per person in units with bath, the higher prices charged in summer. All the bedrooms have color TV, beverage-making facilities, and controllable heaters, while the public rooms are centrally heated. The hotel has a large guest lounge, a small but well-stocked bar, and two acres of gardens.

Queens Hotel, Market Place (tel. 0966/32206), in the heart of the resort, is an old-fashioned and long-established hotel, a family-run place where guests are housed and fed very well. The hotel rents out 30 comfortably furnished bedrooms, 23 of which contain private baths. The charge is £15 ($22.50) per person for a bed and full English breakfast. With a private bath or shower, there is a supplement of £2.50 ($3.75) per person. Since the hotel has two fully licensed bars and restaurants, you may want to stay here on half-board terms, costing from £25 ($37.50) per person nightly. The food is good and hearty, the portions generous. The Queens is open year round and is centrally heated in the winter.

Oaklands, Millans Park (tel. 0966/32525), is a country house hotel run by Hilary A. Prickett. In a quiet setting in pleasant grounds away from the main roads, it is only two minutes' walk from the center of town. The centrally heated hotel has an intimate cocktail bar, separate dining room, spacious lounge where an open fire blazes on cool nights, and ample parking. The bright, comfortable bedrooms all have color TV and hot beverage-making facilities. Most of them have private baths. They rent for £9.50 ($14.25) to £11.50 ($17.25) for B&B in a single, from £9.50 ($14.25) to £20 ($30) per person in a double. For extra luxury, ask for the "Special Occasion" room, with a large, complete bath and a four-poster bed. An excellent four-course dinner is served.

On the Outskirts

The **Britannia Inn,** at Elterwater (tel. 0966/210), just off the B5343 west of Ambleside, is a 400-year-old traditional village inn adjoining the green in the unspoiled village of Elterwater. Views from the inn are over the meadows to the three tarns making up Elterwater (lake of the swan) and the fells beyond. Bar meals are served in the cozy bar where a log fire blazes in cool weather. David Fry, the innkeeper, rents ten well-appointed bedrooms, all with hot and cold water basins and central heating radiators, as well as beverage-making facilities and hair dryers. He charges £17.25 ($25.88) per person for a bed and a full English breakfast in high season, £1 ($1.50) less at other times of year. Evening meals at £10 ($15) are served in a Victorian dining room. The inn receives guests all year except Christmas. Guests enjoy staying in the whitewashed building, with its low-beamed ceilings, stone fireplaces, and country bedrooms.

WHERE TO DINE: In the center of town, **Jacaranda Restaurant,** Compston Road (tel. 0966/32430), with seating for 60 persons, provides traditional English home cooking. A typical three-course meal could include corn on the cob, roast chicken in red wine sauce, and a fruit cheesecake dessert, costing from £5 ($7.50). The restaurant serves from 5 to 9 p.m.

Zeffirellis, Compston Road (tel. 0966/33845), is a drinking, dining, shopping, movie, and café complex right near the center of town. During the day you might enjoy its Garden Room downstairs or a pizzeria upstairs, ordering a selection of freshly made pastas or wheatmeal and sesame seed pizzas. A meal costs from £5 ($7.50). The Garden Room is open from 10 a.m. to 5:30 p.m., and the pizzeria and restaurant serves noon to 3 p.m. and 5 to 9:45 p.m. At night, against a Japanese art deco backdrop in the restaurant and pizzeria, you can order a three-course candlelit dinner for £8.95 ($13.43). There is also a selection of French and Italian wines.

Apple Pie Eating House, Rydal Road (tel. 0966/33679), makes its own apple pie, and does so exceedingly well, a thick slice with fresh cream. The cooks make very good quiches, including the Lorraine classic. Everything tastes better with their freshly ground coffee with cream. The homemade meat pies are also recommended. Lunches cost from £5 ($7.50). A licensed restaurant is upstairs, and out back there's a little terrace. The eating house is also a bakery, and the quality of the baking is so good you may want to take away with you some cakes, pastries, or scones. Hours are 9 a.m. to 5:30 p.m. weekdays, 10 a.m. to 5:30 p.m. on Sunday. Closed in November.

Harvest Wholefood Vegetarian Restaurant, Compston Road (tel. 0966/33151), offers homemade fare, far better than some of the bland vegetarian restaurants opening in England. The home-cooking is pure and simple, and fresh produce is used. Meals, eaten at simple, pine-sheathed tables, cost around £5 ($7.50). The restaurant is open from 10:30 a.m. to noon for morning coffee, noon to 2:30 p.m. for lunch, and 4 to 8:30 p.m. for dinner.

4. Rydal

Between Ambleside (the top of Lake Windermere) and Wordsworth's former retreat at Grasmere is Rydal, a small village on one of the smallest lakes, Rydal Water. **Rydal Mount** (tel. 0966/33002) was the home of William Wordsworth from 1813 until his death in 1850. Part of the house was built as a farmer's lake cottage around 1575. A descendant of Wordsworth's still owns the property, now a museum, and some family portraits are displayed, along with mementos and books. It is open daily from 10 a.m. to 5 p.m. March to October, daily except Thursday from 10 a.m. to 4 p.m. November to February. Admission is £1.50 ($2.25) for adults, 50p (75¢) for children 5 to 16.

The village of Rydal is noted for its sheep-dog trials at the end of summer.

WHERE TO STAY: Beside the roadway between Ambleside and Grasmere, **Rydal Lodge** (tel. 0966/33208) is a good center for walking and touring the whole of the Lake District. The Rothay River runs beside the pleasant and secluded gardens; and Rydal Water, a beautiful lake, is at the end of the garden. Mr. and Mrs. Haughan and family provide meals of high quality, and the menus are well planned. Strawberries and other fruit from the garden are provided in season, and the lodge has a license to serve wine with main meals. The bedrooms are equipped with hot and cold running water, shaving points, electric blankets, heaters, and innerspring mattresses. There are eight bedrooms as well as a private car park. Terms are from £15 ($22.50) for B&B, with dinner costing from £9 ($13.50), including VAT. Rydal Lodge is of historical interest. Matthew Arnold stayed here, and it is connected with Harriet Martineau. The older part of the house was an inn in 1655.

Nab Cottage (tel. 09665/311) is a 300-year-old cottage whose architectural facade is protected by the local building commission. That pleases the owners, Tim and Liz Melling, who maintain seven rooms for paying guests. None of the accommodations contains a private bath, but the shared facilities are adequate. The cottage, dating from 1702, was once the residence of Hartley Coleridge, son of the famous poet, Samuel Taylor Coleridge. The writer, Thomas De Quincey, was also a resident. The cottage is well situated on the shore of Rydal Water, about two miles outside of Grasmere, with views of the lake from many of the bedroom windows. The Mellings charge £11 ($16.50) for B&B, from £17.50 ($26.25) for a well-prepared half board. Much of the original character remains in the in-house pub, where a log fire wards off the cold-weather chill.

5. Grasmere

Grasmere, on the lake that bears its name, was the home of Wordsworth from 1799 to 1813. During his most creative years, the nature poet lived at Dove Cottage, along with his sister, Dorothy, known for her Grasmere Journals. Visitors are given a guided tour around the cottage and the garden which William and Dorothy cultivated. Wordsworth died in the spring of 1850, and was buried in the graveyard of the village church at Grasmere. The other famous tenant of Dove Cottage was Thomas De Quincey *(Confessions of an English Opium Eater)*, who lived there from 1808 to 1835. The house has belonged to the Dove Cottage Trust and has been open to the public since 1891. Nearby is the Grasmere and Wordsworth Museum, with displays of treasures, manuscripts, books, paintings, drawings, photographs, and personalia. There are also special exhibitions throughout the year. Admission to both cottage and museum is £2.50 ($3.75) for adults, £1 ($1.50) for children. They are open April to September from 9:30 a.m. to 5:30 p.m. weekdays, 11 a.m. to 5:30 p.m. Sunday. October to March, weekday hours are 10 a.m. to 4:30 p.m., Sunday from 11 a.m. to 4:30 p.m. Closed in November. For more information, telephone 09665/544.

WHERE TO STAY: An old Lakeland house in the center of town, the **Moss Grove Hotel** (tel. 09665/251), is owned and run by Ken and Shirley Wood. Ken deals with the reception and reservations, and he's a man who always remembers your name, greeting you with a genuine and cheery "good morning." Shirley does the cooking. Ken used to work for a brewery, and she is a physicist. Both loved the area and came here more than a decade ago. They spend at least one day a week walking in their beloved hills and will take guests with them and will advise on walks and special scenery to be viewed. Ken is white-bearded and lean from leading an outdoor life, and his gentle eyes reflect a relaxed attitude to life. The hotel is well furnished and warm. Rooms, all with color TV, costs from £13.50 ($20.25) per person bathless to £16.50 ($24.75) per person with shower and toilet, including VAT and a large, wholesome Lakeland breakfast. There are two lounges, one with TV, the other with a small bar. Dinner during the week is a well-cooked meal with a roast joint or poultry, fresh vegetable, and on Sunday, a cold buffet including various cold meats, some 14 choices of salad, and a quiche, followed by dessert or cheese. Such a meal costs £8.50 ($12.75).

How Foot Lodge at Town End (tel. 09665/366). The house, which once belonged to Wordsworth's friends, lies just along the road from Dove Cottage and Rydal Mount. The bedrooms all have private bath, and cost from £15 ($22.50) to £17 ($25.50) per person for B&B. The country house lounges have open fires, comfortable chairs, and some antiques. An evening meal costs around £10 ($15).

Craigside House (tel. 09665/292), is set in 1½ acres of garden, with views over the lake to the hills beyond. It's just above Dove Cottage, where Wordsworth lived. It was he who pointed out this site to the people who agreed with him that this was an ideal location for a house and built Craigside back in 1839. Ken and Shirley Wood, who operate the Moss Grove Hotel (previewed above), run this guesthouse as well, offering rooms with bath and breakfast from £15 ($22.50) per person. One of the rooms has a Hepplewhite four-poster bed.

Ryelands (tel. 09665/652) is a recently opened guesthouse in a 19th-century building of Lakeland stone, in a tranquil spot looking south down the valley. Surrounding gardens and an adjacent paddock provide privacy and ample parking. The owners, Mr. and Mrs. Le Cornu, are interesting people with discriminating taste. The house is light, airy, and welcoming. The comfortable bedrooms rent for £14.50 ($21.75) to £17.50 ($26.25) per person for B&B in a shared double- or twin-bedded room, £24.50 ($36.75) to £30 ($45) for one person using a double room for single occupancy. The breakfast room is a calm oasis in which to begin the day. A traditional English breakfast is offered, but if you prefer, you can have a vegetarian meal.

Titteringdales, Rye Lane (tel. 09665/439), is a small, private guesthouse run by Edwin and Vera Watson. Away from traffic noise, it opens onto views of Silverhow, Fairfield, and Helm Crag. Surrounded by its own gardens, the house is well run and comfortable, with full central heating. The Watsons have a family room, and children sharing accommodations with their parents are given one-third reductions in prices. The owners take pride in the English home-cookery and personal service, trying and succeeding in achieving that home-away-from-home appeal. B&B costs from £12.50 ($18.75) per night, and an evening meal is provided for another £7 ($10.50). Packed lunches and afternoon tea are available on request.

Silver Lea, Easedale Road (tel. 09665/657), is a small, well-run guesthouse, operated by Ken and Olive Smith. The location is about a three-minute walk from the heart of Grasmere. Their stone house is well kept, and their rooms are comfortable, opening onto mountain views. Some of the accommodations have their own bath and toilet. The rate is from £15.50 ($23.25) to £17 ($25.50) per person nightly for dinner, bed, and breakfast in a double, £17 ($25.50) for single occupancy. Guests take delight in the Lakeland cookery of Mrs. Smith, who receives visitors from February to November.

The **Grasmere Hotel,** on Broadgate (tel. 09665/277). The main feature of this Lakeland hotel is the large, modern dining room at the rear where Ian and Annette Mansie provide mouthwatering evening meals for their guests. Prettily decorated tables cluster around the central buffet on which desserts are displayed along with a huge slate cheeseboard. Both Ian and Annette do the cooking, and their green-and-white kitchen is almost as popular a meeting place for guests as is the sitting room and bar. The four-course meals include such delectable dishes as lamb stuffed with apricots, celery, and walnuts. Upstairs, the pleasantly furnished bedrooms contain private bath or showers, color TV, radios, and direct-dial phones. Dinner, bed, and a full breakfast ranges from £26 ($39) to £32 ($48) per person.

WHERE TO EAT: A cheerful, friendly place, the **Cumbria Carvery** (tel. 09665/515) offers simple food at reasonable prices. They serve some Greek specials but mainly fish, grills, and roasts. Meals cost around £6.50 ($9.75). A snack menu is served from 11:30 a.m. to 3:30 p.m. and dinners from 6 to 10 p.m. The restaurant is under the warm supervision of Elaine and Louis Diomedous, who open it from Easter to mid-November.

Mykonos Taverna, Stock Lane (tel. 09665/515), is also owned by Louis Diomedous, owner of the Cumbria Carvery (above). This small Greek restaurant is the answer to Louis's wish to bring real Greek food and ambience to the English Lake District. A complete opposite to the Carvery, the taverna is small and intimate, with rough plaster walls, wheelback chairs, and warm red table linen. Appetizers include taramasalata and calamaris served with pita bread. Moussaka is good here, as is the aselia, pork marinated in wine served with potatoes and Greek salad. Try the traditional Greek meal of mezdes, with a choice of more than 30 small dishes, for £8 ($12). Louis guarantees you'll never eat it all. There's a piano player nightly except Sunday. The restaurant is open Easter to November seven days a week from 6 to 10:30 p.m.

The **Coffee Bean** on Red Lion Square (tel. 09665/234), right in the center of Grasmere, offers soups, sandwiches (toasted or not), coffee, tea, chocolate, pastries, pies, and cookies. Food can be eaten there or taken away. They will fill flasks of hot tea or coffee for you. Everything is freshly made and much is home-baked. Light meals cost from £2.80 ($4.20). It's open from 9 a.m. to 5:30 p.m. daily in summer, from 10 a.m. to 4 p.m. on Saturday and Saturday only, from November to mid-March.

6. Hawkshead and Coniston

Discover for yourself the village of Hawkshead, with its 15th-century grammar school where Wordsworth went to school for eight years (he carved his name on a desk that still remains). Near Hawkshead, in the vicinity of Esthwaite Water, is the 17th-century **Hill Top Farm,** former home of Beatrix Potter, the author of the Peter Rabbit books, who died during World War II.

At Coniston, four miles away from Hawkshead, you can visit the village famously associated with John Ruskin. Coniston is a good base for rock climbing. The Coniston "Old Man" towers in the background at 2,633 feet, giving mountain climbers one of the finest views of the Lake District.

John Ruskin, poet, artist, and critic, was one of the great figures of the Victorian age and a prophet of social reform, inspiring such diverse men as Proust, Frank Lloyd Wright, and Gandhi. He moved to his home, **Brantwood** (tel. 0966/41396), on the east side of Coniston Water in 1872 and lived there until his death in 1900. The house today is open for visitors to view much Ruskiniana, including some 175 pictures by him. Also displayed are his coach and boat, the *Jumping Jenny*.

An exhibition illustrating the work of W. J. Linton is laid out in his old printing room. Linton was born in England in 1812 and died at New Haven, Connecticut, in 1897. Well known as a wood engraver and for his private press, he lived at Brantwood, where he established his printing business in 1853. He published *The English Republic,* a newspaper and review, before emigrating to America in 1866, where he set up his printing press in 1870. The house is owned and managed by the Education Trust, a self-supporting registered charity. It is open daily from mid-March to mid-November and Wednesday to Sunday in winter, from 11 a.m. to 5:30 p.m. Admission is £1.50 ($2.25) for adults and 75p ($1.13) for children, with a family ticket costing £4 ($6). Part of the 250-acre estate is also open as a nature trail, costing 50p (75¢) for adults, 35p (53¢) for children, if the walk is taken separate from a visit to the house. The Brantwood Stables, designed by Ruskin, have been converted into a tea room and licensed restaurant, the Proserpina Gallery.

There is also the **Ruskin Museum** (tel. 0996/41387), where you can see the personal possessions and relics, sketchbooks, letters, and a collection of mineral rocks collected by Ruskin. It's open April to the end of October from 9:30 a.m. to dusk. Admission is 30p (45¢).

Literary fans may want to pay a pilgrimage to the graveyard of the village church, where Ruskin was buried; his family turned down a chance to have him interred at Westminster Abbey.

The National Trust steam yacht *Gondola*, High Waterhead, Coniston (tel. 0966/41288), will take you on a leisurely **sail on the lake** in old-world comfort, with the added pleasure that travel on a steamboat is comparatively silent. This original steam yacht, launched in 1859, was in constant service on Lake Coniston until 1937. She was laid up until 1980, when she was restored to her full Victorian splendor and entered public service once more. She plies the waters four or five times a day between Coniston Pier and Park-a-Moor from April to the end of October. Passage costs £2 ($3) one way, £3 ($4.50) for a round trip. Family tickets sell for £8.50 ($12.75).

HOTELS IN HAWKSHEAD: Warming the Lake District is the **Ivy House Hotel** (tel. 09666/204), a friendly Georgian house. It's an ideal headquarters from which to branch out for visits on Lake Windermere. The B&B rate ranges from £19.50 ($29.25) to £21.75 ($32.63) per person daily. About half of the 12 rooms rented out by David and Jane Vaughan have private baths. Because of their charming house and lovely situation, they are heavily booked, so it's imperative that you reserve well in advance. Some other points worth noting: All the rooms are centrally heated and have hot and cold water basins. A modern, motel-type annex, with unrestricted electric heating, handles overflow guests. The hotel is known for its good English cookery, including roast turkey with sage and onion stuffing, boiled silverside of beef served with dumplings, and a typical dessert such as blackberry and apple pie with custard. The house is open March to the end of October only. Log fires blaze in the lounge in early and late seasons.

Kings Arms, The Square (tel. 09666/372), is a crooked-fronted old coaching inn in the middle of the village, with leaded windows and sloping roofs. Inside, low beams and whitewashed walls complete the picture, along with a friendly bar patronized by the locals. There is also a neat buttery, and in the rear, a room for bar games. Rosalie Johnson, who runs the inn, offers grills and steaks at mealtimes, and also experiments on the locals with national evenings, including Indian, Oriental, or Greek fare. Dinners start at £8 ($12). A total of six bedrooms, three with private bath, is rented out, a bed and Cumbrian breakfast costing from £13 ($19.50) to £16.50 ($24.75) per person, depending on the plumbing.

On the outskirts, **Field Head House** at Outgate (tel. 09666/240) is a bit hard to find but worth the search. From Hawkshead, take the Ambleside road (B5286), then take the second turning on the left, a mile from Hawkshead (signposted Field Head). After about a quarter of a mile, Field Head is on your right. Once there, you will be welcomed by the Dutch-born owners, Eeke and Bob van Gulik, to this marvelous old Lake District home, whose origins go back to the 1600s when it was built as a hunting lodge for a duke. A friend of William Wordsworth, the artist John Harden lived in this house for about a decade from 1834. On its own six acres of wooded grounds and gardens, Field House offers eight very different accommodations, most with private bath. Accommodations are homelike and well appointed, with B&B rates going from £18 ($27) to £23 ($34.50) per person.

Even if you can't stay here, you might call and see if you can have dinner with them, as their food is considered the best in the area. From 7:30 to 9 p.m., a superb five-course dinner is served for £12.50 ($18.75). The menu changes every night, but a typical meal might include a pear and Stilton savory, mushroom soup, roast shoulder of venison with five different fresh vegetables (often from their own garden), English cheese, and peaches and cream, followed by coffee.

EATING AND DRINKING IN HAWKSHEAD: The most famous pub in the area is **Queens Head** (tel. 09666/271), in the center of this celebrated village. It's really more an inn than a pub, as it also rents out bedrooms. Behind a mock black-and-white timbered facade, it is a 17th-century structure of character, serving Hartley's Ulverston beer from the wood, a local favorite brew. Bar lunches, costing from £3.50 ($5.25), are served from noon to 2 p.m. Or else you can enjoy à la carte dinners from 7 to 9 p.m. for £8 ($12). Try a sizzling sirloin steak, grilled local rainbow trout, or perhaps pheasant in casserole. Nine comfortably old-fashioned bedrooms are rented, costing £17 ($25.50) in a single, £27 ($40.50) in a double.

AN INN AT CONISTON: The most popular, traditional, and attractive pub, restaurant, and hotel in this Lakeland village is the **Coniston Sun Hotel** (tel. 05394/412248). In reality, it is a country house hotel of much character, dating from 1902, although the inn attached to it is from the 16th century. Standing on its own beautiful grounds above the village, it lies at the foot of "Coniston Old Man." Donald Campbell made this place his headquarters during his attempt on the world water speed record. Each of the 11 bedrooms is decorated with style and flair, and four of them contain four-posters. Each unit also has a private bath, color TV, and drink-making facilities. It's best to book in here on half-board terms, costing £36.50 ($54.75) per person nightly. Fresh local produce is used whenever possible in the candlelit restaurant. Log fires take the chill off a winter evening, and guests relax informally in the lounge which is like a library. Many sports can be arranged.

A HOTEL AT FAR SAWREY: A welcoming old country inn, **The Sawrey Hotel,** Far Sawrey, near Ambleside (tel. 09662/3425), is in the village where Beatrix Potter lived the happiest years of her life. The bars are well patronized by locals and travelers alike, and there is a good range of bar food. A five-course meal in the restaurant costs from £8.50 ($12.75). Most bedrooms have color TV, phone, and some private facilities, at rates ranging from £12.95 ($19.43) to £14.75 ($22.13) per person, including a large cooked breakfast. David Brayshaw is your host.

A good headquarters for touring the northern Lake District is:

7. Keswick

Lying 22 miles north of Windermere, Keswick opens onto Derwentwater, one of the loveliest lakes in the district. Robert Southey, poet laureate, lived for four decades at Greta Hall, and was buried at Crosthwaite Church. Coleridge lived there too, depending on Southey for financial aid. Sir Hugh Walpole, the novelist, in a different era also resided near Keswick.

Keswick is the natural geographical starting point for car tours and walks of exploration in the northern Lake District, including the John Peel country to the north of Skiddaw (quiet and little known), Borrowdale, Buttermere, and Crummock Water, as well as Bassenthwaite, Thirlmere, and Ullswater.

And you too, following in the footpaths of Charles Lamb and Shelley, will seek out an accommodation.

WHERE TO STAY: Known to Southey and Coleridge, the **George Hotel,** St. John Street (tel. 07687/72076), is a 400-year-old coaching inn, the oldest inn in town, once known as the George & Dragon. Still offering unvarnished charm, it lies in the middle of town, near the market square, which comes alive on Saturday morning. For B&B, guests are charged £15 ($22.50) per person, plus another £8 ($12) for dinner. The rooms are well appointed and maintained. The inn, particularly the two old-world bars, offers a relaxed atmosphere.

Kings Arms Hotel, Main Street (tel. 0596/72083), right in the middle of Keswick, is a coaching inn dating back more than 200 years to the time of George III. Some bedrooms have private baths, and all have TV and hot-beverage facilities. Bed and a full breakfast cost £18 ($27) per person with bath, £13 ($19.50) per person without bath. Half-board prices are £21 ($31.50) per person with bath, £16 ($24) per person in a bathless unit. Evening meals can be taken in any of the hotel's eating places, costing from £5 ($7.50) to £12 ($18). There is a lounge, and the Beefeater Restaurant offers excellent grills to be eaten by candlelight with soft background music. The oak-beamed bar offers light snacks and bar food, and the old coaching stables and yard have been converted into the delightful Loosebox Bar and Pizzeria. You can enjoy a 12-inch Nosebag pizza seated in what used to be a horse stall or at one of the tables in the yard.

Linnett Hill Hotel, 4 Penrith Rd. (tel. 07687/73109), has been thoroughly modernized, yet it retains oak beams and other typical characteristics. This private town house dates from 1812, and its decorations in the main are Victorian. Jane and Andrew Lysser offer seven bedrooms, most with private baths and all with hot and cold running water, electric shaver points, and central heating. They cost from £11.50 ($17.25) per person for B&B, plus another £6 ($9) for an evening dinner. Meals are not only large, but they're beautifully prepared and served. The hotel has a comfortable lounge with color TV, a small private bar, and a private car park. It is pleasantly situated opposite the River Greta and Fitz Park, with open views of Skiddaw Range and Latrigg, five minutes' walk to the lake shore.

The Bay Tree, 1 Wordsworth St. (tel. 07687/73313), offers B&B to travelers for £12.50 ($18.75) per night. Rooms are comfortable and attractively furnished, and the service is friendly and efficient. The restaurant serves meals both to residents and non-residents. Appreciating the Victorian antiques of its dining room is part of the fun of going there. The owners, Ann and Edward Peill, offer a traditional Sunday lunch with roast beef and Yorkshire pudding. But aside from that, they are open only in the evening for grills. The average meal costs from £7.50 ($11.25). Advance reservations are essential.

Crow Park Hotel, The Heads (tel. 07687/72208). The Langfords' old gray stone house makes a super guesthouse only a short distance from the town center, where it opens onto views of the Borrowdale valley. All well-furnished rooms have private shower or tub and contain many amenities. B&B costs from £12 ($18) to £14 ($21) per person, and half board is £17.50 ($26.25) to £20.50 ($30.75) per person. They close from December to March.

WHERE TO EAT: The most famous pub in Keswick is the **Dog & Gun,** Lake Road (tel. 07687/73463). Inside, there's warmth and character a-plenty, along with tasty bar snacks or else full-size meals. A tavern, right in the center, with two rooms, it offers an atmosphere of low beams (at least in one section) and open fires in winter. Meals include such hearty fare as Hungarian goulash and roast chicken. Service is from 11:30 a.m. to 2 p.m. and 6 to 9:30 p.m.; on Sunday from noon to 1:30 p.m. and 7 to 9:30 p.m. Meals cost from £6 ($9).

FOOD AND LODGING ON THE OUTSKIRTS: At the foot of Whinlatter Pass, west of Keswick, in the village of Braithwaite, stands the **Coledale Inn** (tel. 059682/272), a typical Victorian Lakeland house. It has large old rooms, a busy bar, a comfortable and quiet sitting room, and another bar where darts are played and pub grub provided. On summer evenings drinking is on a terrace, with views of the surrounding peaks and fells. In the dining room, you can order a set dinner, including local lamb or game and the famous Cumberland sausage, perhaps venison in season. Upstairs the bedrooms are large, often with views, all with showers and toilets. Stanley and Helen Hind charge from £14 ($21) per person, including a full breakfast.

In the heart of Thornthwaite Forest close to the top of Whinlatter Pass is **Cottage in the Wood,** Whinlatter Pass (tel. 059682/409), which was once an old coaching inn providing a staging post for coaches and wagons traveling to and from the Cumbrian coast. Now, it is a welcoming small country hotel with full central heating and cozy lounges containing deep armchairs and a warming fire. Comfortable bedrooms, beautifully decorated and furnished in cottage style, all have hot beverage-making facilities, and most have private bathrooms. Bed and a full English breakfast cost from £15 ($22.50) per person nightly. Lunches, from £2 ($3), and evening meals, from £7 ($10.50), are served in the dining room, which has superb views of the Skiddaw mountain range. The emphasis is on traditional English cooking, with Lakeland specialties often featured.

Greenbank, at Borrowdale (tel. 059684/215), is a comfortable guesthouse run by Trevor and Jennifer Lorton. It is up a steep, narrow lane off the main road. They provide a relaxing sitting room, a sparklingly clean dining room, and lots of local information. Some units have private baths. Half-board costs £20.50 ($30.75) to £21.50 ($32.25) per person. For £8 ($12) and up, you can enjoy a dinner that might consist of lamb with Cumberland sauce, fresh vegetables, and, for dessert, a fruit cobbler or apple pie.

8. Bassenthwaite

With its fine stretch of water in the shadow of the 3,053-foot Skiddaw, Bassenthwaite makes a good center for exploring the western Lakeland.

FOOD AND LODGING: A 16th-century inn, the **Pheasant,** Bassenthwaite Lake, near Cockermouth (tel. 059681/234), has a neat exterior set against a wooded mountain backdrop. Inside, the bar is smoke-mellowed. Old hunting prints dot the walls, and real ale is on tap. The beamed dining room is bright and cheerful, with spotless white tablecloths and a menu of good-quality roasts, fish, and poultry with fresh vegetables. There are three pleasant lounges with open log fires, and fresh flowers when possible. The bedrooms are immaculate and bright with chintz. All 20 units have private baths. Prices are £21 ($31.50) in a single and £55 ($82.50) in a double, admittedly splurge prices but worth it for those who want to enjoy the charm of the place. Prices include VAT, service, and an English breakfast. There are three bedrooms in the annex, which is a bungalow on the grounds.

To keep costs low, your best bet is to stay at a local farm that receives paying guests during the summer months. Try **Bassenthwaite Hall Farm** (tel. 059681/393), which dates from the 17th century. The centrally heated farmhouse, on this 200-acre beef and sheep farm, receives paying guests from February to November. Only two bedrooms, accommodating up to six persons, are available, both with hot and cold water basins. The hostess, Mrs. Trafford, charges from £8 ($12) per person for B&B. The farmhouse, brought up to date but keeping such features as its old oak beams, is in a delightful village beside a stream.

9. Penrith

This is an old Lakeland border town with a turbulent history. See the red ruins of Penrith Castle and the ancient church with its Giant's Grave. It is a good area for exploring not only Hadrian's Wall, but the rolling hills of the Lake District, the small and ancient stone hamlets that still carry Norse and Danish names, having been settled by the Vikings, and an occasional Norman tower.

In and around this area—but not in Penrith itself—I have selected a random sampling of accommodations in case you'd like to anchor in and do some exploring. This is an ideal stopping-off place en route to Scotland.

WHERE TO STAY: If you're driving past the Lake District without time to visit the better-known places, come off the M6 at Carlisle or Penrith and go east into the valley of the River Eden. There you can stay at **Nunnery House,** Kirkoswald (tel. 076883), the Armstrongs' 18th-century house, built on the site of an ancient nunnery. Bed and a substantial breakfast costs from £10 ($15). There is a lounge and bar, so after a day's trek in the Nunnery Walks along the Eden and Croglin Rivers, you can sink into a chair with a well-earned drink at your elbow before enjoying a pleasant evening meal. For £5 ($7.50), you are served an appealing appetizer, then a meat or fish course with vegetables, followed by dessert.

Nearer to Kendal, on the A685 in Gaisgill, is **Barbara's Cottage,** Gaisgill, Tebay, near Penrith (tel. 05874/340). Mrs. Chrissy Hill owns this 17th-century cottage, with open beams and roaring log fires. She provides comfortable overnight accommodations where guests have their own bath and dining room and lounge with color TV. The cottage is part of a small holding which provides many fresh vegetables for the wholesome meals. The paddock is home to a number of almost exotic animals such as Jacob sheep and Muscovy ducks and bantams. The overnight charge is £7.50 ($11.25) per person, including a full breakfast. For half board, the rate is £12 ($18) per person. It is a good center for fishing in the River Lune, birdwatching, walking, and sightseeing. Nearby is Appleby Castle with its perfect Norman keep, or you can visit Langrigg Pottery at Winton, or Wetherriggs Country Pottery at Clifton Dykes, an ancient industrial monument where pottery is still produced by means of a steam engine, blunger, settling pans, and pug mill.

Longthwaite Farm, Watermillock, near Penrith (tel. 08536/584), was built in 1695, and it's been modernized with hot and cold running water in the bedrooms along with central heating. The old house is in fine shape with black oak floorboards and some of the original doors. Edward and Mary Graham, the owners, take a limited number of paying guests at any time of the year, charging £8.50 ($12.75) per person, including a full English breakfast. In fact the farm is an ideal center for touring the English lakes. Mr. and Mrs. Graham will direct you to a number of old castles open to the public, as well as to festivals, exhibitions, and sheep-dog trials. If you're writing for reservations and an answer is required, send an International Reply Coupon.

Chapter XIX

YORKSHIRE AND NORTHUMBRIA

1. York
2. North Yorkshire
3. West Yorkshire
4. Durham
5. Tyne and Wear
6. Northumberland

FOR THE CONNOISSEUR, the northeast of England is rich in attractions.

Yorkshire, known to readers of *Wuthering Heights* and *All Creatures Great and Small*, is the Texas of Britain, embracing both the moors of North Yorkshire and the Dales. With the radical changing of the old country boundaries, the shires are now divided into North Yorkshire (the most interesting from the tourist's point of view), West Yorkshire, South Yorkshire, and Humberside.

Away from the cities and towns that still carry the taint of the Industrial Revolution, the beauty is wild and remote. It's characterized by limestone crags, caverns along the Pennines, many peaks, mountainous uplands, rolling hills, the chalkland wolds, heather-covered moorlands, broad vales, lazy rivers, and tumbling streams.

Yorkshire lures not only in inland scenery, but with some 100 miles of shoreline, with its rocky headlands, cliffs, sandy bays, rock pools, sheltered coves, fishing villages, bird sanctuaries, former smugglers' dens, and yachting havens.

Across this vast region came the Romans, the Anglo-Saxons, the Vikings, the monks of the Middle Ages, kings of England, lords of the manor, craftsmen, hill farmers, wool growers, each leaving his mark. You can still see Roman roads and pavements, great abbeys and castles, stately homes, open-air museums, and craft centers, along with parish churches, old villages, and cathedrals. In fact, Yorkshire's battle-scarred castles, Gothic abbeys, great country manor houses (from all periods) are unrivaled anywhere in Britain.

Northumbria is made up of the counties of Northumberland, Cleveland, and Durham. Tyne and Wear is one of the more recently created counties, with Newcastle upon Tyne as its center.

The Saxons who came to northern England centuries ago carved out this kingdom, which at the time stretched from the Firth of Forth in Scotland to the banks of the Humber in Yorkshire. Vast tracts of that ancient kingdom remain natural and unspoiled. Again, this slice of England has more than its share of industrial towns, but you don't go here to see those. Set out to explore the wild hills and open spaces, crossing the dales of the eastern Pennines.

The whole area evokes ancient battles and bloody border raids. Castles, Saxon churches, and monastic ruins abound in Northumbria, none more notable than the Roman wall, one of the wonders of the Western world. The finest stretch of the wall lies within the Northumberland National Park between the stony North Tyne River and the county boundary at Gilsland.

1. York

Few cities in England are as rich in history as York. It is still encircled by its 13th- and 14th-century city walls—about 2½ miles long—with four gates. One of these, Micklegate, once grimly greeted visitors coming up from the south with the heads of traitors. To this day you can walk on the footpath of the walls of the Middle Ages.

The crowning achievement of York is its minster or cathedral, which makes the city an ecclesiastical center equaled only by Canterbury. In spite of this, York is one of the most overlooked cities on the cathedral circuit. Perhaps foreign visitors are intimidated by the feeling that the great city of northeastern England is too far north. Actually, it lies about 195 miles north of London on the Ouse River, and can easily be tied in with a motor trip to Edinburgh. Or after visiting Cambridge, a motorist can make a swing through a too-often-neglected cathedral circuit: Ely, Lincoln, York, and Ripon.

There was a Roman York (Hadrian came this way), then a Saxon York, a Danish York, a Norman York (William the Conqueror slept here), a medieval York, a Georgian York, a Victorian York (the center of a flourishing rail business), and of course, a 20th-century York. A surprising amount of 18th-century York remains, including Richard Boyle's restored Assembly Rooms.

SEEING THE SIGHTS: The best way to see York is to go to the **Tourist Information Centre,** DeGrey Rooms, Exhibition Square (tel. 0904/21756) at 10:15 a.m. and 2:15 p.m. daily from April 1 to the end of October, where you'll be met by a voluntary guide who will take you on a 1½-hour walking tour of the city, revealing its history and lore through numerous intriguing stories. There is no charge. Additional tours are made at 7 p.m. daily during June, July, and August.

At some point in your exploration, you may want to visit **The Shambles,** once the meat-butchering center of York, dating back before the Norman Conquest. But this messy business has given way, and the ancient street survives. It is filled with jewelry stores, cafés, and buildings that huddle so closely together you can practically stand in the middle of the pavement, arms outstretched, and touch the houses on both sides of the street.

Recently, special interest has been focused on discoveries of the Viking era, from 867 to 1066, when the city was known as Jorvik, the Viking capital and major Scandinavian trade center. During excavations under York's Coppergate prior to development, a wealth of artifacts was unearthed in the late 1970s and early 1980s, including entire houses and workshops of the Viking age. For information on the period of history and treasures found in the excavations, inquire at the **Jorvik Viking Centre,** Coppergate (tel. 0904/643211).

Incidentally, the suffix *gate* for streets and sites in York is from the Scandinavian word for street, a holdover from the era when the Vikings held sway here.

York Minster

One of the great cathedrals of the world, York Minster traces its origin back to the early seventh century. The present building, however, was begun in the 13th century and finished in the 15th, when the three great towers were constructed. The architectural styles are thus Early English, Decorated, and Perpendicular.

Perhaps the distinguishing characteristic of the cathedral is its medley of stained and painted glass from the Middle Ages (more than any other church in Britain) in glorious blues, reds, greens, and amber. See in particular the large east window, the work of a 15th-century glass painter from Coventry and the earlier "Five Sisters" window in the North Transept with its five great 13th-century lancets. The choir screen, from the late 15th century, has an impressive line-up of English kings, from William the Conqueror to Henry VI.

Entrance and guided tours are free for individuals. Voluntary guides do not accept tips, but donations toward the maintenance of the minster are always welcome. The Chapter House is open Monday to Saturday from 10 a.m. (9:30 a.m. in summer), and the admission charge is 40p (60¢) for adults, 20p (30¢) for children. The Undercroft hours are the same, with the charge being 80p ($1.20) for adults, 40p (60¢) for children. On Sunday, opening time is 1 p.m. The bookshop is open Monday to Saturday from 9 a.m. to 6:30 p.m. in summer, to 5 p.m. in winter, and from 1 to 4 p.m. on Sunday. For further information, telephone 0904/24426.

The Treasurer's House

In the Minster Yard, the Treasurer's House (tel. 0904/24247) stands on a site where there has been a building since Roman times. The main part of the house was rebuilt in 1620 as the official residence of the treasurers of York Minster, and was lived in as a private home until 1930. The house contains fine furniture, glass, and china of the 17th and 18th centuries. An audio-visual program describes the work of the medieval treasures and some of the personalities with which this famous York house is associated. Hours April to the end of October are daily from 10:30 a.m. to 6 p.m. (last entry at 5:30 p.m.). It's closed Good Friday. Admission is £1.30 ($1.95) for adults, 60p (90¢) for children. On some evenings in summer the house is open from 8 to 9:30 p.m., when you can enjoy coffee by candlelight in the main hall.

York Castle Museum

On Tower Street, York Castle Museum (tel. 0904/53611) is arguably the most popular museum of everyday life in Britain. Its unique feature is Kirkgate, a reconstructed cobblestone street with shops rescued from demolition by the museum's founder, Dr. Kirk, who on his travels through Yorkshire acquired a large collection of antiques and relics.

A series of period rooms ranges from the elegant Georgian dining room through a cluttered and claustrophobic Victorian parlor to a 1953 sitting room, complete with a nine-inch television set for watching the coronation of Queen Elizabeth II. "Every Home Should Have One" is a new gallery showing domestic appliances and how they have changed our lives: vacuum cleaners, amazing washing machines, stylish bathrooms, toilets, radios, and televisions. Reconstructed kitchens, arms and armor, costumes, and jewelry are also displayed. The Debtors' Prison includes a reconstructed Edwardian Street complete with a garage and a pub. Raindale Mill (open April to October only) grinds corn beside the River Foss.

The museum is open from 9:30 a.m. to 6:30 p.m. April to October and 9:30 a.m. to 5 p.m. November to March. Sunday opening all year is at 10 a.m. Last admission is an hour before closing time. Admission is £2.25 ($3.38) for adults, £1.15 ($1.73) for children. The museum is closed December 25, December 26, and January 1.

National Railway Museum

The first national museum to be built away from London, the National Railway Museum, Leeman Road (tel. 0904/21261), was adapted from an original steam locomotive depot. The museum gives visitors a chance to look under and inside steam

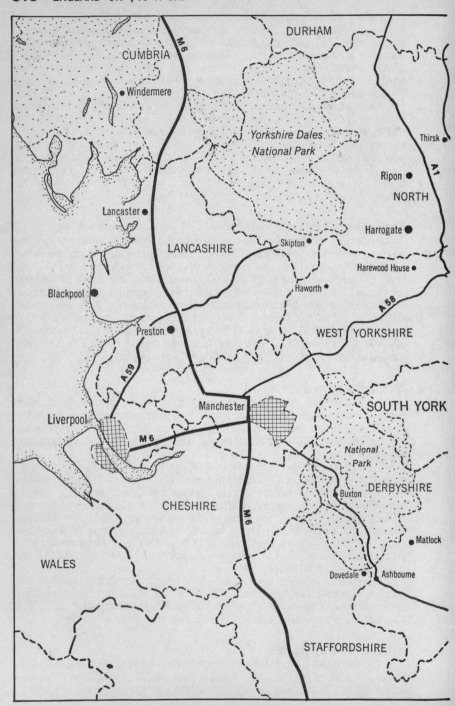

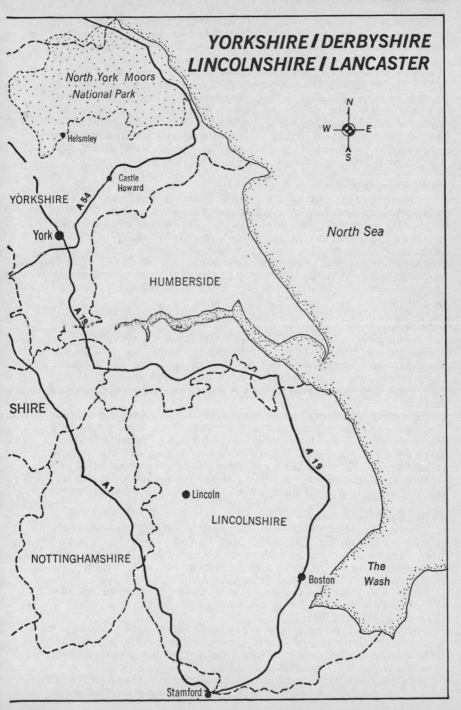

YORKSHIRE / DERBYSHIRE
LINCOLNSHIRE / LANCASTER

North York Moors
National Park

Helsmley

N
W ✦ E
S

YORKSHIRE

A 54

Castle
Howard

York

North Sea

HUMBERSIDE

A 19

SHIRE

A 19

A 1

Lincoln

LINCOLNSHIRE

NOTTINGHAMSHIRE

Boston

The
Wash

Stamford

locomotives or see how Queen Victoria traveled in luxury. In addition, there's a full-size collection of railway memorabilia, with an early 19th-century clock and penny machines for purchasing tickets to the railway platform. On display are more than 20 full-size locomotives including diesel and electric. One, the *Agenoria*, dates from 1829, and is a contemporary of Stephenson's well-known *Rocket*. It's almost identical to the first American locomotive, the *Stourbridge Lion,* brought over from England in 1828. Of several royal coaches, the most interesting is the century-old Royal Saloon, in which Queen Victoria rode until her death. It's like a small hotel, with polished wood, silk, brocade, and silver accessories. Items on exhibition change from time to time, but a popular display is *Mallard,* the fastest steam locomotive in the world. The museum can be visited weekdays from 10 a.m. to 6 p.m. and on Sunday from 2:30 to 6 p.m. Admission is free. It is closed on some public holidays.

Jorvik Viking Centre

At Coppergate (tel. 0904/643211) is the Viking city discovered many feet below the present ground level. It was reconstructed exactly as it was in the year A.D. 948. In a "time car," you can travel back through the ages to 1067 when Normans sacked the city and then ride slowly through the street market peopled by faithfully modeled Vikings. You can go through a house where a family lived and down to the river to see the shipchandlers at work and a Norwegian cargo ship unloading. At the end of the ride you pass through the Finds Hut, where thousands of artifacts discovered are displayed. The center is open from 9 a.m. to 7 p.m. daily (until 5:30 p.m. in summer). Admission is £2.50 ($3.75) for adults, £1.25 ($1.88) for children.

Theatre Royal

Theatre Royal, on St. Leonard's Place (tel. 0904/23568), is an old traditional theater building with modern additions to house the box office bars and restaurant. It is worth inquiring about the current production, as the Royal Shakespeare Company includes York in its tours. The Arts Council presents dance, drama, and opera, and visiting celebrities appear in classics. There is also an excellent resident repertory company.

Seat prices range from £2.50 ($3.75) to £6 ($9). The glass-walled, ground-floor snackbar serves coffee and tea along with such fare as soup, baked potatoes with cheese, and ham and baked beans, priced from £1.25 ($1.88). Upstairs in the Theatre Restaurant is a salad buffet and choice of hot dishes. A three-course meal will cost around £5 ($7.50). The restaurant is open from noon to 2:30 p.m. and 5 p.m. until curtain time. You don't have to buy a ticket to eat here, and it's quite a relaxing experience to sit outside with your drink and a snack, looking out on the world passing by.

An Unguided Walk-About

Starting from York Minster, walk down past Youngs Hotel, the reputed birthplace of Guy Fawkes. Turn right into Stonegate, a pedestrian area with old shops, a 12th-century house on the right, and some old coffeehouses. Continue across Davygate into St. Helen's Square to see the Guildhall and Mansion House, then go left into Coney Street, taking a right into Lower Ousegate.

At the beginning of Ouse Bridge, take the steps down to Kings Staithe, with a pub on the left for refreshment, before continuing on into South Esplanade and St. George's Gardens beside the river.

At the bridge, join the road again, turning left and in front of you stand the Castle Museum, the Assize Courts, and Clifford's Tower. Walk up Tower Street and Clifford Street to Nessgate. Turn right into High Ousegate and continue across Parliament Street to the beginning of the Shambles on the left.

Walk up the Shambles past the attractive shops and ancient buildings to Kings Square, then bear right into Goodramgate. Walk down Goodramgate and, at the end, cross Deangate into College Street with St. William's College on the right. At the end a narrow road leads to the Treasurer's House.

You're now behind the east end of the minster. Walk around to the west end and then up Bootham Bar, through the city gate and turn left into Exhibition Square. The Art Gallery is on the right, the Tourist Information Centre to the left, and beside it, York's Theatre Royal. Continue down St. Leonard's Street to the crossroads, turning right into Museum Street. Cross the river and go right to join part of the old medieval wall which you follow all the way to Skeldergate Bridge. Then follow the river's course upstream again to the center of York.

WHERE TO STAY: In a Georgian brick building, **Galtres Lodge,** Low Petergate (tel. 0904/22478), has cellars containing some beams believed to date back to the 13th century, as well as a beautiful Adam fireplace and three priest holes. It is owned by Mike and Janis Freshney. Janis used to work as a personal secretary to the Prime Minister at No. 10 Downing Street. There are 13 bedrooms, some of which open onto a view of the rose window of the minster. A few contain private showers, toilets, and four-poster or half-tester beds. All accommodations have direct-dial phones, color TV, and hot beverage-making facilities. The tariff is from £15 ($22.50) to £20 ($30) per person for B&B, including VAT. Lunch and dinner are offered à la carte in the restaurant, and the lodge has a cozy, well-stocked bar and a separate guests' lounge. The Galtres is in an excellent position, offering an ideal and centrally located base from which to explore the city and within easy reach of the railway station.

Minster View, 2 Grosvenor Terrace, Bootham (tel. 0904/55034), is a brick Victorian guesthouse run by Audrey and Neville Richardson. The warm, comfortable bedrooms are well appointed, all with color TV, hot and cold water basins, and beverage-making facilities. Some have private baths. The charge is from £12 ($18) per person for B&B, with dinner offered from £6.50 ($9.75). The excellent dinner menu and wine list will add to your pleasure of visiting York. The house has private parking, and it's about a 15-minute walk from the city center.

Arnot House, 17 Grosvenor Terrace, Bootham (tel. 0904/641966), like other houses on the terrace, has views over Bootham Park, and in the distance, you can see the minster. Sue and Rupert Scott welcome guests to the Victorian house, with its original fireplaces, cornices, and fine old staircase. The atmosphere is warm and comfortable. The bedrooms all have color TV, hot and cold water basins, and beverage-making facilities. Singles rent for £12 ($18) and twins or doubles for £23 ($34.50), with a full English breakfast (alternative on request) included. Evening meals are served in the candlelit dining room, allowing you a choice of main dishes and costing £6.50 ($9.75) for a four-course repast. The house is licensed. Grosvenor Terrace is a 15- to 20-minute walk from the train station.

Craig-y-Don, 3 Grosvenor Terrace, Bootham (tel. 0904/37186). Mr. and Mrs. Oliver are some of the most hospitable hosts in the heart of York. They run an immaculately kept and most inviting home, serving a large Yorkshire breakfast. The inclusive rate is from £10 ($15) per person nightly. Mrs. Oliver also welcomes children.

Priory Hotel, 126 Fulford Rd. (tel. 0904/25280), stands on the main route into York from the south. Lying in a residential area, it has many double- and twin-bedded rooms. The rate for a good, comfortable bed and one of their large breakfasts comes to £15 ($22.50) per person nightly. All units with private baths. The location is on the A19. A riverside walk will take you to the heart of "monumental" York.

The **Sycamore Hotel,** 19 Sycamore Pl. (tel. 0904/24712), was built as a private dwelling in 1902, but has been carefully converted to maintain much of its original splendor. Now it's a family-owned and -run hotel, offering a high level of accommodation for £11 ($16.50) per person, including a full breakfast. The location is close to the city center (a 10-minute walk to the minster, a 15-minute walk to the rail station), yet it occupies a position in a quiet cul-de-sac. All rooms have hot and cold running water, central heating, tea/coffee-making facilities, and color TV. There are two toilets, a bathroom, and a shower. Keys are provided each guest, and car parking is available.

Dairy Wholefood Guest House, 3 Scarcroft Rd. (tel. 0904/39367), is a lovely house decorated throughout with ideas and furnishings in the "Habitat, Sanderson, Laura Ashley" style, with emphasis on pine and plants and an enclosed courtyard. It lies only 200 yards south of the medieval city walls, within easy access of car parking. Keith Jackman, proprietor, has some accommodations with private bath or shower. The charge for B&B is from £11 ($16.50) per person nightly. Breakfast choices range from traditional English to whole-food vegetarian. The lounge has a color TV and hot-drink facilities.

Gleneagles Lodge Guest House, 27 Nunthorpe Ave. (tel. 0904/37000), is a handsomely decorated, well-maintained, and comfortable guesthouse which is nicely furnished. On a quiet street, it is within walking distance of the center of York, including the train station, Micklegate Bar, and a number of restaurants serving good but reasonably priced food. The success of Gleneagles has everything to do with the hospitality of Terry and Eni Walker, who go far out of their way to make your stay a memorable one. With them, good conversation comes easy, and they are kind and gracious, as well as sensitive to your needs. Eni will prepare a superb home-cooked evening meal if you make arrangements in advance. For B&B, the charge is from £12 ($18) per person nightly. Children are granted reductions. Don't be surprised if coffee and fresh scones are brought in to greet you one evening.

Grasmead House Hotel, 1 Scarcroft Hill (tel. 0904/29996). One American guest departing was overheard to remark, "This hotel is just like an *Alice in Wonderland* place—so super inside." It doesn't have any white rabbits or mad hatters, but it does boast genuine four-poster beds in all the rooms. It's been refurbished with excellent fabrics and made very comfortable with made-to-measure mattresses. Len and Eileen Spray, the resident owners, give you a real welcome and personal service. Their small family-run hotel lies within easy walking distance of the center, close to the Castle Museum. Some rooms look out toward the city walls and minster. All units have their own private bath, with easy chairs, color TV, and tea- or coffee-making equipment. Prices are from £20 ($30) per person nightly, including an English breakfast and VAT.

Linden Lodge Hotel, 6 Nunthorpe Ave., Scarcroft Road (tel. 0904/20107), is a 15-bedroom accommodation run by Val and John Thompson. The units are color coordinated, with radios and hot and cold water basins. Toilet facilities are quite near the bedrooms, which include twin and double beds. For £11 ($16.50) per person, the Thompsons supply you with a bed and a full breakfast. Evening meals are available for £6 ($9). There is a pleasant TV lounge where you can have a brandy and a chat before bedtime.

Clifton Green Hotel, 8 Clifton Green (tel. 0904/623597), about a 10-minute walk from Bootham Bar, the north gate of old York, is an immaculate small hotel fronting on a green. The seven bedrooms, rented by Ben and Gloria Braithwaite, are carpeted and have central heating, color TV, hot and cold water basins, hot-beverage facilities, bedlights, wardrobes with hangers, dressing tables, nightstands, filled tissue dispensers, and other amenities to make a stay here rewarding. The B&B rates are from £11 ($16.50) in a single, from £21 ($31.50) in a double. Half board costs from £16 ($24) per person daily. The hotel offers private parking, some in covered spaces, and the no. 17 bus comes almost to the door. To find Clifton Green, take the A19 road toward Thirsk.

Adams House Hotel, 5 Main St., in Fulford (tel. 0904/55413), is a family-owned business lying on the A19 York–Selby road, about a five-minute drive from the minster. Sometimes guests have found accommodations here in the peak summer months when the hotels in the city center have been fully booked. Pat and David Johnson run this efficient hotel where the bedrooms are comfortably furnished, each with private bath. The charge, including VAT and a full breakfast, ranges from £13 ($19.50) to £17 ($25.50) per person nightly. The hotel has a residential license. Guests can enjoy the hotel's gardens as well as its proximity to the Fulford Golf Club.

Avenue House Guest House, 6 The Avenue, Clifton (tel. 0904/20575), is a Victorian house in a quiet residential area run by Mr. and Mrs. Roberts and their family. All rooms have hot and cold running water and TV. There are two toilets, a shower room, and a bathroom. B&B costs from £8 ($12) per person, plus another £6 ($9) if you want dinner. Tea and cookies are served at 9:45 p.m. without charge when you return from a theater performance.

Barrington House, 15 Nunthorpe Ave., Scarcroft Road (tel. 0904/34539), is the small, family-run guesthouse of Fred and Greta Cornforth. They have a guest lounge, and each of their bedrooms has hot and cold running water, color TV, shaver points, and tea- and coffee-making equipment. Including a full English breakfast, the charge is from £9.50 ($14.25) per person nightly. Evening meals can be served if arranged in advance.

Feversham Lodge, 1 Feversham Crescent (tel. 0904/23882), was a 19th-century Methodist manse converted to receiving guests. It still retains its lofty dining room and TV lounge. Bob and Jill Peacock charge from £9 ($13.50) per person for B&B in their neatly kept bedrooms, all of which have central heating and hot and cold running water.

Aberford House, 35 E. Mount Rd. (tel. 0904/22694), is a large family home belonging to Paul and Jackie Sanderson. It is just five minutes from the rail station on a quiet road close to the great southern city gateway. There are 14 rooms, all with wash basins; shaver points, color TV, and facilities for making hot beverages. Some of the units have private showers, while some have showers and toilets. B&B costs £11 ($16.50) per person. Large cooked breakfasts and simple evening meals are served in the dining room. Meals are modestly charged according to what you order. They have a well-stocked cellar bar and a private car park.

Hazelwood, 24 Portland St., Gillygate (tel. 0904/26548), lies an easy walk from York Minster. It is the domain of Mr. and Mrs. Cox, who do a fine job of running a B&B. Their place is immaculately kept and well furnished, with rooms costing from £11.50 ($17.25) to £14 ($21) per person nightly. Their breakfast is large and well prepared, and they are always willing to answer your questions about touring in York and the surrounding moors and dales.

The **Railway King Hotel,** George Hudson Street (tel. 0904/55478), is a good choice for those who want to pay slightly more to get the services of a hotel instead of the routine B&B. It is a short block from the bus station and about a seven-minute walk to York Minster and the Shambles. Charges in rooms with private baths, TV, and tea and coffee-makers are £30.50 ($45.75) to £34 ($51) in a single, £44.50 ($66.75) to £49 ($73.50) in a double. A full English breakfast is included, and you have your choice of a morning paper brought to your door. The dining room serves good evening meals at reasonable prices.

WHERE TO EAT: A good all-round eating house, **Bettys Café Tea Rooms,** St. Helens Square (tel. 0904/59142), open from 9 a.m. to 9 p.m. (from 9:30 a.m. to 9 p.m. on Sunday). You can call in for a quick coffee and pastry or treat yourself to a full, cooked English breakfast, a Yorkshire cheese lunch, or a Yorkshire rarebit. Genteel afternoon teas with scones as well as fish and chips high teas are also firm favorites. A selection of healthy salads and whole-food quiches are also on offer. Bettys is famous for its cream cakes, including a fresh strawberry noisette and a summer fruit flan. The light suppers and wide variety of cooked and cold meals makes this a good place to stop in the evening. Families are made especially welcome, and customers drop in for anything from a cup of coffee to a substantial meal, costing from £6.50 ($9.75). You can make this the finishing point to a stroll through York or enjoy a pretheater supper, complete with fine Alsatian wine. A café concert entertains customers as they dine. The concerts range from lute duets to Palm Court trios. Bettys also has cafés in the heart of James Herriot Country, in Northallerton; in the Yorkshire Dales, at Ilkley in Wharfedale; and overlooking the delightful Montpellier Gardens in the old spa town of Harrogate.

St. William's, 3 College St. (tel. 0904/34830), lies within the shadow of the great east window of the minster. With its half timbering and leaded-glass windows, it is a medieval and oak-beamed setting. It serves some of the best of the low-cost food of York. Lunch is offered from noon to 2:30 p.m. daily, costing £5 ($7.50). Selections include much "olde English fayre," including roast rib of beef or one of the "raised pies" such as pork and apricot. A self-service cafeteria, St. William's draws many young people to its precincts, as they know they get good value here. You can also visit for morning coffee (except on Sunday) from 10 a.m. to noon and for afternoon tea from 2:30 to 5 p.m.

York Wholefood Vegetarian Restaurant, 98 Micklegate (tel. 0904/56804), is one of the best of the vegetarian restaurants of York. These so-called whole-food establishments are springing up all over Britain, and York is no exception. This one is entered through a health food store at ground level. Climb the steps in back to reach this pristine little place with plain pine furniture. It is open from noon to 2 p.m. Monday to Saturday and also serves dinner Thursday through Saturday from 7:30 to 10 p.m. It is unlicensed, but you can bring your own wine at dinner. Buffet lunches are a special feature, and you can select from such dishes as a cashew curry, ground chick peas and garlic, and a vegetable and tofu goulash. Meals cost from £4 ($6) to £6 ($9).

Dean Court Hotel, Duncombe Place (tel. 0904/25082), has a coffeeshop entered through the main door of the hotel and a bar with an entrance from a basement door just by the minster. A sandwich and coffee are popular items, and they also do hot foods, including a mug of hot soup, toast, welsh rarebit, or chicken liver pâté. Desserts include peach and banana sundaes, and there is a good selection of afternoon tea specialties, such as scones with cream and strawberry jam. Service and VAT are included in the prices on the menu, so you know exactly what you're paying. Light meals cost from £2 ($3). Hours are daily from noon to 2 p.m. and 6:30 to 9 p.m.

Kooks Bistro, 108 Fishergate (tel. 0904/37553), is an informal, relaxed eating place run by the owner, Angie Cowl. Decorated in dark green with individually painted flamingos and a collection of memorabilia on the same theme given by customers, it features a varied and unusual menu of English, American, Mexican, French, and vegetarian food, with several dishes distinctive to Kooks. Most main courses include in the price a choice of baked potato, french fries, hash browns, or side salad. Meats range from burgers to beef Stroganoff. The service is prompt and friendly and the atmosphere relaxed, with varied background music and a little fun in the form of handmade jigsaws and other puzzles and games on every table. Meals cost from £6 ($9). Kooks is fully licensed and open daily except Monday from 11 a.m. to midnight, with last orders at 11 p.m. It is within walking distance of the city center, and there is plenty of easy parking.

The **Aquarium Seafood Restaurant,** 25 Tanner Row, Rougier Street (tel. 0904/654839), was York's first seafood restaurant when it opened in 1986. Michael and Kathleen Moat offer a nautical atmosphere, with fishnets on the ceiling and a real live aquarium, plus a menu to match. You might enjoy such specialties as smoked haddock (a Yorkshire delicacy), crab, lobster, or salmon. Also there are meat dishes if you're not that fond of fish. Depending on your selection of a main course, you can dine here for only £4 ($6), although you're likely to spend £7.50 ($11.25) or more. Service is from noon to 2:30 p.m. daily and 6 to 9:30 p.m. except on Friday and Saturday when it closes at 11:30 p.m.

Restaurant Bari, 15 The Shambles (tel. 0904/33807), stands in one of York's oldest and most colorful streets, originally the street of the butchers and mentioned in the *Domesday Book*. In a continental atmosphere, you can enjoy a quick single course or a full leisurely meal. Ten different pizzas are offered. Lasagne and cannelloni are superb. Lunch can cost as little as £4 ($6), and dinner from about £6 ($9). A main-dish specialty is escalope Sophia Loren (veal cooked with brandy and cheese with a rich tomato sauce). It is open seven days a week from 11:30 a.m. to 2:30 p.m. and 6 to 11 p.m.

Russells on the Square, Kings Square (tel. 0904/36592), opposite the Shambles, is a typical grill restaurant. Burgers are made from 100% selected beef, which is then double-chopped for extra tenderness. They come in three sizes: the quarter-pounder, half-pounder, and for trenchermen, the "three-quarter-pounder." They're served on a hot toasted sesame seed bun, with a crisp salad, french fries, and American-style relishes. Meals cost from £6 ($9). For dessert, there are eight varieties of ice cream, and Russells serves daily from 10:30 a.m. to 10:30 p.m.

Tullivers, 55 Goodramgate (tel. 0904/51525), is a friendly vegetarian restaurant in the heart of York, serving lunches and dinners. Even meat fanciers are likely to be pleased with such dishes as baked eggplant with onion, pine kernels, cheese, and basil, or why not try cashew and almond roast with spicy tomato sauce? Appetizers include spinach and mushroom pâté and guacamole with pita bread. The Basque omelet with onions, peppers, and fresh herbs is tasty, and a range of good desserts is offered to finish your meal. All dishes are prepared on the premises, using fresh produce and free-range eggs. Lunch is served from noon to 1:45 p.m., costing less than £3.50 ($5.75), with an à la carte dinner, from 7 to 9:30 p.m., going for £7.50 ($11.25) and up. Closed Sunday and Monday.

Raffles Tea Room, Allenby House, Stonegate (tel. 0904/29812), is above the House of Tweed shop. It's a traditional English tea room, offering morning coffee with pastries or toasted buns. Light lunches, including sandwiches, salads, chicken pie, and quiche, cost around £4 ($6). Afternoon teas are a specialty. You can enjoy warm scones with strawberry jam and clotted cream, with a choice among five blends of tea, for less than £2 ($3). The place is open from 9:30 a.m. to 5 p.m. Monday to Saturday, from 10:30 a.m. to 4:30 p.m. on Sunday.

Taylors in Stonegate, 46 Stonegate (tel. 0904/22865). Downstairs the bow-windowed shop is filled with bags and jars of coffee. The old-fashioned till bears the prices of the 36 varieties of teas and coffees for sale. When you see the shop, you'll know that this is no idle boast. Teas come all the way from China and India, including exotic oolongs, souchongs, and passion fruit. Upstairs, the coffeeshop dispenses these same beverages. They advertise a late breakfast for £2.75 ($4.13). You can also order rarebits and omelets with various fillings, and a selection of salads, with meals costing from £5 ($7.50). Spiced Yorkshire tea cakes and cinnamon toast are also on the menu. Service is from 9 a.m. to 5:30 p.m. Monday to Saturday and most Sundays.

A PUB CRAWL: Known for the best location of any pub in York, the **Kings Arms,** King's Straithe (tel. 0904/59435), is a popular riverside pub. Right near the Ouse Bridge, the location is on the left bank of the River Ouse, across from Sweeney Todd's, where you may want to go later for a pizza. This historic public house, one of charm, character, and intimacy, is filled with beamed ceilings, brick walls, and a mellow atmosphere. A board records flood levels of the Ouse. In summer, tables are placed outside along the river. Your hosts serve a full range of Samuel Smith's draft and bottled beers traditionally brewed in Tadcaster, only ten miles from York. Meals cost from £3.50 ($5.25) and include such dishes as the "curry of the day" or roast chicken. Food is not served on Saturday evening, and the pub is open from 11 a.m. to 3 p.m. and 5:30 to 11 p.m.

The Black Swan, Peaseholme Green (tel. 0904/25236), is a fine timbered frame house, the home of the Lord Mayor of York in 1417. The mother of General James Wolfe of Québec also lived here. One of the oldest inns in the city, it offers pub meals Monday to Saturday from noon to 2 p.m., costing £3 ($4.50). Open fires burn in winter, making the place even more atmospheric. You can also go for drinks in the evening from 5:30 to 11.

Olde Starre, Stonegate (tel. 0904/23063), lies on a pedestrian street in the heart of Old York. Considered York's oldest licensed pub, it serves hot and cold pub lunches from 11:30 a.m. to 2 p.m. It is also open for drinks in the evening from 5:30 to 11. Cod, plaice, and scampi appear regularly on the menu, along with chili con carne and shepherd's pie. In fair weather, guests fill the tables in a courtyard. Inside, guests enjoy the old beams and the Edwardian benches.

2. North Yorkshire

For those seeking legendary untamed scenery, I recommend a tour of North Yorkshire, which also takes in the already-previewed historic cathedral city of York.

North Yorkshire contains England's most varied landscape. Its history has been turbulent, often bloody, and many relics of its rich past are still standing, including ruined abbeys. North Yorkshire is little known to the average North American visitor, but many an English traveler knows of its haunting moors, serene valleys, and windswept dales.

The hospitality of the people of North Yorkshire is world renowned, and if a pudding that originated there doesn't accompany a slab of roast beef, the plate looks naked to the British. The people of North Yorkshire, who speak an original twang often imitated in English cinema, are, in general, hardworking and industrious, perhaps a little contemptuous of the easy living of the south. But they are decidedly open and friendly to strangers, providing you speak to them first.

CASTLE HOWARD: In its dramatic setting of lakes, fountains, and extensive gardens, the 18th-century palace designed by Sir John Vanbrugh is undoubtedly the finest private residence in North Yorkshire. Principal location for the TV series, "Brideshead Revisited," this was the first major achievement of the architect who later created the lavish Blenheim Palace near Oxford. Castle Howard was begun in 1699 for the third Earl of Carlisle, Charles Howard, whose descendants still call the place "home." The striking facade is topped by a painted and gilded dome, reaching more than 80 feet into the air. The interior boasts a 192-foot "Long Gallery," as well as a chapel with magnificent stained-glass windows by the 19th-century artist, Sir Edward Burne-Jones. Besides the collections of antique furniture, tapestries, porcelains, and sculpture, the castle contains a number of important paintings, including a portrait of Henry VIII by Holbein, and works by Rubens, Reynolds, and Gainsborough.

The seemingly endless grounds around the palace also offer the visitor some memorable sights, including the domed Temple of the Four Winds, by Vanbrugh, and the richly designed family mausoleum by Hawksmoor. There are two rose gardens, one with old-fashioned roses, the other featuring modern creations. The stable court houses the Costume Galleries, the largest private collection of 18th- to 20th-century costumes in Britain. The authentically dressed mannequins are exhibited in period settings. Castle Howard, just 15 miles northeast of York, is open to the public daily from March 25 through the end of October; the grounds from 10 a.m., the house and Costume Galleries from 11 a.m. to 5 p.m. (last entry at 4:30 p.m.). Admission is £3.50 ($5.75) for adults, £1.75 ($2.63) for children. There is a self-service cafeteria where you can order sandwiches and hot dishes, the latter for around £2.50 ($3.25). Good wines are served. The cafeteria opens at 11 a.m. For information, telephone 065384/333.

HARROGATE: If you head west from York for 20 miles, you reach Harrogate, North Yorkshire's second-largest town after York. In the 19th century, Harrogate was a fashionable spa. Most of the town center is surrounded by a 200-acre lawn called "The Stray." Boutiques and antique shops, which Queen Mary used to frequent, make Harrogate a shopping center of excellence, particularly along Montpellier Parade. Harrogate is called England's floral resort, deserving such a reputation because of its gardens, including Harlow Car Gardens and Valley Gardens. The former spa has an abundance of guesthouses and hotels, including the expensive Swan where Agatha Christie hid out during her mysterious disappearance—still unexplained—in the 1920s.

Where to Stay

Garden House Hotel, 14 Harlow Moor Dr. (tel. 0423/503059), is a handsomely restored Victorian house. It's really more an upmarket guesthouse than most B&Bs in Harrogate. With good car parking and peaceful surroundings, this is an ideal alternative to an accommodation in the heart of Harrogate where parking can be a serious problem. All eight rooms have private baths or shower, color TV, and beverage-making facilities. The B&B charge ranges from £16 ($24) to £18 ($27) per person. Half-board terms go from £22 ($33) to £24 ($36) per person nightly. Full English breakfasts incorporate all sorts of local and natural ingredients and are freshly prepared for guests. Evening meals are simple but tasty. Poultry or meat with a good sauce will be accompanied by crisp fresh vegetables.

Crescent Lodge Guest House, 20 Swan Rd. (tel. 0423/503688), is known for its charm and atmosphere, but since it takes only six guests it might be hard to get in unless you reserve. This is a solid early Victorian building overlooking Crescent Gardens and lying only a short walk from the Royal Pump Room. It has a comfortable family lounge with color TV and a pleasant dining room where a full English breakfast is served. On the landing leading to the bedrooms is a polished mahogany table laden with fresh fruit and Perrier water for guests to help themselves. The B&B rate ranges from £22 ($33) to £16.50 ($24.75) per person in an accommodation with shower and toilet. The owner will also provide a washing machine and dryer, and hair dryers and irons are also available. There is a pleasant peaceful walled garden in which to relax.

Wessex Hotel, Harlow Moor Drive (tel. 0423/65890), is in an attractive part of Harrogate overlooking and with immediate access to the Valley Gardens. It is only a ten-minute walk from the center of town. The family-run hotel provides hospitality in the Yorkshire style, combined with comfort and personal service, with special emphasis on good food served in their spacious dining room. There is central heating throughout the hotel, and all 15 bedrooms are equipped with radio and shaver points. All bedrooms have private showers and toilets, and have been refurbished. A pleasantly decorated and well-furnished television lounge is available for relaxation after a busy day of sightseeing or shopping. Or you can have a drink in the comfortable bar lounge and unwind by getting to know your fellow guests. For £16 ($24) per person, you get a very clean and airy room and a standard English breakfast. The proprietors, Mr. and Mrs. Terence Samuel, will be happy to direct you to the Valley Gardens with its beautiful floral displays; or the facilities for tennis, 18-hole mini-golf course, horseback riding, and if you are a racing fan, there are four racecourses within easy distance of the hotel.

Ashley House Hotel, 36/40 Franklin Rd. (tel. 0423/507474), is a comfortable family-run licensed hotel with excellent food and friendly atmosphere. There are 18 guest rooms, all equipped with coffee- and tea-making facilities, TV, and alarm-clock radios. Some rooms have private showers and toilets. A good selection of wines is available with meals in the spacious dining room, and in the evening guests may relax and meet fellow visitors in the cozy "olde worlde" bar. There are two lounges for guests, both with color TV, and there is full central heating throughout. The hotel is in a quiet, residential part of town, yet only a five-minute walk to the center. It's a convenient site for visiting York and the Yorkshire Dales. Wendy and Richard Wood assure you of every comfort and attention. They charge £12 ($18) per person daily in a double or twin room, including a full English breakfast. Single rooms are £14 ($21) daily. A four-course dinner is served each evening at £7.50 ($11.25) a head, including coffee. All prices are fully inclusive.

The **Manor Hotel,** 3 Clarence Dr. (tel. 0423/503916), is an impressive Victorian stone concoction with complex architectural details—a square tower and off-balance gables, in the secluded Duchy area of Harrogate, yet within walking distance of the town center and the Valley Gardens. The hotel has been extensively modernized and provides a high standard of accommodation for guests in family surroundings. All bedrooms have private baths, remote control color TV, radios, hot beverage facilities, and direct-dial phones. For B&B, the charge is from £19 ($28.50) per person in a double or twin to £24 ($36) in a single, VAT included. The restaurant offers table d'hôte and à la carte menus. There is a private car park.

Alvera Court Hotel, 76 Kings Rd. (tel. 0423/505735), is a fine Victorian stone residence that has been renovated and modernized. Charming architectural features of the Victorian era are enhanced by the furnishings and welcoming atmosphere. Colin and Patricia Kitching, owners and managers, offer ten bedrooms, all with private baths or showers, color TV, direct-dial phones, alarm clock radios, in-house movies, and beverage-making facilities. Rents are £19 ($28.50) in a single and £18 ($27) per person in a double, with breakfast and VAT included. The hotel serves mainly traditional Yorkshire dishes, with dinner, which must be ordered by noon of the day required, costing £8 ($12). A restful lounge and a cocktail bar, plus a private car park, are among the Alvera's attractions. It's directly opposite the International Conference and Exhibition Centre. On warm days, you can sit on the front lawn and watch the world go by.

Where to Eat

Bettys Café Tea Room, 1 Parliament St. (tel. 0423/64659), one of four such places in Yorkshire, is in a Victorian building in the town center, marked by an iron canopy over the pavement and hanging baskets of flowers. Inside, the decor is Victorian with marquetry panels done by the man who decorated the *Queen Mary*. This was the first Bettys, founded by Fred Belmont, a Londoner who allegedly took a train to Highgate but ended up in Harrogate instead. The menu includes sandwiches, salads, toasted muffins, tea cakes, and scones served as a cream tea with masses of cream and strawberry jam. Hot dishes are offered, as well as rich fruit cakes with whipped cream or Wensleydale cheese. Several exotic brands of tea from India and China are available, or you might order a cafetière of coffee for one, choosing Jamaica Blue Mountain, Mexican Maragogipe, or Mocha Harrar Longberry from Ethiopia, even plain old decaf, if you prefer. Meals cost from £7 ($10.50). If you'd like to go on a countryside treasure hunt, ask at the cashier's desk for a Treasure Trail pack, containing a map and a set of directions and clues. James Herriot, the world-famous veterinarian *(All Creatures Great and Small),* has been a regular visitor to Bettys for a number of years. Bettys is open from 9:30 a.m. to 5:30 p.m. Monday to Saturday and 10 a.m. to 6 p.m. on Sunday. Soft music is played Thursday through Sunday. From the Verandah Café, you can look out over the flowers and lawns of the Montpellier Gardens as you enjoy a cup of coffee and one of Bettys famous cream cakes.

The **Open Arms Restaurant,** Royal Parade (tel. 0423/503034), is a neat little place with canopied ceilings, glinting wall lights, brass rails, and red curtains separating some of the tables into alcoves. The menu devised by Barry Holland over the past 20 years is truly a Taste of Yorkshire. Appetizers include Yorkshire pudding with onion , gravy, served before the meat course to cut your appetite a bit. Among main dishes are the traditional roast beef and Yorkshire pudding, fried fish with chips, and the chef's large golden Yorkshire puddings which are served with vegetables and filled with beefsteak with onions, tomatoes, and mushrooms; country game in red wine sauce with celery, onions, and carrots; or seafood tidbits in white sauce. Try apple pie with Wensleydale cheese for dessert. Meals cost around £10 ($15). Open daily except Monday for lunch from noon to 2 p.m. and for dinner in summer from 6 to 10 p.m. Closed Sunday and for dinner on Monday off-season.

Drum and Monkey, 5 Montpellier Gardens (tel. 0423/502650). Come here for some of the best fish dishes in the spa, prepared with skill by chef Patrick Laverack. In the heart of Harrogate, the restaurant is a bustling place. It's usually filled downstairs, where many patrons prefer to eat at the bar. Tables are freely shared with those savoring Dover sole, salmon, grilled mackerel, whatever swims. If you're here for lunch, try the "dressed" crab salad. Meals range in price from £10 ($15), but could go much higher, depending on your fish selection. It is open from noon to 2:30 p.m. and 7 to 10 p.m. Monday to Saturday.

MOORS AND DALES: The rural landscape is pierced with ruins of once-great abbeys and castles. North Yorkshire is a land of green hills, valleys, and purple moors. Both the Yorkshire Dales and the Moors are wide open spaces, two of Britain's finest national parks, with a combined area of some 1,200 square miles. However, the term "national" can be misleading, as the land is managed by foresters, farmers, and private landowners. In fact, more than 90% of the land is in private ownership. The Dales rise toward Cumbria and Lancashire to the east, and the Moors stretch to the eastern coastline.

Of course, York, the major center, has already been previewed. But those with the time may want to explore deeper into the rural roots of England. From Harrogate, our last stopover, you can enjoy the wildest scenery of the region by heading out on day trips, anchoring at one of the inns coming up if you don't want to return to the old spa.

After leaving Harrogate, you can discover white limestone crags, drystone walls, fast-rushing rivers, and isolated sheep farms or else clusters of sandstone cottages.

Malhamdale receives more visitors annually than any dale in Yorkshire. Of the priories and castles to visit, two of the most interesting are the 12th-century ruins of **Bolton Priory,** and a 14th-century pile, **Castle Bolton,** to the north in Wensleydale.

In contrast, the Moors, on the other side of the Vale of York, have a wild beauty all their own, quite different from that of the Dales. They are bounded by the Cleveland and Hambleton Hills. The white horse of Kilburn can be seen hewn out of the landscape.

Both **Pickering** and **Northallerton,** two market towns, serve as gateways to the Moors. Across the Moors are seen primordial burial grounds and stone crosses. The best known trek in moorland is the 40-mile hike over bog, heather, and stream from Mount Grace Priory inland to Ravenscar on the seacoast. It's known as **Lyke Wake Walk.**

Along North Yorkshire's 45 miles of coastline are such traditional seaside resorts as **Filey, Whitby,** and **Scarborough,** the latter claiming to be the oldest seaside spa in Britain, standing on the site of a Roman signaling station. It was founded in 1622, following the discovery of mineral springs with medicinal properties. In the 19th century its Grand Hotel, a Victorian structure, was acclaimed "as the best in Europe." The Norman castle on big cliffs overlooks the twin bays.

In and Around Helmsley

This attractive market town, with a market every Friday, is a good center for exploring the surrounding area. It is called the key to Ryedale and is the mother town of the district, standing at the junction of the roads from York, Pickering, Malton, Stokesley, and Thirsk.

Helmsley is on the southern edge of the North Yorkshire Moors National Park and is well known as a center for walking and "potholing." It is an area among many places and things of interest: remains of Bronze and Iron Age existence on the moors; prehistoric highways, Roman roads, and of course the ruins of medieval castles and abbeys. Beyond the main square of the town are the ruins of its castle with an impressive keep. This castle was built between 1186 and 1227.

A good reason for selecting Helmsley as a stopover is because it is near York and well located, but the hotel rates are far below those of York.

Three miles to the north of Helmsley are the ruins of **Rievaulx** (pronounced "Reevo") **Abbey** (tel. 04396/228). The abbey was named for Rye Vallis, valley of the River Rye. It was the first Cistercian house in northern England and was founded in 1131 by monks who came over from Clairvaux in France. At its peak it had 140 monks and 500 lay brothers. In its size, its architecture, and its setting, even its ruins are among the most impressive in the country. The land was given by Walter l'Espec, a Norman knight, who later entered the community as a novice and died and was buried here.

It is open from 9:30 a.m. to 4 p.m. October to March (on Sunday from 2 to 4 p.m.). From March to October its hours are 9:30 a.m. to 6:30 p.m. (on Sunday from 2 to 6:30 p.m.). Admission is £1 ($1.50) for adults and 50p (75¢) for children.

Rievaulx Terrace, a property of the National Trust, is a landscaped grassy terrace about half a mile long, which was laid out in the mid-18th century by Thomas Duncombe of Duncombe Park. The visitor, after a woodland walk, emerges onto a wide lawn near a circular "temple," known as the Tuscan Temple. The walk along the terrace gives frequent views of the abbey ruins in the valley below. On a windy North Yorkshire spring day, this walk is truly a constitutional.

At the opposite end from the Tuscan Temple is the Ionic Temple, whose interior is beautifully decorated and furnished, with a classically painted ceiling and gilded wood and rose-velvet upholstered furniture. In the basement are two rooms that were originally used by servants to prepare food for guests above. These rooms are now used to display exhibitions on English landscape design and periods, from the Duncombe family album. This temple was planned by Thomas Duncombe III as a banqueting house and a place of rest and refreshment after the long carriage ride from Duncombe Park.

Admission is £1.20 ($1.80), and visits are possible from 10:30 a.m. to 6 p.m. April to October.

Crown Hotel, Market Square at Helmsley (tel. 0439/70297), is a 16th-century inn built of stone. The walls are covered by creepers, giving it charm. The owners, Mr. and Mrs. Mander, have spared no effort to make every room not only attractive but comfortable. Wherever possible in the restoration, old beams have been left exposed. Ten of the bedrooms have showers, and all have hot and cold water basins, color TV, and facilities for making hot beverages. The half-board rate ranges from £26 ($39) to £28.50 ($42.75) per person daily. The dining room is well furnished, the menus offering a roast, two different fresh east coast fish, and at least three other main courses. The hotel has two living rooms and two bars, one public and a better furnished one for residents.

At Coxwold

Coxwold is on the southern border of the park, one of the most attractive villages in the Moors.

Fauconberg Arms, The High (tel. 03476/214), is a fine old Yorkshire inn, on the main street of this village of stone houses. The social center of the village, it attracts residents with a lounge bar, where a fire burns brightly in a stone fireplace topped by a 15-foot oak beam. There are black oak settles, Windsor armchairs, a stone floor, horse brasses, and in spring a bowl of flowers in the wide bay window overlooking the street. Here you can literally settle in for a premeal drink in front of the fire. If it's Thursday, the maid starts her weekly round of polishing the impressive collection of brass and copper. The dining room is cozily decorated, and you can get a set lunch for £6.50 ($9.75). The cuisine is traditional English, including roast pork with apple sauce or roast chicken with bread sauce. Perhaps the cook will make a rhubarb pie served with a dollop of thick cream. Dinners are à la carte and include poultry choices and meat dishes for around £12 ($18) per person. There are three attractively decorated rooms which share a corridor bath, costing £32 ($48), rising to £34 ($51) with shower, in a double. Bathless singles go for £20 ($30), the tariff going up to £22 ($33) with shower. If you can get it, the best room, the fourth one, is a double complete with shower and television.

In and Around Settle

Golden Lion Hotel, Duke Street (tel. 07292/2203), has been accepting overnight guests since 1671 when travelers would arrive via the covered entryway and descend from the carriage in the inner courtyard. Each of the ten attractive guest rooms has hot and cold running water and is centrally heated. The rate for B&B is £12 ($18) per person, including VAT and service. Some have private baths. The rooms have old-style furnishings and are of a good size. There are two lounge bars, each colorful, with open fires in cold weather. They have real ale. Bar snacks include chicken and chips. The menu in the dining room has simple but well-prepared Yorkshire fare, including a roast and a fish dish. A three-course set meal costs about only £4.50 ($6.75). Bernard Houghton is the jovial owner.

Close House, Giggleswick, near Settle (tel. 07292/3540), is a 17th-century farmhouse of great charm with all the required modern amenities, a delightfully relaxing place. The owner, Mrs. B. T. Hargreaves, has tastefully furnished the rooms with antiques and a collection of horse brasses, and other objects, all making it an unusual stopover retreat. Close House and its 230 acres of farmland lie at the end of a tree-lined private drive in the Yorkshire Dales. It's 1½ miles from Settle (off the A65 Lancaster–Skipton road). The rate for B&B is £15.50 ($23.25) to £17.50 ($26.25) per person, depending on your length of stay. A home-prepared evening meal is available for £11 ($16.50), by prior arrangement. The service charge is left to your discretion. Close House does not cater to children.

Near Skipton

The **Buck Inn,** Malham, near Skipton (tel. 07293/317), is a Victorian stone inn where Dale explorers can find excellent ale, a comfortable and cozy room, and a good breakfast and dinner. There are two bars, one especially for hikers, and the other for residents. The inn offers ten centrally heated bedrooms, each with a wash basin, only two with private bath. A single ranges from £15 ($22.50) to £17 ($25.50), and a double goes for £26 ($39) to £30 ($45), the latter for units with private bath or shower. The half-board tariff is in the range of £21 ($31.50) to £23 ($34.50) per person nightly. You can order bar lunches noon and evening if you don't want a full meal.

In and Around Richmond

Richmond, the most frequently used town name in the world, stands at the head of the Dales as the mother of them all. It's an old market town built beside the River Swale and dominated by the striking ruins of its Norman castle. In the center of the cobbled marketplace stands an ancient church and a tall stone pillar known as the Market Cross. It's a good touring center for the surrounding countryside.

The Georgian Theatre here, which was constructed in 1788, has a resident amateur company of the highest quality.

For an accommodation in the area, try the following recommendation:

Whashton Springs Farms, 3 miles from Richmond (tel. 0748/2884), is a 300-acre mixed farm in the heart of Herriot country, set high in the hills. In the stone farmhouse, Fairlie and Gordon Turnbull and their two sons receive guests, who are free to wander around the farm and enjoy the tranquil countryside. Bedrooms in the centrally heated house all have color TV and beverage-making facilities. They're all comfortably furnished, with wall-to-wall carpets. The six units in the stable courtyard have private baths or showers. For B&B, they charge £10 ($15) per person in bathless rooms, £12 ($18) per person in rooms with private plumbing. In the pleasant dining room, which has a bow window overlooking the moors, real Yorkshire farmhouse breakfasts and dinners are served (no evening meal on Thursday). On other days, half board costs from £16 ($24) to £18 ($27) per person, depending on whether the room you occupy has a bathroom. If you come into Richmond from the A1 South, turn right at a traffic light onto the Ravensworth Road, following it for 3 miles. Down a steep hill with woods on either side, you'll come upon the farm at the bottom on the left.

In and Around Bedale

Ainderby Myers, Bedale (tel. 0609/748668). At this 16th-century manor house, Mrs. Anderson offers B&B, charging from £9 ($13.50) per person nightly. There are mentions of the manor in the *Domesday Book*. She offers four rooms with hot and cold running water and good heating, plus a lounge with TV. In the pleasant garden, you can sit and enjoy a view of the rolling Yorkshire countryside. An evening meal can be provided for £7 ($10.50), but there are some very good places to eat out in the area, of which Mrs. Anderson will furnish details if required. To reach the village, turn off the A1 at the Hackforth turning.

Mill Close Farm, Patrick Brompton, near Bedale (tel. 0677/50257), is in the center of James Herriot country, within easy reach of the Yorkshire Dales. This is a dairy and corn-growing farm, run by the Knox family. Mrs. Knox will give you a Yorkshire welcome over a cup of tea and homemade cookies. She has two double rooms and provides B&B at a cost of £10 ($15) per person per night. Evening meals are available on request or may be obtained at several local inns at reasonable charges.

Elmfield House, Arrathorne, near northeast of Bedale (tel. 0677/50558), is a charming house with open views of the surrounding countryside. Mrs. Edith Lillie operates a comfortable, centrally heated house, with a spacious lounge in which guests can watch color TV, and a dining room. She charges £9 ($13.50) for B&B, with an evening meal offered for £6 ($9).

In and Around Ripon

Ripon has an ancient tradition of the watchman blowing a horn in the center of town every night, a custom dating back to 886. This cathedral city, 27 miles north of Leeds by road, was once a Saxon village where a Celtic monastery was founded in 651.

Beneath the central tower of **Ripon Cathedral,** the site of a Norman cathedral dating from 1154, is the original crypt built by St. Wilfrid more than 1,300 years ago. This is one of the oldest buildings in England, and the original plaster is still on the walls. The crypt contains silver chalices and patens dating from 1500 to the present.

Archbishop Roger built the nave of the Norman cathedral, the north transept, and part of the choir stalls. The twin towers of the west front are Early English, from about 1216, and the library (once the "Lady Loft") is from sometime in the 14th century.

The canons stalls were hand-carved and were completed in 1495. Two sides of the tower date from the original construction in 1220, but in 1450 an earthquake caused the other two to collapse. They were reconstructed and the central tower and south transept were added at the beginning of the 16th century. The completion of all the work was never carried out, as King Henry VIII took away all the cathedral endowments. Until 1664 the towers had tall spires, which were removed to prevent fires caused by lightning.

Today the cathedral is a lively Christian Centre, with a study center and a choir school. It is the mother church of the Diocese of Ripon, which spreads over most of the Yorkshire Dales to the fifth-largest city in England, Leeds. For further information, telephone 0765/4108.

Three miles west of Ripon lie the ruins of **Fountains Abbey,** which I consider the most magnificent abbey ruins in England. Founded in 1132, this former abbey was Cistercian in origin. It is set in 100 acres of meadow and woodland, with ornamental gardens, Fountains Hall, and a deer herd. The abbey and garden are open all year. From mid-October until the end of March hours are 9:30 a.m. to 4 p.m. Monday to Saturday (on Sunday from 2 to 4 p.m.). From April until mid-October, hours are daily from 9:30 a.m. to 8 p.m. Admission is £1.70 ($2.55) for adults and 80p ($1.20) for children.

The **Ripon Prison and Police Museum,** St. Marygate (tel. 0765/3706), is a fascinating exhibition of the history of police work from the time of the wakeman of Ripon (the watchman of the town in the Middle Ages) up to the wonders of modern technology as they pertain to fighting crime. The building in which the museum is housed started life as a prison, built in 1815. In 1887, it became a police station and continued so until its retirement in 1956. Now it has displays of life in both phases of its existence, including some of the punishment devices so popular in Victorian days. The museum is open May to the end of September Tuesday to Saturday from 1:30 to 4:30 p.m., plus Sunday and bank holiday Mondays, in July, August, and September. Admission is 50p (75¢) for adults, 25p (38¢) for children.

Newby Hall, lying on the northeast bank of the Ure River between Ripon (4 miles) and Boroughbridge (3½ miles), is a famous Adam house set in 25 acres of grounds, filled with sunken gardens, magnolias, azaleas, and countless flowering shrubs, along with many rare and unusual species. The house, built for Sir Edward Blackett circa 1695, is in the style of Sir Christopher Wren. In the mid-18th century, Robert Adam redesigned the house, extending it to display the antique sculpture, tapestries, and furniture of its then owner, William Weddell, a connoisseur and art collector. Robin Compton is the present owner. Displayed are the Gobelin Tapestries, one of only five sets completed, with medallions by Boucher, appointed first painter to Louis XV.

On the grounds is a miniature railway, the Newby 10¼-inch gauge, providing rides for both children and adults, adventure gardens, and a steamboat that sails on Sunday along the river, a gift shop, a licensed Garden Restaurant, a plant stall, and a Woodland Discovery Walk. From April until late September, the house is open from noon to 5:30 p.m., with last admissions at 5 p.m. The gardens and restaurant open at 11 a.m., and the train runs from 1 p.m. daily except Monday, unless it's a bank holiday. Admission to the hall and gardens is £2.30 ($3.45) for adults, £1.20 ($1.80) for children. For more information, telephone 09012/2583.

Several attractive accommodations are available in the area:

The Nordale, 1 North Parade, Ripon (tel. 0765/3557), is a bargain at the daily per-person rate of from £11 ($16.50), which includes not only a complete full-course breakfast but VAT. All rooms have hot and cold running water, and there is a shower room in the corridor. Some units have showers. Consider having a Yorkshire dinner as well, and this costs from £16 ($24) per person including your room and breakfast.

Mrs. Richmond, the owner, will pack a picnic lunch for you if you are making a day trip. All her bedrooms are attractively furnished, with twins and doubles, according to your wish. Children can stay at reduced rates. The Nordale is a good center for exploring the Yorkshire Dales. Mr. Richmond, who assists in the running of the Nordale, has a keen interest in the city of Ripon and a knowledge of its history and traditions, and he can arrange for the viewing of the "City Regalia" for those who wish. He also has forged links with the Ripons of America, one in Wisconsin and more recently the Ripon in California. You might also ask about his self-catering units.

Black-a-Moor Inn, Risplith, near Ripon (tel. 076586/214), is a stone country inn well known for its hospitality and convivial atmosphere. It's on the Ripon–Pateley Bridge road, the B6265, five miles from Ripon, just perfect for visits to Fountains Abbey, the Brimham Rocks, and the Dales. Owners Joyce and David Beckett have decorated the three bedrooms with taste, installing central heating as well as hot and cold running water. They charge £17 ($25.50) per person for B&B in a single, £22 ($33) in a double, including VAT and the service charge. They offer country grill breakfasts, and some of their specialties include homemade steak-and-kidney pie, venison in black cherries, and chicken with lobster and prawns. Two dessert concoctions they are known for include lemon meringue pie and "Old Perculier Cake" with Wensleydale cheese.

At Thirsk

This pleasant old market town, north of York, has a fine parish church, lying in the Vale of Mowbray. But what makes it such a stopover for visitors is the fame brought to the village by James Herriot, author of *All Creatures Great and Small*. Mr. Herriot still practices in Thirsk, and visitors can photograph his office, perhaps get a picture of his partner standing in the door.

If you'd like to stay over, **Brook House,** Ingramgate (tel. 0845/22240), is a large Victorian house set in 2 acres of land, some of which is filled with flower beds. It overlooks the open countryside, but a three-minute walk brings you to the Market Square. Mrs. Margaret McLauchlan charges from £13 ($19.50) per person for B&B, VAT included, and makes reductions for children. She is charming and kind, and has even been known to do a batch of washing for guests at no extra cost (however, I can't promise that!). She serves a good Yorkshire breakfast, hearty and filling, plus an English tea in the afternoon. She has a spacious and comfortable living room with color TV, and her bedrooms are large and airy. For out-of-season visitors, the house is fully centrally heated, and in the guests' drawing room there is always an open log fire. One major benefit of staying at Brook House is the peace and quiet away from traffic and other noise. There is ample secluded parking for cars. The experience of knowing John and Margaret McLauchlan and enjoying their hospitality will remain long in your memory. They are acquaintanced with Mr. Herriot.

Sheppard's Church Farm, at Sowerby, near Thirsk (tel. 0845/23655), offers rural peace. You can drive there, and it's also reached by a footpath from the town center, about a ten-minute walk from Thirsk Market Square. It is both a Cordon Bleu restaurant and a farm offering accommodations. The owners, Roy and Olga Sheppard, were born in Yorkshire, and they are most helpful to guests touring in the area. Their home is some three centuries old, but it has been brought up-to-date and handsomely furnished, often with family heirloom pieces. Outside stand large lime trees which were planted to honor Queen Victoria's Jubilee. Bedrooms are nicely furnished and have a personalized touch. My favorites are the two double rooms and a family room, all with private bath, installed in a former hayloft. Accommodations with private bath rent for £17 ($25.50) per person, or if you take one of the other double rooms, the charge is lowered to £12 ($18) per person. Tariffs include a full English breakfast.

The six-stall horse barn has been converted into the Sheppard's Table. It is possible to enjoy a quiet drink and a candlelit dinner on the very spot where James Herriot ministered to the horses. The walls are of rough brick, and dark wood and farm equipment make for a rustic atmosphere. The cuisine is excellent because all the ingredients that go into making it are bought fresh daily. The cookery is both imaginative and served with flair. A traditional Sunday lunch is featured for £6.50 ($9.75) and a dinner from £10 ($15) and up. An extensive à la carte dinner menu is available daily from 7 p.m. Reservations are advised.

St. James House, 36 The Green (tel. 0845/22676), is a lovely three-story, 18th-century Georgian brick house on the village green, near the former maternity home where James Herriot's children were born. The guesthouse, operated by Mrs. Liz Ogleby, is tastefully furnished, with some sturdy Regency antiques. (Mr. Ogleby is an antique dealer.) The attractive bedrooms have such touches as good bone china to use with the tea/coffee-makers. B&B rates are £18 ($27) in a bathless single, £25 ($37.50) for double occupancy of a bathless unit, and £32 ($48) for double occupancy in one of the two accommodations with private baths. VAT is included in the prices. The house does not receive guests from November to March.

HAWES: The natural center of the Yorkshire Dales National Park is Hawes, a market town in Wensleydale and home of the cheese of that name. It's on the Pennine Way, which is popular with hikers. Hawes lies on a good road, the A684, about midway between the A1 running on the east and the M6 on the west.

The **Upper Dales Folk Museum** at Station Yard (the old train station) (tel. 09697/494), traces folk life in the area of the Upper Dales. Peat-cutting and cheese-making, among other occupations, are depicted. The museum is open April to September from 11 a.m. to 5 p.m. Monday to Saturday, from 2 to 5 p.m. on Sunday. Admission is 50p (75¢).

Rookhurst Georgian Country House, West End, Gayle, near Hawes (tel. 09697/454), is on the outskirts of the village of Gayle, about five minutes' walk from Hawes. Brian and Susan Jutsum own the handsome stone hotel fronting the Pennine Way. The bedrooms, with views over the surrounding fells, are individually furnished, all with unusual or antique beds, including a brass four-poster and a similar walnut bed, circa 1770. The Georgian rooms, in part of the house (then named West End) which was originally built in 1734 as a farmhouse, are heavily oak beamed. Those in the Victorian wing, added in 1869, are larger and quite elegant. Most have baths or showers. B&B rates are £21 ($31.50) in a single, from £21 ($31.50) to £26 ($39) per person in a double (the higher price being for units with private baths). Charges include a full English breakfast and VAT. Three-course dinners are served in the restaurant for £8.50 ($12.75). Afternoon cream teas are offered in summer.

You don't need to travel far from Rookhurst for beautiful Dales scenery. Gayle, originally a Celtic settlement, is divided by Duerley Beck, with two lovely waterfalls, a ford, and an old stone bridge beloved of artists and photographers.

At Thornton Rust

A little road to the south off the A684 between Worton and Aysgarth, east of Hawes, the tiny hamlet of Thornton Rust, central to all the Yorkshire Dales. The post office for the village is Leyburn, to the east, it is much closer to Hawes.

Thornton Rust Hall (tel. 09693/569) is a handsome listed building of 17th- and

18th-century origin. The main house has been restored to provide a well-appointed country house with such features as exposed beam ceilings and a full height arched stone fireplace in the paneled dining room. The spacious bedrooms, all with large private baths with antique brass fittings and bidets as well as beverage-making facilities, rent for £18 ($27) to £25 ($36.50) per person for B&B, depending on the season. Alan and Gillian Cooper serve home-cooked dinners for £10 ($15) to £12 ($18), the latter including wine and a nightcap. The Coopers also have cottages which they rent by the week to parties of two to four persons.

3. West Yorkshire

HAWORTH: In West Yorkshire, this ancient stone village lying on the high moors of the Pennines—45 miles west of York via Leeds and 21 miles west of Leeds—is world famous as the home of the Brontë family. The three sisters—Charlotte, Emily, and Anne—distinguished themselves as English novelists. They lived a life of imagination at a lonely parsonage at Haworth.

Anne wrote two novels, *The Tenant of Wildfell Hall* and *Agnes Grey,* and Charlotte's masterpiece was *Jane Eyre,* which depicted her experiences as a governess and enjoyed popular success in its day.

But, of course, it was Emily's fierce and tragic *Wuthering Heights* that made her surpass her sisters, as she created a novel of such passion, intensity, and primitive power, with its scenes of unforgettable, haunting melancholy, that the book has survived to this day, appreciated by later generations far more than those she'd written it for.

From Haworth (pronounced "How-worth"), you can walk to Withens, the "Wuthering Heights" of the immortal novel. In Haworth, Charlotte and Emily are buried in the family vault under the church of St. Michael's.

The parsonage where they lived has been preserved as the **Brontë Parsonage Museum** (tel. 0535/42323), housing their furniture, personal treasures, pictures, books, and manuscripts. It may be visited daily from 11 a.m., closing at 5:30 p.m. April to September, at 4:30 p.m. October to March. It is closed the first three weeks in February and on December 24, 25, and 26. Admission for adults is 50p (75¢), rising to £1.50 ($2.25) in July, August, all summer Sundays, and bank holidays. Children's admission costs 25p (38¢) all year.

Haworth is the second most visited literary shrine in England, after Stratford-upon-Avon. Frequent bus and train service is available from Haworth to Keighley and Bradford and Leeds in West Yorkshire. The popular Worth Valley Steam Railway is one of the best preserved steam lines in England. At Keighley it connects with British Rail, running up the Worth Valley to Oxenhope via Haworth. From Haworth you can visit the tiny market town of Settle as well as Skipton with its canal and castle.

Food and Lodging

The **Tourist Information Centre,** 2–4 West Lane (tel. 0535/42329), offers an accommodation booking service for the local area and also a "book a bed ahead" service but cannot recommend individual establishments. The office is open daily throughout most of the year (closed over the Christmas period). If you don't avail yourself of this service, then you might stay at one of the recommendations below.

The **Old White Lion Hotel** (tel. 0535/42313) stands at the top of a cobblestone street. It was built around 1700 with a solid stone roof almost next door to the church where the Reverend Brontë preached and to the parsonage where the family lived. Joyce and Keith Bradford welcome tourists from all over the world to their warm, cheerful, and comfortable hotel. The cost is £30 ($45) for a double room, including breakfast and all taxes. Singles go for £20 ($30). Dinners are available either table d'hôte or à la carte in the candlelit restaurant. Hot and cold bar snacks prepared by the hotel chefs are offered at meal times.

The **Black Bull,** Main Street (tel. 0535/42249), owned by Ron Bennett, stands close to the parish church where Patrick Brontë was incumbent for 41 years and is closely associated with the son, Branwell Brontë. Although renovated and improved since Branwell's day, it is still interesting to spend time within the walls that drew him so strongly and even to sit in the chair that he occupied on his many visits to the inn, still on the premises. Today the Black Bull is as comfortable as inn as you will find. Conversion of the restaurant, which seats 40, has made use of a thick stone wall in forming a central arch. This is the room where Branwell's chair sits and here is the original bell pull and bell which he used to ring for his many drinks. Luncheon and bar snacks are served from noon until 2:30 p.m. A three-course lunch with roast beef and Yorkshire pudding costs around £6 ($9). Dinner is served from 7 until 10:30 p.m. The cuisine is excellent, and the à la carte menu, with a good supporting wine list, given an ample choice. Morning coffee and high tea are served on Sunday. Mr. Bennett charges £28 ($42) for a double room, £18 ($27) in a single, including a good breakfast.

The **Brontë Bookshop,** 1 Church St. (tel. 0535/42243), was the post office in the Brontës' time. Today Mrs. Tricia Richmond runs a spotlessly clean B&B accommodation at the address, charging £10 ($15) per person, including a large Yorkshire breakfast. She and her husband spent many years in Africa before returning to Haworth. Mrs. Richmond admits to being from Lancashire, but "as my father was from Yorkshire, they let me in." She has accommodations for families, couples, or singles, with the best location in town for sightseeing. Next door stands the Chocolate Box, which some have called "the sweetest candy store in England."

Moorfield Guest House, 80 West Lane (tel. 0535/43689), in a rural setting on the edge of town overlooking the moors, is only a 3-minute walk to downtown Haworth and the Brontë Parsonage. Pat and Barry Hargreaves offer four heated bedrooms with electric blankets. For a bed and a full English breakfast, they charge from £9 ($13.50) per person. All the units have hot and cold water basins, and one has a private bath. A four-course evening meal is available for £5 ($7.50). The hospitality of the owners is outstanding.

On the Outskirts

On the Haworth moors stands a Brontë landmark, **Ponden Hall,** Stanbury, near Keighley (tel. 0535/44154), a distance of some three miles from Haworth. A 400-year-old farmhouse, it lies about a third of a mile from the main road between Ponden reservoir and the moors. The wide, rough track which is a part of the Pennine Way long-distance footpath leads to this Elizabethan farmhouse with its traditional hospitality to walkers, visitors by car, children, and pets. The hall was extended in 1801 and is reputedly the model for Thrushcross Grange, Catherine's home after her marriage to Edgar Linton, in Emily Brontë's *Wuthering Heights*. Today it provides farmhouse accommodation that is spacious and homey, with one double, a twin, and a family room. The dining hall has an open fire, traditional flagstone floor, original oak beams, timbered ceiling, and mullioned windows. B&B charges are £8.50 ($11.75) per person per night, and a home-cooked evening meal is offered at £5 ($7.50). Vegetarian and special diets are catered too.

HAREWOOD HOUSE AND BIRD GARDEN: In West Yorkshire, at Junction A61/

659, midway between Leeds and Harrogate, and five miles from the A1 at Wetherby, stands the home of the Earl and Countess of Harewood. One of the "Magnificent Seven" homes of England, this 18th-century house was designed by John Carr and has always been owned by the Lascelles family. The fine Adam interior has superb ceilings and plasterwork, and furniture made especially for Harewood by Chippendale. There are also important collections of English and Italian paintings and Sèvres and Chinese porcelain.

The Capability Brown landscape includes a 4½-acre bird garden which borders the lake. It contains exotic species from all over the world, including penguins, macaws, flamingoes, and snowy owls, and there is an undercover extension. The spacious grounds offer terraces, lakeside and woodland walks, exhibitions, shops, and a restaurant and cafeteria. Car parking is free, and there is a picnic area, plus an adventure playground for the children.

Harewood is open daily from April 1 to October 31 at 10 a.m. The house, bird garden, and adventure playground are also open on Sunday in November, February, and March. Admission is £3.50 ($5.25) for adults, £1.50 ($2.25) for children. For further facts, phone Visitor Information (tel. 0532/886225).

Incidentally, Harewood is on a regular bus route (Leeds/Harrogate/Ripon), but the stop is about a mile from the house. Summer excursions run on varying days from those cities served by the regular buses from York and Bradford among other places. Ask at local tourist information centers and at your hotel for details.

6. Durham

This densely populated county of northeast England was once pictured as a dismal foreboding place, with coalfields, ironworks, mining towns, and shipyards. Now its image has brightened considerably, as intrepid explorers have sought out its valleys of quiet charm and its regions of wild moors in the west. Therefore, if you have the time, it would be interesting to explore the Durham Dales, especially Teesdale with its waterfalls and rare wild flowers and Weardale with its brown sandstone villages.

DURHAM: The county town, which has the same name, is built on a sandstone peninsula. Its treasure is the **Cathedral of Durham,** which ranks among the most beautiful buildings in the world. Its solid towers dominate the surrounding countryside from its sandstone pinnacle surrounded by the River Wear. Inside, the massive and bold incised piers in the nave and the ribbed vaults—one of the first English churches to have this decoration—give it a feeling of solidarity and security. The church was named for St. Cuthbert, the greatest North Country saint who was buried at Lindisfarne in A.D. 687. After being hauled around for many years, his body was interred behind the high altar in 1104 in the new construction begun in 1093. No admission is charged to visit the cathedral. However, to see the glorious gold and wealth and St. Cuthbert's coffin, you must pay 50p (75¢) for adults and 10p (15¢) for children. That admits you to the Treasury, which is open daily from 10 a.m. to 4:30 p.m. (on Sunday from 2 to 4:30 p.m.). Admission to the tower is 50p (75¢) for adults and 25p (38¢) for children. From the top, you'll have a magnificent view over the city and castle.

From Framweigate Bridge, below the massive church, is a peaceful riverside walk, known locally as **The Banks.** It leads you through trees beneath the castle and then up a steep path to the cathedral. It's quite a challenge for the weak-hearted, but well worth the effort for the fit.

In the shadow of the cathedral is the Church of St. Mary le Bow, now containing the **Durham Heritage Centre,** which is open from May until the end of September from 2 to 4:30 p.m. daily. It presents changing exhibitions and audio-visual presentations of the city's past and history, plus rubbing of replicas of monumental brasses. They also organize guided walking tours of the city daily at 2:30 and 3:30 p.m. when, for 50p (75¢) per person, you can join a fascinating and well-informed tour of the major sights, going through the Vennels, the narrow passages joining the old city streets.

Adjoining the cathedral is **Durham Castle** (tel. 091/386-5481), which was founded by the Normans and was the home of the prince-bishops until it was given to Durham University in 1832. Except on the occasion of university or other functions, the castle is open to visitors all year. From July to September, hours are 10 a.m. to noon and 2 to 4:30 p.m. weekdays only. During the rest of the year it is open from 2 to 4 p.m. on Monday, Wednesday, and Saturday. Admission is 90p ($1.35) for adults, 40p (60¢) for children.

Where to Stay

Mrs. Anne Williams, Castle View, 4 Crossgate (tel. 091/386-8852). Crossgate is quite a steep road across the river from the cathedral, and Castle View has just that, a magnificent view across the gorge. There is adequate parking in the street outside the large 250-year-old house beside St. Margaret's Church. Anne and her husband, Michael, have renovated their home, finding lovely old beams and woodwork in the process. Two singles, two doubles, and one family room share two bathrooms at a rate ranging from £10 ($15) to £12 ($18) per person. A large breakfast is served, and there is a residents' lounge.

Crossgate House, 11 Crossgate (tel. 091/386-8070), is the home of Robert and Jane Weil, who love old houses and have turned their home into a showpiece worthy of a magazine layout. Jane says she really just drifted into renting rooms and thoroughly enjoys the experience of meeting overseas visitors. Her two rooms are beautifully furnished, spotless, and warm. The charge for B&B ranges from £12 ($18) per person. The Weils are emphatic that Crossgate is their home, and will do everything they can to make you feel part of it. But they are quick to point out they can't provide the services of a five-star hotel.

Drumforke, 25 Crossgate Path (tel. 091/384-2966), is a modest guesthouse owned and run by Mrs. D. B. Greenwell, who for years has catered to small families. She asks £10 ($15) per person for a room, the rate including a hefty breakfast. She reduces the tariff for children sharing one of the good-size rooms with their parents.

Where to Eat

Market Tavern, Market Place (tel. 091/386-2069), right in the center of town, remembers associations of more than a century ago with one of England's first trade unions, reputedly organized on the premises. Lunchtime finds this pub busy and bustling with people who work in the area. It offers such selections as Durham broth, a special roast dish of the day, and a very popular local dish, "mince" and dumplings. You can finish it off with thieves' pudding. Meals cost from £5 ($7.50). Hours are from 11:45 a.m. to 2 p.m. and 7:30 to 9 p.m. daily.

Undercroft Restaurant, The College (tel. 091/386-3721), is found under the ancient roof and arches of the Cathedral of Durham. It lies in the crypt beside the Treasury, and is open weekdays from 9:30 a.m. to 5 p.m. (on Sunday from 1 to 5 p.m.). In the midst of pine furnishings and stone walls, you can order a hot dish of the day, such as cottage pie and buttered cabbage, followed by apple pie and cream, or perhaps you'd prefer to choose from pastas, pâté, and quiches. You can even order wine by the glass. Meals cost from £4 ($6).

Three Tuns Hotel, New Elvet (tel. 091/386-4326), has a good bar buffet, serving baked ham, chili con carne, and baked potatoes, with meals costing from £3.50 ($5.25). The Tudor Restaurant, serving traditional and vegetarian menus, offers lunch costing from £6.50 ($9.75) and dinner from £9.50 ($14.25). Go for meals from noon to 2 p.m. and 6:30 to 9 p.m. The lower bar is noisy and crowded with students from the

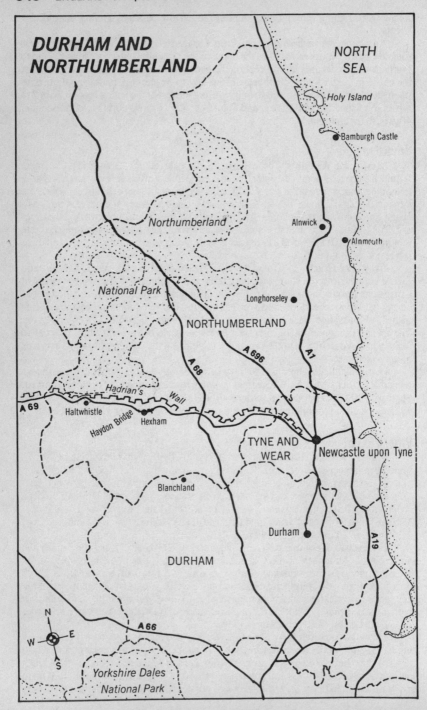

DURHAM AND
NORTHUMBERLAND

NORTH
SEA

Holy Island

Bamburgh Castle

Northumberland

Alnwick

Alnmouth

National Park

Longhorseley

NORTHUMBERLAND

A 696

A 68

A 1

Hadrian's

Wall

A 69

Haltwhistle

Haydon Bridge

Hexham

TYNE AND
WEAR

Newcastle upon Tyne

Blanchland

Durham

A 19

DURHAM

N
W E
S

A 66

Yorkshire Dales
National Park

university, discussing the latest fundraising "rag" event. But then they're the sort of people who know good value when they taste it.

The **Swan and Three Cygnets,** on Elvet Bridge (tel. 091/384-0242), is the domain of Russ and Judith Sharpe, who serve Samuel Smith ale from Yorkshire's oldest brewery in a black-and-white timbered pub at the junction of the bridge and the pedestrian area leading to the cathedral. At lunch, between noon and 2 p.m., you can get "mince" and dumplings, along with steak-and-kidney pie, plus soups and desserts, with meals costing around £4 ($6).

The **Ristorante de Medici,** 12 Elvet Bridge (tel. 091/386-1310), is several small rooms up a flight of steps over a store. This is a gaily decorated place with Chianti bottles, wagon wheels, and warm reds and dark browns. From noon to 2:30 p.m. and 6:30 to 11 p.m. daily except Sunday, you can get a typical Italian menu, including cannelloni and chicken milanese. Meals cost around £7.50 ($11.25).

BARNARD CASTLE: Near the River Tees, in the town of Barnard Castle, stands the **Bowes Museum** (tel. 0833/37139), at the eastern end of town. It was built in 1869 by John Bowes and his wife, the Countess of Montalbo, to house and display their art collection. Here you'll find masterpieces by Goya and El Greco, plus many fine tapestries and porcelains. There are also collections of French and English furniture, superb costumes, musical instruments, a children's gallery, and many other things of interest. A tea room and ample parking are found on the premises. It is open from 10 a.m. to 5:30 p.m. Monday to Saturday, from 2 to 5 p.m. on Sunday, closing at 4 p.m. November to February. Admission is £1.35 ($2.03) for adults, 45p (68¢) for children.

Food and Lodging

Coach & Horses, 22 Galgate (tel. 0833/38369), has a name that commemorates the heyday of the coaching inns of north England, and enjoys an enviable central location in the vicinity of most of the attractions of town. The rooms are full of character, and the pub and restaurant attract many nonresidents. The place is small, with only seven rooms to rent, three of which contain private baths. The B&B charge is £15 ($22.50) in a single, £29 ($43.50) in a double. It's also possible to stay here on half-board terms, costing from £18 ($27) per person nightly.

George & Dragon Inn, at Boldron (tel. 0833/38215), is a local favorite. This well-maintained old inn has a long tradition of welcoming wayfarers to the lovely Teesdale. A friendly place, it offers the traditions of a typical English country inn, with the hospitality of the northeast and good food and ale. Management has only two rooms to rent, a double and a twin, and occupants share the one bathroom. The charge is from £17 ($25.50) to £18 ($27) for two persons. It's also possible to book in here on a half-board rate of £13.50 ($20.25) per person. There is ample car parking.

The Market Place Tea Shop, 28 The Market Place (tel. 0833/37049), is a charming place for good-tasting meals, with a rustic interior and rugged stone walls, along with dark Windsor chairs. It's easy to find, right in the center of the marketplace, with a blue facade and red café curtains. It is also a handcraft center, displaying various articles made locally. Ample parking is available in front of the tea shop. For appetizers, try either the homemade chicken and cheese terrine, served with granary bread, or the prawn and smoked salmon terrine. The owner has widened the range of homemade main dishes to include such offerings as breast of chicken stuffed with homemade mushroom pâté, a traditional Lancashire hot-pot served with red cabbage, and pot roast brisket with Yorkshire pudding. Tempting desserts include syrup and orange sponge served with either cream or custard, as are the assorted fruit pies. Expect to spend from £5 ($7.50), plus the price of your drink. The place has a full table license between 11:30 a.m. and 3 p.m., and carries a fine selection of wines which are only available to those ordering meals. It remains open till 5:30 p.m. if you'd like afternoon tea. Sunday hours are from 2 to 5:30 p.m., but the establishment is closed on Sunday from December through March.

BEAMISH: West of Chester le Street, just a few miles south of Newcastle upon Tyne is Beamish, the **North of England Open Air Museum,** lying off the A693 and the A6076 roads. Here the way of life of the people of this area around the turn of the century has been re-created. You can take a tram ride into the past down a cobblestone 1920s street and visit old shops, houses, printworks, and a public house and Victorian park. Go down a "drift" mine in the colliery area, where you can see bread being baked in a row of pit cottages. Pop into the traditional farmhouse at Home Farm and meet the poultry, pigs, and cattle. There's a North Eastern Railway area, too, with a country station, signal box, and locomotives in steam. An average visit takes about four hours. It is open from the first of the year to mid-April daily except Monday from 10 a.m. to 5 p.m., mid-April to mid-September daily from 10 a.m. to 6 p.m., and mid-September to the end of the year daily from 10 a.m. to 5 p.m. Not all the attractions are open in winter. Admission is £2.95 ($4.43) for adults, £1.95 ($2.93) for children. For further information, phone 0202/231811, or ask at any Tourist Information Centre in England.

5. Tyne and Wear

In the county of Tyne and Wear, industrial Newcastle upon Tyne is the dominant focus, yet outside the city there is much natural beauty. Cattle graze on many a grassed-over mining shaft. There is such scenic beauty as moors and hills of purple-blue. The rugged coastline is beautiful. Americans like to pass through because of their interest in the ancestral home of George Washington (see below), and Newcastle also merits a stopover, particularly from motorists heading to Scotland.

The National Trust administers two sights in the region surrounding Newcastle:

Gibside Chapel, built in the classical style of James Paine in 1760, is an outstanding example of Georgian church architecture. A stately oak-lined avenue leads to the door of the chapel, which is the mausoleum of the Bowes family. The interior is decorated in delicate plasterwork and is furnished with paneled pews of cherrywood and a rare mahogany three-tiered pulpit. The chapel is open Wednesday, Saturday, and Sunday from 1 to 5 p.m. April to the end of October (open Good Friday and bank holiday Mondays). Other times of year, it can be seen by appointment with the custodian (tel. 0207/542255). Admission to the car park avenue and the chapel is £1 ($1.50) for adults, 50p (75¢) for children. There's a small kiosk for refreshments. The location is 6 miles southwest of Gateshead and 20 miles northwest of Durham between Rowlands Gill and Burnopfield.

Washington Old Hall is the ancestral home of the first president of the United States, and the place from which the family took its name. The interior of the house, whose origins date back to 1183, is furnished with period antiques and a collection of Delft ware. Relics of the Washingtons are also on display. The hall is open from 11 a.m. to 5 p.m. daily except Friday from mid-April to September and on Wednesday, Saturday, and Sunday in October. The first two weeks in April, hours are from 1 to 5 p.m. Wednesday, Saturday, and Sunday. Closed Good Friday. Admission is £1 ($1.50) for adults, 50p (75¢) for children. For additional information, telephone 0632/4166879. The location is in Washington on the east side of the A182, five miles west of Sunderland (two miles from the A1). South of Tyne Tunnel, follow signs for Washington New Town District 4 and then Washington Village.

NEWCASTLE UPON TYNE: An industrial city, Newcastle is graced with some fine streets and parks, as well as many old buildings. After crossing its best-known landmark, the Tyne Bridge, you enter a steep city which sweeps down to the Tyne, usually on narrow lanes called "chares." Once wealthy merchants built their town houses right on the quayside, and some of them remain.

For years Newcastle has been known as a shipbuilding and coal-exporting center, and gave rise to the expression of suggesting the absurdity of shipping coals to Newcastle.

Dominating the skyline, the **Cathedral of Newcastle** rises to a beautiful Scottish crown spire. It is England's most northerly cathedral, lying on a downward sweep between the Central Station and the quay. Its provost says that "the cathedral is one of the gems among the glorious churches of Northumberland." The cathedral's date of construction is unknown, but its recorded history predates 1122. The church was rebuilt in the 14th century, and John Knox preached from its pulpit.

The keep of the so-called New Castle, built by Henry II in 1170, contains the **Keep Museum,** on St. Nicholas Street, with an interpretation of the history of the castle site. It's open April to September, on Monday from 2 to 5 p.m.; Tuesday to Saturday, 10 a.m. to 5 p.m. From October to March, its Monday hours are 2 to 4 p.m.; Tuesday to Saturday, 10 a.m. to 4 p.m.

Where to Stay

Chirton House Hotel, 46 Clifton Rd. (tel. 091/2730407), is a substantial hotel, owned and managed by Capt. and Mrs. Hagerty, who have set reasonable rates. They charge from £17.25 ($25.88) to £23 ($34.50) for B&B in a single, VAT included, the higher price being for a room with shower. Doubles cost £27.60 ($41.40) to £32.50 ($48.75). The accommodations are well maintained and comfortable, all with hot and cold water basins. An evening meal can be prepared if requested in advance, costing £7 ($10.50). In the lounge, there's a color TV, and a bar serves residents. Chirton House is nicely located on a quiet street, yet close to the city.

Morrach Hotel, 82–86 Osborne Rd., Jesmond (tel. 091/2813361), is often cited as one of the best of the modestly priced hotels of Newcastle upon Tyne. A tranquil, family-managed establishment, it lies on the border of the city, the Morpeth road or B1309, right off the A6125. The hotel was converted from a series of 19th-century private residences, and today it offers a total of 34 comfortably furnished bedrooms. Depending on the plumbing, the single B&B rate ranges from £19.50 ($29.25) to £31 ($46.50), the double going from £28.50 ($42.75) to £41 ($61.50). This two-story establishment has a Buttery Bar serving meals throughout the day and night, and a more formal restaurant which serves from noon to 2 p.m. and 7 to 9:30 p.m. Meals cost from £5 ($7.50) at lunch, £8 ($12) at dinner. Try, if featured, the Tweed salmon or one of the continental dishes such as coq au vin.

Food and Drink

Dennhofers Blackgate Restaurant, The Side, off Dean Street (tel. 091/2617356), offers a classical range of dishes, mainly European but prepared in a modern style. To please the health-conscious dining public of today, Douglas Gordon, executive chef, and H.G. Seebacher, general manager, offer no fried foods, with only small amounts of oil, cream, and butter used when necessary. Such main courses as fresh poached halibut, braised salmon, roast guinea fowl, and grilled steaks are offered. Lunches change daily, dishes listed on the blackboard. A fixed-price meal costs from £4 ($6) to £6 ($9), and is served from noon to 3 p.m. Dinner, with an à la carte menu changing seasonally, is served from 7:30 to 10:30 p.m., a table d'hôte meal priced at around £10 ($15). The restaurant is open Monday to Friday for lunch and Tuesday to Saturday for dinner.

Ristorante Roma, 22 Collingwood St. (tel. 091/320612), helps you remember that holiday in Italy or your favorite little restaurant in Roma. Food is authentically Italian, prepared with care and thoughtfulness by Chef Pasquale, while the resident guitarist, Eusebio, plays enough live music to make you think you're being serenaded in Naples. A three-course meal, beginning with spaghetti al tonno (with tomatoes and tuna) and followed by saltimbocca alla romana, topped by zabaglione, would come to £10 ($15). A less expensive meal, and almost as good, could be ordered by choosing a pasta as a main course. In that event, the portion will be doubled. Try spaghetti alla pescatora (in a seafood and tomato sauce). There is dancing in the bar downstairs, and hours are from noon to 2 p.m. and 7 to 11:30 p.m. weekdays, from 7 to 11:30 p.m. on Sunday.

Jade Garden, 53 Stowell St. (tel. 091/2615889), is the city's best-known Cantonese restaurant, lying in the old Blackfriars district. Its staff keeps long hours, noon to 11:30 p.m. daily, and Alex Chung oversees everything with a welcoming hospitality. Against a backdrop of pink and green neon, guests order a set lunch for only £3.50 ($5.25), a table d'hôte dinner for £9.50 ($14.25). Vegetarians will find comfort here, and main courses, some 200 selections in all, include such tasty dishes as barbecued pork, lemon chicken, and fresh seafood. Some of the wines came all the way from China, as the song goes.

6. Northumberland

Most motorists zip through this far-northern county on their way to Scotland. Because it lies so close to Scotland, Northumberland was the scene of many a skirmish. The county now displays a number of fortified castles which saw action in those battles. Inland are the valleys of the Cheviot Hills, lying mostly within the Northumberland National Park and the remainder of the Border Forest Park, Europe's largest man-made forest.

Northumberland's coast is one of Britain's best kept secrets. Here are islands, castles, tiny fishing villages, miles of sands, along with golf and fishing among the dunes, birdwatching in the Farne Islands—in all, an area of outstanding natural beauty.

Wallington House Gardens & Grounds, at Cambo, 12 miles west of Morpeth (take the A696 north from Newcastle), dates from 1688, but the present building reflects the great changes brought about in the 1740s when Daniel Garrett completely refashioned the exterior of the house. The interior is decorated with rococo plasterwork and furnished with fine porcelains, furniture, and paintings. Visitors may also visit the museum and enjoy an extensive display of dollhouses. The West Coach House contains an exhibit of ornate carriages. The main building is surrounded by 100 acres of woodlands and lakes, including a beautifully terraced garden and a conservatory. The grounds are open all year, the house from May 1 to September 1 from 2 to 6 p.m. daily except Tuesday, April to October from 2 to 6 p.m. Wednesday, Saturday, and Sunday. Last admission is half an hour before closing time. Admission to the house and gardens is £2.40 ($3.60); to the grounds only £1 ($1.50). Children pay half price. For more information, telephone 067074/283.

The **Farne Islands** are a group of small islands off the Northumbria coast, which provide a summer house for at least 20 species of sea birds as well as for one of the largest British colonies of gray seals. St. Cuthbert died here in 687, and a chapel built in the 14th century is thought to be on the site of his original cell. Only Inner Farne and Staple Island are open to the public. Visiting season extends from April through September, but access is more controlled during the breeding season, from mid-May to the end of July. Admission is £1.50 ($2.25), going up to £2.40 ($3.60) during the breeding season.

The best way to get to this most famous bird and animal sanctuary in the British Isles is to telephone or write Billy Shiel, the Farne Islands boatman, at 4 Southfield Ave., Seahouses, Northumberland (tel. 0665/720308). He has been taking people in his licensed boat for the past 40 years, so he knows the tides and the best places to film seals, puffins, and guillemots. During breeding season, he runs 5½-hour trips daily, weather permitting, leaving at 10 a.m. and costing £6.50 ($9.75) per person. From April 1 to the end of October, 2½-hour trips are offered at 10 a.m. (outside breeding season), 1 p.m., and 3:30 p.m., costing £3 ($4.50). The *Glad Tidings* boats he operates hold from 44 to 72 passengers.

Incidentally, these are the islands where Grace Darling and her father made their famous rescue of men from a foundered ship (see below).

HOLY ISLAND: The site of the Lindisfarne religious community during the Dark Ages, Holy Island is only accessible for ten hours of the day, high tides covering the causeway at other times. For crossing times, check with the local information centers.

Lindisfarne Castle was built on the island about 1550. It is open to the public Wednesday, Saturday, and Sunday the first two weeks in April and daily except Friday mid-April to the end of September from 11 a.m. to 5 p.m. In October, it is open from 11 a.m. to 5 p.m. on Saturday and Sunday only. Last entry is 4:30 p.m. Admission is £2.20 ($3.30) for adults, £1.10 ($1.65) for children. For more information, telephone 0289/89244.

At Lindisfarne on Holy Island, you can stay at the **Lindisfarne Private Hotel** (tel. 0289/89273). This is a fine, substantial frame building with a trio of tall chimneys. It's run by members of the Massey family, who conduct it more like a private home than a hotel. Centrally heated bedrooms contain hot and cold running water and are decorated with personality, providing home-like comfort. The charge is £19 ($28.50) to £22 ($33) per person daily for half board. Boating excursions can be arranged to the Farnes.

BAMBURGH CASTLE: Guarding the British shore along the North Sea, the castle (tel. 06684/20208) stands on a site that has been occupied since the first century B.C. The Craggy Citadel where it stands was a royal center by A.D. 574. The Norman keep has stood for eight centuries, the remainder of the castle having been restored toward the end of the 19th century. This was the first castle to succumb to artillery fire, the guns of Edward IV. You can visit the grounds and public rooms from 1 to 5 p.m. in April, May, June, and September, 1 to 6 p.m. in July and August, and 1 to 4:30 p.m. in October. Admission is £1.60 ($2.40) for adults, 60p (90¢) for children.

Nearby is the **Grace Darling Museum** (tel. 0665/720037), which has various mementoes, pictures, and documents relating to the heroic Grace Darling, including the boat in which she and her father, who was keeper of the Longstone lighthouse in the Farne Islands, rescued nine people from the S.S. *Forfarshire* that foundered in 1838. It's open from Easter to mid-October from 11 a.m. to 6 p.m. Admission is free.

HADRIAN'S WALL: This wall, which extends across the north of England for 73½ miles, from the North Sea to the Irish Sea, is particularly interesting for a stretch of 3½ miles west of Housesteads. Only the lower courses of the wall are preserved intact; the rest were reconstructed in the 19th century with the original stones. From several vantage points along the wall, you have incomparable views north to the Cheviot Hills along the Scottish border, and south to the Durham moors.

The wall was built following a visit of the Emperor Hadrian in A.D. 122. He wanted to see the far frontier of the Roman Empire, and he also sought to build a dramatic line between the so-called civilized world and the barbarians. Legionnaires were ordered to build a wall across the length of the island of Britain, stretching for 73½ miles, going over hills and plains, beginning at the North Sea and ending at the Irish Sea.

The wall is the premier Roman attraction in Europe, ranking with many people up with Rome's Colosseum. The western end can be reached from Carlisle, with a good museum of Roman artifacts, and the eastern end from Newcastle upon Tyne (some remains on the city outskirts and a good museum at the university). South Shields, Chesters, Corbridge, and Vindolanda are all good forts to visit in the area.

At Housesteads you can visit a **Roman fort** (tel. 04984/363), built about A.D. 130 to house an infantry of 1,000 men. Called Vercovicium in Latin, the fort housed a full-scale military encampment, the remains of which can be seen today. There is also a small museum with altars, inscriptions, and models. The fort is open from March 15 to October 15 on weekdays from 9:30 a.m. to 6:30 p.m., on Sunday from 2 to 6:30 p.m. From October 16 to March 14, hours are 9:30 a.m. to 4 p.m. on weekdays, from 2 to 4 p.m. on Sunday. Between April and September, the fort is also open on Sunday from 9:30 a.m. Price of admission is £1 ($1.50) for adults and 50p (75¢) for children.

Just west of Housesteads at Bardon Mill is **Vindolanda** (Chesterholme) (tel. 04984/277), another fort south of the wall at Chesterholm. The building is very well preserved, and there is also a recently excavated civilian settlement outside the fort with an interesting museum of artifacts of everyday Roman life. Admission is £1.40 ($2.10) for adults and 70p ($1.05) for children.

Not far from Vindolanda is the **Roman Army Museum,** Carvoran, on Hadrian's Wall near Greenhead, which traces the growth and influence of Rome from her early beginnings to the development and expansion of the empire, with special emphasis on the role of the Roman army and the garrisons of Hadrian's Wall. A barracks room shows basic Roman army living conditions. Realistic life-size figures make this a striking visual museum experience. Admission is £1 ($1.50) for adults, 55p (83¢) for children. For information, telephone 06972/485.

Within easy walking distance of the Roman Army Museum lies one of the most imposing and high-standing sections of Hadrian's Wall, **Walltown Crags,** where the height of the wall and magnificent views to the north and south are impressive.

HALTWHISTLE: About 20 miles east of Carlisle lies the town of Haltwhistle. There the **Grey Bull Hotel** (tel. 0498/20298) would be a good base of operations for seeing the best sections of Hadrian's Wall and its Roman garrisons. These include Housesteads, Vindolanda (the largest site in Europe), the Chesters, and Carvorum (Roman Military Museum)—all within 15 minutes' drive from the hotel. The Grey Bull has been modernized and reequipped. There are 11 bedrooms, each with its own wash basin with hot and cold running water and tea- and coffee-making facilities. The inclusive price is from £10 ($15) per person for B&B. The bar at the hotel is a lively gathering place for the local people, and "pub grub" is available.

White Craig Farm, Shield Hill (tel. 0498/20565), is a farmhouse just a mile up the hill north of Haltwhistle, and about a mile from the major attraction, Hadrian's Wall. Mrs. J. W. Laidlow, a pleasant, accommodating person, rents rooms in an old house (part from the 17th century) with modern facilities, with a good hillside view. She charges from £9.50 ($14.25) per person in a double with hot and cold running water, from £11 ($16.50) per person in a double- or twin-bedded room with private bath. Two self-catering cottages, sleeping four and seven persons, respectively, rent on weekly terms.

The **Milecastle Inn & Game Restaurant,** Route B6318 off Main, Newcastle to Carlisle A69 (tel. 0498 / 20682), is run by Jennie and Barrie W. Smith, and features such unusual specialties as hunters casserole, venison, jugged hare, grouse, quail, partridge, homemade venison sausages marinated in port, and Pickwick puddings (steak, mushroom, and oyster). The cooks also serve a few grills and fish. Meals start at £12 ($18). Bar lunches cost £4 ($6) and up. The food is prepared with pride and imagination, and the countryside is reminiscent of the days one hunted for his dinner, and with such fare to choose from you could almost believe the Smiths did just that! The place is open from 11 a.m. to 2:30 p.m. and 6 to 10 p.m.

ALLENDALE: In the southwestern sector of the shire, this unspoiled country village is the geographic center of Great Britain. It is well known for its ancient Fire Festival on New Year's Eve in the Market Place. From a base here, some of the finest scenery of Northumbria—heather-clad hills, moor, and woodland—unfolds:

For the best food and lodging in the area, seek out **Bishopfield Farm** (tel. 043483/248), which remains open all year. On some 200 acres of rolling, lovely Northumberland countryside, this farm cum hotel traces its origins back to 1740. The Fairless family, the owners, have owned this homestead for several generations, and their welcome will take some of the chill off a gray day. They rent out a total of nine comfortably furnished and pleasantly equipped bedrooms. Each of these units contains a private shower or bath, and also has a phone and central heating. Two-thirds of the units lie in a courtyard of cobblestones. The most sensible way to book in here is to take half-board terms, costing £21 ($31.50) to £25 ($37.50) per person nightly. The food is one of the attractions of the place. The food is wholesome and fresh, the portions generous, and whenever possible the produce comes from Northumberland. The location is about a mile west of Allendale.

HEXHAM: Above the Tyne River, this historic market town is characterized by its narrow streets, old Market Square, a fine abbey church, and its Moot Hall. It makes a good base for exploring Hadrian's Wall and the Roman supply base of Corstopitum at Corbridge-on-Tyne, the ancient capital of Northumberland. The Tourist Office has masses of information on the wall for walkers, drivers, campers, and picnickers.

The Abbey Church of St. Wilfred is full of ancient relics. The Saxon font, the misericord carvings on the choir stalls, Acca's Cross, and St. Wilfred's chair are well worth seeing.

For a place to stay, try the **Beaumont Hotel,** Beaumont Street (tel. 0434/602331), a family-run place across from the village park. It offers excellent facilities, including handsomely furnished and pleasantly decorated bedrooms, which are in the modern style, the effect livened by bright colors. All 20 accommodations have private baths. The tariff is £25 ($37.50) in a single for B&B and £35 ($52.50) in a double. VAT and service are included in the rates. Lunch is from £6 ($9), and dinner is à la carte. The hotel is owned by Mr. and Mrs. Martin Owen.

Royal Hotel, Priestpopple (tel. 0434/602270), stands just off the Market Place with its "shambles" and Moot Hall. Two buildings are linked together by a central square tower and dome, and the car park is entered through the original coaching arch. Dinner in the restaurant goes from £9 ($13.50). A salad buffet is presented each day in the lounge bar. Bedrooms are comfortable and well appointed, many with private bath and shower and tea- and coffee-making facilities. All have TV. Daily rates include a full English breakfast and VAT, and run from £18 ($30) in a single without bath to £39 ($58.50) in a double with bath.

West Close House, Hextol Terrace (tel. 0434/603307), is a B&B establishment with prize-winning gardens, lying in a private cul-de-sac with parking, only a ten-minute walk from the center of Hexham. Patricia Tomlinson receives guests to her house all year, sheltering them in tastefully and comfortably furnished rooms, each with hot and cold running water. The rate is from £9.50 ($14.25) per person nightly. Guests can enjoy a choice of an English or a continental breakfast, and packed lunches and light snacks are available by arrangement.

CORBRIDGE-ON-TYNE: This is the ancient capital of Northumberland and a good base for exploring the eastern section of Hadrian's Wall. To the west of the historic village is Corstopitum (Corchester), dating from about A.D. 80 to A.D. 400, during which it was a supply town for the Roman wall. Extensive remains have been excavated. The town stood on Agricola's Road, the Dere Street York to the north.

Corbridge was a Saxon town and in medieval days became a place of importance, sending two burgesses to the first English parliaments, in the 13th century.

St. Andrew's Church is on the site of a seventh-century Saxon tower. The present bridge over the River Tyne, built in 1674, was the only Tyne bridge to survive floods of 1771.

For accommodations, try **The Hayes,** Newcastle Road (tel. 043471/2010), set in 7½ acres of flower gardens, neat lawns, and fenced-in pastureland, all owned by Mr. and Mrs. F. J. Matthews. You can stay here on B&B terms at £9 ($13.50) per person, plus another £6 ($9) for dinner. Children are granted reductions according to age. On any arrangement, a cup of hot tea and cookies are provided at 10 p.m. In addition, families may want to inquire about two apartments for rent, a self-contained apartment sleeping four persons and a comfortable caravan housing five.

Clive House, Appletree Lane (tel. 043471/2617), was once a boys' school which was divided into four homes. Mr. and Mrs. E.M. Clarke have made this a charming and architecturally interesting home. Eunice Shears of Vancouver, B.C., says she found the Clarkes to be a stimulating couple. Mr. Clarke was once a Professor of Art at a university and Mrs. Clarke also taught there. Their three comfortable bedrooms all have four-poster beds, lace curtains, and hot-beverage facilities, and rent for £23 ($34.50) to £26 ($39) in a double, with a full breakfast included. The hosts invite guests to relax in their living room around the fireplace. They will direct you to several good places to eat nearby.

OTTERBURN: This mellowed old village on the Rede River was the scene of the famous Battle of Otterburn in 1388. It makes a good base for touring the Cheviot Hills.

The **Percy Arms** (tel. 0830/20261) is one of the finest English country inns to stop over at, for either food or lodging, if you're touring the scenic route between Newcastle and Edinburgh. On the banks of the River Rede, the hotel is attractively furnished and decorated. Several of the rooms open onto views of the hotel gardens. Jean and Carl Shirley are your hosts, welcoming you to patronize their establishment for drinks, bar meals, or dinners in their Garden Restaurant, which most often features classic English specialties along with some local dishes. All their rooms contain private bath or shower, a single going for £26.50 ($39.75), a double or twin ranging from £24 ($36) to £27 ($40.50) per person. Dinners cost from £12 ($18), but bar meals at lunch are much cheaper.

ALNMOUTH: A seaside resort on the Aln estuary, Alnmouth attracts sporting people who fish for salmon and trout in the Coquet River or play on its good golf course.

The **Schooner Hotel,** Northumberland Street (tel. 0665/830216), is a well-preserved Georgian inn, only a few minutes' walk to the water. The hotel is adjacent to the nine-hole Village Golf Course, the second oldest in the country. Bedrooms have private baths or showers, color TV, and direct-dial phones. Singles rent for £15 ($22.50) to £20 ($30) and doubles for £24 ($36) to £40 ($60). Guests count on finding the meals prepared and served at moderate prices. Set luncheons are £5.50 ($8.25), dinners costing £8.50 ($12.75). There are 24 bedrooms, a grill room, dining room, the Sea Hunter bar, the Chase Bar, and the Long Bar as well as a resident's lounge. Resident hostess is Christine Smith, who keeps the Schooner in good and tidy form.

ALNWICK: Set in the peaceful countryside of Northumberland, this ancient market town has had a colorful history. A good center for touring an area of scenic beauty, Alnwick is visited chiefly today by travelers wanting to see—

Alnwick Castle

In the town of Alnwick, 35 miles north of Newcastle, Alnwick Castle (tel. 0665/602207) is the seat of the Duke of Northumberland. This border fortress dates from the

11th century, when the earliest parts of the present castle were constructed by Yvo de Vescy, the first Norman Baron of Alnwick. A major restoration was undertaken by the fourth duke in the mid-19th century, and Alnwick remains relatively unchanged to this day. The rugged medieval outer walls do not prepare the first-time visitor for the richness of the interior, decorated mainly in the style of the Italian Renaissance.

Most of the castle is open to the public during visiting hours. You can tour the principal apartments, including the Armory, Guard Chamber, and Library, where you can view portraits and landscapes painted by such masters as Titian, Canaletto, and Van Dyck. You may also visit the dungeons and the Museum of Early British and Roman Relics. From the terraces within the castle's outer walls, you can look across the broad landscape stretching over the River Aln.

Alnwick is open to the public daily except Saturday (open Saturday on bank holiday weekends) from 1 to 5 p.m. May to September. Admission is £1.80 ($2.70) for adults and 80p ($1.20) for children. For an additional fee you can also visit the Regimental Museum of the Royal Northumberland Fusiliers, within the castle grounds.

Food and Lodging

The **Hotspur Hotel,** Bondgate Without (tel. 0665/602924), started in the 16th century as a coaching inn and was well known as the favorite local rendezvous for the musicians when "Billy Bones," a famed piper to the Duchess of Northumberland, was host. Now it has been extensively modernized, providing much comfort. Percy's restaurant, decorated in the William and Mary style of dark oak, has a fine cuisine. The Cocktail Bar, also in the William and Mary style, is intimate and excellent for a before-dinner drink. The Billy Bones Buttery also has its own character, decorated in elm with Jacobean screens. It is both informal and intimate. You can drink or dine here as well as enjoy the music of Northumbrian folksingers. There are 28 comfortable and stylish bedrooms fitted with oak furniture, radio, and telephone. Eighteen have private baths. Singles are £21 ($31.50) to £26 ($39), with doubles costing £37 ($55.50) to £44 ($66), the higher prices being for chambers with private baths. Tariffs include an English breakfast, service, and VAT. A luncheon goes for £5 ($7.50) and up, dinners from £9.50 ($14.25). Last food orders are at 9 p.m. The cuisine includes such dishes as roast local beef and poached Bulmer salmon.

CRAGSIDE: Designed in the late 19th century by architect Richard Norman Shaw for the first Lord Armstrong, Cragside at Rothbury is a grand estate stretching across 900 acres on the southern edge of the Alnwick Moor. Here groves of magnificent trees and fields of rhododendrons frequently give way to peaceful ponds and lakes. Cragside is 13 miles southwest of Alnwick, the entrance being 3 miles northeast of Rothbury on the B6341 Alnwick–Rothbury road. The grounds are open April to September daily from 10:30 a.m. to 6 p.m. In October hours are daily from 10:30 a.m. to 5 p.m., and from November to March Cragside is open only on Saturday and Sunday from 10:30 a.m. to 4 p.m. Admission is £1 ($1.50). The house is open from 1 to 5 p.m. on Wednesday, Saturday, and Sunday the first two weeks in April and during October; daily except Monday from mid-April to the end of September. Admission to both the house and park costs £2.40 ($3.60). For more information, telephone 0669/20333.

DUNSTANBURGH CASTLE: On the coast northeast of Alnwick, about 1½ miles east of Embleton (which is the castle's address), this castle was begun in 1316 by Thomas, Earl of Lancaster, and enlarged in the 14th century by John of Gaunt. The dramatic ruins of the gatehouse, towers, and curtain wall stand on a promontory high above the sea. You can reach the castle on foot only, either walking from Craster in the south or across the Dunstanburgh Golf Course from Embleton and Dunstan Steads in the north. The castle is open mid-March to mid-October, Monday to Saturday from 9:30 a.m. to 6:30 p.m., on Sunday from 2 to 6:30 p.m. The rest of the year, hours Monday to Saturday are 9:30 a.m. to 4 p.m., on Sunday from 2 to 4 p.m. Admission is 75p ($1.13) for adults, 35p (53¢) for children under 15.

NOW, SAVE MONEY ON ALL YOUR TRAVELS!
Join Arthur Frommer's $35-A-Day Travel Club™

Saving money while traveling is never a simple matter, which is why, over 26 years ago, the **$35-A-Day Travel Club** was formed. Actually, the idea came from readers of the Arthur Frommer Publications who felt that such an organization could bring financial benefits, continuing travel information, and a sense of community to economy-minded travelers all over the world.

In keeping with the money-saving concept, the annual membership fee is low—$18 (U.S. residents) or $20 U.S. (Canadian, Mexican, and foreign residents)—and is immediately exceeded by the value of your benefits which include:

(1) The latest edition of any TWO of the books listed on the following pages.

(2) An annual subscription to an 8-page quarterly newspaper *The Wonderful World of Budget Travel* which keeps you up-to-date on fastbreaking developments in low-cost travel in all parts of the world—bringing you the kind of information you'd have to pay over $35 a year to obtain elsewhere. This consumer-conscious publication also includes the following columns:

Hospitality Exchange—members all over the world who are willing to provide hospitality to other members as they pass through their home cities.

Share-a-Trip—requests from members for travel companions who can share costs and help avoid the burdensome single supplement.

Readers Ask . . . Readers Reply—travel questions from members to which other members reply with authentic firsthand information.

(3) A copy of *Arthur Frommer's Guide to New York*.

(4) Your personal membership card which entitles you to purchase through the Club all Arthur Frommer Publications for a third to a half off their regular retail prices during the term of your membership.

So why not join this hardy band of international budgeteers NOW and participate in its exchange of information and hospitality? Simply send $18 (U.S. residents) or $20 U.S. (Canadian, Mexican, and other foreign residents) along with your name and address to: $35-A-Day Travel Club, Inc., Gulf + Western Building, One Gulf + Western Plaza, New York, NY 10023. Remember to specify which *two* of the books in section (1) above you wish to receive in your initial package of member's benefits. Or tear out the next page, check off any two of the books listed on either side, and send it to us with your membership fee.

Date_____

FROMMER BOOKS
PRENTICE HALL PRESS
ONE GULF + WESTERN PLAZA
NEW YORK, NY 10023

Friends:

Please send me the books checked below:

FROMMER'S $-A-DAY GUIDES™

(In-depth guides to sightseeing and low-cost tourist accommodations and facilities.)

☐ Europe on $30 a Day $13.95	☐ New Zealand on $40 a Day $10.95
☐ Australia on $25 a Day $10.95	☐ New York on $50 a Day............. $10.95
☐ Eastern Europe on $25 a Day $10.95	☐ Scandinavia on $50 a Day........... $10.95
☐ England on $40 a Day.............. $11.95	☐ Scotland and Wales on $40 a Day..... $11.95
☐ Greece on $30 a Day............... $11.95	☐ South America on $30 a Day $10.95
☐ Hawaii on $50 a Day............... $11.95	☐ Spain and Morocco (plus the Canary
☐ India on $15 & $25 a Day........... $10.95	Is.) on $40 a Day $10.95
☐ Ireland on $30 a Day............... $10.95	☐ Turkey on $25 a Day............... $10.95
☐ Israel on $30 & $35 a Day $11.95	☐ Washington, D.C., & Historic Va. on
☐ Mexico on $20 a Day $10.95	$40 a Day $11.95

FROMMER'S DOLLARWISE GUIDES™

(Guides to sightseeing and tourist accommodations and facilities from budget to deluxe, with emphasis on the medium-priced.)

☐ Alaska........................... $12.95	☐ Cruises (incl. Alaska, Carib, Mex,
☐ Austria & Hungary $11.95	Hawaii, Panama, Canada, & US) $12.95
☐ Belgium, Holland, Luxembourg $11.95	☐ California & Las Vegas $11.95
☐ Egypt............................ $11.95	☐ Florida............................ $11.95
☐ England & Scotland $11.95	☐ Mid-Atlantic States $12.95
☐ France........................... $11.95	☐ New England...................... $12.95
☐ Germany......................... $12.95	☐ New York State $12.95
☐ Italy............................. $11.95	☐ Northwest........................ $11.95
☐ Japan & Hong Kong $12.95	☐ Skiing in Europe $12.95
☐ Portugal (incl. Madeira & the Azores) . $12.95	☐ Skiing USA—East $11.95
☐ South Pacific...................... $12.95	☐ Skiing USA—West $11.95
☐ Switzerland & Liechtenstein $12.95	☐ Southeast & New Orleans........... $11.95
☐ Bermuda & The Bahamas........... $11.95	☐ Southwest........................ $11.95
☐ Canada $12.95	☐ Texas............................ $11.95
☐ Caribbean $13.95	

TURN PAGE FOR ADDITIONAL BOOKS AND ORDER FORM.

THE ARTHUR FROMMER GUIDES™

(Pocket-size guides to sightseeing and tourist accommodations and facilities in all price ranges.)

☐ Amsterdam/Holland	$5.95	☐ Mexico City/Acapulco	$5.95
☐ Athens	$5.95	☐ Minneapolis/St. Paul	$5.95
☐ Atlantic City/Cape May	$5.95	☐ Montreal/Quebec City	$5.95
☐ Boston	$5.95	☐ New Orleans	$5.95
☐ Cancún/Cozumel/Yucatán	$5.95	☐ New York	$5.95
☐ Dublin/Ireland	$5.95	☐ Orlando/Disney World/EPCOT	$5.95
☐ Hawaii	$5.95	☐ Paris	$5.95
☐ Las Vegas	$5.95	☐ Philadelphia	$5.95
☐ Lisbon/Madrid/Costa del Sol	$5.95	☐ Rome	$5.95
☐ London	$5.95	☐ San Francisco	$5.95
☐ Los Angeles	$5.95	☐ Washington, D.C.	$5.95

FROMMER'S TOURING GUIDES™

(Color illustrated guides that include walking tours, cultural & historic sites, and other vital travel information.)

☐ Egypt	$8.95	☐ Paris	$8.95
☐ Florence	$8.95	☐ Venice	$8.95
☐ London	$8.95		

SPECIAL EDITIONS

☐ A Shopper's Guide to the Best Buys in England, Scotland, & Wales......... $10.95

☐ A Shopper's Guide to the Caribbean... $12.95

☐ Bed & Breakfast—N. America $8.95

☐ Fast 'n' Easy Phrase Book (Fr/Ger/Ital/Sp in *one* vol.) $6.95

☐ Guide to Honeymoons (US, Canada, Mexico, & Carib)................. $12.95

☐ How to Beat the High Cost of Travel ... $4.95

☐ Marilyn Wood's Wonderful Weekends (NY, Conn, Mass, RI, Vt, NH, NJ, Del, Pa) $11.95

☐ Motorist's Phrase Book (Fr/Ger/Sp) ... $4.95

☐ Swap and Go (Home Exchanging) $10.95

☐ The Candy Apple (NY for Kids)....... $11.95

☐ Travel Diary and Record Book........ $5.95

☐ Where to Stay USA (Lodging from $3 to $30 a night) $9.95

ORDER NOW!

In U.S. include $1.50 shipping UPS for 1st book; 50¢ ea. add'l book. Outside U.S. $2 and 50¢, respectively.

Enclosed is my check or money order for $_____

NAME _____

ADDRESS _____

CITY _____ STATE _____ ZIP _____